INTERNATIONAL HUMAN RIGHTS LAW

International Human Rights Law

Six Decades after the UDHR and Beyond

Edited by

MASHOOD A. BADERIN

School of Oriental and African Studies (SOAS), University of London, UK

MANISULI SSENYONJO

Brunel University, UK

Routledge
Taylor & Francis Group
LONDON AND NEW YORK

First published 2010 by Ashgate Publishing

Published 2016 by Routledge
2 Park Square, Milton Park, Abingdon, Oxfordshire OX14 4RN
711 Third Avenue, New York, NY 10017, USA

First issued in paperback 2016

Routledge is an imprint of the Taylor & Francis Group, an informa business

British Library Cataloguing in Publication Data
International human rights law : six decades after the UDHR
and beyond.
1. Human rights. 2. Human rights--History.
I. Baderin, Mashood A. II. Ssenyonjo, Manisuli.
341.4'8-dc22

Library of Congress Cataloging-in-Publication Data
International human rights law : six decades after the UDHR and beyond / by Mashood A. Baderin and Manisuli Ssenyonjo.
p. cm.
Includes bibliographical references and index.
ISBN 978-1-4094-0359-3 (hardback) -- ISBN 978-1-4094-0360-9 (ebook)
1. Human rights. I. Baderin, Mashood A. II. Ssenyonjo, Manisuli.

K3240.I5795 2010
341.4'8--dc22

2010016243

ISBN 13: 978-1-138-27512-6 (pbk)
ISBN 13: 978-1-4094-0359-3 (hbk)

Contents

PART III MECHANISMS AND IMPLEMENTATION

PART IV RESPONSIBILITIES AND REMEDIES

Foreword

The Universal Declaration of Human Rights is one of the most important documents in human history. Quite apart from its moral and political impact, in international law it has been the catalyst for most later developments in human rights protection and it has been instrumental in abandoning the idea that the treatment of nationals is a matter within a state's sovereignty, or, in Lord Palmerston's words, that nationals can be 'boiled in oil' without this being the proper concern of other states. The Declaration has also been incorporated into national constitutions and extensively applied by national courts, and remains an inspiration for those subject to oppression.

Quite remarkable is the foresight of the drafters in formulating a list of human rights that has fully stood the test of time. With very few exceptions, all human rights are there. Even later third generation human rights such as the rights to development, to the environment and to peace can, in Mr Justice Douglas's phrase in the Griswold case, be found at least in the Declaration's 'penumbra'. What was not so clearly anticipated was the current emphasis upon the positive obligations of states and the related endeavours to bring non-state actors within the reach of international human rights law. It also took later treaty developments to provide measures, however imperfect, for the enforcement of international human rights law. If the division in the two Covenants between civil and political rights and economic, social and cultural rights held back the provision of enforcement mechanisms for some kinds of rights, this was not the fault of the Declaration, which includes both groupings of rights on an equal footing.

All of these are matters that are impressively considered in the chapters of the present book. There are nearly thirty chapters on key rights and issues, written by leading human rights authors, containing many valuable insights and reflections. Particularly notable is the book's critical emphasis, examining realistically both what has been achieved since 1948, and remains to be achieved, and the prospects for the future. It is this critical dimension that will give the book lasting value.

David Harris
Professor Emeritus and Co-Director
Human Rights Law Centre
School of Law
University of Nottingham

List of Contributors

Dr Tawhida Ahmed is Lecturer in Law at the University of Sheffield, UK. She holds the degrees of LL M and Ph.D. from the University of Nottingham, UK. Her research interests lie in doctrinal and normative questions on EU law, international human rights and minority rights law. She has written on the EU's linguistic and cultural policy, as well as on the rights of religious minorities. She is the author of *The Impact of EU Law on Minority Rights* (Hart Publishing, 2010).

Dr Olufemi Amao is a graduate of University College Cork, Ireland (Ph.D. and PG Cert 2009); University of Warwick, UK (LL M, 2005); University of Ibadan, Nigeria (LL M, 2003); Obafemi Awolowo University, Nigeria (LL B, 1997); and University of Ilorin, Nigeria (BA, 1991). He was called to the Nigerian Bar in 1999. Formerly a Lecturer at University College Cork, he joined the Brunel Law School, London, UK, in September 2009. He has published widely on current human rights issues in academic journals.

Professor Mashood A. Baderin, LL B, BL, LL M, Ph.D., is Professor of Law and Head of the School of Law, School of Oriental and African Studies (SOAS), University of London. He is an expert in international human rights and Islamic law. His publications include *International Human Rights and Islamic Law* (Oxford University Press, 2003, 2005), *Economic, Social and Cultural Rights in Action* (co-edited with Robert McCorquodale (Oxford University Press, 2007), *International Law and Islamic Law* (Ashgate, 2008), and *Islam and Human Rights: Selected Essays of Abullahi An-Na'im* (Ashgate, 2010). He is a founding co-editor of the *Muslim World Journal of Human Rights.*

Professor Ilias Bantekas, LL B (Athens, Greece), LL M (Liverpool, UK), Ph.D. (Liverpool), Dip. Theology (Cambridge, UK), is Professor of International Law at Brunel University School of Law, UK. In 1998–2006, he was an Associate Professor and Director of the International Law Unit at Westminster Law School, UK, and during 2003–04 he was a Fellow at Harvard Law School, USA. He is Head of International Law and Arbitration at Mourgelas and Associates Law Firm (Athens), where he specializes also in renewable energy and implementation of the Kyoto Protocol. His publications include *International Criminal Law* (4th edition, Hart, 2010), *Oil and Gas Law in Kazakhstan: National and International Perspectives* (Kluwer, 2004), and *Trust Funds in International Law* (Asser/Cambridge University Press, 2009). He has published widely in leading international journals, including the *American Journal of International Law*, *International and Comparative Law Quarterly*, and others.

Dr Danwood Mzikenge Chirwa is Head of the Public Law Department and an Associate Professor at the University of Cape Town, South Africa. He has published widely on various aspects of human rights. The founder and editor-in-chief of the *Malawi Law Journal*, Dr Chirwa is a contributing editor to the *South African Journal of Criminal Justice* and an editor of the *ESR Review,* and he currently serves on the advisory boards of the *Constitutional Court Review* and the *City of Hong Kong University Law Review*.

Professor Jack Donnelly is Professor at the Graduate School of International Studies, University of Denver, USA. He is the author of several articles and books including *International Human Rights* (3rd edition, Boulder, CO: Westview Press, 2006); *Universal Human Rights in Theory and Practice* (2nd edition, Ithaca, NY: Cornell University Press, 2003); and *Realism and International Relations* (Cambridge: Cambridge University Press, 2000).

Dr Todd Howland is a human rights lawyer with over 20 years of experience. He is presently the director of the Joint UN Human Rights Office in the Democratic Republic of Congo (High Commissioner for Human Rights/MONUC – Peacekeeping Operation). His work experience includes UN, non-governmental organization, and academic posts spanning a number of countries. He has published numerous scholarly pieces and commentaries.

Professor Sarah Joseph is Professor of Law and the Director of the Castan Centre for Human Rights Law, at Monash University, Melbourne, Australia. She is the co-author of *The International Covenant on Civil and Political Rights: Cases Commentary and Materials* (Oxford University Press, 2004), co-editor of *The World Trade Organisation and Human Rights: Interdisciplinary Perspectives* (Edward Elgar, 2009), and co-editor of *Research Handbook on International Human Rights Law* (Edward Elgar, 2010). Her many other publications concern a wide range of human rights issues such as corporate accountability, interactions with trade law, poverty, terrorism, self-determination, extraterritoriality, and human rights institutions.

Professor Robert McCorquodale has been Director of the British Institute of International and Comparative Law since January 2008. He is also Professor of International Law and Human Rights, and former Head (Dean) of the School of Law, at the University of Nottingham, UK. His research and teaching interests are in the areas of public international law and human rights law. He has published widely on these areas. His books include *Cases and Materials on International Law* (with Martin Dixon) (4th edition, Oxford, Oxford University Press, 2003); *Economic, Social and Cultural Rights in Action* (edited with Mashood Baderin) (Oxford, Oxford University Press, 2007); *Human Rights* (Ashgate, 2003); and *Self-Determination in International Law* (Ashgate, 2000).

Professor Alastair Mowbray read law as an undergraduate at Warwick University, UK, and then completed his doctorate in public law at the University of Edinburgh, UK. Since 2003, he has been Professor of Public Law at the University of Nottingham, UK. He has published books on the *European Convention on Human Rights* for academics, students and practitioners; together with numerous articles in a variety of leading journals. For over 20 years, he has taught both postgraduate and undergraduate courses on the Convention.

Professor Rachel Murray is Professor of International Human Rights Law at the University of Bristol, UK. Her specialist areas are human rights in Africa, particularly the African Charter and its Commission on Human and People's Rights and the Organization of African Unity/African Union. She has written widely in this area, including books such as *Human Rights in Africa, from Organization of African Unity to African Union* (Cambridge: Cambridge University Press, 2004); *The African Charter on Human and People's Rights. The System in Practice, 1986–2006*, with Malcolm Evans (Cambridge, Cambridge University Press, 2008); *The African Commission on Human and People's Rights and International Law* (Oxford, Hart Publishing, 2000), and articles in leading legal human rights journals.

Dr Gerd Oberleitner is Lecturer at the Institute of International Law and International Relations at the University of Graz, Austria. From 2002 to 2004, he was Lecturer in Human Rights at the Centre for the Study of Human Rights, London School of Economics. He is a board member of the European Training and Research Centre for Human Rights and Democracy in Graz. His latest book is *Global Human Rights Institutions: Between Remedy and Ritual* (Cambridge: Polity, 2007).

Dr Paul O'Connell is Lecturer in Law at the University of Leicester, UK. His research to date has focused on the protection of socio-economic rights, in particular the right to health, and on the relationship between globalization and law. His most recent published work problematizes the relationship between prevailing economic and political orthodoxies, neo-liberalism or 'the Washington consensus', and commitment to the realization of human rights.

Dr Robert L. Ostergard, Jr. is Assistant Professor of Political Science and Faculty Associate of the Gender, Race and Identity Program at the University of Nevada, Reno, USA. His research focuses on the impact of intellectual property on human security and the impact of HIV/AIDS on issues of national and human security in Africa. His latest research is focused on the impact of women's rights and the HIV/AIDS epidemics in Africa.

Professor Dianne Otto is Director of the International Human Rights Law Program of the Institute for International Law and the Humanities (IILAH) and inaugural Convener of the University of Melbourne Human Rights Forum, Australia. She teaches and supervises higher-degree research candidates in the areas of human rights law and international law. She has edited Special Editions of *Third World Legal Studies* (1998–99) on 'Postcolonialism and Law' and the *Australian Journal of Human Rights* (2004) on 'Housing, Homelessness and Human Rights'. Recent publications include chapters in Vanessa Munro and Carl F. Stychin (eds), *Sexuality and the Law: Feminist Engagements* (2007), and Anne Orford (ed.), *International Law and Its Others* (2006), and 'A Sign of "Weakness"? Disrupting Gender Certainties in the Implementation of Security Council Resolution 1325', *Michigan Journal of Gender and Law, 13* (2006), pp. 113–75.

Professor Jo M. Pasqualucci is Professor of Law at the University of South Dakota, USA. She earned her JD at the University of Wisconsin, USA, and her SJD in International and Comparative Law at George Washington University Law School, USA. She clerked at the Inter-American Court of Human Rights and is the author of *The Practice and Procedure of the Inter-American Court of Human Rights* (Cambridge: 2003) and several articles on the Inter-American Human Rights System.

Dr Jona Razzaque is a barrister and Reader in Law at the University of the West of England (UWE), Bristol, UK. Her research interests include environmental governance and access to environmental justice. She was a member of the UNEP/OHCHR Expert Panel on Human Rights and the Environment (2002). She is the Consultant Editor of the *Journal of Human Rights and the Environment* and serves on the Board of Editors of the *Journal of Environmental Law*.

Professor John Gerard Ruggie is the Berthold Beitz Professor in Human Rights and International Affairs at Harvard's Kennedy School of Government, and Affiliated Professor in International Legal Studies at Harvard Law School, USA. He also serves as the United Nations Secretary-General's Special Representative for Business and Human Rights. A Fellow of the American Academy of Arts and Sciences, he has been identified by *Foreign Policy* magazine as among the 25 most influential international relations scholars in North America.

Professor Arjun Sengupta graduated with a Ph.D. from Massachusetts Institute of Technology, USA. He is one of India's leading economists, who moved between economic research and teaching and policymaking at the highest level. He is currently Member of Parliament and Chairperson of the Inter-governmental Working Group on the Right to Development, UN Human Rights Commission, Geneva, and was formerly Chairman, National Commission for Enterprises in the Unorganized Sector, Government of India, and Adjunct Professor of Development and Human Rights, at the François-Xavier Bagnoud Center of Harvard School of Public Health, USA. He is also a former Professor in the School of International Studies, Jawaharlal Nehru University, India, and served as an Executive Director of the *International Monetary Fund* and the Head of the Technical Team and Administration of the Indian Planning Commission as its Member Secretary.

Professor Rhona Smith is Professor of International Human Rights at Northumbria University, UK, and RWI Visiting Professor in Human Rights at Peking University Law School, Beijing University, China. She has authored and edited various articles and books on International Human Rights including *Textbook on International Human Rights* (4th edition, Oxford University Press, 2009) and *Text and Materials on International Human Rights* (2nd edition, Routledge Cavendish, 2009). She has undertaken human rights capacity-building work in various countries.

Dr Manisuli Ssenyonjo is Senior Lecturer in Law at Brunel University, London. He is the author of *Economic, Social and Cultural Rights in International Law* (Hart Publishing, 2009). His many other publications concern a wide range of human rights issues such as extraterritorial application of human rights treaties, accountability of non-state actors, human rights of women, international crimes, and reservations to human rights treaties.

Professor Sonja B. Starr is a Professor at the University of Michigan Law School, USA. She specializes in US and international criminal procedure and human rights law, with a focus on developing effective remedies for rights violations. Other research interests include sentencing law and policy and re-entry of former offenders. She earned her JD from *Yale Law School*, USA, where she served as senior editor of the *Yale Law Journal* and was awarded the American Bar Association's annual Ross Student Writing Prize. She is the author of numerous articles and books.

Dr Shawna E. Sweeney is an Assistant Professor at the University of Massachusetts, Dartmouth Public Policy Department, and Senior Research Associate at the University of Massachusetts Dartmouth Center for Policy Analysis, USA. She specializes in comparative politics, globalization policies, women's public policy issues, and human rights. Her research focuses on cross-national variations in governments' protection of women's economic, social and political rights. Her current research is centred on gender inequality and the HIV/AIDS epidemic in Africa.

Professor Nsongurua J. Udombana is Professor of International Law and Dean, Faculty of Law, University of Uyo, Nigeria. He is also Visiting Professor in Hungary (Central European University), Italy (International University College of Turin), and South Africa (University of Pretoria). He divides his research interest and time between international law and transitional justice, with a focus on Africa, and publishes globally on these themes. He is a member of several professional bodies, including the Nigerian Bar Association, the Nigerian Society of International Law, and the American Society of International Law.

Dr Anastasia Vakulenko is a Lecturer in Law at the University of Birmingham, UK. Her research is in the areas of human rights, religion and secularism studies, and critical and feminist research theory. Her forthcoming monograph, *Understanding the Islamic Veiling Controversy* (Routledge), examines the topical Islamic dress issue for what it reveals about western perceptions of human rights, gender, autonomy and religion. Her other research explores various ways in which freedom of religion in international and domestic human rights law is configured by a particular secular understanding of religion and its place in society, which does not always reflect the reality of religious experience.

Professor Frans Viljoen obtained the LL B, MA and LL D degrees from the University of Pretoria, South Africa, and the LL M degree from Cambridge University, UK. He is the Director of the Centre for Human Rights, Faculty of Law, University of Pretoria; Professor of International Human Rights Law; and the academic co-coordinator of the LL M programme (Human Rights and Democratisation in Africa), presented by the Centre, in collaboration with seven partner law faculties across Africa. He is the author of numerous articles, especially dealing with human rights issues, and the book *International Human Rights Law in Africa*. He is also editor-in-chief of the *African Human Rights Law Journal* and co-editor of the English and French versions of the *African Human Rights Law Reports*.

Mr Vernor Muñoz Villalobos has been the United Nations Special Rapporteur on the Right to Education since July 2004. He is also a Director of the Human Rights Education Department at the Costa Rican Ombudsman Office, Professor of Civil Rights in the Latina University of Costa Rica, and adviser on human rights education for the Communication School of the University of Costa Rica and other non-governmental organizations. He completed advanced studies in philology, law, human rights, philosophy and education. He is experienced as lecturer, researcher and promoter of human rights education, as well as in informal processes of conflict resolution.

Dr Gentian Zyberi is a senior researcher of the Dutch School of Human Rights Research. His book *The Humanitarian Face of the International Court of Justice: Its Contribution to Interpreting and Developing International Human Rights and Humanitarian Law Rules and Principles* was published by Intersentia in 2008. He has worked for the Defense at the Tribunal for the former Yugoslavia and has acted as Legal Adviser for Albania in the Kosovo case before the International Court of Justice.

PART I
Introduction

Chapter 1

Development of International Human Rights Law Before and After the UDHR

Mashood A. Baderin and Manisuli Ssenyonjo

[I]t is essential, if man is not to be compelled to have recourse, as a last resort, to rebellion against tyranny and oppression, that human rights should be protected by the rule of law.[1]

1. Introduction

The international legal protection of human rights has undergone dramatic growth and evolution since the end of the Second World War, the founding of the United Nations (UN) in 1945, and the subsequent adoption, by the UN General Assembly, of the Universal Declaration of Human Rights (UDHR)[2] on 10 December 1948.[3] Although the historical origins of the concept of human rights are often linked with the idea of natural rights[4] and there had been legal instruments adopted earlier in different states aimed at acknowledging and ensuring the protection of human rights by the rule of law,[5] the proclamation and adoption of the UDHR on 10 December 1948 marked the real beginning of the momentous international journey towards ensuring that human rights are protected universally by the rule of law.[6] Thus, the UDHR is considered today as the legal baseline for modern international human rights law, and 10 December 2008 marked the 60th anniversary of the setting of that legal baseline.

1 Universal Declaration of Human Rights G.A. res. 217A (III), UN Doc. A/810 at 71 (1948), Preamble, para. 3.

2 *Ibid.*

3 On the history and evolution of human rights, see e.g. M.R. Ishay, *The History of Human Rights: From Ancient Times to the Globalization Era* (Berkeley, CA: University of California Press, 2004); T. Buergenthal, 'The Evolving International Human Rights System', *American Journal of International Law*, 100(4) (2006), pp. 783–807; and M. Mutua, 'Standard Setting in Human Rights: Critique and Prognosis', *Human Rights Quarterly*, 29 (2007), pp. 547–630.

4 See e.g. J. Porter, 'From Natural Rights to Human Rights: Or, Why Rights Talk Matters', *Journal of Law and Religion*, 14 (1999), pp. 77–96.

5 E.g. Magna Carta Libertatum (1215), the French Declaration of the Rights of Citizens (1789), and the American Declaration of the Rights and Duties of Man (July 1948). In her speech at the UN General Assembly at the adoption of the UDHR, Eleanor Roosevelt, chairperson of the Human Rights Commission, stated, famously: 'We stand today at the threshold of a great event both in the life of the United Nations and in the life of mankind. This Declaration may well become the international Magna Carta for all men everywhere. We hope its proclamation by the General Assembly will be an event comparable to the proclamation in 1789 [the French Declaration of the Rights of Citizens], the adoption of the Bill of Rights by the people of the US, and the adoption of comparable declarations at different times in other countries'.

6 M.A. Glendon, 'The Rule of Law in the Universal Declaration of Human Rights', *Northwestern Journal of International Human Rights*, 2 (2004), p. 5 [online]. Available from: http://www.law.northwestern.edu/journals/JIHR/v2/5.

Although not intended as a legally binding instrument at the time of its adoption, the UDHR clearly acknowledged in its preamble, as quoted at the beginning of this chapter, the essential need to protect human rights through the rule of law. The UN General Assembly then proclaimed the Declaration to be

> a common standard of achievement for all peoples and all nations, to the end that every individual and every organ of society, keeping this Declaration constantly in mind, shall strive by teaching and education to promote respect for these rights and freedoms and by progressive measures, national and international, to secure their universal and effective recognition and observance, both among the peoples of Member States themselves and among the peoples of territories under their jurisdiction.[7]

From that humble beginning in 1948, international human rights law has evolved tremendously in different perspectives over the last six decades. Commemorating the 60th anniversary of the UDHR in 2008, the former UN High Commissioner for Human Rights, Louise Arbour, observed that 'it is difficult to imagine today just what a fundamental shift the Universal Declaration of Human Rights represented when it was adopted 60 years ago'.[8] Over those years there have been substantive developments in the theoretical, normative and legal perspectives of international human rights law, including debates on several conceptual issues regarding the scope and content of human rights generally. There has also been significant growth in the jurisprudence of different bodies and tribunals responsible for the interpretation and implementation of human rights law, and the human rights role of non-state entities such as non-governmental organizations (NGOs) has increased tremendously. New perspectives have also evolved regarding responsibilities and remedies for human rights violations relating to individual criminal responsibility for serious human rights violations, among others. This tremendous evolution of international human rights law in the past six decades calls for in-depth reflective analyses on the subject. The chapters in this volume, contributed by established human rights scholars and experts from different parts of the world, provide this much needed reflective analyses of the developments in the different areas of international human rights law over the past six decades since the adoption of the UDHR. This chapter provides an introductory background to these chapters.

---

7 UDHR, Preamble, para. 8. On the UDHR, see B.G. Ramcharan (ed.), *Human Rights: Thirty Years After the Universal Declaration.* Commemorative Volume on the Occasion of the Thirtieth Anniversary of the Universal Declaration of Human Rights (The Hague and Boston: Martinus Nijhoff, 1979); A. Eide *et al.* (eds), *The Universal Declaration of Human Rights: Commentary* (Oslo: Scandinavian University Press, 1992); United Nations, *The Universal Declaration of Human Rights* (New York: United Nations, 1998); B. van der Heijden and B. Tahzib-Lie (eds), *Reflections on the Universal Declaration of Human Rights: A Fiftieth Anniversary Anthology* (The Hague and London: Martinus Nijhoff, 1998); Y. Danieli, E. Stamatopoulou, and C.J. Dias (eds), *The Universal Declaration of Human Rights: Fifty Years and Beyond* (Amityville, NY: Baywood, 1999); G. Alfredsson and A. Eide (eds), *The Universal Declaration of Human Rights: A Common Standard of Achievement* (The Hague: Martinus Nijhoff, 1999); W. Korey, *NGOs and the Universal Declaration of Human Rights: A Curious Grapevine* (New York: Palgrave, 2001); and W. Sweet (ed), *Philosophical Theory and the Universal Declaration of Human Rights* (Ottawa, ON: University of Ottawa Press, 2003).

8 United Nations, *Universal Declaration of Human Rights: Dignity and Justice for All of Us.* 60th Anniversary Special Edition (United Nations Department of Public Information, 2009), p. v.

2. The UN Charter and the Development of International Human Rights Law

The UN has been the major international institution that has consistently promoted, within the context of its Charter, the protection of international human rights through the rule of law. The drafting and adoption of the UDHR was itself undertaken within the context of the UN Charter. Thus, the significance of the UDHR as the baseline for international human rights law would be better appreciated with a brief analysis of the UN Charter in relation to the background and development of international human rights law prior to the adoption of the UDHR.

Prior to the creation of the UN after the Second World War in 1945, earlier attempts at including specific human rights provisions in the Covenant of the League of Nations after the First World War in 1919 were unsuccessful. The only substantive human rights provision in the Covenant was on labour rights in its Article 23, stating that members of the League 'will endeavour to secure and maintain fair and humane conditions of labour for men, women, and children, both in their own countries and in all countries to which their commercial and industrial relations extend'[9] and 'undertake to secure just treatment of the native inhabitants of territories under their control'.[10] However, there emerged separate minority protection treaties and state declarations guaranteeing the protection of the rights of minorities, with the League of Nations performing a supervisory role over the obligations created, which were considered of international concern.[11]

Nevertheless, private endeavours continued both within and outside the League of Nations for the realization of an international human rights legal regime. In 1929, the Institute of International Law, a private body of distinguished authorities on international law in Europe, the Americas and Asia, adopted the Declaration of the Rights of Man,[12] in which it considered that it was the duty of every state to recognize, inter alia, the equal rights of every individual to life, liberty and property. The Institute also considered that every state had a duty to accord to everyone within its territory the full and entire protection of these rights without distinction as to nationality, sex, race, language or religion. Although the Declaration was not a legally binding document, it contributed to the popularization of the idea of an international human rights legal regime in the years immediately after its adoption. Commenting on the Declaration, Marshall Brown, writing in 1930, observed:

> This declaration … states in bold and unequivocal terms the rights of human beings, 'without distinction of nationality, sex, race, language and religion,' to the equal right to life, liberty and property, together with all the subsidiary rights essential to the enjoyment of these fundamental rights. It aims not merely to assure to individuals their *international* rights, but it aims also to impose on all nations a standard of conduct towards all men, *including their own nationals*. It thus repudiates the classic doctrine that states alone are subjects of international law. Such a revolutionary document, while open to criticism in terminology and to the objection that it has not juridical value, cannot fail, however, to exert an influence on the evolution of international law. It marks a new era which is more concerned with the interests and rights of sovereign individuals than with the rights of sovereign states.[13]

---

9 Covenant of the League of Nations, Art. 23(a).

10 *Ibid.*, Art. 23(b).

11 See e.g. Article 12 of the Polish Minorities Treaty (1920). See also A. Cassese, *Human Rights in a Changing World* (Cambridge: Polity Press, 1990), pp. 17–21.

12 See G.A. Finch, 'The International Rights of Man', *American Journal of International Law*, 35 (1941), pp. 662–5.

13 P.M. Brown, 'The New York Session of the Institut De Droit International', *American Journal of International Law*, 24 (1930), pp. 126–8, at p. 127 (emphasis in original).

The atrocities committed during the Second World War further provoked significant humanitarian concerns and moved the world community to call for formal international measures aimed at ensuring the legal protection of human rights and achievement of world peace and security. Thus, the Allies determined even before the end of the war that an international commitment to the protection of human rights should be a part of the post-war settlement.[14] Consequently, in the preamble of the UN Charter that emerged after the war, the member states, after declaring their determination 'to save succeeding generations from the scourge of war, which twice in our lifetime has brought untold sorrow to mankind',[15] also declared their determination 'to reaffirm faith in fundamental human rights, in the dignity and worth of the human person, in the equal rights of men and women and of nations large and small'.[16]

The Charter also provided substantively in its Article 1(3) that one of the purposes of the UN would be '(t)o achieve international co-operation in ... promoting and encouraging respect for human rights and for fundamental freedoms for all without distinction as to race, sex, language, or religion'. Futhermore, Article 55 provided that:

> With a view to the creation of conditions of stability and well-being which are necessary for peaceful and friendly relations among nations based on respect for the principle of equal rights and self-determination of peoples, the United Nations shall promote... [*inter alia*] universal respect for, and observance of, human rights and fundamental freedoms for all without distinction as to race, sex, language, or religion.

The UN member states then pledged themselves under Article 56 of the Charter 'to take joint and separate action in co-operation with the Organization for the achievement of the purpose stated in Article 55'.[17]

Although the Charter did not list the specific contents of the human rights and fundamental freedoms referred to, it signalled the dawn of the international human rights legal regime. To take the international human rights initiative forward, the Charter provided for the establishment of an Economic and Social Council (ECOSOC) whose functions included making 'recommendations for the purpose of promoting respect for, and observance of, human rights and fundamental freedoms for all',[18] and the powers to 'set up commissions ... for the promotion of human rights, and such other commissions as may be required for the performance of its functions'.[19] The basic objective of the (now disbanded) International Trusteeship System created under the Charter for the administration of the Trust Territories also included the requirement 'to encourage respect for human rights and for fundamental freedoms for all without distinction as to race, sex, language, or religion, and to encourage recognition of the interdependence of the peoples of the world'.[20]

---

14 See e.g. the Atlantic Charter of 1941 [online]. Available from: http://avalon.law.yale.edu/wwii/atlantic.asp.

15 UN Charter, Preamble, para. 1.

16 *Ibid.*, par. 2.

17 In its opinion on 'the legal consequences for States of the continued presence of South Africa in Namibia, notwithstanding Security Council resolution 260 (1970)', *ICJ Reports*, 58 (1971), para. 29, the ICJ stated: 'To establish instead, and to enforce distinctions, exclusions, restrictions and limitations exclusively based on grounds of race, colour, descent or national or ethnic origin, which constitutes a denial of fundamental human rights, is a flagrant violation of the purposes and principles of the Charter'.

18 UN Charter, Art. 62(2).

19 *Ibid.*, Art. 68.

20 *Ibid.*, Art. 76(c).

By virtue of these Charter provisions, seen in the context of Article 103,[21] the UN member states are obliged to observe, promote and encourage universal respect for human rights. Today, the UN Charter is widely considered as the basis of an international 'constitutional order'[22] that imposes obligations on member states to uphold international co-operation in promoting and encouraging respect for human rights.[23] Louis Henkin has concisely described the development as follows:

> The UN charter ushered in a new international law of human rights. The new law buried the old dogma that the individual is not a 'subject' of international politics and law and that a government's behaviour toward its own nationals is a matter of domestic, not international concern… It gave the individual a part in international politics and rights in international law, independently of his government. It also gave the individual protectors other than his government, indeed protectors and remedies against his government.[24]

Thus did the UN Charter provide a binding legal basis for the development of international human rights law in 1945, a foundation upon which the UDHR was subsequently built in 1948.

As noted above, apart from the Charter's prohibition of discrimination as to race, sex, language, or religion, it did not clearly define what human rights states were obliged to promote and protect. Efforts by some countries and non-governmental organizations (NGOs) attending the San Francisco conference for the inclusion of an international bill of rights in the UN Charter failed mainly because they were opposed by the major powers.[25] Soon after the adoption of the UN Charter, ECOSOC, acting on its mandate and powers under the Charter, established a Commission on Human Rights in 1946 with the mandate to develop the framework for an international bill of rights that set out clearly the specific contents of the international human rights recognized under the Charter. The Commission, appointed a Drafting Committee chaired by Eleanor Roosevelt, which drafted the UDHR between January 1947 and December 1948 as the first part of the so-called international bill of rights.[26]

---

21 Article 103 of the UN Charter states: 'In the event of a conflict between the obligations of the members of the United Nations under the present Charter and their obligations under any other international agreement, their obligations under the present Charter shall prevail'. For a discussion, see R. Liivoja, 'The Scope of the Supremacy Clause of the United Nations Charter', *International & Comparative Law Quarterly*, 57 (2008), pp. 583–612.

22 N. White, 'The United Nations System: Conference, Contract or Constitutional Order?', *Singapore Journal of International and Comparative Law*, 4 (2000), pp. 281–99, at p. 291. *See also* B. Fassbender, 'The United Nations Charter as Constitution of the International Community', *Columbia Journal of Transnational Law*, 36 (1997), pp. 529–619, at p. 594 (claiming that Art. 2(6) and Art. 103 of the Charter 'give a strong hint of its constitutional character'). But see B. Conforti, *The Law and Practice of the United Nations*, 2nd edn (The Hague, London and Boston: Kluwer Law International, 2000), p. 10, noting that '[t]he constitutional aspect of the UN should not be exaggerated. The Charter is and remains a treaty'.

23 See B. Simma (ed.), *The Charter of the United Nations: A Commentary*, 2nd edn, 2 vols (Oxford: Oxford University Press, 2002), vol. 1, at pp. 33–47; vol. 2, at pp. 917–44; Z. Stavrinides, 'Human Rights Obligations Under the United Nations Charter', *International Journal of Human Rights*, 3(2) (1999), pp. 38–48.

24 L. Henkin (ed.), *The International Bill of Rights: The Covenant on Civil and Political Rights* (New York: Columbia University Press, 1981), p. 6.

25 For a discussion, see T. Buergenthal, 'The Normative and Institutional Evolution of International Human Rights', *Human Rights Quarterly*, 19 (4) (1997), pp. 706–7, at p. 703.

26 The so-called International Bill of Rights consists of the UDHR, the International Covenant on Civil and Political Rights (ICCPR), and the International Covenant on Economic, Social and Cultural Rights

3. The UDHR as a Common Standard of Achievement

The UDHR was the first UN instrument adopted that contained a list of internationally recognized human rights. It was adopted unanimously[27] as a simple resolution of the UN General Assembly on 10 December 1948, and it has served, since its adoption, as a framework for subsequent international human rights treaties as well as many regional human rights instruments and national constitutions.[28]

As a common standard of achievement, the rights covered by the UDHR are the following: right to life, liberty and security of person (Art. 3); prohibition of slavery or involuntary servitude (Art. 4); prohibition of torture or cruel, inhuman or degrading treatment or punishment (Art. 5); right to recognition as a person before the law (Art. 6); right to equality before the law, non-discrimination, and equal protection of the law (Art. 7); right to an effective legal remedy (Art. 8); right to freedom from arbitrary arrest, detention, or exile (Art. 9); right in full equality to a fair and public hearing by an independent and impartial tribunal (Art. 10); right to be presumed innocent until proved guilty according to law, right not to be held guilty for any act or omission which did not constitute an offence at the time committed, and right not to be punished with a heavier penalty than applicable at the time of committing an offence (Art. 11); right to freedom from arbitrary interference with privacy, family, home or correspondence and attacks on one's honour and reputation (Art. 12); right to freedom of movement and residence within state borders and right to leave any country and to return to one's own country (Art. 13); right to seek and enjoy asylum (Art. 14); right to nationality and right to change nationality (Art. 15); right to marry and found a family (Art. 16); right to property (Art. 17), right to freedom of thought, conscience and religion (Art. 18); right to freedom of opinion and expression (Art. 19); right to freedom of peaceful assembly and association (Art. 20); right to take part in the government of one's country, have access to public service, and take part in elections (Art. 21); right to social security (Art. 22); right to work, to equal pay for equal work, and to form and join trade unions (Art. 23); right to rest and leisure, limitation of working hours, and periodic holidays with pay (Art. 24); right to a standard of living adequate for health and well-being, including food, clothing, housing and medical care, and necessary social services, and right to security in the event of unemployment, sickness, disability, widowhood, old age or other lack of livelihood in circumstances beyond one's control (Art. 25); right to education (Art. 26); right to participate freely in cultural life and to enjoy the arts and share in scientific advancement, and right to protection of the moral and material interests resulting from any scientific, literary or artistic production of which one is the author (Art. 27); and right to a social and international order in which the rights and freedoms can be fully realized (Art. 28).

Significantly, as can be noted from the above list, the UDHR covered both civil and political rights, as well as economic, social and cultural rights (ESC) rights without distinction, and thus recognized indivisibility, interdependence and interrelatedness of all human rights from the

---

(ICESCR). See notes 42–7 below. For documents and information on the history of the drafting of the UDHR, see e.g. http://www.un.org/Depts/dhl/udhr/ ; J. Morsink, *The Universal Declaration of Human Rights: Origins, Drafting, and Intent* (Philadelphia: University of Pennsylvania Press, 1999), Chapter 1; M.G. Johnson and J. Symonides, *The Universal Declaration of Human Rights: A History of Its Creation and Implementation, 1948–1998* (Paris: UNESCO Publishing, 1998); M.A. Glendon, *A World Made New: Eleanor Roosevelt and the Universal Declaration of Human Rights* (New York: Random House, 2001).

27 With eight states out of the then 58 UN members states abstaining.

28 E.g. H. Hannum, 'The Status of the Universal Declaration of Human Rights in National and International Law', 25 *Georgia Journal of International and Comparative Law*, 25 (1 and 2) (1995–6), pp. 287–396.

beginning.[29] It also recognized that 'everyone has duties to the community in which alone the free and full development of his personality is possible'.[30]

Although the UDHR at the time of its adoption was not a legally binding instrument, over time it has evolved to the extent that some of its provisions now either constitute customary international law and general principles of law or represent elementary considerations of humanity.[31] As noted above, its greatest significance is that it provides an authoritative content, adopted by the UN General Assembly, to the interpretation of the UN Charter in respect of its human rights provisions. Its considerable practical importance, in that regard, has been demonstrated through its invocation by the International Court of Justice (ICJ),[32] the International Criminal Court (ICC),[33] regional and domestic courts as an aid to interpretation of relevant human rights treaties,[34] and national constitutional provisions protecting human rights.[35] The Declaration has also been referred to in a number of cases involving human rights issues.[36] At the regional level, Article 60 of the African Charter on Human and Peoples' Rights (African Charter or ACHPR), ratified by 53 African states, specifically requires the African Commission on Human and Peoples' Rights to draw inspiration, inter alia, from the UDHR when interpreting the African Charter.[37] Some national constitutions also accord the UDHR a special status by their reference to it, with some explicitly providing for the interpretation of the constitutions in conformity with the UDHR. For example, Article 102 of the Spanish Constitution of 1978 provides that 'The norms relative to basic rights and liberties which are recognized by the Constitution shall be interpreted in conformity with the Universal Declaration of Human Rights and the international treaties and agreement on those matters ratified by Spain'. Similarly, Article 75(22) of the Constitution of Argentina (as amended) confers constitutional rank on various human rights instruments, including the UDHR, by declaring that these instruments 'have a higher hierarchy than laws'.

---

29 See, generally, M. Ssenyonjo, *Economic, Social and Cultural Rights in International Law* (Oxford: Hart Publishing, 2009).

30 UDHR, Art. 29(1).

31 I. Brownlie, *Principles of Public International Law*, 7th edn (Oxford: Oxford University Press, 2008), p. 559.

32 The ICJ invoked the UDHR in relation to the detention of hostages 'in conditions of hardship'. See *Case Concerning United States Diplomatic and Consular Staff in Tehran*, *ICJ Reports*, 3 (1980), para. 91, at p. 42.

33 See Pre-Trial Chamber I, Situation in Darfur, Sudan: in the Case of the *Prosecutor* v *Omar Hassan Ahmad Al Bashir*, No. ICC-02/05-01/09 (4 March 2009), para. 156.

34 See e.g. the European Court of Human Rights in the *Golder* case, ILR 57, 201 at pp. 216–17.

35 See e.g. Supreme Court of Uganda, *Attorney General* v *Susan Kigula and 417 Others*, Constitutional Appeal No. 03 of 2006, Judgment of 21 January 2009.

36 See M.N. Shaw, *International Law*, 6th edn (Cambridge: Cambridge University Press, 2008), p. 280, citing the following cases: *In re Flesche* 16 AD, 266, at 269; *The State (Duggan)* v *Tapley* 18 ILR, 336, at 342; *Robinson* v *Secretary-General of the UN* 19 ILR, 494, at 496; *Extradition of Greek National* case, 22 ILR 520 at 524; *Beth El Mission* v *Minister of Social Welfare* 47 ILR, 205 at 207; *Corfu Channel* case, *ICJ Reports*, 4 (1949), at p. 22; *Filartiga* v *Pena-Irala* 630 F.2d 876 (1980).

37 The African Charter on Human and Peoples' Rights, below note 41, Article 60 reads: 'The Commission shall draw inspiration from international law on human and peoples' rights, particularly from the provisions of various African instruments on human and peoples' rights, the Charter of the United Nations, the Charter of the Organisation of African Unity, the Universal Declaration of Human Rights, other instruments adopted by the United Nations and by African countries in the field of human and peoples' rights as well as from the provisions of various instruments adopted within the Specialized Agencies of the United Nations of which the parties to the present Charter are members'.

This confirms the view that over the years the UDHR has indeed acquired a legal or normative character as envisaged by its designation as 'a common standard of achievement for all peoples and all nations' in its preamble when it was adopted in 1948.

4. International Human Rights Law: Six Decades After the UDHR

Since the adoption of the UDHR in 1948, a considerable number of rules of international law, both customary and treaty, have been developed at the international[38] and regional levels – in Europe,[39] the Americas[40] and Africa[41] – with the aim of protecting, promoting, further defining and expanding the content of human rights.[42]

38 The principal UN international human rights instruments include the UDHR, note 1 above; ICCPR, note 44 below; ICESCR note 45 below 3; International Convention on the Elimination of All Forms of Racial Discrimination (CERD), 660 UNTS 195; Convention on the Elimination of All Forms of Discrimination Against Women (CEDAW), UN Doc. A/34/46; Convention Against Torture and Other Cruel, Inhuman or Degrading Treatment or Punishment (CAT), UN Doc. A/39/51 (1984); and the Convention on the Rights of the Child (CRC), UN Doc. A/44/49 (1989). See United Nations, *Human Rights: A Compilation of International Instruments*, UN Doc. ST/HR/1/Rev.6, UN Sales No. E.02.XIV.4 (New York: United Nations, 2002).

39 The European Convention for the Protection of Human Rights and Fundamental Freedoms (ECHR), 1950; UKTS (1953), 213 UNTS 221. For a discussion, see Chapter 14 in this volume and, generally, C. Ovey and R. White, *Jacobs and White: The European Convention on Human Rights*, 5th edn (Oxford: Oxford University Press, 2006); M.W. Janis *et al.*, *European Human Rights Law: Text and Materials*, 3rd edn (Oxford: Oxford University Press, 2010). See also the European Social Charter (ESC) 1961, UKTS 38 (1965), and the European Social Charter (revised), ETS No. 163. For a discussion, see D. Harris and J. Darcy, *European Social Charter*, 2nd edn (Ardsley, NY: Transnational Publishers, 2001). Another key human rights treaty at the European Union level is the Charter of Fundamental Rights of the European Union, 2000 O.J. (C 364) 1, entered into force 7 December 2000.

40 The American Convention on Human Rights 1969 (1970), 9 ILM 673. Additional Protocol to the American Convention on Human Rights in the Area of Economic, Social and Cultural Rights, 'Protocol of San Salvador', OAS Treaty Series No. 69 (1988). See Chapter 13 in this volume and, generally, D. Harris and S. Livingstone (eds), *The Inter-American System of Human Rights* (Oxford: Oxford University Press, 1998); T. Buergenthal and D. Shelton, *Protecting Human Rights in the Americas: Cases and Materials*, 4th edn (Kehl: N.P. Engel, 1995).

41 The African Charter on Human and Peoples' Rights (African Charter or ACHPR) 1981, OAU Doc. CAB/LEG/67/3 rev. 5, 21 ILM 58 (1982); Protocol to the African Charter on the Establishment of the African Court on Human and Peoples' Rights, OAU/LEG/MIN/AFCHPR/PROT.1 rev. 2 (1997); Protocol to the ACHPR on the Rights of Women in Africa, Maputo, 11 July 2003, African Commission on Human and Peoples' Rights [online]. Available from: at http://www.achpr.org/english/_info/women_en.html; African Charter on the Rights and Welfare of the Child, OAU Doc. CAB/LEG/24.9/49 (1990); OAU Convention Governing the Specific Aspects of Refugee Problems in Africa, 1001 UNTS 45. For a discussion of human rights in Africa, see Chapter 12 in this volume and, generally, F. Viljoen, *International Human Rights Law in Africa* (Oxford: Oxford University Press, 2007); F. Ouguergouz, *The African Charter on Human and Peoples' Rights* (The Hague: Martinus Nijhoff, 2003); V. Nmehielle, *The African Human Rights System: Its Laws, Practice, and Institutions* (The Hague: Martinus Nijhoff, 2001).

42 For an overview of the action taken to protect international human rights, see, generally, H. Steiner and P. Alston, *International Human Rights in Context: Law, Politics, Morals – Text and Materials,* 3rd. edn (Oxford: Oxford University Press, 2008); M Nowak, *Introduction to the International Human Rights Regime* (Leiden: Martinus Nijhoff, 2003); M. Haas, *International Human Rights: A Comprehensive Introduction* (London: Routledge, 2008).

In continuance of its mandate of drafting the international bill of rights, the UN Commission on Human Rights commenced, in earnest after the adoption of the UDHR, the drafting of a legally binding international human rights treaty under the UN system. Eventually, two binding covenants were produced after nearly 20 years of drafting debates and disagreements regarding whether or not to combine civil and political rights and ESC rights in one single covenant.[43] The International Covenant on Civil and Political Rights (ICCPR)[44] and the International Covenant on Economic, Social and Cultural Rights (ICESCR)[45] were adopted in 1966 and both entered into force in 1976.[46] As noted above, the two covenants, together with the UDHR, constitute the so-called International Bill of Rights. The rights protected in the two covenants cover and enlarge most of the rights recognized under the UDHR and thereby protect nearly all the basic values cherished by all states and every human society.[47] In addition, many other ancillary international treaties and declarations on the rights of women, children, refugees, stateless persons, diplomatic agents, minorities, persons with disabilities, etc., have been adopted under the UN system. There are also specific international human rights treaties for the protection of a person against atrocities such as genocide, racial discrimination, apartheid, slavery, forced labour, torture, etc.[48] Today, every state in the world (despite a wide variety of historical, political, religious, social and cultural differences) has ratified at least one of these international human rights treaties,[49] indicating the increasing trend towards universal acceptance of human rights in the international legal system.[50] It is in this context that it is recognized that:

> While the significance of national and regional particularities and various historical, cultural and religious backgrounds must be borne in mind, it is the duty of States, regardless of their political, economic and cultural systems, to promote and protect all human rights and fundamental freedoms.[51]

---

43 See e.g. M. Baderin and R. McCorquodale, 'The International Covenant on Economic, Social and Cultural Rights: Forty Years of Development', in M. Baderin and R. McCorquodale (eds), *Economic, Social and Cultural Rights in Action* (Oxford: Oxford University Press, 2007), pp. 4–9, at p. 3.

44 999 UNTS 171.

45 993 UNTS 3.

46 For the drafting history and long-standing contentious debate on the nature of civil and political rights and economic social and cultural rights, see e.g. L.B. Sohn, 'A Short History of United Nations Documents on Human Rights', in *United Nations and Human Rights* (Dobbs Ferry, NY: Oceana, 1968); I. Szabo, 'Historical Foundations of Human Rights and Subsequent Developments', in K. Vasak (ed.), *The International Dimensions of Human Rights*, vol. 1 (Westport, CT: Greenwood Press, 1982).

47 See L. Chen, *An Introduction to Contemporary International Law* (New Haven, CT: Yale University Press, 1989), pp. 209–11.

48 See Office of UN High Commissioner for Human Rights at http://www2.ohchr.org/english/bodies/ratification/.

49 For example, as of 16 January 2010, the total states parties to the following treaties were as follows: ICESCR, 160; ICCPR, 165; ICERD, 173; CEDAW, 186; CAT, 146; CRC, 193. For the current state of ratification, see Office of UN High Commissioner for Human Rights at http://www2.ohchr.org/english/bodies/ratification/.

50 Although many states have ratified various human rights treaties with different reservations and/or interpretive declarations. See e.g. http://treaties.un.org/Pages/Treaties.aspx?id=4&subid=A&lang=en.

51 See Vienna Declaration and Programme of Action, as adopted by the World Conference on Human Rights on 25 June 1993, UN Doc. A/CONF.157/23 9 (12 July 1993), para 5.

At the regional level, organizations such as the Council of Europe, the Organization of American States, the Organization of African Unity/African Union,[52] and the League of Arab States have also adopted different regional human rights treaties in recognition of the noble ideals of international human rights. The basic regional human rights treaties are the European Convention for the Protection of Human Rights and Fundamental Freedoms (1950),[53] the European Social Charter (1961),[54] the American Convention on Human Rights (1969),[55] the African Charter on Human and Peoples' Rights (1981),[56] and the Arab Charter on Human Rights (1994).[57] Specific regional human rights treaties and declarations on the rights of women, children, refugees, and the prohibition of torture, etc., have also been adopted.[58] Although Arab and Asian states have not yet created a regional human rights system, as a result of several factors including vast differences in culture, political ideology and economic development,[59] there are emerging trends that present an opportunity to create a regional system in the Middle East. This is evident, for example, in the adoption of a revised Arab Charter on Human Rights by the League of Arab States in 2004, which, in its preamble, reaffirmed, inter alia, the principles of both the UN Charter and the UDHR.[60]

Over the last six decades since the adoption of the UDHR, human rights have progressively developed into a universal value system, and it is now generally accepted that 'the promotion and protection of all human rights is a legitimate concern of the international community,'[61] and it is against this that states are evaluated today. Evidently, the scope and limits of human rights have enormously transcended the initial rights guaranteed under the UDHR in 1948. While it is certainly impossible to attempt to address all the relevant issues, developments and failures in that regard in a single volume of this nature, this book has been carefully structured and issues carefully selected to cover the principal and most relevant aspects of the developments.

5. Thematic Structure of this Book

This book is structured thematically into five parts, namely: introduction, concepts and norms, mechanisms and implementation, responsibilities and remedies, and the concluding section entitled 'And Beyond'. This structure is aimed at covering relevant developments in the theory and practice of international human rights law as comprehensively and thematically as possible

---

52 The Organization of African Unity was replaced by the African Union (AU) in 2001. See Art. 28 of the Constitutive Act of the African Union, which came into force on 26 May 2001.

53 Adopted on 4 November 1950. E.T.S. No. 005.

54 Adopted on 18 October 1961. E.T.S. No. 035.

55 Adopted on 22 November 1969. O.A.S.T.S. No. 36 at 1.

56 Adopted on 27 June 1981. OAU Doc.CAB/LEG/67/3 rev. 5 (1982) 21 I.L.M. 58.

57 Adopted on 22 May 2004, reprinted in *International Human Rights Reports* 12 (2005), p. 893. Entered into force 15 March 2008. For an overview of the Arab Charter, see M. Rishmawi, 'The Arab Charter on Human Rights and the League of Arab States: An Update', *Human Rights Law Review*, 10(1) (2010), pp. 169–78.

58 See e.g. http://treaties.un.org/Pages/Treaties.aspx?id=4&subid=A&lang=en.

59 See D. Shelton, 'The Promise of Regional Human Rights Systems', in Burns H. Weston and S.P. Marks (eds), *The Future of International Human Rights* (New York: Transnational Publishers, 1999), pp. 351–98, at p. 364.

60 See Preamble, para. 5, Arab Charter on Human Rights, adopted by the League of Arab States, 22 May 2004; reprinted in *International Human Rights Reports*, 12 (2005), p. 893. Entered into force 15 March 2008.

61 Vienna Declaration, note 48 above, para. 4.

in a single volume. A brief summary of the chapters contained in each of the four remaining parts is provided below.

5.1 Concepts and Norms

Part II of this book consists of nine chapters addressing different issues relating to the development of concepts and norms under international human rights law. Theoretically, the question of universality has remained at the heart of international human rights debates since the adoption of the UDHR. While the naming of the UDHR as a 'Universal Declaration' clearly indicated that the international human rights venture was meant to be a universal venture from the beginning, it also raised questions about the meaning and scope of the universality of human rights. For example, one of the earliest questions posed to the UN Commission on Human Rights, then drafting the UDHR, was the statement submitted to the Commission by the American Anthropological Association (AAA) on 24 June 1947 about the proposed universality of human rights and how that would be achieved.[62] Although the UDHR has, today, established itself as an instrument of significant moral and legal influence universally, that theoretical question about the meaning and scope of the universality of human rights has not been fully muted. Traditionally, the universality debate has been generally divided into the 'universalist' and 'cultural relativist' perspectives, and it has oscillated over the last six decades but has influenced, substantively, the conceptual understandings informing the implementation of international human rights law in different parts of the world today.

Part II opens with Jack Donnelly's Chapter 2 entitled 'International Human Rights: Universal, Relative or Relatively Universal?', which provides a refreshing insight into the conceptual debate on universalism and cultural relativism. Jack argues that while each side in the debate rests on important insights about the nature of human rights, the standard terms of the debate are, essentially, misformulated. He asserts that universality and relativity are multifaceted concepts that are not necessarily incompatible, and that human rights are indeed universal in some standard and important senses of that term but also relative in some relevant standard senses of that term. He states that the real issue is not *whether* human rights are universal or relative but *how* they are and are not universal, and also *how* they are and are not relative, and *how* these universalities and relativities interact, in theory and in practice. Jack then proceeds to identify and analyse three different senses in which human rights may be reasonably understood as being universal – that is, 'international legal universality', 'functional universality' and 'overlapping consensus universality' – and two senses, in which human rights are not essentially universal – that is, 'ontological universality' and 'historical (or anthropological) universality'. He also considers some standard relativist arguments before proposing that human rights must rather be seen as being 'relatively universal'. Essentially, the chapter endeavours to bridge the dichotomy between the traditional 'universalist' and 'cultural relativist' theoretical debate through a refreshing perspective of 'relative universality', which he sees as a powerful perspective that can be used to build more just and humane national and international societies through international human rights law. He concludes that there can be little doubt that human rights are both universal and relative and that any reasonable discussion of the

62 See American Anthropological Association (AAA), 'Statement on Human Rights', *American Anthropologist*, 49 (1947), pp. 539–43, at pp. 539 and 542–3. Cf. the 1999 AAA Declaration on Anthropology and Human Rights [online]. Available from: http://www.aaanet.org/stmts/humanrts.htm and K. Engle, 'From Scepticism to Embrace: Human Rights and the American Anthropological Association from 1947–1999' *Human Rights Quarterly*, 23(3) (2001), pp. 536–59, for an analysis of the two statements.

issue of universality today must start from this observation. This perspective can certainly provide a new dimension to the debate on the universality of human rights into the future.

Normatively, while the UDHR contains a mixture of civil and political rights and ESC rights, one of the main normative controversies that confronted the UN Commission on Human Rights in the drafting of an internationally binding human rights covenant, subsequent to the UDHR, was, as noted earlier, the question of whether or not civil and political rights and ESC rights should be combined together in one single legally binding covenant. The compromise in the end was to draft two separate covenants, namely the ICESCR and the ICCPR, both of which were adopted in 1966 and entered into force in 1976.[63] This created the initial division between the two set of rights. Consequently, ESC rights under the ICESCR and civil and political rights under the ICCPR have developed differently over the years. The development of ESC rights had, traditionally, been much slower than that of civil and political rights due to different reasons.[64]

Manisuli Ssenyonjo's Chapter 3, 'Economic, Social and Cultural Rights', provides a comprehensive analysis of the evolution of ESC rights since the adoption of the UDHR. He first shows that despite the fact that ESC rights have received increased positive attention in recent years, they are still very much marginalized and still considered as second class to civil and political rights. This marginalization of ESC rights, Manisuli argues, mostly affects the poor and disadvantaged groups and individuals, and also raises specific questions that the chapter seeks to address; namely, (i) what are the real human rights obligations of states parties to the ICESCR? (ii) are such obligations territorially limited or is there scope for extraterritorial obligations? (iii) are states permitted to derogate from ESC rights during emergencies despite the fact that the ICESCR does not contain a derogation clause either permitting or prohibiting derogations?, and (iv) was it really necessary to adopt, in 2008, an Optional Protocol to the ICESCR providing for the right of complaint by individuals and groups against violations of the rights protected by the ICESCR? In addressing these questions, Manisuli endeavours to demonstrate that the ICESCR lays down clear human rights legal obligations on states parties. He notes that the recent increase in domestic and regional case law on ESC rights and the adoption by the UN General Assembly on 10 December 2008, the 60th anniversary of the UDHR, of an Optional Protocol to the ICESCR, clearly indicates that violations of ESC rights are now clearly established as being justiciable both in theory and practice. The chapter also notes that the absence of a clause allowing derogation in times of public emergency in the ICESCR indicates that the covenant generally continues to apply in the time of armed conflict, war or other public emergencies, and, as a minimum, states cannot derogate from the minimum core obligations of ESC rights. Thus, the chapter analyses clearly that from the humble beginnings in Articles 22–27 of the UDHR in 1948, it has taken more than six long decades to bring ESC rights to the same level of enforcement accorded to civil and political rights under international human rights law, and envisages that, with the entry into force of the Optional Protocol, the enforcement of ESC rights should proceed more effectively than before.

Furthermore, Sarah Joseph's Chapter 4, 'Civil and Political Rights', provides a reflective insight into the development of civil and political rights under international human rights law by analysing their evolution since the adoption of the UDHR. She starts by observing that, while Articles 3 to 21 of the UDHR are concerned with the recognition that all people are entitled to the enjoyment and protection of their civil and political rights, these rights were only specified in greater detail in a legally binding treaty, the ICCPR, 16 years after the UDHR. Over the years, the interpretation

63 While both the ICESCR and ICCPR were adopted on 16 December 1966, the ICESCR entered into force on 3 January 1976 prior to the ICCPR, which entered into force on 23 March 1976.

64 See Baderin and McCorquodale, note 41 above, pp. 6–14.

of these rights has thrown more light on their scope and limits. In that regard, the chapter focuses particularly on the jurisprudence of the Human Rights Committee (HRC), the body established to monitor the implementation of the ICCPR. Sarah analyses the philosophical background of civil and political rights by linking its beginnings to the concept of natural rights but then notes that modern conceptions of civil and political rights have evolved far beyond their libertarian roots. She then goes on to analyse the different ways that civil and political rights may be categorized and also addresses other relevant issues such as civil and political rights versus ESC rights; individual and collective rights; cultural relativism; vertical and horizontal application of the ICCPR; and the various limitations on civil and political rights within the ICCPR such as clawback clauses, Article 20 restriction, and other implied restrictions. The analyses are well illustrated with relevant cases that have evolved over the years. The chapter concludes with an observation that civil and political rights have, over the years, become more complex than perhaps originally conceived under the UDHR, arguing that they are, today, conceived as being both negative and positive, capable of vertical and horizontal application, and do allow room for cultural differences, although breaches of minimum standards cannot be justified by cultural relativist arguments.

Since the adoption of the UDHR, ICCPR, and the ICESCR, some new concepts of rights that were not specifically understood in 1948 and were not provided for in the UDHR have been evolving normatively over time. The remaining chapters in this part of the book explore some of those evolving normative perceptions and developments in international human rights law.

Arjun Sengupta's Chapter 5, 'Simple Analytics of the Right to Development', examines the concept of the right to development in international human rights law. The debate on the right to development has been a very topical one, particularly between developed and developing countries, since the 1980s. One of the main arguments has been about the definition, content and scope of the right to development. Arjun's 'simple analytics' of the right to development provides an insight into the topic, addressing mainly the definitional and contextual issues. He begins by noting that the UDHR did not provide specifically for the right to development, and that a specific concept of the right to development under international human rights law postdates the UDHR. He observes that when the right to development was first recognized in 1986, in the UN Declaration on the Right to Development, it appeared to be a utopian right, but was later appreciated and adopted by academics, civil society leaders and policymakers from both the developed and developing countries. Arjun provides an analytic definition of right to development, identifying, in that regard, the need for an indicator of the realization of the right by combining its different elements or objectives, which in essence relate to defining the right to development in terms of all or some of the rights that have already been recognized in different international human rights instruments. In that way, Arjun argues, the obligations for realizing the right to development would essentially derive from the obligations of realizing all those recognized rights under international human rights law. The chapter then links this to the issue of development policy as a meta-right, positing that the international community must formulate, adopt and implement an appropriate development policy which is grounded in development cooperation as an international obligation. Arjun argues that the implementation of such a development policy, will move the international community steadily towards realizing the right to development. The chapter concludes with the observation that even though it was not specifically addressed in the UDHR, the right to development need no longer remain a utopia, and that if there is sufficient will for international cooperation in today's world, the right to development can genuinely be achieved within the context of the UDHR.

Another important, newly developing norm in international human rights law is the concept of the right to a healthy environment. This is examined in Chapter 6 by Jona Razzaque. The chapter begins with a truism that the right to a healthy environment is indispensable for leading a life in human dignity, and Jona argues that it is a prerequisite for the realization of other human rights. Jona notes that while the UDHR, ICCPR and ICESCR do not specifically mention the right to a healthy environment, it can be argued that the spirit of the UDHR includes this right, and that expansive interpretations of the rights to life, health, property and privacy, among others, have been used to promote the concept of the right to a healthy environment in the jurisprudence of some national and regional institutions. The chapter then analyses how the specific concept of the right to a healthy environment has evolved within international human rights law, particularly since the Draft Declaration of Principles on Human Rights and the Environment proposed in the Ksentini report submitted to the UN Sub-Commission on Human Rights in 1994. Jona further analyses the existing theoretical debates and questions regarding the link between human rights and the environment at the national, regional and international levels of human rights discourse and jurisprudence. She also addresses issues of competing rights and the role of procedural rights in relation to the realization of the right to a healthy environment. Based on the analysis provided, the chapter argues that human rights law does acknowledge the existence of a right to a healthy environment, albeit indirectly, concluding that although the UDHR did not declare a specific right to a healthy environment, human rights law has, nevertheless, evolved over the years to meet the challenges of environmental degradation, and that the link between human rights and environmental protection is now firmly established at the national, regional and international levels of human rights discourse. Jona closes the chapter by stating that there is a need, in the sixth decade since the adoption of the UDHR, for a substantive right to a healthy environment with supporting procedural rights responsive to the challenges of climate change and the sustainable management of the ecosystem.

It is clear that conflict situations contribute significantly to human rights violations in various parts of the world today. This continues to engender debates on the need to recognize the right to a peaceful world order if human rights are to be maximally guaranteed globally. In Chapter 7, Nsongurua J. Udombana examines the evolving concept of the right to a peaceful world order within the context of the general development of international human rights law since the adoption of the UDHR. In doing so, he begins by interrogating 'peace' as a human right and finds that the concept of a universal right to peace appears to be supported by general international law and alluded to by judicial authorities and publicists on the basis of some underlying principles that he identifies and analyses in the first part of the chapter. He notes specifically that Article 28 of the UDHR implicitly guarantees the right to a peaceful world order, and that the UN General Assembly has adopted several resolutions bearing on global peace, particularly the Declaration on Right of Peoples to Peace, adopted in 1984. All these, Nsongurua argues, tend to provide the material evidence for the existence of the right to a peaceful world order under international human rights law. The second part of the chapter then traces the continued search for a peaceful world order and pinpoints some reasons why that goal has largely been elusive, while the third part analyses some factors that contribute to the continuing threats to a peaceful world order and provides suggestions on how to stem these. The chapter concludes with a forceful observation that a peaceful world order is not just an ideal but a foundational and fundamental human right, which the UN must work towards actualizing by promoting 'social progress and better standards of life in larger freedom', and the author proposes some ways that this could be achieved.

Tawhida Ahmed and Anastasia Vakulenko's Chapter 8, 'Minority Rights 60 Years After the UDHR: Limits on the Preservation of Identity?,' examines the question of minority rights in international human rights law. The chapter opens with an assertion that the international response to the question of what to do with 'minorities' has been far from static, oscillating between assimilationist and protectionist attitudes. In proving this assertion, Tawhida and Anastasia first provide an overview of the evolution of minority rights protection since the adoption of the UDHR. They observe that the development of minority rights under international human rights law has been characterized by a move from an assimilationist policy, prevailing at the inception of the UDHR, to a preservation of identity policy from the 1960s onwards. Preservation of identity, they argue, is currently the prevalent policy on minority rights under international human rights law as evidenced by the adoption of specific minority rights provisions in international human rights law and minority-sensitive interpretations of general human rights provisions. They consider this as a welcome sensitization of international human rights law to minority issues and a more sustained commitment to equality. The chapter then proceeds to argue that this commendable policy of preservation of identity is, however, not always maintained in practice by international adjudicating bodies. They use the topical issue of restrictions on the Islamic headscarf as a case study to demonstrate how the preservation of identity policy is ignored in practice, illustrating their arguments with relevant case law and jurisprudence. They conclude that this is a shortcoming that not only weakens the prestige of international adjudicating bodies as protectors of human rights, but also undermines the much-pronounced commitment to the preservation of minority identities in international human rights law. It is noted that this shortcoming certainly indicates a troubling contradiction between rhetoric and reality and should be addressed seriously if, six decades after the UDHR, minority rights are to be given any real content.

While intellectual property rights and the right to health are both recognized under the UDHR, there is concern, particularly in the face of HIV/AIDS pandemic in many parts of the developing world, about the threat posed by intellectual property rights to access to essential medicines in developing countries. Robert Ostergard and Shawna Sweeney's Chapter 9, 'Intellectual Property Rights, the Right to Health, and the UDHR: Is Reconciliation Possible?,' examines this apparent conflict of rights and their possible reconciliation. They note that while there has been growing support in many circles to make health care a universal human right and a 'global public good', since all societies benefit immensely from a healthy population, the present system of intellectual property rights has a detrimental impact on the right to health, as it reduces the availability of pharmaceuticals, especially for individuals suffering from curable diseases in developing countries, hence pitting the needs of the poor who require medicine to live against the profit-maximizing goals of pharmaceutical firms. The chapter discusses the numerous practical impediments to balancing the two values – the right of a creator to protect intellectual property and the right of everyone to enjoy the highest attainable standard of health care. Robert and Shawna argue that to strike a balance between these important values, all countries must work to develop policies that take into account the basic health and developmental interests of developing countries, and also that important changes must be made to the current system, especially with respect to the production and pricing of basic goods and services needed to achieve health subsistence rights. These changes, they argue, must include allowing developing countries access to essential medicines that support the realization of basic health, welfare, and economic development. The chapter concludes with a proposition that the current dominant state-centric paradigm that views the right to health care in strictly nationalistic terms must be replaced with a more cosmopolitan paradigm that reflects the true nature of the relationship between intellectual property rights and human rights as a 'global public good'. Anything short of that goal, they conclude, would leave the universal right to health care unrealized for a significant segment of the world's population.

Part II closes with Paul O'Connell's Chapter 10, 'Brave New World? Human Rights in the Era of Globalization', wherein he engages with the challenges posed by globalization to international human rights law. Paul notes that, like most other social phenomena, human rights have not escaped the gravitational pull of 'globalization speak' even though human rights scholars and practitioners were late entrants to the debate. He identifies, however, that literature on globalization and human rights has since burgeoned, generating a variety of perspectives, both optimistic and pessimistic, about the relationship between globalization and human rights. The chapter provides a critical analysis of the concept of globalization, examining alternative approaches to its definition, the actual impact which globalization has had on human rights to date, the potential long-term implications of globalization for human rights, and the opportunities and obstacles that globalization presents in the realization of the UDHR promise. Paul argues, *inter alia*, that a clear understanding of what globalization is really about reveals that conditions for the violation of human rights are structurally embedded within the global status quo, as evidenced by the fact that neoliberal globalization has, to date, had serious adverse consequences for the protection of the entire catalogue of rights protected by the UDHR, with the effect that six decades after the adoption of the UDHR the promise of human flourishing contained therein remains unfulfilled. He concludes, *inter alia*, that if the next decade of globalization is to see any improvement in the global protection of human rights, it is essential that the ideals of the UDHR be joined with other emancipatory discourses, and be central to the opposition to neoliberal globalization and instrumental in the construction of a genuine alternative. The guiding principle in that regard, he argues, will be the pursuit of a social and international order in which the rights and freedoms set out in the UDHR can be fully realized.

5.2 Mechanisms and Implementation

Part III of this book covers issues relating to human rights mechanisms and implementation. Without relevant mechanisms and specific means of implementation, human rights theory and norms could remain mere rhetoric on paper. Effective mechanisms and means of implementation lead to the practical realization of human rights in the lives of human beings. It is often argued in that regard that the hurdles to implementation are much higher than those of norms and standard setting under international human rights law. While the UDHR did not provide for any specific mechanism of implementation for the rights guaranteed under it, the UN Charter before it and many human rights instruments after it provide for specific mechanisms and means of implementation aimed at ensuring the practical realization of human rights norms and provisions globally. This section thus consists of 10 chapters relating to systems, mechanisms and implementations of international human rights law, ranging from the UN global human rights system, the different regional human rights systems, and the role of National Human Rights Institutions (NHRIs) and non-governmental organizations (NGOs), as well as other relevant factors relating to the practical realization of human rights.

This part opens with Rhona Smith's Chapter 11, 'The United Nations Human Rights System', wherein she examines a complex system described as 'a multitude of entities which vary greatly in their range, remit and composition'. Rhona critically analyses the different mechanisms and means of implementation within the UN human rights system, which she identifies as falling into two main divisions. The first division consists of the UN Charter-based bodies such as the UN Security Council, the UN General Assembly, ECOSOC, the ICJ, and the UN Secretary-General. She examines the processes and procedures of each of these and other sub-bodies in this division. The second division consists of the UN treaty-based bodies created under the respective international human rights treaties. The chapter also examines other UN bodies such as the United Nations Educational, Scientific and Cultural Organization (UNESCO), the International Labour Organization (ILO), the World Health Organization (WHO), the Food and Agricultural Organization (FAO) and United Nations Children's Fund (UNICEF), analysing how their mandates impact on the realization of international human rights globally. Following the overall critical analysis of the system, Rhona concludes that while there is no doubt that, six decades after the UDHR, human rights are now well ingrained in international and national society, transforming the rhetoric of the UDHR into a reality for some 6.7 billion people globally is still a challenge facing everyone and all parts of the UN system into the future.

While the UN system represents the major institutional framework for the universal implementation of international human rights law, the role of the different regional systems in achieving that goal cannot be overemphasized. Thus, the three existing regional human rights systems are also examined.

The African regional human rights system is examined in Chapter 12 by Olufemi Amao. The African system is the youngest of the three existing regional human rights systems and has often been castigated for its relative ineffectiveness over the years. Olufemi notes, however, that despite the grim picture often painted about the system, a potentially viable regional human rights system is emerging in Africa that is progressively making the human rights promises of the UDHR a reality to the people of Africa. The chapter gives a background of the emergence of the system, followed by a critical analysis of the relationship between the African human rights system and the UDHR, the unique features of the African Commission on Human and Peoples' Rights (ACHPR), the expansion of the rights protected under the African system, and the different mechanisms and means of implementation under the system such as the ACHPR, the African Court of Human and Peoples' Rights (ACtHPR), and the newly created African Court of Justice and Human Rights that would replace the ACtHPR in due course, as well as other relevant mechanisms. Olufemi also discusses the influence of the African Charter on domestic courts in Africa, using Nigeria as a case study in that regard. The chapter concludes with the observation that the African human rights system has, from inception, taken a very expansive approach to protection of rights by combining civil and political rights, ESC rights, and group rights. It is also noted that the African Commission has, through its jurisprudence, further widened the scope of rights protected under the African system, and the author hopes that this will further improve with the introduction of the African Court of Justice and Human Rights.

This chapter is followed by Jo Pasqualucci's Chapter 13, 'The Inter-American Human Rights System'. Jo starts with the observation that, prior to the UN General Assembly's adoption of the UDHR in December 1948, the General Assembly of the Organization of American States (OAS) had adopted the American Declaration of the Rights and Duties of Man more than 6 months earlier in April 1948, and that, since then, the OAS has adopted numerous other human rights treaties and declarations. She notes, however, that progress in the actual protection of human rights has not always been evident across the region. The chapter critically examines the American Declaration of the Rights and Duties of Man, the American Convention on Human Rights (ACHR), and the various implementing organs such as the Inter-American Commission on Human Rights, the Inter-American Court of Human Rights (IACtHR), and their processes. Apart from the American Declaration of the Rights and Duties of Man and the ACHR, the chapter also examines other Inter-American human rights instruments and the impediments to the optimal functioning of the Inter-American system. The chapter concludes, *inter alia*, that since the adoption of both the UDHR and the American Declaration of the Rights and Duties of Man in 1948, the OAS has developed a functioning regional system of human rights protection, with all Latin American states being parties to the ACHR and accepting the jurisdiction of the IACtHR. While recognizing the need to strengthen the system, Jo asserts that the Inter-American human rights system is yet serving as a model for human rights protection in other parts of the world, especially as the first system to function in an underdeveloped region.

The third regional system is examined in Alastair Mowbray's Chapter 14 on the European Convention on Human Rights (ECHR). The chapter starts with an analysis of the relationship between the UDHR and ECHR, detailing how the UDHR was a significant component in the formulation of the ECHR and how over the years the member states have gradually widened, via additional protocols, the substantive rights and freedoms guaranteed by the ECHR to cover almost all the rights in the UDHR. He notes, however, that the Committee of Ministers, the dominant institution in the reform process, has retained the fundamental philosophy of the ECHR to ensure that the additional protocols should concentrate upon civil and political – and not ESC – rights. Alastair also analyses the mechanisms and means of implementation under the ECHR, observing that, while the UDHR did not provide any system to enforce its provisions, a major achievement of the ECHR was the provision of organs of implementation for the European regional system, originally in the form of an European Commission of Human Rights and a part-time European Court of Human Rights, which were later merged into the current, single, full-time European Court of Human Rights (ECtHR) under the Protocol 11 reforms in 1994. The chapter analyses the processes of the ECtHR and the role of the Committee of Ministers in supervising the execution of the court's judgements, as well as the issue of the work load crisis of the court and the various proposals to address that problem, which consequently led to the adoption of Protocol 14bis by the Committee of Ministers in May 2009, which is now in force. The judicial expansion of the provisions of the ECHR by the decisions of the ECtHR is also illustrated with relevant case law. The chapter concludes, *inter alia*, that, whatever their problems, the ECHR and the ECtHR are a major achievement for the entire world in relation to the development of international human rights law.

As the main judicial organ of the UN, the role of the ICJ in enhancing the promotion of human rights is well recognized, even though it does not have a specific human rights mandate, and individuals have no *locus standi* to bring cases of human rights violations before it. In Chapter 15, 'Human Rights in the International Court of Justice', Gentian Zyberi examines the ICJ's role. The chapter examines this role through analyses of relevant ICJ case law relating to the UDHR and the court's contribution to the development of human rights generally. Gentian observes that the jurisprudence of the ICJ in the field of international human rights law encompasses many important issues such as the internationalization of human rights, the coining of certain fundamental principles of international human rights law, the characterization of the right of peoples to self-determination as a right *erga omnes*; the interpretation of the prohibition of genocide as including an obligation to prevent genocide, the clarifications on the right to asylum, diplomatic and consular protection, the protection of human rights rapporteurs in order for them to be able to fulfil their duty when in the service of the UN, the applicability of international human rights instruments in situations of armed conflict, clarifications on the issue of individual criminal responsibility for internationally recognized crimes, and some important pronouncements on environmental issues. The chapter concludes with the observation that, although the ICJ does not represent a forum where individuals can claim their human rights, it is, nevertheless, a judicial organ that has contributed and can still contribute to furthering international human rights law in two principal ways. First, it can continue to interpret and thus develop international human rights rules and principles, and, second, by keeping the fabric of international law together, it can ensure a better interaction between the different branches of international law in order to achieve an optimum protection of human rights within the framework of international law. The chapter also provides an annex of a list of cases submitted to the ICJ relating to human rights since 1991.

The role of national human rights institutions (NHRIs) is examined by Rachel Murray in Chapter 16. Rachel begins with the observation that, while states were the main actors on the international human rights stage when the UDHR was adopted, with other players getting only brief mention in the preamble, today the important role of national institutions in the promotion and protection of human rights and the need for states to establish them are well recognized and acknowledged. She notes, however, that with this recognition comes an understanding of the unique and powerful position that these types of bodies hold and the need to consider more their accountability and separate status from governments and civil society. Rachel argues that, while the position of NHRIs as important actors in the field of human rights appears to have been clearly established, there are still many unanswered questions about who exactly should be permitted to be involved and whether the checks and balances in place at present are sufficient to monitor and regulate them. The chapter also examines three important issues in relation to the future role of NHRIs, namely, accreditation, the range of bodies, and their role in monitoring and implementation of international treaties. The chapter concludes, *inter alia*, that NHRIs have come a long way since the adoption of the UDHR, and the human rights field has also changed dramatically in terms of the actors who play a role in the creation, monitoring and implementation of human rights standards. While they are a potential force to be reckoned with, they also need to be considered meticulously and objectively.

This is followed by Dianne Otto's Chapter 17, 'Institutional Partnership or Critical Seepages?: The Role of Human Rights NGOs in the United Nations', wherein she examines the role of NGOs as important non-state actors in the promotion and protection of international human rights. The chapter starts by stating that international human rights NGOs were made possible by the UN Charter's introduction of the term 'non-governmental organizations' in its Article 71 and also by the UDHR, which laid the groundwork for the normative and institutional developments that were to follow. Dianne observes that, today, six decades after the UDHR, there are manifold and diverse accounts of the role of human rights NGOs in the promotion and protection of international human rights. She presents a critical analysis of this role under three main themes, namely, the expanding institutional and normative participation of human rights NGOs, the challenges of such increased institutionalization, and the issue of whether NGOs are institutional partners or critical seepages. The chapter concludes with the observation, *inter alia*, that the UDHR itself recognizes that the realization of its vision cannot be left in the hands of states or intergovernmental institutions when it calls upon 'every individual', as well as 'every organ of society', to strive for the effective recognition and observance of universal human rights and fundamental freedoms. In that regard, Dianne asserts that the primary role of human rights NGOs is to challenge the privileged knowledge and systems of hierarchy that international institutions support, and that, to do this, NGOs need to act dangerously in their engagement with intergovernmental institutions; preserve their autonomy; defend their use of oppositional and confrontational strategies; maintain their character as diverse, creative and often locally based; and take advantage of all manner of seepage to keep emancipatory visions of human rights free from institutional capture.

In Chapter 18, Mashood Baderin examines the impact of Islamic law on the implementation of international human rights law, particularly in Muslim states, using the ICCPR as a case study. He begins with the observation that the relevance and prospective impact of Islamic law on international human rights law had been manifested from the beginning of the UN's human rights venture during the early debates on the draft provisions of the UDHR, when objections were raised on grounds of Islamic law, particularly by Saudi Arabia, regarding the scope of certain provisions of the UDHR. Although the objections were defeated at the drafting stage, Saudi Arabia consequently abstained in the voting for the UDHR at the UN General Assembly in December 1948. While most Muslim states, including Saudi Arabia, have, today, ratified various international human rights treaties, some of them have done so with reservations and/or interpretative declarations on grounds of Islamic law, with others making reference to Islamic law in their periodic reports concerning relevant international human rights treaties. Mashood analyses the importance of domestic law in facilitating the implementation of international human rights law in respective states, highlighting the role of Islamic law in that regard in respect of Muslim states that apply Islamic law as part of their domestic laws. He then examines the nature of Islamic law, distinguishing between its historical and evolutional perceptions, and argues that the adoption of an evolutional perception of Islamic law by Muslim states can help to harmonize apparent areas of contradiction between Islamic law and international human rights law. The chapter then analyses the impact of Islamic law on the implementation of the ICCPR, referring to other relevant human rights treaties in that regard. After engaging with relevant materials in that regard, the chapter notes that international human rights law has, conversely, also affected the development of Islamic law and has led to some relevant reforms to Islamic law in certain Muslim states. The chapter concludes, *inter alia*, that while Islamic law will continue to impact, one way or another, on the implementation of international human rights law in many Muslim states, such impact should not necessarily be negative, and that, through the right political will, Islamic law could be constructively utilized for the positive implementation of international human rights law in Muslim states.

While human rights courts have been created within all the existing three regional human rights systems, no international human rights court currently exists under the UN international human rights system. Gerd Oberleitner examines the need for such a court in Chapter 19, 'Towards an International Court of Human Rights? '. He notes that, while a remarkable global human rights infrastructure has been put in place since the adoption of the UDHR, the one institution conspicuously absent in the assemblage of human rights bodies is a World Court with the mandate to adjudicate human rights on a global scale. Gerd argues that, while the idea of an international human rights court is often dismissed as utopian, regional human rights courts are praised as the crown jewels of human rights protection. The chapter asserts that the time has come to begin a debate on an international court of human rights, especially with recent important steps taken within the UN system such as the replacement of the Commission on Human Rights by the Human Rights Council in 2006 and the creation of the International Criminal Court (ICC) since the Rome Statute came into force in July 2002. Gerd analyses the advantages and disadvantages of creating such a court, weighing all the different propositions in that regard. He concludes that while there is no doubt that the difficulty in setting up an international human rights court is considerable, it seems inconsistent, if not hypocritical, to push for the right to an effective remedy as a core human right on the national level while at the same time negating this right in the UN human rights system and thereby excluding a great number of persons from access to an international court in cases of human rights violations not addressed at national or regional levels. The creation of such a court or, to begin with, the engaged debate over its establishment, he argues, would open a new chapter for the UN and the development of international human rights law generally.

Part III on mechanisms and implementation closes with Todd Howland's Chapter 20, 'Multi-State Responsibility for Extraterritorial Violations of Economic, Social and Cultural Rights'. Todd notes that, six decades after the UDHR, there is still debate on the precise nature and content of extraterritorial human rights obligations, especially when the acts or omissions of states or non-state actors, whether as a result of foreign military intervention, war on terrorism, globalization or otherwise, affect the human rights of individuals in another state. Todd argues that multiple states can and do hold legal responsibility to protect and promote ESC rights beyond their borders. He notes that the idea that multiple states have human rights obligations to the same individual is derived, in part, from his own experience as a UN representative working in 'failed states' and as part of multilateral efforts to bring peace, respect for human rights, and stability to war-torn and dysfunctional states. He notes that these violations can be direct or indirect. The chapter uses Haiti and the Democratic Republic of Congo as reference points, and explores several existing theoretical frameworks that will help situate the idea of multi-state accountability in human rights in current scholarship. He further explores different theories of tort and contract law that can help incorporate the multi-state approach into human rights law and practice, and he also outlines the existing hurdles in the international legal system that the proposal will have to overcome. In conclusion, Todd asserts that defining the extent of states' human rights obligations when intervening in other states will help to improve transparency, accountability and effectiveness in the international protection of human rights. He notes that once there is a growing understanding of this responsibility, the result will be the realization of this obligation whenever states and their agents, such as the UN and the World Bank, operate in another state.

5.3 Responsibilities and Remedies

Part IV of this book contains seven chapters addressing relevant issues relating to human rights responsibilities and remedies. The UDHR acknowledges that the full realization of human rights entails some responsibilities on the part of states, individuals, and every organ of society,[65] as well as the right of victims of human rights violations to an effective remedy.[66]

Since states have the major responsibility for securing human rights, this section opens with Danwood Chirwa's Chapter 21, 'State Responsibility for Human Rights'. In this chapter, Danwood critically analyses the ways in which international human rights law, spearheaded by the UDHR, has fundamentally altered the traditional doctrine of state responsibility in international law. He notes that international human rights law has expanded the conceptual framework of the idea of state responsibility beyond what was initially imagined by international jurists. He explores relevant questions such as the following. Who can invoke the doctrine of state responsibility? Whose rights give rise to state responsibility? Can non-state action give rise to state responsibility? The last question then leads to a discussion of the implications of the doctrine of state responsibility for the position of non-state actors in relation to international human rights law. Danwood observes that international human rights law has altered the traditional conceptions of state responsibility in two fundamental ways. The first is in relation to the status of the individual in international law and the second relates to the range of states which can enforce rights in international law. He argues that for human rights to be secured, non-interference by the state is as critical as protective measures by it, and that failure by the state to take protective measures will lead to its responsibility in international law not necessarily because of the mere occurrence of the violations themselves but because of the state's inaction or failure to prevent the violation. He concludes, inter alia, that, international human rights law has painstakingly developed to extend the scope for holding states responsible for violations of human rights and has also emboldened the status of individuals in international law by arming them with the power to enforce their rights not only against foreign states but also against their own state. A state, he argues, can be held responsible even if not directly connected to the actual violation, and it can be held responsible even for those violations that it fails to exercise due diligence to prevent', investigate, punish the perpetrators, and provide redress to the victims.

This is followed by the specific examination of the question of state compliance in Frans Viljoen's Chapter 22, 'State Compliance with the Recommendations of the African Commission on Human and Peoples' Rights'. This chapter begins by noting that recent years have seen the increased engagement of international human rights law practice and scholarship with issues

65 See Preamble, UDHR.
66 See Art. 8, UDHR.

of implementation and compliance, and argues that this can certainly be reconciled with the vision of the drafters of the UDHR. Frans states that, by examining state compliance with the recommendations of the African Commission, which is a regional treaty body with a quasi-judicial status similar to that of the UN human rights treaty bodies, some light can be shed on the progress made to achieve effective recognition and observance of human rights standards as envisaged under the UDHR. After a brief exploration of the concept of compliance and an introduction to the African Commission's recommendatory mandate, four types of recommendations issued by the Commission are identified and discussed with the aim of placing the literature and available data in an analytical framework and pointing to avenues for further research and gaps that may need to be filled. In that regard, two major questions are explored, namely: do states comply with their formal treaty obligations, and do individuals benefit from the ratification of treaties? The chapter concludes that the overall picture that emerges is that of very limited state compliance in Africa, and it recommends ways that state compliance can be improved to ensure concrete benefits and real improvements in the lives of human beings as envisaged under the UDHR. Compliance with the recommendations of a regional body such as the African Commission, Frans argues, is a small but important part of realizing the UDHR promise.

The question of individual responsibility is examined by Ilias Bantekas in Chapter 23, 'Individual Responsibility and the Evolving Legal Status of the Physical Person in International Human Rights Law'. He notes that, since the adoption of the UDHR, it has become clear over the years that state responsibility for human rights violations ought to be complemented by perpetrators' individual responsibility under criminal and civil law. This chapter focuses on the concept of individual responsibility, according to which the natural corollary of a human rights violation is the criminal liability of the perpetrator under international law. Ilias examines to what degree this concept is applicable to all violations of human rights. He argues that the concept of individual responsibility is inextricably linked to the evolving nature of the status of the physical person in international law and that international human rights law has played a prominent role in this regard, particularly through the establishment of individual complaint mechanisms and the granting of *locus standi* to aggrieved persons. He also examines the employment of extra territorial jurisdiction to give meaning to the existence of criminal liability under international law. He traces the Nuremberg legacy and how this has evolved into individual responsibility in contemporary international human rights law. He concludes, *inter alia*, that the big test for human rights and international criminal law is to sustain prosecutorial activism in more states and to enhance state cooperation in the exercise of universal jurisdiction. This latter type of jurisdiction must not become anathema or the battleground for only a handful of states, but must develop into a real threat against perpetrators of international crimes that also often amount to human rights violations.

In Chapter 24, 'The International Criminal Court and Individual Responsibility of Senior State Officials for International Crimes', Manisuli Ssenyonjo examines the role of the ICC in relation to such criminal responsibility. Manisuli starts with the observation that effective protection of human rights requires that those who commit serious crimes such as genocide, crimes against humanity and war crimes, which amount to serious human rights violations, must be held individually responsible for those crimes without any distinction based on official capacity. This, he argues, will help to end impunity and deter future commission of international crimes that constitute serious violations of human rights. He notes that the ICC was established, 50 years after the UDHR, to operate beyond national courts, which tend to refrain from prosecuting state officials enjoying immunity from prosecution under national law and private individuals suspected of having committed international crimes that national authorities implicitly instigate, or at least tolerate. He makes the important observation that since the ICC became operational, all its active investigations by the end of 2009 have been in Africa, with the Sudanese President Al Bashir's case constituting its highest profile case so far. After a thorough examination of the relevant issues, the chapter concludes, *inter alia*, that the establishment of the ICC is a major step forward in the struggle against impunity and that since there is currently no international court of human rights, the ICC can play an essential role by holding individuals responsible for international crimes within its jurisdiction without any distinction based on official capacity. He argues that, as a permanent judicial institution that aspires to be global in scope and universal in acceptance, the ICC needs to demonstrate that it is not a neo-colonial institution investigating crimes in a few weak states, but should widen its scope of investigation and possible prosecution of crimes committed by the nationals of the most powerful states falling within its jurisdiction, while at the same time acting independently in deciding cases before it.

The right to an effective remedy is addressed by Sonja Starr in Chapter 25, 'The Right to an Effective Remedy: Balancing Realism and Aspiration'. Sonja notes that, of all the rights guaranteed under the UDHR, few have been so transformed over the last six decades as Article 8's right to an effective remedy. While the provision on effective remedy appears to have been an afterthought during the drafting of the UDHR, and the content of the remedy had been little developed for decades thereafter, Sonja identifies that the situation has now changed and that the international human rights community has successfully pushed for the creation of international remedial mechanisms, with international case law and instruments establishing the principles governing reparations. The chapter reviews the developments in that regard and assesses the current state of the law of remedies for human rights violations. Sonja traces the evolution of the individual right to an effective remedy, identifying the major types of remedies granted by international courts in human rights cases. She also discusses the corrective, expressive, structural, and deterrent purposes of remedies and the effectiveness of current remedial practice in accomplishing them. She argues that human rights law, committed in theory to the full remedy ideal but in practice often unable to realize it, is in need of a coherent set of principles governing the permissibility of remedial shortfall and the choice among second-best remedies in situations involving strong competing interests. In conclusion, she observes that six decades after its articulation in the UDHR, the right to an effective remedy remains a rapidly evolving component of human rights law, but its specific content has not been clearly defined. This is illustrated by the differences in remedial approach between the European and Inter-American Courts, two regional human rights courts with similar treaty mandates. Even wider variation is found among the multitude of other domestic and international courts and other remedial institutions. Every new institution with authority to grant reparations, such as the ICC and the African Court, offers the prospect of taking remedial doctrine in new and unexpected directions.

Generally, human rights become more vulnerable during emergency situations and so do human rights responsibilities and remedies. Vernor Muñoz Villalobos examines the respect for human rights in emergency situations in Chapter 26, 'Protecting Human Rights in Emergency Situations: The Example of the Right to Education'. This chapter focuses on the protection of human rights in emergency situations with particular reference to the right to education, since education is not only a human right in itself but also an indispensable means of realizing other human rights. Vernor notes that protecting the right to education in emergency situations can reinforce the protection of other human rights by creating a more favourable environment for the realization of human rights generally – for example, by empowering women, safeguarding children from exploitation, promoting human rights and democracy, and protecting the environment. He observes that six decades after the UDHR the commitment to realizing the human right to education has been a signal failure, especially in situations of emergency and for the vulnerable. He asserts that there remains an urgent need to redouble efforts to safeguard the right to education for the vulnerable – especially children, adolescents and youths – who are denied any possibility of attending school or attaining an education as the result, direct or indirect, of an emergency situation impacting their community. The chapter defines what constitutes emergency situations and stresses the importance of education in such situations. It also analyses the international legal and political framework for the protection of education in emergencies, and the role of donors and education providers, and notes that there is currently no single agency to which states requiring educational assistance can turn in an emergency. He concludes that the tolerance of the international community of the violation of the right to education in times of emergency is under challenge, and that it is our collective responsibility to rise to this challenge and ensure that the principle of an education for all, enshrined in the UDHR, is fully protected in emergency situations.

Part IV closes with by John Ruggie's Chapter 27, 'Protect, Respect, and Remedy: The UN Framework for Business and Human Rights', in which he examines the human rights responsibilities of corporate bodies. John observes that the international community is still in the early stages of adapting the current human rights regime to provide more effective protection to individuals and communities against corporate-related human rights harm. The chapter presents a principles-based conceptual and policy framework intended to help achieve that aim. The framework comprises three core principles; namely, the state duty to protect against human rights abuses by third parties, including business; the corporate responsibility to respect human rights; and the need for more effective access to remedies. John indicates that the three principles form a complementary whole in that each supports the others in achieving sustainable progress. After comprehensive analyses of each of the three principles, he concludes, *inter alia*, that while many countries, including in the developing world, have been able to take advantage of the new economic landscape to increase prosperity and reduce poverty, the rapid market expansion has also created governance gaps in numerous policy domains; the area of business and human rights is one such domain. While there have been a variety of measures, albeit gingerly introduced to date, to promote a corporate culture respectful of human rights, the fundamental problem is that there are too few of them, with none reaching a scale commensurate with the challenges at hand. That, John asserts, is what needs fixing, and that is what the framework of 'protect, respect and remedy' is intended to help achieve.

5.4 'And Beyond'

Part V, which forms the conclusion of this book, is entitled 'And Beyond', a phrase culled from the main title of the book. It aims to project a future for international human rights law beyond the six decades since the adoption of the UDHR. This part consists of Robert McCorquodale's Chapter 28, entitled appropriately, 'A Future for Human Rights Law'. With reference to the final words of the preamble of the UDHR, which indicates that 'every individual and every organ of society' is to promote respect for human rights and that they are to secure the universal and effective recognition and observance of human rights, Robert explores the possibilities that may arise in the future for human rights protections if international human rights law were to be inspired by the UDHR to extend legal obligations to individuals and other organs of society, that is, to non-state actors, and the impact that this could have on the universal and effective protection of international human rights. In that regard, the chapter examines non-state actors and human rights, including corporations, international organizations, opposition groups, social organizations, and the application of human rights to poverty. Robert concludes, *inter alia*, that the UDHR was a remarkable document when it was adopted just as the Cold War began, and, six decades later, it remains a remarkable document. He notes that human rights are only fully effective when they are lived in reality and that the mission of the UDHR was not aimed solely at states, or designed to create an international human rights law in which only states have legal obligations. Rather, its intention was to ensure that 'every individual and every organ of society' have responsibilities to promote respect for human rights and 'secure [the] universal and effective recognition and observance' of human rights. This was an appeal beyond states, and it is in this spirit that human rights law must be carried forward into the future.

6. Conclusion

It is certainly not possible to examine all the ways in which international human rights have developed theoretically and practically over the past six decades since the adoption of the UDHR, and beyond, in just one volume. Nevertheless, this book has endeavoured to capture as far as possible, through these chapters contributed by highly qualified publicists from various states and experts in different fields of international human rights law, the most relevant and significant issues in the development of international human rights law over the past six decades, issues that will certainly continue to influence its development for many decades into the future.

PART II
Concepts and Norms

Chapter 2
International Human Rights: Universal, Relative or Relatively Universal?

Jack Donnelly

1. Introduction

Universality is at the core of the global human rights regime. The foundational document is the UDHR,[1] the six decades of which this volume commemorates. The first operative paragraph of the Vienna Declaration and Programme of Action of the 1993 World Human Rights Conference goes so far as to assert that 'the universal nature of these rights and freedoms is beyond question.'[2] And indeed this is close to true at the level of interstate relations. Virtually every state acknowledges an authoritative body of international human rights law that flows from the UDHR.

Nonetheless, claims of cultural, historical, and socio-political relativity have been and remain central features of international human rights discussions. During the Cold War era, arguments of distinct socialist and Third World conceptions of human rights produced 'three worlds' arguments[3] that persist today in the 'three generations' narrative of the historical development of modern human rights ideas.[4] In the post-Cold War era, 'Asian values' advocates[5] and Islamists have prominently and powerfully challenged the universality of internationally recognized human

1 G.A. res. 217A (III), UN Doc. A/810 at 71 (1948).

2 A/CONF.157/23 of 12 July 1993, para. 1.

3 See e.g. H. Gros Espiell, 'The Evolving Concept of Human Rights: Western, Socialist and Third World Approaches', in B.G. Ramcharan (ed.), *Human Rights: Thirty Years After the Universal Declaration* (The Hague: Martinus Nijhoff, 1979), p. 49; A. Pollis, 'Liberal, Socialist, and Third World Perspectives on Human Rights', in P. Schwab and A. Pollis (eds), *Toward a Human Rights Framework* (New York: Praeger, 1982), p. 1.

4 See S.P. Marks, 'Emerging Human Rights: A New Generation for the 1980s?', *Rutgers Law Review*, 33 (1981), p. 435; K. Vasak, 'Pour une troisième génération des droits de l'homme', in C. Swinarski (ed.), *Studies and Essays on International Humanitarian Law and Red Cross Principles in Honour of Jean Pictet* (The Hague: Martinus Nijhoff, 1984); K. Vasak, 'Les Différentes catégories des droits de l'homme', in A. Lapeyre, F. de Tinguy and K. Vasak (eds), *Les Dimensions universelles des droits de l'homme* (Bruxelles: Émile Bruylant, 1991). M. Ishay, *The History of Human Rights: From Ancient Times to the Globalization Era* (Berkeley, CA: University of California Press, 2004), presents a relatively sophisticated post-Cold War version of this argument. For a counter-argument, see J. Donnelly, 'Third Generation Rights' in C. Brolmann, R. Lefeber and M. Zieck (eds), *Peoples and Minorities in International Law* (The Hague: Kluwer, 1993).

5 A.J. Langlois, *The Politics of Justice and Human Rights* (Cambridge: Cambridge University Press, 2001), offers perhaps the best overview. For useful collections of essays, see J.R. Bauer and D.A. Bell (eds), *The East Asian Challenge for Human Rights* (Cambridge: Cambridge University Press, 1999), and M. Jacobsen and O. Bruun (eds), *Human Rights and Asian Values: Contesting National Identities and Cultural Representations in Asia* (Richmond: Curzon, 2000).

rights. In addition, increasingly popular post-structuralist and post-colonial perspectives stress the contingent particularities of the dominant human rights discourse.[6]

This chapter argues that 'each side' in the universality–relativity debate rests on important insights about the nature of human rights. I argue, however, that the standard terms of the debate – 'Are human rights universal or relative?' – are misformulated. 'Universality' and 'relativity' are multifaceted concepts that are not necessarily incompatible. Human rights are indeed 'universal' in some standard and important senses of that term – but not 'universal' in some equally standard senses. Likewise, human rights both are and are not 'relative' in standard senses of that term. The real issue is not *whether* human rights are universal or relative but *how* they are (and are not) universal, how they are (and are not) relative, and how these relativities and universalities interact, in theory and in practice.

2. 'Universal' and 'Relative'

The first definition of 'universal' in the *Oxford English Dictionary* (*OED*) is 'Extending over, comprehending, or including the whole of something'. Universal, in this sense, is 'relative' to a particular class or group. For example, universal health care, universal primary education, and universal suffrage, as those concepts are ordinarily used, involve providing health care, primary education, and voting rights (only) to all citizens, nationals, or residents of a particular state. Universality, in that sense, is relative to residence or citizenship. Similarly, a universal remote control operates (almost) all types of currently standard home entertainment devices, but not all present, let alone all past or possible, such devices.

'Universal' also is defined as 'of or pertaining to the universe in general or all things in it; existing or occurring everywhere or in all things' (*OED*).[7] Little is universal in this sense, other than formal logical systems of propositions, such as mathematics, and perhaps some of the laws of physics (or God). Thus, the *OED* describes this sense as 'chiefly poetic or rhetorical' (to which, I think, we could add 'philosophical' or 'theological'). This 'occurring everywhere' sense of universal is secondary and specialized. The primary sense of universality is relative to a particular 'universe' of application (rather than everywhere in the universe).

The parallel *OED* definitions of 'relative' are 'arising from, depending on, or determined by, relation to something else or to each other' and 'constituted, or existing, only by relation to something else; not absolute or independent'. Talk of relativity immediately calls forth the question, 'Relative to what?' Something cannot be relative in general but must always be relative to (or dependent on) something else in particular.

Even this simple definitional exercise allows us to identify a number of standard problems in discussions of the universality and relativity of human rights. For example, from a denial of the ontological, 'applies anywhere' universality of human rights, it does not follow that other important forms of universality cannot be defended. And that human rights are not ontologically universal does not entail that they are *culturally* relative. (Below, I will argue that they are instead relative to social structure.) On the 'universalist' side, the nature of the asserted universality of human rights often is either left unspecified or defended in ontological terms (for example, in contemporary

6 See Section 8 below.

7 *The American Heritage Dictionary* has almost identical definitions, although this definition, which is third in the *Oxford*, is first in the *American Heritage*, and the first *Oxford* definition is second in the *American Heritage*.

Roman Catholic natural law social teaching) that are acceptable to only a tiny proportion of those who endorse internationally recognized human rights. And both sides often are unwilling to acknowledge, let alone explore, the insights of the other.

The following sections identify three senses in which human rights are, in the contemporary world, reasonably understood as universal. I call these (1) international legal universality (2) functional universality, and (3) overlapping consensus universality. I then consider two senses, which I call ontological and historical (or anthropological) universality, in which I argue that human rights are not universal. I then consider, more briefly, some standard 'relativist' arguments before, in the final section, defending the summary assessment that human rights are 'relatively universal'. Here I will simply note that the term is not paradoxical. Rather, it recognizes that the universality of human rights is relative to particular contexts (specified in the following sections).

3. International Legal Universality

Virtually all states accept the authority of the UDHR, which has been further elaborated in a series of widely ratified treaties. As of 31 December 2009, the six core international human rights treaties (on economic, social, and cultural rights; civil and political rights; racial discrimination; women's rights; torture; and rights of the child) had on average 170 parties.[8] This truly impressive 87% ratification rate establishes what we can call *international legal universality*. Human rights are universal within the domain of contemporary international law.

The universality of these rights is 'beyond question' not in the sense that no one violates, challenges, or denounces them but rather in the sense that such challenges and violations are treated as beyond the pale. International human rights law can only be rejected by challenging the whole body of contemporary international law. Such challenges are indeed advanced by philosophers, political radicals, revolutionary groups, and even the occasional revolutionary regime. But challenges to the international legal universality of internationally recognized human rights are typically ruled 'out of the question'. They simply are not seriously engaged – in much the same way that in most national legal systems, challenges to a national constitution that has been accepted as authoritative for decades or centuries are dismissed out of hand, rather than seriously considered, by national courts and political authorities.

Such international legal universality is often described as reflecting 'hegemony', a combination of authority and force in which conventional legitimacy plays the central role (although ultimately backed by the coercive resources of dominant power).[9] Whatever the exact mixture of force and authority in maintaining a hegemonic doctrine or order – it varies dramatically with time, place, and issue – the essential point is that in contemporary international society a 'hegemonic'/authoritative system of international legal principles gives an important element of universality to internationally recognized human rights.

---

8 This figure was calculated from the ratification data available at http://www2.ohchr.org/english/bodies/ratification/index.htm. The Convention Against Torture had a low of 146 parties and the Convention on the Rights of the Child had a high of 193 (of a possible 195) parties.

9 This sense of hegemony derives from the work of Antonio Gramsci. See, especially, A. Gramsci, *Selections from the Prison Notebooks* (New York: International Publishers, 1971). Among secondary sources, J.V. Femia, *Gramsci's Political Thought: Hegemony, Consciousness, and the Revolutionary Process* (Oxford: Clarendon Press, 1981), and S. Gill (ed.), *Gramsci, Historical Materialism and International Relations* (Cambridge: Cambridge University Press, 1993), provide very different kinds of useful introductions.

Over the past six decades, the UDHR has indeed become, as it describes itself, 'a common standard of achievement for all peoples and all nations',[10] a standard of international legitimacy. Sovereignty, however, is another standard of international (legal) legitimacy, and one that typically takes priority over human rights. States that systematically violate internationally recognized human rights usually retain their sovereign legitimacy. Nonetheless, their 'legitimacy' is tarnished or diminished. Consider Robert Mugabe's Zimbabwe. Today, those desiring full political legitimacy must be seen as, if not committed to internationally recognized human rights, then not violating them too seriously. For example, China has (very reluctantly) adopted the language (although not too much of the practice) of human rights, seemingly as an inescapable precondition to its full recognition as a great power. And in the case of genocide, human rights violations may even trump sovereignty (e.g. East Timor and Kosovo), something that was unthinkable when the UDHR was drafted.

In the first few decades following the drafting of the UDHR, this international legal universality was rather superficial, both in breadth and depth. It did not penetrate very deeply even in interstate relations. Major progress began in the mid-1970s, however, symbolized by the Helsinki Final Act of 1975,[11] the election of Jimmy Carter as President of the United States in 1976, and the award of the Nobel Peace Prize to Amnesty International in 1977. Another spurt of spread and deepening took place in the 1990s, with the result that today international human rights norms have come to penetrate, surprisingly, deeply in most regions (the Middle East being the principal exception). Particularly notable is the fact that movements for social justice and of political opposition have increasingly adopted the language of human rights. In addition, growing numbers of new international issues, ranging from migration, to global trade and finance, to access to pharmaceuticals are being framed as issues of human rights.[12]

The relativity of this international legal universality deserves note. It holds (only) within a particular universe, namely, among states, who are the principal source and subjects of international law, and political actors who principally target state policy. It is further relative to a particular time. And it is deeply contingent in the sense that this universality was produced by mechanisms that in the past did not and in the future might not produce such widespread endorsement. We might want to relativize this universality even further by stressing its incompleteness, in the sense that a number of states continue to resist, more or less strenuously, these hegemonic international norms.

Nonetheless, international legal universality is of immense theoretical and practical significance. Sovereign territorial states, the designated class, remain by far the most important actors in determining whether people enjoy the human rights that they have. The formal endorsement of international human rights obligations thus is of immense importance. Furthermore, local activists, transnational advocates, and foreign states can appeal to widely endorsed international norms that, in almost all cases, the target state has itself repeatedly accepted as binding. This greatly facilitates the work of human rights advocacy and defence.

Of course, tomorrow, states and movements of political opposition may no longer accept or give as much weight to human rights. Today, however, they clearly have chosen human rights over competing conceptions of national and international political legitimacy. This, I would suggest, is the most important practical legacy of the UDHR.

10 UDHR, Preamble, para. 8.

11 Adopted 1 August 1975, 14 ILM, 1292.

12 A. Brysk, *Human Rights, Private Wrongs* (New York: Routledge, 2005).

4. Overlapping Consensus Universality

Law lies at the intersection of power and justice. We thus should expect to find international legal universality both backed by preponderant political power and reflecting deeper ethical, moral, or religious values. It certainly is not coincidental that the world's leading military and economic powers – the United States, Western Europe, and Japan – all strongly support internationally recognized human rights. I want to focus instead, however, on the cross-cultural ethical foundations of internationally recognized human rights.

The philosopher John Rawls distinguishes 'comprehensive religious, philosophical, or moral doctrines', such as Islam, Kantianism, Confucianism, and Marxism, from 'political conceptions of justice', which address only the political structure of society, defined (as far as possible) as independent of any particular comprehensive doctrine.[13] Adherents of different comprehensive doctrines may be able to reach an 'overlapping consensus' on a political conception of justice.[14] Such a consensus is overlapping; partial rather than complete. It is political rather than moral or religious. But it is real and important. Although Rawls developed the notion to understand liberal national societies, it has obvious application to a culturally and politically diverse international society.[15] International human rights, I want to argue, have what I will call *overlapping consensus universality.*

Human rights can be grounded in a variety of comprehensive doctrines. For example, they can be seen as encoded in natural law, called for by divine commandment, political means to further human good or utility, or institutions to produce virtuous citizens. Over the past few decades, more and more adherents of a growing range of comprehensive doctrines in all regions of the world have come to endorse human rights – (but only) as a political conception of justice.[16]

It is important to note that within the West as well, human rights rest on an overlapping consensus. Thomists and utilitarians, for example, agree about little at the level of comprehensive doctrines; Thomists do not even consider utilitarianism a moral theory. Nonetheless, most contemporary adherents of both comprehensive doctrines endorse human rights as a political conception of justice.

This, however, is a rather recent phenomenon. Aquinas had no conception of natural rights. Bentham, often considered the founder of modern utilitarianism, famously described natural rights as 'simple nonsense' and imprescriptible natural rights as 'nonsense upon stilts'. Until the mid-

---

13 J. Rawls, *The Law of Peoples* (Cambridge, MA: Harvard University Press, 1999), pp. xliii–xlv, 11–15, 174–6; J. Rawls, *Political Liberalism* (New York: Columbia University Press, 1996), pp. 31–3, 172–3.

14 Rawls, *Political Liberalism*, note 13 above, pp. 133–72, 385–96.

15 Rawls, *Law of Peoples*, note 13 above. Rawls's own extension involves both a wider political conception of justice and a narrower list of internationally recognized human rights. The account offered here is Rawlsian in inspiration but not that of John Rawls.

16 H. Bielefeldt, '"Western" versus "Islamic" Human Rights Conceptions?: A Critique of Cultural Essentialism in the Discussion of Human Rights', *Political Theory*, 28 (2000), p. 90, makes a similar argument, illustrated by a discussion of recent trends in Islamic thinking on human rights. See also A.K. Peetush, 'Cultural Diversity, Non-Western Communities, and Human Rights', *The Philosophical Forum*, 34 (2003), p. 1, which deals with South Asian views. For a looser account of cross-cultural consensus, see A. An-Na'im, 'Toward a Cross-Cultural Approach to Defining International Standards of Human Rights: The Meaning of Cruel, Inhuman, or Degrading Treatment or Punishment', in A. An-Na'im (ed.), *Human Rights in Cross-Cultural Perspectives: A Quest for Consensus* (Philadelphia: University of Pennsylvania Press, 1992).

twentieth century, virtually all utilitarians were hostile to natural or human rights[17] and human rights were almost completely foreign to Thomist moral and political thought[18] (which relied almost exclusively on the language of duty). Over the past several decades, however, prominent Thomists have enthusiastically endorsed human rights and human rights have become central to contemporary Catholic social teaching.[19] Utilitarian defences of human rights – especially as second-order rules justified by the principle of utility; that is, as something like a political conception of justice – are also common.[20] And in the domain of ordinary, day-to-day politics, most utilitarians and Thomists have no difficulty in accepting human rights, and often do so with considerable enthusiasm.

In fact, virtually all Western religious and philosophical doctrines through most of their history have either rejected or ignored human rights, understood as equal and inalienable entitlements held by all human beings that can be exercised against the state and society. Today, however, most adherents of most Western comprehensive doctrines endorse human rights. There is no logical reason why a similar transformation could not happen elsewhere. If the medieval Christian world of crusades, serfdom, and hereditary aristocracy could become today's world of liberal and social democratic welfare states, it is hard to imagine a place where a similar transformation would be impossible. And just such a transformation has indeed been taking place over the last several decades.

Perhaps the most unpromising cultural environment is the traditional Hindu caste system, which not only stressed categorical, qualitative moral differences between different descent-based groups (castes) but even denied moral significance to a category of human beings. Gandhi, however, showed that it is possible to reshape Hindu traditions to support a fundamentally egalitarian conception of human rights. And, in practice, India has been, both at home and abroad, one of the leading Third World supporters of internationally recognized human rights.

Or consider claims that '[East] Asian values' are incompatible with internationally recognized human rights.[21] Asian values – like Western values, African values, and most other sets of values – can be, and have been, understood as incompatible with human rights. But they also can be and have been interpreted to support human rights, as they regularly are today in Japan, Taiwan, and South Korea. And political developments in a growing number of Asian countries suggest that ordinary people and even governments are increasingly viewing human rights as a contemporary political expression of their deepest ethical, cultural, and political values and aspirations.[22]

---

17 See e.g. D.G. Ritchie, *Natural Rights: A Criticism of Some Political and Ethical Conceptions* (London: S. Sonnenschein & Co., 1895).

18 On Aquinas in particular, see J. Donnelly, 'Natural Law and Right in Aquinas' Political Thought', *Western Political Quarterly*, 33 (1980), p. 520.

19 See e.g. J. Maritain, *The Rights of Man and Natural Law* (New York: C. Scribner's Sons, 1943); J. Finnis, *Natural Law and Natural Rights* (Oxford: Clarendon Press, 1980); and papal encyclicals such as *Pacem in Terris* (John XXIII, 1963) and *Redemptor Hominis* (John Paul II, 1979).

20 See e.g. D. Lyons, 'Human Rights and the General Welfare', *Philosophy and Public Affairs*, 6 (1977), p. 113; D. Lyons, 'Utility and Rights' in J. Chapman (ed.), *Nomos XXIV: Ethics, Economic and the Law* (New York: New York University Press, 1982); R.G. Frey (ed.), *Utility and Rights* (Minneapolis, MN: University of Minnesota Press, 1984); R. Hardin, 'The Utilitarian Logic of Liberalism', *Ethics*, 97 (1986), p. 47; and R.B. Brandt, *Morality, Utilitarianism, and Rights* (Cambridge: Cambridge University Press, 1992).

21 See note 5.

22 'Confucians can make sense of rights out of the resources of their own tradition', M. Sim, 'A Confucian Approach to Human Rights', *History of Philosophy Quarterly*, 21 (2004), pp. 337, 338. Cf. J. Chan, 'Moral Autonomy, Civil Liberties, and Confucianism', 52 *Philosophy East and West*, 52 (2002), p. 281, and J. Chan, 'Confucian Perspective on Human Rights for Contemporary China', in J. Bauer and D.A. Bell (eds), *The East Asian Challenge for Human Rights* (Cambridge: Cambridge University Press, 1999). On Confucianism and

No culture or comprehensive doctrine is 'by nature', or in any given or fixed way, either compatible or incompatible with human rights. Whatever their past practice, nothing in indigenous African, Asian, or American cultures prevents them from endorsing human rights now. Cultures are immensely malleable, as are the political expressions of comprehensive doctrines. It is an empirical question whether (any, some, or most) members of a culture or exponents of a comprehensive doctrine support human rights as a political conception of justice.

All major civilizations have for long periods treated a significant portion of the human race as 'outsiders' not entitled to guarantees that could be taken for granted by 'insiders'. Few areas of the globe, for example, have never practised and widely justified human bondage. All literate civilizations have for most of their histories assigned social roles, rights, and duties primarily on the basis of ascriptive characteristics such as birth, age, and gender.

Today, however, the moral equality of all human beings is strongly endorsed by most leading comprehensive doctrines in all regions of the world. This convergence, both within and between civilizations, provides the foundation for a convergence on the rights of the UDHR. In principle, a great variety of social practices other than human rights might provide the basis for realizing foundational egalitarian values. In practice, human rights are rapidly becoming the preferred option.

Is this transnational overlapping consensus more voluntary or coerced? Although the power and influence of the United States and Western Europe should not be underestimated, I want to suggest that example has been more powerful than advocacy and that coercion has typically played much less of a role than positive inducements. Human rights dominate political discussions less because of pressure from materially or culturally dominant powers than because they respond to some of the most important social and political aspirations of individuals, families, and groups in most countries of the world. The consensus on the UDHR, it seems to me, principally reflects its cross-cultural substantive attractions. People, when given a chance, usually (in the contemporary world) choose human rights, irrespective of region, religion, or culture. The transnational consensus on the UDHR arises above all from the largely voluntary decisions of people, states, and other political actors that human rights are essential to protecting their visions of a life of dignity.

5. Functional Universality

How can we explain this consensus? Those who focus on culture will find it inexplicable – and thus are likely to appeal to power, imposition, and 'cultural imperialism'. I want to suggest instead that it rests on social-structural features that are relatively universal in the contemporary world. Internationally recognized human rights respond to certain standard threats to human dignity associated with modern markets and modern states in every part of the globe today. This creates what I will call the *functional universality* of internationally recognized human rights.

Natural or human rights ideas first developed in the West. John Locke's *Second Treatise of Government*, published in 1689 in support of the so-called Glorious Revolution in Britain, offers one of the first full-fledged natural rights political theories. The American and French Revolutions first used such ideas to construct new political orders. I want to draw attention, however, to the

---

modern social and political practices, see D.A. Bell and Hahm Chaibong (eds), *Confucianism for the Modern World* (Cambridge: Cambridge University Press, 2003).

social-structural 'modernity' of these ideas and practices, rather than their cultural 'Westernness'.[23] Human rights ideas and practices arose not from any deep Western cultural roots but from the social, economic, and political transformations of modernity. They thus have relevance wherever those transformations have occurred, irrespective of the pre-existing culture of the place.

Nothing in classical or medieval culture specially predisposed Europeans to develop human rights ideas. Even early modern Europe, when viewed without the benefit of hindsight, appears as a particularly unconducive cultural milieu for human rights. No widely endorsed reading of Christian scriptures supported the idea of a broad set of equal and inalienable individual rights held by all Christians, let alone all human beings. Violent, often brutal, internecine and international religious warfare was the norm. The divine right of kings was the reigning orthodoxy. Nonetheless, in early modern Europe, ever more powerful and penetrating (capitalist) markets and (sovereign, bureaucratic) states disrupted, destroyed, or radically transformed 'traditional' communities and their systems of social support and obligation. Rapidly expanding numbers of (relatively) separate families and individuals were thus left to face a growing range of increasingly unbuffered economic and political threats to their interests and dignity. New 'standard threats'[24] to human dignity provoked new remedial responses.

One solution was the absolutist state, which offered a society organized around a monarchist hierarchy justified by a state religion. The newly emergent bourgeoisie, by contrast, envisioned a society in which the claims of property balanced those of birth. And as 'modernization' progressed, an ever widening range of marginalized and dispossessed groups advanced claims for relief from injustices and disabilities. Such demands took many forms, including appeals to scripture, Church, morality, tradition, justice, natural law, order, social utility, and national strength. Claims of equal and inalienable natural/human rights, however, became increasingly central. And the successes of some groups opened political space for others to advance similar claims for their equal rights.

The spread of modern markets and states has globalized the same threats to human dignity initially experienced in Europe. Human rights represent the most effective response yet devised to a wide range of standard threats to human dignity that market economies and bureaucratic states have made nearly universal across the globe. Human rights today remain the only proven effective means to ensure human dignity in societies dominated by markets and states. Although historically contingent and relative, this functional universality fully merits the label 'universal', for us, today.

Arguments that another state, society, or culture has developed plausible and effective alternative mechanisms for protecting or realizing human dignity in the contemporary world certainly deserve serious attention. Today, however, such claims, when not advanced by repressive elites and their supporters, usually refer to an allegedly possible world that no one yet has had the good fortune to experience. The alleged success stories of the Cold War era, for example, have collapsed in tragic failure, often with dreadful human consequences.

The functional universality of human rights depends on human rights providing attractive remedies for some of the most pressing systemic threats to human dignity. Human rights today do precisely that for a growing number of people of all cultures in all regions. Whatever our other problems, we all must deal with market economies and bureaucratic states. Whatever our other

---

23 Cf. M. Goodhart, 'Origins and Universality in the Human Rights Debate: Cultural Essentialism and the Challenge of Globalization' *Human Rights Quarterly*, 25 (2003), p. 935. A. Sharma, *Are Human Rights Western? A Contribution to the Dialogue of Civilizations* (New Delhi: Oxford University Press, 2006), exhaustively explores the wide variety of senses in which human rights have been held to be 'Western'.

24 H. Shue, *Basic Rights: Subsistence, Affluence, and U.S. Foreign Policy* (Princeton, NJ: Princeton University Press, 1980), pp. 29–34.

religious, moral, legal, and political resources, we all need equal and inalienable universal human rights to protect us from those threats.

6. Historical or Anthropological Universality

Human rights are often held to be universal in the sense that most societies and cultures have practised human rights throughout most of their history. 'All societies cross-culturally and historically manifest conceptions of human rights.'[25] This has generated a large body of literature on so-called non-Western conceptions of human rights. 'In almost all contemporary Arab literature on this subject [human rights], we find a listing of the basic rights established by modern conventions and declarations, and then a serious attempt to trace them back to Koranic texts'.[26] 'It is not often remembered that traditional African societies supported and practiced human rights.'[27] 'Protection of human rights is an integral part' of the traditions of Asian societies.[28] 'All the countries [of the Asian region] would agree that "human rights" as a concept existed in their tradition.'[29] Even the Hindu caste system has been described as a "traditional, multidimensional view of human rights.'[30]

Such claims confuse values such as justice, fairness, and humanity, with human rights. Rights – entitlements that ground claims with a special force – are a particular kind of social practice. Human rights – equal and inalienable entitlements of all individuals that may be exercised against the state and society – are a distinctive way to seek to realize social values such as justice and human flourishing. There may be considerable historical/anthropological universality of values across time and culture. No society, civilization, or culture prior to the seventeenth century, however, had a widely endorsed vision, let alone practice, of equal and inalienable individual human rights.[31]

---

25 A. Pollis and P. Schwab, 'Human Rights: A Western Construct with Limited Applicability', in A. Pollis and P. Schwab (eds), *Human Rights: Cultural and Ideological Perspective* (New York: Praeger, 1979), p. 15. Cf. M. Mutua, 'The Banjul Charter and the African Cultural Fingerprint: An Evaluation of the Language of Duties', *Virginia Journal of International Law*, 35 (1995), pp. 339, 358; D.R. Penna and P.J. Campbell, 'Human Rights and Culture: Beyond Universality and Relativism', *Third World Quarterly*, 19 (1998), pp. 7, 21.

26 F. Zakaria, 'Human Rights in the Arab World: The Islamic Context', in UNESCO (ed.), *Philosophical Foundations of Human Rights* (Paris: UNESCO, 1986), p. 228.

27 D.M. Wai, 'Human Rights in Sub-Saharan Africa', in A. Pollis and P. Schwab (eds), *Human Rights: Cultural and Ideological Perspectives* (New York: Praeger, 1980), p. 116.

28 Ibrahim Anwar, Luncheon Address. Paper read at JUST International Conference, 'Rethinking Human Rights', at Kuala Lumpur, 7 December 1994.

29 R. Coomaraswamy, 'Human Rights Research and Education: An Asian Perspective', in *International Congress on the Teaching of Human Rights: Working Documents and Recommendations* (Paris: UNESCO, 1980), p. 224.

30 R. Buultjens, 'Human Rights in Indian Political Culture', in K.W. Thompson (ed.), *The Moral Imperatives of Human Rights: A World Survey* (Washington, DC: University Press of America, 1980), p. 113. Cf. Y. Khushalani, 'Human Rights in Asia and Africa' *Human Rights Law Journal*, 4 (1983), pp. 403, 408; M.L. Stackhouse, *Creeds, Society, and Human Rights: A Study in Three Cultures* (Grand Rapids, MI: William B. Eerdmans, 1984).

31 For detailed support for this claim, see J. Donnelly, *Universal Human Rights in Theory and Practice*, 2nd edn (Ithaca, NY: Cornell University Press, 2003), ch. 5. On Africa in particular, see R.E. Howard, *Human Rights in Commonwealth Africa* (Totowa, NJ: Rowman & Littlefield, 1986), ch. 2.

For example, Dunstan Wai argues that traditional African beliefs and institutions sustained the 'view that certain rights should be upheld against alleged necessities of state'.[32] This confuses human rights with limited government.[33] Government has been limited on a variety of grounds other than human rights, including divine commandment, legal rights, and extralegal checks such as a balance of power or the threat of popular revolt. '[T]he concept of human rights concerns the relationship between the individual and the state; it involves the status, claims, and duties of the former in the jurisdiction of the latter. As such, it is a subject as old as politics.'[34] Not all political relationships, however, are governed by, related to, or even consistent with, human rights. What the state owes those it rules is indeed a perennial question of politics. Human rights provide one answer. Other answers include divine right monarchy, the dictatorship of the proletariat, the principle of utility, aristocracy, theocracy, and democracy.

'[D]ifferent civilizations or societies have different conceptions of human well-being. Hence, they have a different attitude toward human rights issues.'[35] Even this is misleading. Other societies may have (similar or different) attitudes toward issues that we consider today to be matters of human rights. But without a widely understood concept of human rights endorsed or advocated by some important segment of that society, it is hard to imagine that they could have any attitude toward human rights. And it is precisely the idea of equal and inalienable rights that one has simply because one is a human being that was missing not only in traditional Asian, African, Islamic, but in traditional Western societies as well.

The ancient Greeks, for example, distinguished between Hellenes and barbarians, practised slavery, denied basic rights to foreigners, and (by human rights standards) severely restricted the rights of even free adult (male) citizens. In medieval Europe, where the spiritual egalitarianism and universality of Christianity expressed itself in deeply inegalitarian politics, the idea of equal legal and political rights for all human beings, had it been seriously contemplated, would have been seen as a moral abomination, a horrid transgression against God's order. In the 'pre-modern' world, both Western and non-Western alike, the duty of rulers to further the common good arose not from the rights (entitlements) of all human beings, or even all subjects, but from divine commandment, natural law, tradition, or contingent political arrangements. The people could legitimately expect to benefit from the obligations of their rulers to rule justly. Neither in theory nor in practice, though, did they have human rights that could be exercised against unjust rulers. The reigning ideas were natural law and natural right (in the sense of righteousness or rectitude), not natural or human rights (in the sense of equal and inalienable individual entitlements). Arguments of anthropological universality, rather than show cultural sensitivity and respect, misunderstand and misrepresent the

---

32 Wai, note 25 above, p. 116.

33 Cf. A. Legesse, 'Human Rights in African Political Culture', in K.W. Thompson (ed.), *The Moral Imperatives of Human Rights: A World Survey* (Washington, DC: University Press of America, 1980), pp. 125–7; NKAJ Busia, 'The Status of Human Rights in Pre-Colonial Africa: Implications for Contemporary Practices', in E. McCarthy-Arnolds, D.R. Penna and D.J.C. Sobrepena (eds), *Africa, Human Rights, and the Global System: The Political Economy of Human Rights in a Changing World* (Westport, CT: Greenwood Press, 1994), p. 231. For non-African examples, see A.A. Said, 'Precept and Practice of Human Rights in Islam', *Universal Human Rights*, 1 (1979), pp. 63, 65; R. Mangalpus, 'Human Rights Are Not a Western Discovery', *Worldview*, 4 (October) (1978); A. Pollis and P. Schwab, 'Introduction', in A. Pollis and P. Schwab (eds), *Human Rights: Cultural and Ideological Perspectives* (New York: Praeger, 1979), p. xiv.

34 H.-C. Tai, 'Human Rights in Taiwan: Convergence of Two Political Cultures?', in J.C. Hsiung (ed.), *Human Rights in an East Asian Perspective* (New York: Paragon House Publishers, 1985), p. 79.

35 M. Lee, 'North Korea and the Western Notion of Human Rights', in J.C. Hsiung, note 34 above, p. 131.

foundations and functioning of the societies in question by anachronistically imposing an alien analytical framework.

I am not claiming that Islam, Confucianism, or traditional African ideas cannot support internationally recognized human rights. Quite the contrary, I have already argued that in practice today they increasingly do support human rights. My point is simply that Islamic, Confucian, and African societies did not in fact develop significant bodies of human rights ideas or practices prior to the twentieth century – any more than Western societies did prior to the modern era. Throughout most of history in all parts of the world, questions of social justice and human dignity were considered to have nothing at all to do with equal and inalienable rights that all human beings held simply because they were human. Unless we appreciate the historical particularity and contingency of internationally recognized human rights, we cannot understand their essential nature and the functions that they do (and do not) perform in the contemporary world.

7. Ontological Universality

Overlapping consensus implies that human rights can, and in the contemporary world do, have multiple and diverse 'foundations'. A single trans-historical foundation would provide what I will call *ontological universality*.[36] Although a single moral code may indeed be objectively correct and valid at all times in all places, at least three problems make ontological universality substantively implausible and politically unappealing.

First, no matter how strenuously adherents of a particular philosophy or religion insist that (their) values are objectively valid, they are unable to persuade adherents of other religions or philosophies to adopt them. This failure to agree leaves us in pretty much the same position as if there were no objective values at all. We are thrown back on arguments of functional, international legal, and overlapping consensus universality (understood now, perhaps, as imperfect reflections of a deeper ontological universality). Second, all prominent comprehensive doctrines have for large parts of their history ignored or actively denied human rights. It is highly improbable that any objectively correct doctrine has been interpreted incorrectly so widely. Thus, it is unlikely that human rights in general, and the particular list in the UDHR, are ontologically universal. Third, if human rights were ontologically universal, then the fact that virtually all moral and religious theories through most of their histories have rejected human rights would mean that these theories have been objectively false or immoral. Before we embrace such a radical idea, I think we need much stronger arguments than are currently available to support the ontological universality of human rights.

Overlapping consensus, rather than render human rights groundless, gives them multiple grounds. Whatever its analytical and philosophical virtues or shortcomings, this is of great practical utility. Those who want (or feel morally compelled) to make ontological claims can do so with no need to convince or compel others to accept this particular, or even any, foundation. Treating human rights as a Rawlsian political conception of justice thus allows us to address a wide range of issues of political justice and right while circumventing not merely inconclusive but often pointlessly divisive disputes over moral foundations.

---

36 For a recent attempt to defend ontological universality, see W.J. Talbott, *Which Rights Should Be Universal?* (New York: Oxford University Press, 2005). The most cited such argument is that of A. Gewirth, *Human Rights: Essays on Justification and Applications* (Chicago: University of Chicago Press, 1982).

8. Forms of Relativism

Having considered a variety of possible senses of 'universality', I now want to turn, more briefly, to 'relativity'. What makes (or is alleged to make) human rights relative? Relative to what? We have already seen that they are historically relative. Here I consider four other types of relativity.

8.1 National Implementation of International Human Rights

International legal, overlapping consensus, and functional universality are all essentially normative. International human rights law establishes international legal obligations. The practice of states, however, often diverges substantially from these obligations. Overlapping consensus and functional universality identify moral-religious and sociological foundations that point to the value and desirability of the practice of human rights. They do not ensure that such desirable practices actually occur.

Although we *have* human rights universally, simply as human beings, we *enjoy* them as a result of contingent political and legal practices. This relativity of the implementation and enjoyment, however, is not just accidental but also systematic. The global human rights regime relies on national implementation of internationally recognized human rights. Norm creation has been internationalized. Enforcement of authoritative international human rights norms, however, is left almost entirely to sovereign states. Except in the European regional regime, supranational supervisory bodies are largely restricted to monitoring how states implement their international human rights obligations. Transnational human rights NGOs and other national and international advocates engage in largely persuasive activity, aimed at changing the human rights practices of states. Foreign states are free to raise human rights violations as an issue of concern but have no authority to implement or enforce human rights within another state's sovereign jurisdiction. The few and limited exceptions – most notably genocide, crimes against humanity, certain war crimes, and perhaps torture and arbitrary execution – only underscore the almost complete sovereign authority of states to implement human rights in their territories as they see fit. The implementation and enforcement of universally held human rights thus is extremely relative, largely a function of where one has the (good or bad) fortune to live.

There is another dimension of implementation where relativity is not merely a fact but desirable. Human rights are (relatively) universal at the level of the *concept*, broad formulations such as the claims in Articles 3 and 22 of the UDHR that 'everyone has the right to life, liberty and the security of person' and 'the right to social security'. Particular rights concepts, however, have multiple defensible *conceptions*. Any particular conception, in turn, will have many defensible *implementations*. At this level – for example, the design of electoral systems to implement the right 'to take part in the government of his country, directly or through freely chosen representatives' (Article 21) – relativity is not merely defensible but desirable.

Functional and overlapping consensus universality lies primarily at the level of concepts. These concepts, as formulated in the UDHR, set a range of plausible variations among conceptions, which in turn restrict the range of practices that can plausibly be considered implementations of a particular concept and conception. In addition to this relativity, we should also take seriously the idea that even some deviations from authoritative international human rights norms may be, all things considered, (not il)legitimate, especially when they involve one or a few relatively isolated exceptions that are of considerable local importance to active participants in the overlapping consensus.

8.2 Self-Determination and Sovereignty

Self-determination and sovereignty ground a tolerant relativism based on the mutual recognition of peoples/states in an international community. Self-determination, understood as an ethical principle, involves a claim that a free people is entitled to choose for itself its own way of life and its own form of government. The language of 'democracy' is also often used. Democratic self-determination is a communal expression of the principles of equality and autonomy that lie at the heart of the idea of human rights.

Whether a particular practice is in fact the free choice of a free people, however, is an empirical question. And self-determination must not be confused with legal sovereignty. Legally sovereign states need not satisfy the ethical principle of self-determination. Too often, repressive regimes falsely claim to reflect the will of the people. Too often, international legal sovereignty shields regimes that violate both ethical self-determination and most internationally recognized human rights – a fact that brings us back to the relative enjoyment of human rights, based largely on where one happens to live.

Often, the result is a conflict between justice, represented by human rights and self-determination, and order, represented by international legal sovereignty. Non-intervention in the face of even systematic human rights violations dramatically decreases potentially violent conflicts between states. We can also see international legal sovereignty as an ethical principle of the society of states, a principle of mutual toleration and respect for (state) equality and autonomy. However we interpret it, though, legal sovereignty introduces a considerable element of relativity into the enjoyment of internationally recognized human rights in the contemporary world.

8.3 Cultural Relativism

The most common argument for relativity appeals to culture. I have already suggested that human rights are much more closely tied to social structure than to culture, and that numerous particular cultures at different times have variously accepted, rejected, and operated without a thought to human rights ideas and practices. Here I want to consider arguments of cultural relativity directly.

Cultural relativity is a fact: cultures differ, often dramatically, across time and space. Cultural relativism is a set of doctrines that imbue cultural relativity with prescriptive force. For our purposes, we can distinguish methodological and substantive cultural relativism.[37] Methodological cultural relativism was popular among mid-twentieth-century anthropologists. They advocated a radically non-judgmental analysis of cultures in order to free anthropology from biases rooted in describing and judging other societies according to modern Western categories and values.[38] Such arguments lead directly to recognition of the historical or anthropological relativity of human rights.

In discussions of human rights, however, cultural relativism typically appears as a substantive normative doctrine that demands respect for cultural differences.[39] The norms of the UDHR are

---

37 J.J. Tilley, 'Cultural Relativism', *Human Rights Quarterly*, 22 (2000), p. 501, carefully reviews a number of particular conceptions and cites much of the relevant literature from anthropology. Cf. A.D. Renteln, 'Relativism and the Search for Human Rights', *American Anthropologist*, 90 (1988), p. 56.

38 M.J. Herskovits, *Cultural Relativism: Perspectives in Cultural Pluralism* (New York: Random House, 1972).

39 Even Renteln, note 37 above, p. 56, who claims to be advancing 'a metaethical theory about the nature of moral perceptions', thus making her position more like what I have called methodological relativism, insists on 'the requirement that diversity be recognized' and the 'urgent need to adopt a broader view of human rights that incorporates diverse concepts'. A.D. Renteln, 'The Unanswered Challenge of Relativism

presented as having no normative force in the face of divergent cultural traditions. Practice is to be evaluated instead by the standards of the culture in question. As the 1947 Statement on Human Rights of the American Anthropological Association (AAA) put it, 'man is free only when he lives as his society defines freedom'.[40] Rhoda Howard-Hassmann has aptly described this position as 'cultural absolutism'.[41] Culture provides absolute standards of evaluation; whatever a culture says is right is right (for those in that culture). Rather than address the details of such claims, which usually involve arguments that other cultures give greater attention to duties than to rights and to groups than to individuals, I will focus on six very serious general problems with substantive or absolutist cultural relativism.

First, it risks reducing 'right' to 'traditional', 'good' to 'old', and 'obligatory' to 'habitual'. Few societies or individuals, however, believe that their values are binding simply or even primarily because they happen to be widely endorsed within their culture. Without very powerful philosophical arguments (which are not to be found in this cultural relativist literature on human rights), it would seem inappropriate to adopt a theory that is inconsistent with the moral experience of almost all people – especially in the name of cultural sensitivity and diversity.

Second, the equation of indigenous cultural origins with moral validity is deeply problematic. The 1947 AAA statement insists that 'standards and values are relative to the culture from which they derive so that any attempt to formulate postulates that grow out of the beliefs or moral codes of one culture must to that extent detract from the applicability of any Declaration of Human Rights to mankind as a whole.'[42] The idea that simply because a value or practice emerged in place A makes it, to that extent, inapplicable to B is, at best, a dubious philosophical claim that assumes the impossibility of moral learning or adaptation except within (closed) cultures. It also dangerously assumes the moral infallibility of culture.

Third, intolerant, even genocidal, relativism is logically at least as defensible as tolerant relativism. If my culture's values tell me that others are inferior, there is no standard by which to challenge this. A multidimensional, multicultural conception of human rights requires appeal to principles inconsistent with normative cultural relativism.

Fourth, cultural relativist arguments usually either ignore politics or confuse it with culture. The often deeply coercive aspect to culture is simply ignored. As a result, such arguments regularly confuse what a people has been forced to tolerate with what it values.

Fifth, these arguments typically ignore the impact of states, markets, colonialism, the spread of human rights ideas, and various other social forces. The cultures described are idealized representations of a past that, if it ever existed, certainly does not exist today. For example, Roger Ames, in an essay entitled 'Continuing the Conversation of Chinese Human Rights', completely ignores the impact of half a century of Communist Party rule, as if it were irrelevant to discussing human rights in contemporary China.[43]

---

and the Consequences for Human Rights', *Human Rights Quarterly*, 7 (1985), pp. 514, 540. Such substantive propositions simply do not follow from methodological relativism or any causal or descriptive account of moral perceptions.

40 Executive Committee, American Anthropological Association, 'Statement on Human Rights Submitted to the Commission on Human Rights, United Nations', *American Anthropologist*, 49 (1947), pp. 539, 543.

41 R.E. Howard, 'Cultural Absolutism and the Nostalgia for Community', *Human Rights Quarterly*, 15 (1993), p. 315.

42 Executive Committee, American Anthropological Association, note 40 above, at p. 542.

43 R. Ames, 'Continuing the Conversation on Chinese Human Rights', *Ethics and International Affairs*, 11 (1997), p. 177.

Sixth, and most generally, the typical account of culture as coherent, homogeneous, consensual, and static largely ignores cultural contingency, contestation, and change. Culture, in fact, is a repertoire of deeply contested symbols, practices, and meanings over and with which members of a society constantly struggle.[44] Culture is not destiny – or, to the extent that it is, that is only because victorious elements in a particular society have used their power to make a particular, contingent destiny.

The fact of cultural relativity and the doctrine of methodological cultural relativism are important antidotes to misplaced universalism. The fear of (neo-)imperialism and the desire to demonstrate cultural respect that lie behind many cultural relativist arguments need to be taken seriously. Normative cultural relativism, however, is a deeply problematic moral theory that offers a poor understanding of the relativity of human rights.

8.4 Post-Structuralist, Post-Colonial, and Critical Arguments

The growing hegemony of the idea of human rights since the end of the Cold War, combined with the rise of post-structuralist and post-colonial perspectives, has spawned a new stream of relativist, or perhaps more accurately anti-universalist, arguments. They typically are based on a very different sort of anti-foundationalist ontology and epistemology[45] and tend to be specially addressed to the context of globalization. They seek to challenge arrogant, neo-imperial arguments of universality and draw attention to 'the civilizationally asymmetrical power relations embedded in the international discourse', in order to open or preserve discursive and practical space for autonomous action by marginalized groups and peoples across the globe.[46]

Although some versions of such arguments are dismissively critical,[47] many are well modulated. '[T]he seduction of human rights discourse has been so great that it has, in fact, delayed the development of a critique of rights'.[48] They claim that a lack of critical self-reflection has made human rights advocates 'more part of a problem in today's world than part of the solution'.[49]

---

44 For excellent brief applications of this understanding of culture to debates over human rights, see A.-B.S. Preis, 'Human Rights as Cultural Practice: An Anthropological Critique', *Human Rights Quarterly*, 18 (1996), p. 286; A.J. Nathan, 'Universalism: A Particularistic Account' in L. Bell, A.J. Nathan and I. Peleg (eds), *Negotiating Culture and Human Rights* (New York: Columbia University Press, 2001).

45 Critical Marxian perspectives, however, make similar arguments from a foundationalist perspective. See e.g. T. Evans, *US Hegemony and the Project of Universal Human Rights* (Basingstoke: Macmillan Press, 1996).

46 A. Woodiwiss, 'Human Rights and the Challenge of Cosmopolitanism', *Theory, Culture and Society*, 19 (2002), p. 139.

47 For example, Makau Mutua writes of 'the biased and arrogant rhetoric and history of the human rights enterprise', which is simply the latest expression of 'the historical continuum of the Eurocentric colonial project'. M. Mutua, 'Savages, Victims, and Saviors: The Metaphor of Human Rights', *Harvard International Law Journal*, 42 (2001), pp. 201, 202, 204. The hegemony of international human rights norms, in this reading, amounts to granting Western culture 'the prerogative of imperialism, the right to define and impose on others what it deems good for humanity'. *Ibid.*, p. 219.

48 M. Mutua, 'The Ideology of Human Rights', *Virginia Journal of International Law*, 36 (1996), pp. 589, 591.

49 D. Kennedy, 'The International Human Rights Movement: Part of the Problem?', *Harvard Human Rights Journal*, 15 (2002), p. 101.

There *are* 'dark sides of virtue.'[50] The uncomfortable reality, whatever the intentions of Western practitioners, too often is 'imperial humanitarianism'.[51]

In these accounts, universality per se – and more particularly the tendency for difference to be intellectually obscured and politically repressed by universal claims – is targeted more than universal human rights in particular. Conversely, even many fairly radical post-structuralist and post-colonial authors reject normative cultural relativism in favour of a more dialogical approach that is not dissimilar to the overlapping consensus arguments discussed above.[52] The emphasis is on the dangers of false, abusive, or coerced universalism – a theme to which I now turn, from a more universalistic position.

9. Universalism Without Imperialism

My account has emphasized the 'good' sides of universalism, understood in limited, relative terms. The political dangers of arguments of anthropological universality are modest, at least if one accepts functional and international legal universality. In arguing against ontological universality, however, I ignored the dangers of imperialist intolerance when such claims move into politics.

The legacy of colonialism demands that Westerners show special caution and sensitivity when advancing arguments of universalism in the face of clashing cultural values. Westerners must also remember the political, economic, and cultural power that lies behind even their best intentioned activities. Anything that even hints of imposing Western values is likely to be met with understandable suspicion, even resistance. How arguments of universalism and arguments of relativism are advanced may sometimes be as important as the substance of those arguments.[53]

Care and caution, however, must not be confused with inattention or inaction. Our values, and international human rights norms, may demand that we act on them even in the absence of agreement by others – at least when that action does not involve force. Even strongly sanctioned traditions may not deserve our toleration if they are unusually objectionable. Consider, for example, the deeply rooted tradition of anti-Semitism in the West or 'untouchables' and bonded labour in India. Even if such traditional practices were not rejected by the governments in question, they would not deserve the tolerance, let alone the respect, of outsiders. When rights-abusive practices raise issues of great moral significance, tradition and culture are a slight defence.

---

50 D. Kennedy, *The Dark Sides of Virtue: Reassessing International Humanitarianism* (Princeton, NJ: Princeton University Press, 2004).

51 G. Gott, 'Imperial Humanitarianism: History of an Arrested Dialectic', in B.E. Hernández-Truyol (ed.), *Moral Imperialism: A Critical Anthology* (New York: New York University Press, 2002). Cf. S. Koshy, 'From Cold War to Trade War: Neocolonialism and Human Rights', *Social Text*, 58 (1999), p. 1; P. Cheah, 'Posit(ion)ing Human Rights in the Current Global Conjuncture', *Public Culture*, 9 (1997), pp. 233–66, at p. 233. M. Ignatieff, *Human Rights as Politics and Idolatry* (Princeton, NJ: Princeton University Press, 2001), expresses similar worries from within a very traditional Western liberal perspective.

52 See e.g. B. de Sousa Santos, 'Toward a Multicultural Conception of Human Rights', in B.E. Hernández-Truyol (ed.), *Moral Imperialism: A Critical Anthology* (New York: New York University Press, 2002); B.E. Hernández-Truyol and S.E. Rush, 'Culture, Nationhood, and the Human Rights Ideal', *Michigan Journal of Race and Law*, 5 (2000), p. 817.

53 I probably would not object to readers who take this as implicit acknowledgement of certain shortcomings in some of my previous work on relativism, although I suspect that we might disagree about the range of applicability of such criticisms.

I do not mean to minimize the dangers of cultural and political arrogance, especially when backed by great power. US foreign policy often confuses American interests with universal values, with devastating results. Faced with such undoubtedly perverse 'unilateral universalism', even some well-meaning critics have been seduced by misguided arguments for the essential relativity of human rights. This, though, in effect accepts the American confusion of human rights with US foreign policy.

The proper remedy for 'false' universalism is defensible, relative universalism. Functional universality, overlapping consensus universality, and international legal universality, in addition to their analytical and substantive virtues, can be valuable resources for resisting many of the excesses of US foreign policy, and perhaps even for redirecting it into more humane channels. Without authoritative international standards, to what can the USA (or any other great power) be held accountable? If international legal universality has no force, why shouldn't the USA act on its own (often peculiar) understandings of human rights? Although human rights are not a panacea for the world's problem, the relative universality of those rights is a powerful resource that can be used to help to build more just and humane national and international societies.

10. The Relative Universality of Human Rights

I have been using the language of relative universality for over 20 years now.[54] The crucial point was, and I still believe it to be, to escape the idea of a universal–relative dichotomy. And that has been the clear direction of the development of discussions. Most sophisticated defenders of both universality and relativity today recognize the dangers of an extreme commitment, and acknowledge at least some insights in the positions of those 'on the other side'.

The standard representation is of a spectrum of views. At the relatively universalistic end of this spectrum, I have defended 'relative universality'.[55] Towards the relativist end, Richard Wilson argues that ideas of and struggles for human rights 'are embedded in local normative orders and yet are caught within webs of power and meaning which extend beyond the local'.[56] We might call this 'universalistic relativity'. Nearer the centre, Andrew Nathan uses the language of 'tempered universalism',[57] but English, with its standard adjective–noun structure, does not seem to provide a succinct label for a position that wishes to give priority to neither universality nor relativity.

The above discussion, however, suggests that we replace the metaphor of a spectrum – or a scale, with different weights on the two sides – with that of a multidimensional space. Neither

54 See J. Donnelly, *Universal Human Rights in Theory and Practice* (Ithaca, NY: Cornell University Press, 1989), pp. 98, 106, 107.

55 Towards this end of the spectrum, compare Fred Halliday, Relativism and Universalism in Human Rights: The Case of the Islamic Middle East', *Political Studies*, 43 (1995), p. 152; Michael J. Perry, Are Human Rights Universal? The Relativist Challenge and Related Matters, *Human Rights Quarterly*, 19 (1997), p. 461; Charles R. Beitz, Human Rights as a Common Concern, *American Political Science Review*, 95 (2001), p. 269.

56 Richard A. Wilson, ed., *Human Rights, Culture and Context: Anthropological Perspectives* (London: Pluto Press, 1997), p. 23. Cf. Fred Dallmayr, 'Asian Values' and Global Human Rights', *Philosophy East and West*, 52 (2002), p. 173; Charles Taylor, Conditions of an Unforced Consensus on Human Rights, in *The East Asian Challenge for Human Rights*, note 5 above; Penna and Campbell, note 25 above, p. 3.

57 Nathan, note 44 above; cf. Preis, note 44 above; Declan O'Sullivan, 'Is the Declaration of Human Rights Universal?', *Journal of Human Rights*, 4 (2000), p. 25.

universality nor relativity is a single thing. Rather than with *how much* universality or relativity, we should be concerned with *how* human rights are relative and universal.

'Relative universality', 'universalistic relativity', 'tempered universalism', and all such summary labels should be understood to mean simply that human rights are in some senses relative and in other senses not relative, and in some senses universal but in other senses not universal. I have advanced a particular account of which is which. Some may disagree with those judgements. I think, though, that there can be little doubt that human rights are both universal and relative and that any reasonable discussion of the issue of universality today must start from this observation.

Chapter 3
Economic, Social and Cultural Rights

Manisuli Ssenyonjo

1. Introduction

The UDHR[1] declared human rights, both civil and political rights and economic, social and cultural (ESC) rights, as a 'common standard of achievement' for all peoples and all nations, without separating them. In particular, Articles 21–29 of the UDHR declared that 'everyone' has the right to the following: social security; work; rest and leisure including reasonable limitation of working hours and periodic holidays with pay; adequate standard of living including food, clothing, housing and medical care; education; freedom to participate in the cultural life of the community; and a social and international order in which the rights set forth in the UDHR can be fully realized. Clearly, the UDHR contained a comprehensive list of ESC rights. However, as noted by Mrs Eleanor Roosevelt, the US representative to the General Assembly and chairperson of the United Nations (UN) Commission on Human Rights during the drafting of the UDHR, the UDHR 'is not, and does not purport to be a statement of law or of legal obligation', but it is 'a common standard of achievement for all peoples of all nations'.[2] Despite this, the UDHR has had considerable impact in shaping treaties protecting human rights, including ESC rights, at both regional and UN levels.[3] In addition, the UDHR has influenced the content of many national constitutions and decisions of domestic courts.[4]

In recent years, ESC rights have received increasing attention in various international organizations, academic writings and human rights law generally. At the UN level, the Committee on Economic, Social and Cultural Rights (CESCR),[5] which monitors the implementation of ESC rights under the International Covenant on Economic, Social and Cultural Rights (ICESCR),[6] has adopted a number of useful 'general comments', which clarify the contents of specific rights as well as other issues related to the protection of ESC rights.[7] Furthermore, non-governmental

1 GA Res. 217A (III), UN Doc. A/810 at 71 (1948).

2 *US Department of State Bulletin*, 19 (1948), p. 751.

3 Both the International Covenant on Economic, Social and Cultural Rights (ICESCR), 993 UNTS 3, and the International Covenant on Civil and Political Rights (ICCPR), 999 UNTS 171, refer to the UDHR in their preambles, recognizing that 'in accordance with the Universal Declaration of Human Rights, the ideal of free human beings enjoying civil and political freedom and freedom from fear and want can only be achieved if conditions are created whereby everyone may enjoy his civil and political rights, as well as his economic, social and cultural rights'.

4 See *Measures Taken within the United Nations in the Field of Human Rights*, UN Doc. A/CONF.32/5, pp. 28–30.

5 The CESCR was established by the United Nations Economic and Social Council (ECOSOC) Resolution 1985/17 of 28 May 1985.

6 See note 3 above.

7 See 'Compilation of General Comments and General Recommendations Adopted by Human Rights Treaty Bodies', UN Doc. HRI/GEN/1/Rev. 9 (vol. 1) (27 May 2008), pp. 1–171. The General Comments of the CESCR are available from http://www2.ohchr.org/english/bodies/cescr/comments.htm.

organizations (NGOs) are becoming more interested in working with these rights, and the courts in many domestic legal systems are showing a growing willingness to enforce ESC rights in some of their decisions.[8] Despite these positive developments, many actors working with human rights law still focus mainly on issues relating to civil and political rights and tend to pay only lip service to the interdependence and interrelatedness of all human rights. This means that, in practice, ESC rights are still marginalized and still considered, inaccurately, as 'programmatic, aspirational, and not justiciable',[9] and they are honoured more in 'the breach than the observance'.[10] The marginalization of ESC rights affects most the poor and disadvantaged groups and individuals because they lack the resources required for an adequate standard of living (including adequate food, housing, health, and education) and lack a political voice to influence the formulation of government policy. Although ESC rights are protected at an international level by a legally binding international treaty, the ICESCR, and now reinforced by the Optional Protocol (OP) to the ICESCR, adopted in December 2008,[11] there are still, six decades after the UDHR, many substantive questions regarding the status of ESC rights as human rights in international law.

In analysing the evolution of ESC rights since the adoption of the UDHR, the following four key questions regarding these rights are addressed in this chapter: (1) What are the human rights obligations of states parties to the ICESCR? (2) Are such obligations territorially limited or is there scope for extraterritorial obligations? (3) Are states permitted to derogate from (some) ESC rights during emergencies despite the fact that the ICESCR does not contain a derogation clause either permitting or prohibiting derogations? (4) Was it really necessary to adopt an OP to the ICESCR to enable the CESCR to receive and consider communications alleging violations of any of the rights protected by the ICESCR? Apart from the first question, which provides a general overview of state obligations under the ICESCR, the other questions have been selected because, despite their significance, they are not specifically addressed in the ICESCR and few studies have explored them in relation to ESC rights.

In addressing these questions, the chapter aims to demonstrate that since the adoption of the UDHR, ESC rights have evolved over the years and that the ICESCR lays down clear, legal human rights obligations for states parties. Although the ICESCR provides for 'progressive realization' and acknowledges the constraints of limited 'available resources', it also imposes various obligations which are of immediate effect (e.g. the obligation to take steps, and to eliminate discrimination in the enjoyment of ESC rights). This chapter notes that the increase in domestic case law on ESC rights clearly indicates that violations of ESC rights are justiciable, and that states should ensure

8 See e.g. M. Ssenyonjo, *Economic, Social and Cultural Rights in International Law* (Oxford: Hart Publishing, 2009), ch. 4; F. Coomans (ed.), *Justiciability of Economic, and Social Rights: Experiences from Domestic Systems* (Antwerp: Intersentia, 2006). For a survey of cases on ESC rights, see e.g. ESCR-Net [online]. Available from: http://www.escr-net.org/caselaw/caselaw_list.htm [accessed 26 August 2010]; Centre for Housing Rights and Evictions (COHRE), *Leading Cases on Economic, Social and Cultural Rights: Summaries*, Working Paper No. 3 (Geneva: COHRE, 2006); and International Commission of Jurists, *Courts and the Legal Enforcement of Economic, Social and Cultural Rights: Comparative Experiences of Justiciability* (Geneva: International Commission of Jurists, 2008).

9 See e.g. CESCR, *Concluding Observations: Poland*, UN Doc. C.12/POL/CO/5 (20 November 2009), para. 9.

10 D. Bilchitz, *Poverty and Fundamental Rights: The Justification and Enforcement of Socio-Economic Rights* (Oxford: Oxford University Press, 2007), p. 2.

11 See the Optional Protocol to the ICESCR, Human Rights Council, Resolution 8/2, 28th Meeting, 18 June 2008 [online]. Available from: http://ap.ohchr.org/documents/E/HRC/resolutions/A_HRC_RES_8_2.pdf. See also UN Doc. A/63/435, Annex.

their justiciability in practice at a national level. At the international level, it is noted that the adoption of an OP to the ICESCR by the UN General Assembly in 2008 providing for individual and group communications, and interstate communications, as well as an inquiry procedure in cases of grave or systematic violations of any ESC rights, was long overdue. Further, the chapter argues that any state party to the ICESCR could be in violation of its obligations under the ICESCR for actions taken by it extraterritorially, in relation to anyone within the power, effective control or authority of that state, as well as within an area over which that state exercises effective overall control. Finally, the chapter notes that the absence of a clause allowing derogation in times of public emergency in the ICESCR indicates that the it generally continues to apply in the time of armed conflict, war or other public emergency, and, as a minimum, states cannot derogate from the minimum core obligations of ESC rights.

It is hoped that this analysis will encourage states to take their human rights obligations under the ICESCR more seriously and will also help to develop the necessary political will for the ratification of the OP by states parties, as this would contribute to generally strengthening the international legal framework of accountability for violations of ESC rights.

2. ESC Rights: An Overview

ESC rights in international human rights law include a wide range of human rights. For example, the rights to work and to just and favourable conditions of work; to rest and leisure; to form and join trade unions, and to strike; to social security; to protection of the family, mothers and children; to an adequate standard of living, including adequate food, clothing and housing; to the highest attainable standard of physical and mental health; to education; and to participate in cultural life and enjoy benefits of scientific progress.[12] The effective respect, protection, and fulfilment of these rights is an important – but under-explored – component of international human rights law. This is despite the fact that the UDHR, as noted above, recognized two sets of human rights from inception: civil and political rights and ESC rights. In transforming the provisions of the UDHR into legally binding obligations, the UN adopted two separate but interdependent covenants: the International Covenant on Civil and Political Rights (ICCPR)[13] and the ICESCR. As of 31 December 2009, there were 160 states parties to the ICESCR and 165 states parties to the ICCPR. The two covenants, along with the UDHR, constitute the so-called 'international bills of rights'.

At the international level, ESC rights are protected in several international human rights treaties, the most comprehensive of which is the ICESCR. The ICESCR initially did not have an independent treaty-monitoring body, let alone one that could receive individual complaints. This omission was partially addressed by the creation of the CESCR in 1985, to receive and review regular state party reports.[14] Recently, on 18 June 2008, the UN Human Rights Council adopted an OP to the ICESCR that provides the CESCR with three new roles: (1) to receive and consider individual and group communications claiming 'a violation of any of the economic, social and cultural rights set forth in the Covenant'; (2) interstate communications to the effect that a state party claims that another state party is 'not fulfilling its obligations under the Covenant'; and (3)

12 See ICESCR, note 3 above, Art. 6–15.

13 See ICCPR, note 3 above.

14 See ECOSOC Resolution 1985/17, note 5 above.

to conduct an inquiry in cases where the CESCR receives reliable information indicating 'grave or systematic violations' by a state party of any ESC rights set forth in the ICESCR.[15]

Significantly, on the 60th anniversary of the UDHR (10 December 2008), the UN General Assembly unanimously adopted the OP,[16] 42 years after a similar mechanism was adopted for civil and political rights. The signing ceremony for the OP was held on 24 September 2009 during the 2009 Treaty Event at the UN Headquarters in New York. By 23 December 2009, 3 months after it was opened for signature, 31 states had signed the OP, marking a significant beginning towards support for this historic mechanism.[17] The OP will enter into force after ratification by 10 states in accordance with its Article 18. In its preamble, the OP reaffirmed 'the universality, indivisibility, interdependence and interrelatedness of all human rights and fundamental freedoms'. The unanimous adoption of this OP on the 60th anniversary of UDHR is indeed a significant human rights development that ushers in a new era of accountability for violations of ESC rights in international law (once the OP enters into force) and thus dispel claims that ESC rights under the ICESCR were not intended to be justiciable.[18] This means that, more than ever before, it is timely and pertinent to examine the nature and scope of state obligations under the ICESCR in light of the current state of international law, for which states that ratify the OP could be held accountable.

At the regional level, there was largely the same pattern of difference. The European Convention on Human Rights (ECHR) 1950,[19] despite its all-embracing name as a 'human rights convention', is concerned almost exclusively with civil and political rights.[20] Indeed, it may be stated that although the 'interpretation of the European Convention may extend into the sphere of social and economic rights',[21] the ECHR does not protect ESC rights, either explicitly (with the exception of the right to education and possibly the right to property) or implicitly.[22] It took another decade before the European Social Charter was adopted and a further generation before a right of collective (but not individual) complaints was introduced under it.[23] As for the Inter-American Human Rights System, the American Convention on Human Rights (ACHR) 1969,[24] likewise despite its all-embracing name as a convention on 'human rights', emphasizes civil and political rights, and it was only

15 Optional Protocol to the ICESCR, note 11 above, Art. 1, 2, 10, and 11.

16 GA Res. A/RES/63/117 (10 December 2008), UN Doc. A/63/435.

17 The first 32 states to sign the OP were as follows: Argentina; Armenia, Azerbaijan, Belgium, Bolivia, Chile, Congo, Ecuador, El Salvador, Finland, Gabon, Ghana, Guatemala, Guinea-Bissau, Italy, Luxembourg, Madagascar, Mali, Mongolia, Montenegro, The Netherlands, Paraguay, Portugal, Senegal, Slovakia, Slovenia, Solomon Islands, Spain, Timor-Leste, Togo, Ukraine, and Uruguay.

18 See M. Dennis and D. Stewart, 'Justiciability of Economic, Social and Cultural Rights: Should There Be an International Complaints Mechanism to Adjudicate the Rights to Food, Water, Housing and Health', *American Journal of International Law*, 98(3) (2004), p. 462.

19 CETS No. 5, adopted on 4 November 1950. See Chapter 15 in this volume.

20 For a comprehensive discussion of the ECHR, see generally D.J. Harris *et al.*, *Law of the European Convention on Human Rights*, 2nd edn (Oxford: Oxford University Press, 2009).

21 *Airey* v *Ireland* A 32 (1979); 2 EHRR 305 at para. 26.

22 C. Warbrick, 'Economic and Social Interests and the European Convention on Human Rights', in M. Baderin and R. McCorquodale (eds), *Economic, Social and Cultural Rights in Action* (Oxford: Oxford University Press, 2007), p. 241.

23 The European Social Charter was adopted in 1961 and revised in 1996. On the European Social Charter, see generally D.J. Harris and J. Darcy, *European Social Charter*, 2nd edn (Ardsley, NY: Transnational Publishers, 2001); and H. Cullen, 'The Collective Complaints System of the European Social Charter: Interpretative Methods of the European Committee of Social Rights', *Human Rights Law Review*, 9(1) (2009), pp. 61–93.

24 OAS Treaty Series No. 36, 1144 UNTS 123.

later that the Additional Protocol to the American Convention on Human Rights in the Area of Economic, Social and Cultural Rights, 'Protocol of San Salvador',[25] was adopted, with its partial system of individual complaint. The African Charter on Human and Peoples' Rights 1981 (African Charter)[26] was a great improvement in that it included from the outset a comprehensive guarantee of the full range of human rights, including ESC rights alongside civil and political rights, without drawing any distinction between the justiciability or implementation of the two categories of rights. Significantly, the African Charter made all rights subject to a right of individual complaints.

However, until recently, the African Commission on Human and Peoples' Rights (a body with the mandate to promote and protect human rights in Africa and to interpret all the provisions of the African Charter at the request of a state party, an institution of the African Union or an African Organization recognized by the African Union)[27] did not develop any comprehensive ESC rights jurisprudence under the African Charter.[28] Nonetheless, in two important cases, *Purohit and Moore* v *The Gambia*[29] *and The Social and Economic Rights Action Center and the Center for Economic and Social Rights* v *Nigeria*,[30] the African Commission demonstrated the practical application of the principle that the African Charter provisions on ESC rights were justiciable. It has held that 'economic and social rights are essential elements of human rights in Africa' and that 'no right in the African Charter cannot be made effective'.[31] In addition, the African Commission has held that states parties to the African Charter have to take 'concrete and targeted steps', while taking full advantage of their available resources, to 'ensure' that ESC rights such as the right to health are fully realized in all aspects without discrimination of any kind.[32] Although the commission's promotional activities initially paid lip service to ESC rights by being predominantly focused on civil and political rights, the commission later paid attention to ESC rights after concerns were raised by representatives of civil society organizations during several of the commission's sessions about the need for a focus on ESC rights.[33]

---

25 OAS Treaty Series No. 69 (1988), entered into force 16 November 1999. On the justiciability of ESC rights in the Inter-American system, see M.F. Tinta, 'Justiciability of Economic, Social, and Cultural Rights in the Inter-American System of Protection of Human Rights: Beyond Traditional Paradigms and Notions', *Human Rights Quarterly*, 29(2) (2007), pp. 431–59.

26 Adopted 27 June 27 1981, OAU Doc. CAB/LEG/67/3 rev. 5, 21 ILM 58 (1982). For a discussion, see Malcolm D. Evans and R. Murray (eds), *The African Charter on Human and Peoples' Rights: The System in Practice, 1986–2006*, 2nd edn (Cambridge: Cambridge University Press, 2008); F. Ouguergouz, *The African Charter on Human and Peoples' Rights: A Comprehensive Agenda for Human Rights* (The Hague: Kluwer Law International, 2003); and Chapter 12 in this volume.

27 African Charter, note 26 above, Art. 45.

28 See M. Ssenyonjo, 'The Justiciability of Economic, Social and Cultural Rights', *East African Journal of Peace and Human Rights*, 9(1) (2003), pp. 1–36.

29 Communication 241/2001, Sixteenth Annual Activity Report of the African Commission on Human and Peoples' Rights 2002–2003, Annex VII; *African Human Rights Law Reports*, 96 (2003).

30 Communication 155/96, Fifteenth Annual Activity Report of the African Commission on Human and Peoples' Rights 2001–2002, Annex V; *African Human Rights Law Reports*, 60 (2001); (2003)10 IHRR 282. For a comment on this case, see D. Shelton, 'Decision Regarding Communication 155/96: *Social and Economic Rights Action Center and the Center for Economic and Social Rights* v *Nigeria*', *American Journal of International Law*, 96(4) (2002), p. 937.

31 Communication 155/96, note 30 above, para. 68.

32 Communication 241/2001, note 29 above, para. 84.

33 See S. Khoza, 'Promoting Economic, Social and Cultural Rights in Africa: The African Commission Holds a Seminar in Pretoria', *African Human Rights Law Journal*, 4(2) (2004), p. 334. See also Statement

At the national level, the courts of some states have demonstrated that ESC rights can be enforced through the courts. In this regard, the jurisprudence of the Indian courts[34] and South African courts[35] has been particularly useful. Despite some limitations, celebrated judgements by the South African Constitutional Court, such as judgements in the *Grootboom* and *Mazibuko* cases,[36] have been particularly influential, showing that ESC rights are justiciable and providing a public law model for deciding cases in that regard by holding that, when challenged as to its policies relating to ESC rights, the state 'must explain why the policy is reasonable' and that the policy is being reconsidered consistent with the obligation to 'progressively realize' ESC rights.

In sum, what emerges from the foregoing overview is that it is not the nature of the rights that is crucial (i.e. whether rights are considered ESC rights or civil and political rights), but the nature of the obligations that are imposed by international and national law concerning them. It is thus clear that the argument about justiciability has now been resolved. Whenever ESC rights cannot be made fully effective without some role for the judiciary, judicial remedies are 'necessary'.[37] This means that effective judicial remedies must be available for victims of all violations of ESC rights so that such rights can be enforced through the courts. As the CESCR has stated, affirming the principle of the interdependence and indivisibility of all human rights, 'all economic, social and cultural rights are justiciable'.[38] Indeed, ESC rights, both individual and collective, have long been enforced in national courts without difficulty. At times, national (and even regional human rights) courts have in fact been applying ESC rights, such as the rights to health and education, without knowing it, deciding cases that are about these rights (though not necessarily in compliance with them) under different rubrics, such as health or education law or, in the case of the ECHR, under Article 2 of the First Protocol.[39]

---

on Social, Economic and Cultural Rights in Africa, Pretoria, 17 September 2004, *African Human Rights Law Journal*, 5(1) (2005), p. 182.

34 See e.g. Supreme Court of India in the following cases: *Francis Coralie* v *The Union Territory of Delhi* (1981) 1 SCC 608; *Francis Coralie Mullin* v *The Administrator, Union Territory of Delhi* (1981) 2 SCR 516; *Olga Tellis* v *Bombay Municipal Corp.* (1985) 3 SCC 545; *Shantistar Builders* v *Narayan Khimalal Totame and Others* (1990) 1 SCC 520; and *Chamelli Singh and Others* v *State of Uttar Pradesh JT* (1995) 9 SC 380; *Shanti Star Builders* v *Narayan K. Totame* (1990) 1 SCC 520; *Consumer Education and Research Centre (CERC)* v *Union of India* (1995) 3 SCC 42.

35 See e.g. Constitutional Court of South Africa (CC) in the following cases: *Thiagraj Soobramoney* v *Minister of Health, KwaZulu-Natal* 1998 (1) SA 765 (CC); 1997 (12) BCLR 1696 (CC); *Government of the Republic of South Africa and Others* v *Grootboom and Others* 2001 (1) SA 46 (CC); 2000 (11) BCLR 1169 (CC); *Minister of Health and Others* v *Treatment Action Campaign* 2002 (5) SA 721 (CC), 2002 (10) BCLR 1033 (CC).

36 *Government of the Republic of South Africa and Others* v *Grootboom and Others* 2001 (1) SA 46 (CC); *Lindiwe Mazibuko and Others* v *City of Johannesburg and Others*, Case CCT 39/09 [2009] ZACC 28 [online]. Available from: http://www.saflii.org/za/cases/ZACC/2009/28.html, paras. 161–2.

37 CESCR, *General Comment 9: The Domestic Application of the Covenant*, UN Doc. E/C.12/1998/24 (3 December 1998), para. 9.

38 See CESCR, *Concluding Observations: United Kingdom*, UN Doc. E/C.12/1/Add.79 (5 June 2002), para. 24. See also CESCR, *Concluding Observations: Poland*, UN Doc. E/C.12/POL/CO/5 (20 November 2009), para. 9.

39 See Protocol to the Convention for the Protection of Human Rights and Fundamental Freedoms, 213 UNTS 262, entered into force 18 May 1954. Art. 2 reads: 'No person shall be denied the right to education. In the exercise of any functions which it assumes in relation to education and to teaching, the State shall respect the right of parents to ensure such education and teaching in conformity with their own religious and philosophical convictions'. For the analysis, see Harris *et al.*, note 20 above, at pp. 697–709.

3. State Obligations Under Article 2(1) of the ICESCR

In this section, specific human rights obligations of states parties to the ICESCR arising from Article 2(1) are examined, since these directly inform all of the substantive rights protected in Articles 6 to 15 of the ICESCR. Article 2(1) is fundamental to the ICESCR since it is the general legal obligation provision.[40] Article 2(1) provides that:

> Each State Party to the present Covenant undertakes to take steps, individually and through international assistance and co-operation, especially economic and technical, to the maximum of its available resources, with a view to achieving progressively the full realisation of the rights recognised in the present Covenant by all appropriate means, including particularly the adoption of legislative measures.

It has been observed that '[r]elative to Article 2 of the ICCPR, Article 2 of the ICESCR is weak with respect to implementation'.[41] Hence, Craven expressed the position as follows:

> Article 2(1) itself is a somewhat confused and unsatisfactory provision. The combination of convoluted phraseology and numerous qualifying sub-clauses seems to defy any real sense of obligation. Indeed it has been read by some as giving states an almost total freedom of choice and action as to how the rights should be implemented.[42]

The language of Article 2(1) is clearly wide and full of caveats, making it difficult to ascertain the exact nature of legal obligations arising from this provision. However, the nature and scope of the states parties' obligations under the ICESCR, including the provisions of Article 2(1) above, and the nature and scope of violations of ESC rights and appropriate responses and remedies, have been examined by groups of experts in international law who adopted the Limburg Principles on the Implementation of the ICESCR in 1986 (Limburg Principles)[43] and the Maastricht Guidelines on Violations of Economic Social and Cultural Rights in 1997 (Maastricht Guidelines).[44] Although the Limburg Principles and Maastricht Guidelines are not legally binding *per se*, they may arguably

40 M. Craven, *The International Covenant on Economic, Social and Cultural Rights: A Perspective on its Development* (Oxford: Clarendon Press, 1995), pp. 106–52.

41 H. Steiner and P. Alston, *International Human Rights in Context: Law, Politics, Morals – Text and Materials*, 2nd edn (Oxford: Oxford University Press, 2000), p. 275. For the analysis of Article 2(1) of the ICCPR, see D. Harris, 'The International Covenant on Civil and Political Rights and the United Kingdom: An Introduction', in D. Harris and S. Joseph (eds), *The International Covenant on Civil and Political Rights and United Kingdom Law* (Oxford: Clarendon Press, 1995), pp. 1–8; M. Nowak, *U.N. Covenant on Civil and Political Rights: CCPR Commentary*, 2nd edn (Kehl: N.P. Engel, 2005), pp. 37–42.

42 M. Craven, 'The Justiciability of Economic, Social and Cultural Rights', in R. Burchill, D. Harris and A. Owers (eds), *Economic, Social and Cultural Rights: Their Implementation in United Kingdom Law* (Nottingham: University of Nottingham Human Rights Law Centre, 1999), pp. 1–12, at p. 5 (footnotes omitted).

43 UN Doc. E/CN.4/1987/17, Annex; *Human Rights Quarterly*, 9(2) (1987), pp. 122–35; and *Review of the International Commission of Jurists*, 37 (1986), pp. 43–55. The 29 participants who adopted the Limburg Principles came from various states and international organizations.

44 *Human Rights Quarterly*, 20(3) (1998), pp. 691–704. The Maastricht Guidelines were adopted by a group of more than 30 experts. For a commentary on these guidelines, see E. Dankwa, C. Flinterman and S. Leckie, 'Commentary to the Maastricht Guidelines on Violations of Economic, Social and Cultural Rights', *Human Rights Quarterly*, 20(3) (1998), pp. 705–30.

provide 'a subsidiary means' for the interpretation of the ICESCR as 'teachings of the most highly qualified publicists of the various nations' under Article 38(1)(d) of the Statute of the International Court of Justice. Moreover, the participants who adopted the Limburg Principles believed that they 'reflect[ed] the present state of international law, with the exception of certain recommendations indicated by the use of the verb 'should' instead of 'shall'.[45] Also, the participants who adopted the Maastricht Guidelines considered them to 'reflect the evolution of international law since 1986'.[46]

The CESCR has also, in numerous general comments and statements, spelt out the content of state obligations and individual and group rights under the ICESCR. By December 2009, the CESCR had adopted 21 general comments, 14 of which related to substantive rights while seven dealt with other aspects of the ICESCR.[47] In addition, the CESCR had issued 16 statements on several key issues relevant to ESC rights, including, for example, poverty, globalization, intellectual property and the world food crisis.[48] While general comments and statements are not legally binding, they can have a persuasive effect, setting out interpretive positions around which state practice may unite. No state has ever raised any formal objections to the general comments or statements of the CESCR, apparently suggesting wide acceptance by states of the CESCR's interpretation of the ICESCR through its general comments and statements.

Four key human rights obligations arise from Article 2(1); namely, (1) the obligation to 'take steps ... by all appropriate means'; (2) the obligation of 'achieving progressively the full realisation' of ESC rights; (3) the obligation to utilize 'maximum available resources'; and (4) the obligation to seek (or provide) international assistance and cooperation. These obligations are considered below.

3.1 Obligation to 'take steps ... by all appropriate means'

The first obligation is for states to 'take steps' in the field of ESC rights. This is an immediate obligation, which, in itself, is not qualified or limited by other considerations.[49] A failure to comply with this obligation cannot be justified by reference to social, cultural or economic considerations within the state.[50] What 'steps' are required under Article 2(1)? States have a wide margin of discretion in selecting the steps they consider most appropriate for the full realization of ESC rights. Generally, two types of steps are required; namely, legislative and non-legislative steps to respect, protect and achieve ESC rights. There is no doubt that legislative measures are indispensable in the protection of all human rights including ESC rights,[51] since a sound legislative foundation provides a firm basis to protect such rights (e.g. in the fields of housing, employment, and education) and to enforce them in case of violations. By legislation on ESC rights, these rights acquire content at a domestic level, and that content could be developed through judicial review. Legislation is

---

45 See the introduction to the Limburg Principles, note 43 above, para. iii.

46 See the introduction to the Maastricht Guidelines, note 44 above.

47 See CESCR, *General Comments*, note 7 above.

48 Statements of the Committee [online]. Available from: http://www2.ohchr.org/english/bodies/cescr/statements.htm [accessed 26 August 2010].

49 CESCR, *General Comment 3*, para. 2; Limburg Principles, note 43 above, paras. 16 and 21.

50 CESCR, *Concluding Observations: Iraq*, UN Doc. E/1998/22 (20 June 1998), paras. 253 and 281.

51 See e.g. CESCR, *General Comment 3*, para. 3; CESCR, *General Comment 14*, para. 56: 'states should consider adopting a framework law to operationalise their right to health national strategy'. See also, generally, CESCR, *General Comment 20: Non-Discrimination in Economic, Social and Cultural Rights* (Art. 2(2), UN Doc. E/C.12/GC/20 (25 May 2009); and A. Nolan, 'Addressing Economic and Social Rights Violations by Non-State Actors Through the Role of the State: A Comparison of Regional Approaches to the "Obligation to Protect"', *Human Rights Law Review*, 9(2) (2009), pp. 225–55.

particularly essential to combat the formal and substantive discrimination faced by some of the most disadvantaged and marginalized individuals and groups, as in discrimination against women, minorities, children, persons with disabilities, older persons, migrants, indigenous peoples, and persons living in poverty.[52]

Thus, states are obliged to enact, without delay, a comprehensive anti-discrimination law, guaranteeing protection against discrimination in the enjoyment of ESC rights, as stipulated in Article 2(2) of the ICESCR. Anti-discrimination legislation should attribute obligations to public and private actors and cover all the prohibited grounds of discrimination stated in the ICESCR. Article 2(2) obliges each state party 'to guarantee that the rights enunciated in the ... Covenant will be exercised without discrimination of any kind'. It lists the prohibited grounds of discrimination as 'race, colour, sex, language, religion, political or other opinion, national or social origin, property, birth or other status'. The inclusion of 'other status' indicates that this list is merely illustrative and not intended to be exhaustive. It covers other grounds such as disability, age, nationality, marital and family status, place of residence, health status, and sexual orientation and gender identity, as well as economic and social situation.[53] This reflects the fact that the nature of discrimination is not static but 'varies according to context and evolves over time'.[54] Since discrimination undermines the achievement of ESC rights for a significant proportion of the world's population, anti-discrimination legislation must cover not only discrimination in the public sector but also discrimination by non-state actors.[55] Among others, this might help to overcome gender inequalities – for example, by eliminating the wage gap between men and women for work of equal value in all sectors of employment, whether private or public.

It is in this regard that the Committee on the Elimination of Discrimination against Women (CEDAW) has urged states with discriminatory laws against women to accelerate the law-review process and to work effectively with legislatures to ensure that all discriminatory legislation is amended or repealed.[56] However, while legislation is essential, it is not enough *per se* for the realization of ESC rights. Therefore, in addition to legislation, other 'appropriate means' are necessary, such as the adoption and implementation of strategies, policies and plans of action to guarantee the effective enjoyment of ESC rights. These may include measures to stimulate economic growth and development, increased budgetary allocations to ESC rights, and the adoption of measures necessary to eliminate discrimination in ESC rights. In addition, other appropriate means include the provision of judicial or other effective remedies (e.g. compensation, reparation, restitution, rehabilitation, guarantees of non-repetition, and public apologies); administrative, financial, educational, or informational campaigns; and social measures, all of which must be undertaken to achieve the intended result.

---

52 See e.g. CESCR, *Concluding Observations: Iraq*, UN Doc. E/C.12/1/Add.17 (12 December 1997), paras. 13–14; CESCR, *Concluding Observations: Morocco*, UN Doc. E/C.12/1/Add.55 (1 December 2000), paras. 34, 45 and 47; CESCR, *Concluding Observations: United Kingdom*, UN Doc. E/C.12/GBR/CO/5 (22 May 2009), para 16; CESCR, *General Comment 5*, para. 16; CESCR, *General Comment 21*, paras. 25–39.

53 CESCR, *General Comment 20*, paras. 27–35.

54 CESCR, *General Comment 20*, para. 27.

55 See e.g. Committee on the Elimination of Racial Discrimination, *Ylimaz Dogman* v. *the Netherlands*, Communication 1/1984 (29 September 1988); African Commission, *Kevin Mgwanga Gunme et al.* v *Cameroon*, Communication 266/2003, Twenty-sixth Annual Activity Report of the African Commission on Human and Peoples' Rights 2009, Annex 4.

56 CEDAW Committee, *Concluding Observations: Tanzania*, UN Doc. CEDAW//C/TZA/CO/6 (18 July 2008), paras. 16, 17 and 55; CEDAW *Committee, Concluding Observations: Nigeria*. UN Doc. CEDAW/C/NGA/CO/6 (18 July 2008), paras. 13, 14 and 44.

In assessing whether states have complied with the obligation to 'take steps ... by all appropriate means', the CESCR considers whether the steps (strategies and policies) taken are reasonable or proportionate with respect to the attainment of relevant rights, and comply with human rights and democratic principles, and whether such steps are subject to an adequate framework of monitoring and accountability. In this regard, the strategies and policies adopted by states should provide for the establishment of effective mechanisms and institutions where these do not exist, to investigate and examine alleged infringements of ESC rights, identify responsibilities, publicize the results, and offer the necessary administrative, judicial, or other remedies to compensate victims. This calls for putting in place appropriate means of redress, or remedies to any aggrieved individual or group, and appropriate means of ensuring accountability of states and non-state actors.[57] Essentially, this entails making ESC rights justiciable at a national level, and not mere, non-legally enforceable principles and values. The CESCR has stressed this point in its concluding observations on state reports. For example, in May 2009, the CESCR urged the UK 'to ensure that the Covenant is given full legal effect in its domestic law, that the Covenant rights are made justiciable, and that effective remedies are available for victims of all violations of economic, social and cultural rights'.[58] This must be the case for all other states parties to the ICESCR.

3.2 Progressive Realization

The second obligation is to ensure that the steps taken are geared towards a result which is 'achieving progressively the full realization' of ESC rights. The appropriateness of the steps taken should therefore be examined by reference to the standard of 'progressive realization'. But what is meant by 'progressive' realization? Does the word 'progressive' enable the obligations of states parties 'to be postponed to an indefinite time in the distant future', as argued by Hungary during the preparatory work on the ICESCR?[59]

According to its ordinary meaning, the term 'progressive' means 'moving forward'[60] or 'advancing by successive stages'[61] in a manner that is 'continuous, increasing, growing, developing, ongoing, intensifying, accelerating, escalating, gradual, step by step'.[62] Thus, states parties are obliged to improve continuously the conditions of ESC rights, and generally to abstain from taking regressive measures. This notion of progressive realization of ESC rights over a period of time 'constitutes a recognition of the fact that full realisation of all [ESC rights] will generally not be able to be achieved in a short period of time ... reflecting the realities of the real world and the difficulties involved for any country in ensuring full realisation of [ESC rights]'.[63] This obligation contrasts with the immediate obligation imposed by Article 2(1) of the ICCPR that obliges states to 'respect and ensure' the substantive rights under the ICCPR.

57 CESCR, *General Comment 9*, para. 2.

58 CESCR, *Concluding Observations: United Kingdom*, UN Doc. E/C.12/GBR/CO/5 (22 May 2009), para. 13.

59 10 UN GAOR para. 9, UN Doc. A/2910/Add.6 (1955).

60 H.W. Fowler, *The Concise Oxford Dictionary of Current English* (Oxford: Clarendon Press, 1990), p. 954.

61 E.M. Kirkpatrick (ed.), *Chambers Family Dictionary* (Edinburgh: Chambers, 1981), p. 613.

62 P. Hanks (ed.), *The New Oxford Thesaurus of English* (Oxford: Oxford University Press, 2000), p. 754.

63 CESCR, *General Comment 3*, para. 9. Under the Convention on the Rights of the Child (CRC), which includes ESC rights and corresponding state obligations, there is no reference to the qualifying clause 'progressive realization'. Thus, its obligations arise immediately, although implementation is qualified by the phrase 'within their means'.

However, the 'reality is that the full realisation of civil and political rights is [also] heavily dependent both on the availability of resources and the development of the necessary societal structures'.[64] As a result, states are also required to take relative positive measures for the realization of civil and political rights.[65] For example, the right to a fair trial, as protected by Article 14(1) ICCPR and Article 6 of the ECHR, encompasses the right of access to a court in cases of determination of criminal charges and rights and obligations in a suit at law,[66] and the provision of free legal aid if this is 'indispensable for an effective access to court'[67] for individuals who do not have sufficient means to pay for it.[68] Accordingly, fair trial necessitates the provision of independent and accessible organs of justice. Despite this, the obligation under the ICCPR is considered to be immediate rather than progressive.

Since the obligation upon states under Article 2(1) of the ICESCR is the progressive achievement of ESC rights, it might be argued that to demand their immediate implementation is not required by the ICESCR. However, some rights under the ICESCR give rise to obligations of immediate effect. One example, as earlier noted, is the right to be free from discrimination in the enjoyment of all ESC rights. The CESCR has stated:

> The prohibition against discrimination enshrined in article 2(2) of the Covenant is subject to neither progressive realisation nor the availability of resources; it applies fully and immediately to all aspects of education and encompasses all internationally prohibited grounds of discrimination.[69]

Thus, a state cannot argue that it is providing primary education or primary health care to boys immediately but would extend it to girls progressively. Similarly, the argument that a state is paying women less than men for work of equal value until resources are available would not be acceptable, since the right of women to equal remuneration with men for equal work must be implemented immediately.[70]

Moreover, every substantive ICESCR right has a minimum core content which gives rise to minimum core entitlements to individuals and groups and corresponding minimum core state

---

64 P. Alston and G. Quinn, 'The Nature and Scope of States Parties' Obligations Under the International Covenant on Economic, Social and Cultural Rights', *Human Rights Quarterly*, 9(2) (1987), p. 156, at p. 172. See also H. Steiner, 'International Protection of Human Rights', in M. D. Evans, *International Law* (Oxford: Oxford University Press, 2003), pp. 757–87.

65 See A. Mowbray, *The Development of Positive Obligations Under the European Convention on Human Rights by the European Court of Human Rights* (Oxford: Hart Publishing, 2004).

66 Human Rights Committee (HRC), *General Comment 32: Article 14 – Right to Equality before Courts and Tribunals and to a Fair Trial*, UN Doc. CCPR/C/GC/32 (23 August 2007), para. 9; *Golder* v *United Kingdom*, Judgment of 21 February 1975, Series A, no. 18; (1979–1980) 1 EHRR 524, paras. 34–35.

67 *Airey* v *Ireland*, Judgment of 9 October 1979, Series A, No. 32; (1979–1980) 3 EHRR 592, para. 26.

68 HRC, *General Comment 32*, note 66 above, para. 10.

69 CESCR, *General Comment 13*, para. 31. See also Commission on Human Rights Res. 2002/23, para. 4(b).

70 Under the ICESCR, Art. 7(a)(i), 'The States Parties to the ICESCR recognise the right of everyone to the enjoyment of just and favourable conditions of work which ensure, in particular, remuneration which provides all workers, as a minimum, with fair wages and equal remuneration for work of equal value without distinction of any kind, in particular women being guaranteed conditions of work not inferior to those enjoyed by men, with equal pay for equal work'.

obligations of immediate effect.[71] On the latter, the CESCR has found that, with regard to every substantive ICESCR right, there is

> a minimum core obligation to ensure the satisfaction of, at the very least, minimum essential levels of each of the rights is incumbent upon every state party. Thus, for example, a state party in which any significant number of individuals is deprived of essential foodstuffs, of essential primary health care, of basic shelter and housing, or of the most basic forms of education is, prima facie, failing to discharge its obligations under the Covenant.[72]

The CESCR has identified minimum core obligations in several general comments,[73] and held that a state party cannot, under any circumstances whatsoever, justify its non-compliance with these core obligations, which are 'non-derogable'.[74] Otherwise, the ICESCR would be largely deprived of its *raison d'être*. Progressive realization demands that after achieving the minimum core obligations, states have to take appropriate steps to ensure 'the continuous improvement of living conditions' necessary for an adequate standard of living, such as adequate food, health, housing, clothing, water and sanitation.[75]

Furthermore, the CESCR has explained that Article 2 'imposes an obligation to move as expeditiously and effectively as possible' towards the ICESCR's goal of full realization of the substantive rights under it.[76] However, the CESCR has not specified how 'expeditiously and effectively' a state should act in achieving the full realization of all ESC rights, but has established in several general comments[77] that the full realization of ESC rights, like other human rights, imposes three types or levels of multi-layered state obligations: the obligations to *respect*, *protect* and *fulfil*.[78] This approach has also been applied by regional human rights supervisory bodies such

71 For a discussion of minimum core obligations, see, generally, A. Chapman and S. Russell (eds), *Core Obligations: Building a Framework for Economic, Social and Cultural Rights* (Antwerp, Intersentia, 2002).

72 CESCR, *General Comment 3*, para. 10.

73 See e.g. CESCR, *General Comment*, nos 11 (para. 17); 13 (para. 57); 14 (para. 43); 15 (para. 37); 17 (para. 39); 18 (para. 31); and 19 (para. 59); 21 (para. 55), respectively, all available from: www2.ohchr.org/english/bodies/cescr/comments.htm.

74 CESCR, *General Comment*, nos 14, para. 47; and 15, para. 40. See also CESCR, *Poverty and the International Covenant on Economic, Social and Cultural Rights*, UN Doc. E/C.12/2001/10 (10 May 2001), para. 18.

75 A key provision of the ICESCR, Article 11(1) captures the idea of progressive realization when it recognizes a right to an adequate standard of living including adequate food, clothing and housing, 'and to the continuous improvement of living conditions'.

76 See e.g. CESCR, *General Comment 3*, para. 9; *General Comment 13*, para. 44; *General Comment 14*, para. 31; and *General Comment 15*, para. 18; Limburg Principles, para. 21. See also CESCR, *Statement on Poverty and the ICESCR*, UN Doc. E/C.12/2001/10 (4 May 2001), para. 18.

77 See e.g. CESCR, *General Comment 21* (2009), paras. 48–54; *General Comment 19* (2008), para. 43; *General Comment 18* (2005), para. 22; *General Comment 17*, para. 28 (2005); *General Comment 16* (2005), paras. 18–21; *General Comment 15* (2002), paras. 20–29; *General Comment 14* (2000), para. 33; and *General Comment 13* (1999), para. 46.

78 See A. Eide, *The Right to Adequate Food as a Human Right*, UN Doc. E/CN.4/Sub.2/1987/23 (7 July 1987), para. 66; A. Eide, 'Economic and Social Rights', in J. Symonides (ed.), *Human Rights: Concepts and Standards* (Aldershot: UNESCO Publishing, 2000), 109–74.

as the African Commission on Human and Peoples' Rights in some of its decisions,[79] which provide a useful analytical framework to understand state obligations.

In order to comply with the obligation to achieve ESC rights 'progressively', states parties are required to monitor the realization of ESC rights and to devise appropriate strategies and clearly defined programmes (including indicators – carefully chosen yardsticks for measuring elements of the right – and national benchmarks – or targets – for each indicator) for their implementation.[80] Monitoring the progressive realization of ESC rights is important because it helps to identify what steps have been most effective, so that these can be maintained, and what steps have been less effective, so that new steps can be adopted. A human rights approach to government actions must begin with a proper understanding of the actual situation in respect of each right, accurate identification of the most vulnerable groups, and the formulation of appropriate laws, programmes and policies.[81]

The obligation of progressive realization entails a related prohibition of 'any deliberately retrogressive measures'.[82] Unless otherwise justified 'after the most careful consideration of all alternatives' and 'by reference to the totality of the rights provided for in the Covenant in the context of the full use of the state party's maximum available resources',[83] the adoption of measures (legislation or policy) that cause a clear deterioration or setback in the protection of rights hitherto afforded violates the ICESCR.[84] For example, unless justified in accordance with the above criteria, 'the re-introduction of fees at the tertiary level of education … constitutes a deliberately retrogressive step',[85] especially where adequate arrangements are not made for students from poorer segments of the population or lower socio-economic groups.[86] In this respect, while commenting on the UK's policy on tuition fees for tertiary education, which provides for lower fees for the European Union (EU) member state nationals while subjecting nationals of other states (so-called 'international students') to higher levels of fees, the CESCR has stated as follows:

> In line with General Comment No. 13 (1999) on the right to education, the Committee encourages the State party to review its policy on tuition fees for tertiary education with a view to implementing article 13 of the Covenant, which provides for the progressive introduction of free education at all levels. It also recommends that the State party eliminate the unequal treatment between EU

79 See e.g. *The Social and Economic Rights Action Center and the Center for Economic and Social Rights/Nigeria*, Communication 155/96, note 30 above, para. 44.

80 CESCR, *General Comment 14*, paras. 57–58; P. Alston, 'Out of the Abyss: The Challenges Confronting the New UN Committee on Economic, Social and Cultural Rights', *Human Rights Quarterly*, 9(3) (1987), pp. 332–81, at pp. 357–8; Maastricht Guidelines (1997), para. 8. For example, in the 2002 World Summit on Sustainable Development Plan of Implementation, states made a commitment to halve, by the year 2015, the proportion of people who are unable to reach or to afford safe drinking water (as outlined in the Millennium Declaration) and the proportion of people who do not have access to basic sanitation.

81 CESCR, *Concluding Observations*: *Republic of Korea*, UN Doc. E/C.12/1/Add.59 (21 May 2001), para. 34.

82 CESCR, *General Comment 3*, para. 9.

83 CESCR, *General Comment 13*, para. 45; CESCR, *General Comment 14*, para. 32; CESCR, *General Comment 15*, para. 19; *General Comment 21*, para. 65.

84 The Maastricht Guidelines, 14(e); CESCR, *General Comment 21*, paras. 46 and 65.

85 CESCR, *Concluding Observations: Mauritius*, UN Doc. E/C.12/1994/8 (31 May 1994), para. 16.

86 See e.g. CESCR, *General Comment 13: The Right to Education*, UN Doc. E/C.12/1999/10 (8 December 1999), paras. 14, 20, and 45; CESCR, *Concluding Observations: United Kingdom,* UN Doc. E/C.12/1/Add.79 (5 June 2002), paras. 22 and 41.

member State nationals and nationals of other States regarding the reduction of university fees and the allocation of financial assistance.[87]

Since ESC rights under the ICESCR apply to everyone within a state's jurisdiction, including non-nationals, the standard of progressive realization requires that nationality and other prohibited grounds should not be a bar to the equal enjoyment of all ESC rights including the right to higher education.

3.3 Obligation to Utilize 'maximum available resources'

The third obligation is to ensure that 'maximum available resources' are allocated for the protection and fulfilment of ESC rights, especially to the most vulnerable and marginalized individuals and groups. Thus, the steps that a state party is obliged to take under Article 2(1) to realize progressively the enumerated rights must be 'to the maximum of its available resources'.[88] Chapman has noted that evaluating progressive realization within the context of resource availability 'considerably complicates the methodological requirements' for monitoring.[89] There are two practical difficulties in applying this requirement to measure state compliance with the full use of maximum available resources. The first is in determining what resources are 'available' to a particular state to give effect to the substantive rights under the ICESCR. The second difficulty is to determine whether a state has used such available resources to the 'maximum'. It has been suggested that the word 'available' leaves too much 'wriggle room for the state',[90] making it difficult to define the content of the progressive obligation and to establish when a breach of this obligation arises.[91] Nonetheless, it is clear that the ICESCR does not make an absurd demand – a state is not required to take steps beyond what its available resources permit. The implication is that more would be expected from high-income states than low-income states, particularly the least developed states.[92] This means that both the content of the obligation and the rate at which it is achieved are subject to the maximum use of available resources.

The availability of resources refers not only to those which are controlled by or filtered through the state or other public bodies, but also to the social resources which can be mobilized by the widest possible participation in development, as necessary for the realization by every human

87 CESCR, *Concluding Observations: United Kingdom*, UN Doc. E/C.12/GBR/CO/5 (22 May 2009), para. 44.

88 See CESCR, *General Comment 3*, para. 9; *General Comment 13*, para. 44; and *General Comment 14*, para. 31; Limburg Principles, para. 21.

89 A. Chapman, 'A "Violations Approach" for Monitoring the International Covenant on Economic, Social and Cultural Rights', *Human Rights Quarterly*, 18(1) (1996), pp. 23–66, at p. 31; A. Chapman and S. Russell, 'Introduction' in A. Chapman and S. Russell (eds), *Core Obligations: Building a Framework for Economic, Social and Cultural Rights* (Antwerp: Intersentia, 2002), 1–19, at p. 5.

90 See R. Robertson, 'Measuring State Compliance with the Obligation to Devote the "Maximum Available Resources" to Realising Economic, Social and Cultural Rights', *Human Rights Quarterly*, 16(4) (1994), p. 693, at p. 694.

91 S. Joseph *et al.*, *The International Covenant on Civil and Political Rights: Cases, Materials and Commentary* (Oxford: Oxford University Press, 2000), p. 7.

92 In 2004, the UN identified 50 states as the 'Least Developed Countries'. See UN LDCs List at http://www.un.org/special-rep/ohrlls/ldc/list.htm; UNCTAD, *The Least Developed Countries Report 2004* (New York and Geneva: United Nations, 2004), p. 318.

being of ESC rights.[93] In this respect 'available resources' refer to resources available within the society as a whole, 'from the private sector as well as the public. It is the state's responsibility to mobilize these resources, not to provide them all directly from its own coffers'.[94] As shown below, available resources also include those available through international cooperation and assistance.

Given that one of the major issues in the realization of ESC rights is not resource availability but rather resource distribution, states should demonstrate that the available resources are used equitably and are effectively targeted to subsistence requirements and essential services,[95] and targeted towards those that are most in need, including women, children, older persons, persons with disabilities, minorities, migrants, indigenous peoples, and persons living in poverty. To this end, the CESCR requires states to adopt strong, efficient and time-framed measures to promote good governance and combat the corruption that negatively impacts on the availability of resources.[96] Corruption may be combated by adopting and strictly applying anti-corruption legislation and measures; intensifying efforts to prosecute cases of corruption and reviewing sentencing policy for corruption-related offences; and raising the awareness of politicians, lawmakers, national and local civil servants, and law enforcement officers on the negative impact of corruption, as well as adopting effective mechanisms to ensure transparency in the conduct of public authorities, in law and in practice. At the same time, states should demonstrate that they are developing societal resources to achieve ESC rights.[97] In this respect, it is important to note that although states generally have a 'margin of discretion'[98] to decide how to allocate the available resources, 'due priority' must be given to the realization of human rights including ESC rights.[99] Thus, it is important for the state to make appropriate choices in the allocation of the available resources in ways which ensure that the most vulnerable are given priority.[100] All domestic resources must be considered for use by the state because human rights generally deserve priority over all other considerations.[101]

In determining state compliance with the obligation to utilize the 'maximum available resources', the CESCR has developed in its 'Concluding Observations' some useful indicators.

93 See A. Eide, 'Economic and Social Rights', in J. Symonides (ed.), *Human Rights: Concepts*; *Declaration on the Right to Development* (GAR 41/128 of 4 December 1986), Art. 2, stating in part: '1. The human being is a central subject of development and should be the active participant and beneficiary of the right to development. 2. All human beings have a responsibility for development, individually and collectively'.

94 Chapman and Russell, note 89 above, p. 11.

95 Limburg Principles, paras. 23, 27 and 28.

96 See e.g. CESCR, *Concluding Observations: Nigeria*, UN Doc. E/1999/22, paras. 97 and 119; *Mexico*, UN Doc. E/2000/22, paras. 381 and 394; CESCR, *Concluding Observations: Cambodia*, UN Doc (22 May 2009), para. 14; CESCR, *Concluding Observations: Democratic Republic of Congo*, UN Doc. E/C.12/COD/CO/4 (20 November 2009), para. 11; CESCR, *Concluding Observations: Madagascar*, UN Doc. E/ C.12/MDG/CO/2 (20 November 2009), para. 11.

97 Limburg Principles, 24.

98 CESCR, *General Comments 14, 15, 16* and *21*, paras. 53, 45, 32 and 66 respectively. See also CESCR, statement, note 108 below, para. 11, stating that 'in accordance with the practice of judicial and other quasi-judicial human rights treaty bodies, the Committee always respects the margin of appreciation of states to take steps and adopt measures most suited to their specific circumstances'.

99 Limburg Principles, para. 28. See also CRC, *Concluding Observations: Rwanda*, UN Doc. CRC/C/15/Add.236 (4 June 2004), para. 18.

100 See A. Eide, 'The Use of Indicators in the Practice of the Committee on Economic, Social and Cultural Rights', in A. Eide, C. Krause and A. Rosas (eds), *Economic, Social and Cultural Rights: A Textbook*, 2nd edn (Dordrecht: Martinus Nijhoff Publishers: 2001), pp. 545–51, at p. 549.

101 Robertson, note 90 above, p. 700.

One indicator is to consider the percentage of the national budget allocated to specific rights under the ICESCR (such as health, education, housing, and social security) relative to areas outside it (such as military expenditure or debt-servicing). Many resource problems revolve around the misallocation of available resources: for example, to purchase expensive military weapons systems rather than to invest in primary education or primary or preventive health services.[102] In 2001, for example, with respect to Senegal, the CESCR stated:

> The Committee [was] concerned that funds allocated by the state party for basic social services … fall far short of the minimum social expenditure required to cover such services. In this regard the Committee note[d] with regret that more is spent by the state party on the military and on servicing its debt than on basic social services.[103]

Similarly, in 2009, the CESCR expressed its concern about the continuous decrease over the past decade of the resources allocated to social sectors in the Democratic Republic of Congo (DRC), notably health and social protection, whereas budgetary allocations to defence and public security had increased considerably to reach 30% of the state expenditures.[104] The CESCR concluded that 'unbalanced budgetary allocations constitute *serious breaches* in the State party's obligations under article 2.1 of the Covenant', and it recommended that the DRC substantially increase its national spending on social services and assistance such as housing, food, health and education, so as to achieve, in accordance with Article 2, paragraph 1, the progressive realization of the ESC rights provided for in the ICESCR.[105]

It follows that where a state spends more on the military than on basic social services, it would have a high burden to convince the CESCR that it had utilized available resources to the 'maximum' as required by the ICESCR. It is, accordingly, imperative to consider the priority or rate of resource allocation to military expenditure in comparison to the expenditure on ESC rights.[106] A reordering of priorities and an increase in budgetary allocations for ESC rights may alleviate some of the resource burden of any state. Another indicator that may be applied is to consider the resources spent by a particular state in the implementation of a specific ICESCR right and that which is spent by other states at the same level of development.

It is striking to note that when the OP to the ICESCR enters into force, it would be possible for the CESCR to receive and consider communications submitted by or on behalf of individuals or groups of individuals under the jurisdiction of a state party, claiming to be victims of a violation of any of the ESC rights set forth in the ICESCR against states parties to the OP.[107] If a communication

---

102 See e.g. CESCR, *Concluding Observations: Philippines*, UN Doc. E/C.12/1995/7 (7 June 1995), para. 21, stating that 'in terms of the availability of resources, the Committee notes with concern that a greater proportion of the national budget is devoted to military spending than to housing, agriculture and health combined'.

103 CESCR, *Concluding Observations: Senegal*, UN Doc. E/C.12/1/Add.62 (24 September 2001), para. 23.

104 CESCR, *Concluding Observations: Democratic Republic of Congo*, UN Doc. E/C.12/COD/CO/4 (20 November 2009), para. 16.

105 *Ibid.* (emphasis added).

106 Eide rightly argued that 'The "expenditure of death" should be turned into "expenditure of life" (public action to combat poverty)'. See A. Eide, 'Economic, Social and Cultural Rights as Human Rights', in A. Eide, C. Krause and A. Rosas (eds), *Economic, Social and Cultural Rights: A Textbook*, 2nd edn (Dordrecht: Martinus Nijhoff Publishers, 2001), pp. 9–28, at p. 28.

107 Optional Protocol to the ICESCR, note 11 above, Art. 1 and 2.

was brought against a state party to the ICESCR and its OP, and the state used 'resource constraints' as an explanation for any retrogressive steps taken, the CESCR has indicated that it would consider such information on a country-by-country basis in the light of objective criteria such as:

(a) the country's level of development;
(b) the severity of the alleged breach, in particular whether the situation concerned the enjoyment of the minimum core content of the Covenant;
(c) the country's current economic situation, in particular whether the country was undergoing a period of economic recession;
(d) the existence of other serious claims on the state party's limited resources; for example, resulting from a recent natural disaster or from recent internal or international armed conflict;
(e) whether the state party had sought to identify low-cost options; and
(f) whether the state party had sought cooperation and assistance or rejected offers of resources from the international community for the purposes of implementing the provisions of the Covenant without sufficient reason.[108]

The obligation to take steps to the maximum of a state's 'available resources' means that in making any assessment as to whether a state is in breach of its obligations to achieve the rights recognized under the ICESCR of a particular individual or group, an assessment must be made as to whether the steps taken were 'adequate' or 'reasonable' by taking into account, *inter alia*, the following considerations:

(a) the extent to which the measures taken were deliberate, concrete and targeted towards the fulfilment of economic, social and cultural rights;
(b) whether the state party exercised its discretion in a non-discriminatory and non-arbitrary manner;
(c) whether the state party's decision (not) to allocate available resources is in accordance with international human rights standards;
(d) where several policy options are available, whether the state party adopts the option that least restricts Covenant rights;
(e).the time frame in which the steps were taken;
(f) whether the steps had taken into account the precarious situation of disadvantaged and marginalized individuals or groups and, whether they were non-discriminatory, and whether they prioritized grave situations or situations of risk.[109]

In the context of an OP communication, where the CESCR considers that a state party has not taken reasonable or adequate steps, the CESCR could make recommendations, *inter alia*, along four principal lines:

(a) recommending remedial action, such as compensation, to the victim, as appropriate;
(b) calling upon the state party to remedy the circumstances leading to a violation. In doing so, the Committee might suggest goals and parameters to assist the state party in identifying

108 CESCR, *Statement: An Evaluation of the Obligation to Take Steps to the 'Maximum of Available Resources' Under an Optional Protocol to the Covenant*, UN Doc. E/C.12/2007/1 (10 May 2007), para. 9.

109 *Ibid.*, para. 8.

appropriate measures. These parameters could include suggesting overall priorities to ensure that resource allocation conformed with the state party's obligations under the Covenant; provision for the disadvantaged and marginalised individuals and groups; protection against grave threats to the enjoyment of economic, social and cultural rights; and respect for non-discrimination in the adoption and implementation of measures;

(c) suggesting, on a case-by-case basis, a range of measures to assist the state party in implementing the recommendations, with particular emphasis on low-cost measures. The state party would nonetheless still have the option of adopting its own alternative measures;

(d) recommending a follow-up mechanism to ensure ongoing accountability of the state party; for example, by including a requirement that in its next periodic report the state party explain the steps taken to redress the violation.[110]

From the above, it is clear that the obligation to use 'maximum available resources' may be subjected to judicial or quasi-judicial scrutiny, and, as such, it is not a bar to justiciability. As noted in Section 2 above, domestic courts have dealt with cases that aim at the protection of ESC rights. In South Africa, for example, under the Constitution of the Republic of South Africa (Act 108 of 1996), which guarantees numerous ESC rights, the justiciability of ESC rights has been demonstrated through constitutional case law.[111] For example, the case of *Minister of Health* v *Treatment Action Campaign* concerned state provision of nevirapine, an antiretroviral drug used to prevent mother-to-child-transmission of HIV.[112] Applying the concepts of progressive realization and resource availability, the South African Constitutional Court declared that

> Sections 27(1) and (2) of the Constitution require the government to devise and implement within its available resources a comprehensive and co-ordinated programme to realise progressively the rights of pregnant women and their newborn children to have access to health services to combat mother-to-child transmission of HIV.[113]

The programme to be realized progressively within available resources had to include reasonable measures for counselling and testing pregnant women for HIV, counselling HIV-positive pregnant women on the options open to them to reduce the risk of mother-to-child transmission of HIV, and making appropriate treatment available to them for such purposes.[114] Simply put, through the institution of the courts, governments can be called upon to account for their decisions affecting ESC rights, and this may impact beneficially on the policymaking process.

Therefore, although the 'availability of resources' is an important qualifier to the realization of ESC rights, it does not alter the immediacy of the obligation to 'take steps', including legislative and other measures, to achieve the 'progressive realization' of these rights. Similarly, resource

110 *Ibid.*, para. 13. See also the Optional Protocol to the ICESCR, note 11 above, Art. 9.

111 For a discussion, see D. M. Davis, 'Socioeconomic Rights: Do They Deliver the Goods?', *International Journal of Constitutional Law*, 6(3–4) (2008), pp. 687–711.

112 CCT 8/02, [2002] ZACC 15; 2002 (5) SA 721; 2002 (10) BCLR 1033 (5 July 2002).

113 *Ibid.*, para. 135. Section 27 reads: '1) Everyone has the right to have access to (a) health care services, including reproductive health care; (b) sufficient food and water; and (c) social security, including, if they are unable to support themselves and their dependants, appropriate social assistance. (2) The state must take reasonable legislative and other measures, within its available resources, to achieve the progressive realization of each of these rights. (3) No one may be refused emergency medical treatment'.

114 *Ibid.*

constraints alone should not justify inaction and certainly should not be seen as a bar to judicial review. Where the available resources are demonstrably inadequate, the obligation remains for a state to ensure the widest possible enjoyment of ESC rights by taking reasonable or adequate steps under the prevailing circumstances. It follows therefore that even in times of severe resource constraints the state must protect the most disadvantaged and marginalized members or groups of society by adopting relatively low-cost targeted programmes for the realization of ESC rights.

3.4 Obligation to Seek (or Provide) International Assistance and Cooperation

The fourth state obligation is to seek or provide international assistance and cooperation whenever it is necessary to do so. The ICESCR refers to international assistance and cooperation, or similar formulations, in five articles.[115] International assistance and cooperation may be regarded as one element of the more extensive right to development that was affirmed in the Declaration on the Right to Development (1986)[116] and the Vienna Declaration and Programme of Action (1993).[117] More recently, 191 states recognized explicitly in the Millennium Declaration the link between the realization of the right to development and poverty reduction, and committed themselves to make 'the right to development a reality for everyone' and to free 'the entire human race from want'.[118]

Does 'international assistance and cooperation' oblige developed states to transfer resources to developing states? And are developing states obliged to seek such 'assistance and cooperation'? In general, while most developed states give assistance to developing states,[119] developed states have consistently denied the existence of any clear legal obligation to transfer resources to the developing states.[120] It has further been argued that 'although there is clearly an obligation to cooperate internationally, it is not clear whether this means that wealthy States Parties are obliged to provide aid to assist in the realisation of the rights in other countries'.[121] In the debates surrounding the drafting of the OP to the ICESCR, the representatives of the UK, the Czech Republic, Canada, France and Portugal believed that international cooperation and assistance was an 'important moral obligation' but 'not a legal entitlement', and they did not interpret the ICESCR to impose a legal obligation to provide development assistance or give a legal right to receive such aid.[122] It

115 See ICESCR, Art. 2(1), 11, 15, 22 and 23. For a discussion of these articles, see S.I. Skogly, *Beyond National Borders: States' Human Rights Obligations in International Cooperation* (Antwerp, Intersentia, 2006), pp. 83–98. See also UN Charter, Art. 1, 55, and 56; UDHR, Art. 22 and 28; Convention on the Rights of the Child, Arts. 4, 7(2); 11(2), 17(b), 21(e), 22(2), 23(4), 24(4), 27(4), 28(3), 34 and 35.

116 GA Res. 41/128, annex, 41 UN GAOR Supp. (No. 53) at 186, UN Doc. A/41/53 (1986).

117 Vienna Declaration (1993), paras. 9, 12 and 34.

118 Office of the UNHCHR, *Draft Guidelines: A Human Rights Approach to Poverty Reduction Strategies* (2002), para. 215 [online]. Available from: http://www.unhchr.ch/pdf/povertyfinal.pdf [accessed 26 August 2010].

119 P.S. Heller and S. Gupta, *Challenges in Expanding Development Assistance* (Washington, DC: IMF, 2002) [online]. Available from: http://www.imf.org/external/pubs/ft/pdp/2002/pdp05.pdf [accessed 1 May 2009]. For the designation of a state as 'developed' and 'developing', see United Nations, Standard Country or Area Codes for Statistical Use, Series M, No. 49, Rev. 4 (United Nations publication, Sales No. M.98. XVII.9) [online]. Available in part from: http://unstats.un.org/unsd/methods/m49/m49regin.htm.

120 Alston and Quinn, note 64 above, at pp. 186–91.

121 M. Craven, 'The International Covenant on Economic, Social and Cultural Rights', in R. Hanski and M. Suksi (eds), *An Introduction to the International Protection of Human Rights: A Textbook*, 2nd edn (Åbo: Åbo Akademi University, 1999), pp. 101–23.

122 See Report of the Open-ended Working Group to Consider Options Regarding the Elaboration of an Optional Protocol to the International Covenant on Economic, Social and Cultural Rights on Its Second

is not surprising, then, that the final text of the OP contained a weaker provision on 'international assistance and cooperation' in its Article 14 by referring only to the 'need for technical advice or assistance' in Article 14(1) and establishing a trust fund with a view to 'providing expert and technical assistance to States Parties' without prejudice to the obligations of each state party to fulfil its obligations under the ICESCR in Article 14(3) and (4) of the OP. Significantly, however, the OP did not exclude other possible forms of international cooperation and assistance. Although these were not stated in either the ICESCR or its OP, other possible forms of assistance could include the conclusion of international agreements; the provision of human resources, enabling access to literature; the development of collaborative research agendas that enable researchers in developed states to address issues affecting developing states; educational and academic scholarships and exchanges; direct investment; and joint venture programmes in the creation of various projects relating to various aspects of ESC rights.

But if there is no legal obligation underpinning the human rights responsibility of international assistance and cooperation, then, inescapably, all international assistance and cooperation fundamentally rests upon charity.[123] Is such a position tenable and acceptable in the twenty-first century? Increasingly, human rights scholars have argued for a legal obligation to underpin international assistance and cooperation.[124] The CESCR's approach also seems to suggest that the economically developed states parties to the ICESCR are under an obligation to assist developing states parties to realize the core obligations of ESC rights. Thus, the CESCR has stressed that 'it is particularly incumbent on all those who can assist, to help developing countries respect this international minimum threshold'.[125] By implication, where a developing state is in need of assistance to comply with its minimum core obligations there is an obligation to seek assistance and cooperation from 'all those who can assist'.

For example, after identifying core obligations in relation to the right to water, the CESCR emphasized that 'it is particularly incumbent on states parties, and other actors in position to assist, to *provide* international assistance and cooperation, especially economic and technical which enables developing countries to fulfil their core obligations'.[126] In the course of examination of state reports, the CESCR has enquired into the percentage of gross domestic/national product (GDP/GNP) that developed reporting states dedicate to international cooperation[127] and Official Development Assistance (ODA).[128] The UN-recommended target/benchmark of 0.7% GDP[129] was reiterated along with other targets in the Monterrey Consensus, arising from the 2002 International

Session, UN Doc. E/CN.4/2005/52 (10 February 2005), para. 76.

123 See Report of the Special Rapporteur on the Right of Everyone to the Enjoyment of the Highest Attainable Standard of Physical and Mental Health. Paul Hunt, Addendum: Missions to the World Bank and the International Monetary Fund in Washington, DC (20 October 2006) and Uganda UN Doc. A/HRC/7/11/Add.2 (5 March 2008), para. 133.

124 *Ibid.*

125 CESCR, UN Doc. E/C.12/2001/10, note 74 above, para. 17.

126 CESCR, *General Comment 15*, para. 38 (emphasis added).

127 See e.g. CESCR, *Summary Record: Ireland*, UN Doc. E/C.12/1999/SR.14, para. 38.

128 See e.g. CESCR, *Summary Records: Japan*, UN Doc. E/C.12/2001/SR.42, para. 10; *Germany*, UN Doc. E/C.12/2001/SR.48, para. 37.

129 This was originally proposed by the Pearson Commission in 1968 and adopted in 1970. See GA Res. 2226, 25 UN GAOR Supp. (No. 28), para. 43, UN Doc. A/8028 (1970); K. Tomasevski, *Development Aid and Human Rights Revisited* (London: Pinter, 1993), p. 32. This target was reaffirmed in the Copenhagen Declaration on Social Development 1995, Commitment 9, UN Doc. A/CONF.166/9 (14 March 1995), para. 1.

Conference on Financing for Development.[130] This was reaffirmed at the Follow-up International Conference on Financing for Development to Review the Implementation of the Monterrey Consensus, held in Doha on 29 November–2 December 2008.

However, by 2000, only five states had reached or exceeded the target of 0.7% of GDP in ODA.[131] Most developed states (particularly the Group of Eight (G8) industrialized states) were far below the level of 0.7%, with an average of 0.22%.[132] In 2008–09, for example, Australia devoted only 0.32% of its gross national income (GNI) to ODA.[133] In 2007, the only states to reach or exceed the UN's target of 0.7% of their GNI were Denmark, Luxembourg, The Netherlands, Norway and Sweden.[134] The average for all member countries of the Development Assistance Committee (DAC) of the Organization for Economic Cooperation and Development (OECD) was just 0.09%.[135]

Despite this state practice, the CESCR commonly 'recommends' and 'encourages' developed states parties 'to increase ODA as a percentage of GNP to a level approaching the 0.7 per cent goal established by the United Nations'.[136] States have been criticized where the levels devoted to international assistance and cooperation fall below this target,[137] and urged to 'review ... budget allocation to international cooperation'[138] with a view 'to ensure ... as quickly as possible, the UN target of 0.7% GNP'.[139] Other states that have donated more than this target have been commended.[140] Similarly, the CESCR has considered as a 'positive aspect' a state's commitment to achieve the granting of 0.7% of GDP by a specific date. For example, in May 2009, the CESCR acknowledged

---

130 Report of the International Conference on Financing for Development Monterrey, Mexico, 18–22 March 2002, A/Conf.198/11.

131 These states are Denmark (1.06%), The Netherlands (0.82%), Sweden (0.81%), Norway (0.80%) and Luxembourg (0.70%). See OECD, Press release, 20 April 2001.

132 *Ibid.* Examples are Belgium (0.36%); Ireland (0.30); Japan, Germany and Australia (0.27%); New Zealand and Portugal (0.26); Canada and Austria (0.25); Spain (0.24%); Greece (0.19%); Italy (0.13%) and the USA (0.10%). See also U.N. Wire, 'World Bank Head Blasts Rich Nations for Record on Aid', 5 May 2004.

133 CESCR, *Concluding Observations: Australia*, UN Doc. E/C.12/AUS/CO/4 (22 May 2009), para. 12.

134 See the MDG Gap Task Force Report 2008, *Millennium Development Goal 8: Delivering on the Global Partnership for Achieving the Millennium Development Goals* (New York: United Nations, 2008), p. vii.

135 *Ibid.*

136 See e.g. CESCR, *Concluding Observations: Belgium*, UN Doc. E/C.12/1/Add.54 (2000), paras. 16 and 30; *Finland*, E/C.12/1/Add.52 (2000), paras. 13 and 23; *Ireland*, E/C.12/1/Add.77 (2002), para. 38; *Spain*, E/C.12/1/Add.99 (2004), para. 27. In May 2008, the CESCR recommended that France 'increase its official development assistance to 0.7 per cent of its GDP, as agreed by the Heads of State and Government at the International Conference on Financing for Development, held in Monterrey (Mexico) on 18–22 March 2002'. See CESCR, *Concluding Observations: France*, UN Doc. E/C.12/FRA/CO/3 (2008), para. 32. See also Committee on the Rights of the Child, *General Comment 5, General Measures of Implementation for the Convention on the Rights of the Child,* UN Doc. CRC/GC/2003/5 (3 October 2003), para. 61.

137 See e.g. CESCR, *Concluding Observations: Spain*, UN Doc. E/C.12/1/Add.99 (2004), paras. 10 and 27; *France*, UN Doc. E/C.12/FRA/CO/3 (May 2008), para. 12.

138 CESCR, *Concluding Observations: Belgium*, UN Doc. E/C.12/1/Add.54, para. 30.

139 CESCR, *Concluding Observations: Ireland*, UN Doc. E/C.12/1/Add.77 (17 May 2002), para. 38. See also CESCR, *Concluding Observations: Korea*, UN Doc. E/C.12/KOR/CO/3 (20 November 2009), para. 7.

140 See e.g. CESCR, *Concluding Observations: Denmark*, UN Doc. E/C.12/1/Add.34, para. 11, commended for devoting 1% of GDP to international assistance and cooperation. See also CESCR, *Luxembourg*, UN Doc. E/C.12/1/Add.86 (2003), para. 6.

the UK's 'commitment to achieve by 2013 the granting of 0.7% of its Gross Domestic Income as official development assistance in accordance with internationally agreed policies'.[141]

Given the large and growing gap between developed and developing states, and the fact that half the world – nearly 3 billion people – live on less than $2 a day,[142] economically developed states can play a key role in enhancing the enjoyment of ESC rights by granting further assistance, especially technical or economic, to developing states targeted to ESC rights. The large investment requirements of developing states imply that a successful transition to increased reliance on domestic resources and private capital inflows will require more, rather than less, ODA.[143] Interestingly, the European Union (EU) member states have made commitments to increase ODA over a period of time. The targets were stated as follows: (1) 0.33% by 2006, according to the EU Barcelona commitment; and (2) 0.51% by 2010 and 0.7% by 2015, according to the May 2005 EU Council agreement.[144] While this progressive commitment to increase ODA is a step in the right direction, it should be noted that many activities undertaken in the name of development have subsequently been recognized as 'ill-conceived and even counter productive in human rights terms',[145] partly because ODA is not necessarily linked to respect, protect and fulfil human rights including ESC rights. Thus, it is necessary to ensure that states giving ODA and states receiving it relate ODA to the progressive realization of ESC rights. In particular, states receiving international development aid should ensure that there are sustainable institutional frameworks for its absorption and utilization and that such aid is not mismanaged, since the 'mismanagement of international cooperation aid … constitutes *serious breaches* in the State party's obligations under article 2.1 of the Covenant'.[146]

It has to be acknowledged that international assistance and cooperation, including economic aid, entails procedural fairness. Thus, donor states have a responsibility not to withdraw critical aid without first giving the recipient state reasonable notice and opportunity to make alternative arrangements.[147] In addition, states providing aid must refrain from attaching conditions to such aid that are reasonably foreseeable to result in the violation of international human rights law in other states. This is consistent with international law providing a general duty on states not to act in such a way as to cause harm outside its territory.[148]

In order to monitor the use of transferred resources, the CESCR has sought to establish whether resources transferred are used to promote respect for the ICESCR and whether such resources are

---

141 CESCR, *Concluding Observations: United Kingdom*, UN Doc. E/C.12/GBR/CO/5 (22 May 2009), para. 9.

142 UNDP, *The Human Development Report 2007/2008* (New York: Palgrave Macmillan, 2007), p. 25 [online]. Available from: http://hdr.undp.org/en/reports/global/hdr2007-2008/chapters/. The report notes that 'There are still around 1 billion people living at the margins of survival on less than US$1 a day, with 2.6 billion – 40 percent of the world's population –living on less than US$2 a day'.

143 See UNCTAD, 'The Challenge of Financing Development in LDCs', 3rd United Nations Conference on the Least Developed Countries, Brussels, 14–20 May 2001, http://r0.unctad.org/conference/e-press_kit/financing.pdf.

144 See *OECD Journal on Development*, 7(3) (2006), p. 38.

145 CESCR, *General Comment 2: International Technical Assistance Measures*, UN Doc. E/1990/23 (2 February 1990), para. 7.

146 CESCR, *Concluding Observations: Democratic Republic of Congo*, UN Doc. E/C.12/COD/CO/4 (20 November 2009), para. 16 (emphasis added).

147 See Report of the Special Rapporteur, note 123 above, para. 29.

148 See e.g. *The Rainbow Warrior (New Zealand* v *France)* (Arbitration Tribunal) (1990), 82 ILR 449.

contingent upon the human rights record of the receiving country.[149] The CESCR has also asked whether states had formulated a policy on the objective of allocating 0.7% of GDP to ODA.[150]

While the CESCR can investigate all such issues, it is questionable whether it can find a particular developed state to be in violation of Article 2(1) for the failure to devote 0.7% of its GDP on international assistance. Similarly, it is inconceivable that the CESCR can direct or identify a specific developed state to assist a particular developing state party, since the criteria for doing so are not yet clearly drawn, and seem to be difficult to justify. For example, there is no legal basis for directing Canada to assist any of the least developed states. Nonetheless, it is important to note that international assistance and cooperation should not be understood as encompassing only financial and technical assistance: it also includes a responsibility to work actively towards equitable multilateral trading, investment and financial systems that are conducive to the realization of human rights and the elimination of poverty.[151] This may entail genuine special and preferential treatment of developing states so as to provide such states with better access to developed states' markets.[152]

This equitable system is yet to be realized. In 2006, for example, Joseph Stiglitz, former Chief Economist of the World Bank, noted that:

> We see an unfair global trade regime that impedes development and an unsustainable global financial system in which poor countries repeatedly find themselves with unmanageable debt burdens. Money should flow from the rich to poor countries, but increasingly, it goes in the opposite direction.[153]

Therefore, ODA alone without an equitable multilateral trading system would not lead to meaningful realization of ESC rights in poorer developing states. As Oxfam International estimated in 2002, an increase of 5% in the share of world trade by low-income states 'would generate more than $350 billion – seven times as much as they receive in aid'.[154]

3.5 Extraterritorial Human Rights Obligations

This section considers briefly whether states parties' human rights obligations arising under the ICESCR are limited to individuals and groups within a state's territory or whether a state can be liable for the acts and omissions of its agents which produce effects on ESC rights or are

149 See e.g. CESCR, *Summary Records*: *Ireland* E/C.12/1999/SR.14 (2 February 2000), para. 38; *Germany*, UN Doc. E/C.12/2001/SR.48 (31 August 2001), para. 19; and *Finland*, UN Doc. E/C.12/2000/SR.61 (21 November 2000), para. 48.

150 See CESCR, *Summary Records*: *Finland*, UN Doc. E/C.12/2007/SR.11 (15 May 2007), para. 11.

151 P. Hunt, 'Mission to the WTO', UN Doc. E/CN.4/2004/49/Add.1, para. 28.

152 Report of the High Commissioner, UN Doc. E/CN.4/2004/40, para. 40. For a summary of issues relating to the participation of developing countries in the multilateral trading system, see S. Lester and B. Mercurio, *World Trade Law: Text, Materials and Commentary* (Oxford: Hart Publishing, 2008), pp. 779–817; M Matsushita *et al.*, *The World Trade Organization: Law, Practice and Policy*, 2nd edn (Oxford: Oxford University Press, 2006), pp. 763–84.

153 J. Stiglitz, 'We Have Become Rich Countries of Poor People', *Financial Times*, 7 September 2006.

154 Oxfam, *Rigged Rules and Double Standards*: *Trade, Globalisation and the Fight against Poverty* (Oxford: Oxfam, 2002), p. 48. For a further discussion of the intricacies of foreign aid, see, generally, R.C. Riddle, *Does Foreign Aid Really Work?* (Oxford: Oxford University Press, 2008).

undertaken beyond national territory (e.g. to those individuals and groups who are not within the state's territory but who are subject to a state's jurisdiction).[155] Although the ICESCR refers to 'international assistance and cooperation', it does not make any explicit reference to territory or jurisdiction, in contrast to the ICCPR.[156]

The general territorial scope of treaties is stated in Article 29 of the Vienna Convention on the Law of Treaties[157] as follows: 'Unless a different intention appears from the treaty or is otherwise established, a treaty is binding upon each party in respect of its entire territory'. If we apply this provision to the ICESCR, it can be stated that the ICESCR is binding upon each state party in respect of the entire territory of each state party unless a different intention appears or is otherwise stated. However, limiting state obligations to the territory of each state party is inadequate in an increasingly globalized world especially in the post-9/11 environment where some states have waged a 'war on terrorism' abroad, often leading to violations of human rights including ESC rights. Thus, it is argued below that the text of the ICESCR, while primarily providing for territorial obligations, leaves some scope for extraterritorial application.

The International Court of Justice (ICJ) has acknowledged some space, albeit in a restrictive way, for the extraterritorial application of the ICESCR. In its Advisory Opinion of 9 July 2004, *Legal Consequences of the Construction of a Wall in the Occupied Palestinian Territory* (*The Wall*), the ICJ held:

> The International Covenant on Economic, Social and Cultural Rights contains no provision on its scope of application. This may be explicable by the fact that this Covenant guarantees rights which are essentially territorial. However, it is not to be excluded that it applies both to territories over which a state party has sovereignty and to those over which that state exercises territorial jurisdiction. Thus Article 14 makes provision for transitional measures in the case of any state which 'at the time of becoming a Party, has not been able to secure in its metropolitan territory or other territories under its jurisdiction compulsory primary education, free of charge'.[158]

This position was confirmed by the ICJ in its decision in *Democratic Republic of Congo v Uganda*, in which the court stated that 'international human rights instruments are applicable in respect of acts done by a state in the exercise of its jurisdiction outside its own territory, particularly in occupied territories'.[159] Thus, human rights treaties extend state obligations to those within their

155 For a detailed discussion of the term 'jurisdiction' in public international law, see, generally, M. Shaw, *International Law*, 6th edn (Cambridge: Cambridge University Press, 2008), pp. 645–96; I. Brownlie, *Principles of Public International Law*, 7th edn (Oxford: Oxford University Press, 2008), pp. 299–321; V. Lowe, 'Jurisdiction', in M. Evans (ed.), *International Law*, 2nd edn (Oxford: Oxford University Press, 2006), p. 335; and M. Akehurst, 'Jurisdiction in International Law', *British Year Book of International Law*, 46 (1972–3), p. 145.

156 Article 2(1) of the ICCPR provides: '1. Each state Party to the present Covenant undertakes to respect and to ensure to all individuals *within its territory* and *subject to its jurisdiction* the rights recognised in the present Covenant ...'. For a comment, see H. King, 'The Extraterritorial Human Rights Obligations of States', *Human Rights Law Review*, 9(4) (2009), pp. 521–56.

157 1155 UNTS 331, 8 ILM 679, entered into force 27 January 1980.

158 *Legal Consequences of the Construction of a Wall in the Occupied Palestinian Territory*, ICJ Reports (2004), p. 4, para. 112. For a discussion of this Advisory Opinion, see S.R.S. Bedi, *The Development of Human Rights Law by the Judges of the International Court of Justic*e (Oxford: Hart Publishing, 2007), pp. 337–51.

159 *Armed Activities on the Territory of the Congo (Democratic Republic of the Congo* v. *Uganda)* (Merits), Judgment of 19 December 2005, 2006 45 ILM 271, para. 217.

territory and jurisdiction, the latter term not being limited by a state's territorial boundaries. State responsibility can, for example, be incurred by the acts or omissions by a state's authorities which produce effects outside their territories.[160] This means that a state party to the ICESCR must respect, protect and fulfil the ESC rights laid down in the ICESCR to anyone within the power or effective control of that state, even if not situated within the territorial boundaries of the state party.

The extraterritorial application of the ICESCR is reflected in a number of general comments of the CESCR that interpret state obligations as extending to individuals under its jurisdiction. General Comment 1 indicates that states parties to the ICESCR have to monitor the actual situation with respect to each of the rights on a regular basis and thus be aware of the extent to which the various rights are, or are not, being enjoyed by 'all individuals within *its territory* or *under its jurisdiction*'.[161] For example, in its 'Concluding Observations' of 1998 on Israel, the CESCR confirmed that 'the state's obligations under the Covenant apply to all territories and populations under its effective control';[162] and that 'the Covenant applies to all areas where Israel maintains geographical, functional or personal jurisdiction'.[163] Similarly, in General Comment 20, on non-discrimination in ESC rights, the CESCR confirmed that 'States parties should also ensure that they refrain from discriminatory practices in international cooperation and assistance and take steps to ensure that all actors under their *jurisdiction* do likewise'.[164]

Therefore, state obligations with respect to the ICESCR apply to individuals and groups within a state's territory and to those individuals who are subject to a state's jurisdiction. Thus, under the OP to the ICESCR '(c)ommunications may be submitted by or on behalf of individuals or groups of individuals, *under the jurisdiction* of a state Party'.[165] This anticipates that a state can be found to be in violation of its obligations under the ICESCR for actions taken by it extraterritorially, in relation to anyone within the power, effective control or authority of that state, as well as within an area over which that state exercises effective overall control.[166]

The extraterritorial application of the ICESCR is further supported by its reference to 'international assistance and cooperation'. As a minimum, international assistance and cooperation can be understood as entailing obligations to respect ESC rights at an international level. The obligation to *respect* at an international level requires states to refrain from interfering directly or

---

160 See the European Court of Human Rights (ECtHR), *Drozd and Janousek* v. *France and Spain* (App. No. 12747/8), Judgment of 26 June 1992 (1992) 14 EHRR 745, para. 91; *Loizidou* v *Turkey* (Preliminary Objections) (App. No. 15318/89) 1995 20 EHRR 99, para. 52 (confirmed in *Cyprus* v *Turkey* (App. No. 25781/94) (2002) 35 EHRR 30, paras. 76–81).

161 CESCR, *General Comment 1*: *Reporting by States Parties* (Third Session, 1989), UN Doc. E/1989/22, annex III at 87 (1989), para. 3 (emphasis added). See also CESCR, *General Comment 8*: *The Relationship Between Economic Sanctions and Respect for Economic, Social and Cultural Rights*, UN Doc. E/C.12/1997/8 (12 December 1997), para. 10; CESCR, *General Comment 14*: *The Right to the Highest Attainable Standard of Health,* UN Doc. E/C.12/2000/4 (11 August 2000), para. 12(b); CESCR, *General Comment 15: The Right to Water*, UN Doc. E/C.12/2002/11 (20 January 2003), para. 12(c).

162 CESCR, *Concluding Observations: Israel*, UN Doc. E/C.12/1/Add.27 (4 December 1998), para. 8. See also CESCR, *Concluding Observations: Israel*, UN Doc. E/C.12/1/Add.90 (23 May 2003), paras. 15 and 31.

163 CESCR, *Concluding Observations: Israel*, UN Doc. E/C.12/1/Add.27 (4 December 1998), para. 6.

164 CESCR, *General Comment 20*, para. 14 (emphasis added).

165 See Optional Protocol to the ICESCR, note 11 above, Art. 2(1) (emphasis added).

166 See, generally, R. McCorquodale and P. Simons, 'Responsibility Beyond Borders: State Responsibility for Extraterritorial Violations by Corporations of International Human Rights Law', *The Modern Law Review*, 7(4) (2007), pp. 598–625.

indirectly with the progressive realization of ESC rights in other states;[167] and not to impose on another state measures that might be foreseen to work against the progressive realization of ESC rights. This means that states must refrain from causing harm to ESC rights extraterritorially – for example, by refraining from imposing unilateral economic sanctions on other states without taking full account of the provisions of the ICESCR; by refraining from dumping unsafe food or toxic waste in other states; by refraining from imposing embargoes or similar measures restricting the supply of another state with essential goods and services, including adequate food, medicines and medical equipments; by not supporting armed conflicts in other states in violation of international law; and by not providing assistance to corporations and other actors to violate ESC rights in other states.

It should be recalled that the object and purpose of the ICESCR, as a human rights treaty, requires that its provisions be interpreted so as to make its safeguards practical and effective. Effectiveness requires that the human rights obligations to 'respect, protect and fulfil' extends beyond a state's borders to include individuals and groups subject to a state's jurisdiction in other states.[168] Although 'from the standpoint of public international law, the jurisdictional competence of a state is primarily territorial',[169] a state's human rights obligations, as noted above, are not territorially limited. Human rights obligations may extend beyond a state's borders to areas where a state exercises power, authority or effective control over individuals, or where a state exercises effective control of an area of territory within another state.[170] States are legally responsible for their policies that violate human rights beyond their own borders, and for policies that indirectly support violations of ESC rights by third parties. It follows, then, that states may, under certain circumstances, be required to respect, protect and fulfil ESC rights in other states.

While there is some debate over precisely when a state should protect human rights in other states, international law permits a state to exercise extraterritorial jurisdiction provided there is a recognized basis, as, for example, where the actor or victim is a national, where the acts have substantial adverse effects on the state, or where specific international crimes are involved.[171] For example, with respect to economic sanctions, when a state imposes unilateral economic sanctions upon another state and such sanctions lead to violations of ESC rights in another state,[172] the state imposing such sanctions 'unavoidably assumes a responsibility to do all within its power to *protect* the economic, social and cultural rights of the affected population'.[173] Although the CESCR has not consistently inquired into the issue of extraterritorial jurisdiction, it has been raised in the course of examining some state reports. For example, in 1999, one CESCR member asked 'whether

167 CESCR, *General Comment 19: The Right to Social Security*, UN Doc. E/C.12/GC/19 (4 February 2008), para. 53.

168 See CESCR, *Concluding Observations: Cameroon*, UN Doc. E/C.12/1/Add.40 (8 December 1999), para. 38.

169 ECtHR, *Bankovic* v *Belgium and Others*, 12 December 2001, Decision, No. 52207/99, Reports 2001–XII, para. 59.

170 See McCorquodale and Simons, note 166 above, at p. 624.

171 See J. Ruggie, *Business and Human Rights: Mapping International Standards of Responsibility and Accountability for Corporate Acts*, UN Doc A/HRC/4/35 (19 February 2007), para. 15.

172 Economic sanctions often 'cause significant disruption in the distribution of food, pharmaceuticals and sanitation supplies, jeopardize the quality of food and the availability of clean drinking water, severely interfere with the functioning of basic health and education systems, and undermine the right to work'. See CESCR, *General Comment 8: The Relationship between Economic Sanctions and Respect for Economic, Social and Cultural Rights*, UN Doc. E/C.12/1997/8 (12 December 1997), para. 3.

173 *Ibid.*, para. 13 (emphasis added).

Germany exercised extraterritorial jurisdiction over German nationals who committed crimes against children abroad'.[174]

The extraterritorial obligation includes, *inter alia*, adopting the necessary and effective legislative and other measures to restrain, for example, third parties within a state's jurisdiction from any activities that might be foreseen to cause harm to the progressive realization of ESC rights in other states. For example, with respect to the right to social security, the CESCR stated that

> states parties should extraterritorially protect the right to social security by preventing their own citizens and national entities from violating this right in other countries. Where states parties can take steps to influence third parties (non-state actors) within their jurisdiction to respect the right, through legal or political means, such steps should be taken in accordance with the Charter of the United Nations and applicable international law.[175]

In principle, a similar duty to protect ESC rights extraterritorially should apply to all substantive rights. Extraterritorial protection of ESC rights offers an important means to strengthen the protection and enforcement of ESC rights, especially where host states lack the ability to effectively regulate non-state actors and monitor their compliance yet home states are able to do so.

Importantly, states which are members of international economic institutions, notably the International Monetary Fund (IMF), the World Bank, the World Trade Organization (WTO) and regional development banks can also protect ESC rights in other states by paying greater attention to the protection of these rights in the strategies, policies, programmes and decisions of these institutions. As part of international cooperation, states have to ensure that international agreements and policies of these institutions are not enforced in a way that adversely affect ESC rights in other states. For example, gradual privatization of social services including health care, education, water and electricity supply should not make privatized services such as health care less accessible and affordable, in particular for the disadvantaged and marginalized individuals and groups.

4. Non-derogability of ESC Rights

A derogation of a right or an aspect of a right is its complete or partial elimination as an international obligation.[176] Some international treaties on human rights allow states unilaterally to derogate temporarily from (suspend) *certain* human rights guarantees in times of emergency which 'threatens the life of the nation', but only to the extent strictly required by the situation.[177] However, permissible derogations, in addition to being officially proclaimed, must not

174 See CESCR, *Summary Record of the 49th Meeting: Germany*, UN Doc. E/C.12/2001/SR.49 (30 August 2001), para. 48.

175 CESCR, *General Comment 19*, para. 54. See also CESCR, *General Comment 15*, para. 33.

176 D. McGoldrick, 'The Interface Between Public Emergency Powers and International Law', *International Journal of Constitutional Law*, 2 (2004), 380 at p. 383.

177 For example, Article 4(1) ICCPR states: 'In time of public emergency which threatens the life of the nation and the existence of which is officially proclaimed, the States Parties to the present Covenant may take measures derogating from their obligations under the present Covenant to the extent strictly required by the exigencies of the situation, provided that such measures are not inconsistent with their other obligations under international law and do not involve discrimination solely on the ground of race, colour, sex, language,

conflict with the state's other international law obligations and must be non-discriminatory.[178] The predominant objective of a state party derogating from some human rights must be the 'restoration of a state of normalcy' where full respect for human rights can again be secured.[179] Thus, derogation from a particular right must be necessary (strictly required) by the prevailing exceptional threat to protect or restore a (democratic) public order essential for the protection of human rights. It is crucial to note that unlike some other human rights treaties, there are no clauses in the UN treaties protecting ESC rights allowing for or prohibiting derogations in a state of emergency, as in the situation of a failed state, armed conflict or institutional collapse post-conflict.[180] Although the CESCR has acknowledged that the persistent instability and recurrent armed conflicts in some areas of a state party to the ICESCR 'pose great challenges to the State's ability to fulfil its obligations under the Covenant',[181] it has not indicated whether a state can derogate from its obligations under such circumstances. This leaves the question of derogations unclear under the ICESCR. Does the ICESCR apply fully in time of armed conflict, war, natural disasters or other public emergency? Or can states derogate from the ICESCR in such emergencies?

The absence of specific derogation clauses from a treaty is not, *per se*, determinative of whether derogations are permitted or prohibited. In the case of the ICESCR, this may be taken to mean either that derogations from ESC rights are not permissible (since they are not provided for[182] and would seem inherently less compelling given the nature of ESC rights), or that they may be permissible for non-core obligations where the situation appears to be sufficiently grave as to warrant derogation (since they are not explicitly prohibited). The *travaux préparatoires* of the ICESCR do not reveal any specific discussion on the issue of whether or not a derogation clause was considered necessary, or even appropriate.[183] Thus, the possible reasons for its omission are open to speculation. It is possible that this could have been as a result of a combination of factors, including (1) the nature of the rights protected in the ICESCR; (2) the existence of a general limitations clause in the ICESCR in its Article 4, which allows states to respond flexibly to extraordinary situations of tension within a democratic society, including situations of emergencies, without a

religion or social origin'. See Human Rights Committee, *General Comment 29: States of Emergency* (Art. 4), UN Doc. CCPR/C/21/Rev.1/Add.11 (31 August 2001).

178 *Ibid.*

179 *Ibid.*, para. 1.

180 Such derogation clauses may be found in, e.g., ICCPR, Art. 4(1); ECHR, Art. 15; and the American Convention on Human Rights, Art. 27.

181 See CESCR, *Concluding Observations: Democratic Republic of Congo*, UN Doc. C.12/COD/CO/4 (20 November 2009), para. 6.

182 In *Constitutional Rights Project, Civil Liberties Organisation and Media Rights Agenda* v. *Nigeria*, Communications Nos. 140/94, 141/94, 145/95, 13th Annual Activity Report (1999), para. 41, the African Commission stated: 'In contrast to other international human rights instruments, the African Charter does not contain a derogation clause. Therefore limitations [derogations] on the rights and freedoms enshrined in the Charter cannot be justified by emergencies or special circumstances…'. This view was also stated in *Commission Nationale des Droits de l'Homme et des Libertes* v. *Chad*, Communication No. 74/92, 9th Annual Activity Report (1995–96), para. 21; and *Malawi African Association and Others* v. *Mauritania*, Communication Nos. 54/91, 61/91, 98/93, 164/97–196/97 and 210/98, 13th Annual Activity Report (1999–2000), Annex V, para. 84.

183 Alston and Quinn, note 64 above, at p. 217.

need for derogations;[184] and (3) the fact that the general obligation contained in Article 2(1) was 'more flexible and accommodating'.[185]

In General Comment 3, the CESCR confirmed that states parties have a core obligation to ensure the satisfaction of minimum essential levels of each of the rights enunciated in the ICESCR, such as essential health care, basic shelter and housing, water and sanitation, foodstuffs, and the most basic forms of education. Accordingly, the CESCR has taken the view that core obligations arising from the rights recognized in the ICESCR are non-derogable. In General Comment 14 on the highest attainable standard of health, the CESCR stated: '[i]t should be stressed, however, that a state party cannot, under any circumstances whatsoever, justify its non-compliance with the core obligations set out in paragraph 43 above, which are non-derogable'.[186] In General Comment 15, on the right to water, the CESCR stated that a 'state party cannot justify its non-compliance with the core obligations set out ... which are non-derogable'.[187]

It can thus be argued that without a clause providing for derogation in the ICESCR, core obligations arising from ESC rights cannot be derogated from in an emergency including a situation of military occupation.

In *The Wall*,[188] the ICJ asserted the applicability of the ICESCR in Occupied Palestinian Territory. It cited 'Concluding Observations' of the CESCR and also stated that

> territories occupied by Israel have for over 37 years been subject to its territorial jurisdiction as the occupying Power. In the exercise of the powers available to it on this basis, Israel is bound by the provisions of the International Covenant on Economic, Social and Cultural Rights. Furthermore, it is under an obligation not to raise any obstacle to the exercise of such rights in those fields where competence has been transferred to Palestinian authorities.[189]

The ICJ also stated that, save through the effect of provisions for derogation, 'the protection offered by human rights conventions does not cease in case of armed conflict'.[190]

Similarly, the UN General Assembly confirmed in 1970 the applicability of human rights norms in times of armed conflict, stating that '(f)undamental human rights, as accepted in international law and laid down in international instruments, continue to apply fully in situations of armed conflict'.[191] In principle, this position applies to ESC rights as protected by the ICESCR. Some of the general comments of the CESCR have confirmed this position. For example, in General Comment 15, on the right to water, the committee noted that 'during armed conflicts, emergency situations and natural disasters, the right to water embraces those obligations by which states

184 Article 4 of the ICESCR provides that 'The States Parties to the present Covenant recognise that, in the enjoyment of those rights provided by the State in conformity with the present Covenant, the State may subject such rights only to such limitations as are determined by law only in so far as this may be compatible with the nature of these rights and solely for the purpose of promoting the general welfare in a democratic society'. For a discussion, see A. Müller, 'Limitations to and Derogations from Economic, Social and Cultural Rights', *Human Rights Law Review*, 9(4) (2009), pp. 557–601.

185 Alston and Quinn, note 64 above, at p. 217.

186 CESCR, *General Comment 14*, para. 47.

187 CESCR, *General Comment 15*, para. 40.

188 ICJ Reports 2004, p. 136 (Advisory Opinion of 9 July 2004).

189 *Ibid.*, para. 112 (emphasis added).

190 *Ibid.*, para. 106.

191 See Basic Principles for the Protection of Civilian Populations in Armed Conflicts, UN General Assembly Resolution 2675 (xxv), 9 December 1970, para. 1.

parties are bound under international humanitarian law'.[192] This includes protection of objects indispensable for survival of the civilian population, including drinking water installations and supplies and irrigation works, protection of the natural environment against widespread, long-term and severe damage, and ensuring that civilians, internees and prisoners have access to adequate water.[193] Indeed, it is hard to imagine a situation in which the suspension of core obligations under the ICESCR corresponding to minimum core entitlements to basic subsistence rights (inherently linked to the non-derogable right to life and the right to freedom from torture and inhuman and degrading treatment),[194] such as rights to basic health care, water, adequate food, and housing, can be said to be 'strictly required' in order to maintain or restore the (democratic) public order indispensable for the protection of human rights.[195]

Thus, the absence of a clause allowing derogation in times of public emergency in the ICESCR indicates that the ICESCR generally continues to apply,[196] and, at the minimum, states can not derogate from its core obligations. In the words of the CESCR, 'because core obligations are non-derogable, they continue to exist in situations of conflict, emergency and natural disaster'.[197] Does this mean that states can derogate from non-core obligations under the ICESCR provided they comply with the general rules of derogation? The CESCR's use of the word 'non-derogable' in relation to core obligations might be interpreted as implying that other non-core obligations are indeed derogable. However, it is vital to note that the statement of the CESCR was not a general reference to derogations under the ICESCR but a specific example of the non-derogable nature of core obligations. It cannot therefore be taken as being conclusive on the question of whether or not states can derogate from non-core aspects of ESC rights. Given the nature of the rights protected in the ICESCR, the existence of a general limitations clause in Article 4, and the fact that states are not required to do more than what the maximum available resources permit, derogations from the ICESCR in situations of conflict, war, emergency and natural disaster would appear to be unnecessary. In General Comment 21, on the right of everyone to take part in cultural life, the CESCR appears to have affirmed this view by stating in paragraph 50(a) that state parties to the ICESCR are obliged to 'respect and protect cultural heritage in all its forms, in times of war and peace, and natural disasters'.

---

192 CESCR, *General Comment 15*, para. 22. For the interrelationship of human rights law and humanitarian law, the CESCR noted the conclusions of the International Court of Justice on the legality of the threat or use of nuclear weapons (Request by the General Assembly), ICJ Reports (1996), p. 226, para. 25.

193 *Ibid.*, citing Art. 54 and 56, Additional Protocol I to the Geneva Conventions (1977); Art. 54, Additional Protocol II (1977); Art. 20 and 46 of the third Geneva Convention of 12 August 1949; and common Art. 3 of the Geneva Conventions of 12 August 1949.

194 Under the ICCPR, the following rights or protections are non-derogable: the right to life (Art. 6); the prohibition of torture, inhuman and degrading treatment (Art. 7); the prohibition of slavery and servitude (Art. 8, paras. 1 and 2); the prohibition of detention for debt (Art. 11); the prohibition of retroactive criminal laws (Art. 15); the recognition of legal personality (Art. 16); and freedom of thought, conscience, religion and belief (Art. 18).

195 Müller, note 184 above, at p. 593.

196 See E. Mottershaw, 'Economic, Social and Cultural Rights in Armed Conflict: International Human Rights Law and International Humanitarian Law', *International Journal of Human Rights*, 12(3) (2008), pp. 449–70.

197 CESCR, *Poverty and the ICESCR*, note 74 above, para. 18.

5. The OP to the ICESCR

Was it really necessary to adopt the OP to the ICESCR to provide for the competence of the CESCR to receive and consider communications alleging violations of any of the rights protected by the ICESCR? To answer this question, it is important to consider some background to the OP and to examine its contents, significance and limitations.

5.1 Historical Background

By the year 2008, only two of the seven major UN human rights treaties – the Convention on the Rights of the Child and the ICESCR – lacked a complaints procedure that would allow individuals and groups to submit complaints involving alleged violations of rights recognized in these treaties. With respect to the ICESCR, the effect of this lacuna meant that the CESCR could not carry out an extensive and more in-depth inquiry into the real problems confronting specific individuals and groups, which would in turn lead to the development of international jurisprudence or case law on ESC rights that would prompt states to ensure the availability of more effective remedies at the national level.[198] Where national remedies for violations of ESC rights were either not available or ineffective, the absence of a complaints procedure under the ICESCR greatly limited 'the chances of victims of abuses of the Covenant obtaining international redress'.[199] In this respect, the system based exclusively on a state reporting system, and the making of non-binding 'Concluding Observations' after examination of state reports, was clearly a very weak system of holding states responsible for violations of ESC rights.

Accordingly, it was recognized that there was a need to strengthen the supervision of the ICESCR by providing for a complaint procedure to complement the existing supervisory mechanism in the form of an OP to the ICESCR.[200] This need for an OP (in some respects similar to the OP procedure to the ICCPR), providing for a complaint/communication procedure for individuals and groups seeking redress in instances where they consider their human rights guaranteed under the ICESCR to have been violated, had been a subject of discussion before the CESCR from its fifth session in 1990 until its fifteenth session in 1996.[201] The length of this debate at the CESCR reflected the fact that not all CESCR members were in agreement about the need for an OP, or about the content of the proposed protocol.

198 The 1993 World Conference on Human Rights, UN Doc. A/CONF.157/PC/62/Add.5 (26 March 1993), paras. 32–8.

199 See CESCR, Fact Sheet No. 16 (Rev. 1).

200 See e.g. CESCR, 'Towards an Optional Protocol to the ICESCR', UN Doc. E/1993/22; P. Alston, 'Establishing a Right to Petition Under the Covenant on Economic, Social and Cultural Rights', IV(2), *Collected Courses of the Academy of European Law* (Dordrecht: Kluwer Law International, 1995), at p. 107; International Network for Economic, Social and Cultural Rights (ESCR-Net), *Resource Page on the Optional Protocol to the ICESCR* [online]. Available from: http://www.escr-net.org/resources/resources_show.htm?doc_id=431553.

201 Report of the Fifth Session of the CESCR, UN Docs. E/1991/23, para. 25, and E/CN.4/1997/105, para. 2. At the CESCR's meeting, member Philip Alston reported four times on the OP in UN Docs. E/C.12/1991/WP.2 (25 October 1991); E/C.12/1992/WP.9 (27 November 1992); E/C.12/1994/12 (9 November 1994); E/C.12/1996/CRP.2/Add.1. For a background to the OP, see the International Commission of Jurists, *The Evolution of an Optional Protocol Complaints Mechanism Under the ICESCR* (Geneva: International Commission of Jurists, no date) [online]. Available from: http://www.icj.org/IMG/pdf/1.pdf; C. Mahon, 'Progress at the Front: The Draft Optional Protocol to the International Covenant on Economic, Social and Cultural Rights', *Human Rights Law Review*, 8(4) (2008), pp. 617–46.

The 1993 World Conference on Human Rights, held in Vienna, encouraged the UN Commission on Human Rights (CHR), replaced by the Human Rights Council in March 2006,[202] to continue, in cooperation with the CESCR, the examination of the question of an OP to the ICESCR.[203] The CESCR worked on an OP to enable complaint procedures under the ICESCR. In December 1992, the CESCR adopted an 'analytical paper' that examined the various modalities of such protocol, and, *inter alia*, the possibility of the collective and individual complaints.[204] Through this paper, the CESCR strongly supported the development of an OP. The Commission on Human Rights, in paragraph 6 of its Resolution 1994/20, took note of the 'steps taken by the Committee ... for the drafting of an optional protocol ... granting the right of individuals or groups to submit communications concerning non-compliance with the Covenant, and invite[d] the Committee to report thereon to the Commission'. A draft OP was finally adopted in 1996 at the CESCR's fifteenth session.[205]

The draft OP to the CESCR was submitted to the UN Commission on Human Rights during its fifty-third session in 1997, but, for the next decade, its future largely remained uncertain.[206] For four consecutive years (1997–2000), the commission called for comments from states, the UN, intergovernmental organizations and non-governmental organizations (NGOs) but did not take any decision.[207] While NGOs were strongly in favour of an OP,[208] only a limited number of states submitted comments.[209] This partly manifested the considerable lack of enthusiasm and political will on the part of most states to be held accountable for the progressive realization of ESC rights

202 On 15 March 2006, the General Assembly adopted resolution A/RES/60/251 to establish the Human Rights Council. The Commission on Human Rights concluded its 62nd and final session on 27 March 2006 before the OP was adopted.

203 World Conference on Human Rights, Vienna Declaration and Programme of Action, UN Doc. A/CONF.157/23, Part II, para. 75.

204 See Contribution of the Committee on Economic, Social and Cultural Rights to the World Conference on Human Rights, 26 March 1993, UN Doc. A/CONF.157/PC/62/Add.5, Annex I, at para. 18, and Annex II.

205 Draft Optional Protocol to the ICESCR, UN Doc. E/CN.4/1997/105. The draft provided for: (1) the justification for the OP in the Preamble; (2) the complaints to the competent supervisory body from individuals, and groups who are alleged victims or who act on behalf of alleged victims of violations of all rights in the ICESCR contained in Art. 1–15; (3) interim and follow-up measures; and (4) a friendly settlement procedure. For comments on the draft, see UN Doc. E/CN.4/1998/84, and for the analysis, see K. Arambulo, *Strengthening the Supervision of the International Covenant on Economic, Social and Cultural Rights, Theoretical and Procedural Aspects* (Antwerp, Intersentia, 1999), pp. 199–342, and Report on the Workshop on the Justiciability of Economic, Social and Cultural Rights, with Particular Reference to the Draft Optional Protocol to the International Covenant on Economic, Social and Cultural Rights, UN Doc. E/CN.4/2001/62/Add.2 (22 March 2001).

206 See Reports of UNHCHR, Draft Optional Protocol to the ICESCR, UN Docs. E/CN.4/2001/62/Add.2 (2001); E/CN.4/2000/49 (2000); E/CN.4/1997/105.

207 UN Docs. E/CN.4/RES/1997/17; E/CN.4/RES/1998/33; E/CN.4/RES/1999/25; E/CN.4/RES/2000/9.

208 UN Docs. E/CN.4/1998/84 and E/CN.4/2001/62.

209 Most of those who submitted (11 out of 14) were in favour. See e.g. Croatia, UN Doc. E/CN.4/1999/112; Cyprus, UN Doc. E/CN.4/1998/84; Czech Republic, UN Doc. E/CN.4/2000/49; Ecuador, UN Doc. E/CN.4/1998/84; Finland, UN Doc. E/CN.4/1999/112; Georgia and Germany, UN Doc. E/CN.4/2000/49; Lebanon and Lithuania, UN Doc. E/CN.4/2000/49; Mauritius, UN Doc. E/CN.4/2001/62; Mexico, UN Doc. E/CN.4/1999/112/Add.1; Norway and Portugal, UN Doc. E/CN.4/2001/62; Syrian Republic, UN Doc. E/CN.4/1998/84.

by an independent international body. Some states expressed doubts on the desirability of an OP.[210] Some commentators were strongly critical of the proposal to provide for a complaints procedure under the ICESCR. For example, two US State Department legal advisers, writing in their personal capacities, stated that the 'proposal for a new individual-complaints mechanism remains an ill-considered effort to mimic the structures of the ICCPR – and largely for mimicry's sake' – and that the rights and obligations contained in the ICESCR were 'never intended to be susceptible to judicial or quasi-judicial determination'.[211]

However, in 2001, the commission took an important step and appointed an Independent Expert (Professor Hatem Kotrane) to examine the question of the draft OP to the ICESCR.[212] The Independent Expert made two reports[213] and concluded that 'there is no longer any doubt about the essentially justiciable nature of all the rights guaranteed by the Covenant'.[214] As shown above (in Section 2 of this chapter), some examples from domestic jurisdictions and regional human rights systems demonstrate that the above conclusion is tenable. The Independent Expert also noted that the procedure envisaged under the OP would be both beneficial and practical because it would, *inter alia*:

> ensure that effect was given to every individual's right to appeal, and contribute to the development of international law by producing a coherent body of principles covering all the rights set forth in the Covenant; these principles could gradually acquire an authority that would be recognised by all, both at the international level and in the various countries where they could be used in the drafting of national legislation. It would also be beneficial in that it would provide more vigorous support for the principle of the indivisibility and interdependence of all human rights.[215]

Thus, he recommended that the commission establish an open-ended working group mandated to elaborate an OP in the light of the draft OP as prepared by the CESCR, comments by states, intergovernmental and NGOs, and the report of the Independent Expert.[216]

The commission took a further significant step in 2003 by establishing an 'Open-Ended Working Group on an optional protocol to the International Covenant on Economic, Social and Cultural Rights' to 'considering options' regarding the elaboration of an OP.[217] Pursuant to Human Rights Council resolution 1/3 of 29 June 2006, the chairperson-rapporteur, Catarina de Albuquerque, submitted a first draft OP to the fourth session of the Open-Ended Working Group. Based on the discussions held and proposals for amendments made during that session, the chairperson prepared

---

210 Notably, Canada, UN Doc. E/CN.4/1998/84/Add.1, and Sweden, UN Doc. E/CN.4/1999/112/Add.1.

211 Dennis and Stewart, note 18 above, at p. 514.

212 Commission on Human Rights Res 2001/30, 20 April 2001, UN Doc E/CN.4/RES/2001/30, para. 8(c).

213 Report by Mr Hatem Kotrane, Independent Expert on the Question of a Draft Optional Protocol to the ICESCR, UN Doc. E/CN.4/2002/57 (12 February 2002); UN Doc. E/CN.4/2003/53 and Corr. 1 and Corr. 2 (13 January 2003).

214 *Ibid.*, UN Doc. E/CN.4/2003/53 para. 2.

215 *Ibid.*, para. 3.

216 Kotrane, Corrigendum UN Doc. E/CN.4/2003/53/Corr.2 (7 April 2003), para. 76.

217 CHR Resolution 2003/18, paras. 12–13. The open-ended working group met in February–March 2004 but 'did not reach consensus on whether to start drafting an Optional Protocol'. See UN Doc. E/CN.4/2004/44 (15 March 2004), para. 76. See Analytical Paper by C. de Albuquerque, *Elements for an Optional Protocol to the ICESCR*, UN Doc. E/CN.4/2006/WG.23/2 (2005).

a revised draft,[218] which was considered at the first part of the working group's fifth session. Based on discussions held at the first part of the fifth session, the chairperson prepared a new revised version[219] as a basis for negotiations at the second part of the fifth session.

Subsequently, the UN Human Rights Council and the General Assembly adopted the OP to the ICESCR in 2008.[220] As noted above, the OP would enter into effect 3 months after 10 states deposit instruments of ratification with the UN Secretary-General.[221]

5.2 Contents of the OP

It is important to note that in the OP debate there were several contentious issues including the following: (1) the scope of the complaints mechanism – whether the mechanism would allow states to pick and choose the particular right the CESCR had the competence to adjudicate, or whether a comprehensive approach would be adopted giving the CESCR competence to consider all rights under the ICESCR; (2) *locus standi* (standing) – the question of who would have standing to bring complaints under the protocol – individuals only or even groups including NGO-generated complaints or other collective complaints; (3) admissibility – the question of what admissibility criteria were to be applied, of whether applicants should exhaust regional remedies, and whether applications should disclose that victims have suffered a 'clear disadvantage'; (4) criteria for review – the question of what criteria the CESCR should apply when examining complaints: reasonableness, appropriateness, or margin of appreciation; (5) international cooperation and assistance – how appropriate reference should be made to the crucial role of 'international assistance and cooperation' in the realization of ESC rights as enshrined in Article 2(1) of the ICESCR, and whether this would require the establishment of a trust fund; and (6) reservations – whether to allow or prohibit reservations in an express provision.

It is essential to note that the OP contains a number of progressive provisions. For example, under the OP, states parties to the ICESCR that become parties to the OP recognize the competence of the CESCR to receive and consider communications of three types, namely: (1) communications by or on behalf of individuals or groups of individuals; (2) interstate communications; and (3) inquiry procedure. While the first one applies to all states parties to the protocol, the last two are optional, binding only on states that would declare that they have recognized the competence of the CESCR in respect of interstate communications and to conduct an inquiry. These methods are outlined below.

5.2.1 Communications by or on behalf of individuals or groups of individuals The first type involves communications submitted by or on behalf of 'individuals or groups of individuals' or other persons on their behalf, under the jurisdiction of a state party, claiming to be victims of violations of any of the ESC rights set forth in the ICESCR (Article 2). This has several advantages. First, this provision is not limited to individuals only but also extends to groups of individuals such as minority groups, trade unions, or NGOs. Thus, it offers a wider locus standi before the CESCR. Second, communications are not limited to individuals or groups within a state's territory. Communications could be submitted by or on behalf of individuals or groups of individuals under the jurisdiction of a state party. This means that communications could be brought by anyone within

218 Contained in UN Doc. A/HRC/8/WG.4/2 (24 December 2007).

219 Contained in UN Doc. A/HRC/8/WG.4/3 (25 March 2008).

220 See notes 15–18 above and accompanying text.

221 *Ibid.*, Art 18. Ecuador was the first state to ratify the OP on 11 June 2010 followed by Mongolia on 1 July 2010.

the power, effective control or authority of a state. Third, communications under the OP could be brought alleging a violation of any provision of the ICESCR and not only some provisions. Although some states[222] had argued for the exclusion of Part I of the ICESCR (which includes the right to economic, social and cultural self-determination) from the scope of a communications procedure under the OP, the reference in the OP to 'any' of ESC rights in the ICESCR does not appear to exclude the right to self-determination. This confirms that all rights under the ICESCR are justiciable. Therefore, like other existing communication procedures, the approach adopted in the OP is comprehensive and not selective or limited.

5.2.2 Interstate communications The second type involves interstate communications. Under this type, the CESCR can receive and consider communications to the effect that a state party claims that another state party is not fulfilling its obligations under the ICESCR (Article 10). This can only take place where a state party has made a declaration recognizing in regard to itself the competence of the CESCR to receive interstate communications. This means that a state may not recognize this procedure. The interstate communications mechanism reflects the fact that every state party has a legal interest in the performance by every other state party of its human rights obligations.[223] However, even if some states were to make Article 10 declarations, the interstate communications mechanism is unlikely to be widely used because of the perceived diplomatic and political implications of such an action; states might fear retaliatory attacks on their own human rights records.[224] Similar procedures for interstate complaints under other human rights treaties have not been used so far.[225] For example, despite the fact that Article 11 of the International Convention on the Elimination of All Forms of Racial Discrimination (ICERD)[226] provides for a mandatory interstate communication procedure that had entered into force in 1970, not one of the 173 state parties to the ICERD (as of 31 December 2009) had invoked the interstate communication procedure against any of the other states parties where systematic racial discrimination and ethnic cleansing had even led to genocide. Since the contractual dimension of the ICESCR involves any state party to it being obligated to every other state party to comply with its human rights obligations under the ICESCR, it is desirable that states parties to the ICESCR should sign and ratify the OP and make the declaration contemplated in Article 10. But even if the interstate procedure would not be (widely) used, its mere existence provides useful tools for international diplomacy and leaves the door wide open for possible future developments in international human rights litigation. It is better to have it rather than to omit it.

5.2.3 Inquiry procedure The third type of communication is an inquiry procedure. This can be invoked by the CESCR on its own initiative under Article 11 of the OP if the CESCR 'receives reliable information indicating grave or systematic violations by a state party of any of the

---

222 These states were Australia, Greece, India, Morocco, Russia and the USA. See Report of the Fourth Session of the Open-Ended Working Group, UN Doc. A/HRC/6/8 (30 August 2007), para. 36.

223 See also HRC, *General Comment No. 31 [80]: The Nature of the General Legal Obligation Imposed on States Parties to the Covenant*, adopted on 29 March 2004 (2187th meeting), UN Doc. CCPR/C/21/Rev.1/Add.13 (2004), para. 2.

224 See Joseph *et al.*, note 91 above, at p. 21.

225 See CAT, Art. 21; the International Convention on the Protection of the Rights of All Migrant Workers and Members of Their Families, GA Res. 45/158, annex, 45, UN Doc. A/45/49 (1990), entered into force 1 July 2003, Art. 74; ICERD, Art. 11–13; and ICCPR, Art. 41–43.

226 GA Res. 2106 (XX), Annex, 20 UN GAOR Supp. (No. 14) at 47, UN Doc. A/6014 (1966), 660 UNTS 195, entered into force 4 January 1969.

economic, social and cultural rights set forth in the Covenant'. There is no definition of what violations would be considered as 'grave or systematic', and this is left to the CESCR to determine. The origin of such information is not specified, it is likely that in most cases this would be derived from NGOs or media reports. A similar procedure is provided for in Article 20 of the Convention Against Torture (CAT)[227] and Article 8 of the OP to the Convention on the Elimination of All Forms of Discrimination against Women (CEDAW)[228] provided the relevant committees have received indications of grave or systematic practice of torture or forms of discrimination against women.

The inquiry procedure involves, as a first step, an invitation of the state party concerned to submit observations with regard to the information concerned. In addition, the CESCR may designate one or more of its members to conduct a confidential inquiry, which may include a visit to a state's territory with the consent of the state party. The CESCR then transmits the findings of an inquiry to the state party concerned together with any comments and recommendations. A state may then submit its observations to the CESCR within 6 months of receiving the findings, and the CESCR may, after consultations with the state party concerned, decide to include a summary account of the results of the proceedings in its annual report. A follow-up to the inquiry procedure is provided for under Article 12 of the OP, allowing the CESCR to invite the state party concerned to inform it of the measures taken in response to such an inquiry. Thus, the success of the inquiry procedure would depend largely on the positive support and cooperation by states. It is likely that if this procedure is used, it would provide an opportunity to address grave or systematic violations of ESC rights. However, a state may, at any time, withdraw its declaration under Article 11 of the OP by notification to the UN Secretary-General. Accordingly, the success of this procedure would depend on the willingness of states to cooperate.

In practice, the inquiry procedure has been rarely used. This has been the case with respect to both CEDAW and CAT. By 2008, the CEDAW committee had only completed one inquiry under Article 8 of the OP; it was conducted in July 2004 regarding the abduction, rape and murder of women in the Ciudad Juárez area of Chihuahua, Mexico.[229] The CAT had initiated inquiries on systematic practice of torture in seven states parties only and had published the results of six procedures (against Turkey, Egypt, Peru, Sri Lanka, Mexico and Brazil).

5.3 Significance of the OP

Although some states and some authors are generally sceptical as to the viability of the complaints mechanism in relation to ESC rights that are regarded, incorrectly, as 'non-justiciable', the adoption of the OP to the ICESCR that allows complaints from both individuals and groups is a vital step forward to enhance the effective protection of ESC rights at an international level. The complaints procedure under the OP could contribute to the implementation by states parties of the obligations under the ICESCR in several ways including the following:

---

227 Convention against Torture and Other Cruel, Inhuman or Degrading Treatment or Punishment, GA Res. 39/46, annex, 39 UN GAOR Supp. (No. 51) at 197, UN Doc. A/39/51 (1984), entered into force 26 June 1987.

228 GA Res. 54/4, annex, 54 UN GAOR Supp. (No. 49) at 5, UN Doc. A/54/49 (Vol. I) (2000), entered into force 22 December 2000.

229 See Report on Mexico produced by the Committee on the Elimination of Discrimination Against Women Under Article 8 of the Optional Protocol to the Convention, and reply from the Government of Mexico, UN Doc. CEDAW/C/2005/OP.8/MEXICO (27 January 2005).

> First, concrete and tangible cases would be discussed by the Committee in a framework of inquiry that is otherwise absent under the abstract discussions that arise under the State reporting procedure.... Second, the views of a treaty monitoring body on a complaint can be more specific than General Comments on how provisions should be understood [and applied in a specific context]. In this way, the views of the Committee on ESCR can contribute to clarifying the content of the obligations from the provisions of the Covenant. Third, the mere possibility that complaints might be brought before an international forum could encourage governments to ensure that more effective local remedies are made available.[230]

The fact that the protocol provides for the CESCR to request a state concerned to take interim measures in 'exceptional circumstances' if a victim or victims of alleged violations faces possible 'irreparable damage' (Article 5) provides an opportunity to protect ESC rights before determination of a communication. This would in turn positively influence national legislation and administrative policy to give effect to these rights. It would stimulate the formulation of precise claims, attract political concerns of states, and contribute to clarify the scope and content of the rights under the ICESCR. Such a protocol should be signed and 'ratified without delay'.[231] When it enters into force, it would strengthen the ICESCR, and the bringing of appropriate cases before the CESCR under the OP would lead to the development of 'detailed jurisprudential scrutiny at the international level'.[232] In the words of one organization in favour of the OP:

> An OP [Optional Protocol] to the ICESCR allowing individuals and groups of individuals to submit claims against violations of economic, social and cultural rights and providing for an inquiry procedure would advance the principle that all human rights are universal, indivisible and interdependent. Additionally it would help overcome the common misconception that economic, social and cultural rights are not 'justiciable'– that their controversies cannot be decided by a court.[233]

As the former UN High Commissioner for Human Rights stressed in March 2008, the establishment of communication procedure under the ICESCR will truly be a milestone in the history of universal human rights, sending a strong and unequivocal message about the equal value and importance of all human rights and putting to rest the notion that legal and quasi-judicial remedies are not relevant for the protection of ESC rights.[234] Indeed, to the extent that there was still a need for further clarification of the meaning of ESC rights, the early adoption of the OP was more necessary.[235] For this reason, the adoption of the OP, its signature and ratification by states parties to the ICESCR

---

230 ESCR-Net, Benefits of an OP-ICESCR [online]. Available from: http://www.escr-net.org/resources_more/resources_more_show.htm?doc_id=426659. See also P. Alston, 'Establishing a Right to Petition Under the Covenant on Economic, Social and Cultural Rights', *Collected Courses of the Academy of European Law*, 4(2) (1995), at p. 107.

231 Maastricht Guidelines, 31.

232 See UN Doc. A/CONF.157/PC/62/Add.5, para. 24.

233 ESCR-Net, Benefits of an OP-ICESCR, note 230 above.

234 See Statement by Ms Louise Arbour, High Commissioner for Human Rights to the Open-ended Working Group on an Optional Protocol to the International Covenant on Economic, Social and Cultural Rights, Fifth Session, Salle XII, Palais des Nations, 31 March 2008 (on file).

235 W. Vandenhole, 'Completing the UN Complaint Mechanisms for Human Rights Violations Step by Step: Towards a Complaints Procedure Complementing the International Covenant on Economic, Social and Cultural Rights', *The Netherlands Quarterly of Human Rights*, 21(3) (2003), p. 459.

so that it enters into force without delay, makes an important addition to the existing UN system protecting ESC rights.[236]

5.4 Beyond the OP

It should be noted that even if the OP comes into force, such a protocol has its own limitations. Two such limitations are significant. First, although the protocol requires states to give 'due consideration to the views of the Committee' (Article 9(2)), the CESCR's views, like those of the Human Rights Committee (HRC), are likely to be considered by states as non-binding; thus, states might simply ignore the CESCR's recommendations. Yet, firstly, there is no political body in the UN that feels responsible to supervise the implementation of treaty bodies' decisions by states parties, and this is left to the relevant treaty bodies. Secondly, the existing UN treaty monitoring bodies have not handled many cases compared to the regional human rights courts, which grant binding judgements. For example, while the full-time European Court of Human Rights (ECtHR) decides by a binding judgement on some 1,000 individual complaints per year (in relation to 46 states parties to the ECHR), all existing UN bodies competent to deal with individual communications together (the HRC, the Racial Discrimination Committee, the CAT, and the CEDAW) had, by 2007, handled down only little more than 500 non-binding decisions on the merits ('final views') within almost 30 years in relation to more than 100 states parties![237] Therefore, the ultimate goal should be to establish a World Court of Human Rights so that right-holders are able to hold duty bearers (states or non-state actors (NSA)s) accountable for not living up to their legally binding human rights obligations before a fully independent international human rights court with the power to render legally binding judgements and to grant adequate reparation to the victims of human rights violations.[238]

6. Conclusion

This chapter has considered how the concept of state obligations with respect to ESC rights has evolved since the UDHR was adopted in 1948. It has noted that states parties to the ICESCR are obliged to 'take steps by all appropriate means' to achieve 'progressively' the full realization of ESC rights. As noted above, the goal of full realization entails the obligation to respect, protect and fulfil ESC rights. The 'appropriate means' required to achieve this goal include the adoption of legislative measures to protect ESC rights in national law, as well as the adoption of non-legislative measures including the provision of judicial or administrative remedies for violations of ESC rights.[239] Although some states have claimed that a greater part of the ICESCR reflects

236 See Kotrane, UN Doc. E/CN.4/2002/57, para. 56(a).

237 M. Nowak, 'The Need for a World Court of Human Rights', *Human Rights Law Review*, 7(1) (2007), pp. 251–9, at p. 253.

238 *Ibid.*, p. 254.

239 See e.g. CESCR, *Concluding Observations: Kenya*, UN Doc. E/C.12/1993/6 (3 June 1993), para. 10. The CESCR noted 'with concern that the rights recognised by Kenya as a state party to the International Covenant on Economic, Social and Cultural Rights are neither contained in the constitution of Kenya nor in a separate bill of rights; nor do the provisions of the Covenant seem to have been incorporated into the municipal law of Kenya. Neither does there exist any institution or national machinery with responsibility for overseeing the implementation of human rights in the country'.

statements of 'principles' and 'objectives', rather than justiciable legal obligations,[240] the CESCR has affirmed 'the principle of the interdependence and indivisibility of all human rights, and that all economic, social and cultural rights are justiciable'.[241]

The adoption of the OP to the ICESCR by the UN General Assembly on 10 December 2008 on the 60th anniversary of the UDHR is, therefore, a significant and welcome development that was long overdue. This largely brings ESC rights on the same footing and the same emphasis as civil and political rights in terms of enforcement at an international level. Indeed, there is nothing in the ICESCR to indicate that the rights recognized therein are merely 'principles' and 'objectives'. On the contrary, it is clear from Article 2(1) of the ICESCR that, although the rights protected in it have to be realized 'progressively', some rights under the ICESCR, such as freedom from discrimination in the enjoyment of all ESC rights and core obligations, give rise to obligations of immediate effect. As noted above, in any case, the CESCR has explained that Article 2 'imposes an obligation to move as expeditiously and effectively as possible' towards the goal of full realization of the substantive rights under the ICESCR.[242]

It has also been established that states have to use the 'maximum available resources' to realize ESC rights and that this includes resources made available through international assistance and cooperation. As argued above, international assistance and cooperation encompasses more than financial and technical assistance; it must also be understood as entailing the responsibility of states to work actively towards equitable multilateral trading, investment and financial systems that are conducive to the realization of ESC rights. This includes finding ways to allow developing countries to participate effectively in the relevant international organizations (such as the WTO),[243] as well as ways in which they can raise necessary resources to implement their human rights obligations. This may entail genuine special and preferential treatment of developing states so as to provide such states with fairer and better access to developed states' markets.

The chapter has also argued that the human rights obligations of states under the ICESCR may extend to anyone within the power, effective control or authority of a state, as well as within an area over which that state exercises effective overall control. In this respect, human rights obligations with respect to ESC rights, though essentially territorial, are not necessarily territorially limited. There is a possibility of extraterritorial application, as, for example, where a state is an occupying power; or where a state directly or indirectly causes harm to ESC rights extraterritorially. In addition, it has been shown that the absence of a clause in the ICESCR allowing derogation in times of public emergency indicates that the ICESCR's human rights obligations, particularly its core obligations, are non-derogable – they continue to exist in situations of conflict, emergency and natural disaster.

Finally, the chapter has argued that the adoption of the OP to the ICESCR on the 60th anniversary of the UDHR is an important step forward because, when it enters into force, it will provide an avenue to get redress at the UN level to victims of violations of ESC rights who have exhausted all available domestic remedies . As such, it corrects the long-standing and the well-known imbalance in the protection of human rights in the UN system, which has marginalized ESC rights by providing a complaint system for civil and political rights but not for ESC rights. Thus, it is important for states

240 See e.g. the United Kingdom of Great Britain and Northern Ireland (3rd periodic report), UN Doc. E/1994/104/Add.11 (17 June 1996), para. 9.

241 CESCR, *Concluding Observations: United Kingdom*, note 38 above, para. 24.

242 See e.g. CESCR, *General Comment 3*, para. 9; *General Comment 13*, para. 44; *General Comment 14*, para. 31; and *General Comment 15*, para. 18; Limburg Principles, para. 21.

243 D. McRae, 'Developing Countries and the Future of the WTO', *Journal of International Economic Law*, 8(3) (2005), pp. 603–10.

parties to the ICESCR to consider signing and ratifying the OP without delay. However, given the reluctance of many states to implement ESC rights as human rights, it is likely that it may take quite some time before a substantial number of states ratify the OP. From the humble beginnings in Articles 22–27 of the UDHR in 1948, it has taken more than four long decades to bring ESC rights to the same level of enforcement accorded to civil and political rights under international human rights law. Hopefully, with the entry into force of the OP, the enforcement of ESC rights will proceed on a more equal footing than before to civil and political rights.

Chapter 4
Civil and Political Rights

Sarah Joseph

1. Introduction

Articles 3 to 21 of the UDHR are concerned with the recognition of the right of all peoples to the enjoyment and protection of their 'civil and political rights'. These rights were then specified in greater detail in a legally binding treaty adopted 18 years after the UDHR in 1966, the International Covenant on Civil and Political Rights (ICCPR).[1] Over the years the interpretation of these rights has thrown more light on their scope and limits. The focus of this chapter is on the development of civil and political rights under the ICCPR, particularly in the jurisprudence of the Human Rights Committee (HRC), the body established to monitor and supervise the implementation of the ICCPR. This analysis will illustrate the practical evolution of civil and political rights since the adoption of the UDHR in 1948.

2. Philosophical Background

Notions of civil and political rights can be traced to Western liberal philosophies of the seventeenth and eighteenth centuries. Specifically, John Locke's *Second Treatise of Government* proposed that men in a 'state of nature' had 'natural rights' to life, liberty and property.[2] Similar ideas emerged in the Age of Enlightenment in France with the ideas of Rousseau, de Montesquieu and Voltaire, though the Continental European theorists tempered rights more with limitations, duties, and ideas of fraternity and equality along with liberty.[3] They argued that such rights are rooted in the inherent dignity and rationality of human beings (or rather, 'men'), a departure from the 'irrational' religious and scientific dogma that had predominated in earlier societies.[4] These natural rights theories were to be highly influential in the formulation of the first constitutional guarantees of civil and political rights, which emerged in the United States (USA) and France at the end of the eighteenth century.

In classical Lockean theory, societies were formed under a 'social contract', under which 'men' maintained their natural rights subject to the qualification that they did not threaten or harm each other's rights. The role of government was minimal, and was essentially confined to enforcement of that social contract. Otherwise, early conceptions of civil and political rights construed them as freedoms from government action, rather than entitlements to government-provided goods or services.

---

1 Opened for signature 16 December 1966, 999 UNTS 171 (entered into force 23 March 1976).

2 John Locke, *The Second Treatise of Government*, reprinted in P. Laslett (ed.), *Locke, Two Treatises of Government*, 2nd edn (Cambridge: Cambridge University Press, 1988), at pp. 265ff.

3 Mary Ann Glendon, *A World Made New: Eleanor Roosevelt and the Universal Declaration of Human Rights* (New York: Random House, 2002), p. xvii.

4 See Burns Weston, 'Human Rights', *Human Rights Quarterly*, 3 (1984), p. 259.

Despite numerous criticisms of natural rights theories from thinkers such as Karl Marx[5] or Jeremy Bentham,[6] natural rights theories endured and came to dominate the language of the UDHR in 1948. However, as discussed below, modern conceptions of civil and political rights have evolved far beyond their libertarian roots.

3. Categories of Civil and Political Rights

Civil and political rights can be categorized in numerous ways. They may be categorized as encompassing (1) rights of physical and spiritual autonomy; (2) rights of fair treatment; and (3) rights to participate meaningfully in the political process.[7] Category 1 would include the rights to life and freedom from torture and other ill- treatment, freedom of movement, and the right to privacy. Spiritual autonomy is ensured by rights such as freedom of religion, belief and thought. Category 2 encompasses fairness in a narrow procedural sense, such as the right to a fair trial, and in a broader sense, such as a general right of equal protection of the law and freedom from discrimination. Category 3 obviously encompasses the right to vote and to stand for election, but also includes rights which are essential to a healthy political process, such as the freedoms of assembly and association. These categories overlap considerably. For example, freedom of expression can fall into all three categories. It is clearly relevant to the preservation of spiritual autonomy, to allow one to express one's own ideas and to receive the ideas of others. It is also relevant to fair treatment: one cannot be treated fairly and equitably if one's needs and desires cannot be heard, or if one does not have access to relevant information. Finally, freedom of expression is essential to a functional political system, so that there can be a free flow of communication between the elected and those that they represent, and within society to ensure governmental accountability.

Rene Cassin, one of the key drafters of the UDHR, categorized Articles 3–21 in the following way. Articles 3–11 concern rights to life, liberty and personal security, encompassing rights of physical liberty and fairness within the criminal process. Articles 12–17 concerned rights in civil society, including rights regarding one's home and family. Articles 18–21 concerned rights in the polity, including political rights, rights essential to engagement within the political process, and freedom of religion.[8] However, Cassin's categories are no more watertight than the categories proposed directly above. For example, freedom of religion is surely important to one's participation in civil society, contrary to Cassin's characterization.

There are few consequences attached to the characterization of a right within some sub-category of civil and political rights. In contrast, civil and political rights are often juxtaposed against economic social and cultural rights, the subject matter of Articles 22–27 of the UDHR and of the other covenant, the International Covenant on Economic, Social and Cultural Rights (ICESCR),[9]

---

5 Marx, for example, dismissed natural rights as egoistic and based on antisocial premises pitting man against man: see e.g. Karl Marx, 'On the Jewish Question', reprinted in D. McClellan (ed.), *Marx: Selected Writings* (Oxford: Oxford University Press, 1977), pp. 51–7.

6 Bentham famously dismissed natural rights theories as 'anarchical fallacies' and 'nonsense upon stilts': Jeremy Bentham, 'Anarchical Fallacies', reprinted in Jeremy Waldron (ed.), *Nonsense upon Stilts: Bentham, Burke and Marx on the Rights of Man* (London: Methuen, 1987), pp. 46ff.

7 See also Scott Davidson, 'Introduction', in Alex Conte, Scott Davidson and Richard Burchill, *Defining Civil and Political Rights: The Jurisprudence of the United Nations Human Rights Committee* (Aldershot: Ashgate, 2004), p. 2.

8 See Glendon, note 3 above, ch. 10.

9 Opened for signature 16 December 1966, 993 UNTS 3 (entered into force 3 January 1976).

with significant consequences. And yet, as with the sub-categories of civil and political rights, the strict cleavage of civil and political rights and economic social and cultural rights is flawed and simplistic, for reasons discussed directly below.

4. Civil and Political Rights 'Versus' Economic, Social and Cultural Rights

The UDHR did not purport to set up a hierarchy of rights, and it was initially intended that the follow-up treaties would not split up the various UDHR rights. However, Cold War politics, as well as perceptions of fundamental differences between the two sets of rights, led to a decision to split the rights into two covenants.[10] Nevertheless, the preambles to the covenants each proclaim both sets of rights as interdependent, indivisible and equally important. Formal equality may be evidenced in that both covenants came into force in 1977, and both have roughly the same number of states parties as at 31 December 2009.[11] The equal importance and interdependence of both sets of rights was affirmed in the Vienna Declaration and Programme of Action of 1993.[12]

Nevertheless, the norms in the ICCPR are far more developed than those in the ICESCR. This is not surprising, as the former have legal and historical advantages over the latter. Civil and political rights have a longer legal pedigree, having generated much jurisprudence under domestic constitutional documents, such as the US Bill of Rights, for over 200 years. Therefore, there was significant source material from domestic law for the development of civil and political rights at the international level. In contrast, economic, social and cultural rights do not have the same long history of domestic legal protection and justiciability, so those norms were less legally developed.[13]

Another 'advantage' for civil and political rights arises at the advocacy level. Those human-rights non-governmental organizations (NGOs) that have most engaged in domestic and international legal and political processes, such as Amnesty International and Human Rights Watch, have historically focused on civil and political rights. NGOs in the economic, social and cultural rights arena tended to be organizations that facilitated service delivery to disadvantaged groups, such as charitable organizations.[14] Thus, there has historically been greater agitation for states by human rights advocates to 'do something' about civil and political rights abuses, both at home and abroad, and less pressure to address deficiencies regarding economic, social and cultural rights. Of course, historically, there has been much political agitation around economic and social issues, but not in terms of economic and social rights, and certainly not in terms of economic and social rights in other states. This distinction has broken down in the last 20 years. For example, Amnesty

10 See e.g. Dominic McGoldrick, *The Human Rights Committee: Its Role in the Development of the International Covenant on Civil and Political Rights*, 2nd edn (New York: Oxford University Press, 1994), para. 1.16.

11 As at 31 December 2009, the ICCPR had 165 states parties and the ICESCR had 160 states parties.

12 *Vienna Declaration and Programme of Action: Report of the World Conference on Human Rights*, UN Doc A/CONF.157/23 (12 July 1993), para. 5.

13 Significant domestic jurisprudence is now being generated in a number of jurisdictions. See, generally, Malcolm Langford (ed.), *Social Rights Jurisprudence: Emerging Trends in International and Comparative Law* (Cambridge: Cambridge University Press, 2008), Part 2. See also M. Ssenyonjo's Chapter 3 in this book.

14 J. Oloka-Onyango, 'Beyond the Rhetoric: Reinvigorating the Struggle for Economic and Social Rights in Africa', *California Western International Law Journal*, 26(1) (1995), pp. 38–9.

International no longer ignores economic, social and cultural rights issues.[15] And classical service NGOs, such as World Vision, Oxfam and Médecins Sans Frontières, are now more politically active.[16] Nevertheless, civil and political rights had a significant 'head start' over economic social and cultural rights in capturing the attention and agendas of global and domestic human rights activists.

The infrastructure for civil and political rights established by the ICCPR was, and remains, superior to that in the ICESCR. The ICCPR established an independent expert body, the HRC, to oversee its implementation. No such body was established by the ICESCR, with oversight left initially to the United Nations Economic and Social Council (ECOSOC), a political body with political agendas. Only after almost 10 years of inadequate performance did ECOSOC finally establish an independent expert body in 1985, the Committee on Economic, Social and Cultural Rights, to supervise the implementation of the ICESCR.[17] Again, the theme of civil and political rights being 'ahead' of economic social and cultural rights is evident. The HRC had a 10-year head start over its ICESCR counterpart in developing its practices, procedures, institutional culture, and substantive jurisprudence.

Of even greater consequence are key differences between the respective obligations of states under the two covenants. The key obligation provision in the ICCPR, Article 2(1), reads:

> Each State Party to the present Covenant undertakes to respect and to ensure to all individuals within its territory and subject to its jurisdiction the rights recognised in the present Covenant, without distinction of any kind such as race, colour, sex, language, religion, political or other opinion, national or social origin, property, birth, or other status.

Therefore, the ICCPR requires states to immediately respect and ensure to all the enjoyment of the rights therein.

The parallel provision in the ICESCR, Article 2(1), reads:

> Each State Party to the present Covenant undertakes to take steps, individually and through international assistance and co-operation, especially economic and technical, to the maximum of its available resources, with a view to achieving progressively the full realization of the rights recognized in the present Covenant by all appropriate means, including particularly the adoption of legislative measures.

The obligation provision in the ICESCR is distinctly muddier than that in the ICCPR. The obligation is progressive rather than immediate, and is qualified by a state's 'available resources'.[18]

A key to the rationale behind the different obligations is the perception, dating back to their natural rights origins, that civil and political rights are 'negative rights', requiring only that states refrain from rights-violating behaviour, while economic, social and cultural rights are 'positive' in

---

15 See, generally, http://www.amnesty.org/en/economic-social-and-cultural-rights and also http://www.amnesty.org/en/demand-dignity [accessed 8 October 2009].

16 For example, Oxfam International now engages in advocacy, in the form of pressuring decision-makers to 'change policies and practices that reinforce poverty and injustice' as a means of achieving its objectives. Available from: http://www.oxfam.org/en/about/what. See also Oloka-Onyango, note 14 above, p. 39.

17 ECOSOC Resolution 1985/17 of 28 May 1985.

18 This point is further elaborated in the context of economic, social and cultural rights by M. Ssenyonjo in Chapter 3 of this book.

that they require states to take actions to fulfil the rights therein. Negative rights seem to require a state to do nothing, a requirement that is inexpensive and simple, justifying the more onerous ICCPR obligation. Positive rights are expensive and difficult to perform, justifying the leeway given to states under the ICESCR.[19]

However, the reality is somewhat different. Civil and political rights are not wholly negative: they cannot be implemented simply by a state refraining from conduct. For example, the right to a fair trial in Article 14 of the ICCPR clearly requires the establishment of adequate judicial infrastructure. Article 25, covering the right to vote, entails the establishment of the necessary apparatus to run a fair election. Articles 23(1) and 24(1) explicitly call for measures from the state to protect, respectively, families and children. Indeed, all human rights entail both positive and negative characteristics. Freedom from torture fundamentally requires states to refrain from torture; thus, it seems to be a quintessentially negative right. However, a state cannot possibly prevent torture by simply doing nothing. States must take positive steps to ensure that the opportunities for torture are minimized, that systems are in place to prevent torture, and that it is punished in the instances where it occurs. These positive duties have been confirmed by the HRC in its jurisprudence on Article 7 of the ICCPR,[20] and are made explicit in the Convention Against Torture and Other Cruel, Inhuman and Degrading Treatment or Punishment (CAT).[21] In General Comment 31,[22] the HRC confirmed at paragraph 6 that the 'legal obligation under article 2, paragraph 1, is both negative and positive in nature." The same is true of the ICESCR: its norms, too, entail both negative and positive aspects.[23]

Indeed, there is an element of progressiveness also in some of the obligations in the ICCPR. For example, Article 23(4) states, in part:

> States Parties to the present Covenant shall take appropriate steps to ensure equality of rights and responsibilities of spouses as to marriage, during marriage and at its dissolution.

The reference to 'appropriate steps' suggests that this obligation is not immediate, recognizing that states may take some time to erode cultural norms that dictate against equality within the family. However, no such concession is made by the HRC in the General Comment on Article 23.[24]

Indeed, the interdependence and indivisibility of the two sets of rights promoted in the respective covenants' preambles has not been an empty promise. Some economic social and cultural aspects

---

19 See also Craig Scott, 'The Interdependence and Permeability of Human Rights Norms: Towards a Partial Fusion of the International Covenants on Human Rights', *Osgoode Hall Law Journal*, 27 (1989), pp. 769–878, at pp. 832–3.

20 See e.g. General Comment 20, which replaced General Comment 7 concerning prohibition of torture and cruel treatment or punishment (Art. 7), CCPR/C/74/CRP.4/Rev.6. (1992), paras. 11 and 13.

21 Adopted by GA Res 39/46 of 10 December 1984. Opened for signature 10 December 1984, 1465 UNTS 85 (entered into force 26 June 1987).

22 General comments are issued by all treaty bodies and are directed to all states parties. They generally entail expanded interpretations of particular rights in the relevant treaty, or other miscellaneous issues. General Comment 31, UN Doc CCPR/C/21/Rev.1/Add.13 (26 May 2008), concerned the 'Nature of the General Legal Obligation Imposed on States Parties to the Covenant'.

23 See e.g. The Maastricht Guidelines on Violations of Economic, Social and Cultural Rights, reprinted in *Human Rights Quarterly*, 20 (1998), pp. 691–704, especially at para. 15.

24 General Comment 19: Article 23 (The Family), Thirty-Ninth Session, 27 July 1990, reprinted in Compilation of General Comments and General Recommendations Adopted by Human Rights Treaty Bodies, UN Doc HRI/GEN/1/Rev.9 (vol. 1) at 198 (27 May 2008).

have been uncovered within ICCPR rights. The right to join a trade union is explicitly covered in both covenants.[25] Furthermore, the right to life in Article 6 entails a state duty to combat socio-economic threats to life, such as epidemics and malnutrition; states should also adopt measures to promote life expectancy and reduce infant mortality.[26] Minority rights in Article 27 clearly have an important cultural component. Indeed, there are numerous examples of true indivisibility and permeability, such as the links between the right to life and the socio-economic right to an adequate standard of health care, and the right to freedom of expression and the socio-economic right to education.[27]

Arguably, the most significant permeation of economic, social and cultural rights into ICCPR rights has arisen in regard to Article 26, which reads:

> All persons are equal before the law and are entitled without any discrimination to the equal protection of the law. In this respect, the law shall prohibit any discrimination and guarantee to all persons equal and effective protection against discrimination on any ground such as race, colour, sex, language, religion, political or other opinion, national or social origin, property, birth or other status.

The Article 26 guarantee of non-discrimination has famously been interpreted so as to prohibit discrimination in relation to 'any field regulated and protected by public authorities'.[28] For example, in *Broeks* v *Netherlands*,[29] Mrs Broeks alleged a violation of Article 26 entailed in her ineligibility as a married woman for an unemployment benefit, in circumstances where a married man would have received that benefit. The Netherlands responded by arguing that Article 26 only guaranteed non-discriminatory treatment in relation to civil and political rights, and was therefore inapplicable to Mrs Broeks' claim, which concerned a social security right.[30] The HRC rejected the Netherlands' contention, and instead confirmed a broad application of Article 26. Article 26 has since been a vehicle for complaints regarding discrimination in relation to numerous economic, social and cultural rights.[31]

One of the biggest perceived differences between the two sets of rights was the contention that economic, social and cultural rights were not justiciable. Their non-justiciable nature was a function of the vague obligation provision, which hampered findings of violation, and the flawed positive/negative dichotomy. Civil and political rights have long been recognized as justiciable, and may be the subject of individual complaints before the HRC under the First Optional Protocol

25 See ICCPR, Article 22, and ICESCR, Article 8.

26 General Comment 6: Article 6 (Right to Life), Sixteenth Session, 30 April 1982, para. 5, reprinted in Compilation of General Comments and General Recommendations Adopted by Human Rights Treaty Bodies, UN Doc HRI/GEN/1/Rev.9 (vol. 1) at 176 (27 May 2008).

27 See, regarding these socio-economic rights, Articles 12, 13 and 14 of ICESCR.

28 General Comment 18: Non-Discrimination, Thirty-Seventh Session, 10 November 1989, para. 12, reprinted in Compilation of General Comments and General Recommendations Adopted by Human Rights Treaty Bodies, UN Doc HRI/GEN/1/Rev.9 (vol. 1) at 195 (27 May 2008).

29 CCPR/C/29/D/172/1984, 9 April 1987.

30 The right to social security is protected in Article 9, ICESCR.

31 See Sarah Joseph, Jenny Schultz and Melissa Castan, *The International Covenant on Civil and Political Rights: Cases, Commentary and Materials*, 2nd edn (New York: Oxford University Press, 2004), para. 23.13.

to the ICCPR.[32] The existence of an individual complaints system under the ICCPR, and the absence of one under the ICESCR, have exacerbated the gap in normative material on the two sets of rights. While the HRC has decided over 1,500 cases (including inadmissible cases, which can nevertheless be instructive with regard to the normative content of a right), which help to concretize the meaning of ICCPR rights, the Committee on Economic, Social and Cultural Rights has decided none.

On 10 December 2008, the 60th anniversary of the UDHR, the UN General Assembly adopted an Optional Protocol to ICESCR which will come into force when 10 states have ratified it.[33] Its coming into force will usher in a new era of justiciable global economic social and cultural rights. Thus, one of the most important, yet incorrect, perceived differences between the two sets of rights will finally be dispelled.

5. Individual and Collective Rights

The rights in the ICCPR are essentially rights of individuals. The exception is the right of self-determination, a right of peoples in Article 1.[34] The HRC has found that this right is not justiciable under the Optional Protocol, on the basis that that instrument only envisages complaints by individuals.[35] This interpretation is unnecessarily conservative, and has significantly weakened the effectiveness of Article 1.[36]

While the other rights are cast as individual rights, some of them necessarily envisage enjoyment by groups of individuals, such as the Article 22 right of freedom of association, Article 23 family rights and minority rights under Article 27. Furthermore, the inherent individualism in the ICCPR is tempered by the fact that most of the rights therein can be limited by proportionate measures designed to fulfil the legitimate countervailing interests of society, such as promotion of public order, public health, national security, or public morals.[37]

6. Cultural Relativism

The notion of cultural relativism poses a significant challenge to the universality of human rights. Cultural relativist arguments postulate that the application of human rights varies according to the different cultures of states. Such arguments have tended to target civil and political rights more than economic social and cultural rights. Such arguments generally emanate from non-Western states, which is perhaps unsurprising given the Western philosophical origin of civil and political rights.

---

32 *Optional Protocol to the International Covenant on Civil and Political Rights*, adopted by GA Res 2200A (XXI) of 16 November 1966, opened for signature 19 December 1966, 999 UNTS 171 (entered into force 23 March 1976).

33 Optional Protocol to the International Covenant on Economic Social and Cultural Rights, adopted by GA Res A/RES/63/117 of 10 December 2008.

34 The right is found in identical form in Article 1 ICESCR.

35 See e.g. *Kitok* v *Sweden*, CCPR/C/33/D/197/1985, 27 July 1988, para. 6.3.

36 Article 1 issues can be raised in other HRC procedures beyond consideration of cases under the Optional Protocol.

37 Joseph, Schultz, and Castan, note 31 above, para. 1.89. These qualifications to civil and political rights are discussed below.

The text of the ICCPR indicates that the rights therein are universal. Furthermore, states have freely ratified the treaty, so it is perhaps unconvincing for states to subsequently claim some sort of cultural exemption from the rights therein. However, some room for cultural difference in application is given.[38] For example, reservations to the ICCPR are allowed.[39] Furthermore, the application of various permissible limitations can vary according to the circumstances of a state. In particular, the limitations allowed for 'public morals' must vary according to the prevailing moral climate in a state.[40] Article 27 confers cultural rights on minorities, confirming that human rights in fact promote cultural diversity. Finally, the HRC has occasionally conceded cultural differences in application of rights. For example, in *Aumeeruddy-Cziffra et al.* v *Mauritius*, it stated that the rights of family protection in Article 23(1) would 'vary from country to country and depend on different social, economic, political and cultural conditions and traditions'.[41] Similarly, regarding the age of majority for the purposes of Article 24, the right of a child to protection, the HRC has stated that that age is determined by each state in accordance with 'relevant social and cultural conditions'.[42]

On the other hand, the HRC has condemned certain cultural practices as breaches of the ICCPR, implicitly rejecting cultural defences of those practices. For example, it has condemned discrimination against gays and lesbians, female genital mutilation, *hudūd* punishments and prohibitions on apostasy in Islamic states, polygamy, and prohibitions on abortion.[43] Its strongest rejection of cultural relativism arose in General Comment 28, which addressed equality of rights between men and women:

> Inequality in the enjoyment of rights by women throughout the world is deeply embedded in tradition, history and culture, including religious attitudes.... States parties should ensure that traditional, historical, religious or cultural attitudes are not used to justify violations of women's right to equality before the law and to equal enjoyment of all Covenant rights ....[44]

A related argument is that of 'economic relativism'.[45] This theory postulates that economic development is the legitimate priority of developing states, so civil and political freedoms can be delayed while a state develops its economy to a satisfactory level.[46] This argument suggests that civil and political freedoms somehow undermine the promotion of economic development

38 See, generally, Douglas Lee Donoho, 'Relativism Versus Universalism in Human Rights: The Search for Meaningful Standards', *Stanford Journal of International Law*, 27 (1991), p. 345.

39 However, note the restrictions suggested by the HRC to the states parties' rights of reservation in General Comment 24: Issues Relating to Reservations, CCPR/C/21/Rev.1/Add.6 (4 November 1994).

40 See e.g. *Delgado Páez* v *Colombia*, CCPR/C/39/D/195/1985, 12 July 1990 and *Hertzberg* v *Finland*, CCPR/C/15/D/61/1979, 2 April 1982.

41 *Aumeeruddy-Cziffra et al.* v *Mauritius*, CCPR/C/12/D/35/1978, 9 April 1981, para. 9.2(b)2(ii)1.

42 General Comment 17: Article 24 (Rights of the Child), Thirty-Fifth Session, 7 April 1989, para. 4, reprinted in Compilation of General Comments and General Recommendations Adopted by Human Rights Treaty Bodies, UN Doc HRI/GEN/1/Rev.9 (vol. 1) at 193 (27 May 2008).

43 Joseph, Schultz and Castan, note 31 above, para. 1.99.

44 General Comment 28: Article 3 (The Equality of Rights Between Men and Women), CCPR/C/21/Rev.1/Add.10 (29 March 2000), para. 5.

45 Joseph, Schultz and Castan, note 31 above, para. 1.92.

46 For example, this type of argument formed a part of the rationale adopted by leaders of a number of Asian states during the 1990s against the applicability of 'Western' civil and political rights in the Asian context. For a brief outline of the 'Asian Values Debate', see Leena Avonius and Damien Kingsbury, 'Introduction', in Leena Avonius and Damien Kingsbury (eds), *Human Rights in Asia: A Reassessment of the Asian Values Debate* (New York: Palgrave Macmillan, 2008), pp. 1–2.

in vulnerable economies. For example, it might be argued that opposition groups with a free rein distract or undermine governments in achieving their economic goals, and might prompt unhelpful U-turns in economic policy. While developed states can withstand and absorb subsequent economic pressures, developing states do not have that luxury. On the other hand, civil and political rights facilitate government accountability, which helps to guard against corruption and bad governance, both of which can have devastating economic effects.[47]

The HRC has strongly rejected any hint of economic relativism in the application of the ICCPR. For example, it has not permitted states to justify poor prison conditions,[48] court delays,[49] or arbitrary restrictions on restitution schemes[50] on the basis of budgetary constraints. Exceptionally, the HRC has indicated that the right of the family to measures of protection does vary according to a state's economic circumstances.[51]

In its 'General Comment 31 on the Nature of the General Legal Obligation of States Parties to the Covenant', the HRC rejected cultural and economic relativism unambiguously:

> The requirement under article 2, paragraph 2, to take steps to give effect to the Covenant rights is unqualified and of immediate effect. A failure to comply with this obligation cannot be justified by reference to political, social, cultural or economic considerations within the State.[52]

7. Vertical and Horizontal Application of Civil and Political Rights

Human rights, including civil and political rights, are traditionally held by individuals against governments. Under the ICCPR, a state is responsible for the actions of all of its agents, whether they be part of the executive, legislative, or judicial arm of government,[53] and whether they be national, regional or local authorities.[54] The ICCPR obligations extend to all parts of a federal state:[55] even if a federal government is constitutionally unable to control the actions of a provincial government, the former is responsible for the actions of the latter under the ICCPR.[56] Furthermore, states are responsible for the actions of their agents even when they act in excess of their official authority.[57] The HRC has also held that states are responsible for the rights violating actions of their agents abroad noting: 'This means that a State party must respect and ensure the rights laid down in the Covenant to anyone within the power or effective control of that State Party, even if not situated

47 See Amartya Sen, 'Human Rights and Asian Values: What Lee Kwan Yew and Le Peng Don't Understand About Asia', *The New Republic*, 217(2–3) (1997), pp. 33–40.

48 See e.g. *Mukong* v *Cameroon*, CCPR/C/51/D/458/1991, 21 July 1994, General Comment 21: Article 10 (Humane Treatment of Persons Deprived of their Liberty, Forty-Fourth Session, 10 April 1992, para. 4, reprinted in Compilation of General Comments and General Recommendations Adopted by Human Rights Treaty Bodies, UN Doc HRI/GEN/1/Rev.9 (vol. 1) at 202 (27 May 2008).

49 See e.g. *Lubuto* v *Zambia*, CCPR/C/55/D/390/1990, 31 October 1995, *Ashby* v *Trinidad and Tobago*, CCPR/C/74/D/580/1994, 21 March 2002.

50 See e.g. *Adam* v *Czech Republic*, CCPR/C/57/D/586/1994, 23 July 1996.

51 *Aumeeruddy-Cziffra* v *Mauritius*, CCPR/C/12/D/35/1978, 9 April 1981, para. 9.2(b)2(ii)1.

52 General Comment 31: The Nature of the General Legal Obligation Imposed on States Parties to the Covenant, CCPR/C/21/Rev.1/Add.13 (26 May 2004), para. 14.

53 *Ibid.*, para. 4.

54 *Ibid.*

55 Article 50, ICCPR. See also, e.g. *Toonen* v *Australia*, CCPR/C/50/D/488/1992, 31 March 1994.

56 See *Waldman* v *Canada*, CCPR/C/67/D/694/1996, 3 November 1999.

57 See *Jegatheeswara Sarma* v *Sri Lanka*, CCCPR/C/78/D/950/2000, 16 July 2003.

within the territory of the State Party'.[58] For example, states have been found to violate the ICCPR by arbitrarily refusing to reissue individuals with passports at overseas consulates,[59] and when state agents have kidnapped a person in another country.[60]

However, governments are certainly not the only threat to civil and political rights. Private bodies, whether they are individuals, companies, or some other private organizations, are all capable of acting in ways that detrimentally affect an individual's enjoyment of human rights.

The ICCPR has been interpreted so as to have some effect in the private sphere. That is, they have been interpreted as having indirect horizontal effect. In General Comment 31, the HRC stated at paragraph 8:

> The article 2, paragraph 1, obligations are binding on States [Parties] and do not, as such, have direct horizontal effect as a matter of international law. The Covenant cannot be viewed as a substitute for domestic criminal or civil law. However the positive obligations on States Parties to ensure Covenant rights will only be fully discharged if individuals are protected by the State, not just against violations of Covenant rights by its agents, but also against acts committed by private persons or entities that would impair the enjoyment of Covenant rights in so far as they are amenable to application between private persons or entities. There may be circumstances in which a failure to ensure Covenant rights as required by article 2 would give rise to violations by States Parties of those rights, as a result of States Parties' permitting or failing to take appropriate measures or to exercise due diligence to prevent, punish, investigate or redress the harm caused by such acts by private persons or entities.... The Covenant itself envisages in some articles certain areas where there are positive obligations on States Parties to address the activities of private persons or entities. For example, the privacy-related guarantees of article 17 must be protected by law. It is also implicit in article 7 that States Parties have to take positive measures to ensure that private persons or entities do not inflict torture or cruel, inhuman or degrading treatment or punishment on others within their power. In fields affecting basic aspects of ordinary life such as work or housing, individuals are to be protected from discrimination within the meaning of article 26.][61]

Therefore, the ICCPR does not impose direct obligations on private bodies. However, states parties are required, as part of their positive obligations under the treaty, to take measures to protect individuals from harm to their ICCPR rights by private bodies, insofar as those rights 'are amenable to application between private persons or entities'. The general comment does not clarify when such 'amenability' arises. Similar vagueness is evident in the allusion to 'circumstances' in which states must exercise due diligence, suggesting that there are circumstances where a state does not have to exercise due diligence, and in the restriction of Article 26 rights in the private sector to 'basic aspects of ordinary life', rather than, presumably, extraordinary aspects of life. The vagueness of the general comment reflects the fact that the horizontal application of the ICCPR, and of human rights in general, is an underdeveloped area. The outer boundaries of a state's obligations with regard to private bodies cannot be presumed to map its obligations over its own agents. This is because public bodies and private bodies have inherently different societal roles, which impact on the appropriate human rights duties that should be imposed within the respective public and private spheres. Private bodies are

---

58 General Comment 31: The Nature of the General Legal Obligation Imposed on States Parties to the Covenant, CCPR/C/21/Rev.1/Add.13 (26 May 2004), para. 10.

59 *Montero* v *Uruguay*, CCPR/C/18/D/106/1981, 31 March 1983; *Vidal Martins* v *Uruguay*, CCPR/C/15//D/57/1979, 23 March 1982. See also *Munaf* v *Romania*, CCPR/C/96/D/1539/2006, 21 August 2009.

60 *López Burgos* v *Uruguay*, CCPR/C/13/D/52/1979, 29 July 1981.

61 The square brackets are contained in the original.

free, to an extent, to pursue their self-interests unlike public bodies, which have no independent self-interest beyond promoting the interests of the people they represent.[62]

In *Nahlik* v *Austria*,[63] the HRC stated that discrimination by private bodies was prohibited in the 'quasi-public' sphere under Article 26, noting that 'employment' was within that sphere. This decision implies that discrimination in the wholly private sphere, such as within a household or family, may be beyond the scope of the ICCPR: one is permitted to act according to one's prejudices at home so long as those actions do not escalate to egregious levels, such as in the case of domestic violence.[64]

8. Limitations to Civil and Political Rights

Most of the jurisprudence surrounding civil and political rights, whether it is at the global, regional, or domestic level, has concerned restrictions to those rights. That is, the key question in a case has not generally been whether a right is relevant or has been engaged by a certain situation. Rather, the key issue has generally been whether the right at issue can be legitimately limited or qualified in the circumstances. Hence, analysis of the limitations to civil and political rights is often the key to understanding the jurisprudence of those rights.

Most civil and political rights are qualified by permissible limitations and restrictions. First, most civil and political rights are subject to the possibility of derogation under Article 4 of the ICCPR, which permits the suspension of rights in times of public emergency so long as the relevant measures are proportionate. However, Article 4(2) lists certain non-derogable rights.[65] There have been few international cases on the issue of derogation, which only arises in exceptional circumstances.[66] Unfortunately, most notices of derogation submitted regarding the ICCPR have failed to properly justify the adoption of derogatory measures. Furthermore, many states routinely abuse so-called states of emergency to justify illegitimate oppressive measures.[67] However, it may be noted that few states have notified the UN of derogations to the ICCPR in light of the war on terror, despite the number of unusually restrictive provisions adopted by numerous states since 11 September 2001 ostensibly to combat terrorism; this circumstance may indicate that many states believe that their counterterrorism measures fall within the ordinary permissible limits to ICCPR rights, discussed directly below.[68]

62 See also Sarah Joseph, 'Human Rights Committee: Recent Jurisprudence', *Human Rights Law Review*, 4(2) (2004), pp. 277–94, at pp. 278–9.

63 CCPR/C/57/D/608/1995, 22 July 1996.

64 Joseph, Schultz and Castan, note 31 above, p. 734.

65 No derogation is permitted from Articles 6 (right to life), 7 (freedom from torture and other ill treatment), 8(1) (freedom from slavery), 8(2) (freedom from servitude), 11 (freedom from imprisonment for failure to fulfil a contract), 15 (prohibition on retroactive criminal law), 16 (right to recognition as a person before the law), and 18 (freedom of religion and belief).

66 See, generally, on derogation, General Comment 29: Article 4: Derogations During a State of Emergency, CCPR/C/21/Rev.1/Add.11 (31 August 2001).

67 See Sarah Joseph, 'Human Rights Committee: General Comment 29', *Human Rights Law Review*, 2(1) (2002), pp. 81–98, at pp. 96–8.

68 Only the UK has explicitly derogated from the ICCPR in respect of measures adopted in the 'war on terror'. That derogation was withdrawn on 15 March 2005, due to the repeal of the relevant legislative provisions.

Beyond the issue of derogation, most civil and political rights can be legitimately restricted anyway: very few ICCPR rights are absolute. Freedom from torture, cruel inhuman and degrading treatment (Article 7) is such an absolute right. The absolute nature of the freedom from torture is also confirmed in Article 2 of the CAT. Thus, while there has been academic debate over whether torture should in fact be permissible in some circumstances, prompted by the supposed exigencies of the 'war on terror',[69] the legal position is clear: torture is not legally permissible in any circumstance. Other examples of absolute rights in the ICCPR include freedom from slavery (Article 8(1)) and servitude (Article 8(2)).

8.1 Unlawful and Arbitrary Interferences with Rights

There are various ways in which ICCPR rights are qualified. One approach is found in Article 17(1) on the right to privacy, which reads:

> No one shall be subjected to arbitrary or unlawful interference with his privacy, family, home or correspondence, nor to unlawful attacks on his honour and reputation.

Therefore, one's privacy may be interfered with if it is lawful and non-arbitrary to do so. The requirement of 'lawfulness' has generally been interpreted as requiring a limit to be prescribed in a state's law. Regarding privacy, the HRC has stated in General Comment 16, that

> relevant legislation must specify in detail the precise circumstances in which such interferences may be permitted. A decision to make use of such authorised interference must be made only by the authority designated under the law, and on a case-by-case basis.[70]

Therefore, a law which specifies a limit to an ICCPR right, such as privacy, must specify that limit with reasonable precision, rather than, for example, conferring broad discretions on authorities to apply a limit as when they see fit. For example, in *Pinkney* v *Canada*, an early HRC decision in 1981, the HRC stated that a law regarding the censorship of a prisoner's mail was unsatisfactory as it did not specify the grounds upon which the censorship would arise: too much discretion was vested in prison authorities in that regard.[71]

The requirement that interference with rights be 'lawful' is also found in Article 9 regarding one's right to liberty,[72] and ensures that the limits to one's rights are predictable and ascertainable, as they are governed by laws rather than the whims of authorities. However, the proviso that interference

69 See, for an argument that torture should be permitted in certain circumstances, Alan Dershowitz, 'Should the Ticking Bomb Terrorist Be Tortured?: A Case Study in How a Democracy Should Make Tragic Choices', in *Why Terrorism Works: Understanding the Threat, Responding to the Challenge* (New Haven, CT: Yale University Press, 2002), ch. 4. For a response, see Sarah Joseph, 'Torture: The Fallacy of the Ticking Bomb', in Andrew Lynch and George Williams (eds), *Law and Liberty in the War on Terror* (Sydney: Federation Press, 2007), pp. 147–54.

70 General Comment 16: Article 17 (Right to Privacy), Thirty-Second Session, 8 April 1988, para. 8, reprinted in Compilation of General Comments and General Recommendations Adopted by Human Rights Treaty Bodies, UN Doc HRI/GEN/1/Rev.9 (vol. 1) at 191 (27 May 2008).

71 *Pinkney* v *Canada*, CCPR/C/14/D/27/1977, 29 October 1981.

72 Article 9(1) reads: 'Everyone has the right to liberty and security of the person. No one shall be subjected to arbitrary arrest or detention. No one shall be deprived of his liberty *except on such grounds and in accordance with such procedures as are established by law*' [emphasis added].

with a right be 'lawful' does not protect one against a wholly unreasonable law. For example, numerous cases have been submitted against Australia regarding the application of laws prescribing mandatory detention for persons arriving unlawfully in the country.[73] Yet, detentions under this law are undoubtedly 'lawful' in Australia, having been found constitutional by Australia's highest court.[74]

Article 17 also prohibits 'arbitrary' interferences with privacy'.[75] Similarly, Article 9(1) prohibits arbitrary detention. The concept of 'arbitrariness' extends beyond 'lawfulness' to encompass notions of reasonableness and proportionality.[76] Therefore, the above-mentioned detention regime in Australia has been found to be arbitrary and in breach of Article 9(1), even though it is clearly lawful in Australian domestic law. Similarly, anti-gay laws in Tasmania, which were clearly prescribed by law, were found to be arbitrary and in breach of Article 17 in *Toonen* v *Australia*.[77]

However, it does seem that the HRC has morphed the meanings of 'arbitrary' and 'unlawful' somewhat. With regard to the requirement of lawfulness under Article 17, the HRC has stated that a relevant law 'must comply with the provisions, aims and objectives of the Covenant'.[78] This comment indicates that a relevant law must comply with international human rights law, rather than only with municipal constitutional requirements. In *A* v *Australia*,[79] the HRC had to decide on the meaning of Article 9(4), which states:

> Anyone who is deprived of his liberty by arrest or detention shall be entitled to take proceedings before a court, in order that that court may decide on the lawfulness of his detention and order his release if his detention is not lawful.

Article 9(4) seems to require only that one has a right to challenge the lawfulness of one's detention under domestic law. There is no explicit requirement that one be permitted to challenge the reasonableness or arbitrariness of one's detention. Yet, the HRC has in fact interpreted Article 9(4) as a right to challenge the lawfulness of one's detention under both domestic law and the ICCPR itself.[80] The HRC has essentially interpreted Article 9(4) as incorporating a right to challenge both the lawfulness *and* the arbitrariness of one's detention.[81]

---

73 *A* v *Australia*, CCPR/C/59/D/560/1993, 3 April 1997; *C* v *Australia*, CCPR/C/76/D/900/1999, 28 October 2002; *Bakhtiyari* v *Australia*, CCPR/C/79/D/1069/2002, 29 October 2003.

74 See *Chu Kheng Lim* v *Minister for Immigration, Local Government and Ethnic Affairs* (1992) 176 CLR 1, *Al-Kateb Godwin* (2004) 219 CLR 562.

75 Note that only unlawful attacks on honour and reputation are apparently prohibited: arbitrary attacks thereon are not mentioned in Article 17.

76 See e.g. *Toonen* v *Australia*, CCPR/C/50/D/488/1992, 31 March 1994, para. 8.3; General Comment 16: Article 17 (Right to Privacy), Thirty-Second Session, 8 April 1988, para. 4, reprinted in Compilation of General Comments and General Recommendations Adopted by Human Rights Treaty Bodies, UN Doc HRI/GEN/1/Rev.9 (vol. 1) at 191 (27 May 2008).

77 *Toonen* v *Australia*, CCPR/C/50/D/488/1992, 31 March 1994.

78 General Comment 16: Article 17 (Right to Privacy), Thirty-Second Session, 8 April 1988, para. 3, reprinted in Compilation of General Comments and General Recommendations Adopted by Human Rights Treaty Bodies, UN Doc HRI/GEN/1/Rev.9 (vol. 1) at 191 (27 May 2008).

79 *A* v *Australia*, CCPR/C/59/D/560/1993, 3 April 1997.

80 *A* v *Australia*, CCPR/C/59/D/560/1993, 3 April 1997, para. 9.5. This finding has been upheld in numerous similar cases, such as *C* v *Australia*, CCPR/C/76/D/900/1999, 28 October 2002. In *C* v *Australia*, Messrs Rodley and Kretzmer issued separate opinions where they refrained from endorsing the HRC's interpretation of Article 9(4) on the basis that there was no need in the case to address the issue. See also *Baban* v *Australia*, CCPR/C/78/D/1014/2001, 6 August 2003.

81 See also the concurring opinion of Mr Bhagwati in *A* v *Australia*, note 80 above, Appendix.

Even Article 6, the right to life, is not an absolute right. Articles 6(2) to 6(6) set out an explicit limit to that right, outlining the circumstances in which capital punishment is permissible.[82] Further, Article 6(1) reads:

> Every human being has the inherent right to life. This right shall be protected by law. No one shall be arbitrarily deprived of his life.

Therefore, one may lose one's life in circumstances that are not arbitrary; that is, in circumstances that are reasonable and proportional. Of course, there are very few circumstances in which loss of life could be deemed reasonable. Killing in self-defence or in defence of another would be permissible. It is uncertain if the risk being averted in such a situation has to equate with danger to life. In *Suárez de Guerrero* v *Colombia*,[83] a blatant violation of the right to life arose when persons that were mere suspects in a kidnapping were ambushed and killed by police, without being given the opportunity to surrender. There was 'no evidence that the action ... was necessary in their own defence or that of others, or that it was necessary to effect the arrest or prevent the escape of the persons concerned'.[84] The HRC later commented that the killings 'were disproportionate to the requirements of law enforcement'.[85] Therefore, the HRC arguably implied that one could be killed in order to prevent any criminal or suspected criminal from resisting arrest and escaping. At the least, lethal force could only be used against a resistor suspected of a very serious crime, rather than, for example, a fleeing pickpocket. At the most, the 'proportionate requirements of law enforcement' can justify the use of lethal force only against a person who is reasonably suspected of posing an imminent lethal risk to at least one other person.[86]

---

82 The death penalty is prohibited under the Second Optional Protocol to the ICCPR: Second Optional Protocol to the ICCPR, aiming at the abolition of the death penalty, adopted by GA Res 44/128 of 15 December 1989, opened for signature 15 December 1989, 1642 UNTS 414 (entered into force 11 July 1991).

83 *Suárez de Guerrero* v *Colombia*, CCPR/C/15/D/45/1979, 31 March 1982.

84 *Ibid.*, para. 13.2.

85 *Ibid.*, para. 13.3.

86 This standard is imposed by the UN Basic Principles on the Use of Force and Firearms by Law Enforcement Officials, Adopted by the Eighth United Nations Congress on the Prevention of Crime and the Treatment of Offenders, Havana, Cuba, 27 August to 7 September 1990, A/CONF.144/28/Rev.1 at 112 (1990), especially Basic Principle 9.

The equivalent right to life in the Convention for the Protection of Human Rights and Fundamental Freedoms (European Convention on Human Rights), opened for signature 4 November 1950, 213 UNTS 221 (entered into force 3 September 1953), as amended by Protocols 3, 5, 8 and 11, in Article 2 reads:

1. Everyone's right to life shall be protected by law. No one shall be deprived of his life intentionally save in the execution of a sentence of a court following his conviction of a crime for which this penalty is provided by law.
2. Deprivation of life shall not be regarded as inflicted in contravention of this article when it results from the use of force which is no more than absolutely necessary:
   a. in defence of any person from unlawful violence;
   b. in order to effect a lawful arrest or to prevent escape of a person lawfully detained;
   c. in action lawfully taken for the purpose of quelling a riot or insurrection.

The law enforcement exceptions to Article 2 were interpreted strictly by a narrow majority in the European Court of Human Rights in *McCann* v *UK* Series A/342, judgment of 27 September 1995.

Finally, it may be noted that Article 25 which prescribes rights of participation in public affairs, may not be subjected to 'unreasonable restrictions', so 'reasonable' or proportionate restrictions are permissible.[87]

8.2 Clawback Clauses

The second way in which limitations to rights are expressed in the ICCPR is through the use of so-called clawback clauses. Article 19 contains an example. Article 19(2) contains the general right to freedom of expression, while Article 19(3) permits states to limit those rights. Article 19(3) reads:

> The exercise of the rights provided for in paragraph 2 of this article carries with it special duties and responsibilities. It may therefore be subject to certain restrictions, but these shall only be such as are provided by law and are necessary:
>
> (a) For respect of the rights or reputations of others;
>
> (b) For the protection of national security or of public order (*ordre public*), or of public health or morals.

Similar clauses are found in Articles 12(3) (limits to freedom of movement), 18(3) (limits to the right to manifest religion and belief), 21 (limits to freedom of assembly), and 22(2) (limits to freedom of association).

Generally, clawback clauses contain two overriding requirements: they must be prescribed by law and must be necessary to the purpose of promoting one of a list of legitimate ends. These two overriding requirements mirror the limits outlined above relating to 'lawfulness' and 'arbitrariness'. The requirement of prescription by law corresponds to the requirement that limits to Articles 9(1) and 17 be 'lawful'. The requirement that limits be 'necessary' is a proportionality requirement, and corresponds to the prohibition on arbitrary restrictions in Articles 9(1), 17, and 6.

Therefore, clawback clauses are distinguished by the listing of the legitimate ends to which a restriction may be applied. The list of legitimate ends is similar across the relevant rights. They may generally be limited by measures which are prescribed by law and proportionate to the end of promoting national security,[88] public order (*ordre public*),[89] public health, public morals, and the rights and freedoms of others.[90] Article 19 rights may additionally be restricted to protect the reputations of others. Given that reputation is an aspect of one's right to privacy in Article 17, the limitation adds nothing as it is encompassed within the notion of 'rights of others'. Similarly, while

---

87 See e.g. General Comment 25: Issues Relating to Reservations, CCPR/C/21/Rev.1/Add.6 (4 November 1994), para. 4, on the permissibility of 'reasonable and objective' limits to the right to vote.

88 Article 18 omits 'national security' as a legitimate restriction to the right to manifest religion or belief.

89 '*Ordre public*', a civil law concept, is a broader concept than 'public order', for which there is no perfect English language translation. *Ordre public*, unlike the common law concept of public order, permits the variation of private law obligations. No ICCPR case has shed light on the consequences of the extra depth of *ordre public* compared to public order. See Joseph, Schultz and Castan, note 31 above, para. 18.29. See also B. Lockwood Jr., J. Finn, and G. Jubinsky, 'Working Paper for the Committee of Experts on Limitation Provisions', *Human Rights Quarterly*, 7(1) (1985), pp. 35–88, at pp. 57–9.

90 Article 18 refers to the 'fundamental rights and freedoms of others', but jurisprudence to date does not indicate the significance, if any, of the additional word 'fundamental'.

Article 21 adds an apparent additional ground of limitation in referring to 'public safety', that notion is probably encompassed within 'public order'.

The HRC has indicated on numerous occasions that the restrictions to rights should be construed narrowly.[91] However, a conceptual problem arises here with regard to limits designed to promote 'the rights of others'. Rights occasionally clash with each other. The 'rights of others' restriction allows for the appropriate balancing of rights on a case-by-case basis. Sometimes a person's right in fact must be limited in order to allow for the enjoyment by another of his or her rights. For example, a law which prohibits defamation is a law which restricts freedom of expression. It is also a law which is necessary to promote one's right to reputation in Article 17. Contempt-of-court laws also restrict freedom of expression. However, such laws are sometimes necessary to ensure that an accused person enjoys his or her right to a fair trial.[92] Therefore, the deliberate narrow construction of limits to a particular human right cannot take place in every instance, as doing so might unduly restrict a countervailing human right. In such cases, a careful balancing act must take place in order to determine the right that will prevail in a particular instance of clash. Such determinations can only be made on a case-by-case basis.

It is arguable that the limitations allowed under clawback clauses are more constrained than those permitted by the allowance of 'lawful' and 'non-arbitrary' restrictions. However, it is submitted that the two different formulations of permissible restrictions are in fact very similar to each other. It is difficult to conceive of a restriction, for example, to the right to be free from detention (Article 9) or the right to privacy (Article 17) that is not arbitrary and which is designed to achieve an end that is not found in a clawback clause. Indeed, the limits to the right to life (Article 6) are likely to be far narrower than those permitted under clawback clauses. It is, for example, inconceivable that a life could be legitimately terminated in order to promote 'public morals'.

8.3 Article 20

Article 20 is a unique provision, in that it is expressed as a mandatory restriction on rights. It reads:

> 1. Any propaganda for war shall be prohibited by law.
>
> 2. Any advocacy of national, racial or religious hatred that constitutes incitement to discrimination, hostility or violence shall be prohibited by law.

Thus Article 20 is simultaneously a mandatory restriction on freedom of expression and a right that hate speech, as well as war propaganda, be restricted. There have been no substantive cases on Article 20, but relevant cases have been brought under Article 4, the equivalent provision in the International Convention on the Elimination of all Forms of Racial Discrimination (CERD).[93]

---

91 See e.g. *Lee* v *Republic of Korea* CCPR/C/90/D/1296/2004, 20 July 2005 and *Belyatsky* v *Belarus* CCPR/C/90/D/1296/2004, 24 July 2007.

92 For example, a breach of the right to be presumed innocent (Article 14(2)) was found in *Karimov et al.* v *Tajikistan* CCPR/C/89/D/1108 & 1121/2002, in part due to the prejudicial comments against the accused made by a high-ranking official. By implication, the official should not have been allowed to make such statements in court, so the official's expression should in fact have been limited.

93 Adopted by GA Res 2106 (XX) of 21 December 1965, opened for signature 21 December 1965, 660 UNTS 195 (entered into force 4 January 1969). Article 4 only targets hate speech based on race, as one would expect in a treaty concerned specifically with racial discrimination.

For example, a violation of Article 4 was found in *L.K.* v *Netherlands* entailed in the Netherlands' failure to properly investigate and punish credible allegations of threats of racial violence.[94]

Given its clear impact on rights of freedom of expression, Article 20 was a controversial inclusion in the ICCPR. It has been the subject matter of numerous reservations, particularly by liberal Western democracies.[95] However, history bears witness to the devastating effects of unconstrained hate speech, such as its role in the escalation of rampant discrimination against Jews into the Holocaust under the Nazis, and the Rwandan genocide of 1994, which was prompted by homicidal urgings in the media.[96]

On the other hand, a worrying incursion into the domain of freedom of expression may be seen in the promotion by political bodies in the UN, namely the Human Rights Council and its predecessor, the Commission on Human Rights, of freedom from 'defamation of religion' as a human right.[97] The concept of defamation of religion indicates that speech must be limited on the basis that it might criticize or offend the religious sensibilities of others. In many ways, the relevant resolutions target behaviour that is already prohibited under Article 20 of the ICCPR. However, the prohibition of defamation of religion seems to go further and may construct a right to be free from critical or offensive speech on particular (religious) grounds. Censorship of criticism or offensive speech, even on religious grounds, shuts down an important avenue for societal debate, progress and development. Of course, much offensive speech of yesteryear raises few eyebrows and is in fact applauded today. It is therefore to be hoped that the concept of 'defamation of religion' does not entrench itself in the human rights system.[98]

8.4 Implied Restrictions

Beyond express restrictions to ICCPR rights, restrictions have been read into certain rights. For example, Article 26 (reproduced above in Section 4) does not mention any limits to one's right to equality before the law and to be free from discrimination, arguably indicating that no distinctions may be permissibly adopted in legislation. However, the HRC has outlined an exception:

> the Committee observes that not every differentiation of treatment will constitute discrimination, if the criteria for such differentiation are reasonable and objective and if the aim is to achieve a purpose which is legitimate under the Covenant.[99]

---

94 *L.K.* v *Netherlands*, CERD/C/42/D/4/1991, 16 March 1993. See also *Ahmad* v *Denmark*, CERD/C/56/D/16/1999, 13 March 2000 and *Hagan v Australia*, CERD/C/62/D/26/2002, 20 March 2003.

95 For example, Australia, Denmark, Finland, France, Iceland, Ireland, Luxemburg, Malta, the Netherlands, New Zealand, Norway, Sweden, Switzerland, the UK, and the USA have all made reservations against Article 20: see http://treaties.un.org/Pages/ViewDetails.aspx?src=TREATY&id=322&chapter=4&lang=en .

96 See e.g. the judgments concerning the Rwanda 'media trial' in *Prosecutor* v *Nahimana, Barayagwiza, and Ngeze*, Judgment and Sentence, ICTR Case No. 99052-T (3 December 2003); *The Prosecutor* v *Ferdinand Nahimana, Jean-Bosco Barayagwiza, Hassan Ngeze (Appeal Judgment)*, ICTR-99-52-A, International Criminal Tribunal for Rwanda (ICTR), 28 November 2007.

97 Human Rights Council Resolution 13/16: Combating Defamation of Religions, 15 April 2010.

98 See also John Cerone, 'Inappropriate Renderings: The Danger of Reductionist Resolutions', *Brooklyn Journal of International Law*, 33(2) (2008), pp. 357–78, at pp. 373–8.

99 General Comment 18, note 28 above, para. 13.

Thus, differentiations are allowed if they are 'reasonable and objective' and designed to achieve a legitimate purpose. Such differentiations are deemed not to be discrimination, and therefore are outside the ambit of Article 26. Alternatively, such distinctions could be viewed as 'permissible' instances of discrimination, and therefore qualifications and limitations to the right to be free from discrimination.

Article 27 is also expressed in absolute language. It states:

> In those States in which ethnic, religious or linguistic minorities exist, persons belonging to such minorities shall not be denied the right, in community with the other members of their group, to enjoy their own culture, to profess and practise their own religion, or to use their own language.

However, limitations have also been implied in Article 27. Numerous communications have been submitted to the HRC by minority indigenous groups alleging that certain economic development projects have infringed their cultural practices in breach of Article 27. In response, the HRC has noted that 'measures that have a certain limited impact on the way of life of persons belonging to a minority will not necessarily amount to a denial of the right under article 27',[100] especially if the relevant community has been consulted about the relevant development. Therefore, minority rights are not absolute: measures with a limited negative impact on their cultural practices are not deemed to be breaches of their cultural rights. However, once impacts cross a certain threshold, they are held to breach Article 27. For example, in *Poma Poma* v *Peru*,[101] the state's action in diverting water from an indigenous community's lands to a Peruvian city, resulting in the deaths of thousands of livestock and the collapse of the community's traditional economy, without any consultation with the relevant community, was held to be a breach of Article 27.

9. Conclusion

Civil and political rights have long been recognized in numerous domestic constitutions. Their recognition constitutes the bulk of the provisions of the UDHR, and they are, of course, the subject matter of the ICCPR. Civil and political rights are, or have become, more complex than perhaps originally conceived under the UDHR. For example, they are both negative and positive, and they are capable of vertical and horizontal application. They do allow room for cultural differences, but breaches of minimum standards are not, in international law, justified by cultural relativist arguments. Finally, the outer perimeters of most civil and political rights are uncertain, as they may be legitimately restricted in order to promote societal benefits, such as the maintenance of public order, or must on occasion be balanced against the countervailing individual rights of other individuals.

---

100 *Länsman et al.* v *Finland*, CCPR/C/52/D/511/1992, 26 October 1994, para. 9.4; *Länsman et al.* v *Finland*, CCPR/C/58/D/671/1995, 30 October 1996, para. 10.3. See also *Länsman et al.* v *Finland*, CCPR/C/83/D/1023/2001, 17 March 2005, para. 10.3.

101 CCPR/C/95/D/1457/2006, 24 April 2009.

Chapter 5
Simple Analytics of the Right to Development

Arjun Sengupta

1. Introduction

The UDHR did not provide specifically for the right to development.[1] Thus, a specific concept of right to development under international human rights law postdates the UDHR. When the right to development was first recognized in 1986 in the United Nations (UN) Declaration on the Right to Development,[2] it appeared as a utopian 'right of all rights', encompassing almost all the desirable objectives of human society. Although it was initially championed by the developing countries, it was soon adopted by academics, civil society leaders and also many policymakers from both the developed and developing countries. They all joined the effort to give a precise formulation of this right so that it becomes realizable in the real world. A huge literature built up, and when I was appointed the UN Independent Expert on Right to Development, I was overwhelmed by the complexity of the views often conflicting with each other, and extending over the fields of economics, politics and law, not to speak of the basic philosophical underpinnings of the concept of human rights generally. I was deeply influenced by Philip Alston, who was responsible for some of the major human rights studies at the time, Professor Abi-Saab and Stephen Marks of Harvard University. But the commentators on the subject were many, and although I shall not be referring to them by name here, my previous articles have recorded most of them.[3]

In this chapter, I shall present the bare structure of the arguments I have developed over the last 10 years that I have been engaged in reading and writing about the right to development. It is naturally not exhaustive, not even comprehensive, but it is spelled out to facilitate discussions so that an international consensus can be built up to make the right to development a legal right like all other human rights recognized in international human rights law.

2. What Is the Right to Development?

We have to begin with a definition of the right to development which has been accepted by the international community through its different instruments, and I will try to build on a definition as given in the Declaration on the Right to Development (DRD) itself. Article 1 of the DRD states:

---

1 However the Declaration on the Right to Development observed in its preamble that 'under the provisions of the Universal Declaration of Human Rights everyone is entitled to a social and international order in which the rights and freedoms set forth in that Declaration can be fully realized.'

2 A/RES/41/128, adopted by the UN General Assembly on 4 December 1986.

3 A. Sengupta, 'On the Theory and Practice of the Right to Development', *Human Rights Quarterly*, 24(4) (2002), pp. 837–89; A. Sengupta, 'The Human Right to Development', *Oxford Development Studies*, 32(2) (2004), pp. 179–203; A. Sengupta, 'The Human Right to Development' in B.A. Andreassen and S.P. Marks (eds), *Development as a Human Right: Legal, Political, and Economic Dimensions*. A Nobel Symposium Book (Cambridge, MA: Harvard University Press, 2006), pp. 9–36.

> The Right to Development is an inalienable human right by virtue of which every person and all peoples are entitled to participate in, contribute to, and enjoy economic, social, cultural and political development, in which all human rights and fundamental freedom can be fully realized.

It clearly refers to an entitlement to a process of 'development', which is economic, social, cultural and political and which everybody 'can participate in, contribute to and enjoy'. It is also a process in which all human rights and fundamental freedoms can be fully realized.[4]

This definition was obviously a package of a number of concepts arrived at as a negotiated compromise. It has to be given a precision to enable it to be realized through a legal process of carrying out the obligations of the agents, to whom this right is addressed. For this, the most important requirement is that the right should be so defined as to enable us to identify when the right is realized or when there is an improvement in the realization of the right. This is required not only of the right to development but of all rights, so that one can ascertain from empirical evidence if a right is being realized or not.

It is, of course, not a very easy task because all rights, like any desirable objective, consist of a number of elements, some of which are steadily realized while others are not. It means, we need an indicator of the realization of a right by combining its different elements or objectives, so that we can say when the value of the indicator improves, there is an improvement in the realization of the right. If there are two states, X and Y, and if R_i is the indicator of the ith right, then if the value of R_i in X is higher than in Y, X has a better realization of the right.I have put it in this way to underline the need for formulating an indicator for every right, to assess its extent of realization. Furthermore, since a right has a number of dimensions, composed of many different elements, the exercise of building an indicator is the first step of a consensual process of its realization. It is consensual because there is no mechanical way of combining the values of the different elements, which affect different people differently and which may be combined into a single measure through a consensus among the right holders, about the weights to be attached to the different elements of the right.

There is a growing literature on constructing indicators of rights. For us, there are three characteristics that such indicators must accommodate. First, it should be possible to unequivocally identify an improvement in these rights. If it is represented as a 'scalar' quantity,[5] then an increase in its value would mean an increase in the level of realization of the rights. If it is a 'vector',[6] then additional constraints may have to be applied, to identify its increase. Secondly, these indicators must accommodate five basic characteristics of human rights, both as goals and as a process of realizing the goals, as has been recognized in the human rights literature. I have described them as 'ENPAT' in reference to the principles of *E*quity, *N*on-discrimination, *P*articipation, *A*ccountability and *T*ransparency. Each of these characteristics may require formulating sub-indicators, again through a process of consensus and public discussions. But such an exercise is essential for identifying the rights which have to be fulfilled in a 'rights-based-manner'; this essentially means, following the principles of ENPAT. Thirdly, the rights have to be so defined as to make them enjoyable individually. They may be provided collectively or through an exercise that addresses the needs of groups, but they have to be enjoyed individually. I have elaborated this point in my reports, as UN

---

4 The preamble of the declaration defines development along the same line, 'recognizing that development is a comprehensive economic, social, cultural and political process, which aims at the constant improvement of the well-being of the entire population and of all individuals on the basis of their active, free and meaningful participation in development and in the fair distribution of benefits resulting therefrom'.

5 A quantity that has magnitude but no direction.

6 A quantity that has both direction and magnitude.

Independent Expert on the Right to Development,[7] reflecting on the debate about individual rights, collective rights and group rights, and I think that all the apparent conflicts between them can be reconciled provided the enjoyment of the rights is clearly identifiable at the level of an individual. In other words, a right cannot be recognized as a right unless it can be shown that an individual who is entitled to it and in a position to exercise it will be able to enjoy the right. In formulating an indicator of the right to development, the elements should be so defined that although the right is provided collectively, it would be enjoyable by all the individuals forming the collective.

It is possible to accommodate the principles of 'indivisibility' and 'universality' of the rights by stipulating other conditions. A right is indivisible, if an element of the right (which is included in the indicator) cannot have an increase in its value (which means improved realization) if another element of the right deteriorates (i.e. takes on a negative value). The rights are universal in the sense that if any individual can exercise and enjoy that right, then all other individuals in a similar position can also, if they so wish, exercise and enjoy that right.

Once such an indicator of the level of realization, such as R_i for the *i*th right can be identified, the value of an improvement of that level, ΔR_i, can also be identified. We should also be able to identify the value that is realized by each individual, ΔR_{ij} (where *i* refers to a specific right and *j* refers to a specific individual). Similarly, we can also estimate the level of that right at a particular time, $t(\Delta R_{it})$. If ΔR_{it} is greater than 0, the level of R_i is improving overtime. If ΔR_{it} is less than 0, the right is regressing or is being violated. Otherwise, when ΔR_{it} is equal to 0, then there is no change in the level of realization of that right over time.

With this simple definitional clarification, it is possible to give a precise formulation of the right to development in the light of Article 1 and the preface of the DRD as follows.

Development is a process of 'constant improvement of the well-being' of all individuals, and when such well-being is identified with enjoyment of 'all human rights and fundamental freedom', we shall have a process of right-based-development (because all those human rights and fundamental freedom conform to the principles of ENPAT). When such a rights-based process of development is recognized as a right in international human rights law, we have the right to development. Such a right may have to be delivered collectively, for a group or a country. But each individual belonging to the group or the country should be able to exercise and enjoy that right. The recognition of that right in international human rights law would mean that the international community of states accepts the obligations of delivering that right.

---

7 Reports of the Independent Expert (1999–2004): First Report: E/CN.4/1999/WG.18/2, 27 July 1999; Second Report: A/55/306, 17 August 2000; Third Report: E/CN.4/2001/WG.18/2, 2 January 2001; Fourth Report: E/CN.4/2002/WG.18/2, 20 December 2001; Fourth Report of the Independent Expert on the Right to Development – Mission, E/CN.4/2002/WG.18/2/Add.1, 5 March 2002; Fifth Report: E/CN.4/2002/WG.18/6, 16 September 2002 and E/CN.4/2002/WG.18/6/Add.1, 30 December 2002; Preliminary study of the Independent Expert on the right to development on the impact of international economic and financial issues on the enjoyment of human rights, E/CN.4/2003/WG.18/2, 27 January 2003; Review of progress and obstacles in the promotion, implementation, operationalization, and enjoyment of the right to development, E/CN.4/2004/WG.18/2, 17 February 2004 [online]. Available from: http://www.unhchr.ch/html/menu2/7/b/mdev.htm. Reports of the Working Group (1993–1998): Report on its 1st session, UN Doc. E/CN.4/1994/21; Report on its 2nd session, UN Doc. E/CN.4/1995/11; Report on its 3rd session, UN Doc. E/CN.4/1995/27; Report on its 4th session, UN Doc. E/CN.4/1996/10; Report on its 5th session, UN Doc. E/CN.4/1996/24. The first four of these reports, together with some critical and explanatory comments, were reproduced in *The Right to Development: Reflections on the First Four Reports of the Independent Expert on the Right to Development* (Geneva: Franciscans International, 23 January 2003).

It is now possible to go over, quickly, the formalization of this right as I spelt out in my Expert reports.[8] I found it simpler to keep to those rights that have already been recognized in international human rights law such as the civil and political rights and the economic, social and cultural rights as constituent elements of the right to development. If ΔR_{it} denotes an improved realization of *i*th right at a time *t*, the right to development can be described as a 'vector' composed of the simultaneous realization of all the rights, civil, political, economic, social and cultural, that the international community has already recognized. In other words, an improvement in the right to development can be described as:

(1) $\Delta R_{dt} = (\Delta R_{1t,}\ \Delta R_{2t,}\ (\Delta R_{3t}\ \ldots\ \Delta R_{nt})$ when there are '*n*' such rights (All ΔR_{It}s are non-negative).

If we stick to such an indicator as a 'vector', its improvement can be clearly identified as a situation when at least one of these rights improves, but no other right deteriorates. This Paretian approach does not require the comparison between the relative increases of the different rights, so that we do not have to say that, for example, the right to food is more important than the right to free speech. We only have to assert that the right to food has improved without regressing the right to free speech.

But if we consider such a constraint to be too restrictive, we may try to convert this 'vector' to a 'scalar' quantity by attaching weights to the different rights and getting a weighted sum of them. The weighting process, of course, will have to be based on a consensual, 'rights-based process' of public discussions. But once that is done, we can get an unequivocal estimate of an improvement of the right to development such as:

(2) $\Delta R_{dt} = \Sigma W_i \Delta R_{it}\ (i = 1 - n)$ where W_i is the weight attached the *i*th right.

It should be obvious that in these formulations we take account of all rights, civil, political, economic, social and cultural, together with the stipulation that no right can be violated if a right has to be improved, following the principle of indivisibility that we have spelt out above. But it would allow us to attach different weights to different rights, according to a public consensus arrived at in different countries. There is no reason to suggest that W_is of one country should be the same as the W_is of another country, except that every right should have a weight attached through a 'rights-based process' in every country. Some countries may attach much more weight to the right to food and other economic rights than the weight attached to right to freedom of expression or other civil rights. In this way we can avoid all the debates about civil and political rights as real rights and economic, social and cultural rights as aspirational and therefore non-legal rights. All we need is to be able to identify the characteristics of the different rights and construct indicators for them whose values indicate the level of realization of those rights. We shall, of course, have to identify the obligations related to those rights and the methods of their implementation. But that is a common exercise, applicable to all rights: civil and political rights or economic, social and cultural rights, and has to be settled through a consensual process.

When I put the definition in this way, the right to development does appear as utopian, as a process of realization of all human rights and fundamental freedoms. But our definition also is amenable to adjustment, again through a process of consensus. For example, a society may choose to deal with a few rights, say, right to food, right to education, right to health, right to freedom of speech and

8 *Ibid.*

association, and right not to be tortured. It would require that the values of all other rights individually cannot be negative and can remain equal to or greater than 0 (i.e. non negative). This would subject the community of stakeholders to the constraint that no right is regressed or violated.

In this form, we can easily accommodate Henry Shue's 'basic rights' theory. If a society considers that those basic rights should be realized in the form of the right to development, we can substitute these basic rights in our equation 2 above with the stipulation that no other right will be regressed or violated. A better alternative might be to think of a few foundational rights such as rights to life, liberty and livelihood, which are not only desirable in themselves but are also necessary for the fulfilment of all other rights, and can be shown to span or generate all other rights. The basic rights of Henry Shue are described as highly important human rights which, in some cases, have to be fulfilled prior to the exercise of any other right. But the foundational rights that I am talking about go beyond that and can be shown as a vector of rights that generate other important rights.

It is possible to speak about three fundamental rights to life, liberty, and livelihood, which are themselves composites of other rights and through permutation and combination among themselves can generate most other rights. This exercise of permutation and combination can be conducted through a process of consultation and public scrutiny in any society. If these are then recognized through a norm-creating process in the society, such as a declaration or framework legislation, fulfilment of these rights may then be regarded as the fulfilment of right to development.

In other words, our definition would allow any set of rights as the components of the right to development provided they are realized as a vector or a composite right, where all the elements are simultaneously realized without violating any particular right. This follows directly from the definition that development is a process of realization of all fundamental rights and freedoms, and not just of a single or a few isolated rights. The only requirement for accepting such a definition is that the composite or a vector of right, and not just one or two rights, or a simple aggregate of a number of rights, will demonstrate a distinct value. In my Expert reports on the right to development, I have tried to demonstrate this value addition, which not only enhances the levels of the realization of the different rights but also improves the possibility of realizing each of the rights when attempts are made to implement them together.

In line with the above arguments, trying to define the right to development in a manner that can be realistically pursued for fulfilment, I introduced an additional element as a component of a vector of right to development, which can stand as a proxy for the realization of all the rights that are not explicitly included in the definition. I described that variable as *g**, which is a rights-based process of economic growth, conforming to the principles of ENPAT. This *g** not only increases the availability of the resources needed to realize all those rights but also creates an environment where such rights are realized. In that case, if we concentrate, say, on three rights, and *g** as the proxy for improved fulfilment of other rights, our equation can be rewritten as:

$$\Delta R_{dt} = (\Delta R_{1t,} \Delta R_{2t,} \Delta R_{3t,} g^*)$$

To avoid any misunderstanding, I must say that this does not detract in any way from the role of the instrumentality of economic growth. It is now generally agreed that economic growth for increase in income is not a goal in itself; it is nothing more than an instrument for increasing the welfare of the people and cannot be treated as an objective until we spell out how such an instrument can generate increase in welfare. In our discussions, we have treated income growth as having just this instrumental value. The only difference we have introduced is that a rights-based equitable and participatory process of income growth has a direct correspondence with the increasing value of component rights, and this would allow us to use it as a proxy for all other rights. Such a g^* will, of course, have to be separately estimated, after operationalizing the elements of ENPAT. One such example could be $g^* = g\,(1 - \text{gini})$, where 'gini' stands for index of inequality. It should not be difficult for us to find alternative ways of estimating g^* to be exercised as a human right. But if we do and we are able to establish the policy to expand the g^*, our exercise would be comparable with a manageable estimation of the different rights.

3. Obligations Corresponding to Right to Development

All human rights entail corresponding obligations on the authorities to whom the human rights are addressed. If the right to development is to be recognized as a human right, we should be able to identify these obligations, fulfilment of which fulfils the right to development.

One advantage of defining the right to development in terms of the realization of all or some of the rights that have already been recognized by different covenants and instruments is that the obligations for realizing the right to development are based on the obligations of realizing all those recognized rights. There are treaty bodies which are supposed to monitor those rights and there are general comments which have spelt out the nature of the obligations corresponding to those rights and the methods of their implementation.

From this perspective, the identification of obligations corresponding to the right to development and the process of their implementation may not require any additional deliberation other than the process of realizing the existing human rights instruments. The justiciability and the feasibility of the right to development would not be different from these characteristics of the recognized rights. All the innovations, international arrangements and optical protocols that have been accommodated in international human rights law would be applicable in equal measure in the implementation of the right to development.

However, one major difference which distinguishes the process of implementation (and therefore the nature of obligations for the right to development) is that this is a composite right where all the rights are supposed to be realized together and simultaneously. The full implications of this distinction have not been always carefully assessed. If they were appropriately analysed, the richness of the right to development as a right would become apparent.

First, it has now been accepted in the human rights discourse that all the rights are to be progressively realized. Asbjorn Eide introduced the concept of obligations to 'protect, promote and fulfil', initially for the right to food.[9] It was later extended to all economic, social and cultural rights on the assumption that these rights have to be 'progressively' realized because of the constraints of the available resources and appropriate institution. But a closer scrutiny of this issue suggests that this process of progressive realization is not the result of the constraints of resources and institutional services but of the nature of human rights themselves. Therefore, it should be applicable also to civil and political rights, the moment it is accepted that the implementation of the rights does not depend only on the state and other authorities being restrained from violating the rights but also includes the obligation of ensuring that they are not violated by any other agent in the society. Then the distinction between the negative and the positive rights gets diluted. The obligations

---

9 For all these, see A. Sengupta, A. Eide, S. Marks and B.A. Andreassen: 'The Right to Development and Human Rights in Development', presented in the Nobel Symposium, Oslo, October 2003. Reprinted in the Oslo University Website [online]. Available from: http://www.humanrights.uio.no/forskning/publikasjoner/arkiv/rn/2004/0704.pdf (accessed 31 December 2009).

would expand beyond protection, to promotion and fulfilment, necessarily over a period of time. So the notion of progressive realization applies to all rights, whether they are civiland political or economic, social and cultural rights.

Secondly, progressive realization would also involve two major policy considerations, one related to coordination of the policies between different periods and the other related to relaxing the resource constraint over time. Both of these considerations are especially relevant to the right to development. It will be necessary to coordinate the policies at the realization over different periods through an appropriate sequence of policies – the policies of time t would depend upon on policies adopted in time $(t - 1)$ and evolve into policies at time $(t + 1)$. But in addition to this, for the right to development, it will be necessary to coordinate the policies to realize the different rights, taking fully into account the interdependence between the rights and externalities that result from simultaneous application of the different policies. In other words, the policies for realizing the right to development would require the adoption of a programme of policies described in summary as 'development policy'.

Thirdly, such a 'development policy' will have to be built on a policy for promoting economic growth that would not only increase the incomes of the country relating to the constraint of resources but also bring about far-reaching changes in the institutions. If we were concerned only about realizing one single right or only a few important rights, they could probably be fulfilled by reallocating and redistributing the existing resources and institutional services. But when all the rights are expected to be realized together, they are bound to hit the resource constraint that cannot be overcome without sustainable economic growth. This point is important to note because the implementation of any right would involve the use of an investment of resource, either for protecting or for promotion and fulfilling those rights. For example, even a straightforward right like the right not to be tortured would have substantial cost of resources. It would require not only that the state authorities not torture or allow any one else to indulge in torturing. But if the authorities indulge in it as an instrument of policy to acquire information or to prevent some unacceptable development, giving up that policy of torture would also require that the state should adopt alternative policies to secure those objectives, and this would definitely require substantial investment of resources.

It should be clear from this discussion that all rights which are progressively realized call for relaxation of the resource constraint, and when attempts are made to realize several rights together, the removal of resource constraint or a policy of economic growth would be an integral part of a development policy. In other words, the crucial obligation to fulfil the right to development in any country would require the adoption of a coordinated and well-designed development policy including growth.

The primary responsibility for adopting such a development policy, properly designed and coordinated, will, of course, lie with the state authorities. But in the modern, globalized world, no state authority now has the necessary manoeuvrability and sovereignty and over all its policies without international cooperation. On fiscal, monetary, trade and debt, and technology policies, the state today has to depend on the policies of other states and on international cooperation. This would be the case for any country, even when it does not need foreign aid or financial assistance. But many developing countries with a substantial resource constraint of their under-developed economies would require transfer of resources, either as capital flows or foreign aid. That would very much depend on coordinated development cooperation.

Therefore, one of the principal obligations associated with the right to development and carrying out an appropriate development policy would be the obligation of international cooperation. While for other rights, even for important economic, social and cultural rights, development cooperation in the fields of trade technology and finance and transfer of resources may be helpful and sometimes necessary, in the case of the right to development, which involves carrying out a development policy with the objective of achieving a higher rate of economic growth, international cooperation is an integral part of international obligations.

4. Development Policy as a Meta-Right

This brings us to the latest innovation in the literature on the right to development, which invokes the concept of meta-right, which was first formulated by Amartya Sen as follows: 'A meta right to something can be defined as the right to have P(x) that genuinely pursues the objective of making the right to x realizable.'[10] I have applied this to the right to development, which is a right to all rights and which may not be realized within a short span of time, and no agent could be held responsible for that. The right then remains unfulfilled as a background 'moral right' influencing the behaviour of the agent without becoming a justiciable and enforceable legal right. But 'even if the right to x (e.g. right to development) remains unfulfilled or immediately unrealizable, the meta right to x, P(x) can be a fully valid realizable right, if all the obligations associated with this P(x) can be clearly specified with the identification of the agents to carry out those obligations and held accountable for non-compliance. The right to x (i.e. a right to development) in this case may remain a moral right or an abstract background right of general political aim providing justification for political decision, but a right to P(x) can be a real legal right to make x achievable in the future.'[11] An appropriately designed development policy can be regarded as P(x) for realizing the right to development and can be accepted as a meta-right in the full sense of the term.

By one stroke, this concept changes the whole nature of discourse on the right to development. The obligations of the international community and of the different state authorities then revolve around the formulation, adoption and implementation of an appropriate development policy which is grounded in development cooperation as an international obligation. If such a development policy gets implemented, even step by step over time, the international community will move steadily towards the implementation of the right to development.

5. Conclusion

Even though it was not specifically addressed in the UDHR, the right to development need no longer remain utopian. We have by now understood the intricacies of the policies that are involved as obligations to realize that right. If there is sufficient will for international cooperation in today's world of substantial expansion of global resources, the right to development has genuinely become a realized human right, even within the context of the UDHR.

10 A. Sen, 'The Right Not to Be Hungry', in P. Alston and K. Tomaševski (eds), *The Right to Food* (Boston: M. Nijhoff and Utrecht: SIM Netherlands Institute of Human Rights, 1984), pp. 69–81.

11 A. Sengupta, 'The Human Right to Development', note 3 above, pp. 9–36.

Chapter 6
Right to a Healthy Environment in Human Rights Law

Jona Razzaque

1. Introduction

The human right to a healthy environment is indispensable for leading a life with human dignity. It is a prerequisite for the realization of other human rights. The fact that the environment and human rights are intrinsically linked, and that environmental degradation leads to poverty and human indignity, is not a contested issue. Since 1994, after the Ksentini report on 'human rights and the environment',[1] there has been an expectation in both the human-rights and the environmental legal communities that this link would be discussed at policy-making levels. In 2002, experts from around the world were invited to assess the link between human rights and the environment and to clarify the scope of this linkage.[2] It was the first time that the two United Nations (UN) bodies – the then Office of the High Commissioner for Human Rights (OHCHR) and the UN Environment Programme (UNEP) – decided to combine their efforts to explore the link between human rights and the environment. However, the meeting ended with the issuing of a very loosely worded statement.[3] Similarly, only one sentence in the Johannesburg Declaration, adopted after the 2002 World Summit on Sustainable Development (WSSD), took account of the link between the environment and human rights.[4] Before 2002, this link had been addressed in academic writings[5]

1 Final report on the Human Rights and the Environment for the Sub-Commission on Prevention of Discrimination and Protection of Minorities. E/CN.4/Sub.2/1994/9, 6 July 1994. The noted that environmental damage has direct effects on the enjoyment of a series of human rights, and human rights violations, in turn, may damage the environment; and the Rapporteur recommended that the human rights component of environmental rights immediately be incorporated into the work of various human rights bodies.

2 United Nations Environment Programme/Office of the High Commissioner for Human Rights, Meeting of Experts on Human Rights and Environment (2002), Background papers [online]. Available from: http://www.unhchr.ch/environment/index.html [accessed 20 June 2009].

3 The Conclusions of the 2002 Meeting of Experts on Human Rights and the Environment, 16 January 2002 [online]. Available from: http://www.unhchr.ch/environment/conclusions.html [accessed 10 December 2008].

4 Paragraph 152: 'Acknowledge the consideration being given to the *possible relationship* between environment and human rights …'. [emphasis added], World Summit on Sustainable Development (WSSD), Johannesburg Plan of Implementation (2002) [online]. Available from: http://www.un.org/jsummit/html/documents/summit_docs/2309_planfinal.htm [accessed 20 June 2009].

5 D. Shelton, 'Human Rights, Environmental Rights and the Right to Environment', *Stanford Journal of International Law*, 103 (1991), p. 104; A. Kiss, 'Concept and Possible Implications of the Right to Environment', in K. Mahoney and P. Mahoney (eds), *Human Rights in the Twenty-First Century: A Global Challenge* (Dordrecht: Martinus Nijhoff, 1993), pp. 551, 553; A. Boyle and M. Anderson (eds), *Human Rights Approaches to Environmental Protection* (Oxford: Clarendon Press, 1996); D. Shelton, 'Environmental Rights', in P. Alston, *People's Rights* (Oxford: Oxford University Press, 2001), p. 185.

and in treaties such as the UN Convention on the Rights of the Child,[6] the International Labour Organization (ILO) Convention 169 concerning Indigenous and Tribal Peoples in Independent Countries,[7] and the Aarhus Convention.[8] At the regional level, the African Charter on Human and Peoples' Rights (ACHPR)[9] and the Protocol of San Salvador to the American Convention on Human Rights (ACHR)[10] expressly recognize the right to a healthy environment. Recently, a Resolution of the UN Human Rights Council (UNHRC) also asserted that 'a democratic and equitable international order requires' the realization of the 'right of every person and all peoples to a healthy environment…'.[11]

While the three core human rights instruments – the UDHR,[12] the International Convention on Civil and Political Rights (ICCPR),[13] and the International Convention on Economic, Social and Cultural Rights (ICESCR)[14] – unequivocally guarantee the right to life and a right to health, there is no specific mention of a right to a healthy environment.[15] Article 3 of the UDHR states that 'Everyone has the right to life, liberty and security of person', and Article 25 adds, 'Everyone has the right to a standard of living adequate for the health and well-being of himself and of his family,

6 Convention on the Rights of the Child, adopted 20 November 1989, 1577 UNTS 3 (1989) 28 ILM 1448 (entered into force 2 September 1990). Article 24(2)(c) states: 'States Parties shall pursue full implementation of this right and, in particular, shall take appropriate measures … To combat disease and malnutrition, including within the framework of primary health care, through, *inter alia*, the application of readily available technology and through the provision of adequate nutritious foods and clean drinking-water, taking into consideration the dangers and risks of environmental pollution'.

7 Convention (No. 169) concerning Indigenous and Tribal Peoples in Independent Countries, adopted 27 June 1989, 328 UNTS 247 (entered into force 5 September 1991). Article 4(1): 'Special measures shall be adopted as appropriate for safeguarding the persons, institutions, property, labour, cultures and environment of the peoples concerned'. Article 7(4) adds that: 'Governments shall take measures, in co-operation with the peoples concerned, to protect and preserve the environment of the territories they inhabit'.

8 Convention on Access to Information, Public Participation in Decision Making and Access to Justice in Environmental Matters, adopted 25 June 1998, 2161 UNTS 447 (entered into force 30 October 2001). Article 1: 'In order to contribute to the protection of the right of every person of present and future generations to live in an environment adequate to his or her health and well-being, each Party shall guarantee the rights of access to information, public participation in decision-making, and access to justice in environmental matters in accordance with the provisions of this Convention'.

9 African Charter on Human and Peoples' Rights, adopted 27 June 1981, 1520 UNTS 217 (1981) 21 I.L.M 59 (entered into force 21 October 1986). Article 24: 'All peoples shall have the right to a generally satisfactory environment favourable to their development'.

10 Additional Protocol to the American Convention on Human Rights in the Area of Economic, Social and Cultural Rights, 'Protocol of San Salvador', adopted 17 November 1988, OAS Treaty Series No. 69; (1989) 28 ILM 156 (entered into force 16 November 1999. Article 11(1): 'Everyone shall have the right to live in a healthy environment and to have access to basic public services'.

11 Paragraph 3 (m), Human Rights Council Resolution 8/5: Promotion of a democratic and equitable international order (18 June 2008). A similar rights-based approach was adopted in resolutions 2002/72 (25 April 2002), 2004/64 (21 April 2004), and 2008/9 (18 June 2008), and also in UN GA Resolution 60/163 (16 December 2005).

12 Universal Declaration of Human Rights, adopted 10 December 1948, UNGA Res. 217 (AIII), UN GAOR, Third Session, pt 1, at 71, UN Doc A/ 810 (1948).

13 Adopted 16 December 1966, entered into force 23 March 1976; 999 UNTS 171.

14 Adopted 16 December 1966, entered into force 3 January 1976; 993 UNTS 3.

15 However, Article 6 of the ICCPR provides that 'Every human being has the inherent right to life', and Article 12 of the ICESCR provides for the 'right of everyone to the enjoyment of the highest attainable standard of physical and mental health'.

including food, clothing, housing and medical care and necessary social services', but does not include any specific reference to a right to a healthy environment nor does it link the human right to life or health and well-being to the right to a healthy environment. Nevertheless, it can be argued that the spirit of the UDHR includes the right to a healthy environment. For example, the preamble of the UDHR recognizes 'the inherent dignity and inalienable rights of all members of the human family', and, according to Kiss, the inherent dignity of human beings is closely related to a right to a healthy environment.[16] In the absence of any explicit mention of such a right in the global human rights treaties, environmental protection largely depends on an expansive interpretation of the substantive rights to life, health, property and privacy. At the national level, for example, the content of right to life has been interpreted in some states to include the right to live in a balanced and healthy environment, the right to be free from pollution, and the right to have clean, unpolluted water and air.[17]

The anthropocentric and individual nature of human rights is argued to be unsuitable to protect the environment (discussed in Section 2 below). The argument is that a human-rights approach does not take into account the intrinsic value of nature – it only protects human well-being and prioritizes human needs where human beings are the victims and right holders.[18] This anthropocentric bias can be seen in the title of the 1972 UN Conference on the Human Environment (Stockholm Declaration),[19] the 1992 UN Conference on Environment and Development (Rio Declaration),[20] and the 2002 WSSD (Johannesburg) Declaration.[21] However, human beings are an integral part of the environment, some human activities are treated as a part of the ecosystem (e.g. Millennium Ecosystem Assessment),[22] and substantive human rights (e.g. right to life, right to health) are linked to environmental protection. For example, in General Comment 14, the UN Committee on Economic, Social and Cultural Rights (CESCR) interpreted the right to 'the highest attainable standard of physical and mental health' in Article 12(1) of the ICESCR as 'not confined to the right to health care' but as also embracing a wide range of socio-economic factors that promote conditions in which people can lead a healthy life, and extending to the underlying determinants of health, such as potable water and adequate sanitation, safe and healthy working conditions, and a healthy environment.[23]

A number of non-binding instruments, while interpreting human rights treaties, and UN agencies in their policy documents, make explicit reference to the right to a healthy environment (discussed in Section 3 below). There are ample cases in which the regional and national courts have interpreted the right to life liberally to accommodate the right to a healthy environment (discussed

---

16 Kiss, note 5 above, pp. 552–3.

17 Rosaleen O'Gara *et al.*, *Human Rights and the Environment* (Geneva: Earthjustice, 2007).

18 P. Birnie, A. Boyle and C. Redgwell, *International Law and the Environment* (Oxford: Oxford University Press, 2009), p. 280.

19 Principle 1, Stockholm Declaration on the Human Environment, Principle 1, UN Doc. A/CONF.48/14/Rev.1 (16 June 1972).

20 Principle 3, Rio Declaration on Environment and Development, UN Doc. A/CONF.151/26/Rev.1 (14 June 1992).

21 Johannesburg Declaration of Sustainable Development and Plan of Implementation (2002).

22 E. Blanco and J. Razzaque, 'Ecosystem Services and Human Well-Being in a Globalized World: Assessing the Role of Law', *Human Rights Quarterly,* 31 (2009), pp. 692–720. See http://www.millenniumassessment.org/en/index.aspx.

23 S. Kravchenko and J.E. Bonine, *Human Rights and the Environment: Cases. Law and Policy* (Durham, NC: Carolina Academic Press, 2008), pp. 23–66. See e.g. CESCR, General Comment 14, note 57 below, para. 4.

in Sections 4 and 5 below). In addition, the procedural rights (e.g. information, participation and justice) strengthen the substantive right to a healthy environment (discussed in Section 6 below). Noting these developments in international, regional and national law, this chapter concludes that there are some acknowledgements of the existence of a right to a healthy environment in human rights law.

2. Existing Debates and the Question of Existence

While the normative development is slow at the international level, the link between human rights and the environment is elaborately debated by scholars and explored in national application. Scholars have highlighted that there is a common philosophical and political ground between human rights and environmental discourses as well as some important distinctions and areas of apparent dissonance.[24] On the one hand, it would be artificial to conceptualize human and environmental rights as identical, since not all violations of human rights have a direct link to an environmental context, and vice versa. Moreover, there are cases in which environmental rights and rights of particular individuals or groups may come into conflict. On the other hand, failure to protect the environment may interfere with individual rights, and, in some cases, the right of the future generations.[25] Clearly, environmental degradation presently has a direct impact on the rights of vulnerable human beings and communities, such as indigenous populations.[26] There are also arguments in favour of a self-standing 'right to environment' that is not part of the human rights regime.[27] This chapter, however, explores the development of a 'right to a healthy environment' within human rights law.

The first issue is whether there is a need to have a rights-based approach to protect the environment – be it within the human rights framework or as a self-standing right. On the one hand, it has been argued that if human beings are an inseparable part of the environment, a rights-based approach would provide better compliance, monitoring and dispute-settlement mechanisms and ensure priority over non-rights-based objectives.[28] However, a distinct right to a healthy environment may not be acceptable globally, as it creates a corresponding duty for governments, the private sector and even individuals.[29] Further, there are certain challenges linked to a strictly rights-based approach to environmental protection. For example, many states may not implement treaty-based rights in their domestic legal framework; policies and practices at the domestic level

24 P. Taylor, 'Ecological Integrity and Human Rights', in L. Westra, K. Bosselmann and R. Westra (eds), *Reconciling Human Existence with Ecological Integrity: Science, Ethics, Economics and Law* (London: Earthscan, 2008), p. 89.

25 L. Collins, 'Environmental Rights for the Future? Intergenerational Equity in the EU', *Review of European Community and International Environmental Law*, 16(3) (2007), pp. 321–31.

26 See, generally, L. Westra, *Environmental Justice and the Rights of Indigenous Peoples: International and Domestic Legal Perspectives* (London: Earthscan, 2008).

27 L. Collins, 'Are We There Yet? – The Right to Environment in International and European Law', *McGill International Journal on Sustainable Development Law*, 3 (2007), p. 119. The author discusses the status of self-standing environmental right.

28 D. Shelton, 'Human Rights and the Environment: Problems and Possibilities', *Environmental Policy and Law*, 38(1–2) (2008), p. 41.

29 For example, the 1998 Aarhus Convention (discussed below) demonstrates a right/duty-based approach.

may vary; and developing countries may not have efficient and cost-effective monitoring systems.[30] In addition, the international human rights response mechanisms may be inadequate to minimize environmental degradation, and may, to some extent, be undermined by the political agendas of the UN member states (e.g. 2002 Johannesburg Declaration). This is complicated by the fact that there is not yet an independent international court to assist in enforcing human rights internationally.

The second issue relates to the need to have a right to a healthy environment. It is true that a conservative interpretation of the right to a healthy environment will not be able to deal with the issues of biological diversity and protection of non-human species, harm caused to future generations by environmental degradation, and the trans-boundary impact of environmental degradation (e.g. climate change, deforestation, trans-boundary watercourses pollution). Is it possible to have a right to a healthy environment that includes biodiversity protection?[31] Redgwell argues that a rights-based approach may not be ideal to protect the intrinsic value of the ecosystems if non-human value is not integrated into the interpretation and exercise of human rights.[32] To her, the issue is not so much about recognition of a human right to a 'clean, healthy or decent environment' that includes non-human rights; it is more about 'reconciling a diverse environmental and human rights agenda'.[33] This reconciliation is now reflected in several resolutions of the UN Human Rights Council.[34]

Along with the advantages of using a human rights approach to protect the environment, Shelton adds that a rights-based approach may provide an 'elevated environmental protection in the process of balancing it against economic consideration and property rights' and an 'enhanced recognition of the affirmative duties implicit in civil and political rights'.[35] A rights-based approach to a healthy environment indicates that environmental protection is a precondition to the enjoyment of certain human rights (e.g. right to life, health, private life, and home and cultural rights).[36] Moreover, the existing regional, human rights courts provide some remedies when there is no local remedy or weak international compliance mechanisms to protect the environment.[37] Additionally, the human rights regime can benefit from the development in international environmental law. For example, the definition of information in the 1998 Aarhus Convention can be used to interpret the human right to information.[38]

---

30 Shelton, note 28 above, p. 42.

31 J.J. Bruckerhoff, 'Giving Nature Constitutional Protection: A Less Anthropocentric Interpretation of Environmental Rights', *Texas Law Review*, 86 (2008), p. 615. Bruckerhoff argues that it is possible to integrate 'biodiversity considerations into human rights jurisprudence' by linking the concept of environmental rights to a broader definition of environmental health.

32 C. Redgwell, 'Life, Universe and Everything: A Critique of Anthropocentric Rights', in Boyle and Anderson (eds), note 5 above, pp. 71–88.

33 *Ibid*., p. 87.

34 E.g. Human Rights Council Resolution 7/22, Human Rights and Access to Safe Drinking Water and Sanitation (adopted 28 March 2008); Resolution 7/23, Human Rights and Climate Change (adopted 28 March 2008), Resolution 9/1, Mandate of the Special Rapporteur on the Adverse Effects of the Movement and Dumping of Toxic and Dangerous Products and Wastes on the Enjoyment of Human Rights (2008).

35 Shelton, 'Environmental Rights', note 5 above, p. 191.

36 D. Shelton, 'Human Rights and the Environment: Problems and Possibilities', *Environmental Policy and Law*, 38(1) (2008), pp. 41–9, 42.

37 H.M. Osofsky, 'Learning from Environmental Justice: A New Model for International Environmental Rights', *Stanford Environmental Law Journal*, 24(1) (2005), pp. 71–150, at pp. 107–18.

38 Article 2(3) of the 1998 Aarhus Convention (note 8 above) provides that:

> 'Environmental information' means any information in written, visual, aural, electronic or any other material form on:

There is a perception that the strong individualism in human rights discourse is a barrier to the collective action necessary to protect the environment from human activities that degrade its quality – but is this entirely fair? Engaging with this view, Holder and Lee note that '[p]utting in place substantive rights to environmental quality involves difficult questions of prioritisation between different environmental goods, and between environmental protection and other private goods'.[39] If the right to a healthy environment is considered as a collective right, the identity of the right holders remains crucial; for example, do they have to fulfil certain criteria of eligibility, or who has the right to speak on behalf of the group?[40] This raises the issue of whether the unborn (i.e. the future generations) can be possible holders of such a right and, in that case, who would be competent to assert that right on their behalf?[41] One criticism of the collective right approach (also known as 'third-generation' right or solidarity right) is that such rights 'are so vast that they encompass anything and anybody'[42] and can be 'nationalist'.[43] Boyle adds that the collective right approach devalues 'the concept of human rights' and diverts 'attention from the need to implement the civil, political, economic and social rights fully'.[44] However, the concept of collective rights is recognized in several treaties, such as the ICCPR (Articles 27 and 47), the ICESCR (Article 25), the ILO Convention 169 concerning 'Indigenous and Tribal Peoples in Independent Countries' (Article 4), the ACHPR (Article 24), and the 1998 Aarhus Convention (Article 1). In a recent resolution of the UN Human Rights Council, the right to a healthy environment is recognized as an individual as well as a collective right.[45]

Others believe that the right to environment with different qualifications (e.g. safe, healthy, clean, and satisfactory) would be difficult to conceptualize as an inalienable right,[46] or fit into a

---

(a) The state of elements of the environment, such as air and atmosphere, water, soil, land, landscape and natural sites, biological diversity and its components, including genetically modified organisms, and the interaction among these elements;
(b) Factors, such as substances, energy, noise and radiation, and activities or measures, including administrative measures, environmental agreements, policies, legislation, plans and programmes, affecting or likely to affect the elements of the environment within the scope of subparagraph (a) above, and cost-benefit and other economic analyses and assumptions used in environmental decision-making;
(c) The state of human health and safety, conditions of human life, cultural sites and built structures, inasmuch as they are or may be affected by the state of the elements of the environment or, through these elements, by the factors, activities or measures referred to in subparagraph (b) above.

39 J. Holder and M. Lee, *Environmental Protection, Law and Policy: Text and Materials* (Cambridge: Cambridge University Press, 2007), pp. 99–100.

40 J.G. Merrills, 'Environmental Rights', in D. Bodansky *et al.* (eds), *The Oxford Handbook of International Environmental Law* (Oxford: Oxford University Press, 2007), p. 670.

41 *Ibid.*, p. 670.

42 Fitzmaurice highlights the following collective human rights that can be linked to environmental protection: right to development, right to peace, and right to co-ownership of the common heritage of mankind. M. Fitzmaurice, *International Protection of the Environment.* Recueil des cours, vol. 293, 2001 (The Hague: Martinus Nijhoff, 2002), p. 170.

43 P. Alston, 'A Third Generation of Solidarity Right: Progressive Development or Obfuscation of International Human Rights Law', *Netherlands International Law Review*, 29 (1982), p. 307.

44 A. Boyle, 'Human Rights or Environmental Rights – A Reassessment', *Fordham Environmental Law Review*, 18 (2007), p. 472.

45 Paragraph 3 (m). UN Human Rights Council Resolution 8/5, Promotion of a Democratic and Equitable International Order (adopted 18 June 2008).

46 Fitzmaurice, note 42 above, pp. 169–71.

single category of human right. According to Boyle, first, the right to a healthy environment, as part of civil and political rights, can be used to give individuals, groups and non-governmental organizations (NGOs) access to environmental information, judicial remedies and political processes.[47] Second, the right to a healthy environment as part of a social or economic right 'would privilege environmental quality as a value, comparable to those whose progressive attainment is promoted by the 1966 United Nations (UN) Covenant on Economic, Social and Cultural Rights'.[48] Third, the right to a healthy environment as part of a collective or solidarity right would give 'communities ("peoples") rather than individuals a right to determine how their environment or natural resources should be protected and managed'.[49] Boyle opines that the first approach is clearly anthropocentric, and the second approach makes the right 'vulnerable to tradeoffs against other similarly privileged but competing objectives'.[50] Boyle favours the economic and social rights approach that will require the national governments to adopt policies to enable individuals to develop their full potential and to ensure progressive realization.[51] Both the ICESCR and the ICCPR, however, use qualified language allowing states parties either a margin of discretion in implementing these rights[52] or to derogate from some rights in times of public emergency.[53]

Anderson and Boyle list a number of existing rights that play an important role in environmental protection.[54] The realization of certain civil and political rights – such as rights to life, association, expression, property, political participation, personal liberty, equality and legal redress – can make an important contribution to protecting the environment and natural resources. Churchill adds that certain economic, social and cultural rights – such as the right to health – can be linked to decent living or working conditions and may also include the protection of ecosystems.[55] This is clear from the text of Article 12 of the ICESCR. Under Article 12(2)(b), the steps to be taken by the states parties to the ICESCR to achieve the full realization of the right to the highest attainable standard of health include those necessary for the 'improvement of all aspects of environmental and industrial hygiene'.[56] Thus, the improvement of environmental hygiene enhances human health and other human rights such as the rights to water, adequate housing, safe and hygienic working conditions, and adequate food. As explained by the Committee on Economic, Social and Cultural Rights (CESCR):

---

47 Boyle, note 44 above, p. 471.

48 *Ibid.* He notes the main criticisms of this approach as being the relatively weak supervisory mechanisms under the ICESCR. On the positive side, conceptualizing the right to a healthy environment as an economic or social right makes it comparable to other rights recognized in the ICESCR.

49 *Ibid.*, 471–2.

50 *Ibid.*, 472.

51 *Ibid.*, 508–9. Kiss also recognized that a 'clean and safe environment . . . is closely linked to economic and social rights in so far as the environment affects the quality of life and safety of the individual'. Kiss, note 5 above, p. 553.

52 For example, under Article 2 of the ICESCR, each party has the obligation 'to take steps … *to the maximum of its available resources* with a view to achieving progressively the full realization of the rights recognized in the present Covenant'. See Chapter 4 of this book for a discussion.

53 ICCPR, Article 4. Merrills, note 40 above, p. 675. A separate expert panel now monitors the national level compliance, raising the possibility of cautious application of the provisions by member states.

54 M. Anderson, 'Human Rights Approaches to Environmental Protection: An Overview', in Boyle and Anderson (eds), note 5 above, pp. 4–7.

55 R. Churchill, 'Environmental Rights in Existing Human Rights Treaties', in Boyle and Anderson (eds), note 5 above, pp. 89–108.

56 *Ibid.*

> 'The improvement of all aspects of environmental and industrial hygiene' comprises, *inter alia*, preventive measures in respect of occupational accidents and diseases; the requirement to ensure an adequate supply of safe and potable water and basic sanitation; the prevention and reduction of the population's exposure to harmful substances such as radiation and harmful chemicals or other detrimental environmental conditions that directly or indirectly impact upon human health. Furthermore, industrial hygiene refers to the minimization, so far as is reasonably practicable, of the causes of health hazards inherent in the working environment. Article 12.2 (b) also embraces adequate housing and safe and hygienic working conditions, an adequate supply of food and proper nutrition, and discourages the abuse of alcohol, and the use of tobacco, drugs and other harmful substances.[57]

Anderson also considers that the right to self-determination, a collective right, can protect the environment in two ways: providing permanent sovereignty over natural resources and the right of the indigenous community over natural resources.[58] While the state may not always apply the permanent sovereignty in an environmentally friendly manner, the right of the indigenous community has been addressed positively within the UN.[59]

While the status (e.g. as civil and political right or economic, social and cultural right), nature (e.g. moral or legal), and content of the right to a healthy (clean, safe, satisfactory or sustainable) environment are still unclear, that does not make the right itself non-existent. This, however, certainly leads to practical problems in the application of the right to a healthy environment at the national level, as well as 'disagreement as to what it means to have such a right'.[60]

3. Substantive Discussion at the International Institution Level

With the 1994 UN report (Ksentini Report) clearly demonstrating the link between human rights and the environment,[61] many international organizations have also addressed the connection between human rights and the environment in their organizational structures, activities and policies. The UNEP, World Health Organization (WHO) and UN Development Programme (UNDP) all accept the link between human rights and the environment.[62] According to the 'Draft Principles on Human Rights and the Environment' annexed to the Ksentini Report of 1994, 'All persons have the right to a secure, healthy and ecologically sound environment', and 'This right and other human rights, including civil, cultural, economic, political and social rights, are universal, interdependent and indivisible'.[63] But while linkages between the protection of human rights and the protection of the environment are now increasingly recognized, the institutional arrangements and inter-institutional linkages (e.g. between the UNHRC and the UNEP) remain very much under-developed.

57 See CESCR, *General Comment 14: The Right to the Highest Attainable Standard of Health*, UN Doc. E/C.12/2000/4 (11 August 2000), para. 15 (footnotes omitted).

58 Anderson, note 54 above, p. 6.

59 Preamble and Article 29, Declaration on the Rights of Indigenous Peoples (2007), UN Doc A/61/L67.

60 Merrills, note 40 above, p. 675.

61 See note 1 above.

62 O'Gara *et al.*, note 17 above, pp. 25, 27, 35.

63 Draft Principles on Human Rights and the Environment, E/CN.4/Sub.2/1994/9, Annex I (1994), Part I(2).

At the UN level, several non-binding reports outline the serious threat that human rights and the environment face, and confirm the links between human rights and environmental degradation.[64] For example, Resolution 2001/57 highlights the impact of large-scale or major development projects on the human rights of indigenous people and their environment (depletion of resources, destruction and pollution of the traditional environment, etc.).[65] The Special Rapporteur of the report on the right to food links implementation of the right to food with sound environmental policies and notes that problems related to food shortages 'can generate additional pressures upon the environment in ecologically fragile areas'.[66]

In several general comments, the CESCR has confirmed that environmental policies impact on other human rights such as the right to food, health and water. For example, in General Comment 12,[67] the CESCR stated that the right to food is 'inseparable from social justice, requiring the adoption of appropriate economic, environmental and social policies, at both the national and international levels, oriented to the eradication of poverty and the fulfilment of all human rights for all'.[68] Sustainability is one of the key components of the concept of the right to food, as stated in General Comment 12, 'implying food being accessible for both present and future generations'.[69] Similarly, in General Comment 14,[70] the CESCR stated that the 'underlying conditions of health' include 'food and nutrition, housing, access to safe and potable water and adequate sanitation, safe and healthy working conditions, and a healthy environment'.[71] Moreover, General Comment 15[72] on the right to water noted that water is a limited natural resource and 'should be treated as a social and cultural good, and not primarily as an economic good'.[73] Enjoyment of the right to safe drinking water is equally recognized as dependent upon the realization of other human rights, particularly the rights to housing, health, and food, as well as freedom of expression, freedom of association, and participation in public decision-making.[74] In 2005, the Sub-Commission for the Promotion and Protection of Human Rights adopted the draft guidelines for the realization of the right to drinking water supply and sanitation, which refer to a clear link between the right to water and environmental protection.[75]

---

64 Sub-Commission on the Promotion and Protection of Human Rights, Norms on the responsibilities of transnational corporations and other business enterprises with regard to human rights, E/CN.4/Sub.2/2003/12/Rev.2 (26 August 2003). Strengthening international cooperation for alternative development, including preventive alternative development, with due regard for environmental protection, UN Doc E/2006/33 (26 July 2006). Resolution 2005/4 on Right to Development expressed recognition of growing jurisprudence in this field, including the right's constituent elements such as environmental security and sustainability (para. 4).

65 Report of the Special Rapporteur on the situation of human rights and fundamental freedoms of indigenous people, E/CN.4/2003/90, 21 January 2003. Executive Summary, at 2.

66 Paragraph 3. Commission on Human Rights Resolution 2000/10 on Right to Food [online]. Available from: http://ap.ohchr.org/documents/dpage_e.aspx?m=101 [accessed 20 June 2009].

67 CESCR, General Comment 12: The Right to Adequate Food (Art.11), E/C.12/1999/5, 12 May 1999.

68 *Ibid.*, para. 4.

69 *Ibid.*, para. 7.

70 CESCR, General Comment 14, note 57 above.

71 *Ibid.*, para. 4.

72 CESCR, 'The Right to Water', Articles 11 and 12, E/C.12/2002/11 (20 January 2003).

73 *Ibid.*, para. 11.

74 See CESCR, General Comment 4, 'The Right to Adequate Housing' (Article 11 (1) of the Covenant), UN Doc. HRI\GEN\1\Rev.1 (1994) 53 (para. 12). General Comment 12 (n 67). General Comment 14, note 57 above, paras. 4, 11, 16, 36.

75 Guideline 1.2: 'Everyone has the right to have access to adequate and safe sanitation that is conducive to the protection of public health and the environment'. 'Realisation of the Right to Drinking Water and

In addition, two resolutions of the UN Commission on Human Rights deal expressly with human rights and the environment. Resolution 2005/60 stressed the importance for states, when developing their environmental policies, to take into account how environmental degradation may affect all members of society, in particular women, children, indigenous peoples and disadvantaged members of society.[76] Moreover, the resolution 'calls upon States to take all necessary measures to protect the legitimate exercise of everyone's human rights when promoting environmental protection and sustainable development'.[77] However, weak wording makes the impact of these resolutions insignificant. For example, Resolution 2003/71 states that environmental degradation can have '*potentially* negative effects on the enjoyment of some rights' and requests the Commission on Human Rights to produce a report on the '*possible* relationship between the environment and human rights'.[78] Also, Resolution 2005/60 considers that environmental damage, including that caused by natural circumstances or disasters, can have *potentially* negative effects on the enjoyment of human rights and on a healthy life and a healthy environment'.[79]

Noting these resolutions and decisions in different UN fora, we can safely confirm that the link between human rights and the environment is acknowledged, albeit not always in a forceful or succinct manner. The question remains of the impact of these non-binding documents. Perhaps, they create a moral obligation, reaffirm commitments of the international community to protect the environment, establish an accepted standard of behaviour, and highlight a consensus on content of norms (e.g. actors, obligations). The normative value of a declaration or resolution cannot be ignored if one considers the UDHR, which is a declaration and provides an example of hardened 'soft law'. While it may be too early to conclude that there is an established right to a healthy environment within the UN fora, the resolutions linking environmental protection to indigenous people's rights; water, food and housing rights; climate change; toxic waste; and weapons of mass destruction make it easier to outline the content of the right to a healthy environment.[80]

4. Discussing the Link in International Courts

The inseparable link between human rights and the environment was summarized in the *Gabcíkovo-Nagymaros* case[81] by Justice Weeramantry (as he then was) in the International Court of Justice (ICJ) as follows:

> The protection of the environment is … a vital part of contemporary human rights doctrine, for it is a sine qua non for numerous human rights such as the right to health and the right to life itself. It

Sanitation': report of the Special Rapporteur, El Hadji Guissé (E/CN.4/Sub.2/2005/25, 11 July 2005).

76 Paragraph 4. UN Commission on Human Rights, Human Rights Resolution 2005/60: 'Human Rights and the Environment as Part of Sustainable Development', 20 April 2005, E/CN.4/RES/2005/60 [online]. Available from: http://www.unhcr.org/refworld/docid/45377c759.html [accessed 25 June 2009].

77 *Ibid.*, para. 3.

78 *Ibid.*, paras. 2 and 11. UN Commission on Human Rights, Resolution 2003/7, 'Human rights and the environment as part of sustainable development', 25 April 2003.

79 Resolution 2005/60, note 76 above, Preamble.

80 See e.g. Commission on Human Rights Resolutions 2000/10 and 2001/57, and Commission on Human Rights, 'Human rights and weapons of mass destruction, or with indiscriminate effect, or of a nature to cause superfluous injury or unnecessary suffering', E/CN.4/Sub.2/2002/38, 27 June 2002.

81 *Case Concerning the Gabčíkovo-Nagymaros Project (Hungary* v. *Slovakia)*, 1997 ICJ Rep. 85, 91–92 (25 September) (Separate Opinion of Vice-President Weeramantry).

> is scarcely necessary to elaborate on this, as damage to the environment can impair and undermine all the human rights spoken of in the Universal Declaration and other human rights instruments.

This recognition of sound environment as a basic condition of right to life and that the deterioration of environmental quality can impair the fulfilment of other human rights, such as right to health, right to family life and right to property, is not an isolated comment from the ICJ. Regional human rights bodies in Europe, the Americas and Africa have examined cases that allege violation of human rights and environmental degradation and have assessed the link between human rights and the environment.[82] Within the European Court of Human Rights (ECtHR), the claims for environmental protection are primarily based on the violation of the right to private life and home.[83] However, the application of this right does not include a general right to protect the environment. In addition, Article 8 can be restricted if the activity falls under Article 8(2) of the 1950 European Convention on Human Rights and Fundamental Freedoms (ECHR)[84] (e.g. authorized economic activity). The only ground for solace is that the activity must have a legitimate aim, and must be lawful and proportionate to the legitimate aim pursued. In the *Hatton* case,[85] the ECtHR, when faced with competing interests (e.g. right to respect for private life versus the right to development), applied the 'fair balance' test while balancing the economic interests (e.g. economic contribution from flights) of the country with the rights of the affected individuals (e.g. noise pollution).[86] These decisions by the ECtHR show that there is a positive duty of the government to take measures to prevent environmental pollution, and this duty is owed only to the individuals whose rights are affected.[87]

A bolder approach has been taken by the African Commission on Human and Peoples' Rights in its interpretation of the ACHPR that expressly links environmental quality and human rights. Article 24 of the ACHPR provides: 'All peoples shall have the right to a general satisfactory environment favourable to their development'. The African Commission dealt with the scope of

---

82 Boyle, note 44 above, p. 471; D. Shelton, 'Human Rights, Health and Environmental Protection: Linkages in Law and Practice', *Human Rights and International Legal Discourse*, 1 (2007), pp. 9–59; M. Fitzmaurice and J. Marshall, 'The Human Right to a Clean Environment – Phantom or Reality? The European Court of Human Rights and English Courts Perspective on Balancing Rights in Environmental Matters', *Nordic Journal of International Law*, 76 (2007), pp. 103–51.

83 Article 8(1) provides that 'everyone has the right to respect for his private and family life, his home and his correspondence'. Article 8(2) provides the permissible grounds for limiting the exercise of the right.

84 European Convention for the Protection of Human Rights and Fundamental Freedoms, opened for signature 4 November 1950, 213 UNTS 222 (entered into force 3 September 1953).

85 *Hatton and Others* v. *The United Kingdom*, Judgment of 8 July 2003. The case deals with noise pollution from Heathrow Airport. The initial Chamber judgment found that the noise from increased flights at Heathrow airport between 4 a.m. and 6 a.m. violated the rights of the applicants to respect for their home and family life (Article 8). This judgment was overturned by a Grand Chamber decision (12–5) on 8 July 2003. Thus, there was no violation of Article 8. At the same time, the Grand Chamber (with one dissenting vote) upheld the Chamber's judgment finding a violation of Article 13 (right to a remedy) and awarded some costs and compensation to the applicants.

86 See discussion of these cases in D.J. Harris, M. O'Boyle, E. Bates and C. Buckley, Law of the European Convention on Human Rights, 2nd edn (Oxford: Oxford University Press, 2009), pp. 390–1.

87 Birnie, Boyle and Redgwell, note 18 above, pp. 282–5. (In their view, 'the duty is not one of protecting the environment, but of protecting human beings from significantly harmful environmental impacts', at p. 285, footnote omitted.)

this guarantee, in the *Ogoniland* case,[88] which involved the disposal of toxic waste that poisoned soil and water, and affected human health. The commission noted that the right to a general satisfactory environment (Article 24) 'imposes clear obligations upon a government', requiring the state 'to take reasonable and other measures to prevent pollution and ecological degradation, to promote conservation, and to secure an ecologically sustainable development and use of natural resources'.[89] In addition, the commission outlined various procedural tools that may facilitate the enforcement of substantive right to environment, such as environmental impact assessment, public information and participation, access to justice for environmental harm, and monitoring of potentially harmful activities.[90]

Several conclusions can be drawn from a brief survey of the cases outlined above. First, there is a need for express provision on environmental quality in binding instruments (e.g. the ACHPR). Second, states and non-state actors can be held responsible for action or inaction causing environmental degradation. Third, strong procedural techniques are required to enhance the enforcement of substantive rights (e.g. *Ogoniland* case). Finally, it is essential to develop remedies for violations of environmental rights such as remedial action or compensation (e.g. the *Hatton* case). Express provisions on the right to a healthy environment or the right to natural resources may make it easier for the affected individuals to bring a claim in the court and less challenging for the court to reach a fair balance between two competing rights.

5. Issue of Competing Rights at the National Level

There are questions regarding the role of human rights in relation to the protection and management of the ecosystem that create competing interests among different stakeholders. For example, there are conflicts over the rights to access and manage natural resources. Tropical forest is such a natural resource that is usually subject to state sovereignty but attracts competing claims from both internal and external actors (e.g. government agencies, environmental activists, the timber industry, and local communities) in respect of its management. The importance of tropical forest as a source of ecosystem services (e.g. fuel wood, energy, food and shelter) for local communities, as a carbon sink, and as a biodiversity reserve makes its management a challenging task.

Another example of competing interests among various stakeholders is the growing of grains for biofuels in large parts of America that is said to be endangering the food security of millions of people.[91] As in the regional courts, there are examples at the national level where environmental policies, rights and responsibilities conflict, such as with human rights to development, food, privacy, and private property. The question is, how might these conflicts and tensions be resolved? Whose interests will be prioritized in a conflict between the right to food and the use of biofuel, or

88 Decision Regarding Communication 155/96 (*Social and Economic Rights Action Center/Center for Economic and Social Rights* v *Nigeria*), Communication No. ACHPR/COMM/A044/1 (African Commission on Human and Peoples' Rights, 27 May 2002). The African Commission found Nigeria to have violated, *inter alia*, the right to life (Article 4), right to property (Article 14), right to health (Article 16), and right to satisfactory environment favourable to development (Article 24) of the ACHPR.

89 *Ibid.*, para. 52.

90 *Ibid.*, para. 53.

91 A. Chakrabortty, 'Secret Report: Biofuel Caused Food Crisis', *The Guardian*, 4 July 2008 [online]. Available from: www.guardian.co.uk/environment/2008/jul/03/biofuels.renewableenergy [accessed 20 June 2009].

the right to property and restrictions on shrimp cultivation?[92] Should states maximize the potential of natural resources (e.g. extraction of energy from natural resources) or should they protect the resources for the benefit of future generations? The balancing of competing interests (e.g. economic interests and health problems) is common in many of the cases brought before the regional human rights courts.[93] The human rights approach seeks to resolve these conflicts with accessible redress, albeit not always successfully.

Approximately 60 national constitutions include provisions to protect the environment.[94] These constitutional provisions recognize the state's obligations to prevent environmental damage, outline duties for citizens to protect the environment, prohibit the use of property in a manner that harms the environment, and establish a right to compensation for those suffering from environmental injury.[95] The constitutional enactment offers an opportunity to promote environmental and resource concerns at the highest and most visible level of the domestic legal order. Addressing environmental concerns and resource protection at the constitutional level as human *right*s means that their protection does not depend on the liberal or conservation interpretation of the judiciary.

Constitutional provisions protecting the right to a healthy environment respond to the two crucial arguments regarding the anthropocentric nature of the human rights approach. First, the protection of the ecosystem and natural resources; and, second, the protection of present and future generations. Several constitutional provisions deal with the sustainable exploitation and management of natural resources (e.g. Afghanistan (2004), Albania (1998), Bahrain (1973), Bolivia (1967), Cambodia (1993), China (1982), Cuba (1992), Peru (1993), Portugal (1976), South Africa (1996)) and the management of species and ecosystems (e.g. Brazil (1998), Colombia (1991), Ecuador (1998), Namibia (1990), Panama (1972)). Some of these constitutions create a justiciable right and some contain purely aspirational provisions.[96] Constitutional provisions (e.g. Albania (1998), Argentina (1994), Bolivia (1967), Brazil (1998), Iran (1979), Malawi (1994), Norway (1814), South Africa (1996), Uganda (1995)) recognize the rights of future generations by means of environmental protection and the sustainable development of natural resources. With constitutional provisions on its side, the community affected by a development decision (e.g. the *Oposa* case[97]) may argue that the principle of intergenerational responsibility is legally justiciable, and that the express provision in the constitution provides them with legal capacity to sue on behalf of the present and future generations.

It is also true that the conceptual difficulty undermines the very notion of a human right to a healthy environment. In India, for example, there is a judiciary-created right to a healthy environment. The Indian Constitution protects the right to life (Article 21) but does not include any mention of environmental protection. The state has a duty to protect and preserve the environment

92 Human Rights Council, Promotion and Protection of All Human Rights, Civil, Political, Economic, Social and Cultural Rights Including the Right to Development, Report of the Special Rapporteur on the Right to Food, Jean Ziegler, A/HRC/7/5, 10 January 2008 (para. 14, 57). *S. Jagannath* v *Union of India* (1997) 2 SCC 87.

93 For example, in the *Lopez Ostra* case, the court took into account the economic interests of the community. It ruled that the activities of the tannery waste treatment plant had produced severe environmental pollution that affected the enjoyment of basic human rights. *Lopez-Ostra* v *Spain*, ECHR (1994), Series A, No. 303C.

94 O'Gara *et al.*, note 17 above.

95 *Ibid.*

96 *Ibid.*

97 *Oposa* v *Factoran*, GR No. 101083, 224 SCRA 792 (30 July 1993, Philippines).

– this is part of the directive principle of state policy and not a fundamental right.[98] However, the nature and extent of this right are not similar to the self-executory and actionable right to a healthy environment prescribed in the constitution of the Philippines or South Africa.[99] That means, in the absence of any explicit right to a healthy environment in the constitution, that the community or individual affected by an adverse environmental decision must depend on a liberal interpretation of the 'right to life' by the judiciary. The Indian judiciary has interpreted the right to life in a diversified manner: that is, the right to survive as a species, the quality of life, the right to live with dignity, and the right to livelihood.[100]

In India, with a long history of public interest environmental litigation and constitutional approval, the link between human rights and the environment is not contested. Moreover, it is difficult to have a clear-cut division between human rights cases and environmental cases. Examples of public interest litigation show that it is not always possible to separate environmental issues from human rights issues.[101] Examples include large-scale, infrastructure projects that displace indigenous people from their land and adversely affect the natural resources; in such cases, the Indian Supreme Court had to balance the development aspects, human rights and the environmental concerns.[102] Another example is activities undertaken by a multinational company that were challenged in the national courts, and the court restricted the way resources were being extracted or utilized.[103]

The lack of an express provision in the constitution means that if the right to a healthy environment is defined inadequately or imprecisely, there is a possibility that it will not be enforced effectively by the public agencies. Express provision in the constitution also makes it somewhat easier to implement the right without recourse to an expansive or broad interpretation of the right to life. Is it easier if the judiciary has to balance two competing rights (e.g. the right to property

98 Constitution of India, Article 48A ('The State shall endeavour to protect and improve the environment and safeguard the forests and wildlife of the country'). Article 51A (g) imposes responsibility on every citizen to protect and improve the environment.

99 The 1986 Constitution of the Philippines provides that 'the State shall protect and advance the right of the people to a balanced and healthful ecology in accord with the rhythm and harmony of nature'. Article II, Section 16. The 1996 Constitution of South Africa provides that 'everyone has the right to an environment that is not harmful to their health or well-being,' and 'to have the environment protected, for the benefit of present and future generations' (Chapter 2, Article 24).

100 J. Razzaque, 'Human Rights and the Environment: National Experiences', *Environmental Policy and Law*, 32(2) (2002), pp. 99–111.

101 J. Razzaque, 'Linking Human Rights, Development and Environment: Experiences from Litigation in South Asia', *Fordham Environmental Law Review*, 18(3) (2007), pp. 587–608.

102 *Narmada Bachao Andolan* v *Union of India*, A.I.R. 1999 S.C. 3345. The Supreme Court, in 2006, dismissed the litigation filed by an activist group and upheld the government decision to go ahead with the construction even though the progress on rehabilitation is not satisfactory and the construction of the dam was outpacing the rehabilitation process.

103 *Perumatty Grama Panchayat* v *State of Kerala* 2004(1)KLT731. In India, the local village council of Kerala refused to renew the licence of the Coca-Cola Company on the ground that the over-exploitation of groundwater by the company had created severe water shortages for the community. Noting that groundwater belongs to the general public, the High Court of India ordered the village council to renew the licence in terms that would allow the company to extract only a limited quantity of groundwater. The village council renewed the licence on the condition that the company not use groundwater for industrial purposes, or for producing soft drinks, aerated (carbonated) beverages or fruit juice. These conditions made it impossible for the company to operate. Water Aid, the Right to Water Under the Right to Life: India [online]. Available from: http://www.righttowater.info/code/legal_7.asp [accessed 25 June 2009].

and the express right to a healthy environment)? Probably not – much would depend on the nature of the constitutional provision (binding or aspirational) and, once challenged, whether the court would give more emphasis to environmental protection.

6. Role of the Procedural Rights

Procedural rights deal with the process through which an administrative or judicial decision is made and include the right to information, participation and access to courts.[104] Since the 1970s, the environmental movement has drawn political and legal attention to the frequently deleterious impacts of human activities and the right/value-based discourses on biodiversity and ecosystems. This has contributed to the adoption of important global environmental initiatives such as the 1992 Rio Declaration, the 2000 Millennium Development Goals, and the 2002 Johannesburg Declaration. The complex interplay between human well-being and the ecosystem is in urgent need of reconsideration in an age of climate change and increasing environmental degradation. At the same time, there is an emphasis on procedural rights that would enable peoples (or individuals and communities) to seek enforcement of the right to a healthy environment.[105] Several interrelated factors influence the growth of procedural rights;[106]for example, the growing relationships between environmental health and human well-being,[106] the lack of political consensus for a human right to a healthy environment,[107] and the prevalent concerns of the international community for 'good governance' and the strengthening of civil societies.[108] An effective procedural rights regime allows individuals and communities to challenge the failure of a country to enforce regional laws (e.g. ECtHR), or breach of international law (e.g. the World Trade Organization Dispute Settlement Panel), or the failure of an organization to enforce its own policies (e.g. World Bank Inspection Panel).

6.1 Procedural Rights at the International Level

Prior to 1992, most human rights treaties included provisions on procedural rights. The UDHR declared the rights of access to information (Article 19) and justice (Articles 8 and 10). Similarly, Article 19(2) of the ICCPR guarantees citizens the 'freedom to seek, receive and impart information and ideas of all kinds'. The period between the 1972 Stockholm Declaration and 1992 Rio Declaration has seen a growing recognition of procedural tools to protect the environment.[109] The 1992 Rio Declaration elaborated on the three pillars of public participation in its Principle 10:

104 J. Ebbesson, 'The Notion of Public Participation in International Environmental Law', *Yearbook of International Environmental Law*, 8 (1997), pp. 70–5.

105 For example, para. 5, Resolution 2005/60 on Human Rights and the Environment as Part of Sustainable Development (note 76 above).

106 B. Barton, 'Underlying Concepts and Theoretical Issues in Public Participation in Resource Development', in D. Zillman *et al.* (eds), *Human Rights in Natural Resource Development: Public Participation in the Sustainable Development of Mining and Energy Resources* (Oxford: Oxford University Press, 2002), pp. 81–3.

107 Shelton, note 5 above, p. 198.

108 J. Steffek *et al.* (eds), *Civil Society Participation in European and Global Governance: A Cure for the Democratic Deficit?* (Basingstoke: Palgrave Macmillan, 2007).

109 Preamble of the 1972 Stockholm Declaration; 1982 World Charter for Nature; 1986 WCED Experts Group on Environmental Law for Environmental Protection and Sustainable Development.

participation of all concerned citizens at the relevant level of decision making; *access to information* concerning the environment; *access to judicial and administrative proceedings* including redress and remedy.[110] At the same time, access to information, public participation, and access to justice appear throughout Agenda 21 (1992).[111] Several non-binding[112] and binding[113] instruments have incorporated specific provisions on information, participation and access to justice. The 1994 Draft Declaration of Principles on Human Rights and Environment affirms that procedural rights (e.g. information, participation, justice) are essential for the realization of the substantive rights.[114]

Strong procedural rules make it easier for individuals and communities to claim the substantive right to a healthy environment in a court of law. At the international level, procedural rules of some of the international courts and tribunals allow people to participate in the court proceedings. For example, the World Bank Inspection Panel allows individuals and NGOs who believe that their rights have been or could be directly harmed by a project financed by the World Bank to bring their action.[115]

6.2 Procedural Rights at the Regional Level

Also, some regional non-binding and binding instruments include provisions on information, participation and justice. For example, the right of communities to participate in consultation on major new projects is entrenched in the environmental impact assessment (EIA) processes.[116] The ACHPR also guarantees that every individual has the rights of access to information (Article 9(1), participation (Article 13), and justice (Articles 3 and 7). Similar provisions on information (Article 10) and justice (Article 6) can be found in the ECHR. The Inter-American Commission on Human Rights has also observed that

> [c]onditions of severe environmental pollution, which may cause serious physical illness, impairment and suffering on the part of the local populace, are inconsistent with the right to be respected as a human being .... *The quest to guard against environmental conditions which threaten*

110 *Emphasis added.* Principle 10: 'Environmental issues are best handled with participation of all concerned citizens, at the relevant level. At the national level, each individual shall have appropriate access to information concerning the environment that is held by public authorities, including information on hazardous materials and activities in their communities, and the opportunity to participate in decision-making processes. States shall facilitate and encourage public awareness and participation by making information widely available. Effective access to judicial and administrative proceedings, including redress and remedy, shall be provided'. Rio Declaration (note 20 above).

111 Chapters 12, 19, 27, 36, 37, and 40. Agenda 21, Report of the UNCED, I (1992) UN Doc. A/CONF.151/26/Rev.1 (1992) 31 ILM 874.

112 OAS, Inter-American Strategy for the Promotion of Public Participation in Decision-Making for Sustainable Development (2000). CIDI Res 98 (V 0/00, OEA/Ser W/II.5, CIDI Doc 25/00 (25 April 2000).

113 1992 UN Framework Convention on Climate Change, 1992 Convention on Biological Diversity, 1993 Convention on Civil Liability for Damage Resulting from Activities Dangerous to the Environment, 1994 Convention to Combat Desertification.

114 Draft Principles, note 63 above.

115 D. Hunter, 'Using the World Bank Inspection Panel to Defend the Interests of Project-Affected People', *Chicago Journal of International Law*, 4 (2003), p. 201.

116 For example, the 1991 UNECE Convention on Environmental Impact Assessment in a Transboundary Context provides provisions on participation (Articles 2, 3) and information (Articles 3, 4, 6). 30 ILM (1991), 802.

> *human health requires that individuals have access to: information, participation in relevant decision making processes, and judicial recourse*.[117]

Similarly, the African Commission on Human and Peoples' Rights[118] and the Inter-American Court of Human Rights[119] have highlighted the importance of meaningful opportunities for individuals to be heard and to participate in the development decisions affecting their health and environment. Several regional courts and tribunals (e.g. ECtHR,[120] Inter-American Court of Human Rights[121]) allowed individuals, NGOs or groups of individuals to have access to the court if they are victims of any violation. In addition, the ECtHR allows NGOs to submit *amicus curiae* briefs during the written procedure and, in some cases, take part in oral hearings.[122]

The Aarhus Convention[123] is the only regional treaty that adopts a rights-based approach to information, participation and justice, and allows people to enforce their procedural and substantive environmental rights in court.[124] The convention recognizes that 'adequate protection of the environment is essential to human well-being and the enjoyment of basic human rights, including the right to life itself',[125] and that there is a duty 'both individually and in association with others, to protect and improve the environment for the benefit of present and future generations'.[126] While these points are in the preamble (i.e. non-binding), Article 1 reiterates that the objective of the convention is 'to contribute to the protection of the right of every person of present and future generations to live in an environment adequate to his or her health and well-being…'.[127] The convention enables 'public authorities and citizens to assume their individual and collective responsibility to protect and improve the environment for the welfare and well-being of present and

117 *Emphasis added.* IACtHR, *Report on the Situation of Human Rights in Ecuador*, OEA/Ser.L/V/II.96, doc. 10 rev. 1 (1997), 92, 93.

118 Decision Regarding Communication 155/96, note 88 above, para. 53.

119 Awas Tingni Mayagna (Sumo) Indigenous Community v Nicaragua. Judgment of 31 August 2001, IACtHR (Ser. C) No. 79 (2001). The complaint protested government-sponsored logging of timber on indigenous forest lands in Nicaragua and argued that the government failed to consult the community before granting concession rights to the exploitation of natural resources in their land. The court held that the government violated the right to judicial protection (Article 25) and the right to property (Article 21).

120 The court has dealt with the rights to information, privacy and family life; e.g. *Guerra and Others* v *Italy* (1998) 26 EHRR 357; *Lopez-Ostra* v *Spain* (1994) 20 EHRR 277; *Hatton* v *UK* (Judgment of the Grand Chamber, 8 July 2003), 37 EHRR 28; *Kyrtatos* v *Greece* (2003) ECHR 242; *Öneryildiz* v *Turkey* (2004) ECHR 657; *Fadeyeva v Russia* (2005) ECHR 376; *Taskin* v *Turkey* (2006) 42 EHRR 50.

121 O'Gara *et al.*, note 17 above, pp. 54–6.

122 J. Razzaque, 'Changing Role of Friends of the Court in the International Courts and Tribunals', *Non-State Actors and International Law*, 1 (2001), pp. 169–200.

123 UN Economic Commission for Europe Convention on Access to Information, Public Participation and Access to Justice in Environmental Matters, *International Legal Materials*, 38 (1999), p. 515. Although the Convention is regional in scope, it is open to accession by any UN member state [Article 19(3)].

124 S. Stec and S. Casey-Lefkowitz, *Aarhus Convention: An Implementation Guide* (Geneva: UNECE, 2000), pp. 29–30. It is interesting to note that the Almaty Declaration refers to an 'entitlement' to live in a healthy environment instead of a right. Para. 3, Economic Commission for Europe, Almaty Declaration, ECE/MP.PP/2005/2/Add.1 (20 June 2005).

125 Preamble, para. 6.

126 *Ibid.*, para. 7.

127 In the interpretative statement upon ratification, the UK noted that the 'right' mentioned in Article 1 is aspirational and limited only to the three pillars of the convention. Declaration upon ratification by the UK (25 June 1998).

future generations'.[128] While the convention provides a useful framework for public participation – and the participatory rights are linked to the legal, political and administrative arrangements at the national level – successful national implementation will require strong political support. In addition, developing countries may not be willing to ratify this convention, as it contains a detailed impact assessment procedure for development projects (e.g. power plants, pipelines, and infrastructure projects), and the EIA procedure may be expensive and time-consuming.

The development of procedural rights at the regional level has considerably influenced lawmaking at the European level.[129] The effect of the Aarhus Convention is not limited within the European Union (EU).[130] For example, the 1999 (London) Protocol on Water and Health of the 1991 Espoo Convention expressly incorporates the Aarhus Convention provisions in the context of environmental health. However, in the EU Charter of Fundamental Rights, the affirmation of a responsibility of states to integrate environmental protection into various policies falls short of a right.[131]

6.3 Procedural Rights at the National Level

At the national level, procedural rights (i.e. access to court, information and participation in the decision-making process) facilitate the application of the right to a healthy environment and promote better environmental governance. In many developing countries, Principle 10 of the 1992 Rio Declaration influences the procedural laws and policies.[132] Some constitutions accommodate provisions on right to information and public participation. For example, the constitutions of Uganda (1995), South Africa (1996), and Thailand (1991) guarantee the right of the public to information.[133] The right to access courts is included in the constitutions of several EU member states such as France (1958), Germany (1949), Ireland (1937), Portugal (1976) and Spain (1978).[134] These procedural rights can be found in general laws (administrative law, civil code and penal

128 Para. 2, Economic Commission for Europe, Almaty Declaration, ECE/MP.PP/2005/2/Add.1 (20 June 2005); *emphasis added.*

129 The EU signed the Aarhus Convention in 1998 and approved it in early 2005. Directive 2003/4/EC on Public Access to Environmental Information (2003) OJL 41, at 26; Directive 2001/42/EC on the Assessment of the Effects of Certain Plans and Programmes on the Environment (2001) OJL 197, at 30; Directive 2003/35/EC, providing for public participation in respect of the drawing up of certain plans and programmes relating to the environment and amending with regard to public participation and access to justice (2003) OJL 156, at 17.

130 2003 UNECE Protocol on Strategic Environmental Assessment to the 1991 Espoo Convention; 2000 Biosafety Protocol to the 1992 Convention on Biological Diversity.

131 Article 37 of the charter states: 'A high level of environmental protection and the improvement of the quality of the environment must be integrated into the policies of the Union and ensured in accordance with the principle of sustainable development'. Articles 2, 6 and 174 of the EC Treaty created an obligation for member states to take into account environmental protection when defining or implementing policies. Charter of Fundamental Rights of the European Union (2000) OJ C 364/1. A. Kiss, 'Environmental and Consumer Protection', in S. Peers and A. Ward (eds), *The European Union Charter of Fundamental Rights: Politics, Law and Policy* (Oxford: Hart, 2004), pp. 247–68, at p. 252.

132 UNECE, Global and Regional Developments on Issues Related to Principle 10 of the Rio Declaration on Environment and Development, ECE/MP.PP/2008/8 (23 May 2008) [online]. Available from: http://www.unece.org/env/documents/2008/pp/mop3/ece_mp_pp_2008_8_e.pdf [accessed 25 June 2009].

133 E. Petkova, C. Maurer, N. Henninger and F. Irwin, *Closing the Gap: Information, Participation, and Justice in Decision-Making for the Environment* (Washington, DC: World Resources Institute, 2002).

134 J. Ebbesson, *Access to Justice in Environmental Matters in the EU* (The Hague: Kluwer, 2002).

code), as well as in specific environmental legislation or other specific laws (sectoral law dealing with air and water; framework environmental law, information law and EIA procedures). General laws may provide formal (judicial reviews, class action, and public inquiries), informal or quasi-judicial forums (mediation and arbitration) for legal redress. In addition, they outline procedural issues such as standing in public interest litigation or class action and legal aid. Examples of public interest litigation and judicial activism can be found in Africa (Uganda, South Africa), Asia (Pakistan, Philippines) and Latin America (Argentina, Peru), enabling poorer sections of the community to enforce their constitutional rights, including a substantive right to a healthy environment.[135]

7. Conclusion

While human beings are responsible for much environmental degradation – they are part of the ecosystem. Strictly speaking, human rights and environmental regulation tend to inhabit distinct institutional regimes, but the two legal systems increasingly share a set of common concerns such as the impact of globalization and market economy. Both legal systems address issues of quality of life and sustainable development, trade and right to development, the access and management of natural resources, and the need to safeguard the planet for present and future generations.

Although the UDHR did not specifically declare a specific right to a healthy environment, over the years, human rights law has evolved to meet the challenges of environmental degradation. The link between human rights and environmental protection is established at the international (e.g. soft law), regional (e.g. human right treaties) and national levels (e.g. constitutional provisions, case laws). A number of domestic and international legal and political developments connect well-established rights, such as the right to life and the right to health, with the requirement of a healthy environment. The human right to a healthy environment is expressed as a separate right (e.g. in the Aarhus Convention, regional conventions, and national constitutions), or as a necessary corollary to other human rights (e.g. in UN non-binding documents). National constitutional provisions and the judiciary (both national and regional) show that it is possible, to a certain extent, to integrate concerns related to nature conservation and the right of the future generations within the right to a healthy environment. It is true that there is no simple way to categorize the right to a healthy environment: it can be part of civil and political rights (e.g. right to life, right to participation, information, due process), since it is central to the full and effective realization of those rights as well, or part of 'an economic right, a social right and a cultural right at the same time'.[136] It is all of these. In this way, the right to a healthy environment epitomizes the indivisibility and interdependence of all human rights. The realization of the substantive right to a healthy environment requires adequate information and the participation of affected communities to protect and manage natural resources. Environmental justice demands that there should be a right to a healthy environment for all, and the vulnerable communities should be integrated in the decision-making processes.

The lack of an enforcement mechanism within the environmental realm makes it more urgent to adopt a human rights approach to protect the environment. The Intergovernmental Panel on Climate Change stated that climate change will 'exacerbate inequities in health status and access to

135 Examples of relevant cases are available from: www.elaw.org.

136 Kiss, note 5 above, p. 559.

adequate food, clean water and other resources'.[137] The issue of climate change is closely linked to right to life (e.g. right to live in an unpolluted environment) and to the right to health.[138] In 2005, a case was filed by the Inuit community against the USA, challenging the impact of global warming on human health.[139] The basis of their argument was that the government of the USA has failed to address the consequences of global warming and its action or omission violated the human rights of the Inuit.[140] Criticisms aside, other national cases also show how human rights approach can provide some benefits to the future climate change regime.[141]

The right to a healthy environment contributes to the sustainable realization of other human rights, such as the rights to development, or clean water, and property. If states want to maximize natural resources to benefit the most people, they need to decide on the basis of long-term sustainability, as opposed to short-term profit. That goes for liberalizing markets or adopting an ecosystem approach in managing natural resources. As an integral part of ecosystems, human beings benefit from the services that the ecosystem provides.[142] Ecosystem services, such as water and food, are directly linked with security (e.g. secured resource access), basic material for a good life (e.g. sufficient nutritious food), and health (e.g. access to clean water).[143] Human beings have increased the production of some ecosystem services, such as food crops and freshwater, through technological advances in extracting groundwater or increasing areas dedicated to food crop cultivation. While the world population doubled between 1960 and 2000, food production increased by 160% and water use doubled.[144] There is an increasing pressure on the forest and mountain ecosystems that are the largest provider of freshwater. In recent years, market instruments (e.g. payment for ecosystem services) are promoted as a useful tool to manage ecosystem services. The problem with the introduction of market instruments is that they often do not offer adequate protection to those who are vulnerable and directly dependent on the resources.

Human rights, with established mechanisms (e.g. monitoring, compliance, dispute settlement), can play an important role in preserving ecosystem services. At the same time, human rights cannot be fully realized without the environmental aspects of ecosystem services that are essential to the right to life and all other rights that contribute to and constitute the preconditions of its enjoyment

---

137 R. Watson *et al.* (eds), *Climate Change 2001: Synthesis Report – Questions* (IPCC, 2001) [online]. Available from: http://www.ipcc.ch/ipccreports/tar/vol4/english/index.htm [accessed 20 June 2009].

138 Human Rights Council, 'Human Rights and Climate Change', A/HRC/RES/7/23 (28 March 2008). Y. von Schirnding and C. Mulholland, 'Health in the Context of Sustainable Development: Background Document', WHO/HDE/HID/02.6 (Geneva: WHO, 2001).

139 Petition to the Inter-American Commission on Human Rights Seeking Relief from Violations Resulting from Global Warming Caused by Acts and Omissions of the United States, Submitted by Sheila Watt-Cloutier, with the Support of the Inuit Circumpolar Conference, on Behalf of All Inuit of the Arctic Regions of the United States and Canada (7 December 2005) [online]. Available from: http://www.inuitcircumpolar.com/index.php?Lang=En&ID=316 [accessed 20 June 2009].

140 The list of rights includes, *inter alia*, rights to enjoy the benefits of their culture, to use and enjoy the lands they have traditionally occupied, to use and enjoy their personal property, and to preserve health and life. The Inter-American Commission on Human Rights rejected this petition in 2006.

141 S. Humphreys and R. Archer (eds), *Climate Change and Human Rights: A Rough Guide* (Geneva: International Council on Human Rights Policy, 2008) pp. 3–5. Examples of cases from Nigeria, the USA, Australia and Germany are in www.climatelaw.org [accessed 25 June 2009].

142 Millennium Ecosystem Assessment, Ecosystems and Human Well-Being: Synthesis (Washington. DC: Island Press, 2005), Preface, p. v [online]. Available from: http://www.millenniumassessment.org/documents/document.356.aspx.pdf [accessed 25 June 2010].

143 *Ibid.*, p. 10.

144 *Ibid.*

such as the right to health and the right to property). For example, serious impacts from ecosystem degradation are affecting indigenous peoples, the majority of whom live in extremely vulnerable ecosystems. As we reach the sixth decade since the adoption of the UDHR, there is a need to ensure that the substantive right to a healthy environment and the supporting procedural rights are responsive to the challenges of climate change and the sustainable management of ecosystem services.

Chapter 7
The Right to a Peaceful World Order

Nsongurua J. Udombana

> From the moment when Hitler's invasion of Poland revealed the bankruptcy of all existing methods of preserving peace, it became evident … that we must begin almost immediately to plan the creation of a new system.'[1]

> Sooner or later, all the people of the world will have to discover a way to live together in peace, and thereby transform this pending cosmic elegy into a creative psalm of brotherhood.'[2]

1. Introduction

This chapter interrogates the right to a peaceful world order (PWO) within the context of the general development of international human rights law since the adoption of the Universal Declaration of Human Rights (UDHR).[3] The concept of a 'world order' is often used to indicate a rearrangement of world-view based on distinctive changes in political, economic and social attitudes and structures. Goldstein defines 'world order' as 'rules that govern – albeit in a messy and ambiguous way – the most important relationships of the interstate system in general, and the world's great powers in particular'.[4] The world system does not always go in the same route; indeed, history is replete with several world orders. The political world orders have mostly alternated between empires/ hegemony and balance, leading to the current 'multipolar and multicivilizational' era.[5]

The break-up of the former Soviet Union and the fall of the Berlin Wall ushered in the 'New World Order' (NWO) – also known as the 'post-Cold War world order'. The NWO marks a shift in the balance of power between states, with wider implications on the Westphalia international order. This NWO, which 'replaces the relatively simple, broad disagreements of the superpowers with a seemingly endless array of dormant ethnic and national rivalries',[6] is anchored on three hemispheric pan-regions, longitudinal zones – led by the USA, the European Union (EU), and

1 Cordell Hull, *Memoirs* (New York: Macmillan, 1948), vol. 2, p. 1628.

2 Martin Luther King, Jr., 'Nobel Prize Acceptance Speech', in James M. Washington (ed.), *A Testament of Hope: The Essential Writings and Speeches of Martin Luther King, Jr.* (New York: HarperCollins, 1986), p. 225.

3 Universal Declaration of Human Rights 1948, GA Res. 217A (III), UN Doc. A/810 at 71 (1948) (hereinafter UDHR).

4 J. Goldstein, *International Relations*, 6th edn (New York: Longman, 2002), p. 43.

5 S. Huntington, *The Clash of Civilizations and the Remaking of World Order* (New York: Touchstone, 1997), pp. 19ff, arguing that civilizations based primarily on ethnic, linguistic, and religious heritage will clash with competing civilizations.

6 Thematic Essay: 'The History of American Foreign Policy', *Encarta* [online]. Available from: http://encarta.msn.com/encyclopedia_461575607_5/Thematic_Essay_The_History_of_American_Foreign_Policy.html [accessed 1 February 2009].

China – what Hessbruegge calls 'a "medievalization" of international relations'.[7] Securing and maintaining 'global peace' is one of the goals of the NWO.

'Globalization' – the buzzword for today's intricate, interdependent, interwoven, intensely dangerous world[8] – also represents a 'new international economic order (NIEO)'. The campaign for a NIEO, which began in the early 1970s, led to the elaboration of the Declaration on the Establishment of a NIEO.[9] The NIEO was a paradigm shift from concepts based on nation states. It replaced the preceding international economic order (IEO) where states were the 'be all' and 'end all' of power, trade, and wealth.[10] The NIEO had three goals. First, it sought to eliminate developing countries' economic dependence on developed countries. Second, it sought to accelerate the development of economies in developing countries based on the principle of self-reliance. Lastly, it sought to introduce appropriate institutional changes for the global management of world resources in the interest of mankind as a whole.

Meanwhile, the current global financial meltdown that begun in late 2007 – the worst since the Great Depression – is leading to a full-scale rethink of financial regulatory infrastructures and a reconsideration of economic theory. Some G-20 member states, especially France, Germany and Russia, are lobbying for a new 'grand bargain' to reorder the global balance of financial power, a euphemism for a 'new world financial order'.

The title of this chapter assumes that a PWO is a human right. According to Beetham, an entitlement qualifies as a human right if it is fundamental and universal, is definable in justiciable form, is clear on who has the duty to uphold or implement it, and has a responsible agency with capacity to fulfil its obligation in relation to the right.[11] Beetham's characterization is defective to the extent that he fails to distinguish between normativity and justiciability. An entitlement remains a human right if it is normative, though not legally enforceable or justiciable. Normativity deals with questions of whether a particular standard or principle is binding on members of a group and is guiding and regulating acceptable behaviour in a society. Justiciability deals with questions of whether courts can, and at least sometimes will, provide a remedy for aggrieved individuals claiming a violation of certain standards.

If we assume Beetham's criteria, however, several questions demand answers. What qualifies peace as a human right? Otherwise stated, what are the justifications for classifying a PWO as a human right? Who are the beneficiaries of this right and who are the duty-bearers? Which agencies have responsibilities and capacities to ensure compliance with obligations entailed therein or to sanction non-compliance? If a PWO is a human right, why has its realization been largely elusive? Is world peace realizable? How?

The first segment of this chapter interrogates 'peace' as a human right. The second segment traces the search for a PWO and spotlights reasons why that search has largely been elusive. The

7 Jan Hessbruegge, 'Human Rights Violations Arising from Conduct of Non-State Actors' *Buffalo Human Rights Law Review*, 11 (2005), pp. 21ff, at p. 21.

8 See Chapter 10 on globalization in this volume.

9 See Declaration on the Establishment of a New International Economic Order, GA Res. 3201 (S-VI), at 3–4, UN Doc. A/9559 (1 May 1974) (hereinafter Declaration on NIEO).

10 See, generally, Mohammed Bedjaoui, *Towards a New International Economic Order* (New York: Holmes & Meier, 1979), discussing the role of international law in shaping the IEO.

11 See D. Beetham, 'What Future for Economic and Social Rights?', *Political Studies*, 43 (1995), pp. 41–60, at pp. 41–2. Cf. E.W. Vierdag, 'The Legal Nature of the Rights Granted by the International Covenant on Economic, Social and Cultural Rights', *Netherlands Yearbook of International Law*, 9 (1978), p. 69 ('In order to be a legal right, a right must be legally definable; only then can it be legally enforced, only then can it be said to be justiciable').

third segment examines the continuing threats to a PWO, embedding therein suggestions for its realization. In general, it urges the global community to unite around the common values that bind – human dignity, freedom, democracy, rule of law, and justice – in order to achieve a PWO. The last segment concludes with brief annotations.

2. Peace as a Human Right

The noun 'peace' lacks any lexical exactitude; it could denote 'calm', 'quiet', 'stillness', 'tranquillity', 'silence', 'harmony', or 'serenity.' As an ideal state, peace may be defined as the absence of fear, though not necessarily the absence of conflict.[12] In its traditional political connotation, peace is defined as the absence of war; that is, *pax* as *absentia belli*. It connotes the absence of violence or other disturbances within a state. Others see peace as a collective good[13] or as 'a dynamic process of cooperation among all States and peoples' founded on principles of 'respect for freedom, independence, national sovereignty, equality, and human rights, as well as on a fair and equitable distribution of resources to meet the needs of peoples'.[14] Lasting peace, declares the United Nations (UN) Educational, Scientific and Cultural Organization (UNESCO),

> is a prerequisite for the exercise of all human rights and duties. It is not the peace of silence, of men and women who by choice or constraint remain silent. It is the peace of freedom – and therefore of just laws – of happiness, equality, and solidarity, in which all citizens count, live together and share.[15]

The concept of a universal right to peace appears to be supported by general international law. Judicial authorities and publicists also allude to it. Peace is the infrastructure on which the UN erects the legal, political, economic, social and other superstructures. As Joyce argues, 'the moral and legal rule established by the UN is itself a "peace" system.'[16] The UN represents an attempt to establish law and order within the modern state system. Its principal aim is '[t]o maintain international peace and security, and, to this end, to take effective collective measures for the prevention and removal of threats to the peace' and to achieve 'international co-operation in solving international problems of [a] … humanitarian character'.[17] This function accords with the general purpose of international

---

12 Declaration and Programme of Action on a Culture of Peace 1999, GA Res. A/RES/53/243, 6 October 1999 (hereinafter Declaration on a Culture of Peace), Preamble, stating, 'peace not only is the absence of conflict…'.

13 See, generally, Ruben P. Mendez, 'Peace as a Public Good', in Inge Kaul, Isabelle Grunberg and Marc A. Stein (eds), *Global Public Goods: International Cooperation in the 21st Century* (Oxford: Oxford University Press, 1999), p. 382.

14 O. Vandekerckhove, 'Peace Through Solidarity: A Priority for the Next 125 Years', *Dissemination*, 11 (1988), pp. 1ff.

15 The Human Right to Peace. Declaration by the Director-General of UNESCO Federico Mayor, January 1997 (hereinafter UNESCO Declaration) [online]. Available from: www.wagingpeace.org/articles/1997/01/01_human-right-to-peace_mayor.htm [accessed 2 February 2009]).

16 J.A. Joyce, 'Is There a Right to Peace?', *Christian Century*, 24 February 1982, p. 202 [online]. Available from: www.religion-online.org/showarticle.asp?title=1284.

17 Charter of the UN, San Francisco, 26 June 1945, entered into force 24 October 1945, Cmd 7015 (hereinafter UN Charter), Art. 1(1) and (3).

law, which seeks to 'safeguard international peace, security and justice in relations between states'.[18] Consequently, the 'peoples' of the UN undertake to 'practice tolerance and live together in peace with one another as good neighbours' and to unite their strength 'to maintain international peace and security'.[19]

The UDHR, adopted by the UN General Assembly in 1948 'as a common standard of achievement for all peoples and all nations',[20] is the authoritative interpretation of the UN Charter.[21] Its preamble speaks of the 'disregard and contempt for human rights [that] have resulted in barbarous acts which have outraged the conscience of mankind',[22] a euphemism for the dreadful acts of World War II, including the Holocaust. Kennedy justly describes the UDHR as 'one of the greatest political statement in world history',[23] 'an outstanding document, with an outstanding range',[24] though he sincerely adds that '[t]he vast majority of colonial peoples in Africa, Asia, the Caribbean, and other regions had no chance to vote on this solemn declaration of their inherent rights'.[25]

The UDHR does not specifically guarantee the right to a PWO, but its preamble notes that 'recognition of the inherent dignity and of the equal and inalienable rights of all members of the human family is the foundation of freedom, justice and peace in the world.'[26] The declaration references 'peace' in the context of the right to education; it provides that 'Education ... shall promote understanding, tolerance and friendship among all nations, racial or religious groups, and shall further the activities of the United Nations for the maintenance of peace.'[27] Article 28 implicitly guarantees the right to a PWO thus: 'Everyone is entitled to a social and international order in which the rights and freedoms set forth in this Declaration can be fully realized.'

Some judicial authorities, such as *Filartiga* v *Pena-Irala*,[28] consider the UDHR as reflective of customary international law. In the *United States Diplomatic and Consular Staff in Tehran* case, the ICJ treated fundamental human rights principles, as defined by the UDHR, as legal norms capable of application against a sovereign state.[29] The UN Security Council, General Assembly and other principal organs of the UN have severally relied on the UDHR norms either in elaborating particular resolutions or in mapping out their political actions. The Security Council has invoked the UDHR to dispatch military operations, impose economic sanctions, mandate arms inspections, and deploy human rights and election monitors, and take other actions.

The General Assembly, for its part, has adopted several resolutions bearing on global peace, all of which tend to provide the material evidence for the existence of the right to peace. In 1981, the Assembly declared that the opening day of its regular session in September 'shall be

18 C. Tomuschat, 'International Law: Ensuring the Survival of Mankind on the Eve of the New Century', *Recueil des Cours*, 23 (1999), pp. 1ff.

19 UN Charter, note 17 above, Preamble.

20 UDHR, note 3 above, Preamble.

21 See Louis Henkin *et al.*, *International Law: Cases and Materials*, 2nd edn (St. Paul, MN: West Publishing, 1987), p. 987.

22 UDHR, note 3 above, Preamble.

23 Paul Kennedy, *The Parliament of Man: The Past, Present, and Future of the United Nations* (New York: Random House, 2006), p. 180.

24 *Ibid.*, p. 179.

25 *Ibid.*, p. 181.

26 See UDHR, note 3 above, Preamble.

27 *Ibid.*, Art. 26(2). Cf. International Covenant on Economic, Social and Cultural Rights, adopted 16 December 1966, entered into force 23 March 1976, 993 UNTS 3 (hereinafter ICESCR), Art. 13(1).

28 *Filartiga* v *Pena-Irala,* 630 F.2d 876 (2n Cir. 1980).

29 *United States Diplomatic and Consular Staff in Tehran (U.S.* v *Iran)*, 1980 I.C.J. 3, at 42.

officially dedicated and observed as the International Day of Peace (IDP) and shall be devoted to commemorating and strengthening the ideals of peace both within and among all nations and peoples'.[30] In 1984, the Assembly adopted the Declaration on the Right of Peoples to Peace[31] expressing, *inter alia*, 'the will and the aspirations of all peoples to eradicate war from the life of mankind and, above all, to avert a world-wide nuclear catastrophe'.[32] Such resolutions are material sources for the future formation of custom.

The right to peace is predicated on some underlying principles. The first principle is the *a priori* and indisputable universal desirability of peace; that is, the importance of humane values in both historic concepts of peace and calculations for the future. The second principle is the implied proposition that all rationally acceptable political purposes can be achieved without aggression. These principles give rise to the concept of the unity of humankind, a 'common humanity', in an increasingly complex and interdependent world.[33] Principles of humanity 'have obvious connections with general principles of law and with equity'.[34] In the *Corfu Channel* case, the International Court of Justice (ICJ) acknowledged 'elementary considerations of humanity, even more exacting in peace than in war'.[35]

Some publicists believe that there is emerging a 'culture of peace'; that is, 'an approach to life that seeks to transform the cultural roots of war and violence into a culture where dialogue, respect, and fairness govern social relations'.[36] The Declaration on a Culture of Peace defines a 'culture of peace' as 'a set of values, attitudes, traditions and modes of behaviour and ways of life' based on certain factors and fostered by an enabling national and international environment conducive to peace.[37] The factors that underpin this culture are respect for life, ending of violence, and promotion and practice of non-violence through education, dialogue and cooperation; full respect for the principles of sovereignty, territorial integrity and political independence of states, and non-intervention in matters which are essentially within the domestic jurisdiction of any state; full respect for and promotion of all human rights and fundamental freedoms; commitment to peaceful settlement of conflicts; and efforts to meet the developmental and environmental needs of present and future generations. Others are respect for and promotion of the right to development; respect for and promotion of equal rights and opportunities for women and men; respect for and promotion of the right of everyone to freedom of expression, opinion and information; and adherence to the principles of freedom, justice, democracy, tolerance,

30 General Assembly Resolution 36/67 (1981). The IDP received a reaffirmation by another assembly resolution of 4 June 1998. See GA Res. 52/232 (1998).

31 Declaration on the Right of Peoples to Peace, GA Res. 39/11 of 12 November 1984 (hereinafter 'Declaration on the Right to Peace').

32 *Ibid.*, Preamble.

33 See John Fried, 'The United Nations' Report to Establish a Right of the Peoples to Peace', *Pace Yearbook of International Law*, 2 (1990), pp. 24ff.

34 Ian Brownlie, *Principles of Public International Law* (Oxford: Oxford University Press, 2003), p. 27. Cf. Peter Macalister-Smith, *International Humanitarian Assistance: Disaster Relief Actions in International Law and Organization* (Dordrecht: Martinus Nijhoff, 1985), p. 55, stressing that considerations of humanity have become 'the principles of the UN Charter'.

35 *Corfu Channel*, I.C.J. Rep. 4, para. 22 (9 April 1949).

36 Douglas Roche, 'The Human Right to Peace: Ethics and Policy', 4th World Summit of Nobel Peace Laureates, Rome, 28 November 2003 [online]. Available from: www.gsinstitute.org/docs/Rome03_Roche.pdf [accessed 8 October 2009].

37 Declaration of a Culture of Peace, note 12 above, Art. 1.

solidarity, cooperation, pluralism, cultural diversity, dialogue and understanding at all levels of society and among nations.[38]

If we assume the existence of the right to a PWO, who are its beneficiaries? Vasak, in his now largely discredited 'generations' metaphor,[39] classifies the right to peace among the 'third generation of solidarity rights', alongside the rights to development, to environment, to the ownership of the common heritage of mankind, and to communication.[40] If we maintain Vasak's division, then the right to peace is a collective, albeit unenforceable, right within the category of human needs.[41] Indeed, the Declaration on the Right to Peace '[s]olemnly proclaims that the *peoples* of our planet have a sacred right to peace' (emphasis added).[42] The African Charter on Human and Peoples' Rights (ACHPR)[43] equally vests the right to peace on 'peoples', guaranteeing to all peoples the right to national and international peace and security.[44] The ACHPR further provides that the principles of solidarity and friendly relations implicitly affirmed by the UN Charter and reaffirmed by the Charter of the Organization of African Unity (OAU) 'shall govern relations between states'.[45] The recognition of these 'collective rights' is 'a reply to the new challenges and ambitions which are placed before us'.[46] Peace is probably the greatest human need today.

The right to a PWO educes a correlative obligation of conduct and result. The obligation of conduct entails non-interventionist behaviour from the state, such as refraining from carrying out, sponsoring or tolerating any practice, policy or legal measures violating the integrity of the individual.[47] The obligation of result entails 'a positive expectation on the part of the State to move its machinery towards the actual realisation of the rights'.[48] These obligations – to preserve, promote and realize peace – fall on the international community as a whole, including states. Thus, the Declaration on the Right to Peace obligates states to preserve peace and promote its implementation, including the renunciation of the use of force in international relations.[49] States must also direct their policies towards eliminating the threat of war, particularly nuclear war.[50]

---

38 *Ibid.*

39 E.g. Cees Flinterman, 'Three Generations of Human Rights', in Jan Berting *et al.* (eds), *Human Rights in a Pluralist World* (London: Meckler, 1990), p. 76, describing the periodization of human rights as misleading – as it implies a hierarchy within human rights standards – and insisting that such periodization is incompatible with the indivisibility of human rights, which is a necessary concomitant of inclusive universality.

40 See Karel Vasak, 'For the Third Generation of Human Rights: The Right of Solidarity', Inaugural Lecture, Tenth Study Session, International Institute of Human Rights, July 1979, p. 3. See also Karel Vasak, 'A 30-Year Struggle', *UNESCO Courier*, 11 (1977), pp. 29ff.

41 See Joyce, note 16 above.

42 Declaration on the Right to Peace, note 31 above, para. 1.

43 African Charter on Human and Peoples' Rights, adopted 27 June 1981, entered into force 21 October 1986, OAU Doc CAB/LEG/67/3/rev. 5, reprinted in (1982) 21 *I.L.M.* 59 (hereinafter African Charter).

44 *Ibid.*, Art. 23.

45 *Ibid.*

46 Flinterman, note 39 above, p. 78.

47 See *Social & Economic Rights Action Center* v *Nigeria*, Comm. No. 155/96, 2001–2002 African Annual Activity Report, Annex V (hereinafter *SERAC*), para. 52.

48 *Ibid.*, para. 47.

49 See Declaration on the Right to Peace, note 31 above, para. 3.

50 *Ibid.*

3. The Perpetual Search for a 'Perpetual Peace'

The two gruesome world wars of the twentieth century[51] induced the international community to invent peace as a policy goal, perhaps the most important change in international relations in the second half of that century.[52] The Great Powers adopted the UN Charter in the twilight of World War II to hammer out a post-1945 new world order, in the same way that the constellation of large victor powers led to the League of Nations to regulate the post-1919 world order. The UN Charter was adopted, *inter alia*, to save succeeding generations from another scourge that could threaten not just 'untold sorrow' but, with the invention of atomic and nuclear weapons, the 'ultimate doom'. The charter replaces the anarchy of nations with the hegemony of a world government or, at least, a collective security system.[53] It creates a strict rule against the use of force and an almost inviolable presumption favouring state sovereignty.

The UN Charter obligates its member states to 'settle their international disputes by peaceful means' and to 'refrain in their international relations from threat or use of force'.[54] It prohibits threats to peace, breaches of peace and acts of aggression, and vests the Security Council with authority to determine when these thresholds are crossed and the power to recommend appropriate measures to prevent or suppress them,[55] including, where inevitable, 'war for peace'.[56] The principles of solidarity and friendly relations contained in the Declaration on Principles of International Law Concerning Friendly Relations and Co-operation Among States in Accordance with the Charter of the United Nations of 1970[57] similarly prohibits threat or use of force by states in settling disputes. Principle 1 provides:

> Every state has the duty to refrain in its international relations from the threat or use of force against the territorial integrity or political independence of any state, or in any other manner inconsistent with the purposes of the United Nations. Such a threat or use of force constitutes a violation of international law and the Charter of the United Nations and shall never be employed as a means of settling international issues.

The constitutive instruments of regional organizations also prohibit the use of force in inter-state relations. The Charter of the Organization of American States (OAS)[58] provides: 'The American States bind themselves in their international relations not to have recourse to the use of force,

51 World War II, in particular, claimed 40 million lives [online]. Available from: www.worldwar2database.com/html/frame5.htm.

52 Cf. Robert Cooper, *The Breaking of Nations: Order and Chaos in the Twenty-First Century* (London: Atlantic Books, 2004), p. 111.

53 Cf. *Ibid.*, p. 23.

54 UN Charter, note 17 above, Art. 2(4). On non-use of force, see Lori Fisler Damrosch and David J. Scheffer (eds), *Law and Force in the New International Order* (Boulder, CO: Westview Press, 1991).

55 See UN Charter, note 17 above, Art. 39. See also Art. 24 (vesting the Security Council with responsibility to maintain international peace and security).

56 *Ibid.*, Art. 42 (permitting the Security Council to authorize the use of force to secure international peace and security).

57 Declaration of Principles of International Law Concerning Friendly Relations and Co-operation Among States in Accordance with the Charter of the United Nations, adopted 24 October 1970, GA Res. 2625 (XXV), UN GAOR, 25th Session, Suppl. No. 28, UN Doc. A/8028/ (1970), reprinted in (1970) 9 *I.L.M.* 1292 (hereinafter Friendly Relations Declaration).

58 Charter of the Organization of American States, 30 April 1948, 2 UST 2394, 119 UNTS 3, entered into force 13 December 1951), reprinted in 33 ILM 981 (1994) (hereinafter OAS Charter).

except in the case of self-defence in accordance with existing treaties or in fulfillment thereof.'[59] The Constitutive Act of the African Union (AU)[60] equally prohibits the use or threat of force against any member state.[61] These treaty obligations, which form the essence of contemporary world legal order, 'are incompatible with any claims of a self-asserted right to violence in the interest of any specific State or group of persons'.[62]

The perpetual peace paradigm is based on the theory of multi-polarity, which posits that a PWO is possible when numerous systems of power rely on interdependence, interconnection, and cooperative interaction.[63] However, the adversarial decade of the Cold War slowed down any modest advance towards a PWO.[64] The Western bloc created the North Atlantic Treaty Organization (NATO) in 1949 while the Eastern bloc established the Warsaw Pact – officially called 'Treaty of Friendship, Cooperation and Mutual Assistance' – in 1955. This 'war system', which institutionalized violence, was opposed to the UN 'peace system'. Thus, '[t]he strategic interests of the superpowers superseded the altruism of the [UN's] original mandate. Development assistance became a tool of ideological propaganda, while the defence of territorial rights became a pretext for proxy wars and elaborate balancing games.'[65] President Roosevelt's idea of the Security Council as 'a board of directors of the world', responsible for 'enforcing the peace against any potential miscreant',[66] fell flat.

Superpower politics and policies, coupled with realpolitik (foreign policy based on considerations of power as opposed to ideals), complicated the process of state making in many developing countries. World powers unashamedly engaged in backstabbing and infighting, with little or no concern for ex-colonies struggling with state or nation building. The USA was a primary obstacle in preventing the spread of democracy. Its goal to contain Soviet influence and suppress the proliferation of communism resulted in increased foreign aid and political alliances, including aid to rogue regimes such as that of Zaire's (now the Democratic Republic of Congo (DRC)) Mobutu Sese Seku.[67] Such overt acts or wilful indifference paved the way for dictatorships, coups, and wars. The Cold War bipolarity might have prevented World War III, but it certainly contributed to state failures and collapse in such countries such as Somalia, Liberia, the DRC, Haiti, Sri Lanka, and Lebanon.

The end of the Cold War saw the dismantling of alliances and the beginning of globalization. The post-Cold War world order not only 'widened possibilities for strengthening a culture of peace',[68] but also provided the global community with a platform to construct a new paradigm for

---

59 *Ibid.*, Art. 21.

60 Constitutive Act of the African Union (AU), adopted 11 July 2000, entered into force 26 May 2001, OAU Doc. CAB/LEG/23.15 (2000).

61 See *ibid.* Art. 4(f).

62 Fried, note 33 above, p. 22.

63 See Tyler Moselle, 'The Concept of World Order', 19 June 2008 [online]. Available from: www.hks.harvard.edu/cchrp/research/ConceptOfWorldOrder_Moselle.pdf [accessed 6 October 2009].

64 See Secretary-General, *An Agenda for Peace: Preventive Diplomacy, Peacemaking, and Peace-Keeping,* U.N, Doc. S/24111, A/47/277 (17 June 1992) (hereinafter *An Agenda for Peace*), para. 2.

65 Takashi Inoguchi, 'The United Nations' Role in Global Security: Peace Builder or Peace Enforcer?', in Muthiah Alagappa and Takashi Inoguchi (eds), *International Security Management and the United Nations* (Tokyo: UN Press, 1999), pp. 1ff, at p. 2.

66 Henry Kissinger, *Diplomacy* (New York: Simon & Schuster, 1995), p. 395.

67 See, generally, R. Falk, *Explorations at the Edge of Time: The Prospects for World Order* (Philadelphia: Temple University Press, 1992).

68 Declaration on a Culture of Peace, note 12 above, Preamble.

world peace. The period enabled the UN Security Council to broaden its interpretation of threats to international peace and security. The phrase has come to include matters that hitherto would have been deemed to be within the domestic domain of states, such as extreme human rights violations.[69] The authorization of force against Iraq to liberate Kuwait in 1991 was a watershed in terms of Security Council activism under Chapter VII of the UN Charter,[70] but other milestones include the authorization of humanitarian military interventions in Somalia[71] and Rwanda[72] and the use of force to restore democratic government in Haiti.[73] The end of the Cold War also enabled the UN to bring an end to several protracted wars in Central America and parts of Africa.[74]

An Agenda for Peace,[75] *A More Secure World*,[76] and similar strategic documents embody the global community's hunger for security in an increasingly insecure world. *A More Secure World* – a Report of the High-Level Panel on Threats, Challenges and Change – addressed key security concerns, including collective security, the use of force, sustainable development, peacekeeping, and terrorism. Recognizing past failures at collective security, the report recommended changes that could be made within the UN system to enable it to address contemporary security challenges. It called on the global community to step in to assist in providing or developing capacity to provide protection where needed.

The development of advanced capitalist democracies at the 'end of history' was expected to lead to a perpetual peace model – similar to Emmanuel Kant's vision – predicated on trade, economic interdependence and the avoidance of war.[77] According to Kant,

> the *spirit of commerce* sooner or later takes hold of every people, and it cannot exist side by side with war. And of all the powers (or means) at the disposal of the power of the state, *financial power* can probably be relied on most. Thus states find themselves compelled to promote the noble cause of peace, though not exactly from motives of morality [original emphasis].[78]

---

69 See, generally, S. Chesterman, *Just War or Just Peace: Humanitarian Intervention and International Law* (Oxford: Oxford University Press, 2001).

70 See C. Gray, 'From Unity to Polarisation: International Law and the Use of Force against Iraq', *European Journal of International Law*, 13 (2001), pp. 1–19, at p. 2–3.

71 See Security Council Resolution 794 (Granting the Secretary-General Discretion in the Further Employment of Personnel of the UN Operation in Somalis), SC Res. 794, 47 UN SCOR at 63, UN Doc. S/Res/794 (1992).

72 See Security Council Resolution 978 (On Arrest and Detention of Persons Responsible for Acts Within the Jurisdiction of the International Tribunal for Rwanda), S/Res/978(1995).

73 See Security Council Resolution 841, UN Doc. S/Res/841 (1993).

74 See *Report of the High-Level Panel on Threats, Challenges and Change: A More Secure World: Our Shared Responsibility*, UN Doc. A/59/565 (17 November 2004) (hereinafter *A More Secure World*), para. 12.

75 See the Secretary-General, *An Agenda for Peace: Preventive Diplomacy, Peacemaking and Peace-Keeping*, UN Doc. S/24111, A/47/277 (17 June 1992) (hereinafter *An Agenda for Peace*).

76 See *A More Secure World*, note 74 above (putting forward a new vision of collective security that addresses all of the major threats to international peace and security felt around the world).

77 See Francis Fukuyama, *The End of History and the Last Man* (New York: Free Press, 1992).

78 See Immanuel Kant, 'Perpetual Peace: A Philosophical Sketch', in Hans Reiss (ed.), *Kant's Political Writings* (New York: Cambridge University Press, 1970), p. 114. Cf. Bruce Russett and John Oneal, *Triangulating Peace: Democracy, Interdependence, and International Organizations* (New York: Norton, 2001), p. 154 ('Higher levels of economically important trade, as indicated by the bilateral trade-to-GDP ratio, are associated with fewer incidences of militarized international disputes').

Thus, Kant 'relied upon international commerce to create ties of mutual advantage that would help make republics pacific'.[79]

Why, despite the UN Charter, the UDHR, and the 'end of history', has the perpetual search for peace produced a perpetual war?[80] Why has the bright new dawn perceived years ago by the post-World War II global community turned into a rather cloudy, if not to say, drizzly, day with occasional thunderstorms? What are the threats to a PWO and how should the global community confront them? The next section attempts to answer these and related questions.

4. Continuing Threats to a PWO

Everything has changed; nothing has changed. That is the paradox in which the world finds itself. This final section examines some factors – including aggression, conflicts, poverty, and inequality – that continue to threaten the realization of a PWO and offers some prescriptions. Mindful that '[e]very threat to international security today enlarges the risk of other threats',[81] this chapter calls on the global community as a whole to rise to the challenge of cooperation and proffer realistic and realizable solutions to economic, social, health and related problems, including higher standards of living, full employment, social progress and development. We all desire peace, but willing the end is one thing and willing the means quite another.

4.1 Aggression and Erosion of Human Rights

The incessant use of armed force against the sovereignty and territorial integrity of other states[82] contravenes the well-established principle of international law that states should settle their disputes by peaceful means in such a manner that international peace, security and justice are not endangered. Powerful states increasingly wage a war of aggression against weaker states, notwithstanding that such an act 'constitutes a crime against the peace, for which there is responsibility under international law'.[83] Many consider the contemporary human rights project as an American project;[84] indeed, George W. Bush described the USA as '*the* beacon of freedom

---

79 Michael W. Doyle, 'Kant, Liberal Legacies, and Foreign Affairs', *Philosophy and Public Affairs*, 12 (1983), pp. 205–35, 323–53, at p. 350.

80 See, *passim*, Robert A. Divine, *Perpetual War for Perpetual Peace* (College Station, TX: A&M University Press, 2000).

81 *A More Secure World*, note 74 above, para. 20.

82 See Definition of Aggression, GA Res. 3314 (XXIX), UN GAOR, 2319th Meeting (1974), Art. 1 (defining aggression as 'the use of armed force by a State against the sovereignty, territorial integrity or political independence of another State, or in any other manner inconsistent with the Charter of the United Nations'). Cf. AU Non-Aggression and Common Defence Pact, adopted 31 January 2005 (not yet in force), Art. 1(c) [online]. Available from: www.africa-union.org (defining aggression as 'the use, intentionally and knowingly, of armed force or any other hostile act by a State, a group of States, an organization of States or non-State actor(s) or by any foreign or external entity, against the sovereignty, political independence, territorial integrity and human security of the population of a State Party to this Pact, which are incompatible with the Charter of the United Nations or the Constitutive Act of the African Union').

83 Friendly Relations Declaration, note 57 above, Principle 1.

84 E.g. Tony Evans, *US Hegemony and the Project of Universal Human Rights* (Basingstoke: Macmillan, 1996), arguing that while the USA was instrumental in establishing the 'idea of human rights as a dominant theme in international relations', rhetoric, powerful political and economic interests undermined the emergence of a strong international regime for the protection of human rights.

in the world' (original emphasis).[85] Yet, in recent years, the USA has embraced illiberal policies, propelled by the erroneous belief that 'one power capable of exerting international influence can stabilize the world and function as a quasi-international enforcer of laws and order in a more adequate manner than other alternative forms'.[86]

The arrogant claims of the USA to supremacy in world-views have resulted in 'hegemonic globalization'[87] verging on empire.[88] One explanation is that the weakening of the Soviet power led to 'fewer physical constraints on the excesses of U.S. Liberalism'.[89] Balance of power, some argue, is the best guarantee for a PWO.[90] Another explanation is that the central objective of the USA is to prevent, at all cost, the re-emergence of a new global rival, which could emerge if a hostile power or coalition gained hegemony over a critical region.

Most of the world's raging infernos have leaped from US and European campfires, aided by the technological sophistication of cruelty that now defines the great democracies of the earth. The West has deliberately locked the world in a state of permanent emergency by melding World War II with the Cold War and the Cold War with the war on terror. In this terrifying new world, '[a]ll values are becoming subsumed within the value of security, justifying the use of force in an ever-broadening set of circumstances'.[91] The so-called 'war on terror' has eroded human rights worldwide and rubbished international law.[92] In spite of – or, not inconceivably, because of – this 'war paradigm', 'We are not more secure. We are more divided, and peoples are more cynical about the operation of laws.'[93] The concept of human rights, like the law, has become an ass,[94] whereby universality results in a 'permanent battlefield of political power between or within states, in which the rich "good guys" interfere in the affairs of the poor "bad guys"'.[95]

Powerful states increasingly deploy human rights to justify their brutality and hide their capacity for bloodthirsty acts, just as the Nazi nightmares resulted from Hitler's project to create a better world! Human rights were some of the justifications for the 1991 Gulf War, in which an estimated

---

85 Quoted in Bob Woodward, *Plan of Attack* (New York: Simon & Schuster, 2004), p. 88.

86 Moselle, note 63 above (continuing: 'This template is similar to arguments justifying Empires (particularly the Roman model) where laws, transportation, communication, and a host of other issues were standardized, protected, and enforced by a single, unified power').

87 The term refers to the USA as 'a hegemonic power that oversees and orchestrates world order partially as a result of, and enhanced by, the current phase of globalization'. See *ibid.*

88 See Michael C. Desch, 'America's Liberal Illiberalism: The Ideological Origins of Overreaction in U.S. Foreign Policy', *International Security*, 32(3) (2007–8), pp. 7–43.

89 *Ibid.*, p. 9.

90 E.g. K.R. Cox and T.J. Sinclair, *Approaches to World Order* (Cambridge: Cambridge University Press, 1996), chapters. 2 and 3.

91 Jutta Brunnée and Stephen Toope, 'The Use of Force: International Law After Iraq', *International Comparative Law Quarterly*, 53 (2004), pp. 785–806, at p. 787.

92 See Nsongurua Udombana, 'Battling Rights? International Law and Africa's War on Terrorism', *African Yearbook of International Law*, 13 (2006), pp. 67ff, p. 70, observing: 'The war on terrorism has made so many inroads into the rule of law and human rights as to render both concepts almost meaningless'.

93 Laura MacInnis, 'U.S. "War on Terror" Eroded Rights Worldwide: Experts', *Reuters*, 16 February 2008 (quoting Mary Robinson) [online]. Available from: http://news.yahoo.com/s/nm/20090216/ts_nm/us_counterterrorism.

94 The phrase 'The law is an ass' originates in Charles Dickens, *Oliver Twist* (1838). When the character, Mr Bumble, is informed that 'the law supposes that your wife acts under your direction', he replies, 'if the law supposes that, the law is a ass – an idiot'.

95 Ulrich Beck, *Power in the Global Age* (Cambridge: Polity Press, 2005), p. 66.

100,000 Iraqis died.[96] Human rights also figured prominently during the 2003 US aggression against Iraq, preceded by a tsunami of propaganda for a war of aggression contrary to international law. The so-called coalition forces involved in that aggression committed and still commit inexcusable atrocities against non-combatants,[97] not to mention harsh detentions and interrogations and the rendition policy. Among the most elementary of moral truisms is the principle of universality, which posits that one should apply to himself the same standards he applies to others, if not more stringent ones. For the USA, says Chomsky, '[t]here is a straightforward single standard: *their* terror against us and our clients is the ultimate evil, while *our* terror against them does not exist – or, if it does, is entirely appropriate.'.[98]

The USA under President George W. Bush engaged in a reinterpretation of laws and treaties that once seemed immutable, including something as fundamental as the lawfulness of using torture to interrogate terrorist suspects.[99] Basic rules of international humanitarian law (IHL) that the international community had long taken as representing customary law, even *jus cogens*, were given new interpretations, influenced by mere expediency. Moral philosophers invent the theory of 'consequentialist' ethics to explain such a phenomenon.[100] The theory posits that good or moral ends may justify the morally questionable means by which they are achieved, but such a vile philosophy hurts human rights, encourages impunity around the world, and endangers world peace.[101]

The global community must come together to restore the universal human rights that have been bartered for the soggy mess of political opportunism and military adventurism. The use of torture and extralegal imprisonment in fighting terrorism creates a breach of the rule of law, accelerates the race to the bottom in human rights, and ties anti-terrorism policies in knots.[102] Refreshingly, President Barack Obama has reversed some of Bush's obnoxious policies and shifted the paradigm of US diplomacy from unilateralism to multilateralism. This 'new climate in international politics' has justly won Obama the Nobel Peace Prize,[103] but the award is a call to further action on human rights, including closing the Guantánamo Bay detention camp and ending the abuses of US counterterrorism policy.[104] No precedent can justify absurdity.

---

96 See Joy Gordon, 'The Concept of Human Rights: The History and Meaning of Its Politicization', *Brooklyn Journal of International Law*, 23 (1998), pp. 689ff, at p. 789.

97 See Joan Fitzpatrick, 'Speaking Law to Power: The War Against Terrorism and Human Rights', *European Journal of International Law*, 14(2) (2003), pp. 241–64.

98 See Noam Chomsky, *Failed States: The Abuse of Power and the Assault on Democracy* (London: Hamish Hamilton, 2006), p. 5.

99 See Karen Greenberg and Joshua Dratel (eds), *The Torture Papers: The Road to Abu Ghraib* (New York: Cambridge University Press, 2005) (a shocking account of how the Bush administration's policy of torture in the questioning of prisoners held on suspicion of terrorist activities evolved).

100 See, generally, S. Darwall (ed.), *Consequentialism* (Oxford: Blackwell, 2003); T. Mulgan, *The Demands of Consequentialism* (Oxford: Clarendon Press, 2001).

101 A report on counter-terrorism and human rights recently released by the Geneva-based International Commission of Jurists (ICJ) found that many democratic states have referred to US counter-terrorism practices to justify their own abuses. See MacInnis, note 93 above.

102 See Udombana, 'Battling Rights?', note 92 above, p. 70.

103 Mark Silva, 'President Obama Wins a Nobel Peace Prize', *Los Angeles Times*, 9 October 2009 (quoting the Nobel Committee) [online]. Available from: www.latimes.com/news/nationworld/world/la-fg-obama-nobel10-2009oct10,0,7971377.story.

104 See 'Nobel Spotlight Need for Obama to Act on Human Rights', *Human Rights Watch*, 9 October 2009 (calling on President Obama to stand up for persecuted human rights activists and to end the debacle at Guantánamo) [online]. Available from: www.hrw.org/en/node/86028?tr=y&auid=5442678 [accessed 10 October 2009].

4.2 Conflicts

Civilization and conflicts are antithetical concepts; yet inter- and intra-state conflicts have continued unabated in this modern age. The Middle East remains the most war-torn region in the world, and its instability is a persistent threat to a PWO. Africa, for its part, accounts for nearly 40% of all current international wars.[105] War of any nature is never without its atrocities, never without its casualties among the innocent, its abuses of human rights, and its general debasement of humanity. All contemporary wars, like the previous ones, violate the basic protections afforded by IHL, including –

> (a) violence to life, health, or physical or mental well-being of persons, in particular: i) murder; ii) torture of all kinds, whether physical or mental; iii) corporal punishment and iv) mutilation; (b) outrages upon personal dignity, in particular, humiliating and degrading treatment, enforced prostitution and any form of indecent assault.[106]

In *Democratic Republic of the Congo* v *Burundi, Rwanda and Uganda*,[107] the African Commission on Human and Peoples' Rights held the armed occupation of the DRC by neighbouring African states and the subsequent acts of vandalism as contravening 'the well-established principle of international law that states shall settle their disputes by peaceful means in such a manner that international peace and security and justice are not endangered'.[108]

The Security Council has a greater role to play towards achieving a PWO. However, it will require a united and tougher action, particularly by the veto-wielding members, to confront the common threats to universal peace. As noted earlier, the council, in several of its resolutions, has held that internal and international conflicts could constitute threats or breaches of the peace, depending on their intensity and their impacts on regional and international security. The council has held that the conflict in Darfur, Sudan, constitutes a threat to peace,[109] but the council has failed to take tougher action to force the government of Sudan to end the atrocities. More than 300,000 civilians have died in state-sponsored violence since 2003. Yet, '[a]s in Rwanda, the world watches while the catastrophe worsens. The Security Council is busy playing dice with lives, holding endless closed-door meetings and passing countless, often self-serving, but utterly meaningless resolutions.'[110] Meanwhile, another crisis is looming in the southern flank of Sudan, as the global

105 See Nsongurua Udombana, 'The Unfinished Business: Conflicts, the African Union and the New Partnership for Africa's Development', *George Washington International Law Review*, 35 (2003), pp. 55ff, at p. 63.

106 Protocol Additional to the Geneva Conventions of August 12, 1949, and Relating to the Protection of Victims of International Armed Conflicts, 15 August 1977, 16 *I.L.M.* 1391 (hereinafter First Protocol), Art. 75(2).

107 *Democratic Republic of the Congo* v *Burundi, Rwanda and Uganda* (2004) AHRLR 19 (finding the respondent states in violation of several articles of the African Charter on Human and Peoples' Rights and urging them to abide by their obligations under conventional and other applicable international principles of law and to withdraw their troops immediately from the complainant's territory).

108 *Ibid.*, para. 75.

109 E.g. Security Council Resolution 1706, adopted at its 5519th meeting, 31 August 2006, S/Res/1706 (2006), Preamble ('*Determining* that the situation in the Sudan continues to constitute a threat to international peace and security') (original emphasis).

110 Nsongurua Udombana, 'Still Playing Dice with Lives? Darfur and Security Council Resolution 1706', *Third World Quarterly*, 28(1) (2007), pp. 97ff, at p. 110 (continuing: 'These failings in stopping mass atrocities across the globe cast a shadow over the UN's policing mechanism').

community fails to find a Solomonic solution to the thorny question of the ownership of oil wells in Abieye.

Some have also argued, chillingly, that without progress towards peace in the Middle East, the festering Israeli/Palestinian-Arab conflict could 'precipitate a military confrontation involving the use of nuclear weapons'.[111] If the parties to the conflict show progress in lighting the fires of moderation, the international community should encourage them by fanning the flames. The Security Council, in particular, should not only energize the Middle East peace process but also come up with a more effective strategy to roll back Iran's, as well as North Korea's, nuclear programmes. Otherwise, the UN could become another League of Nations, a naïve, toothless enterprise that provided a tragic wellspring of World War I.

The international community as a whole should do more to strengthen global and regional institutions for conflict prevention and peace-building. There is currently no mechanism in the UN system explicitly designed to avoid state collapse and slide into war or to assist countries as they move from war to peace. The High-Level Report proposes the creation of three interlinked organs: a Peace-Building Commission, a Peace-Building Support office in the UN Secretariat, and a second deputy secretary-general for peace and security matters.[112] It further recommends that the UN Secretariat should have a Strategic Analysis staff, who should have autonomous eyes and ears to scan ahead and a capacity to follow up.[113] These operational innovations, if faithfully implemented, could be of much value to states while simultaneously protecting the sovereignty of individuals.[114] The UN should collaborate more with regional organizations particularly in the area of early response to conflicts.

The global community should expedite and conclude negotiations on a treaty on the marking and tracing, brokering and transfer of small arms and other light weapons.[115] Arms control agreements between the big world powers have focused on weapons of mass destruction (WMD) and sophisticated weapons system, such as nuclear and chemical weapons, but it is light weapons – rocket-propelled grenades, landmines, mortars, etc. – that cause most casualties in dirty 'little' internal conflicts.[116] International financial institutions (IFIs), including the Bretton Woods sisters, should provide material support for mechanisms involved in conflict prevention, management, resolution, and peacekeeping initiatives. In the past, such processes have not brought real peace because the community – donors and multilateral institutions – failed to fully meet the challenge of engaging to consolidate the processes. Donors should also invest in building a strong civil society network for regional peace-building.

The collapse of authoritarianism in many states put many developing and former socialist states on the path to becoming robust, if somewhat confusing, democracies, and provided hope for achieving political integration between and within democracies. Democracy may not be a perfect system; it 'is not even a system of government that fully embodies all democratic ideals, but [it is] one that approximates them to a reasonable degree'.[117] Human rights flourish the most under

---

111 Jimmy Carter, *Palestine: Peace Not Apartheid* (New York: Simon & Schuster, 2006), p. 12.

112 See *A More Secure World*, note 74 above, Recommendations 82–5 and 95.

113 *Ibid.*, para. 294.

114 See Gwyn Prins, 'Lord Castlereagh's Return: The Significance of Kofi Annan's High Level Panel on Threats, Challenges and Change', *International Affairs*, 81(2) (2005), pp. 373–91, at p. 390.

115 *A More Secure World*, note 74 above, para. 96.

116 See Kumer Rupesinghe, 'Conflict Transformation', in Kumer Rupesinghe (ed.), *Conflict Transformation* (New York: St. Martin's Press, 1995), pp. 65ff, at p. 70.

117 Arend Lijphart, *Democracy in Plural Societies: A Comparative Exploration* (New Haven, CT: Yale University Press, 1977), p. 4.

a democratic government, with independent judiciaries to safeguard individual freedoms. Letting people rule themselves – which is what democracy does – advances world peace as well. Peace is further advanced through the creation of 'a positive, dynamic participatory process where dialogue is encouraged and conflicts are solved in a spirit of mutual understanding and cooperation'.[118]

To be sustainable, democracy must take each nation's historical and cultural idiosyncrasies as its point of reference. Peace flourishes only in an inclusive and audacious environment – an environment that advances understanding, tolerance and solidarity among all civilizations, peoples and cultures, including ethnic, religious and linguistic minorities. The 'clash of civilizations' must give way to a 'universal cultural legitimacy', given the world's varied cultural milieux. Democracy might be a universal ideal, but it should not be seen as an antithesis to religion and culture, which 'are the most important sources of restraint in a society'.[119] 'Liberalism,' writes Owen, 'is no final solution to the problem of war, it must not be allowed to efface all other values in international life.'[120]

4.3 Poverty and Inequality

The increased polarization of wealth and poverty is one of the incidences of globalization, and one that threatens its sustainability.[121] Certainly, globalization has improved the quality of life and lifted millions of people out of poverty; it has created opportunities to expand wealth, acquire knowledge and skills, improve access to goods and services, and increase life expectancy in some countries. Private capital circulating the world economy has created new opportunities, but it has also destroyed old ones, 'thereby giving rise to both employment and unemployment in both the developing and the developed world'.[122] Large numbers of the world's population have been pushed to the fringe of society, and no institutional finance is available to overcome the social security needs arising from globalization.[123]

There are many causes of poverty in the world, but the contemporary neo-liberal economic order is a prime cause of this evil in developing countries. The global economic disorder created by unfair international trade has complicated developing countries' efforts at economic self-reliance. Although many developing countries attained *de jure* independence many decades ago, they are still under the *de facto* economic domination of developed countries. Massive outlay of government support for Western industries imperils the movement towards free trade. Developed countries' requirements of developing countries' primary commodities have dwindled due to the former's protectionist policies. A PWO is possible only in a world of equitable spread of the wealth,

---

118 Declaration on a Culture of Peace, note 12 above, Preamble.

119 Thomas Friedman, 'No Way, No How, Not Here', *New York Times*, 18 February 2009, p. A27 [online]. Available from: www.nytimes.com/2009/02/18/opinion/18friedman.html?em [accessed 18 February 2009].

120 John M. Owen IV, 'International Law and the "Liberal Peace"', in Gregory H. Fox and Brad R. Roth (eds), *Democratic Governance and International Law* (New York: Cambridge University Press, 2000), pp. 343ff, at p. 385.

121 See New Partnership for Africa's Development Framework Document (2001) [online]. Available from: www.iss.co.za/AF/RegOrg/unity_to_union/pdfs/oau/keydocs/NEPAD.pdf (hereinafter NEPAD), para. 35.

122 Commission on Human Rights, Sub-Commission on the Promotion and Protection of Human Rights, U.N. ESCOR, 53rd Session, 20th meeting at para. 20, UN Doc. E/CN.4/Sub.2/2001/SR.20 (2001) (hereinafter ECOSOC, Summary Record of 20th Meeting).

123 *Ibid.* See also Report of the United Nations High Commissioner for Human Rights, para. 6, U.N. ESCOR, 51st Session, UN Doc. E/1999/96.

ownership and control of productive resources that would eventually guarantee a movement away from the circles of poverty, squalor and dependency.[124]

Realizing the right to a PWO demands policies directed at eliminating the threat to war, particularly nuclear war,[125] and the spread of WMD. Eradicating poverty and illiteracy and reducing inequalities within and among nations will aid a PWO. The ability of the North to integrate the South may help mitigate a host of these and other problems – including disease, and sexual and racial discrimination – and generally advance human security. According to Slaughter, human security is –

> the security of each individual from death or violence, not the state worrying about its own existence as a state, but the actual security of each individual within a state. From this perspective – of human security – it really doesn't matter if you die from a bullet or you die from AIDS or you die from hunger. What matters is that you die.[126]

'Everyone is crying out for peace, yes. None is crying out for justice.' In those opening lyrics of *Equal Rights*,[127] the legendary singer Peter Tosh opted for 'justice' rather than 'peace', not that peace and justice are mutually exclusive, but because there can be no peace without justice. A more equitable IEO, for example, could engender peace by advancing prosperity and reducing poverty.[128] Economic misery anywhere threatens peace and security everywhere, whereas economic justice begets peace, absolutely. Contrary to Kant's 'perpetual peace' model, there is nothing inherent in the current globalization process that automatically reduces poverty and inequality;[129] and inequality polarizes the world society. Hatred exploits the brutalities of poverty and oppression; and terrorism 'flourishes in environments of despair, humiliation, poverty, political oppression, extremism and human rights abuse'.[130] Humans are driven to desperation and extremism by a sense of denial and closure. The most dangerous creation of any society is the man who has nothing to lose.

Governments 'should be sensitive to the root causes of social unrest and dislocations and should correct observed anomalies, especially those relating to better opportunities, justice and equity'.[131] No society can flourish when the greater part of its members are poor and miserable. One measure of a nation's greatness lies in the scrupulousness with which it ensures that justice is served to

---

124 See Shadrack Gutto, 'Modern "Globalisation" and the Challenges to Social, Economic and Cultural Rights for Human Rights Practitioners and Activists in Africa', *African Legal Aid*, Oct.–Dec. (2000), pp. 12ff, at p. 13.

125 See Declaration on the Right to Peace, note 31 above, para. 3.

126 Anne-Marie Slaughter, 'A New U.N. for a New Century', *Fordham Law Review*, 74 (2006), pp. 2961ff, p. 2963. Cf. UNDP, *Human Development Report 1994* [online]. Available from: www.undp.org/hdro/e94over.htm [hereinafter *Human Development Report 1994*] ('Most people instinctively understand what security means. It means safety from the constant threats of hunger, disease, crime and repression. It also means protection from sudden and hurtful disruptions in the pattern of our daily lives – whether in our homes, in our jobs, in our communities or in our environment').

127 Peter Tosh, *Equal Rights* (1977) (a musical album advocating human rights and political equity and calling on oppressed people to 'Get Up, Stand Up' for their rights).

128 See Nsongurua Udombana, 'A Question of Justice: The WTO, Africa, and Countermeasures for Breaches of International Trade Obligations', *John Marshall Law Review*, 38 (2005), pp. 1153–1204, at p. 1178.

129 See NEPAD, note 121 above, para. 40.

130 *A More Secure World*, note 74 above, p. 145.

131 Nsongurua Udombana, 'Life, Dignity, and the Pursuit of Happiness: Human Rights and Living Standards in Africa', *University of Tasmania Law Review*, 28(1) (2008), pp. 47–82, at p. 81.

all its citizens, regardless of their station. Politics or public choice that discounts the people is unsustainable; in the end, the conditions lead to cleavages that provoke social collapse. In contrast, improvements in living standards of the marginalized offer massive potential for increasing economic capacities and growth, 'stability on a global scale, [and] ... a sense of economic and social well-being'.[132]

The global community must take active measures to 'make the world safe for democracy', to use Woodrow Wilson's famous phrase. There can be no democracy without peace and no peace without development. As the UNESCO Declaration puts it, 'Peace, development and democracy form an interactive triangle. They are mutually reinforcing. Without democracy, there is no sustainable development: disparities become unsustainable and lead to imposition and domination.'[133] A culture of peace supports cooperation and social justice. It 'promotes sustainable development for all, free human rights, and equality between men and women. It requires genuine democracy and the free flow of information. It leads to disarmament.'[134]

5. Conclusion

The right to a PWO is not just an ideal; it is a foundational and fundamental right. As the Declaration on Right to Peace puts it, 'life without war serves as the primary international prerequisite for the material well-being, development and progress of countries, and for the full implementation of the rights and fundamental human freedoms proclaimed by the United Nations.'[135] The establishment of a lasting peace in this nuclear age 'represents the primary condition for the preservation of human civilization and the survival of mankind'.[136] The emerging security issues – civil war, disease, climate change, nuclear proliferation, poverty, terrorism, money laundering, and transnational criminality – demand '[a] new kind of international law and internationalist spirit'.[137] These global challenges require a global response, because if nuclear proliferation is allowed to take hold, the losers will be not only the West but 'all those people who have an interest in an orderly world'.[138] No price is too high to pay for peace.

The global community must play the whole keyboard in order to establish an international society where shared goals and interests, rather than aggression or threat thereof, fertilize inter-state relations; where the lights of the UDHR and its progenies illuminate state and non-state activities; and where ideals of justice animate global economic enterprise. The UN (including its member states) and other institutions of global and regional governance – the World Trade Organization, IMF, World Bank, EU, African Union, OAS, *etc.* – must collaborate to promote 'social progress and better standards of life in larger freedom'.[139] Systems of governments do not exist in the abstract, but in their consequences for peoples in the present and in succeeding generations.

132 See NEPAD, note 121 above, para. 38.

133 UNESCO Declaration, note 15 above.

134 Roche, note 36 above.

135 Declaration on the Right to Peace, note 31 above, Preamble.

136 *Ibid.*

137 Anne Orford, *Reading Humanitarian Intervention: Human Rights and the Use of Force in International Law* (Cambridge: Cambridge University Press, 2003), p. 2.

138 Cooper, note 52 above, p. ix.

139 UN Charter, note 17 above, Preamble.

The choice facing the world is 'stark and dreadful and inescapable: shall we put an end to the human race; or shall mankind renounce war?'[140] Who knows! The world could renounce war in the next few decades and end the perpetual search for a perpetual peace. This is no more than a possibility, really, but one thing is certain: no state, no matter how powerful, can achieve a PWO alone. It is easier to win a war alone than to win a peace alone. Only in an environment of cooperative interaction may this age of violence mellow into peace.

140 Bertrand Russell and Albert Einstein, *New York Times*, 10 July 1955, quoted in Chomsky, note 98 above, p. 3.

Chapter 8

Minority Rights 60 Years after the UDHR: Limits on the Preservation of Identity?

Tawhida Ahmed and Anastasia Vakulenko

1. Introduction

The international response to the question of what to do with 'minorities' has been far from static, oscillating between assimilationist and protectionist attitudes. The current trend rests on a sharp turn from international law's previously passive attitude towards diversity to one which values pluralism and recognizes the need to preserve identities of all groups in society. The impetuses for this were numerous, not least the stark recognition that unity of identities which the nation-state model pursued was simply not working either to protect the basic rights of some individuals or, fundamentally, to address the types of tensions and conflicts in the world which the international community sought to prevent. There have been signs, therefore, since the 1970s and 1980s that the international community has incorporated into its human rights rhetoric, activities and instruments, the ideal of respect for plurality of identities. Nonetheless, as this chapter demonstrates, the recent case law before the Human Rights Committee (HRC) and the European Court of Human Rights (ECtHR) do not always follow a preservation of identity approach. Although international law appears to have a pluralist vision, on closer examination this is rather limited.

That this resistance to the concrete recognition and protection of minority rights, even today, pervades the – still Western state-centric – international arena is not surprising, given the practical implications that the recognition of minority rights holds for the autonomy with which the modern nation state can regulate its own territory. These practical implications are perhaps more far-reaching than those involved in the recognition of any other set of human rights. Minority rights go to the heart of what defines the very essence of individuals, their beliefs and belongingness. Negotiating the boundaries and legitimacy of such beliefs in legal terms is indeed an insurmountable challenge at times, which may not always produce an outcome favourable to the minority. This chapter argues that even where this is the case, international courts and tribunals, at the very least, need to be more transparent and elaborate in more detail the grounds on which they reach their decisions than they have done to date. A failure to do so puts forward an image of an international judicial body that is reluctant to uphold the pluralist identity agenda projected by international law.

The chapter proceeds in two sections. Section 2 provides an outline of the development of minority rights in international law. Particular attention is paid to the fluidity of strategies adopted at the international level, especially between the objective of preserving identities and that of individual rights and equal citizenship. Section 3 provides an analysis on how the use – or lack of use – of these ideas plays out in one controversial case facing the world today – that of the religious and cultural rights of women who wear the Islamic headscarf or other forms of Islamic dress. The chapter aims at interrogating the underlying reasoning and the practical impact of the decisions in international case law on this topic. It thus also provides a current picture of the extent to which international law is effective in addressing the contemporary identity problems faced by Muslim women.

The analysis asserts that the ECtHR's and the HRC's attention to diversity and pluralism has been expanded in recent years, as shown by their approach to other minority issues. However, in relation to the Islamic headscarf cases, their interpretations are more restrictive. Further, the particular ways in which the two institutions have been restrictive also fail to do justice to the preservation of identity strategy that the international community seems to have explicitly adopted. They fail to do this justice either because they do not accommodate the idea of 'preservation of identity' or because the reasoning of the judgements fails to explain clearly the link between the manifestation of religion through the wearing of the headscarf and the harm it supposedly entails.

2. Development of Minority Rights in International Law: An Overview

While a comprehensive commentary on the development of minority rights is not feasible, a brief overview of milestones and the situation as it presently stands is given here in order to frame the subsequent analysis of the Islamic dress cases. The historical development of minority rights, both domestically and internationally, has been imbued by two opposing philosophies[1] – assimilation[2] and preservation of identity.[3]

The UDHR[4] adopted in the first years of the United Nations (UN) system for international cooperation makes no mention of the rights of minorities. It embodies instead a range of other rights, such as the rights to life, liberty, security of persons, fair trial, freedom of expression, privacy and family life. This lack of explicit reference to minority rights reflected the overall attitude of the UN at the time of its creation. The UN system provided no legal guarantees to preserve minorities as separate or different from the rest of the population of a state. Minority rights were not addressed in the UN Charter and were in fact on the UN agenda as a whole in only a small measure.[5] This bears a strong contrast to the targeted nature of minority rights protection which existed before 1948, arising from the post-Reformation European peace treaties and also from the subsequent League of Nations system (1919), which monitored various (*ad hoc*) treaty obligations through legal and political mechanisms.[6]

Instead, the UN's approach to rights focused on two different goals: first, facilitating self-determination in the colonial context; and, second, on a more universal level, promoting individual human rights, in particular non-discrimination, for all persons in all states. The implied rationale for the latter was that members of minority groups would be adequately protected by rights to individual equality and that recognition of any special rights beyond that would accentuate

1 Although the reality of legal policies is not as clear-cut as this classification suggests, the model is useful in assisting in identifying the underlying essence of the case law concerning Islamic dress.

2 Assimilation refers to the absorption of minority groups into the majority society, so that differences between groups in society are not maintained.

3 P. Thornberry, 'An Unfinished Story of Minority Rights', in A. Biro and P. Kovacs (eds), *Diversity in Action: Local Public Management of Multi-Ethnic Communities*. Local Government and Public Service Reform Initiative (Budapest: Open Society Institute, 2001), pp. 45–73, at p. 52; K. Henrard, *Devising an Adequate System of Minority Protection, Individual Human Rights, Minority Rights and the Right to Self-Determination* (The Hague: Martinus Nijhoff, 2000), pp. 11–13.

4 GA Res. 217A (III), UN Doc. A/810 at 71 (1948).

5 The Convention on the Prevention and Punishment of the Crime of Genocide 1948; the establishment of the Sub-Commission on Prevention of Discrimination and Protection of Minorities 1946.

6 See e.g. H. Rosting, 'Protection of Minorities by the League of Nations', *American Journal of International Law*, 17(4) (1923), pp. 641–60.

differences and provoke political instability and disorder. Thus, homogeneity, and not pluralism, was the intention of the international community, which mirrored the concerns of states. The same attitude prevailed across the European sphere, culminating in the adoption of the European Convention for the Protection of Human Rights and Fundamental Freedoms (ECHR) in 1950, which neglected to include a minority rights provision.

The homogeneous basis of human rights is, however, problematic for minorities on theoretical and practical levels alike. A basic level of non-discrimination leaves no room for plurality and access to rights over and above or different from those available under equal citizenship. Further, because the equal citizen is usually modelled on the dominant majority group in the state, minorities are entitled to only those rights that are available to the majority group. This inevitably leads to some level of assimilation, which, contrary to the belief of the state, fosters ill-feeling of the minority towards the majority and leads to conflicts. As such, attempts by the international community to de-emphasize the differences between groups did not lead to homogeneous societies living in harmony. Ethnic minority tensions in Africa, the Balkans and the Mediterranean provide testimony to this.

Consequently, the international community underwent a certain re-evaluation with respect to minority concerns. Two main types of international law developments that essentially entail the better preservation of identity reflect this process.

The first type is the development of minority-specific instruments and institutions, and the second is the interpretation of general human rights in a minority rights-friendly manner. The introduction of minority-specific instruments and institutions signalled a move away from the sole reliance on general human rights and anti-discrimination. The UN Sub-Commission on Prevention of Discrimination and Protection of Minorities, which was established in 1946,[7] began to pay more attention to minorities directly.[8] A specific minority rights provision was introduced in one of the most significant general human rights treaties adopted to date: Article 27 of the International Covenant on Civil and Political Rights (ICCPR).[9] This article, the UN's explicit provision on minority rights protection, asserts that

> In those States in which ethnic, religious or linguistic minorities exist, persons belonging to such minorities shall not be denied the right, in community with the other members of their group, to enjoy their own culture, to profess and practice their own religion or to use their own language.

Article 27 of the ICCPR is directed at ensuring the survival and continued development of the minority identity.[10] It requires both negative and positive measures of support from states,[11] which are intended to achieve real equality: ‘minorities are dependent on active support from their States in order to preserve their cultural, linguistic and religious identity. Otherwise, they cannot over the long run withstand the assimilationist pressure normally exercised by the dominant

---

7 The name was changed from Sub-Commission on Prevention of Discrimination and Protection of Minorities to Sub-Commission on the Promotion and Protection of Human Rights in July 1999 by ECOSOC decision 1999/256 of 27 July 1999. The Sub-Commission on the Promotion and Protection of Human Rights was also replaced by the Human Rights Council Advisory Committee in 2006.

8 In its early years, it largely ignored minority issues. For an analysis of the role of the sub-commission, see P. Thornberry, *International Law and the Rights of Minorities* (Oxford: Clarendon Press, 1991), ch. 12.

9 999 UNTS 171, adopted on 16 December 1966, entered into force on 23 March 1976.

10 General Comment 23(50), para. 9.

11 *Ibid.*, paras. 6.1 and 6.2.

majority.'[12] Indeed, although Article 27 is phrased as a right of individuals, it has a group element: 'in community with other members of their group'. This has been confirmed by the jurisprudence of the HRC.[13]

In addition to Article 27 of the ICCPR and largely due to the experiences of the Cold War, the (non-binding) UN Declaration on the Rights of Persons Belonging to National or Ethnic, Religious and Linguistic Minorities was adopted in 1992,[14] the Working Group on Minorities was established in 1995,[15] and an Independent Expert on Minority Issues was introduced in 2005 to promote the implementation of the UN Declaration within states, by engaging both with governments and non-governmental organizations. Further, the 1981 Declaration on the Elimination of All Forms of Intolerance and of Discrimination Based on Religion or Belief[16] represents the UN's attempt to provide the right to freedom of religion some specialist legal protection. Additional relevant mechanisms include the UN Convention on the Prevention and Punishment of the Crime of Genocide (1948),[17] the International Labour Organization (ILO) Convention on Indigenous and Tribal Peoples (No. 169) of 1989,[18] the UN Declaration on the Rights of Indigenous Peoples of 2007,[19] and the continuing efforts of the UN Permanent Forum on Indigenous Issues, which promotes the rights of indigenous communities. The general objective of these developments was, and remains, the preservation of identity through a preventive approach to breaches of minority rights.[20]

At the same time as these global developments, the Council of Europe (CoE) has produced legal and policy instruments affecting minority rights both generally and under specialized minority units. It introduced the European Charter for Regional or Minority Languages (ECRML)[21] in 1992 and the Framework Convention for the Protection of National Minorities (FCNM)[22] in 1994. Although these instruments contain escape clauses and weak phraseology, the underlying language is still in sharp contrast to the previous equality stance of the CoE in relation to diversity within states.[23] The CoE also has a group of experts on the Roma minority as well as the European Commission against Racism and Intolerance. Moreover, Protocol 12

12 M. Nowak, *UN Covenant on Civil and Political Rights: CCPR Commentary* (Kehl: N.P. Engel, 1993), p. 662.

13 *Chief Ominayak and the Lubicon Lake Band* v *Canada*, CCPR Communication No. 167/1984; *Ivan Kitok* v *Sweden*, CCPR Communication No. 197/1985.

14 Adopted by General Assembly Resolution 47/135 of 18 December 1992.

15 The Working Group on Minorities was established in 1995 as a subsidiary organ of the Sub-Commission on the Promotion and Protection of Human Rights (previously called the Sub-Commission on Prevention of Discrimination and Protection of Minorities). In 2007, the Working Group was replaced by the Forum on Minority Issues, established by Human Rights Council Resolution 6/15.

16 Adopted by General Assembly Resolution 36/55 of 25 November 1981.

17 78 UNTS 277, adopted on 9 December 1948, entered into force on 12 January 1951.

18 72 ILO Official Bulletin 59, adopted on 27 June 1989, entered into force on 5 September 1991.

19 Adopted by General Assembly Resolution 61/295 of 13 September 2007.

20 G. Pentassuglia, *Minorities in International Law* (Strasbourg: Council of Europe Publishing, 2002), p. 34.

21 ETS No. 148, adopted by the Committee of Ministers of the Council of Europe on 25 June 1992, entered into force on 1 March 1998.

22 ETS No. 157, adopted by the Committee of Ministers of the Council of Europe on 10 November 1994, entered into force on 2 January 1998.

23 For instance, Article 5 of FCNM mandates states to promote essential elements of minority identity. Article 7 of ECRML promotes the teaching and study of regional and minority languages, as well as facilitating their use in private and public life.

to the ECHR guarantees an independent right of non-discrimination to persons on grounds of membership of national minority groups, thus finally overcoming the limits of Article 14 of the ECHR.[24]

There is thus an array of international law mechanisms in place for the protection of minority rights which attempt to support a preservation of identity approach. Although there is no legally binding definition of the term 'minority',[25] an important point to note is the emphasis by, *inter alia*, the HRC[26] and the CoE[27] in some aspects of their activities, on self-identity. Self-identity essentially connotes autonomy. It refers to the right of individuals to decide whether or not they belong to a minority (although an individual cannot choose arbitrarily to belong to any minority without some objective links to that identity).

The second type of development at international level concerning minorities is the interpretation of general human rights provisions in a manner which takes into account their minority dimensions. Thus, the particular interpretation given in a decision or judgement is informed by the fact that the applicant is a member of a minority group. For example, In Lovelace v Canada,[28] the HRC considered that a law which restricted residence in Indian reserves to certain Indian groups was a breach of the freedom of residence of others (Article 12 of the ICCPR) but that, together with Article 27, it was justified by reference to the need to protect and preserve the identity of the Indian indigenous community. Article 12 was therefore given a certain minority dimension. Under Article 14 of the ICCPR, procedural rights within states have also been interpreted with a minority dimension. Thus, states must take into account the effect that financial penalties in judicial proceedings may have on disadvantaged minority groups.[29] In addition, Article 14 provides linguistic minorities with the right to conduct court proceedings in the language of their choice if they are insufficiently proficient in the official language of the court.[30]

With respect to freedom of expression and association, international decisions have been protective of the political activity of minorities.[31] A democratic society cannot automatically dissolve a political party just because it seeks solutions for the needs of a minority group, even if that party calls for secession. Any exceptions to this under Articles 10 and 11 of the ECHR, together with the state's margin of appreciation in the field, are strictly construed.[32] Similarly, taking measures against a group for materials they published in relation to the situation or claims of a minority group is disproportionate to Article 10 of the ECHR.[33] The ECtHR in *Sidiropoulos and Others*

24 Article 14 is only operative in conjunction with a substantive convention right.

25 The most authoritative definition is that provided by F. Capotorti, *Study on the Rights of Persons Belonging to Ethnic, Religious and Linguistic Minorities* (New York: UN, 1991), para. 568.

26 *Lovelace* v *Canada*, CCPR Communication No. 6/24.

27 Article 3(1) FCNM.

28 Note 26 above.

29 *Aarela and Nakkalajarvi* v *Finland*, CCPR Communication No. 779/1997.

30 *Guesdon* v *France*, CCPR Communication No. 219/1986.

31 Article 19 ICCPR and Article 10 ECHR. See e.g. at the UN, *Aduayom et al.* v *Togo*, CCPR Communications Nos 422–424/90, and *Kivenmaa* v *Finland*, CCPR Communication No. 412/90, and, at the ECHR, *Incal* v *Turkey* (1998), 29 EHRR 449, which confirm that state arguments concerning security and territorial integrity will be strictly scrutinized.

32 See e.g. *Socialist Party and Others* v *Turkey* (1999), 25 EHRR 51; *Freedom and Democracy Party* v *Turkey*, Reports of Judgements and Decisions 1999-VIII; and *Stankov and the United Macedonian Organisation Ilinden* v *Bulgaria* (1998), 26 EHRR CD 10.

33 *EK* v *Turkey*, Judgement of 7 February 2002, Application No. 28496/95, and *Association Ekin* v *France*, Judgement of 17 July 2001, Application No. 39288/98. The ECtHR in *Gorzelik and Others* v

v *Greece*[34] maintained that 'the existence of minorities and different cultures in a country was a historical fact that a "democratic society" had to tolerate and even protect and support according to the principles of international law'.[35]

Further, international law principles have emerged on the right to a way of life of a minority. The right to privacy, family life and the home[36] allows for a broad spectrum of minority lifestyle features to be brought into play in the human rights field. Under Article 17 of the ICCPR (privacy and family life), the HRC has held that minorities are entitled to register names in accordance with their religious affiliation.[37] The HRC has given a broad interpretation to the term 'family', to include ancestors based on 'family' as understood in the cultural traditions of an indigenous group.[38] With regard to Article 8 of the ECHR, 'home' is widely interpreted to include the caravan site of gypsies,[39] and, as illustrated in *Connors* v *UK*,[40] it imposes a positive obligation on states to facilitate the gypsy way of life. To this end, freedom of movement provisions in the ECHR[41] can facilitate a right to practise nomadic lifestyles by guaranteeing non-discrimination in relation to movement. Finally, in relation to anti-discrimination, the *D and H* case (at the ECtHR)[42] indicates a willingness to recognize indirect discrimination of state policies against minority groups. In this case, pupils who fell below a certain level of an intelligence test were placed in special schools which demanded less in terms of academic ability and hence affected their eventual employment prospects. The fact that the overwhelming majority of the children placed in these schools were of Roma origin constituted indirect discrimination.

All of these factors indicate that while the international community is committed to an individual and equality-based protection of human rights, there is accommodation within that and beyond that for the protection of the diverse needs of different groups in society. The preservation of identity

---

Poland, Judgement of 20 December 2001, Application No. 44158/98 has provided that an exception to this is only acceptable where there is a clear demonstration that the applicant association is hiding its violent objectives. Although this is based on speculation, *Sidiropoulos and Others* v *Greece*, Judgement of 10 July 1998, Application No. 26695/95 ensures that this exception is strictly construed.

34 *Ibid.*

35 *Sidiropoulos*, note 33 above. While issues such as seeking language rights, or even a federal system or the advocacy of secession, were not regarded as threatening democracy in order to justify dissolving a party, a political system based on the religious divisions was regarded as automatically contrary to the needs of a democratic society (here involving an Islamic group). See *Refah Partisi (the Welfare Party) and Others* v *Turkey*, Judgement of 13 February 2003, Application Nos 41340/98, 41342/98, 41343/98 and 41344/98.

36 Articles 17 and 23 ICCPR; Article 8 ECHR.

37 *Coeriel and Aurik* v *The Netherlands*, Communication No. 453/1991.

38 *Hopu and Bessert* v *France,* CCPR Communication No. 594/93. See U. Kilkelly, *The Right to Respect for Family and Private Life: A Guide to the Implementation of Article 8 of the European Convention on Human Rights.* Human Rights Handbook No. 1 (Strasbourg: Council of Europe, 2001), pp. 18–19, for relevant cases; also ECHR cases *Marckx* v *Belgium,* Judgement of 13 June 1979, Application No. 6833/74, para. 31; *Al-Nasif* v *Bulgaria*, Judgement of 20 June 2002, Application No. 50963/96, para. 112; *Johnstone and Others* v *Ireland,* Judgement of 18 December 1986, Application No. 9697/82, para. 55. See, further, S. Holt, 'Family, Private Life and Cultural Rights', in Weller (ed.), *Universal Minority Rights: A Commentary on the Jurisprudence of International Courts and Treaty Bodies* (Oxford: Oxford University Press, 2007), pp. 203–52, at pp. 208–9.

39 *Burton* v *United Kingdom* (1996), 22 EHRR CD 135; *Buckley* v *United Kingdom* (1997), 23 EHRR 101. See also *Connors* v *UK* (2005), 40 EHRR 9; *Chapman* v *United Kingdom* (2001), 33 EHRR 399.

40 *Connors* v *UK* (2005), 40 EHRR 9.

41 Protocol 4, Articles 2, 3 and 4, especially Article 2.

42 *DH and others* v *The Czech Republic* (2008), 47 EHRR 3.

thus frames the rhetoric and values of the system of international protection of human rights in the present. International courts and tribunals have been implementers of this approach and, at times, initiators in that regard. As noted at the outset, however, the case of the Islamic headscarf contradicts this approach and provides little support for the elements which require preservation of identity. It is to this case study that the chapter now turns.

3. The Islamic Headscarf as a Case Study

For some years, various prohibitions on the wearing of the Islamic headscarf have been the stuff of international news as well as human rights litigation within the UN and Council of Europe systems. Current international human rights law tends to view such cases under the more general, 'universal rights' heading of religious freedom, protected by Article 9 of the ECHR and Article 18 of the ICCPR respectively. Yet, the Islamic headscarf is also an obvious minority issue as it is a uniquely Muslim practice. This part of the chapter will show how international human rights law provides a less than robust form of protection against national assimilationist policies in respect of the headscarf. This is an arguably incompatible outcome with the currently prevalent preservation of identity rhetoric.

The failure is twofold. First, where some sort of understanding of preservation of identity can be found in the cases, the adjudicating bodies' approach still falls short of the international community ideal (as explained in the previous part of the chapter). There is a big question mark over the acceptance of the headscarf as a manifestation of the Islamic religion (in other words, a minority identity). Second, the adjudicating bodies fail to clearly spell out their reasons for refusing the applicant's claim; in other words, to explain the link between the manifestation of religion through the wearing of the headscarf and the harm it supposedly entails. The chapter proceeds accordingly.

3.1 The Headscarf as a Manifestation of Islamic Identity

To begin with, there has been a reluctance in international human rights jurisprudence to accept that Islamic headscarves could even be an issue of freedom of religion, as protected by human rights law. In *Senay Karaduman* v *Turkey*,[43] a university graduate could not obtain a provisional certificate confirming her qualifications because the university rules required her to submit a photograph with an uncovered head in order for such a certificate to be issued. She alleged breaches of Article 9 of the ECHR (freedom to manifest one's religion, 'in public or private', in 'worship, teaching, practice and observance') and Article 14 of the ECHR, which prohibits discrimination in the exercise of other ECHR rights on a number of grounds – in this case nationality. The case originated in Turkey. Although Turkey's population is overwhelmingly Muslim, in a certain sense Muslims are a minority in Turkey. Numerical status is not decisive in determining whether a group qualifies as a minority, with vulnerability and political non-dominance being more important factors.[44] Practising Muslims have thus been a consistently disadvantaged group in Turkey since

43 (1993) 74 DR 93. See also *Bulut* v *Turkey*, Admissibility Decision of 3 May 1993, Application No. 18371/91.

44 Thus, the black majority were a non-dominant minority in apartheid South Africa. Likewise, the Shi'ite majority lacked political power and were suppressed by the numerically inferior Sunnis in pre-2003 Iraq.

the change of regime in 1923, when Turkey embraced Western-style democratic secular values.[45] The wearing of Islamic headscarves is considered to be antithetical to these, and has been legally restricted since the 1930s as part of Turkey's thorough secularization.[46] Thus, Muslims who want to wear a headscarf are a minority – as opposed to the officially endorsed 'modern' secular(ized) Turkish identity – if not numerically.

The *Karaduman* case did not pass the admissibility stage, having been declared 'manifestly unfounded'. As regards the Article 9 complaint, the European Commission on Human Rights (ECmHR) was of the opinion that the article in question 'does not always guarantee the right to behave in public in a way dictated by this conviction', and that 'the term "practice", in the sense of paragraph 1 of Article 9 … does not denote any act motivated or inspired by a religion or a conviction'.[47] This essentially meant casting Islamic headscarves outside the scope of Article 9 (which was the primary legal basis on which the case was decided).

This stance can be contrasted with previous decisions of the HRC under the UN human rights system. In one decision, a turban worn by a Sikh man was accepted by the committee as a manifestation of his religion.[48] In Boodoo v Trinidad and Tobago,[49] the beard of a Muslim man was regarded as one element of his manifestation of the Islamic religion. In addition, in General Comment 22, the HRC stated that '[t]he observance and practice of religion or belief may include not only ceremonial acts but also such customs as ... the wearing of distinctive clothing or headcoverings ...'.[50]

The ECmHR's ruling that the headscarf worn by the applicant in *Karaduman* does not in this case represent a manifestation of the Islamic religion seems out of line with this approach, particularly because the applicant's contention that she wore the headscarf for religious purposes was ignored. This reluctance at the initial step of human rights protection is problematic for the preservation of identity approach. It takes away the right of the individual to decide which aspects of his or her actions are of a religious representation and therefore the autonomy and freedom to shape his or her own identity.

In 2001, the ECtHR delivered its decision as to the admissibility of the case of *Dahlab* v *Switzerland*,[51] which involved a teacher in a state school who had been wearing an Islamic headscarf to work for five years before she was asked to remove it. The reasons for the objection were similar to the Turkish ones; that is, the need to protect the constitutionally embedded principles of denominational neutrality (the Swiss equivalent of secularism) and gender equality. Before the ECtHR, *Dahlab* relied on Articles 9 and 14 of the ECHR (alleging discrimination on the grounds of sex). Like Karaduman's, Dahlab's case was also declared 'manifestly ill-founded', but the

45 The principle of secularism received constitutional recognition in Turkey as long ago as 1937. Gender equality provisions were also introduced around that time. According to Article 2 of the current, 1982 constitution, '[t]he Republic of Turkey is a democratic, secular (*laik*) and social state governed by the rule of law; bearing in mind the concepts of public peace, national solidarity and justice; respecting human rights; loyal to the nationalism of Atatürk' (English translation [online]. Available from: http://www.byegm.gov.tr/mevzuat/anayasa/anayasa-ing.htm).

46 See the Dress Regulations Act of 3 December 1934, Law No. 2596.

47 See *Senay Karaduman* v *Turkey*, note 43 above, p. 100.

48 *Singh Bhinder* v *Canada*, Communication No. 208/1986, UN Doc. CCPR/C/37/D/208/1986 (9 November 1989).

49 Communication No. 721/1996, CCPR/C/74/D/721/1996 (2 April 2002).

50 HRC, *General General Comment 22*, Article 18 (Forty-Eighth Session, 1993), UN Doc. CCPR/C/21/Rev.1/Add.4 (30 July 1993), para. 4.

51 2001-V 447.

ECtHR's reasoning in this decision is more detailed, and is generally regarded as a critical point in the development of the ECHR jurisprudence on Islamic headscarves.

In contrast to Karaduman, Dahlab argued that she wore the headscarf for aesthetic, and not for religious, reasons. The Federal Court in Switzerland was unwilling to accept this, describing the headscarf as a 'manifest religious attribute in this case',[52] which derives from passages of the Koran,[53] and which 'may even be said to constitute a "powerful" religious symbol'.[54] The ECtHR seemed to be in agreement with these findings. There are two implications of this. First, the ECHR institutions demonstrate incoherency and contradiction: in *Karaduman*, the headscarf was regarded as not necessarily a manifestation of religion, whereas in *Dahlab* it was considered to be so without doubt. Secondly, the passages of the Koran in *Dahlab* are taken at face value, even though the interpretation of the Koran is not so straightforward and the significance attached to each religious practice varies among individuals. Again, therefore, as in *Karaduman*, the views of the particular applicant in the case were dismissed. Although affiliation to an identity must also have an objective dimension,[55] that identity is not sustainable without subjective input from the individual whose identity is being examined. Courts thus ought to integrate the views of the applicant more seriously or justify in detail any rejection of the subjective element of identity formation. *Dahlab* is all the more concerning as the case was declared inadmissible despite the ECtHR's views that wearing a headscarf was an expression of a religious identity.

An interesting argument was advanced in the case of *Şen and Others* v *Turkey*, in which the applicants had been discharged from the Turkish Army for their alleged fundamentalist leanings.[56] Among other claims, they invoked Article 8 of the ECHR (which protects the right to respect for private and family life), referring to their wives' headscarves as 'their families' and their wives' way of life and behaviour'.[57] This arguably brings out the minority dimension of the issue, as minority rights protection in international human rights law includes protecting a distinctive way of life. The ECtHR did not respond to this argument, appearing to accept the Turkish government's contention that 'their wives' and relatives' Islamic scarves had not been taken as the sole basis for their discharge from the army',[58] thus declaring the complaint inadmissible. Arguably, a court committed to the preservation of identity would have been more forthcoming in scrutinizing this claim, even if it were only one of the reasons for the applicants' dismissal.

In *Şahin* v *Turkey*,[59] the applicant was a medical student at Istanbul University. In accordance with the Vice Chancellor's circular, she was prevented from attending some lectures and examinations because she wore an Islamic headscarf, and was eventually suspended. The ECtHR, although retaining the right to find that not every wearing of a headscarf amounts to a manifestation of religion, finally conceded that prohibitions on wearing Islamic headscarves in educational establishments *could* raise an issue under Article 9 of the ECHR. It thus accepted that the Islamic headscarf is an element of the Islamic identity of sufficient significance to fall within the parameters of Article 9.

52 *Ibid.*, 6–7.

53 *Ibid.*, 2–3.

54 *Ibid.*, 2–3.

55 See e.g. HRC, General Comment 23, UN Doc. CCPR/C/21/Rev.1/Add.5 (8 April 1994), para. 5.2.

56 Admissibility Decision of 8 July 2003, Application No. 45824/99 at 9. See also *Dal and Özen* v *Turkey*, Admissibility Decision of 3 October 2002, Application No. 45378/99; and *Baspinar* v *Turkey*, Admissibility Decision of 3 October 2002, Application No. 45631/99.

57 *Şen*, *ibid.*, p. 9.

58 *Ibid.*

59 (2007) 44 EHRR 5.

This should not, however, be seen as the beginning of settled jurisprudence on the issue. Şahin also pleaded a violation of Article 14, claiming that she had been discriminated against on the basis of her religion. This was rejected as 'the regulations on the Islamic headscarf were not directed against the applicant's religious affiliation',[60] a ruling that suggests obliviousness to the complex discriminatory effects that a facially neutral provision might have. Furthermore, the ECtHR accepted that Şahin's headscarf threatened Turkey's secularism, although the dissenting opinion of Judge Tulkens pointed out that there appeared to be 'no evidence to show that the applicant, through her attitude, conduct or acts, contravened that principle'.[61] The majority of the ECtHR did 'not lose sight of the fact that there are extremist political movements in Turkey which seek to impose on society as a whole their religious symbols and conception of a society founded on religious precepts ...'.[62] The applicant, however, did not belong to any such movements or seek to impose her religious views on others.[63]

Thus, the dissenting judge pointed out that the majority 'paternalistically' denied the applicant's 'right to personal autonomy [developed] on the basis of Article 8'[64] – in other words, the right to identity at the core of minority rights. The majority's approach seems to suggest that Şahin is not able to be religious, without also being fundamentalist. It forced an identity upon her that is not hers. This runs contrary to the importance given by other elements of the international minority rights discourse to the right of self-identification, as shown earlier.

Like earlier cases, the more recent *Ilicak* v *Turkey*[65] case demonstrates the ECtHR's tendency to ignore the minority element of Islamic headscarf cases. The wearing of a headscarf by a member of the Turkish National Assembly (who belonged to an 'extremist' political party, *Fazilet Partisi*) in parliament was argued to raise a freedom of expression issue under Article 10 of the ECHR. Although this complaint was declared admissible,[66] the ECtHR considered that it was not necessary to examine it in the judgement on the merits, in view of its finding of a violation, based on the wider facts of the case, of Article 3 of Protocol 1, which guarantees voting rights. By circumventing the Article 10 aspect, the minority dimension of the case was unfortunately removed from the picture.

The cases of *Dogru* v *France*[67] and *Kervanci* v *France*[68] are the more recent ECHR cases on the issue of Islamic headscarves. Like Turkey, France has a long history of opposing the wearing of Islamic headscarves in public educational institutions. A distinctive feature of the French debate is the ideology of *laïcité*, the French version of secularism, which denotes a normative aspiration of near-total banishing of religion from the public sphere. At present, Muslims constitute the largest religious minority in France, amounting to approximately 10% of the population.

Although France takes pride in its tradition of respect for human rights and individual liberty, it is notorious for not recognizing the possibility that individual situations may be shaped by historical injustices resulting from group affiliations. Although a party to the ICCPR, France does not consider

---

60 *Ibid.*, para. 165.

61 *Ibid.*, para. 7 of the dissenting opinion of Judge Tulkens.

62 *Ibid.*, para. 115.

63 *Ibid.*, para. 14. See also para. 10 of the dissenting opinion.

64 *Ibid.*, para. 12 (citations omitted).

65 Judgement of 5 April 2007, Application No. 15394/02. See also *Silay* v *Turkey*, Application No. 8691/02, and *Kavakci* v *Turkey*, Application No. 71907/01, decided on the same day.

66 Admissibility Decision of 6 April 2004.

67 Judgement of 4 December 2008, Application No. 27058/05.

68 Judgement of 4 December 2008, Application No. 31645/04.

itself bound by Article 27 of the ICCPR.[69] Although the HRC has accepted France's declaration to this effect as a valid reservation under international law,[70] it has expressed disagreement with the official French position that there are no ethnic, religious or linguistic minorities in France.[71]

In the *Dogru* and *Kervanci* cases, in contrast, the ECtHR seems to endorse the assimilationist drive behind France's anti-Islamic headscarf policies. Both cases involved Muslim schoolgirls who had been expelled from school for refusing to remove their headscarves for physical education classes. They alleged violations of Article 9 of the ECHR and Article 2 of Protocol 1 to the ECHR (access to education). The ECtHR declared the case admissible, but found no violation of either of these provisions. It noted that the French secular model properly addresses the concern that the manifestation by pupils of their religious beliefs on school premises does not 'take on the nature of an ostentatious act that would constitute a source of pressure and exclusion'.[72] Ironically, this resulted in the applicants' own exclusion from the school and the secular model more generally. The court accepted that their expulsion from school was 'merely the consequence' of their refusal to comply with school rules 'and not of their religious convictions, as they alleged',[73] a position that appears to ignore the fact that a facially neutral provision may have a discriminatory effect on minorities and that the pupils had chosen to act on their religious convictions. There was no effort to uphold the identities desired by the applicants.

As far as the UN system of human rights protection is concerned, the leading case is *Hudoyberganova* v *Uzbekistan*,[74] which was decided by the HRC in 2005. As in Turkey, the majority of Uzbekistan's population are Muslim. However, Uzbekistan's policies in respect of Islam are clearly restrictive, making practising Muslims a 'minority', in a similar way to Turkey. The government in this post-Soviet, central Asian state is trying to reassert an official version of Uzbek identity, which implies a certain, rather 'moderate' understanding of Islam. In contrast, various proliferating, independent Islamic practices (including opening mosques and selecting imams) are perceived as a political threat. In this way, Islamic headscarves that are of a solid colour and clasped at the front are perceived as 'foreign' (in contrast with patterned scarves that loosely cover the head, which are considered to be traditional Uzbek headgear). 'Foreign' forms of Islamic apparel are prohibited in public educational institutions.

The author of the communication in *Hudoyberganova* was a student at the Farsi Department of the Faculty of Languages at the Tashkent State Institute for Eastern Languages. In her second year at university, she began to wear what is referred to as '*hijab*' in the HRC's views. She alleged that since September 1997 the administration of the institute began to seriously limit students' right to freedom of religion, including the introduction of new regulations that prohibited Islamic headscarves. Hudoyberganova was eventually excluded from the Institute. In her petition to the HRC, Hudoyberganova complained of breaches of Article 18 of the ICCPR, which protects

---

69 On accession to the ICCPR, France entered a reservation, *inter alia,* to Article 27, stating: 'In the light of article 2 of the Constitution of the French Republic, the French Government declares that article 27 is not applicable so far as the Republic is concerned.'

70 See *TK* v *France*, Annual Report of the Human Rights Committee, UN Doc. A/45/40, 118; *SG* v *France*, Annual Report of the Human Rights Committee, UN Doc. A/47/40, 346, cited in D. McGoldrick, *Human Rights and Religion: The Islamic Headscarf Debate in Europe* (Oxford: Hart, 2006), p. 46.

71 Concluding Observations on the French Report of 1997, 4 August 1997, UN Doc. CCPR/C/79/Add 80, para. 24. See also HRC General Comment 23, The Rights of Minorities, 8 April 1994, UN Doc. CCPR/C/21/Rev/1/Add.5.

72 Para. 71.

73 Para. 73.

74 UN Doc. CCPR/C/82/D/931/2000, views of 18 January 2005.

freedom of religion, and Article 19, which protects freedom of expression. The HRC found the Article 19 complaint to be unsubstantiated, but it did find a violation of Article 18. The structure of Article 18 of the ICCPR is slightly different from that of Article 9 of the ECHR, as it contains a separate provision (in paragraph 2) that prohibits coercion 'which would impair [one's] freedom to adopt a religion or belief of [one's] choice'. It is this part of Article 18 that Uzbekistan was found to be in breach of.

The HRC considered that 'the freedom to manifest one's religion encompasses the right to wear clothes or attire in public which is in conformity with the individual's faith or religion' and that, in accordance with paragraph 5 of its General Comment 22, restrictions on religious dress 'that have the same intention or effect as direct coercion, such as those restricting access to education', are inconsistent with Article 18(2).[75] The HRC felt that preventing individuals from wearing certain clothes would amount to coercion which would impair the individual's freedom to have or adopt a religion in accordance with Article 18(2). Thus, the autonomy of the individual was given importance in this case.

To sum up, the cases discussed demonstrate that the decisions of international bodies are not altogether satisfactory with respect to deciding whether the Islamic headscarf is a manifestation of a religious identity. They are based on an assessment which sometimes recognizes the right of individuals to determine their own identities, sometimes accepts the authority of the court to determine this, and sometimes makes assumptions about the headscarf based on the Koran, without any coherent policy as to when each is to be taken into account and without acknowledging the controversial nature of interpreting religious texts such as the Koran. In this first issue, therefore, insufficient attention has been paid to the right of self-identity. There is a lack of clear reasoning given for the assumptions made by the judiciary in that regard. The ECtHR, in particular, has underestimated the complex nature of religious belief and identity. It does not fully acknowledge that religion and identity are open to different interpretations and therefore are also very much dependent on the self-perception of each individual.

Is this the best outcome that the judiciary could have pursued in such a controversial issue as the Islamic headscarf? Even if so, it is difficult to reach such conclusions where opaque and insufficiently explained judgements leave little evidence in their support. Let us now consider the adjudicating bodies' justifications for their findings of no breach of the right to freedom of religion in those cases.

3.2 Justifying Restrictions on Islamic Identity

Although the Islamic headscarf may be recognized as a manifestation of Islamic religion, the freedom to wear it may still be lawfully restricted by states under international human rights law. In relation to the Islamic headscarves cases, the justifications have revolved around the need to protect the rights and freedoms of others and public order. These justifications have been given very broad interpretations at international level, placing the preservation of identity in a precarious position.

As noted earlier, in *Karaduman*, the ECmHR did not believe that the wearing of a headscarf was even covered by Article 9 of the ECHR. Yet, it was also persuaded by the state's need to prohibit the individual's wearing the headscarf on her photograph for her degree certificate. The ECmHR referred to the applicant's 'choice' to study at a secular university, and noted that such a

75 *Ibid.*, at para. 6.2, citing HRC, General Comment 22, The Right to Freedom of Thought, Conscience and Religion (Article 18), 30 July 1993, UN Doc. CCPR/C/21/Rev/1/Add.4.

status 'naturally' implied submission to certain rules (i.e. not to wear a headscarf), established in order 'to ensure respect for the rights and freedoms of others'.[76] The ECmHR also explained that such protection was justified in view of 'certain religious fundamentalist currents',[77] implying that wearing a headscarf *per se* may amount to pressure on others. The ECmHR did not provide clear reasons as to how a photograph for the purposes of the issuance of a degree certificate could amount to pressure on others, nor did it explain the link between such a photograph and the existence of certain fundamentalist currents. There is thus a glaring gap in the reasoning of the commission.

In *Dahlab*, the ECtHR agreed with the Swiss Federal Court that the measure prohibiting the schoolteacher from wearing the headscarf in school was justified by the principles of denominational neutrality and gender equality, protected by the Swiss Constitution. It did not directly address the applicant's argument that the fact that she had worn the headscarf for more than five years without attracting any complaints was sufficient proof that the beliefs of others were not interfered with. Instead, it appeared to be in tacit agreement with the Swiss Federal Court's speculation that 'some may well have decided not to take any direct action so as not to aggravate the situation, in the hope that the education authorities will react of their own motion.'[78] As an improvement on the *Karaduman* decision, there was some attempt here to provide a link between the headscarf and the rights of others. Nonetheless, that speculation – that others failed to react in order not to aggravate matters – is less than satisfactory.

The Swiss court went on to say about the applicant, '[a]dmittedly, she is not accused of proselytising or even of talking to her pupils about her beliefs'. What was the problem then? It went on to explain:

> However, the appellant can scarcely avoid the questions which her pupils have not missed the opportunity to ask. It would seem somewhat awkward for her to reply by citing aesthetic considerations or sensitivity to the cold – the approach she claims to have adopted to date, according to the file – because the children will realise that she is evading the issue.[79]

Thus, even if there is no active use of the teacher's religious views, the very fact of the display of the religion is considered sufficiently antithetical to the benefit of the pupils in the school. The ECtHR reinforced the perception of the Islamic headscarf as a threat to others, especially to Dahlab's pupils aged between 4 and 8.[80] It also considered that 'it cannot be denied outright that the wearing of a headscarf might have *some kind of proselytising effect*, seeing that it appears to be imposed on women by a precept which is laid down in the Koran.'[81] The court felt it unproblematic to reach these conclusions, even though it itself admitted that it is very difficult to assess this impact. The court thus accepted the views of the Swiss Federal Court that the wearing of the headscarf itself is sufficient for such a finding. The case thus echoes *Refah Partisi* in that any system based on religion is considered automatically problematic for ECHR rights.[82] In other words, the very notion of Islam is considered to be against human rights. In the headscarf issue, there are thus very limited avenues for the assertion of one's identity as a Muslim.

76 *Karaduman*, note 43 above, p. 101.
77 *Ibid.*
78 *Dahlab*, note 51 above, p. 450.
79 *Ibid.*, Federal Court, pp. 6–7.
80 *Ibid.*, p. 463.
81 *Ibid.*
82 *Refah Partisi*, note 35 above.

The court was also concerned that the headscarf 'is hard to square with the principle of gender equality'.[83] This was not further clarified and is at odds with Dahlab's own sex discrimination complaint.[84] As in *Karaduman*, one can question whether this link is justified by any evidence cited in the judgement. The ECtHR seems to be easily convinced that the *hijab* prescription in the Koran amounts to gender inequality. However, the gender dimension of Islam is a complex issue intertwined with cultural and historical contexts, which would have required further, more intelligent scrutiny from the court before it pronounced such a conclusion (which then itself serves as evidence of the incompatibility of the headscarf with gender equality in further cases). The philosophy of the preservation of identity would at least require a genuine attempt to understand the religious and cultural rationales behind the minority identity in question, as well as its gender and individual dimensions. Arguably, this was done by the HRC in *Lovelace* v *Canada*, in which a Maliseet Indian woman lost her Indian status when she married a non-Indian (whereas an Indian man married to a non-Indian woman would not have lost his). The HRC found the concrete rule in question to be a violation of Lovelace's Article 27 rights, which inevitably meant an acknowledgement of its discriminatory nature. This finding, however, was based on clear evidence of concrete discrimination – and this was not at all the case in *Dahlab*.

Thus, in dealing with Islamic headscarves, the ECtHR seems to follow its previously criticized commission, which found it justifiable to prohibit a Buddhist prisoner's growing his beard, to deny a rosary, or to refuse to provide a prisoner with meals commensurate with his religious faith.[85] From *Şahin* onwards, there has been some improvement, but still questions can be raised regarding the genuineness of the judiciary's attempts to preserve identity.

In *Şahin*, the restrictions imposed by the university were deemed justified in view of Article 9(2), which provides that the right to manifest one's religion is subject to 'limitations as are prescribed by law and are necessary in a democratic society ... for the protection of public order ... or for the protection of the rights and freedoms of others'. Thus, no violation of Article 9 was found, as the ban was put 'in its legal and social context'; that is, Turkey's long-standing commitment to the democratic principles of secularism and gender equality, on the one hand, and the backdrop of burgeoning extremist currents, on the other hand. The message of the headscarf was thus interpreted as clearly antagonistic to the constitutionally embedded principles of secularism and gender equality.[86] The significant point is that it is the wearing of the headscarf *per se* which is

83 *Dahlab*, note 51 above, p. 463.

84 The latter was dismissed, as the ECtHR considered that the measure 'was not directed against her as a member of the female sex' and that the law 'could also be applied to a man who, in similar circumstances, wore clothing that clearly identified him as a member of a different faith' (*ibid.*, p. 460). This is a distinctly 'formal equality', comparator-based type of reasoning, attributable to the generally underdeveloped nature of Article 14 jurisprudence. Despite Dahlab's suggestion of a Muslim man as the appropriate comparator, the ECtHR went for an abstract, 'clearly identifiable' male 'member of a different faith'. As to the ECtHR's approach to Article 14, see *Abdulaziz, Cabales and Balkandali* v *UK* (1985), 7 EHRR 471, in which the applicants, whose husbands were precluded from joining them in the UK, alleged discrimination on the grounds of both race and sex. The ECtHR approached the complaint as implying two distinct types of discrimination, despite the interaction of the two, as the immigration rule in question relied on gendered stereotypes of immigrants of Asian descent. Only sex (and not race) discrimination was found to have taken place, thus denying the applicants their minority status.

85 See Nowak, note 12 above, pp. 421 and 428. E.g. *Grandrath* v *Germany*, Application No. 2299/64 YB 626.

86 See paras. 112–13.

regarded as detrimental to democracy. The court took a broad-brush approach without requiring any further evidence of antidemocratic practice.

As noted earlier, the applicant's practice of wearing the headscarf was believed to threaten the principle of secularism, with only rhetorical statements in place of concrete evidence. Thus, the majority's approach here contrasts with that to Article 11 of the ECHR: as discussed earlier, the ECtHR usually requires *evidence* that a party or political activity is a threat to democracy, before upholding national restrictions on freedom of association. On the other hand, it is in line with the ECtHR's pronouncement in the *Refah Partisi* case that 'sharia is incompatible with the fundamental principles of democracy'.[87]

The majority's stance is also incompatible with its Article 10 case law. The incongruity is pointed out by Judge Tulkens:

> The Court has never accepted that interference with the exercise of the right to freedom of expression can be justified by the fact that the ideas or views concerned are not shared by everyone and may even offend some people. Recently, in *Gündüz v. Turkey* ... the Court held that there had been a violation of freedom of expression where a Muslim religious leader had been convicted for violently criticising the secular regime in Turkey, calling for the introduction of the sharia and referring to children born of marriages celebrated solely before the secular authorities as "bastards". Thus, manifesting one's religion by peacefully wearing a headscarf may be prohibited whereas, in the same context, remarks which could be construed as incitement to religious hatred are covered by freedom of expression.[88]

Judge Tulkens also criticizes the lack of the majority's reasoning on the link between the ban of the headscarf and sex discrimination and also its failure to take into account women's views, as mirrored in the *Dahlab* decision, examined earlier. According to her,

> It is not the Court's role to make an appraisal of this type – in this instance a unilateral and negative one – of a religion or religious practice, just as it is not its role to determine in a general and abstract way the signification of wearing the headscarf or to impose its viewpoint on the applicant. ... I fail to see how the principle of sexual equality can justify prohibiting a woman from following a practice which, in the absence of proof to the contrary, she must be taken to have freely adopted. Equality and non-discrimination are subjective rights which must remain under the control of those who are entitled to benefit from them .... Finally, if wearing the headscarf really was contrary to the principle of equality between men and women in any event, the State would have a positive obligation to prohibit it in all places, whether public or private.[89]

All these shortcomings in the ECtHR's majority reasoning significantly weaken its image of an international adjudicating body committed to human rights which are practical and effective, rather than theoretical and illusory.

The recent cases of *Dogru* v *France* and *Kervanci* v *France* hardly improve the position. As a positive development, the ECtHR in these cases noted that 'the wearing of religious signs was not inherently incompatible with the principle of secularism in schools'.[90] However, the effect of

---

87 *Refah Partisi*, note 35 above, para. 123.

88 *Şahin*, note 59 above, Dissenting Opinion of Judge Tulkens, para. 10 (citations omitted).

89 *Ibid.*, para. 12 (citations omitted).

90 See notes 67 and 68 above, para. 70.

this was undone by the subsequent, largely unscrutinized assertion that it 'became so according to the conditions in which they were worn and the consequences that the wearing of a sign might have'.[91] As in previous cases, there was very little scrutiny of the link between the applicants' own behaviour and the 'legitimate aim' behind the restriction, with the ECtHR simply concluding that expulsion was not a disproportionate penalty as the applicants had been able to continue their education by correspondence classes.

Dogru argued that

> Despite her proposal to wear a hat or balaclava instead of her headscarf, she had continually been refused permission to participate in sports classes. The teacher had refused to allow her to take part in the class on grounds of her safety. However, when the teacher had been asked, at the session of the pupil discipline committee, how wearing the headscarf or a hat during his classes would endanger the child's safety, he had refused to answer the question. The Government had not provided any further explanations on this point.[92]

These contentions were not addressed. Instead, the court gave a very wide margin of appreciation to the state, allowing it both to introduce and assess its own evidence,[93] noting that 'an attitude which fails to respect [the] principle [of secularism] will not necessarily be accepted as being covered by the freedom to manifest one's religion and will not enjoy the protection of Article 9 of the Convention'.[94]

While the ECtHR's attitude may at some level be linked to the absence of minority rights in the ECHR, the UN system does have a minority provision and thus it should be easier to see progress there. Nonetheless, that is not necessarily the case. Following an acceptance of religious clothing as a manifestation of Islamic religion in *Hudoyberganova*, the HRC in that case went on to say that the freedom to manifest one's religion is not absolute and may be subject to limitations listed in paragraph 3 of Article 18. These are, as in Article 9(2) of the ECHR, limitations 'as are prescribed by law and are necessary to protect public safety, order, health, or morals or the fundamental rights and freedoms of others'. However, in the present case, the state party failed to advance any specific grounds in Article 18(3) on which the restriction could be justified, as its argument simply was that the author's expulsion was as a result of her non-compliance with domestic rules. Therefore, the HRC was 'led to conclude, in the absence of any specific justification provided by the State party, that there has been a violation of article 18, paragraph 2'.[95]

This has been described as a 'default decision',[96] meaning that a violation was found essentially due to the state party's poor arguments. However, the HRC emphasized in *Hudoyberganova* that it did not wish to prejudge 'the right of a State party to limit expressions of religion and belief' or 'the right of academic institutions to adopt specific regulations relating to their own functioning'.[97]

It was also noted that it was unclear from the evidence before the HRC what kind of Islamic dress exactly Hudoyberganova wore, as both parties referred to her apparel as simply '*hijab*'. In particular, Ms Ruth Wedgwood in her individual opinion considered that the 'facts of this case remain too obscure to permit a finding of a violation of the Covenant' and took the view that 'a

---

91 *Ibid.*
92 See note 67 above, para. 44.
93 *Ibid.*, paras. 72–7.
94 *Ibid.*, para. 72.
95 *Hudoyberganova*, note 74 above, para. 6.2.
96 McGoldrick, note 70 above, p. 230.
97 *Hudoyberganova*, note 74 above, para. 6.2.

state may be allowed to restrict forms of dress that directly interfere with effective pedagogy'.[98] She cited the ECtHR in *Şahin,* as an example of circumstances in which 'a particular garb might cause other persons of the same faith to feel pressure to conform'.[99]

This indicates a certain rationale deficit in the HRC's reasoning. Although Hudoyberganova succeeded with her case, the opinions of the HRC members indicate the possibility of a less favourable outcome in future cases, if the state parties' arguments are more skilled.

To sum up, there are several points of significance that arise from these cases in relation to the question of what justifies a restriction on the freedom to wear the headscarf. Most importantly, the cases discussed indicate that the place of preservation of identity in the Islamic headscarf cases has taken a back seat in favour of state concerns relating to respect for the rights and freedoms of others and the curbing of fundamentalism. The evidence required to demonstrate a link between the wearing of the headscarf and the effect on these other issues has been given a disappointingly low content. This treatment contrasts with the stricter stance of both the ECtHR and the HRC in relation to other aspects of minority rights, in particular those relating to free association and expression. The reasoning of the cases discussed indicate a neglect by international courts and tribunals of the personal autonomy of individuals in the formation of their own identities. There is also ostensible neglect of the fact that Islamic beliefs could be anything but fundamentalist, proselytizing and discriminatory for women.

4. Conclusion

This chapter has pursued a twofold task. On the one hand, it has traced the evolution of minority rights protection over the six decades since the adoption of the UDHR. In brief, this evolution is characterized by a marked move from the assimilationist philosophy, common at the time of the inception of the UDHR, to an express commitment to the preservation of identity, as has been practised from the 1960s onwards. The latter attitude is currently the prevalent policy on international human rights levels. This is evidenced by the adoption of specific minority rights provisions in international human rights law, as well as minority-sensitive interpretations of general human rights provisions. All these testify to a welcome sensitization of international human rights law to minority issues and a more sustained commitment to equality.

On the other hand, the chapter has shown how this commendable commitment may not always be lived up to. It has used the currently topical issue of Islamic headscarf restrictions to demonstrate how the obvious minority dimensions of this issue are commonly ignored and, as a result, assimilationist policies are upheld. The problem has been examined in two stages. First, international jurisprudence shows incoherence as to the recognition that wearing an Islamic headscarf may constitute a religious minority identity. The individual's own views (the subjective dimension of the minority identity) are often disregarded as inconsequential. Second, there is inadequate reasoning as to the link between the justifications for the contested restrictions (commonly the rights and freedoms of others and public order) and the minority practice in question. These shortcomings not only weaken the prestige of international adjudicating bodies as protectors of human rights, but also undermine international human rights law's much-pronounced commitment to the preservation of minority identities.

---

98 *Ibid.*, Individual Opinion by Committee Member Ms. Ruth Wedgwood.

99 *Ibid.*

Although this one case study may not be representative of the attitude of international human rights bodies on the whole, it certainly indicates a troubling contradiction between rhetoric and reality. This is an alarm to be taken seriously if, six decades after the UDHR, minority rights are to be given any real content.

Chapter 9

Intellectual Property Rights, the Right to Health, and the UDHR: Is Reconciliation Possible?

Robert L. Ostergard, Jr. and Shawna E. Sweeney

1. Introduction

Since the signing of the 1994 Marrakesh Agreement establishing the World Trade Organization (WTO) and the included Agreement on Trade-Related Aspects of Intellectual Property (TRIPS), activists, scholars and policymakers have expressed concerns over how the global protection of intellectual property rights (IPR) may affect access to essential medicines. On 31 March 2009, the United Nations (UN) Human Rights Council's Special Rapporteur on the Right of Everyone to the Enjoyment of the Highest Attainable Standard of Physical and Mental Health, Anand Grover, issued his report on the right to health and TRIPS.[1] Grover concluded that the TRIPS and Free Trade Agreements (FTAs) had negatively affected pharmaceutical prices and availability, making it difficult for states to meet their obligations to fulfil the right to health.[2] The report was the latest volley in the debate over what appears to be two contradictory aspects of human rights protection: the right to health and the right to intellectual property. As such, reaction to the special rapporteur's report, predictably, has been split between developed and developing countries. While states such as Egypt and India were supportive of the findings, and particularly critical of the evergreening[3] of existing patents, the USA and Switzerland were particularly critical of the findings, arguing that intellectual property has *not* had an adverse effect on the availability of pharmaceuticals and that the report did not take into account the concerns of states that manufacture medicines.[4]

1 A. Grover, *Promotion and Protection of All Human Rights, Civil, Political Economic, Social and Cultural Rights, Including the Right to Development: Report of the Special Rapporteur on the Right of Everyone to the Enjoyment of the Highest Attainable Standard of Physical and Mental Health* (New York: UNGA, 2009).

2 *Ibid.*, p. 28. Grover's findings were subsequent to the 2001 Doha WTO Declaration on the TRIPS agreement and public health that affirmed states' rights to implement flexible arrangements for access to medicines, particularly for critical medicines related to public health emergencies. See World Trade Organization, Declaration on the TRIPS agreement and public health WTO Doc WT/MIN(01)/DEC/2 [online]. Available from: http://www.wto.org/english/theWTO_e/minist_e/min01_e/mindecl_trips_e.htm [accessed 22 December 2009].

3 'Evergreening' refers to obtaining a new patent on a medicine by making relatively minor changes to it; Grover, note 1 above, p. 13. The practice effectively gives companies the ability to extend the life of a medicine's patent for a greater period than the original patent provides.

4 International Service for Human Rights, 'Special Rapporteur on the Right to the Highest Attainable Standard of Health, 11th Session', Council Monitor [online]. Available from: http://www.ishr.ch/content/view/471/513/ [accessed 19 October 2009]; see also United Nations Human Rights Council, *Archived Video: Human Rights Council Eleventh Session* (Geneva: United Nations, 2009) for individual state responses to the rapporteur's report.

While it is likely that no country would deny the human right to health care, the interpretation of its scope is certainly in dispute. For instance, regarding the USA's response to the rapporteur's report, Chargé d'Affaires Mark C. Storella stated:

> While the United States recognizes this right, we do not agree, as a legal and policy matter, with the way in which the contours of the right are described in the report. The United States believes in the importance of non-discriminatory access to medicines as an integral component of an effective health care system. We note, however, that the report focuses on a narrow aspect of health: medicines that are patented in certain countries. We strongly disagree with the report's contention that intellectual property protections, as embodied in TRIPS and Free Trade Agreements, have had an adverse impact on access to medicines. The report's perspective fails to acknowledge intellectual property protections as highly positive to the availability of medicines, of health innovations, and of improving health care. The United States also believes that the report also raises serious institutional concerns related to the interpretation of WTO agreements, in particular the TRIPS agreement.[5]

Following the rapporteur's report, Brazil introduced a resolution (sponsored by several countries, including Cuba, Egypt, India and South Africa among others) that

> *Calls upon* States, at the international level, to take steps, individually and/or through international cooperation, in accordance with applicable international law, including international agreements, to ensure that their actions as members of international organizations take into due account the right of everyone to the enjoyment of the highest attainable standard of physical and mental health, and that the application of international agreements is supportive of public health policies that promote broad access to safe, effective and affordable medicines.[6]

France, speaking on behalf of the European Union (EU), objected that the resolution did not focus on other aspects of health care such as systems to provide health care.[7] The US chargé d'affaires, Douglas Griffiths, expressed regrets that the resolution was so narrowly drawn as to emphasize only intellectual property and trade.[8] The resolution highlights the significant differences in perspectives that the two groups of countries have on the right to health and how IPR affects it. In part, the differences in policies can be explained by structural differences in the economies of developed and developing countries. Developed countries experiencing shifts in the nature of their national economies from a manufacturing base to a services base see intellectual property as a key means to protect domestic employment and expanding overseas markets for their IPR-dependent

5 M.C. Storella, 'Comments Before the Human Rights Council Eleventh Session, 3rd Plenary Meeting' (United Nations Human Rights Council, 3 June 2009).

6 United Nations Human Rights Council, *Resolution 12/24 Access to Medicine in the Context of the Right of Everyone to the Enjoyment of the Highest Attainable Standard of Physical and Mental Health* (Geneva: United Nations, 25 September 2009).

7 International Service for Human Rights, 'Council Update – Decisions and Resolutions, Human Rights Council, 12th Session, 1 and 2 October 2009', Council Monitor [online]. Available from: http://www.ishr.ch/content/view/471/513/ [accessed 30 October 2009].

8 D. Griffiths, 'UN Human Rights Council – 12th Session Resolution: Access to Medicine in the Context of the Right of Everyone to the Enjoyment of the Highest Attainable Standard of Physical and Mental Health' (United States Government, 2 October 2009) [online]. Available from: http://geneva.usmission.gov/2009/10/02/item-3-decision-adoption/ [accessed 30 October 2009].

products (i.e. software, pharmaceuticals, mp3 audio files, movie DVDs, etc.). Developing countries experiencing economic and social difficulties that hinder providing basic health care to their populations see global IPR protection as a further impediment to health care for their people. Given these differences, the question that has to be asked is: can these two perspectives on human rights be reconciled?

In recent years, there has been growing support in many circles to make health care a universal human right and a 'global public good' since all societies benefit immensely from a healthy population. Yet, the present IPR system has a detrimental impact on the right to health, since it reduces the availability of pharmaceuticals, especially for individuals suffering from curable diseases in developing countries, hence pitting the needs of the poor who require medicine to live against the profit-maximizing goals of pharmaceutical firms.

Though few publicists and policymakers would argue against the right to health care on moral grounds, this chapter argues that the greater problem has been over the feasibility of such an idea, especially where the 'right to health' has never been clearly defined. We discuss the numerous practical impediments to balancing the two values – the right of creators to protect their intellectual property and the right of everyone to enjoy the highest attainable standard of health care. We argue that to strike a balance between these important values, all countries must work to develop policies that take into account the basic health and developmental interests of developing countries. We also argue that important changes must be made to the current IPR system, especially with respect to the production and pricing of basic goods and services needed to fulfil health subsistence rights. These changes must include allowing developing countries access to essential medicines that support the realization of basic health, welfare, and economic development. Since one of the goals of development is the improvement of people's physical well-being and the expansion of their capabilities, the restricted production of particular medicines under the current IPR system conflicts with these important goals. The implementation of international agreements must also be made more consistent with the goals of public health policies that promote broad access to safe, effective and affordable medicines, and conflicts between the types of rights enumerated in these agreements must be worked out for the broader benefit of human society if the right to health will ever be fully realized. For example, the UDHR[9] declares both intellectual property and health to be human rights.[10] A number of incentives exist for pharmaceutical and biotechnology companies to focus more of their research on the development of drug protocols that treat diseases afflicting poor people in developing countries. However, there are a number of important drawbacks to these proposals, which we discuss.

Before elaborating on the arguments outlined above, this chapter explores the differences between traditional property rights and intellectual property, as well as the benefits and drawbacks of supporting stronger IPR for developed and developing countries, which tend to have differing national priorities over the issue of IPR protection. We explore the historical origins of the concept of 'right to health' in human rights discourse and how this right received greater attention during the 1990s. During this period, an important conceptual shift occurred in this discourse that increasingly emphasized the promotion of basic subsistence rights. Yet, this shift in focus has not been without controversy, as some writers are opposed to the idea of the right to health, not necessarily on moral grounds since one would be hard-pressed to advocate profits over human life, but on more practical grounds since such rights are, arguably, not easily implementable and are costly. This chapter reviews a number of criticisms of viewing health care as a basic subsistence right (or a

9 GA Res. 217A (III), UN Doc A/810 at 71 (1948).

10 Art. 25 and 27 UDHR.

type of positive right) on a par in importance with civil and political rights (negative rights), the latter of which have been historically considered morally superior to the former, and less costly and easier to implement. As this chapter illustrates, subsistence and civil and political rights do not fit neatly into the positive/negative dichotomy, since all human rights require both positive action and restraint by the state if they are to be effectively implemented, and all human rights require governments to take costly action.[11] Hence, the argument that health subsistence rights are impossible to implement in developing countries that experience significant resource constraints should not be used as a reason to continue denying more than half the world's population access to basic health care.

This chapter concludes with the potentially controversial argument that we need to replace the dominant state-centric paradigm that views the right to health care in strictly nationalistic terms (as simply problems of the state) with a more cosmopolitan paradigm that reflects the true nature of the relationship between IPR and human rights as a 'global public good'. Anything short of that goal would leave the universal right to health care unrealizable for a significant segment of the world's population.

2. The Nature and Variable Importance of IPR

Traditional property theory holds that property is equated with individual possession. However, property represents a relationship between the owner and other individuals relative to some item. The relationship is a right that can protect the owner's property. What makes intellectual property (IP) unique in this regard is its intangible nature. With traditional forms of tangible property, formal law is not necessary to protect it; people may protect their property from encroachment by others. IP differs from simple tangible property in this sense because there is no way to protect it; or, rather, the only way to protect IP completely is to keep it secret. Hence, one of the primary characteristics of IP is that it is non-exclusive because a person cannot prevent others from using the property once it is disclosed. In the case of IP, the state must guarantee the exclusive ownership of the idea or work, artificially creating a relationship of exclusion (or monopoly) between IP owners and others who may want to utilize the IP.[12] For instance, if plans for a new invention are disclosed, there is no way to prevent a person from utilizing the idea.

Another distinction between traditional property and IP is supply. For instance, no one can use land that has already been appropriated. Furthermore, the supply of land is finite, which means that market forces of supply and demand have a significant (though not final) role in determining real-estate prices. Contrast this with the chemical formula for a particular medicine. Individuals can use that formula repeatedly and its supply will remain unchanged. No matter how many people pass along the formula, its supply will never diminish. Likewise, there is absolutely no cost involved in an additional person using the formula, and, as Hettinger points out, modern technology

11 See also Chapters 3 and 4 in this volume.

12 The issue of whether patents or other forms of IP create a relationship of exclusion or a monopoly condition has been a point of concern in the debate surrounding the justification of IPR. But, as Mossoff aptly notes, whether one perceives IPR as an exclusionary or monopolistic element, the debate itself does not say much about the nature of IPR as an intangible form of property. Without such an approach, it is difficult to dismiss the claims that IPR promote monopolistic conditions. See A. Mossoff, 'What Is Property? Putting the Pieces Back Together', *Arizona Law Review*, 45 (2003), pp. 371–443, at pp. 415–16.

has made the transmission of such ideas practical with few limitations.[13] Hence, without state protection, IP possesses fundamental differences from simple property. The state establishes laws to protect people's property from others. These laws assign rights to exclude others from using one's property. Similarly, IPR give individuals the right to exclude others from using their ideas, works, and inventions. IP laws alter the essential nature of intangible property by eliminating non-exclusive property. To this end, IPR grant exclusive control over some object (whether it is literary, mechanical, or procedural). The possessor is then able to exclude others, to control the output, and to establish a monopoly price within the limits that product demand will allow.[14] The supply of the intangible object has thus been artificially limited by the introduction of exclusive control over distribution. As Hettinger points out, it is the non-excludable attribute of intellectual objects that is key to understanding the nature of and justifications for IP.[15] Without formal protections of IPR that the state can impose and enforce, IPR producers are left with no guaranteed ways to 'secure' their property against infringement. This situation can present real problems of investment return for producers who may spend millions of dollars developing a product only to have the product mass-produced by producers who did not incur the initial start-up cost of production. Or, to put it relative to pharmaceuticals, the first pill of a new medication may cost $200 million to produce; each pill after that initial pill may have a production cost of a few cents. Nonetheless, the pharmaceutical producer still has to make up the $200 million for the first pill.

From a practical, macro-perspective, strong IPR supporters tend to focus on the economic benefits that states and societies can derive from protecting IPR. Most often, supporters cite Joseph Schumpeter's research, which focuses on innovation and technology as *the* driving forces of industrial development for modern states.[16] Those supporting stronger IPR protection argue that it has several benefits, including increased domestic research and development, increased flows of new products, enhanced value in patent rights, greater inward investment and technology transfers, and improved local knowledge.[17] These benefits, however, are most often associated with *developed* countries that do not face some of the specific, and more pressing, issues that confront developing countries. Most developing countries do not have the capacity for domestic research and development; in fact, the notion of product variety for developing countries is, in the short term, limited to the variety of ways that they can feed and care for their people. Even if developing

---

13 E.C. Hettinger, 'Justifying Intellectual Property', *Philosophy & Public Affairs*, 18 (1989), pp. 31–52, at p. 34. As Stiglitz puts it, 'there is no marginal cost associated with the use of knowledge.' See J.E. Stiglitz, 'Economic Foundations of Intellectual Property', *Duke Law Journal*, 57 (2008), pp. 1693–1724, at p. 1700.

14 E.T. Penrose, *The Economics of the International Patent System* (Baltimore, MD: Johns Hopkins University Press, 1951), pp. 1–2.

15 Hettinger, note 13 above, p. 34.

16 A.S. Gutterman, 'The North–South Debate Regarding the Protection of Intellectual Property Rights', *Wake Forest Law Review*, 28 (1993), p. 89; J.A. Schumpeter, *Capitalism, Socialism, and Democracy*, 2nd edn (New York and London: Harper & Brothers, 1942); on the relationship between technology and economic growth, see, more generally, D.C. Mowery and N. Rosenberg, *Paths of Innovation: Technological Change in 20th Century America* (Cambridge: Cambridge University Press, 1998); N. Rosenberg and L.E. Birdzell, Jr., *How the West Grew Rich: The Economic Transformation of the Industrial World* (New York: Basic Books, 1986); N. Rosenberg, *Technology and American Economic Growth* (New York: Harper & Row, 1972); N. Rosenberg, *Schumpeter and the Endogeneity of Technology: Some American Perspectives* (New York: Routledge, 2000).

17 Gutterman, note 16 above, p. 120. Stiglitz has argued that 'Ordinarily, property rights are argued for as a means of achieving economic efficiency; intellectual property rights, by contrast, result in a static inefficiency which can only be justified by the dynamic incentives. These examples suggest that the static inefficiencies may be greater than is often thought.' See Stiglitz, note 13 above, p. 1704.

countries want and can afford new products, the more pressing issue is whether those products are necessarily appropriate for countries that are seeking simply to provide basic provisions, such as food, water, shelter, and health care, to their people. Does a country such as Mali or Namibia need the latest Windows software on new laptops when the available resources could be better used to ensure the right of access to health facilities; access to minimum essential food which is nutritionally adequate and safe; access to basic shelter, housing and sanitation; and an adequate supply of safe and potable water, especially for vulnerable or marginalized groups? The example is a bit extreme, but it serves to highlight the disjoint in national priorities between developed and developing states overall.

While national-level IPR may provide this incentive structure for innovation in developed countries, when IPR protection is provided equally across all countries, such as the case with TRIPS under the WTO, the incentive structures become much more complex for developed states and may actually work against their interests. For instance, if copyright protection is provided to producers no matter where they are located, it is in the interest of producers to take advantage of lower production costs if they are afforded equal protection no matter where they produce their product. Thus, while IPR may be critical for long-term state economic advancement, in the short term, IPR may, in fact, be detrimental to advanced states. For instance, if a software producer such as Apple or Microsoft can get the same copyright protection in India as they would in the USA, all else being equal, the labour market dynamics would promote the shifting of production from the USA to India. Engineers and programmers in India make a relatively small amount of money compared to their counterparts in the USA or the UK.[18] But this situation is not just a problem for easily copied software or music. Even the pharmaceutical industry has displayed patterns of shifting high-paying pharmaceutical development jobs to areas around the globe that have a lower prevailing wage. The shift in employment can be attributed to several factors, but prominent among them is the emergence of strong IPR regimes in states such as Singapore, India and China.[19] Hence, while the IPR incentive structure may promote innovation, it may also promote certain negative externalities for developed countries seeking to promote job growth and overall economic growth.

3. Prioritizing Rights: The Right to Health as a Subsistence Right

One of the emerging areas in the discourse on human rights is the right to health. The concept has a long history, dating to the nineteenth-century Industrial Revolution.[20] Edwin Chadwick, a student of Jeremy Bentham, had argued that disease promoted poverty and that poverty promoted social ills, disorder and ultimately higher taxes. Friedrich Engels, Karl Marx's friend and collaborator, reversed Chadwick's causal relationship and promoted the idea that poverty caused disease in his *Condition of the Working Class in England*.[21] The modern incarnation of the right to health as an institutionalized 'human right' dates only from the UDHR of 1948.[22] But what this right to health

---

18 C.A. Rarick, 'India: Employment Black Hole?', SSRN eLibrary [online]. Available from: http://papers.ssrn.com/sol3/papers.cfm?abstract_id=1123151 [accessed 14 November 2009].

19 A. Scott, 'Major Report Forecasts Growth in Pharma Outsourcing', *Chemical Weekly*, 28 (2008) [online]. Available from: www.chemweek.com [accessed 8 November 2009].

20 M. Susser, 'Health as a Human Right: An Epidemiologist's Perspective on the Public Health', *American Journal of Public Health*, 83 (1993), pp. 418–26, at p. 419.

21 *Ibid.*

22 *Ibid.*

means is not clear, and scholars and practitioners have been struggling to define its scope for some time now.

In early work on the concept, scholars debated what was termed the 'absurdity' of the term, which, some argued, implied a right to 'perfect health'.[23] Such debates led to discussions that made the concept more precise in meaning such that the concept of a 'right to health' implied a 'right to health care' or a 'right to health protection'.[24] By the 1990s, a shift in the human rights discourse started to give greater attention to economic, social and cultural (ESC) rights (so-called second-generation or positive human rights). Prior to this expansion in the discourse, the primary objective of human rights specialists was working toward the protection of civil and political rights (so-called first-generation or negative human rights).[25] As the concept received greater attention from international organizations, the idea of feasibility began to enter into the discourse. The UN recognized the growing importance of rights to health when it appointed the UN special rapporteur on the right to the highest attainable standard of health in 2002. Brazil had pushed to appoint this special rapporteur, and the UN approved the post despite the two votes against it from the USA and Australia.[26] The first special rapporteur, Paul Hunt, began to shape the context of the right to the highest attainable standard of health, which has been shortened to the 'right to health'.[27] As Hunt contended:

> While the right to health includes the right to health care, it goes beyond health care to encompass the underlying determinants of health, such as safe drinking water, adequate sanitation, and access to health-related information. The right includes freedoms, such as the right to be free from discrimination and involuntary medical treatment. It also includes entitlements, such as the right to essential primary care. The right has numerous elements including child health, maternal health and access to essential drugs. Like other human rights, it has a particular concern for the disadvantaged, the vulnerable and those living in poverty. The right requires an effective, inclusive health system of good quality.[28]

The rights listed by Hunt require state action that includes provisions for these rights and the monitoring of indicators and benchmarks. In short, they are implicitly recognized rights that must

---

23 B. Toebes, 'Towards an Improved Understanding of the International Human Right to Health', *Human Rights Quarterly*, 21 (1999), pp. 661–79, at p. 662; V.A. Leary, 'The Right to Health in International Human Rights Law', *Health and Human Rights*, 1 (1994), pp. 24–56, at p. 31 [online]. Available from: http://www.hhrjournal.org/archives-pdf/4065261.pdf.bannered.pdf. On this point, Susser refutes the idea that a person could be entitled to some form of perfect health or the guarantee of a healthy state for each person (effectively eliminating this as a right to each person). 'The mere existence of congenital or hereditary impairment renders such a hope naïve.' See Susser, note 20 above, p. 419.

24 Toebes, note 23above, p. 662. See also Committee on Economic, Social and Cultural Rights, General Comment 14: 'The Right to the Highest Attainable Standard of Health', UN Doc. E/C.12/2000/4 (11 August 2000).

25 Some scholars have written on the emergence of a 'third generation' of human rights that incorporates rights to peace, a healthy environment, development and even humanitarian assistance. See D. Forsythe, *Human Rights in International Relations*, 2nd edn (Cambridge: Cambridge University Press, 2006), p. 31.

26 P. Hunt, 'The Human Right to the Highest Attainable Standard of Health: New Opportunities and Challenges', *Transactions of the Royal Society of Tropical Medicine and Hygiene*, 100 (2006), pp. 603–7, at p. 604.

27 *Ibid.*

28 *Ibid.*

be worked towards, meaning that they are 'expressly subject to both progressive realisation and resource availability'.[29]

While the right to health may be gaining traction in international discourse and attention from non-governmental and intergovernmental organizations, it has been subject to criticism, along with the whole category of ESC rights, from liberal scholars, who contend that ESC rights are not rights, but goals or objectives for states to achieve.[30] Since the post-World War II era, the normative foundations of human rights have been expanded to include not only civil and political rights, but also a broad array of other types of human rights, notably ESC rights.[31] Both types of rights form two subsets of the broader concept of human rights.[32] International declarations, covenants, and treaties, notably the International Bill of Rights, list a wide catalogue of civil, political, economic, social, and cultural human rights.[33] Notable examples include the right to life and liberty and security; the rights to freedom of speech, conscience, and religion; the right to education; the right to participate in community affairs; the right to vote; the right to health care and social insurance; the right to work; and the right to property, among others.[34]

Despite the obvious grounding in international human rights law and in national constitutions, some commentators criticize support for a full menu of human rights because of factors of impracticability; cultural insensitivity; and difficulty in implementation, identifying duty bearers, and specifying the division of labour of duties.[35] For example, for many years, scholars and practitioners studying Asia have argued that some international human rights norms are fundamentally incompatible with 'Asian values', which, in their view, should receive priority over so-called Western-oriented rights.[36] Others have challenged the notion that ESC rights are genuine human rights or on a par, in significance, with civil and political rights. As Donnelly notes,

> Such critics argue that economic, social, and cultural rights, entitlements to socially provided goods, services, and opportunities such as food, health care, social insurance, and education, are at best less important than civil and political rights, such as due process, freedom of speech, and the right to vote, and probably not human rights at all.[37]

---

29 *Ibid.*

30 See also Chapter 3 in this volume.

31 A. Sen, *Development as Freedom* (New York: Alfred A. Knopf, 1999); A. Sen, 'Elements of a Theory of Human Rights', *Philosophy & Public Affairs*, 32 (2004), pp. 315–56. Human dignity is widely recognized in numerous international covenants as the key normative foundation that justifies all human rights.

32 Human rights are moral rights of the highest order that apply to all human beings simply by virtue of being human.

33 The International Bill of Rights includes the UDHR, the International Covenant on Civil and Political Rights (ICCPR), and the International Covenant of Economic, Social, and Cultural Rights (ICESCR). See Chapter 1 in this volume.

34 J. Donnelly, *International Human Rights*, 3rd edn (Boulder, CO: Westview Press, 2007), p. 24. See also Chapters 3 and 4 in this volume.

35 S. Hertel and L. Minkler (eds), *Economic Rights: Conceptual, Measurement, and Policy Issues* (Cambridge: Cambridge University Press, 2007).

36 Donnelly, note 34 above. Sen also has argued that human rights are not uniquely Western and that there are strains of Asian thought that place value on human rights. Moreover, he contends that human rights are not incompatible with economic growth, as some observers have argued. See A. Sen 'Human Rights and Asian Values: Sixteenth Annual Morgenthau Memorial Lecture on Ethics and Foreign Policy' (New York: Carnegie Council for Ethics in International Affairs, 1997) [online]. Available from: http://www.cceia.org/resources/publications/morgenthau/254.html [accessed 29 November 2009].

37 Donnelly, note 34 above, p. 25.

Henry Shue disputes the notion that ESC rights are not really human rights or that they are lesser rights in his seminal work, *Basic Rights: Subsistence, Affluence, and U.S. Foreign Policy*.[38] He identifies both civil and political rights and ESC rights as forming a set of 'basic rights' to which all individuals are entitled. For Shue, basic rights are those minimal reasonable demands that everyone can place on the rest of humanity to ensure personal self-respect and survival.[39] Because of this, Shue argues that 'basic rights are necessary for the enjoyment of all other rights, and it is this link that justifies basic rights.'[40] There are two kinds of basic rights: security rights and subsistence rights. Security rights refer to freedom from murder, torture, rape and assault and correspond primarily to civil and political rights. Subsistence rights, which are meant to provide minimal economic security, refer to the rights to unpolluted air and water; adequate food, clothing, and shelter; and minimal preventive health care.[41] These rights correspond primarily with ESC rights.[42] Taken together, both kinds of rights – security and subsistence – are indivisible in the sense that both are equally necessary for the enjoyment of any other right.[43] Basic rights are interdependent in the sense that all other rights are dependent on security and subsistence rights being fulfilled.[44] While Shue does not elaborate on how basic rights are dependent upon one another, interdependence clearly follows from his arguments. One cannot enjoy subsistence rights if one is not also free from murder, torture, and incarceration, just as one cannot enjoy security rights if one is malnourished or has starved to death. As Shue observes,

> In the absence of physical security people are unable to use any other rights that society may be said to be protecting without being liable to encounter many of the worst dangers they would encounter if society were not protecting the rights.[45]

---

38 H. Shue, *Basic Rights: Subsistence, Affluence, and U.S. Foreign Policy*, 2nd edn (Princeton, NJ: Princeton University Press, 1996).

39 *Ibid.*, p. 19.

40 L. Minkler and S. Sweeney, 'On the Indivisibility and Interdependence of Basic Rights in Developing Countries' (University of Connecticut Human Rights Institute's Economic Rights Working Group Annual Meeting, 12–13 April 2008).

41 Shue, note 38 above, p. 23.

42 Shue does not give a clear characterization of what constitutes subsistence rights and the conditions necessary to secure subsistence, but at least it is to be understood as having 'available for consumption what is needed for a decent chance at a reasonably healthy and active life of more or less normal length, barring tragic interventions', Shue, note 38 above, p. 23. What would clearly not constitute an environment where subsistence rights were being met, for example, is a 20% infant mortality rate or 'a life expectancy of 35 years of fever-ridden, parasite-ridden listlessness'. At the other extreme, a right to subsistence would not mean that every baby born with a heart defect requiring open-heart surgery has a right to such surgery. It is the grey area between these two extremes upon which Shue needs to elaborate.

43 While Shue does not use the word 'indivisibility', that is what he means when he writes: 'The only parallel being relied upon is that guarantees of security and guarantees of subsistence are equally essential to providing for the actual exercise of any other rights.' See Shue, note 38 above, p. 23. For a good, short treatment of the distinctions between 'indivisibility' and 'interdependence' (and 'interrelatedness') of human rights, see also D. Whelan, 'Untangling the Indivisibility, Interdependency, and Interrelatedness of Human Rights' (Economic Rights Working Paper Series, University of Connecticut, 2008) [online]. Available from: http://ideas.repec.org/p/uct/ecriwp/7.html [accessed 18 November 2009].

44 For instance, Shue argues that all liberties depend on basic rights, and also that basic rights depend on some liberties. See Shue, note 34 above, pp. 70–1.

45 Shue, note 38 above, p. 21.

Similarly,

> Deficiencies in the means of subsistence can be just as fatal, incapacitating, or painful as violations of physical security. The resulting damage or death can at least as decisively prevent the enjoyment of any right as can the effects of security violations.[46]

However, as stated earlier, there have been numerous criticisms of Shue's basic rights thesis, particularly with respect to his emphasis on subsistence rights. If they recognize these rights at all, critics see them as less important than civil and political rights. This belief in the superiority of the latter type of rights is based upon the assumption that there is a significant moral difference between so-called positive rights (subsistence rights) and so-called negative rights (civil and political rights), and that negative rights are more important than positive rights, and are less costly and easier to implement since they simply require refraining from certain types of actions whereas positive rights require undertaking certain types of actions. Negative rights supposedly require only the forbearance of others to be realized.[47] Commonly cited examples include the right to be free from restrictions on speech, movement, association, and so forth. On the other hand, positive rights require that others provide active support for the realization of these rights such as the provision of shelter, food and clothing. Liberals argue that universal human rights are limited to negative rights, and positive rights are limited to being the aspiration of all peoples.[48] The best way to achieve these aspirations is through the realization of negative rights that promote greater levels of economic growth, higher income and lower unemployment. Hence, the priority is negative rights, with positive rights being 'aspirations'.[49]

Likewise, Maurice Cranston harshly criticized subsistence rights as devaluing real human rights (civil and political), because the former depend on a government's ability to pay, especially for health care, which is a significant public expense.[50] He claims that it is relatively easy to transform civil and political into positive rights, but that in most countries it is 'utterly impossible' to do the same for ESC rights.[51] Moreover, the identities of those holding negative obligations are clear: the government and everyone else have the obligation not to interfere with others' exercise of their civil and political rights. Supposedly, the same cannot be said for positive obligations. The important question is this: who is obligated to provide the aid required to fulfil subsistence rights?[52] In the case of health care, is it the government, taxpayers, employers, or a combination of all three? Less well-off governments (and even their more affluent counterparts) have difficulty meeting the obligations associated with positive subsistence rights, and this is recognized under the concept of 'progressive realization' in international human rights law, as specifically found in the International Covenant on Economic, Social, and Cultural Rights (ICESCR),[53] as fully discussed in Chapter 3 of this volume.

---

46 *Ibid.*, p. 24.

47 T. Evans, 'A Human Right to Health?', *Third World Quarterly*, 23 (2002), pp. 197–215, at pp. 200–1.

48 *Ibid.*, p. 201.

49 See Evans, note 47 above, for one of the best general discussions on the liberal approach to positive and negative rights.

50 M. Cranston, 'Human Rights, Real and Supposed', in D. Raphael (ed.), *Political Theory and the Rights of Man* (Bloomington, IN: Indiana University Press, 1967).

51 Quoted in Donnelly, note 34 above, p. 26.

52 Hertel and Minkler, note 35 above.

53 993 UNTS 3.

Despite the priority given to civil and political rights, the reality in much of the world, with regard to human rights, revolves around problems of socio-economic deprivation more than problems of civil and political freedoms. More people die worldwide from famine, hunger, poverty, and lack of access to basic health care than from security rights violations, even including those that occur during military conflicts, major wars, and genocide. For instance, in 2001 alone, 22 million people died from preventable deaths due to poverty and other deprivations.[54] In that same year, almost 1.1 billion people lived on $1 a day or less, and over 2.7 billion lived on $2 a day or less, both combined equalling more than half the world's population.[55] Although many countries have registered significant health progress in recent years, health gains have been unevenly shared.[56] As a result, health gaps between countries and among social groups within countries have widened, with a negative impact on the realization of human rights in many cases, especially for those living in poverty. Hence, to lack a reasonably adequate diet or minimum level of health care can be as incapacitating or fatal as violations of physical security, and it also creates a crippling environment in which rights-bearers cannot enjoy any of their rights. For Shue, then, all rights are founded on basic rights, and basic rights are founded on the reasonable, minimal demands required for self-respect.

Moreover, Shue refutes the assumption that there is a sharp and significant distinction between rights to subsistence and rights to security via the positive/negative dichotomy that is unquestionably accepted by some.[57] He does this by illustrating how all human rights require both positive action and restraint by the state if they are to be effectively implemented, and all human rights require governments to take costly actions. For example, as Donnelly notes, the right to vote requires a costly electoral/legal system and extensive positive efforts, not forbearance, on the part of government.[58] So does the right to due process, the right to a fair trial, and the right to access legal remedies for violations of basic rights. In fact, the types of positive actions that are required to ensure physical security are actions that establish police forces, criminal courts, penitentiaries, schools and universities, and so on. Importantly, all these social institutions are supported through taxes, which also count as positive actions with the goal of ensuring security rights. In a similar vein, the right to subsistence requires both positive actions and restraint on the part of others. Not only does one's right to subsistence require others to provide those commodities that are necessary to health and economic security, but this right also sometimes requires people to refrain from engaging in activities that might interfere with others' ability to provide for their own subsistence. For example, in many countries, the right to food would be more secure if governments simply refrained from encouraging the production of cash crops such as coffee, cocoa, flowers, and fruits

54 Hertel and Minkler, note 35 above.

55 Pogge, for example, estimates that the death toll from all wars (civil and interstate), genocides, and other forms of government repression was 200 million in the twentieth century alone. By his estimate, it took only 11 years at the end of the century for approximately the same number of deaths to result from poverty. See T. Pogge, 'Severe Poverty as a Violation of Negative Duties', *Ethics and International Affairs*, 19 (2005), pp. 55–83.

56 See World Health Organization, The World Health Report 2008 – Primary Health Care: Now More Than Ever [online]. Available from: http://www.who.int/whr/2008/whr08_en.pdf.

57 Shue, note 38 above. Similarly, Shue does not claim that there is a right to the prevention and eradication of all illness and death. There are illnesses that are incurable and fatal to which people do not have a right to protection.

58 Donnelly, note 34 above.

for export, which infringe on the lands and livelihoods of indigenous populations, and decrease the availability (and increase the price) of local food staples, causing severe economic hardship.[59]

Shue takes his argument further by redefining the obligations or duties associated with basic rights. He claims that there are three primary types of duties – both negative and positive – that are correlated with both security and subsistence rights. This tripartite array of duties includes obligations to: (1) avoid depriving someone of his or her right; (2) protect others from deprivation of the right; and (3) aid those who have been deprived of the substance of the right. This taxonomy applies to both subsistence and security rights. So, for example, with subsistence rights there are duties not to deprive people of their only available means of subsistence, to protect their means of subsistence from deprivation from other actors, and to provide subsistence for those unable to provide for themselves, such as children or the physically infirm.[60] Shue's formulation clearly shows that subsistence and security rights do not fit neatly into the positive/negative dichotomy, and, moreover, there is not a sharp and significant distinction between negative and positive obligations, since both types of obligations are inherent to all human rights.

Shue's basic rights thesis has been revived in recent years in support of global public health initiatives and the drive to make health care a universal human right. The right to health means that everyone has the right to the highest attainable standard of physical and mental health, without discrimination of any kind.[61] This includes, at a minimum, access to all medical services including preventive ones (i.e. immunizations), access to sanitation, adequate food, decent housing, healthy working conditions and a clean environment.[62] Advocates of universal health care argue that the right to health care underscores the importance of viewing all human rights as interdependent and indivisible, since without basic health care people will not be able to enjoy any other rights. For example, if people are suffering from the most basic and curable diseases (such as malaria) and deprivation (malnutrition, hunger), they will not be able to participate in the civil and political life of their community. What good is having the right to vote and freedom of speech, conscience, and assembly if someone is too weak to go to the polls, or to organize a political rally, speak in public, or worship in a church or mosque? If mothers cannot survive childbirth because they lack simple maternal care, or if their children do not live past the age of 5, as in many of the least developed countries today, what good to them is being able to participate in politics ? Without basic health care, people cannot ensure their own well-being and that of their family, and cannot enjoy other fundamental rights and freedoms.

Numerous provisions of international human rights law explicitly recognize this fact in guaranteeing everyone the human right to health care. These include the UDHR, the ICESCR, the Convention on the Elimination of All Forms of Discrimination Against Women (CEDAW),[63] and the Convention on the Rights of the Child (CRC),[64] among others. The majority of the world's governments have also made firm commitments to ensuring the realization of this right at a number of international conferences and forums, including commitments made at the Earth Summit in Rio, the World Summit for Social Development in Copenhagen, and the 1995 Beijing World Conference on Women, among others. For example, the Beijing Platform for Action that emerged out of the 1995 conference states in paragraph 106 that nation states must

59 *Ibid.*

60 Hertel and Minkler, note 35 above.

61 Cairo Programme of Action (13 September 1994), LT/, Principle 8, para. 8.6 [online]. Available from: http://www.iisd.ca/Cairo/program/p08000.html [accessed 20 November 2009].

62 See UDHR, Art. 25; ICESCR, Art. 12.

63 1249 UNTS 13.

64 1577 UNTS 3.

> reaffirm the right to the enjoyment of the highest attainable standards of physical and mental health, protect and promote the attainment of this right for women and girls ... provide more accessible, available and affordable primary health care services of high quality ... in order to ensure universal access to health services ... reduce maternal mortality by at least 50 percent of the 1990 levels by the year 2000 and a further one half by the year 2015. ... by the year 2000, the . . . mortality rates of infants and girls under five [must be reduced to] one third of the 1990 level.[65]

Despite these numerous international guarantees to which the majority of nation states have committed themselves, vast inequalities exist in terms of individual access to health-care services and quality of care. It is well known that the gap between those who receive the best health care in the world and those who receive the worst is absolutely staggering,[66] and that the country or world region one lives in (national health-care system versus private or hybrid health-care system; affluent versus developing country) makes a significant difference in the length and quality of one's life. In part, the disparity between what is guaranteed by international agreements and what is seen at the individual level is a function of how policymakers and scholars perceive the notion of development.

Scholars and practitioners often view the concept of economic development as a macro-level process, but with this conception of development, the focal point is on the national level, which often lacks a focus on who the development process is targeting. Development policies ultimately target individuals, and policies are created for the improvement of the general conditions for those individuals. Subsistence rights and positive rights are not about giving everyone luxuries that states can ill afford; rather, they are focused on providing everyone with the *basic* necessities that human beings need to carry on with their daily lives – clean air, food, water, and shelter.[67] They concern basic elements that give people the capacity to function. Development, therefore, is not just a state concept; its focus is on the individuals that reside in a particular state. In this sense, development can be considered to be an expansion of people's capabilities.[68] This conception of development concentrates on individuals rather than all of society, and is carefully constructed to incorporate three often-cited definitions and components of development: expansion of commodities, an increase in utility, and basic needs.[69] This approach to development that stresses capabilities is an attempt to integrate all of these components into the broader development framework while at the same time demonstrating the deficiencies of defining development solely within the context of *one* of these concepts.

Capability theorists define people's capabilities in terms of their functions, which 'vary from such elementary physical [needs] as being well-nourished, being adequately clothed and sheltered, avoiding preventable morbidity, and so forth, to more complex social achievements such as

---

65 The Fourth World Conference on Women, the Beijing Platform for Action (adopted 15 September 1995) [online]. Available from: http://www.un.org/womenwatch/daw/beijing/platform/ [accessed 20 November 2009].

66 E.g. World Health Organization, *World Health Statistics* (Geneva: WHO, 2009); D. Acheson *et al.*, 'Health Inequalities and the Health of the Poor', *Bulletin of the World Health Organization*, 78 (2000), p. 75; D. Gwatkin, 'Health Inequalities and the Health of the Poor: What Do We Know? What Can We Do?', *Bulletin of the World Health Organization*, 78 (2000), p. 3.

67 On this point, see Shue, note 38 above, pp. 25–6.

68 A. Sen, 'Goods and People', in W. Aiken and H. LaFollette (eds), *World Hunger and Morality*, 2nd edn (New York: Prentice-Hall, 1996), p. 187; A. Sen, *Resources, Values and Development* (Cambridge, MA: Harvard University Press, 1984), pp. 510–11.

69 See, generally, Sen (1996), note 68 above, for an analysis of these three individual components.

taking part in the life of a community, being able to appear in public without shame, and so on'.[70] Through this lens, the basis of positive and negative rights takes on greater meaning than simply the state's actions or inactions. That is, positive and negative rights are equally important in the larger development process. Sen has asserted that people's capabilities depend, though not entirely, on access to commodities, which is their entitlement as human beings.[71] Through exercising their agency, people are able to contribute to the development process because the actualization of positive and negative rights contributes to overall development. A person's entitlements in this development process are a reflection of the entitlement system itself. This means that while people are entitled to access to certain commodities, their access is a reflection of a social entitlement system. In this sense, IPR and the right to health are a subset of the rules of the entitlement system, as they grant and restrict access to commodities. Yet, one important proviso must be made with regard to having access to commodities that affect one's physical well-being: the emphasis is not on the actual possession of the object itself, but rather on the *availability* of the commodity. The importance of access to commodities therefore becomes a major issue of concern when trying to balance IPR, which theoretically and practically limit access to a commodity, and the right to health, which theoretically and practically demands greater access to commodities and services.

For instance, few could argue that medicines are not important for the realization of the highest attainable standard of health conducive to living a life in dignity and to the improvement of physical well-being; they promote health and allow individuals or groups to survive medical conditions that would otherwise be devastating. Obviously, the restricted production of particular medicines has an impact on life. But it is not just the restricted production that is problematic for particular individuals or groups; often the demand for pharmaceuticals is inelastic – individuals or groups cannot find alternatives and they must purchase the product even if the cost escalates. If they cannot afford the manufacturer's price, they must do without the product, compromising their well-being. One could easily argue that this is not an issue of IPR, but rather an issue of human rights obligations or social welfare policy; if the vulnerable members of society cannot afford health care, it is incumbent upon the government to take positive measures that enable and assist individuals and communities to enjoy the right to health. However, this obligation may be difficult to fulfil by governments that do not have the economic base or available resources to meet human rights obligations. Moreover, what this amounts to is the state subsidizing industry profits. The state is put in the bizarre circumstance of providing financial assistance to individuals and communities who cannot afford medicines because the state granted the firm a monopoly on the production of the medicine.

4. IPR, Health and the Paradox of the UDHR

Under Article 27(2) of the UDHR, IP is designated as a universal human right:

> Everyone has the right to the protection of the moral and material interests resulting from any scientific, literary, or artistic production of which he is the author.

---

70 *Ibid.*, p. 192. Complex social achievements are closely linked to societal norms and will not be addressed here. For our purposes, the concern is with physical functioning or physical well-being, both of which may be related to societal norms, but are also subject to a series of other conditions, such as entitlement systems.

71 Sen (1996), note 68 above, p. 187.

In identical language, Article 15(1)(c) of the ICESCR provides: 'The States Parties to the present Covenant recognize the right of everyone: To benefit from the protection of the moral and material interests resulting from any scientific, literary or artistic production of which he is the author.' Similarly, this right is recognized in regional human rights instruments, such as Article 13(2) of the American Declaration of the Rights and Duties of Man of 1948,[72] Article 14(1)(c) of the Additional Protocol to the American Convention on Human Rights in the Area of Economic, Social and Cultural Rights of 1988,[73] and, albeit not explicitly, Article 1 of Protocol No. 1 to the Convention for the Protection of Human Rights and Fundamental Freedoms (ECHR) of 1952.[74]

The basis for such a claim without doubt lies in the Western conception of property rights. What this implies is that, as with the ownership of property, people also have an exclusive right to their ideas, creations, and inventions. However, the UDHR's position on IP and its duty to carry out agreements promoting universal IP protection are incompatible with other important goals, particularly the promotion of human physical well-being, particularly the right to health, which is also guaranteed in Article 25 of the UDHR:

> (1) Everyone has the right to a standard of living adequate for the health and well-being of himself and of his family, including food, clothing, housing and medical care and necessary social services, and the right to security in the event of unemployment, sickness, disability, widowhood, old age or other lack of livelihood in circumstances beyond his control. (2) Motherhood and childhood are entitled to special care and assistance. All children, whether born in or out of wedlock, shall enjoy the same social protection.[75]

The conflict between Articles 27 and 25 occurs when IP protection raises barriers to commodity access that would improve the physical well-being of everyone. By promoting IP as a guaranteed right, the UDHR gives IP producers significant latitude in abrogating any responsibility to promote national development, though producers often argue for greater access to foreign markets and the protection of IP in those markets. The conflict becomes more convoluted when we consider Article 28 of the UDHR, which states: 'Everyone is entitled to a social and international order in which the rights and freedoms set forth in this Declaration can be fully realized.' The article is, as Pogge states, 'peculiar' relative to the rest of the Universal Declaration.[76] It does not prescribe another right or set of rights; rather, it lays the conditions under which rights should be realized as 'claims on the institutional order of any comprehensive social system'.[77] Hence, the question that arises is whether the pursuit of Article 27 through the current system of IPR protection embodied in the TRIPS agreement constitutes a barrier to the realization of health rights under Article 25.

---

72 OAS Doc. OEA/Ser. L./ V/II.23, doc. 21 rev. 6 (1948).

73 OAS Treaty Series No. 69 (1988), entered into force 16 November 1999.

74 CETS No. 009.

75 This issue is made more convoluted when we consider the United Nations Economic and Social Council's comments on Article 12 of the International Covenant on Economic, Social and Cultural Rights. These comments guarantee availability of, accessibility to, acceptability of and quality of health care. See Article 12, United Nations Economic and Social Council, Substantive Issues Arising in the Implementation of the International Covenant on Economic, Social and Cultural Rights, General Comment No. 14 E/C.12/2000/4 (25 April–12 May 2000) [online]. Available from: http://www.unhchr.ch/tbs/doc.nsf/%28Symbol%29/40d009901358b0e2c1256915005090be?Opendocument [accessed 22 December 2009].

76 T.W. Pogge, 'Human Rights and Global Health: A Research Program', *Metaphilosophy*, 36 (2005), pp. 182–209.

77 *Ibid.*, p. 196.

The declaration of IP as a universal human right is problematic within the established framework of physical well-being and subsistence rights, because the UN position does not recognize the hierarchy of IP that exists. Under the UDHR, the registered trademark for a multinational corporation is accorded the same importance and protection as a patent for medicinal purposes. This position has been challenged emphatically by the developing nations with the issue again centred on the profits versus physical well-being and subsistence rights argument. Prime Minister Indira Gandhi of India echoed these concerns:

> Affluent societies are spending vast sums of money understandably on the search for new products and processes to alleviate suffering and to prolong life. In the process, drug manufacture has become a powerful industry, subject to the same driving considerations of other big industries, that is, concentration on profit, fierce competition and recourse to hard-sell advertising. Medicines, which may be of the utmost value to poorer countries, can be bought by us only at exorbitant prices, since we are unable to have adequate independent bases of research and production. This apart, sometimes dangerous new drugs are tried out on populations of weaker countries although their use is prohibited within the countries of manufacture. It also happens that publicity makes us victims of habits and practices which are economically wasteful or wholly contrary to good health. … My idea of a better ordered world is one in which medical discoveries would be free of patents and there would be no profiteering from life or death.[78]

Fundamentally, the reconciliation of Articles 27 and 25 would have to recognize a hierarchy of rights that states pursue. As Pogge notes, the current system under which states protect IPR is morally problematic, particularly with regard to the right to health, because it puts the needs of the poor, who need medicine to live, against the needs of pharmaceutical firms, who are trying to recoup their investments and earn a profit.[79] From a moral perspective, states that support stronger IPR protection for profits over the subsistence needs of poor and impoverished people will *never* be able to win this argument outright. Such a strong statement is predicated on the idea that health and the goods and services needed to maintain it are *common goods* or *public goods* to which everyone would want access due to the broad societal benefits that emanate from a minimally healthy population. To place property rights and the pursuit of profits over the common good, in this context, becomes morally problematic, as it places a price on human life, but also constitutes a form of economic blackmail that is cruel. The HIV/AIDS problem in Africa is the best example. Until recent agreements between African states and pharmaceutical companies to lower the cost of anti-retroviral therapies, the cost of treatment to extend people's lives was prohibitively exorbitant for most Africans.

The situation could best be summarized as follows. Without any other known treatments, at the time of writing, antiretroviral medicines are the only treatments that can extend the lives of HIV/AIDS patients. The granting of exclusive patents for these drugs meant that pharmaceutical firms could dictate the price of the drugs, putting them out of reach of, not just Africans, but even the average Westerner without health insurance or government assistance. The pricing scheme was tantamount to dangling a treatment in front of dying people and telling them they could

78 Address by Prime Minister Indira Gandhi, 34th World Health Assembly, quoted in Editor's Introduction, in S. Patel (ed.), *Pharmaceuticals and Health in the Third World* (Oxford: Pergamon, 1983), p. 165.

79 Pogge, note 76 above, p. 187.

not have it simply because they were poor. Faced with a global public outcry[80] and the possible issuing of compulsory licences for antiretroviral therapies, the pharmaceutical firms agreed to a restructuring of the prevailing production and pricing scheme. In general, the HIV/AIDS case points to the need for a restructuring of production and pricing of the basic goods and services needed to fulfil subsistence rights. As David Hollenbach has stated,

> The growing *de facto* interdependence of both national and international life requires a stronger vision of the goods and services we share in common. It calls for the exploration of how the well-being of individual people might be advanced by seeking goods we must share in common if we are to have them at all.[81]

In other words, if we are to reconcile the guarantees of the UDHR with regard to the right to IPR and the right to health, a common vision of the goals we seek as *humans* must emerge, irrespective of nationalist state objectives and corporate quarterly goals. These goals must focus on what is, in the long-term, better for humans. The difficult part of this conception of these goals is not what is important for humans – few would disagree that health is a priority. The more critical factor is the notion of the long term, a concept that is embedded in humans as part of the psychology of survival, but is near non-existent as a concept in both political and corporate institutions. As human beings, our notion of the long term is simply a survival instinct. But for politicians and corporations, the long term is difficult to conceptualize because of the institutional constraints. Western politicians define the long term as the period up until the next election, while corporations see the long term as a reflection of their yearly profit margin. Politicians want strong corporate performance because it promotes job creation, a key indicator in their electoral fortunes. Corporations want higher profits because they are a key indicator for shareholders, who elect the board of directors. People are a part of this short-term vision, but only as segmented constituents of electoral votes and shareholders, not as a singular group of *human beings*. The point to be made here is that decision-making is mostly on a short-term basis such that we do not have a clear vision of what society should embody in the long term. While it is unrealistic to change the constitutional arrangements of states, how we view corporate performance is less immutable. In this sense, we can begin to change the way in which we measure corporate performance and health from a short-term profit rate to a measure that reflects long-term stability and profit consistency. In doing so, corporations, health rights proponents and people can benefit. One way to do this is to begin examining alternative IPR structures that could benefit all the stakeholders in the now globalized IPR system. Thomas Pogge has proposed one such way.

5. IPR Incentives for Promoting the Right to Health?

Pogge has proposed a new IPR system for incentivizing medical research that is predicated on the needs and demands of the wider world populace. As the system is right now, medical research seeks out what is most profitable. So, long before we have a treatment for malaria, we

80 For an account of the pharmaceutical patent dispute, the lawsuits and global public reaction, see R.L. Ostergard, 'The Political Economy of the South African-US Patent Dispute', *Journal of World Intellectual Property*, 2 (1999), pp. 875–88.

81 D. Hollenbach, 'The Common Good and Globalisation', in R. Gill (ed.), *A Textbook of Christian Ethics*, 3rd edn (London: T&T Clark, 2006).

have products to help with baldness, erectile dysfunction and acne. While these medicines treat conditions, these conditions generally are not life-threatening. Likewise, when treatments are available for conditions that afflict the poor, those treatments are often priced above what these people can afford. Pogge's approach tries to give pharmaceutical and biotechnology companies incentives to tackle conditions and diseases that afflict poor people and not just conditions that afflict the wealthy, while also providing a monetary incentive to provide medicines that already exist to the poor. As Pogge notes, there are two methods to deal with the problems of incentivizing research for diseases that are under-researched and for providing medicines that already exist to the poor. The first is a differential-pricing strategy that would reduce costs to poor countries for medicines while increasing costs to wealthier countries.[82] However, as Pogge notes, the idea has practical problems. The greatest drawback to a differentiated pricing scheme for pharmaceuticals is that such a system would create an incentive to import cheaper drugs from countries that are purchasing the pharmaceuticals at a lower price into countries that are paying the higher prices.[83] This problem alone would create a production and research disincentive for pharmaceutical and biotechnology and defeat the idea of providing incentives that are needed.

The second approach that Pogge establishes is a public-good strategy.[84] The strategy consists of three component parts. First, the development of *essential* drugs (defined as medicines for diseases that destroy human lives) would be provided as a public good so that all pharmaceutical firms would have access to the research for free. The idea here would be to eliminate monopolistic pricing practices under the current IPR regime. As Pogge notes, by itself this would be a disincentive generally to do research.[85] To mitigate this problem, Pogge introduces the second component of the public-good strategy, which is that corporations would be entitled to a multiyear patent on any essential drug they invent. Patent compensation, however, would be awarded out of public funds proportionate to the impact that the drug has on the global disease burden.[86] The objective would be to incentivize research on diseases that have a widespread impact on global health, but may not be as lucrative because of the target population – poor people. Incentives for second-party producers would be enhanced under this scheme because copying the drug would increase the number of users and thus the drug's impact on the global disease burden. The result would be to align the interests of research pharmaceutical firms with generic producers. Under the current system, these interests are diametrically opposed, as pharmaceutical firms perceive generic producers as profiting from their research without absorbing any of the research cost. Drugs for non-essential conditions could remain under the existing regime without incentive losses.[87]

---

82 Pogge, note 76 above, pp. 186–7.

83 This idea is not just a social welfare reallocation to help the poor. In fact, the idea of a differential responsibility for international public goods has a basis in international law, particularly with regard to environmental regulations and pollution control. Hence, the application of the idea to IPR is not far-fetched theoretically. See P.H. Sand, 'International Cooperation: The Environmental Experience', in J.T. Mathews (ed.), *Preserving the Global Environment: The Challenge of Shared Leadership* (New York: W.W. Norton, 1991) for an elaboration on differential responsibility in international environmental negotiations.

84 Pogge, note 76 above, p. 188.

85 *Ibid.*

86 *Ibid.*, p. 189.

87 *Ibid.*, p. 190. As Stiglitz notes, 'Indeed, I believe one of the main reasons the pharmaceutical industry was pushing TRIPS was that they wanted to reduce access to generic medicines. These are so disliked by the drug companies for the same reason that they are so liked by everybody else: the prices of generic drugs are very low.' See Stiglitz, note 13 above, p. 1701.

Of course, the remaining issue would be how the public funds option would be supported. This issue is the third component that Pogge establishes, which is to develop 'a fair, feasible, and politically realistic allocation of these costs, as well as compelling arguments in support of this allocation'.[88] Pogge elaborates on how to make the approach feasible and politically realistic, and, just as importantly, why developed states should engage in this approach voluntarily. While too long to expound in this chapter, Pogge's arguments on the moral imperative for such a system are compelling.[89] But, as discussed earlier, few people that would argue that providing better health for everyone around the world is a bad thing. Any objections would not be moral objections; instead they would be practical objections predicated on the system that is currently in place. But when one takes a closer look at the potential problems with Pogge's scheme, these issues are tied more to the nature of the corporate perception of the world than to any objection to providing everyone with better health care.

The key part of Pogge's scheme is the patent that firms would be awarded with compensation from public funds. Pogge estimates that the funding for new essential drugs would be in the US$45–90 billion range globally.[90] Undoubtedly, these funds would have to be funded on a differential basis by developed states. Even with such funding, there is no guarantee that such a system could provide enough incentive to entice pharmaceutical research firms to move funding toward essential drugs. To put the issue in perspective, one of Pfizer's best-selling drugs, the cholesterol-fighting drug Lipitor, had sales in 2005 in excess of US$11 billion. In that same year, Pfizer posted overall *profits* of US$11.4 billion.[91] Taken in perspective for one year, Pfizer's profit was between 11% and 24% of the global cost that Pogge estimated for essential drug funding under his scheme. With such *short-term* profits available in sales of non-essential drugs, it would seem that pharmaceutical firms would need greater incentives over the *long term* to entice them to enter into a research programme for essential drugs.[92] A possible way to extend the view of corporations would be to maintain the patent system, as Pogge proposes, but with two amendments.

First, pharmaceutical firms would be eligible to apply for subsidization of research on essential drugs through Pogge's public fund. This reimbursement would reduce some of the risk that firms assume when pharmaceutical firms undertake research on *new drugs*, not derivative drugs.[93] Of course, the subsidization would not be automatic, and funding reviews would have to be

88 Pogge, note 76 above, p. 191.

89 See *Ibid.*, pp. 191–200 for an elaboration on these principles.

90 *Ibid.*, p. 191.

91 D. Teather, 'Pfizer Profits Up 470% on Year Despite Wilting Viagra Sales', *The Guardian*, 20 January 2005 [online]. Available from: http://www.guardian.co.uk/business/2005/jan/20/highereducation.businessofresearch/print [accessed 18 November 2009].

92 In part, this idea is based on the assumption that the *true* cost of pharmaceutical research can be ascertained. For instance, critics of the pharmaceutical industry suggest that the industry has inflated its estimate of the cost of developing new drugs by incorporating marketing and the opportunity costs of spending research money on a new drug as opposed to investing it. For a scathing indictment of pharmaceutical industry pricing practices, see M. Angell, *The Truth About the Drug Companies: How They Deceive Us and What to Do About It* (New York: Random House, 2005).

93 This point is critical. As one pharmaceutical firm executive said, 'If I'm a manufacturer and I can change one molecule and get another twenty years of patent rights, and convince physicians to prescribe and consumers to demand the next form of Prilosec, or weekly Prozac instead of daily Prozac, just as my patent expires, then why would I be spending money on a lot less certain endeavor, which is looking for brand-new drugs?' See M. Angell, 'The Truth About the Drug Companies', *The New York Review of Books* (15 July 2004) [online]. Available from: http://www.nybooks.com/articles/17244#fn1 [accessed 15 November 2009].

conducted in conjunction with an independent body, most likely the World Health Organization (WHO). Second, firms that produce successful essential drugs would be eligible for an extended patent that would double the term of the patent. However, the royalty from the use of the research and product would not set the drug's price at a monopoly level. Instead, a small royalty attached to the *actual* production of the essential drug could be assessed as part of the production cost. That royalty would then be paid to the firm for a longer period of time. The benefits of such a scheme would be that pharmaceutical firms would be able to derive income over the long term, but at a smaller rate in the short term. With half of the research cost subsidized by Pogge's public fund, the profitability of the research on essential drugs would be more secure, but over a longer period. Such long-term patents would be held as long-term assets by the firm, improving its yearly income stream and further building the long-term assets of the firm. An international body, such as the WHO, would set the royalty compensation rate for the use of the essential drug. As with Pogge's scheme, a multidisciplinary group of specialists in economics, public health, biotechnology and other fields would need to work on many of the details. However, the focus would be to restructure compensation such that firms are willing to make a long-term investment in the essential drugs needed to fulfil the human right to subsistence health.

6. Conclusion

The argument set forth in this chapter has focused on the idea that there is not necessarily a disagreement over the right to health as a human right; instead, the greater problem has been over the feasibility of such an idea. Governments that are already strapped for money, particularly during periods of economic decline, are naturally reluctant to guarantee any positive rights that commit them to a massive financial investment. Moreover, governments that can barely afford to feed their own people simply do not have the resources to commit to such activities. The dichotomy between IPR and the right to health will never be resolved on a moral plane, as few could or would make the argument that profits trump human lives; instead the solution needs to be found in how the two ideas can conceivably work together. The market for innovation cannot remain structured in such a way that a limited number of individuals and groups who can afford to pay benefit from those innovations. When those innovations pit monopoly profits against human lives, the end result for the poor and impoverished individuals and groups is a cruel form of blackmail in which a cure for a disease is dangled in front of individuals and groups who then learn that they are too poor to purchase it. However, changes to these problems will only come about when governments, policymakers and corporations stop thinking of these problems in strictly nationalistic terms (as simply problems of the state) and instead start conceptualizing them as issues that affect all individuals and groups. That is, the right to health is a global public good that should be supplied to the best of humankind's ability. If this is done, citizens of all states can benefit from this level of cooperation.

The starting point for this reassessment of health as a public good must be how we approach the imbalance in research and the funding of that research. While an incentive structure is needed to entice private firms to engage in this research, the compensation under the current patent regime pits corporate interest against human interest. The objective should be to merge these two sets of interests into a long-term partnership that is beneficial to humankind and to the private interests that are the engines of innovation. While Pogge's framework is an excellent jumping-off point for this, the returns that corporations are realizing by engaging in predominantly non-essential drug research are greater than the type of compensation that would be feasible under a public funding framework. Instead, what we have suggested is that some of the development cost could be borne by a global public fund and that the rest of the development cost, plus a small, but long-term royalty payment, could define corporate interests to entice them into this line of research. Without addressing the current compensation structure in the patent system, the right to health under the UDHR will never be fully realized.

Chapter 10
Brave New World? Human Rights in the Era of Globalization

Paul O'Connell*

1. Introduction

Globalization is the meta-narrative of our age.[1] Few, if any, contemporary social phenomena, whether migration, global warming, or the present global economic crisis, are deemed intelligible outside the easy, intuitively appealing explanatory shorthand of globalization. As one of the other pervasive discourses of the post-war years, the subject of human rights has not escaped the gravitational pull of 'globalization speak', although it is fair to say that human rights scholars, like lawyers in general, have come somewhat late to the debate.[2] Indeed, writing earlier on the occasion of the 50th anniversary of the UDHR,[3] Philip Alston noted that globalization 'poses a variety of challenges which demand our attention but have not been receiving it'.[4] Thankfully, the literature on globalization and human rights has since burgeoned, generating a variety of perspectives, both optimistic and pessimistic, about the relationship between globalization and human rights.[5] It is the aim of this chapter to contribute to the development of this discourse, by offering a snapshot of the impact which globalization has had to date on human rights, and to assess what future obstacles and opportunities globalization presents for the realization of the UDHR promise.

This chapter begins by setting out the 'promise of globalization'; that is to say, the purported benefits for human rights from the process of globalization, as a starting point for the broader discussion which will follow. We then take one step back, as it were, to get a clearer analytical understanding of what exactly 'globalization' is, by examining alternative approaches to defining

---

*My thanks to Conor Gearty for generously reading an earlier draft of this chapter, and for his helpful, and typically insightful, comments; and to the editors of the present volume, both for the invitation to contribute to such a valuable collection and for their comments and suggestions throughout. As ever, responsibility for any shortcomings or omissions that remain rests solely with the author.

1 In the sense of being a 'global or totalizing cultural narrative schema which orders and explains knowledge and experience'; John Stephens, 'Pre-Texts, Metanarratives and the Western Metaethic', in John Stephens and Robyn McCallum (eds), *Retelling Stories, Framing Culture* (London: Routledge, 1998), pp. 3–55, at p. 6.

2 Gavin Anderson, *Constitutional Rights After Globalization* (Oxford: Hart Publishing, 2005), p. 1.

3 GA Res. 217A (III), UN Doc. A/810 at 71 (1948).

4 Philip Alston, 'The Universal Declaration in an Era of Globalisation', in Barend Van Der Heijden and Bahia Tahzib-Lie (eds), *Reflections on the Universal Declaration of Human Rights: A Fiftieth Anniversary Anthology* (The Hague: Martinus Nijhoff, 1998), p. 29.

5 For a useful introductory sampling of the literature, see Matthew J. Gibney (ed.), *Globalizing Rights* (Oxford: Oxford University Press, 2003); Alison Brysk (ed.), *Globalization and Human Rights* (Los Angeles: University of California Press, 2002); and Roger Brownsword (ed.), *Global Governance and the Quest for Justice. Vol. 4: Human Rights* (Oxford: Hart Publishing, 2004).

globalization. Then, with the benefit of greater definitional clarity, the remainder of the chapter is devoted to a consideration of the actual impact which globalization has had on human rights to date, before drawing some conclusions as to the potential long-term implications of globalization for human rights, and the obstacles and opportunities which globalization presents for the realization of human rights.

Before proceeding, I wish, at this juncture, to say a word about the analytical approach adopted in this chapter. According to Tony Evans, there are, broadly speaking, three different approaches to the analysis of human rights: (1) the philosophical (2) the legal and (3) the political; and, historically, the first two approaches have tended to marginalize the political discourse of human rights.[6] In contrast, this chapter explicitly privileges the politics of human rights. This is so because, given the nature of globalization, an over-reliance on a purely abstract philosophical or positivist legal discourse may tend to obscure 'the dynamics of human rights violations'.[7] In contrast, a more contextualized account of human rights, which accords prominence to the socio-political contexts in which the discourse of human rights is conducted, is more likely to 'reveal ... inequalities based on race or ethnicity, gender, religious creed, *and – above all – social class* [as] the motor force behind most human rights violations'.[8] This is to say that explicitly approaching the politics of globalization and human rights allows us to identify more clearly the power relations which underpin globalization, and how they interact with human rights. As David Held and Anthony McGrew note, '[power] relations are deeply inscribed in the dynamics of globalization';[9] therefore, it is essential to adopt an analytical framework which brings these relations to the fore.

2. The Promise of Globalization

With respect to human rights, proponents of globalization make two important, interrelated claims: firstly, globalization will, through the spread of 'free market' capitalism, generate economic growth, which in turn will lead to the eventual amelioration of poverty throughout the world; and, secondly, this reduction in poverty will ultimately lead to the development of civil society constituencies that will, in time, advance claims for democracy and human rights. In this way, globalization is presented as being a positive agent for the promotion of human rights and the general improvement of human well-being on a global scale. These two propositions, taken together, constitute the 'promise of globalization'. Matthew Gibney notes that the promise of globalization is 'an article of faith' for most government and corporate leaders in the West.[10] In this section, we will briefly relate the terms of these propositions, as articulated by the advocates of globalization, and leave to a later point in the chapter an interrogation of the veracity of these dual claims. At the outset, and for reasons that will become apparent in the next section of this chapter, it should be noted that for advocates of globalization the extension of free market capitalism is the *sine qua non* of globalization, and the precondition for the promise of globalization to be realized.

6 Tony Evans, *The Politics of Human Rights: A Global Perspective*, 2nd edn (London: Pluto Press, 2005), pp. 6–8.

7 Paul Farmer, *Pathologies of Power: Health, Human Rights and the New War on the Poor* (Los Angeles: University of California Press, 2005), p. 219.

8 *Ibid.* (emphasis added).

9 David Held and Anthony McGrew, *Globalization/Anti-Globalization* (Cambridge: Polity Press, 2002), p. 8.

10 Matthew Gibney, 'Introduction', in Gibney, note 5 above, p. 5.

If we assume the greater integration of national markets into the functioning of the global capitalist system, and the steady removal of barriers to trade, the logic then is straightforward for the proponents of globalization. As Thomas Friedman argues:

> [it is an] irrefutable fact that more open and competitive markets are the only sustainable vehicle for growing a nation out of poverty, because they are the only guarantee that new ideas, technologies, and best practices will easily flow into your country and that private enterprises, and even government, will have the competitive incentive and flexibility to adopt those new ideas and turn them into jobs and products. That is why ... nonglobalizing countries ... saw their per capita GDP growth shrink in the 1990s, while countries that moved ... to a globalizing model saw their per capita GDP grow in the 1990s.[11]

In similar terms, Andrew Berg and Anne Krueger argue that 'the weight of evidence is overwhelming on the positive effect of openness on growth', and they go on to argue that there are 'strong reasons to suppose that trade liberalization will benefit the poor at least as much as it benefits the average person'.[12] Going one step further, David Dollar and Aart Kraay argue that between 1980 and 2000 those countries that integrated most with the global economy witnessed both significant reductions in absolute poverty, and a generally egalitarian distribution of the benefits of economic growth and increased prosperity.[13] Furthermore, they argue that the 'real losers from globalization are those developing countries that have not been able to seize the opportunities' of globalisation.[14]

One of the best known advocates of globalization, Jagdish Bhagwati, makes the link between growing prosperity and human rights explicit, by arguing that greater integration into the global economy will, along with reducing poverty, lead to the gradual overcoming of practices which are considered contrary to human rights, such as gender discrimination (in pay and other fields) and child labour.[15] A more expansive version of this argument is presented by Daniel Griswold:

> Economic freedom and rising incomes ... help to nurture a more educated and politically aware middle class. A rising business class and wealthier civil society create leaders and centers of influence outside government. People who are economically free over time want and expect to exercise their political and civil rights as well. In contrast, a government that can seal its citizens off from the rest of the world can more easily control them and deprive them of the resources and information they could use to challenge its authority .... In other words, governments that grant their citizens a large measure of freedom to engage in international commerce find it increasingly difficult to deprive them of political and civil liberties, while governments that 'protect' their citizens behind tariff walls and other barriers to international commerce find it much easier to deny

---

11 Thomas L. Friedman, *The World Is Flat: The Globalized World in the Twenty-First Century* (London: Penguin Books, 2006), pp. 409–10.

12 Andrew Berg and Anne Krueger, 'Lifting All Boats: Why Openness Helps Curb Poverty', *Finance & Development*, 39(3) (2002), p. 18.

13 David Dollar and Aart Kraay, 'Trade, Growth and Poverty', *Finance & Development*, 38(3) (2001), pp. 16–18.

14 *Ibid.*, p. 19.

15 See Jagdish Bhagwati, 'Coping with Antiglobalization: A Trilogy of Discontents', *Foreign Affairs*, 81 (2002), p. 2; Jagdish Bhagwati and T.N. Srinivasan, 'Trade and Poverty in the Poor Countries', *American Economic Review*, 92(2) (2002), p. 180; and Jagdish Bhagwati, 'Why the Critics of Globalization Are Mistaken', *Der Tagesspiegel*, 14 September 2008.

> those same liberties. Of course, the correlation between economic openness and political freedom across countries is not perfect, but the broad trends are undeniable.[16]

Griswold concludes that for 'the past three decades, globalization, human rights, and democracy have been marching forward together ... in a way that unmistakably shows they are interconnected. By encouraging globalization ... we not only help to raise growth rates and incomes ... we also spread political and civil freedoms.'[17] This view is echoed by Erich Weede, who argues that globalization engenders a 'virtuous circle' in which human rights and increasingly liberalized international trade reinforce one another.[18] Significantly, this view is also shared by the World Bank and the International Monetary Fund (IMF),[19] which might go some way to explaining its prevalence. Later in this chapter we will look at the extent to which globalization has or is likely to deliver on its promise; however, before that, we will use the next section to gain some greater clarity about what we mean when we talk about globalization.

3. Definitional Clarity

Precisely because of the all-encompassing nature of the term 'globalization', it defies easy definition. Much ink has been spilt on debates over the precise genesis, nature and content of the phenomenon referred to as globalization. Indeed, so extensive is the disagreement that Jan Aart Scholte has concluded that 'the only consensus about globalization is that it is contested'.[20] In somewhat more exasperated terms, Gerald Helleiner has argued that the 'term globalization has become so slippery, so ambiguous, so subject to misunderstanding and political manipulation that it should be banned from further use, at least until there is precise agreement as to its meaning,'[21] Notwithstanding this extensive and ongoing disagreement, there is an analytical imperative to adopt a definite understanding of globalization before we can reflect on its implications for human rights. Put simply, it is entirely unsatisfactory to posit an analysis of the impact of *x* on *y*, without having a clear understanding of the nature of the two phenomena under discussion. In the same way, we cannot discuss the implications of globalization for human rights, without first clearly setting out our understanding of human rights and globalization.[22] For the purposes of this chapter, human rights are to be understood as the catalogue of fundamental rights set out in the UDHR.[23]

16 Daniel T. Griswold, 'Globalization, Human Rights and Democracy', *eJournal USA* (February 2006), pp. 40–1.

17 *Ibid.*, p. 41.

18 Erich Weede, 'Human Rights, Limited Government and Capitalism', *Cato Journal*, 28 (2008), pp. 35–52, at p. 49.

19 See World Bank, *Development and Human Rights: The Role of the World Bank* (Washington, DC: World Bank, 1998); and Sérgio Pereira Leite, 'Human Rights and the IMF', *Finance & Development*, 38(4) (2001).

20 Jan Aart Scholte, *Globalization: A Critical Introduction* (London: Palgrave Macmillan, 2000), p. 39.

21 Gerald K. Helleiner, 'Markets, Politics and Globalization: Can the Global Economy Be Civilized?', *Global Governance*, 7 (2001), p. 243.

22 Or, as Helleiner puts it, 'those involved in economic and political policymaking and debate must clarify their meaning [of globalization] if they are to be taken seriously'; *ibid.*

23 This is not to argue that the idea of human rights is, or should be, limited to the rights identified, explicitly or by implication, in the UDHR. Similarly, it is not intended here to dismiss or diminish the significance of the ongoing debates about the 'nature' of human rights. Rather, for the purposes of argumentation in this

In the paragraphs that follow, we will seek some definitional clarity with respect to globalization, by looking at two distinct approaches to defining and comprehending it, before adopting the most satisfactory account, and reflecting on its implications for human rights.

3.1 Globalization Simpliciter

The first approach to defining globalization which we look at, and the one which has held sway in many respects, is what I will refer to as the lowest-common-denominator definition of globalization, or globalization *simpliciter*. These simplistic definitions of globalization tend to proffer a vague, descriptive account of the objectively observable phenomena associated with the era of globalization as equivalent to a satisfactory definition of globalization. For example, in a recent article, John Glenn defines globalization as 'the intensification of economic relations between states'.[24] In similar terms, Nicholas Stern, the former Chief Economist of the World Bank, defines globalization as 'the growing integration of economies and societies around the world',[25] while Eduardo Aninat refers to it as 'the process through which an increasingly free flow of ideas, people, goods, services, and capital leads to the integration of economies and societies'.[26] In the same vein, albeit with a move away from the purely economic dimensions, Manfred Steger refers to globalization as 'a multidimensional set of social processes that create, multiply, stretch, and intensify worldwide social interdependencies and exchanges while at the same time fostering in people a growing awareness of deepening connections between the local and the distant'.[27] Jost Delbrück goes one further and imputes a positive, moral character to the process when he notes that 'globalization ... may be defined as the process of denationalization of markets, laws and politics in the sense of interlacing peoples and individuals for the sake of the common good.'[28] In one sense this approach to defining globalization is not objectionable. As a *descriptive* account, it is perfectly fine; however, it is sorely lacking as a useful *explanatory* definition of the process.[29]

With respect to human rights, it is interesting to note that while human rights lawyers have begun to develop evaluative positions on the relationship between globalization and human rights,[30] they have thus far failed to adopt an adequate or satisfactory analytical conception of globalization. Instead, they have tended, by and large, to embrace definitions of globalization akin to the globalization *simpliciter* account. For example, Allison Brysk defines globalization

chapter, the term 'human rights' is understood as encompassing, at least, the catalogue of rights contained in the UDHR.

24 John Glenn, 'Globalization's Alternatives: Competing or Complementary Perspectives?', *Government and Opposition*, 43 (2008), pp. 79–110, at p. 79.

25 World Bank, *Globalization, Growth and Poverty* (New York: Oxford University Press, 2002), p. ix.

26 Eduardo Aninat, 'Surmounting the Challenges of Globalization', *Finance & Development*, 39(1) (2002), p. 4.

27 Manfred Steger, *Globalization: A Very Short Introduction* (Oxford: Oxford University Press, 2003), p. 13.

28 Jost Delbrück, 'Globalization of Law, Politics, and Markets – Implications for Domestic Law – A European Perspective', *Indiana Journal of Global Legal Studies*, 1 (1993), pp. 9–36, at p. 11.

29 See Justin Rosenberg, 'And the Definition of Globalization Is ...?', *Globalizations*, 4 (2007), pp. 417–21.

30 As Shelton has noted, 'Two opposing views of globalization and its relationship to human rights have emerged: some see the two topics as mutually reinforcing and positive in improving human well-being, while others view globalization as posing new threats not adequately governed by existing international human rights law'; Dinah Shelton, 'Protecting Human Rights in a Globalized World', *Boston College International and Comparative Law Review*, 25 (2002), pp. 273–322, at p. 273.

as 'the growing interpenetration of states, markets, communications, and ideas across borders'.[31] For Dinah Shelton, globalization 'is a multidimensional phenomenon, comprising numerous complex and interrelated processes that have a dynamism of their own. It involves a deepening and broadening of rapid transboundary exchanges ... at all levels ... creating a more interdependent world.'[32] Again, these simplistic, descriptive accounts are unobjectionable at one level; however, if we are to seriously enquire into the relationship between globalization and human rights, the globalization *simpliciter* account is unsatisfactory, principally because such a definition fails to adequately address the values which underpin contemporary globalization and the agents which drive the process.[33] This failure, in turn, leads to the reification of the process, whereby it is presented as a natural, neutral inevitable process,[34] and this, in turn, seriously impairs our ability to interrogate and respond to globalization's impact on human rights.[35]

3.2 Neo-Liberal Globalization

The simplistic definitions of globalization given above assume, or at least imply, that globalization is in some respect, a natural and neutral phenomenon. This is revealed by Friedman when he argues that 'the flattening of the world [Friedman's euphemistic phrase for what globalization is about] is connecting all the knowledge centres of the planet together into a single global network, which – *if politics and terrorism do not get in the way* – could usher in an amazing era of prosperity, innovation, and collaboration, by companies, communities, and individuals.'[36] This idea that globalization somehow exists and develops independently of politics, that it has its own agency and momentum, and that, if left to its own devices, it will deliver its own form of utopia, is the fundamental flaw at the heart of the optimistic account of globalization and of globalization's likely impact on human rights. The simple reality is that politics is a possessive mistress, and globalization is very much a creature of politics. Appreciating this fact sharpens our understanding of globalization, and allows us to better analyse the relationship of globalization to human rights. Therefore, this section sets out the contours of a normative, political account of the nature of globalization, which in turn frames the subsequent discussion of globalization's impact on human rights.

It is useful at this point to note an important distinction here, one helpfully made by Eric Hobsbawm, between globalization as an objective material process, and globalization as a political and ideological construct.[37] While both are, of course, products of human agency, the former, which is marked by greater global interconnectedness in every sphere of life, is in some respects now beyond control, in the sense that it cannot be 'undone' (the clock cannot be unwound, as it were). In contrast, the latter form is fundamentally a historically contingent and mutable dispensation, one which can be altered and remade in myriad ways. The globalization *simpliciter* approach is perhaps least objectionable when addressing itself to the former form of globalization, although such clear

31 Allison Brysk, 'Introduction: Transnational Threats and Opportunities', in Brysk (ed.), *Globalization and Human Rights* (Los Angeles: University of California Press, 2002), p. 1.

32 Shelton, note 30 above, p. 275 (internal references omitted).

33 Philip Alston, 'The Myopia of the Handmaidens: International Lawyers and Globalization', *European Journal of International Law*, 3 (1997), pp. 435–48, at p. 447.

34 See Rhoda Howard-Hassmann, 'The Second Great Transformation: Human Rights Leapfrogging in the Era of Globalization', *Human Rights Quarterly*, 27 (2005), pp. 1–40.

35 This argument is developed further in Paul O'Connell, 'On Reconciling Irreconcilables: Neo-liberal Globalisation and Human Rights', *Human Rights Law Review*, 7(3) (2007), pp. 483–509.

36 Friedman, note 11 above, p. 8 (emphasis added).

37 See Eric Hobsbawm, *The New Century* (London: Abacus Books, 2000), p. 69.

distinctions are rarely drawn, whereas it is completely inappropriate as an optic through which to view the latter form of globalization. The rest of this section is concerned with an exposition of the political and ideological nature of contemporary globalization, or at least the politically and ideologically dominant form, as providing a necessary starting point for adequately conducting an interrogation of the impact of globalization on human rights.

It follows from this that, contrary to the implicit view of the globalization *simpliciter* thesis, the consensus among the majority of globalization scholars is that throughout the modern era of globalization 'the ideologically hegemonic position has been the neoliberal agenda.'[38] As James Mittelman notes, 'Globalization ... has been normalized as a dominant ideology that joins with neoliberalism to extol the virtues of individualism, efficiency, competition, and minimal state intervention in the economy. Neoliberalism also forms a policy framework, whose instruments of deregulation, liberalization, and privatization centre on heightened market integration.'[39] Jan Aart Scholte sets out in detail the extent of the influence of neo-liberalism on the dominant actors who have shaped globalization:

> Neoliberalism has generally prevailed as the reigning policy framework in contemporary globalization ... Most governments ... have promoted neoliberal policies towards globalization, especially since the early 1980s ... agencies such as the IMF, the WTO and the [OECD] have continually linked globalization with liberalization. Champions of neoliberal globalization have also abounded in commercial circles, particularly in the financial markets and among managers of transborder firms. Business associations like the International Organization of Employers and the World Economic Forum ... have likewise figured as bastions of neo-liberalism. In the mass-media, major business-orientated newspapers ... have generally supported neoliberalism. In academic quarters, mainstream economists have extolled the virtues of global free markets .... Given this widespread hold on centres of power, neoliberalism has generally ranked as policy orthodoxy in respect of globalization. Indeed in the late twentieth century neoliberal ideas gained widespread unquestioned acceptance as 'commonsense'.[40]

Given this assessment, the contemporary era is best understood as one in which neo-liberal globalization has been pre-eminent. With this understanding, we can now fruitfully move on to look at the impact of neo-liberal globalization on human rights; however, before that we will take the time to spell out what we mean by neo-liberalism, and what has contributed to its emerging as the 'commonsense' world-view over the last quarter-century.

Neo-liberalism[41] emerged as a coherent ideological and political programme in the early 1970s, a time at which global profit rates were either stagnating or falling. What neo-liberalism proposed

---

38 William Tabb, *Economic Governance in the Age of Globalization* (New York: Columbia University Press, 2005), p. 3; see also Held and McGrew, note 9 above, p. 4.

39 James H. Mittelman, *Whither Globalization?* (London: Routledge, 2004), p. 5.

40 Scholte, note 20 above, p. 35; see also Hilde Eileen Nafstad, Rolv Mikkel Blakar, Erik Carlquist, Joshua Marvle Phelps and Kim Rand-Hendriksen, 'Ideology and Power: The Influence of Current Neo-liberalism in Society', *Journal of Community & Applied Psychology*, 17 (2007), pp. 313–27.

41 The account of neo-liberalism and neo-liberal globalization presented here draws heavily on David Harvey, *Neoliberalism: A Brief History* (Oxford: Oxford University Press, 2005); Gérard Duménil and Dominique Lévy, *Capital Resurgent: Roots of the Neoliberal Revolution* (Cambridge, MA: Harvard University Press, 2004); Andrew Glyn, *Capitalism Unleashed: Finance, Globalization, and Welfare* (Oxford: Oxford University Press, 2006); Jeff Faux, *The Global Class War* (Hoboken, NJ: Wiley, 2006); and David Kotz, 'Globalization and Neoliberalism', *Rethinking Marxism*, 14(2) (2002), pp. 64–79.

was a break with the post- World War II consensus, which placed limits on corporate activity and also provided for a relatively strong welfare state. The *raison d'être* of neo-liberalism was to roll back this social state, although, as Leo Panitch notes, the neo-liberal rhetoric of rolling back the state belies the fact that neo-liberal globalization has relied heavily on strong, activist states; it augments the manner and reasons for which the state intervenes, but does not, in truth, diminish the state's power. What neo-liberal globalization has really been about is rolling back the state's involvement in social provision (education, health care, etc.) and opening up these fields to profit-making while at the same time strengthening the state's coercive capacities and its pro-capital, market-friendly regulatory functions.[42]

However, the subsequent influence enjoyed by neo-liberal doctrine within the so-called 'halls of power' did not develop in a vacuum. The point is made cogently by William Tabb:

> [to date] globalization has been overwhelmingly the result of a political project, an agenda of the most internationalized fractions of capital in the leading states of the world carried on in significant measure through both private consultations between peak organizations of the business community in the most powerful economies and through the agencies of their governments, actualized above all through the leadership of the executive branch of the American government.[43]

Thus, neo-liberal globalization has, first and foremost, been 'part of a hegemonic project concentrating power and wealth in elite groups around the world, benefiting especially the financial interests within each country, and US capital internationally'.[44] This is the understanding of globalization adopted here.

Clearly, as David Harvey notes, an open project around the concentration of economic and political power in the hands of a small elite would be unlikely to gain much popular support or forbearance.[45] Therefore, in order to advance its central agenda, the rhetoric of neo-liberalism has virtually promised the sun, moon and stars to those who would adopt its orthodoxy. Based on the cardinal belief that 'the market works perfectly and should be extended to as many areas of life as possible',[46] neo-liberals urged the 'liberalization of cross-border transactions; deregulation of market dynamics; and privatization of both asset ownership and the provision of social services',[47] arguing that if governments followed this general policy prescription the 'magic of laissez-faire',[48] as Scholte sardonically termed it, would result in rapid economic growth, stable economies, a generalized reduction in poverty and improvement in material well-being, among other things (i.e. the promise of globalization). While the rhetorical promise of an eventual 'trickle down' may have been presented as the public rationale, the real driving force behind neo-liberal globalization has been its powerful

42 Leo Panitch, 'Globalization and the State', in L. Panitch, C. Leys, A. Zuege and M. Konings (eds), *The Globalization Decade: A Critical Reader* (London: Merlin Press, 2004), p. 9.

43 Tabb, note 38 above, pp. 41–2.

44 Alfredo Saad-Filho and Deborah Johnston, 'Introduction', in A. Saad-Filho and D. Johnston (eds), *Neoliberalism: A Critical Reader* (London: Pluto Press, 2005), p. 1.

45 Harvey, note 41 above, p. 40.

46 Ben Fine, 'Examining the Ideas of Globalisation and Development Critically: What Role for Political Economy?', *New Political Economy*, 9 (2004), p. 216.

47 Scholte, note 20 above, p. 284.

48 *Ibid.*, p. 213.

backers, chief among them the governments of the USA and the UK and the various financial institutions which govern the global economy, both formally and informally.[49]

Following the Reagan–Thatcher revolution of the 1980s, the virtues of neo-liberalism were persistently extolled by two of the world's leading economic, political and military powers.[50] The support of these governments also ensured that the leading institutions of global economic regulation, the IMF, the World Bank, and the World Trade Organization (WTO), made governments throughout the world 'safe' for liberalized, mobile capital and imposed neo-liberal orthodoxy, with respect to small government,[51] in return for access to the putative benefits of the global economy. Thus, since the purge of the Keynesian influence in the early 1980s, these institutions have been 'centres for the propagation and enforcement of "free market fundamentalism" and neo-liberal orthodoxy'.[52] In concert with the most dominant Western governments, they have advanced the neo-liberal global project in two principal ways. In dealing with underdeveloped and impoverished countries, they have used structural adjustment programmes (SAPs) to compel neo-liberal reforms from governments in return for much needed capital.[53] In contrast, when dealing with more affluent countries, the agents of neo-liberalism have extended the project's hegemony through enforcing international trade rules which keep transnational capital 'disembedded' from the societies in which it operates. The consequence of these policies is that all governments are now subject to a generalized 'market discipline', which ensures that they augment their legal and policy structures so that they are more conducive to the generation of profits for global and domestic economic elites. In turn, this makes states subject to the whims of transnational corporations.[54] As Held and McGrew have noted,

> [The] increased mobility of capital ... shifts the balance of power between markets and states and generates powerful pressures on states to develop market-friendly policies, including restricted public deficits and curbs on expenditure, especially on social goods; lower levels of taxation that are internationally competitive; privatization and labour market deregulation.[55]

Thus, the agents of neo-liberal globalization have crafted a global market which, first and foremost, is geared towards the interests of economic elites. Individual states are reduced to the role of mere 'facilitators' in the operation and expansion of global capital.[56]

---

49 While the World Bank and other interstate fora set the formal rules of the global order, private organizations in the service of big business also play a key role in shaping policy at the global level. On the workings of the private forums which play a massive role in the shaping of the global order, including the Trilateral Commission, the World Economic Forum, etc., see Tabb, note 38 above, pp. 141–83; and Tom Hanahoe, *America Rules: US Foreign Policy, Globalization and Corporate USA* (Kerry: Brandon Books, 2003).

50 Harvey, note 41 above, pp. 9–29.

51 As Thomas puts it, these institutions all tend to 'understand the world through neoliberal tinted glasses'; Caroline Thomas, 'International and Financial Institutions and Social and Economic Human Rights: An Exploration', in Tony Evans (ed.), *Human Rights Fifty Years On: A Reappraisal* (Manchester: Manchester University Press, 1998), p. 166.

52 Harvey, note 41above, p. 29.

53 See Alejandro Colas, 'Neoliberalism, Globalisation and International Relations', in Saad-Filho and Johnston, note 44 above, pp. 75–9.

54 Evans, note 6 above, p. 43.

55 Held and McGrew, note 9 above, pp. 22–3.

56 Claire Sjolander, 'The Rhetoric of Globalization: What's in a Wor(l)d?', *International Journal*, 51 (1996), pp. 603–16, at p. 608.

Contrary, then, to the simplistic accounts of globalization, which present it as a generally benevolent, natural and neutral phenomenon, globalization, or at least the dominant form thereof, is best understood as neo-liberal globalization: a consciously undertaken political project to privilege private economic power over public power, in the interests of global and local economic elites. Globalization has, thus, been fundamentally about the creation of a global, deregulated, privatized economy subservient to the interests of dominant transnational capital, based primarily in the USA and Western Europe. Before going on to consider the impact to date of neo-liberal globalization on human rights, we will briefly highlight two important contextual factors that are central to an assessment of globalization's impact on human rights; the actual effect which globalization has had on poverty and inequality and the role of political and military force in the era of neo-liberal globalization.

3.2.1 Neo-Liberal Globalization and Poverty As one of the central promises of globalization is that it will result in the reduction of poverty and inequalities, with the concomitant raising of living standards and eventual embrace of human rights, it is important at this juncture to reflect on the actual impact of neo-liberal globalization on global poverty. As a preliminary, it should be noted that significant controversy surrounds the methodology of poverty measurement, analysis, etc.; and determining whether or not it has increased or decreased is fraught with problems and controversies.[57] Nonetheless, there is a great quantity of empirical research which can provide the basis for, at the very least, tentative conclusions about the impact of globalization on poverty and, of equal importance, inequality, to date. In keeping with the promise of globalization, the World Bank has consistently claimed that globalization has contributed to significant decreases in global levels of absolute poverty (as determined by the very crude measure of the number of people living on less than $1 a day) and that it has also contributed to reducing levels of inequality.[58] There is, however, a wealth of literature which argues to the contrary on both points. Interestingly, the World Bank, in a recent report, has revealed that its own methodology had, heretofore, under estimated the number of people around the world living in absolute poverty; and, having revised its approach, the bank revealed that there are approximately 400 million more people living in absolute poverty than was previously thought to be the case.[59] This, taken with the fact that the World Bank has been and remains one of the central institutional architects of neo-liberal globalization, lends greater credence to the alternative accounts of globalization's impact on poverty and inequality, and encourages a healthy scepticism when viewing World Bank accounts of global poverty levels.

Following a survey of a number of competing studies on levels of global poverty over time, Raphael Kaplinsky concludes that, contrary to the optimistic predictions of the World Bank, the preponderance of evidence suggests absolute poverty levels (people living on less than $1 a day) have remained static, and that, if one takes China out of the equation, the number of people in absolute poverty has in fact increased. Kaplinsky also notes that the number of people living on

57 See, for example, the ongoing work of the UN Statistics Division in compiling a handbook for measuring, assessing and acting on poverty data [online]. Available from: http://unstats.un.org/unsd/methods/poverty/default.htm [accessed 18 November 2009].

58 See World Bank, note 25 above.

59 See Shaohua Chen and Martin Ravallion, 'The Developing World Is Poorer Than We Thought, But No Less Successful in the Fight Against Poverty', *Policy Research Working Paper 4703* (2008); and Nicolo Tomaselli, 'World Bank New Poverty Estimates: More Confusing Than Ever' [online]. Available from: http://www.brettonwoodsproject.org/art-562473 [accessed 17 December 2009].

less than $2 a day has increased markedly during the era of neo-liberal globalization.[60] In this context China is significant, as the 'poster child' of globalization. The rapid economic growth of China in many respects skews global statistics on poverty and inequality, but, as Kaplinsky and others note, once China is taken out of the equation, global poverty and inequality have both increased throughout the last 30 years of globalization.[61] Furthermore, while China tends to skew the global aggregate figures on poverty and inequality, China itself has seen growing levels of poverty and inequality, and greater entrenchment of poverty, throughout the years of its 'miracle' economic growth, thus giving the lie to the assumed correlation between free-market growth and shared prosperity.[62] As to the question of inequality, various studies attest to the fact that while the impact of free trade on poverty reduction might be somewhat unclear, it is perfectly clear that such policies inexorably result in greater and greater inequalities in wealth distribution, both within and between countries.[63] Indeed, a recent study by the Organization for Economic Cooperation and Development (OECD) found that during the years of neo-liberal globalization, poverty and inequality increased in three-quarters of all OECD member states.[64]

Ostensibly, the persistence of high levels of absolute poverty, and, by some accounts, the increase in the number of people living in absolute poverty, coupled with marked increases in inequality within and between countries, might be viewed as a failure of globalization to deliver on its promise. This, however, ignores the reality of the political project of neo-liberal globalization. From the outset, neo-liberal globalization has been about strengthening and enhancing the position of global economic elites. This, of necessity, is achieved at the expense of others. The point is made, in a roundabout way, by Thomas Pogge when he notes that the persistence of extreme poverty, and by extension inequality, is not a natural phenomenon, but rather is a result of the 'ways that economic interactions are structured by interlocking national and international institutional arrangements'.[65] Or, as Susan Marks puts it,

> [the] processes which impoverish the bottom billion [people in the world] are not just dysfunctions, mishaps or signs of local problems or weaknesses. Rather, they belong with the logics of a world that is structured around multiple and shifting forms of exploitation. This has important strategic implications, inasmuch as poverty reduction then appears to hinge not just on changing policies, nor even on implementing institutional reforms, but on curbing the power and curtailing the privileges of those on the 'winning' side of current global relations.[66]

---

60 Raphael Kaplinsky, *Globalization, Poverty and Inequality* (Cambridge: Polity Press, 2005), pp. 27–51; see also Robert Hunter Wade: 'On the Causes of Increasing World Poverty and Inequality, Or Why the Matthew Effect Prevails', *New Political Economy*, 9(2) (2004), pp. 164–88.

61 E.g. Thomas Pogge, 'Growth and Inequality: Understanding Recent Trends and Political Choices', *Dissent*, 55(1) (2008), pp. 66–75.

62 See Fei Yan, 'The Rising Urban Poverty and Political Resentment in Transitional China: The Experience of Shanghai', *Journal of Politics and Law*, 1(1) (2008), pp. 15–24.

63 See Frances Stewart and Albert Berry, 'Globalization, Liberalization and Inequality: Expectations and Experiences', in A. Hurrell and N. Woods (eds), *Inequality, Globalization and World Politics* (Oxford: Oxford University Press, 1999), pp. 150–86, at p. 186; and the United Nations Development Programme, *Human Development Report 2005 – International Cooperation at a Crossroads: Aid, Trade and Security in an Unequal World* (New York: Oxford University Press, 2005).

64 OECD, *Growing Unequal? Income Distribution and Poverty in OECD Countries* (OECD, 2008).

65 Thomas Pogge, 'Introduction', in Pogge (ed.), *Freedom From Poverty as a Human Right* (Oxford: Oxford University Press, 2007), p. 3.

66 Susan Marks, 'Human Rights and the Bottom Billion', *European Human Rights Law Review*, no. 1 (2009), pp. 37–49, at p. 47.

Put simply, the reasons for the persistence of poverty in the era of globalization are embedded in the very structures of the global economic, political and legal *status quo*. Similarly, Kaplinsky notes that while the World Bank and other institutions of neo-liberal globalization insist that the persistence of poverty is a result of states failing to globalize enough, the reality is that entrenched and increasing poverty and inequality are endemic within the economic, political and social structures of neo-liberal globalization.[67]

3.2.2 Neo-Liberal Globalization and Imperialism According to Stephen Gill, the current global conjuncture is maintained through a 'combination of market discipline and the direct application of political power'.[68] The idea of 'market discipline' correlates with the hegemony of neo-liberal economic orthodoxy discussed above; the second point, however, 'the direct application of political power', opens the door for a discussion of the use of force in the maintenance of the current global order. More specifically, Gill's aphorism brings into focus the place of imperialism in the world today; while the language of imperialism is somewhat out of vogue in mainstream social science, and is almost unknown to the contemporary discourse of human rights, there is an extensive and growing literature on the subject, and in particular on the place of imperialism in the era of globalization.[69] In the space available here, it is impossible to do full justice to all of the aspects of this literature; instead, I will set out briefly the contours of the argument relating contemporary globalization to imperialism. Samir Amin stresses the centrality of imperialism in the modern era.[70] For him, the contemporary world order is dominated above all by the military and economic power of the USA, with junior partners in Europe and Japan. In this context, globalization is simply an aspect of the contemporary imperialist project which has as its aim the subordination of the rest of the world to the interests of the US ruling class, and consequently can 'produce only an organized system of apartheid on a world scale'.[71]

It is interesting to note that for many mainstream US commentators the fact that America is an imperial power is taken for granted. However, these commentators view American imperialism as a benign, benevolent force ('empire lite', as Michael Igantieff puts it) maintaining the global public interest, through advancing America's interests.[72] This is surely a highly self-serving assessment; nonetheless, their acknowledgement of the imperial nature of the USA in the current global order lends weight to the account presented by Amin and others. If we adopt this perspective, then 'globalization' may also be understood as the hegemonic discourse of contemporary imperialism.

67 Kaplinsky, note 60, p. 235; and see Jeremy Seabrook, 'In a World of Wealth, Poverty Has Become a Necessity', *The Guardian*, 27 July 2006.

68 Stephen Gill, *Power and Resistance in the New World Order* (Basingstoke: Palgrave Macmillan, 2003), p. 118.

69 E.g. Leo Panitch and Colin Leys (eds), *The New Imperial Challenge: Socialist Register 2004* (London: Merlin Press, 2003); Stephen Hartnett and Laura Ann Stengrim, *Globalization and Empire: The U.S. Invasion of Iraq, Free Markets, and the Twilight of Democracy* (Tuscaloosa, AL: University of Alabama Press, 2006); and Manfred B. Steger, 'From Market Globalism to Imperial Globalism: Ideology and American Power After 9/11', *Globalizations*, 2(1) (2005), pp. 31–46.

70 This very rough synopsis of Samir Amin's account of contemporary imperialism draws on the following works of his: *Capitalism in the Age of Globalization: The Management of Contemporary Society* (London: Zed Books, 1997); *The Liberal Virus* (London: Pluto Press, 2004) (hereinafter: *Liberal Virus*); and *Beyond US Hegemony: Assessing the Prospects for a Multipolar World* (London: Zed Books, 2006).

71 Amin, *Liberal Virus*, note 70 above, p. 20.

72 Thomas L. Friedman, 'Manifesto for a Fast World', *New York Times Magazine*, 28 March 1998; Michael Igantieff, 'The Burden', *New York Times Magazine*, 5 January 2003; and Ivo Daalder and James Lindsay, 'American Empire, Not "If" But "What Kind"', *New York Times*, 10 May 2003.

Whether or not globalization completely embraces imperialism, or vice versa, this line of argument at least highlights the important role of imperialism, be it 'soft' (economic and ideological hegemony) or 'hard' (projection of force), in the contemporary world order and helps us to appreciate the consequences for human rights which flow from it.

4. Neo-Liberal Globalization and Human Rights

A number of years ago, and writing without a clearly articulated, analytical conception of globalization, Asbjørn Eide nonetheless warned that 'the present direction of the process of globalization ... if not properly redirected can become an increasing threat to many human rights.'[73] In this section of the chapter, we will look at the extent to which this concern has been borne out by the actual processes of neo-liberal globalization. The UDHR contains a comprehensive catalogue of human rights; in this section, however, we consider separately the impact of neo-liberal globalization on civil and political rights on the one hand, and socio-economic rights on the other hand. Drawing this distinction is not meant to detract in any way from the inherent interdependence of all human rights; rather, the point is to demonstrate clearly the way in which different practices characteristic of neo-liberal globalization have impacted on human rights in their totality.

4.1 Civil and Political Rights

The attacks on New York and Washington on 11 September 2001 marked a watershed in recent history. They provide the starting point for what Conor Gearty has referred to as an incipient 'age of terrorism or ... at the very least an age of counter-terrorism'.[74] The attacks themselves, and the response of the US administration, are common knowledge and the intricacies of each will not be recounted here. Instead, what I want to do here is locate the contemporary terrorist threat and the US response in the context of neo-liberal globalization, and to give an indication of the implications which the interaction between the two have had for the enjoyment of basic civil and political rights. The first point to note is the close relationship between the practices of neo-liberal globalization and terrorism. As James Mittelman points out, 'terrorism and globalization are closely intertwined ... while global terrorism feeds on marginalization, globalization spawns it.'[75] A similar point is made by Amin, who notes that faced with the failure of globalization to deliver on its promise, the marginalized of the world react in what they perceive to be the only ways open to them; 'in the absence of ... positive utopias the peoples of the world invariably react to their desperate circumstances by reviving other types of utopia',[76] including absolutist, religious fundamentalism. The persistence of officially defined terrorism also has to be seen as an inevitable concomitant of US imperialism.

Another noteworthy point, made by Gary Teeple, is that the attacks of 11 September can be viewed as providing the necessary pretext for US imperial 'business as usual'. The response of the USA, in the form of the ill-defined and seemingly boundless 'war on terror', provides *carte blanch* for the USA to exert coercive force both domestically and internationally, and in this way maintain and defend the inequalities of the global, imperial *status quo*. On this account, the attacks of 11 September, indeed the terrorist threat itself (both perceived and actual), are structural requirements

73 Asbjørn Eide, 'Obstacles and Goals to Be Pursued', in A. Eide, C. Krause and A. Rosas (eds), *Economic, Social and Cultural Rights: A Textbook*, 2nd edn (The Hague: Martinus Nijhoff, 2001), pp. 554–5.

74 Conor Gearty, 'Terrorism and Human Rights', *Government and Opposition*, 42 (2007), p. 340.

75 Mittelman, note 39 above, p. 96.

76 Amin, *Liberal Virus*, note 70 above, p. 29.

of an imperial system built on massive global inequalities and maintained, in large part, through staggering levels of military spending.[77] To paraphrase Voltaire, if the attacks had not taken place, there would have been a need for the USA to invent some form of threat in order to justify both its military spending and its routine intervention in foreign countries.

In any event, the attacks on New York and Washington have provided the pretext for 'a general attack on civil rights both domestically and internationally on the part of the Bush administration and US military and intelligence, including the sanctioning of assassination as a potential CIA tool, the establishment of secretive military tribunals, the ongoing detainment of Arab men [and] open discussion of torture as a "necessary" interrogation measure'.[78] Gearty makes a similar point, in noting that the US-declared war on terror has also provided cover for governments throughout the world to row back on human rights guarantees, in order to confront perceived threats to national security.[79] He goes on to note that the counter-terrorism policies of the US government have involved

> the rejection or unilateral redefinition of international human rights law; the refusal to abide by international humanitarian law ... the detention of 'unlawful combatants' at Guantánamo and elsewhere, and of course, notoriously, the prisoner abuse at Abu Ghraib and elsewhere, and the rendition of suspected terrorists to friendly countries where torture is used as a means of interrogation is routine.[80]

Coupled with its activities against international terrorism, the US government has also used the threat of terrorism to greatly erode the protection of the basic civil liberties (privacy, freedom of expression and association) of its own citizens, principally through the adoption of the unashamedly Orwellian 'Patriot Act';[81] this approach has been mimicked by governments throughout the world, contributing to a generalized, global assault on basic civil and democratic rights.[82] In addition to this, the US government has, in the ultimate act of mendacity, co-opted the language of human rights to justify in part the continued prosecution of its war on terror, and as an *ex post facto* rationale for its imperial foray into Iraq.[83]

In sum, the age of counter-terrorism, which can be understood as a structural imperative in a world divided by the injustices and inequalities engendered by neo-liberal globalization, is, contrary to the optimistic accounts of Weede and others, engendering a vicious circle leading to the steady erosion of the core civil and political rights enshrined in the UDHR, whether it is privacy, physical integrity, freedom of expression or association, and, in far too many instances, the right to life itself. It does so in a number of ways: in the first instance, the human rights-denying injustices caused by neo-liberal globalization and US imperial activities generate the sort of resentment and

77 Gary Teeple, *The Riddle of Human Rights* (London: Merlin Press, 2005), pp. 167–211.

78 Ruth Reitan, 'Human Rights in U.S. Policy: A Casualty of the "War on Terrorism"?', *International Journal of Human Rights*, 7(4) (2003), pp. 51–62, at p. 55.

79 Gearty, note 74 above, p. 347.

80 *Ibid.* pp. 350–1.

81 See Julie Mertus and Tazreena Sajjad, 'Human Rights and Human Insecurity: The Contributions of US Counterterrorism', *Journal of Human Rights*, 7 (2008), pp. 2–24, at pp. 7–9.

82 Michael Head, 'The Global "War on Terrorism": Democratic Rights Under Attack', in Brownsword, note 5 above, p. 11.

83 See Tom Farer, 'Un-Just War Against Terrorism and the Struggle to Appropriate Human Rights', *Human Rights Quarterly*, 30 (2008), p. 356; and Amy Bartholomew and Jennifer Breakspear, 'Human Rights as Swords of Empire', in L. Panitch and C. Leys (eds), *The New Imperial Challenge: Socialist Register 2004* (London: Merlin Press, 2003), p. 125.

hatred that fuels terrorist organizations,[84] which, in turn, commit massive human rights violations in their attacks. In response, governments throughout the world invoke the spectre of terrorism as the basis for rowing back on basic civil liberties and democratic rights, ostensibly to counter terrorism but also to suppress any inconvenient opposition. Furthermore, the co-optation by the US government of the language of human rights to justify its worldwide interventions, which invariably entail further human rights violations, serves to rob human rights of legitimacy in the eyes of many oppressed people throughout the world.

4.2 Socio-Economic Rights

Two factors that are characteristic of neo-liberal globalization combine to contribute to a generalized undermining of the enjoyment of socio-economic rights by the majority of the people in the world: (1) the small state rhetoric and (2) the persistence of poverty and inequality. As to the first of these points, the simple reality is that all human rights, but in particular socio-economic rights, require significant state involvement for them to be fully and meaningfully realized. Consequently, the neo-liberal rhetoric of the small state and the global neo-liberal practice of rolling back the social state through privatization, deregulation and trade liberalization run counter to the meaningful enjoyment of socio-economic rights. Related to the small state rhetoric, and also to the issue of poverty, the privatization of fundamental social services (availability to consumers versus entitlement of individuals) has resulted in the widespread denial of the basic rights to food, shelter, health and education. Referring specifically to the issue of poverty, Eide argues that the 'most dramatic obstacle to the enjoyment of economic and social rights is the steep increase in income-specific inequality, both among nations and within nations, and the spread of poverty in the midst of plenty.'[85]

This apprehension is borne out by the actual experience of neo-liberal globalization to date. The work of a number of UN special rapporteurs, on the rights to health, education, housing and food, has revealed a tension between the practices of neo-liberal globalization and the protection of socio-economic rights.[86] The general concern intimated by the various special rapporteurs is spelt out quite explicitly by the former special rapporteur on the right to food, Jean Zeigler:

> the Bretton Woods institutions [the World Bank and the IMF], along with the government of the United States of America and the World Trade Organization, refuse to recognize the mere existence of a human right to food and impose on the most vulnerable States the 'Washington Consensus' emphasizing liberalization, deregulation, privatization and the compression of State domestic budgets, a model which in many cases produces greater inequalities. In particular, three aspects of the general process of privatization and liberalization create catastrophic consequences for the right to food; the privatization of institutions and public utilities, the liberalization of agricultural trade, and the market-assisted model of land reform.[87]

84 As Richard Falk puts it, 'globalisation-from-above is definitely encouraging a resurgence of support for right-wing extremism'; Richard Falk, 'Resisting "Globalisation-from-Above Through "Globalisation from Below"', *New Political Economy*, 2 (1997), pp. 17–24, at p. 21.

85 Eide, note 73 above, p. 555.

86 The work of the special rapporteurs on the rights to health, education and housing is considered in more detail in O'Connell, note 35 above, pp. 501–7.

87 Report of the Special Rapporteur on the Right to Food, Jean Ziegler, 10 January 2008, A/HRC/7/5, para. 24; for a related argument, see Jacqueline Mowbray, 'The Right to Food and the International Economic System: An Assessment of the Rights-Based Approach to the Problem of World Hunger', *Leiden Journal of International Law*, 20 (2007), pp. 545–69.

Previously, Zeigler had raised concerns that the economic policies imposed by the IMF and the World Bank had contributed to and further exacerbated food crises in Niger, and that in an environment which demanded greater privatization of essential services and liberalization of trade rules, large multinational corporations could abuse their monopoly positions to the detriment of the rights of the world's citizens.[88]

Ultimately, the work of these special rapporteurs on fundamental rights lends itself to the conclusion (albeit more directly in some cases than others) that the practices associated with neo-liberal globalization are detrimental to the protection of socio-economic rights. The various common issues that the rapporteurs have highlighted as being inimical, either potentially or actually, to the protection of the rights with which their respective mandates are concerned include the following: state failure (or inability) to act, privatization and deregulation, poverty and the imposition of fees for essential services, and the way in which these various policy stances interact with entrenched poverty and inequality. These factors are all direct consequences of the project of neo-liberal globalization and the result of the structural logic of that project. The conclusion to be drawn, then, is that the 'current global economic structure cannot deliver economic and social rights for all of humankind'.[89] In light, then, of the impact which neo-liberal globalization has had on the entire catalogue of human rights to date, it is difficult not to agree with Teeple:

> In the world today, the principles of most human rights appear to be increasingly transgressed, subordinated, or usurped. In general human rights seem to be more in decline than ascendant. The seeming promise of the postwar years, of a world based on clearly established human rights, lies unfulfilled ... the consolidation of the global economy and regulatory structures seem to be taking place more in the violation than in the realization of human rights.[90]

The promise of globalization is a hollow one, for the very simple reason that globalization is not, as its apologists would have it, a natural, neutral, benevolent phenomenon. Rather, neo-liberal globalization, the dominant form of globalization in our age, is a political project constructed to serve the economic interests of a small global elite. Precisely because of this, the conditions for the violation of the human rights of the world majority are embedded within the processes of contemporary globalization.

5. Globalization and the UDHR at 70?

The argument presented in this chapter, in sum, is that once we gain a clear understanding of what globalization is really about, we can see that the conditions for the violation of human rights are structurally embedded within the global *status quo*. Furthermore, the evidence presented above shows that neo-liberal globalization has, to date, had serious adverse consequences for the protection of the entire catalogue of rights protected by the UDHR and that six decades after its adoption, the promise of human flourishing contained therein remains unfulfilled. Unfortunately, we can also conclude from the above that if 'globalization, underpinned by neo-liberalism, expands and intensifies, an increasing number of people will be marginalized and the entire complex of rights will be abused'.[91] We could then reasonably expect that, assuming the continued pre-eminence of

88 Report of the Special Rapporteur on the Right to Food, Jean Ziegler, 16 March 2006, E/CN.4/2006/44, paras. 13–16 and 46–51.

89 Thomas, note 51 above, p. 182.

90 Teeple, note 77 above, p. 1.

91 Adamantia Polis, 'Human Rights and Globalization', *Journal of Human Rights*, 3 (2004), p. 355.

neo-liberal globalization, the 70th anniversary of the UDHR will witness the continued failure to meet 'the highest aspirations of the common people',[92] and, instead, confront us with even greater structural denials of human rights.

The really positive thing, however, is that in taking the step of actually defining globalization, we move from the paralysing, powerlessness engendered by those accounts which reify globalization, and towards the liberating realization that if 'globalization was made by humankind, then it can be unmade or remade by political agency. As with slavery, feudalism, and mercantile capitalism, there is no reason to believe that neoliberal globalization is eternal.'[93] Furthermore, the current global economic crisis potentially presents us with a unique historical moment, within which both globalization and human rights can be reclaimed by the global majority. At the risk of historical over-simplification, it can be said that the Great Depression of the 1930s led, ultimately, to the adoption of the UDHR.[94] In the same way, the present economic crisis, while it has not yet reached the depths of the 1930s, presents us with a potentially epoch-changing moment. One of the great fallacies accompanying the current global economic crisis is that the credit crunch and attendant economic recession were unforeseeable, and that nobody, as such, is culpable. The reality is that the deregulation of the global financial sector, the lifting of restrictions on cross-border movement of capital, etc. (in short the neo-liberal prescription), made the current economic crisis inevitable.[95]

The consequences of these failed policies will undoubtedly lead to hardship and suffering for hundreds of millions of people around the world,[96] and intensified denial of basic socio-economic rights.[97] However, the hardship caused by this crisis may also lead, but by no means necessarily, to the emergence of new political possibilities and realities. Already the active agents for an alternative to neo-liberal globalization are present in the multifarious dimensions of the subaltern globalization movement,[98] and it is possible that these groups will be galvanized by the crisis and contradictions of the current economic collapse. It is possible, then, that popular dissatisfaction engendered by the crisis of neo-liberal globalization, and the inability of neo-liberal orthodoxy to resolve these problems, will

92 UDHR, second preambular paragraph.

93 Mittelman, note 39 above, p. 89.

94 This is so in two respects: (1) in so far as the standard narrative portrays the adoption of the UDHR as a response to the atrocities of World War II, in particular the Nazi atrocities, and many historical accounts point to the Great Depression as providing the objective conditions which contributed to the breakout of the war (the rise of Fascism etc.); (2) Franklin D. Roosevelt's response to the Great Depression, the New Deal, and his 'Second Bill of Rights' are held to have significantly influenced the content and the subsequent adoption of the UDHR. See Jeffrey A. Frieden, *Global Capitalism: Its Fall and Rise in the Twentieth Century* (New York: W.W. Norton, 2006), pp. 173–229; Johannes Morsink, 'World War Two and the Universal Declaration', *Human Rights Quarterly*, 15 (1993), p. 357; and Cass R. Sunstein, *The Second Bill of Rights* (New York: Basic Books, 2004).

95 See Robert Wade, 'Financial Regime Change', *New Left Review*, 53 (2008), p. 5; John Bellamy Foster, 'The Financialization of Capitalism', *Monthly Review*, 58(11) (2008), p. 1; and Paulo dos Santos, 'The World Bank, the IFC and the Antecedents of the Financial Crisis' [online]. Available from: http://www.brettonwoodsproject.org/art-563119 [accessed 23 October 2009].

96 See Stephany Griffith-Jones and Jenny Kimmis, 'International Financial Volatility', *Journal of Human Development*, 4(2) (2003), pp. 209–25; they note how financial crises invariably lead to serious social hardship for the most vulnerable.

97 This much was recently acknowledged by the Council of Europe's Commissioner for Human Rights, Thomas Hammerberg: 'In times of economic crisis it is particularly essential to ensure the protection of social rights' [online]. Available from: http://www.coe.int/t/commissioner/Viewpoints/081117_en.asp [accessed 22 December 2009].

98 For an introductory discussion of subaltern globalization, see O'Connell, note 35 above, pp. 493–5.

lead to the rolling back of the privatization agenda, and the 're-socialization' of the various fields of human interaction that had been surrendered to the market.[99] As David Kotz argued a number of years ago, the 'macroinstability of neoliberal global capitalism might produce a major economic crisis at some point, one that could spin out of the control of the weakened regulatory authorities. This would almost certainly revive the politics of the regulationist state.'[100] While, in the closing months of 2008 and throughout 2009, we certainly witnessed the arrival of the economic crisis suggested by Kotz, it is not yet clear what the political outcome will be, but there will almost certainly be global agitation for an alternative to the 'common sense' of neo-liberalism. Such political mobilization will present a real opportunity to reclaim both human rights and globalization for the benefit of the world's majority.

6. Conclusion

One of the great and tragic ironies of the contemporary era of globalization is that it has involved, through the agency of the UN and numerous NGOs, and, belatedly, the rhetoric of the World Bank and others, the diffusion on a truly global scale of the language of human rights, while at the same time witnessing the continued, and, as argued above, intensified, systemic violation of human rights. As Anthony McGrew puts it, 'contemporary patterns of globalization are associated with a growing set of disjunctures between the global diffusion of the idea of universal human rights and the social, political and economic conditions necessary for their effective realization.'[101] The reason for this disjuncture between rhetoric and reality may be largely the fact that during the era of neo-liberal globalization, the language of human rights was, as Evans argues, co-opted as an *apologia* for the negative consequences of globalization.[102] However, as Gearty argues, in conditions where the denial of human rights is structurally embedded within the social, economic and political *status quo*, human rights must be 'subversive rather than supportive of such a brutal *status quo*'.[103]

The current global economic crisis presents a critical historical juncture; if the greater interdependence of the world's people which globalization has engendered is to deliver anything other than more suffering and oppression, it is essential that all of us concerned with human rights make common cause with the social and political movements that emerge from the milieu of the current crisis, and work to create alternative national, regional and international institutions which privilege the interests of the world's majority, as opposed to the interests of economic elites. If the next decade of globalization is to see any improvement in the global protection of human rights, it is essential that the animating ideals of the UDHR are joined with other emancipatory discourses, and are central to the opposition to neo-liberal globalization and instrumental in the construction of a genuine alternative. Perhaps the guiding principle in going forward will be the pursuit of 'a social and international order in which the rights and freedoms set out in [the UDHR] can be fully realized'.[104] Such an order will either be the antithesis of the neo-liberal global order, or it will not be at all.

---

99 See Gunther Teubner, 'Justice Under Global Capitalism?', *Law and Critique*, 19 (2008), pp. 329–34.

100 Kotz, note 41 above, p. 78.

101 Anthony McGrew, 'Human Rights in a Global Age: Coming to Terms with Globalization', in Evans, note 51 above, p. 194; see also Brownsword, 'Introduction: Global Governance and Human Rights', note 5 above, p. 2.

102 Evans, note 6 above, pp. 129–30.

103 Conor Gearty, *Can Human Rights Survive?* (Cambridge: Cambridge University Press, 2006), p. 141.

104 UDHR, Article 28. See also the discussion in Chapter 7 of this volume.

PART III
Mechanisms and Implementation

Chapter 11
The United Nations Human Rights System

Rhona K.M. Smith

1. Introduction

While the last 60 years has witnessed a dramatic expansion in the tabulation of international human rights and in state acceptance of international human rights, the existence of rights and freedoms can only go so far. Few would question the importance of the UDHR[1] in establishing a 'common standard of achievement' for all peoples and all nations. However, what use are human rights to you, me or any of the millions whose rights are violated, if there is no possibility of enforcing them? Part of the General Assembly Resolution by which the UDHR was adopted, requested further examination of the 'problem of petitions' when considering measures of implementation. A piecemeal approach evolved, lacking coherence – as the former Chief of the United Nations (UN) Human Rights Communications Branch comments wryly, '[c]ould it be that, while all governments are ready at all times to talk about human rights, most find it difficult to walk their talk?'.[2]

Six decades after the adoption of the UDHR, the laudable aspirations of the international community seem intangible. As some entries in this book have shown, many human rights remain unrealized. Undoubtedly, considerable advancements have been made in promoting and protecting human rights at the national, regional and international level. As Steiner and Crawford remarked at the dawn of this millennium, '[i]n human rights terms the twentieth century yielded a valuable legacy of internationally agreed standards and the creation of a set of institutional arrangements designed to monitor compliance with those standards. But the overriding challenge for the future is to develop the effectiveness of those monitoring systems'.[3] The chapters in this part of the book consider the progress made towards implementing human rights and identify many of the challenges faced in the twenty-first century.

This chapter will focus on the UN Human Rights system, 'a multitude of entities which vary greatly in their range, remit and composition. Established *ad hoc* in response to concrete needs rather than as part of any master plan, such institutions have experienced sustained, yet mostly unplanned and uncoordinated, growth and internal development'.[4] Much of the UN's system fits this description, although, in its defence, human rights as agreed international standards have proliferated to an extent hitherto unforeseeable. The systems discussed herewith are more involved with monitoring than enforcing, in accordance with the extent to which states allow limitations to their sovereignty.

---

1 GA Res. 217A (III), UN Doc. A/810 at 71 (1948).

2 J. Moller, 'The Right of Petition: General Assembly Resolution 217B', in G. Alfredsson and A. Eide (eds), *The Universal Declaration of Human Rights: A Common Standard of Achievement* (The Hague: Martinus Nijhoff, 1999), p. 699.

3 P. Alston and J. Crawford (eds), 'Editors' Preface' to *The Future of UN Human Rights Treaty Monitoring* (Cambridge: Cambridge University Press, 2000), p. xv.

4 G. Oberleitner, *Global Human Rights Institutions* (Cambridge: Polity Press, 2007), p. 1.

Over six decades, what was once a novel concept, that states could be held accountable on the international stage for how they treat individuals, has been transformed into accepted, if sometimes controversial, policy and practice. Government leaders, previously considered to enjoy sovereign immunity, are now increasingly being indicted for atrocities committed during their term of office: Slobodan Milošević, former president of Yugoslavia, died during his trial before the International Criminal Tribunal for the Former Yugoslavia;[5] Saddam Hussein was executed following conviction by the Iraqi High Tribunal;[6] and Donald Rumsfeld was challenged over the detention of individuals in Guantánamo Bay.[7] National laws have also been used to secure a form of justice for victims of international human rights law abuses.[8] Beyond the scope of criminal prosecutions, continuing attempts are being made to monitor state compliance with human rights in an attempt to raise the threshold of the standard of rights and freedoms worldwide. How does the UN actively promote and protect human rights within its institutional framework?

Gudmundur Alfredsson suggested that early UN human rights work was characterized by 'the "minimum flying speed" necessary for barely keeping the human rights plane aloft',[9] though now due to '[p]opular support, democracy trends and demands for good governance as prerequisites for development and economic well-being [such perceptions are changing with calls for] faster implementation and more effective monitoring'.[10] Taking a more idealistic approach, Zdzisław Kędzia remarks that effective protection of human rights is indispensable to the UN goal of saving succeeding generations from the devastating scourge of war, and thus 'human rights standards should not remain simply 'law in books' – just a beautiful promise', and that an 'impressive international human rights framework has developed'.[11] International mechanisms should not be deemed a panacea for global ills – 'they are not a substitute for effective national mechanisms. At best international mechanisms can only supplement effective domestic mechanisms'.[12]

Implementation of human rights under the auspices of the UN generally falls into two divisions: UN Charter-based bodies and treaty-based bodies. The former refers to those entities deriving their authority from the UN Charter and bodies founded thereunder, and the latter to those bodies established by the core human rights treaties concluded under the auspices of the UN. Obviously, the charter systems apply to all UN member states while the treaty bodies only have authority over those states which have accepted their jurisdiction through ratifying the relevant treaty (or, as appropriate, the relevant optional protocol).

---

5 *Prosecutor* v *Milošević*, Case IT-02-54, International Criminal Tribunal for the Former Yugoslavia.

6 http://www.iraq-iht.org/en/aboutthecourt.html (November 2007 – on file).

7 *Hamdan* v *Rumsfeld* (No. 05-184) 415 F. 3d 33 (US Supreme Court); see also *Hamdi* v *Rumsfeld*, 542 U.S. 507, 518, 588–589, and *Boumediene et al.* v *Bush* Nos. 06-1195 and 06-1196) 476 F. 3d 981.

8 E.g. *Romagoza* v *Garcia.* Upheld in the Court of Appeals, D.C. Docket No. 99-08364-CV-DTKH, compensation for victims of torture in El Salvador; *DPP* v *Zardad*, 18 July 2005 [online]. Available from: http://www.redress.org/news/zardad%207%20apr%202004.pdf [accessed October 2009].

9 'Concluding Remarks: More Law and Less Politics', in G. Alfredsson *et al.* (eds), *International Human Rights Monitoring Mechanisms. Essays in Honour of Jakob Th. Moller* (The Hague: Kluwer 2001), p. 925.

10 *Ibid.*

11 Z. Kędzia, 'United Nations Mechanisms to Promote and Protect Human Rights', in J. Symonides (ed.), *Human Rights: International Protection, Monitoring, Enforcement* (Aldershot: Ashgate, 2003), p. 3.

12 M. Gomez, 'Monitoring and Enforcing Human Rights', in R. Smith and C. van den Anker (eds), *The Essentials of Human Rights* (London: Hodder Arnold, 2005).

2. Charter Bodies

The principal organs of the UN are the Security Council, the General Assembly, the International Court of Justice (ICJ), the Economic and Social Council (ECOSOC), and the (now disbanded) Trusteeship Council. None of these bodies are explicitly responsible for human rights monitoring. Indeed, their competency to consider human rights is mired in controversy – the UN Charter explicitly provides that '[n]othing contained in the present Charter shall authorize the United Nations to intervene in matters which are essentially within the domestic jurisdiction of any State or shall require the Members to submit such matters to settlement under the present Charter'.[13] The inclusion of 'human rights' in the Charter (e.g. Articles 1(3), 13(1), 55) thus was seen as tangential to the foremost issues surrounding the maintenance of peace and security, and therefore human rights were not something the UN organs would directly comment on. That changed in 1971 when the ICJ found South Africa in violation of its charter obligations to observe and respect human rights for all without discrimination in its *South West Africa* opinion: 'To establish [...] and to enforce, distinctions, exclusions, restrictions and limitations exclusively based on grounds of race, colour, descent or national or ethnic origin which constitute a denial of fundamental human rights is a flagrant violation of the purposes and principles of the Charter'.[14] Those 'scattered, terse, even cryptic'[15] clauses in the UN Charter were metamorphosing into legal commitments. While politics may preclude a comprehensive system of monitoring and enforcing human rights, there is ever more evidence of human rights emerging as a pillar of twenty-first-century international law.

2.1 Security Council

The Security Council has primary responsibility for ensuring the maintenance of international peace and security,[16] though this includes international human rights given that so many conflicts escalate from or with human rights abuses.[17] Therefore, the Security Council cannot avoid being enmeshed in human rights discussions. A more intractable problem is the power of veto enjoyed by the permanent members of the Security Council (France, the People's Republic of China, the Russian Federation, the UK and the USA), the last-named a power which, regrettably, has so often paralysed the decision-making process, by producing 'weak' conciliatory compromises, rather than penetrating condemnations of human rights infringements. Nevertheless, the powers of the Security Council to authorize action (whether passive or active) offer an important 'last resort': the Security Council declared the (former) Constitution of South Africa null and void on account of racial discrimination[18] – although the legal effect of such a resolution is debatable; it authorized

---

13 Article 2(7), UN Charter.

14 *Legal Consequences for States of the Continued Presence of South Africa in Namibia (South West Africa) Notwithstanding Security Council Resolution 276*, Advisory Opinion [1971], ICJ Reps 16, p. 57, para. 131.

15 H. Steiner *et al.* (eds), *International Human Rights in Context – Law, Politics and Morals*, 3rd edn (Oxford: Oxford University Press, 2008), p. 135.

16 Article 24, UN Charter.

17 See, generally, B. Ramcharam, *The Security Council and the Protection of Human Rights* (The Hague: Martinus Nijhoff, 2002).

18 UNSC Res 554 (1984).

the establishment of the Special Court for Sierra Leone;[19] and has extended mandates for nation-building work in Iraq.[20]

There is also evidence that the Security Council acknowledges humanitarian concerns when approving enforcement actions,[21] notably sanctions – contrast the broad raft of sanctions imposed on Iraq,[22] with those imposed more recently on North Korea.[23] Not all such measures are successful – the Oil for Food Programme[24] in Iraq was introduced to mitigate the civilian impact of the sanctions, while action on Somalia has not resulted in any major improvements.[25]

As the foregoing demonstrates, the Security Council has tentatively embraced human rights, cultivating a broad approach to peace and security, and recognizing the significant role adherence to internationally agreed human rights standards plays in realizing the purposes of the UN. However, although politics presently precludes it from human rights enforcement, there are mounting indications of a 'responsibility to protect' justifying deployment of military force as a last resort to prevent crimes such as genocide.[26]

2.2 General Assembly

A radical breakthrough in promoting human rights was undoubtedly the General Assembly's adoption of the UDHR in 1948, since supplemented by a raft of human rights resolutions and treaties.[27] Monitoring and enforcing those rights is inevitably a different matter. As Tomuschat notes, '[p]olitical bodies have great difficulties in satisfying the requirement to act in a fair and objective manner, above all when they are called upon to assess the situation in a given country. On the other hand, their voice carries much more weight than assessments by expert bodies'.[28] This paradox shapes much of the work of the General Assembly – greater political weight reinforces its declarations and resolutions yet precludes agreement on monitoring and enforcement. In general, human rights fall within the remit of the Third Committee of the General Assembly, but, inevitably, human rights issues penetrate deeper, and it is not uncommon for other committees and indeed the main assembly to discuss human rights issues.

In 1949, the General Assembly used the UDHR to condemn the USSR's restrictions on Russian wives of foreign diplomats leaving the Soviet Union – Articles 13 and 16 of the UDHR were explicitly cited.[29]

---

19 UNSC Res 1315 (2000).

20 UNSC Res 1859 (2008).

21 E.g. L. Oette, 'A Decade of Sanctions Against Iraq: Never Again! The End of Unlimited Sanctions in the Recent Practice of the UN Security Council', *European Journal of International Law*, 13(1) (2002), pp. 93–103; M. Craven, 'Humanitarianism and the Quest for Smarter Sanctions', *European Journal of International Law*, 13 (2002), pp. 43–61; and related articles in symposium collection.

22 UNSC Res 687 (1991).

23 UNSC Res 1718 (2006).

24 UNSC Res 986 (1995).

25 E.g. UNSC Res 814 (1993) acting under Chapter VII of the Charter, but note UNSC Res 1863(2009) – Security Council remains seized of matter.

26 Secretary-General's High Level Panel on Threats, Challenges and Change, *A More Secure World: Our Shared Responsibility* (2004), para. 203 [online]. Available from: http://www.un.org/secureworld/ [accessed October 2009].

27 E.g. UN General Assembly Resolution 55/2, adopting the Millennium Declaration.

28 C. Tomuschat, *Human Rights – Between Idealism and Realism* (Oxford: Oxford University Press, 2003), p. 113.

29 UNGA, Res. 285(III) (1949).

Frequently, the General Assembly is not seized of human rights issues *ab initio*; rather, the matter being discussed will have stemmed from a report submitted by the Office of the High Commissioner for Human Rights (OHCHR), the Secretary-General, the treaty bodies, or any of the other agencies which report to the General Assembly. However, the agenda of the General Assembly suffers from overload, and many of its resolutions are passed without open debate, yet they impact on monitoring and enforcing of human rights.[30] The power of the General Assembly to raise the political profile of human rights is unparalleled.[31] It has made commendable use of its powers to 'initiate studies and make recommendations' on human rights.[32]

2.2.1 Office of the High Commissioner for Human Rights (OHCHR) The General Assembly also established the OHCHR.[33] Under the leadership of the High Commissioner for Human Rights,[34] the OHCHR has grown in importance, and it (and its website) is now the first port of call for those seeking information on human rights. The OHCHR provides vital secretariat support for the treaty bodies[35] though it has been deemed to work within a 'mandate between servant and shield'.[36]

2.3 Economic and Social Council (ECOSOC)

In terms of the UN Charter, ECOSOC can initiate studies and reports on 'economic, social, cultural, education, health and related matters' as well as making recommendation for 'promoting respect for … human rights and fundamental freedoms'.[37] Given the scope of the workload, ECOSOC lost little time in establishing a number of functional commissions to assist in carrying out its mandate. The first communications concerning human rights were circulated to ECOSOC in 1946,[38] though responding to them was a task soon delegated to the Commission on Human Rights, which largely eclipsed ECOSOC in raising the profile of human rights. The Commission on Human Rights, politicized though it was, enjoyed the most transparently human rights-focused mandate.[39] However, ECOSOC repeatedly undermined the work of the Commission (e.g. on individual communications) but generally endorsed its standard-setting initiatives.[40]

Gender-mainstreaming and promotion of the equal enjoyment of rights for men and women were singled out for particular attention, and they form the focal point of the work of the Commission on the Status of Women.[41] This commission has made considerable progress in a number of fields for the advancement of women and girl children within the framework set by the World Conferences

30 E.g. the adoption of the Optional Protocol to the International Covenant on Economic, Social and Cultural Rights (permitting individual communications) – UN Doc. A/63/435.

31 E.g. world summits on human rights.

32 Article 13, UN Charter.

33 See P. Alston, 'Neither Fish Nor Fowl: The Quest to Define the Role of the UN High Commissioner for Human Rights', *European Journal of International Law*, 8(2) (1997), pp. 321–35; A. Clapham, 'Creating the High Commissioner for Human Rights', *European Journal of International Law*, 5 (1994), pp. 556–68.

34 Created UNGA Res. 48/141 (1993); from 2008 the High Commissioner is Navanethem Pillay.

35 All treaty bodies since 1 January 2008.

36 Oberleitner, note 4 above, p. 88.

37 Article 62, UN Charter.

38 UN Doc. E/HR/2, 23 April 1946, cited in J. Moller, 'The Right of Petition: General Assembly Resolution 217B', in Alfredsson and Eide (eds), note 2 above, p. 653.

39 Discussed below under Human Rights Council.

40 See D. O'Donovan, 'The Economic and Social Council', in P. Alston (ed.), *The United Nations and Human Rights: A Critical Appraisal* (Oxford: Clarendon Press, 2002), p. 105.

41 UNECOSOC Res. II(II) (1946).

on Women.[42] Until recently, the commission secretariat serviced the Committee on the Elimination of Discrimination Against Women (CEDAW), a practice which some commentators felt alienated women's rights from mainstream human rights.[43]

2.3.1 ECOSOC Initiative A number of other fora established under the auspices of ECOSOC strengthen human rights promotion and protection. Erica-Irene A. Daes,[44] former Chairperson of the UN Working Group on Indigenous Populations,[45] has long led the call for a Permanent Forum on Indigenous Peoples. This call was answered in 2000.[46] Given that the General Assembly rejected the Draft Declaration on the Rights of Indigenous Peoples, despite its adoption by the Human Rights Council in June 2006, this body provides a welcome voice for indigenous peoples within the UN system.

More recently, the Forum on Minority Rights was established,[47] *inter alia,* to identify and analyse best practices and challenges for implementing the Declaration on the Rights of Persons Belonging to National or Ethnic, Religious or Linguistic Minorities.[48] The forum will complement the work of the independent expert on minority issues. Its first session (December 2008) focused on the perennial matter of realizing the right to education, while its second session (November 2009) focused on effective political participation.

2.4 Human Rights Council

Arguably, the principal body with responsibility for monitoring compliance with human rights is now the Human Rights Council[49] (established in 2006), following the dissolution of the derided Commission on Human Rights. The principal criticisms of the commission included the charges that it was biased and secretive[50] and that it had become excessively politicized, causing a 'credibility deficit',[51] perhaps not so unsurprising for a body comprised of member states. Nevertheless, it did achieve considerable success, especially in standard-setting (not least in drafting the UDHR) and profiling human rights, by itself or through the work of its Sub-Commission on the Promotion and Protection of Human Rights (initially titled for discrimination and minorities).

The Human Rights Council is a subsidiary body of the UN General Assembly, to which it reports (status to be reviewed in 2011). Its 47 elected states are 'responsible for promoting universal respect for the protection of all human rights and fundamental freedoms for all, without any distinction

42 E.g. UNECOSOC Res 1987(22), 1996(6): Beijing Platform for Action [online]. Available from: http://www.un.org/womenwatch/daw/beijing/platform/ [accessed October 2009].

43 E.g. L. Reanda, 'The Commission on the Status of Women', in Alston, note 40 above, p. 265.

44 E.g. E. Daes, 'A United Nations Permanent Forum for the World's Indigenous Peoples – A Global Imperative', in Alfredsson *et al.*, note 9 above, p. 371.

45 Established by UNECOSOC Res 1982/34.

46 UNECOSOC Res. 2000/22.

47 UNHRCl Res. 6/15(2007).

48 UNGA Res. 47/135 (1992), based on Article 27, International Covenant on Civil and Political Rights.

49 See, generally, Oberleitner, note 4 above .

50 See H. Boekle,'Western States, the UN Commission on Human Rights, and the "1235 Procedure": "The Question of Bias" Revisited', *Netherlands Quarterly of Human Rights*, 13 (1995), pp. 367–402; T. Frank, 'Is There a Double Standard in the United Nations?', *American Journal of International Law*, 78 (1984), p. 811.

51 K. Annan, 'In Larger Freedom: Towards Development, Security and Human Rights for All', UN Doc. A/59/2005, para. 182.

of any kind and in a fair and equal manner'.[52] Most states seeking election to the council produce written commitments to human rights rhetoric, and the resultant membership reflects geographical, political and cultural diversity. It is thus not a guaranteed body of states persons bestowing or indeed offering a panoply of wisdom in the manner being evinced by, for example, 'The Elders'.[53] As a monitor of human rights, the impact of the Human Rights Council has yet to be determined.[54] It can draw not only on the undoubted expertise of the OHCHR secretariat but also on the Human Rights Council Advisory Committee – 18 independent experts operating as a 'think tank' – which, in contrast to the former sub-committee, has little autonomous authority, reinforcing the inter-governmental nature of the Human Rights Council.

2.4.1 Universal Periodic Review A significant innovation is the Human Rights Council's mandate to undertake a universal periodic review of the fulfilment by each state of its human rights obligations and commitments. States will be specifically reviewed while serving as members of the council, though all states will be reviewed in each 4-year cycle.[55] This system is heralded as complementing the work of the treaty bodies (see below) and not 'overly burdensome' to those involved.[56] Compliance with international human rights law and, more controversially, international humanitarian law will be examined. States will submit a report, the OHCHR will compile relevant reports of treaty bodies and special procedures, and additional credible and reliable information provided by 'other relevant stakeholders' as summarized by the OHCHR may be used when drafting the outcome document.

If we consider the initial outcomes (2008/9), the fact that a cross-section of countries can contribute by tabling questions and recommendations is clearly positive, while the litany of 'predictable' comments is perhaps less helpful. In the case of the UK, key topics were extrapolated from the UK report[57] and from external sources with frank responses elucidated from the UK authorities.[58] Although an exchange of rhetoric has some merit, the real test will be whether any of the recommendations are followed by the state concerned and whether the recommendations are followed up – in other words, whether the council's work is complementary to, and integrated into, existing human rights systems which examine states periodically.[59] The sheer range of rights and freedoms, policies and laws conceivably falling within the remit of the council may prove a major obstacle, as there is no benchmarking *per se*, and the examination cannot be thorough. Its very existence is an exciting

52 UNGA Res. 50/251 at 2.

53 'The Elders are an independent group of eminent global leaders, brought together by Nelson Mandela, who offer their collective influence and experience to support peace building, help address major causes of human suffering and promote the shared interests of humanity' [online]. Available from: http://www.theelders.org/ [accessed October 2009].

54 C. Callejon, 'Developments at the Human Rights Council in 2007: A Reflection of Its Ambivalence', *Human Rights Law Review*, 8 (2008), pp. 323–42.

55 The process will be reviewed after 2011.

56 UN Human Rights Council Resolution 5/1 at 3(f) + (h.)

57 *National Report Submitted in Accordance with Paragraph 15(a) of Annex to Human Rights Council Resolution 5/1*. UN Doc.A/HRC/WG.6/1/GBR/1.

58 *Report of the Working Group on the Universal Periodic Review. United Kingdom of Great Britain and Northern Ireland*, UN Doc. A/HRC/8/25. See also Human Rights Council Decision 8/107, *Outcome of the Universal Periodic Review: United Kingdom of Great Britain and Northern Ireland* (June 2008).

59 E.g. F. Gaer, 'A Voice Not an Echo: Universal Periodic Review and the UN Treaty Body System', *Human Rights Law Review*, 7 (2007), pp. 109–39.

development, as, in effect, all states are now having their policies and practices scrutinized against the web of rights and freedoms stemming from the UDHR. States can no longer avoid UN monitoring.

2.4.2 Special Mechanisms The Human Rights Council assumed responsibility for the country and thematic rapporteurs (the special mechanisms), which had previously operated under the auspices of the Commission on Human Rights. These are currently being reviewed and a number of changes are currently being implemented to render the system more transparent: general criteria have now been published for nominating, selecting and appointing mandate holders,[60] and thematic mandates are now initially approved for three years, and country mandates for only one year. Hurst Hannum suggests that the mandates are 'an important part of the overall scheme of human rights protection and promotion within the UN system'.[61] Arguably, the country mandates have emerged from the original 1253 public process,[62] through which ECOSOC charged the former commission with investigating violations of human rights at a time before the treaty bodies were established (indeed, before core treaties were drafted and/or ratified). Most mandate-holders receive individual petitions although their investigative powers are limited.

Perhaps inevitably, the fate of individual mandates is tied to the identity and enthusiasm of its holder. However, finance is always tricky – the special mechanisms are not operated by salaried employees of the UN, and this, although positive for ensuring independence, exacerbates existing UN funding problems. A further impediment is the need for consent. Visits can only be carried out with the prior approval of the state concerned. However, some states issue standing (open) invitations.[63] In 2005, Manfred Nowak, special rapporteur on torture and two colleagues,[64] after four years of negotiations, rejected outline permission to visit Guantánamo Bay detention facility in Cuba due to the strictures placed on the visit by the USA. When governments refuse to cooperate, other sources of information are drawn upon to provide as accurate as possible information on the human rights situation of the state concerned.[65] Fact-finding has considerable value: the late Sergio Vieira de Mello commented that the special mechanisms are 'a constructive, critical approach to imperfect human rights standards'.[66]

2.4.3 Special Sessions The council can also act swiftly in response to evolving situations. Many special sessions have been held in the short period since the council was inaugurated. For example, it authorized the dispatch of a fact-finding mission to investigate violations of international human

60 HRC Res. 5/1 at 39.

61 H. Hannum, 'Reforming the Special Procedures and Mechanisms of the Commission on Human Rights', *Human Rights Law Review*, 7 (2007), pp. 73–92, at p. 82.

62 UNECOSOC Res 1235 (XLII) 1967.

63 For the current list, see <http://www2.ohchr.org/english/bodies/chr/special/invitations.htm> [accessed November 2009].

64 Leandro Despouy and Asma Jahangir, rapporteurs on, respectively, independence of judges and freedom of religion. Note that the USA refused access to the rapporteurs on health and on arbitrary detention.

65 See UNHRCl Res. 5/2(2007), *Code of Conduct for Special Procedures Mandate-Holders of the Human Rights Council.*

66 S. Vieira de Mello, 'Membership Entails Responsibility', Human Rights Features 22–25 April 2003, cited in O. Hoehne, 'Special Procedures and the New Human Rights Council – A Need for Strategic Positioning', *EssexHumRR*, 4(1), at n21 [online]. Available from: http://projects.essex.ac.uk/ehrr/V4N1/Hoehne.pdf .

rights law throughout the Occupied Palestinian Territory in January 2009.[67] There has been some criticism that Israel and the Palestinian Occupied Territories have been singled out for criticism.[68] While that region has been the subject of a number of special session resolutions, the US power of veto has rendered the Security Council virtually impotent; thus, the Human Rights Council opens an avenue of public discussion and scrutiny, albeit not with substantive enforcement powers. It is nevertheless true that many other areas are experiencing devastating human rights violations but eliciting no response from the council. Other special sessions have considered the human rights situation in Myanmar,[69] Sudan (Darfur),[70] Sri Lanka[71] and the Democratic Republic of the Congo.[72]

2.4.4 Investigations The Human Rights Council also has competence to receive complaints addressing 'consistent patterns of gross and reliably attested violations'[73] of human rights and freedoms. This procedure draws heavily on its predecessor (the former commission's 1235/1503/2000 procedures[74]), the original international human rights investigation system. Now the council follows in the footsteps of the commission which initially restricted itself to condemnatory comments on South African apartheid and the ongoing tensions and human rights violations in south-west Africa (Namibia) and Southern Rhodesia (Zimbabwe)[75] before including Israel and the Occupied Territories in spreading the geographical net, thereby freeing the 'entire human rights system … of its one-sided orientation towards South Africa … and Israel'.[76] The 1503/2000 process has now been revamped, apparently to increase its efficiency as the Human Rights Council builds on it with expectations of greater objectivity and impartiality, though with the confidential nature of the former mechanism maintained. The threshold for admissibility remains high, but it must be remembered that this system operates alongside the special mechanisms and the treaty bodies.

Communications undergo an initial admissibility review by a working group of independent experts (from the Human Rights Council Advisory Committee), consideration by a working group on situations (drawn from council members), and review and/or action by the Human Rights Council. No information on the nature of the complaints or the discussions of the council will be

---

67 HRCl ResL.1/Rev.2 (2009) UN Doc. A/HRC/S-9/L.1/Rev.2 at para. 14 – 'The Goldstone Report', UN Doc. A/HRC/12/48 (released September 2009). For information on the fact-finding mission, see http://www2.ohchr.org/english/bodies/hrcouncil/specialsession/9/FactFindingMission.htm [accessed October 2009].

68 E.g. 12th Session followed by 12th Special Session (October 2009) discussing the 'Goldstone Report' on the Occupied Palestinian Territory and East Jerusalem. See the US statement at http://geneva.usmission.gov/2009/09/30/posner/ [accessed October 2009].

69 Fifth Special Session, which adopted Resolution S-5/1: *Situation of Human Rights in Myanmar*, October 2007.

70 Fourth Special Session, which adopted Decision S-4/101: *Situation of Human Rights in Darfur*, December 2006.

71 Eleventh Special Session, which adopted Resolution S-11/1: *Assistance to Sri Lanka in the Promotion and Protection of Human Rights.*

72 Eighth Special Session, which adopted Resolution S-8/1*: Situation of Human Rights in the East of the Democratic Republic of the Congo*, November 2008.

73 UNHRCl Res. 5/1 at 85.

74 UNECOSOC Res. 1235 (XLII) 1967, followed by UNECOSOC Res. 1503(XLVIII) 27 May 1970; amended by UNECOSOC Res. 2000/3, 16 June 2000.

75 As per UNECOSOC Res. 1235 (XLII) 1967.

76 Tomuschat, note 28 above, p. 120.

made public (unless, of course the state consents).[77] The entire process is required to take no more than two years[78] with the complainant informed of progress, welcome improvements on the former system. The range of options open to the council reflects the *status quo ante* under the commission, including review of the situation and request for further information from the state, appointment of an independent expert to monitor and report on the situation, and recommendation to the OHCHR on technical cooperation or capacity-building assistance.[79]

2.5 International Court of Justice (ICJ)

The ICJ is tasked with determining contentious disputes raised before it with the consent of the parties (and/or delivering Advisory Opinions). Human rights appear tangential at best to this jurisdiction. Its initial engagement with human rights offered opinions on the status of reservations to the Genocide Convention,[80] and more recently comments on the application of the Genocide Convention, holding that Serbia was in violation thereof by failing to prevent genocide in Srebrenica.[81] In 1971, as noted above, it highlighted human rights in the *South West Africa* case.[82] Yet, many decisions of the ICJ concern (albeit indirectly) human rights issues. Interim measures have been ordered to protect individuals (directly or indirectly realizing human rights) in various regions including Pakistan,[83] Nicaragua,[84] and, more recently, the Balkans.[85] The court even ordered, ultimately unsuccessfully, a stay of execution for a Paraguayan national on death row in the USA: 'The United States should take all measures at its disposal to ensure that Angel Francisco Breard is not executed pending the final decision in these proceedings, and should inform the Court of all the measures which it has taken in implementation of this Order.'[86] Clearly, the court is willing to consider provisional measures to protect human rights.[87]

---

77 UNHRCl Res. 5/1 (2007).

78 UNHRCl Res. 5/1 at 105.

79 UNHRCl Res. 5/1 at 109.

80 *Reservations to the Convention* on *Genocide, Advisory Opinion* [1951], ICJ Rep. 15.

81 *Application of the Convention on the Prevention and Punishment of the Crime of Genocide (Bosnia and Herzegovina* v *Serbia and Montenegro*), judgement of 26 February 2007 [online]. Available from: http://www.icj-cij.org/docket/files/91/13685.pdf; see also *Case Concerning Application of the Convention on the Prevention and Punishment of the Crime of Genocide (Croatia* v *Serbia)*, 1999 general list No. 118. On 18 November 2008, the court indicated that it had jurisdiction, under Article IX of the Genocide Convention, to entertain the case on the merits [online]. Available from: http://www.icj-cij.org/docket/files/118/14883.pdf. See, generally, Symposium: *Genocide, Human Rights and the ICJ, European Journal of International Law*, 18(4) (2007).

82 Note 14 above.

83 *Trial of Pakistani Prisoners of War (Pakistan* v *India), Interim Protection Order*, [1973] ICJ Rep. 328 – case ultimately removed from the list of the court by the parties.

84 *Military and Paramilitary Activities in and Against Nicaragua (Nicaragua* v *USA) Provisional Measures Order* [1984], ICJ Rep. 169.

85 *Application of the Convention on the Prevention and Punishment of the Crime of Genocide (Bosnia and Herzegovina* v *Yugoslavia) Provisional Measures Order* [1993], ICJ Rep. 3.

86 *The Vienna Convention on Consular Relations (Paraguay* v *USA) Provisional Measures Order* [1998], ICJ Rep. 248, at p. 258, para. 41.

87 Art. 41, Statute of the ICJ; e.g. Measures refused as necessity not proven in *Certain Criminal Proceedings in France (Republic of the Congo* v *France), Provisional Measure* [2003], ICJ Rep. 102.

Individuals have no *locus standi* to institute proceedings against a state in the ICJ but inevitably, the court has competence to adjudicate on treaty disputes, assuming the parties elect to refer the case.

The first case based on a core human rights treaty (the International Convention on the Elimination of All Forms of Discrimination (ICERD)[88]) was lodged before the ICJ in 2008. This contentious dispute between Georgia and the Russian Federation follows the procedure in Article 22 ICERD. Georgia instituted proceedings against the Russian Federation in August 2008, claiming violation of the convention and reserved the right to include the Genocide Convention in future proceedings. As of 15 October 2008, provisional measures were ordered to alleviate the plight and prevent escalation of racial discrimination in South Ossetia, Abkhazia and adjacent areas in Georgia, with emphasis on ensuring 'without distinction as to national or ethnic origin, security of persons; the right of persons to freedom of movement and residence within the border of the State; [and] the protection of the property of displaced persons and of refugees'.[89]

A number of commentators have discussed the possibility of individual *locus standi* before the ICJ and/or the establishment of a world (single) court for human rights.[90] This could be an additional jurisdiction for the ICJ or (preferably) a distinct body assuming aspects of the roles currently discharged by the Human Rights Council and/or treaty bodies.[91] The creation of the International Criminal Court (ICC)[92] has prompted a re-examination in some quarters of the role of individuals under international law.[93] While the corollary of duties and responsibility is rights, the debate on judicial mechanisms for enforcing those rights against states continues. Undoubtedly, progress has been made, but the numbers of communications are but a trickle compared to the flood lodged before the regional courts, corroborating the demand for a global 'court'.

2.6 Secretary-General

As 'Chief Administrative Officer of the Organisation',[94] the UN Secretary-General can also exert influence over human rights. Increasingly, of recent years, each incumbent Secretary-General has regularly spoken on human rights matters, advocating compliance with human rights standards. The good offices of the Secretary-General are regularly extended to obviate conflict and minimize infringements of human rights. The former UN Secretary General, Kofi Annan (1997–2006), implemented a review of the entire UN system with a view to ensuring its continued viability in the future,[95] a process which culminated in the establishment of the Human Rights Council.

---

88 660 UNTS 195.

89 *Case Concerning Application of the International Convention on the Elimination of All Forms of Racial Discrimination (Georgia* v *Russian Federation)* 15 October General List No. 140, p. 41, para. 149 [online]. Available from: http://www.icj-cij.org/docket/files/140/14803.pdf.

90 E.g. T. Buergenthal, 'A Court and Two Consolidated Treaty Bodies', in A. Bayefsky (ed.), *The UN Human Rights System in the 21st Century* (The Hague: Kluwer, 2000); M. Nowak, 'The Need for a World Court of Human Rights', *Human Rights Law Review*, 7 (2007), pp. 251–9. See also Chapter 19 in this volume.

91 Human Rights Council discussed above; treaty bodies, discussed below.

92 Statute of Rome 1998, UN Doc. A/CONF.183/9.

93 See Chapters 23 and 24 in this volume.

94 Article 97, UN Charter.

95 *Strengthening of the United Nations: An Agenda for Further Change*, UN Doc. A/57/387; High Level Panel note 26 above; Annan, note 51 above.

3. Treaty Bodies

In addition to the UN Charter bodies discussed above, there are a range of additional bodies which consider the extent to which states have complied with their human rights obligations under the UN human rights system. Each of these bodies has primary responsibility for monitoring specified rights and freedoms and assessing state compliance therewith.

These treaty bodies should complement the work of the Human Rights Council, its special mechanisms and other international bodies.[96] Their focus is on promoting and monitoring compliance with a particular human rights treaty, specific rather than generic. However, in view of the nature of human rights treaties with overlapping obligations,[97] the patent benefits to be derived from a cross-treaty, inter national approach are apparent. Undeniably, there are significant benefits to fusing the systems, and indeed there are now regular meetings of the chairpersons of treaty bodies, and evidence is increasing of some coordination of efforts.

The Committee on Elimination of Racial Discrimination (CERD) was the first such body to be established, and it pioneered many aspects of committee work. The treaty bodies also can deploy a wide range of technical cooperation (assistance with compiling reports, creating rule of law institutions, etc.) offered under the auspices of the OHCHR. These resources offer public and private support to states genuinely struggling to meet their treaty obligations.

3.1 Composition, Status and Powers of the Treaty Bodies

First and foremost, all treaty bodies are limited by the terms of their constitutive treaty.[98] Each treaty specifies the composition and powers of its committee, although some procedural issues may be altered via the committee's own rules of procedure. Numbers are generally compact and sessions short and infrequent (when viewed in light of the number of states parties – up to 193 to the Convention on the Rights of the Child). Members of the committees need not be legally qualified; that is a criterion preserved for the ICJ. Committee members are generally unremunerated, and the lack of funds precludes expansion of fact-finding missions and other activities.[99]

Membership of the committees is not prescribed in a way, suggesting a quasi-judicial function. This was intended. The committees are, in effect, a 'light' touch, reviewing state compliance with their treaty obligations on the basis of evidence primarily submitted by the states themselves. While some committee members have a strong political background, many are academics or practitioners. All committee work is supported by the OHCHR with its experienced and well-qualified secretariat. The Human Rights Committee, another early creation, has, as Steiner states, 'transformed what was a novel and in some ways radical mandate into one that now appears

---

96 E.g. N. Rodley, 'United Nations Human Rights Treaty Bodies and Special Procedures of the Commission on Human Rights – Complementarity or Competition?', *Human Rights Quarterly*, 25 (2003), pp. 882–908.

97 E. Tistounet, 'The Problem of Overlapping Among Different Treaty Bodies', in Alston and Crawford (eds), note 3 above, p. 383.

98 The Committee on Economic, Social and Cultural Rights was established subsequently – UNECOSOC – Res 1985/17.

99 See E. Evatt, 'Ensuring Effective Supervisory Procedures: The Need for Resources', in Alston and Crawford, note 3 above, p. 461.

conventional'.[100] As a semi-collegiate entity, the work of all the treaty bodies reflect this, and the establishment of a committee is a *sine qua non* of modern human rights treaties.[101]

There are three main mechanisms by which the committees monitor compliance with human rights: periodic reports; inter-state and individual complaints; and *in situ* investigations.

3.2 Periodic Reports

Monitoring of state compliance with human rights treaties is primarily done in periodic reports. The Committee on Economic, Social and Cultural Rights identified seven objectives of the periodic report system: ensure a comprehensive review of national legislation, policy and practices to ensure the fullest possible conformity with the treaty; monitor the actual situation of human rights within national territory; implement principled policy-making by the government to prioritize realization of rights; public scrutiny of government policies; evaluate progress made towards realizing the rights (particular to the International Covenant on Economic, Social and Cultural Rights' 'progressive realization of rights'); help states develop a better understanding of difficulties it encounters; and facilitate the exchange of information among states.[102] These objectives are generally the same for each treaty body.

The process is essentially cyclical: the state submits a periodic report; the committee draws up a list of questions based on issues identified from the report, news coverage, etc.; the state may elect to send in written responses to some or all the issues raised; the state's delegates meet with the committee in Geneva at a predetermined scheduled session of the committee; the committee drafts its concluding observations, comments and recommendations for transmission to the state and publication; the state may issue a response; follow-up mechanisms may be deployed; and the state submits its next periodic report, hopefully taking into account the dialogue prompted by the previous periodic report. This process is continuous. Some states, such as Pakistan,[103] have now filed their twentieth periodic report under ICERD.

The international system is often regarded as 'toothless', as states claim acceptance of treaty obligations for diplomatic benefits without adequately improving their human rights practices. Indeed, the reporting process has been described as 'a lecture in the anatomy of human rights'.[104] Certainly, dissecting the process reveals a number of latent issues: many countries ratify treaties and then negate the impact by the deployment of reservations and declarations; others thwart the process of periodic reporting by failing to submit timely reports; others submit minimalistic reports that fall far below the ideal of a self-evaluation upon which constructive dialogue can build. Undoubtedly, the contracting parties are not entirely to blame: what started with a UN of 58 states adopting the UDHR has evolved into a web of treaties binding on sometimes nearly 200 states. A state ratifying all the core treaties with entry into force on the 60th anniversary of the UDHR would

100 H. Steiner, 'Individual Complaints in a World of Massive Violations: What Role for the Human Rights Committee?', in Alston and Crawford, note 3 above, p. 18; D. McGoldrick, *The Human Rights Committee: Its role in the Development of the International Covenant on Civil and Political Rights* (Oxford: Clarendon Press, 1994).

101 Most recently, the 2006 Convention on the Rights of Persons with Disabilities.

102 CESCR General Comment 1, *Reporting by States Parties*, 24/2/89, UN Doc. E/1989/22.

103 UN Doc. CERD/C/PAK/20.

104 Joaquim Fonseca, former Timor L'este Human Rights Reporting Liaison Officer, cited (from an interview), in A. Devereux and C. Anderson, 'Reporting Under International Human Rights Treaties: Perspectives from Timor Leste's Experience of the Reformed Process', *Human Rights Law Review*, 8(1) (2008), pp. 69–104, at p. 69.

have the following timetable for reports: five reports due December 2009, and then a further two the following year, by which time the second report under ICERD may be due and the entire vortex requires reports due most years for at least one treaty. This is clearly onerous on states and, given the current situation, unworkable for the committees. Accordingly, alterations have been made to practice; for example, the Human Rights Committee sets dates in each report, usually with a 4-year periodicity; CERD altered its rules of procedure to allow for periodic reports; the Committee on the Rights of the Child meets more frequently; and the Committee on Elimination of All Forms of Discrimination Against Women increased its membership. Unfortunately, each committee has accrued a significant but inevitable backlog of reports. Thus, it is not uncommon for one report to be discussed when submission of the next is imminent, or, indeed, for two consecutive reports to be considered simultaneously.

The lack of a follow-up mechanism and the fact that some states have failed to respond to repeated adverse comments by various committees suggest that the concept of periodic reporting was not fulfilling any function other than a public record. States can avoid the system entirely by failing to submit reports, although now committees such as the CERD deploy a 'back-up' mechanism, considering states *in absentia*. The role of non-governmental organizations (NGOs) has also been extended, and many states now find themselves being quizzed on the material presented by NGOs, rather than only their own mechanistic, lacklustre, positive self-analysis. It appears that few states consult widely with diverse national stakeholders and/or NGOs before compiling their reports; thus, the 'whole picture' is not necessarily presented.

Perhaps it was not anticipated that the treaty systems would be so successful, yet the UN human rights system is predicated on the oft-repeated goal of universal ratification of all core treaties. While perhaps it is overstating it to comment that '[t]he treaty bodies have been successful in pursuing their mandates, in particular by engaging States in open and frank discussion on the problems of implementing human rights treaties through the reporting process', undoubtedly, '[t]he treaty bodies have been continuously engaged in seeking ways to enhance their effectiveness'.[105]

Strengthening the treaty body system is on the international agenda. Attempts are being made to streamline the system of reporting, rendering it less onerous for states (e.g. an expanded core document with all the general information supported by treaty-specific information where required rather than repeating information to different committees).[106] Greater integration of the procedures should ensure that committees adopt similar approaches to violations, a crucial factor given overlapping treaty obligations (i.e. the same right in several different treaties). As Henkin noted in 1994, following on from the Vienna World Conference on Human Rights, the major task facing the international system is that '[a]ll states have committed themselves to respect human rights standards, but they have not been prepared to see them implemented or enforced, to accept communal scrutiny of the condition of human rights in their own countries to scrutinize others, to establish monitoring bodies, or to welcome and respond to non-governmental monitoring'.[107] More than 15 years later, the tenor of those comments has resonance.

105 OHCHR, *The United Nations Human Rights Treaty System: An Introduction to the Core Human Rights Treaties and the Treaty Bodies* (Geneva: OHCHR, 2005), Fact Sheet no. 31, p. 32.

106 See UN Doc. HRI/GEN.2/Rev. 2 (2004).

107 L. Henkin, 'Preface' to L. Henkin and J. Hargrove (eds), *Human Rights: An Agenda for the Next Century* (Washington, DC: American Society of International Law, 1994), p. xvii.

3.3 Communications and Complaints

3.3.1 Inter-State complaints Until 2008, the system for inter-state complaints was viewed as virtually redundant, an almost archaic (through twenty-first- century eyes) throwback to the concept that human rights formed part of traditional inter national law, something which states would enforce *inter se*. Political reality rendered the inclusion of an inter-state process inevitable in the earlier treaties, while it became less relevant in later treaties, though an important 'threat' to states and an integral part of treaty law. Only the ICERD contains a mandatory inter-state procedure for complaints (Articles 11 and 12). For a well-established litany of reasons (diplomatic and political), states would always prove reluctant to open their human rights record to scrutiny by instituting proceedings against another state unless relations have declined to an unsustainable level. As noted above, Georgia engaged Article 22 of ICERD to bring its dispute with the Russian Federation before the ICJ. Even the regional systems demonstrate a dearth of inter-state complaints.[108]

3.3.2 Individual communications The provision for individual communications, albeit optional, is a real advance in international human rights law. From tentative beginnings and few state acceptances of the jurisdiction (e.g. ICERD), individual complaints have become acceptable in international human rights, even now for the International Covenant on Economic, Social and Cultural Rights (ICESCR) subsequent to the adoption of an Optional Protocol to the ICESCR by the UN General Assembly on 10 December 2008. Yet, they remain, in effect, a very weak and underutilized remedy. The terminology deployed – communications submitted by authors, opinions of committees, etc. – is redolent of diplomacy rather than adjudication, a move clearly intended to assuage the fears of contracting parties. Even now, the UK,[109] the USA, and the People's Republic of China, permanent members of the Security Council, generally do not permit individual communications against them under the UN system – hardly a stunning endorsement for an international system.

Although individual communications can offer some succour to victims of human rights abuses, remedies are effectively unenforceable and usually non-pecuniary,[110] interim/provisional measures may not be heeded,[111] and it is a disparate range of states which accept the competence of committees to receive reports. Moreover, states may elect not to engage with the committee once a communication is lodged.[112] As states may be selective in recognizing jurisdiction to receive communications, individuals must be innovative, 'playing' concurrent treaty obligations to their advantage, and bringing communications under whichever treaty the state so permits. A further peculiarity of the system is that the decisions of the committees 'constitute part of what is known as "hard law". And yet, case law is not considered as potent as the normative rule itself ... because the application of a norm may

108 The European Court of Human Rights has adjudicated two contentious inter-state complaints: *Ireland* v *UK*, Ser. A, No. 25 (1978) 2 *EHRR* 25, and *Cyprus* v *Turkey*, Application 25781/94(1997), 23 *EHRR* 244.

109 A 'trial' of acceptance of individual communications in CEDAW is currently being evaluated after only a couple of communications were lodged, and none were deemed admissible.

110 *Dung Thi Thuy Nguyen* v *Netherlands*, UN Doc. CEDAW/C/36/D/3/2004, maternity provision discriminatory.

111 *Piandiong* v *Philippines*, UN Doc. CCPR/C/70/D/869/1999, executions carried out contrary to request by committee.

112 *Nikolic & Nikolic* v *Serbia and Montenegro*, UN Doc. CAT/C/35/D/174/2000; son's unexplained death.

vary … from expert committee to expert committee'.[113] Most commentators agree that, ideally, the forum for raising violations of human rights should be internalized within the state concerned.[114] Indeed, the committees all require exhaustion of domestic remedies (unless unreasonably prevented by the state) before proceedings can be brought to the international level.[115]

3.4 In Situ and Other Investigations

Some core treaties enable the committee to undertake *in situ* investigations. Thus, the Committee Against Torture can request visits,[116] and for those states bound by the Optional Protocol to the Convention Against Torture, a sub-committee can undertake regular visits to detention centres.[117] However, most visits are undertaken through the special mechanisms of the Human Rights Council, rather than by treaty bodies.

3.5 General Comments

Not strictly a monitoring mechanism, but nevertheless important, each committee adopts General Comments ('General Recommendations' for CEDAW) which elaborate on rights and freedoms and articulate the committee's perception of the extent of the treaty obligations. The quality (and, accordingly, the usefulness) of these vary. Much depends on the committee in question, the author of the General Comment, and the political sensitivity of the topic (indicating the extent to which the content may have been diluted prior to adoption). The General Comments are not 'hard' law – they are not agreed by all states as an amendment to the salient treaty – and thus they operate around the fringes of 'soft' law. However, this perhaps misrepresents their value. Some comments clarify the nature or extent of the treaty obligations, indicating the likely approach being taken by the committee to periodic reports.[118] Others provide detail on what information is required in the reports.[119]

3.6 Reform

The two principal protagonists in the debate over the treaty bodies are Philip Alston and Ann Bayefsky.[120] Both agree that treaty monitoring has arrived at a critical crossroads[121]; their debate

---

113 A. de Zayas, 'The Examination of Individual Complaints by the United Nations Human Rights Committee Under the Optional Protocol to the International Covenant on Civil and Political Rights', in Alfredsson *et al.*, note 9 above, p. 73.

114 E.g. C. Heyns and F. Viljoen, 'The Impact of the United Nations Human Rights Treaties on the Domestic Level', *Human Rights Quarterly*, 23 (2001), pp. 483–535; D. Cassel, 'Does International Human Rights Law Make a Difference?', *Chicago Journal of International Law*, 2 (2001), pp. 121–35.

115 Each regional court has a similar requirement.

116 Article 20, Convention Against Torture and Other Cruel, Inhuman or Degrading Treatment or Punishment.

117 Optional Protocol to the Convention Against Torture and Other Cruel, Inhuman or Degrading Treatment or Punishment 2002, Article 1.

118 E.g. General Comment 8 (2006) on corporal punishment, UN Doc.CRC/C/GC/8.

119 E.g. General Comment 30 (2002) on reporting obligation under Article 40 ICCPR, UN Doc. CCPR/C/21/Rev.2/Add.12.

120 P. Alston, *Effective Functioning of Bodies Established Pursuant to United Nations Human Rights Instruments – Final Report on Enhancing the Long-Term Effectiveness of the United Nations Human Rights Treaty System* (1997), UN Doc. E/CN.4/1997/74; A. Bayefsky, *Universality at the Crossroads* (The Hague:

is set against the detailed examination of the treaty-monitoring system, and indeed the effective functioning of the UN generally. Former UN Secretary-General, Kofi Annan, instituted a detailed review process aimed at increasing the efficiency of the UN generally, including in the area of human rights.[121]

Calls have been made for a single consolidated periodic report and for a single unified treaty body.[122] Neither has found support. Certainly, now the report system is simplified and now that treaty monitoring is firmly embedded in international practice, the treaty bodies perform a valuable function. The expertise of many committee members is unparalleled and their independence is rarely questioned now. As the committees have evolved into their mandates, boundaries have been pushed. Changes have been made to the periodicity of the reporting cycle to facilitate efficiency, more effective follow-up mechanisms are being introduced as committees consider advances (if any) made by the reporting state since its previous report, and general comments and recommendations have gained value as (with a few exceptions) they provide useful guidance. Supported by the OHCHR secretariat, improvements are occurring. Although, conceptually, the system may be far from perfect, six decades after the UDHR, states are recognizing the importance of human rights rhetoric and the benefits of engaging therewith.

4. Other UN Bodies (UNESCO, ILO)

The UN encompasses a range of additional bodies, many of which have some bearing on human rights, including the core treaties and the Millennium Development Goals. Human rights are being so successfully mainstreamed within the UN that few international organizations (if any) can ignore them, and apathy is the only reason for eschewing rights.

The Constitution of the World Health Organization (WHO) alludes to the links between health and respect and the promotion of human rights. Health can be affected by infringements of human rights (torture, slavery, violence against women, etc.), while many human rights directly impact on health concerns (e.g. non-discrimination in accessing medical aid). Although the WHO provides technical and policy guidance in the field of health and human rights and works closely with other UN agencies, its involvement in strengthening compliance with human rights is primarily through collaboration with the special mechanism and pertinent treaty bodies. The same is true of the UN Food and Agriculture Organization (FAO). It works with special mechanism mandate-holders and various treaty bodies monitoring human rights and contributes to standard-setting. The United Nations Children's Fund (UNICEF) was a powerful and successful advocate of children before the adoption of the United Nations Convention on the Rights of the Child. From an organization primarily responding to children's needs to one

---

Kluwer); P. Alston, 'Beyond "Them" and "Us": Putting Treaty Body Reform into Perspective', in Alston and Crawford, note 3 above, p. 503.

121 Reports cited *ibid.*, note 120; High Commissioner Concept Paper HRI/MC/2006/CR.P.1.

122 E.g. Bayefsky, note 121 above, pp. 142–7; M. O'Flaherty and C. O'Brien,'Reform of UN Human Rights Treaty Monitoring Bodies: A Critique of the Concept Paper on the Hugh Commissioner's Proposal for a Unified Standing Treaty Body', *Human Rights Law Review*, 7 (2007), pp. 141–72; R. Johnstone, 'Cynical Savings or Reasonable Reform? Reflections on a Single Unified UN Human Rights Treaty Body', *Human Rights Law Review*, 7 (2007), pp. 173–200; M. Bowman, 'Towards a Unified Treaty Body for Monitoring Compliance with UN Human Rights Conventions? Legal Mechanisms for Treaty Reform', *Human Rights Law Review*, 7 (2007), pp. 225–49.

addressing responsibilities and rights,[123] UNICEF has undoubtedly exercised tremendous impact on children's rights. It also plays a notable role in education, rendering human rights accessible to children worldwide through a host of media. A more recent creation, the United Nations Development Programme (UNDP), currently spearheads work on the Millennium Development Goals, drawing on a number of organizations and funds in furtherance of advancing the eradication of extreme poverty, combating HIV/AIDS, democratization, and sustainable development. Its annual Human Rights Development Report is a key indicator of the practical impact of human rights (includes life expectancy and literacy rates).

The United Nations High Commissioner for Refugees (UNHCR) was established in 1950 with a mandate to lead and coordinate action for the protection of refugees. From a focus on European refugees displaced during the Second World War, its remit has expanded to the global organization it is today. Sadly, it has worked with ever more refugees and internally displaced peoples over the last six decades. UNHCR is primarily a humanitarian organization, responding to crises as they unfold, ensuring the full realization of the Convention Relating to the Status of Refugees 1951[124] and its 1967 Protocol. Its work is unsurpassed for the right to seek asylum while it makes considerable practical contributions to work on the rule of law, child soldiers, right to health, etc. However, as with the foregoing agencies and organizations, UNHCR has no mechanism for securing affected human rights.

The International Monetary Fund (IMF) and the World Bank, though not strictly part of the UN, clearly have a role to play in promoting respect for human rights.[125] Poverty reduction is a key goal of the UN. The financial decisions made by these organizations have obvious implications for government capacity-building, as strong financial institutions bring stability and prosperity to states and combat corruption. There is, however, no direct system for monitoring human rights compliance, and politics or economics, rather than human rights, is the principal factor considered when making decisions.

Alone, the International Labour Organization (ILO) and UNESCO have distinct systems for ensuring the protection of rights protected by treaties concluded under their auspices – hence the specific focus on them in this section.

4.1 United Nations Educational, Scientific and Cultural Organization (UNESCO)

Article I (1) of UNESCO's constitution obliges the organization to further human rights. UNESCO also operates a system for considering communications concerning rights within its jurisdiction.[126] UNESCO Decision 104 EX/3.3 (1978) prescribes the procedures which should be followed in the examination of cases and questions which might be submitted to UNESCO concerning the exercise of human rights in the spheres of its competence.[127] These proceedings are generally confidential. A comparable (to the treaty bodies) number of communications have been brought.

---

123 M. Santos Pias, *A Human Rights Conceptual Framework for UNICEF* (Florence: UNICEF, 1999) [online]. Available from: http://www.unicef-icdc.org/publications/pdf/essay9.pdf [accessed October 2009].

124 189 UNTS 150.

125 S. Skogly, *The Human Rights Obligations of the World Bank and the International Monetary Fund* (London: Cavendish, 2001)..

126 K. Partsch and K. Hufner, 'UNESCO Procedures for the Protection of Human Rights', in Symonides, note 11 above, p. 111.

127 See also D. Weissbrodt and R. Farley, 'The UNESCO Human Rights Procedures – an Evaluation', *Human Rights Quarterly*, 16 (1994), pp. 391–414.

4.2 International Labour Organization (ILO)

The ILO is one of the oldest international organizations addressing major human rights issues. It dates from the Treaty of Versailles of 1919 when the terminology used was 'social justice' rather than 'human rights'.[128] Now it has almost 400 treaties and recommendations. With a focus centrally on social justice, the ILO trail-blazed standard-setting for workers' rights and has a tripartite system with workers, employers and states represented on its governing body.[129] Compliance with its treaties is by state report, compliance monitoring and individual or group complaints.

Reports are required every two or five years, depending on whether the treaty is a core or high priority one (thus demanding biennial reports) or not. The Committee of Experts on the Application of Conventions and Recommendations meets annually to review these state progress reports. A range of technical assistance is available to states in furtherance of workers' rights. Article 24 of the constitution of the ILO allows for complaints by industrial associations of employers/workers that any of the members has failed to secure effective observance of any ILO treaty.

5. Conclusions

As Tomuschat notes, 'international protection of human rights is a chapter of legal history that has begun at a relatively late stage in the history of humankind'.[130] Is it too late to make a difference? It would seem not, though Alston,[131] Annan,[132] Robinson[133] and Hathaway,[134] among others, emphasize that with universal ratification of many instruments approaching, improving the effectiveness of treaty obligations is inevitably the next hurdle to securing human rights. While states exhibit considerably less reticence when ratifying treaties today, reservations remain a problem and the controversial (many would say, futile) arguments of cultural relativism still rage as the bastions of state sovereignty are broached. Few would counter the argument that, six decades years after the UDHR was formally adopted, human rights are ingrained in international and national society.[135]

Not everyone enjoys all rights and freedoms, but there is a greater consciousness thereof. Human rights are accepted in principle but want full realization. No longer is diplomatic pressure and fear of 'adverse publicity' sufficient to ensure full compliance with human rights treaties. If the UN human rights system cannot be made to work, then there is a risk that the rhetoric will

---

128 L. Swepston, 'The International Labour Organization's System of Human Rights Protection', in Symonides, note 11 above, p. 91.

129 ILO Constitution, Article 7.

130 Tomuschat, note 28 above, p. 7.

131 Alston, note 120 above.

132 Annan, note 51 above.

133 M. Robinson, 'From Rhetoric to Reality: Making Human Rights Work', *European Human Rights Law Review*, 1 (2003).

134 O. Hathaway, 'Why Do Countries Commit to Human Rights Treaties?', *Journal of Conflict Resolution*, 51 (2007), pp. 588–621.

135 An interesting discussion in E. Petersmann, 'Time for a United Nations "Global Compact" for Integrating Human Rights into the Law of Worldwide Organizations: Lessons from European Integration', *European Journal of International Law*, 13 (2002), pp. 621–50.

never become a reality. The regional systems, NGOs and National Human Rights Institutions all have their role to play, roles that gain in importance as the UN system is strained. Transforming the rhetoric of the UDHR into a reality for some 6.7 billion people is the challenge facing everyone and all parts of the UN system in the future.

Chapter 12

The African Regional Human Rights System

Olufemi Amao

1. Introduction

Owing to its turbulent history, the African continent has faced tremendous challenges in the human rights sphere. The continent frequently makes international news for protracted and catastrophic civil wars, interstate conflicts, ethnic cleansing, coup d'états, corruption of gargantuan proportions, chaotic elections, toxic waste dumping, famine, diseases, child labour and the like. This state of affairs ensures that human right abuses on a massive scale continue across the continent. The current dire situations in Sudan, Somalia, Democratic Republic of Congo and Zimbabwe are glaring examples. The First Organization of African Unity Ministerial Conference on Human Rights in Africa (1999) correctly identified the causes of human rights violations in Africa. These included the following: contemporary forms of slavery, neo-colonialism, racism, religious intolerance, poverty, conflicts, mismanagement and bad governance, corruption, monopoly of power, lack of judicial and press autonomy, environmental degradation, terrorism and nepotism.[1] Despite that grim outlook, a potentially viable regional human rights system is emerging in Africa which is progressively making the human rights promises of the UDHR[2] a reality to the people of Africa.

2. The African Regional Human Rights System

The African Charter on Human and Peoples' Rights (ACHPR)[3] is at the core of the African human rights system. However, it must be noted that there are other instruments (though some of these are not wholly human rights instruments) created within Africa before and after the African Charter which have bearing on the system. These include the Convention on Specific Aspects of the Refugee Problems in Africa 1969,[4] the African Charter on the Rights and Welfare of the Child 1990,[5] the Protocol on the Establishment of an African Court on Human and Peoples' Rights 1998,[6] the Protocol to the African Charter on Human and People's Rights on the Rights of Women

1 See Paragraph 8 of the *Grand Bay (Mauritius) Declaration and Plan of Action*, adopted by the First OAU Ministerial Conference on Human Rights, meeting from 12 to 16 April 1999 in Grand Bay, Mauritius. Available on the African Union website from: http://www.achpr.org/english/declarations/declaration_grand_bay_en.html [accessed 26 December 2009].

2 GA Res. 217A (III), UN Doc. A/810 at 71 (1948).

3 Adopted 27 June 1981, entered into force on 21 October, 1986 OAU. Doc. CAB/LEG/67/3 Rev. 5.

4 1001 UNTS 45. Adopted by the Assembly of Heads of State and Government at its 6th Ordinary Session in Addis Ababa on 10 September 1969 and entered into force on 20 June 1974.

5 OAU Doc. CAB/LEG/24.9/49 (1990). Adopted on 11 July 1990, and entered into force on 29 November 1999.

6 OAU Doc. OAU/LEG/EXP/AFCHPR/PROT (III). Adopted on 10 June 1998, and entered into force on 25 January 2004.

in Africa 2003,[7] and the Protocol on the Statute of the African Court of Justice and Human Rights 2008.[8] To a greater or lesser degree, each of the instruments incorporates the peculiarities of Africa in the protection of human rights.

3. Relationship Between the African Human Rights System and the UDHR

The emergence of 'an African regional human rights system' can be traced back to the establishment of the Organization of African Unity (OAU). The OAU was established in 1963 with the aim of fighting colonialism and apartheid in South Africa.[9] The OAU did not engage much with human right issues except in the context of self-determination and apartheid in South Africa.[10] The lack of emphasis on human rights under the OAU was due to the strong bias in favour of non-interference in other states' internal affairs. Nonetheless, the preamble of the OAU Charter makes specific reference to the UDHR. It asserts, *inter alia,* that OAU states are

> [p]ersuaded that the Charter of the United Nations and the Universal Declaration of Human Rights, to the Principles of which we reaffirm our adherence, provide a solid foundation for peaceful and positive cooperation among States

The OAU Charter further provides in Article 2 that one purpose of the OAU, among others, was to:

> promote international cooperation, having due regard to the Charter of the United Nations and the Universal Declaration of Human Rights.

It was therefore not the case that African leaders were completely uninterested in human rights issues. To the contrary, after the summit in 1963 at which the OAU Charter was signed, African leaders started considering the possibility of adopting a Convention on Human Rights in line with the UN Charter and the UDHR. Despite the fact that at the time of the making of the UDHR, only two African states (Ethiopia and Liberia) were members of the UN, with the rest under colonial or apartheid rule, the UDHR was the main inspiration underlying the creation of the African human rights system. The process culminated in the introduction of the African Charter on Human and Peoples' Rights in 1981. The African Charter is the continent's principal human rights instrument. It has its independent commission in Banjul, Gambia. As will be explained later in this chapter, the African Charter has unusual features that set it apart from other regional and international human rights instruments. These include the coverage of economic, social and cultural rights alongside

---

7 CAB/LEG/66.6 (13 September 2000), adopted by the 2nd Ordinary Session of the Assembly of the Union, Maputo on 11 July 2003, and entered into force on 25 November 2005.

8 Adopted on 1 July 2008. This protocol merges the African Court on Human and Peoples' Rights and the Court of Justice of the African Union into one single court (Articles 1 and 2). It thus replaces both the Protocol to the African Charter on Human and Peoples' Rights on the Establishment of an African Court on Human and Peoples' Rights (adopted in 1998) and the Protocol of the Court of Justice of the African Union (adopted in 2003). See Section 4.4 of this chapter below.

9 See the Charter of the Organization of African Unity, adopted 25 May 1963 and entered into force 13 September1963, 479 UNTS 39.

10 A. Lloyd and R. Murray, 'Institutions with Responsibility for Human Rights Protection Under the African Union', *Journal of African Law*, 48(2) (2004), pp. 165–86, at p. 166.

civil and political rights, inclusion of third-generation rights, inclusion of people's rights, and specific duties of individuals and states.

In 2001, the African Union (AU) was established as a successor to the OAU. The purposes that the AU is designed to serve include the securing of the continent's democracy, human rights and sustainable economy. The Constitutive Act of the AU incorporated all of the objectives and principles of the OAU in its provisions. However, it went further than the OAU Charter by providing for the promotion of democratic principles and institutions, popular participation and good governance, and, most importantly in the context of this chapter, the promotion and protection of human rights.[11] The AU thus seems to take a more rigorous and robust approach to human rights promotion and protection. The principles of the Constitutive Act also expressly include respect for democratic principles, human rights, the rule of law, and the promotion of social justice to ensure balanced economic development.[12]

To improve the efficacy of its human rights system, the AU departed from the earlier emphasis placed on non-interference with the internal affairs of member states under the OAU by making provision for the imposition of sanctions on member states that fail to comply with the decisions and policies of the AU.[13] The AU Constitutive Act provides for the following institutions: an Assembly and Executive Council, a Pan-African Parliament, an African Court of Justice, a Permanent Representatives Committee, an Economic, Social and Cultural Council, a Peace and Security Council, and specialized technical committees and financial institutions. Many of these institutions have the potential to deal with human rights issues.[14]

3.1 The African Charter and UDHR

A comparison of the African Charter with the UDHR reveals great similarities. Articles 2 and 19 embody the right to non-discrimination in similar terms to Article 2 of the UDHR. The right of equality before the law guaranteed under Article 3 of the African Charter can also be inferred from Article 2 of the UDHR. Article 4 of the African Charter guarantees the right to life in similar terms to Article 3 of the UDHR. Article 20(1) of the African Charter provides further elaboration on the right to life. Article 5 of the Charter guarantees the right to the respect of the dignity inherent in a human person and the right to the recognition of his legal status. The article goes on to prohibit all forms of exploitation and degradation with particular reference to slavery, the slave trade, torture, and cruel, inhuman or degrading treatment. These guarantees are covered by Articles 3, 4 and 5 of the UDHR. The right to liberty is guaranteed in Article 6 of the African Charter and is more elaborate on the subject than Article 3 of the UDHR, which, among other things, also guarantees the right to liberty. Article 7 of the African Charter protects the right to a fair trial, combining various provisions of Articles 7, 8 and 11 of the UDHR. Article 8 of the Charter protects 'freedom of conscience, the protection and free practice of religion' in similar terms to Article 18 of the UDHR. However, the UDHR elaborates more on the right to freedom of religion. Other provisions of the African Charter that are similar to those of the UDHR are as follows: Article 9 of the African Charter and Article 19 of the UDHR on freedom to information; Articles 10 and 11 of the African Charter and Article 20 of the UDHR on the right to association and assembly; Article 12 of the African Charter and Articles 13 and 14 of the UDHR on the right to movement and to seek

11 Article 3, Constitutive Act of the African Union, OAU Doc. CAB/LEG/23.15, entered into force 26 May 2001.

12 *Ibid.*, Article 4.

13 Lloyd and Murray, note 9 above, p. 172.

14 *Ibid.*, p. 173.

asylum; Article 13 of the African Charter and Article 21 of the UDHR on the right to participate in government and to access public service; Article 14 of the African Charter and Article 17 of the UDHR on the right to property; Article 15 of the African Charter and Article 23 of the UDHR on the right to work and employment; Article 16 of the African Charter and Article 25 of the UDHR on the right to health; Article 17 of the African Charter and Article 26 of the UDHR on the right to education; Article 18 of the African Charter and Articles 16 and 25 of the UDHR on the rights of the family, women and child; Article 19 of the African Charter and Article 1 of the UDHR on equality of all human beings; Article 22 of the African Charter and Article 22 of the UDHR on the right to development; Article 23 of the African Charter and Article 28 on the right to national and international peace and security; Articles 25 and 29 of the African Charter and Article 29 of the UDHR on the duties of the individual and the state.

Notwithstanding the many similarities between the African Charter and the UDHR, some commentators have contended that the African Charter's provisions are inadequate with respect to freedom from slavery, freedom from compulsory or forced labour, the prohibition of the death penalty, marital rights, and the right to privacy.[15]

3.2 The African Charter's Unique Features

The African Charter combines elements of international law with African concepts of rights. The drafters of the charter were guided by the principle that the Charter 'should reflect the African conception of human rights and should take as a pattern the African philosophy of law and meet the needs of Africa'.[16] There was a conscious effort to rationalize African perspectives on the relationship between the individual and society with international human rights standards. According to Udombana, the African Charter is 'more than just a matter of public international law or international customary law; it is a synthesis of universal and African elements. Its organizing principle is the balance between tradition and modernity, not only between African tradition and the modernity of international law, but also between African modernity and the tradition of international law.'[17] Perhaps this combination of elements explains the unique features of the African Charter.

The charter recognizes not only civil and political rights but also economic, social and cultural rights. It provides for the unconditional realization of these rights. According to Heynes and Killander, this approach emphasizes the indivisibility of human rights and the importance of developmental issues within the African context.[18] The socio-economic rights that are expressly mentioned in the charter include the right to work under equitable and satisfactory conditions (Art. 15), the right to health (Art. 16), and the right to education (Art. 17).

The African Commission has interpreted the provisions of the charter to include unenumerated rights. The commission in *SERAC* v *Nigeria*[19] held that there are rights which are not explicitly

---

15 E.g. C. Heynes and M. Killander, 'The African Regional Human Rights System', in F. Gomez Isa and K. De Feyter (eds), *International Protection of Human Rights: Achievements and Challenges* (Bilbao: University of Deusto, 2006), pp. 514–15.

16 Meeting of Experts for the Preparation of the Draft African Charter of Human and Peoples' Rights, Dakar 28 November 1979, OAU CAB/LEG/67/3 Rev. 1, p. 1.

17 J. Udombana, 'Between Promise and Performance: Revisiting States' Obligations Under the African Human Rights Charter', *Stanford Journal of International Law*, 40 (2004), p. 110.

18 Heynes and Killander, note 15 above, pp. 507 and 516.

19 *Social and Economic Rights Action Centre (SERAC) and The Centre for Economic and Social Rights (CESR)* v *Nigeria* (2001), Communication No. 155/96, University of Minnesota Human Rights Library

mentioned in the charter but which should be regarded as being implicitly included. Such rights identified in the SERAC case include:

> The right to housing or shelter deduced from the provisions on health, property and family in the Charter.[20]

> The right to food deduced from the right to life, right to dignity, right to health and right to economic, social and cultural development.[21]

The commission went on to hold that all rights under the African Charter are enforceable. It would thus not matter whether the rights are civil and political rights or economic, social and cultural rights. Any right specified under the charter would be enforceable through the communication procedure of the commission. Shelton observed in this regard:

> The Commission's decision that all rights in the African Charter are enforceable and may be subject to the system's communication procedure advances the African system well ahead of other regional systems – which have moved tentatively toward allowing petitions for economic, social and cultural rights, and which only partially recognize a right to environment.[22]

Another distinctive feature of the African Charter is its recognition of 'people's rights'. Though the concept is not defined under the charter, it is generally understood to mean collective or group rights. The rights include equality of people (Article 19), the right of people to existence and self-determination (Article 20), the right of people to freely dispose of their wealth and national resources (Article 21), the right to development (Article 22), the right to national and international peace and security (Article 32), and the right to 'a generally satisfactory environment' favourable to development (Article 24).

Furthermore, the charter imposes correlative duties on individuals contained in many human rights instruments and goes further to impose autonomous duties not connected with rights.[23] Perhaps more unique is the imposition of wider and specific duties upon states. These duties are contained in Articles 20, 21, 22, 25 and 26 of the African Charter. States' duties include duties to assist in liberation struggles, to eliminate foreign economic exploitation, to ensure the exercise of the right to development, to promote the rights and freedoms contained in the charter, to guarantee the independence of courts, and to establish and improve national institutions entrusted with the promotion and protection of human rights.

A notable difference between the charter and the UDHR is the employment of clawback clauses in many of the substantive provisions of the African Charter (Articles 6–14), in contrast with the UDHR, which includes a derogation clause. The UDHR employs a general derogation clause in

---

[online]. Available from: http://www1.umn.edu/humanrts/africa/comcases/155-96b.html [accessed 27 May 2009].

20 Articles 14, 16 and 18 of the African Charter. See Paragraph 60 of *SERAC* v *Nigeria*, note 19 above.

21 Articles 4, 5, 16 and 22 of the African Charter.

22 D. Shelton, 'Decision Regarding Communication 155/96 (Social and Economic Rights Action/ Center for Economic and Social Rights v Nigeria). Case No. ACHPR/ Comm. A044/1', *American Journal of International Law*, 96(4) (2002), pp. 937–42, at p. 942.

23 The Preamble and Articles 27 through 29 of the African Charter recognize private duties. See also Udombana, note 17 above, p. 111.

Article 29(2), which permits derogation from the rights protected when necessary for the purposes of securing the rights of others, or meeting the just requirements of morality, public order and the general welfare. On the face of it, it would appear that the non-inclusion of a derogation clause in the African Charter provides a more secure framework for rights protection by not allowing for derogation from the rights protected. The reality, however, is that many of the clawback clauses subordinate the provisions of the charter to municipal laws and to the discretion of states in that they qualify the observance of the principles in the charter under certain circumstances.[24] The use of these clauses has been widely criticized by human rights scholars.[25]

On a positive note, the commission in its jurisprudence has contained the effects of the use of clawback clauses by interpreting the provisions in harmony with international human rights standards.[26]

3.3 Expansion of the Rights Protected Under the African Human Rights System

Over the years, there has been a progressive expansion of the rights protected under the African system. This expansion has accentuated the similarities between the rights protected under the African system and the UDHR. An example is the protection of the rights of children. Children are generally entitled to the rights guaranteed under the UDHR. However, the UDHR makes direct references to children only in Articles 25 and 26. Later instruments made pursuant to the UDHR, especially the UN Convention on the Rights of the Child 1989,[27] broadened the rights of the child under the UN framework. Similarly, under the African Charter, with the exception of Article 18(3), there is no special or specific provision for the rights of children. Article 18(3) does not, however, confer any specific right on children but only provides for 'the protection of the rights of ... the child as stipulated in international declarations and conventions'. The African Charter on the Rights and Welfare of the Child (ACRWC) was introduced to fill this gap in the African system. Its provisions are very similar to the UN Convention on the Rights of the Child, and in some instances the ACRWC provides a higher level of protection.

Similarly, the African Convention on the Ban on the Import into Africa and the Control of Transboundary Movement of Hazardous Waste in Africa (the Bamako Convention) 1991[28] complements the provisions of the African Charter on the right to a general satisfactory environment (Article 24), right to life (Article 4), right to security of a person (Article 6), and right to health (Article 16). The dumping of toxic wastes impinges on the aforementioned rights. The convention was adopted to strengthen the framework for the control of the movement of hazardous wastes within Africa.

---

24 C.M. Shaw, 'The Evolution of Regional Human Rights Mechanisms. A Focus on Africa', *Journal of Human Rights*, 6 (2007), pp. 209–32, at p. 214.

25 K. Hopkins, 'A New Human Rights Era Dawns on Africa?', *SA Publiek/SA Public Law*, 18 (2003), pp. 349–70.

26 E.g. *Amnesty International* v *Zambia*, 12th Annual Activity Report, 1994–2001 Compilation (Banjul: IHRDA, 2002), pp. 371–82; *Civil Liberties Organization (in respect of Nigerian Bar Association)* v *Nigeria*, 8th Annual Activity Report, 1994–2001 Compilation (Banjul: IHRDA, 2002), pp. 200–2; *Sir Dawda K. Jawara* v *The Gambia*, 13th Annual Activity Report, 1994–2001 Compilation (Banjul: IHRDA, 2002), pp. 108–21.

27 GA Res. 44/25, annex, 44 UN GAOR Supp. (No. 49) at 167, UN Doc. A/44/49 (1989), entered into force 2 September 1990.

28 (1991) 30 *ILM* 773. Adopted in January 1991, entered into force 22 April 1998.

African states also adopted the Protocol to the African Charter on Human and Peoples' Rights on the Rights of Women in Africa (Maputo Protocol) 2003[29] to expand the rights of women under the African Charter. Many of the rights guaranteed under the Protocol can also be found in the African Charter, but the Maputo Protocol is more comprehensive and specific to issues relating to women.[30] The rights include respect for dignity (Article 3), freedom from discrimination (Article 2), right to physical and emotional security (Article 4), right to participate in the political process (Article 9), right to peace (Article 10), economic and social welfare rights (Article 13), health and reproductive rights (Article 14), environmental rights (Article 18), and the right to sustainable development (Article 19). However, the protocol introduces some new rights that were not contained in the African Charter. These include governments' duty to integrate a women perspective in policy development (Article 2); the right of vulnerable groups of women, including elderly women, widows, disabled women and women in distress (Articles 20, 21, 22 and 24); rights to food security and housing (Articles 15 and 16); the right to live in a positive cultural environment (Article 17); prohibition of female genital mutilation (Article 5); and the reproductive rights of women (Article 14).

4. The Control Mechanisms Under the African Human Rights System

Unlike the UDHR, which does not provide for a mechanism for enforcing its provisions, enforcement mechanisms are included in the principal human rights instrument in Africa.

4.1 The African Charter's Mechanism

The two main mechanisms provided for under the African Charter are the African Commission's procedure and the reporting procedure. Originally, the African Commission was established under the African Charter for the purposes of ensuring compliance with the provisions of the charter.[31] The commission was modelled on the European Human Rights Commission (since abolished)[32] and the Inter-American Commission on Human Rights.[33] As stated in Article 45 of the charter, the commission's functions include the promotion of human rights, the protection of human rights under the African Charter, the interpretation of the African Charter, and any other functions assigned to the commission by the Assembly of Heads of State. The commission also has the additional task of preparing cases for submission to the African Court on Human and Peoples' Rights.[34] The commission thus has both protective and promotional responsibility. Its protective responsibility involves receiving communications on violations of rights protected under the

---

29 See note 7 above.

30 The African Charter made specific reference to women only in Article 68.

31 Article 30 of the African Charter.

32 The European Commission on Human Rights was abolished by Protocol 11 to the European Convention for the Protection of Human Rights and Fundamental Freedoms (213 UNTS 222 as amended).

33 The Inter American Commission on Human Rights is an autonomous organ of the Organization of American States (OAS). It was created in 1959 to promote and protect human rights in the Americas pursuant to the OAS Charter (119 UNTS 3 as amended) and the American Convention on Human Rights (O.A.S. Treaty Series No. 36, 1144 UNTS 123).

34 Article 5 of the Protocol to the African Charter on Human and Peoples' Rights on the Establishment of an African Court on Human and Peoples' Rights, 1998, OAU Doc. OAU/LEG/EXP/AFCHPR/PROT (III) (hereafter 'ACtHPR Protocol'.

charter, communicating them to states and investigating them with the view to reconciling the parties. The decisions are also included in the commission's activity report. Although the African Charter directly refers only to communications from states, the commission also accepts communications from non-state actors under the provision for 'Other Communications'.[35] This makes it possible for individuals and non-governmental organizations (NGOs) to bring complaints before the commission. However, a communication can only be brought against a state party to the charter and not against private persons or individuals.[36] Hence, a private person or individual can only be implicated when a state is held liable for the violation of human rights. Significantly, specific provision was made for legal aid for the first time under the recently adopted Interim Rules of Procedure of the African Commission on Human and Peoples' Rights (Interim Rules).[37] Rule 107 provides that the commission may by itself or at the request of the author of a communication facilitate legal aid to the author in connection with the case. Such legal aid will be facilitated where the commission is convinced that the facilitation is essential for the proper discharge of its duties and the author has no sufficient means to meet all or part of the costs of proceedings. The commission does not by itself enforce its decisions but occasionally grants interim or provisional measures to avoid irredeemable harm.[38] In *International PEN and Others* v *Nigeria*, the commission held that such provisional measures are binding.[39] The commission has produced world- leading decisions in the area of economic, social and cultural rights, thereby refuting the widely canvassed argument that such rights cannot be dealt with through a judicial process.[40] The commission is also setting the pace in translating collective rights (such as the right to development, the right of people to dispose of their wealth and natural resources freely, the right to peace and security, the right to self-determination, and cultural rights) into enforceable rights.[41]

Despite its potential as an institution to protect and promote human rights, the commission has its limitations. State parties generally refuse to cooperate with the commission during investigations, hearings of cases and implementations of decisions. In relation to the implementation of its decisions, it has been suggested that the commission, in most of its decisions, has failed to enunciate clear and specific remedies that may effect compliance.[42] This places a question mark over the commission's effectiveness.[43] The commission has also been criticized for its lack of independence. This is because of its close links with African heads of state and government.[44] Under Article 33 of the African Charter, the 11 members of the commission are elected by secret ballot by the Assembly of Heads of States and Government, from a list of persons nominated by

35 Articles 55–59 African Charter.

36 *Ibid.*, Article 47.

37 Adopted at the Commission's 44th Ordinary Session in November 2008.

38 See U.O. Umozorike, 'The African Charter on Human and Peoples' Rights: Suggestions for more Effectiveness', *Annual Survey of International and Comparative Law*, 13 (2007), p 186.

39 Communication No. 137/94, 139/94, 154/96 and 161/97 (1998). See also R. Wright, 'Finding an Impetus for Institutional Change at the African Court on Human and Peoples' Rights', *Berkeley Journal of International Law*, 24 (2006), pp. 463–98, at p. 471.

40 S. Sceats, 'Africa's New Human Rights Court: Whistling in the Wind?', Chatham House Briefing Paper (IL BP 09/01), March 2009, p. 7.

41 E.g. *Social and Economic Rights Action Centre (SERAC) and Centre for Economic and Social Rights (CESR)* v *Nigeria*, Communication No. 155/96, 2001; *Democratic Republic of Congo* v *Burundi, Rwanda and Uganda*, Communication No. 227/99, 2006.

42 R. Murray, *The African Commission on Human and Peoples' Rights and International Law* (Oxford: Hart Publishing, 2000), p. 32.

43 Wright, note 39 above, pp. 471–2.

44 *Ibid.*, p. 472.

the states parties to the charter. This means that states have significant control over the commission. An attempt was made to address this issue in the recently adopted Interim Rules. However, the attempt did not address the manner of election of members. Rather, Rule 7 provides that it is incompatible to be a member of government, a minister or under-secretary of state, a diplomatic representative, a director of a ministry or one of his subordinates, or the legal adviser to a foreign office, or any other political binding function and at the same time be a member of the commission. A major limitation on the commission's authority is the provision in Article 59 of the charter, which directs that measures taken within the provisions of the charter are to remain confidential until the Assembly of Heads of State and Government decide otherwise. Considering that one of the major weapons in the enforcement of human rights is the attendant publicity, this provision whittles down the power of the commission. Another major drawback is the restriction on access by non-state actors such as NGOs and individuals. Under Article 58 of the charter, communications received from non-state parties must 'relate to special cases which reveal the existence of a series of serious or massive violations of human and peoples' rights'.[45] The charter does not define what are 'special cases' or 'serious or massive violations of human and peoples' rights'. This provision could be used to deny access to an otherwise relevant application. Furthermore, such communications must not be 'written in disparaging or insulting language'.[46] The determination of what is considered a disparaging or insulting language is left to the commission. However, the commission has generally interpreted these provisions liberally.[47]

4.2 State Reporting

Under Article 62 of the African Charter, each state party undertakes to submit every two years, from the date the charter comes into force, a report on the legislative or other measures introduced with a view to giving effect to the rights and freedoms recognized and guaranteed under the charter. State reporting under the charter is designed to monitor state compliance with the provisions of the charter and establish dialogue with states on the promotion and protection of human rights. The reporting mechanism is also designed to encourage states to learn from each other's experiences in the implementation of the provisions of the charter. In practice, the reporting mechanism has had little success. There is a very high default record by state parties. Where parties have submitted reports, the reports have generally been lacking in depth, quality and consistency.[48]

At its Fourth Ordinary Session in 1998, the commission adopted a general guideline on the form and content of the report in order to encourage compliance. The guideline is not helpful because

45 Article 58, African Charter.

46 Article 56, African Charter. The commission sometimes applies this rule strictly to deny the admissibility of a petition. In *Ligue Camerounaise des droits de l'homme* v *Cameroon*, Communication No. 65/92 (1997), the commission ruled that phrases such as 'regime of torturers' and 'government barbarisms' are insulting language under Article 56 that rendered the communication inadmissible.

47 E.g. *Social and Economic Rights Action Centre (SERAC) and Centre for Economic and Social Rights (CESR) v Nigeria*, Communication No. 155/96, 2001, *Zimbabwe Human Rights NGO Forum* v *Zimbabwe*, Communication 245/02, Annexure 3 to the African Commission on Human and Peoples' Rights 21st Activity Report (July–December 2006).

48 Rule 78(3) of the Interim Rules now provides that where a state party fails to comply with its reporting obligations under Article 62, the commission shall fix a new date and communicate this to the state concerned.

of its complexity, repetitiveness, length and lack of coherent organization.[49] The commission's attempt to address the problem by adopting an 11-point guideline went to the other extreme. It was too brief to be meaningful and has not improved compliance with Article 62. As of May 2009, 23 states had submitted one or two reports, owing further reports and 12 had not submitted any.[50] As a way of providing feedback, the African Commission is currently refining its system of providing concluding observations on reports submitted to it. Under Rule 81(2) of the Interim Rules, the commissioners are required to follow up the implementation of concluding observations.

Furthermore, to enhance the robustness of the African system, Rule 30 of the Interim Rules provides that a state proposing to host a session of the commission should not be under any African Union (AU) sanction or be in arrears of its reporting obligations, and if it is a party to a communication of which the commission had issued recommendations, it should have complied with the recommendations.[51]

4.3 The African Court on Human and Peoples' Rights (ACtHPR)

In order to strengthen the mechanism for the protection of human rights and to address the limitations of the African Commission's procedure, there was a push for the creation of a court for human rights within the African system. The first attempt in this regard was the establishment of the African Court on Human and Peoples' Rights (ACtHPR). However, the lifespan of the court is going to be short because it will soon be replaced by the African Court of Justice and Human Rights when the protocol establishing the latter comes into force. This development is discussed further later in this chapter. The ACtHPR was therefore established by an additional protocol to the African Charter adopted by the Assembly of Heads of State and Governments of the OAU in 1998.[52] The protocol came into force in 2004. The first set of judges was appointed in 2006. The court consists of an independent, 11-member panel. Under the protocol, the court is empowered to exercise jurisdiction over all human rights instruments 'ratified by the States concerned'.[53] It has been suggested that this may include regional, sub-regional, bilateral and multilateral international treaties.[54] This means that a person whose rights are not adequately protected under the African Charter can invoke other treaties which state parties have signed up to.[55] This is in contrast to the jurisdiction of the commission which is limited to the interpretation and application of the African Charter. The jurisdiction of the court covers wide-ranging human rights areas, including violations of civil and political rights, economic, social and cultural rights and collective rights of people.

---

49 T.S. Bulto, 'Beyond the Promises: Resuscitating the State Reporting Procedure Under the African Charter on Human and Peoples' Rights', *Buffalo Human Rights Law Review*, 12 (2006), pp. 57–92, at p. 77.

50 25th Activity Report of the ACHPR (2008), EX.CL/490(XIV); G. Bekker, 'Recent Developments in the African Human Rights System 2008–09', *Human Rights Law Review*, 9(4) (2009), pp. 668–89, at p. 680.

51 It is ironic that the Commission is currently based in Banjul, Gambia, a country which is becoming increasingly autocratic. See C. Heyns, 'Some thoughts on Challenges facing the International Protection of Human Rights in Africa', *Netherlands Quarterly of Human Rights*, 27(4) (2009), p. 448.

52 See note 6 above.

53 *Ibid.*, Article 3(1).

54 R.W. Eno, 'The Jurisdiction of the African Court on Human and Peoples' Rights', *African Human Rights Law Journal*, 2 (2002), pp. 223–33, at p. 226; N.J. Udombana, 'Towards the African Court on Human and Peoples' Rights: Better Late Than Never', *Yale Human Rights and Development Law Journal*, 45 (2000), pp. 85–110.

55 *Eno*, note 54 above, p. 226.

The court has both advisory and contentious jurisdiction. The court is generally empowered to receive complaints alleging violations of human rights submitted by states, the African Commission, African Intergovernmental Organizations, and (subject to certain restrictions) NGOs and individuals.[56] It has jurisdiction to entertain requests for advisory opinion on any legal matter relating to the charter or any other relevant human rights instrument from member states, the AU and its organs, or any other organization recognized by the regional body.[57]

For the purpose of exercising its contentious jurisdiction, the court can exercise compulsory (automatic) or optional jurisdiction. Under its compulsory jurisdiction, Article 5(1) provided that the following are entitled to submit cases to the court:

a. the African Commission;
b. the State which has lodged a complaint to the African Commission;
c. the State Party against which the complaint has been lodged at the Commission;
d. the State Party whose citizen is a victim of a human rights violation;
e. African Intergovernmental Organizations.

Furthermore, under Article 5(2), matters may be referred to the court by a state party that has an interest in a case in which it was not originally involved.

The court's optional jurisdiction is for other claimants such as individuals and NGOs that have observer status with the African Commission. The access of such non-state actors is severely restricted in comparison with access to the commission. The court may only allow cases brought by other claimants, first, where a state party had made an express declaration accepting the court's jurisdiction to hear such a case.[58] Second, the court reserves a discretionary power to grant or deny access as it deems fit in particular cases.[59] Juma has described these hurdles placed on the access to the court as an 'assault on the African human rights system'.[60]

The approach of the African system in requiring state declaration is in line with the procedural law of other human rights systems.[61] However, it has been posited that the lack of direct access under the Inter-American Court System has been one of its greatest weaknesses because it limits the role of the victim and requires the intervention of the Inter-American Commission to refer individual cases to the court.[62] The position is different under the European system. Under Protocol 11 of the European Convention, 'the Court may receive applications from any person, non-governmental organization or group of individuals claiming to be the victim of a violation by one of the High Contracting Parties of the rights set forth in the Convention or the protocols thereto.'[63] The provision in the African Court's protocol may have been included to encourage countries to

56 ACtHPR Protocol, Article 5.

57 *Ibid.*, Article 4.

58 *Ibid.*, Article 34(6).

59 *Ibid.*, Article 5(3).

60 D. Juma, 'Access to the African Court on Human and Peoples' Rights: A Case of the Poacher Turned Gamekeeper', *Essex Human Rights Review*, 4(2) (2007), pp. 1–21, at p. 3.

61 E.g. Article 41 of International Covenant on Civil and Political Rights, 999 UNTS 171; Article 21(1) Convention Against Torture, 1465 UNTS 85; Articles 25(1) and 46(1), European Convention for the Protection of Human Rights and Fundamental Freedoms, 213 UNTS 222 (as amended); Article 44(1) of the American Convention on Human Rights, 1144 UNTS 123.

62 Wright, note 39 above, p. 478.

63 Protocol No. 11 to the Convention for the Protection of Human Rights and Fundamental Freedoms, Article 34, which replaced Article 44 of the European Convention.

sign up to it without fear that that the platform would be used against them by non-state entities. According to Eno,

> While the limitation under article 5(3) of the Protocol on the African Court may be necessary to bring states on board to ratify the Protocol, it is nevertheless disappointing and a terrible blow to the standing and reputation of the African Court. After all, it is individuals and NGOs, and not the African Commission, regional intergovernmental organizations or state parties who would be the primary beneficiaries and users of the African Court. The Court is not an institution for the protection of rights of states. A human rights court exists primarily for protecting citizens against the state and other government agencies.[64]

Another area where access to the court is unduly restrictive is the provision that only 'relevant Non Governmental Organizations with observer status before the (African) Commission' have access to the court.[65] As Eno correctly notes, this is a unique and potentially dangerous restriction.[66] There is no guide to determine what is meant by a relevant NGO. Eno therefore argues that the determination may be left within the competence of the commission, which may consider those NGOs that have been submitting periodic reports to it. The implication of this is that NGOs which do not have observer status with the commission would be excluded completely.[67] This is significantly different from the position under the Inter-American system, which permits any NGO legally recognized in one or more member states to lodge a petition with the American Commission, which may transmit the case to the Inter-American Court for determination where necessary.[68]

However, if the ACtHPR adopts a liberal attitude to the interpretation of these provisions, as the African Commission did, the provisions may not necessarily constitute impediments in this regard.

The requirement for the exhaustion of local remedies is also problematic. Under Article 6 of the protocol establishing the court, the court is required to take into consideration the provisions of Article 56 of the African Charter when ruling on the admissibility of cases. Article 56 requires that domestic remedies must be exhausted before communications (in relation to the procedure of the commission) are accepted. If this provision is applied restrictively by the court, it may discourage access to the court by individuals and NGOs. For example, where domestic remedies are not effective and adequate, it may be unjust to require the exhaustion of such remedies. It has therefore been suggested that the rules of procedure for the court should contain explicit reference to the fact that domestic remedies must be both effective and adequate or exhaustion will not be required.[69] Such provision could follow the example of the Inter-American Commission's rules of procedure, which provide as follows:

1. In order to decide on the admissibility of a matter, the Commission shall verify whether the remedies of the domestic legal system have been pursued and exhausted in accordance with the generally recognized principles of international law.

---

64 Eno, note 54 above, p. 231.
65 ACtHPR Protocol, Article 5(3).
66 Eno, note 54 above, p. 231.
67 *Ibid.*
68 Article 44, American Convention on Human Rights; Eno, note 54 above, p. 231.
69 Wright, note 39 above, p. 479.

2. The provisions of the preceding paragraph shall not apply when:
   a. the domestic legislation of the State concerned does not afford due process of law for protection of the right or rights that have allegedly been violated;
   b. the party alleging violation of his or her rights has been denied access to the remedies under domestic law or has been prevented from exhausting them; or,
   c. there has been unwarranted delay in rendering a final judgment under the aforementioned remedies.
3. When the petitioner contends that he or she is unable to prove compliance with the requirement indicated in this article, it shall be up to the State concerned to demonstrate to the Commission that the remedies under domestic law have not been previously exhausted, unless that is clearly evident from the record. [70]

A minor concession was made in this regard under Rule 40(1) of the Interim Rules of Procedure of the African Court.[71] It provides that application to the court shall 'be filed after exhausting local remedies, if any, unless it is obvious that this procedure is unduly prolonged'. This concession is not as comprehensive as the provision under the Inter-American Commission's rules of procedure quoted above.

The African Commission has been inconsistent in its decisions on the application of Article 56 to its processes. It has insisted on effective domestic remedies in some cases.[72] In others it has not, interpreting the provision strictly.[73] If the court adopts a restrictive approach, further access to the court will be hampered.

To date, only two cases have been brought before the court.[74] The Court delivered its first judgment in December 2009 rejecting a case on the ground of lack of jurisdiction.[75]

---

70 Rules of Procedure of the Inter-American Court of Human Rights, Annual Report of the Inter-American Court of Human Rights, 1991, OAS Doc. OEA/Ser.L/V/III.25 doc.7 at 18 (1992), reprinted in Basic Documents Pertaining to Human Rights in the Inter-American System, OEA/Ser.L.V/II.82 doc.6 rev.1 at p. 145 (1992).

71 Adopted and entered into force on 20 June 2008. The Interim Rules cover matters such as membership of the court, sessions of the court, jurisdiction, default judgement, independence of judges, relationship between the court and the commission, legal aid, proceedings of the court and judgement.

72 Constitutional Rights Project v Nigeria (in respect of *Wahab Akamu, G. Adega, and Others, African Commission on Human and Peoples' Rights,* Communication No. 60/91 (1995); *International PEN and Others* v *Nigeria, African Commission on Human and Peoples' Rights*, Communication Nos.137/94, 139/94, 154/96 and 161/97 (1998), *Media Rights Agenda, Constitutional Rights Project* v *Nigeria*, Communication Nos. 105/93, 128/94, 130/94, 152/96 (1998).

73 In *Legal Defence Centre* v *The Gambia,* Communication No. 219/98 (2000), the commission held that there was a failure to exhaust local remedies even though the petitioner was barred from re-entering the state and therefore could not access the local court. A similar approach was followed in *Kenya Human Rights Commission* v *Kenya,* Communication No. 135/94 (1985); *Mohammed Lamine Diakite* v *Gabon,* Communication No. 73/92 (2000).

74 M.K. Mbondenyi, 'Invigorating the African System on Human and Peoples' Rights Through Institutional Mainstreaming and Rationalisation', *Netherlands Quarterly of Human Rights*, 27(4) (2009), pp. 451–83, at p. 472.

75 *Michelot Yogogombaye* v *The Republic of Senegal,* Application No. 001/2008, Judgment of December 2009.

4.4 The African Court of Justice and Human Rights

The Court of Justice of the African Union is one of the organs of the AU specified under Article 5(1) of the Constitutive Act of the AU, and it was originally intended to be the principal judicial organ of the AU. The protocol setting up the court was adopted in 2003, but before it could come into force it was superseded by subsequent events. At its Third Ordinary Session in July 2004, the Assembly of Heads of State and Government of the African Union adopted a resolution to the effect 'that the African Court of Human and Peoples' Rights and the Court of Justice should be integrated into one Court'.[76] At the African Union Summit in July 2008, a protocol was adopted for the purpose of merging the Court of Justice with the ACtHPR and renaming the merged entity the 'African Court of Justice and Human Rights'.[77] The reason for the decision was the need to save costs and to reduce the proliferation of human rights institutions within the African system. The court is divided into two sections, a general affairs section and a human rights section. The former deals with matters such as breaches of treaty obligations by state parties and the exercise of the powers of the AU, while the latter is devoted exclusively to human rights matters. The court takes over the adjudicatory duties of the African Commission on Human and Peoples' Rights. The protocol establishing the court will come into force 30 days after 15 member states have deposited their instrument of ratification.[78] The merger of the Court of Justice and the ACtHPR and the incorporation of the adjudicatory functions of the commission are significant because these changes affect some of the issues discussed earlier in this chapter. These include access to the court, scope of jurisdiction and enforcement of decisions.

Under the statute establishing the African Court of Justice and Human Rights, individuals and NGOs are eligible to submit cases to the court in respect of rights guaranteed by the Charter on the Rights and Welfare of the Child, the Protocol to the African Charter on Human and Peoples' Rights on the Rights of Women in Africa, or any other legal instrument relevant to human rights ratified by the states parties concerned.[79] However, there is no direct access for NGOs and individuals to the court unless the state party against which a complaint is made has made a special declaration to accept the court's competence to hear cases brought by NGOs and individuals.[80] This provision is similar to the requirement under Article 34 (6) of the protocol establishing the ACtHPR. The provision is more restrictive than the restriction placed by Article 58 of the African Charter in respect of access of non-state parties to the commission discussed earlier in this chapter. It is unlikely that states will be eager to make such voluntary declaration that will potentially expose them to more litigation. A similar provision in the ACtHPR has received very little patronage from states. In fact, only two states (Burkina Faso and Mali) have made the necessary declaration to allow access. Furthermore,

---

76 See Decision on the Seats of the Organs of the African Union, Assembly/AU/Dec. 45 (III) Rev.1; Decision on the Merger of the African Court on Human and Peoples' Rights and the Court of Justice of the African Union. Doc. Assembly/ AU/Dec.83(v). Adopted in Sirte, Libya, 4–5 July 2005.

77 Protocol on the Statute of the African Court of Justice and Human Rights Adopted by the Eleventh Ordinary Session of the Assembly of the African Union, held in Sharm El-Sheikh, Egypt, 1 July 2008.

78 The old Protocol to the African Charter on Human and Peoples' Rights on the Establishment of an African Court on Human and Peoples' Rights will, however, remain in force for a transitional period not exceeding one year, or any other period determined by the assembly, after entry into force of the new protocol, to enable the African Court on Human and Peoples' Rights to take the necessary measures for the transfer of its prerogatives, assets, rights and obligations to the African Court of Justice and Human Rights (Article 7).

79 Article 30 of the Statute of the African Court of Justice and Human Rights.

80 Article 8(3) of the Protocol on the Statute of the African Court of Justice and Human Rights and Article 30(f) of the Statute of the African Court of Justice and Human Rights.

NGOs are required to be accredited to the AU or its organs before they can be allowed access to the court. Direct access to the court is available to the state parties, the Pan-African Parliament and other organs of the AU, the African Commission, the African Committee of Experts on the Rights and Welfare of the Child, African Intergovernmental Organizations accredited to the AU or its organs, and African National Human Rights Institutions.[81]

There are provisions in the protocol establishing the court which may potentially make it more effective than the current ACtHPR and the African Commission. The court has competence to exercise jurisdiction over the following: the Constitutive Act of the AU; union treaties and other subsidiary legislation; international law; all acts, decisions, regulations and directives of the AU; and agreements concluded between parties among themselves or with the AU.[82] The jurisdiction of the court is thus very wide when compared to the European Court of Human Rights and the Inter-American Court of Human Rights, which each enforce one treaty. The court is further empowered either on its own motion or on an application by the parties to grant provisional measures (such as injunctions) to preserve the respective rights of the parties.[83]

The enforcement of the judgement of the African Court of Justice and Human Rights is more robust than that of the current ACtHPR and the African Commission. State parties are obliged to comply with the decisions of the court.[84] However, where a party fails to comply, the court may upon application by either party to a dispute refer the matter to the AU Assembly, which may decide upon measures to be taken to give effect to the judgement.[85] Under Article 46(5), such measures may include sanctions.

4.5 Other Control Mechanisms

There are other control mechanisms established for specific instruments. These include the African Committee of Experts on the Rights and Welfare of the Child (ACERWC), which receives and examines state reports on the measures adopted to implement the Children's Charter and progress achieved. The body also has the power to investigate issues covered by the Children Charter. Based on Article 46 of the African Charter, the commission has also appointed special rappoteurs to investigate and report on specific issues. These include the right to life and protection from extrajudicial killings, the rights of women, the rights of prisoners, press freedom and the right to information, refugees and internally displaced persons, and the matter of human rights defenders. Regional Courts of the Economic Community of West Africa (ECOWAS), the South African Development Community (SADC), and the East African Community (EAC) are also taking on significant human rights roles in their jurisprudence.[86]

5. The African Charter's Influence on Domestic Courts: The Example of Nigeria

There is ample evidence that the provisions of the African Charter (and, by extension, the UDHR) are influencing the shape and direction of human rights norms and enforcement in domestic courts

81 *Ibid.*, Article 29.
82 *Ibid.*, Article 31.
83 *Ibid.*, Article 35.
84 *Ibid.*, Article 46.
85 *Ibid.*, Article 46(4).
86 See Heyns, note 51 above, p. 448.

in Africa.[87] For the purpose of this chapter, the case of Nigeria shall be used as an example. Nigeria has ratified the African Charter on Human and People's Rights and incorporated it into domestic law through the African Charter on Human and Peoples' Rights (Ratification and Enforcement) Decree.[88] It has thus been held to be part of Nigerian domestic law,[89] which can be enforced through the procedure provided under the Nigerian constitution.[90]

In *Abacha* v *Fawehinmi*,[91] the Nigerian Supreme Court had the opportunity to clarify the status of the African Charter under Nigerian law. This was the case of Gani Fawehinmi, a human rights activist and lawyer in the country, who had been arrested and detained for a week without being presented with an arrest warrant or given reasons for his arrest. He was held in total isolation before being transferred to another prison. Fawehinmi challenged the detention on the ground that it violated his fundamental rights under Articles 4, 5, 6 and 12 of the African Charter (equivalents in UDHR: Articles 3, 5, 13 and 14). The Supreme Court held that since the African Charter had been incorporated into the Nigerian domestic legal system, it was a statute with international flavour. Therefore, if there were a conflict between it and another domestic statute, its provisions will prevail over those other statutes because it is presumed that the legislature does not intend to breach an international obligation. It was thus held that the African Charter possesses greater vigour and strength than any domestic statute. The implication of this approach was manifested clearly in the later decision of the Federal High Court in *Gbemre* v *Shell and 2 Others*.[92]

The *Gbemre* case was brought by Jonah Gbemre, on behalf of himself and the Iwhereken Community in Delta State in the Niger Delta area of Nigeria, against Shell Petroleum Development Company Nigeria Ltd, the Nigerian National Petroleum Corporation, and the Attorney General of the Federation. The case was brought under the fundamental rights enforcement procedure in the Nigerian constitution, alleging violations of both constitutional provisions and the African Charter. The plaintiffs claimed that the oil exploration and production activities of Shell, which led to incessant gas flaring, had violated their right to life and the dignity of the human person under Sections 33(1) and 34(1) of the Constitution and Articles 4, 16 and 24 of the African Charter (equivalents in the UDHR: Articles 3 and 25). The plaintiffs alleged that the continuous gas flaring by the company had led to poisoning and pollution of the environment, which exposed the community to the risk of premature death, respiratory illnesses, asthma and cancer. They also alleged that the pollution had affected their crop production, thereby adversely affecting their food security. They claimed that many of the natives had died and many more were suffering from various illnesses. The community was therefore left in a state of gross underdevelopment. The defendants opposed the case on several grounds, including that the Articles of the African Charter referred to did not create enforceable rights under the Nigerian Fundamental Rights Enforcement procedure. However, they failed to follow up their arguments during the proceedings due to procedural issues. The trial judge therefore proceeded to judgement without any findings of fact, leaving the judgement bereft of any in-depth legal analysis. In its judgement, the Federal High Court held that the constitutionally protected rights include rights to clean, poison-free, pollution-free environment, and that the actions of Shell in continuing to flare gas in the course of their oil

87 F. Viljoen, 'Application of the African Charter on Human and Peoples' Rights by Domestic Courts in Nigeria', *Journal of African Law*, 43 (1999), pp. 1–17.

88 Cap 10, vol. 1, Laws of the Federation of Nigeria, 1990.

89 *Garba* v *Lagos State Attorney General*, Suit ID/599m/91, and *Agbakoba* v *Director State Security Services* (1994), 6 NWLR (Pt 351) 475.

90 *Nemi* v *The State* (1994), 1 LRC 376 (Nigeria, SC). See also Viljoen, note 86 above.

91 (2000) 6 NWLR (Pt. 660) 228.

92 Suit No. FHC/B/CS/53/05, Federal High Court, Benin Judicial Division, 14 November 2005.

exploration and production activities in the applicant's community violated the plaintiffs' right to life and/or their dignity of the human person under the constitution and the African Charter. Even though there is no apparent justiciable right to a 'clean poison-free, pollution-free and healthy environment' under the Nigerian constitution, the court relied on a cumulative use of constitutional provisions with the provisions of the African Charter (especially Article 24) to recognize and apply a fundamental right to a 'clean poison-free, pollution-free and healthy environment'.[93] This is in line with the decision of the African Commission in the *SERAC* case, although the court did not refer to the case in its judgement.[94] The implication of this decision is that there is a possibility of resorting to the African Charter for rights that are not available under national law.

6. Conclusion

The African human rights system demonstrates how the UDHR has influenced and continues to influence the perception of human rights globally. This is remarkable in itself because the increasing importance placed on human rights in Africa is taking place against the backdrop of widespread human rights violations across the continent. In spite of the fact that many African countries are wary of signing up to human rights standards because of their poor human rights records, they have realized that they cannot buck the global trend. It is interesting to note that from its inception the African human rights system has taken a very expansive approach to protection of rights by covering not only civil and political rights but also economic, social and cultural rights and third-generation rights. In its jurisprudence, the African Commission has further widened the scope of rights protected under the African system. The impact of the African human rights system is trickling down to the national level, as shown by the example of Nigeria. The control system under the African system seems to be in flux at the moment because of the proliferation of mechanisms, many of which are not effective. However, it is noted that a more focused control system may be emerging with the introduction of the African Court of Justice and Human Rights.

93 G. Fortman, '"Adventurous" Judgments: A Comparative Exploration into Human Rights as a Moral-Political Force in Judicial Law Development', *Utrecht Law Review*, 2 (2006), pp. 22–43.

94 The African Commission on Human Rights held, in *SERAC* v *Nigeria*, Communication No. 155/96, 2001, that the failure of the Nigerian government to prevent the escape of toxic waste from oil reserves violated the right to health (Article 16) and the right to a clean environment (Article 24) of the African Charter on Human and Peoples' Rights. The Nigerian government had argued that the rights are vague and incapable of legal enforcement.

Chapter 13
The Inter-American Regional Human Rights System

Jo M. Pasqualucci

1. Introduction

The Inter-American human rights system has evolved over time, despite setbacks, into a force for human rights protection in the Americas. In 1948, prior to the United Nations (UN) General Assembly's adoption of the UDHR,[1] the General Assembly of the Organization of American States (OAS) adopted the American Declaration of the Rights and Duties of Man.[2] Since that time, the OAS has promulgated other human rights treaties and declarations. Progress in the actual protection of human rights, however, has not always been evident across the region.

Some states in the Americas, particularly in the 1970s and early 1980s, struggled under repressive regimes that freely violated human rights. These governments used gross and systematic human rights violations to intimidate sectors of the population and to maintain the status quo. Torture, forced disappearances and extrajudicial executions were deliberate policy in certain countries. Subsequently, when democracies regained control in those states, they ratified regional and international human rights treaties and accepted the jurisdiction of international monitoring organs with the aspiration that 'never again' would their countries descend into depths of human rights abuse.

Over time, civil and political rights have improved in most countries of the Americas, although impunity still exists for violations. Conversely, economic, social and cultural rights have not yet shown significant development in the Inter-American system. Nonetheless, much of the progress that has been made in human rights can be attributed to the growth and efforts of the Inter-American human rights system. The challenges still to be met are vast, but the groundwork has been laid and the system is evolving.

The Inter-American human rights system was established under the auspices of the OAS, an international organization comprising all 35 independent states of the Western hemisphere, namely, Antigua and Barbuda, Argentina, the Bahamas, Barbados, Belize, Bolivia, Brazil, Canada, Chile, Colombia, Costa Rica, Cuba, Dominica, the Dominican Republic, Ecuador, El Salvador, Grenada, Guatemala, Guyana, Haiti, Honduras, Jamaica, Mexico, Nicaragua, Panama, Paraguay, Peru, Saint Kitts and Nevis, Saint Lucia, Saint Vincent and the Grenadines, Suriname, Trinidad and Tobago, United States, Uruguay, and Venezuela. In 1962, Cuba was suspended from participating in the OAS because it adopted a Marxist-Leninist form of government. Cuba's suspension was withdrawn on 3 June 2009 when the OAS General Assembly voted by acclamation to revoke the 1962 resolution that barred Cuba's participation in the OAS. The OAS has, however, set certain conditions before Cuba is fully reinstated; first, Cuba must request readmission to the OAS and, second, it must take part in negotiations. It is hoped that Cuba will eventually play a more active role in the OAS human rights system by ratifying human rights treaties, nominating members

1 GA Res. 217A (III), UN Doc. A/810 at 71 (1948).

2 OAS Res. XXX, International Conference of American States, 9th Conference, OAS Doc. OEA/Ser. L./ V/II.23, doc. 21 rev. 6 (1948).

to the Inter-American Commission and judges to the Inter-American Court, and accepting the jurisdiction of the Inter-American Court.

The OAS adopted both the American Declaration of the Rights and Duties of Man[3] and the OAS Charter at the Ninth Conference of American States in 1948. Although the OAS Charter, the constituent instrument forming the OAS, proclaimed that one of the basic principles of the OAS is the 'fundamental rights of the individual',[4] it did not enumerate or define those rights in any detail.[5] That role was fulfilled by the American Declaration of the Rights and Duties of Man.

2. The American Declaration of the Rights and Duties of Man

The American Declaration of the Rights and Duties of Man (American Declaration) was the first international statement of human rights. It was adopted in April 1948, more than 6 months before the UN General Assembly adopted the UDHR. The American Declaration remained the only human rights instrument in the Inter-American system until 1978, when the American Convention on Human Rights entered into force. The Inter-American Commission on Human Rights, which began examining individual human rights complaints under the amended OAS Charter in 1965,[6] initially applied the American Declaration as the only source of legal norms of what constituted human rights within the Inter-American system.

The American Declaration is not a treaty, and was not originally intended to be binding on states. In its advisory opinion *Interpretation of the American Declaration of the Rights and Duties of Man Within the Framework of Article 64 of the American Convention on Human Rights*,[7] the Inter-American Court of Human Rights clarified the current normative value of the declaration in the Inter-American system. In doing so, the court did not look solely to the normative value and significance that the declaration was believed to have had when it was adopted in 1948.[8] Rather, it determined the legal status of the declaration by considering the evolution of the Inter-American system since the adoption of the declaration.[9] The court advised that

> [t]he Declaration contains and defines the fundamental human rights referred to in the Charter. Thus the Charter of the Organization cannot be interpreted and applied as far as human rights are concerned without relating its norms, consistent with the practice of the organs of the OAS, to the corresponding provisions of the Declaration.[10]

---

3 See *ibid.*

4 Charter of the Organization of American States (as amended) 30 April 1948, entered into force 13 December 1951, 2 UST 2394, TIAS No. 2361, amended effective 1970, 21 UST 607, TIAS No. 6847, Art. 3(i).

5 Charter of the Organization of American States, Preamble (para. 3) and in Arts. 3(j), 16, 43, 47, 51, 112 and 150; Preamble (para. 4), Arts. 3(k), 16, 44, 48, 52, 111 and 150 of the charter revised by the Protocol of Cartagena de Indias). See I/A Court H.R., *Interpretation of the American Declaration of the Rights and Duties of Man Within the Framework of Article 64 of the American Convention on Human Rights*, Advisory Opinion OC-10/89, 14 July 1989, para. 39.

6 OAS Charter as amended by the Protocol of Cartagena de Indias, Arts. 111 and 150.

7 I/A Court H.R., note 5 above, para. 33. Court cases and documents can be found at www.corteidh.or.cr.

8 *Ibid.*, para. 37.

9 *Ibid.*

10 *Ibid.*, para. 43.

The court emphasized that the OAS General Assembly has repeatedly recognized the American Declaration as a source of legal obligations for OAS member states.[11] Moreover, the Statute of the Inter-American Commission, which was approved by the OAS General Assembly, provides that '[f]or those States that have not ratified the American Convention, the Commission continues to apply the norms of the American Declaration.[12]

This interpretation of the legal effects of the American Declaration of the Rights and Duties of Man is similar to the assertion that the UDHR has come to have binding effects on the states parties to the UN Charter. Louis Sohn and other international law experts have maintained that the UDHR is an authoritative interpretation of the human rights protected by the UN Charter, which is a treaty, and that the failure to observe those rights is a violation of the UN Charter.[13] Sohn's vision of the status of the UDHR was reflected in the Proclamation of Tehran, adopted by the 1968 International Conference on Human Rights, which proclaimed that the 'Universal Declaration of Human Rights states a common understanding for the peoples of the world concerning the inalienable and inviolable rights of all members of the human family and constitutes an obligation for the members of the international community.'[14] This proclamation was later endorsed by the UN General Assembly[15] and emphasized by the UN Secretary-General.[16] Subsequently, the Inter-American Court employed similar reasoning when determining the status of the American Declaration.

Like the UDHR, the American Declaration recognizes both civil and political rights as well as economic, social and cultural rights. It establishes 27 substantive human rights which must be protected by the state. The freedoms and rights protected include the rights to life, religious freedom, assembly, association, property, equality before the law, a fair trial, asylum, the inviolability of the home and correspondence, education, work with fair remuneration, social security, leisure time, the benefits of culture, political participation, nationality, protection for mothers and children, freedom of expression, and the right to take part in the cultural life of the community.

Whereas the UDHR focuses on rights and makes only a brief statement that '[e]veryone has duties to the community', the American Declaration focuses on both the rights and the duties of persons. It puts special emphasis on the duties of the individual stating, '[t]he fulfillment of duty by each individual is a prerequisite to the rights of all.'[17] The preamble to the American Declaration also asserts that 'duties of a juridical nature presuppose others of a moral nature, and that man has the duty to 'preserve, practice and foster culture by every means within his power' and to develop spiritually.[18] In addition, the individual duties imposed by the American Declaration include, *inter*

11 *Ibid.*, para. 42.

12 Statute of the Inter-American Commission on Human Rights, Article 1, approved by Resolution No. 447, adopted by the General Assembly of the OAS at its Ninth Regular Period of Sessions, held in La Paz, Bolivia, in October 1979. Commission documents and reports can be found at www.cidh.oas.org.

13 L.B. Sohn, 'John A. Sibley Lecture: The Shaping of International Law', *Georgia Journal of International and Comparative Law*, 8 (1978), pp. 1–25, at pp. 18–19. See Jo M. Pasqualucci, 'Louis Sohn: Grandfather of International Human Rights Law in the United States', *Human Rights Quarterly*, 20 (1998), pp. 924–44, at pp. 938–9.

14 Final Act of the International Conference on Human Rights, UN Doc. A/Conf.32/41, U.N. Pub.E.68. XIV.2 at 3, 4, Π 2.

15 GA Res. 2442, 23 UN GAOR, Supp. (No. 18) 49, UN Doc. A/7218 (1969). See Sohn, note 13 above, pp. 20–1 for a more comprehensive discussion of the Universal Declaration as binding on states.

16 Introduction to the Annual Report of the Secretary General on the Work of the Organization, September 1968, 23 UN GAOR, Supp. (No. 1A) 13, UN Doc. A/7201/Add.1 (1968).

17 American Declaration, note 2 above, preamble.

18 *Ibid.*

alia, the duty of parents to care for their children and children to honour their parents, and the duty of every individual to acquire at least an elementary education, and to vote, obey the law, pay taxes, work, and serve the community and the nation.

Initially, there was no organ charged with monitoring state observance of the human rights guaranteed under the American Declaration. Progress was made in enforcement of human rights when the Inter-American Commission on Human Rights was created in 1959.[19] Six years later, the OAS explicitly authorized the commission to examine individual human rights complaints.[20] The Inter-American Commission became a principal organ of the OAS when the OAS Charter was amended by the 1967 Protocol of Buenos Aires. Until 1969, the American Declaration was the sole human rights instrument of the Inter-American system and, consequently, the commission applied it to all OAS member states.[21] Since the adoption of the American Convention on Human Rights, the commission only applies the American Declaration to those member states that have not yet ratified the American Convention.

3. American Convention on Human Rights

Subsequent to the adoption of the American Declaration and the creation of the Inter-American Commission, the OAS followed the lead of the UN by promulgating binding human rights treaties. The first and most comprehensive OAS human rights treaty is the American Convention on Human Rights.[22] The American Convention recognizes in its preamble that the principles set forth in the UDHR, the OAS Charter, and the American Declaration reflect the aspirations, purposes and goals for the American Convention.[23] As of 31 December 2009, 24 of the 35 OAS member states are states parties to the American Convention.[24] All Latin American states have ratified the American Convention. The USA, Canada and some English-speaking Caribbean states are not parties to the treaty. Trinidad and Tobago denounced the American Convention in 1998.

19 Organization of American States, Fifth Meeting of Consultation of Ministers of Foreign Affaires, Santiago Chile, 12–18 August 1959, Final Act. Document OEA/Ser.C/II.5., Resolution, Part II.

20 Resolution XXII of the Second Special Inter-American Conference. Rio de Janeiro, November 1965, Final Act, OEA/Ser.C/I.13, 32–4.

21 See C.M. Cerna, 'Reflections on the Normative Status of the American Declaration of the Rights and Duties of Man', *University of Pennsylvania Journal of International Law*, 30 (2009), pp. 1211–38 (for a critique of the Inter-American's Commission's application of the American Declaration of Human Rights to State Parties to the American Convention on Human Rights).

22 American Convention on Human Rights 1969, OAS Treaty Series No. 1, reprinted in Basic Documents pertaining to Human Rights in the Inter-American System, preamble, OEA/Ser.L/V/I.4 rev. 12, 31 January 2007 at Basic Documents pertaining to Human Rights in the Inter-American System. OEA/Ser.L/V/I.4 rev. 12, 31 January 2007 [online]. Available from: http://www.cidh.org.

23 The Preamble to the American Convention on Human Rights reads as follows:

> *considering* that these principles have been set forth in the Charter of the Organization of the American States, in the American Declaration of the Rights and Duties of Man, and in the Universal Declaration of Human Rights, and that they have been reaffirmed and refined in other international instruments, worldwide as well as regional in scope. *Ibid.*, preamble, para. 3.

24 States parties to the American Convention are Argentina, Barbados, Bolivia, Brazil, Chile, Colombia, Costa Rica, Dominica, the Dominican Republic, Ecuador, El Salvador, Grenada, Guatemala, Haiti, Honduras, Jamaica, Mexico, Nicaragua, Panama, Paraguay, Peru, Suriname, Uruguay, and Venezuela.

While the drafting of the American Convention was in progress, the UN General Assembly approved the texts of the International Covenant on Civil and Political Rights[25] and the International Covenant on Economic, Social and Cultural Rights.[26] At that time, the OAS member states were canvassed to establish whether or not they remained committed to the promulgation of a separate Inter-American human rights treaty. The delegates voted in favour of an OAS treaty that would not simply replicate the UN covenants. Aware of the realities of the region, the drafters adapted the regional instrument to enhance human rights protections within the unique circumstances of the Americas.[27] When some state delegates suggested that the drafters more closely follow the wording of the UN covenants, the majority of delegates disagreed with that suggestion.[28] In response, they argued that if the American states were to conclude a regional human rights treaty subsequent to the adoption of the UN treaties, 'it was appropriate to introduce any modifications that were desirable in the light of circumstances prevailing in the American Republics.'[29]

The American Convention focuses almost exclusively on the protection of civil and political rights. The scope of the human rights enshrined in the convention is much broader than the original rights in the European Convention on Human Rights 1950[30] but narrower than the rights recognized by the UDHR or the American Declaration. The American Convention obligates states to respect and ensure 23 substantive rights. It protects traditional rights such as life, humane treatment, personal liberty, a fair trial, equal protection of the law, peaceful assembly, association, property, movement and residence, and the freedoms of religion, thought and expression, as well as freedom from slavery and *ex post facto* laws. It also protects the rights of the family and the child, and the rights to nationality, to a name, to compensation from the state when the person has been sentenced through a miscarriage of justice, and to the right to reply in the same medium in which an inaccurate or offensive statement has been made about the person. The convention's only provision for economic, social and cultural rights specifies that states parties undertake progressive development by adopting legislative and other measures to achieve the 'economic, social, educational, scientific and cultural standards' set forth in the amended OAS Charter.[31]

After the adoption of the convention but before it received the requisite number of ratifications and accessions, Thomas Buergenthal, then Professor of Law at the University of Texas, was concerned that the broad reach of the convention would jeopardize state acceptance of the treaty.[32] Although Buergenthal was strongly in favour of the American Convention, he believed that it should have concentrated on fewer and more basic rights in order to obtain the 11 state ratifications necessary for it to enter into force. He even published a critical essay on what he considered to be

25 Adopted 16 December 1966, entered into force 23 March 1976; 999 UNTS 171.

26 Adopted 16 December 1966, entered into force 3 January 1976; 993 UNTS 3.

27 T. Buergenthal and R. Norris, Human Rights, The Inter-American System, Part 2, the Legislative History of the American Convention on Human Rights, Chap. III, Reports on the Conference, at 88.

28 Council of Europe, Report on the Inter-American Specialized Conference on Human Rights, in Thomas Buergenthal and Robert Norris, 2 Human Rights, The Inter-American System, Part 2, the Legislative History of the American Convention on Human Rights, ch. III, Reports on the Conference, at 71.

29 *Ibid.*

30 CETS No. 5, adopted on 4 November 1950.

31 American Convention, note 22 above, Art. 26.

32 See Jo M. Pasqualucci, 'Thomas Buergenthal: Holocaust Survivor to Human Rights Advocate', *Human Rights Quarterly*, 18 (1996), pp. 877–99, at pp. 884–5, taken from Thomas Buergenthal, Address at George Washington University Law School to a human rights class (22 September 1995).

the unnecessarily ambitious American Convention,[33] and he expressed this viewpoint in his human rights classes. The American Convention received the necessary ratifications in 1978, sooner than had been anticipated. The states parties to the convention were then to nominate the first judges to the Inter-American Court of Human Rights, an enforcement organ established by the American Convention. One day, while working in his office, Buergenthal received a telephone call from a very formal-sounding gentleman with a Spanish accent, who informed him that he was calling from the Costa Rican Embassy in Washington, DC, to inquire whether Buergenthal would allow Costa Rica to nominate him as a candidate for a seat on the Inter-American Court. Buergenthal was convinced that one of his students was playing a joke on him, but he could not be certain. He cautiously asked whether he could return the call. He then hung up and immediately verified the number the caller had given him. It was the number of the Costa Rican Embassy. He called back and accepted the nomination.[34] He was elected, and he eventually served two terms, becoming the president of the court. In this way, Buergenthal became the first and only US citizen to serve on the Inter-American Court.

4. Enforcement Organs of the American Convention

Unlike the UDHR and the American Declaration, the American Convention empowered enforcement organs modelled on the organs of the already-established European human rights system. Like the original European system, the American Convention provided for two bodies to oversee compliance with the rights protected by the convention – the pre-existing Inter-American Commission on Human Rights and the newly constituted Inter-American Court of Human Rights.[35] The American Convention, however, did not establish a means, such as that implemented by the Council of Europe's Committee of Ministers, to monitor state compliance with Inter-American Court judgements.

The human rights enforcement authority of the Inter-American Commission and the Inter-American Court is subsidiary to the authority of the states' domestic judicial systems. Individual petitioners must first exhaust domestic remedies, whenever possible, before bringing a complaint to the organs of the Inter-American system. Although international courts and quasi-judicial bodies may be empowered by treaty to enforce international human rights law, the first and foremost authorities to deal with claims of human rights abuse are the national authorities. The principle of subsidiarity, which underlies the Inter-American human rights system, 'requires that problems be solved where they occur, by those who understand them best, and by those who are most affected by them'.[36] Only when there are defects in the domestic system and its efforts are not effective can the case be referred to the regional enforcement bodies. The role of the Inter-American Commission and Court is to determine whether a state violated its internationally contracted human rights obligations. The commission and the court may not overturn domestic court decisions that applied national law, unless the procedures followed by the national courts were in violation of the international obligations that the states in their

33 Thomas Buergenthal, 'The American Convention on Human Rights: Illusions and Hopes', *Buffalo Law Review*, 21 (1971), p. 121.

34 See Pasqualucci, note 32 above.

35 American Convention, note 22 above, Art. 33.

36 D. Shelton, 'Subsidiarity, Democracy and Human Rights', in Donna Gomien (ed.), *Broadening the Frontiers of Human Rights: Essays in Honour of Asbjørn Eide* (Oslo: Scandinavian University Press, 1993), pp. 43–4, quoting J.E. Linnan, 'Subsidiarity, Collegiality, Catholic Diversity, and Their Relevance to Apostolic Visitations', *The Jurist*, 49 (1989), pp. 399, 403.

sovereignty agreed to assume by becoming parties to the treaties. If an individual alleges that there has been a violation of his or her rights under the American Declaration or the American Convention, the alleged victim can take his complaint to the Inter-American Commission on Human Rights. One of the principal advances of the American Convention is that it permits broadened individual access to the Inter-American Commission on Human Rights. In a reversal of traditional international law, the American Convention allows individuals to file complaints with the commission against a state upon the state's ratification of the convention.[37] Conversely, the American Convention provides that a state party must make an express declaration recognizing the competence of the commission to deal with state-against-state complaints.[38] Thomas Farer, a former president of the Inter-American Commission, observed, '[s]urely this was to swallow a camel and shrink from a fly.' He explained that it was inevitable that states would be confronted by individual complaints, whereas state-filed complaints 'were improbable at any time, much less among members of a political and military alliance waging a Cold War'.[39]

Another progressive feature of the American Convention that is especially relevant to states that suffer from gross and systematic violations of human rights is that the *locus standi* to petition the Inter-American Commission is not limited to the individual victim or family members of the victim. Any person, group of persons, or non-governmental entity that is legally recognized in an OAS member state, even though it is not the direct victim of the abuse, may file a petition alleging that human rights have been violated.[40] This provision has proved to be especially important in the Inter-American system, where victims or their family members may be too intimidated or indigent to submit a petition. As complainants and their lawyers have, at times, become victims of human rights abuse, non-governmental organizations (NGOs) often file the petitions with the commission, as they are less susceptible to threats of retaliation. NGOs are also more likely to have the necessary resources to carry a case forward than the individuals involved.

4.1 The Inter-American Commission on Human Rights

The Inter-American Commission on Human Rights represents all member states of the OAS. It is composed of seven commissioners who are elected at the OAS General Assembly by secret ballot of all OAS member states. Commissioners serve in their individual capacities;[41] they do not represent states. Although commissioners must be nationals of an OAS member state, no two commissioners can be from the same state.[42] The Inter-American Commission is located in Washington, DC, at the OAS headquarters. The commission's secretariat, composed of attorneys and human rights specialists, works full-time, but the commission meets on only a part-time basis. The commission fulfils many roles in the Inter-American human rights system. The American Convention charges the commission with promotion of respect and defence of human rights in the

37 American Convention, note 22 above, Art. 44.

38 *Ibid.*, Art. 45.

39 T. Farer, 'The Rise of the Inter-American Human Rights Regime: No Longer a Unicorn, Not Yet an Ox', in John Harris and Stephen Livingstone (eds), *The Inter-American System of Human Rights* (Oxford: Clarendon Press, 1998), pp. 31–64, at p. 36. As Farer accurately predicted, to date only two inter-state complaints have been filed in the inter-American system. Even when concerned about human rights violations, political reality often inhibits a state from making accusations about another for fear of jeopardizing its economic interests or of having its own practices evaluated.

40 American Convention, note 22 above, Art. 44.

41 *Ibid.*, Arts. 34–6.

42 *Ibid.*, Arts. 36–7.

Americas. The commission has interpreted this authority broadly and creatively to have the most impact possible. The commission conducts country studies of the human rights situation in states where there are reports of massive human rights violations; prepares thematic studies focusing on the violations of particular rights throughout the Americas, and submits an annual report to the OAS General Assembly.[43] Commissioners may serve as thematic rapporteurs for issues such as freedom of speech or religion, or the rights of particularly vulnerable groups such as migrant workers, incarcerated persons, indigenous groups, and women and children.

A primary function of the commission is the consideration of individual petitions complaining of human rights violations in any OAS member state. In 2008, the Inter-American Commission received 1,323 petitions.[44] All individual complaints alleging human rights violations against states must first be brought to the Inter-American Commission. States and petitioners do not have the option to waive proceedings before the commission.[45] If the state named in the complaint has not ratified the American Convention on Human Rights, as is the case with the USA and Canada, the commission will determine whether the state violated the protections set forth in the American Declaration. If the state has ratified the American Convention, the commission will determine whether the state violated the rights protected by the American Convention.

When the commission receives a petition alleging human rights abuse in the jurisdiction of an OAS member state, the commission will determine whether the petition meets its admissibility requirements. To be admissible, the petition must state facts that establish a violation of the rights set forth in the American Convention, or, for those states that have not yet ratified the Convention, of the rights delineated in the American Declaration. In addition, petitioners must provide the required personal information and must show that the victim, when possible, has exhausted all available remedies in the state where the violation occurred. The petition must be lodged with the commission within 6 months from the date of notification of the final domestic decision, and the subject of the petition cannot be pending before another international proceeding.[46] If the petition does not meet the requirements of admissibility, the commission may request that the petitioner provide any necessary additional information. The commission will communicate with both the petitioners and the state before making a formal decision on admissibility.

Should the commission determine that a petition is admissible, it will engage in fact-finding procedures, possibly including a hearing, and will be available to aid the parties to reach a friendly settlement. If the parties do not enter into a friendly settlement, the commission will draw up a report stating the facts of the case and its conclusions.[47] The commission may make proposals and recommendations to the state in its report. If the state does not comply with the commission's recommendations, and if the state has accepted the jurisdiction of the Inter-American Court, the commission or the state may submit the case to the court.[48]

The convention specifically mandates that '[o]nly the States Parties and the Commission shall have the right to submit a case to the Court.'[49] Consequently, short of a protocol to the American Convention, the victim or petitioner will never have the right to seize the court. To circumvent this limitation, when the state involved has accepted the court's jurisdiction, the commission's rules of

---

43 *Ibid.*, Art. 41.

44 2008 Annual Report of the Inter-American Commission on Human Rights [online]. Available from: www.cidh.oas.org.

45 In the Matter of Viviana Gallardo *et al.*, IACtHR, Series A, No. G101/81 (1981).

46 American Convention, note 22 above, Arts. 47(a) and 46(2).

47 *Ibid.*, Art. 50(1).

48 *Ibid.*, Art. 51(1).

49 *Ibid.*, Art. 61(1).

procedure provide for automatic referral of a case to the court 'unless there is a reasoned decision by an absolute majority of the members of the Commission to the contrary'.[50] A primary criterion in the commission's decision is the petitioner's position on the matter.[51] If the petitioner is in favour of carrying the case forward, the commission usually does so. As a result, most cases in which the commission finds that the state has violated the victim's rights, and in which the state has not followed the recommendations of the commission, are referred to the court. The commission no longer represents victims before the Court. The victims' legal representatives present their case. If the victim does not have legal counsel, the Court may appoint an Inter-American public defender to represent the victim. The Inter-American Court signed an agreement with the Inter-American Association of Public Defenders (Asociación Interamericana de Defensorías Públicas (AIDEF)) to provide for free legal assistance to alleged victims of human rights abuse who lack the financial means to hire counsel to represent them.

4.2 Inter-American Court of Human Rights

The Inter-American Court of Human Rights is the sole judicial organ of the OAS. The American Convention authorizes the court to adjudicate contentious cases alleging state violations of human rights, to issue advisory opinions, and to order states to take provisional measures to protect persons who are in grave and imminent danger.[52]

The seat of the court is in San José, Costa Rica, although the court may convene in any OAS member state, at the invitation of the state and with the agreement of the majority of the judges. In recent years, the court has attempted to increase public awareness of the Inter-American human rights system by holding special sessions in states parties to the convention, with the state's approval. The court meets on a part-time basis, but, like the commission, it has a full-time secretariat. The official languages of the court are Spanish, English, Portuguese, and French. Each year, the judges decide on the working languages. Any person appearing before the court may use his or her own language, which will be interpreted into one of the court's working languages.

The court is composed of seven judges who are elected to a 6-year term by a vote, not of all OAS member states, as is the case with the election of the members of the commission, but exclusively by the states parties to the convention. Although the judges must be nationals of OAS member states, the election of a judge is not limited to nominees from states that have ratified the American Convention or accepted the jurisdiction of the court. The judges serve in their individual capacity and do not represent states parties. They may be re-elected once. Judges are to be chosen from 'jurists of the highest moral authority' who are recognized for their competence in human rights law, and who possess the qualifications to be a judge in the nominating state or the state of the nominee's nationality. There is no formal vetting procedure in the OAS to guarantee that candidates meet these qualifications. The plenary bench hears and rules on all contentious cases that come before the Inter-American Court, unlike the European Court of Human Rights, which often decides cases in chambers. In addition to the seven sitting judges, the bench may also include an *ad hoc* judge for a specific case.

The court's contentious jurisdiction empowers it to adjudicate those cases, referred to it by the commission or the state, that involve allegations of violations of the individual human rights

---

50 2009 Rules of Procedure of the Inter-Am. Com. H.R., Art. 45.

51 *Ibid.*, Art. 45(2).

52 See Jo M. Pasqualucci, *The Practice and Procedure of the Inter-American Court of Human Rights* (Cambridge: Cambridge University Press, 2003).

protected by the American Convention. Only states that have ratified the American Convention and have accepted the jurisdiction of the court are subject to the court's contentious jurisdiction. The 21 of the 24 states parties to the American Convention that also filed declarations accepting the jurisdiction of the Inter-American Court are Argentina, Barbados, Bolivia, Brazil, Chile, Colombia, Costa Rica, the Dominican Republic, Ecuador, El Salvador, Guatemala, Haiti, Honduras, Mexico, Nicaragua, Panama, Paraguay, Peru, Suriname, Uruguay, and Venezuela. Trinidad and Tobago denounced the court's jurisdiction when it denounced the American Convention in 1998. Other states parties to the American Convention may accept the court's jurisdiction by special agreement for specific cases.

Initially, the commission did not refer contentious cases to the court, and the court was limited to issuing advisory opinions. Subsequently, however, the cases brought before the court involved egregious human rights violations including disappearances, torture and extra-judicial executions. With time, the court's jurisprudence expanded and now includes decisions on most of the rights set forth in the American Convention. The court's jurisprudence on the rights of children, communal property rights of indigenous peoples, amnesty laws, due process rights, and freedom of expression, especially in relation to domestic laws criminalizing allegedly defamatory statements, is precedent-setting. The court had issued 213 judgements on contentious cases as of 26 May 2010, although there were multiple judgements issued in some cases.

The role of the victim before the Inter-American Court has evolved to the full extent possible under the American Convention and the Statute of the Inter-American Court. In the original contentious cases, victims played no official part in the written or oral proceedings before the court, other than as witnesses. Since that time, the court and the commission have repeatedly amended their rules of procedure to enhance the victim's role. Although the American Convention provides that only the commission or states can refer a case to the court, once an application is submitted, the victim has standing under the court's rules of procedure to present his or her case autonomously at all stages of the proceedings.[53] In 2001, the court defined the term 'parties to the case' to include the 'victim or the alleged victim, the State and, only procedurally, the Commission'.[54] This alteration permits the alleged victim to participate at all stages of the proceedings before the court once the application has been filed by the commission or the state.[55] The representatives of the victims file written memoranda, propose and examine witnesses, and make final arguments independent of the position of the commission and on an equal footing with the attorneys for the commission and the state. The separation of roles is important to the victim because his or her objective may differ from that of the commission. The victim's position is to protect his or her individual interests, while that of the commission is to fulfil its mandate under the convention.

The stages of proceedings before the Inter-American Court include preliminary objections, if any are filed, merits, and reparations. The court now combines the stages of the proceedings whenever possible to expedite the cases and reduce costs for the parties. The state may make preliminary objections to the admissibility of the application or to the court's jurisdiction to hear a case. If a state does not submit preliminary objections or the case is not dismissed at the preliminary

53 Rules of Procedure, IACtHR, approved at LXXXV Regular Period of Sessions, held 16–28 November 2009, Art. 25(1) during its LXXXII Ordinary Period of Sessions, held 19–31 January 2009. See Christina M. Cerna, 'Are We Headed in the Right Direction? Reflections on the New (2001) Rules of Procedure of the Inter-American Commission on Human Rights in Light of the Experience of the European System', in Anne F. Bayefsky (ed.), *Human Rights and Refugees, Internally Displaced Persons, and Migrant Workers: Essays in Memory of Joan Fitzpatrick and Arthur Helton* (Leiden: The Netherlands: Nijhoff, 2006), pp. 387–442. .

54 2001 Rules of Procedure, Inter-American Court of Human Rights, Art. 2(23).

55 *Ibid.*, Art. 23.

objections stage, the court will reach the merits of the case. At the merits stage of the proceedings, the court considers written briefs as well as affidavits from witnesses and other documentary evidence. In addition, although it is not mandatory, the court will often hold public hearings to take oral testimony from witnesses and experts. In recent years, the court has shortened the time expended on public hearings and has accepted much testimony in the form of written affidavits. Although this results in savings of time and expense, it detracts from the victim's opportunity to be heard and from the media value of the proceedings. Media coverage has a deterrent value and often supports the work of grass-roots human rights activists.[56]

At the conclusion of the proceedings, the judges hold private deliberations, which remain confidential. A judgement of the court is final and not subject to appeal, although a party may ask the court to interpret its judgement. The court's judgement is binding on the parties to the case.

4.2.1 Reparations and Compliance The American Convention authorizes the Inter-American Court to order state reparations to the victim, when it determines that the state is liable for a violation of the victim's human rights, or when the state voluntarily accepts responsibility for the violation. The convention's broad provision on reparations allows the court to specify innovative forms of reparations in an attempt to make full restitution to the victims. Reparations often include financial compensation, although money alone could never compensate for death or injury to the victim. Financial compensation traditionally includes, but is not limited to, loss of earnings, restitution of material property taken or destroyed, and payment for moral damages for emotional harm to the victim. States have complied with approximately 80% of the financial reparations ordered by the court.[57] Generally, the state must pay the costs and expenses of the successful victim. The court, however, has not ordered a state to pay punitive damages for even the most egregious violations.

The court can 'also rule that the injured party be ensured the enjoyment of his right or freedom that was violated'.[58] Pursuant to this authority, the court ordered Peru to release Maria Elena Loayza Tamayo, a university professor who had been wrongfully imprisoned in Peru for several years.[59] Peru complied with the court's order and released the prisoner.[60]

The convention also authorizes the court to rule that the consequences of the measure or situation that constituted the breach be remedied. In accordance with this provision, the court may mandate that the state amend, adopt or repeal domestic legislation so as to comply with obligations the state voluntarily assumed on becoming a party to the American Convention. Costa Rica amended its code of criminal procedure to permit the challenge and review of both legal and factual findings in lower court criminal convictions in response to the Inter-American Court's reparations order in *Herrera-Ulloa* v *Costa Rica*.[61] Herrera-Ulloa, a journalist, had been found guilty of criminally defaming an honorary diplomat by quoting and reproducing newspaper articles from Belgium

56 J. L. Cavallaro and S.E. Brewer, 'Reevaluating Regional Human Rights Litigation in the Twenty-First Century: The Case of the Inter-American Court', *American Journal of International Law*, 102 (2008), pp. 768–27.

57 2008 Annual Report, IACtHR [online]. Available from: http://www.corteidh.or.cr/docs/informes/eng2008.pdf at 73.

58 American Convention, note 22 above, Art. 63(1).

59 *Loayza Tamayo* v *Peru*, IACtHR Series C, No. 33 (17 September 1997).

60 *Chicago Tribune*, 17 October 1997, section 1, p. 28.

61 *Herrera-Ulloa* v *Costa Rica*, IACtHR (Series C), No. 107 (2 July 2004); see Carlos Ayala, 'Conference on Reparations in the Inter-American System: A Comparative Approach', *American University Law Review*, 56(6) (2007), pp. 1375–1468, at pp. 1413, 1415–16.

which alleged that the Costa Rican representative had engaged in drug trafficking and fraud.[62] The Inter-American Court held that the Costa Rican appeal process did not satisfy the requirements of the American Convention. In its judgement the court ordered Costa Rica to nullify the judgements against the victim and to take the necessary measures to conform its domestic laws to the state's responsibilities under the American Convention.[63]

Likewise, Peru complied with an Inter-American Court judgement by amending its anti-terrorism and treason laws to conform to the American Convention following the court's judgements in the *Loayza Tamayo* and *Castillo Petruzzi* cases.[64] The court has also ordered states to repeal domestic judgements or convictions.[65] These changes were necessary so that states would be in compliance with the human rights obligations they have undertaken in ratifying or acceding to the American Convention.

The court's remedies may be centered on the victim, or on repairing the injury to the community or to society as a whole.[66] The court may require that the state apologize to the victim for the human rights abuse and undertake some public act such as creating a memorial to the victim, publishing the judgement of the court, or participating in a ceremony in honour of the victims. In the *Kawas Fernández* v *Honduras* case, in which an environmental activist was murdered in Honduras, the court ordered, as one form of reparations, that the state implement a national campaign to educate the public about the work of environmental activists and their contributions to the defence of human rights.[67] In an effort to avoid future human rights violations, the court may require that the state provide human rights training to police and the military.

To combat impunity, the court consistently specifies as a form of reparations that the state must investigate the facts of the violation and identify, prosecute and punish those responsible. States have not been as willing to comply with these court orders as they have with financial reparations. In some cases, governments lack the power to bring influential persons to justice. In other cases, government officials may be complicit or fear that they could be charged with other violations in the future. Until impunity is eradicated and states willingly arrest and try the perpetrators of human rights abuse, the court's docket will continue to be over-burdened because it monitors state compliance with most of its judgements.

If the state does not comply with an Inter-American Court's judgement in a contentious case or with its order of provisional measures, the only external recourse for the court is to specify the state failure in its annual report to the OAS General Assembly. The political pressure of one's peers to coerce compliance, foreseen by the drafters of the American Convention, has not materialized. The OAS political bodies, in general, and the General Assembly, in particular, have lacked the political will to impose any sanction on states that fail to comply with their human rights obligations. The court also maintains the case on its docket until the state complies with its judgement, and it holds private compliance hearings.

---

62 *Herrera-Ulloa* v *Costa Rica*, note 61 above, para. 95(d)–(i).

63 *Ibid.*

64 *Loayza Tamayo* v *Peru* (Reparations), IACtHR, 27 November 1998, Series C, No. 42, operative para. 5; *Castillo Petruzzi et al.* v *Peru* (Merits), IACtHR, 30 May 1999, Series. C, No. 52, operative para.14.

65 See *Raxcacó Reyes* v *Guatemala*, Monitoring Compliance with Judgement, 2008 Annual Report, IACtHR. at 18. (The Inter-American Court ordered Guatemala to annul the victim's death sentence, and the state complied.)

66 See Thomas Antkowiak, 'Remedial Approaches to Human Rights Violations: The Inter-American Court of Human Rights and Beyond', *Columbia Journal of Transnational Law*, 46 (2008), pp. 351–419.

67 *Kawas Fernández* v *Honduras* (Merits, Reparations and Costs), IACtHR, 3 April 2009, Series C, No. 196, operative para. 14.

4.2.2 Advisory Jurisdiction In addition to its jurisdiction to resolve contentious cases, the Inter-American Court has a broad advisory jurisdiction. Under its advisory jurisdiction, OAS member states and certain OAS organs can consult the court regarding the interpretation of the American Convention or of other treaty provisions that create human rights obligations for American states.[68] OAS member states may also request advisory opinions as to whether their domestic laws are compatible with the American Convention and other treaties to which they are parties.[69] Its advisory competence allows the court to address many doctrinal human rights questions that have not arisen in the contentious cases that have come before the court. Thus, through its advisory opinions, the court has contributed to the conceptual framework of the international law of human rights. Some fundamental concepts addressed by the court in the context of its advisory jurisdiction include non-discrimination, the incompatibility of reservations to non-derogable rights, democracy as the basis of human rights, the non-reciprocal nature of human rights treaties, and the universal character of human rights.[70] Through its advisory opinions, the Inter-American Court has also contributed to the uniformity and consistency of the interpretation of the American Convention and other human rights treaties to which American states are parties.

Advisory opinions are not binding but they carry a certain moral force. States have revised their laws in response to advisory opinions issued by the Inter-American Court. The Argentine Supreme Court, relying on the advisory opinion *Enforceability of the Right to Reply or Correction*, held that the American Convention on Human Rights creates a directly enforceable right of reply in Argentina without the need for separate domestic legislation.[71] The applicable provision of the American Convention provides that a person 'injured by inaccurate or offensive statements or ideas disseminated to the public in general by a legally regulated medium of communication has the right to reply or to make a correction using the same communications outlet, under such conditions as the law may establish'.[72] The Inter-American Court stated in its advisory opinion that 'any State Party that does not already ensure the free and full exercise of the right to reply or correction is under an obligation to bring about that result, be it by legislation or whatever other measures may be necessary under its domestic legal system.'[73] Advisory opinions, although nonbinding, are contributing to the harmonization of international human rights law.

5. Interim Measures

Another innovation of the Inter-American human rights system is broad access to interim measures to protect persons who are in grave and urgent danger of irreparable harm or death. Traditional

---

68 American Convention, note 22 above, Art. 64(1).

69 *Ibid.*, Art. 64(2).

70 See Jo M. Pasqualucci, 'Advisory Practice of the Inter-American Court of Human Rights: Contributing to the Evolution of International Human Rights Law', *Stanford Journal of International Law*, 38 (2002), p. 241.

71 Thomas Buergenthal, 'International Tribunals and National Courts: The Internationalization of Domestic Adjudication', in Ulrich Beyerlin (ed.), *Recht zwischen Umbruch und Bewährung. Festschrift für Rudolf Bernhardt* (Berlin: Springer-Verlag, 1995), pp. 695–99, at p. 687 (citing *Ekmekdjian* v *Sofovich*, No. E. 64. XXIII, 315 Fallos 1492, 1511–15 (Arg., CSJN, 1992).

72 American Convention, note 22 above, Art. 14(1).

73 Enforceability of the Right to Reply or Correction (Arts. 14(1), 1(1) and 2 of the American Convention on Human Rights), Inter-Am. Ct. H.R., Advisory Opinion OC-7/86 of 29 August 1986, Series A, No. 7, para. 33.

international proceedings may take too long to avoid the death or injury of the victim. In urgent situations, the commission and the court have the authority to call upon the state to take special measures immediately to prevent human rights violations and to protect potential victims. Interim measures are referred to as 'precautionary measures' when ordered by the commission and 'provisional measures' when ordered by the court.

The American Convention provides that 'in cases of extreme gravity and urgency, and when necessary to avoid irreparable damage to persons, the court shall adopt such provisional measures as it deems pertinent.'[74] Pursuant to this authority, the Inter-American Court can order a state to take immediate action or to refrain from some action if an individual's life or physical integrity is threatened. For instance, the court may order a state to stay the execution of a prisoner or to protect persons who have been threatened. Beneficiaries of court-ordered provisional measures include journalists and news organizations that have exposed corruption or human rights abuse, human rights activists and organizations, and witnesses who have been threatened for testifying before the Inter-American Commission or Court. The court also may order the state to take provisional measures when the person or persons to be protected are petitioners or witnesses before the commission, but the case is not yet on the docket of the court. The court's provisional measures orders are binding and can be issued only to states that are states parties to the American Convention and that have accepted the jurisdiction of the court.

6. Other Inter-American Human Rights Instruments

The Inter-American Democratic Charter was adopted by the OAS General Assembly on 11 September 2001.[75] It reaffirms the essential connection between democracy and human rights in the Americas in stating that '[d]emocracy is indispensable for the effective exercise of fundamental freedoms and human rights'.[76] On 5 July 2009, in reliance on the Democratic Charter, the OAS General Assembly suspended Honduras from OAS participation after the constitutionally elected president of the country was deposed in a military coup.[77]

The OAS has also promulgated other human rights instruments to protect specific rights in the Americas. It has adopted two protocols to the American Convention. The first, the Additional Protocol to the American Convention on Human Rights in the area of Economic, Social and Cultural Rights, also referred to as the 'Protocol of San Salvador', entered into force in 1999.[78] Fifteen states were parties to the protocol as of 1 July 2010. The preamble to the Protocol of San Salvador recognizes that 'the ideal of free human beings enjoying freedom from fear and want can only be achieved if conditions are created whereby everyone may enjoy his economic, social and cultural rights as well as his civil and political rights.' Some of the rights protected by the protocol, which is binding on the states that ratify it, include the right to work, to unionize, and to have just, equitable and satisfactory working conditions, as well as the rights to social security, essential health care,

74 American Convention, note 19 above, Art. 63(2). The commission's authority to issue orders to states to take precautionary measures is based on the commission's rules of procedure.

75 Adopted by the OAS General Assembly at its special session held in Lima, Peru, on 11 September 2001, 40 ILM 1289.

76 *Ibid.*, Art. 7.

77 OAS Press Release, OAS Suspends Membership of Honduras, 5 July 2009 [online]. Available from: http://www.oas.org/OASpage/press_releases/press_release.asp?sCodigo=E-219/09 [accessed 12 September 2009].

78 Adopted on 17 November 1988 at the 18th regular session of the OAS General Assembly.

adequate nutrition, basic public services to create a healthy environment, and free, compulsory, and accessible primary education The protocol also requires the special protection of families, children, the elderly, and the handicapped. States must submit periodic reports explaining the measures they have taken to protect the rights set forth in the protocol. Violation of specified rights in the protocol allows the victims to have recourse to the Inter-American Commission and Court. Those rights include the right to organize or join a trade union, the right to free primary education, and the right of parents to select the type of education for their children. A second protocol, the Protocol to the American Convention on Human Rights to Abolish the Death Penalty, entered into force in 1991 and has been ratified or adhered to by 11 states as of 1 July 2010.[79]

The OAS also promulgated the 1994 Inter-American Convention on Forced Disappearance of Persons which entered into force in 1996.[80] It had 13 states parties as of 1 July 2010. The convention defines 'forced disappearance' as 'the act of depriving a person or persons of his or their freedom, in whatever way, perpetrated by agents of the state or by persons or groups of persons acting with the authorization, support, or acquiescence of the state, followed by an absence of information or a refusal to acknowledge that deprivation of freedom or to give information on the whereabouts of that person, thereby impeding his or her recourse to the applicable legal remedies and procedural guarantees'. States parties to the convention commit themselves to criminalize forced disappearances and to prosecute or extradite a person accused of the crime. The Inter-American Commission and Court have jurisdiction under the convention to consider allegations of disappearances.[81]

The 1985 Inter-American Convention to Prevent and Punish Torture[82] reaffirms that acts of torture 'are violations of the fundamental human rights and freedoms proclaimed in the American Declaration of the Rights and Duties of Man and the Universal Declaration of Human Rights'.[83] Article 2 of the Convention defines torture as 'any act intentionally performed whereby physical or mental pain or suffering is inflicted on a person' for certain purposes. The prohibited purposes include criminal investigation, personal punishment, and intimidation. Even when there is no physical or mental pain, the convention identifies as torture, methods which attempt to 'obliterate the personality of the victim or to diminish his physical or mental capacities'. The existence of war, state of emergency, political instability or disaster may never be used to justify torture. Moreover, the convention specifically negates the validity of the common justification that the torturer was merely acting 'under orders of a superior'. States parties to the convention commit themselves to exclude evidence obtained through torture and to emphasize the prohibition of torture in the training of police officers. The Convention entered into force in 1987, and, as of 1 July 2010, has 18 states parties.

The 1994 Inter-American Convention on the Prevention, Punishment, and Eradication of Violence against Women,[84] also known as the Convention 'Belém Do Pará' for the city in Brazil where it was adopted, defines violence against women to include physical, psychological, and

79 Adopted at the 20th regular session of the OAS General Assembly on 8 July 1990.

80 Adopted on 9 June 1994, at the 24th regular session of the General Assembly of the OAS, entered into force on 28 March 1996, 33 ILM 1529.

81 *Ibid.*, Art. 13.

82 OAS Treaty Series, No. 67, Adopted on 9 December 1985.

83 Inter-American Convention to Prevent and Punish Torture signed at Cartagena de Indias, Colombia, Art. 5, adopted 9 December 1995, at the 15th regular session of the General Assembly of the OAS, entered into force on 28 February 1987, 25 ILM 519.

84 33 ILM 1534, adopted on 9 June 1994, at the 24th regular session of the General Assembly of the OAS.

sexual violence within or outside of the home.[85] The treaty, which entered into force in 1995, had been ratified by 32 states as of 1 July 2010, more ratifications than those of any other OAS human rights treaty. Individuals, groups, or NGOs legally recognized in any OAS member state may file a complaint with the Inter-American Commission alleging the violation of state duties set forth in the treaty. Also, states parties to the treaty authorize the Inter-American Commission of Women and the Inter-American Commission on Human Rights to request advisory opinions from the Inter-American Court on questions of interpretation of the convention. The 1999 Inter-American Convention on the Elimination of All Forms of Discrimination Against Persons with Disabilities, has been ratified by 18 states and entered into force in 2001.[86] A special committee was created to oversee state compliance with the treaty.

The OAS has also adopted non-binding resolutions and declarations in the area of human rights. The most significant are the Declaration of Principles on Freedom of Expression, the Principles and Best Practices on the Protection of Persons Deprived of Liberty in the Americas, the proposed American Declaration on the Rights of Indigenous Peoples, and the draft Inter-American Convention Against Racism and All Forms of Discrimination.

7. Impediments to the Optimal Functioning of the Inter-American System

Lack of universality in the ratification and accession to the American Convention on Human Rights and to the acceptance of the jurisdiction of the Inter-American Court weakens and needlessly complicates the functioning of the Inter-American human rights system. The commission applies the American Declaration to OAS member states that have not ratified the American Convention and applies the American Convention to those states that are parties to the convention. Furthermore, only cases involving those states that have accepted the jurisdiction of the Inter-American Court can be referred to the court. The USA and Canada, two of the most powerful states that have not ratified the American Convention, set a negative precedent for those that have. Fortunately, the states of Latin America can look to the example of the Western European democracies such as Great Britain, Germany, and France, which agree to be bound by international human rights norms and comply with the decisions of the European Court of Human Rights.

Even the universal ratification of the Inter-American human rights treaties will be ineffective unless states domestically implement Inter-American Court judgements and follow commission recommendations. Some American states have made strides in domestic implementation but others lag behind. Certain types of court orders are regularly followed, such as orders of provisional measures or financial reparations, whereas others such as the duty to investigate and punish, are not.

Moreover, inadequate financial support from the OAS continues to impose constraints on the functioning of the Inter-American Commission and Court. Under-funding results in an inadequate number of staff attorneys and insufficient commission and court sessions to handle complaints expeditiously. The court meets on an average of 10 weeks a year for regular and special sessions, and, in addition, judges must dedicate significant time while they are away from the court to reviewing cases and evidence, writing draft judgements and resolutions, and

85 *Ibid.*, Art. 1

86 Adopted at Guatemala City, Guatemala, at the 29th regular session of the General Assembly of the OAS, held on 7 June 1999. Available from: http://www.oas.org/juridico/english/treaties/a-65.html. Haiti was the most recent state to ratify the treaty on 29 May 2009.

overseeing precautionary measures or the enforcement of judgements.[87] The duration of public hearings in which victims give testimony has been reduced; thus, not giving all victims the opportunity to testify live before the court. Formerly, legal aid was not available, which limited the access of impoverished victims who cannot find NGOs to take their cases. The commission and the court rely on voluntary contributions to supplement their funding under the OAS. Some of the contributions come from OAS member states, which are subject to the jurisdiction of the court.[88] These contributions may appear to compromise the integrity of the organs. Financial constrains do not allow the commission and court to become permanent sitting bodies, although their increasing work load cannot be handled expeditiously on the current part time basis. The OAS General Assembly has resolved to examine the possibility that the Inter-American Commission and Court come to operate on a permanent basis, but insufficient funding is one of the major draw backs to this consideration.[89]

8. Conclusion

Since 1948 and the adoption of both the UDHR and the American Declaration of the Rights and Duties of Man, the OAS has developed a functioning regional system of human rights protection. All Latin American states are parties to the American Convention and have accepted the jurisdiction of the Inter-American Court. The primary holdouts are the USA, Canada, and some non-English-speaking Caribbean nations. Much has changed since the 1970s and 1980s when the mention of 'human rights' was considered communist by many in power. To a great extent, this change has come about through the replacements of dictatorships with democracies and the efforts of the OAS, Inter-American Commission on Human Rights, and the Inter-American Court of Human Rights. If the improvements are to continue, the Inter-American human rights system needs to be strengthened – an issue that is under consideration by the OAS, the court and the commission, as well as in civil society.

The Inter-American human rights system is serving as a model for human rights in other parts of the world. As the first system to function in an under developed region, the commission's recommendations and the court's jurisprudence deal with the types of human rights abuses that can take place in states that are not accustomed to the rule of law. Other regional organizations, such as the Council of Europe, which has admitted member states from the former Soviet Republics; the African human rights system; and the developing ASEAN system will likely find valuable precedents in Inter-American human rights decisions.

---

87 Permanent Council of the Organization of American States, Committee on Juridical and Political Affairs, Presentation by the Executive Secretary of the Inter-American Court of Human Rights, Dr Pablo Saavedra, During the Joint Meeting of the Committee on Juridical and Political Affairs and the Committee on Administrative and Budgetary Affairs, 5 February 2009, OEA/Series G, CP/CAJP-2695/09, 18 February 2009.

88 Some parties that have contributed are Canada, Chile, Colombia, Costa Rica, Mexico, the USA, Denmark, Finland, France, Ireland, Italy, Norway, the Republic of Korea, Spain, Sweden, the European Union, the Inter-American Development Bank, the Office of the United Nations High Commissioner for Refugees, the Save the Children Foundation, and the University of Notre Dame. Draft Resolution, OEA/Ser. P AG/doc. 4839/08, 22 May 2008.

89 OAS General Assembly, Strengthening of Human Rights Systems Pursuant to the Mandates Arising from the Summit of the Americas, 39th Regular Session, OEA/Ser.P, AG/doc 5006/09 (4 June 2009).

Chapter 14
The European Convention on Human Rights

Alastair Mowbray

1. The Relationship Between the UDHR and the ECHR

The close interconnection between the UDHR[1] and the Convention for the Protection of Human Rights and Fundamental Freedoms,[2] generally known as the European Convention on Human Rights (ECHR/Convention), is clearly expressed in the preamble to the latter treaty. The signatory states begin by 'considering the UDHR' and, 'being resolved, as the governments of European countries which are like-minded and have a common heritage of political traditions, ideals, freedom and the rule of law, to take the first steps for the collective enforcement of certain of the rights stated in the Universal Declaration', agree to respect the rights and freedoms elaborated in the ECHR. If we compare the ECHR guarantees with those contained in the UDHR, we see that Article 2 (right to life) of the ECHR replicates, in greater detail, the first element of Article 3 of the UDHR. Article 3 of the ECHR (prohibition of torture) contains almost identical wording to that of Article 5 of the UDHR. Article 4 (prohibition of slavery and forced labour) of the ECHR proscribes, at greater length, the content of Article 4 of the UDHR. Article 5 of the ECHR (right to liberty and security) repeats, again in a more elaborate form, the latter part of Article 3 and two-thirds of Article 9 of the UDHR. Article 6 (right to a fair trial) of the ECHR covers the same rights as Article 10 and Article 11(1) of the UDHR, while Article 7 (no punishment without law) of the ECHR encompasses Article 11(2) of the UDHR. Article 8 of the ECHR (right to respect for private and family life) safeguards the rights in Article 12 of the UDHR, with the latter's protection of a person's reputation falling under Article 10 of the ECHR. Article 9 (freedom of thought, conscience and religion) of the ECHR uses almost identical terminology to Article 18 of the UDHR. Article 10 of the ECHR (freedom of expression) covers the same matters as Article 19 of the UDHR. Article 11 of the ECHR (freedom of assembly and association) elaborates the rights contained in Article 20(1) and Article 23(4) (right to form and join trade unions) of the UDHR. Article 12 of the ECHR (right to marry) is similar to the first element of Article 16(1) of the UDHR. Article 13 of the ECHR requires all member states to establish effective domestic remedies for everyone whose rights and freedoms under the ECHR have been violated, while Article 8 of the UDHR provides for such remedies in respect of violations of fundamental rights derived from the constitution or law. Article 14 of the ECHR prohibits discrimination in the enjoyment of the rights and freedoms defined in the ECHR; likewise, Article 2 of the UDHR states that 'everyone is entitled to all the rights and freedoms set forth in this Declaration without distinction of any kind.'. Both Article 17 of the ECHR and Article 30 of the UDHR state that nothing in the respective instruments provides any right for persons, groups or states to engage in any activity aimed at the destruction of the rights and freedoms elaborated in the convention and declaration respectively.

---

1 UNGA Res 217 A(III), 10 December 1948.
2 CETS No. 005.

So we have seen there is considerable overlap between the ECHR and the UDHR. However, it must also be appreciated that the ECHR was shaped and drafted in accordance with European constitutional history and ideas.[3] For example, seven months before the UDHR was proclaimed, the 'Congress of Europe', a gathering of over 1,000 politicians and representatives of civil society in The Hague, issued a pledge expressing a desire for a Charter of Human Rights that would guarantee liberty of thought, assembly, expression and the right to form a political opposition. The congress also wanted a court of justice, possessing appropriate sanctions, to implement the charter. These aims were subsequently refined into a draft European Convention on Human Rights and Statute of the European Court of Human Rights by a committee of the European Movement chaired by Pierre-Henri Teitgen. Soon after the foundation of the Council of Europe, in May 1949,[4] the European Movement's drafts were submitted to the Committee of Ministers (the executive body of the Council of Europe). The dialogue between the Council of Europe's Consultative Assembly (representing national parliaments and now known as the Parliamentary Assembly) and the Committee of Ministers refined the content of the ECHR. Early on in the drafting process, it became clear that the ECHR would have a narrower scope in its coverage of rights than the UDHR. As Sir David Maxwell-Fyfe, who had been a member of the Teitgen Committee, said in the Consultative Assembly:

> Our list, it is true, contains none of the so-called economic or social rights which appear in the U.N.O. Declaration. Such rights would, in my view, be too controversial and difficult of enforcement even in the changing state of social and international development in Europe, and their inclusion would jeopardise the acceptance of the Convention. Examples, on which I need not expatiate, are the right to free choice of employment, and the right, unknown to you, I am sure, Mr. President, of rest or leisure.[5]

Secondly, the ECHR differs from the UDHR in that many of its rights and freedoms, together with their associated limitations, are expressed in much greater detail than the latter. An example is the right to life, the most fundamental of all human rights; in the UDHR, it is proclaimed in six words; 'everyone has the right to life.'[6] In contrast, the corresponding Article 2 of the ECHR takes over 100 words to elaborate the right and its permitted exceptions.

> 2(1) Everyone's right to life shall be protected by law. No one shall be deprived of his life intentionally save in the execution of a sentence of a court following his conviction of a crime for which this penalty is provided by law.
>
> (2) Deprivation of life shall not be regarded as inflicted in contravention of this article when it results from the use of force which is no more than absolutely necessary:
> (a) in defence of any person from unlawful violence;
> (b) in order to effect a lawful arrest or to prevent the escape of a person lawfully detained;
> (c) in action lawfully taken for the purpose of quelling a riot or insurrection.

3 See S. Greer, *The European Convention on Human Rights: Achievements, Problems and Prospects* (Cambridge: Cambridge University Press, 2006), p. 56.

4 Statute of the Council of Europe CETS, No. 001.

5 H.A. Robertson (ed.), *Collected Edition of the 'Travaux Préparatoires'*, Vol. 1 (The Hague: Martinus Nijhoff, 1975), p. 116.

6 Article 3.

One explanation for these different approaches is that the UDHR contains a general limitation clause in Article 29:

> 2. In the exercise of his rights and freedoms, everyone shall be subject only to such limitations as are determined by law solely for the purpose of securing due recognition and respect for the rights and freedoms of others and of meeting the just requirements of morality, public order and the general welfare in a democratic society.

In contrast, the ECHR articulates exceptions to its rights and freedoms on an article-by-article basis. During the drafting of the ECHR, the UK successfully took the lead in advocating the need for specificity in defining the rights and freedoms guaranteed by the convention.[7]

2. Additional Protocols

The substantive guarantees of the ECHR have been expanded by later additional protocols, some of which echo rights and freedoms contained in the UDHR. The first protocol[8] was opened for signature within two years of the ECHR being promulgated. The protocol contains three controversial rights which the member states could not agree upon including in the original text of the ECHR.[9] The 'Protection of property' (Article 1) and the 'Right to education' (Article 2) have strong socio-economic aspects. The former was politically sensitive to governments, such as the 1945 Labour administration in Britain, which had undertaken large-scale nationalization of basic industries such as coal mining. Hence, the text formulated did not expressly safeguard the right to property, as found in Article 17 of the UDHR.[10] Furthermore, Article 1, following the style of the ECHR, includes a number of limitations.

> Every natural or legal person is entitled to the peaceful enjoyment of his possessions. No one shall be deprived of his possessions except in the public interest and subject to the conditions provided for by law and by the general principles of international law.
>
> The preceding provisions shall not, however, in any way impair the right of a State to enforce such laws as it deems necessary to control the use of property in accordance with the general interest or to secure the payment of taxes or other contributions or penalties.

The right to education obviously has extensive cost implications for states (e.g. what financial contributions are parents and students expected to make?), so it is perhaps not surprising that the first limb of Article 2 was defined in negative terms:

---

7 See E. Wicks, 'The United Kingdom Government's Perceptions of the European Convention on Human Rights at the Time of Entry' [2000], PL 438.

8 Protocol to the Convention for the Protection of Human Rights and Fundamental Freedoms, Paris, 20 March 1952, CETS No. 009.

9 See P. van Dijk, F. van Hoof, A. van Rijn and L. Zwaak (eds), *Theory and Practice of the European Convention on Human Rights*, 4th edn (Antwerp: Intersentia, 2006), p. 864.

10 '1. Everyone has the right to own property alone as well as in association with others. 2. No one shall be arbitrarily deprived of his property.'

> No person shall be denied the right to education. In the exercise of any functions which it assumes in relation to education and to teaching, the State shall respect the right of parents to ensure such education and teaching in conformity with their own religious and philosophical convictions.

The corresponding Article 26 of the UDHR,[11] reflecting a wider spectrum of state economic development, elaborated a more extensive set of goals. The third element of the protocol, Article 3 the 'Right to free elections',[12] was also drafted in cautious terms with the democratic obligation being placed on member states rather than express rights being conferred on citizens. In comparison, Article 21 of the UDHR, again, has a broader scope.[13] The protocol came into force in 1954, and by 2009 all but two member states, Switzerland and Monaco, had ratified it.

In 1963 the member states agreed the text of Protocol No. 4 to the ECHR.[14] Part of the motivation behind this protocol was to take account of the ongoing work at the United Nations (UN) to draft the International Covenant on Civil and Political Rights (ICCPR).[15] Furthermore, Article 2, 'Freedom of movement', of the Protocol provided that:

> 1. Everyone lawfully within the territory of a State shall, within that territory, have the right to liberty of movement and freedom to choose his residence.
> 2. Everyone shall be free to leave any country, including his own.
> 3. No restrictions shall be placed on the exercise of these rights other than such as are in accordance with law and are necessary in a democratic society in the interests of national security or public safety, for the maintenance of *ordre* public, for the prevention of crime, for the protection of health or morals, or for the protection of the rights and freedoms of others.
> 4. The rights set forth in paragraph 1 may also be subject, in particular areas, to restrictions imposed in accordance with law and justified by the public interest in a democratic society.

---

11 '1. Everyone has the right to education. Education shall be free, at least in the elementary and fundamental stages. Elementary education shall be compulsory. Technical and professional education shall be made generally available and higher education shall be equally accessible to all on the basis of merit. 2. Education shall be directed to the full development of the human personality and to the strengthening of respect for human rights and fundamental freedoms. It shall promote understanding, tolerance and friendship among all nations, racial or religious groups, and shall further the activities of the United Nations for the maintenance of peace. 3. Parents have a prior right to choose the kind of education that shall be given to their children.'

12 'The High Contracting Parties undertake to hold free elections at reasonable intervals by secret ballot, under conditions which will ensure the free expression of the opinion of the people in the choice of the legislature.'

13 '1. Everyone has the right to take part in the government of his country, directly or through freely chosen representatives. 2. Everyone has the right to equal access to public service in his country. 3. The will of the people shall be the basis of the authority of government; this will shall be expressed in periodic and genuine elections which shall be by universal and equal suffrage and shall be held by secret vote or by equivalent free voting procedures.'

14 Protocol No. 4 to the Convention for the Protection of Human Rights and Fundamental Freedoms Securing Certain Rights and Freedoms Other Than Those Already Included in the Convention and in the First Protocol Thereto, Strasbourg 16 September 1963, CETS No. 046.

15 999 UNTS 171. Adopted 16 December 1966, entered into force 23 March 1976. See the Explanatory Report to Protocol No. 4.

This article is the ECHR equivalent to Article 13 of the UDHR.[16] The protocol entered into force in 1968. However, neither Greece nor Switzerland had signed Protocol No. 4 by 2009. The UK and Turkey had signed but not ratified the protocol.

After the adoption of the ICCPR in December 1966, by the UN General Assembly, the Committee of Ministers of the Council of Europe began a programme to compare the coverage of the ECHR with that of the covenant. This eventually led to the promulgation of Protocol No. 7 to the ECHR.[17] Article 5 of the protocol states:

> Spouses shall enjoy equality of rights and responsibilities of a private law character between them, and in their relations with their children, as to marriage, during marriage and in the event of its dissolution. This Article shall not prevent States from taking such measures as are necessary in the interests of the children.

In so providing, the protocol addresses the second limb of Article 16(1) of the UDHR.[18] The protocol entered into force in 1988. But, the UK had not signed Protocol No. 7 by 2009 and Belgium, Germany, The Netherlands and Turkey had not ratified it.

The most recent protocol which broadens the ECHR to encompass another UDHR right is Protocol No. 12.[19] The protocol provides a general prohibition of discrimination[20] that echoes Article 7 of the UDHR.[21] The protocol was inspired by the UDHR's basic belief that '[a]ll human beings are born free and equal in dignity and rights'[22] and the guarantee contained in Article 7.The Council of Europe's programmes to promote equality between men and women and combat racism and intolerance also underpinned the creation of the protocol.[23] The protocol entered into force in 2005. However, by 2009, it had been ratified by only 17 member states, and a number of states, including Denmark, France, Poland, Sweden, Switzerland and the UK, had not signed it.

We have seen how over 50 years the member states have undertaken a step-by-step process of widening, via additional protocols, the substantive rights and freedoms guaranteed by the ECHR to provide further protection for UDHR provisions. This is to be commended, although the negotiation and ratification stages can be lengthy. However, the Committee of Ministers, the dominant institution in the reform process, has retained the fundamental philosophy of the

---

16 '1. Everyone has the right to freedom of movement and residence within the borders of each State. 2. Everyone has the right to leave any country, including his own, and to return to his country.'

17 Protocol No. 7 to the Convention for the Protection of Human Rights and Fundamental Freedoms, Strasbourg 22 November 1984, CETS No. 117.

18 '1. Men and women of full age, without any limitation due to race, nationality or religion, have the right to marry and to found a family. They are entitled to equal rights as to marriage, during marriage and at its dissolution.'

19 Protocol No. 12 to the Convention for the Protection of Human Rights and Fundamental Freedoms, Rome, 4 November 2000, CETS No. 177.

20 Article 1(1) The enjoyment of any right set forth by law shall be secured without discrimination on any ground such as sex, race, colour language, religion, political or other opinion, national or social origin, association with a national minority, property, birth or other status. (2) No one shall be discriminated against by any public authority on any ground such as those mentioned in paragraph (1).

21 'All are equal before the law and are entitled without any discrimination to equal protection of the law. All are entitled to equal protection against any discrimination in violation of this Declaration and against any incitement to such discrimination.'

22 Article 1 of the UDHR.

23 See the Explanatory Report to Protocol 12.

ECHR to ensure that the protocols should concentrate upon civil and political, not economic and social, rights.[24]

3. The Control System of the ECHR

While the UDHR sought to proclaim the rights and freedoms enshrined in the text, it did not provide any system to enforce those provisions. A major achievement of the ECHR was that it created an international system to adjudicate upon whether member states had infringed any of the guarantees elaborated in the convention and to provide redress if a breach had occurred. This involved a considerable international intrusion into the traditionally sacrosanct domestic affairs of member states. However, given the earlier gross violations of human rights by the Nazis and their allies, it was considered necessary to establish an international system to protect basic rights and freedoms in those states belonging to the Council of Europe in order to prevent further atrocities in the future. But, in order to respond to the sensitivities of member states on this topic, the original control system established under the ECHR was subject to parties to the convention undertaking optional recognition of (1) the right of a person claiming to be the victim of a violation of convention guarantees by a member state to bring a complaint against that state before the European Commission of Human Rights (Commission)[25] and (2) to recognize the jurisdiction of the European Court of Human Rights (Court).[26] As time passed, more states made those declarations,[27] and by the early 1990s all members states were under a political obligation, within the Council of Europe, to recognize the jurisdiction of the court.

The original control system, physically located in Strasbourg, was institutionally complex. Membership of the commission was limited to a number of persons equalling the total of states parties to the ECHR.[28] Lists of three candidates for each place on the commission were drawn up by the Parliamentary Assembly and one candidate was elected by the Committee of Ministers. Once appointed, members of the commission were required to act as independent persons, not as representatives of any particular state.[29] They held office for a period of 6 years and were eligible for re-election. The commission determined the admissibility of applications, mainly from individuals who claimed to be the personal victims of violations by member states. If a complaint was found to be admissible, the commission then sought to determine the facts of the dispute; generally, this was a documentary process with the applicant and respondent state submitting supporting written

24 The Council of Europe has a separate system for securing social and economic rights in the European Social Charter, Turin, 18 October 1961, CETS No. 035. Further rights were added through the Additional Protocol to the European Social Charter, Strasbourg, 5 May 1988, CETS No. 128, and supervisory reforms were contained in the Protocol Amending the European Social Charter, Turin, 21 October 1991, CETS No. 148. For a study of this system, see D.J. Harris and J. Darcy, *The European Social Charter*, 2nd edn (Ardsley, NY: Transnational Publishers, 2001) and H. Cullen, 'The Collective Complaints System of the European Social Charter: Interpretative Methods of the European Committee of Social Rights', *Human Rights Law Review*, 9 (2009), pp. 61–93.

25 ECHR, original Article 25.

26 ECHR, original Article 46.

27 For example, the UK first recognized the competence of persons to bring complaints against it before the commission in 1966; see Lord Lester, 'UK Acceptance of the Strasbourg Jurisdiction: What Really went on in Whitehall in 1965' [1998], PL 237.

28 ECHR, original Article 20.

29 ECHR, original Article 23.

evidence. At the same time, the commission sought to see whether it could achieve a negotiated 'friendly settlement' between the parties. If no such settlement could be agreed, the commission would produce its opinion as to whether there had been a breach of the ECHR. The commission was a quasi-judicial body that performed its functions in secret and did not make binding decisions. Its opinions were normally sent to the Committee of Ministers. The ministers, generally acting through their ambassadors, decided (by a two-thirds majority) whether there had been a breach of the convention. The complainant had no involvement in this process. Where, however, a case was considered to be legally significant – for example, because it raised a novel issue concerning the interpretation of the ECHR, or was otherwise important – the commission, a state concerned in the complaint, or the individual complainant[30] could refer the case to the court for determination.

The original court created by the ECHR was a part-time body, like the commission, with a membership equal to the number of states belonging to the Council of Europe. The judges were elected by the Parliamentary Assembly from a shortlist of candidates submitted by each state. The judges had to be 'of high moral character' and must either possess the qualifications required for appointment to high judicial office or be jurisconsults (i.e. academics or other types of experts) of recognized competence.[31] On appointment, the judges were to act independently and were forbidden to hold any positions incompatible with their impartiality.[32] The idea of a 'national judge' was to enable a member of the court to be fully cognizant of each state's domestic legal order. The judges held office for periods of 9 years and were eligible for re-election. When a case was referred to the court, it examined the merits of the complaint in a fully judicial manner and normally held an oral hearing at which the parties could submit their arguments via legal representatives. In the early decades of the court's existence, individual complainants had no standing before the court, as the ECHR did not confer such procedural rights on individuals. However, in 1983, the court sought to partially redress this omission, through an amendment to the Rules of the Court, by allowing persons whose cases had been referred to the court to appoint their own lawyers to represent their interests. After the completion of written and oral proceedings, the court would deliver its judgement (dissenting opinions could be issued). If the court found a breach of the rights and freedoms guaranteed by the ECHR, it could award the successful complainant 'just satisfaction'.[33] This was a sum of money the respondent state was obliged to pay to compensate the complainant for (1) pecuniary damage (e.g. in respect of the unlawful seizure of a complainant's property[34]), (2) non-pecuniary damage (e.g. pain and anxiety suffered by a detainee subject to police maltreatment[35]) suffered, and (3) the reasonable legal costs incurred by complainants in seeking to protect their convention rights via domestic and Strasbourg proceedings. The court tended to be cautious in making such awards.[36]

The Committee of Ministers was[37] (and remains today[38]) responsible for supervising the execution of judgements made by the court. If a respondent state had been found in breach of the

30 Under Protocol No. 9 to the Convention for the Protection of Human Rights and Fundamental Freedoms, Rome, 20 November 1990, CETS No. 140.

31 ECHR, former Article 39.

32 ECHR, former Article 40.

33 ECHR, former Article 50.

34 *Hentrich* v *France* (1994), 18 EHRR 440.

35 *Ribitsch* v *Austria* (1995), 21 EHRR 573.

36 See A. Mowbray, 'The European Court of Human Rights' Approach to Just Satisfaction' [1997], *Public Law* 647.

37 ECHR, former Article 54.

38 ECHR, Article 46.

convention, it was required to notify the committee when it had paid any just satisfaction awarded and what 'individual' measures (i.e. those concerning the successful applicant) and 'general' measures (i.e. those affecting other persons in a similar situation to the applicant) had been taken to remedy the breach identified by the court. Until the Committee of Ministers was satisfied with the responses from the relevant state, it would keep the case open on its agenda. The committee relied upon political pressure to require member states to comply with adverse judgments. It could take several years for judgements to be fully executed, especially when constitutional or legislative changes were required to be made.

3.1 The Protocol 11 Reforms

By the 1980s, the member states began to contemplate fundamental reforms of the Strasbourg control system to improve its efficiency. Two alternatives were proposed: to convert the commission into a first-instance judicial body with the court exercising a selective appellate jurisdiction (an idea advocated by Switzerland), or to merge the commission and the court (supported by The Netherlands and Sweden). In 1993, the Committee of Ministers decided in favour of the latter, single court, solution (this was also favoured by the Parliamentary Assembly).[39] Protocol No. 11[40] established a new full-time court that possesses different powers and undertakes the admissibility, fact-finding and friendly settlement duties previously carried out by the commission. Controversially, the judges of the new court had their (renewable) terms of office reduced to 6 years. Also, Protocol 11 created a *de facto* appellate process whereby either party to a case can request the court's Grand Chamber, composed of 17 judges, to reconsider the merits of important cases, such as those raising serious legal issues, after a judgement has been delivered by a seven-judge chamber.[41] However, the Grand Chamber exercises this jurisdiction with circumspection and accepts only about 10 cases per year for reconsideration.[42]

From the perspective of persons who consider that a member state has violated their convention rights, the great benefit of Protocol 11 is that it has established a fully judicial international mechanism of redress for them. Under the protocol, all states parties to the ECHR (over the last two decades, all states wishing to join the Council of Europe[43] have been required to become a party to the ECHR as a condition of membership of the council) recognize the jurisdiction of the court to receive and determine individual applications.[44] These can be made by natural persons, legal persons[45] or non-governmental organizations (NGOs)[46] who claim to be the victims of such infringements. However, such applicants must first exhaust effective domestic remedies before making an application to the court.[47] Unfortunately, most complainants to Strasbourg fail to satisfy

39 See A. Mowbray, 'Reform of the Control System of the European Convention on Human Rights' [1993], 419.

40 Protocol No. 11 to the Convention for the Protection of Human Rights and Fundamental Freedoms, Strasbourg, 11 May 1994, CETS No. 155.

41 ECHR, Article 43.

42 See A. Mowbray, 'An Examination of the Work of the Grand Chamber of the European Court of Human Rights' [2007], *Public Law* 507.

43 Currently, the Council of Europe comprises 47 states.

44 ECHR, Article 34.

45 For example, *Société Colas Est* v *France* (2004), 39 EHRR 17.

46 For example, *Liberty and Others* v *United Kingdom* (application no. 58243/00) Judgement of 1 July 2008.

47 ECHR, Article 35.

this or the other admissibility criteria;[48] as a result, over 90% of applications are determined to be inadmissible by the court.[49] In regard to admissible cases, the relevant chambers seek to encourage the parties to agree friendly settlements.[50] Where such an agreement cannot be obtained, the chamber will provide a judgement on the merits.[51] Around 95% of these judgements will find at least one violation of the convention by the respondent state.[52] As discussed above, the Committee of Ministers has responsibility for supervising the execution of the court's judgements.

3.2 The Workload Crisis

The establishing of direct access to the court for aggrieved individuals, combined with growing awareness, among both lawyers and laypersons, of the rights and freedoms guaranteed by the ECHR, along with an expanding number of member states, has generated an ever increasing volume of applications. Although the court, aided by its registry staff of lawyers and administrators, has significantly expanded its productivity,[53] there has been a growing backlog of applications awaiting determination by the court. At the end of 2008, the court was faced with 97,300 pending applications.[54] Soon after the full-time court began to function, its then president, Luzius Wildhaber, asked the Committee of Ministers to appoint a group of experts to examine further institutional and legal reforms to secure the long-term viability of the Strasbourg enforcement system. An 'Evaluation Group', including President Wildhaber, was established and reported in 2001. The report[55] contained a number of proposals that the court could implement under the existing convention (such as developing a procedure for dealing with 'repetitive' applications where different applicants complained about the same defect in a particular state's legal order) and others (e.g. giving the court greater discretion to select the cases it would determine) that required amendments to the convention. The Committee of Ministers endorsed the report and directed that its Steering Committee of Human Rights should consider detailed reform proposals. In due course, the Steering Committee drafted Protocol 14. Despite criticisms of the draft by the Parliamentary Assembly,[56] the Committee of Ministers agreed on the final text and opened the protocol for signature in May 2004.

---

48 Including lodging their application within 6 months of the final domestic determination of their complaint and not making 'manifestly ill-founded (unsubstantiated) or "incompatible' (legally irrelevant) complaints.

49 *European Court of Human Rights: Annual Report 2008*, p. 131 [online]. Available from: www.echr.coe.int.

50 In 2008, six cases were resolved through friendly settlements: *ibid.*, p. 131.

51 If a case raises serious questions of law, the chamber may decide to relinquish jurisdiction over the case to the Grand Chamber under ECHR, Article 30.

52 See A. Mowbray, 'No Violations But Interesting: A Study of the Strasbourg Court's Jurisprudence in Cases Where No Breach of the Convention Has Been Found', *European Public Law*, 14(2) (2008), pp. 237–60.

53 In 1995, the original court delivered 56 judgements; in 1999 (the first complete year of the full-time court), 177 judgements were given; and in 2008, the court pronounced 1,543 judgements. See note 50 above, p. 131.

54 See note 49 above, p. 129.

55 *Report of the Evaluation Group to the Committee of Ministers on the European Court of Human Rights* (EGCourt(2001)1).

56 Opinion No. 251, 28 April 2004.

Protocol 14[57] seeks to increase the efficiency of the court while maintaining the basic structures introduced under Protocol 11. Under the new protocol, 'single-judge formations', comprising a judge assisted by a rapporteur from the court's registry, will be empowered to determine clearly inadmissible applications. Committees of three judges will be authorized to determine the merits of straightforward applications which do not raise novel points of law. More controversially, an additional admissibility criterion will be imposed for applications brought by persons (but not for the very rare inter-state complaints[58]). Where an application has been considered by a domestic tribunal and the Strasbourg Court believes that the applicant has 'not suffered a significant disadvantage',[59] the court will be able to declare the application inadmissible even though a formal breach of the convention may have occurred. This limited discretion is designed to allow the court to focus its precious resources on cases of greater magnitude. It is believed that these reforms will allow the court to increase its productivity by about 25%. The Committee of Ministers and the court hoped that all the member states would have ratified the protocol so that it could be brought into effect by the summer of 2007. However, the Russian Duma failed to approve the ratification process,[60] and so it has not been possible for the protocol to be implemented.

One year after Protocol 14 was opened for signature, the Heads of State and Government of the Council of Europe agreed to the establishment of a 'group of wise persons' to examine more fundamental long-term reforms of the Strasbourg control system. This group, chaired by the former president of the European Union's European Court of Justice, Mr Gil Carlos Rodriguez Iglesias, submitted its final report in November 2006.[61] The major institutional reform proposed was the creation of a 'Judicial Committee' that would be subordinate to the Strasbourg Court. Members of the Judicial Committee, of judicial stature, would take over responsibility for determining the admissibility of applications and the merits of routine well-founded cases. Relieving the court of these burdens would enable it to focus on the most complex and important cases. While the Committee of Ministers formally welcomed the final report, a great deal of support for fundamental re-engineering of the Strasbourg control system in the short term was not displayed at a high-level colloquy on the report organized by the Chair of the Committee of Ministers.[62]

In the autumn of 2008, the President of the Court, Jean-Paul Costa, suggested to the Committee of Ministers that because of the serious workload crisis facing the court the member states should consider the provisional application of two of Protocol 14's reform measures (the creation of single-judge formations and extending the powers of committees). The Committee of Ministers acted swiftly to consult its expert Steering Committee on Human Rights (CDDH) and the Committee of Legal Advisers on Public International Law (CAHDI) on the feasibility of this proposal. By the spring of 2009, the expert committees had reported back that there were

57 Protocol No. 14 to the Convention for the Protection of Human Rights and Fundamental Freedoms, amending the control system of the Convention, Strasbourg, 13 May 2004, CETS No. 194.

58 Brought under ECHR Article 33; see e.g. *Cyprus* v *Turkey* (2002), 35 EHRR 731.

59 Article 12 of Protocol 14.

60 There appears to be significant Russian hostility to adverse court judgements concerning extrajudicial killings in Chechnya, refusals to extradite Chechens from Georgia, and Russian involvement in the self-proclaimed 'Transdniestria' area of Moldova. See L.R. Helfer, 'Redesigning the European Court of Human Rights: Embeddedness as a Deep Structural Principle of the European Human Rights Regime', *European Journal of International Law*, 19(1) (2008), pp. 125–59, at p. 157.

61 CM(2006)203.

62 In San Marino on 22–23 March 2007.

two mechanisms, compatible with public international law, that would enable the provisional application of the identified Protocol 14 reform measures.[63] These were a new protocol specifying the two measures (requiring only a small number of ratifications to bring it into effect in respect of ratifying states) and a formal agreement among the parties to Protocol 14 allowing the provisional application of the specified measures in cases brought against states that so consented. The Committee of Ministers then drafted a new Protocol 14bis. A copy of the draft protocol was sent to the Parliamentary Assembly for urgent consideration during its April session. The assembly approved an opinion[64] endorsing draft Protocol 14bis. At the next meeting of the Committee of Ministers, in Madrid on 12 May 2009, a separate conference of all the states parties to the ECHR was held. The parties agreed to the text of Protocol 14bis and also to allow parties to Protocol 14 to formally declare their provisional acceptance of the two reform measures. Protocol 14bis was opened for signature later that month.[65] It only required the ratification of three states to come into force and states which ratified Protocol 14bis could accept its provisional application after 1 month. By the end of June 2009, Denmark, Norway and Ireland had ratified Protocol 14bis, and it was being provisionally applied by July 2009. On 1 October 2009, Protocol 14bis entered into force, and at that time seven states had ratified it.[66] In addition, by the same date, nine states had formally declared their acceptance of the provisional application of the specified reform measures under Protocol 14.[67] So the court was able to utilize more efficient means to process complaints against 16 states within a year of President Costa's plea for urgent action to tackle the backlog of cases.

It is clear that the Protocol 11 control system cannot cope with the current levels of individual applications. Therefore, member states must make greater efforts to ensure that their administrative and legal systems effectively respect and protect the rights and freedoms guaranteed in the convention. Furthermore, they need to muster the political will to agree on fundamental institutional reforms to enable the Strasbourg control system to both provide redress for individuals where it is not available domestically, and to continue the progressive development of the court's jurisprudence. The speed with which Protocol 14bis was agreed and the formal declaratory mechanism introduced under Protocol 14 were positive developments with respect to short-term reforms of the court's working methods. The Swiss government has undertaken to hold a major conference on the future of the court in February 2010, during its chairmanship of the Committee of Ministers. President Costa has publicly urged the member states to use the conference as an opportunity to start planning for the radical reforms needed in the control system by 2019 – the sixtieth anniversary of the court.[68]

63 CDDH, 'Final Opinion on Putting into Practice Certain Procedures Envisaged to Increase the Court's Case-Processing Capacity', CM(2009)51, and 'Opinion of the CAHDI', CM(2009)56.

64 Opinion No. 271, 30 April 2009.

65 Protocol No. 14bis to the Convention for the Protection of Human Rights and Fundamental Freedoms, Strasbourg, 27 May 2009, CETS No. 204.

66 Denmark, Georgia, Iceland, Ireland, Monaco, Norway and Slovenia.

67 Albania, Azerbaijan, Estonia, Germany, Liechtenstein, Luxembourg, The Netherlands, Switzerland and the UK.

68 Memorandum of the President of the European Court of Human Rights to the States with a View to Preparing the Interlaken Conference, 3 July 2009.

4. Judicial Elaboration of the ECHR

Both the original court and its full-time successor have adopted an expansive attitude towards the interpretation of the ECHR.[69] They have developed doctrines including the evolutive/living instrument approach,[70] which requires the rights/freedoms guaranteed by the convention to be interpreted in the light of contemporary social/scientific standards, and the need for ECHR Articles to be applied in a manner that ensures the practical and effective benefit of the rights/freedoms to persons.[71] These techniques have facilitated the extension of the literal text of the convention and its protocols to encompass other rights enshrined in the UDHR. A classic example is the gradual recognition by the court of a negative right not to belong to an association like that set out in Article 20(2) of the UDHR. In *Young, James and Webster* v *United Kingdom*,[72] the applicants had been dismissed from employment by British Rail (the state-owned railway operator) because they refused to join one of the unions which had negotiated closed shop agreements with British Rail. Two of the applicants objected to the political aims of the relevant unions. As their dismissals were lawful under domestic law, the applicants complained to Strasbourg, alleging a breach of their implied negative right to freedom of association under Article 11 of the ECHR. The respondent government – paradoxically, it was the Conservative administration led by Mrs Thatcher that had to defend the dismissals, which had occurred under the previous Labour administration – sought to argue that the drafters of the convention had consciously excluded such a right, as was shown by the *travaux préparatoires:*

> On account of the difficulties raised by the 'closed-shop system' in certain countries, the Conference in this connection considered that it was undesirable to introduce into the Convention a rule under which 'no one may be compelled to belong to an association' which features in [Article 20(2)] of the United Nations Universal Declaration.[73]

The court decided that it was not necessary, in this case, to determine whether there was a negative right. However,

> [a]ssuming for the sake of argument that, for the reasons given in the above-cited passage from the *travaux préparatoires*, a general rule such as in Article 20(2) of the Universal Declaration of Human Rights was deliberately omitted from, and so cannot be regarded as itself enshrined in, the Convention, it does not follow that the negative aspect of a person's freedom of association falls completely outside the ambit of Article 11 and that each and every compulsion to join a particular trade union is compatible with the intention of that provision. To construe Article 11 as permitting every kind of compulsion in the field of trade union membership would strike at the very substance of the freedom it is designed to guarantee.[74]

---

69 See J.G. Merrills, *The Development of International Law by the European Court of Human Rights* (Manchester: Manchester University Press, 1993), and A. Mowbray, 'The Creativity of the European Court of Human Rights', *Human Rights Law Review* (2005) 5(1): 57–79.

70 First applied in *Tyrer* v *UK* (1979–80), 2 EHRR 1.

71 As in *Airey* v *Ireland* (1979–80), 2 EHRR 305.

72 (1981), 4 EHRR 38.

73 Report of 19 June 1950 of the Conference of Senior Officials, Collected Edition of the '*Travaux Préparatoires*', vol. IV, p. 262 cited *ibid.*, para. 51.

74 *Ibid.*, para. 52.

The court went on to conclude that the interferences with the applicants' Article 11 rights were 'not necessary in a democratic society', as permitted under Article 11(2), and therefore amounted to a violation of the convention. Judges Sorensen, Thor Vilhjalmsson and Lagergren issued a dissenting opinion in which they expressed their belief that no technique of interpretation could justify extending an article to cover a matter deliberately excluded by the framers of the convention.

A decade later, the court strengthened its recognition of the negative element within Article 11. In *Sigurdur A Sigurjonsson* v *Iceland*,[75] the applicant complained to Strasbourg regarding his statutory obligation to join a designated trade union in order to be eligible for a licence to operate a taxi. The government contended that the negative aspect identified in *Young, James and Webster* should be interpreted narrowly. However, the court noted that during the intervening years developments had occurred at the international level. These included the EC adopting the Community Charter of the Fundamental Social Rights of Workers, which provided that employees should have the freedom to join or not join trade unions, and the recognition of a similar negative rights under the European Social Charter by the Committee of Independent Experts. Consequently, the court, subject to the dissent of Judge Thor Vilhalmsson, held that

> it should be recalled that the Convention is a living instrument which must be interpreted in the light of present-day conditions (see, *Soering* v *UK* [(1989) 11 EHRR 439]). Accordingly, Article 11 must be viewed as encompassing a negative right of association. It is not necessary for the court to determine in this instance whether this right is to be considered on an equal footing with the positive right.[76]

Applying this approach, the court found the applicant's negative right had been infringed and the compulsory trade union membership requirement could not be justified under Article 11(2).

The Grand Chamber of the full-time court found a violation of 'the negative right to trade union freedom'[77] in *Sorensen and Rasmussen* v *Denmark*.[78] The two applicants objected to their obligation to join designated trade unions as a condition of gaining employment (pre-entry closed shop arrangements) and argued that the negative right under Article 11 should be accorded the same status as the positive right. In response, the government contended that the negative right should not be recognized as having the same weight and, because of the complex social and political issues involved, governments should be granted a wide margin of appreciation (i.e. discretion) to regulate closed shops. The court found a breach of the applicants' negative right, but the Grand Chamber was still unwilling to rule definitively that the negative and positive rights were of equal stature. Nevertheless, the Grand Chamber rejected the government's argument that states should be accorded a wide margin of appreciation to allow closed shops.

Another illustration of the court developing the scope of convention rights in a manner that encompassed aspects of the UDHR not directly replicated in the text of the ECHR was the protection accorded to single-parent families and their illegitimate children in *Marckx* v *Belgium*.[79] Article 25(2) of the UDHR provides that

---

75 (1993), 16 EHRR 462.

76 *Ibid*., para. 35.

77 See note 78 below, para. 76.

78 (2008), 46 EHRR 29.

79 (1979), 2 E.H.R.R. 330. See M.D. Goldhaber, *A People's History of the European Court of Human Rights* (Piscataway, NJ: Rutgers University Press, 2007) for an insight into the background to the case.

> Motherhood and childhood are entitled to special care and assistance. All children, whether born in or out of wedlock, shall enjoy social protection.

Marckx, a single mother, complained on her own behalf and for her baby daughter to Strasbourg, alleging that various elements of Belgian law, such as the need for single mothers to formally recognize their children, unlawfully discriminated against illegitimate children in breach of Articles 8 and 14 of the ECHR. The court held:

> 31. ... By guaranteeing the right to respect for family life, Article 8 presupposes the existence of a family. The Court concurs entirely with the Commission's established case-law on a crucial point, namely that Article 8 makes no distinction between the 'legitimate' and the 'illegitimate' family. Such a distinction would not be consonant with the word 'everyone', and this is confirmed by Article 14 with its prohibition, in the enjoyment of the rights and freedoms enshrined in the Convention, of discrimination grounded on 'birth'. In addition, the Court notes that the Committee of Ministers of the Council of Europe regards the single woman and her child as one form of family no less than others (Resolution (70) 15 of 15 May 1970 on the social protection of unmarried mothers and their children, para. I-10, para. II-5, etc.).

Article 8 thus applies to the 'family life' of the 'illegitimate' family as it does to that of the 'legitimate' family. Besides, it is not disputed that Paula Marckx assumed responsibility for her daughter Alexandra from the moment of her birth and has continuously cared for her, with the result that a real family life existed and still exists between them.

> 41. ... It is true that, at the time when the Convention of 4 November 1950 was drafted, it was regarded as permissible and normal in many European countries to draw a distinction in this area between the 'illegitimate' and the 'legitimate' family. However, the Court recalls that this Convention must be interpreted in the light of present-day conditions (*Tyrer* judgment of 25 April 1978, Series A no. 26, p. 15, para. 31). In the instant case, the Court cannot but be struck by the fact that the domestic law of the great majority of the member States of the Council of Europe has evolved and is continuing to evolve, in company with the relevant international instruments, towards full juridical recognition of the maxim '*mater semper certa est*'.

Consequently, by varying majorities, the court went on to find that the Belgian laws on affiliation and family relationships violated both applicants' rights under Article 8 and Article 14 in conjunction with Article 8. This was a highly important judgement in establishing the court's attitude towards the treatment of single-parent families and relied heavily upon the living instrument method of interpretation. In later cases the court built upon Marckx to require states to demonstrate 'very weighty reasons'[80] if they were to be capable of justifying the lawfulness of different treatment of children born out of wedlock under the convention.

The obligation upon member states to hold regular free elections contained in Article 3 of Protocol No. 1 has been interpreted by the court to contain the implied rights for individuals to stand for elected office and to vote. These implied rights echo those found in Article 21(1) of the UDHR.[81] The applicants in *Mathieu-Mohin and Clerfayt* v *Belgium*[82] were French-speaking

80 For example, in *Inze* v *Austria* (1987), 10 EHRR 394 at para. 41.

81 See note 13 above.

82 (1987), 10 EHRR 1.

politicians who were unable to participate in the decision-making of the Flemish Council due to the linguistic constitutional arrangements in that divided country. They contended that the restrictions violated their individual rights under Article 3. The court ruled as follows:

> 51. As to the nature of the rights thus enshrined in Article 3, the view taken by the Commission has evolved. From the idea of an 'institutional' right to the holding of free elections (decision of 18 September 1961 on the admissibility of application no. 1028/61, *X v. Belgium*, Yearbook of the Convention, vol. 4, p. 338), the Commission has moved to the concept of 'universal suffrage' (see particularly the decision of 6 October 1967 on the admissibility of application no. 2728/66, *X v. the Federal Republic of Germany*, *op. cit.*, vol. 10, p. 338) and then, as a consequence, to the concept of subjective rights of participation – the 'right to vote' and the 'right to stand for election to the legislature' (see in particular the decision of 30 May 1975 on the admissibility of applications nos. 6745-6746/76, *W, X, Y and Z v. Belgium*, *op. cit.*, vol. 18, p. 244). The Court approves this latter concept.
>
> 52. The rights in question are not absolute. Since Article 3 recognises them without setting them forth in express terms, let alone defining them, there is room for implied limitations (see, *mutatis mutandis*, the *Golder* judgment of 21 February 1975, Series A no. 18, pp. 18–19, § 38). In their internal legal orders the Contracting States make the rights to vote and to stand for election subject to conditions which are not in principle precluded under Article 3 (Collected Edition of the 'Travaux Préparatoires', vol. III, p. 264, and vol. IV, p. 24). They have a wide margin of appreciation in this sphere, but it is for the Court to determine in the last resort whether the requirements of Protocol No. 1 have been complied with; it has to satisfy itself that the conditions do not curtail the rights in question to such an extent as to impair their very essence and deprive them of their effectiveness; that they are imposed in pursuit of a legitimate aim; and that the means employed are not disproportionate (see, amongst other authorities and mutatis mutandis, the *Lithgow and Others* judgment of 8 July 1986, Series A no. 102, p. 71, § 194). In particular, such conditions must not thwart 'the free expression of the opinion of the people in the choice of the legislature'.

Given the complex constitutional history of the linguistic splits in Belgium, a large majority of the court determined that the applicants had not suffered a breach of their implied rights under Article 3.

While the court has been sensitive to states' arguments that their particular electoral arrangements reflect the needs of their societies, it has nevertheless sometimes found a violation of the implied rights of individuals. A dramatic example is the case of *Matthews* v *United Kingdom*,[83] which had its origins in Spain's claim of sovereignty over Gibraltar, a dependent territory of the UK. The UK's policy was that the people of Gibraltar should determine their own future, and in several votes they had opposed becoming part of Spain. Against this background, Spain would not approve changes to European Union law that could enable the people of Gibraltar to elect a Member of the European Parliament. Matthews, a resident of Gibraltar, applied in 1994 to the Gibraltar Electoral Registration Officer for a vote in the forthcoming European Parliamentary elections. This was rejected as the residents of Gibraltar did not have such a right to vote. Subsequently, she brought a complaint against the UK, as the state responsible for guaranteeing ECHR rights in Gibraltar, alleging a breach of her right to vote under Article 3 of the Convention. The Grand Chamber, by 15 votes to 2, dismissed the British government's submission that the European Parliament did not constitute a 'legislature' within the meaning of Article 3. The majority believed that the European Parliament had sufficient

83 (1999), 28 EHRR 361.

involvement in the legislative process to fall within the ambit of Article 3. Therefore, as 'the very essence of the applicant's right to vote'[84] had been denied, the UK was determined to have violated Article 3. This judgement firmly signalled the court's support for democratic accountability within the European Union. Britain sought to comply with the judgement by incorporating Gibraltar in the European Parliamentary constituency for the South-West of England at the next election.

Over time, the court has also interpreted Article 1 of Protocol No. 1 as guaranteeing a 'right to property'[85] which can be invoked by persons. The range of interests that fall within the Article's concept of 'possessions' has been continually expanded by the court, and it now includes such diverse property rights as welfare benefits[86] and corporate intellectual property rights (such as trademark applications and registered marks).[87] However, the court has also recognized that states have a wide margin of appreciation in interfering with or even depriving persons of their property, under the limitations provided for by Article 1, where national parliaments have enacted socio-economic programmes (such as leasehold enfranchisement) that adversely affect some types of property.[88] Generally, the court requires the payment of appropriate compensation by such programmes if they are to be lawful under Article 1.[89] The obligations imposed upon member states depriving persons of their property under Article 1 constitute an elaboration of the limitation on the right to property contained in Article 17(2)[90] of the UDHR.

A highly innovative feature of the court's jurisprudence has been its willingness to find an ever-growing spectrum of positive obligations upon member states contained within the ECHR.[91] Initially, the original court had focused upon elaborating the requirements of positive obligations expressly included in the text of the convention. Examples include the nature of the duty of states to provide free interpretation for defendants in criminal trials who do not speak the language used in court[92] and the provision of effective legal assistance for impecunious defendants facing serious criminal charges.[93] Later, a range of positive obligations, extending from states' responsibility to protect the homes of persons from severe environmental pollution[94] to granting full legal recognition of the new identity of post-operative transsexuals,[95] have been developed by the court from the ambiguous term 'respect' in Article 8 of the Convention. Furthermore, in order to enhance the efficacy of the ECHR's guarantees of the right to life, prohibition of torture, and the right to liberty, the court has imposed procedural obligations upon states, mandating the holding of rigorous investigations into allegations of breaches of these substantive guarantees.[96]

---

84 *Ibid.*, para. 65.

85 *Stec and Others* v *UK* (2005), 41 EHRR SE 18, para. 56.

86 *Ibid.*

87 *Anheuser-Busch Inc.* v *Portugal* (2007), 45 EHRR 36, and see L.R. Helfer, 'The New Innovation Frontier? Intellectual Property and the European Court of Human Rights', *Harvard International Law Journal*, 49 (2008), pp. 1–52.

88 For example, in *James* v *UK* (1986), 8 EHRR 123.

89 For example, in *The Former King of Greece and Others* v *Greece* (2001), 33 EHRR 21.

90 See note 10 above.

91 See A. Mowbray, *The Development of Positive Obligations Under the ECHR by the European Court of Human Rights* (Oxford: Hart, 2004).

92 ECHR Article 6(3)(e) as defined in *Luedicke, Belkacem and Koc* v *Germany* (1978), 2 EHRR 149.

93 ECHR Article 6(3)(c) elaborated in *Artico* v *Italy* (1980), 3 EHRR 1.

94 The court first found a breach of this obligation in *Lopez Ostra* v *Spain* (1994), 20 EHRR 277.

95 *Christine Goodwin* v *UK* (2002), 35 EHRR 18; cf. Article 6 of UDHR.

96 See A. Mowbray, 'Duties of Investigation Under the ECHR', *International & Comparative Law Quarterly*, 51 (2002), pp. 437–48.

In the context of elaborating the extent of positive obligations under the convention, the court has addressed the issue of the connection between rights/freedoms protected by the ECHR and social/economic rights. In *Airey* v *Ireland*,[97] the court was confronted with the complaint that a wife, who had suffered physical violence from her husband, was unable to obtain an order of judicial separation from him due to the absence of legal aid in Ireland (Mrs Airey's limited education prevented her from personally seeking such an order under the complex Irish judicial process, and she could not afford to pay for a lawyer to make the application on her behalf). At Strasbourg, it was argued on behalf of Mrs Airey that Ireland was in breach of both Article 6(1), by denying her access to a court, and Article 8, through failing to respect her right to family life (by enabling her to obtain a judicial separation order). The court observed that

> 26. ... Whilst the Convention sets forth what are essentially civil and political rights, many of them have implications of a social or economic nature. The Court therefore considers, like the Commission, that the mere fact that an interpretation of the Convention may extend into the sphere of social and economic rights should not be a decisive factor against such an interpretation; there is no water-tight division separating that sphere from the field covered by the Convention.

By varying majorities, the court then determined that Ireland had failed to comply with its positive obligations to Mrs Airey under both articles.

Although the court in *Airey* acknowledged some overlap between convention rights and social/economic rights, it has been circumspect in finding breaches of the convention in cases where the complaint primarily concerned the latter category of rights.[98] For example, in *Botta* v *Italy*,[99] the physically disabled applicant complained that public authorities had failed to take adequate measures to ensure that private beach owners provided suitable facilities for him (and other disabled holidaymakers). The court, unanimously, concluded that Mr Botta's complaint did not fall within the state's duty to respect his private life under Article 8. Indeed, the commission had earlier characterized Botta's claim as involving social rights (participation in recreation and leisure activities[100]) that were more appropriately dealt with under the European Social Charter. Nevertheless, one area of overlap where the full-time court has found a number of states to have breached the ECHR concerns the failure of domestic authorities to provide adequate health care for detained persons.[101] An illustration is *Keenan* v *UK*,[102] where the court found that serious failings in the provision of medical treatment for the applicant's mentally ill son while he served a prison sentence (he committed suicide before it was completed) contributed to his suffering inhuman and degrading treatment and punishment, violating Article 3 of the ECHR.

97 See note 72 above.

98 C. Warbrick has argued that the ECHR does not generally protect economic and social rights: 'Economic and Social Interests and the ECHR', in M.A. Baderin and R. McCorquodale (eds), *Economic, Social and Cultural Rights in Action* (Oxford: Oxford University Press, 2007).

99 (1998), 26 EHRR 241.

100 Cf. Article 24 of UDHR.

101 Cf. Article 25(1) of UDHR.

102 (2001), 33 EHRR 913.

5. Conclusion

We have examined how the UDHR was a significant component in the formulation of the ECHR together with the constitutional heritage of the original member states. However, those states decided to focus on civil and political rights when drafting the ECHR and its later additional protocols. Nevertheless, in some areas, the protocols have extended beyond the UDHR. For example, Protocol 6[103] abolished the death penalty in peacetime and Protocol 13[104] provides for its complete abolition. Our study also analysed how the jurisprudence of the Strasbourg Court has widened the scope of convention articles to encompass UDHR rights not expressly incorporated in the text of the convention, such as the implied negative right of association found within Article 11 of the ECHR.[105] A pioneering feat of the ECHR has been its creation of a system of international adjudication which enables aggrieved persons to assert their convention rights and freedoms against member states. The ongoing institutional challenges created by this mechanism have been scrutinized in our exposition. It is illuminating to conclude with a non-European commentator's global perspective on the ECHR:

> The Convention was founded by visionaries, and, to date, their vision is being carried out. So, whatever its problems (a charitable characterization might be that they are growing pains), the existence of the Convention and the Strasbourg Court is a major achievement for the entire world.[106]

103 Protocol No. 6 to the Convention for the Protection of Human Rights and Fundamental Freedoms, Concerning the Abolition of the Death Penalty, Strasbourg, 28 April 1983, CETS No. 114. By 2009, all the member states, except Russia, had ratified the protocol.

104 Protocol No. 13 to the Convention for the Protection of Human Rights and Fundamental Freedoms, Concerning the Abolition of the Death Penalty in all Circumstances, Vilnus, 3 May 2002, CETS No. 187. The protocol had been ratified by 41 states, but not signed by Russia or Azerbaijan, by 2009.

105 See note 75 above.

106 P.L. McKaskle, 'The European Court of Human Rights: What It Is, How It Works, and Its Future', *University of San Francisco Law Review*, 40(1) (2005), pp. 1–84, at pp. 72–3.

Chapter 15

Human Rights in the International Court of Justice

Gentian Zyberi

1. Introduction

> It is a truism that since the end of the Second World War there has been both a deepening of the substantive law of human rights and a broadening of what is perceived as human rights entitlements.... It is inevitable – and welcome – that all of this should over time have an impact on the International Court of Justice (ICJ). Article 34 of the Statute provides that the Court may only deal with cases between states. Until comparatively recently the Court was a 'Court of sovereign States'. But, as it is above all a court of international law, it has in recent years become also a court concerned with human rights, as human rights law has finally found its proper place within international law. Advisory Opinions, and interstate cases which claim human rights treaty violations *inter se*, have provided the vehicle for this development within the Court.[1]

It should be noted beforehand that there is some literature on the contribution of the International Court of Justice (ICJ) to the development of human rights,[2] and a greater amount of literature on specific judgements or advisory opinions delivered by the court.[3] Even a quick glance at the case law of the court reveals the variety of issues with clear implications for the development of

1 R. Higgins, 'Human Rights in the International Court of Justice', *Leiden Journal of International Law*, 20(4) (2007), pp. 745–51 See Appendix 1 for a list of relevant cases brought before the ICJ since 1991.

2 See, *inter alia*, E. Schwelb, 'The International Court of Justice and the Human Rights Clauses of the Charter', *American Journal of International Law*, 66 (1972), pp. 337–51; N.S. Rodley, 'Human Rights and Humanitarian Intervention: The Case-Law of the World Court', *International & Comparative Law Quarterly*, 38 (1989), pp. 321–33; S.M. Schwebel, 'Human Rights in the World Court', in R.S Pathak (ed.), *International Law in Transition: Essays in Memory of Judge Nagendra Singh* (The Hague: Martinus Nijhoff, 1992), pp. 267–90; S.M. Schwebel, 'The Treatment of Human Rights and of Aliens in the International Court of Justice', in V. Lowe and M. Fitzmaurice (eds), *Fifty Years of the International Court of Justice: Essays in Honour of Sir Robert Jennings* (Cambridge: Cambridge University Press, 1996), pp. 327–50; R. Higgins, 'The International Court of Justice and Human Rights', in K. Wellens (ed.), *International Law: Theory and Practice: Essays in Honour of Eric Suy* (The Hague: Kluwer Law International, 1998), pp. 691–705; A. Duxbury, 'Saving Lives in the International Court of Justice: The Use of Provisional Measures to Protect Human Rights', *California Western International Law Journal*, 31 (2000), pp. 141–76; J. Grimheden, 'The International Court of Justice in Furthering the Justiciability of Human Rights', in G. Alfredsson *et al.* (eds), *International Human Rights Monitoring Mechanisms* (The Hague: Kluwer Law International, 2001), pp. 469–84; G. Zyberi, 'The Development and Interpretation of International Human Rights and Humanitarian Law Rules and Principles Through the Case-Law of the International Court of Justice', *Netherlands Quarterly of Human Rights*, 25 (2007), pp. 117–39; S.R.S. Bedi, *The Development of Human Rights Law by the Judges of the International Court of Justice* (Oxford: Hart Publishing, 2007); G. Zyberi, *The Humanitarian Face of the International Court of Justice: Its Contribution to Interpreting and Developing International Human Rights and Humanitarian Law Rules and Principles* (Antwerp: Intersentia, 2008), especially pp. 65–258.

3 See Zyberi, *The Humanitarian Face*, note 2 above, pp. 473–506.

international human rights law rules and principles that it has dealt with. Nevertheless, assessing the contribution of the court to the interpretation and development of these rules and principles is no easy task. Human rights encompass an array of civil, political, economic, social, and cultural rights whose promotion and protection are considered to be one of the fundamental aims of the United Nations (UN), of which the ICJ is the principal judicial organ. While it is difficult to do justice to such a broad topic in the space available, this chapter tries to provide an overall picture through four components, namely the internationalization of human rights, their development and codification, the case law relating to the 1948 UDHR,[4] and a brief general overview of the court's contribution to the development of human rights.[5] That is followed by some concluding remarks.

For our purposes, the international law of human rights is understood as being that part of international law comprising numerous international instruments and to a significant extent also reflected in customary international law norms. They comprise a rather detailed normative framework and give rise to a considerable number of protection mechanisms. Indeed, over a relatively short period of time, international human rights law has developed to 'create a body of universal standards and values at the service of human dignity, equality and non-discrimination, and human freedoms'.[6] It is obvious, not only to the human rights scholar, but also to any layperson, that the body of international human rights law has experienced a large and substantial growth in the decades following the Second World War.[7] As Judge Buergenthal has rightly noted, the idea that the protection of human rights knows no international boundaries, and that the international community has an obligation to ensure that governments guarantee and protect human rights wherever they may be violated, has gradually captured the imagination of mankind.[8] However, against this impressive development in conceptualization, standard-setting and institutionalization of protection of human rights, practice shows that still quite a lot remains to be done to fully implement these commonly agreed human rights standards.

2. Internationalization of Human Rights

Understanding the ICJ's contribution to the interpretation and development of the rules and principles of international human rights law requires, besides an analysis of the court's case law, also knowledge of the development of this branch of law. By way of illustration of the court's contribution, suffice it to mention here the *obiter dictum* in the *Barcelona Traction* case[9] about the

---

4 GA Res. 217A (III), UN Doc. A/810 at 71 (1948).

5 These cases are the *Tehran Hostages* case (1979), the *Armed Activities* case (1999), and the *Diallo* case (1998). Although the UDHR was not issued as a binding legal document, over time it has acquired such binding force. All cases are available online in the official website of the court: *http://www.icj-cij.org/docket/index.php?p1=3* [accessed 15 July 2010].

6 J. Symonides (ed.), *Human Rights: Concept and Standards* (Aldershot: Ashgate Dartmouth and UNESCO Publishing, 2000), p. xi.

7 For a list of core international human rights instruments and their monitoring bodies, see Office of the High Commissioner for Human Rights [online]. Available from: http://www.ohchr.org/EN/HRBodies/Pages/HumanRightsBodies.aspx [accessed 26 April 2009].

8 T. Buergenthal, 'International Human Rights in an Historical Perspective', in Symonides, note 6 above, p. 4.

9 ICJ, *Barcelona Traction* (Belgium *v* Spain) (*Merits*), judgement of 5 February 1970, ICJ Reports, 1970, p. 32, para. 33.

erga omnes nature of fundamental human rights which lies at the roots of the development and the acquired importance of the international law of human rights. Although the ICJ is restricted in this respect due to the lack of *locus standi* for individuals, it has been seized with cases where issues of international law of human rights either form the subject matter of the dispute or are closely related to it.

The development of international human rights, like that of any branch of international law, is a process that takes place within the international legal and political framework with its own laws, procedures, and institutions that shape the form and content of human rights. As Steiner and Alston assert, 'it would be impossible to grasp the character of the human rights movement without a basic knowledge about international law and its contributions to it.'[10] Indeed, the development of rules and principles of international human rights law is intrinsically linked with international law and international institutions. National and international human rights promotion and protection represent, respectively, the horizontal and the vertical strands where the attainment of commonly agreed human rights standards takes place. Since the ICJ, which is the focal point of this chapter, is an international judicial body, our focus remains primarily on the vertical strand of the international law of human rights that is meant to bind states. Today, human rights are characteristically imagined as a movement involving international law and institutions, as well as a movement involving the spread of liberal constitutions among states.[11] Although, understandably, national governments have a primary responsibility to promote and protect the human rights of persons under their jurisdiction, international promotion and protection of human rights have been and continue to be an essential element of the human rights system.

The importance of human rights, illustrated, among other ways, also by the *jus cogens* status that certain human rights have achieved, is largely due to the emergence, the development, and the acquired importance of the human rights discourse in the international arena. This development stems from the human rights clauses of the UN Charter and, obviously, from the moral and legal weight that command the duty to respect and to ensure respect for human rights. There is a huge difference between the former situation, in which the individual was considered to be just an object of international law, and now when few would dispute that the individual is a participant in the international legal system.[12] Indeed, at present, every individual enjoys a set of rights guaranteed by numerous international human rights instruments, while at the same time also bearing certain duties and responsibilities. While usually individuals do not have specific duties under human rights treaties, international law provides for individual criminal responsibility for violations that constitute internationally recognized crimes such as genocide, war crimes, crimes against humanity, and torture.[13] The latest developments in the field of international criminal law seem to suggest that the above-mentioned crimes have come to be subject to universal jurisdiction, just like piracy and the slave trade.

The question of the possibility of individuals being subjects of international law has come before the predecessor of the ICJ, the Permanent Court of International Justice (PCIJ), and has been answered in the positive. In the advisory opinion of the PCIJ in the *Jurisdiction of the Courts*

10 H.J. Steiner and P. Alston, *International Human Rights in Context: Law, Politics, Morals*, 2nd edn (Oxford: Oxford University Press, 2000), p. 57.

11 *Ibid.*

12 The term 'participant' as opposed to 'object' or 'subject' of international law was first introduced by Rosalyn Higgins; see R. Higgins, *Problems and Process. International Law and How We Use It* (Oxford: Clarendon Press, 1994), pp. 48–55.

13 See, *inter alia*, T. Meron, *War Crimes Law Comes of Age* (New York: Oxford University Press, 1999). See also Chapters 23 and 24 in this volume.

of Danzig case,[14] the court admittedly accepted that the contracting parties might create rights and obligations for private parties. At earlier stages, the exertion by states of the right to diplomatic protection on behalf of their citizens caused, necessarily, a shift of attention to the rights of the individual, better reflected in the words of the PCIJ: 'the fact that the beneficiary of rights is not authorized to take independent steps in his own name to enforce them does not signify that he is not a subject of the law or that the rights in question are vested exclusively in the agency which possesses the capacity to enforce them.'[15] That paradigm shift has paved the way for further advancements regarding the position and the standing of individuals under international law. Whether entitlement is accompanied with the capacity of enforcement of these human rights is an issue which should be answered by a case-by-case approach through reference to the given situation and to the relevant international instrument. While individuals do not have specific duties under human rights treaties, gross violations of human rights entail individual criminal responsibility for internationally recognized crimes such as genocide and crimes against humanity.

3. The ICJ and the Development and Codification of International Human Rights Law

While, on the one hand, the work of the court has exerted a considerable influence upon the development of the international law of human rights, on the other hand, the development of this branch of law itself has also exerted a considerable influence on the jurisprudence and the caseload of the court. Obviously, that mutual interaction takes place in a political, socio-economic, and legal environment, which has formed and continues to form and shape our society. Thus, the findings of the court cannot be properly assessed, or even understood if taken out of the context of the development of our society and the laws in force at that given time. In an advisory opinion, the court stated that an international instrument has to be interpreted and applied within the framework of the entire legal system prevailing at the time of the interpretation.[16] Certainly, that very legal system the court refers to is itself the product of political and societal needs and human development and thus, eventually, would have to serve those needs. The development of the international law of human rights has gone through three main phases which have conditioned, to a large extent, the contribution rendered by the court to this branch of international law. The number of cases being brought before the court dealing with human rights issues differs from one period to another. However, it is noteworthy that this number has notably increased since the *Nicaragua* case,[17] and the fall of the Iron Curtain.

A distinguishing characteristic of the first phase of the development of the international law of human rights is the process of standard setting. This important process started in 1945 with the establishment of the UN, which made the protection and the promotion of human rights one of its

14 PCIJ, *Jurisdiction of the Courts of Danzig*, Advisory Opinion, Series B, No. 15, pp. 17–21 stating: 'It might be readily admitted that, according to a well established principle of international law, the *Beamteabkommen*, being an international agreement, cannot, as such, create direct rights and obligations for private individuals. But it cannot be disputed that the very object of an international agreement, *according to the intention of the contracting Parties* [emphasis added], may be the adoption by the parties of some definite rules creating individual rights and obligations and enforceable by the national courts.'

15 PCIJ, *Appeal from a Judgment of the Hungaro-Czechoslovak Mixed Arbitral Tribunal* (*The Peter Pázmány University* v *The State of Czechoslovakia*), Series A/B, No. 61, 1933, p. 231.

16 ICJ, *Legal Consequences for States of the Continued Presence of South Africa in Namibia*, Advisory Opinion of 21 June 1971, ICJ Reports 1971, p. 31, para. 53.

17 ICJ Reports 1986.

main purposes.[18] In fact, in this period the court's involvement with human rights issues was at a very low level, as instruments of international law of human rights were scarce. But two of the first advisory opinions, although concerned mainly with treaty interpretation, allowed the court to propagate the concept of internationalization of human rights,[19] and of the civilizing purpose of such human rights treaties.[20] Furthermore, in this first phase the court helped to clarify a very important principle of human rights law, namely the right of peoples to self-determination.[21] This right was to be embedded in Article 1 of both the International Covenant on Civil and Political Rights (ICCPR)[22] and the International Covenant on Economic, Social and Cultural Rights (ICESCR)[23] adopted in 1966. The latter year marked the beginning of the second phase, namely that of implementation and enforcement of the standards already set by that still small body of international law of human rights. That does not mean that the standard-setting process and the body of international law of human rights instruments stopped developing – for that is an ongoing process accompanying the development of human society – but the main foundations of this branch of law were finally laid with the International Bill of Human Rights[24] and the 1948 Genocide Convention. During this period, the court was faced with a considerable number of cases which touched upon many intricate and contentious issues, such as decolonization, immunity of human rights rapporteurs, and diplomatic protection. That second phase of the development of international law of human rights finished in 1989 with the end of the Cold War, which marked an important shift in the international world order.

Indeed, the end of the Cold War marked the beginning of a new phase in the activity of the ICJ when developing countries had shown an increased willingness to have their disputes settled by the court. Furthermore, as mentioned above, the end of this era saved the court from the lurking risk of being trapped in that ideological debate or being perceived as taking sides in it, a perception that would have resulted in undesirable repercussions for its work. From the fall of the Berlin Wall in 1989 to the present, we have entered the third phase of the development of human rights, namely that of the mainstreaming of human rights. According to the UN High Commissioner for Human Rights, mainstreaming human rights refers to the concept of enhancing the human rights programme and integrating it into the broad range of UN activities, including the areas of development and humanitarian action. The contribution that the court can render to mainstreaming human rights from the position of one of the main organs of UN and the principal judicial organ needs no explanation.

The development of international human rights law through the adoption of many international and regional treaties and the ensuing recognition of direct entitlements of individuals to these rights have influenced the frequency of cases dealing with human rights brought before the court. Commenting upon this development, Higgins observed that 'this vast explosion of human rights conventions could, it might have been thought, lead to a heavy human rights component in the Court's

18 UN Charter, Article 1(3).

19 Namely the advisory opinion on the *Interpretation of the Peace Treaties*, ICJ Reports 1950, p. 65.

20 Namely the advisory opinion on the *Reservations to the Genocide Convention*, ICJ Reports 1951, p. 15.

21 G. Zyberi, 'Self-determination through the Lens of the International Court of Justice', *Netherlands International Law Review*, 56 (2009), pp. 429–53.

22 999 UNTS 171.

23 993 UNTS 3.

24 As observed in Chapter 1 of this volume, the 'International Bill of Human Rights' comprises the UDHR, the ICCPR and the ICESCR.

work. The reality, however, is different.'[25] It should be noted though that, while not amounting to an 'explosion', the human rights component of cases brought before the ICJ has increased considerably over time. Suffice it to mention here the substantial increase in cases touching upon human rights brought before the court since the 1990s.[26] Consequently, a distinguishable and strong human rights element has been present in proceedings before the court both in contentious cases and requests for an advisory opinion. Potentially, the court will receive more cases arising from violations of human rights committed whether in peacetime or during armed conflicts. However, any increased role of the court with regard to the interpretation and development of international human rights rules and principles necessitates also a change in state behaviour, a change in substantive and procedural international law, and, last but not least, a substantial increase of the capacities of the court.

The adoption of numerous instruments of international law of human rights and the importance attached to the protection and promotion of human rights contributed to an upsurge in the case law of the court dealing with issues concerning human rights. While for reasons of space it is not possible to analyse in detail the relevant case law, suffice it to say that the court has generally taken a firm position in favour of human rights and clarified how certain human rights rules and principles were to be understood and applied. Indeed, since the beginning of its work, the court coined and emphasized the importance of *elementary considerations of humanity*,[27] which lie at the foundation of international human rights law. In the words of Judge Weeramantry:

> The enormous developments in the field of human rights in the post-war years, commencing with the Universal Declaration of Human Rights in 1948, must necessarily make their impact on assessments of such concepts as 'considerations of humanity' and 'dictates of the public conscience'. This development in human rights concepts, both in their formulation and in their universal acceptance, is more substantial than the developments in this field for centuries before. The public conscience of the global community has thus been greatly strengthened and sensitized to 'considerations of humanity' and 'dictates of public conscience'. Since the vast structure of internationally accepted human rights norms and standards has become part of common global consciousness today in a manner unknown before World War II, its principles tend to be invoked immediately and automatically whenever a question arises of humanitarian standards.[28]

Although not an exhaustive list, issues concerning human rights which have come before the court include the right of peoples to self-determination, the status and treatment of special UN rapporteurs, consular relations or diplomatic protection, the application of the Genocide Convention, the immunity of senior state officials, the right to asylum, and the application of human rights treaties in territories under occupation. By interpreting and developing rules and principles of human rights related to these issues the court has contributed to creating more clarity and ultimately to improvement of the human rights protection system.

---

25 Higgins, note 2 above, p. 693.

26 Suffice it to mention here the *East Timor* case, the *Diplomatic Protection* cases, the *Arrest Warrant* case, the *Armed Activities in the Territory of the Congo* cases, the *Certain Criminal Proceedings* case, the advisory opinions on the *Legality of Threat or Use of Nuclear Weapons* case, the *Difference Relating to Immunity from Legal Process of a Special Rapporteur of the Commission on Human Rights* case, and the *Wall* case.

27 *Corfu Channel* Case (UK *v* Albania) (Merits), ICJ Reports 1949, p. 22.

28 ICJ, *Legality of the Threat or Use of Nuclear Weapons*, Dissenting Opinion of Judge Weeramantry, ICJ Reports 1996, p. 493.

Some of the above-mentioned issues have been the subject of the work of the International Law Commission (ILC), whose mission is to work towards the codification and progressive development of international law in general. Some of the issues considered by the ILC are diplomatic protection, nationality including statelessness, formulation of the Nuremberg Principles, international criminal jurisdiction, the definition of aggression (as included in the draft code of crimes against the peace and security of mankind), and state responsibility. When identifying diplomatic protection as a topic appropriate for codification and progressive development by the ILC, this body acknowledged the useful dialogue with the ICJ on this issue.[29] In clarifying the relation between human rights and diplomatic protection, the ILC referred to quite a few cases decided by the ICJ.[30] In fact, the special rapporteur of the ILC on this topic has gone as far as to propose making it obligatory for states to exercise diplomatic protection where a norm of *jus cogens* has been violated in respect of the individual.[31] If this proposal were to be endorsed and further upheld by the ICJ in its case law, it would decisively qualify as a progressive development for the international law of human rights.

A look at the summaries of the work of the ILC reveals that some important issues under consideration are reservations to treaties, the effect of armed conflicts to treaties, the obligation to extradite or prosecute (*aut dedere aut judicare*), the responsibility of international organizations, and the expulsion of aliens.[32] Given the important ramifications that the ILC work on these issues can have for the international law of human rights, the case law of the ICJ can provide some guidance in choosing the right approach and vice versa.[33] Indeed, the interaction between the ILC, as a body entrusted with the codification and progressive development, and the ICJ, as an organ of international law, creates the necessary background for the further development of international law in general and human rights norms and principles in particular.

4. ICJ Case Law Relating to the UDHR

A simple search on the official website of the ICJ shows that the UDHR comes up a considerable number of times in the legal proceedings before the ICJ.[34] It should be mentioned, however, that while the UDHR has been used in applications instituting proceedings or written statements submitted to the court, rarely, if ever, has the court mentioned it in the judgements it has issued. In its 1993 application, Bosnia–Herzegovina asked the court to adjudge and declare that Serbia and Montenegro had violated and continued to violate Articles 1, 2, 3, 4, 5, 6, 7, 8, 9, 10, 11, 12, 13, 15, 16, 17, 18, 19, 20, 21, 22, 23, 25, 26 and 28 of the UDHR with respect to the citizens of Bosnia–Herzegovina. In Bosnia–Herzegovina's view, these fundamental human rights protected by the UDHR are binding upon all states of the world community as a matter of customary international law and *jus cogens,* and in accordance with the requirements of the UN Charter Article 1(3), Article

---

29 Yearbook of ILC, 1998, vol. 2, Part II, p. 16.

30 Yearbook of ILC, 1998, vol. 2, Part II, pp. 46–8.

31 A/CN.4/506 and Corr. 1 and Add.1.

32 For a detailed overview on the work of the ILC, see the 'Analytical Guide to the Work of the ILC' [online]. Available from: http://untreaty.un.org/ilc/guide/gfra.htm [accessed 15 July 2010].

33 See the Speech by H.E. Judge Rosalyn Higgins, President of the International Court of Justice, at the 59th Session of the International Law Commission, 10 July 2007, in Statements by the President [online]. Available from: http://www.icj-cij.org/presscom/files/9/13919.pdf [accessed 15 July 2010].

34 A search using the exact phrase 'Universal Declaration of Human Rights' and the English version of documents yielded a result of 71 hits.

55, and Article 56.[35] That is the strongest submission with regard to the applicability and status of UDHR norms and principles ever made. However, since jurisdiction in this case was based only on the 1948 Genocide Convention, the court did not pronounce on this claim.[36] Specific attention will be devoted here to the only case where the UDHR has been used in a judgement on merits, namely the *Tehran Hostages* case (1979).[37] It is noteworthy that in this case the violation of UDHR principles was raised by the court *proprio motu*, without the applicant having made specific claims in this regard.

4.1 United States Diplomatic and Consular Staff in Tehran (United States v Iran)

In the beginning of November 1979, a group of radical Iranian students attacked the US embassy and took everyone inside hostage. The events unfolded with Ayatollah Khomeini's support, in retaliation for the USA agreeing to shelter the Shah of Iran. The USA filed an application with the ICJ on 29 November 1979, requesting from it the indication of provisional measures relating to the fact that staff of the American embassy in Tehran were being kept hostage. Although this case is primarily about inviolability of diplomatic envoys, which is a distinct category of persons, the 1979 Order of the Court indicating provisional measures referred explicitly to the safeguarding of the right to life and health of these persons. In the court's words: '[c]ontinuance of the situation ... exposes the human beings concerned to privation, hardship, anguish and even danger to life and health and thus to a serious possibility of irreparable harm.'[38] Obviously, besides diplomatic immunity, this category of persons enjoys the same general protection under international human rights law as any individual.

For our purposes, the court's judgement in this case is rather important for the findings made on the applicability of fundamental human rights principles to the actions that had taken place. Firstly, the court pointed out the importance of the principle of the inviolability of the diplomatic envoys and embassy premises as a precondition to the conduct of good and friendly relations between states. Further, in its judgement, considering the circumstances of the case, the court held:

> Wrongfully to deprive human beings of their freedom and to subject them to physical constraints in conditions of hardship is in itself manifestly incompatible with the principles of the Charter of the

35 *Application of the Convention on the Prevention and Punishment of the Crime of Genocide* (Bosnia and Herzegovina *v* Serbia and Montenegro), Application of 20 March 1993, para. 132 [online]. Available from: http://www.icj-cij.org/docket/files/91/7199.pdf [accessed 15 July 2010].

36 See *Application of the Convention on the Prevention and Punishment of the Crime of Genocide* (Bosnia and Herzegovina *v* Serbia and Montenegro), Judgement of 26 February 2007, paras. 142–9 [online]. Available from: http://www.icj-cij.org/docket/files/91/13685.pdf [accessed 15 July 2010].

37 Also in the *Armed Activities* case (1999), the Democratic Republic of the Congo contended that Uganda had violated the rules set out in the 1948 UDHR. See Application of 23 June 1999, p. 15 [online]. Available from: http://www.icj-cij.org/docket/files/116/7151.pdf [accessed 15 July 2010]. While Uganda was found in breach of a number of articles of the international covenants, the court did not pronounce on the violation of the UDHR; see judgement of 19 December 2005[online]. Available from: http://www.icj-cij.org/docket/files/116/10455.pdf [accessed 15 July 2010].

38 ICJ, *Case Concerning United States Diplomatic and Consular Staff in Tehran* (United States of America *v* Iran) (*Request for the Indication of Provisional Measures*), Order of 15 December 1979, ICJ Reports 1979, p. 20, para. 42 (*Tehran Hostages* case).

> United Nations, as well as with the fundamental principles enunciated in the Universal Declaration of Human Rights.[39]

That wording seems to be a direct reference to Articles 3 and 5 of the UDHR. While Article 3 guarantees everyone's right to life, liberty and security of person, Article 5 provides for the prohibition of 'torture or cruel, inhuman or degrading treatment or punishment'. The importance of referring to the principles of the UN Charter and those of the UDHR increases when taking into account the fact that for ensuring the safety and protection of US citizens the court could have simply referred to the 1955 Treaty of Amity between the two states. This finding seems to support the conclusion that certain fundamental principles from the UDHR are part of customary international law, thus, creating obligations on the part of states for the protection of those individual human rights they provide for. It is noteworthy that this finding was made 7 years before the Convention Against Torture entered into force.[40] Thus, it can be reasonably concluded that in the eyes of the court wrongful deprivation of liberty, as well as conditions amounting to torture or cruel and inhuman treatment, represented such fundamental principles, whose violation gives rise to state responsibility.

5. The ICJ's Contribution to the International Law of Human Rights in a Nutshell

Having no limitations over its subject matter jurisdiction, the ICJ offers a judicial forum in which much interpretation and progressive development of different branches of international law can take place. As Teson has pointed out, international law must be wed to notions of political legitimacy associated with consent, individual rights and human dignity.[41] The court's judgements and advisory opinions, which have contributed to the interpretation and development of the international law of human rights rules and principles, encompass a period of over 60 years. As is the case with every human activity, this contribution does not represent an immaculate record, as the work of the court has been subject to both praise and criticism. Two of the main obstacles in the way of the court's progression towards a greater contribution to developing and interpreting human rights rules and principles have been the lack of compromissory clauses in instruments of international law of human rights and the lack of standing before the court of individuals. Fortunately, the court's jurisdiction *ratione materiae* is unlimited; thus, human rights violations, as a breach of international law, would obviously fall under the court's jurisdiction. As shown by the court's case law, despite these considerable obstacles, the court has been able to progressively develop and interpret norms of international law of human rights, hence contributing to an international legal order where human rights protection is given a prominent place.

---

39 *Tehran Hostages* case, judgement of 24 May 1980, ICJ Reports 1980, p. 42, para. 91.

40 While this judgement was rendered on 24 May 1980, the Convention Against Torture was adopted on 10 December 1984 and entered into force only on 26 June 1987. However, the prohibition on torture and cruel and inhuman treatment was already laid down in a number of international instruments, namely the 1948 UDHR, the 1949 Geneva Conventions, and the two Additional Protocols of 1977, the 1966 International Covenant on Civil and Political Rights, and the UN Declaration on the Protection of All Persons from Being Subjected to Torture and Other Cruel, Inhuman or Degrading Treatment or Punishment, adopted by the General Assembly on 9 December 1975 (Resolution 3452 (XXX).

41 F.R. Teson, 'Le Peuple, C'est Moi! The World Court and Human Rights', *American Journal of International Law*, 81(1) (1987), pp. 173–83.

That prominent place that international human rights law occupies is due to the entrenchment of the promotion and protection of human rights as part of the purposes and aims of the UN. The court has referred to the weight and place in the international law of human rights of the human rights clauses of the UN Charter on two occasions.[42] In a remarkable passage, the ICJ declared that conduct by a state, which violates the fundamental rights of individuals, is contrary to the principles of the UN Charter. In this way, the Court confirmed that respect for the human rights clauses of the UN Charter is an important substantive obligation among all other obligations undertaken by states under this legal instrument. As mentioned above, in the *Tehran Hostages* case, the court asserted that to wrongfully deprive human beings of their freedom and to subject them to physical constraints in conditions of hardship is in itself manifestly incompatible with the principles of the UN Charter, as well as with the fundamental principles enunciated in the UDHR.[43] Further, in the advisory opinion on Namibia concerning the actions of South Africa, the court held that 'denial of fundamental human rights is a flagrant violation of the purposes and principles of the [UN] Charter'.[44] Certainly, these findings point to the obligations incumbent upon states under both the UN Charter and the UDHR to respect the human rights of individuals.

The court's clarification of what constitutes customary international law carries evident relevance in the assessment of the possible achievement by certain human rights principles of the status of customary international law. In the *North Sea Continental Shelf* cases, the ICJ held that for a rule to qualify as part of customary international law it has be supported by an extensive and virtually uniform state practice. This process should have occurred in such a way so as to show the involvement of a general recognition of a rule of law or legal obligation.[45] Consequently, the recognition of many principles of human rights, such as the prohibition of genocide, torture, slavery and racial discrimination, as part of customary international law, is strengthened by the findings of the court. Evidently, the conclusion of the process of solidifying of these principles of human rights into becoming part of customary international law is based, *inter alia*, on the strength of the civilizing power these principles embody – a strength stemming from the more general principle of elementary considerations of humanity.

While considering the relationship between customary and treaty law in the context of the sources of international law, the court stated, 'Even if two norms belonging to two sources of international law appear identical in content, and even if the States in question are bound by these rules both on the level of treaty-law and on that of customary international law, these norms retain a separate existence.'[46] Therefore, human rights principles, which have achieved the status of customary international law, such as the prohibition of torture, the prohibition of genocide, and so on, are to be respected as part of the obligations a state has under customary international law, besides the obligations undertaken by a state under the relevant international human rights instruments. This finding is very important for the system of international protection of human

42 Namely the *Hostages* case (US *v* Iran), ICJ Reports 1980, p. 42, para. 91, and the Advisory Opinion on *Legal Consequences for States of the Continued Presence of South Africa in Namibia (South-West Africa) notwithstanding Security Council Resolution 276 (1970)*, ICJ Reports 1971, p. 57, para. 13.

43 *Hostages* case (US *v* Iran), Judgement of 24 May 1980, ICJ Reports 1980, p. 42, para. 91.

44 ICJ, *Legal Consequences for States of the Continued Presence of South Africa in Namibia (South-West Africa) Notwithstanding Security Council Resolution 276 (1970)*, Advisory Opinion of 21 June 1971, ICJ Reports 1971, p. 57, para. 131.

45 ICJ, *North Sea Continental Shelf* (Federal Republic of Germany *v*. Denmark, Federal Republic of Germany *v*. The Netherlands), Judgment, ICJ Reports 1969, p. 44, para. 77; see also the *Nicaragua* case (*Merits*), ICJ Reports 1986, pp. 97–8, para. 184.

46 *Nicaragua* case (*Merits*), ICJ Reports 1986, para. 178.

rights, as the separate existence of customary and treaty law rules or principles ensure a double-layered obligation to respect these human rights. That enhances, considerably, the protection accruing to individuals under international human rights law.

The court's contribution to developing and interpreting rules and principles of international law of human rights can be briefly, though not exhaustively, summarized as follows:

1. The human rights clauses of the UN Charter contain binding legal obligations (*South West Africa* cases and *Tehran Hostages* case).
2. The principles and rules of international law concerning the fundamental rights of the human beings engender obligations *erga omnes* (*Barcelona Traction* case).
3. The right of peoples to self-determination is a right which has an *erga omnes* character under international law (*Western Sahara*, *East Timor*, and *Legal Consequences of the Construction of a Wall in the Occupied Palestinian Territory*).
4. Seemingly, not only international human rights treaties, but also other international instruments, such as the 1963 Vienna Convention on Consular Relations, create individual rights for natural persons (*LaGrand* and *Avena and other Mexican Nationals* cases).
5. The protection afforded to individuals under international human rights instruments does not cease in situations of armed conflict except for derogations of the kind to the found under Article 4 of the ICCPR (*Legal Consequences of the Construction of a Wall in the Occupied Palestinian Territory* and *Armed Activities* cases (DRC v Uganda)).
6. The substantive obligations arising under Articles I (prevent and punish genocide) and III of the 1948 Genocide Convention are not on their face limited by territory, and state responsibility can arise under the convention for genocide and complicity, without an individual being convicted of this crime or an associated one (*Application of the Genocide Convention* (Bosnia–Herzegovina v Serbia and Montenegro)).
7. Immunity does not mean impunity; therefore, perpetrators of gross violations of human rights can be held accountable either before domestic courts or before international courts (*Arrest Warrant* case (DRC v Belgium)).

Obviously, the court's position, as expressed through its case law, is that fundamental human rights, as provided for in several international human rights instruments, are to be respected and promoted by all states for they have a civilizing and humanitarian character. This conclusion is reinforced by the fact that the court itself introduced the concept of 'obligations *erga omnes*' in its judgement in the *Barcelona Traction* case, emphasizing the interest of the international community in ensuring respect for certain fundamental human rights.[47] The importance for the international law of human rights of these two concepts, namely that of 'elementary considerations of humanity' and that of 'obligations *erga omnes*' cannot be overemphasized, for, together, they provide a basic, but solid foundation for the human rights protection system. It can be said that these two concepts represent the essence of international human rights law.

The importance of international human rights law instruments and the work of their monitoring bodies in ensuring better protection of human rights worldwide has been acknowledged and utilized by the court in several of its judgements and advisory opinions. Its remarkably important findings with regard to the applicability of these instruments and the legal consequences of their application with regard to states and the UN, and also to the rights accruing to individuals, are an important contribution of the court to international human rights law. However, despite calls from

47 *Barcelona Traction* case (*Merits*), judgement of 5 February 1970, ICJ Reports 1970, p. 32, para. 33.

civil society for a better use of such international instruments in order to bring perpetrators of gross violations of human rights to justice, there is also a fear, expressed even by members of the court, of what is commonly referred to as a 'cacophony of voices'.[48] Far from a cacophony of voices, a proper application of these instruments at the domestic level would bring about an improved and strong culture of respect for human rights.

Under the court's case law it has been established not only that states should respect human rights, but also that states have an obligation under international law to ensure respect for human rights. Long ago the court found that the physical control of a territory, and not sovereignty or legitimacy of title, is the basis of state liability for wrongful acts affecting other states.[49] In the *Barcelona Traction* case, the ICJ pointed out that enforcement mechanisms established by treaty are a means to ensure respect for human rights regardless of nationality.[50] The incorporation of human rights in international treaties is in itself a reflection of the growing awareness of the need to address social inequalities at a worldwide level. The formation of worldwide human rights networks and the media have brought to the fore several issues which need to be addressed such as redress for victims of wars, child labour, the disabled, the rights of indigenous people and so on. Through its case law, the court has rendered its contribution to the strengthening of this movement. Further, it has, on several occasions, clarified that human rights rapporteurs while on duty enjoy immunity and that states are under a duty to assist them to the maximum extent possible and respect their immunity from judicial proceedings.

Quite a few cases have been brought before the court on the basis of diplomatic protection. Besides acknowledging the protection accruing to individuals on the basis of the 1961 Vienna Convention on Diplomatic Relations,[51] a protection having a strong basis in customary law, the court seems to have taken a broader view by referring to the other layer of the protection of diplomatic personnel which they enjoy as every other human being under the principles of the UN Charter and certain international human rights instruments, including the UDHR.[52] Cases relating to consular relations, such as *Breard*, *LaGrand* and *Avena*, are a distinct subgroup of cases brought under diplomatic protection. While the latter is a right of a state, the right to consular assistance has a dual nature as it is a right of a state to assist its national, but also an individual right of the individual concerned to receive such assistance, creating obligations owed to both the state and the individual, as the court itself has acknowledged. In the operative paragraph of the *LaGrand* case, the court stated that by not informing the LaGrand brothers about their rights under the Vienna Convention on Consular Relations, Article 36, paragraph 1(b), the USA breached its obligations to Germany *and to the LaGrand brothers* (emphasis added).[53] Thus, with regard to the

---

48 See Separate Opinion of President Guillame, *Arrest Warrant* case (DRC *v* Belgium), ICJ Reports 2002, p. 43, para. 15. There he stated: 'International criminal courts have been created. But at no time has it been envisaged that jurisdiction should be conferred upon the courts of every State in the world to prosecute such crimes, whoever their authors and victims and irrespective of the place where the offender is to be found. *To do this would, moreover, risk creating total judicial chaos* [emphasis added]. It would also be to encourage the arbitrary for the benefit of the powerful, purportedly acting as agent for an ill-defined "international community". Contrary to what is advocated by certain publicists, such a development would represent not an advance in the law but a step backward.'

49 ICJ, *Legal Consequences for States of the Continued Presence of South Africa in Namibia (South-West Africa) Notwithstanding Security Council Resolution 276 (1970)*, Advisory Opinion of 21 June 1971, ICJ Reports 1971, p. 54, para. 118.

50 *Barcelona Traction* case (*Merits*), ICJ Reports 1970, p. 47, para. 91.

51 500 UNTS 95.

52 *Tehran Hostages* case (US *v* Iran), ICJ Reports 1980, p. 42, para. 91.

53 *LaGrand* case (Germany *v* United States of America) (*Merits*), ICJ Reports 2001, p. 514, para. 128.

right to consular assistance the court has at one point acknowledged that the Vienna Convention on Consular Relations creates individual rights.

6. Conclusion

As mentioned above, the jurisprudence of the ICJ in the field of international human rights law encompasses many important issues for international human rights law, starting with the internationalization of human rights; the coining of certain fundamental principles of international human rights law; the characterization of the right of peoples to self-determination as a right *erga omnes*;[54] the interpretation of the prohibition of genocide as including an obligation to prevent genocide;[55] the clarifications on the right to asylum, and the diplomatic and consular relations cases;[56] the protection to be awarded to human rights rapporteurs in order for them to fulfil their duty when in the service of the UN;[57] the applicability of international human rights instruments in situations of armed conflict; clarifications on the issue of individual criminal responsibility for internationally recognized crimes; and, although not discussed here, some important pronouncements on environmental issues.[58] Although not dealt with here, environmental issues are prone to come before the court more often in the years to come, especially in the form of trans-border environmental hazards or trans-border pollution. Certainly, given that the quality of the environment affects our quality of life and because states are interdependent in preserving the environment from further deterioration, the right to a clean environment is likely to receive increased attention.[59]

That famous pronouncement in the *Barcelona Traction* case on the *erga omnes* character of certain basic human rights was to lay the foundation both for a huge development in the field of human rights and for their central place in international relations.[60] It is a truism that the ICJ's

---

54 See the following cases: *South-West Africa Cases*; *Western Sahara*; *East Timor*; *Legal Consequences of the Construction of a Wall in the Occupied Palestinian Territory*.

55 See the following cases: *Application of the Convention on the Prevention and Punishment of the Crime of Genocide* (Bosnia-Herzegovina *v* Serbia and Montenegro); *Application of the Convention on the Prevention and Punishment of the Crime of Genocide* (Croatia *v* Serbia and Montenegro); *Application for Revision of the Judgment of 11 July 1996 in the Case concerning Application of the Convention on the Prevention and Punishment of the Crime of Genocide (Bosnia–Herzegovina* v *Serbia and Montenegro)*, Preliminary Objections (Serbia and Montenegro *v* Bosnia and Herzegovina)

56 *Case Concerning the Vienna Convention on Consular Relations* (Paraguay *v* United States of America); *Ahmadou Sadio Diallo* case (Republic of Guinea *v* Democratic Republic of the Congo); *LaGrand* case (Germany *v* United States of America); *Case Concerning Avena and Other Mexican Nationals* (Mexico *v* United States of America).

57 *Reparation for Injuries*; *Applicability of Article VI, Section 22, of the Convention on the Privileges and Immunities of the United Nations* (Advisory Opinion of 15 December 1989); and *Difference Relating to Immunity from Legal Process of a Special Rapporteur of the Commission on Human Rights* (Advisory Opinion of 29 April 1999).

58 *Legality of Threat or Use of Nuclear Weapons*, ICJ Reports 1996, pp. 241–3, paras. 27–33.

59 See Chapter 6 in this volume.

60 The court in the *Barcelona Traction* case held that the obligations of a state towards the international community are obligations *erga omnes*, noting that 'Such obligations derive, for example, in contemporary international law from ... principles and rules concerning the basic rights of the human person, including protection from slavery and racial discrimination. Some of the corresponding rights of protection have entered into the body of general international law ... others are conferred by international instruments of a universal

contribution stands also in that it has read and interpreted international law instruments according to the dictates of human rights.

> It is self-evident that no system of law can depend for its operation or development on specific prohibitions *ipsissimis verbis*. Any developed system of law has, in addition to its specific commands and prohibitions, an array of general principles which from time to time are applied to specific items of conduct or events which have not been the subject of an express ruling before. The general principle is then applied to the specific situation and out of that particular application a rule of greater specificity emerges.[61]

By relying upon or coining concepts such as elementary considerations of humanity, the sacred trust of civilization, and obligations *erga omnes*, the ICJ has contributed in a larger sense to the creation of a worldwide common culture of respect for human rights and human dignity. The underlying idea behind these concepts is that whenever human rights are violated our common humanity is targeted, and thus every state has, simultaneously, the right and the duty to take action to address the wrongdoing. Further, as Ragazzi has pointed out, the court has generally adopted a 'value-oriented' approach;[62] an approach which aims at giving certain fundamental human rights the maximum legal support.

Human rights are a rare and valuable intellectual and moral resource in the struggle to right the balance between society (and the state) and the individual.[63] The implementation of human rights principles is a struggle that is carried on in different arenas and levels. Although the ICJ is not a forum where individuals themselves can bring their claims, it is, nevertheless, a judicial body that has offered and can offer its contribution to furthering the human rights cause through a twofold function. First, through interpreting and developing rules and principles of international human rights law, the court enforces and further clarifies this part of international law. Second, by keeping the fabric of international law together, it can ensure a better interaction between the different branches of international law in order to achieve an optimum protection of human rights within the framework of international law. It can be said that through its pronouncements the ICJ has helped in the creation of an environment more conducive to the realization of full enjoyment of human rights worldwide. Further, the increased involvement of the UN Security Council in putting a stop to human rights violations, the emergence of the doctrine of 'responsibility to protect', and the increased sensitivity and willingness by states to deal with gross human rights violations are some of the factors which can eventually lead to a further increase in the court's involvement and thus its contribution to the interpretation and development of human rights rules and principles.

---

or quasi-universal character as a whole.' See *Barcelona Traction*, judgement of 5 February 1970, ICJ Reports 1970, p. 32, para. 33.

61 *Legality of the Threat or Use of Nuclear Weapons*, Dissenting Opinion of Judge Weeramantry, ICJ Reports, 1996, p. 493.

62 M. Ragazzi, *The Concept of International Obligations Erga Omnes* (Oxford: Oxford University Press, 1997), p. 72.

63 J. Donnelly, 'Human Rights, Individual Rights and Collective Rights', in Jan Bertin *et al*., *Human Rights in a Pluralist World: Individuals and Collectivities* (London: Meckler, 1990), p. 49.

Appendix 15.1 List of Cases Submitted to the International Court of Justice Relating to International Human Rights Law Since 1991

No.	Parties	Name of the case	Year of filing
1.	Portugal *v* Australia	*East Timor*	1991
2.	Bosnia–Herzegovina *v* Serbia and Montenegro	*Application of the Convention on the Prevention and Punishment of the Crime of Genocide*	1993
3.	World Health Organization (Advisory Opinion)	*Legality of the Use by a State of Nuclear Weapons in Armed Conflicts*	1993
4.	General Assembly (Advisory Opinion)	*Legality of the Threat or Use of Nuclear Weapons*	1995
5.	Paraguay *v* United States of America	*Vienna Convention on Consular Relations*	1998
6.	Economic and Social Council (Advisory Opinion)	*Difference Relating to Immunity from Legal Process of a Special Rapporteur of the Commission on Human Rights*	1998
7.	Republic of Guinea *v* Democratic Republic of the Congo	*Ahmadou Sadio Diallo*	1998
8.	Germany *v* United States of America	*LaGrand*	1999
9.	Serbia and Montenegro *v* 10 NATO countries	*Legality of Use of Force* (10 cases)	1999
10.	Democratic Republic of the Congo *v* Burundi	*Armed Activities on the Territory of the Congo*	1999
11.	Democratic Republic of the Congo *v* Rwanda	*Armed Activities on the Territory of the Congo*	1999
12.	Democratic Republic of the Congo *v* Uganda	*Armed Activities on the Territory of the Congo*	1999
13.	Croatia *v* Serbia	*Application of the Convention on the Prevention and Punishment of the Crime of Genocide*	1999
14.	Democratic Republic of the Congo *v* Belgium	*Arrest Warrant of 11 April 2000*	2000
15.	Liechtenstein *v* Germany	*Certain Property*	2001
16.	Democratic Republic of the Congo *v* Rwanda	*Armed Activities on the Territory of the Congo (New Application : 2002)*	2002
17.	Mexico *v* United States of America	*Avena and Other Mexican Nationals*	2003
18.	Republic of the Congo *v* France	*Certain Criminal Proceedings in France*	2003
19.	General Assembly (Advisory Opinion)	*Legal Consequences of the Construction of a Wall in the Occupied Palestinian Territory*	2003

20.	Ecuador *v* Colombia	*Aerial Herbicide Spraying*	2008
21.	Mexico *v* United States of America	*Request for Interpretation of the Judgment of 31 March 2004 in the Case concerning Avena and Other Mexican Nationals*	2008
22.	Georgia *v* Russian Federation	*Application of the International Convention on the Elimination of All Forms of Racial Discrimination*	2008
23.	Jurisdictional Immunities of the State	*Proceedings instituted by the Federal Republic of Germany Against the Italian Republic*	2008
24.	General Assembly (Advisory Opinion)	*Accordance with International Law of the Unilateral Declaration of Independence by the Provisional Institutions of Self-Government of Kosovo*	2008
25.	Belgium *v* Senegal	*Questions relating to the Obligation to Prosecute or Extradite*	2009

Chapter 16
The Role of National Human Rights Institutions

Rachel Murray

1. Introduction

When the UDHR[1] was adopted in 1948 the main actors on the international human rights stage were states, with other players getting only brief mention in the preamble.[2] Contrast the recognition in 1993 at the Vienna World Conference to 'the important and constructive role played by national institutions for the promotion and protection of Human Rights' and the need for states to establish them,[3] and then, later, to the direct reference by the United Nations (UN) High Commissioner for Human Rights to National Human Rights Institutions (NHRIs) as part of the 60th anniversary of the UDHR and their role in prevention of torture.[4] Statements such as those from the UN Secretary-General in March 2008 that 'NHRIs compliant with the Paris Principles are key elements of strong and effective national human rights protection systems. They can also be important partners in the international human rights system, especially through the Human Rights Council, the human rights treaty bodies and special procedures mandate holders',[5] reflect the significant role that NHRIs are perceived now to play in the human rights field.

We are now at a position where NHRIs occupy as important a position as states, NGOs and international bodies, in drafting treaties and other international documents, having separate standing before the UN and regional bodies, submitting *amicus* briefs before regional human rights courts,[6] and forming influential groups at the international and regional levels. Yet, with this recognition comes an understanding of the unique and powerful position these types of bodies hold and a need to consider more their accountability and separate status from governments and civil society. While their position as actors appears to have been clearly established on the international plane, there are still many unanswered questions about who exactly should be permitted to be involved and whether the checks and balances in place at present are sufficient.

1 GA Res. 217A (III), UN Doc. A/810 at 71 (1948).

2 'Every individual and every organ of society … shall strive by teaching and education to promote respect for these rights and freedoms'; preamble, UDHR.

3 Vienna Declaration and Programme of Action, 12 July 1993, UN Doc. A/CONF.157/23, at para. 36.

4 Resolution 2005/74, para. 9. Statement on the Universal Declaration of Human Rights 60th Anniversary Initiatives, Ms Kyung-wha Kang, UN Deputy High Commissioner for Human Rights, ICC 20th Session, April 2008, Geneva, Draft Report of the Twentieth Session of the International Coordinating Committee of National Institutions for the Promotion and Protection of Human Rights (ICC) [online]. Available from: http://nhri.net/2008/ICC20_Final_Record_of_Proceedings.DOC.

5 United Nations, Report of the Secretary-General on National Institutions for the Promotion and Protection of Human Rights to the Human Rights Council, UN Doc.A/HRC/7/69, para. 81.

6 For example, the European Group of National Human Rights Institutions was involved as a third party in a case before the European Court of Human Rights – see Draft Report of the Twentieth Session of the International Coordinating Committee of National Institutions for the Promotion and Protection of Human Rights (ICC), Geneva, 14–18 April 2008, p. 7 [online]. Available from: www.nhri.net [accessed 18 July 2010].

This chapter will examine the place now occupied by NHRIs in the international human rights arena, and focus on three emerging themes that are important to consider in relation to their future role.

2. What Are National Human Rights Institutions?

The term 'national human rights institution' (NHRI) has been defined as 'a body which is established by a government under the constitution, or by law or decree, the functions of which are specifically defined in terms of the promotion and protection of human rights'.[7] It can refer to a number of different institutions: human rights commissions or commissioners, ombudspersons or hybrid bodies, although ombudspersons are only properly being considered under this heading more recently.[8] The Paris Principles, adopted in 1993 by the UN General Assembly,[9] are seen as the checklist against which these types of bodies are assessed. These principles refer to the need for the institution to be independent, that members be appointed through an appropriate process, and that the institution have independent funding and a stable mandate. A NHRI should also have 'as broad a mandate as possible' and have a range of responsibilities including advising government and other bodies, making recommendations on existing or proposed legislation, preparing reports on violations, encouraging ratification of international instruments, contributing to reports submitted to the UN or other bodies, cooperating with international bodies, and promoting, educating and publicizing on human rights issues.

The Paris Principles, despite being a non-binding UN General Assembly Resolution, are now the benchmark applied to the variety of bodies at the national, regional and international levels, almost to the extent that, despite their being soft law, compliance with them is determinative of a range of rights and privileges then accorded to that institution. Yet, there is now a growing body of evidence and research which finds that compliance with the Paris Principles alone will not guarantee an effective or even independent institution and that what is needed is a more nuanced and sophisticated approach to an evaluation of the role of a NHRI.[10] These include the need to examine the broader context in which they exist, the extent to which they use their powers and resources appropriately and to the full, how they are perceived by others, and their credibility and legitimacy.[11] But the international system has still to catch up. UN and regional bodies are

---

7 United Nations, *National Human Rights Institutions. A Handbook on the Establishment and Strengthening of National Institutions for the Promotion and Protection of Human Rights*, Professional Training Series No. 4, 1995, at para. 39.

8 L.C. Reif, 'Building Democratic Institutions: The Role of National Human Rights Institutions in Good Governance and Human Rights Protection', *Harvard Human Rights Journal*, 13 (2000), pp. 1–59.

9 Principles relating to the Status and Functioning of National Institutions for the Protection and Promotion of Human Rights (the Paris Principles), Resolution 1992/54, as endorsed by the General Assembly Resolution 48/134 of 20 December 1993, Annex.

10 International Council on Human Rights Policy, *Performance and Legitimacy: National Human Rights Institutions*, ICHRP, Geneva, 2000; International Council on Human Rights Policy, *Assessing the Effectiveness of National Human Rights Institutions*, ICHRP, Office of the High Commissioner for Human Rights, Geneva, 2005; S. Livingstone and R. Murray, 'The Effectiveness of National Human Rights Institutions', in S. Halliday and P. Schmidt (eds), *Human Rights Brought Home: Socio-Legal Perspectives on Human Rights in the National Context* (Oxford: Hart Publishing, 2004).

11 See all works cited in note 10 above.

continuing to propound the idea that all states should establish a human rights commission[12] and that as long as the Paris Principles are complied with, this is sufficient to ensure an independent, effective and appropriate body.

The role of NHRIs is an interesting one, as their potential contribution comes from the fact that they are neither governmental, nor non-governmental bodies.[13] In reality, they sit in the uneasy ground between what are often seen as opposing factions in the human rights arena, with some erring more on the government side, some towards the NGOs. The need for them to have a clearly defined role that separates them from, on the one hand, the governments they were supposed to be watching and, on the other, the non-statutory and constitutional bodies, has gained increasing importance as NHRIs have sought to affirm their status at national and international fora.

NHRIs have formed a range of groupings, some of which have become increasingly important and influential. At the level of the UN, NHRIs meet under the International Coordinating Committee (ICC) of NHRIs, a forum representing their interests. Article 5 of its statute states that the role of the ICC is 'an international association of NHRIs which promotes and strengthens NHRIs to be in accordance with the Paris Principles and provides leadership in the promotion and protection of human rights'. The ICC was established in 1994 and since then has gained more credibility and status. It is now supported by a secretariat at the UN Office of the High Commissioner for Human Rights (OHCHR) and the National Institutions Unit, and through its work and presence and the recognition of the Unit, it has developed a profile for these institutions throughout the UN structures. It has recently registered itself as a non-governmental entity in Geneva under Swiss law.[14] Its tasks include coordinating NHRI activities with the UN bodies, collaborating with NHRIs, and providing communication and information sharing among them as well as good practice.[15] Yet, it also has a role expressly provided in its statute now to 'promote the establishment and strengthening of NHRIs in conformity with the Paris Principles', through processes of accreditation, by providing assistance and training.[16] The ICC also now has a presence in Geneva, which, it is hoped, will facilitate the relationship between the ICC and UN bodies.

NHRIs have also grouped themselves together both under the regional groupings of the ICC and in other fora, some of which are more active than others. The Asia-Pacific Forum on National Human Rights Institutions is the most prominent and visible of these regional groupings, with a secretariat based in Sydney, Australia. It has spearheaded a significant amount of work on NHRIs including, more recently, on the UN Convention on Disabilities[17] and has assisted in

12 E.g. Committee on the Rights of the Child, General Comment No. 2, The Role of Independent National Human Rights Institutions in the Promotion and Protection of the Rights of the Child, HRI/GEN/1/Rev.7, at para. 2. See also Committee on the Elimination of Racial Discrimination, Concluding Observations on Egypt, 59th Session, A/56/18, para. 292.

13 See R. Murray, *The Role of National Human Rights Institutions at the International and Regional Levels: Lessons from Africa* (Oxford: Hart Publishing, 2008).

14 Statute of the International Coordinating Committee of National Human Rights Institutions, adopted Nairobi, October 2008 [online]. Available from: www.nhri.net.

15 Article 7(1), ICC Statute.

16 Article 7(2) ICC Statute.

17 E.g. Asia-Pacific Forum, Annual Conference, Disability Issues Paper, 12th Annual Meeting of the APF, Sydney, Australia, 24–27 September 2007 [online]. Available from: http://www.asiapacificforum.net/about/annual-meetings/12th-australia-2007/downloads/disability-issues/Disability%20Issues%20Paper.pdf [accessed 18 July 2010].

pushing forward the role of NHRIs on a formal basis at the international level. The Coordinating Committee of African National Human Rights Institutions has been less active, although it does have a secretariat, based in Kenya, and its meetings have produced some important declarations.[18] An additional network of West African NHRIs has also been created.[19] For the Americas, there is a Network of National Human Rights Institutions for the Americas and networks of ombudsmen,[20] and, in Europe, a European Coordinating Committee of NHRIs and European Group of National Human Rights Institutions have also held a number of events including various roundtables.

It is through these various groupings, in particular the ICC, that NHRIs have managed to use their collective weight to give themselves greater formal recognition and a status separate from those of governments and NGOs. While NHRIs used to sit with governments or NGOs at UN committee meetings and in other sessions, with the changes brought about by the work of the ICC, as will be described below, NHRIs now have a separate standing and are able to participate in their own right, with specific seating at these international and regional meetings.

Regionally, the African Commission on Human and Peoples' Rights has recognized NHRIs with its creation of the category of 'affiliated status' open to application by NHRIs who comply with the Paris Principles.[21] Applications are assessed by commissioners in open forum, and NHRIs have to provide paperwork including the legislative documents establishing them, a financial statement, and a recent activity report and its composition.[22] In return, they may participate in the sessions of the commission and make statements, and they are obliged to submit reports every two years on their activities in this regard. Although this sounds like a relatively sophisticated approach on paper, and over 20 NHRIs have made use of this affiliated status category, in reality few actually participate in the African Commission's sessions or attend its meetings. The Commission in turn has not felt it necessary to challenge those who have such status to engage more fully with it, and it has never held NHRIs to account for their total failure to submit any reports. As a result, although the potential for its use is there, at this stage the African Commission cannot be said to have contributed a great deal to the debate at the African level.

The Asia-Pacific Forum (APF), operating in a region which does not have a human rights treaty, has spent considerable time in developing its approach to membership. There are three categories of membership: full, candidate and associate.[23] Full members are those that are deemed by the Forum Council to comply with the Paris Principles. As the ICC develops its more robust approach to accreditation, however, the APF is bringing its approach more in line with that of the ICC.

---

18 E.g. Abuja Declaration, Fifth Conference of African National Human Rights Institutions, Abuja, Nigeria, 8–10 November 2005.

19 See 'ECOWAS Establishes a Network of African NHRIs in West Africa', 13 November 2006 [online]. Available from: http://www.nhri.net/news.asp?ID=1084 [accessed 10 December 2008].

20 E.g. Ibero American Federation of the Ombudsman (FIO) and Ombudsnet.

21 African Commission on Human and Peoples' Rights, Resolution on Granting Observer Status to National Human Rights Institutions, African Commission on Human and Peoples' Rights, 1998.

22 See Murray, note 13 above, p. 84.

23 Asia Pacific Forum of National Human Rights Institutions, Constitution [online]. Available from: http://www.asiapacificforum.net/about/governance/downloads/constitution.pdf.

3. Emerging Issues

Given the increased recognition of NHRIs, a number of challenges and issues have also arisen.

3.1 Accreditation

Because of the unique position NHRIs occupy, being neither government nor NGO, but a possible additional voice in international and regional fora, over the years greater attention has been paid to the need to accredit or assess these NHRIs against some form of benchmark. The Paris Principles have been used as the criteria against which these institutions are assessed in order to determine the level of their involvement in international bodies in particular, but also at the regional level. The ICC set up a Sub-Committee on Accreditation, whose task is to assess applications from NHRIs. It is composed of one NHRI from each of four regions: Europe, Africa, Americas and Asia-Pacific.[24] With the replacement of the Human Rights Commission by the Human Rights Council and the general process of reform in the UN, the ICC used the opportunity of change to assert the role of NHRIs and ensure their formal recognition before the UN Human Rights Council and many of the treaty bodies.[25] Over recent years, there have been a number of changes made to the way in which NHRIs are accredited[26] with the aim of ensuring 'transparency, rigour and independence'.[27]

An NHRI applying for accreditation must produce a number of written documents including the legislation or document by which the NHRI was established, its organizational structure, staff and budget, a copy of its recent annual report, and 'a detailed statement showing that the organization complies with the Paris Principles'.[28] This statement of compliance covers a range of issues including its pluralist representation, the manner in which its members are appointed, its relationship with civil society and others including UN bodies, its working methods, and how it is accessible. The National Institutions Unit of the OHCHR, acting as the secretariat to the ICC, will receive this documentation, and it is also now permitted to seek information from civil society and other actors, including OHCHR field missions, to give alternative views on the compliance of the NHRIs with the Paris Principles. The National Institutions Unit produces a summary document which is presented to the Sub-Committee on Accreditation, and the NHRI is given the opportunity to comment on its contents. This has introduced a more objective analysis into the process of accreditation compared to previously when it was only information submitted by the NHRI itself that was taken into account in the accreditation process.

Two categories of accreditation can be granted: (A) compliance with the Paris Principles; (B) observer status – not fully in compliance with the Paris Principles or insufficient information

24 Rules of Procedure of the ICC Sub-Committee on Accreditation, para. 2.

25 E.g. 17th Session of the International Coordinating Committee of NHRIs, Agenda item 9a–9d. The Role of NHRIs in the UN System. Discussion Paper on NHRIs in UN Reform Process [online]. Available from: www.nhri.net [accessed 18 July 2010].

26 See Decision Paper on the Review of ICC Accreditation Procedures for National Human Rights Institutions (NHRI) of March 2008 [online]. Available from: www.nhri.net [accessed 10 December 2008].

27 *Ibid.*, p. 5.

28 Guidelines for Accreditation and Re-Accreditation of National Human Rights Institutions to the International Coordinating Committee of National Human Rights Institutions, Version 3 – April 2008, para. 2.

provided to make a determination.[29] Each NHRI is now reviewed every 5 years or when necessary if there is a change of circumstances.

The ICC managed to attain the position before the former UN Human Rights Commission whereby 'national institutions that are accredited by the Accreditation Subcommittee of the International Coordinating Committee ... under the auspices of the UN Office of the High Commissioner, and coordinating committees of such institutions, are permitted 'to speak ... within their mandates, under all items of the Commission's agenda ... to allocate dedicated seating to national institutions for this purpose...'.[30] In adopting the approach that 'participation of and consultation with observers, including ... national human rights institutions ... shall be based on arrangements and practices observed by the Commission on Human Rights',[31] NHRIs have now consolidated this standing before the Human Rights Council on the basis that 'accreditation of national institutions in international forums could be commensurate with the institution's accreditation to the ICC'.[32]

Now only those NHRIs who have category 'A' accreditation can address the Human Rights Council, and it is apparent that the UN treaty bodies and others take the accreditation very seriously.[33] Indeed, as a result of the changes to the accreditation process, a number of NHRIs have been downgraded from category A to B status.[34]

This process, although it is vastly improved from previously, still has a number of difficulties with it. Firstly, just because a NHRI can fulfil the Paris Principles does not mean that it will be effective or even independent on the ground. In contrast, even those that appear not to fulfil Paris Principles criteria can still be champions of human rights. The ICC accreditation process at present does not take into account the effectiveness of the institutions, but simply their compliance with the Paris Principles. Secondly, this is still peer review. Although civil society can give some input now, it is still NHRIs making assessments on other NHRIs. While the new process does seem to have

29 Two additional categories were available in the past: A (R), accreditation with reservation, and C, not compliant, Rules of Procedure of the International Coordinating Committee of National Human Rights Institutions Sub-Committee on Accreditation, as adopted by members of the International Coordinating Committee at its 15th Session, Seoul, Republic of Korea, 14 September 2004, para. 5. Since 2006 and 2008, respectively, these categories are no longer used by the ICC.

30 Human Rights Commission, Resolution National Institutions for the Promotion and Protection of Human Rights, Resolution 2005/74, para. 11(a).

31 Resolution of the General Assembly, UN Doc. A/RES/60/251, at para. 11.

32 Process Currently Utilised by the International Coordinating Committee to Accredit National Human Rights Institutions in Compliance with the Paris Principles and Ensure That the Process Is Strengthened with Appropriate Periodic Review and on Ways and Means of Enhancing Participation of National Human Rights Institutions in the Work of the Commission, Report of the Secretary-General, 25 January 2006, UN Doc. E/CN.4/2006/102, para. 22.

33 See Conclusions of the International Roundtable on the Role of National Human Rights Institutions and Treaty Bodies (Berlin, 23 and 24 November 2006), UN Doc. HRI/MC/2007/3.

34 The Human Rights Commission of Sri Lanka (A status placed under review in March 2007, reviewed in October 2007); Commission Nationale des Droits de l'Homme of Burkina Faso, reviewed March 2007, A(R) status; Cameroon's National Commission on Human Rights and Freedoms, previous A status, reviewed October 2006 to B status. Nigerian Human Rights Commission, placed under review in March 2007, from A to B. Slovakia National Centre for Human Rights, B Status, reviewed October 2007. Madagascar, Commission Nationale des Droits de l'Homme de Madagascar, A status withdrawn in April 2006, reviewed October 2006, now C. See Chart of the Status of National Institutions Accredited by the International Coordinating Committee of National Institutions for the Promotion and Protection of Human Rights, Annex I, A/HRC/7/70 [online]. Available from: www.nhri.net [accessed 18 July 2010].

become more robust and has downgraded some NHRIs, as it is still a process primarily of peer review, it cannot be as objective as many would wish it to be. Thirdly, there is still considerable mismatch with the process adopted by the ICC and that adopted regionally. Although some of the regional bodies are now moving away from their own system of accreditation based on the belief that this ICC system is sufficient on its own,[35] this is not the case with all of them. The African Commission is less robust in ensuring its system of consideration fits with that of the ICC. In assessing applications for affiliated status, for example, it is clear that African Commissioners do have comments and concerns from NGOs and others before them, but they have seemed reluctant to engage in an in-depth critical examination of the institution and on some occasions have granted affiliated status to an institution which at that time had not acquired accreditation by the ICC.[36]

In addition, even though ICC accreditation is now taken as the licence for participation in UN bodies, UN committees and institutions still differ in their approach to NHRIs. There is still the assumption made by some that all states need a NHRI and that a government that decides to select one is doing the right thing. In fact, whether a NHRI is necessary or even desirable in a state is a question that must be determined by a detailed examination of the situation in any given country. This takes us to the next issue.

3.2 Range of Bodies

In one state there may be a range of different constitutional or statutory bodies that are supposed to be independent and fulfil a watchdog function over government. These may range from a prison ombudsman, public or parliamentary ombudsman, commissioners with a specific mandate, such as information commissioners and children's commissioners, to human rights commissions or commissioners. It may be that some states do not need a human rights commission if there is a range of other bodies that fulfil the broader functions of promoting and protecting human rights. In addition, the political climate may be such that to create a human rights commission would be counterproductive, taking funding and other resources away from civil society organizations who are carrying out the necessary functions effectively, or other statutory or constitutional bodies who are already embedded within the system. A newly created human rights commission may then become simply another mouthpiece for government. Yet some UN committees and regional bodies are still pushing states to create a human rights commission where none exist, without proper consideration of the influences and difficulties this may raise or the need for them to operate in the first place.

In part, this drive for more human rights commissions seems to be based on the presumption that human rights commissions are different types of institutions from, say, ombudsmen or theme-specific commissions, or commissioners, such as a children's commissioner or parliamentary commission. Indeed, they are. But, conversely, when it comes to assessing and considering and accrediting these institutions at the international level, they are all treated the same. The ICC, for example, has by and large dealt with applications from human rights commissions, although it has now started to take more applications from ombudspersons. It is clear that it treats them the same. Similarly, commissioners are treated the same as commissions, and the international and regional bodies treat those with broader mandates (e.g. such as the Commission on Human Rights and Administrative Justice (CHRAJ) in Ghana) the same as those with more narrow functions (e.g. public defenders). But, in practice, there are some important differences between these various institutions that need further exploration and research. For example, a human rights commissioner,

35 This is the approach now being taken by the Asia Pacific Forum.

36 See Murray, note 13 above, pp. 83–4.

headed by a single individual who acts as the public face of the institution, will have its legitimacy and credibility inevitably assessed in part by the reputation of that particular individual. A human rights commission, on the other hand, composed of a number of individuals who front the organization, has a range of people on which to base its reputation and also to give the impression of representativeness. This plurality is more difficult to achieve if only one individual is visible.

Similarly, as noted above, although ombudspersons have not always been included within the term 'NHRI', this is increasingly changing. Yet there may in practice be differences between a national human rights commission and an ombudsman. In many states an ombudsman often has a reactive role, responding to complaints that are submitted to it, rather than the more proactive or promotional role that is the norm with human rights commissions. Ombudspersons also may often not be set up as 'human rights' institutions, but as public administration institutions with a different ethos and less knowledge about human rights than an organization set up specifically to deal with human rights issues in general. This may also have an impact on the expertise and background of the staff and those who head the institutions as well.

Different regions have illustrated trends towards the types of institution they select. So, for example, in the Americas, there are a considerable number of ombudspersons, yet, in Africa, this role has been taken by national human rights commissions. The reasons for creating a human rights institution vary from state to state. In some, it is the result of a peace agreement or an emergence from conflict,[37] in others, it is part of a government's own desire to be proactive in the human rights field;[38] and, in others, because it is a useful tool for suggesting compliance but one over which the government can retain some influence.[39]

Despite the above, the ICC and others have tended to treat all institutions the same, applying the Paris Principles and a process that is not adapted to take account of these subtle differences.

3.3 Role in Monitoring and Implementation of International Treaties

A final trend apparent in relation to NHRIs is their role in implementing and monitoring treaties. Although, legally, states are responsible for implementing human rights treaties, and, arguably, a body such as a NHRI is responsible for monitoring that implementation, a number of recently adopted treaties bring the apparent clear division between monitoring and implementation into question. These new instruments move beyond the simple recognition of the existence of such bodies, such as one might find in Article 26 of the African Charter on Human and Peoples' Rights,[40] to requiring them to carry out certain tasks as set out in the provisions of the instrument itself.

The Optional Protocol to the UN Convention on Torture (OPCAT) was adopted in 2006 and came into force in 2007. With the aim of preventing torture, it set up a two-tier system of visits to places of detention, firstly, by an international Sub-Committee for the Prevention of Torture (SPT) and, secondly, by National Preventive Mechanisms (NPMs) in each signatory state. The latter are 'designated' by states, from among existing or newly created national institutions. They

37 E.g. as in South Africa, Northern Ireland and the Republic of Ireland.

38 E.g. in Ghana, see Human Rights Watch, Protectors or Pretenders? Government Human Rights Commissions in Africa (New York: Human Rights Watch, 2001), p. 29.

39 E.g. as was the case in Nigeria; see O.C. Okafor and S.C. Agbakwa, 'On Legalism, Popular Agency and "Voices of Suffering": The Nigerian National Human Rights Commission in Context', *Human Rights Quarterly*, 24 (2002), pp. 662–720.

40 Article 26 reads: 'States parties to the present Charter shall have the duty to guarantee the independence of the Courts and shall allow the establishment and improvement of appropriate national institutions entrusted with the promotion and protection of the rights and freedoms guaranteed by the present Charter.'

are required to be independent, both functionally and in relation to their personnel,[41] and to have a number of minimum powers and protection from sanctions.[42] There is express reference in OPCAT to the Paris Principles and the need for 'due consideration' to be given to them in establishing these national mechanisms.[43] Of those NPMs that have been designated, there are national human rights commissions,[44] ombudspersons,[45] newly established bodies, and commissions or ombudspersons with NGO formal involvement. Some states have chosen a single body to act as the NPM, and others a group.[46]

It is clear, then, that it is these bodies that are to carry out these visits to places of detention and that once the state has designated them it is they who are in part responsible for the OPCAT implementation. While the state therefore should have the obligation to establish, designate or maintain the NPM, and provide it with the necessary powers, resources, mandate and protection, if that NPM is truly independent and properly resourced, it must take some responsibility itself. This may include carrying out its functions effectively and using its resources appropriately, for example. This has raised some difficulties for the SPT, which has an express mandate to advise and assist states and to 'maintain direct [...] contact' with the NPM itself and assist it 'in the evaluation of the needs and the means necessary to strengthen the protection of persons deprived of their liberty against torture and other cruel, inhuman or degrading treatment or punishment'.[47] It has yet to decide whether it should be accrediting those institutions and so far, sensibly, it has relied on engaging on quiet diplomacy with states and the NPMs to give advice. It is a difficult line to tread, however. This is made more complex by the fact that some of those NPMs who have been designated or the bodies which are being considered as NPMs have already been accredited by the ICC. Indeed, it seems to be the trend of the ICC to suggest that if a national body has been accredited by them and if a national human rights commission exists already within an OPCAT member state, then that body should automatically become the NPM.[48] This puts the SPT in a difficult position and fails to recognize that just because an institution complies with the Paris Principles does not necessarily mean it will be well suited to perform the functions required of OPCAT; it may not have the particular expertise needed by OPCAT, such as medical staff, and while the ICC may now be looking more broadly at the way in which a NHRI functions in its determination of accreditation, it is not equipped to consider the appropriateness of any particular institution to visit places of detention and fulfil the mandate as set out under OPCAT.[49]

Although it is not yet as far advanced as the OPCAT, the UN Convention on the Rights of Persons with Disabilities[50] raises very similar issues. As one of the most recently adopted UN

41 Article 18, OPCAT.

42 Articles 20–21, OPCAT.

43 Article 18(4), OPCAT.

44 E.g. New Zealand, as one among five bodies.

45 E.g. as in Denmark.

46 For example, in New Zealand, where five bodies have been chosen to act collectively as the NPM; the model being proposed in the UK is an NPM of over 20 bodies.

47 Article 11(b)(iii) OPCAT. See also APT, 'The International Subcommittee on Prevention Under the Optional Protocol to the Convention Against Torture', APT Position Paper, Geneva, May 2006, p. 9.

48 See OPCAT project team, *The Relationship Between Accreditation by the International Coordinating Committee of National Human Rights Institutions and the Optional Protocol to the UN Convention Against Torture*, November 2008 [online]. Available from: http://www.bristol.ac.uk/law/research/centres-themes/opcat/index.html.

49 *Ibid.*

50 UN Doc.A/61/611.

human rights convention,[51] NHRIs were able to have a prominent role in the drafting of this instrument,[52] and in doing so inserted for themselves a role in its monitoring and implementation.[53] Article 33 of the Convention provides:

> 1. States Parties, in accordance with their system of organization, shall designate one or more focal points within government for matters relating to the implementation of the present Convention, and shall give due consideration to the establishment or designation of a coordination mechanism within government to facilitate related action in different sectors and at different levels.
> 2. States Parties shall, in accordance with their legal and administrative systems, maintain, strengthen, designate or establish within the State Party, a framework, including one or more independent mechanisms, as appropriate, to promote, protect and monitor implementation of the present Convention. When designating or establishing such a mechanism, States Parties shall take into account the principles relating to the status and functioning of national institutions for protection and promotion of human rights.
> 3. Civil society, in particular persons with disabilities and their representative organizations, shall be involved and participate fully in the monitoring process.

There has been some discussion over what the roles of these various national actors are likely to be.[54] Article 33(1) provides for government focal points and coordinating bodies, and some have already proposed that this role be played by a NHRI. There are also concerns that a NHRI may be seen as having sole responsibility for promoting, protecting and monitoring implementation of the convention even though Article 33 envisages a 'framework'.[55] This blurs the line between implementation and monitoring so clearly marked by the Convention. Similarly, 'the "promotional" element of national monitoring may indeed lead NHRIs to make recommendations for appropriate regulation…'.[56]

---

51 It was adopted on 13 December 2006 and came into force on 3 May 2008.

52 See Report of the Ad Hoc Committee on a Comprehensive and Integral International Convention on Protection and Promotion of the Rights and Dignity of Persons with Disabilities, 7 August 2002, UN Doc. A/AC.265/2. See also the first session of the Ad Hoc Committee where it 'extend[s] an invitation to National Human Rights Institutions to participate in its future sessions', UN Doc. A/57/357, para. 11.

53 Interventions by National Human Rights Institutions on Articles 1–24 of the working group draft [online]. Available from: http://www.un.org/esa/socdev/enable/rights/ahc3nhricomments.htm.

54 E.g. G. Quinn, 'The UN Convention on the Rights of Persons with Disabilities. National Institutions as Key Catalysts of Change', in *National Monitoring Mechanisms of the Convention on the Rights of Persons with Disabilities*, William & Mary Law School Research Paper No. 09-30 (2008), pp. 123–32; G. Quinn, 'NHRIs and the Next Steps Under the UN Convention on the Human Rights of Persons with Disabilities', 19th Session of the Annual Meeting of the International Coordinating Committee (ICC), Geneva, 23 March 2007 [online]. Available from: www.nhri.net; Asia Pacific Forum, *Annual Conference Disability Issues Paper, 12th Annual Meeting of the Asia Pacific Forum of National Human Rights Institutions*, Sydney, Australia, 24–27 September 2007; R. Kayess and P. French, 'Out of Darkness into Light: Introducing the Convention on the Rights of Persons with Disabilities', *Human Rights Law Review*, 8(1) (2008), pp. 1–34;

55 Asia Pacific Forum, *Annual Conference Disability Issues Paper, 12th Annual Meeting of the Asia Pacific Forum of National Human Rights Institutions*, Sydney, Australia, 24–27 September 2007, p. 6.

56 G. Quinn, 'NHRIs and the Next Steps Under the UN Convention on the Human Rights of Persons with Disabilities', 19th Session of the Annual Meeting of the International Coordinating Committee (ICC), Geneva, 23 March 2007, p. 5 [online]. Available from: www.nhri.net.

Just as under OPCAT, where its UN committee, the SPT, has faced difficulties in how it should deal with NPMs, that is, whether it should be accrediting them or assessing their performance in some way, so the UN Committee on the Rights of Persons with Disabilities is likely to face similar challenges in its consideration of compliance with the Convention by states.

Furthermore, the same issues will not necessarily be confined to these two treaties. With the reference in recent instruments, such as Article 28 of the International Convention for the Protection of All Persons from Enforced Disappearances, which requires the Committee on Enforced Disappearances to 'cooperate (…) with all relevant State institutions, agencies or offices working towards the protection of all persons against enforced disappearances', the formal role of NHRIs and similar bodies in international treaties is likely to become a more common feature.

4. Conclusion

NHRIs have come a long way since the adoption of the UDHR, but then so has the human rights field changed dramatically in terms of the actors who play a role in the creation, monitoring and implementation of human rights standards. Just as NGOs have developed a role for themselves,[57] so have NHRIs come to make their presence felt at the national, regional and international levels. Yet, not all of this is a force for good. Despite the rhetoric from the UN and regional bodies that states should be establishing a national human rights commission if a similar body does not exist, there are dangers inherent in jumping on this bandwagon. There is recognition that NHRIs should be home-grown and that it shall be the 'right of each State to choose the framework which is best suited to its particular needs at the national level'.[58] But equally, there must be a greater honesty in the discussion over whether a NHRI is needed in the first place. A careful consideration of the political context, the likelihood of the institution being given the necessary support by the government without interference, and whether there are other institutions in the country which already fulfil the tasks that any such body can do, are only some of the many issues that must be examined by those considering setting up a national human rights institution.

It was not seen as appropriate for independent NHRIs to sit alongside governments and NGOs in various international and regional fora, and those who do act independently and effectively can play a very valuable role as a voice which is neither governmental nor non-governmental. But this is not the case for all institutions, some of which are the mouthpiece of government, and providing them with standing at the international and regional levels gives them a worrying legitimacy.

There have been significant developments by the ICC in its assessment of NHRIs, and its ability to act as the gateway to representation of NHRIs at the UN is an improvement. Including civil society opinions in the accreditation process clearly addresses the criticism that the ICC was ineffective in peer review. While independence may be the most important consideration in determining whether a NHRI should then have the ability to sit on UN committees and separate from governments, accreditation is not used only for this purpose by NHRIs and others. Accreditation by the ICC and other regional bodies, such as the APF and the African Commission, can be a powerful tool to obtain more funding, and lobby for formal roles under OPCAT or the Disability Convention. The Paris Principles and the process of accreditation do not address these issues or whether a NHRI is actually an effective body.

57 See Chapter 17 in this volume.

58 Vienna Declaration and Programme of Action, para. 36.

With the OPCAT and the Disability Convention, the role of NHRIs has entered a new phase. Not only are they now another voice in the civil society arena that can challenge government and act as watchdogs on state activities, but they now have formal roles to play under these international instruments. This adds another dimension to their work. OPCAT requires states to set up National Preventive Mechanisms that are independent and protected, but once it has done so, there are, arguably, obligations on the NPMs to carry out visits effectively and to maintain contact with the UN SPT. Similarly, under the Disability Convention, the blurring of the boundaries between monitoring and implementation is already apparent and may become increasingly so. There is a need for further examination of the challenges these types of instruments raise.

Academically, the importance of an actor at the international plane has been played out in the discussion on who are subjects of international law and who are not.[59] Debate has raged about the role of civil society and NGOs[60] challenging the traditional notion that states are the only subjects of international law, with their rights and duties at the international level and the ability to enforce those rights.[61] In applying the same criteria to NHRIs, they, arguably, have come as far if not further. Accreditation provides certain rights before international bodies, and instruments such as the OPCAT and Disability Convention, arguably, address duties directly to NHRIs. Moreover, the opportunities that some have taken to bring litigation and challenge accreditation, for example, suggest they also have the ability to enforce those rights. Whether one agrees with the debate on subjects/objects of international law or the importance of such a discussion, there is little doubt that NHRIs are now important actors in human rights law. They are a potential force to be reckoned with, but, equally, one that should be considered, as with any actor, meticulously and objectively.

59 P. Alston, *Non-State Actors and Human Rights*, Oxford University Press, 2005; R. Higgins, *Problems and Process: International Law and How We Use It* (Oxford: Oxford University Press, 1994).

60 M. Kamminga, The Evolving Status of NGOs Under International Law: A Threat to the Inter-State System?', in Alston, note 60 above, 93–112; H. Cullen and K. Morrow, 'International Civil Society in International Law: The Growth of NGO Participation', *Non-State Actors in International Law*, 1 (2001), pp. 7–39.

61 B. Cheng, 'Introduction to Subjects of International Law', in M. Bedjaoui (ed.), *International Law: Achievements and Prospects* (Paris: UNESCO, 1991), p, 23; Reparations for Injuries, Advisory Opinion, ICJ Rep. 1949, 174.

Chapter 17
Institutional Partnership or Critical Seepages? The Role of Human Rights NGOs in the United Nations

Dianne Otto

1. Introduction

In 1945, international human rights non-governmental organizations (NGOs) were made possible by the United Nations (UN) Charter, which recognized the universality of human rights for the first time[1] and introduced the terminology of NGOs,[2] and by the UDHR,[3] which laid the groundwork for the normative and institutional developments that were to follow. Today, six decades after the adoption of the UDHR, the accounts of the role of human rights NGOs in the promotion and protection of universal human rights are manifold. The majority of commentators describe a considerably more expansive role than the consultative function, limited to the economic and social field, which was envisaged in the UN Charter. Many accounts celebrate human rights NGOs as indispensable to the operation of the UN systems for promoting the domestic implementation of human rights.[4] They have been credited with playing a major role in critical global transformations, such as the fall of the Berlin Wall and the ending of apartheid in South Africa.[5] Human rights NGOs have also been depicted as part of the vanguard of an emergent international civil society, helping to shape new forms of global governance that are more democratic and inclusive.[6] In this role, NGOs have been variously described as bringing 'the voice of the people' or 'the conscience of the world' to international law and governance.[7] There are also less celebratory accounts. Stalwarts of the realist tradition have always maintained that the impact of human rights NGOs is negligible, while others have suggested that they are merely a mouthpiece for 'global elites',[8] a neo-imperial tool

---

1 Charter of the United Nations (adopted 26 June 1945, entered into force 24 October 1945) (UN Charter), preamble para. 1, Arts. 1(3), 10, 13(1)(b), 22, 55, 56, 58 and 62(2).

2 *Ibid.*, Art. 71.

3 Adopted 10 December 1948, UNGA Res. 217 A(III).

4 Helena Cook, 'Amnesty International at the United Nations', in Peter Willetts (ed.), *The 'Conscience' of the World: The Influence of Non-governmental Organisations in the UN System* (London: Hurst and Co, 1996), pp. 181, 198.

5 William Korey, *NGOs and the Universal Declaration of Human Rights: A Curious Grapevine* (New York: Palgrave Macmillan, 1998), pp. 8–9.

6 Thomas G. Weiss and Leon Gordenker (eds), *NGOs, the UN, and Global Governance* (London: Lynne Reinner, 1996).

7 Willetts, note 4 above.

8 Kenneth Anderson, 'The Ottawa Convention Banning Landmines, the Role of International Non-governmental Organizations, and the Idea of International Civil Society', *European Journal of International Law*, 11 (2000), pp. 91–120, at p. 118.

for the promotion of Western liberal values aimed at 'civilizing savage cultures,'[9] and themselves 'part of the problem'.[10]

The following account of the role of human rights NGOs has relatively modest goals. It will focus on the proliferation of both formal and informal institutional developments in the UN that have enabled human rights NGOs to participate in increasing numbers in a very broad array of intergovernmental forums, and examine how this has shaped and challenged both the way that institutions have approached the development of international human rights law and its implementation, and the ways that NGOs have sought to influence institutional processes. After outlining many of the developments I have in mind, my discussion will focus on the challenges that increased institutional interaction presents, on the one hand, to multilateral institutions and their member states and, on the other hand, to the way that human rights NGOs conceive of their role. For the institutions, while there is much to gain, there are many unresolved problems about how to deal with those states who fear criticism by NGOs, and how to formalize NGO involvement in a way that is controllable and does not displace states from their 'primary' role. For NGOs, there are problems associated with the institutional privileging of Western NGOs, the extent of compromise that engagement extracts, and the dangers of institutional cooption.

Six decades after its adoption, it is clear that the UDHR has inspired thousands of diverse, creative and insistent movements for change, which organize locally and internationally, and from many in-between vantage points. Yet, there is very little agreement about how to conceptualize the role of the NGOs of these movements in the UN's promotion and protection of human rights. There are many possible roles on the table: as providers of expert advice and technical assistance; as partners with states, multinational corporations and other international actors; as advocates for oppressed and powerless people(s); as adversaries bent on challenging the primary position of states in the international system; or as apologists for a state-based system sorely in need of the legitimacy that human rights NGOs can provide. I conclude that while human rights NGOs have become indispensable to the operation of all the UN human rights systems as we know them today, this has endangered many of their aims and the aspirations of the UDHR. I urge a revitalization of the emancipatory goals that have inspired human rights movements over the centuries and are reflected in the UDHR and, in pursuit of those goals, a critical engagement with the institutional openings that are on offer today.

2. The Expanding Institutional and Normative Participation of Human Rights NGOs

The UN Secretary-General's Panel of Eminent Persons on UN-Civil Society Relations reported in 2004 that the participation of civil society in the UN had been 'growing exponentially',[11] to the point that it is now 'pivotal' to 'managing globalization' so that it is inclusive and equitable.[12] Building strong 'partnerships' between states, civil society and other global actors with vested interests is

9 Makau Mutua, 'Human Rights International NGOs: A Critical Evaluation', in Claude E. Welch, Jr (ed.), *NGOs and Human Rights: Promise and Performance* (Philadelphia: University of Pennsylvania Press, 2001), pp. 151–66.

10 David Kennedy, 'The International Human Rights Movement: Part of the Problem?', *Harvard Human Rights Journal*, 15 (2002), pp. 101–25.

11 Report of the Panel of Eminent Persons on United Nations-Civil Society Relations, *We the Peoples: Civil Society, the United Nations and Global Governance* (Cardoso Report), UN Doc A/58/817, 11 June 2004, para. 1.

12 Ibid., para. 5.

recommended as a means of enhancing the quality of intergovernmental deliberative processes, making the UN more responsive and accountable and therefore more effective.[13] In opting for a 'partnership' model, the panel's report (Cardoso Report)[14] took a neo-corporatist approach that recognizes the significance of engagement with organized sectional interests but, in the process, ignores the general public interest.[15] Although the report treats 'international civil society' as a single undifferentiated entity and therefore does not give human rights NGOs specific treatment,[16] it nevertheless provides a useful backdrop to a discussion of their present engagement in the UN system. Like other civil society actors, human rights NGOs have proliferated in the period of post-Cold War globalization, vastly expanding the scope of their participation in UN forums, extending well beyond the consultative role envisaged by Article 71 of the UN Charter, which, as the Cardoso Report observes, implies they 'can speak only when invited and are not participants in their own right'.[17] Also in common with other civil society actors, formal accreditation arrangements have been completely outpaced by informal practices, and the influence of human rights NGOs is no longer confined to matters within the ECOSOC's sphere.[18]

However, the Cardoso Report fails to identify the many distinctive features of the expanding engagement of human rights NGOs with the UN, two of which I want to highlight. First, while the panel suggests a cautious approach to removing the restrictions of Article 71,[19] it is clear that human rights NGOs have already forged many new institutional practices within the UN's human rights systems, which allow them to participate, at least to some extent, 'in their own right'. Second, human rights NGOs have carved out an increasingly central role in normative development, something that, in the panel's view, should remain firmly in the hands of states.[20] I also question whether the concept of 'partnership' is accurate, or even desirable, as a description of these interactions.

2.1 Institutional Developments

Many systems for the promotion and protection of human rights have developed under the broad umbrella of the UN, including through its specialized agencies and funds. However, in this section, I will focus on the institutional practices that have developed in the two most important schemes – the charter-based system developed pursuant to the UN Charter's recognition of the link between the universal enjoyment of human rights and international peace and security, and the treaty-based system under which states have assumed specific human rights obligations. As they have developed, both systems have gradually given human rights NGOs a much more substantial role than consultation that, at least on the surface, might be described as partnership.

13 *Ibid.*, paras. 68–78.

14 The panel was chaired by Fernando Henrique Cardoso, the former president of Brazil.

15 Peter Willetts, 'The Cardoso Report on the UN and Civil Society: Functionalism, Global Corporatism, or Global Democracy?', *Global Governance*, 12 (2006), pp. 305–24, at p. 317.

16 The report does define 'non-governmental organization' in its glossary to include organizations devoted to human rights, Cardoso Report, note 11 above, p. 13.

17 *Ibid.*, para. 43.

18 Chadwick Alger, 'The Emerging Roles of NGOs in the UN System: From Article 71 to a People's Millennium Assembly', *Global Governance*, 8 (2002), pp. 93–117.

19 Cardoso Report, note 11 above, para. 43.

20 *Ibid.*, para. 24.

In the charter-based system, the Commission on Human Rights was the major human rights body until 2006, when it was replaced by the Human Rights Council.[21] Much of the work of the commission would simply not have been possible without the involvement of NGOs, many of which built significant capacity to provide it with credible information about alleged human rights violations.[22] They also put pressure on the commission to establish procedures that would enable it to publicly address the concerns they were raising, hoping thereby to 'shame' states into changing their violative practices. Those NGOs with ECOSOC accreditation[23] were able to attend the commission's annual sessions, and large numbers of NGOs, many of whom were not officially accredited, regularly participated in the NGO forums that were held contemporaneously. While the hope that the commission's membership of 53 states would develop procedures capable of subjecting individual states to serious scrutiny might well be dismissed as utopian, the recent establishment of the Human Rights Council to replace the commission could be seen as motivated by the same hope.

In the shadow of the often shameless political jockeying by states to avoid scrutiny of their human rights record by the commission, two types of procedures were eventually adopted in order to do just that. The first crack in the edifice of state sovereignty was the establishment by ECOSOC of two petition procedures – a public procedure in 1967[24] and a confidential procedure in 1970[25] – which would address 'situations which appear to reveal a consistent pattern of gross and reliably attested violations of human rights'.[26] Human rights NGOs have always had standing to submit communications under these procedures, and these are, in practice, their most important source of information.[27] The second type of procedure developed by the commission was to appoint independent human rights experts with country-specific or thematic mandates, able to respond to individual communications, provide research and advice, and monitor and publicly report on matters within their mandates.[28] These 'special procedures' were described by the former UN Secretary-General, Kofi Annan, as the 'crown jewel' of the UN's human rights system.[29] Many of them were established as the direct result of NGO lobbying,[30] and they, too, rely heavily on information from NGOs;[31] indeed, many of the positions are occupied by experts from the NGO sector. Of special significance for NGOs is the work of the Secretary-General's Special Representative on Human Rights Defenders, whose position was created in 2001.[32] While mandated to investigate individual human rights abuses suffered by human rights defenders, the vast majority of concerns that the special rapporteur has raised with governments have been about individuals who have been

21 GA Res., A/RES/60/251, 2 April 2006. See also Chapter 11 in this volume.

22 Korey, note 5 above, p. 9.

23 The ECOSOC accreditation arrangements will be discussed further below.

24 ECOSOC Res. 1235(XLII), 6 June 1967.

25 ECOSOC Res. 1503(XLVIII), 27 May 1970.

26 *Ibid.*, para. 1.

27 Nigel Rodley, 'Human Rights NGOs: Rights and Obligations', in Theo van Boven *et al.* (eds), *The Legitimacy of the United Nations: Towards an Enhanced Legal Status of Non-State Actors* (Utrecht: Netherlands Institute of Human Rights, SIM Special, 1997), pp. 41, 58.

28 The first special procedure was the Working Group on Enforced or Involuntary Disappearances, established in 1980.

29 National Committee on American Foreign Policy, *The United Nations Human Rights Council: A US Foreign Policy Dilemma*, Report of a Roundtable held in New York City, 28 May 2008, p. 11.

30 Rodley, note 27 above, p. 45.

31 *Ibid.*, p. 58.

32 E/CN.4/RES/2000/61, Human Rights Defenders, 27 April 2001, para. 3.

targeted in their capacity as members of human rights NGOs.[33] While this work does not formally make NGOs subjects of international law, it comes close.

Another key site, where the formal prescriptions for NGO participation have been pushed beyond their limits, was the Commission's Sub-Commission on the Promotion and Protection of Human Rights,[34] also disbanded in the process of establishing the Human Rights Council. The Sub-Commission's role included standard-setting and the preparation of working papers and studies aimed at keeping the commission abreast of current human rights issues. It was made up of 26 experts, nominated and elected by member states of the commission for 4-year terms, enabling it to adopt more creative procedures for NGO participation than the commission, and to be more outspoken in condemning human rights violations.[35] A particularly far-reaching practice, developed by the Sub-Commission's Working Group on Indigenous Populations during the 1980s and later formalized by the commission, was to allow the full participation of organizations of indigenous peoples in its drafting of the Declaration on the Rights of Indigenous Peoples.[36] The process was hailed by one indigenous leader as transformational,[37] and the experience led eventually to ECOSOC establishing, in 2000, a new advisory body, the Permanent Forum on Indigenous Issues, whose membership comprises equal numbers of representatives of states and indigenous peoples.[38] The Cardoso Report describes the forum as an example of 'innovation in governance', promoting it as a model for the type of future system-wide, 'multi-stakeholder' advisory bodies that it supports.[39]

Future opportunities for NGO participation rely heavily on the approach of the new Human Rights Council, which was established to replace the commission in an attempt to 'depoliticize' the UN's human rights work, in the sense of making it possible to address human rights violations more impartially.[40] With the introduction of the universal periodic review procedure, under which all states must report on their human rights compliance on a rotating 4-year schedule,[41] new opportunities for NGO participation have been created, described as making 'stakeholder submissions' by the UN Office of the High Commissioner for Human Rights (OHCHR).[42] However, while the formal understanding is that NGO participation will continue to be based on the same arrangements and practices of the commission, including retention of the existing ECOSOC accreditation procedures, there are already signs that the Human Rights Council may be less amenable to NGO involvement in practice with, for example, the discontinuation of the commission's public petition procedure, the limited 'advisory' role given to its Advisory Committee of 18 experts, and the emphasis on

33 Anna-Karin Lindblom, *Non-Governmental Organisations in International Law* (Cambridge: Cambridge University Press, 2004), p. 154.

34 The Sub-Commission was known as the Sub-Commission on Prevention of Discrimination and Protection of Minorities until its name was changed in 1999.

35 David Weissbrodt, Mayra Gomez and Bret Thiele, 'An Analysis of the Fifty-First Session of the United Nations Sub-Commission on the Promotion and Protection of Human Rights', *Human Rights Quarterly*, 22 (2000), pp. 788–837, at p. 789.

36 Lindblom, note 33 above, p. 389. See also Draft Declaration on the Rights of Indigenous Peoples, E/CN.4/Sub.2/1994/2/Add.1, 26 August 1994.

37 Mick Dodson, Aboriginal and Islander Social Justice Commissioner, 'Comment', in Sarah Pritchard (ed.), *Indigenous Peoples, the United Nations and Human Rights* (Sydney: Federation Press, 1998), pp. 63, 64–5.

38 Establishment of a Permanent Forum on Indigenous Issues, E/RES/2000/22, 28 July 2000.

39 Cardoso Report, note 11 above, para. 52.

40 Human Rights Council, GA Res. 60/251 (2006).

41 *Ibid.*, para. 5(e).

42 Office of the High Commissioner for Human Rights (OHCHR), *Working with the United Nations Human Rights Programme: A Handbook for Civil Society* (New York and Geneva: OHCHR, 2008), pp. 147–9.

dialogue and cooperation rather than condemnation.[43] Even the semblance of 'partnership' with human rights NGOs in the charter-based system may prove to be ephemeral.

The UN's second main human rights system, based on monitoring states parties' treaty obligations, is also 'heavily reliant' on information provided by NGOs,[44] and many innovative processes for increasing the participation of NGOs have been developed. All bar one of the nine major human rights treaties establishes an expert committee which is empowered to monitor its implementation. The exception is the International Covenant on Economic, Social and Cultural Rights (ICESCR).[45] To fill this gap, ECOSOC created the ICESCR Committee as a subsidiary body in 1985, modelled on the committee that monitors the International Covenant on Civil and Political Rights (ICCPR).[46] It follows that the ICESCR committee is the only treaty body subject to the ECOSOC accreditation system, although this has not stopped it from establishing its own additional procedures. The treaty bodies have all developed informal practices that encourage and facilitate both national and international NGO participation.[47] Many of these initiatives have later been adopted by other treaty bodies, a process that has been supported by the Meeting of the Chairpersons of the Human Rights Treaty Bodies. In 1995, the chairpersons emphasized the importance of information provided by NGOs,[48] and in 1996 they encouraged NGOs to critically examine the work of the treaty bodies, as a means of enhancing their effectiveness.[49] The more recent human rights treaties provide an explicit legal basis for cooperation with NGOs – the Convention on the Rights of the Child (CRC),[50] the Convention on the Protection of the Rights of All Migrant Workers and Members of their Families (CRMW),[51] and the Convention on the Rights of Persons with Disabilities (CRPD).[52]

The primary monitoring method available to the treaty bodies is their mandate to review the periodic reports that states parties are required to submit every 4–5 years. All the treaty bodies have come to welcome parallel or shadow reports from national as well as international NGOs, which are then formally distributed to committee members and taken into account when reviewing states parties' reports.[53] As Nigel Rodley explains, this puts treaty body members in a better position to

43 Institution-Building, HRC Res. 5/1, 18 June 2007.

44 Claude E. Welch, Jr, 'Conclusion', in Welch, note 9 above, pp. 261–80, at p. 275.

45 A16 December 1966, entered into force 3 January 1976, 993 UNTS 3.

46 Adopted 16 December 1966, entered into force 23 March 1976) 999 UNTS 171 (ICCPR). The Human Rights Committee is established pursuant to ICCPR, Art. 28. I shall refer to it as the ICCPR committee for clarity.

47 Shanthi Dairiam, 'From Global to Local: The Involvement of NGOs', in Hanna Beata Schopp-Schilling (ed.), *The Circle of Empowerment: Twenty-Five Years of the UN Committee on the Elimination of Discrimination Against Women* (New York: Feminist Press, City University of New York, 2007), pp. 313, 316. The CEDAW Committee first developed informal arrangements for NGO participation in 1988.

48 Report of the Sixth Meeting of Persons Chairing the Human Rights Treaty Bodies, A/50/505 (1995), para. 23.

49 Report of the Seventh Meeting of Persons Chairing the Human Rights Treaty Bodies, A/51/482 (1996) paras. 35 and 36.

50 Adopted 20 November 1989, entered into force 2 September 1990, 1577 UNTS 3 (CRC), Arts. 45(a) and (b).

51 Adopted 18 December 1990, entered into force 1 July 2003, reprinted in 30 ILM 1517 (1991) (CRMW), Art. 74(4).

52 Adopted 13 December 2006, not yet entered into force (CRPD), Arts. 38(a) and 33(3).

53 Andrew Clapham, 'UN Human Rights Reporting: An NGO Perspective', in Philip Alston and James Crawford (eds), *The Future of UN Human Rights Treaty Monitoring* (Cambridge: Cambridge University Press, 2000), pp. 175–200, at p. 176.

question the 'usually self-serving' claims of the official reports of states.[54] The ICESCR committee has even adopted a procedure for soliciting reports from NGOs once it has received a state party's report and, because it is a subsidiary body of ECOSOC, NGO shadow reports are issued as official UN documents and translated into the working languages of the committee.[55] Many of the treaty bodies also make provision for formal discussions with NGOs. Pre-sessional working groups of the Convention on the Elimination of All Forms of Discrimination Against Women (CEDAW),[56] ICCPR and CRC committees, for example, meet with NGOs as they prepare for dialogue with states parties about the information provided in their reports,[57] while the ICESCR committee devotes the first day of each of its reporting sessions to hearing oral submissions from NGOs.[58] Many additional practices have been crafted by particular treaty bodies. For example, the ICESCR committee initiated the practice of involving NGOs in days of general discussion on particular aspects of the covenant and in preparing drafts of general comments (authoritative interpretations) on specific provisions,[59] and the CRC committee has requested a number of NGOs to undertake specific research for the committee.[60]

A second monitoring method available to some of the treaty bodies is their capacity to consider individual and, in some cases, group complaints.[61] The procedures provide another avenue for NGO participation. The starting point for all of them is that complaints must be made by the victim of the alleged human rights violation(s) or, with the group procedures, by the group of individual victims,[62] but not NGOs. This point was underlined during the drafting of the Optional Protocol to the ICCPR, which establishes the ICCPR procedure, when a US proposal that NGOs with ECOSOC consultative status be permitted to author communications was rejected.[63] However, the practice has developed that in exceptional circumstances there may be some scope for an NGO to submit a communication on behalf of the victim if the victim is unable to submit personally, and there is also the capacity for an NGO to act as the victim's representative.[64] According to Lindblom, it is not common for NGOs to represent a victim in communications brought under the ICCPR procedure,[65] but it happens more frequently with complaints made under the Convention for the

54 Rodley, note 27 above, p. 55.

55 Lindblom, note 33 above, p. 398. In order for shadow reports to be issued as official UN documents, they must have been submitted by an NGO in general or special consultative status with ECOSOC, or by an NGO that has the support of an NGO in consultative status.

56 Adopted 18 December 1979, entered into force 3 September 1981, 1249 UNTS 13 (CEDAW).

57 Lindblom, note 33 above, pp. 396, 401 and 405.

58 *Ibid.*, p. 398.

59 *Ibid.*, p. 399.

60 Cynthia Price Cohen, 'The United Nations Convention on the Rights of the Child: Involvement of NGOs', in van Boven, note 27 above, pp. 169–84.

61 Convention for the Elimination of Racial Discrimination (adopted 21 December 1965, entered into force 4 January 1969), 660 UNTS 195 (CERD), Art. 14; Optional Protocol to the ICCPR (adopted 16 December 1966, entered into force 23 March 1976), 999 UNTS 171 (OP ICCPR); Convention Against Torture and Other Cruel, Inhuman or Degrading Treatment or Punishment (adopted 10 December 1984, entered into force 26 June 1987), 1465 UNTS 85 (CAT), Art. 22; Optional Protocol to CEDAW (adopted 6 October 1999, entered into force 10 December 1999) (OP CEDAW); Optional Protocol to CRPD (adopted 13 December 2006, GA Res. 61/106) (OP CRPD); Optional Protocol to ICESCR (adopted 10 December 2008, GA Res. 63/117) (OP ICESCR).

62 Groups of victims are able to complain under CERD, Art. 14, OP CRPD and OP ICESCR.

63 Lindblom, note 33 above, p. 225.

64 *Ibid.*, pp. 227–8.

65 *Ibid.*, p. 229.

Elimination of Racial Discrimination (CERD)[66] and the Convention Against Torture (CAT)[67] procedures.[68] In practice, it is likely that NGOs are much more involved in encouraging victims to make complaints, and supporting them through the process than is formally recorded. The more recently established CEDAW, ICESCR and CRPD procedures take a broader view, formally recognizing that a complaint may be made by someone acting on the victim's behalf, giving NGOs standing to bring a complaint, provided the victim has consented or the NGO can otherwise justify bringing the complaint. While NGOs may themselves be victims of human rights abuses – for example as a result of threats to collective associational or free speech rights – they do not have standing to bring a complaint in their own case, and, in any event, the human rights treaties only recognize individual rights, with few exceptions.[69]

Another feature of the treaty-based system is that it has generated dynamic NGO constituencies in each of the substantive issue areas covered by human rights treaties, creating many opportunities for international and national NGOs to network and link in their efforts to engage with the treaty bodies. I offer three examples. First, International Women's Rights Action Watch Asia-Pacific (IWRAW-AP), based in Kuala Lumpur, Malaysia, offers training about CEDAW to local and national NGOs in the Asia-Pacific region, and coordinates a global programme that has enabled it to assist over 100 NGO delegations to prepare shadow reports and attend the CEDAW sessions when the report of their state is discussed.[70] Second, the Anti Racism Information Service (ARIS) is an NGO that was founded in 1992 to keep national and regional NGOs informed about the work of the CERD committee and help them in the preparation of shadow reports or individual complaints. The ARIS maintains a substantial database pertaining to all states that have ratified CERD and more than 180 minority groups.[71] Third, the NGO Group for the Convention on the Rights of the Child, established in 1983, coordinates a network of over 80 international and national non-governmental organizations to support and assist the work of the CRC committee.[72]

In sum, it is clear that the information provided by human rights NGOs is indispensable to the operation of all the UN's human rights machineries, whether charter or treaty based, and that there have been many institutional developments aimed at enhancing the availability of this information, although there are more recent signs that states may resile from some of these practices, at least in the charter-based system. In addition to strengthening their role as informants, these developments have helped NGOs to become active participants by enabling them to submit petitions and communications on behalf of or as representatives of victims alleging violations; to table and, in some forums, speak to critical reports that shadow states' periodic reports to the treaty bodies and the Human Rights Council; to participate directly in many treaty-body processes, including the drafting of General Comments and pre-sessional preparations for the review of periodic reports; and to put pressure on intergovernmental bodies to develop better accountability mechanisms that NGOs can, in turn, utilize to draw attention to human rights violations and to bring pressure

---

66 CERD, note 61 above.

67 CAT, note 61 above.

68 Lindblom, note 33, above, pp. 234–5.

69 The main exception is the right of peoples to self-determination, which is recognized by the ICCPR and ICESCR, common article 1.

70 Dairiam, note 47 above. See further: http://www.iwraw-ap.org/ [accessed 26 July 2010].

71 Due to lack of funding, the Anti-Racism Information Service (ARIS) was forced to close in April 2009 [online]. Available from: http://www.antiracism-info.org/Public/pageQueFaitARIS.php [accessed 21 April 2009].

72 NGO Group for the Convention on the Rights of the Child [online]. Available from: http://www.crin.org/NGOGroup/ [accessed 21 April 2009].

for change. Although many of these institutional developments may look like partnerships, they are controlled ultimately by states, and human rights NGOs continue to be unable to formally participate in intergovernmental forums. However, there are seepages everywhere. Using informal processes that are hard for the institution to control, NGOs have often been able to substantially influence formal decision-making and participate in their own right in many UN forums.

2.2 Normative Influence

The participation of human rights NGOs in the UN's human rights systems has also had a significant normative impact, perhaps more than in any other area of engagement of civil society with the UN. As Rodley describes it, 'NGOs have been an engine, perhaps the engine ... in the evolution of laws, norms and standards in the field of human rights'.[73] While only states and intergovernmental organizations are formally able to 'make' international law, NGOs have been very influential in the shaping of international human rights law, both directly in the drafting of treaties and indirectly in their interpretation and application, and also in fostering the development of customary international law. Playing a role in normative development exceeds the limits of 'consultation', bringing NGOs into a relationship that can closely resemble 'partnership' with states but which, I argue, is of a different quality.

There are many instances of direct involvement of human rights NGOs in drafting treaty texts, to the point where today, it would be unthinkable to embark on such a project without them. Two examples will suffice for present purposes – the role that Amnesty International and other NGOs[74] played in securing the adoption of CAT in 1984, which brought NGOs from the sidelines to the table of drafting negotiations, and the involvement of NGOs in drafting the CRC from 1979 to 1989, which demonstrated the power that can come from the coordination of NGO efforts. Since then, NGOs have been actively involved in all the commission's working groups that have drafted human rights instruments.[75]

The first step that Amnesty International took towards having the UN take up the issue of torture was to launch an international Campaign for the Abolition of Torture in December 1972, aimed at persuading governments to establish legal mechanisms that would enforce the prohibition against torture, as set out in Article 5 of the UDHR.[76] The campaign led to the adoption of a General Assembly resolution in late 1973 which condemned torture and other cruel treatment.[77] At the same time, the problem of torture was highlighted by world events, with the brutality of the regime that overthrew the Allende Government in Chile in 1973 and evidence of widespread torture practised in Portugal that was uncovered by the 1974 coup.[78] These events, and the sustained contributions of NGOs, led to the promulgation of a number of soft-law instruments,[79] including the Declaration

73 Rodley, note 27 above, p. 45.

74 *Ibid.*, p. 42, noting that the International Commission of Jurists and the International Association of Penal Law were particularly involved.

75 E.g. Claire Breen, 'The Role of NGOs in the Formulation of and Compliance with the Optional Protocol to the Convention on the Rights of the Child on Involvement of Children in Armed Conflict', *Human Rights Quarterly*, 25 (2003), pp. 453–81.

76 Cook, note 4 above, p. 189.

77 GA Res. 3059(XXVIII), 2 November 1973.

78 Cook, note 4 above, pp. 189–90.

79 Theo van Boven, 'The Role of Non-Governmental Organizations in International Human Rights Standard-Setting: A Prerequisite of Democracy', *California Western International Law Journal*, 20 (1990), pp. 207–25, at p. 214.

Against Torture which was adopted by the General Assembly in 1975.[80] Increasingly concerned about the actions of the South African apartheid regime, the General Assembly called on the Commission on Human Rights in 1977 to draft a convention.[81] The NGOs worked initially in the margins of the commission's drafting sessions, but gradually assumed a more central role. Although Amnesty, unlike most other NGOs, has a policy of not proposing or supporting specific text in order to maintain its independence, it lobbied governments to include a number of key principles in the text which contributed to 'strengthening some aspects of the final Convention', in the rather conservative estimate of Amnesty activist Helena Cook.[82] The procedural advance, which would have lasting institutional effect, was that the distinction between states and NGOs largely disappeared in the drafting process – something that would have been inconceivable in 1948 when NGOs were reliant on states' representatives to present their proposals during the drafting of the UDHR.[83]

The first step towards the adoption of the CRC can be traced back to 1924, when an NGO called Save the Children International Union (SCIU) composed the first international declaration of the rights of the child, known as the Declaration of Geneva, which was adopted by the League of Nations the same year.[84] In 1948, the UDHR recognized in Article 25 that children 'are entitled to special care and assistance' and in 1950 the Commission on Human Rights began drafting the UN Declaration of the Rights of the Child,[85] which was eventually adopted unanimously by the General Assembly in 1959.[86] It took another 20 years, the designation of 1979 as the International Year of the Child, and a proposal for a convention by Poland, before the General Assembly requested the commission to establish a Working Group to draft a convention on the rights of the child.[87] From the beginning, NGOs participated in the drafting sessions by making written and oral presentations, although they were not included in the attendance records until 1981, and then only those with ECOSOC consultative status were listed.[88] In 1983, some of the NGOs took the inspired initiative to establish the Informal Ad Hoc Group on the Drafting of the Convention on the Rights of the Child to coordinate their various inputs to the drafting process. The group, initially comprising 23 NGOs, started to produce reports, based on consultations with participating NGOs, which reviewed the draft text and, on the basis of consensus, expressed support for the text, suggested changes, or, in some cases, recommended entirely new articles.[89] The reports were distributed to participating delegations, and the proposals were promoted by all members of the group.[90] The result was a break-through. The NGOs were increasingly integrated into the drafting processes, and at least one of them was always included in the informal groups tasked with

80 Declaration on the Protection of All Persons from being Subjected to Torture and Other Cruel, Inhuman or Degrading Treatment or Punishment, GA Res. 3452 (XXX), 9 December 1975.

81 GA Res. 32/62, 8 December 1977.

82 Cook, note 4 above, p. 191.

83 van Boven, note 79 above, p. 211.

84 Michael Longford, 'NGOs and the Rights of the Child', in Peter Willetts (ed.), *The 'Conscience' of the World: The Influence of Non-Governmental Organisations in the UN System* (London: Hurst and Co, 1996), pp. 214, 215–16.

85 *Ibid.*, p. 217.

86 GA Res. 1386(XIV), 20 November 1959.

87 Longford, note 84 above, p. 218.

88 Cynthia Price-Cohen, 'The Role of NGOs in the Drafting of the Convention on the Rights of the Child', *Human Rights Quarterly*, 12 (1990), pp. 137–47, at p. 139.

89 *Ibid.*, pp. 140–1.

90 *Ibid.*

resolving particularly troublesome issues.[91] Cynthia Price-Cohen calculates that 'the imprint of the NGO Group can be found in almost every article',[92] and she also observes that most government statements to the commission, supporting the adoption of the draft, made approving reference to the substantial role played by NGOs in arriving at the final text.[93] Thus, by the end of the 1980s, human rights NGOs had broken through the institutional barrier that had previously kept them at arm's length, becoming full participants, and at times principal actors, in the drafting of human rights treaties;[94] although further up the chain of UN decision-making their influence continued to rely on informal discussions in the labyrinthine corridors and crowded cafes of the UN's meeting facilities.

Human rights NGOs have also made significant indirect normative contributions by their interpretation and application of human rights treaties. One very influential practice has been the production of detailed interpretations of particular human rights treaty provisions, arrived at through intensive deliberative processes involving a range of NGO experts and activists. The 'Siracusa Principles', which interpret the meaning and scope of the derogations and limitations provisions in the ICCPR, are an early example.[95] They were drawn up in 1984 at a meeting organized by the International Commission of Jurists, the International Association of Penal Law, and the Urban Morgan Institute of Human Rights. Similar instruments have been elaborated interpreting the implementation obligations and sex equality provisions of the ICESCR[96] and the application of international human rights law in relation to sexual orientation and gender identity.[97] In addition, some of the activities of NGOs that I have already mentioned, such as drafting General Comments and assisting victims of alleged human rights violations to frame their petitions and communications, also contribute to normative development. In a field that lacks a judicial mechanism to clarify the scope and detailed content of human rights obligations, there are many openings for NGOs to foster developments in the law through their monitoring, lobbying, shaming and educational activities.

Human rights NGOs have also played an important catalytic role in the development of customary international law, operating on what Antonio Cassesse has described as the 'level of imagination'.[98] One dynamic aspect of this work has involved urging the General Assembly's adoption of human rights declarations which, like the UDHR, can serve as evidence of emerging custom and as precursors to the negotiation of binding treaties. The website of the OHCHR lists 24 such declarations adopted, usually unanimously, by the General Assembly.[99] Most of them have been shaped in significant ways by NGOs. I have already made reference to the inclusive initial drafting processes of the Declaration on the Rights of Indigenous Peoples, which was finally

91 *Ibid*., p. 145.

92 *Ibid*., p. 142. See also Longford, note 84 above, p. 224.

93 Price-Cohen, note 88 above, p. 145.

94 van Boven, note 79 above, p. 218.

95 The 'Siracusa Principles', reprinted in *Review of the International Commission of Jurists*, 36 (June 1986), pp. 47–56.

96 The 'Limburg Principles', elaborating the nature and scope of the implementation obligations of the ICESCR *International Commission of Jurists Review*, 37 (December 1986), p. 43; 'Maastricht Guidelines on Violations of Economic, Social and Cultural Rights', *Human Rights Quarterly*, 20 (1998), p. 691; 'Montreal Principles on Women's Economic, Social and Cultural Rights', *Human Rights Quarterly*, 26 (2004), p. 760.

97 The Yogyakarta Principles, adopted at an experts' meeting held in Yogyakarta, Indonesia, 6–9 November 2006.

98 Antonio Cassese, 'How Could Nongovernmental Organizations Use UN Bodies More Effectively?', *Universal Human Rights*, 1 (1979), pp. 73–80, at p. 76.

99 OHCHR [online]. Available from: http://www2.ohchr.org/english/law/ [accessed 22 April 2009].

adopted by the General Assembly in 2007,[100] and to the 1959 Declaration of the Rights of the Child and the 1975 Declaration Against Torture. General Assembly statements can also be an important means of building consensus towards the formal acknowledgement of previously unrecognized or new human rights violations. Notable in this regard was a statement read in the General Assembly by Argentina, on 18 December 2008, and supported by 66 member states, confirming that international human rights protections prohibit discrimination on the basis of sexual orientation and gender identity.[101]

In part through the work of human rights NGOs, it is increasingly true that the groundswell of global opinion is 'not without legal relevance', as Judge Weeramantry remarked in his dissenting opinion in the Nuclear Weapons Advisory Opinion.[102] This groundswell, in the form of transnationally organized human rights movements, has been an important ingredient in the success that NGOs have had, working 'inside' intergovernmental institutions, in promoting normative development – whether it is concern about the widespread use of torture with impunity, the epidemic levels of violence against women, the generations of suffering of dispossessed indigenous peoples, or the deadly consequences of homophobia. However, even these developments, significant as they are, fall well short of the equality, mutuality and self-interest that are deeply embedded in the idea of 'partnership'. I say this partly because these interactions remain institutionally constrained and, more importantly, because there is a significant public interest element driving the participation of NGOs, which is not captured by the concepts of stakeholder and partnership.

3. The Challenges of Increased Institutionalization

It is clear that the role played by NGOs in the UN human rights systems has moved well beyond the consultative status envisaged in the UN Charter. Once 'inside', human rights NGOs forged institutional practices that have increased their power to draw institutional attention to human rights violations and demand an institutional response. They also assumed an increasingly influential role in normative development, making significant contributions to interpreting existing conventions and drafting new ones, and drawing attention to new or as yet unrecognized human rights abuses. To this point in my discussion, I have assumed that these developments are beneficial, both for intergovernmental institutions and for human rights NGOs. Indeed, the Cardoso Report emphasizes the positive effects for the UN, insisting that further enhancing the participation of NGOs and other civil society actors will make it more democratic and therefore more effective, while also strengthening its unique intergovernmental character.[103] Peter Urvin identifies another institutional advantage that flows from engagement with NGOs, which is that NGOs build local constituencies for institutional policies and policies, enhancing their visibility and legitimacy.[104] Kenneth Anderson argues that international organizations have cynically embraced the notion of partnerships with

100 GA Res. 61/295, 2 October 2007.

101 The text of Argentina's statement [online]. Available from: http://www.ilga.org/news_results.asp?LanguageID=1&FileID=1211&FileCategory=1&ZoneID=7 [accessed 22 April 2009]. An alternative statement was also submitted by nearly 60 states, principally from the Islamic world, sub-Saharan Africa and Oceania.

102 *Legality of the Use by a State of Nuclear Weapons in Armed Conflict*, 8 July 1996, Dissenting Opinion of Judge Weeramantry (1996), ICJ Rep 438.

103 Cardoso Report, note 11, para. 24.

104 Peter Uvin, 'Scaling Up the Grassroots and Scaling Down the Summit: The Relations Between Third World NGOs and the UN', in Weiss and Gordenker, note 6 above, pp. 159, 164.

international NGOs because they '*themselves* are in desperate need of [democratic] legitimacy'.[105] The foregoing discussion of the participation of human rights NGOs in the UN supports the view that their involvement has enhanced the effectiveness of its human rights work, at least in the sense of pushing institutional and normative developments that make effectiveness more possible. Their participation has also helped to build new local, national, regional and international constituencies that look to the UN to address human rights violations. Because NGOs are usually in a better position than states to be informants about human rights violations and advocates for victims, they have enhanced the legitimacy of the UN's human rights work by improving, at least in appearance, the system's openness and responsiveness to the concerns of those who experience human rights violations.

However, the Cardoso Report sheds little light on what NGOs might have to gain from enhanced participation in UN institutions, although it does recognize the frustration of many in civil society who are able to speak in UN forums 'but feel they are not heard and that their participation has little impact on outcomes'.[106] In Urwin's view, one of the benefits for NGOs is that they are able to play a role in shaping the international laws and policies that directly concern them and to influence national governments through the international institutions.[107] For Anderson, it is 'obvious' that the inclusion of NGOs increases 'their power and authority within international organizations, international elites, and beyond'.[108] The foregoing discussion supports the view that human rights NGOs have pursued institutional engagement with the UN human rights machineries because of the opportunities they present – to make those machineries more effective, to pursue the human rights goals that matter to them and to the victims who have sought their assistance, and to influence laws, policies and practices at both the international and the national levels to reflect the aspirations of the UDHR.

However, exploring the challenges that institutional incorporation of human rights NGOs present, for both the institutions and for NGOs, allows a more complete evaluation of these institutional interactions and their effects, than does examining only the benefits. The Cardoso Report makes only brief reference to institutional challenges, notably 'governance' problems with the accountability and support base of NGOs and practical problems such as overcrowding and time-management, which it deals with perfunctorily.[109] Yet, there are many significant challenges that the report fails to acknowledge, to some of which I will now turn – first to those facing the institutions and then to those confronting NGOs.

3.1 The Challenges for Intergovernmental Institutions

Increased participation by human rights NGOs has frequently not been welcomed by many member states of UN institutions, especially those who fear becoming the focus of NGO criticism. Through the Cold War, the political sensitivities of states on both sides of the ideological divide created volatility in the UN's relationship with human rights NGOs, as they named states who were alleged violators and became increasingly adept at influencing global public opinion. For decades, states in their capacity as members of international institutions resisted naming the states who were subject to the Human Rights Commission's procedures, confining the commission's role to making public recommendations of a 'objective and general character', which, as Philip Alston

105 Anderson, note 8 above, p. 113.
106 Cardoso Report, note 11 above, 'Executive Summary', p. 7.
107 Urvin, note 103 above, p. 164.
108 Anderson, note 104 above, p. 117.
109 Cardoso Report, note 11 above, paras. 123 and 140.

observes, was a euphemism for non-country-specific comments.[110] Violator states also worked hard to protect themselves through election to the commission, with the result that those few states that were publicly criticized, reflected UN politics rather than independent assessment.[111] Against this backdrop, even the treaty bodies adopted 'general comments' that identified general trends emerging from states parties' reports without naming names. It was only after the Cold War ended that the practice of adopting state-specific 'concluding observations' commenced.[112] Even so, many treaty body members continue to treat states in a highly deferential manner when examining their periodic reports, refraining from outright criticism for fear of alienating them.[113]

Many states also fear that the participation of human rights NGOs presents a threat to the primacy of states in the UN system, despite the Cardoso Report's insistence that it will strengthen the UN's unique intergovernmental quality. The accreditation rules adopted by ECOSOC to regulate consultative arrangements with NGOs have, from the start, been very clear that there is a 'fundamental' and 'deliberately made' distinction between the 'consultative' status that is accorded to NGOs and the capacity to 'participate without vote' in ECOSOC and its subsidiary bodies, which is enjoyed by non-member states and UN specialized agencies.[114] Yet the distinction is often blurred, as when human rights NGOs play a formative role in normative development. The sensitivity of states to what they see as the usurpation of their sovereign powers is also evident in the Declaration on the Rights of Human Rights Defenders, where the General Assembly makes it clear that it is the domestic legal framework that determines what amounts to acceptable conduct for human rights defenders.[115] In some respects, states do have legitimate concerns about the power of NGOs, particularly in the developing world. For example, as Antonio Donini observes, a few large NGOs have together become a larger source of development and relief assistance than the UN itself, assuming functions which have hitherto been considered the sole responsibility of states, such as the provision of public services like education and health.[116] This, as he warns, can further weaken already fragile state structures and thwart the development of indigenous coping mechanisms and autonomy.[117] Also, as Margaret Keck and Kathryn Sikkink argue, the doctrines of sovereignty and non-intervention remain an important defence against foreign interventions that limit the ability of

110 Philip Alston, 'The Historical Origins of the Concept of "General Comments" in Human Rights Law', in Vera Gowlland-Debbes and Laurence Boisson de Chazournes (eds), *The International Legal System in Quest of Equity and Universality* (Dordrecht: Martinus Nijhoff, 2001), pp. 763, 771–2.

111 Felice D. Gaer, 'Reality Check: Human Rights NGOs Confront Governments', in Weiss and Gordenker, note 6 above, pp. 51–66, at p. 53.

112 Thomas Buergenthal, 'The Human Rights Committee', *Max Planck Yearbook of United Nations Law*, 5 (2001), pp. 341, 348.

113 Scott Leckie, 'The Committee on Economic, Social and Cultural Rights: Catalyst for Change in a System Needing Reform', in Alston and Crawford, note 53 above, pp. 129, 132.

114 Representation of Non-Governmental Bodies on the Economic and Social Council, GA Res. 4(I), 14 February 1946; Arrangements for Consultation with Non-Governmental Organisations, ECOSOC Res. 288B(X) 1950; *Arrangements for Consultation with Non-Governmental Organisations*, ECOSOC Res. 1296(XLIV), 23 May 1968, para. 12; *Consultative Relationship between the United Nations and Non-Governmental Organisations*, ECOSOC Res. 1996/31, UN Doc E/1996/31, 25 July 1996, paras. 18–19.

115 Declaration on the Rights and Responsibilities of Individuals, Groups and Organs of Society to Promote and Protect Universally Recognised Human Rights and Fundamental Freedoms, GA Res. 53/144, 9 December 1998, Art. 3.

116 Antonio Donini, 'The Bureaucracy and the Free Spirits: Stagnation and Innovations in the Relationship Between the UN and NGOs', in Weiss and Gordenker, note 6 above, pp. 83, 88–9.

117 *Ibid.*, p. 90.

states in the developing world to fully realize their right to self-determination.[118] These fears are compounded by the Western location and orientation of the majority of international human rights NGOs.

Consequently, there has been a counter-flow of efforts to limit the formal access of human rights NGOs to UN institutions, focusing in particular on the ECOSOC rules for NGO accreditation, and decision-making under the rules by the ECOSOC Committee for NGOs. Since the initial arrangements were established in 1950, they have been reviewed three times, and, each time, concern about criticisms of governments by human rights NGOs was one of the issues precipitating the review.[119] The first review in 1968 led to the introduction of new mechanisms for the committee to control accreditation,[120] granting it the power to review quadrennial reports from NGOs in consultative status[121] and suspend or withdraw accreditation in certain circumstances, including where an NGO has 'systematically engage[d] in unsubstantiated and politically motivated acts against [s]tates',[122] a provision that was patently aimed at human rights NGOs. The second review in 1978, initiated by Argentina, questioned the consultative status of a whole group of human rights NGOs, but in the end did not lead to any change.[123] As Chiang Pei-heng observed in 1981, 'NGO criticism of human rights violations seems to be one of the few issues which cause many governments of both the right and left to close ranks, ignoring ideological differences.'[124] The primary stimulus for the third review, which commenced in 1994, was concern about the proliferation of formal and informal arrangements for NGO participation operating outside the restrictive ECOSOC rules, effectively enabling NGO participation in all aspects of the UN's work,[125] but the hostility of many states to human rights NGOs and continuing concern about the arrangements favouring Western-dominated NGOs were other factors.[126] The result was to hold the line against broadening the accreditation criteria, with the single exception of making it easier for southern NGOs to gain accreditation by allowing regional and national organizations to apply.[127]

Many of the states who fear being targeted by human rights NGOs have sought election to the ECOSOC Committee for NGOs in order to determine the outcome of accreditation applications and participate in reviewing NGO reports, resulting in a situation that Jurij Aston has aptly described as 'the fox … guarding the henhouse'.[128] The politicization of accreditation decision-making about human rights NGOs in particular was evident in the failure of the committee to reach consensus about applications from Human Rights Watch and the International Gay and Lesbian Association in 1993, forcing it to a vote for the first time.[129] More recent examples include its refusal to accredit

118 Margaret Keck and Kathryn Sikkink, *Activists Beyond Borders: Advocacy Networks in International Politics* (Ithaca, NY: Cornell University Press, 1998), p. 215.

119 Dianne Otto, 'Nongovernmental Organizations in the United Nations System: The Emerging Role of International Civil Society', *Human Rights Quarterly*, 18 (1996), pp. 107–41.

120 Chiang Pei-heng, *Non-Governmental Organizations at the United Nations* (New York: Praeger, 1981), pp. 175–9.

121 ECOSOC Res. 1296(XLIV), 23 May 1968, para. 40(b).

122 *Ibid.*, para. 36(b).

123 Pei-heng, note 119 above, p. 187; Gaer, note 110 above, p. 54.

124 *Ibid.*, p. 193.

125 Otto, note 118 above, p. 120.

126 *Ibid.*, p. 121.

127 ECOSOC Res. 1996/31, 25 July 1996, paras. 18 and 19.

128 Jurij Daniel Aston, 'The United Nations Committee on Non-Governmental Organizations: Guarding the Entrance to a Politically Divided House' 12 *European Journal of International Law* (2001), pp. 943, 950.

129 Otto note 118, p. 116.

the international NGO Human Rights in China founded by Chinese scientists and scholars living outside China;[130] its 3-year suspension of the consultative status of the International Council of the Association for Peace in the Continents, a Spanish-based human rights organization, at the instigation of Cuba;[131] and the continual deferment of applications from Hadassah, an American-Jewish women's charity, and Freedom House, a US-based NGO promoting global democracy and civil rights, because of complaints by the Sudan and China respectively.[132] This is hardly the 'constructive engagement' and 'partnership' that the Cardoso Report envisages.

In sum, states have complex relationships with human rights NGOs, which can be friendly and cooperative but are often marked by hostility, suspicion, volatility and confrontation. The 1994 review of ECOSOC consultative arrangements recommended to the General Assembly that it consider establishing arrangements for NGO participation in all the UN's areas of work,[133] but it received a cool response.[134] The Cardoso panel's similar and more detailed recommendation has also not been taken up,[135] attesting to the continuing perception by many states that NGOs present a threat. Paradoxically, the reluctance of intergovernmental institutions to liberalize their NGO accreditation rules encourages the proliferation of informal arrangements, which often give NGOs more power than they would enjoy in formal activities. This is particularly so today, when much of the work of the UN is done in informal and off-the-record meetings. Yet the informal character of their participation works to the disadvantage of NGOs in other respects, and to the advantage of those states that fear criticism by NGOs or feel their privileged position in intergovernmental forums may be threatened. Institutional attempts to arrive at a satisfactory compromise, which will allay the concerns of states, yet 'reshape multilateralism' in ways that will increase the legitimacy and effectiveness of UN institutions, seem inevitably to reach a stalemate. It can be anticipated that the proliferation of informal interactions will continue as states, and the intergovernmental institutions they inhabit, resist change that they fear will threaten their authority as international actors and erode their sovereignty over domestic matters.

3.2 The Challenges for Human Rights NGOs

Increased institutional involvement also raises many dilemmas for human rights NGOs. One problem, which also concerns some states, is that the accreditation rules, and the demands of organization and access, are more easily fulfilled by northern NGOs. The concern is not just about location, but about the conception of human rights that NGOs adopt and promote within intergovernmental institutions. At a retreat of human rights activists held in 1991, participants agreed that while there were many commonalities between southern and northern NGOs, there were also significant differences.[136] Southern human rights NGOs placed considerably more emphasis on the realization of economic and social rights than their northern counterparts, and generally identified (neo)imperialism and other forms of northern intervention as an underlying

130 Lindblon note 33, p. 383

131 Aston, note 127, pp. 952–3.

132 *Ibid.,* p. 950 (especially footnotes 44 and 45 and pp. 956–7).

133 E/1996/297, 25 July 1996.

134 Alger, note 18, p. 96.

135 Cardoso Report, note 11, paras. 120–8.

136 Henry J. Steiner, *Diverse Partners: Non-governmental Organizations in the Human Rights Movement*, The Report of a Retreat of Human Rights Activists, co-sponsored the Harvard Law School Human Rights Program and Human Rights Internet (1991).

problem.[137] Their goals were more likely to challenge overall development plans and aim for social transformation, involving them more in community-based political processes than in law reform and legal advocacy.[138] While many northern NGOs investigated human rights violations primarily in the south, their ideological orientation was nevertheless shaped by traditional liberal values, which led them to focus on civil and political rights violations and individual human rights advocacy, rather than exploring the underlying causes of violations.[139] Although generalizations, these differences have proved to be enduring, despite many international NGOs extending their mandates to include economic and social rights, and the change in ECOSOC accreditation rules to make it easier for non-Western NGOs to participate. As Makau Mutua argues, northern human rights NGOs still need to admit to their ideological bias towards promoting liberal ideals and norms, and stop dressing it up as 'neutrality' and 'objectivity'[140] and, as Maria Grahn-Farley contends, the deep colonial structure of international law continues to reinforce European prerogative.[141] Chidi Odinkalu despairs about the lack of community-based membership of many African human rights NGOs, which are modelled on the watchdog NGOs of the north, and the consequent inability of these organizations to popularize human rights concerns and mobilize movements for change.[142] These competing ideas about the role of human rights NGOs – as legal experts or as grass-roots organizers – continue to be hotly debated in human rights circles,[143] and they have different implications for the role human rights NGOs might seek to play in intergovernmental institutions. The provision of expert advice is consistent with the functionlist role imagined by the UN Charter,[144] while seeking transformative change is the critical role that is best placed to realize the aspirations of the UDHR.

A second major issue for human rights NGOs is the extent of compromise that they are expected to make in order to be perceived as institutionally relevant and effective. Even the 'successful' collaboration between NGOs and states in the drafting of the CRC involved considerable compromise for many of the NGOs involved. As Price-Cohen explains, NGOs constrained themselves from pursuing further improvements in the text, as it made its way through the processes of adoption by the Human Rights Commission, ECOSOC and finally the General Assembly, because they were afraid to upset the delicate balance of state interests that it represented.[145] In a similar vein, Cook explains Amnesty International's acceptance that the price of the General Assembly adopting a consensus resolution, establishing the position of High Commissioner for Human Rights in 1993, was a weaker and vaguer mandate than the one Amnesty had worked for.[146] In the intergovernmental

137 *Ibid.*, p. 28.

138 *Ibid.*, pp. 32–3.

139 *Ibid.*, p. 18. See further, James Gathii and Celestine Nyamu, 'Note, Reflections on United States based Human Rights NGOs' Work on Africa', 9 *Harvard Human Rights Journal* (1996), p. 285.

140 Mutua, note 9, p. 159.

141 Maria Grahn-Farley, 'Neutral Law and Eurocentric Lawmaking: A Postcolonial Analysis of the UN Convention on the Rights of the Child' 34 *Brook Journal International Law* (2008), 1, p. 30.

142 Chidi Anselm Odinkalu, 'Why More Africans Don't Use Human Rights Language' 2(1) *Human Rights Dialogue* (1999), p. 3.

143 See, for example, Kenneth Roth, 'Defending Economic, Social and Cultural Rights: Practical Issues Faced by an International Human Rights Organization', 26 *Human Rights Quarterly* (2004), p. 63; Leonard S. Rubenstein, 'How International Human Rights Organizations Can Advance Economic, Social and Cultural Rights: A Response to Kenneth Roth', 26 *Human Rights Quarterly* (2004), p. 845.

144 Willetts, note 15, p. 312.

145 Price-Cohen, note 88, p. 144.

146 Cook, note 4, p. 195.

setting of the UN, which operates by the rules of diplomacy involving compromise, negotiation and many private discussions, refusal to compromise can be counter-productive. The compromise that is extracted by the institution can create tensions between an NGO's public campaigning and what it is able to achieve through quiet diplomacy.[147] The result is a familiar dilemma; that is, to borrow Audre Lorde's framing of it in the context of the African-American struggle for freedom, whether it is possible to use the 'master's tools' to dismantle the 'master's house'.[148] Those NGOs who have chosen to work from 'inside' the UN's institutions have the hope, if not the conviction, that dismantling and reconstruction from within is possible, but it does require that they play by the rules of the institution, which inevitably demands a diminution of their aspirations.

In some situations, the price of institutional cooption may be too high and this is when NGOs may themselves become 'part of the problem', as David Kennedy has suggested.[149] One of his concerns is that institutional engagement with human rights serves to 'delegitimize' other emancipatory strategies that may more effectively challenge the status quo, and that NGOs can become, in effect, handmaidens to the conservatizing hegemony of international institutions.[150] Donini provides an example, in the context of UN development projects, when he observes that NGOs are increasingly losing their independence as they are implicated in promoting and implementing the institutional policies of northern donors and UN programmes.[151] At the same time, he notes the disappearance of developing world militancy and the muting of the quest for a more equitable international economic order.[152] Uvin, too, describes how NGO participation in intergovernmental policymaking can change the organization's style of functioning to the point where it loses contact with its grass-roots base and 'softens' its positions so that transformative goals such as empowerment and structural change fall off its agenda.[153]

In sum, institutional inclusion creates many dilemmas for human rights NGOs. They become implicated in the institution's overall agenda, which is underpinned by a colonial history that continues to shape relationships in the international community and the development and application of human rights law. They must also compromise their more radical aspirations in order to become institutionally acceptable. Such compromises can lead to a blurring of the distinction between NGOs and the institutions that they initially sought to change, leading NGOs to tone down their commitment to structural change. The 'professionalization' that comes with institutionalization can separate human rights advocates from those they represent, and human rights can become tools of the state and of international governmental institutions, rather than a force for liberation from domination and oppression.

4. Institutional Partnership or Critical Seepages?

Six decades after the adoption of the UDHR, human rights NGOs are engaging with UN human rights institutions through many formal and informal processes, in numbers unanticipated by the drafters of the UN Charter in 1945 and often in a more substantial capacity than the consultative

147 *Ibid.*, p. 209.

148 Audre Lorde, 'The Master's Tools Will Never Dismantle the Master's House' in *Sister Outsider: Essays and Speeches* (Freedom Press, Crossing CA 1984), p. 110.

149 Kennedy, note 10, p. 101.

150 *Ibid.*, pp. 108–9.

151 Donini, note 115, p. 90.

152 *Ibid.*, p. 99.

153 Uvin, note 103, p. 169.

function that was imagined. Increasing institutional engagement has created at least as many challenges for the intergovernmental institutions as for the NGOs. On the one hand, the institutions have taken up the cause of human rights, defining and using them to serve institutional purposes, which threatens to divest human rights of their emancipatory potential and diminish the space for conceptions of human rights 'outside' their institutional form. On the other hand, the institutions can never completely occupy this ground, and human rights NGOs have found seepage points that enable them to breach the comfort zone of states, forcing the institutions to be more critical and to develop mechanisms that offer the possibility of holding more states more accountable for human rights violations.

The Cardoso Report completely sidesteps the many challenges of interaction between NGOs and intergovernmental institutions when it describes the relationship as one of 'partnership'. The panel imagines an international community of 'stakeholders' who can participate on an equal footing in pursuit of their interests, and where intergovernmental institutions provide the forum for the political resolution of any conflicts between stakeholder interests that arise. This model papers over present and historical inequities and the struggles that need to occur over power and distribution and, at times, the preservation of life itself. The panel does not own up to its own ideological bias, which prioritizes private interest over public good.

Seeking to fulfil the aspirations of the UDHR is not just a technical exercise or a process of legally monitored implementation. It involves keeping alive the idea of human rights as an emancipatory discourse founded in the idea of natural rights, which were born to challenge oppression. Pursuing the aspirations of the UDHR involves struggle at many levels – at the grass roots and at the summit, inside intergovernmental institutions and outside them. The UDHR itself recognizes that the realization of its vision cannot be left in the hands of states or intergovernmental institutions when it calls upon 'every individual', as well as 'every organ of society', to strive for the effective recognition and observance of universal human rights and fundamental freedoms.[154]

As the French philosopher Michel Foucault once said, while nothing is in itself evil, everything is dangerous.[155] Engagement with international human rights institutions in order to realize the aspirations of the UDHR is a dangerous endeavour for human rights NGOs because the institutions have the power to turn the discourse of human rights to their own ends.[156] However, institutions can never entirely contain resistive imaginations and energies, especially if they are inspired by and answerable to local movements struggling against inequality and tyranny. Institutions need continual reinvention to remain in the service of such movements, rather than in the power of those seeking to preserve interests vested in hierarchy and privilege. For me, the primary role of human rights NGOs is to challenge the privileged knowledge and systems of hierarchy that international institutions support. To do this, NGOs need to act dangerously in their engagement with intergovernmental institutions, preserve their autonomy, defend their use of oppositional and confrontational strategies, maintain their character as diverse, creative and often locally based, and take advantage of all manner of seepage to keep emancipatory visions of human rights free from institutional capture.

---

154 UDHR (n. 3) preamble, para 8.

155 Colin Gordon, 'Government Rationality: An Introduction' in Graham Burchell, Colin Gordon and Peter Miller (eds), *The Foucault Effect: Studies in Governmentality* (University of Chicago Press, Chicago 1991), p. 46.

156 Costas Douzinas, *The End of Human Rights: Critical Legal Thought at the Turn of the Century* (Hart, Oxford 2000).

Chapter 18

Islamic Law and the Implementation of International Human Rights Law: A Case Study of the International Covenant on Civil and Political Rights

Mashood A. Baderin

1. Introduction

Using the International Covenant on Civil and Political Rights (ICCPR)[1] as a case study, this chapter provides a general analysis of the impact of Islamic law on the implementation of international human rights law in Muslim states where the *Shari'ah* is a source of law, and Islamic law (or elements thereof) is applied as part of the domestic law of the state. The relevance and prospective impact of Islamic law on international human rights law had been manifested from the very beginning of the United Nations (UN) human rights venture during the early debates on the draft provisions of the UDHR before its adoption on 10 December 1948. During the UN General Assembly's Third Committee article-by-article consideration of the draft provisions of the UDHR in November 1948, there were objections, particularly from Saudi Arabia, about the scope of the draft provisions of the UDHR on equal rights of spouses within marriage and at its dissolution, and the right to freedom of religion including freedom to change one's religion or belief. The scope of the provisions that eventually became Articles 16 and 18 of the UDHR, respectively, was considered by the objecting Muslim states to be contrary to Islamic law.[2] For example, among the Muslim states represented at the Third Committee deliberations on the draft provisions, only Lebanon voted in favour of Article 18 of the UDHR on the right to freedom of religion, including the right to change one's religion or belief, for which Lebanon was criticized by the other Muslim states present.[3] Although the objections of the Muslim states in that regard were defeated in the end, and eight[4] of the 48 UN member states who eventually voted affirmatively in the UN General Assembly for the adoption of the UDHR on 10 December 1948 were Muslim states in which Islamic law had some domestic influence, Saudi Arabia maintained its stand and abstained from the voting, apparently in pursuance of its earlier objection to the scope of Articles 16 and 18 of the UDHR respectively, on grounds of Islamic law.

---

1 999 UNTS 171.

2 See UN Doc. A/C.3/SR.125–7 (1948). See also, generally, J. Kelsay, 'Saudi Arabia, Pakistan, and the Universal Declaration of Human Rights', in D. Little, J. Kelsay and A.A. Sachedina (eds), *Human Rights and the Conflict of Cultures: Western and Islamic Perspectives on Religious Liberty* (Columbia, SC: University of South Carolina Press, 1988), pp. 33–52.

3 See M. Ganji, *International Protection of Human Rights* (Geneva: Droz, 1962), p. 145.

4 Afghanistan, Egypt, Iran, Iraq, Lebanon, Pakistan, Syria and Yemen.

Over time, most Muslim states that apply Islamic law, including Saudi Arabia, have become states parties to different international human rights treaties after the adoption of the UDHR. It has, however, been noted that Saudi Arabia's contentions during the 1948 debates on the provisions of the UDHR 'has resonated ever since in Islamic encounters' with international human rights law.[5] Today, many Muslim states have entered interpretive declarations and/or reservations, on grounds of the *Shari'ah* or principles of Islamic law, to some of the human rights treaties they have signed or ratified. Many more states that may not have entered interpretive declarations or reservations have made references to the *Shari'ah* or principles of Islamic law in their periodic human rights reports to relevant UN treaty bodies, all of which certainly has significant impact on the implementation of international human rights law generally and in the respective Muslim states particularly.

This chapter critically analyses such references to the *Shari'ah* or Islamic law in the interpretive declarations, reservations and periodic human rights reports of relevant Muslim states, with particular reference to the ICCPR. At the end, the chapter also highlights the challenges that international human rights law has, conversely, posed to Islamic law over the years and how this has impacted on the application of Islamic law and led to reforms in the law in relevant Muslim states. The scope of enquiry will be limited to those Muslim states that apply Islamic law (or elements of it) as part of their domestic law and/or have made references to the *Shari'ah* or Islamic law in their interpretive declarations, reservations or human rights reports. While the main human rights treaty to be examined in that regard, owing to constraints of space, is the ICCPR, references may be made to other relevant international human rights treaties for further illustration of relevant points where necessary.

2. Implementation of International Human Rights Law

It is evident that the international human rights venture initiated by the UN after the Second World War was not meant to be a mere theoretical exercise but a venture aimed at touching and improving human lives through its practical implementation universally. Although it is often highlighted that the UDHR did not provide for a specific implementation mechanism, it is important to note that in proclaiming the declaration as a common standard of achievement for all peoples and nations, the UN General Assembly also expressed a clear implementational intention by stating that effort must be made at all levels of society to 'promote respect for these rights and freedoms and by progressive measures, national and international, to secure their universal and effective recognition and observance, both among the peoples of Member States themselves and among the peoples of territories under their jurisdiction'.[6] The UDHR was the first part of the so-called international bill of rights and was subsequently followed by binding human rights treaties with provisions for specific implementation mechanisms. The implementational intention initially expressed in the UDHR has now materialized in two main ways, in the form of state obligations, under the different international human rights treaties adopted after the UDHR.

5 M. Ignatieff, 'The Attack on Human Rights', *Foreign Affairs*, 80(6) (2001), pp. 102–16, at p. 103 (Although Ignatieff refers to 'Western human rights', this is apparently in reference to the international human rights system).

6 UDHR, Preamble, para. 8.

Firstly, the different human rights treaties normally contain an implementational undertaking by respective states parties to ensure the enjoyment of the rights provided under the respective treaties by all individuals within their respective territories and subject to their respective jurisdictions, and that the states will, where not already provided, adopt such laws or other necessary measures to give effect to the rights recognized under the respective treaties.[7] Secondly, relevant mechanisms in the form of implementation committees are created by different human rights treaties to monitor and facilitate the practical implementation of the respective treaties by states parties.[8] In both ways, states are the primary obligation holders that are expected to ensure the implementation of human rights within their respective territories and jurisdictions. The universal implementation of international human rights law is thus achieved through the combined implementation of respective human rights treaties by individual states parties in their respective territories and jurisdictions. Such implementation of human rights treaties by states parties normally occurs within their respective domestic legal systems, and it would be difficult to guarantee the implementation of any international human rights treaty without the facilitating aid of the domestic laws of respective states parties.

The importance of domestic law in facilitating the implementation of international human rights law is reflected, for example, in Article 2(2) of the ICCPR, which provides that '[w]here not already provided for by existing legislation or other measures, each State Party to the present Covenant undertakes to take the necessary steps, in accordance with its constitutional processed and with the provisions of the present Covenant, to adopt such laws or other measures as may be necessary to give effect to the rights recognized in the present Covenant.' This is complemented by the general rule on the law of treaties that 'a party may not invoke the provisions of its internal law as justification for its failure to perform a treaty',[9] whereby states are expected to change or amend any existing domestic laws that are inconsistent with the provisions of any human rights treaty to which they are parties.[10] On the contrary, states may, except where a treaty prohibits it, enter interpretative declarations or reservations to modify or limit their treaty obligations in relation to their domestic laws, provided such declarations or reservations are not incompatible with the object and purpose of the treaty.[11]

It is in the context of domestic law that Islamic law becomes legally and formally relevant with regard to the implementation of international human rights treaties in many Muslim states.[12]

---

7 E.g. Article 2 of the ICCPR, the International Convention on Economic, Social and Cultural Rights (ICESCR); the Convention on the Elimination of Racial Discrimination (CERD); the Convention on the Elimination of All Forms of Discrimination Against Women (CEDAW); the Convention Against Torture and Other Cruel, Inhuman or Degrading Treatment or Punishment (CAT); and the Convention on the Rights of the Child (CRC), and Article 7 of the Convention on the Protection of the Rights of Migrant Workers and Their Families (CMW), and the Convention on the Rights of Persons with Disabilities (CRPD), respectively.

8 E.g. Part IV of ICCPR and ICESCR; Part II of CERD, CAT and CRC; Part V of CEDAW; Part VII of CMW; and Articles 34–9 of CRPD, respectively.

9 Art. 27, Vienna Convention on the Law of Treaties (1969), 1155 UNTS 331.

10 E.g. HRC General Comment 31[80], UN Doc. CCPR/C/21/Rev.1/Add.13, para. 13.

11 Art. 19, Vienna Convention on the Law of Treaties (1969), 1155 UNTS 331.

12 Apart from the legal relevance, Islamic law also has a socio-cultural relevance in relation to human rights in Muslim states. See M.A. Baderin, 'Islam and the Realization of Human Rights in the Muslim World: A Reflection on Two Essential Approaches and Two Divergent Perspectives", *Muslim World Journal of Human Rights*, 4(1) (2007), Art. 5.

3. Islamic Law As Part of Domestic Law in Muslim States

Islamic law remains one of the major legal systems in the world today. It is applicable in different forms as part of state law in many countries of the Middle East, Asia and Africa. In some of these countries, such as Saudi Arabia, Yemen, Iran, Pakistan, Libya, and Sudan, and in northern Nigeria, Islamic law (or elements thereof) applies in both the areas of criminal law and personal status laws, while in most others Islamic law applies only in the areas of personal status laws[13] applicable to Muslims. The constitutions of some Muslim states further provide that any laws contrary to the *Shari'ah* shall be null and void in the respective states.[14]

Traditionally, Islamic law is usually stated as having four sources, namely the Qur'an,[15] the *Sunnah*,[16] the *Ijmā'*,[17] and the *Qiyās*.[18] One major misunderstanding, in that regard, is the erroneous view that all the sources of the law and the Islamic legal system generally are completely divine, immutable, monolithic and inflexible. Such misconceptions of Islamic law can create serious difficulties in its relationship with international human rights law. For example, such a misconception is reflected in the decision of the European Court of Human Rights (ECtHR) in the case of *Refah Partisi (Welfare Party) and Others* v *Turkey*,[19] wherein the court emphatically expressed its (mis)understanding that Islamic law is static and invariable and thus incompatible with human rights.

The first step to a better understanding of the nature of Islamic law is to appreciate that the terms '*Sharī'ah*' and 'Islamic law' are not technically synonymous concepts. Rather, the *Sharī'ah,* strictly speaking, refers to the fundamental sources of Islam, namely, the Qur'an and the authenticated traditions (*Sunnah*) of the Prophet Muhammad (pbuh),[20] both of which Muslims consider to be divine and immutable sources from which Islamic religious, moral, social, economic, political and legal norms are derived. Thus, the *Sharī'ah,* in the context of these two divine sources, covers more than just law – it is law plus. Conversely, Islamic law refers to the law or rulings (*Ahkām*; singular: *Hukm*) that are derived from the *Sharī'ah* (i.e. the Qur'an and the *Sunnah*) by Muslim jurists and applied by judges. Muslim jurists therefore normally talk of '*Ahkām al-Sharī'ah*' (singular: '*Hukm al-Sharī'ah*'), meaning '*Sharī'ah* rulings' or '*Sharī'ah* law', i.e. rulings derived from the *Sharī'ah,* when referring to Islamic law as applied law. The '*Ahkām al-Sharī'ah*' (or 'Islamic law') are reached through a human juristic method called '*Fiqh*' (which literally means 'understanding' and technically means 'jurisprudence'), based on the process of *Ijtihād* (legal reasoning); that is, human juristic understanding of the divine sources using different, well-defined classical and post-classical jurisprudential methods and principles formulated by Muslim jurists over time. Thus, it was through the medium of *Fiqh,* based on the process of *Ijtihād,* that the early Islamic jurists transformed the provisions of the *Sharī'ah* into applied law in the form of *Ahkām al-Sharī'a* or Islamic law. Ahmad Qadri has observed in that regard that the Islamic jurists were emphatic in saying that 'though God has given us a revelation He also gave us brains to understand it; and

13 Covering matters relating to marriage, divorce, maintenance, custody, and inheritance.

14 E.g. Art. 227(1) of the Constitution of the Islamic Republic of Pakistan (1973 as amended); Art. 10(b) of the Constitution of the Republic of Maldives (2008); Art. 4 of the Constitution of the Islamic Republic of Iran (1979 as amended), and Art. 48 of the Saudi Arabian Basic Law of Government.

15 The Holy Book of Islam.

16 Traditions of the Prophet Muhammad (pbuh, note 20 below).

17 Jurisitic consensus.

18 Analogical deductions.

19 *European Human Rights Review*, 37 (2003), p. 1.

20 The abbreviation (pbuh) means 'Peace be upon him', and is normally inserted after the name of the Prophet Muhammad.

He did not intend to be understood without careful and prolonged study.'[21] Based on their human understandings of the provisions of the *Sharī'ah* through careful and prolonged study, the classical Islamic jurists compiled books of *Fiqh* (jurisprudence) containing the *Ahkam al-Sharī'ah* or Islamic law as derived by the different Islamic schools of law (*Madhāhib*) that were consequently established around the tenth century, namely the *Māliki, Hanafī, Shāfi'ī* and *Hanbalī Sunnī* schools of law, as well as the different *Shī'ah* schools of law that are followed respectively in different Muslims countries today. These jurisprudential rulings by the classical Islamic jurists, unlike the *Sharī'ah* itself, are neither divine nor immutable, but have become accepted by Muslims as established legal treatises of Islamic law in different Muslim countries today.

In that regard, Islamic law as derived rulings from the *Sharī'ah* can be perceived either in a historical or evolutional sense. Perceived in a historical sense, Islamic law is often restricted to the traditional rulings of the classical jurists as if those rulings were immutable, like the *Sharī'ah* itself. This creates a reductionist perception of Islamic law that is hinged on the disputed theory of the 'closing of the gate of legal reasoning *(Ijtihād)*' around the thirteenth century. This theory is to the effect that Islamic law must be restricted to the legal rulings of the classical jurists as recorded in the legal treatises of the established schools of Islamic jurisprudence dating back to the tenth century, a theory that, in essence, represents Islamic law as a system stuck in the past. A strict and blind adherence to the historical perception of some aspects of Islamic law can lead to contradictions between some traditional Islamic jurisprudential views and international human rights law. Conversely, the evolutional perception of Islamic law is the opposite of the historical perception, and it is to the effect that while the legal rulings of the classical jurists provide a rich source of jurisprudence they do not stop the continual development of Islamic law based on modern jurisprudence *(Fiqh)* through the process of continual legal reasoning *(Ijtihād)* by qualified jurists in Islamic law. In essence, the evolutional perception represents Islamic law as a system that evolves in necessary response to the dynamic nature of human life. Adoption of the evolutional perception of Islamic law helps to positively harmonize the apparent contradictions between some aspects of Islamic law and international human rights law.

While there are Muslim and non-Muslim commentators on Islamic law who advance a strict, historical perception of Islamic law, there is abundant theoretical and practical evidence to establish that Islamic law as '*hkām al-Sharī'ah*' (i.e. rulings derived from the *Shari'ah*) through *Fiqh* has not actually been inherently static or immutable, but has responded and adjusted to the factors of time and circumstances since its inception. This is particularly so in respect of temporal matters pertaining to human relations (*Mu'āmalāt*), which are more affected by the dynamic nature of human life, in contrast to matters relating to religious observances and acts of worship *(Ibādāt)*, which are relatively stable. It is in the different aspects of human relations (*Mu'āmalat*) that the evolutional nature of Islamic law has been well manifested in theory and practice over the years, since its emergence in the seventh century. There are many relevant established jurisprudential principles and maxims of Islamic law depicting its evolutional and flexible nature in both theory and practice. A relevant Islamic legal maxim in that regard is that Islamic legal rulings may change with relevant changes in time within the context of the *Sharī'ah*.[22]

21 A.A. Qadri, *Islamic Jurisprudence in the Modern World* (New Delhi: Taj Co., 1986), p. 199.

22 This is expressed as *Lā yunkar taghayyur al-Ahkām bi taghayyur al-Azman* [it is an accepted fact that legal rulings vary with the change in times] See e.g. Art. 38 of *Majallah* [online]; available from: http://www.ummah.net/Al_adaab/fiqh/majalla/index.html; M.T. al-Ghunaimi, *Durūs fī Usūl al-Qānūn al Wada'ī* (1961), p. 150, cited in M.T. al-Ghunaimi, *The Muslim Conception of International Law and the Western Approach* (The Hague: Nijhoff, 1968), p. 101. See also the following Arabic sources in that regard, F.U. al-Zayla'i, *Tabyin al-Haqa'iq* (Cairo: Dar al-Kutub al-Islamiyyah, 1313AH), vol. 1, p. 140; A. al-Zarqa,

Contrary to a strict historical perception, the evolutional nature of Islamic law is currently reflected in different degrees in the practices of most Muslim states and communities as well as in the views of contemporary Muslim jurists and scholars in the Muslim world and among Muslim communities generally. Kamali illustrates this as follows:

> In modern times legal interpretation or reasoning [in Islamic law] has occurred in the following three ways: statutory legislation, judicial decision and learned opinion (*fatwa*), and scholarly writings. Instances of legislative interpretation, which Noel Coulson referred to as 'neo-*ijtihad*,' can be found in the modern reforms of family law in many Muslim countries, particularly with reference to polygyny and divorce, both of which have been made contingent upon a court order, and therefore are no longer the unilateral privilege of the husband. Current reformist legislation on these subjects derives some support from the jurists' doctrines of the *Maliki* and *Hanafi* schools, but these reforms are essentially based on novel interpretation of the Quran's relevant portions. Numerous instances of independent reasoning are also found in the views of the *ulama* [religious scholars], such as the collections of published opinions of Muhammad Rashid Rida in the 1920s and those of the late *shaykh* of Azhar, Mahmud Shaltut, in the 1950s. In the 1967 case of *Khursid Bibi* vs. *Muhammad Amin*, the supreme court of Pakistan's decision to validate a form of divorce, known as *khula*, that can take place at the wife's initiative, even without the consent of the husband, can be cited as an example of judicial *ijtihad*. Another example of ongoing reinterpretation is the scholarly contribution of the Egyptian scholar Yusuf al-Qaradawi, who validated air travel by women unaccompanied by male relatives. According to the rules of *fiqh* that were formulated in premodern times, women were not permitted to travel alone. Al-Qaradawi based his conclusion on the analysis that the initial ruling was intended to ensure women's physical and moral safety, and that modern air travel fulfills this requirement. He further supported this view with an analysis of the relevant *hadiths* on the subject and arrived at a ruling better suited to contemporary conditions.[23]

Thus, current Islamic jurisprudential trends clearly demonstrate that the humane objectives of the *Shari'ah* can be better realized through the evolutional perception of Islamic law in a continually changing world, especially in relation to international human rights law, as will be further argued below.

4. The Impact of Islamic Law on the ICCPR in Muslim States[24]

The ICCPR, adopted in 1966 and entered into force in 1976, guarantees 24 substantive civil and political rights, generally reflecting basic ideals of freedom, liberty, equality and security. The

---

Sharh al- Qawa'id al-Fiqhiyyah, 4th edn (Damascus: Dar al-Qalam, 1996/1417), pp. 227–9; A.A. al-Nadwi, *al-Qawa'id al-Fiqhiyyah, Mafhumuha, Nash'atuha, Tatawwuruha, Dirasatuha, Mu'allafatiha, Adillatuha, Muhimmatuha, Tatbiqatuha*, 4th edn (Damascus: Dar al-Qalam, 1998/1418), p. 158; M.S.A. al-Burnu, *al-Wajīz fi Idah Qawa'id al-Fiqhiyyah al-Kuliyyah* 5th edn (Beirut: Mu'assasah al-Risalah, 2002/1422), p. 310; S. al-Sidlan, *al-Qawa'id al-Fiqhiyyah al-Kubra wama Tafarra' 'anha* (Riyadh: Dar Balnasiyah, 1417 AH), pp. 426–49.

23 H.M. Kamali, 'Law and Society: The Interplay of Revelation and Reason in the Shariah', in J.L. Esposito (ed.), *The Oxford History of Islam* (Oxford: Oxford University Press, 1999), pp. 107–54, at p. 118.

24 All information on ratification, reservation, declarations, etc., has been gathered from the UN Treaty Collection Database [online]. Available from: http://treaties.un.org/Pages/ViewDetails.aspx?src=TREATY&mtdsg_no=IV-2&chapter=4&lang=en [accessed 23 January 2010].

rights guaranteed under the covenant are the right of self-determination; the equality of rights between men and women; the right to life; the right to freedom from torture or cruel, inhuman or degrading treatment or punishment; the right to freedom from slavery, servitude and forced labour; the right to liberty and security of person; the right to a humane incarceration system; the right to freedom from imprisonment for contractual obligation; the right to liberty of movement and choice of residence; the right of aliens to freedom from arbitrary expulsion; the right to a fair hearing and the due process of law; the right to freedom from retroactive criminal laws; the right to recognition as a person before the law; the right to privacy; the right to freedom of thought, conscience and religion; the right to freedom of opinion and expression; the prohibition of propaganda for war and incitement to hatred; the right to peaceful assembly; the right to freedom of association; the right to marry and found a family; the rights of the child; the right to political participation; the right to equality before the law; and the rights of ethnic, religious or linguistic minorities.

Over the years, many Muslim states that apply Islamic law (or elements of it) as part of their domestic laws have become states parties to the ICCPR. These include countries such as Afghanistan, Algeria, Bahrain, Bangladesh, Djibouti, Egypt, Gambia, Indonesia, Iran, Iraq, Jordan, Kuwait, Lebanon, Libya, Maldives, Mali, Mauritania, Morocco, Nigeria, Sudan, Syria, Tunisia and Yemen. Conversely, some prominent Muslim states in which Islamic law applies significantly as part of domestic law, such as Brunei, Comoros,[25] Malaysia, Oman, Pakistan,[26] Qatar, Saudi Arabia and the United Arab Emirates have not yet ratified the covenant. While it could be postulated that Islamic religious considerations and the role of Islamic law in the domestic laws of these Muslim states might have an apparent role in their non-ratification of the ICCPR, it is difficult to make a definite conclusion in that regard without the respective states specifically stating so. It has been rightly observed that, regardless of the influence of the *Shari'ah* or Islamic law on the ratification practices of Muslim states, there are still many ambiguous reasons, other than Islamic law, why a particular Muslim state may or may not ratify a particular human rights treaty.[27]

It is evident, however, that some of the Muslim states parties to the ICCPR, such as Algeria, Bahrain, Egypt, Maldives, Mauritania and Kuwait, have entered interpretative declarations or reservations to the covenant on grounds of the *Shari'ah* or Islamic law, which definitely impacts, in one way or another, on the implementation of the covenant in the respective states. Generally, such declarations and reservations relate mainly to Article 3 on equality of rights between men and women; Article 18 on the right to freedom of thought, conscience and religion; and Article 23 on the right to marry and found a family, particularly the equal rights of spouses within a marriage and at its dissolution,[28] all of which reflects the objection made by Saudi Arabia, on grounds of Islamic law, against Articles 16 and 18 of the UDHR earlier in 1948. The declarations and reservations are analysed below.

---

25 Comoros signed the ICCPR on 25 September 2008 but has not yet ratified it and thus is not yet a state party.

26 Pakistan signed the ICCPR on 17 April 2008 but has not yet ratified it and thus is not yet a state party.

27 N. Abiad, *Sharia, Muslim States and International Human Rights Treaty Obligations: A Comparative Survey* (London: BIICL, 2008), p. 82.

28 Specifically, Art. 23(4) ICCPR.

4.1 Article 3 Reservations and Declarations on Grounds of Islamic Law

Under Article 3 of the ICCPR, the state parties 'undertake to ensure the equal rights of men and women to the enjoyment of all civil and political rights' guaranteed under the covenant. Bahrain is the only state that, on accession to the covenant, entered a reservation to Article 3 specifically on grounds of Islamic law, stating that it will interpret the article 'as not affecting in any way the prescriptions of Islamic Shari'ah'. Although this reservation is specific to Article 3, it has a far-reaching effect that extends to all the other articles of the covenant. The consequence of this reservation is that Bahrain does not undertake to ensure the equal rights of men and women within its territory and jurisdiction to enjoy all the civil and political rights guaranteed under the covenant, if that is considered violative of its interpretation of Islamic law. This could lead to discriminatory application of the provisions of the ICCPR principally to women, but also to men, depending on the state's interpretation of the prescriptions of Islamic Shari'ah on particular provisions of the covenant, especially where a historical rather than evolutional perception of Islamic law is adopted by the state.[29] Bahrain's reservation was, however, rejected by the UN Secretary-General, as depository of multi-lateral treaties, owing to objections received from other states parties to the covenant in that regard.[30] As Bahrain has not yet submitted any periodic report to the Human Rights Committee (HRC) in respect of the ICCPR, it is not possible to appraise its position for the time being on the reservation and its rejection by the UN Secretary-General.

Of relevance also is the interpretive declaration entered by Kuwait to Article 3 to the effect that the rights guaranteed under Article 3 would be 'exercised within the limits set by Kuwaiti law'. While Islamic law is not specifically referred to in this interpretive declaration, the reference to 'Kuwaiti law' indirectly relates to Islamic law, as Kuwait made it clear in its other interpretive declaration to Article 23 that its personal status laws are based on Islamic law. This indirect relation to Islamic law was identified in the consideration of Kuwait's 1999 initial periodic report to the HRC, whereby the committee concluded that this interpretive declaration contravenes the state party's essential obligations under the covenant, and it thus urged the state to withdraw it.[31] The committee referred in particular to the Kuwaiti Personal Status Code, expressing concern that the code accommodated discriminative practices against women, and it thus urged the state to ensure equality between men and women both in law and practice, to prohibit polygamy, and 'to

29 See, generally, M.A. Baderin, *International Human Rights and Islamic Law* (Oxford: Oxford University Press, 2003), pp. 58–66.

30 'The reservation was lodged with the Secretary-General on 4 December 2006 by Bahrain, following its accession to the Covenant on 20 September 2006. In keeping with the depositary practice followed in similar cases, the Secretary-General proposed to receive the reservation in question for deposit in the absence of any objection on the part of any of the Contracting States, either to the deposit itself or to the procedure envisaged, within a period of 12 months from the date of the relevant depositary notification. In the absence of any such objection, the above reservation would be accepted in deposit upon the expiration of the above-stipulated 12 month period, that is on 28 December 2007. In view of the … objections [received from The Netherlands, Latvia, Portugal, Czech Republic, Estonia, Canada, Australia, Ireland, Italy Poland, Sweden, Hungary, Mexico, Slovakia, and the UK], the Secretary-General did not accept the reservation made by Bahrain in deposit.' See note 15 to Status of Ratification of the ICCPR [online]. Available from: http://treaties.un.org/Pages/ViewDetails.aspx?src=TREATY&mtdsg_no=IV-4&chapter=4&lang=en#15.

31 HRC Concluding Observations on 1999 Initial Periodic Report of Kuwait, UN Doc. CCR/CO/63/KWT of 27 July 2000, para. 4.

take all necessary measures to sensitize the population, so as to eradicate attitudes that lead to discrimination against women in all sectors of daily life and society'.[32]

Contrary to the reservation and declaration to Article 3 by Bahrain and Kuwait, respectively, other Muslim states parties to the ICCPR, who also apply Islamic law as part of their domestic law, generally indicate in their periodic reports to the HRC that their compliance with Article 3 of the covenant is not impeded by their interpretations and applications of Islamic law.[33] This does not, however, detract from the fact that some traditional historical interpretations of Islamic law may facilitate substantial gender discrimination in practice in almost all Muslim states, contrary to the envisaged scope of Article 3 of the ICCPR and similar equality of rights provisions such as Article 3 of the International Covenant on Economic, Social and Cultural Rights (ICESCR)[34] and Article 3 of the Convention on the Elimination of all Forms of Discrimination Against Women (CEDAW).[35]

4.2 Article 18 Reservations on Grounds of Islamic Law

Article 18 of the ICCPR guarantees freedom of thought, conscience and religion. The initial draft of the article included 'freedom to change one's religion or belief' as in Article 18 of the UDHR, which was opposed by Muslim states such as Afghanistan, Egypt, Saudi Arabia and Yemen.[36] As a compromise, this was changed to include, instead, 'freedom to have or to adopt a religion or belief of [one's] choice'.[37] The HRC has, however, indicated in its General Comment 22 that the freedom to have or to adopt a religion of one's choice includes the freedom to change one's religion or belief.[38] The Saudi Arabian representative who had proposed the change during the debates on Article 18 at the Third Committee meeting is recorded to have indicated after the amendment that he did recognize that the freedom to change one's belief or religion was still implicit in Article 18 of the ICCPR, despite the amendment.[39] It is this understanding that has, perhaps, influenced the declarations and reservations entered to the article by some Muslim states on grounds of Islamic law.

Bahrain's reservation mentioned earlier above also referred to Article 18 with the effect that it will interpret Article 18 'as not affecting in any way the prescriptions of Islamic Shari'ah'. Similarly, on accession to the ICCPR, Maldives entered a reservation stating that 'the application of the principles set out in Article 18 of the covenant shall be without prejudice to the Constitution of

32 *Ibid*., para. 5.

33 E.g. Fifth Periodic Report (Morocco) UN Doc. CCPR/C/MAR/2004/5 of 11 May 2004, para. 58ff; Third Periodic Report (Libya), UN Doc. CCPR/C/102/Add.1 of 15 October 1997, para. 91ff; Combined Third and Fourth Periodic Report (Egypt) UN Doc. CCPR/C/EGY/2001/315 April 2002, para. 150ff.

34 993 UNTS 3. Article 3 of the ICESCR states: 'The States Parties to the present Covenant undertake to ensure the equal right of men and women to the enjoyment of all economic, social and cultural rights set forth in the present Covenant.'

35 1249 UNTS 13. Article 3 of CEDAW states: 'States Parties shall take in all fields, in particular in the political, social, economic and cultural fields, all appropriate measures, including legislation, to ensure the full development and advancement of women, for the purpose of guaranteeing them the exercise and enjoyment of human rights and fundamental freedoms *on a basis of equality with men*' (emphasis added).

36 See K.J. Partsch, 'Freedom of Conscience and Expression, and Political Freedoms', in L. Henkin (ed.), *The International Bill of Rights: The Covenant on Civil and Political Rights* (1981), p. 211; and Baderin, note 25 above, p. 119.

37 See UN Doc. A/C.3/SR.1026 (1960), para. 26; and B.G. Tahzib, *Freedom of Religion or Belief: Ensuring Effective International Legal Protection* (The Hague: Martinus Nijhoff Publishers, 1996), p. 86.

38 HRC General Comment 22, para. 5.

39 See Tahzib, note 37 above,

the Republic of Maldives'. This can be considered as an indirect reference to Islamic law, as Article 10 of the constitution of Maldives provides that 'Islam shall be one of the bases of all the laws of Maldives' and that 'No law contrary to any tenet of Islam shall be enacted in the Maldives'. Further, the fundamental rights and freedoms under the Maldivian constitution are themselves guaranteed to all persons 'in a manner that is not contrary to any tenet of Islam'.[40] Thus, in its objection to the Maldivian reservation, Slovakia noted, *inter alia*, that '[a]ccording to the Maldivian legal system, *mainly based on the principles of Islamic law*, the reservation raises doubts as to the commitment of the Republic of Maldives to its obligations under the Covenant, essential for the fulfilment of its object and purpose.'[41] Another Muslim country that has entered a reservation to Article 18 on grounds of Islamic law is Mauritania, which stated that its application 'shall be without prejudice to the Islamic *Shari'ah*', meaning, in essence, that the scope of the article will be curtailed by the provisions of Islamic law on freedom of religion.

Islamic law does acknowledge the general concept of freedom of religion based on specific provisions of the Qur'an such as 'Let there be no compulsion in religion: Truth stands out clearly from Error'[42] and 'Had your Lord willed so everyone on earth would have believed; would you then compel people to become believers?'[43] Yet, under traditional historical interpretations of Islamic law, apostasy from Islam is prohibited and is a serious, punishable crime. Under that historical interpretation, Muslims are not allowed to change their religion within the context of Article 18 of the ICCPR. Apparently, it is this traditional prohibition of apostasy by Islamic law that engendered Saudi Arabia's objection to Article 18 of the UDHR in 1948 and has also engendered the reservations of the Muslim states to Article 18 of the ICCPR on grounds of Islamic law.

Like Bahrain, both Maldives and Mauritania have not yet submitted any periodic reports to the HRC on the ICCPR, and thus their submissions on their reservations to Article 18 cannot be appraised for the time being. However, in its engagement with other Muslim states that have submitted periodic reports to the ICCPR, the HRC has expressed concern regarding the impact of Islamic law on the application of Article 18 of the ICCPR in the respective Muslim states, as referred to in Section 4.5 below.

4.3 Article 23 Reservations and Declarations on Grounds of Islamic Law

Generally, Article 23 guarantees the 'right of men and women of marriageable age to marry and to found a family' based on the 'free and full consent of the intending spouses', states parties to the covenant undertaking under Article 23(4) to 'take appropriate steps to ensure equality of rights and responsibilities of spouses as to marriage, during marriage and at its dissolution'. Apparently, it is this provision to ensure equality of rights and responsibilities of spouses as to marriage, during marriage and at its dissolution that has engendered reservations on grounds of Islamic law from the Muslim states mentioned in the following discussion.

Bahrain has entered reservation in respect of Article 23 generally 'as not affecting in any way the prescriptions of Islamic Shari'ah', while Mauritania has also entered reservation specifically to Article 23(4) of the covenant to the effect that its application will not affect 'in any way the prescriptions of the Islamic Shari'ah'. Algeria has also entered an interpretive declaration to Article 23(4) to the effect that it will interpret the provision 'regarding the rights and responsibilities of

40 Article 16, Constitution of the Republic of Maldives (2008).

41 See note 28 to the Status of Ratification of the ICCPR, note 24 above (emphasis added).

42 Q2:256.

43 Q10:99.

spouses as to marriage, during marriage and at its dissolution as in no way impairing the essential foundations of the Algerian legal system'. Although Algeria makes no direct reference to Islamic law in this interpretive declaration, its representatives indicated in response to questions in that regard before the HRC that the declaration was entered on the basis of Islamic law provisions applicable under the Algerian Family Code.

However, Algeria appears to have adopted an evolutionary perspective of Islamic law in the reform of its old Family Code, which was based on traditional Islamic jurisprudence, and upon which it had entered the interpretive declaration to the ICCPR in 1989. In its third periodic report to the ICCPR, submitted in 2006, Algeria indicated that while the old Family Code had not been revised since its promulgation in 1984, 'the many social changes that had taken place in Algerian society, combined with the need to bring domestic legislation into line with the international conventions ratified by Algeria ... made it natural that the Code should be revised.' Thus, in October 2003, the commission set up by the Algerian government to revise the old Family Code 'found that Algerian families had evolved from being patriarchal families, in which the husband was head of household, to families based on the mutual support of family members' and thereby proposed urgent amendments, in line with both the constitution and Islamic law, which establish the equality of all citizens, combat injustice, and advocate equality, and which 'can adapt to various transformations of society by opening the gate of *ijtihad* (exegesis of Islamic law)'.[44] This raises the question of whether, based on the amendments introduced by the Ordinance of 27 February 2006 to the Algerian Family Code,[45] through the evolutionary perspective of Islamic law, Algeria should now be able to withdraw the interpretive declaration to Article 23(4), which it entered in 1989 on the basis of the old Family Code, that code being essentially based on a historical perspective of Islamic law. In response to a relevant question by the HRC probing the full compatibility of the revised Family Code with the ICCPR, the Algerian representative noted that the interpretive declarations were still maintained to safeguard the state in respect of any remaining perceived contradictions between the provisions of Article 23(4) and the application of Islamic law in Algeria.[46]

Kuwait has also entered an interpretive declaration to Article 23, declaring that the matters addressed by Article 23 are governed by personal-status law, which is based on Islamic law in Kuwait, and, thus, '[w]here the provisions of that article conflict with Kuwaiti law, Kuwait will apply its national law.' During the consideration of Kuwait's 1999 initial report to the HRC, the representatives of Kuwait 'asserted that the purpose of the interpretive declaration was to protect the primacy of the shariah' in Kuwait; however, a member of the HRC expressed the view that 'such primacy did not appear to be the sole objective; for example, [the Kuwaiti] Parliament's refusal to adopt the Amir's bill introducing political rights for women caused her to think that the reservation might not be motivated by religious reasons alone.' The committee also expressed concern that the Kuwaiti representatives could not specifically indicate 'which articles of the covenant were affected by the shariah' in Kuwait, leading the committee to note that the 'interpretative declaration was therefore manifestly inconsistent with the Covenant."[47]

In contesting the position of the Kuwaiti representatives, a member of the HRC, Mr Abdelfattah Amor, noted:

44 See Third Period Report (Algeria), UN Doc. CCPR/C/DZA/3 CCPR/C/DZA/3, 7 November 2006, paras. 123–30 and para. 351.

45 *Ibid.*, para. 353.

46 See Summary Record of the 2495th Meeting, UN Doc. CCPR/C/SR.2495, 31 October 2007, paras. 16 and 47.

47 Summary Record of 1854th Meeting of the HRC on the 1999 Initial Report of Kuwait, UN Doc. CCPR/C/SR.1854, of 24 July 2000, para. 19.

> There was no doubt that the Islamic shariah possessed the flexibility to contribute to social development and renewal in the human rights context. Rather than being a dogmatic instrument, it offered a doctrine that could be applied to all walks of life. Moreover, contrary to what many believed, Islam was characterized by a continual process of flux and change, providing a context for helpful interpretations of the shariah that in certain countries had led to developments in important areas of social life. One example concerned polygamy, in regard to which Islam had actually improved women's situation, since in the pre-Islamic period they had merely existed as chattels. While it was still possible to have more than one wife, Islam placed great emphasis on their equal treatment and on the importance of not having several wives if such treatment could not be assured. Islam had also brought other improvements to women's situation; it was important to understand the historical context in each case. That said, the Committee had a duty to determine the extent to which the shariah was invoked as a pretext in Islamic States in order to impede the implementation of human rights.[48]

The Kuwaiti representatives agreed that Islamic laws were open to interpretation and that, for example, 'abortion and adoption were permitted for humanitarian reasons, and attempts were made to take into account the rights of the women in question' in relevant circumstances.[49]

> It is obvious that the interpretive declarations and reservations in respect of Articles 3, 18 and 23 all mirror the objection made by Saudi Arabia, on grounds of Islamic law, against Articles 16 and 18 of the UDHR earlier in 1948. In the same vein, many more Muslim states, including Algeria, Bahrain, Bangladesh, Brunei, Egypt, Iraq, Jordan, Kuwait, Lebanon, Libya, Malaysia, Maldives, Mauritania, Morocco, Oman, Pakistan, Qatar, Saudi Arabia, Syria, Tunisia, and the United Arab Emirates, have entered reservations to different paragraphs of Articles 2 and 16 of CEDAW,[50] both of which also require states parties to eliminate discrimination against women and ensure equality of men and women generally and in all matters relating to marriage and family relations in a more far-reaching way.

There is no doubt that a strict, historical perspective and adherence to the traditional Islamic jurisprudential views on gender rights, and the rights and responsibilities of spouses 'as to marriage, during marriage and at its dissolution' will reveal differences between the rights and responsibilities of spouses, which will amount to discrimination and inequalities under Articles 3 and 23 of the ICCPR and Articles 2 and 16 of CEDAW, respectively. Also, the historical jurisprudential view on the crime of apostasy under traditional Islamic law would limit the scope of freedom of thought, conscience and religion under Article 18 of the covenant. It is submitted, however, that these apparent limitations could be positively addressed through an evolutionary perspective of Islamic law as analysed earlier above and as currently employed by some Muslim states, albeit cautiously.

---

48 Summary Record of 1852nd Meeting on the HRC on the 1999 Initial Report of Kuwait, UN Doc. CCPR/C/SR.1852 of 24 July 2000, para. 13.

49 *Ibid.*, para. 38.

50 Also, Singapore, although not a Muslim state, has entered a religious reservation to Articles 2 and 16 as follows: '(1) In the context of Singapore's multi-racial and multi-religious society and the need to respect the freedom of minorities to practise their religious and personal laws, the Republic of Singapore reserves the right not to apply the provisions of Articles 2 and 16 where compliance with these provisions would be contrary to their religious or personal laws.' This obviously relates to the application of Islamic religious and personal laws in Singapore.

Such a perspective has, for example led countries such as Bangladesh[51] and Malaysia[52] to withdraw substantive parts of their reservations to CEDAW.

4.4 Generic Declarations and Reservations on Grounds of Islamic Law

Apart from the specific declarations and reservations to Articles 3, 18 and 23, Egypt also entered a general declaration on its ratification of the ICCPR and ICESCR, stating that 'taking into consideration the provisions of the Islamic Sharia and the fact that they do not conflict with the text annexed to the instrument, we accept, support and ratify it.' During the consideration of its combined 2002 third and fourth periodic reports to the HRC, representatives of Egypt indicated that this 'general reservation … was intended to ensure there was no deviation from the principles of Islamic Shariah law, which according to the Constitution was the principal source of Egyptian law', noting, however, that 'there was no contradiction between those principles and the provisions of the Covenant',[53] but also stressing a 'need for the careful study of any possible conflicts between the Shariah and treaty provisions'.[54] The HRC, however, expressed concern that this declaration was confusing and that the committee 'needed to be told exactly how far the declaration affected the implementation of the Covenant within Egypt'.[55] The committee referred to its General Comment 24 'to the effect that it was not possible to enter a general reservation modifying or rendering inapplicable whole groups of rights set forth in the Covenant without infringing the purpose of the Covenant as a whole'.[56] In its concluding observations the HRC noted 'the general and ambiguous nature of the declaration' and urged Egypt either to 'clarify the scope of its declaration or withdraw it'.[57] There are similar generic reservations entered on grounds of the *Shari'ah* or Islamic law by other Muslim states parties to other international human rights treaties such as CEDAW,[58] the Convention on the Rights of the Child (CRC),[59] and the International Convention on the Elimination of Racial Discrimination (CERD),[60] which have been criticized as being imprecise and

51 Upon accession to the CEDAW, Bangladesh entered a reservation that: 'The Government of the People's Republic of Bangladesh does not consider as binding upon itself the provisions of articles 2, 13 (a) and 16 (1) (c) and (f) as they conflict with *Sharia* law based on Holy Quran and Sunna." On 23 July 1997, Bangladesh withdrew the reservation relating to Articles 13(a) and 16(1)(f). See note 5, Status of Ratification to CEDAW [online]. Available from: http://treaties.un.org/Pages/ViewDetails.aspx?src=TREATY&mtdsg_no=IV-8&chapter=4&lang=en#5.

52 On 6 February 1998, Malaysia partially withdrew its reservation in respect of Article 2(f), 9(1), 16(b), 16(d), 16(e) and 16(h) of CEDAW. See note 36, Status of Ratification to CEDAW, *ibid.*

53 Summary Record of the 2048th Meeting of the HRC on the 2002 Combined Third and Fourth Periodic Reports of Egypt, UN Doc. CCPR/C/SR.2048 of 23 October 2002, para. 11.

54 *Ibid.*, para. 12.

55 *Ibid.*, para. 38.

56 *Ibid.*, para. 39.

57 HRC Concluding Observations on the 2002 Combined Third and Fourth Periodic Report of Egypt, UN Doc. CCPR/CO/76/EGY of 28 November 2002, para. 5.

58 E.g. M. Brandt and J.A. Kaplan, 'The Tension Between Women's Rights and Religious Rights: Reservations to CEDAW by Egypt, Bangladesh and Tunisia', *Journal of Law and Religion*, 12 (1995–6), pp. 105–42.

59 1577 UNTS 3.

60 660 UNTS 195. See, generally, N. Abiad, note 23 above, pp. 67–71.

their compatibility with the object and purpose of the relevant treaties questioned by the respective treaty bodies as well as by academic commentators.[61]

4.5 References to Islamic Law in the Periodic Reports of Muslim States Parties to the ICCPR

Apart from reservations and declarations on grounds of Islamic law as analysed above, references have also been made to Islamic law in respect of different issues, in relation to the implementation of the covenant, in the periodic reports of Muslim states parties to the ICCPR such as Algeria,[62] Egypt,[63] Libya,[64] Iran,[65] Jordan,[66] Kuwait,[67] Morocco,[68] Sudan,[69] Syria,[70] and Yemen.[71] The HRC has engaged critically with these Muslim states in respect of those references to Islamic law in the consideration of those reports.[72]

For example, during the consideration of Algeria's 2007 third periodic report by the HRC, the representatives of Algeria stated generally that Algeria 'had exercised its legitimate right to express its reservations to the Covenant regarding contradictions with Islamic sharia' and that the 'reservations did not undermine the substance of the Covenant, but rather related to the sociological situation in Algeria'.[73] This was apparently in reference to its interpretative declaration to Article 23(4) discussed earlier. Even though Algeria had not entered a declaration or reservation in respect of Article 18 of the ICCPR, in engaging with the representatives on the scope of freedom of religion in Algeria, a member of the HRC noted, in relation to Islamic law, as follows:

> Freedom of religion as defined in article 18 included freedom to change one's religion or faith. It was claimed that the sharia did not permit such action, but that depended on how the sharia was interpreted. The question of apostasy (ridda) in Islam was not a doctrinal but a socio-political issue. ... A person might decide to change his or her religion on account of personal conviction or in response to peaceful proselytism. Moreover, Islam itself engaged in proselytism through a multitude of organizations. He therefore requested information regarding the legal situation in Algeria with respect to changing one's religion.[74]

---

61 E.g. N. Abiad, note 23 above., and CRC Concluding Observation on the 2001 First Periodic Report to the CRC, UN Doc. CRC/C/15/Add.148, paras. 7–8.

62 See Third Periodic Report (Algeria), UN Doc. CCPR/C/DZA/3 of 7 November 2006.

63 See Combined Third and Fourth Periodic Report (Egypt), UN Doc. CCPR/C/EGY/2001/3 of 15 April 2002.

64 See Fourth Periodic Report (Libya), UN Doc. CCPR/C/LBY/4 of 10 May 2007.

65 See Summary Record of Meeting, UN Doc. CCPR/C/SR.1252 of 27 June 1994.

66 See Third Periodic Report (Jordan), UN Doc. CCPR/C/JOR/3 of 30 March 2009.

67 See Initial Report (Kuwait), UN Doc. CCPR/C/120/Add.1 of 3 December 1999.

68 See Fourth Periodic Report (Morocco), UN Doc. CCPR/C/MAR/2004/5 of 11 May 2004.

69 See Third Periodic Report (Sudan), UN Doc. CCPR/C/SDN/3 of 10 January 2007.

70 See Third Periodic Report (Syria), UN Doc. CCPR/C/SYR/2004/3 of 19 October 2004.

71 See Fourth Periodic Report (Yemen), UN Doc. CCPR/C/YEM/2004/4 of 23 February 2004.

72 E.g. Summary Record of the 2050th Meeting of the HRC on the 2002 Combined Third and Fourth Periodic Report of Egypt, UN Doc. CCPR/C/SR.2050 of 24 October 2002, para. 39; Summary Record of 1852nd Meeting on the HRC on the 1999 Initial Report of Kuwait, UN Doc. CCPR/C/SR.1852 of 24 July 2000, paras. 49 and 53.

73 Summary Record of the 2495th Meeting of the HRC on the 2006 Third Periodic Report of Algeria, UN Doc. CCPR/C/SR.2495 of 31 October 2007, para. 47.

74 *Ibid*., para. 76.

In its concluding observations, the HRC expressed concerns 'that some activities leading persons to convert from Islam to another religion have been criminalized and that article 11 of [Algerian] Ordinance No. 06-03 establishing the conditions and rules for the practise of faiths other than Islam does not specify exactly which activities are prohibited.[75]

Also, in considering Iran's second periodic report, the HRC noted that '[i]t seemed that the implementation of the Covenant was causing problems for Iran, which very frequently invoked the argument that the Covenant was in conflict with the precepts of Islam', and that it would be interested 'to know what precepts of Islamic law were in conflict with the Covenant'.[76] The committee raised specific questions on different issues in relation to Islamic law as applied in Iran, such as freedom of expression, freedom of religion, freedom of assembly and the issue of women's testimony. It noted that on the basis of Islamic law 'Iranian legislation stipulated that the testimony of two women was equivalent to that of one man' and urged Iran that [w]hile the principles enshrined in Islamic law must be upheld ... the problem of their interpretation should be looked at more closely.'[77] The committee expressed its impression that even though Iran had not entered any reservation to the ICCPR, the state appeared to have 'mental reservations about the implementation of the Covenant, since it seemed to find it normal to impose restrictions or to fail to enforce certain rights if the shariah so required'.[78] A member of the committee, Mr Sadi, however, noted that he 'categorically rejected any argument that there was an inherent contradiction between Islam and the Covenant [because the] elaboration of the Covenant had taken place with the direct support and participation of the Islamic world', and that 'one of the essential principles of Islam was the need to continue to interpret its precepts', and thus he requested that the Iranian interpretation of the relevant Islamic injunctions be made clearer.[79] The Iranian representative responded generally that those restrictions on grounds of Islamic law were in strict conformity with relevant provisos of the covenant that clearly state that the exercise of those freedoms was subject to certain restrictions necessary 'for respect of the rights or reputations of others' and 'for the protection of national security or of public order (ordre public), or of public health or morals'.[80] The representative also argued that there was 'need for flexibility in interpreting some of the articles in the Covenant to make allowance for cultural differences between the various States parties', especially in respect of equality of rights and responsibilities in marriage, which Iran argued could be viewed quite differently from European countries.[81]

In its list of issues on Libya's fourth periodic report, the HRC raised questions regarding issues on women's rights, criminal punishments, equal rights of men and women, and other issues that relate to the application of Islamic law in Libya. Libya's representative noted during the consideration of the report that '[t]he human rights that constituted the core content of the revealed religions were inalienable [and that] Islamic sharia guaranteed human rights through an

75 HRC Concluding Observations on the 2006 Third Period Report of Algeria, UN Doc. CCPR/C/DZA/CO/3 of 12 December 2007, para. 23.

76 Summary Record of 1252nd Meeting of the HRC on the Second Periodic Report of Iran, UN Doc. CCPR/C/SR.1252 of 27 June 1994, para. 32.

77 Summary Record of 1251st Meeting of the HRC on the Second Periodic Report of Iran, UN Doc. CCPR/C/SR.1251 of 29 July 1993, para. 19.

78 Summary Record of 1252nd Meeting of the HRC on the Second Periodic Report of Iran, UN Doc. CCPR/C/SR.1252 of 27 June 1994, para. 33.

79 *Ibid.*, paras. 36–8.

80 *Ibid.*, paras. 45 and 47.

81 Summary Record of 1253rd Meeting of the HRC on the Second Periodic Report of Iran, UN Doc. CCPR/C/SR.1253 of 30 July 1994, para. 4.

all-embracing and consistent framework that was applicable everywhere and for all time', and he elaborated on the principles of Islamic law of inheritance as an example.[82] The representative noted that Libya's domestic legislation 'was consistent with the provisions of the Covenant unless those provisions were at variance with the sharia, an approach based on the principle of freedom of belief and worship which was guaranteed by the Covenant',[83] even though Libya had not entered any interpretive declaration or reservation to the covenant in that regard. In response to the HRC's question on the penalties of flogging and amputation imposed for adultery, theft and highway robbery, Libya responded that the *Shari'ah* was the source of the relevant Libyan legislation but that 'imposition of such penalties was subject to extremely strict conditions so as to safeguard the rights of the accused [and that] an offender who repented was exempted from such punishment.'[84] They also noted that 'the provisions governing *qisas* and *diyah* [payment of blood money] could be invoked to prevent the imposition of the death penalty for premeditated homicide', arguing that '[t]he provisions in question were not incompatible with the Covenant because they were applied in accordance with the requirements of a fair trial and were based on the sharia.'[85] A member of the HRC, Mr Amor, noted that Libya 'had ratified the Covenant without any reservations, and he wondered whether the treatment of women under the sharia and the provisions on *qisas* and *diyah* could be considered consistent with the provisions of the Covenant.'[86] In its concluding observation, the HRC responded to Libya's arguments by a general statement that Libya 'should recognize that according to the 1969 Vienna Convention on the Law of Treaties, the provisions of its internal law cannot be invoked as a justification for its failure to fulfil its obligations under a treaty to which it is a party.'[87] With specific reference to women's rights, the committee urged Libya to 'review its laws in order to ensure equality between men and women in matters of personal status, in particular regarding divorce and inheritance [and should] ... guarantee that equality is ensured in law and in practice.'[88] Also, the committee stated that it 'remains deeply concerned that corporal punishment such as amputation and flogging are prescribed by law even if rarely applied in practice'. noting that the punishments 'constitute a clear violation of article 7 of the Covenant'. It thus urged Libya to 'immediately stop the imposition of all corporal punishment and repeal the legislations for its imposition without delay',[89] [and that] the state 'should review the laws and practice of *qisas* and the *diyah* in light of the Covenant'.[90]

During the consideration of Jordan's 1993 third periodic report, a member of the HRC observed, *inter alia*, that 'a number of matters of great importance to women still appeared to be subject to religious courts [and that] some of the religious laws appeared to have provisions which were unequal in their impact, such as inheritance laws which distinguished between sons and daughters, divorce laws, and laws which gave the Islamic husband the right to discipline his wife'.[91] She

82 Summary Record of the 2487th Meeting of the HRC on the 2007 Fourth Periodic Report of Libya, UN Doc. CCPR/C/SR.2487 of 26 October 2007, para. 4.

83 *Ibid.*, para. 5.

84 *Ibid.*, para. 16.

85 *Ibid.*, para. 19.

86 *Ibid.*, para. 21.

87 HRC Concluding Observations on the 2007 Fourth Periodic Report of Libya, UN Doc. CCPR/C/LBY/CO/4 of 15 November 2007, para. 8.

88 *Ibid.*, para. 11.

89 *Ibid.*, para. 16.

90 *Ibid.*, para. 17.

91 Summary Record of the 1321st Meeting of the HRC on the 1993 Third Periodic Report of Jordan, UN Doc. CCPR/C/SR.1321 of 8 July 1994, para. 28.

'wondered whether that right meant that, in general, the community considered violence against women to be a matter of private concern' and asked 'whether a woman was required to obtain permission from her husband in order to travel abroad or to take their children abroad and, if so, whether that rule applied reciprocally to the husband.'[92] Other committee members raised questions regarding the value of women's testimony and other relevant issues.[93] In response to the issues raised, the Jordanian representatives stated that the testimonies of both men and women were treated equally before Jordanian courts, and that 'any judgement which accorded less value to a woman's testimony would be quashed by a higher court'.[94] They also noted in respect of inheritance laws that, 'a woman's share of any immovable property inherited was equal to that of a man but [only] less in the case of movable property',[95] and that 'in Jordan no difficulties arose with regard to freedom of religion'.[96] The representatives further emphasized that while there was no division between Church and state, 'and hence in many countries of the Islamic world Islamic precepts were incorporated into national law', yet, under Islamic law, 'the human rights of all should be safeguarded, all should have equal access to justice, and the well-being of all, regardless of race, colour or community, should be secured.'[97]

In its 2009 third periodic report, Jordan highlighted that, under its Personal Status Code, marriage is a contract which a man and a woman enter into freely with full consent and that the code grants women and men the same rights in that regard. The report noted that 'either partner may withdraw from the engagement and may add conditions to the contract and women may also initiate a divorce at their own instance.'[98] On the question of polygamy, the report further noted that 'although Muslim men are allowed more than one wife under Islamic law, polygamy is not widely practised in Jordan, where 93.2 per cent of husbands have only one wife. Jordanian law imposes restrictions on a man's right to take more than one wife, requiring the courts to verify the husband's financial status and stipulating that the second wife must be informed, before marriage, of the existence of the other wife and that the first wife must be notified of the marriage after it is concluded.'[99] Reference was eventually made to the Amman Message launched on 9 November 2004, which 'reflects Jordan's determination to portray an accurate image of Islam, a religion which advocates tolerance, dialogue and equality and which preaches moderation'.[100]

In its concluding observation on the 2004 fourth periodic report of Morocco, the HRC commended Morocco, noting 'with appreciation that since the submission of its fourth periodic report ... Morocco has pursued democratic reforms, adopted legislation in this regard (including the new Family Code) and created the office of Ombudsman (*Diwan Al Madhalim*).'[101] The committee,

---

92 *Ibid.*

93 *Ibid.*, para. 35.

94 Summary Record of the 1322nd Meeting of the HRC on the 1993 Third Periodic Report of Jordan, UN Doc. CCPR/C/SR.1322 of 16 March 1994, para. 11.

95 *Ibid.*, para. 12.

96 Summary Record of the 1323rd Meeting of the HRC on the 1993 Third Periodic Report of Jordan, UN Doc. CCPR/C/SR.1323 of 12 July 1994 para. 6.

97 *Ibid.*, para. 21.

98 See Third Periodic Report (Jordan), UN Doc. CCPR/C/JOR/3 of 30 March 2009, para. 27.

99 *Ibid.*, para. 28.

100 *Ibid.*, para. 85.

101 HRC Concluding Observations on the 2004 Fourth Periodic Report of Morocco, UN Doc. CCPR/CO/82/MAR of 1 December 2004, para. 3. I have proposed the establishment of the Islamic institution of Diwan al-Madhalim as a human rights mechanism by Muslim states in my earlier works. E.g. M.A. Baderin, note 25 above, pp. 229–30, and M.A. Baderin, 'Identifying Possible Mechanisms Within Islamic Law for the

however, noted that it was 'concerned about the de facto limitations on the freedom of religion or belief, including the fact that it is impossible, in practice, for a Muslim to change religion', recalling that 'article 18 of the Covenant protects all religions and all beliefs, ancient and less ancient, major and minor, and includes the right to adopt the religion or belief of one's choice.' It then urged Morocco to 'take steps to ensure respect for freedom of religion or belief and to ensure that its legislation and practices are fully in conformity with article 18 of the Covenant'.[102] The committee also expressed concern 'about the legal ban on marriages between women of the Muslim faith and men from other religions or with other beliefs', which it considered as violating Articles 3, 23 and 26 of the covenant, and which Morocco should comply with by revising the legislation concerned.[103] Morocco had highlighted its new Family Code adopted in January 2004 as an important step in ensuring equality between men and women in its personal status laws based on Islamic principles.[104] The report stated that the reformed Family Code 'will enable half of the Moroccan population [i.e. women] to reclaim their rights, remove the injustice and inequity that weighed down on them and guarantee respect for the rights of women and children, for the benefit of the stability of the family unit. The joint responsibility of the husband and wife in running the family home is set out in the Code, which introduces new social practices that will affect people's daily lives.'[105] However, the committee regretted that 'the new Family Code, while placing limitations on the practice of polygamy, nevertheless does not ban it, despite the fact that it is detrimental to women's dignity'[106] and violates Articles 3, 23 and 26 of the covenant. The committee thus noted that the state 'should ban polygamy clearly and definitively'[107] and that while it welcomed the adoption of the Family Code, it, nevertheless, 'notes with concern that inequalities between women and men persist in the area of inheritance and divorce. The State party should [therefore] review its legislation and ensure that any gender-based discrimination in the area of inheritance or divorce is eliminated.'[108]

In its concluding observation on the report of Sudan, the HRC considered that 'corporal punishment including flogging and amputation is inhuman and degrading', noting 'with concern the continued practice of, and legislation concerning, *diya* (blood money) which may be paid in exchange for less severe punishment'; thus, it urged Sudan to 'abolish all forms of punishment that are in breach of articles 7 and 10 of the Covenant'. The committee also indicated that Sudan 'should also review the practice of the payment of *diya* (blood money) for murder and similar crimes [and] ensure that sentences are proportional to the crimes and offences committed'.[109] It further expressed its concern that 'apostasy is a crime under the [Sudanese] 1991 Penal Code' and urged that the state 'should abolish the crime of apostasy, which is incompatible with article 18

Promotion and Protection of Human Rights in Muslim States', *Netherlands Quarterly of Human Rights*, 22(3) (2004), pp. 1–18, at pp. 12–14.

102 HRC Concluding Observations on the 2004 Fourth Periodic Report of Morocco, UN Doc. CCPR/CO/82/MAR of 1 December 2004, para. 21.

103 *Ibid.*, para. 27.

104 See Fifth Periodic Report (Morocco) UN Doc. CCPR/C/MAR/2004/5, para. 58ff.

105 *Ibid.*, para. 22.

106 HRC Concluding Observations on the 2004 Fourth Periodic Report of Morocco, UN Doc. CCPR/CO/82/MAR of 1 December 2004, para. 30.

107 *Ibid.*, para. 30.

108 *Ibid.*, para. 33.

109 HRC Concluding Observations on the 2007 Third Periodic Report of Sudan, UN Doc. CCPR/C/SDN/CO/3 of 29 August 2007, para. 10.

of the Covenant'.[110] The HRC had also raised questions on almost all the different issues earlier discussed above in relation to the application of Islamic law in Sudan. There have been similar engagements and expression of concern by the HRC regarding the impact of Islamic law on the implementation of the ICCPR in other Muslim states such as Yemen[111] and Gambia,[112] and also by the other treaty bodies in respect of other international human rights treaties such as the ICESCR, CEDAW, ICERD and CRC.

One can expediently adduce from the above analyses that most Muslim states parties that apply Islamic law as part of their domestic law have adopted, on grounds of their application of Islamic law, a sort of Islamic relativist position in respect of their international human rights obligations. It, must, however, be noted that despite the tenacity of the different Muslim states in relation to their application of Islamic law as part of domestic law, the position has also been challenging in relation to their international human rights obligations. It is evident from the submissions of the different Muslim states before the different treaty bodies that they seek cautiously to find ways of meeting the challenges that their international human rights obligations pose to their domestic application of Islamic law. In that regard international human rights law has also impacted on the development of Islamic law in various Muslim states in different ways, and this now, conversely, brings us to a brief analysis of the impact of international human rights law leading to some relevant reforms of Islamic law in Muslim states.

5. The Impact of International Human Rights Law on Islamic Law in Muslim States

In the interaction between international human rights law and Islamic law over the years, the impact has not only been, unilaterally, that of Islamic law on international human rights law, but, conversely, international human rights law has also challenged Islamic law and impacted on its evolution and reform in various Muslim states. Theoretically, the challenge of international human rights law has engendered much legal scholarship proposing new approaches to Islamic jurisprudence in relevant areas of Islamic law, such as women's rights, minority rights and freedom of religion, freedom of expression, and Islamic criminal justice among others.[113] Practically, the challenges of international human rights law have also led to diverse reforms to traditional historical Islamic jurisprudence in different Muslim states. For example, during the consideration of Egypt's first initial report on the ICESCR, the country's representative described such reforms by Egypt in response to the challenges of international human rights law as 'enlightened interpretation of the Islamic shariah that [has] emerged from recent debates'.[114] The challenges of international human rights law have

110 *Ibid.*, para. 26.

111 HRC Summary Record of 2282nd Meeting, UN Doc. CCPR/C/SR.2282 of 15 July 2005, para. 38.

112 Concluding Observations of the Human Rights Committee on the Gambia, UN Doc. CCPR/CO/75/GMB of 12 August 2004, para. 16(c).

113 E.g. H.M. Kamali, 'Freedom of Religion in Islam', *Capital University Law Review*, 21 (1992), pp. 63–81; J.S. Nielsen, 'Contemporary Discussions on Religious Minorities in Muslim Countries' *Islam and Christian–Muslim Relations*, 14(3) (2003), pp. 325–35; and A. Ahmad, 'Extension of Shari'ah in Northern Nigeria: Human Rights Implications for Non-Muslim Minorities', *Muslim World Journal of Human Rights*, 2(1) (2005), Art. 6.

114 Summary Record of the 11th Meeting of the ESCR Committee on the Initial Report of Egypt, E/C.12/2000/SR.11 of 8 May 2000, para. 64.

also influenced courts in different Muslim states, such as the Egyptian Constitutional Court, to adopt an evolutional perspective in their interpretations of Islamic law.[115]

One of the most significant recent reforms in that regard is the 2004 reform to the Moroccan Family Law code, to which the state referred in its 2004 fifth periodic report to the HRC[116] and its 2006 combined third and fourth periodic reports to CEDAW.[117] Morocco indicated in the 2004 fifth periodic report to the HRC that the reforms in the new Family Code covered the following issues: (1) equality within the family, whereby both spouses were now responsible for the family; (2) recognition of the emancipation of married women, whereby matrimonial guardianship has been extended to adult women; (3) uniform age of marriage, whereby the marriageable age of both men and women has been set uniformly at 18 years; (4) tight restrictions on polygamy, whereby polygamy is subjected to approval of the courts on proof of the man's ability to treat the wives equitably, and a woman may insert a condition in the marriage contract that the man agrees not to take any other wives; (5) simplification of procedures for expatriate marriages; (6) joint right to divorce, whereby the dissolution of the marriage may be exercised by either the husband or wife subject to judicial supervision; (7) greater balance within the marriage, whereby the wife has a right to seek judicial divorce where the husband does not comply with any condition in the marriage contract or where she suffers harm or violence in the marriage; (8) recognition of children's rights, whereby relevant provisions of international human rights instruments ratified by Morocco have been incorporated into the Family Code; (9) protection of the right to establish paternal filiation, whereby a child's right to paternal recognition is protected where there was no formalized marriage contract between the parents; (10) equality in inheritance, whereby a man's daughter can inherit from their grandfather on an equal footing with the man's son; (11) regulation of the administration of property, whereby property acquired by a couple during the marriage, may without prejudice to the principle of separate ownership of their personal property, be based on post-marital agreements.[118] The preamble of the new Family Code states, obviously in response to the challenges of international human rights law to traditional historic interpretations on Islamic family law, that its provisions are 'in conformity with Islam's tolerant rules and exemplary purposes while providing balanced, fair and pragmatic solutions resulting from enlightened open *ijtihad* (juridical reasoning)'.[119]

Among other Muslim states that have undertaken relative reforms of relevant Islamic laws within their domestic system in response to the challenges of international human rights law are Algeria, which also adopted a new Family Code in January 2006,[120] and Saudi Arabia, which first

---

115 E.g. C.B. Lombardi and N.J. Brown, 'Do Constitutions Requiring Adherence to *Shari'a* Threaten Human Rights?: How Egypt's Constitutional Court Reconciles Islamic Law with the Liberal Rule of Law', *American University International Law Review*, 21 (2006), pp. 379–435.

116 Fourth Periodic Report (Morocco) UN Doc. CCPR/C/MAR/2004/5 of 11 May 2004.

117 Third and Fourth Combined Periodic Report (Morocco), UN Doc. CEDAW/C/MAR/4 of 18 September 2006. See also L.A. Weingartner, 'Family Law and Reform in Morocco – the *Mudawana*: Modernist Islam and Women's Rights in the Code of Personal Status', *University of Detroit Mercy Law Review*, 82 (2004–05), pp. 687–713.

118 Fourth Periodic Report (Egypt), UN Doc. CCPR/C/MAR/2004/5 of 11 May 2004, para. 60–71.

119 See 5th Preambular Paragraph to the Moroccan Family Code (Moudawana) of 5 February 2004 [online]. Available from: http://www.hrea.org/moudawana.html#preamble.

120 See Third Period Report (Algeria), UN Doc. CCPR/C/DZA/3 CCPR/C/DZA/3 of 7 November 2006, paras. 123–30 and para. 351.

adopted a Basic Law of Government in 1993 with a specific chapter on rights and duties,[121] a Law of Procedure before the Shari'ah Courts in 2000,[122] and a Human Rights Commission Regulation in 2005,[123] establishing a Human Rights Commission 'to protect and enhance human rights according to international standards for human rights in all aspects, and to promote public awareness thereof and participate in ensuring implementation of the same in light of the provisions of *Shari'ah*'.[124]

The impact of international human rights law on Islamic law is also apparently reflected by the withdrawal of some Muslim states, such as Bangladesh, Egypt and Malaysia, of previous reservations they had entered to different human rights treaties on grounds of traditional historic interpretations of Islamic law. Thus, while Islamic law has definitely impacted on the implementation of international human rights in Muslim states, the ideals and challenges of international human rights law have, conversely, encouraged movement towards an evolutional interpretation of Islamic law in Muslim states.

6. Conclusion

Based on a case study of the ICCPR, this chapter has demonstrated how Islamic law as applicable domestic law in Muslim states impacts on the implementation of international human rights law in Muslim states. It is clear that owing to its continued strong influence in many parts of the Muslim world, Islamic law will certainly continue to impact, one way or another, on the implementation of international human rights law in many Muslim states into the future. However, such impact should not necessarily be negative. Rather, future endeavours, particularly on the part of Muslim states, should be in the direction of constructively using Islamic law, through an evolutional perception as analysed herein, for the positive implementation of international human rights law in the Muslim world.

121 See Chapter 5 of the Saudi Arabian Basic Law of Government (1993) [online]. Available from: http://servat.unibe.ch/icl/sa00000_.html.

122 Adopted by Royal Decree No. (M/21) on 19 August 2000 [online]. Available from: http://www.lexadin.nl/wlg/legis/nofr/oeur/lxwesau.htm.

123 Adopted by Council of Ministers Resolution No. 207 of 12 September 2005 [online]. Available from: http://www.lexadin.nl/wlg/legis/nofr/oeur/lxwesau.htm.

124 See Art. 1, Saudi Arabian Human Rights Commission Regulation, *ibid.*

Chapter 19
Towards an International Court of Human Rights?

Gerd Oberleitner

1. Introduction

Since the adoption of the UDHR[1] six decades ago, a remarkable global human rights infrastructure has been put in place. What started as a 'common standard of achievement for all peoples and all nations'[2] is now transformed into a complex web of institutions tasked with promoting and protecting human rights and preventing human rights violations. The remit and mode of operation of these institutions differ, as do their legal basis, composition and impact. Their sustained growth and development, indeed their sheer existence in the absence of any overarching master plan, remains an intriguing feature of an international legal order which rests firmly on state sovereignty, yet keeps creating and entrusting such institutions with the very mandate to intrude into that sovereignty.

The one institution which is, however, conspicuously absent in this assemblage of human rights bodies is a World Court with the mandate to adjudicate human rights on a global scale. While human rights courts have been created in Europe, the Americas and Africa,[3] no such court exists as part of the United Nations (UN) human rights system. Unlike in the area of genocide, war crimes and crimes against humanity, no coalition in support of such a court has ever formed and no like-minded group of states has stepped forward to push for the creation of such an institution. In a way, this seems easily explicable, self-evident even: what more of a utopian idea could one float than setting up an independent world court to adjudicate on the whole range of human rights and with respect to all states, given their insistence on sovereignty, their reluctance to accept even less demanding supervisory procedures, the multitude of cases such a court would have to hear, and the deep divisions in the international community over many fundamental principles of human rights in spite of the rhetoric of their universality? This may well explain the near complete silence on even the idea of such a court for the past six decades, not only in governmental circles and human rights non-governmental organizations (NGOs), but also in academia.

On the other hand, such a court is like the proverbial elephant in the room: while we hush up its mere possibility, we carry in us a steadfast conception that, where injustice is done and all else fails, it is in the authoritative words of a judge that we hope to find justice, be it on the national or international level. While we dismiss the idea of an international human rights court as utopian, we praise, at the same time, regional human rights courts as the crown jewels of human rights

1 GA Res. 217A (III), UN Doc. A/810 at 71 (1948).

2 *Ibid.*, Preamble.

3 There is the European Court of Human Rights under the European regional human rights system, the Inter-American Court of Human Rights under the Inter-American regional human rights system, and the recent African Court on Human and Peoples' Rights under the African regional human rights system (The African Court on Human and Peoples' Rights will merge with the African Court of Justice, transforming the two courts into a single African Court of Justice and Human Rights, when the Protocol on the Statute of the African Court of Justice and Human Rights, adopted on 1 July 2008, enters into force).

protection, and we consider the way in which the international legal order has relied ever since on dispute settlement through judicial procedures (from arbitration panels to the International Court of Justice (ICJ)) in many fields of the law as perfectly normal.

This chapter seeks to break this silence of the past decades and question the assumption that such a world court for human rights would be utopian at best and detrimental at worst. It explores the potential of and pitfalls in creating such an institution, asks whether its establishment would be a desirable goal, and sketches the contours of such a court. The time to begin a debate on an international court of human rights seems to have come: with some important steps in the UN reform process taken (such as the replacement of the Commission on Human Rights by the Human Rights Council) and the International Criminal Court (ICC) having commenced its work since the Rome Statute came into force in July 2002,[4] there seems a space to reflect on the future global human rights infrastructure in a more visionary and long-term manner. In December 2008, a Panel of Eminent Persons, convened by Switzerland, used the 60th anniversary of the UDHR to do precisely that, and the proposal for an international human rights court is part of the 'Agenda for Human Rights' which came out of their deliberations.[5]

2. 1945: Proposals for a Comprehensive Infrastructure

In the years after 1945, the visions for a new world included, quite boldly, a fairly holistic, universal and robust human rights infrastructure with interlinking institutions, but the respective ideas evaporated all too soon. The human rights mandate of the UN, as contained in the UN Charter ('promoting and encouraging respect for human rights and for fundamental freedoms for all'[6]) was to be realized through the adoption of standards and by setting up a number of specific institutions. The only such body which eventually found its way into the Charter was the Commission on Human Rights,[7] set up by the Economic and Social Council (ECOSOC) in 1946.[8] The mandate, functions and composition of the commission were decided after lengthy debates,[9] but the idea put forward by Eleanor Roosevelt (who was so influential in setting up this body) to allow the commission to assist the UN Security Council in deciding when a human rights violation amounted to a breach of or threat to the peace was not acceptable to the UN member states then, so that early attempt at an institutional link between security and human rights in the UN was thwarted.[10]

Likewise, the creation of a High Commissioner for Human Rights, as proposed by Uruguay and Costa Rica in 1950,[11] did not find support and could only be realized later at the Vienna World

4 See Chapter 24 in this volume.

5 See http://www.udhr60.ch/agenda.html and (specifically on the establishment of a court and on first research activities carried out in this respect) http://www.udhr60.ch/research.html [accessed 14 October 2009].

6 Article 1(3), Charter of the United Nations 1945.

7 Article 68, Charter of the United Nations: 'the Economic and Social Council shall set up commissions in economic and social fields and for the promotion of human rights…'.

8 Economic and Social Council Resolution 5(1) of 16 February 1946.

9 See Howard Tolley, Jr., *The U.N. Commission on Human Rights* (Boulder, CO: Westview Press, 1987), pp. 4–13.

10 See Philip Alston, 'The Commission on Human Rights', in Philip Alston (ed.), *The United Nations and Human Rights: A Critical Appraisal* (Oxford: Clarendon Press, 1992), pp. 127–8.

11 See Philip Alston, 'Neither Fish nor Fowl: The Quest to Define the Role of the High Commissioner for Human Rights', *European Journal of International Law*, 8(2) (1997), pp. 323–35.

Conference on Human Rights in 1993. An international criminal tribunal to prosecute international crimes was set up in a more specific form when the drafters of the 1948 UN Genocide Convention[12] inserted Article VI on such a tribunal for the crime of genocide.[13] Such a body, however, remained a legal fiction for half a century until the ICC was established in 1998.

Finally, an International Court of Human Rights was proposed by Australia in 1947 to complement the Commission on Human Rights, the Criminal Tribunal, and the High Commissioner for Human Rights.[14] Had all these proposals been realized, a comprehensive and mutually reinforcing structure would have been set up, with the commission setting standards as well as alerting the UN Security Council on human rights violations, the High Commissioner promoting human rights and coordinating UN initiatives, a Criminal Tribunal punishing individual perpetrators of not only genocide but also other crimes against humanity, and an International Court of Human Rights specifically for adjudication of human rights violations. With the exception of the commission's standard-setting activities, which eventually resulted in the adoption of the UDHR in 1948 and subsequent treaties, none of this could be realized for many decades to come.

3. The International Court of Justice (ICJ)

The ICJ was established in 1945 as the UN's principal judicial organ and as such was never meant to hear human rights cases. While, in principle, the court's mandate covers human rights law, its role in human rights litigation is restricted in many ways, as only states have access to the court, while individuals, judicial persons and non-governmental organizations cannot address it. The ICJ has no special mandate to adjudicate claims on human rights violations, and it deals with individual rights only to the extent that they are implicated in an inter-state dispute brought before it by states or in a requested advisory opinion, a function which pertains only to the other principal organs of the UN, most importantly the General Assembly and the Security Council.

The ICJ has nevertheless taken some decisions on human rights in both its adjudicatory and advisory capacities.[15] Out of the 144 cases the court has been confronted with,[16] human rights concerns figured in a rather limited range of these cases. While the court's predecessor, the Permanent Court of International Justice (1921–45) had to deal with the rights of minorities (very much in line with the predominant interwar concern with national minorities rather than individual rights),[17] the ICJ could draw on a greater range of human rights provisions, but did so cautiously.

12 Convention on the Prevention and Punishment of the Crime of Genocide, 78 UNTS 277, adopted by the UN General Assembly on 9 December 1948, entered into force 12 January 1951.

13 *Ibid.* Article VI provides: 'Persons charged with genocide or any of the other acts [...] shall be tried by [...] such international penal tribunal as may have jurisdiction with respect to those Contracting Parties which shall have accepted its jurisdiction'.

14 See Manfred Nowak, *Protecting Dignity: An Agenda for Human Rights. Progress Report of the Eminent Persons Panel*, 36 (2009) [online]. Available from: http://www.udhr60.ch/agenda/Nowak-Agenda.pdf [accessed 14 October 2009].

15 See also Chapter 15 in this volume.

16 As of October 2009 [online]. Available from: http://www.icj-cij.org/docket/index.php?p1=3 [accessed 14 October 2009].

17 See Rosalyn Higgins, 'The International Court of Justice and Human Rights', in Frances Butler (ed.), *Human Rights Protection: Methods and Effectiveness* (The Hague: Kluwer, 2002), pp. 163–6.

In some areas, it referred directly to fundamental rights, as in the *South West Africa* case[18] of 1971, where it found the introduction of apartheid in what today is Namibia a denial of fundamental human rights,[19] and in the case of *Bosnia and Herzegovina* v *Yugoslavia*[20] (Serbia and Montenegro) of 2007, where it found the latter responsible for breaches of the Genocide Convention, but not liable for committing genocide.[21] In its advisory opinion of 2004 on the legal consequences of the construction of a wall in the Occupied Palestinian Territory, the court invoked specific provisions of human rights treaties and found that the wall erected by Israel violates, inter alia, the liberty of movement as guaranteed under the International Covenant on Civil and Political Rights (ICCPR)[22] and the right to work, health, education and an adequate standard of living as proclaimed in the International Covenant on Economic, Social and Cultural Rights (ICESCR)[23] and in the Convention on the Rights of the Child (CRC).[24]

Other than that, human rights have never taken centre-stage before the ICJ but were seen as being folded into issues such as diplomatic protection, armed conflict, interpretation of treaty law, and immunity[25] Only in adopting interim measures (in a string of death penalty cases in the USA, where the court asked the government to stay executions until the court could take a final decision) has the ICJ ever attempted directly to protect human rights.[26] The utmost the court did was to 'fix the coordinates for any discussion on the relevance of human rights'[27] in some of its decisions. It may have successfully used human rights law to develop international law but has not used international law to promote human rights. It cannot, and (given its importance as the UN's principal judicial organ) should not, stand in for an international human rights court.

4. Regional Human Rights Courts

In three regions of the world, human rights courts have been set up.[28] The European Court of Human Rights (ECtHR) was set up in 1959 pursuant to the European Convention on Human Rights

18 *Legal Consequences for States of the Continued Presence of South Africa in Namibia (South West Africa) notwithstanding Security Council Resolution 276 (1970)*, Advisory Opinion, ICJ Reports 1971, p. 16.

19 See Rosalyn Higgins, 'The International Court of Justice and Human Rights', in Karel Wellens (ed.), *International Law: Theory and Practice* (The Hague: Kluwer, 1998), p. 694.

20 *Application of the Convention on the Prevention and Punishment of the Crime of Genocide (Bosnia and Herzegovina v. Serbia and Montenegro*), judgement of 26 February 2007 [online]. Available from: http://www.icj-cij.org/docket/index.php?p1=3&k=8d&p3=4&case=91 [accessed 14 October 2009].

21 See Claus Kress, 'The International Court of Justice and the Elements of the Crime of Genocide', *European Journal of International Law*, 18(4) (2007), pp. 619–29.

22 999 UNTS 171.

23 993 UNTS 3.

24 1577 UNTS 3. See *Legal Consequences of the Construction of a Wall in the Occupied Palestinian Territory*, Advisory Opinion, ICJ Reports 2004, p. 136; and Gentian Zyberi, *The Humanitarian Face of the International Court of Justice. Its Contribution to Interpreting and Developing International Human Rights and Humanitarian Law Rules and Principles* (Antwerp: Intersentia, 2008), pp. 308–21.

25 See Gerd Oberleitner, *Global Human Rights Institutions – Between Remedy and Ritual* (Cambridge: Polity, 2007), pp. 152–7.

26 See Alison Duxbury, 'Saving Lives in the International Court of Justice. The Use of Provisional Measures to Protect Human Rights', *California Western International Law Journal*, 31(1) (2000), pp. 141–76.

27 Christian Tomuschat, *Human Rights Between Idealism and Realism* (Oxford: Oxford University Press, 2003), p. 192.

28 See Chapters 12, 13 and 14, respectively, in this volume.

(ECHR)[29] and delivers binding judgements on the ECHR. In 1979, the Inter-American Court of Human Rights (IACtHR) was created under the Inter-American Convention on Human Rights so as to issue binding judgements and advisory opinions for the inter-American human rights system. While, in the African region, earlier attempts (in 1961) to set up a court as part of an envisaged African human rights convention had failed,[30] a protocol to the African Charter on Human and People's Rights on the establishment of a court was adopted in 1998.[31] The protocol entered into force in 2004. However, the court – 15 years after the process was initiated to establish such a tribunal – has not yet delivered any judgement, and is still to finalize its operational documents such as the rules of procedure. A new treaty – Protocol on the Statute of the African Court of Justice and Human Rights – is creating a new court (the African Court of Justice and Human Rights) because of a decision of the African Union Summit in 2008 to merge the court with the newly established African Court of Justice.[32] As soon as this treaty enters into force, the current court will be transformed, and will have to find its feet again. Until such a merger takes place, the African Court of Human and Peoples' Rights (ACtHPR) will continue to function at its seat in Arusha, Tanzania.[33] As one commentator has noted, the creation of an integrated regional African court has several advantages in the African context:

> First, it will avoid the splitting of resources towards maintaining two courts. Secondly, an integrated court will result in simplicity and is an antidote to the ongoing proliferation of regional institutions. Thirdly, it will assist in concentrating efforts, energy and focus on one institution rather than two. Finally, an integrated regional court will offer the opportunity to develop unified and cohesive human rights jurisprudence for Africa.[34]

The rationale for establishing regional courts was to move forward with the effective enforcement of human rights in line with regional needs, experiences and legal traditions. These courts forcefully demonstrate that international human rights jurisdiction is not a utopian concept. Altogether, 94 European, American and African states (as of October 2009) have submitted themselves to the jurisdiction of their respective regional human rights court.[35] While the existence of these courts and (as for the European and Inter-American system) their successful handling of a great number of cases make questionable the added value of yet another international human rights court, these

29 The court was reconstituted in 1998 pursuant to Protocol 11 to the European Convention of 1994.

30 See Scott Lyons, 'The African Court on Human and Peoples' Rights', *ASIL Insights*, 10(24) (2006) [online]. Available from: http://www.asil.org/insights060919.cfm [accessed 14 October 2009].

31 Protocol to the African Charter on Human and People's Rights on the Establishment of an African Charter on Human and People's Rights, adopted 9 June 1998[online]. Available from: http://www.african-court.org/fileadmin/documents/Court/Court%20Establishment/africancourt-humanrights.pdf [accessed 14 October 2009].

32 See African Union Document AU/Dec.83 (V), 5th Ordinary Session of the African Union, Sirte, 4–5 July 2005. See also Protocol on the Statute of the African Court of Justice and Human Rights [online]. Available from: http://www.africa-union.org/root/au/Documents/Treaties/text/Protocol%20on%20the%20Merged%20Court%20-%20EN.pdf.

33 See http://www.african-court.org/en [accessed 14 October 2009].

34 See M.K. Mbondenyi, 'Invigorating the African System on Human and Peoples' Rights Through Institutional Mainstreaming and Rationalisation', *Netherlands Quarterly on Human Rights*, 27(4) (2009), pp. 451–83, at p. 474.

35 See http://conventions.coe.int; and http://www.cidh.org/Basicos/English/Basic4.Amer.Conv.Ratif.htm; and http://www.africa-union.org/root/AU/Documents/Treaties/treaties.htm [all accessed 14 October 2009].

same facts, together with decades of legal and practical lessons learned on adjudicating human rights, can also be used as arguments in favour of replicating this exercise on the universal level.

5. 1993 and Beyond

In the years after the Vienna World Conference on Human Rights in 1993, all the proposals made in the years after 1945 to create a comprehensive human rights infrastructure could finally be realized, with the exception of an international human rights court. The UN High Commissioner for Human Rights now acts as the focal point for the UN's human rights activities; the ICC can deliver judgements on genocide, war crimes and crimes against humanity; and the UN Security Council (although not formally linked to the human rights system as suggested in 1945) has become more sensitive to human rights matters than the drafters of the charter would perhaps have imagined. The idea to establish an international court of human rights was once more floated around the time of the World Conference,[36] but whatever (little) enthusiasm there may have been vanished in the years after, not least because of the anticipation which the imminent establishment of the ICC generated.

The international human rights court remains the missing piece of the 1945 blueprint, and the potential duties of the court to monitor states' compliance with human rights obligations continue to be carried out by the UN treaty bodies and the UN Human Rights Council. Yet, neither the state reporting, inter-state and individual complaints procedure of the treaty bodies nor the complaints procedures, special procedures, and the newly created Universal Periodic Review of the Council can deliver results as a judicial procedure before an international court would.

The ICC (with its statute having attracted 110 ratifications as of July 2009) does not remedy this situation, either. Yes, there is strong emphasis on human rights violations as part of international crimes in the ICC statute, just as there was in the statutes of its precursors, the International Criminal Tribunal for the Former Yugoslavia and the International Criminal Tribunal for Rwanda. Indeed, commentators have pointed out that the focus of these two institutions is on 'human rights crimes'.[37] Such a list of the most serious crimes of concern to the international community in the ICC statute is impressive: genocide and war crimes are accompanied by crimes against humanity, which encompass acts such as murder; extermination; enslavement; deportation and forcible transfer of population; imprisonment or other severe deprivation of physical liberty; torture; rape; sexual slavery; enforced prostitution; forced pregnancy; enforced sterilization; persecution of groups on political, racial, national, ethnic, religious, gender, or other grounds; enforced disappearance; apartheid; and other similar acts.[38] Yet, the ICC is an entirely different kind of court from an international human rights court. It establishes individual criminal responsibility and puts an end to the impunity of dictators, *génocidaires* and war criminals but is not meant to hold states accountable for the much greater range of violations of civil, cultural, economic, political and social human rights as laid down in the respective treaties.

---

36 E.g. Christian Strohal, 'The Development of the International Human Rights System by the United Nations', in Franz Cede and Lilly Sucharipa-Behrmann (eds), *The United Nations – Law and Practice* (The Hague: Kluwer, 1999), p. 166.

37 William Schabas, 'Criminal Responsibility for Violations of Human Rights', in Janusz Symonides (ed.), *Human Rights: Protection, Monitoring, Enforcement* (Aldershot: Ashgate, 2003), p. 281.

38 Article 7, Statute of the International Criminal Court 1998, 2187 UNTS 90.

6. An International Court of Human Rights: Necessary and Realistic?

The mere fact that no international court of human rights exists does not necessarily mean that it ought to be established. In order to be a desirable and realistic option, the realization of which would merit the considerable energy and resources necessary, an international court of human rights must comply with four core requirements: it must provide added value in comparison to existing institutions and procedures, and must be legal, politically feasible, and able to produce effective results. Added value means that the court should be able to remedy existing shortcomings and fill gaps in the present international human rights framework, supplement – and not duplicate or contradict – those procedures which at present function effectively, and enhance such procedures rather than endanger their further functioning.

The shortcomings of the UN treaty bodies are obvious and have been described in detail.[39] To name but the most striking: the respective procedures are not well known outside expert circles, their impact on the ground is limited, their proceedings are no match for proper court proceedings, their conclusions are mere recommendations and there is no follow-up to their decisions. Interstate complaints have rarely been used before treaty bodies and the number of final conclusions on individual complaints is minute in comparison to the judgements regularly handed down by the ECtHR: an average of 1,000 decisions on individual complaints per year before the European Court compete against some 500 final views of all treaty bodies together in the more than 30 years of their existence.[40]

An international human rights court could fill many of these gaps. In line with the law and practice of existing regional human rights courts, it would have to be mandated to render legally binding judgements in an adjudicatory procedure, it could be authorized to authoritatively settle human rights disputes in advisory opinions, and it would be able to compensate victims for damages suffered. It would bring to bear judicial independence and procedural rules (for example, on evidence), provide consistency in jurisprudence, and could cover all human rights, civil-political as well as social, economic and cultural, in a comprehensive way. As the highest judicial UN body in the field of human rights, it could be expected to exercise the visibility and the intellectual and societal impact which existing procedures do not. In terms of its geographical coverage, the court would be able to allow for decisions on cases from all regions of the world, including Asia, which has no regional human rights system.

The establishment of an international human rights court is legally possible if one follows the model suggested recently by Manfred Nowak[41] and Martin Scheinin,[42] who – based on the example of the ICC – suggest adoption of a treaty to set up the court, which should be open to all states and allow them, upon accepting the court's jurisprudence, to indicate which human rights obligations they are willing to have scrutinized by the court. The treaty on the court's statute would enter into force after a certain number of ratifications. It would be left to states whether or not to accept the court's jurisdiction, and they would be free with regard to the scope of rights that could be invoked before such a court. The court would be an option for those states willing to abide

39 E.g. Anne Bayefsky, *The UN Human Rights Treaty System: Universality at the Crossroads* (Ardsley, NY: Transnational Publishers, 2001). See also Chapter 12 in this volume.

40 See Manfred Nowak, 'The Need for a World Court of Human Rights', *Human Rights Law Review*, 7(1) (2007), pp. 251–9, at p. 253.

41 *Ibid.*, 251–9.

42 Martin Scheinin, Interim research paper submitted within the framework of the Swiss initiative to commemorate the 60th anniversary of the Universal Declaration of Human Rights [online]. Available from: http://www.udhr60.ch/report/hrCourt_scheinin.pdf [accessed 14 October 2009].

by it. This would mean a gradual phasing in of the court, would leave the existing human rights infrastructure untouched, would not require amendments to existing treaties, and would not need the introduction of new human rights norms. The original idea of 1945 to make the court a judicial organ of the UN on par with the ICJ would today require amending the UN Charter. Although this proposal has briefly been discussed,[43] it seems unrealistic to find the support of states to amend the UN Charter to create a 'world' court, as opposed to an 'international' court along the lines of the Nowak/Scheinin model.

Placing the court in the existing human rights system, fencing off its competences from other bodies, securing cooperation with them, and avoiding duplication and contradiction will be more difficult to achieve than setting up the court in the first place. With regard to the UN treaty bodies, it has been suggested that the court should gradually replace the individual complaints procedure, so that states that accept the court's jurisprudence would withdraw, for example, from the individual complaints protocol of the ICCPR.[44] Given that the court's jurisprudence would, in principle, cover all human rights treaties, this would include those treaties which so far have no complaints procedure. Whether this might extend to monitoring procedures under UN specialized agencies, programmes and funds – such as the UN Educational, Scientific and Cultural Organization (UNESCO) or the International Labour Organization (ILO) – is another question. While the long-term vision is to phase out individual complaints before treaty bodies and at the same time gradually introduce the judicial procedure, the treaty bodies would continue to fulfil all other functions. This would leave untouched the mandate of treaty bodies to examine state reports and, where applicable, on-site inquiries.

An alternative approach, suggested by Scheinin, would be to allow for appeals against the concluding views of treaty bodies before the international court.[45] It is not quite clear what would be gained from such an approach, as it would mean that appellants would still have to go through the much criticized treaty body procedure before finally being allowed to go where they would most likely have headed anyway, namely to the court.

A third alternative would be to use the treaty bodies as some sort of filtering mechanism which, at their discretion or according to predetermined criteria, would pass on important cases to the court. This could be done along the lines of the European Commission of Human Rights (which, however, was abandoned in 1998 precisely in order to make room for a proper court procedure before the European Court), or it could (preferably) follow the more complex relationship between the Inter-American Commission and the IACtHR, and the African Commission and the ACtHPR, which are more 'partners' in handling complaints than set in a hierarchic structure.[46] When individual complaints are allowed before the international court of human rights, some sort of filtering mechanism might be necessary in any case, with or without the involvement of treaty bodies. Commentators with experience in the European human rights system have already warned that easy access to the court for individuals would be opening the floodgates, as in the ECtHR,

---

43 Stefan Trechsel, 'A World Court for Human Rights?', *Northwestern University Journal of International Human Rights*, 1(3) (2003) [online]. Available from: http://www.law.northwestern.edu/journals/jihr/v1/3/trechsel.pdf, 7, [accessed 14 October 2009].

44 See Nowak, note 40 above, p. 255.

45 See Martin Scheinin, 'The Proposed Optional Protocol to the Covenant on Economic, Social and Cultural Rights: A Blueprint for UN Human Rights Treaty Body Reform – Without Amending the Existing Treaties', *Human Rights Law Review*, 6(1) (2006), pp. 131–42.

46 For greater detail on the Inter-American Court, see Chapter 13 in this volume and Jo M. Pasqualucci, *The Practice and Procedure of the Inter-American Court of Human Rights* (Cambridge: Cambridge University Press, 2003), and see the African Court [online]. Available from: http://www.african-court.org/en/court/mandate/general-information [accessed 14 October 2009].

where the overload with individual cases has made the court a victim of its own success and in need of yet another reform.[47] If the proposal to unify all UN treaty bodies into one is turned into reality, the situation might present itself in a different light again, depending on the mandate of such a unified body.[48] The linkage between treaty body reform and the idea of an international human rights court may thus become an issue.

The relationship between the international court of human rights and regional human rights courts may be even thornier. Ideas of a 'pyramid model' in which the court is an appellate body or court of last instance, not only for the UN treaty bodies but also for the regional courts, have rightly met with scepticism.[49] While appealing in its hierarchical structure in analogy to national jurisdictions, such a proposal seems unrealistic given the way it intrudes into the remit of existing bodies. It seems unlikely that member states of the European or Inter-American Convention on Human Rights would accept an appeal from the European or Inter-American Court to an international court. It would probably mean amending the respective treaties and prolong the length of trials and – for the European system – it may mean transmitting the case overload of the European Court directly to the international court (assuming that complainants would most likely want to take advantage of an appeals procedure when they do not succeed before the European Court). The easiest way forward seems to be to ensure that the regional courts are left untouched by the introduction of the international court of human rights, but such an approach risks the potential for 'forum-shopping' by potential victims in search of the most convenient court and might also lead to contradictory human rights jurisprudence.

Is the establishment of an international court of human rights politically realistic? What seems *a priori* to be the biggest obstacle – the political will of states – might at the end be less difficult to overcome than the legal and practical issues mentioned above, strange as this may sound. In addition to the 94 states that have accepted the jurisprudence of regional courts, a considerable number of states have submitted themselves to the individual complaints procedure before treaty bodies – 113 under the Optional Protocol to the ICCPR; 98 under the Optional Protocol to the Convention on the Elimination of all Forms of Discrimination Against Women; 69 under Article 22 of the Convention Against Torture and Other Cruel, Inhuman or Degrading Treatment and Punishment; and 53 under Article 14 of the Convention on the Elimination of All Forms of Racial Discrimination.[50] To this list, one may add states that have accepted complaints procedures under UNESCO or ILO conventions. Notwithstanding the differences between all these procedures and an international human rights court, a considerable number of states should thus have no reason to come forward with a principled objection to an international body which scrutinizes their performance on the basis of individual complaints.

Finally, will an international human rights court be effective? This will depend on giving the court a realistic mandate in line with sufficient resources and some formalized political backing to see its decisions implemented on the ground. Whatever solid procedure one might devise, the ultimate test for the court will be the implementation of its decisions at the national level. This is not specific for the international court of human rights – the European and Inter-American courts are also affected by the problem of non-implementation of their decisions. While the European Court

---

47 See Trechsel, note 43 above, p. 6.

48 A concept paper for treaty body reform is on the table but has not found general acceptance; see Concept Paper of the High Commissioner's Proposal for a Unified Standing Treaty Body, UN Doc. HRI/MC/2006/2 of 22 March 2006.

49 See Trechsel, note 43 above, p. 6.

50 See the ratification database [online]. Available from: http://treaties.un.org [accessed 14 October 2009]. In addition, more than 30 states have signed the new complaints protocol to the International Covenant on Economic, Social and Cultural Rights (see Chapter 4 in this volume).

relies on the Committee of Ministers to enforce its decisions,[51] the Inter-American Court keeps following up states' responses to its judgements with a consistent monitoring and, if necessary, calls the states to the court again until a satisfactory implementation is achieved.[52] One would have to study the experiences of the two regional courts carefully and apply them in the UN setting. Innovative suggestions to secure the political follow-up, such as using the Human Rights Council's new monitoring procedure, the Universal Periodic Review, have already been made.[53]

7. Mandate and Procedure

On the crucial questions of *locus standi* of potential petitioners and the admissibility requirements for complaints, the court can build on the divergent procedural rules of the regional courts, but it should go beyond those established principles in an innovative way so as to better respond to today's realities. Cases could, of course, be brought by states, but in light of the experiences with inter-state complaints, one should not raise expectations: states have never used the inter-state complaints mechanisms before UN treaty bodies, and only in a handful of cases have they resorted to it before the ECtHR.[54]

Allowing individuals to address the court, along the model of the ECtHR, is certainly the most appropriate way to realize access to justice in the UN human rights system. It might, however, not only mean the introduction of some filtering mechanism but also begs the question of what the exhaustion of domestic remedies (a core requirement before all individual complaints procedures before international bodies) would be in the case of the international court. Should a regional mechanism be considered a 'domestic' remedy? Should there be new intermediate layers? Manfred Nowak, for example, suggests the creation of domestic human rights courts,[55] a proposal that is likely to be opposed by many states.

In many complaints procedures, NGOs are heavily involved and often bring the majority of cases to international bodies. The respective rules of an international court will have to provide for this reality, but, most likely, states would want to see the introduction of criteria for NGOs entitled to bring cases to the court. One should also go beyond NGOs and explicitly include other organizations, such as National Human Rights institutions. Hitherto unrepresented groups, such as indigenous and tribal groups, have recently gained much better access to the UN,[56] and the court cannot be allowed to stand back in acknowledging this development. Intergovernmental organizations and human rights bodies might also have preferred access to the court. Some of these actors might be allowed to ask for advisory opinions from the court (although it remains to be seen whether such opinions could not conflict with the general comments issued by the UN treaty bodies in their capacity to interpret the respective treaty provisions).

Rationae materiae, the court would, as mentioned, decide on those human rights obligations which states have accepted. Any other option (such as following the example of the ICC and

51 For greater detail, see Theodora Christou and Juan-Pablo Raymond (eds), *European Court of Human Rights: Remedies and Execution of Judgements* (London: British Institute of International and Comparative Law, 2003).

52 See Pasqualucci, note 46 above.

53 See Nowak, note 40 above, p. 259.

54 See Trechsel, note 43, pp. 7–8.

55 See Nowak, note 14), p. 37.

56 For example, see the UN Permanent Forum on Indigenous Issues [online]. Available from: http://www.un.org/esa/socdev/unpfii [accessed 14 October 2009].

including a list of human rights in the court's statute that the court would be allowed to monitor) would most likely politicize negotiations and prolong, if not render impossible, the creation of an international human rights court. *Rationae personae*, it has been suggested that the court's core competence to scrutinize states' implementation of human rights norms could be extended to other entities, including the UN itself and organizations such as the World Bank or NATO, trans-national business corporations, or other non-state actors.[57] Despite being innovative, whether this is realistic is yet another question.

The most important value the court would add to the existing UN human rights system is its ability to hand down legally binding, final judgements, which include reparations for the victims of human rights violations. One could, and should, go well beyond the financial compensation which the ECtHR regularly grants, and resort to broader means of compensation. The IACtHR has, for example, recently compensated the Sarawaka people of Suriname for damages (incurred in the course of decades of logging, gold-mining and hydropower infrastructure projects) not only in financial terms, but also by ordering many practical measures, including the demarcation of land, the establishment of a communal development fund with an independent supervisory committee, and the repeated broadcasting of the court's judgement by the local radio.[58]

8. Alternatives?

Can one achieve the kind of consolidation of the international human rights system which the establishment of an international court of human rights would allow with other means? Given that neither the ICJ nor the ICC can be turned into a human rights court along the lines sketched above, two other approaches remain possible. The first one is to upgrade and reform the UN treaty bodies in a way which enables them to deliver the kind of results a court would. Given the necessity to amend the respective treaties and taking into account the cumbersome process of treaty body reform over the past years, this seems less realistic and less desirable than to add an optional institution to the system, such as the court.[59]

The second, and perhaps more feasible way, would be to achieve the kind of jurisprudence envisaged above in the three existing regional courts. This seems a more attractive choice because it can build on established systems and avoid the irritations a new institution such as the international court of human rights may introduce, but it would require a series of reforms in the regional systems to introduce the kind of broad and innovative mandate the international court would have (and which makes the court attractive as an addition to existing procedures). Such reforms will be more difficult to set in motion than the gradual phasing in of an international court of human rights. As for the Asian region, the setting up of a regional court remains unlikely in the near future, so that this approach would have no value added at all for that region, as opposed to the establishment of an international human rights court.

57 See Nowak, note 40, p. 256.

58 Inter-American Court of Human Rights, Case of the Saramaka People *v* Suriname, judgement of 28 November 2007, Series C, No. 172, paras. 186–214.

59 See also Scheinin, note 42 above, p. 142.

9. Conclusion

No doubt, the difficulties in setting up an international human rights court are considerable. Such a new court will have to be anchored in the existing human rights framework in a way that is intellectually and practically attractive to interested states and the human rights movement alike.

'Judicial romanticism',[60] which overestimates the role of courts in the protection of human rights, is certainly inappropriate. Like all institutions, courts have defects of their own, and the way in which they transform the promise of human rights into a bureaucratic and legalized undertaking carried out by lawyers acting in the straitjacket of international law and concern for procedure may well be criticized. Human rights remain an essentially political issue, and the kind of justice a court offers may not always respond to the need of victims and societies affected by human rights violations. The international court of human rights will be no exception in facing this kind of critique and having to respond to it.

Yet, the way in which the development of international human rights law benefits from the cases and precedents of courts, both international and domestic, makes them an indispensable tool in the array of human rights institutions. Beyond the immediate advantages sketched above, and notwithstanding the difficulties ahead, two overarching reasons speak for such an international human rights court. First, it seems inconsistent, if not hypocritical, to push for the right to an effective remedy as a core human right on the national level while at the same time negating this right in the UN system and excluding a great number of persons from access to an international court. There is no better way to make this right a reality than to allow access to a court composed of independent judges, not only at the domestic and regional levels but also in the UN system. Second, what the international human rights system requires to become meaningful and attractive in the eyes of ordinary people is not so much endless tinkering with procedural details of this or that sub-committee in the basement of the *Palais de Nations* in Geneva as some visionary ideas on how to realize human rights in the twenty-first century. Just as the ICC is important not only as a legal institution but also as a symbolic herald of a new era, so could an international human rights court (or, to begin with, the engaged debate over its establishment) open a new chapter for the UN and for the development of international human rights law generally into the future.

60 David P. Forsythe, *Human Rights in International Relations*, 2nd edn (Cambridge: Cambridge University Press, 2006), p. 90.

Chapter 20

Multi-State Responsibility for Extraterritorial Violations of Economic, Social and Cultural Rights

Todd Howland

1. Introduction

Six decades after the adoption of the UDHR,[1] there is still debate on the precise nature and content of extraterritorial human rights obligations, especially when the acts or omissions of states or non-state actors (whether as a result of foreign military intervention, war on terrorism, globalization or otherwise) affect the human rights of individuals in another state. This chapter posits that multiple states can and do hold legal responsibility to protect and promote economic, social and cultural (ESC) rights beyond state borders. States parties to the International Covenant on Economic, Social and Cultural Rights (ICESCR) are obliged to take steps individually or through 'international assistance and cooperation' to achieve progressively the full realization of ESC rights.[2] The idea that multiple states have human rights obligations to the same individual is derived, in part, from the author's own experience working in 'failed states' and as part of multilateral efforts to bring peace, respect for human rights, and stability to war-torn and dysfunctional states. These violations can be direct or indirect, and this chapter discusses both.

Often, ESC rights violations are direct as states fail to ensure that state revenues are maximized and in turn invested in improving the full spectrum of human rights. A clear example of this is illegal mining and mineral exploitation. State elites may use informally collected revenue from these enterprises for personal gain and effectively divert resources away from public budgets that protect a range of ESC rights such as education and health care. The diversions can be created by the state where the minerals are located, by neighbouring states that allow the minerals into their own territory without verifying their legitimacy, and by the states that allow trading in the illegally obtained minerals. Even non-state actors, such as rebel groups and corporate actors, can take part in such diversions.

The other type of violation discussed in this chapter can be described as indirect, in that revenues are not prevented from reaching the state coffers but nonetheless are not used to maximize resources available to measurably improve the situation of human rights in a given state. These efforts are often cloaked in good intentions or designed to appear to be responding to human suffering. Often the resources at the disposal of the 'host state', such as power and financial capacity, are extremely limited, while other actors such as the United Nations (UN) member states choosing to intervene in that state, either bilaterally or multilaterally, have extensive resources and at times more political power than the host state. Such resources and political power may be used to contribute to, as opposed to minimize, human rights violations.

1 GA Res. 217A (III), UN Doc. A/810 at 71 (1948).

2 Art. 2, International Covenant on Economic, Social and Cultural Rights, 993 UNTS 3. See also Chapter 3 in this volume.

Thus, indirect violations can be committed by states, international entities (such as the UN), and even non-governmental organizations.

Oddly, considering legal developments in other fields and the nature of human rights, actors continue to place all legal obligations for violations of human rights on the state where such violations occur. Those governments that contribute to instability and deficient protection of ESC rights through poor service provision, or that have voluntarily joined in efforts to rehabilitate failed states, have enjoyed total impunity for their acts. This impunity is enjoyed regardless of the relative power and financial capacity brought to bear in what these states would call a collective endeavour to bring peace, respect for human rights and stability to war-torn and dysfunctional countries.[3]

This chapter begins with some brief background information on Haiti and the Democratic Republic of Congo (DRC), as reference is made to these two states throughout this chapter. It then explores several existing theoretical frameworks that will help situate the idea of multi-state accountability in current human rights scholarship. This section will move from a discussion of human rights and human rights actors, to humanitarian law and how it is different from human rights. It will then explore several theories of tort and contract law that can help incorporate the multi-state approach. Next, the chapter will outline several existing hurdles in the international legal system that the proposal will have to overcome, such as a very state-centric approach to international law, the marginalization of ESC rights, and other logistical difficulties that would arise when holding multiple states accountable for a single action. Finally, the theoretical framework will be applied to the human rights situations in the DRC to illustrate in which contexts the international system could benefit from the multi-state accountability approach to human rights.

2. Haiti and the Democratic Republic of Congo (DRC)

Haiti and the DRC provide salient examples of why a broader, non-state-centric approach is necessary to create respect for human rights. Both states demonstrate why it is not tenable to continue to assert that multi-state or non-state actors are immune from human rights accountability.

---

3 In fact, the UN was founded for this reason. E.g. Preamble, UN Charter:

We the Peoples of the United Nations Determined to save succeeding generations from the scourge of war, which twice in our lifetime has brought untold sorrow to mankind, and to reaffirm faith in fundamental human rights, in the dignity and worth of the human person, in the equal rights of men and women and of nations large and small, and to establish conditions under which justice and respect for the obligations arising from treaties and other sources of international law can be maintained, and to promote social progress and better standards of life in larger freedom, *And for these Ends* to practice tolerance and live together in peace with one another as good neighbors, and to unite our strength to maintain international peace and security, and to ensure by the acceptance of principles and the institution of methods, that armed force shall not be used, save in the common interest, and to employ international machinery for the promotion of the economic and social advancement of all peoples, *Have Resolved to Combine our Efforts to Accomplish these Aims.* Accordingly, our respective Governments, through representatives assembled in the city of San Francisco, who have exhibited their full powers found to be in good and due form, have agreed to the present Charter of the United Nations and do hereby establish an international organization to be known as the United Nations.

2.1 Haiti

After the ouster of President Aristide in February 2004,[4] the UN mounted its fifth UN peacekeeping operation to Haiti.[5] Haiti was considered a 'failed state' and had a temporary or interim administration that was established extra-constitutionally with a good deal of influence from important states such as the USA. Against the counsel of experts, the USA intervened to facilitate Aristide's removal and the 'restoration' of order when regional actors were against the idea and most favoured preventive measures.[6] The USA obtained UN Security Council support for the US-led 'multinational interim force' intervention and quickly turned the intervention over to the UN.[7] The overall power and resources that were brought to bear by various member states to achieve the common objectives of bringing peace, respect for human rights and stability were massive. They brought resources that were much greater than those of the government of Haiti.[8] Haiti is not the exception. For example, in post-genocide Rwanda, those states participating in the international intervention were much better resourced than the post-genocide government. Following the genocide, the Rwandan Ministry of Justice, tasked with responding to the genocide, had almost no resources and most of its infrastructure had been destroyed. The only vehicle the ministry had was the minister's old, worn-out private car, which on most days needed to be push-started.

In the absence of a war, a ceasefire, a peace process, or a peace accord, the UN Stabilization Mission to Haiti (MINUSTAH)[9] was a clear example of a well-resourced peacekeeping mission to a state with extreme poverty and a long history of bad governance. There was no hot war in Haiti, so it was unclear why the main response of the UN Security Council was to send troops. Making change on the ground is no easy task,[10] but sending the wrong tool does not make it any easier. Even without considering multilateral, bilateral or other sources of government funding,

4 President Aristide had been deposed once before. In fact, Haiti never had a democratic transition until 1994, when President Aristide handed power to René Préval, who won the presidential vote. Aristide was barred from running for a second consecutive term, but was elected again in 2001 in the context of growing instability. E.g. Paul Farmer, 'Haiti's Wretched of the Earth', *Tikkun Magazine*, May–June 2004; Walt Bogdanich and Jenny Nordberg, 'Democracy Undone – Mixed U.S. Signals Help Tilt Haiti to Chaos', *New York Times*, 29 January 2006, p. A1.

5 See SC Res. 1542, UN Doc. S/RES/1542 (30 April 2004); see, generally, United Nations Stabilization Mission in Haiti [online]. Available from: http://www.un.org/depts/dpko/missions/minustah/index.html [accessed 31 December 2009].

6 US interventions in failed states have basically been failures and should be used rarely instead of being invoked without trying many alternatives. E.g. Anatol Lieven, 'Failing States and US Policy', Stanley Foundation, *Policy Analysis Brief*, September 2006 [online]. Available from: http://www.stanleyfoundation.org/publications/pab/pab06failingstates.pdf.

7 SC Res. 1529, UN Doc. S/RES/1529 (29 February 2004).

8 T. Howland, 'Peacekeeping and Conformity with Human Rights Law: How MINUSTAH Falls Short in Haiti', *International Peacekeeping*, 13 (2006), pp. 462–76, at p. 470.

9 On 30 April 2004, the UN Security Council decided to establish the United Nations Stabilization Mission in Haiti (MINUSTAH) and requested that authority be transferred from the Multinational Interim Force (MIF), authorized by the Security Council on 29 February 2004, to MINUSTAH on 1 June 2004. See SC Res. 1542, note 4 above; SC Res. 1529, note 6 above.

10 See J. Benomar, 'Rule of Law Technical Assistance in Haiti: Lessons Learned, a World Bank Conference: Empowerment, Security and Opportunity Through Law and Justice', St Petersburg, Russia (8–12 July 2001) [online]. Available from: http://haiticci.undg.org/uploads/Lessons%20Learned%20Justice_2001.pdf (discussing how to advance reform in a political environment not conducive to change and characterized by protracted political crisis and paralysis).

MINUSTAH's annual budget was larger than that of the government of Haiti. For example, the USA in 2004 and 2005 disbursed US$352 million in assistance for Haiti, most of it through US-based NGOs.[11] The Haitian government had annual revenues of about US$400 million and expenditures of about US$600 million in 2005,[12] whereas the approved 2005 MINUSTAH budget was US$518.30 million.[13]

Remarkably, President Aristide's former prime minister was elected president a little more than two years following Aristide's ouster.[14] His election brought about a reduction in political violence, perhaps indicating that international intervention may have contributed to, as opposed to minimized, the political violence. Nonetheless, it is difficult to determine whether the international intervention, with all its expenditures, has measurably improved the human rights situation in Haiti. Do bilateral or multilateral participants in the international intervention actually have an obligation to create programmes in a way that improves the human rights situation? At present, there is a gulf between those scholars who convincingly assert that such human rights obligations exist,[15] and operational entities that seem to begrudge being bound even by humanitarian law after a directive from the UN Secretary-General,[16] let alone take their human rights obligations seriously.

2.2 Democratic Republic of Congo (DRC)

The DRC has had a turbulent history of war, exploitation, and European colonization ever since the Stanley–Livingstone expeditions of the 1870s. Since the intervention of King Leopold and the Belgium Empire, the DRC has had a complicated and often violent and exploitative relationship with outside interveners. Of particular import is mining in the DRC. The DRC is a naturally rich nation with resources such as gold, copper, diamonds and coltan.[17] Little progress has been made in holding human rights violators accountable – whether member states, individuals, rebels, or corporations – for the impact of their illegal mining involvement on the DRC.[18]

11 US Department of State, *Background Note: Haiti*, January 2007 [online]. Available from: http://www.state.gov/r/pa/ei/bgn/1982.htm [accessed 31 December 2009].

12 *CIA World Factbook*, 'Haiti' [online]. Available from: https://www.cia.gov/cia/publications/factbook/geos/ha.html [accessed 31 December 2009].

13 The Secretary-General, *Report of the Secretary-General on the Revised Budget for the United Nations Stabilization Mission in Haiti for the Period from 1 July 2005 to 30 June 2006*, UN Doc. A/60/176 (1 August 2005).

14 L. Aucoin, 'Haiti's Constitutional Crisis', *Boston University International Law Journal*, 17 (1999), pp. 115–40, at p. 118.

15 M. Salomon and A. Sengupta, 'The Human Rights Obligations of Multilateral Institutions and of States as Members of the MLI', in *The Right to Development: Obligations of States and the Rights of Minorities and Indigenous Peoples* (2003), pp. 39–40 [online]. Available from: http://www.minorityrights.org/admin/Download/pdf/IP_RTD_SalomonSengupta.pdf [accessed 31 December 2009].

16 The Secretary-General, *Observance by United Nations Forces of International Humanitarian Law*, UN Doc. ST/SGB/1999/13 (6 Aug. 1999); E.g. R. Murphy, 'An Assessment of UN Efforts to Address Sexual Misconduct by Peacekeeping Personnel', *International Peacekeeping*, 13 (2006), pp. 531–46, at p. 532.

17 D. Renton *et al.*, *The Congo: Plunder and Resistance* (London: Zed Books, 2007).

18 *Ibid.*

3. Theoretical Considerations

In many economies around the world, short-term profit-seeking trumps individual ESC rights, and even long-term business interests, creating a catch-22 short-sighted business arrangement. Legally binding ESC human rights laws have, thus far, failed to change this calculation as international organizations and member states have not created regimes designed to reinforce the respect for ESC human rights by making these types of deals less profitable and more risky. This has been especially clear in the DRC and Haiti.

As odd as it may sound, political and bureaucratic concerns trump human rights obligations in the organization of international missions, mainly because member states and multilateral and bilateral bureaucrats do not consider themselves bound by human rights law in the organization and operation of an intervention.[19] Of course, private actors, such as armed rebels and corporations, are even less likely to consider themselves bound, and act accordingly. How human rights organizations can more effectively organize mission resources and hold accountable those directly and indirectly linked to violations of ESC rights must be better defined. The questions, 'Who holds human rights?' and 'Who has the obligation to respect human rights?', are increasingly complex.

3.1 The Essence of Human Rights Law

It is well established in international human rights law that human rights derive from the inherent dignity and worth of all persons, with the human person as the central subject and primary beneficiary of human rights.[20] Thus, human rights are not derived from being a national of a particular state but are based upon attributes of human personality. During the Vienna Conference on Human Rights, states declared that 'Human rights and fundamental freedoms are the birthright of all human beings; their protection and promotion is the first responsibility of Governments.'[21] What is noteworthy in this language is that it reiterates attachment of rights to the individual, and the use of the plural form of government infers that more than one government can be concerned with the rights of a particular individual. But for years there has been theoretical debate and practical confusion about the application of human rights. To some degree, growing out of the state-centric reality of international law, it is understandable how many continually attempt to limit human rights to the relationship between the individual and the state. Focusing on the individual without linking him or her to a particular state seems fanciful, but if the objective of human rights law is the protection of individual/group rights and the creation of a just world, that is the logical outcome.[22]

19 Some scholars have described how the structure of public organizations can lead to questionable ethical decisions and behaviours. E.g. G. Adams and D. Balfour, 'Human Rights, the Moral Vacuum of Modern Organisations, and Administrative Evil', in T. Campbell and S. Miller (eds), *Human Rights and the Moral Responsibilities of Corporate and Public Sector Organisations* (Dordrecht: Kluwer Academic Publishers, 2004), ch. 11.

20 E.g. the Preambles to the Universal Declaration of Human Rights; the International Covenant on Economic, Social; Cultural Rights and the International Covenant on Civil and Political Rights; and the American Declaration of the Rights and Duties of Man, O.A.S. Res. XXX, reprinted in Basic Documents Pertaining to Human Rights in the Inter-American System, OAS/Ser.L/V/I.4 Rev. 9 (2003); *American Journal of International Law*, 43 Suppl. 133 (1949).

21 World Conference on Human Rights, 14–25 June 1993, *Vienna Declaration and Programme of Action*, I(1), UN Doc A/CONF.157/23 (12 July 1993).

22 In many ways, this is already a well-established principle; for example, 'Aliens shall enjoy, in accordance with domestic law and subject to the relevant international obligation of the State in which they

The failure of entities with the capacity to effect positive changes in human rights to be bound by human rights principles reinforces the idea that human rights law has no restraining normative content and may be manipulated simply for political ends.[23] The more often human rights law is applied to those with power, the closer we are to a place where the individual person becomes of the essence of law's purpose.[24]

The fact that all laws are broken, however, does not mean there is no law – but it does affect the law's acceptance and effective enforcement. What is most problematic, however, is the relative difficulty of getting the most powerful entities to accept and comply with their human rights obligations in practice. While a lack of mechanisms, effective forums and third-party oversight does not negate the existence of rights, these deficiencies certainly present challenges for human rights advocates. The traditional realist's view of human rights is grounded in a tight-knit community or nation, where a contract between governed and governors defines these rights. This idea, in times of little movement between one nation and another, worked adequately enough to ground human rights law. But today, human rights law is about protecting individuals and groups from those who have the capacity to violate their rights.[25] The 'community' is heterogeneous and international, and therefore laws ought to apply globally. In that regard, the International Court of Justice (ICJ) observed in the *Reservations to the Genocide Convention* case:

> [T]he contracting states do not have any interests of their own; they merely have, one and all, a common interest, namely, the accomplishment of those high purposes which are the raison d'être of the convention.... The high ideals which inspired the Convention provide, by virtue of the common will of the parties, the foundation and measure of all its provisions.[26]

Indeed, in 1993, the Vienna Conference affirmed the idea that human rights are universal, indivisible, interdependent and interrelated, yet, we have not achieved full acceptance of human rights as a constant limitation of power. Historically, human rights law has been viewed too narrowly and has been portrayed as a dichotomy of good or evil intentions. In fact, because human rights apply to everyone, people with evil intentions are not the only ones who can violate them. Often organizations created to do good, such as the UN, NGOs and even human rights groups, can violate human rights of individuals and groups. The idea that violators must be evil limits the understanding and application of human rights law.[27]

---

are present ...'. See Declaration on the Human Rights of Individuals Who Are Not Nationals of the Country in Which They Live, GA Res. 40/144, Art. 5, Annex, UN GAOR, Suppl. No. 53, UN Doc. A/40/53 (13 December 1985).

23 M. Koskenniemi, *From Apology to Utopia: The Structure of International Legal Argument* (Cambridge: Cambridge University Press, 2005), pp. 251–4.

24 J. Elisabeth Nijman, *The Concept of International Legal Personality: An Inquiry into the History and Theory of International Law* (The Hague: T.M.C. Asser Press, 2004), pp. 457–73.

25 E.g. Alon Harel, 'How (and Whether) to Rethink Human Rights', *International Legal Theory*, 9 (2003), pp. 87–104, at p. 88; and Chapter 28 in this volume.

26 Reservations to the Convention on the Prevention and Punishment of the Crime of Genocide, 1951 I.C.J. 3, 23 (28 May).

27 D. Kennedy, 'The International Human Rights Movement: Part of the Problem?', *Harvard Human Rights Journal*, 15 (2002), pp. 101–25, at pp. 109, 111. One should question the effectiveness of international interventions and of the overriding usefulness of the dominant paradigm, given that the world should be better off than we are. *Review Essay Symposium: Philip Allott's* Eunomia *and the Health of Nations. Thinking Another World: 'This Cannot Be How the World Was Meant to Be'*, Discussion, *European Journal of International Law*, 16(2) (2005), pp. 255–6, 260. For a discussion of why NGOs should be accountable under human rights

3.2 Multiple Actors and Human Rights

Many theories regarding the accountability of multiple actors have been developed and are in use throughout the world. Most of these theories allow for degrees of responsibility or fault, distinguishing the actions of one wrongdoer from another involved in the same action. Theories and practice, ranging from simple to very sophisticated, have developed to allocate or apportion fault, responsibility and liability. These theories include co-defendant and co-conspirator liability, agency, contract, vicarious liability, *respondent superior*, market share liability, joint and several liability, enterprise liability, and comparative fault.[28]

Even in international law, multiple actors can be held responsible. The ICJ, humanitarian and environmental law, and even trade law allow for multiple actor liability, even though international law otherwise usually focuses on the state actor. This traditional thinking of international law provides an incomplete framework for examining human rights obligations. Human rights law should not be held prisoner by the dated idea that only one state at a time can violate international law, that a state is only bound by law regarding its own citizens. In fact, human rights treaties ratified by a vast majority of states are very open. They apply not just to citizens but to everyone within a state's jurisdiction.[29] Thus, a state and any other powerful entity can violate the human rights of someone under its jurisdiction.

Unfortunately, human rights and humanitarian law are often lumped together within the public international law field. Practitioners often practise both, and human rights lawyers are far from immune from the phobia that human rights law may be more fantasy than fact. Because humanitarian law is the more developed discipline, practitioners often wrongly apply its obsessive concerns with jurisdiction to human rights cases. However, no such hurdle need be crossed in human rights law. This desire to determine first whether human rights law applies has created a problem for its extraterritorial application, when, in fact, human rights law is not territorially limited. Human rights are distinct from most international law or law between nations. For example, whether refugee law is a distinct discipline within international law, or, rather, a part of human rights law, makes a difference as to how these laws are interpreted. Laws relating to refugee rights use language about such laws applying in the territory of the contracting state.[30] The territorial limits included in the Convention Relating to the Status of Refugees[31] have been interpreted narrowly by contracting states. The US Supreme Court, in a narrow interpretation of refugee law as traditional international law, as opposed to a part of human rights law, found that detention of Haitians in Guantánamo, Cuba, was not covered by the Refugee Convention, since that would be an 'uncontemplated'

---

law, see K. Nowrot, 'Legal Consequences of Globalization: The Status of Non-Governmental Organizations Under International Law', Symposium: The Rule of Law in the Era of Globalization, *Indiana Journal of Global Legal Studies*, 6(2) (1999), pp. 579–645.

28 See, generally, K. Abraham, *Concise Restatement of Torts* (American Law Institute, 2000); Donald Harris and Denis Tallon (eds), *Contract Law Today: Anglo-French Comparisons* (Oxford: Clarendon Press, 1989); European Group on Tort Law, *Principles of European Tort Law* (New York: Springer-Verlag/Wien, 2005); Rebecca Attree and Patrick Kelly (eds), *European Product Liability* (London: Butterworths, 1992); Fowler V. Harper *et al.*, *The Law of Torts* (New York: Aspen Publishers, 2005); William M. Sage, 'Enterprise Liability and the Emerging Managed Health Care System', *Law and Contemporary Problems*, 60 (1997), pp. 159–210.

29 See also Chapter 3 in this volume.

30 Convention Relating to the Status of Refugees, Arts. 10 and 40, 28 July, 1951, 189 UNTS 150.

31 *Ibid.*

extraterritorial obligation.[32] Viewing the Refugee Convention as protecting the human rights of individuals first, rather than as simply an agreement between states, would have resulted in a different decision that protected the rights of the refuge-seeking Haitians.[33]

Again, human rights law focuses on the rights of individuals and groups, and its purpose is to protect individuals and groups against human rights violations. Such violations may be by states or actors other than states. International organizations have gained their legitimacy from participation of states, but are losing their credibility after failing to live up to the principles they were founded to uphold. Accountability to their principles – beyond toothless self-review – should be enforced, and legal developments support this change.[34] Human rights law should and does apply to international organizations.[35] However, the realization of this principle has been difficult, given that such organizations are not currently parties to human rights treaties.

Human rights law is not humanitarian law, with all its jurisdictional definitions. Humanitarian lawyers spend countless hours in mental contortions attempting to show how humanitarian law either applies or does not apply to a particular circumstance.[36] Is it an international conflict? Were the participants engaged in combat? Were they wearing uniforms? And, recently, is he or she an enemy combatant? Such a practice appears to help these lawyers comfort themselves that humanitarian law is really law. Human rights apply and belong to humans. Although this may be a stark and sweeping statement, this is the nature of human rights law, and this is why human rights law should now apply to non-state actors,[37] to corporations and in the private sphere (e.g. discrimination).[38] It is out of step with these developments, which represent the essence of human

32 *Sale* v *Haitian Centers Council, Inc.*, 113 S. Ct. 2549, 2564 (1993), cited in G. Neuman, 'Extraterritorial Violations of Human Rights by the United States', *American University Journal of International Law and Policy*, 9 (1993), pp. 213, 219.

33 Neuman, note 32 above, p. 219.

34 E.g. S. Herz, 'International Organizations in U.S. Courts: Reconsidering the Anachronism of Absolute Immunity', *Suffolk Transnational Law Review*, 31 (2008), pp. 471–532, at p. 471. For additional support for peacekeeping operations to be held accountable when they fall short of what they promise to do, see A. Raven-Roberts, 'Gender Mainstreaming in United Nations Peacekeeping Operations: Talking the Talk, Tripping over the Walk', in Dyan Mazurana *et al.* (eds), *Gender, Conflict, and Peacekeeping* (London: Rowman & Littlefield, 2005), p. 43.

35 E.g. Menno T. Kamminga, *Inter-State Accountability for Violations of Human Rights* (Philadelphia: University of Pennsylvania Press, 1992). For a more limited view of multi-state responsibility for human rights violations, one scholar outlines how the UN should be responsible for its human rights violations in the context of its administrative missions. See B. Knoll, *The Legal Status of Territories Subject to Administration by International Organisation* (Cambridge: Cambridge University Press, 2008).

36 A clear example of this is US government lawyer efforts to show that somehow humanitarian law does not apply to its war on terror. For an effective critique of this mental yoga, see Human Rights Watch, *Briefing Paper, International Humanitarian Law Issues in a Potential War In Iraq* (20 February 2003) [online]. Available from: http://www.hrw.org/backgrounder/arms/iraq0202003.htm [accessed 31 January 2009].

37 Nigel S. Rodley, 'Can Armed Opposition Groups Violate Human Rights?', in Kathleen E. Mahoney *et al.* (eds), *Human Rights in the Twenty-First Century: A Global Challenge* (Dordrecht: Martinus Nijhoff, 1993), p. 297. See, generally, A. Clapham, *Human Rights Obligations of Non-State Actors* (Oxford: Oxford University Press, 2006).

38 E.g. A. Clapham, *Human Rights in the Private Sphere* (Oxford: Clarendon Press, 1996); M. Gibney and R.D. Emerick, 'The Extraterritorial Application of United States Law and the Protection of Human Rights: Holding Multinational Corporations Accountable to Domestic and International Standards', *Temple International and Comparative Law Journal* 10 (1996), pp. 123ff; Steven R. Ratner, 'Corporations and Human Rights: A Theory of Legal Responsibility', *Yale Law Journal*, 111 (2001), pp. 443–545.

rights law, to limit the extraterritorial application of human rights law and to presume that only one state may be held responsible for violating individual or group human rights. To some degree, these limits have been based on the desire to avoid the difficult task of evaluating government policy in a war abroad. In addition, the international law state-based approach appears to helpfully limit the inquiry to one state at a time. However, these limitations are mainly due to an enculturation from humanitarian law and traditional international law, in which we review the actions of one state at a time and where some sort of jurisdictional hurdle must be crossed before the law applies. Human rights law is relevant whenever individual or group rights are violated whether by one state, several states or non-state actors.

3.3 Humanitarian Purpose Versus the Intervention Industry

Historically, linked to the work of the International Red Cross and the content of humanitarian law or the rules of war, interventions with a humanitarian purpose have developed a certain mystique. They enjoy international protection, not only in the form of limited scrutiny, but as full affirmative privileges. The problem is that interventions with an ostensibly humanitarian purpose now regularly include a full range of operations, from aid programmes to sending troops (known informally as 'blue helmets').[39] This complicates any effort to hold individual states responsible, since a state may easily avoid scrutiny by claiming a humanitarian purpose.[40]

In the ICJ's consideration of the complaint by the Nicaraguan government regarding the covert war the USA was waging against it, the court even entertained the US argument that its activities in Nicaragua should be considered of humanitarian nature and, therefore, legitimate. The ICJ stated:

> the provision of humanitarian aid cannot be regarded as an unlawful intervention or in any way contrary to international law … if [implemented] to avoid violations of sovereignty and limited to the purpose 'to prevent and alleviate human suffering' and 'to protect life and health' and to ensure respect for human beings and given without discrimination.[41]

Although the ICJ did not find the US intervention in Nicaragua to have a humanitarian purpose, its tautological statement that humanitarian aid cannot be regarded as contrary to international law is consistent with the mystique that has developed around humanitarian purpose. Humanitarian intention is now used instrumentally by governments and NGOs as a means to avoid seriously evaluating whether their intervention actually contributes to measurably improving the human rights situation. This allows for the disease of 'appearing to be doing' to replace 'actually doing'. If the intervention can be classified as having a humanitarian purpose, intervening states can avoid scrutiny. The question should be not whether there is a humanitarian purpose, but whether interventions have a measurable impact on human rights.

---

39 D. Rieff, *A Bed for the Night: Humanitarianism in Crisis* (London: Random House, 2002), pp. 308, 328.

40 Adding to the complexity is the fact that more and more state functions, such as delivering foreign aid, are being contracted to private entities (both for profit and non-profit). See Laura A. Dickinson, 'Government for Hire: Privatizing Foreign Affairs and the Problem of Accountability Under International Law', *William and Mary Law Review,* 47 (2005), pp. 135, 146–60.

41 Military and Paramilitary Activities (*Nicar.* v *U.S.*), 1986 I.C.J. 14, 242–3 (27 June).

Within many international NGOs, there has been a question in reaction as to whether good intentions are good enough.[42] There has not been a similar process for states and international organizations. Scholars of humanitarianism have discussed the need for human rights to be respected and promoted by NGOs.[43] All actors would be assisted, most specifically the intended beneficiary, if all interveners were truly held to human rights standards. The reality that international interventions have become a major industry begs for the legal framework to be reconsidered. The fact that public monies fuel this industry is not a reason to avoid scrutiny, but rather a reason for it. If one were to sum up all the entities which contribute to work that may fall into the vaguely worded humanitarian purpose, the number would be significant.[44] The international intervention industry offers goods and services and should be treated like any other industry. Having good intentions should not be a reason for arguing that such industry has no human rights obligations. The public policy behind holding those who manufacture goods or provide services responsible for their quality applies to all actors, including those with the ostensible intention to do good. In fact, given that some of these 'do-gooders' are working for organizations that promote the respect for principles, they may have a duty to do good. The fact that governments have a long history of enacting laws or signing international treaties and not applying those laws or treaties at the domestic level simply highlights the historical challenge, but it does not negate the importance of holding governments to accept their freely accepted legal obligations.

3.4 Duty to Act

General principles of tort, contract and criminal law create a number of situations requiring an affirmative duty to act. A duty to act may be based on the relationship of the parties (e.g. parent to child, pilot to passenger) or in contract; a duty may be based on a voluntary assumption of care; a duty may arise from the fact that a person created a risk from which a need for protection arose (for example, the good Samaritan principle,[45] in which no duty exists to intervene, but once a person intervenes he or she has a duty to intervene appropriately); a duty may arise from a special relationship that makes the non-acting partner criminally responsible for the actor's criminal action (for example, one person beats the other and leaves the victim lying on the ground injured); a duty can arise from the fact that one owns the real property upon which the victim is injured; and the duty to act and the resulting criminal liability for failing to act, may be based on statute.[46] If one borrowed and applied these general principles of law to instances of states intervening in

---

42 See, generally, Mary B. Anderson, *Do No Harm: How Aid Can Support Peace or War* (Boulder, CO: Lynne Rienner, 1999); H. Slim, 'Doing the Right Thing: Relief Agencies, Moral Dilemmas and Moral Responsibility in Political Emergencies and War', *Disasters*, 21 (1997), pp. 244ff.

43 Hugo Slim, 'Not Philanthropy But Rights: The Proper Politicisation of Humanitarian Philosophy in War', *International Journal of Human Rights*, 6 (2002), pp. 1, 8.

44 For example, all the foreign aid budgets, the budgets of international organizations (e.g. UN, World Bank), and even some parts of defence budgets designated for this purpose, as well as NGOs and private foundations for this purpose.

45 Other scholars have attempted to impute liability or accountability in circumstances where the law has not yet done so; for example, C. Barry, 'Applying the Contribution Principle', in C. Barry, and T.W. Pogge (eds), *Global Institutions and Responsibilities: Achieving Global Justice* (Oxford: Blackwell, 2005).

46 E.g. D.C. Biggs, 'The Good Samaritan Is Packing: An Overview of the Broadened Duty to Aid Your Fellowman, with the Modern Desire to Possess Concealed Weapons', *University of Dayton Law Review*, 22 (1997), pp. 225, 229–30.

another state in any way (from invasion, to peacekeeping, to development work), a duty would often exist.

Perhaps the strongest basis to assert a duty is the good Samaritan principle, given that states would argue that they had no duty in the first place to intervene. Just as in general principles of law, a good Samaritan has no obligation to intervene, but if he or she does, he or she is held to certain legal obligations.

Another basis for an affirmative duty could be asserted depending on circumstances. For example, considering Chapter IX of the UN Charter and various human rights agreements,[47] it could be argued that a contractual or statutory duty exists. Or where a state has intervened in another state – for example, militarily or economically – and damage has been done and attributed to the intervening state, a duty could arise. The idea is established rhetorically and intellectually that a human rights duty applies to protect the 'target beneficiaries' of international actors involved in development projects. This understanding, however, has yet to be accepted or realized by most states and other international actors. It is notable that, on paper, the World Bank already recognizes this duty:

> Human rights foster accountability of all actors involved in development by locating duty for particular development outcomes on duty-bearers (usually States). This advances accountability to the poor and a consequent empowerment of the poor. In short, human rights improve the processes through which development occurs for those it is designed to benefit.[48]

3.5 An Agent or Subcontractor Cannot Avoid Legal Obligations

In general principles of law, it is clear, whether under contract, agency or tort law, that an individual or entity cannot escape legal responsibility by forming an association with others. In these cases, one is held to be liable for the acts or omissions of the other. Similarly, international organizations have human rights obligations, and entities that created these organizations do not escape liability by acting through the international organization. Indeed, as Shelton notes,

> International organizations are entities created by states delegating power to achieve certain goals and perform specified functions.... It would be surprising if states could perform actions collectively through international organizations that states could not lawfully do individually.[49]

International organizations are subjects of international law and, as such, they are bound by any obligations incumbent upon them under general rules of international law.[50] Case law interpreting the European Convention of Human Rights (ECHR)[51] has consistently held states to be responsible

47 UN Charter, Arts. 55–60.

48 Robert Danino, 'Legal Opinion on Human Rights and the Work of the World Bank', para. 2 (27 January 2006) (on file with the author). For more on the IMF and World Bank human rights obligations, see Gazi Bahram, *The IMF, The World Bank and the Question of Human Rights* ((New York: Transnational Publishers, 2005). See also World Bank [online]. Available from: http://go.worldbank.org/72L95K8TN0.

49 D. Shelton, 'Protecting Human Rights in a Globalized World', *Boston College International and Comparative Law Review*, 25 (2002), pp. 273–322, at p. 309; see also Reparations for Injuries Suffered in the Service of the United Nations, Advisory Opinion, 1949 I.C.J. 174 (11 April).

50 Interpretation of the Agreement of March 25, 1951 Between the WHO and Egypt, 1980 I.C.J. 73, 89 (20 December).

51 ETS No. 005.

for their actions, regardless of the banner or entity through which such actions were carried out.[52] It has been held that it would be incompatible with the purposes of the ECHR (and indeed other human rights treaties) to absolve states from responsibility when acting through international organizations.[53]

4. Specific Hurdles

Ending obligations to respect human rights at a state's borders severely limits human rights law's capacity to effectuate positive change. A state-based interpretation is anachronistic and flows against an actual trend of globalization of commerce as well as conflicts. In contrast to the old state-centric model of international relations, the present world is amazingly interconnected.[54] Trade, international investment and economic immigration have accelerated the reach of the global economy, and eroded the power of the state to govern.[55] Corporations increasingly perform roles state governments were previously responsible for, and their impacts on social life have broadened and deepened in countries around the world. Corporations have expanded their influence in countries around the world, and with great power comes great responsibility. In principle, corporations therefore have obligations to respect human rights wherever they operate. But when human rights principles apply in the private sphere across borders, can states claim that only a host state has human rights obligations? Can they claim that their domestic human rights obligations do not apply when that state is working in another, either directly or through an agent (e.g. the UN, OAS or World Bank)?[56] Some aspects of this issue have received academic attention.[57]

The prevalence of illegal mining in some states shows how a state-based approach to human rights enforcement is ineffective. Illegal mining constitutes a crime of conversion, but it goes well beyond a crime as it infects and inhibits the development of sustainable peace and true human-centred development. Unfortunately, legal developments to address this problem are well behind the understanding of the damage it creates.

There is a growing understanding of the application of human rights law to individuals serving in international operations. For instance, human rights principles forbid 'blue helmets' to torture or

52 M. Kearney, 'Extraterritorial Jurisdiction of the European Convention on Human Rights', *Trinity College Law Review*, 5 (2002), pp. 126, 139.

53 *Waite and Kennedy* v *Germany*, 30 Eur. Ct. H.R. 261, 262 (1999).

54 Some scholars have developed theories of responsibility based on this interconnectedness; e.g. I.M. Young, 'Responsibility and Global Justice: A Social Connection Model', *Social Philosophy and Policy*, 23(1) (2006), pp. 102–30.

55 See also Chapter 10 in this volume.

56 For example, both home and host states have an obligation to regulate multinational corporations. E.g. Shelton, note 49 above. It is a general principle that those with power must be accountable for the way in which they exercise it. International organizations have developed limited and limiting ways to hold themselves to account. E.g. Daniel D. Bradlow, 'Private Complainants and International Organizations: A Comparative Study of the Independent Inspection Mechanisms in International Financial Institutions', *Georgia Journal of International Law and Comparative Law*, 36 (2005), pp. 403–94.

57 Professor Ved Nanda has been sitting on a Committee of the International Law Association that has been grappling with this topic for a number of years and has already caught the wave in a recently published article. See Ved Nanda, 'Accountability of International Organizations – Some Observations', *Denver Journal of International Law and Policy*, 33 (2005), pp. 379ff.

rape those they have been sent to protect.[58] At the same time, mechanisms to create accountability for these violations are underdeveloped.[59] However, while there is also a growing understanding and acceptance of the international responsibility to protect,[60] there is still again an underdevelopment of the collective responsibility for failing to act or to fail while acting.[61]

An understanding of how human rights law applies when member states organize their interventions in another state, and how they spend their money, is also underdeveloped.[62] There are, however, attempts to address this. For example, Zanmi Lasante (Partners in Health), the Robert F. Kennedy Memorial Center for Justice and Human Rights, and the International Human Rights Clinic at the New York University School of Law requested and received a hearing on the human rights obligations, specifically economic and social rights, that members of the OAS have when implementing projects in Haiti.[63] The purpose of the hearing was to remind the commissioners of the confusion regarding this issue and the ripeness for further clarification.

4.1 Extraterritorial Application of Human Rights Law

Extraterritorial responsibility has been well established in international law for decades. The seminal case, the *Trail Smelter Arbitration*, held that 'no state has the right to use or permit the use of *its* territory in such a manner as to cause injury … in or to the territory of another' (emphasis added).[64] Do these principles also apply to human rights violations arising from decisions taken in one state that result in actions carried out in another? A number of forums and scholars have argued that this should be the case. Many scholars argue that decisions against the extraterritorial

58 E.g. Ray Murphy, 'An Assessment of UN Efforts to Address Sexual Misconduct by Peacekeeping Personnel', *International Peacekeeping*, 13 (2006), pp. 531–46, illustrating how human rights laws are serving in international operations.

59 Some scholars see a more gradual acceptance by the UN and member states of their human rights obligations – for example, when acting as a quasi-sovereign. E.g. F. Mégret and F. Hoffmann, 'The UN as a Human Rights Violator? Some Reflections on the United Nations Changing Human Rights Responsibilities', *Human Rights Quarterly*, 25 (2003), pp. 314–42.

60 The United Nations Security Council Resolution 1674, adopted on 28 April 2006, 'Reaffirm[ed] the provisions of paragraphs 138 and 139 of the 2005 World Summit Outcome Document regarding the responsibility to protect populations from genocide, war crimes, ethnic cleansing and crimes against humanity', and committed the Security Council to action to protect civilians in armed conflict.

61 Seumas Miller, 'Collective Responsibility and Armed Humanitarian Intervention', in Tony Coady and Michael O'Keefe (eds), *Righteous Violence: The Ethics and Politics of Military Intervention* (Melbourne: Melbourne University Press, 2005), p. 51.

62 Some scholars believe the general principles of state responsibility apply to human rights law and that the host state would be justified in approaching the intervening state for compensation for the violation of the rights of its citizens. The logical extension of this argument is that Haiti could bring a case in the ICJ against various states for violating the ESC rights of those in its jurisdiction. E.g. D.M. Chirwa, 'The Doctrine of State Responsibility as a Potential Means of Holding Private Actors Accountable for Human Rights', 5 *Melbourne Journal of International Law*, 5(1) (2004), pp. 1–65, at pp. 26–7, and Chapter 21 in this volume.

63 *Statement of Partners in Health/Zanmi Lasante* before the Inter-American Commission on Human Rights (3 March 2006) [online]. Available from: http://www.rfkmemorial.org/human_rights/2002_Loune/PIHStatement.pdf.

64 *The Smelter Arbitral Tribunal Decision, American Journal of International Law*, 35 (1941), pp. 684ff, quoted in Rebecca M. Bratspies, 'Trail Smelter's (Semi)Precautionary Legacy', in Rebecca M. Bratspies and Russell Miller (eds), *Transboundary Harms in International Law: Lessons from the Trail Smelter Arbitration* (Cambridge: Cambridge University Press, 2006).

application of human rights law actually works against the protection of individual rights, the very purpose of human rights law.[65]

Notably, states take interest in the impact of their corporate actors abroad (e.g. product liability)[66] or acts of individuals (e.g. paedophiles, money launderers, tax dodgers), and international humanitarian law attaches to the actor, not the place.[67] Yet, human rights NGOs and advocacy groups have not spent much time looking at the extraterritorial impact of state actions. One author has stated that '[g]reater commitment is needed to the complex and broad-ranging business of transforming the political culture both nationally and internationally in order to create greater transparency and accountability in relation to state actions overseas.'[68] The human rights advocate's position, and one that has significant theoretical support, is that it is unconscionable to interpret human rights treaty obligations in such a way that would permit the violation of human rights by a contracting party extraterritorially, but find that same violation condemnable when done in its own territory.[69] The issue has been litigated often in the European Court on Human Rights (ECtHR). These cases turn mainly on the definition of 'jurisdiction' found in Article 1 of the ECHR.[70]

There have been many critiques of the ECtHR's approach to extraterritorial application of the convention, a number of which show what appears to be somewhat inconsistent judgements that tend to support the idea that the court has placed the higher interests of the state parties above examining serious human rights violations.[71] Cases against Turkey and Russia have tended to support

65 E.g. T. Meron, 'Extraterritoriality of Human Rights Treaties', *American Journal of International Law*, 89(1) (1995), pp. 78–82. See also J. Creone, 'Minding the Gap: Outlining KFOR Accountability in Post-Conflict Kosovo', *European Journal of International Law*, 12(3) (2001), pp. 469–88, at p. 475.

66 In fact, some have argued that various states, including the USA, have gone too far in asserting extraterritorial jurisdiction or application of their laws in other countries. (This is a far cry from the US position on the application of human rights to its actions extraterritorially.) E.g. Note, 'Extraterritorial Application of the Export Administration Act of 1979 Under International and American Law', *Michigan Law Review*, 81(5) (1983), pp. 1308–36, at p. 1309; see also Jerry W. Cain, Jr., 'Extraterritorial Application of the United States' Trade Embargo Against Cuba: The United Nations General Assembly's Call for an End to the U.S. Trade Embargo', *Georgia Journal of International and Comparative Law*, 24 (1994), pp. 379, 380; see, generally, Note, 'Constitutional Law – Extraterritorial Application of the Fourth Amendment to Actions Taken by or at the Direction of United States Agents Against Aliens Residing in Foreign Nations', *Wayne Law Review*, 21 (1974–5), pp. 1473, 1479, and R.L. Sarosdy, Comment, 'Jurisdiction Following Illegal Extraterritorial Seizure: International Human Rights Obligations as an Alternative to Constitutional Stalemate', *Texas Law Review*, 54 (1975–6), pp. 1439–70, at p. 1468, discussing the ebb and flow of the extraterritorial application of the individual rights guaranteed in the U.S. Constitution; see also A. Fisher and M. Satterthwaite, *Beyond Guantánamo: Transfers to Torture One Year After Rasul* v. *Bush*, Center for Human Rights and Global Justice, 28 June 2005 [online]. Available from: http://www.nyuhr.org/docs/Beyond%20Guantanamo%20Report%20FINAL.pdf (providing a more recent example of the ebb and flow of the extraterritorial application of the individual rights guaranteed in the U.S. Constitution).

67 E.g. D. Kritsiotis, 'The Kosovo Crisis and NATO's Application of Armed Forces Against the Federal Republic of Yugoslavia', *International and Comparative Law Quarterly*, 49 (2000), pp. 330ff.

68 R. Wilde, 'Legal "Black Hole"? Extraterritorial State Action and International Treaty Law on Civil and Political Rights', *Michigan Journal of International Law*, 26(3) (2005), pp. 739–806, at p. 770.

69 M. Kearney, '*Extraterritorial Jurisdiction of the European Convention on Human Rights*', *Trinity College Law Review*, 5 (2002), pp. 126–9.

70 Convention for the Protection of Human Rights and Fundamental Freedoms, Art. 1, 11 April 1950, 213 UNTS 221. 'The High Contracting Parties shall secure to everyone within their jurisdiction the rights and freedoms defined in Section 1 of this Convention.'

71 E.g. Kearney, note 69 above, pp. 126–57, providing an analysis of several decisions of the European Court regarding the extraterritorial application of international human rights laws.

the extraterritorial application, while cases against core European states do not.[72] In the context of the Turkish occupation of Cyprus, the court stated: '[A] Contracting State to the Convention could not, by way of delegation of powers to a subordinate and unlawful administration, avoid its responsibility for breaches of the Convention, indeed of international law in general.'[73] The term 'jurisdiction' is not limited to the national territory of the high contracting parties; their responsibility can be involved because of acts of their authorities producing effects outside their own territory.[74]

One line of cases clearly does not limit jurisdiction to territorial boundaries and uses the 'effective control' or 'degree of control' test based on power or authority to determine whether the ECHR should be applied extraterritorially.[75] While the 'control entails responsibility' principle is well established in international law,[76] the limits become evident when control is shared or complex. In the *Bankovic* case, plaintiffs attempted to hold states responsible for a bombing in Belgrade by NATO forces, but the ECtHR narrowed the applicability of the convention extraterritorially to the territories of the contracting states. By taking this tack, the court avoided the more interesting question regarding the degree to which state parties are responsible for actions carried out within the framework of NATO.[77] The court stated:

> [T]he Convention is a multi-lateral treaty operating, subject to Article 56 of the Convention, in an essentially regional context and notably in the legal space (*espace juridique*) of the Contracting States. The FRY [Federal Republic of Yugoslavia] clearly does not fall within this legal space. The Convention was not designed to be applied throughout the world, even in respect of the conduct of Contracting States. Accordingly, the desirability of avoiding a gap or vacuum in human rights protection has so far been relied on by the Court in favour of establishing jurisdiction only when the territory in question was one that, but for the specific circumstances, would normally be covered by the Convention.[78]

Although this reading of the ECHR moves away from extraterritorial application, the '*espace juridique*' concept would reinforce the notion that regional human rights instruments apply throughout the territories of the contracting states. If we take this line of thinking a logical step further, the International Covenant on Civil and Political Rights (ICCPR) and the International Covenant on Economic, Social and Cultural Rights (ICESCR) were designed to apply throughout the world, so it is not a stretch to define '*espace juridique*' to be global.[79]

---

72 Some scholars have pointed to the odd development of jurisprudence in this area as related to Europe's colonial past. Louise Moor and A.W. Brian Simpson, 'Ghosts of Colonialism in the European Convention on Human Rights', *British Yearbook of International Law*, 76 (2005), pp. 121ff.

73 *Cyprus* v *Turkey*, App. No. 25781/94, Eur. Ct. H.R., para. 71 (10 May 2001).

74 *Drozd & Janousek* v *France & Spain*, 240 Eur. Ct. H.R. (ser. A) at 91 (1992); see also *Loizidou* v *Turkey*, 310 Eur. Ct. H.R. (ser. A) at 62 (1995).

75 See *Cyprus* v *Turkey*, note 73 above, at 71; *Loizidou v Turkey*, note 74 above, at 62; *Ocalan v Turkey*, App. No. 46221/99, Eur. Ct. H.R. (2003); Issa v Turkey, App. No. 31821/96, Eur. Ct. H.R. (2004); *Ilascu* v *Moldova & Russia*, App. No. 48787/99, Eur. Ct. H.R (2004).

76 G. Kreijen (ed.), *State, Sovereignty, and International Governance* (Oxford: Oxford University Press, 2002).

77 E.g. A. Ruth and M. Trilsch, 'International Decision: *Bankovic* v *Belgium* (Admissibility)', *American Journal of International Law*, 97 (2003), pp. 168, 172.

78 *Bankovic* v *Belgium*, App. No. 52207/99, 2001-XII Eur. Ct. H.R. 333 para. 80 (12 December 2001).

79 It should be noted that the Human Rights Committee has not been so expansive in its view of extraterritorial application. In its General Comment 31 on Article 2, it stated, 'that a State Party must respect and ensure the rights laid down in the Covenant to anyone within the power or effective control of that

Many scholars have become understandably fixated on the ECHR *Bankovic* case and appear to accept this humanitarianization of human rights law. We create hurdles like 'effective control' and 'military occupation'.[80] Other scholars have managed to show how even in the ECHR framework, the ECtHR could hold multiple state parties responsible for the same act.[81] The court could have looked first at the victims and analysed who had power over them and who could violate their rights.

Other scholars use the text of the ICCPR to argue that its Article 2(1) limits its jurisdiction to its territory.[82] Others argue that '[it] does not imply that the State ... cannot be held accountable for violations of rights under the Covenant which its agents commit upon the territory of another State, whether with the acquiescence of the Government of that State or in opposition to it.'[83] Rising above this debate, the ICESCR speaks of the collective obligation of states parties.

Regarding extraterritorial application of the American Convention on Human Rights (ACHR), the Inter-American Commission for Human Rights has taken a position that is conceptually consistent with the essence of human rights law. It has held that '[g]iven that individual rights inhere simply by virtue of a person's humanity, each American state is obliged to uphold the protected rights of any person subject to its jurisdiction.'[84] This appears to suggest that all OAS members are bound by inter-American human rights law when intervening in Haiti. The Inter-American Commission has also specified the non-nationality basis for conceiving human rights.[85] If human rights law cannot support a distinction between nationals and foreigners domestically, should it be able to do so extraterritorially?

Part of the problem is the continued focus on the duty bearer and not the rights holder. In other areas of law there are some interesting developments regarding the extraterritorial application of law. The dominant approach in Europe has often focused on a territory-based approach, while the approach in the USA uses an interest-based analysis.[86] But in some areas of law, such as antitrust, doctrines such as that of 'effects', carry great weight in both the USA and in Europe.[87] In many ways, the exaggerated notion of sovereignty and state impedes development of the extraterritorial application of human rights law to be coherent with other areas of law related to rights holders. Part of the problem is that some find multi-party extraterritorial jurisdiction for human rights violations

State Party, even if not situated within the territory of the State Party.' U.N. Human Rights Comm., *General Comment No. 31 [80]: The Nature of the General Legal Obligation Imposed on State Parties to the Covenant*, para. 10, UN Doc. CCPR/C/21/Rev.1/Add.13 (26 May 2004).

80 A. Tarik, 'The Long Arm of the European Convention on Human Rights and the Recent Development of *Issa* v *Turkey*', *Human Rights Brief*, 12(2) (2005), pp. 9–11.

81 E. Guild, *Security and European Human Rights: Protecting Individual Rights in Times of Exception and Military Action* (Nijmegen: Wolf Legal Publishers, 2007).

82 M. Milanović, 'From Compromise to Principle: Clarifying the Concept of State Jurisdiction in Human Rights Treaties', *Human Rights Law Review*, 8 (2008), pp. 411ff; Michael J. Dennis, 'Application of Human Rights Treaties Extraterritorially in Times of Armed Conflict and Military Occupation', *American Journal of International Law*, 99 (2005), pp. 119ff.

83 Wilde, note 68 above.

84 *Coard* v *United States*, Case 10.951 Inter-Am. C.H.R., Report No. 109/99 OEA/Ser.L/V/II.106, doc. 3 rev., ¶ 37 (1999).

85 Wilde, note 68 above, p. 791.

86 Karl M. Meessen (ed.), *Extraterritorial Jurisdiction in Theory and Practice* (The Hague: Kluwer Law International, 1996).

87 Vladimir Pavic, *Extraterritoriality in the Matters of Antitrust* (Fucecchio: European Press Academic Publishing, 2001).

difficult to reconcile with 'normal thinking about government'.[88] But this 'normal thinking' dates to a time when government decisions were designed to impact those in its territory. Now, often government and corporate decisions have an impact on individuals and groups that do not share a common political system and have no way other than law to hold those decision-makers responsible for their actions. As some scholars have pointed out, international law is dynamic and adaptable, and will continue to change until it can properly address this type of human rights violation.[89] Indeed, international law has already evolved in such a way that human rights law now trumps sovereignty. Eventually, a concept of sovereignty will develop that allows for trans-border and collective human rights obligations, as is required to make individual rights real.[90]

The 'jurisdiction' limitation that exists in the ECHR, the ICCPR and the ACHR is conspicuously absent in the ICESCR. It should be noted that only Article 14 of the ICESCR specifies that each state party must have a plan for securing free primary education in its territory or under its jurisdiction. Otherwise, the ICESCR requires international cooperation to achieve the progressive realization of ESC rights. The Committee on Economic and Social Rights clarified this point by stating:

> The Committee wishes to emphasize that in accordance with Articles 55 and 56 of the Charter of the United Nations, with well-established principles of international law, and with the provisions of the Covenant itself, international cooperation for development and thus for the realisation of economic, social and cultural rights is an obligation of all States. It is particularly incumbent upon those States which are in a position to assist others in this regard.[91]

This certainly can be read as an attempt to create an obligation to provide foreign assistance, but it also supports the idea that if a state or states choose to intervene in another nation, the intervening states continue to be bound by the ICESCR. It follows therefore that state obligations under the ICESCR are not territorially limited.

4.2 Marginalization of ESC Rights

ESC rights are still marginalized in practice. Many governments and a number of leading NGOs see ESC rights more as the equivalent of letters to Santa Claus than as justiciable rights. A few states, such as the USA, still cling to the outdated notion that human rights are limited to civil and political rights. Those in the advocacy community also are part of the problem,[92] as their focus on civil and political rights has helped to marginalize ESC rights. Importantly, violations of ESC

88 E.g. J.A. Rabkin, *Law Without Nations? Why Constitutional Government Requires Sovereign States* (Princeton, NJ: Princeton University Press, 2005).

89 J. Cerone, 'Holding Military and Paramilitary Forces Accountable', in Julie Mertus, and Jeffrey Helsing, *Human Rights and Conflict: Exploring the Links Between Rights, Law, and Peacebuilding* (Washington, DC: United Nations Institute of Peace, 2006), p. 217.

90 S. Besson, 'Sovereignty in Conflict', in C. Warbrick, and S. Tierney (eds), *Towards an 'International Legal Community'?: The Sovereignty of States and the Sovereignty of International Law* (London: British Institute of International and Comparative Law, 2006).

91 CESCR, *General Comment 3: The Nature of States Parties Obligations (Art. 2, para. 1 of the Covenant)*, UN Doc. (14 December 1990), para. 14.

92 See Kenneth Roth, 'Defending Economic, Social and Cultural Rights: Practical Issues Faced by an International Human Rights Organization', *Human Rights Quarterly*, 26(1) (2004), pp. 63–71; Leonard S. Rubenstein, 'How International Human Rights Organizations Can Advance Economic, Social and Cultural Rights: A Response to Kenneth Roth', *Human Rights Quarterly*, 26(4) (2004), pp. 545–6.

rights affect women disproportionately since women tend to be marginalized in terms of political power.[93] This is especially noteworthy as more conflicts are driven, at least in part, by access to natural resources and the money derived from them. Oddly, this human rights framework for viewing and resolving conflict is stunningly absent. For example, UN Security Council resolutions about the DRC do not use ESC rights language, and even reports of the UN human rights presence in the DRC and Human Rights Watch reports do not use the language.[94] This needs to change.

Currently, most academic and convention-based discussions of the extraterritorial application of human rights law have related to civil and political rights. The marginalization of ESC rights can be seen partly from this fact, especially considering the distinct wording between the ICCPR and ICESCR, which favours the extraterritorial application of ESC rights. Some states, such as Canada and Brazil, have developed very sophisticated ways of measuring positive change in the level of respect for ESC rights.[95] When intervening abroad, these states should bring this experience with them in order to demonstrate whether money being spent is actually improving the human rights situation.[96]

There is a growing understanding of the many ways of conceptualizing and working internationally. However, too often when considering human rights problems, reference is made to only the criminal aspect of the law, and its social justice component is neglected; thereby, there is a failure to include a focus on the obligations to improve the ESC rights in the state where the international entities are intervening. Often, for example, in the field of transitional justice, ESC rights are marginalized.[97] In short, peacekeeping and peace-building efforts are lagging well behind in terms of measuring their impact on ESC rights. Whereas human rights are normally included in the report of the UN Secretary-General to the UN Security Council related to a specific peacekeeping operation, these reports almost always focus on civil and political rights and contain minimal, if any, discussion of ESC rights.

---

93 See J. Oloka-Onyango, 'Reinforcing Marginalized Rights in an Age of Globalization: International Mechanisms, Non-State Actors, and the Struggle for Peoples' Rights in Africa', *American University International Law Review*, 18 (2002–3), pp. 857–84, at pp. 876–9.

94 E.g. MONUC Human Rights Division Report, 6 July 2006 [online]. Available from: http://74.6.146.127/search/cache?ei=UTF-8&p=MONUC+human+rights+report&fr=yfp-t-501&u=www.unhcr.org/refworld/pdfid/46caab060.pdf&w=monuc+human+rights+report+reports&d=XUxZ00xISpdm&icp=1&.intl=us [accessed 31 December 2009]. E.g. Human Rights Watch, *We Will Crush You*, 25 November 2008 [online]. Available from: http://www.hrw.org/en/reports/2008/11/25/we-will-crush-you-0.

95 E.g. T. Landman, 'Measuring Human Rights: Principle, Practice and Policy', *Human Rights Quarterly*, 26 (2004), pp. 906–31; K. Tomasevski, 'Measuring Compliance with Human Rights Obligations', in *Human Rights in Domestic Law and Development Assistance Policies of the Nordic Countries* (Dordrecht: Martinus Nijhoff, 1989), p. 109; R.E. Robertson, 'Measuring State Compliance with the Obligation to Devote the "Maximum Available Resources" to Realizing Economic, Social, and Cultural Rights', *Human Rights Quarterly*, 16 (1994), pp. 693ff.

96 Tools have been created that are useful in determining if a state is taking steps to the maximum of its available resources. E.g. Claudio Schuftan, 'Dignity Counts: A Guide to Using Budget Analysis to Advance Human Rights', *Human Rights Quarterly*, 27 (2005), pp. 134ff.

97 L. Arbour, *Economic and Social Justice for Societies in Transition* (25 October 2006) [online]. Available from: http://www.ictj.org/en/news/features/1025.html.

4.3 Multi-State Responsibility

Roman law offers one of the first examples of how a legal system is renovated under the influence of equitable ideas.[98] It is time for our thinking about multi-state responsibility for violations of ESC rights to be renovated. In general principles of law, for example, we find co-defendants and co-conspirators in criminal law, and joint enterprises and joint enterprise liability in civil law.[99] Many actors (e.g. states, multilateral organizations and NGOs) are part of the joint enterprise of bringing sustainable peace and the respect of the full spectrum of human rights to Haiti and the DRC. There should therefore be shared responsibility and accountability.[100] Not only general principles of law, but also general principles of international law support this position.[101]

The Committee on ESC Rights has already held that if states fail to abide by their obligations in the ICESCR when entering bilateral or multilateral agreements, they may violate their obligations under the covenant.[102] It is a logical step to consider states bound by the covenant in the implementation of these agreements. Certainly, states are individually and collectively bound by human rights law, but the question remains as to how to achieve acceptance of this principle. The Sub-Commission on the Promotion and Protection of Human Rights has noted that in the case of 'decisions … made collectively, one cannot disaggregate such actions and attribute them to individual member States. Member States are then obliged to discharge their obligations undertaken *qua* members pursuant to those collective decisions, and will be held … responsible under international law for the breach thereof.'[103]

In places such as Haiti and the DRC where the governments are not trusted or have a limited capacity to absorb funds from international donors, a different way of looking at human rights obligations needs to be developed. Importantly, in Haiti and the DRC, most money flows from a donor directly to UN missions, NGOs or corporations (implementing projects approved by the donor). However, the governments of Haiti and the DRC are held responsible for improving the human rights situation and are accountable for violations that occur, whether or not these projects actually benefit the people, and regardless of the government's ability to influence their execution. Something is wrong with this position; the UN peacekeeping missions to Haiti and the DRC, the OAS mission, the Inter-American Development Bank, the World Bank, and all the member states' missions and projects to Haiti and the DRC, and NGOs and corporations, as well as rebel groups,

---

98 M.J. Schermaier, 'Bona Fides in Roman Contract Law', in R. Zimmermann and S. Whittaker (eds), *Good Faith in European Contract Law* (Cambridge: Cambridge University Press, 2000), pp. 63–92, at p. 65.

99 E.g. G.C. Keating, 'The Idea of Fairness in the Law of Enterprise Liability', *Michigan Law Review*, 95 (1996–7), pp. 1266–1380.

100 More has been written on the obligations of UN and multilateral entities than on holding multiple states responsible for the same violation; however, more work is needed to flush out how states must abide by their human rights obligations while acting collectively. E.g. Kritsiotis, note 67 above.

101 See Legal Consequences for States of the Continued Presence of South Africa in Namibia (South West Africa) Notwithstanding Security Council Resolution 276 (1970), 1971 I.C.J. 15 (29 January). See also Salomon and Sengupta, note 15 above.

102 CESCR, *General Comment 14: The Right to the Highest Attainable Standard of Health,* UN Doc. E/C.12/2000/4 (2000) para. 50; CESCR, *General Comment 12: Right to Adequate Food*, UN Doc. E/C.12/1999/5 (1999), para. 19.

103 UN Economic and Social Council [ECOSOC], Sub-Commission on the Promotion and Protection of Human Rights, *Progress Report: Globalization and Its Impact on the Full Enjoyment of Human Rights,* UN Doc. E/CN.4/Sub.2/2001/10 (2 August 2001), para. 58 (prepared by J. Oloka-Onyango and Deepika Udagama).

are often better resourced than the governments. Often, their decisions have a more direct impact on the human rights of everyone in Haiti and the DRC than their governments.

Numerous entities have the power to impact on the lives of Haitians and Congolese. In multiple ways, the relative power of each entity should be examined when determining levels of responsibility to respect and promote the human rights of everyone in Haiti and the DRC. Interestingly, all of those entities, except corporations, would accept that one of their missions is to improve the human rights situation in Haiti and the DRC. The problem is that the expectation and measurement of each entity's contribution to improving the human rights situation remains undeveloped. All accountability still flows to the entity considered by many to be corrupt and ineffective – the Haitian and the DRC governments – while other relevant actors, including intervening states and their agents, enjoy the moral high ground and no accountability. As noted above, even 'do-gooders' need to examine carefully to see whether their work is actually producing a human rights benefit, including the human rights components of UN missions.

It is not simply the international interveners' responsibility; obviously the host member state has significant obligations. However, it is time to begin constructing a process to define each intervener's human rights obligations based on how the interventions are structured and how their impact is measured. Rights also *have addressees* who are assigned duties or responsibilities. A person's human rights are not primarily rights against the UN or other international bodies; they primarily impose obligations on the government of the state in which the person resides or is located. International agencies, and the governments of states other than one's own, are secondary or 'back-up' addressees. A growing acceptance of the responsibility to protect highlights the significance of 'back-up' responsibility; the principle makes it an obligation of UN member states to intervene to end massive human rights violations.[104]

Contemporary practice makes it hard to see how states other than the primary state have duties in a Hohfeldian legal sense (to have a real right, one needs a duty bearer), but such practice is out of step with other areas of law that clearly contemplate multiple duty holders. There is nothing in human rights law that prevents us from using a similar analysis. In fact, the call for state cooperation to achieve full respect for human rights seems to highlight the duty. The main hurdle is overcoming the perception that a group of actors do not have an obligation to take action to protect human rights. This is clear in cases of international intervention when a state has not acted on a legal responsibility to protect, but has done so voluntarily. In this case, we can simply borrow from the general principles of law. Just as in the case of the good Samaritan, there may be no duty to intervene, but the act of an intervention, or voluntary operation in another state, creates legal duties to respect human rights law in that intervention.

Once we get over the duty hurdle, it is also not clear what standard should be applied. Until now, states could point to their good intentions as a reason why they should not be held responsible. However, given that *mens rea* or bad intention is only required in some cases of criminal law, other standards need to be looked at, such as recklessness, negligence and strict liability. In many ways, a violation of human rights law is a *malum prohibitum* or a prohibited wrong. When such a wrong happens, the parties involved are liable. This should be the case in human rights law generally. In sum, once a violation of human rights can be established, liability and responsibility should be divided on the basis of relative power and ability to have ended the violation.

---

104 E.g. Mukesh Kapila, United Nations Humanitarian Coordinator in Sudan, 'The Responsibility to Protect: Moving from Words to Action' (25 January 2006) [online]. Available from: http://www.aegistrust.org/index.php ?option=comcontent&task=view&id=318&Itemid=147.

5. Multi-State Responsibility for Exterritorial Violations in the DRC

Mining exploits in the DRC have led directly and indirectly to a drastic fall in the nation's GDP,[105] increased poverty,[106] and grave violence.[107] Traditional theories in tort may help create solutions as the international community seeks to find ways to create human rights accountability. Of particular relevance to the DRC are the good Samaritan principle, multi-state responsibility, and states' contractual duties of care to foreign nations.

5.1 The Good Samaritan Principle

In an international context, the good Samaritan principle would mean that once a state actor intervenes, such an actor can be held to certain legal obligations. In the DRC, this means that intervening state actors, multi-state actors, and NGOs would all be liable on the basis of their initial intervention in the conflict. For example, states such as Belgium and France would and could be held responsible for the corrupt mining practices in the DRC because they noted but failed to stop the actions after becoming involved in the conflicts in the DRC. In response to a *Report on Exploitation of Resources of the DRC*, France's representative, Jean-David Levitte, stated that his 'country had initiated the creation of the UN panel to put an end to illegal exploitation, because such plundering was morally unacceptable and also because the plundering of the Congo had become one of the main engines of the conflict.'[108] Levitte's statement clearly indicates that the French government via its support for the UN Panel had concrete knowledge of mineral exploitation and criminal activity in the DRC. Given that the Panel may not have been created without the French government's support, it can be said that the French state possessed such knowledge (and any accompanying responsibility) as well (for questions, refer to section 3.5). In light of this, if French firms continue to export and trade in natural resources obtained illegally from the DRC, France's previous impunity should end. Even if France had not admitted responsibility, its involvement in the UN Panel and knowledge of the exploitation of resources in the DRC may be enough to hold France liable [in the event of continued criminal exploitation].[109]

A line connecting direct involvement, relative resources and power must be drawn for the use of the good Samaritan principle. If taken too far, the good Samaritan argument might even dissuade NGOs and multi-state intervention forces from attempting to stop a conflict or problem in the first place, for fear of being punished for unexpected consequences later. However, if carefully and narrowly applied, the good Samaritan principle could be used to punish actors who had become involved in a conflict with knowledge of the human rights violations, and who did nothing (or did too little) to stop the violations. Using the principle to expand liability in this way would mean that member states and multi-state forces could no longer hide behind vague mandates, and will have to measurably improve the situation they stated as their objective.

105 *Ibid.*

106 *Ibid.*

107 *Ibid.*

108 'Report on the Exploitation of Resources of Democratic Republic of Congo Is Challenged in Security Council, Neighbouring Countries, Denying Allegations by Expert Panel, Call for More Evidence; Others Stress Serious Effects on Peace Process', Press Release SC/7561, 5 November 2002 [online]. Available from: http://www.un.org/News/Press/docs/ 2002/SC7561.doc.htm.

109 D. Johnson and C. Kayser, 'Democratic Republic of Congo: Shadow Economies in the "Heart of Darkness"', in M. Basedau and A. Mehler (eds), *Resource Politics in Sub-Saharan Africa* (Hamburg: Institute of African Affairs, 2005), p. 52.

5.2 Multi-State Responsibility

Multi-state responsibility is another form of liability that might prove useful in evaluating the exploitation of natural resources in the DRC. Multi-state responsibility argues for shared accountability, regardless of actors' agreements with one another. Just as in criminal law, where joint criminal enterprise and co-conspirators work to hold multiple actors liable for a single act, so, too, should human rights law. The government of the DRC should not solely be responsible for the exploitation of resources within its borders, but the multiple states and actors involved should also be held responsible. For example, neighbouring states such as Rwanda, Uganda, and Zimbabwe could be held liable for their part in the exploitation. Reports from the UN Panel of Experts revealed that officials from each of these states were benefiting from deals related to DRC mineral exploitation.[110] Further confidential reports from the panel revealed that Rwanda 'continued to help Lubanga's UPC [a force largely in control of DRC gold mines] in Ituri with advice, military training and the delivery of ammunition'.[111] Similar claims have also been made against Uganda and Zimbabwe.[112]

A multi-state responsibility approach could also hold international financial institutions (IFIs) accountable for the consequences of the support they provide. On the issue of resource exploitation in the DRC, the International Monetary Fund (IMF) and the World Bank have both remained, perhaps strategically, silent. Even though both encourage transparency and government accountability globally, both have seemed to evade the regional trade of illicit materials from the DRC, perhaps because this would implicate these institutions' success story of economic development in Uganda.[113] The World Bank itself concluded that it should consistently 'requir[e] audits and accurate public disclosure of revenues and expenditures' in extractive industries around the world.[114] The role of the IFIs could also be scrutinized by the approach put forward in this chapter.

Multi-state responsibility argues that to efficiently address the rights violations stemming from the exploitation of resources in the DRC, all actors involved must be held accountable. While this may mean some actors will be punished more than others for deeper, more direct, or more consistent involvement, all should nevertheless be exposed and held liable for their involvement.

5.3 Contract Theory

States can also be held liable to ESC violations by virtue of contractual obligations arising from their participation in treaties or other agreements, such as international contracts mandating a duty of care. care, that party can be held liable in tort for the violation of that duty.

---

110 *Ibid.*, p. 118.

111 *Ibid.*, p. 124. See also P. Schwab, *Africa: A Continent Self-Destructs* (New York: Palgrave, 2001), p. 57.

112 Johnson and Kayser, note 109 above, pp. 122–3. See also S. Rich Dorman, 'Studying Democratization in Africa: A Case Study of Human Rights NGOs in Zimbabwe', in J. Igoe and T. Kelsall (eds), *Between a Rock and a Hard Place: African NGOs, Donors and the State* (Durham, NC: Carolina Academic Press, 2005), p. 52; Schwab, note 111 above, p. 57.

113 Johnson and Kayser, note 109 above, pp. 126–7.

114 *Ibid.*, p. 127. In addition to the financial institutions ignoring the panel's recommendations, other multi-state organizations followed suit. No UN Security Council action followed the panel's last report, a Belgian Senate Committee cleared all Belgian companies involved, and no sanctions recommended in the panel's last report were ever enacted. See Johnson and Kayser, note 109 above, p. 150.

Within the context of mining in the DRC, parties that can be held liable for violations of a contractual duty of care are state parties to international treaties or agreements, private actors who are members of contracting states, and private actors who are engaged in private contracts within the DRC. Currently, the two most prominent international human rights treaties creating a possible duty of care for state parties are the ICCPR and the ICESCR. According to the preamble of the ICCPR, human rights are rights that derive from the inherent dignity of every human being and the equal and inalienable rights of all members of the human family, as well as the foundation of freedom, justice, and peace for the world.[115] Furthermore, parties to the ICESCR can be said to have a contractual duty of care to respect ESC rights created by Articles 3 and 28. According to Article 3, 'The States Parties to the present Covenant undertake to ensure the equal right of men and women to the enjoyment of all economic, social and cultural rights set forth in the present Covenant.'[116] Article 28 offers an extensive jurisdiction for the treaty stating, 'The provisions of the present Covenant shall extend to all parts of federal States without any limitations or exceptions.'[117]

A more direct and stronger contractual duty to respect ESC rights in the context of mining in the DRC is found in the Organization for Economic Co-Operation and Development (OECD). According to the UN Security Council Report, member states are responsible for citizens' extraterritorial violations of the OECD Guidelines for Multinational Enterprises.[118] Therefore, states are held accountable for monitoring the actions of the extraterritorial business endeavours of their citizens.[119] Also, the UN Security Council Report indicates that when states do not hold private actors liable for violations of OECD guidelines, they, too, are complicit in the violations of ESC rights.[120] According to the final report of the Panel of Experts on the Illegal Exploitation of Natural Resources and Other Forms of Wealth of the Democratic Republic of the Congo, 'The Governments of the countries where the individuals, companies and financial institutions that are systematically and actively involved in these activities are based should assume their share of the responsibility.' The report claims that 'governments have the power to regulate and sanction those individuals and entities' and that 'the OECD Guidelines offer a mechanism for bringing violations of them by business enterprises to the attention of home Governments, that is, Governments of the countries where the enterprises are registered.'[121] The report concludes, 'Governments with jurisdiction over these enterprises are complicit themselves when they do not take remedial measures.'[122]

Applying the contract theory of tort liability to the instance of mining in the DRC shows how duties are placed on both state and non-state (private) actors in international agreements and organizations, to respect extraterritorial human rights. In the instance of the DRC, liability for the violation of ESC rights can be extended to both states parties to the ICCPR, the ICESCR, and OECD and to private, individual actors. The concept of contractual duties can be imputed to the

115 International Covenant on Civil and Political Rights, Preamble.

116 International Covenant on Economic Social and Cultural Rights, Art. 3.

117 *Ibid.*, Art. 28.

118 UN Security Council, Final Report of the Panel of Experts on the Illegal Exploitation of Natural Resources and Other Forms of Wealth of the Democratic Republic of the Congo, dated 15 October 2002, para. 170.

119 Some member states, such as Canada and Australia, have attempted to enact domestic laws on this subject. E.g. Sara L. Seck, 'Home State Responsibility and Local Communities: The Case of Global Mining', *Yale Human Rights and Development Law Journal*, 11 (2008), pp. 177ff.

120 See note 118 above, p. 32.

121 *Ibid.*

122 *Ibid.*

area of international human rights law by holding state and non-state actors accountable for their extraterritorial failures to respect human rights. The good Samaritan principle, liability of multi-state actors, and contractual duties of care offer different ways to view human rights violations in the DRC as it relates to the illegal exploitation of natural resources.

6. Conclusion

Recently, member states of the UN, including most notably the USA, have been preoccupied with the concept of the UN's accountability. But the system needs to begin enforcing accountability to the UN's guiding principles rather than accountability to the agenda of particular member states. Defining the extent of states' human rights obligations when intervening in other states will help to improve transparency, accountability and effectiveness in the international protection of human rights. This chapter has only begun to explore this process. Once there is a growing understanding of this responsibility, the result will be the realization of this obligation whenever states and their agents (such as the UN and the World Bank) operate in another state.

PART IV
Responsibilities and Remedies

Chapter 21

State Responsibility for Human Rights

Danwood Mzikenge Chirwa

1. Introduction

The adoption of the UDHR[1] in 1948 was a watershed in the development of international human rights law principally because it provided the moral axis on which international law and international relations would from henceforth revolve. A plethora of international and regional treaties have since been adopted. They form a phalanx of safeguards against intrusion into individual freedoms or group identity and autonomy, and provide a launch pad for claiming certain goods and services from the state or for participating in the polity. One of the key principles of international law which have been affected radically by international human rights law is the long-standing doctrine of state responsibility. This doctrine assigns liability to a state that breaches its international obligations. In its traditional sense, it provided remedies to a state for internationally wrongful acts committed by another state. This chapter seeks to explore the ways in which international human rights law, spearheaded by the UDHR, has fundamentally altered the doctrine of state responsibility in international law. The discussion will dwell on the following questions. Who can invoke the doctrine? Whose rights give rise to state responsibility? Can non-state action give rise to state responsibility? The last question will lead to a discussion of the implications of the doctrine of state responsibility for the position of non-state actors in relation to human rights.

2. State Responsibility

2.1 Meaning and Basis

State responsibility is a general principle of international law that is as old as international law itself. One of its early progenitors is the concept of just war and reprisals developed in the fourteenth and fifteen centuries, which posited that a state was entitled to wage war, as a matter of last resort, to enforce its rights against another state and, conversely, that a state which waged an unjust war had the obligation to pay damages to the injured state.[2] Hence, state responsibility has long encapsulated the simple but vital principle that to every legal wrong must attach legal responsibility. Judge Huber in the *Spanish Zone of Morocco Claims (Spain* v *United Kingdom)* stated: 'Responsibility is the necessary corollary of a right. All rights of an international character involve international responsibility. If the obligation in question is not met, responsibility entails the duty to make reparation.'[3] In *Chorzów Factory (Indemnity)*, the Permanent Court of International Justice (PCIJ)

---

1 GA Res. 217A (III), UN Doc. A/810 at 71 (1948).

2 I. Brownlie, *System of the Law of Nations: State Responsibility*, Part I (Oxford: Clarendon Press, 1983), p. 3.

3 (1923) 2 RIAA 615, 641.

observed that 'any breach of an engagement involves an obligation to make reparation ... reparation is the indispensable complement of a failure to apply a convention, and there is no necessity for this to be stated in the convention itself.'[4]

State responsibility is therefore essential to the authority and effectiveness of international law. Without any form of legal responsibility, the obligations created by international law would not command respect from states. Furthermore, state responsibility emanates from the nature of the international legal system, which relies on states as a means of formulating and implementing its rules, and arises out of the twin principles of state sovereignty and equality of states.[5] Consequently, to establish state responsibility, one must demonstrate that one state owes another an international obligation, that the duty-bound state has breached the obligation, and that the breach has caused damage to the state to which the duty was owed.

The rules on state responsibility are embodied in customary international law. However, the International Law Commission (ILC) adopted the Draft Articles on the Responsibility of States for Internationally Wrongful Acts (Draft Articles) on 9 August 2001, which seek to codify these rules. The ILC referred them to the United Nations (UN) General Assembly (GA) for the latter to take note of them and at a later stage decide whether they should be adopted in the form of a convention or declaration.[6] The GA has not yet taken a decision on the manner in which the Draft Articles should be adopted. Consequently, the Draft Articles have no legal authority, save to the extent to which they simply restate the existing rules of customary international law.

2.2 Traditional Parameters

Before the UDHR was adopted, the doctrine of state sovereignty served as a shield to protect states from international scrutiny in matters concerning the domestic protection of human rights. Issues of human rights within the domestic sphere fell within the boundaries of state sovereignty, and, by operation of its sister doctrine of the equality of all states, no state had a right to question the status of human rights in another state.[7] The incursion by one state into the sovereignty of another state was permissible only where that state sought to protect the rights of its nationals threatened or violated in that other state. The doctrine of state responsibility was thus developed as a device aimed principally at protecting the rights of aliens in a foreign state.[8] Although there was no common international standard for the treatment of citizens, its basic premise was that foreign nationals were entitled to be treated equally with nationals or at least in accordance with minimum international standards of justice.[9] The doctrine was enforced by states through diplomatic means and at times through international arbitration/adjudication or force.[10]

---

4 *Chorzów Factory (Germany* v *Poland) (Claim for Indemnity)* (1928) PCIJ (Ser. A) No. 9, 21.

5 M.N. Shaw, *International Law*, 5th edn (Cambridge: Cambridge University Press, 2003), p. 694.

6 J. Crawford, *The International Law Commission's Articles on State Responsibility: Introduction, Text and Commentaries* (Cambridge: Cambridge University Press, 2002), p. 60.

7 However, international law recognized some exceptions to this general rule. One of them was the doctrine of humanitarian intervention developed in the seventeenth century, which allowed the use of force by a state or a group of them to protect another state from abusing its own nationals. It is a doctrine that still exists, but controversy still abounds the doctrine, especially with regard to the question of the circumstances in which it can be properly and legitimately invoked.

8 F.V. Garcia Amador, 'State Responsibility: International Responsibility', *Yearbook of the International Law Commission*, 2 (1956), pp. 173–231, at pp. 199–200, UN Doc. A/CN.4/SER.A/1956/Add.1.

9 *Ibid.*, p. 201.

10 Brownlie, note 2 above, p. 3.

The adoption of the UN Charter[11] was a milestone in that it placed human rights, which were later set out *ad seriatim* in the UDHR, the International Covenant on Civil and Political Rights (ICCPR)[12] and its Protocols, and the International Covenant on Economic, Social and Cultural Rights (ICESCR)[13] – the so-called International Bill of Rights – at the centre of international relations in the new world order.[14] Since then, human rights have evolved into something of vital international concern. They are no longer constrained by the notion of state sovereignty, as states cannot rely on this doctrine to fend off international opprobrium in the face of serious violations of human rights occurring within their jurisdictions. By accepting that all human beings have human rights irrespective of the state they are in, the basis for the international protection of human rights ceased to rest on the nationality of the individual. Human rights are now understood to inhere in individuals independently of their nation state, binding the latter as well as other states. Inversely, states now incur international responsibility for the rights of non-nationals as well as for those of their own citizens. We explore in detail the implications of these changes below.

3. To Whom Is Responsibility Owed?

3.1 The Dwindling Importance of Nationality

Under the traditional conception of state responsibility, the duty to afford minimum protection to the rights of non-nationals was owed by the host state of the non-nationals to the state to which the latter owed their nationality. The non-nationals themselves did not have any recourse or rights of their own against the foreign state. As Anzilotti argued, when a state violated the rights of non-nationals, it was not the right of the individual which was violated, 'but rather the right of the State to see that the individual be treated in accordance with international law'.[15] The Permanent Court of International Justice (PCIJ), in the *Mavrommatis Palestine Concessions* case, echoed this view:

> It is an elementary principle of international law that a State is entitled to protect its subjects, when injured by acts contrary to international law committed by another State, from whom they have been unable to obtain satisfaction through the ordinary channels. By taking up the case of one of its subjects and by resorting to diplomatic action or international judicial proceedings on his behalf, a State is in reality asserting its own rights – its right to ensure, in the person of its subjects, respect for the rules of international law.[16]

This viewpoint flows from the conventional understanding of subjects of international law as limited to states. None other than states can claim rights or be burdened by obligations in international law, if only because international law is based on the consent of states and develops from state conduct and relations. Individuals, according to this line of thinking, can only be indirect beneficiaries of international rights.

---

11 Adopted 26 June 1945, entered into force 24 October 1945, 59 Stat 1031, TS 993, 3 Bevans 1153.

12 Adopted 16 December 1966, entered into force 23 March 1976, 999 UNTS 171.

13 Adopted 16 December 1966, entered into force 3 January 1976, 993 UNTS 3.

14 See Articles 1(3) and 55.

15 Quoted in Amador, note 8 above, p. 181.

16 (1924) PCIJ, Series B, No. 3. Confirmed in *Case Concerning Payment of Various Serbian Loans Issues in France*, Series A, Nos 20/21, 29) PCIJ, Series A No. 21, 17; the *Panevezys-Saldutiskis Railway* case, Judgement, Orders and Advisory Opinions (1939) PCIJ, Series A/B No. 76.

The consequence of the doctrine of state responsibility for injury to aliens was also to deny any other state than the *national state* of the alien a right to act for the rights of that alien. In the *Panevezys-Saldutiskis Railway* case, the PCIJ stated:

> In the opinion of the Court, the rule of international law on which the first Lithuanian objection is based is that in taking up the case of one of its nationals, by resorting to diplomatic action or international judicial proceedings on his behalf, a State is in reality asserting its own right, the right to ensure in the person of its nationals respect for the rules of international law. This right is necessarily limited to intervention on behalf of its own nationals because, in the absence of a special agreement, it is the bond of nationality between the State and the individual which alone confers upon the State the right of diplomatic protection, and it is as a part of the function of diplomatic protection that the right to take up a claim and to ensure respect for the rules of international law must be envisaged. Where the injury was done to the national of some other State, no claim to which such injury may give rise falls within the scope of the diplomatic protection which a State is entitled to afford nor can it give rise to a claim which that State is entitled to espouse.[17]

International human rights law has altered these traditional conceptions of state responsibility in two fundamental ways. The first concerns the status of the individual in international law and the second relates to the range of states which can enforce rights in international law.

3.2 Individuals

The formulation of human rights in the UDHR leaves no scope for doubt that individuals are direct beneficiaries of human rights in international law. For example, it guarantees every human being the inherent right to life, liberty and security of person or the right of all persons to equality before the courts.[18] The same guarantees are explicit in the ICCPR. Other treaties reveal a rather abstruse way of protecting international human rights whereby states are obligated to recognize certain prescribed rights.[19] Nevertheless, these treaties not only establish reciprocal rights for contracting states but also obligate all states to respect and protect the rights of individuals within their jurisdictions. The Inter-American Court of Human Rights (IACtHR) fittingly stated:

> The Court must emphasize, however, that modern human rights treaties in general, and the American Convention in particular, are not multilateral treaties of the traditional type concluded to accomplish the reciprocal exchange of rights for the mutual benefit of the contracting States. Their object and purpose is the protection of the basic rights of individual human beings irrespective

17 *Ibid.*, *Panevezys-Saldutiskis Railway* case, p. 16.

18 See Articles 3 and 7, UDHR.

19 E.g. Article 6(1) of the ICESCR provides: 'The States Parties to the present Covenant recognise the right to work', while Article 8 of the same Covenant provides that 'States Parties to the Present Covenant undertake to ensure' the right of everyone to form trade unions and to join trade unions. The provisions of the following treaties are defined in a similar manner: Convention on the Rights of the Child (CRC) [(adopted 20 November 1989, entered into force 2 September 1990) GA Res. 44/25, annex, 44 UN GAOR Supp. (No. 49) at 167, UN Doc. A/44/49 (1989)]; Convention on the Elimination of All Forms of Discrimination Against Women (CEDAW) [(adopted 18 December 1979, entered into force 3 September 1981) GA Res. 34/180, 34 UN GAOR Supp. (No. 46) at 193, UN Doc. A/34/46]; and Convention on the Elimination of All Forms of Racial Discrimination (CERD) [(adopted 21 December 1965, entered into force 4 January 1969) GA Res. 2106 (XX), Annex, 20 UN GAOR Supp. (No. 14) at 47, UN Doc. A/6014 (1966), 660 UNTS 195].

> of their nationality, both against the State of their nationality and all other contracting States. In concluding these human rights treaties, the States can be deemed to submit themselves to a legal order within which they, for the common good, assume various obligations, not in relation to other States, but towards all individuals within their jurisdiction.[20]

Moreover, the prominence, which has been given to individual petitions, communications or complaints procedures since the UDHR was adopted, has underscored the status of the individual as a direct beneficiary, claimant and enforcer of rights in international law.[21]

3.3 Other States

As noted above, the second impact of human rights jurisprudence which has evolved since the UDHR was adopted relates to the relaxation of the rule that only the state which is the nationality of the injured person has the right to enforce that person's rights. All states irrespective of nationality can enforce international human rights. The International Court of Justice (ICJ) in the *Barcelona Traction* case explained this principle thus:

> an essential distinction should be drawn between obligations of a State towards the international community as a whole, and those arising vis-à-vis another State in the field of diplomatic protection.

---

20 *The Effect of Reservations on the Entry into Force of the American Convention on Human Rights* (Articles 74 and 75), Advisory Opinion OC-2/82, 24 September 1982, Inter-Am Ct HR (Series A) No. 2 (1982), para. 29, endorsing the views of the European Commission on Human Rights in *Austria* v *Italy*, Application No. 788/60, *European Yearbook of Human Rights*, 4 (1961), p. 140.

21 Examples of treaties which provide for individual complaints include the ICCPR [through the Optional Protocol to the International Covenant on Civil and Political Rights (adopted 16 December 1966, entered into force 23 March 1976) GA Res. 2200A (XXI), 21 UN GAOR Supp. (No. 16) at 59, UN Doc. A/6316 (1966), 999 UNTS 302]; CEDAW [through the Optional Protocol to the Convention on the Elimination of Discrimination Against Women (adopted 6 October 1999, entered into force 22 December 2000) GA Res. 54/4, annex, 54 UN GAOR Supp. (No. 49) at 5, UN Doc. A/54/49 (Vol. I) (2000)]; the Convention Against Torture and Other Cruel, Inhuman or Degrading Treatment or Punishment [(adopted 10 December 1984, entered into force 26 June 1987) GA Res. 39/46, annex, 39 UN GAOR Supp. (No. 51) at 197, UN Doc. A/39/51 (1984) (Article 22)]; the Convention on the Protection and Promotion of the Rights and Dignity of Persons with Disabilities [(adopted 13 December 2006, entered into force 3 May 2008) GA Res. 61/106, Annex I, UN GAOR, 61st Session, Supp. No. 49 at 65, UN Doc. A/61/49 (2006) (through the First Optional Protocol to the International Convention on the Protection and Promotion of the Rights and Dignity of Persons with Disabilities (adopted 12 December 2006, entered into force 3 May 2008) GA Res. 61/106, Annex II, UN GAOR, 61st Session, Supp. No. 49, at 80, UN Doc. A/61/49 (2006)]; the CERD (Article 14); the Convention on the Protection of the Rights of All Migrant Workers and Members of Their Families [(adopted 18 December 1990, entered into force 1 July 2003) GA Res. 45/158, annex, 45 UN GAOR Supp. (No. 49A) at 262, UN Do. A/45/49 (1990) (Article 77)]. All the three regional systems of human rights now have human rights courts with powers to consider individual complaints or petitions. See Protocol to the African Charter on Human and Peoples' Rights on the Establishment of an African Court on Human and Peoples' Rights [adopted 9 June 1998, entered into force 25 January 2004) OAU Doc. OAU/LEG/EXP/AFCHPR/PROT (III)]; Statute of the Inter-American Court on Human Rights [(adopted 1 October 1979, entered into force 1 January 1980) OAS Res. 448 (IX-0/79), OAS Off Rec OEA/Ser.P/IX.0.2/80, vol. 1 at 98, Annual Report of the Inter-American Court on Human Rights, OEA/Ser.L/V.III.3 Doc. 13 corr. 1 at 16 (1980)]; and Protocol No. 11 to the Convention for the Protection of Human Rights and Fundamental Freedoms, restructuring the control machinery established thereby [(adopted 11 May 1994, entered into force 1 November 1998) (ETS No. 155), Strasbourg, 11.V.1994].

> By their very nature the former are the concern of all States. In view of the importance of the rights involved, all States can be held to have a legal interest in their protection; they are obligations erga omnes. Such obligations derive, for example, in contemporary international law, from the outlawing of acts of aggression, and of genocide, and also from the principles and rules concerning the basic rights of the human person, including protection from slavery and racial discrimination. Some of the corresponding rights of protection have entered into the body of general international law; others are conferred by international instruments of universal or quasi-universal character.[22]

It is clear therefore that under international human rights law state responsibility can be claimed by any state within the community of nations as opposed to the nation state of the injured person.[23] This right is implicit in the notion of inter-state complaints. It is also embodied in the charter-based mechanisms for the protection of human rights, which tend to enforce rights in a disinterested manner guided only by common interests of the international community.[24]

The Draft Rules on State Responsibility postulate a broader concept of an 'injured state' for purposes of invoking the responsibility of a state. It defines an injured state as one which has suffered a breach of a duty owed to it individually or as part of a group of states or the international community as a whole.[25] To this extent, these rules are abreast of the developments of international law as regards the widening of the standing to enforce international human rights. However, they completely ignore the idea of state responsibility to individuals as direct beneficiaries and claimants of rights, thereby ignoring the practice and jurisprudence in international human rights law over the past six decades establishing that individuals can and have been enforcing their international human rights through international fora and mechanisms.

4. Whose Acts Give Rise to State Responsibility?

The rules of state responsibility are anchored within the state action paradigm.[26] The Draft Articles codify this tradition by insisting that only acts of the state can give rise to state responsibility. In terms of these articles, state responsibility is incurred when two elements are proved: first, there must be conduct consisting of an act or omission that is attributable to the state under international law; second, the conduct must constitute a breach of an international obligation of the state.[27]

---

22 *Case concerning the Barcelona Traction Light and Power Company Ltd (Second Phase, Belgium* v *Spain)* (1970), ICJ Reports 32.

23 See also T. van Boven, 'Study Concerning the Right to Restitution, Compensation and Rehabilitation for Victims of Gross Violations of Human Rights and Fundamental Freedoms', Final Report Submitted by Mr Theo van Boven, Special Rapporteur, E/CN.4/Sub.2/1993/8, 2 July 1993.

24 For example, the 1235 procedure empowers the Commission on Human Rights (now the Human Rights Council) to examine information relevant to gross violations of human rights and fundamental freedoms, make a thorough study of situations which reveal a consistent pattern of violations of human rights, and report with recommendations thereon. The confidential 1503 procedure allowed the commission to consider communications revealing a consistent pattern of gross violations of human rights and fundamental freedoms. These are examples of collective procedures by the international community for enforcing international human rights.

25 See Article 42.

26 See, generally, Brownlie, note 2 above.

27 Article 2 of the Draft Articles. See also *Phosphates in Morocco (Italy* v *France)* (Preliminary Objections) [1938] PCIJ (Ser. A/B), No. 74, 28; *United States Diplomatic and Consular Staff in Tehran*

The rules of attribution fall into two broad categories. The first encompasses the rules relating to the conduct of acts or omissions of the state itself, its officials, its organs, or the organs of another state placed at its disposal.[28] In respect of these, the state may still be responsible even when the conduct of an organ of state, or of a person or entity empowered to exercise elements of governmental authority, is in excess of authority.[29]

The second category deals with state responsibility in respect of the acts of non-state actors. Such acts may qualify as acts of state in certain defined circumstances.[30] Firstly, Article 5 of the Draft Articles stipulates that the conduct of a person or entity that is not an organ of the state 'empowered by the law of that State to exercise elements of the governmental authority' can give rise to state responsibility provided that the person was acting in that capacity in the particular instance in issue. This rule encompasses a wide range of bodies which are not state organs, but are empowered by state law to exercise elements of governmental authority, such as public corporations, quasi-public entities, and private companies.[31]

Secondly, in terms of Article 8 of the Draft Articles, the conduct of a person or group of persons acting on the instructions of, or under the direction or control of, a state can be attributed to the state in question. Where conduct is authorized by the state, liability is incurred regardless of whether the person to whom authorization is given is a private individual.[32] It also does not matter whether the conduct involves public functions or governmental activity.[33] What is required is proof of state authorization.

Thirdly, Article 9 of the Draft Articles provides that the conduct of private persons or groups exercising elements of governmental authority 'in the absence or default of the official authorities and in circumstances such as to call for the exercise of those elements of authority' can be attributed to the state. To rely on this rule, the conduct must relate to the exercise of public functions or governmental authority, there must be absence or default of official authorities, and the circumstances must have justified the exercise of those powers.

Fourthly, Article 10(1) of the Draft Articles provides that '[t]he conduct of an insurrectional movement which becomes the new government of a State shall be considered an act of that State under international law.' Similarly, '[t]he conduct of a movement, insurrectional or other, which succeeds in establishing a new State in part of the territory of a pre-existing State or in a territory under its administration' amounts to an act of the new state.[34] These provisions clearly envisage state responsibility for acts or omissions of non-state actors such that where rebellion succeeds, all wrongful acts or omissions committed by it or its members are attributed to the new state. However, where the insurrection or rebellion is not successful, the state will not be responsible for violations of international law by the members of the insurrection. In such an instance, the state is only liable if it is guilty of a lack of good faith or negligence in suppressing the insurrection.[35]

Lastly, under Article 11 of the Draft Articles, a state may be responsible for conduct which is otherwise not attributable to it where the state acknowledged such conduct or adopted it as its

---

(United States of America v *Iran)* (judgement) [1980] ICJ Rep. 3, 30 (*Diplomatic and Consular Staff* case); *Dickson Car Wheel Company (USA)* v *United Mexican States* (1931) 4 RIAA 669, 678.

28 See Articles 4 and 6 of the Draft Articles.

29 Article 6 of the Draft Articles.

30 See Brownlie, note 2 above, pp. 159–66.

31 Crawford, note 6 above, p. 100.

32 *Ibid.*, p. 110.

33 *Ibid.*

34 Article 10(2) of the Draft Articles.

35 *GL Solis (USA)* v *United Mexican States* (1928), 4 RIAA 358, 361.

own. Thus, where a state acknowledges or adopts the conduct of non-state actors, the state will be responsible.[36]

In short, the general rules of state responsibility in international law remain wedded to the state-centric conception of state responsibility in that state responsibility is based on the notion of state action. State responsibility is incurred for acts of non-state actors only where a sufficient nexus is established between the state and the acts of the non-state actor such that the conduct of the latter is deemed to be that of the former.

5. Due Diligence, Positive Obligations and Non-State Actors

5.1 Positive Obligations of States

Insofar as the rules of state responsibility are steeped in the state action paradigm, they mirror the traditional view of international law as the law regulating state relations and conduct. Because only states owe obligations in international law, no other actor can violate those obligations; only state conduct can give rise to responsibility in international law.

The rules of attribution discussed above correspond to the state action doctrine in the constitutional law of the USA, which posits that constitutional rights can be infringed only through state action and not private action. In *Virginia* v *Rives*, the US Supreme Court stated that 'the provisions of the Fourteenth Amendment of the Constitution … all have reference to State action exclusively, and not to any action of private individuals.'[37] Likewise, it was stated in the *Civil Rights Cases* that 'it is state action of a particular character that is prohibited. Individual invasion of individual rights is not the subject matter of the Amendment.'[38] The rules that govern the attribution of conduct to the state under US constitutional law are strikingly similar to those under state responsibility in international law.[39]

However, the state action doctrine is framed within a school of thought that regards the obligations of states in relation to human rights as limited to the negative injunction. The state has no positive obligations in relation to constitutional rights.[40] By contrast, international human rights law has developed to impose positive obligations on states in relation to human rights. The UDHR cleared the path for the development of such duties by proclaiming that the UDHR was 'a common standard of achievement for all peoples and all nations', and obligating every individual and every organ of society 'to promote respect for these rights and freedoms and by progressive measures, national and international, to secure their universal and effective recognition and observance'.[41] In concretizing this obligation, Article 2 of the ICCPR enjoins states parties 'to respect and to

36 See *Diplomatic and Consular Staff* case, note 27 above.

37 100 US 313, 318 (1879).

38 109 US 3, 11 (1883).

39 Discussed in D.M. Chirwa, 'The Horizontal Application of Constitutional Rights in a Comparative Perspective', *Law, Democracy and Development*, 10(2) (2006), pp. 21–48, at pp. 22–6; H. Strickland, 'The State Action Doctrine and the Rehnquist Court', *Hastings Constitutional Law Quarterly*, 18 (1981), pp. 587, 645.

40 According to Strickland, note 39 above, p. 608, 'The state generally has no constitutional obligation to intervene in private disputes either to protect individuals from harm inflicted by other private entities or to force the wrongful private entities to compensate the victims of their wrong doing. See also *DeShaney* v *Winnebago County Department of Social Services*, 489 US 189 (1989).

41 See opening para., Preamble, UDHR.

ensure to all individuals within its territory and subject to its jurisdiction the rights recognized in the Covenant'. The duty to 'ensure' suggests that states have the obligation to take positive steps to guarantee the enjoyment of human rights. Similar provisions can be found in regional instruments.[42]

However, the precise nature of these positive obligations took time to take shape. Henry Shue was probably the first scholar to argue that every basic right entails three duties: 'to avoid depriving', 'to protect from deprivation', and 'to aid the deprived'.[43] This classification of duties was adopted and refined by Asbjørn Eide in 1987, who termed these duties, the duty 'to respect', 'to protect' and 'to fulfil' respectively.[44] International and regional human rights monitoring bodies and domestic constitutions have popularized Eide's typology.[45] Of particular relevance to the current discussion is the duty to protect, to which we now turn.

5.2 The Duty to Protect

The provisions of Article 2 of the ICCPR cited above suggest that this duty has two limbs. The first is the duty to take preventive measures against occurrences of violations of human rights by private actors. The second is the duty to take remedial measures once the violations have occurred.[46] The Committee on Economic, Social and Cultural Rights (CESCR), which monitors the implementation of the ICESCR, has stated that the ICESCR imposes an obligation on states parties to prevent violations of these rights by non-state actors.[47]

A further obligation implicit in the duty to protect is the obligation to control and regulate private actors. The Human Rights Committee (HRC), which monitors the implementation of the ICCPR, has stated, for example, that states have the duty to provide a legislative framework prohibiting acts constituting arbitrary and unlawful interference with privacy, family, home or correspondence by natural and legal persons.[48] The CESCR has also stated that states have the duty to 'ensure that

42 E.g. Article 1(1) of the European Convention for the Protection of Human Rights and Fundamental Freedoms [adopted 4 November 1960, entered into force 3 September 1953, ETS No. 5, 213 UNTS 222]; Article 1(1) of the American Convention on Human Rights [adopted 29 April 1982, entered into force 18 July 1978, OAS Treaty Series No. 36, 1144 UNTS 123]; and, in relation to the African Charter on Human and Peoples' Rights [adopted 27 June 1981, entered into force 21 October 1986, OAU Doc. CAB/LEG/67/3 Rev 5, 21 ILM 58 (1982)], *Commission Nationale des Droits de l'Homme et des Libertés* v *Chad*, Communication No. 74/92 (1995) (2000) AHRLR 66 (ACHPR 1995).

43 H. Shue, *Subsistence, Affluence, and US Foreign Policy* (Princeton, NJ: Princeton University Press, 1980), p. 52.

44 See A. Eide 'Final Report on the Right to Adequate Food as a Human Right', UN Doc. E/CN.4/Sub.2/1987/23; A. Eide, 'Economic, Social and Cultural Rights as Legal Rights', in A. Eide *et al.* (eds), *Economic, Social, Cultural Rights: A Textbook* (Dordrecht: Martinus Nijhoff, 1995), pp. 21, 35–40.

45 E.g. *Social and Economic Rights Action Centre and the Centre for Economic and Social Rights* v *Nigeria*, Communication No. 155/96 (2001) AHRLR 60 (ACHPR 2001) (*SERAC* case); CESCR, General Comment No. 13: The Right to Education (Article 13 of the Covenant, 3 December 1999, E/C.12/1999/10, para. 46; CESCR, General Comment No. 14: The Right to the Highest Attainable Standard of Health (Article 12 of the Covenant), 11 August 2000, E/C.12/2000/4, para. 33; and Section 7 of the South African Constitution, which provides that the state 'must respect, protect, promote and fulfil the rights in the Bill of Rights'.

46 See especially Articles 2(2) and (2(3), ICCPR.

47 CESCR, General Comment No. 15: The Right to Water (Articles 11 and 12 of the Covenant), 20 January 2003, E/C.12/2002/11, para. 24.

48 E.g. HRC, CCPR General Comment No. 16: Article 17 (Right to Privacy), The Right to Respect of Privacy, Family, Home and Correspondence, and Protection of Honour and Reputation, 8 April 1988,

activities of the private business sector and civil society are in conformity with the right to food'.[49] Accordingly, 'failure to regulate activities of individuals or groups so as to prevent them from violating the right to food' amounts to a violation by states of the right to food.[50]

When violations occur, the state has the duty to react to them. The HRC has therefore stated in connection with the right to life that the state should 'establish effective facilities and procedures to investigate thoroughly cases of missing and disappeared persons'.[51]

5.3 State Responsibility and Positive Obligations

The Draft Rules on State Responsibility lay emphasis on state action and in so doing tend to ignore inaction as a basis for state responsibility. In overlooking omissions as a basis of state responsibility, the Draft Rules epitomize the conventional view of human rights as injunctions against the state. This oversight is unfortunate not only because international human rights law has now developed to the extent that states have positive obligations, the least of which is the duty to protect those within their jurisdiction, but also because earlier arbitral decisions in international law recognized the notion of due diligence. In the *Youmans Claims*, for example, the General Claims Commission observed that the Mexican government had the obligation to exercise due diligence 'to protect the father of the claimant from the fury of the mob at whose hands he was killed', and to take proper steps to apprehend and punish the persons implicated in the crime.[52] These arbitral decisions have not received as much attention as the *Velásquez Rodríguez* v *Honduras* case,[53] in which the IACtHR stated that a human rights violation that is initially not directly imputable to a state can lead to the international responsibility of the state 'not because of the act itself, but *because of the lack of due diligence to prevent the violation or to respond to it*'.[54] Due diligence requires the state to 'take *reasonable steps* to prevent human rights violations and to use the means at its disposal to carry out a *serious* investigation of violations committed within its jurisdiction, to identify those responsible, to impose the appropriate punishment and to ensure the victim adequate compensation' (emphasis added).[55]

Overall, one can conclude that international human rights law has contributed to the development of positive obligations of states, especially the duty to protect. This duty entails an obligation to exercise due diligence to take such preventive measures as the enactment of legislation and the establishment of regulatory and monitoring mechanisms aimed at preventing occurrences of human rights violations. The state must also take reactive measures once the violations have taken place. As a result, the reach of human rights to non-state conduct has been extended more than under the

---

UN GAOR, 43rd Session, Annex VI, UN Doc. A/43/40 (1988), paras. 1, 2, and 9–10; HRC, CCPR General Comment No. 10: Article 19 (Freedom of Opinion), 29 June 1983, UN GAOR, 38th Session, Annex VI, UN Doc. A/38/40 (1983), paras. 2–3.

49 CESCR, General Comment No. 12: The Right to Adequate Food (Article 11 of the Covenant), adopted by CESCR at its 20th session, 12 May 1999, E/C.12/1999/5, para. 27.

50 *Ibid.*, para. 19. See also CESCR, General Comment No. 14, note 45 above, para. 35; CESCR, General Comment No. 5: Persons with Disabilities, 9 December 1994, E/1995/22, para. 11.

51 HRC, CCPR General Comment No. 6: Article 6 (Right to Life), 30 April 1982, para. 4.

52 RIAA iv, 110, cited in Brownlie, note 2 above, p. 161. See also the *Janes Claim* and the *Massey Claim*, also cited in Brownlie, note 2 above, p. 161.

53 [1988] Inter-Am Court HR (Ser. C) No. 4.

54 *Ibid.*, para. 172.

55 *Ibid.*, para. 174. Other cases endorsing the due diligence paradigm include the *SERAC* case, note 45 above.

traditional conception of state responsibility. Unlike under the latter, where proof of state action was required, responsibility falls on the state for violations of human rights by non-state actors even though the acts violating the rights have no direct or indirect correlation to the state. The state's responsibility springs from the state's actions or inactions before and after the violations, not necessarily from the physical violations themselves. Therefore, where violations of human rights occur because of conduct which cannot be classified as state action, the state might still be held responsible for them if it can be established that it failed to prevent or redress those violations.

6. State Responsibility and Non-State Actors: An Appraisal

The doctrine of state responsibility – as reinforced by the duty to protect and the notion of due diligence – underscores the continuing centrality of the state to modern political life and governance at a time when the authority of the state is in sharp decline and non-state actors are correspondingly gaining more and more influence, exercising the functions which were once regarded as public functions and exerting enormous policy, legislative and political influence at both international and municipal levels.[56] The shift from a minimalist conception of human rights duties as negative edicts to an acceptance of positive obligations, especially the duty to protect, signifies the realization that state inaction or non-interference, far from being the guarantor of freedom, can leave individuals prone to human rights violations and, consequently, form a potential basis for state responsibility where the violations were preventable and 'redressible'. For human rights to be secured, non-interference by the state is as critical as protective measures by it. The failure by the state to take protective measures will lead to its responsibility in international law not necessarily because of the mere occurrence of the violations themselves but because of the state's inaction or omission to prevent the violations.

In requiring states to respect human rights as well as protect them, international human rights law has imposed a responsibility on states which operates in binary opposition to the liberal conception of the state which dominates current global economic thought, as reflected in the notion of globalization demanding a minimal, non-interventionist state.[57] The relevance of this to our current discussion is that states in the globalizing environment – espoused within the World Trade Organization (WTO) establishment, with the World Bank and the International Monetary Fund (IMF) as its high priests – are supposed to adopt a *laissez-faire* approach, allowing the rules of the market to reign in economics and international trade, with minimal regulation of the private sector. For the doctrine of state responsibility to make a meaningful impact on curbing violations of human rights by non-state actors, it would have to overcome this opposing current of thought on the role of the state.

Quite apart from this, the success of the doctrine of state responsibility is contingent on the capacity of the state to establish an effective framework for regulating and monitoring non-state

---

56 See P. Alston, 'The Myopia of the Handmaidens: International Lawyers and Globalisation', *European Journal of International Law*, 8 (1997), pp. 435–48, at p. 435; W.M. Reisman, 'Designing and Managing the Future of the State', *European Journal of International Law*, 8 (1997), pp. 409–20, at pp. 409, 412; S. Sur, 'The State Between Fragmentation and Globalization', *European Journal of International Law*, 8 (1997), pp. 421–34, at p. 422; R. Walker and S. Mendlovitz, 'Interrogating State Sovereignty', in R. Walker and S. Mendlovitz (eds), *Contending Sovereignties: Redefining Political Community* (Boulder, CO: Lynne Rienner Press, 1990), p. 1.

57 See also Chapter 10 in this volume.

actors. This task is onerous, involving considerable financial and human resources.[58] The operational methods of such non-state actors as transnational corporations and terrorist organizations often defy national regulatory mechanisms.[59] The recent credit crunch and resultant global recession has also shown that the task of regulation is not as easy to fulfil as it appears for both rich and poor states, but it certainly is more challenging for poor states, especially those involved in internal armed conflict.

The Draft Articles purport to draw a useful distinction between internationally wrongful acts and state responsibility. The occurrence of an internationally wrongful act does not *per se* lead to state responsibility unless that act is attributed to a particular state. This means that not all internationally wrongful acts can be attributed to a state. Someone else must be held responsible for these. Moreover, state responsibility is not coterminous with vicarious liability in civil law in that the state under the duty to protect is held responsible for its own failings, not for the actual wrongs of the non-state actor.

Hence, the actual violations must be dealt with by other means such as the direct responsibility of the violators themselves. At the domestic level, non-state actors are typically constrained through corporate law, consumer protection laws, employment and labour laws, environmental protection and regulatory laws, competition law, and criminal law. What has been lacking are direct links between these legal mechanisms to human rights, mainly because most constitutions do not recognize the horizontal application of human rights.

The third-party-effect doctrine, developed in Germany offers an interesting example of how constitutional rights can influence the development of private law. This doctrine allows the courts to interpret certain provisions of private law innovatively to infuse the spirit and objects of human rights into private law.[60] In so doing, human rights are considered in the development of private law in ways that permit the indirect horizontal application of human rights. Curiously, even in states where human rights are constitutionally recognized to have horizontal effect, as in South Africa and Ireland, the practice seems to be that courts must first use private law and statutory remedies before they can invoke direct horizontal application of constitutional rights.[61] This practice is dictated by the need to avoid duplication of remedies, and thus, unless private and statutory remedies are inadequate, one cannot rely on direct constitutional remedies to address private wrongs entailing human rights violations. The doctrine of state responsibility serves the useful role of providing the

58 E.g. C. Grossman and D. Bradlow, 'Are We Being Propelled Towards a People-Centred Transnational Legal Order?', *American University Journal of International Law and Policy*, 9 (1993), pp. 1–25, at pp. 8–9.

59 E.g. D. Kokkini-Iatridou and P. de Waart, 'Foreign Investments in Developing Countries: Legal Personality of Multinationals in International Law', *Netherlands Yearbook of International Law*, 14 (1983), pp. 87–131.

60 See K.M. Lewan, 'The Significance of Constitutional Rights for Private Law: Theory and Practice in West Germany', *International and Comparative Law Quarterly*, 17 (1968), pp. 571–601; S. Oeter, 'Fundamental Rights and Their Impact on Private Law – Doctrine and Practice Under the German Constitution', *Tel Aviv University Studies in Law*, 12 (1994), p. 7; B. Markesinis, 'Privacy, Freedom of Expression, and the Horizontal Effect of the Human Rights Bill: Lessons from Germany', *Law Quarterly Review*, 115 (1999), p. 47.

61 Direct horizontal application occurs when a person is allowed to commence an action against a non-state actor based directly on a constitution or to defend an action based on a constitutional right. For some literature on the South African and Irish constitutions on this issue, see G. Hogan and G. White, *The Irish Constitution (J.M. Kerry)* (Dublin: Butterworths, 1994); C. Sprigman and M. Osborne, 'Du Plessis Is Not Dead: South Africa's 1996 Constitution and the Application of the Bill of Rights to Private Disputes', *South African Journal on Human Rights*, 15 (1999), p. 25; S. Woolman, 'Application', in M. Chaskalson *et al.* (eds), *Constitutional Law of South Africa* (Cape Town: Juta, 2005), p. 31.

anchorage for developing private law and statutory remedies and regulatory mechanisms for non-state actors, but, without the recognition of binding human rights obligations of these actors in the constitution, its importance in the context of globalization shrinks significantly.

At the international level, international criminal law has thus far offered the most promising avenue for holding individuals responsible for gross human rights violations that qualify as international crimes. However, corporations cannot be held criminally responsible within the existing body of international criminal law, and avenues for civil liability against non-state actors generally are sharply limited. Thus far, only soft-law mechanisms, arising from declarations or other non-binding international efforts, have been relied upon with varying degrees of success.[62] The most formidable step towards a binding human rights framework for non-state actors was halted when the UN Commission on Human Rights refused to take further action on the UN Norms on the Responsibilities of Transnational Corporations and Other Business Enterprises with regard to Human Rights,[63] and instead appointed, in April 2005, a Special Representative of the UN Secretary-General on the issue of human rights and transnational corporations and other business with a convoluted remit, among other things, to identify and clarify standards of corporate responsibility and accountability, define the notions of complicity and sphere of influence, and compile a compendium of best practices of states and transnational corporations and other business enterprises.[64] In his reports, the special representative has, for good reasons, accentuated the importance of state responsibility in curbing violations of human rights committed by non-state actors.[65] Nevertheless, it would be a weighty mistake to downplay the need for other complementary mechanisms, not least because of the challenges discussed above entailed by state regulation of the private sector, conceptual contradictions between the liberal vision of the state which dominates current global economic policies and an interventionist perspective of the state demanded by current human rights standards, and the need to redress violations directly against

62 These include the UN Global Compact, the Organization for Economic Co-operation and Development Guidelines for Multinational Enterprises, the International Labour Organization Tripartite Declaration of Principles Concerning Multinational Enterprises, and the World Bank Inspection Panel. For a discussion of these, see e.g. D.M. Chirwa, 'The Long March to Binding Obligations of Transnational Corporations in International Human Rights Law', *South African Journal on Human Rights*, 22(1) (2006), pp. 76–98; N. Jägers, *Corporate Human Rights Obligations: In Search of Accountability* (Antwerp: Intersentia, 2002).

63 UN Doc. E/CN.4/Sub.2/2003/12/Rev.2 (2003). The UN norms were adopted by the Sub-Commission's Working Group on the Working Methods and Activities of Transnational Corporations, on 13 August 2003. Discussed in S. Deva, 'UN's Human Rights Norms for Transnational Corporations and Other Business Enterprises: An Imperfect Step in the Right Direction?', *ILSA Journal of International & Comparative Law*, 10 (2004), pp. 493–523; D. Weissbrodt and M. Kruger, 'Norms on the Responsibilities of Transnational Corporations and Other Business Enterprises with Regard to Human Rights', *American Journal of International Law*, 97 (2003), p. 901.

64 See 'Human Rights and Transnational Corporations and Other Business Enterprises', Human Rights Resolution 2005/69, ch. 17, E/CN.4/2005/L.10/Add.17 (2005).

65 E.g. J. Ruggie, 'Promotion and Protection of Human Rights', Interim Report of the Special Representative of the Secretary General on the Issue of Human Rights and Transnational Corporations and Other Business Enterprises, 22 February 2006, E/CN.4/2006/97; J. Ruggie, 'Implementation of General Assembly Resolution 60/251 of 15 March 2006 Entitled "Human Rights Council"', Report of the Special Representative of the Secretary General on the Issue of Human Rights and Transnational Corporations and Other Business Enterprises, 19 February 2007, A/HRC/4/35; J. Ruggie, 'Implementation of General Assembly Resolution 60/251 of 15 March 2006 Entitled "Human Rights Council"', Report of the Special Representative of the Secretary General on the Issue of Human Rights and Transnational Corporations and Other Business Enterprises, 13 February 2007, A/HRC/4/35/Add.1. See also Chapter 27 in this volume.

non-state actors, especially where the state lacks capacity and where the non-state actor unjustly or unfairly enriched itself from the violation.

7. Conclusion

In conclusion, international human rights law has expanded the conceptual framework of the idea of state responsibility beyond what was initially imagined by international jurists. Conceived for the protection of aliens, this doctrine now applies for the benefit of all individuals, non-nationals and nationals. Previously, it could be invoked only by the state which was the nationality of the alien; at present, it is open to claims by all states. Nationality is not the link between the victim of a violation and the state that enforces it. States were in the past the only actors in international law with legal personality to enforce the obligations of other states. International human rights law has emboldened the status of individuals in international law by arming them with the power to enforce their rights not only against foreign states but also against their own state.

Significantly, international human rights law has painstakingly developed to extend the scope for holding states responsible for violations of human rights by private parties. Under the traditional doctrine, state responsibility only emanated from acts of the state. This meant that acts of non-state actors had to be of a kind that admitted the classification of state action for them to give rise to state responsibility. All acts which could not be so categorized could not be censured through legal means in international law. International human rights law has expanded the scope for addressing such acts by holding that even if the state is not directly connected to the actual violation, it may still be held responsible for those violations where it fails to exercise due diligence to prevent those violations, investigate them, punish the perpetrators, and provide redress to victims.

The ideas of due diligence and positive obligations in human rights are still in their formative stages. It remains to be seen how courts in international and domestic fora will use them to bolster the protection of human rights. In principle, they herald better prospects for the protection of human rights. However, it would be a grave oversight to treat due diligence and the duty to protect as the be-all and end-all of efforts to enhance the accountability of non-state actors for human rights. This chapter has pointed out some of the limitations of state responsibility in redressing human rights violations committed by non-state actors. The fulfilment of the vision of the UDHR will remain elusive unless all forms of human rights violations – by states and non-state actors alike – are eliminated and the perpetrators of the violations – whether state or non-state actors – are liable to be held responsible for them.

Chapter 22

State Compliance with the Recommendations of the African Commission on Human and Peoples' Rights

Frans Viljoen

1. Introduction

Recent years have seen the increased engagement of international human rights law practice and scholarship with issues of 'implementation' and 'compliance'. These terms and others, such as impact, follow-up, realization, correspondence, convergence and enforcement, all verbalize in different ways an expectation that maturing human rights systems need to produce results and should be judged by the outcomes of their monitoring activities. Even if its adoption six decades ago marks the first building block of the present international system, it is not difficult to reconcile these apparently more recent concerns with the UDHR.[1] One of the often-referred-to features of the UDHR is that it sets a 'common standard'. Less focus has been given to the preambular phrase following those two words: 'of achievement'. What needs to be achieved, the UDHR continues, is the 'universal and effective *recognition* and *observance* of its provisions'(emphasis added).[2] In similar vein, the UDHR provides for a right to an 'effective remedy'.[3] By examining state compliance with the recommendations of the African Commission on Human and Peoples' Rights (African Commission or Commission), a regional treaty body with a quasi-judicial status similar to that of the UN human rights treaty bodies, this chapter aims to shed some light on the progress made to achieve 'effective recognition and observance' of human rights standards.

This chapter deals as much with the concept of compliance as with *assessing* state compliance. After a brief exploration of the concept of compliance and an introduction to the Commission's recommendatory mandate, four types of recommendations issued by the Commission are identified and discussed. The aim is not to provide new empirical research findings or data on compliance, but to place the literature and available data in an analytical framework, to point to avenues for further research and identify gaps that may need to be filled.

2. Implementation, Compliance and Assessing Compliance

Scholars engaged with international human rights law are increasingly interested in the question of whether treaty ratification 'makes a difference'.[4] In this contribution, 'implementation' is used as an umbrella term combining all elements constituting the domestic application and realization

1 GA Res. 217A (III), UN Doc. A/810 at 71 (1948).

2 Preamble, UDHR.

3 Art. 8, UDHR.

4 E.g. D. Cassel, 'Does International Human Rights Law Make a Difference?', *Chicago Journal of International Law*, 2 (2001), pp. 121–35; and the seminal article by O.A. Hathaway, 'Do Human Rights Treaties Make a Difference?', *Yale Law Journal*, 101 (2002), pp. 1935–2041.

of a treaty and its provisions. Assessing implementation poses questions about the extent to which the main obligations of states under the relevant treaty have been adhered to. To make the most convincing claims about the impact (actual domestic effect or 'implementation') of a treaty, and to hold states accountable for non-observance of their treaty obligations, one should ideally be able to establish some evidence of a change in state practice, and of the positive benefit in peoples' lives, traceable back to (or 'resulting from') the treaty itself. While changes in state practice would best be gauged by way of process indicators (such as the adoption of laws and setting up of institutions), the actual effect on people's lives would depend more on outcome-based indicators (such as statistical data about the actual enjoyment of rights).

Assessing implementation may therefore be viewed as an effort to answer the following two main questions: (1) Do states comply with their formal treaty obligations? (2) Do individuals benefit from the ratification of treaties? Implementation can be *de jure* (related to the element of 'recognition' in the UDHR) or *de facto* (related to 'observance'). While legal or other measures taken by states may be identified with relative ease, assessing the broader impact of a treaty on the lives of a population is obviously much more problematic. Quantitative studies that have endeavoured to do so at the macro-level, by drawing comparisons between states,[5] have been criticized.[6] Perhaps more reliable claims can be made if the focus falls on an in-depth analysis of a particular country,[7] and if these studies use a combination of quantitative and qualitative techniques.

The main reason why the accent in this chapter falls on implementation by states is because the state is, as party to the relevant treaties, the first guarantor of international human rights. However, the mere fact that states have the primary obligation under a treaty does not mean that implementation is only dependent on state action. This emphasis should therefore not be understood as, in any way, negating the necessity to involve a broad array of national and international role players, including civil society organs and the international community, in the process of accomplishing or improving implementation.[8] If implementation comes about primarily through the 'mobilization of shame', the role of civil society, the media and the international community in inducing and coaxing implementation cannot be underestimated.

'Compliance' is, for the purpose of this chapter, distinguished from 'implementation', and is accorded a more narrow and specific meaning. Although the verb 'comply' (and thus the term 'compliance') does not have a universally accepted meaning, it is here understood, in the ordinary understanding of the word, as obedience to a request or command.[9] The inquiry is therefore directed at tangible steps these states are *required to take in response to specific directives by a treaty-monitoring body*, in this case, the African Commission. State compliance may take the form of action taken by any of the branches of government. The executive may, for example,

---

5 Hathaway, note 4 above; see also L.C. Keith and A. Ogundele, 'Legal Systems and Constitutionalism in sub-Sahara Africa: An Empirical Examination of Colonial Influences on Human Rights', *Human Rights Quarterly*, 29 (2007), pp. 1065–97.

6 E.g. R. Goodman and D. Jinks, 'Measuring the Effect of Human Rights Treaties', *European Journal of International Law*, 14 (2003), pp. 171–83; see also O.A. Hathaway, 'Testing Conventional Wisdom', *European Journal of International Law*, 14 (2003), pp. 185–200.

7 C. Heyns and F. Viljoen, 'The Impact of the UN Human Rights Treaties on the Domestic Level', *Human Rights Quarterly*, 23 (2001), pp. 483–535; and country studies in C. Heyns and F. Viljoen, *The Impact of the United Nations Human Rights Treaties on the Domestic Level* (The Hague: Martinus Nijhoff, 2002).

8 See O.C. Okafor, *The African Human Rights System: Activist Forces and International Institutions* (Cambridge: Cambridge University Press, 2007).

9 *Concise Oxford Dictionary*, 8th edn (Oxford: Clarendon Press, 1990), p. 233.

release a detainee, pay compensation, or appoint a Commission of inquiry; the legislature may enact legislative changes; and the judiciary may reopen domestic proceedings.

The main obligation of a state party is, in the shorthand of Article 1 of the African Charter on Human and Peoples' Rights (African Charter), to *recognize* the Charter rights and to *give effect* to them (and the rights provided for under the Protocol to the African Charter on the Rights of Women in Africa (African Women's Protocol)) by adopting *legislative* and *other measures*. In essence, states are required to undertake a general process of domestication (which may precede ratification, and may be the outcome of a compatibility study), and to ensure the implementation (or observance) of these provisions in its practice. It is when domestic laws, policies and practices fail or allegedly fail to live up to this standard that the African Commission enters the fray.

The concept of *compliance* implies the evident possibility of *non-compliance*. One of the functions of the African Commission is therefore to draw a dividing line between these two situations. Through the performance of its monitoring function, the African Commission is mandated to hold states accountable to their treaty promises by pointing out instances where domestic law and practice do not live up to the ideal of fully giving effect to the Charter. To an extent, the Commission's monitoring role is dependent on the opportunities provided by the submission of communications and state reports. Considering a communication or examining a state report provides an opportunity to establish instances (or examples) of non-implementation. Required state action will then be set out in the recommendations contained in the Commission's finding or concluding observations. Adherence to these requirements constitutes compliance, as the term is used here. Moreover, the Commission may also take the initiative by adopting recommendations as part of on-site investigative or promotional missions (although these visits only take place with the consent of the state), or when it adopts country-specific resolutions containing recommendations.

The nature and formulation of the remedial 'order' contained in the recommendation is of great importance in the assessment exercise. To a large extent, one cannot discuss compliance with recommendations in the abstract, but rather as compliance with specific remedies. The expectations and modalities of compliance may, for example, be quite distinguishable in respect of an order for monetary compensation, compared to a recommendation to change a law or release a detainee. The extent to which the government perceives the required action to make inroads into its 'sovereignty' is further likely to be an important factor in its reaction to a recommendation, and the greater the precision of the remedial action required by the recommendation, the easier it becomes to assess state compliance with those recommendations.

It cannot be denied that numerous methodological difficulties beset the process of assessing compliance. A few of these concerns are now raised in relation to the endeavour to establish a reliable picture of state compliance with the African Commission's recommendations.

An exhaustive picture of compliance is almost impossible to achieve. In the more than 22 years of its existence, since its establishment in 1987, the Commission has adopted numerous communications, resolutions and other statements containing recommendations. Considerable resources would be required to provide an exhaustive analysis of compliance by all states in all these instances. Owing to the specific conditions of each case, capturing a sample may also not be sufficiently representative of general trends.

A plethora of methodological difficulties is bound to detract from the accuracy and reliability of claims about state compliance. Although methodologies to assess compliance may differ, they would inevitably entail an empirical element, comprising the collection and analysis of information on steps taken by states in relation (or in response) to the relevant recommendations. In addition to interviewing government officials, such a study may also comprise interviews with individuals or lawyers involved in communications and NGOs operating in a particular country, and may analyse media reports on these issues. Practical obstacles such as the following are bound to hamper this form of research: communication difficulties, reluctance of governments to engage on the issue, insufficient and inaccessible records, inability to trace victims and authors of communications, lack of quality and continuity in state representatives attending the Commission's sessions, divergent views about compliance by those involved in the process, and the lack of media coverage.[10]

Compliance can be described along a sliding scale, rather than in absolute terms. Even if the factual circumstances surrounding compliance could be established with some accuracy, the data still need to be analysed and categorized. The following question arises: to what extent did the state comply – fully, partially, or not at all?[11] A major factor complicating attempts at such categorization is the lack of precision in the formulation of recommendations. If it is not clear what exactly the state was required to do, it would be difficult to know whether it did what was required (and thus 'complied'). It comes as no surprise that the UN Human Rights Committee, after more than 10 years of following up on compliance with its views, remarked, 'Attempts to categorize follow-up replies are necessarily imprecise.'

A further problem with the categorization process is the determination of a causal link between the Commission's recommendation and subsequent state conduct. If one wants to make reliable claims about state compliance with the Commission's recommendations, strict logic requires that one demonstrate that conduct *subsequent to* the adoption of the recommendation came about *as a result of* the recommendation rather than because of some other factor or factors. Reality is multi-faceted, and state conduct is complex, making it inevitable that numerous factors will simultaneously influence the course taken. Where a highly publicized case, for instance, caused significant international pressure to be exerted on a state party, the question may be posed: is state compliance the result of a recommendation by the Commission or did it come about as a result of international pressure? Only rarely would a state explicitly articulate the motivation for its actions. The approach taken here is therefore one that lowers the horizon of expectation, by considering the motivation for state action to be irrelevant. In objective circumstances, compliance is viewed as state action in line with and subsequent to the adoption of the recommendation. However, one should point out that the issue of causality is complicated considerably when state conduct occurs after a fundamental change in circumstances, as, for instance, when a civil war existed during the submission of the complaint or where a military dictator was in power at the time, but the situations had changed considerably at the time compliance (or non-compliance) became an issue.

10 In July 1990, during the committee's 39th Session, it established a follow-up procedure to its views under Article 5(4) of the Optional Protocol to the International Covenant on Civil and Political Rights, and created the mandate of a Special Rapporteur on Follow-Up (see *Official Records of the General Assembly*, 45th Session, Supplement No. 40 (A/45/40), annex XI. With reference to the difficulties in categorizing follow-up replies, see *Report of the Human Rights Committee*, Official Records of the General Assembly, 54th Session, No. 40 (A/54/40), para. 459).

11 Categorization can be done on different bases: see e.g. the Annual Report 2008 of the Inter-American Commission on Human Rights, para. 43, in which the categories 'total', 'partial' and 'pending' compliance are used [online]. Available from: http://www.cidh.org/annualrep/2008eng/Chap3.f.eng.htm [accessed 12 June 2009].

3. The African Commission's Recommendations

As was stated, the African Commission oversees and monitors not only the implementation of the African Charter, but also the African Women's Protocol.[12] Four kinds of recommendations adopted by the Commission are identified here: (1) On the basis of communications (complaints) submitted to it, the Commission makes findings and issues recommendations. (2) The Commission further examines periodic reports submitted by state parties and adopts recommendations as part of its concluding observations on these reports. (3) In its resolutions, the Commission may also direct recommendations to state parties. (4) Other reports on the Commission's activities, such as those emanating from protective on-site and promotional missions and visits or studies by special mechanisms, also routinely contain 'recommendations' to states.

Over the years, neither the Commission nor its Secretariat has conducted any systematic follow-up to find out whether these recommendations have actually been complied with. The reasons for the Commission's long-standing inaction in respect of following up its findings, in particular, are related to its competence to adopt recommendations and undertake follow-up enquiries.

Although some states have questioned the Commission's competence to consider individual communications (as opposed to cases revealing a series of serious or massive violations), the Commission has dismissed these arguments and established a widely accepted practice of considering complaints.[13] Neither the African Charter nor the Commission's rules of procedure explicitly requires follow-up. Questions may therefore be raised regarding the Commission's institutional competence to undertake follow-up measures or actions. A narrow reading of the word 'consider' in Article 55 of the Charter would suggest that it does not have such competence. To 'consider' – such an argument would go – is to 'examine the merits of' or to 'give attention to', and not to 'implement' findings of communications.[14] In other words, the argument would be that the Charter does not mandate follow-up measures in respect of communications. Such an argument is reinforced by the complementarity between the African Commission and the African Union (AU) Assembly. The Commission's mandate is restricted to addressing reports that contain its conclusions and recommendations to the Assembly. It is for the Assembly to decide what needs to be done, in the sense of which action needs to be taken.

However, the preferable view is that the Charter implicitly allows for, and in fact, requires, follow-up. Implicit in the concept 'consider' must be 'careful thoughts' and 'attention' given to the implementation of a decision. If implementation is not regarded as intrinsically part of the consideration of a decision, the following question arises: why does the Commission consider communications in the first place, if it remains unconcerned about their implementation and effect? Adopting views is not a purposeless, formulaic exercise. Adopting a teleological approach, the aim of the communications procedure must be to grant relief (in the form of a remedy) to a complainant, or to change laws or practices. Follow-up is therefore integral to the process of individual communications, and making sense of the overarching duty of states to give effect to the

12 The mandate of the African Commission is to promote and protect the rights guaranteed in the African Charter. The African Commission held its first session in Addis Ababa, Ethiopia, in November 1987. With the transformation of the OAU into the AU in July 2002, the African Commission was retained and the AU Assembly took over the tasks previously performed by the OAU Assembly.

13 See the Commission's response to the Gambian government's arguments that it could only make findings on series of serious or massive violations: Communication 147/95, 149/95 (joined), *Jawara* v *The Gambia* (2000), AHRLR 107 (ACHPR 2000), para. 42.

14 *Concise Oxford Dictionary*, note 9 above, p. 244.

rights in the Africa Charter.[15] Because measures taken to follow up findings may be considered a form of investigation in the context of the communications procedure, the Commission's extensive competence to 'resort to any appropriate method of investigation'[16] also applies here. Furthermore, according to Article 60, the Commission 'shall draw inspiration' from international human rights law, and in terms of this drawing of inspiration from the UN human rights treaty bodies that also deal with communications, and from the inter-American human rights system, one observes a trend to use institutionalized follow-up procedures.[17]

Although the Commission has made some efforts in respect of individual communications, these were few and far apart and have not developed into an established or consistent practice. On occasion, the Commission has, for example, made use of promotional visits or visits for protective reasons to follow up, with government representatives, the status of state compliance with recommendations adopted after the consideration of communications.[18] On other occasions, the Commission has incorporated follow-up measures as part of its findings in deciding individual communications by calling on states parties to report back to it upon submitting their next periodic report, in terms of Article 62 of the African Charter, on the measures they had taken to comply with the Commission's recommendations.[19] In theory, at least, states submit reports at regular intervals. It follows that this provides an ideal opportunity for feedback about the implementation of findings on communications. When the state subsequently reports, the Commission reminds it of this obligation and asks for the required information. In this way a practice has evolved whereby Commissioners use the state reporting procedure to enquire about the implementation of decisions, even in the absence of a specific recommendation to the state to report on this issue.[20] In at least one instance, the Commission detached the requirement to provide information about the implementation of the state reporting procedure, when it recommended that the Swazi government inform it 'in writing within six months on the measures it has taken to implement' the remedies indicated.[21] Such an approach seems preferable, given the irregularity of state reporting.

At its 40th session, in November 2006, the Commission placed assessment of compliance on a much firmer footing, when it formalized its ad hoc approach by adopting the 'Resolution on the Importance of the Implementation of the Recommendations of the African Commission on Human and Peoples' Rights' (Resolution on Implementation).[22] In this resolution, the Commission calls on states to 'respect without delay' its 'recommendations', and to indicate – within 90 days

15 African Charter, Art. 1.

16 African Charter, Art. 46.

17 For example, initially, the UN Human Rights Committee held that its role in the examination of communications comes to an end when it adopts a final decision, including a view on the merits of a case. By 1990, however, it had appointed a Special Rapporteur on the Follow-up of Views.

18 See objectives of the *Report of the African Commission's Promotional Mission to Burkina Faso*, 22 September to 2 October 2001, DOC/OS(XXXIII)/324b/I.

19 Communication 211/98, *Legal Resources Foundation Centre* v *Zambia*, 14th Annual Activity Report (2001), AHRLR 84 (ACHPR 2001), para. 76; and Communication 241/2001, *Purohit and Another* v *The Gambia*, 16th Annual Activity Report (2003), AHRLR 96 (ACHPR 2003), para. 85.

20 As was done by Commissioner Johm in respect of the state reports of Mauritania, examined during the Commission's 31st session; see also objectives of the 'Report of the African Commission's Promotional Mission to Burkina Faso', 22 September to 2 October 2001, DOC/OS(XXXIII)/324b/I.

21 Communication 251/2002, *Lawyers for Human Rights* v *Swaziland*, 18th Annual Activity Report) (2005) AHRLR 66 (ACHPR 2005), para. 53.

22 Doc. ACHPR/Res.97(XXXX)06: Resolution on the Importance of the Implementation of the Recommendations of the African Commission on Human and Peoples' Rights by States Parties; see also Final Communiqué of the Commission's 40th Session.

of being notified of these recommendations – the measures taken and 'obstacles' experienced in implementing them. The Commission further decided that it would attach an annex to future activity reports to the AU Executive Council, setting out the state of compliance with 'recommendations' by state parties. Because the resolution uses the generic term 'recommendation', all four forms of recommendations identified above are included in its ambit. In other words, the requirements above apply to recommendations emanating from individual communications, state reporting, promotional visits, visits and reports of special procedures, and those contained in all other resolutions.

Unfortunately, there is no evidence that the Commission has so far translated the Resolution on Implementation into practice. One searches in vain in subsequent activity reports for any information about state compliance. Most likely, the problem is that states are not 'indicating' to the Commission what measures they have taken. Even so, one would expect the Commission to react to this disregard of its resolution by calling on states to do so, and to bring this to the attention of the AU organs. It may even appoint one of its members as a special rapporteur on follow-up to ensure that this issue receives consistent attention. Its Secretariat should also be more proactive in establishing a dedicated section devoted to the systematic collection of data and follow-up of recommendations.

It is encouraging that the Commission's interim rules of procedure, which are in the process of being considered at the time of writing, speak to many of the concerns raised here, and seek to further institutionalize the procedure set out in the Resolution on Implementation. If finally adopted in its current form, the procedure on follow-up of recommendations would be as follows.[23] Violator states have to inform the Commission, within six months of receipt of a finding,[24] of measures taken 'or being taken' to 'implement the decision'.[25] The Commission may, within three months thereafter, request supplementary information. The Commissioner responsible for the communication, or another Commissioner 'designated for this purpose', must 'ascertain the measures' taken, may 'make such contacts and take such action as may be appropriate',[26] and must make recommendations for the Commission's further action. This information and recommendations will be tabled at the public sessions of the Commission. It will then draw the attention of the Sub-Committee of the Permanent Representatives Committee and the Executive Council on the Implementation of Decisions of the AU to instances of non-compliance.[27] The interim rules of procedure further stipulate that information on follow-up activities must be included in the Commission's activity reports.[28] In the main, the interim rules of procedure confirm and build on the advances contained

23 Rule 115 of the Commission's Interim Rules of Procedure (www.achpr.org, assessed 12 June 2009).

24 The corresponding period in the Resolution on Implementation is 90 days (3 months). The extension of the period to 6 months is more realistic.

25 The Resolution on Implementation provides for 'measures taken and/or the obstacles in implementing' the Commission's recommendations by states. The inclusion of the element of continuity ('is being taken') introduces an opening for states to contend that vague steps are under way. While the retention of this phrase has some merit, the Commission should be vigilant against potential abuse of this aspect.

26 This formulation would allow the Commission to conduct hearings on implementation/ compliance, as the Inter-American Commission on Human Rights has done (e.g. its Annual Report 2008, para. 73) [online]. Available from: http://www.cidh.org/annualrep/2008eng/Chap3.f.eng.htm [accessed 12 June 2009].

27 The corresponding referral institution in the Resolution on Implementation is the Executive Council.

28 For the practice of the Inter-American Commission on Human Rights, see its Annual Report 208, paras. 38–97.

in the Resolution on Implementation. The sooner the Commission's amended rules of procedure are finalized, the better will be the prospect for improved compliance.

3.1 Recommendations on Individual Communications

Addressing the need for empirical evidence on compliance with recommendations on individual communications, Lirette Louw, at the time a doctoral student at the Centre for Human Rights, University of Pretoria, conducted a survey of 44 communications in which the Commission found violations of the Charter between 1987 and mid-2003.[29] The results of her study revealed that the assumption is only partly correct that states fail to implement the Commission's recommendations.[30] Non-implementation seems to be the rule when one juxtaposes instances of 'full implementation' (recorded in 6 cases, or 14% of all cases) against 'non-implementation' (recorded in 13 cases, or 30%). However, in a significant number of cases (14 cases, or 32%), 'partial' implementation was recorded. 'Situational' compliance, occasioned by a far-reaching change in circumstances, such as a change of government, occurred in 7 (or 16%) of the cases.

As Louw's study shows, Nigeria is the setting of some of the most spectacular instances of both compliance and non-compliance. In *Constitutional Rights Project* v *Nigeria*,[31] the five complainants were arrested in June 1995 and were detained without being charged or tried for more than two years before a complaint was lodged with the African Commission. This situation had not changed by the time the Commission finally decided the case in November 1999. The Commission found Nigeria in violation of the right to a fair trial and to be tried within a reasonable time. The Commission appealed to the government of Nigeria to charge the detainees or release them.[32] The government of Nigeria complied and charged the detainees. In *Centre for Free Speech* v *Nigeria*,[33] four journalists were tried in secret by a military tribunal and were not allowed access to counsel of their choice. Under military decrees, the jurisdiction of regular courts to hear appeals from military tribunals was ousted, leaving the journalists without any right to appeal their sentences. The Commission found that Nigeria had violated the right to a fair trial and the principle of the independence of the judiciary, and urged the government of Nigeria to release the four journalists. The journalists were eventually released.[34]

In contrast to these two cases, the Nigerian government ignored the Commission's interim order, taken under the authority of Rule 111 of its rules of procedure, to stay the execution, and executed

29 L. Louw, 'An Analysis of State Compliance with the Recommendations of the African Commission on Human and Peoples' Rights'. Unpublished LLD thesis, University of Pretoria, January 2005.

30 See also F. Viljoen and L. Louw, 'An Assessment of State Compliance with the Recommendations of the African Commission on Human and Peoples' Rights between 1993 and 2004', *American Journal of International Law*, 101 (2007), pp. 1–34. 'Full' compliance denotes the implementation of all aspects of the remedy indicated; 'non-compliance' is used if a state did not implement any of the recommendations; 'partial' compliance indicates that a state implemented some but not all elements of the recommended remedy; and 'situational' compliance came about as a result of changed circumstances and not from a government's response as such.

31 Communication 153/96, 13th Annual Activity Report (2000) AHRLR 248 (ACHPR 1999).

32 Final paragraph of the communication.

33 Communication 206/97, 13th Annual Activity Report (2000) AHRLR 250 (ACHPR 1999).

34 According to Kolawole Olaniyan, previously a legal officer at Constitutional Rights Project (established during an interview at the 33rd ordinary session of the African Commission in Niamey, Niger).

Ken Saro-Wiwa and the other Ogoni men.[35] In its finding on this matter, the Commission held that the state's non-compliance with its directive constituted a violation of Article 1 of the African Charter. However, in a subsequent finding,[36] the Commission did not reach the same conclusion in an analogous case concerning the execution by Botswana of Mariette Sonjaleen Bosch pending the finalization of a communication submitted to the Commission. Instead, and without reference to the case involving Saro-Wiwa, the Commission found that Article 1 was not violated. Although the recommendations directing states to take precautionary measures are not binding,[37] ignoring them displays bad faith and undermines the very act of ratifying the Charter. Even if the Commission's final finding on the merits are not binding, the state should comply with the interim measures so that, at the very least, the Commission's determination of the issues involved may be taken into account, albeit as recommendations. In other words, the state must allow the possibility of being persuaded by the non-binding finding on the merits of the case. By disregarding an interim order, especially when it irrevocably excludes even the possibility of ultimate compliance, the state undermines the very basis of the Charter system – even accepting that such an order is only recommendatory in nature.[38]

Which factors influence the prospect of compliance in these and other instances? Postulating a number of hypotheses, a study building on that of Louw investigated the statistically significant correlation between a number of factors (both legal and political), on the one hand, and the level of compliance by states, on the other hand.[39] This study concluded that the most important variables responsible for state compliance are political, rather than legal. Legal factors, such as the nature of the right concerned and the comprehensiveness of legal reasoning in a finding, were not found to be good predictors of compliance. The only relevant indicators related to the treaty and the treaty body itself was the extent of involvement by the African Commission in following up a particular recommendation.

It is also arguably important that the findings of the Commission on communications are non-binding. Formally, the Commission's recommendations are recommendatory, and are not legally binding. However, there is some debate about the binding nature of the Commission's decisions.[40] States may argue that they are not legally bound to comply with 'decisions', as they are not decisions at all but merely 'recommendations'. However, once these 'recommendations' have been adopted as 'decisions' by the AU Assembly, states should have difficulty in arguing convincingly that they need not comply. Denying an obligation to comply with recommendations would also stand in stark contrast to the principal (and *bona fides*-based) undertaking of states to give effect to the Charter and to guarantee its provisions. Because this factor, in principle, affected all findings and recommendations in the same way, it may explain why findings and recommendations, in

35 Communication 137/94, 139/94, 154/96, 161/97 (joined), *International PEN and Others* v *Nigeria (on behalf of Saro-Wiwa)*, 12th Annual Activity Report (2000) AHRLR 212 (ACHPR 1998).

36 Communication 240/2001, *Interights and Others (on behalf of Bosch)* v *Botswana*, 17th Annual Activity Report (2003) AHRLR 55 (ACHPR 2003).

37 The matter is even further complicated because the core treaty, the African Charter, is silent about interim measures. The competence to issue interim (precautionary) measures is derived from the Commission's rules of procedure, issued under the authority of Article 42(2) of the Charter.

38 See also F. Viljoen, *International Human Rights Law in Africa* (Oxford: Oxford University Press, 2007), p. 327.

39 See Viljoen and Louw, note 31 above .

40 E.g. F. Viljoen and L. Louw, 'The Status of Findings of the African Commission: From Moral Persuasion to Legal Obligation?', *Journal of African Law*, 28 (2004), pp. 1–22.

general, are not complied with. However, it will be of limited value to explain why one particular recommendation was given effect, and another not.

The above-mentioned study found that 'extra-legal' factors are more significant in predicting compliance, in particular the following: (1) the type of government in place in a respondent state (how 'democratic' is it?; how much 'freedom' is allowed?); (2) the level of political stability within the respondent state; (3) the extent of internationalization of exposure to the issues raised in the case and the campaign surrounding implementation; (4) the engagement of the media; and (5) the involvement of NGOs in submitting and arguing the communication and their continuing engagement in the follow-up of recommendations.

Underscoring the importance of the last two factors, Okafor identifies and discusses evidence of 'activist forces' such as activist lawyers, human rights NGOs and activist journalists, who 'deploy the African system's norms and processes to produce the desired outcomes'[41] (including implementation of recommendations) in Nigeria (and some other African states). One of the most prominent of these 'activist forces' has been the Constitutional Rights Project (CRP), which was involved not only in one of the cases discussed above, but also, for example, in the *Zamani Lekwot* case.[42] In this case, the CRP successfully litigated to accomplish the 'domestication' of an interim order by the Commission, thus ensuring that the government did not execute the complainants.[43]

Subsequent to the completion of Louw's study, the Commission has finalized numerous further communications. The expectation created by the adoption of the Resolution on Implementation, namely that information about compliance with communications made public after November 2006 would be available, has unfortunately not been fulfilled. In any event, even if the Resolution on Implementation were given effect to, the state of compliance with findings published between mid-2003 and the end of 2006 would remain unclear. Thorough research therefore has to be undertaken to obtain a more current picture of the state of compliance subsequent to mid-2003.

In some prominent cases, some information about state compliance can be gauged from the Commission's activity reports. In response to the Commission's finding that the Zimbabwean Clemency Order No. 1 of 2000 violates the African Charter, in that it grants pardon to every person liable to criminal prosecution for any politically motivated crime committed between January and July 2000, the government of Zimbabwe replied as follows: 'While Zimbabwe does not question the ability, and competency of the ACHPR to adopt rules, guidelines and principles, *it holds* that the AU declaration on general amnesties does not, and should not apply in this case as the same were pronounced some 2 years after the amnesty had been declared [emphasis added].'[44] From these and other remarks in its response, it appears that the government had no intention of abiding by the Commission's finding.

Another factor that affected all recommendations, equally, is the lack of political engagement by the OAU/AU political organs. As the primary regional political institution responsible for implementing decisions regarding AU members, the AU organs (in particular, the Assembly and

41 Okafor, note 8 above, p. 124; see also F. Viljoen, 'Exploring the Theory and Practice of the Relationship Between International Human Rights Law and Domestic Actors', *Leiden Journal of International Law*, 22 (2009), pp. 177–90.

42 Communication 87/93, *Constitutional Rights Project (in Respect of Lekwot and Others)* v *Nigeria*, 8th Annual Activity Report (2000) AHRLR 183 (ACHPR 1995).

43 Okafor, note 8 above, pp. 98–101.

44 Zimbabwe's response to the African Commission's decision on communication 245/02 – Zimbabwe Human Rights NGO Forum/Zimbabwe, AU Doc. Ex.CL/322(X), Annexure III.

Executive Council) has a crucial role to play in bringing pressure to bear on violator states, including the possible application of sanctions for non-compliance to be enforced by the Assembly.[45]

With the advent of the newly established African Court on Human and Peoples' Rights (African Human Rights Court), it seems likely that the Commission will amend its rules of procedure to provide that cases are to be referred to the African Court in all instances where states have not, within a fixed period, complied with the Commission's recommendations.[46] For such a referral system to become workable, the Commission should ensure that its monitoring of implementation becomes functional and credible. To this extent, then, the future operation of the Court depends on improvements of the Commission's system of monitoring implementation.

3.2 Recommendations on State Reports (Concluding Observations)

When it examines state reports, the African Commission inspects the overall human rights record of states. Critical questions posed by Commissioners may imply but do not establish non-compliance with treaty obligations. Non-compliance is more likely to be established by the official record of the proceedings, the concluding observations, where areas of concern are noted and recommendations made. These concluding observations operate both retrospectively and prospectively, in that they provide indications of non-compliance of previously issued recommendations, and create a framework of expectations for the future.

Assessing compliance with the recommendations contained in concluding observations leads to a conclusion even bleaker than in respect of individual communications. To a great extent, tracking compliance with these recommendations is almost impossible. As is the case with communications, no systematic record of follow-up has been or is being kept. This position is due to a number of failings in the Commission's procedure of examining state reports. Any compliance assessment presupposes a yardstick. In the case of state reporting, this yardstick is the concluding observations, or, more precisely, the recommendations contained therein. The main drawback curtailing follow-up and compliance assessment is that it has been unclear to what extent the Commission actually adopts such concluding observations.

The problem only partially lies in the lack of a clear legal basis for adopting such conclusions. Article 62 of the African Charter, on which the legal status of these recommendations is based, does not provide an unequivocal mandate to adopt concluding observations. However, the rules of procedure, adopted in 1988 and retained in the 1995 amended rules, already provided for the possibility of adopting concluding observations. Rule 85(3) reads as follows:

> If, following the consideration of the reports, and the information submitted by a State party to the Charter, the Commission decides that the State has not discharged some of its obligations under the Charter, it may address all general observations to the State concerned as it may deem necessary.

Rule 86(1) takes the matter further:

> The Commission shall, through the Secretary, communicate to States parties to the Charter for comments, its general observations made following the consideration of the reports and the information submitted by States parties to the Charter which shall be public documents. The

45 See Art. 23(2) of the AU Constitutive Act.

46 Commission's Interim Rules of Procedure, Rule 119(1).

> Commission may, when necessary fix a time limit for the submission of the comments by the States parties to the Charter.

Even the initial 'Recommendation on periodic reports', also adopted in 1988, makes preambular reference to the African Commission 'making pertinent observations to States Parties'.

If concluding observations are to serve as yardsticks for compliance, they must be publicly accessible to all concerned. Even when the Commission as part of its practice adopted concluding observations, they were not made public or disseminated systematically. Publicity is the key to ensure domestic impact, and to ensure that implementation or compliance may be gauged against a clear yardstick. The African Commission's concluding observations should be made public, and should be publicly accessible. Because they have so far not been included in the Commission's activity reports, no official record exists. It is also not sufficient merely to declare that they are public, without taking steps to disseminate them or to allow free access thereto. Neither is it adequate to merely make them public, some time after their adoption, as part of the activity report. Concluding observations should be made public at the same session where the report is examined, and should be contained *in full* in the final communiqué of each session, and on the Commission's website. This is not the case at present. Given the importance of this aspect, concluding observations themselves should contain a recommendation that states give wide publicity to those recommendations, as has been done by other treaty bodies. Publicly accessible and widely disseminated concluding observations are indispensable to enable civil society involvement in the process of ensuring domestic implementation.[47]

Recommendations in concluding observations should be sufficiently clear and precise, requiring definite action that allows for later assessment. At a minimum, they should be in *clear* and *understandable* language. Their fulfilment should be *ascertainable*, enabling the Commission to assess, on a later occasion, compliance or non-compliance with recommendations. Recommendations should not be too vague, or so lofty and idealistic as to be meaningless. States can only respond effectively to recommendations that are clear and directed. A continuing dialogue will be maximized if the recommendations contain clear assessment criteria.

From a perusal of available concluding observations, it appears that in some instances, the recommendations therein are sufficiently precise to allow for an adequate compliance assessment. Recommendations requiring the amendment or adoption of clearly identified legislation fall into this category. A good example is the recommendation that Ghana should amend Article 270 of its Constitution and should ratify the Protocol on the Establishment of the African Court as well as the African Charter on the Rights and Welfare of the Child.[48] In its recommendations adopted as part of the concluding observations on the initial report of the Democratic Republic of Congo

---

47 There is also no sound reason to argue that these observations should remain confidential until the Commission's activity report in which they are contained is approved and made public. The concluding observations are already referred to as 'public documents' in the rules of procedure. They emanate from a public process of examination, in which the issues contained in the observations would have been raised orally in front of everyone attending the Commission's session. They are not 'measures taken' within the ambit of Article 59(1) of the Charter. In all these respects, concluding observations differ from individual communications, and should not be shrouded behind any temporary veil of unnecessary confidentiality. On the contrary, the very purpose of highlighting public concern and awareness of the Charter and its potential will be enhanced domestically if publicity is given both to the examination of state reports and subsequent concluding observations. Local media should be involved to achieve this goal.

48 Reprinted in C. Heyns and M. Killander, *Compendium of Key Human Rights Documents of the African Union* (Pretoria: Pretoria University Law Press, 2007), p. 170.

(DRC),[49] the Commission urged the government to take 'urgent measures to ensure the protection of the rights of the Pygmy/Batwa people in the whole territory of the DRC and move particularly to stop the serious violations of the rights of these people in the Eastern Districts', and it added that it should 'put in place as quickly as possible legislation recognising the rights of the Pygmy/Batwa people'. In its concluding observations in respect of South Africa's first periodic report, the African Commission recommended that South Africa make a declaration under Article 34(6) of the African Human Rights Court Protocol, and that it 'considers lifting' the reservation made on Article 6(d) of the African Women's Protocol.[50] In these instances, the specificity of the recommendations enables a compliance assessment of the Constitution and legislation subsequently adopted. A limited enquiry reveals that the relevant governments had not adhered to any of these recommendations.

These examples may be juxtaposed with the recommendation in the concluding observations on the periodic report on Cameroon,[51] calling on the government to 'take measures to protect and integrate the pygmies and Mbororo who constitute minority groups so that these groups can enjoy the rights prescribed in the African Charter'. The recommendation to Ghana to amend 'its national laws' and to bring 'them in line with the Charter' is so wide-ranging as to be meaningless. The Namibian government is urged to 'continue cultivating a culture of respect for human rights in order to reduce tension in the conflict areas and among the vulnerable groups'. In similar vein, Ghana should 'continue working closely with NGO's'. If a certain trend is required to continue, there must be clarity about the starting point and some benchmarks to move towards. None of these are clearly indicated in the Commission's observations in these cases.

Given these constraints, it is perhaps not surprising that no study similar to the Louw study, discussed above, has been conducted in respect of the Commission's concluding observations. From the Commission's own practice and from the concluding observations at my disposal, it appears that the Commission has articulated numerous instances of both *implementation* (under the heading 'positive factors') and *non-implementation* (under the headings 'areas of concern' and 'recommendations') with aspects of states' treaty obligations. In the first report submitted by the DRC,[52] for example, the Commission identified the success of the peace process, which has culminated in the establishment of a transitional government, 'thereby creating an environment under which the rights under the Charter may be protected for the entire territory of the DRC', and noted 'with appreciation that the DRC has already made serious efforts to put in place legislation for the protection of human rights in line with her obligations under Article 1 of the Charter'.

The Commission's practice is much less informative when it concerns assessment of *compliance* by states with specific recommendations contained in concluding observations. The obvious opportunity for the Commission to assess such compliance is when it examines a state's subsequent report. However, the lack of an official record of the examination of state reports makes nonsense of the notion that the state reporting process forms part of a continuing dialogue with states, and thus for providing an opportunity to assess compliance. Some states noted this when they submitted second or subsequent reports. Initially, these reports were treated as if they were initial reports, with no reference to the prior reporting exercise. In treating subsequent reports as *de novo* submissions rather than as part of a continuous dialogue with the Commission, the

49 Adopted at the Commission's 34th Ordinary Session held in Banjul, Gambia, 6–20 November 2003.

50 Adopted at the Commission's 38th session, 21 November–5 December 2005.

51 Presented to the 39th Ordinary Session African Commission, held in Banjul, Gambia, 11–25 May 2005.

52 Report consolidating its initial to seventh reports, examined at the Commission's 34th Ordinary Session held in Banjul, Gambia, 6–20 November 2003.

opportunity to challenge states about their compliance with previously issued recommendations is not grasped.

Any possibility of assessing compliance is also excluded when states do not report at all, or if they do not submit subsequent reports. Unfortunately, many states fall into this category.[53] When states do not report at all, or submit reports but fail to send a delegation to present the report, the Commission is also deprived of an opportunity to examine the report in the presence of government representatives. Although the Commission has adopted resolutions criticizing these states, it has only once scheduled an examination of a country situation in the absence of a report, namely in respect of the Seychelles. This state party has for many years failed to send a representative to formally present its report, first scheduled to take place in 2004. Eventually, in 2006, the Commission proceeded to examine the report in the absence of a government delegation.[54]

3.3 Recommendations in Resolutions

Article 45(1)(a) of the African Charter, which mandates the African Commission to give its views or make recommendations to governments, provides the legal basis of the Commission's competence to adopt resolutions. Although they are not, as such, binding, they have a strong persuasive value, and may provide evidence to establish the existence or emergence of a rule of customary international law.[55] Under this mandate, the Commission adopts procedural, thematic and country-specific resolutions. These three categories of resolutions will now be taken under review. As will transpire, however, the delineating lines are not always fixed. When it comes to the assessment of compliance, the nature of the resolution does not determine the action required. Irrespective of the categorization of the resolution, the specific recommendations therein should be analysed to determine what state obligation it entails.

Procedural (or operational) resolutions mainly order the internal affairs of the Commission, and regulate the interaction of states and human rights institutions with the Commission. Examples of procedural or operational resolutions include the Resolution on the Protection of Human Rights Defenders in Africa;[56] the Resolution on the Designation of the Special Rapporteur on the Rights of Women in Africa;[57] the Resolution on the Extension of the Mandate of the Special Rapporteur on Prison and Condition of Detention in Africa;[58] and the Resolution on the Mandate of the Special Rapporteur on Refugees, Asylum Seekers and Internally Displaced Persons in Africa.[59] As these resolutions are directed at the Commission itself, rather than state parties, they fall outside the

---

53 As at March 2008, 16 states have not submitted any reports; and 16 states have submitted only one report [online]. Available from: www.achpr.org.

54 Concluding Observations of the African Commission on the Initial Report of the Republic of Seychelles, adopted at its 39th ordinary session. Steps should be taken if a state fails to report. An examination of the country should be scheduled in the persistent absence of a report. It is suggested that on-site investigations (country visits or missions) be undertaken to implement recommendations for such states, with the specific mandate to follow up recommendations made after examination of state reports.

55 *The Legality of the Threat or Use of Nuclear Weapons*, 1996 ICJ Reports, 226.

56 ACHPR Res. 69 (XXXV) 04.

57 ACHPR/Res. 38 (XXV) 99, adopted on 5 May 1999 at the Commission's 25th Ordinary Session held in Bujumbura, Burundi, 26 April–5 May 1999.

58 ACHPR/Res. 37 (XXV) 99 adopted at the African Commission's 25th Ordinary Session held in Bujumbura, Burundi, 26 April–5 May 1999.

59 ACHPR/Res. 72 (XXXVI) 04, adopted at the African Commission's 36th Ordinary Session held in Dakar, Senegal, 23 November–7 December 2004.

scope of the present enquiry. (That does not mean that it is not of interest whether the Commission itself does what it requires itself to do.)

Some resolutions have both a procedural and substantive element, and are sometimes directed at both the Commission and state parties. The Resolution on Implementation falls into this group. None of the subsequent activity reports contain any details of compliance by states. If one accepts that no state has provided any such information, it is clear that they have not complied with this 'procedural' resolution. However, non-compliance with the resolution can also be ascribed to the failure of the Commission to undertake a systematic follow-up of the resolution – for example, by assigning a member of the Secretariat to monitor compliance, by establishing a follow-up unit in the Secretariat, or by using other mechanisms to take action against states or remind them of their obligations.

The focus falls on the other two categories of resolutions. Again, there are no available data, research studies or indications in the Commission's practice to assist one in tracking compliance with these recommendations.

Thematic resolutions deal with pervasive human rights problems affecting most countries on the continent. The majority of the Commission's resolutions fall into this category. These resolutions often elaborate in greater detail upon the substantive rights mentioned in the Charter, playing a role similar to that of 'general comments' adopted by UN human rights treaty bodies. They provide more clarity to states about the content of the legislative and policy measures that they should adopt to give effect to the African Charter. Examples of key thematic resolutions include the Declaration of Principles on Freedom of Expression in Africa (2002); the Resolution on Guidelines and Measures for the Prohibition and Prevention of Torture, Cruel, Inhuman or Degrading Treatment or Punishment in Africa (2002) (Robben Island Guidelines); and the Principles and Guidelines on the Right to a Fair Trail and Legal Assistance in Africa (2003).[60] Assessing compliance with these resolutions is rendered difficult by their very comprehensive scope and content. Other thematic resolutions, such as the Commission's resolution urging states to envisage a moratorium on the death penalty,[61] the Resolution on the HIV/AIDS Pandemic,[62] and the Resolution on Ending Impunity in Africa,[63] are narrower in scope, and the obligations on states more precise. It would be possible to ascertain whether a state has complied with these recommendations, even if the requirement for action was not directed at a specific state, but at all state parties to the Charter.

Country-specific resolutions have been adopted in respect of numerous state parties, including Algeria, Burundi, Comoros, Côte d'Ivoire, DRC, Eritrea, Ethiopia, Gambia, Guinea-Bissau, Liberia, Niger, Nigeria, Rwanda, Somalia, Sudan, Togo, Tunisia, Uganda and Zimbabwe. Resolutions directed

60 ACHPR/Res. 61 (XXXII) 02, adopted at the Commission's 32nd Ordinary Session held in Banjul, Gambia, 17–23 October 2002.

61 ACHPR/Res. 42 (XXVI) 99, adopted on 15 November 1999 at the 26th Ordinary Session held 1–15 November 1999 in Kigali, Rwanda.

62 ACHPR/Res. 53(XXIX)01: Resolution on HIV/AIDS Pandemic – Threat Against Human Rights and Humanity (2001), para. 2, calling on state parties 'to allocate national resources that reflect a determination to fight the spread of HIV/AIDS, ensure human rights protection of those living with HIV/AIDS against discrimination, provide support to families for the care of those dying of AIDS, devise public health care programmes of education and carry out public awareness especially in view of free and voluntary HIV testing, as well as appropriate medical interventions'.

63 ACHPR/Res. 87(XXXVIII)05: Resolution on Ending Impunity in Africa and on the Domestication and Implementation of the Rome Statute of the International Criminal Court, e.g. para. 2: the Commission urges AU member states 'that have not yet done so to ratify the Rome Statute and to adopt a national action plan for the effective implementation of the Rome Statute at the national level'.

at particular states in which pertinent human rights violations are addressed may serve a quasi-protective function, especially in the absence of individual communications against those states.

Country-specific resolutions have also been used as a vehicle to encourage compliance with decisions. In response to Eritrea's failure to implement the finding in the *Eritrean Detention* case,[64] the Commission condemned the continued detention of the victims and called on the government to 'immediately free' the victims, who 'have been arrested and detained without trial for many years'.[65] In this resolution, the Commission makes it clear that non-compliance with its finding and recommendations constitutes a breach of the state's obligations under the African Charter and the AU Constitutive Act.

As is the case in respect of other categories of resolutions, the ease of assessing compliance depends on the extent of their precision. Some country-specific resolutions are so imprecise that they are almost meaningless. In 2004, after ethnic violence erupted in northern Nigeria, the Commission, for example, called on the Nigerian government to bring the perpetrators of 'any human rights violation' to justice and to ensure 'full compliance with the provisions of the African Charter on Human and Peoples' Rights and other international human rights instruments'.[66] Other resolutions are much more specific; such as the Commission's call, in its resolution on the human rights situation in Gambia, for the 'immediate and unconditional release of Chief Ebrima Manneh and Kanyie Kanyiba and all prisoners of conscience',[67] and to 'immediately and fully comply with the 5th June 2008 judgement of the ECOWAS Community Court of Justice in respect of the release of Chief Ebrima Manneh from unlawful detention and pay the damages awarded by the Court'.[68]

States have increasingly contested the content of country-specific resolutions, contending that these resolutions sometimes amount to findings of violations in individual cases. Arguably, when the Commission calls on states to 'stop' violations, its premise is evidently that the states have actually been committing these violations. On this basis, states sometimes justify non-compliance. The greater engagement of states demonstrates better awareness on the part of states of the activities of the Commission, but also highlights the uneasy relationship between states and the NGO community, and the sensitivity of states to criticism of their human rights record.[69] In addition, these debates also sharpened the Commission's insight into the importance of accurate fact-finding.[70]

Uganda's reaction to a resolution dealing with the atrocities of the Lord's Resistance Army (LRA) in northern Uganda, adopted at the Commission's 38th session, provides an illustration of a state's ambiguity about country-specific resolutions. In this resolution, the Commission called upon

---

64 Communication 250/2002, *Zegveld and Another* v *Eritrea*, 17th Annual Activity Report (2003) AHRLR 85 (ACHPR 2003).

65 Resolution on the Human Rights Situation in Eritrea, adopted at the Commission's 38th session, 21 November–5 December 2005, paras. 1 and 4.

66 ACHPR/Res. 70(XXXV)04: Resolution on Nigeria (2004).

67 ACHPR/Res. 134 (XXXXIIII) 08: Resolution on the Human Rights Situation in the Republic of the Gambia.

68 *Ibid.*

69 Inspired by the 'brave new world' of human rights under the AU, the Commission at its 38th session adopted 17 resolutions, only to be faced with a backlash of resistance by states.

70 Report of the Brain-Storming Meeting on the African Commission, 9–10 May 2006, Banjul, Gambia (Brain-Storming Meeting), para. 58(b) (NGOs should provide accurate information in their draft resolutions and the Commission should set up a verification mechanism).

the LRA to free women and children and to demobilize its combatants.[71] Directing itself directly to the state, the Commission called on Uganda to guarantee the independence of the judiciary and to amend laws that allow civilians to be tried before military courts. When given the opportunity to comment on this resolution at the time its publication was being withheld as part of the 19th Activity Report, the Ugandan government denied that it had ever threatened the independence of the judiciary, while at the same time advising the Commission about a constitutional challenge to civilian trials before military courts and an ongoing process of law reform.[72] It finally requested that parts of the resolution 'not based on facts' be 'expunged' and assured the Commission of its willingness to continue a 'constructive dialogue'.[73]

On the same occasion, country-specific resolutions were also adopted on Eritrea, Ethiopia, Sudan and Zimbabwe. With the exception of Eritrea, which did not respond at all, the other three states took issue with various aspects of these resolutions.

In response to a resolution deploring the killing of civilians 'during confrontations with security forces' and requesting the release of arbitrarily detained political prisoners, Ethiopia argued that the 'ill-conceived' resolution should be excluded from the activity report.[74] The government expressed the view that the resolution did not take into account 'the environment in which Ethiopia's freest and most democratic election has taken place'. Although it concedes that 35 civilians were killed, the government blamed their deaths on action instigated by the opposition, the Coalition for Unity and Democracy (CUD).[75] Replying to the issue of arbitrary detention, the government further provided details of the applicable legal framework and of ongoing trials. As for the Commission's procedures, the government identified similarities between the Commission's resolution and that adopted by the NGO workshop prior to the session as an indication that the Commission had adopted the NGO proposal without 'further scrutiny and assessment'.[76]

Invoking grounds similar to those raised by Ethiopia, Zimbabwe called for the exclusion from the Commission's activity report of the resolution on Zimbabwe.[77] The government criticized the Commission for relying on a draft resolution submitted by Amnesty International, and for pre-judging the 13 communications against Zimbabwe pending before the Commission. It proposed that the Commission amend its procedure of adopting resolutions by allowing 'equity and fair play during the exercise of the right response in the public sessions'.[78] This last suggestion is valid, and should lead to a 'verification' process; however, it should not be used as a mechanism to delay the publication of resolutions. It is essential that the Commission is not intimidated and does not revert to a situation in which it adopts resolutions but withholds them from the public eye until such time that their content no longer matters.

71 'Resolution on the Human Rights Situation in Uganda', adopted on 5 December 2005, 20th Activity Report, Annex III.

72 Executive Summary of Uganda's Response to the African Commission Resolution on the Human Rights Situation in Uganda, Presented at the 39th Session of the African Commission, Banjul, Gambia, 18 May 2006, 20th Activity Report, Annex III, paras. 6–8.

73 *Ibid.*, 'prayer'.

74 Submission by Ethiopia in accordance with Resolution EX/CL/Dec.257(VIII) concerning the 16th Activities Report (*sic*) of the African Commission, 20th Activity Report, Annex III (Ethiopian Submission), para. 11.

75 *Ibid.*, para. 5.

76 *Ibid.*, para. 2.3.

77 Response of Zimbabwe to the Resolution of the African Commission adopted during its 38th session, 20th Activity Report, Annex III (Zimbabwean Response).

78 Zimbabwean Response, note 45 above, para. 4.2.

Illustrating how the resolutions of the Commission may play a role at the national level, an opposition member of parliament tabled a motion commending the Commission for its adoption of the resolution on Zimbabwe.[79] This action not only provoked a debate in parliament, but also led to publicity being given to the Commission's work in the targeted country.

3.4 Other Recommendations

The competence of the African Commission to undertake on-site protective missions is found in Article 46 of the African Charter, while Article 45 provides it with the competence to undertake promotional missions and establish special mechanisms. Recommendations to states are contained in the reports of each of these missions and mechanisms.

Although most of these reports are not included in the Commission's activity reports, they are better disseminated than concluding observations and nowadays appear regularly on the Commission's website. Tracking the status of compliance of these recommendations would be an arduous task, because they are mostly articulated in extensive and wide-ranging terms. As is the case with the Commission's other recommendations, little systematic information is available about state compliance with these recommendations. No follow-up procedure has been put in place. Reference is here made, rather eclectically, to a few examples in this category of recommendations.

Promotional visits provide an opportunity to follow up or reinforce recommendations to states. As part of the 2004 promotional visit to Sierra Leone, the Commission, for example, took up the issue of the country's failure to report. In its report of the mission, the Commission recommended that effect be given to the promise 'by the authorities, including, His Excellency, the Vice-President, Mr. Solomon Berewa, the Government of the Republic of Sierra Leone' to speed up 'its internal processes to draft and submit the Republic's Initial State Report'.[80] However, to date, Sierra Leone has not yet submitted a report. The Commission also called on the government of Sierra Leone to 'act upon its de facto moratorium on the application of death penalty by legally abolishing the punishment'.[81] Sierra Leone has not yet complied with this recommendation. The Commission's related thematic resolution has, however, been used as part of ongoing civil society efforts in favour of abolition.[82]

As part of its promotional visit to Mauritania,[83] the Commission called on the government to improve the conditions of detention and to invite the Special Rapporteur on Prisons and Conditions of Detention in Africa to visit the country. However, to date, no visit of the special rapporteur has taken place to Mauritania.

---

79 L. Guma, 'War of Words in Parliament over African Commission Report', 14 February 2006 [online]. Available from: www.swradioafrica.com, [accessed 27 February 2006].

80 Draft Report of the Promotional Mission to the Republic of Sierra Leone, 23-29 February 2004, Commissioner E.V.O. Dankwa.

81 *Ibid.*

82 Amnesty International, Sierra Leone: President Koroma must commute the sentences of all death-row prisoners, 27 April 2009 [online]. Available from: www.amnesty.org: 'Sierra Leone is a state party to the African Charter on Human and Peoples' Rights. In November 2008, the African Commission on Human and Peoples' Rights at its 44th Ordinary Session in Abuja, Nigeria, adopted a resolution calling on state parties to the African Charter on Human and Peoples' Rights to observe a moratorium on the death penalty.'

83 Projet de rapport de mission de promotion du commissaire Yasir sid Ahmad el Hassan, Vice-président de la Commission africaine des droits de l'homme et des peuples, en République Islamique de Mauritanie (3–7 octobre 2004).

Promotional visits also provide an opportunity to address recommendations on issues encountered on the ground during such a visit. In respect of the Seychelles,[84] for example, the Commission's delegation recommended that an independent electoral Commission comprised of several persons, rather than a single person serving as an electoral Commissioner, be established. The Commission further requested that the state makes a copy of the initial report under the Charter available to the opposition parties and other interest groups. It is not clear whether these recommendations were complied with.

The Special Rapporteur on Women in Africa has adopted numerous reports after visits to countries.[85] The accompanying recommendations cover a broad array of topics, sometimes extending beyond the scope of the Rapporteur's mandate. She, for example, recommended that Sudan take steps towards the abolition of death penalty, 'given that it has not been enforced in the country for a long time'. Among the pointed and topical recommendations in the same report are the following: the elimination of 'the discriminatory practice compelling women to present the authorization of their husband before travelling abroad'; a change to the law that would 'ensure equal and indiscriminate access of men and women to employment'; and the encouragement and financial assistance to NGOs 'working in the field of the fight against FGM [female genital mutilation]'. In another recommendation, the Rapporteur encouraged the Sudanese government to establish a system to follow up the programmes put in place, in collaboration with NGOs and other civil society organizations. Perhaps this may be criticized as hypocritical in requiring a domestic standard that the Commission itself has not been able to meet. In any event, in the absence of any follow-up or assessment of compliance, the status of compliance with these recommendations remains a matter of speculation.

4. Conclusion

In the more than 22 years of its existence, the African Commission has directed numerous recommendations to states. These recommendations may be grouped into those adopted after the finalization of communications (forming part of the Commission's protective mandate); those adopted after the examination of state reports (as part of concluding observations); those forming part of thematic and country-specific resolutions; and recommendations issued in mission report of Commissioners or the Commission's special mechanisms. Even if recommendations in these different categories pose broadly similar concerns, it is not so much the identification of a recommendation with one of the categories, but rather the precision and expectation created by the resolution that has a major effect on the likelihood of establishing compliance. Other factors, such as the nature of the required state action (or remedy) and the perceived level of threat that compliance with the recommendation poses to state sovereignty, will also affect compliance.

With the exception of some research pertaining to recommendations emanating from its protective mandate, the available information on state compliance with the Commission's recommendations is scanty. Although there are many methodological difficulties in the way of reliably assessing state compliance with these recommendations, efforts should be increased to track the actual 'observance' by states. Such information will not only serve to enhance states'

84 Report of the Promotional Mission to the Seychelles, July 2004, Doc. ACHPR/37/OS/11/432/Draft.

85 Promotional mission report of Commissioner Angela Melo, Special Rapporteur on the Rights of Women in Africa in the Republic of the Sudan (30 March–4 April 2003), Doc. ACHPR/37/OS/11/443/Draft.

accountability, but will also advance debates about the significance and role of international human rights law.

As far as a picture does emerge, it is one of very limited state compliance. As much as this state of affairs may be ascribed to the unwillingness of states, the African Commission itself should also shoulder part of the blame. By not giving effect to its Resolution on Implementation, an opportunity has been missed both to obtain more accurate data and exert additional pressure on states.

The rather spectacular lack of follow-up under the African Commission further highlights the potential benefits of a future African Human Rights Court. However, it may be overly optimistic to anticipate that the advent of the African Human Rights Court would necessarily improve the position. It is correct that the Court's judgements will be binding,[86] that state parties will guarantee the 'execution' of judgements,[87] and that a formal process of follow-up involving the AU Executive Council is prescribed.[88] However, these formally legal changes still have to elicit political will. In addition, the proposed procedure for referral of cases to the Court reinforces the importance for improvement in the Commission's competence to establish compliance with its recommendations in findings on complaints.

While this chapter has focused on compliance by states, it should be firmly kept in mind that many other role players – including national and international civil society organizations; national and international media; and the AU organs, such as the Assembly, the executive council, the Pan-African Parliament, and the African Commission itself – have important roles to play in ensuring improved compliance. To this list should be added the community of scholars working in and on human rights in Africa. In essence, scholarly debate about compliance within the African regional human rights system is an attempt to fill the void left due to the failure of the African Commission and the other AU organs to establish a record about or to provide for a system to monitor compliance with the Commission's recommendations. There is an obvious need for the Commission to take responsibility for monitoring compliance of its recommendations.

The goal of the UDHR that states should actually observe the rights of all, in the form of national remedies that provide concrete benefits and real improvements in people's lives, will remain a distant ideal if the concerns raised in this chapter are not addressed. Compliance with recommendations of a regional body such as the African Commission is a small but important part of realizing the promise of the UDHR.

---

86 Protocol to the African Charter on the Establishment of the African Human Rights Court, Art. 28(2).

87 *Ibid.*, Art. 30.

88 *Ibid.*, Art. 29.

Chapter 23
Individual Responsibility and the Evolving Legal Status of the Physical Person in International Human Rights Law

Ilias Bantekas

1. Introduction

Since the adoption of the UDHR[1] in 1948 it has become clear over the years that state responsibility for human rights violations ought to be complemented by perpetrators' individual responsibility under criminal and civil law. This chapter focuses on the concept of individual responsibility, according to which the 'natural' corollary of a human rights violation is the criminal liability of the perpetrator, not under domestic law, but under international law. We shall examine to what degree this concept is applicable to all violations of human rights, and not simply in respect to some of them. This involves an examination of the legal basis of human rights violations – as these are contained in human rights treaties – in order to assess whether they can substantiate a degree of criminal liability. In the opinion of this author, the concept of individual responsibility is inextricably linked to the evolving nature of the status of the physical person in international law. International human rights law has played a prominent role in this regard, particularly through the establishment of individual complaint mechanisms and the granting of *locus standi* to aggrieved persons. Another theme examined is the employment of extraterritorial jurisdiction by the family of nations in order to give meaning to the existence of criminal liability; promulgating offences and establishing criminal liability, but without any efforts to prosecute the accused gradually weakens the argument in favour of individual responsibility as a matter of acquiescence.

2. The Concept of Individual Responsibility and Relevance of 'Space'

In contemporary international relations it may seem natural, and without serious challenge, that persons accused of serious violations of human rights or humanitarian law should be held criminally accountable for their actions. Indeed, to the layman, international criminal justice is no other than a natural extension of domestic criminal justice to the international arena. In reality, none of these assumptions are natural or granted. In fact, if one tries to separate the 'national' from the 'international', this will turn out to be an impossible exercise, for the sole reason that the only truly international spaces are located in the seabed beneath the high seas, the high seas themselves, and outer space. Apart from piracy *jure gentium*, relatively few battles are waged on the high seas by sovereign armies, thus leaving few truly international offences, in terms of spatial characteristics at least. In this respect, the only natural line of reasoning suggests that, in fact, the concept of

1 GA Res. 217A (III), UN Doc. A/810 at 71 (1948).

international crime is a matter of fiction and that in reality crimes, even of a large magnitude, are domestic – except of course for inter-state armed conflicts, or incursions by elements of one state into the territory of another.

This line of reasoning, however, only defines the territoriality of crime (the *locus delicti commissi*), but tells us nothing about the other contours of criminal activity, such as its impact on the population of the target state, or that of other states and their governments, the threat to international peace and security, its possible financial cost, and other factors. These elements serve to internationalize both our interest in what are otherwise domestic crimes, but they moreover tend to internationalize, in fact, the crimes themselves. Accordingly, since space is an integral part of sovereignty, its potential irrelevance in favour of other contours necessarily signals also the erosion of sovereignty in the field of criminal justice. This type of erosion is only of recent vintage and its legal and political nature will occupy us throughout this chapter. Given that nations hold on to all elements of their sovereignty with vigour, if criminal justice is to be internationalized it will not become so without a struggle from the forces that keep it from this condition.

The concept of individual criminal responsibility in international law essentially entails that he who has committed an international crime bears not only domestic criminal responsibility, but also, and moreover, international criminal responsibility. There are two distinct, but interwoven, elements applicable to this concept. The first is that the accused is liable under the definition of the crime as this is found in international law and not in accordance with that crime's definition in domestic law. For example, the act of beating prisoners in order to attain a confession may merely constitute a minor assault in the country where the offence took place, but because this act constitutes the international offence of torture, the domestic definition is irrelevant. The criminal liability of the accused will thus be measured in accordance with the definition of the offence under international law.[2] The second element of the concept of individual responsibility relates to jurisdiction. Jurisdiction in this context refers to the power of a state or an inter-state institution (such as an international tribunal) to prescribe and enforce its laws or statutes vis-à-vis natural persons. Hence, even if the torturer in our previous example is liable under international, rather than national, law, we still need to determine a forum in which he or she may be prosecuted. The fact that a person accused of an international crime is prosecuted before a domestic criminal court does not render the offence itself less 'international' than had the case been referred to an international criminal tribunal. Jurisdiction for international crimes has become very complex in the last two decades, particularly with the rise of ad hoc tribunals, some with wide-ranging and others with limited powers; a permanent international criminal court that shares complementary, yet secondary, jurisdiction with its member states; internationalized domestic tribunals; and an interest from some states to enforce universal jurisdiction. In any event, none of the international crimes prosecuted in these tribunals or national courts have been described as a domestic offence.

2 A state's international obligations, whether these have been assumed through treaty or custom, supersede any other obligation assumed under domestic law. In fact, a state cannot invoke its domestic law in order to avoid compliance with an international obligation (see the Vienna Convention on the Law of Treaties, 1155 UNTS 331, 8 ILM 679, entered into force 27 January 1980, Art. 27). For this reason, obligations assumed under international human rights or other treaties, supersede the definition of the same behaviour in that country's internal legislation.

3. International Legal Personality Versus Sovereignty

In the previous section we determined in what ways an otherwise domestic crime may become internationalized, other than by its spatial characteristics. It was also pointed out that when an offence is also defined under international law, it is that definition which supersedes all its domestic counterparts in terms of normative superiority. The two aforementioned elements of individual responsibility, however, are without meaning if the legal status of the physical person is not such that allows him or her to be physically prosecuted under international law. The answer to this question turns on the amount of legal personality granted to physical persons. Legal personality itself means being granted rights and duties under a particular legal system and subsequently possessing the power to enforce one's rights or have one's obligations enforced against oneself. Human, or other, rights prescribed under constitutional or statutory instruments in any domestic legal system provide the right holder with a legitimate entitlement and a capacity to enforce such rights before the full gamut of that country's national courts. The same is true in respect of obligations, and a person will be prosecuted if he fails to fulfil his military duty where he is obliged to do so, or where a person commits an offence prescribed by that country's criminal laws. Domestic legal personality, that is, the granting of rights and duties, is not the same for all the citizens within a given state. Workers in a particular industry will benefit from privileges that are not enjoyed by the entire national workforce, certain persons will be exempt from paying taxes or from being enlisted in the armed forces, and minors as well as the mentally handicapped will not be allowed to exercise the full range of the contractual freedoms that are generally open to those above a certain age or of sound mind.

Legal personality exists also in the international legal system, but is differentiated by the fact that, unlike the vertical power structures of domestic legal systems, its formulation takes place within a largely horizontal power structure.[3] Apart from the binding authority of the UN Security Council, international rules are borne by the consensus of interested nations and are not unilaterally imposed. The entities with 'primary' international legal personality are states, followed by international organizations and lastly by physical persons (and to some degree by constructions or extensions of physical persons, such as non-governmental organizations (NGOs) and multinational corporations). It is only natural that the rights and duties granted upon physical persons in the international legal system are granted by states and to a lesser degree by international organizations. Individuals, or associations of individuals, cannot confer on themselves rights or duties under international law, since this would require the conclusion of a treaty or a customary rule,[4] which is the exclusive domain of states. States have reluctantly been conferring rights and duties on individuals in the international legal system since at least the middle of the nineteenth century, albeit to a very limited degree and in a very selective manner. Piracy *jure gentium* was the primary hallmark, followed by war crimes committed in international armed conflicts, and then only as a matter of entitlement for the winning belligerent power. Although there was no doubt that the consistent practice of states in the field of piracy *jure gentium* gave rise to an international crime and international criminal liability, this was not the case with war crimes. For one thing, piracy *jure gentium* took place on the high seas (i.e. an international space), whereas war crimes

3 See, generally, R. Higgins, *Problems and Process: International Law and How We Use It* (Oxford: Oxford University Press, 1994), pp. 48–55.

4 Exceptionally, physical persons can actively contribute to the formation of particular commercial customary rules if the customary practice of a particular industry is codified in statute, treaty or in the practice of at least two states. See I. Bantekas, 'The Private Dimension of the International Customary Nature of Commercial Arbitration', *Journal of International Arbitration*, 25 (2008), pp. 449–61.

took place within national boundaries. In a time of constant inter-state armed conflicts, states were thus keen not to render war criminals generally subject to international law, but only exceptionally. The objective, of course, was to avoid creating a general rule of liability, which could later be used to prosecute one's own military or civilian personnel before an international or domestic tribunal. In this state of affairs, the physical person was an entity inextricably linked to the legal person of the state, in the same manner as the state's ships, land and immovable property. Every act of the individual was attributable to the state, and he or she had no separate or distinct identity in the international legal sphere.

This position is well reflected in the early treaties addressing humanitarian concerns that were concluded in two rounds at The Hague, in 1899 and 1907, as well as in the views of the victorious delegates following the end of World War I and the setting up of a commission in 1919 to assess whether those who committed crimes during the war were liable under international law and should be punished by an international tribunal.[5] The Hague Peace Conferences of 1899 and 1907 culminated in the adoption of a substantial number of conventions regulating, *inter alia*, military conduct in land and sea warfare. Despite the detailing of prohibitions and acceptable practices, especially in the 1907 Hague Convention IV[6] and the Regulations annexed thereto, no sanctions were expressly prescribed.[7] A number of international agreements enacted in the next two decades failed to circumscribe appropriate penal mechanisms. Instead, they obliged states parties to pass implementing criminal legislation,[8] some promulgated new prohibitions,[9] and, in one case, reference was made to a limited personal liability through the means of universal jurisdiction.[10] The common understanding of the international community at the time with respect to these general conventions was that the obligations addressed therein were addressed to states at the international level, with a subsequent obligation to transpose the criminal aspects of these provisions at the domestic level. This is not apparent in the text of the conventions themselves! Thus, the prohibition of denying quarter in the 1907 Hague Regulations effectively meant that if quarter was denied to an enemy combatant (i.e. an enemy combatant's surrender was not accepted by the capturing entity), liability befell the capturing state under international law and not the individual(s) that committed the offence. This responsibility is obviously one of the state and not a criminal one. The responsibility of the state to criminalize all conduct prohibited in these conventions and punish the perpetrators at the domestic level must have been presumed as part of the signatories' general

5 G. Manner, 'The Legal Nature and Punishment of Criminal Acts of Violence Contrary to the Laws of War', *American Journal of International Law*, 37 (1943), pp. 407–35, at p. 414. Manner noted that the US delegates to the 1919 commission argued that the applicable law with regard to suspected German war criminals was the military legislation of the country against whose nationals the violations were committed. This view, according to the USA and Japan, was justified in the absence of an international penal law upon which a criminal indictment of offenders against the rules of warfare could be predicated.

6 1907 Convention Respecting the Laws and Customs of War on Land, 1 *Bevans* 631.

7 The 1906 Convention for the Amelioration of the Condition of the Wounded and Sick in Armies in the Field provided for the repression of the convention's infractions and abuses regarding the Red Cross emblem in the form of injunctions in order that member states adopt appropriate legislation. 2 (3rd) *Martens NRTG* 620.

8 Art. 29, 1929 Geneva Convention for the Amelioration of the Condition of the Wounded and Sick in Armies in the Field, 118 LNTS 303.

9 1925 Protocol for the Prohibition of the Use in War of Asphyxiating, Poisonous or Other Gases, and of Bacteriological Methods of Warfare, 94 LNTS 65.

10 Art. 3, 1922 Washington Treaty Relating to the Use of Submarines and Noxious Gases in Warfare, 25 LNTS 202. This provision assimilated every unlawful destruction of merchant vessels to acts of piracy *jure gentium*. The convention never entered into force.

obligations under the terms of the convention. It is clear, however, that the criminal elements of the prohibited conduct were reserved only for the domestic legal orders.[11]

Exceptionally, and despite the absence of direct criminal provisions in any international *jus in bello* convention, and the reluctance of the Allies to establish a tribunal throughout and shortly after World War I, a significant number of war crimes trials were conducted by French, Russian, British and US military tribunals against captured German combatants.[12] Moreover, the 1920 Peace Treaty of Sèvres, which made provision for the trial of those Turkish officials responsible for violating the laws and customs of war and of engaging in the Armenian massacres during their 1915 campaign of annihilation,[13] was superseded by the 1923 Treaty of Lausanne, which contained a declaration of amnesty for all offences committed in 1914–22.[14] The granting of an amnesty, however, can only mean that criminal liability at the international level must have somehow existed. Following the Armenian genocide, the governments of Great Britain, France and Russia had issued a declaration denouncing the atrocities as 'crimes against humanity and civilization', further noting the criminal culpability of all members of the Turkish government and its agents.[15] Similar pronouncements of a criminal nature at the international level were introduced in other specialized treaties, particularly Articles 228–30 of the Treaty of Versailles of 28 June 1919,[16] Article 173 of the Treaty of St. Germain of 10 September 1919,[17] and Article 157 of the Treaty of Trianon of 4 June 1920.[18] These agreements recognized the personal liability of offenders and the right of the allies to try them before military tribunals.[19]

It is thus obvious that despite the shared understanding of the then international community regarding the lack of individual criminal responsibility for violations of humanitarian law, there was room for some exceptions. These were victor's justice exceptions and were by no means presumed to form, let alone crystallize, a new rule of international law. However, as we shall see in the following section, once one allows some exceptions and allows the floodgates to open, it is a matter of time before there are demands that the exception become an entrenched rule. Under pressure from public opinion and the rapid flow of events, it inevitably becomes extremely difficult

11 This shared assumption by the then community of nations is confirmed by their practice and their general shielding of the individual in the international legal system, not only evinced in the field of international criminal law, but also in the field of diplomatic protection, among others. This proposition as to a shared understanding finds support in the 'interpretative communities' theory, which articulates the notion that, within an institutional setting, the various actors share common assumptions and beliefs (interpretative community), such that the meaning of a text is constrained by providing the assumptions and understanding relating to the practice at hand. See S. Fish, *Is There a Text in This Class? The Authority of Interpretative Communities* (Cambridge, MA: Harvard University Press, 1982); I. Johnstone, 'Security Council Deliberations: The Power of the Better Argument', *European Journal of International Law*, 14 (2003), pp. 437–80, at p. 444.

12 See T.L.H. McCormack and G.J. Simpson (eds), *The Law of War Crimes: National and International Approaches* (Leyden: Sijthoff, 1997), p. 44.

13 Arts 226, 230, Treaty of Peace Between the Allied Powers and Turkey (Treaty of Sèvres), *American Journal of International Law*, 15 (Suppl.) (1921), p. 179.

14 1923 Treaty of Peace Between the Allied Powers and Turkey (Treaty of Lausanne), 28 LNTS 12.

15 R. Clark, 'Crimes Against Humanity at Nuremberg', in G. Ginsburg and V.N. Kudriavtsev (eds), *The Nuremberg Trial in International Law* (Dordrecht: Martinus Nijhoff, 1990), p. 177.

16 TS. No. 4 (1919).

17 TS. No. 11 (1919).

18 TS. No. 10 (1920).

19 See 15 LRTWC 23; E. Colby, 'War Crimes', *Michigan Law Review*, 23 (1925), pp. 482ff, at pp. 496–7, argued that the agreement ending hostilities in the Boer War granted the right to prosecute enemy combatants who violated the laws of war.

to justify the maintenance of the exceptional rule. This was exactly the effect of the Nuremberg legacy.

4. The Nuremberg Legacy and the 'Rebirth' of Individual Responsibility

In the previous section we detected the gradual, yet expressly exceptional, erosions to an otherwise international system that saw no place for the physical person. This is not detrimental in itself and one should not make too much out of it, but instead one should strive to assess why and to what degree individual criminal responsibility is required at the international, rather than the national, level. Ideally, prosecutions for international crimes should take place in the country where the offence was committed, with the assistance of those other states that possess material evidence, witnesses or other co-accused. In this manner, local knowledge and familiarity with the terrain and the circumstances will aid prosecutorial efforts and the sovereignty of the *locus delicti commissi* will not be compromised. Moreover, from a logistical point of view, such a process will minimize expenses. We do not, however, live in an ideal world, and as a result a vital ingredient is usually lacking in the inter-relations of states; trust. The practice of states during the course of the twentieth century suggests that the prosecution of one's own nationals for serious violations of international human rights law, such as crimes against humanity, genocide or torture, leads to a perceived assimilation of the state, its people, and its government with the perpetrators.[20] This is not far off the mark, and the media and popular culture have contributed to this perception.

In yet other circumstances, as is the case with the USA, the prospect of international prosecution of its armed forces members is perceived as a disincentive for serving on US military missions abroad and is deemed an anathema.[21] Conversely, even a sophisticated democracy such as the USA, with a thorough and liberal legal system, falls prey to its own prejudices and refuses to grant fundamental human rights to persons captured in the course of the 'war on terror'.[22] It is thus obvious that prosecutions for international crimes before domestic courts have the potential to suffer from local biases where the perpetrators are nationals of the forum state. Given that the vast majority of human rights infringements, such as the rights to life, liberty of person, family life, etc., can only be committed by state actors (although increasingly non-state actors are also prominent violators), or by their connivance, it is no surprise that it is in the national interests of some states to deny justice to victims and to avoid recognizing the criminal liability of the perpetrators.

As a result of the inherent inadequacies of even the most sophisticated legal systems to deal with serious human rights violations that take place on their territory, it is necessary for the international legal system to remove some of these biases by taking the individual out of the domestic 'space'. In this manner, the behaviour may be adjudged independently of its setting, context and national sentiments, if any. However, in order to internationalize the domestic space, it is required that the domestic space be eroded by the consent of said interested state. This 'consent to erode' came about inadvertently in the immediate aftermath of World War II. The word 'inadvertently' is purposefully employed in order to illustrate the fact that while the victorious Allies intended to

20 See M. Byron-Hartwell, 'Perceptions of Justice, Identity and Political Processes of Forgiveness and Revenge in Early Post-Conflict Transitions' [online]. Available from: http://www.jha.ac/articles/a187.pdf.

21 See the American Service Members Protection Act (known also as the Hague Invasion Act), which provides authority to the US executive branch to use all necessary means to free US service members that may potentially be prosecuted before the International Criminal Court.

22 See UN Commission on Human Rights, Report on the Situation of Detainees at Guantánamo Bay, UN Doc. E/CN.4/2006/120 (15 February 2006).

prosecute only members of the Axis throughout the world, in order to do so they first had to unlock their aforementioned 'shared understanding' as to the lack of individual criminal responsibility in the 1907 Hague Conventions. Had the Allies decided to adhere to Winston Churchill's opinion of liquidating the Nazi civilian and military leadership without going through the process of a trial, the shared understanding need not have been unshackled at all, and Allied courts could have simply tried lower-ranking Axis officials on the basis of the territoriality principle, without invoking the liability of the physical person in international law. This was not to be, however, because the Allies had already issued a series of declarations from 1942 onwards by which they resolved to try the highest Axis officials before a court comprised of judges from Allied nations. More importantly, when the time finally arrived, in order to avoid unilateral interferences in the process, legality was seen as the best possible standard for the process. Legality dictated that, since the Nuremberg (otherwise known as the International Military Tribunal) tribunal was premised on a multilateral treaty,[23] the charges against the accused persons themselves must be predicated on international law, whether treaty or custom. The problem, of course, was that the shared understanding of the post-World War I era excluded personal liability in the international sphere, and this necessarily meant that if legality were to prevail, the accused persons would have had to be tried under domestic law, their liability thus being domestic in character.

The Nuremberg Tribunal was, therefore, forced by events to disregard the shared understanding, not as a matter of exception, however, but as a general rule, because the relevant provisions were enshrined in multilateral treaties, particularly the 1907 Hague Conventions, the 1928 Pact of Paris (Kellogg–Briand Pact),[24] and the 1929 Geneva Conventions. Thus, the Nuremberg Tribunal rejected the existence of only a state obligation in the Hague Conventions, famously declaring that crimes are committed by men and not abstract entities. This is where our contemporary story begins. The outcome of the Nuremberg process was that the humanitarian law treaties identified above, as well as customary international law, involved obligations at the international level that pertained to natural persons and that these, moreover, could be enforced against them. The absence of a permanent international criminal court meant that whereas international enforcement was exceptional, individual responsibility was no longer exceptional. The Nuremberg principles were soon after enshrined in a UN General Assembly resolution,[25] and clear references to criminal liability were contained in the four 1949 Geneva Conventions (on the basis of their grave breaches provisions)[26] and the 1948 Genocide Convention.[27] In fact, there is mention in the Genocide Convention of even the jurisdiction of an international criminal tribunal, a testament to the imminent expectations of its drafters.

The more poignant question for the purposes of this chapter is to what degree the enunciation of individual responsibility in the post-Nuremberg era has filtered into the various international

23 Charter of the International Military Tribunal, annexed to London Agreement for the Prosecution and Punishment of the Major War Criminals of the European Axis, 8 August 1945, 82 UNTS 280.

24 Treaty Providing for the Renunciation of War as an Instrument of National Policy, 46 Stat. 2343.

25 Affirmation of the Principles of International Law Recognized by the Charter of the Nürnberg Tribunal, GA Res. 95 (I), UN GAOR, 1st Sess., Pt. 2, at 1144, UN Doc. A/236 (1946).

26 Art. 50, Convention for the Amelioration of the Condition of the Wounded and Sick in Armed Forces in the Field (No. I), 75 UNTS 31; Art 51, Convention for the Amelioration of the Condition of the Wounded, Sick, and Shipwrecked Members of Armed Forces at Sea (No. II), 75 UNTS 85; Art. 130, Convention Relative to the Treatment of Prisoners of War (No. III), 75 UNTS 135; Art. 147, Convention Relative to the Protection of Civilian Persons in Time of War (No. IV), 75 UNTS 287.

27 1948 Convention on the Prevention and Punishment of the Crime of Genocide, 78 UNTS 277.

human rights treaties and if such responsibility can be read therein. This is the object of the next section.

5. Individual Responsibility in Contemporary Human Rights Treaties

For reasons of academic convenience, we have tended to distinguish between three international legal disciplines; human rights, laws of war (humanitarian law) and criminal law. None can truly exist without the others, and in this sense they complement the whole, which is the protection and welfare of the human being. A typical human rights convention will focus on the granting of rights, as well as the enforcement of such rights at both the domestic and the international level. On the other hand, a criminal law convention will seek ways to prohibit particular behaviour, criminalize it and oblige participating states not only to take sufficient measures to bring this about, but also to promise to cooperate among themselves. Criminalization (and punishment) is not an aim within itself,[28] but is a necessary ingredient for the primary aim, which is the protection of human beings. International criminal law is thus supposed to complement and promote the goals of international human rights law. Increasingly, the utility of punishment is being questioned, and other alternatives are proposed, such as the use of truth commissions, the granting of amnesties that seek to enhance national reconciliation, and other facets of restorative justice.[29]

From a positivist point of view, the existence or not of individual criminal responsibility in respect of particular prohibited behaviour will depend on whether the relevant treaty (or customary rule) sufficiently criminalizes said behaviour. This effectively means that human rights treaties, such as the International Covenant on Civil and Political Rights (ICCPR),[30] do not give rise to individual criminal responsibility, because they do not explicitly oblige member states to criminalize infractions against protected rights. One could well argue that a corollary of human rights protection in a number of cases is, in fact, direct criminalization, where absent. This is true and is well reflected in Article 2(2) of the ICCPR, according to which state parties are obligated 'to adopt such legislative or other measures as may be necessary to give effect to the rights recognized in the present Covenant'. Two things are evident from this provision. The first thing is that it is up to each signatory to decide whether criminalization is warranted in each case. State authorities may well determine that such a measure would not provide the best effect to a particular right. The absence, therefore, of a general and concrete obligation to criminalize may run contrary to the principle of legal certainty, although in recent years the boundaries of this principle have been widely construed in the sphere of international criminal law.[31] The second thing is that even if we were to take the view that the obligation contained in Article 2(2) suggests a concrete duty to criminalize, this is, in fact, limited to domestic criminal liability because member states are asked

28 C.M. Bassiouni, 'The Penal Characteristics of Conventional International Law', *Case Western Reserve Journal of International Law*, 15 (1983), pp. 27ff.

29 See E. Daly, 'Between Punitive and Reconstructive Justice: The Gacaca Courts in Rwanda', *New York University Journal of International Law and Politics*, 34 (2002), pp. 355–96; K. Asmal, 'International Law and Practice: Dealing with the Past and the South African Experience', *American University International Law Review*, 15 (2000), pp. 1211ff, at p. 1228.

30 999 UNTS 171.

31 See, generally, K.S. Gallant, *The Principle of Legality in International and Comparative Criminal Law* (Cambridge: Cambridge University Press, 2008); M. Shahabudeen, 'Does the Principle of Legality Stand in the Way of Progressive Development of Law?', *Journal of International Criminal Justice*, 2(4) (2004), pp. 1007–17.

to adopt legislative or other measures internally. The conclusion, therefore, is that human rights treaties *per se* do not provide a sufficient legal basis for individual criminal responsibility.

The fact that human rights treaties cannot be relied upon directly to substantiate the existence of a particular prohibition as an international crime, does not mean that such treaties cannot and have not aided local and international courts in the pursuit of that aim indirectly. Let us look at two particular rights, the right to life and the right to be free from torture and other cruel, inhuman or degrading treatment. The formulation and wording of the right to life in Article 6 of the ICCPR is clearly aimed at addressing violations caused by state agents, as was the primary concern when the covenant was being developed and formulated, although there is nothing in paragraph 1 that excludes protection against non-state actors. War crimes, crimes against humanity, and genocide (which result in death) deny the victims the right to life. The international criminal character of these human rights infractions is very well recognized in both treaty and customary law, as well as in the statutes of all contemporary international criminal tribunals. The definition of the right to life in the ICCPR can, however, be employed to support the case that not all takings of life are prohibited (such as the infliction of the death penalty under controlled circumstances), but cannot give anything else more substantial to an already well-entrenched international criminal prohibition. The prohibition of torture runs along the same lines, given the existence of regional and global treaties that criminalize the infliction of torture, thus rendering redundant any effort to extrapolate an indirect criminalization from the ICCPR or human rights law. However, in the *Furundzija* case before the International Criminal Tribunal for the former Yugoslavia (ICTY), the tribunal was unable to determine whether forced oral penetration was to be classified in international law as rape or merely as a form of sexual assault. The tribunal eventually relied on the inherent dignity of the human person, which the relevant provisions aim to protect, as clearly evident in the human rights treaties, in order to conclude that a classification of rape best served that purpose.[32]

The global and regional human rights treaties have done much more in the international criminalization process than serve as minute details of the criminal treaties. It was on the basis of the human rights treaties and standard setting that came about since the adoption of the UDHR that states began to slowly adopt criminal legislation in order to give effect to the recognized rights. Despite the significant reservations made by states during the passage of time, the definitions adopted in domestic legislation did not differ substantially in terms of the core offence, paving the way in the early 1990s for the ad hoc tribunals to declare the existence of a good number of general principles of national criminal laws, by virtue of their coherency and uniformity worldwide.[33]

Another important, yet indirect, contribution of the human rights treaties to the international criminalization process has been their enhancement of the international legal personality of natural persons. Although the relevant obligations are addressed to states, the recipients of the rights are granted *locus standi* to bring claims before both national courts and international judicial or quasi-judicial bodies. Although these bodies do not have the authority to investigate criminal offences or impose criminal sanctions, they give weight to the relevant entitlements by recognizing the recipients as having a right of equal value to the legal personality of the state. It would be hard to imagine the unprecedented emergence of individual criminal responsibility in the post-Cold-War era without the increased international legal personality granted to individuals through the human rights treaties.

---

32 *ICTY Prosecutor* v *Furundzija*, Trial Chamber Judgment (10 December 1998), 38 ILM (1999), 317, paras. 182ff.

33 See I. Bantekas, 'Reflections on Some Sources and Methods of International Criminal and Humanitarian Law', *International Criminal Law Review*, 6 (2006), pp. 121–36.

6. The Current Situation on Individual Responsibility

In the previous sections we demonstrated that individual criminal responsibility is not possible on the basis of human rights treaties. The legal basis for individual responsibility should, instead, be sought in the realm of custom as well as specialized criminal law treaties. Even until the early 1990s, it was not clear whether all treaties concerning the criminal aspects of prohibited behaviour established international crimes. Today, this issue is somewhat moot, given that even transnational crimes are essentially international offences, and, depending on the range of jurisdictional possibilities in a particular treaty, a transnational crime may well involve more than two countries. Three concerns had served to disillusion all those that promoted the cause of individual responsibility; the prevalence of immunity claims, the lack of jurisdictional avenues and prosecutorial vigour, and, finally, claims of domestic jurisdiction where human rights violations had taken place solely within the territory of a single nation. Several historic events helped remove many of these obstacles.

Immunity is not an altogether negative function of inter-state relations. It serves to shield states, through their senior representatives, from being sued before the courts of other states, and, as such, it is a procedural bar to prosecution. Its application does not absolve the offence (nor the liability of the offender), but merely prevents the accused from being prosecuted as long as he or she holds that office. As a result, it protects current office holders. Abuses of the system are far less frequent than the general public believes, but they do occur. The practice of states suggests that the privilege of immunity is enjoyed even by those leaders and their entourage that have gained power illegally – that is, without the benefit of fair elections. Such persons may well stay in power for the rest of their lives, or enact laws that give them the right to enjoy immunity as honorary heads of state. As a result of the work of the ICTY, but particularly after the *Congo* case[34] and the *Pinochet* case,[35] the following is currently accepted about immunity. Immunity continues to shield incumbent heads of state, heads of government, and foreign ministers (immunity *ratione personae*) irrespective of the nature of the contested act. Conversely, it is no longer accepted that persons otherwise enjoying immunity *ratione materiae* are immune from criminal prosecution for acts involving human rights violations, because these can never be deemed official acts. Immunity *ratione personae* will always trump human rights for the sake of international relations,[36] unless the international community decides to make an exception, either by establishing an ad hoc tribunal (as was the case with ex-President *Milošević* of Yugoslavia), or by surrendering such a person to the International Criminal Court (ICC) through an act of the United Nations (UN) Security Council, as was the case with President Al-Bashir of Sudan.[37] Thus, very few people can any longer claim to enjoy immunity and feel safe in travelling across the globe.

---

34 *Democratic Republic of Congo* v *Belgium* (Arrest Warrant of 11 April 2000), Judgement (14 February 2002).

35 *R* v *Bow Street Metropolitan Stipendiary Magistrate and Others ex p Pinochet Ugarte (No. 3)* [1999] 2All ER 97.

36 *Al-Adsani* v *UK*, Judgement (21 November 2001) (2002) 34 EHRR 11, paras. 55–66; for an overview, see E. Voyakis, 'Access to Court v State Immunity' (2003) 52 *ICLQ* 279. In *Jones and Others* v *Saudi Arabia*, [2006] UKHL 26, paras. 30–1, the House of Lords dismissed the argument upheld by the Court of Appeals whereby the state enjoys immunity but not the agent. Equally, in *Bouzari* v *Islamic Republic of Iran* (2004), 124 ILR 427, the Ontario Court of Appeals could find no exception to the general rule of immunity for acts of torture committed outside the forum state.

37 ICC Prosecutor's Statement on Application for a Warrant of Arrest under Art. 58 against Al-Bashir (14 July 2008) [online]. Available from: http://www.icc-cpi.int/library/organs/otp/ICC-OTP-ST20080714-ENG.pdf.

In the past, states were wary of exercising extraterritorial jurisdiction in order to prosecute accused persons. Apart from the obvious logistical problems involved in such exercises, the fear of jeopardizing international relations prevented national prosecutions in situations with an extra-territorial element. Until the establishment of the ICTY and the International Criminal Tribunal for Rwanda (ICTR), prosecutions of war crimes, particularly those committed during World War II, were the sole order of the day, but as time passed since the end of that war, prosecutions had become relatively few and the ageing Nazi associates were increasingly hard to identify. No other international crimes were pursued. In the immediate aftermath of the ICTY, many European states actively sought to prosecute persons associated with the war crimes and other crimes against humanity committed in Yugoslavia and Rwanda.[38] This was not wholly surprising, as both countries were by that time failed states, and such prosecutions could not inflict harm on inter-state relations. Nonetheless, this provided an impetus for activating other jurisdictions for similar offences, including also genocide, in the form of the Sierra Leone Special Court,[39] the East Timor Special Panels,[40] the Cambodian Extraordinary Chambers,[41] and the Iraqi Special Tribunal for Crimes Against Humanity.[42] The latter is also empowered to examine offences that were not committed during armed conflict and is not confined to Iraqi territory alone, but extends to offences committed by the Saddam Hussein regime in Kuwait and Iran. Exceptionally, other jurisdictions have been set up to prosecute international crimes other than war crimes, crimes against humanity and genocide. The *Lockerbie* trial concerned state-sponsored terrorism,[43] whereas the UN-appointed Hariri Commission is to determine the criminal and other aspects of the former Lebanese president's assassination.[44] National prosecutors are also now more inclined to prosecute transnational corruption offences, although such prosecutions are still in their infancy and concern almost entirely those accused of active corruption.[45] We should not be misled into the belief that there has been an explosion in the prosecution of extraterritorial crimes, or in the employment of universal jurisdiction by national prosecutors. This is not the case even in those jurisdictions that are

38 *Public Prosecutor* v *Djajic* (German), *American Journal of International Law*, 92 (1998), p. 528; *Public Prosecutor* v *Grabec* (Swiss), *American Journal of International Law*, 92 (1998), p. 78; *Re Javar and Re Munyeshyaka*, *American Journal of International Law*, 93 (1999), p. 525.

39 Report of the Secretary General on the Establishment of a Special Court for Sierra Leone, UN Doc S/2000/915 (4 October 2000). See A. McDonald, Sierra Leone's Shoestring Special Court (2002) 84 *IRRC* 121.

40 UNTAET/REG/2000/15 (6 June 2000), on the Establishment of Panels with Exclusive Jurisdiction over Serious Criminal Offences. See H. Strohmeyer, 'Collapse and Reconstruction of a Judicial System: The United Nations Missions in Kosovo and East Timor', *American Journal of International Law*, 95 (2001), pp. 46–63.

41 'Law on the Establishment of Extraordinary Chambers in the Courts of Cambodia for the Prosecution of Crimes Committed During the Period of Democratic Cambodia', translation reprinted in *Critical Asian Studies*, 34 (2002), pp. 611ff.

42 See I. Bantekas, 'The Iraqi Special Tribunal for Crimes Against Humanity', *International & Comparative Law Quarterly*, 54 (2005), pp. 237–52.

43 Agreement Between The Netherlands and UK Concerning a Scottish Trial in The Netherlands, 38 ILM (1999), 926. See also SC Res. 1192 (27 August 1998).

44 SC Res. 1595 (7 April 2005). See Report of the International Independent Investigation Commission established pursuant to Security Council Resolution 1595 (2005), UN Doc. S/2005/662 (19 Oct. 2005).

45 See I. Bantekas, 'Corruption as an International Crime and Crime Against Humanity: An Outline of Supplementary Criminal Justice Policies', *Journal of International Criminal Justice*, 4 (2006), pp. 466–84.

traditionally judicially active, particularly the USA and the UK.[46] All these developments, however, evince that individual criminal responsibility exists in respect of all international crimes, whether large or small, and that the only obstacle in their prosecution is immunity *ratione personae* and the lack of prosecutorial action. Moreover, there is currently no doubt that all international criminal law treaties establish individual responsibility in respect of the offences they promulgate, so long as an offence is actually established therein, irrespective of whether the said offence is described as international. This characterization is not required because this new treaty genre provides for a multiplicity of jurisdictional possibilities (as, in fact, did its predecessors) and modes of inter-state cooperation, and explicitly renders the prohibited behaviour a crime, at least, in the domestic legal order of participating states.

Finally, whereas in the pre-ICTY era, claims of domestic jurisdiction precluded other states or international organizations from any sort of intervention even in respect of large-scale violations of human rights, such claims are currently without legal merit. In short, the conclusion is that large-scale, internally perpetrated violations of human rights are tantamount to international crimes and the perpetrators incur criminal responsibility under international law. The impetus for this development was the creation of the ICTY and ICTR themselves, which, after all, must have been designed to deal with what were essentially domestic conflicts, but this idea was not widely shared by international law academics and states alike. For the former, it was mostly aspirational and it had to be proved in practice. This took place with the handing down of the historic Interlocutory Decision on Jurisdiction in *Prosecutor* v *Tadic*, in which the Appeals Chamber of the ICTY held that violations of humanitarian law in non-international armed conflicts are international crimes and the perpetrators incur individual responsibility under customary international law.[47] In fact, not only was there very limited opposition to this statement of law, but also the issue was not seriously debated during the deliberations on the creation of the ICC, and the relevant provision was inserted easily in Article 8 of the ICC Statute. Thus, within a space of only a few years, a poignant obstacle to international human rights law had passed into oblivion.

7. Epilogue

Although we have determined that the pioneering human rights treaties that lack an obligation of states to criminalize do not constitute a sufficient legal basis for establishing individual criminal responsibility, in practice, whether through customary law or subsequent criminal treaties, all human rights violations by now possess an international criminal law counterpart. International criminal tribunals have also proved very inventive in this respect, particularly the ICTY and ICTR, by declaring many human rights violations to possess also an international criminal law character. We have now reached a common consensus according to which all violations of humanitarian law, whether in internal or international armed conflicts, are considered as incurring individual responsibility under international law. The same is true of genocide and crimes against humanity. Given that the concept of crimes against humanity encompasses many other offences, such as torture, enslavement, rape, etc., it stands to reason that all such offences are by themselves of an

46 These countries have in the last 20 years entertained a significant number of tort claims in respect of international crimes. These are not, however, criminal prosecutions entailing individual criminal responsibility. E.g. *Smith* v *Socialist People's Libyan Arab Jamahiriya* (1997) 113 ILR 534; *Lafontant* v *Aristide* (1994) 103 ILR 581.

47 *ICTY Prosecutor* v *Tadic*, Appeals Chamber Interlocutory Decision on Jurisdiction (2 October 1995), para. 134.

international nature and incur the international liability of the perpetrator. This same result has also been expressly confirmed by the adoption in the last 30 years by a plethora of conventions that criminalize, at the international level, all those offences that existed in theory under customary international law.

The big test for human rights and international criminal law is to sustain prosecutorial activism in more states and to enhance state-cooperation in the exercise of universal jurisdiction. This latter type of jurisdiction must not become an anathema or the battleground for only a handful of states, but must develop into a real threat to perpetrators of international crimes. We cannot expect the ICC to deal with all human rights violations taking place around the world, and we should be realistic about expecting all those states where violations take place to prosecute the accused, since corrupt and undemocratic regimes are the instigators of some of the most serious human rights violations in their respective territories. Moreover, states should not shy away from prosecuting what to some are not 'serious' crimes, such as corruption, or human trafficking. It is incredible that, until recently, the vast majority of states did not consider transnational corruption an indictable offence and that the victims of human trafficking were viewed not as victims, but as accomplices to the main offence and were thereafter offered no protection! This is because our perception of international crime and of human rights violations depends on the number of 'obvious' victims, particularly when they are dead. We tend to disregard behaviour that has no obvious and immediate victims as not being tantamount to a crime against humanity or a war crime, something which is clearly not the case, as most of the evils plaguing many states today are a direct result of the corrupt policies exercised by their leaders.

Chapter 24
The International Criminal Court and Individual Responsibility of Senior State Officials for International Crimes

Manisuli Ssenyonjo

1. Introduction

The effective protection of human rights requires that individuals who commit serious crimes (such as genocide, crimes against humanity and war crimes), amounting to serious human rights violations, must be held individually criminally responsible for those crimes without any distinction based on official capacity. This helps to end impunity, deter the future commission of international crimes and deter serious violations of human rights. Although the United Nations (UN) General Assembly, in Resolution 260 of 9 December 1948 adopting the Convention on the Prevention and Punishment of the Crime of Genocide (Genocide Convention), invited the International Law Commission (ILC) 'to study the desirability of establishing an international judicial organ for the trial of persons charged with genocide', it was not possible to establish a permanent international criminal court until 17 July 1998, 50 years after the UDHR1 and the Genocide Convention, when the Rome Statute of the International Criminal Court (hereinafter 'Rome Statute' or 'Statute')2 was adopted in Rome by 120 votes against 7 (Iraq, Israel, Libya, China, Qatar, the USA, and Yemen) and 21 abstentions.

The Rome Statute, which entered into force on 1 July 2002, has been ratified by the vast majority of states, demonstrating an increasing international recognition by states of the need to hold individuals accountable for international crimes within the jurisdiction of the International Criminal Court (ICC or the court).[3] However, it is important to note that some of the world's most powerful states, including three of the five permanent members of the UN Security Council (the

1 GA Res. 217A (III), UN Doc. A/810 at 71 (1948).

2 2187 UNTS 90. The International Criminal Court (ICC) has been the subject of several studies. E.g. R. Lee (ed.), The International Criminal Court: the Making of the Rome Statute – Issues, Negotiations, Results (The Hague: Kluwer Law International, 1999); A. Cassese, P. Gaeta and John R.W.D. Jones (eds), The Rome Statute of the International Criminal Court: A Commentary (Oxford: Oxford University Press, 2002); B. Broomhall, International Justice and the International Criminal Court: Between Sovereignty and the Rule of Law (Oxford: Oxford University Press, 2003); O. Bekou and R. Cryer (eds), The International Criminal Court (Aldershot: Ashgate/Dartmouth, 2004); W.A. Schabas, An Introduction to the International Criminal Court, 3rd edn (Cambridge: Cambridge University Press, 2007); O. Triffterer (ed.), Commentary on the Rome Statute of the International Criminal Court: Observers' Notes. Article by Article, 2nd edn (Baden-Baden: Nomos, 2008); M. Politi and F. Gioia (eds), The International Criminal Court and National Jurisdictions (Aldershot: Ashgate, 2008).

3 As of 18 August 2010, 113 states (out of 192 UN member states) were parties to the Rome Statute of the International Criminal Court. Out of them, 31 were African states, 15 were Asian states, 17 were Eastern

USA, China, and the Russian Federation), and other states such as India, Pakistan and Iran have not yet ratified the Rome Statute. In accordance with Articles 11 and 12 of the Rome Statute, the ICC can only prosecute crimes committed on or after it entered into force, and it is subject to the principle of complementary jurisdiction, which means it only has competence over situations and cases where competent national courts are 'unwilling' or 'unable' genuinely to carry out the investigation or prosecution. Thus, like other international criminal tribunals, the ICC was established to fill in for national courts, which tend to refrain from prosecuting state officials enjoying immunity from prosecution under national law and private individuals suspected of having committed international crimes that national authorities implicitly instigate, or at least tolerate. These crimes are often committed by state officials or with their complicity or acquiescence.[4]

As shown below, since the ICC became operational, all its active investigations carried out by the Office of the ICC Prosecutor by the end of 2009 were in Africa in four situations in the Democratic Republic of Congo (DRC), northern Uganda, the Darfur region of Sudan, and the Central African Republic. Other situations were under preliminary examination by the Office of the ICC Prosecutor in Afghanistan, Colombia, Côte d'Ivoire, Georgia, Guinea, Kenya, and Palestine.[5] By 2009, the ICC's highest-profile case, which is examined in this chapter, was the case against Omar Hassan Ahmad Al Bashir (hereinafter Al Bashir),[6] the president of the state of Sudan, Africa's largest country, since 16 October 1993 and commander-in-chief of the Sudanese armed forces. The ICC Pre-Trial Chamber I issued the first arrest warrant on 4 March 2009 against President Al Bashir as an indirect (co)perpetrator of war crimes and crimes against humanity. This arrest warrant has raised several key questions related to the individual criminal responsibility of serving senior state officials of non-state parties to the Rome Statute examined in this chapter, particularly in relation to the following three issues: (1) the personal immunities accruing to senior state officials, in particular the head-of-state immunity of non-state parties to the Rome Statute; (2) criminal responsibility for indirect (co)perpetration under the Rome Statute; and (3) the standard of evidence required to prove genocide at the pre-trial stage under the Rome Statute.

The structure of this chapter is as follows. Section 2 provides a background to the situation in Darfur giving rise to Al-Bashir's arrest warrant. Brief consideration is given to the armed conflict in Darfur, and the Security Council referral of the situation in Darfur to the ICC. It is argued that while the Security Council in Resolution 1593 urged 'all states' to 'cooperate fully' with the ICC, it discriminates on the basis of nationality, a fact that undermines the independence of the ICC. It is noted that since the Security Council has to exercise its powers in accordance with the provisions of the UN Charter, which prohibits discrimination, it must not make discriminatory referrals to the ICC. Section 3 examines the decision of the chamber for a warrant of arrest against Al Bashir, focusing on his official capacity as a sitting head of state and his immunity thereby; Al Bashir's alleged criminal responsibility as an indirect (co)perpetrator; the chamber's approach to the crime of genocide; and how arresting Al Bashir remains a challenge and an obstacle to the intended trial. It is concluded in Section 4 that given that there is currently no international court of human rights,

---

European states, 25 were Latin American and Caribbean states, and 25 were Western European and other states.

4 See A. Cassese, *International Criminal Law*, 2nd edn (Oxford: Oxford University Press, 2008), p. 435, noting that, for example, 'war crimes are committed by servicemen, or torture is perpetrated by police officers, or genocide is carried out by state officials or paramilitary groups or at any rate with the tacit approval of state authorities.'

5 See Office of the Prosecutor, *ICC Prosecutor Confirms Situation in Guinea Under Examination*, ICC-OTP-20091014-PR464 (14 October 2009).

6 See ICC-02/05-01/09, *The Prosecutor* v *Omar Hassan Ahmad Al Bashir*.

the ICC can play an essential role by holding individuals responsible for international crimes within its jurisdiction. For this to be successful, the ICC requires the full cooperation of all states parties to the Rome Statute, which is still lacking. It is also observed that while the warrant of arrest for Al Bashir is a major step in the struggle against impunity, a deferral might be desirable if such a deferral of the case and the warrant is used to bring about broader accountability measures in Sudan, end a conflict that has devastated the lives of millions, and transform the internal politics of Sudan so as to end the cycles of conflict that have prevailed for decades.

2. Background: The Armed Conflict in Darfur and UN Security Council Referral of the Situation in Darfur to the ICC

On 31 March 2005, the UN Security Council determined that the situation in Darfur, Sudan, constituted 'a threat to international peace and security'.[7] Acting under Chapter VII of the UN Charter and in accordance with Article 13(b) of the Rome Statute,[8] the UN Security Council adopted Resolution 1593, referring 'the situation in Darfur since 1 July 2002' to the ICC prosecutor for investigation and prosecution.[9] Darfur thereby became the first (and so far the only) situation referred by the UN Security Council to the ICC.[10] The ICC prosecutor opened an investigation into the situation in Darfur on 1 June 2005. On 14 July 2008, the ICC prosecutor sought the issue of an arrest warrant for Al Bashir on charges of the alleged crimes of genocide, crimes against humanity and war crimes in the Darfur region.[11]

After eight months of consideration, on 4 March 2009, Pre-Trial Chamber I of the ICC (herein after 'chamber') held that it was satisfied that there were 'reasonable grounds to believe' that Al Bashir was criminally responsible under Article 25(3)(a) of the Rome Statute as an indirect perpetrator, or as an indirect co-perpetrator, of war crimes and crimes against humanity.[12] The chamber issued a warrant for the arrest of Al Bashir, on two counts of war crimes and five counts

7 UN Security Council Resolution 1593, UN Doc. S/RES/1593 (2005), 31 March 2005, p. 1. The resolution was adopted by 11 votes to none, with four abstentions by China, Algeria, Brazil and the USA. Two African states, Benin and Tanzania, voted for the resolution and one, Algeria, abstained. For a discussion, see M. Happold, 'Darfur, the Security Council, and the International Criminal Court', *International and Comparative Law Quarterly*, 55(1) (2006), pp. 226–36.

8 Article 13(b) provides that the ICC may exercise its jurisdiction with respect to a crime within its jurisdiction if '[a] situation in which one or more of such crimes appears to have been committed is referred to the Prosecutor by the Security Council acting under Chapter VII of the Charter of the United Nations'.

9 UN Security Council Resolution 1593, note 7 above.

10 The other three situations before the ICC – Uganda, Democratic Republic of the Congo (DRC) and Central African Republic (CAR) – were all referred to the ICC prosecutor by the relevant states parties.

11 Application under Article 58 of the Rome Statute, requesting that Pre-Trial Chamber I issue a Warrant of Arrest for Omar Hassan Ahmad Al Bashir, ICC-02/05-151-US-Exp, and its annexes, ICC-02/05-151-US-Exp-Anxl-89; ICC-02/05-151-US-Exp-Corr and its annexes, ICC-02/05-151-US-Exp-Corr-Anxl-2. Public Redacted Version of Prosecution's Application under Article 58 of the Rome Statute filed on 14 July 2008, ICC-02/05-157 and its annex ICC-02/05-157-AnxA (Arrest Application).

12 ICC-02/05-01/09, Decision on the Prosecution's Application for a Warrant of Arrest Against Omar Hassan Ahmad Al Bashir, *The Prosecutor* v. *Omar Hassan Ahmad Al Bashir* [online]. Available from: www2.icc-cpi.int/iccdocs/doc/doc639096.pdf. See also ICC-02/05-01/09, Second Decision on the Prosecution's Application for a Warrant of Arrest, *The Prosecutor* v. *Omar Hassan Ahmad Al Bashir* (Pre-trial Chamber I issued a second warrant of arrest for genocide) on 12 July 2010.

of crimes against humanity (but not for genocide).[13] In particular, Al Bashir was suspected of being criminally responsible, as an indirect (co-)perpetrator, for intentionally directing attacks against an important part of the civilian population of Darfur; murdering, exterminating, raping, torturing and forcibly transferring large numbers of civilians; and pillaging their property.[14] The chamber issued the warrant after noting that the arrest of Al Bashir appeared necessary under Article 58(1) of the Rome Statute to ensure that he (1) will appear before the court; (2) will not obstruct or endanger the investigation into the crimes for which he is allegedly responsible; and (3) will not continue with the commission of the above-mentioned crimes.[15] Thus, on 4 March 2009, Al Bashir joined a growing list of individuals (all, so far, exclusively in sub-Saharan Africa) against whom the ICC has issued warrants of arrest, accused mainly of crimes against humanity and war crimes.[16]

The ICC has continued with its focus on investigating and prosecuting crimes in Africa, in some cases even when national courts may well have been an option.[17] Since the ICC was set up in 2002, all the 13 warrants it had issued by March 2009 had been for political or rebel leaders on the African continent: five for the Lord's Resistance Army (LRA) senior commanders in Uganda;[18] four for rebel leaders from the DRC;[19] one for the alleged president and commander-in-chief of the Movement for the Liberation of Congo, arising out of the situation in the Central African Republic;[20] two for Sudanese government officials, arising out of the situation in Darfur, Sudan;[21] and one for the alleged militia (Janjaweed) commander in the Sudan.[22] The ICC had issued one summons to appear against the president of the United Resistance Front (URF), rebel leader Bahar Idriss Abu Garda, on three counts of war crimes;[23] and was considering two new summonses against rebel leaders in Darfur. Rebel leader Bahar Idriss Abu Garda voluntarily appeared in the court on 18 May 2009. It is striking to note that, so far, all other individuals against whom warrants

13 See Warrant of Arrest for Omar Hassan Ahmad Al Bashir, No. ICC-02/05-01/09, 4 March 2009 [online]. Available from:www.icc-cpi.int/iccdocs/doc/doc639078.pdf.

14 *Ibid.*

15 *Ibid.* and see discussion in Section 3.2 in this chapter.

16 See ICC, *Situations and Cases* [online]. Available from: www.icc-cpi.int/Menus/ICC/Situations+and+Cases/.

17 See O. Fiss, 'Within Reach of the State: Prosecuting Atrocities in Africa', *Human Rights Quarterly*, 31(1) (2009), pp. 59–69.

18 See ICC-02/04-01/05, *The Prosecutor* v *Joseph Kony, Vincent Otti, Okot Odhiambo and Dominic Ongwen* currently being heard before Pre-Trial Chamber II. The name of Raska Lukwiya was removed from the case following the confirmation of his death, in accordance with the decision of Pre-Trial Chamber II, No. ICC-02/04-01/05-248 of 11 July 2007, to terminate the proceedings against Raska Lukwiya. The four remaining suspects are still at large.

19 Three cases are being heard before the relevant chambers: ICC-01/04-01/06, *The Prosecutor* v *Thomas Lubanga Dyilo*; ICC-01/04-02/06, *The Prosecutor* v *Bosco Ntaganda*; and ICC-01/04-01/07, *The Prosecutor* v *Germain Katanga and Mathieu Ngudjolo Chui*. The accused Thomas Lubanga Dyilo, Germain Katanga and Mathieu Ngudjolo Chui are currently in the custody of the ICC. The suspect Bosco Ntaganda remains at large.

20 See ICC-01/05-01/08, *The Prosecutor* v *Jean-Pierre Bemba Gombo*, which is at the pre-trial stage of the proceedings, and at the time of writing it was being heard before Pre-Trial Chamber III.

21 Two cases are being heard before Pre-Trial Chamber I: ICC-02/05-01/07, *The Prosecutor* v *Ahmad Muhammad Harun ('Ahmad Harun')* and *Ali Muhammad Ali Abd-Al-Rahman ('Ali Kushayb*'); and ICC-02/05-01/09, *The Prosecutor* v *Omar Hassan Ahmad Al Bashir.*

22 Note 21 above, Ali Kushayb.

23 ICC-02/05-02/09, *The Prosecutor* v *Bahar Idriss Abu Garda.*

of arrest or summons to appear have been issued are leaders of armed rebel movements except for Al Bashir and his Minister of State for Humanitarian Affairs – Ahmad Harun.[24]

The warrant of arrest for Al Bashir is particularly important because it is the first warrant ever issued for a sitting head of state and/or government by the ICC and the first case involving an allegation of the crime of genocide before the ICC. In addition, such a warrant, if applied without discrimination to other leaders who are alleged to have committed crimes within the jurisdiction of the ICC (in case there is a reasonable basis to proceed), is an important signal that everyone, including a head of state, can be held accountable for international crimes within the jurisdiction of the ICC. It is not surprising that human rights organizations welcomed the warrant.[25]

2.1 The Armed Conflict in Darfur

Since Sudan achieved independence from the UK in 1956, it has experienced several armed conflicts.[26] The most recent armed conflict, in which widespread and systematic serious human rights violations have been committed, possibly amounting to war crimes and crimes against humanity, has been in Darfur, western Sudan.[27] The population of Darfur is Muslim, but recent political developments have stressed ethnic divisions between 'Arabs' and 'Africans'.[28] The division of Darfur into racial identities had its roots in the British colonial period. As early as the late 1920s, the British tried to organize two confederations in Darfur: one 'Arab', and the other 'Zurga' or black.[29] Identities based on race were incorporated in the census and provided the frame for government policy and administration.[30] In spite of official policy, Arabs never constituted a single racial group.[31] The conflict in Darfur began as a localized civil war in 1987–9 (before Al

24 Note 21 above, Ahmad Harun.

25 E.g. Amnesty International, 'ICC Issues Arrest Warrant for Sudanese President Al Bashir', 4 March 2009 [online]. Available from:www.amnesty.org/en/news-and-updates/news/icc-issues-arrest-warrant-sudanese-president-al-bashir-20090304. Amnesty International's secretary-general, Irene Khan, stated that '[t]his announcement [of the ICC warrant of arrest for Al Bashir] is an important signal – both for Darfur and the rest of the world – that suspected human rights violators will face trial, no matter how powerful they are.' Human Rights Watch stated that the ICC warrant indicates that '[n]ot even presidents are guaranteed a free pass for horrific crimes.' See Human Rights Watch, 'ICC: Bashir Warrant Is Warning to Abusive Leaders', 4 March 2009 [online]. Available from:www.hrw.org/en/news/2009/03/04/icc-bashir-warrant-warning-abusive-leaders.

26 For an overview, see, generally, A.H. Idris, *Conflict and Politics of Identity in Sudan* (New York: Palgrave Macmillan, 2005); I. Elnur, *Contested Sudan: The Political Economy of War and Reconstruction* (New York: Routledge, 2008); and D.H. Johnson, *The Root Causes of Sudan's Civil Wars* (Oxford: James Currey, 2003).

27 E.g. UN High Commissioner for Human Rights, *Situation of Human Rights in the Darfur Region of the Sudan*, UN Doc. E/CN.4/2005/3, 7 May 2004; Warrant of Arrest for Omar Hassan Ahmad Al Bashir, No. ICC-02/05-01/09 (4 March 2009); Human Rights Committee, *Concluding Observations: Sudan*, UN Doc. CCPR/C/SDN/CO/3/CRP.1, 26 July 2007, para. 9; *Centre on Housing Rights and Evictions (COHRE)* v *The Sudan*, Communication 296/05 [online]. Available from: http://www.cohre.org/Sudan.

28 See A. de Waal, *Famine That Kills: Darfur, Sudan* (Oxford: Oxford University Press, 2005), p. xiv.

29 M. Mamdani, 'Beware of Human Rights Fundamentalism (Part one)', *Daily Monitor*, 1 April 2009.

30 *Ibid.*

31 *Ibid.*, noting that 'Contemporary scholarship has shown that the Arab tribes of Sudan were not migrants from the Middle East but indigenous groups that became Arabs starting in the 18th century.'

Bashir became the president of Sudan) and had turned into a rebellion by 2003.[32] The warrant of arrest for Al Bashir arose out of this armed conflict in Darfur which began in 2003 when rebel ethnic African groups, complaining of discrimination and neglect, took up arms against the Arab-dominated government in Khartoum.[33]

The immediate cause of the armed conflict was a conflict over land, triggered by four different but related causes: the land system, environmental degradation, the spill-over of the four-decade-long civil war in Chad, and the brutal counter-insurgency waged by the Al-Bashir government in 2003 and 2004.[34] However, the long-term cause was the colonial system, which reorganized Darfur as a discriminatory patchwork of tribal homelands where settled peasant tribes were granted large homelands in which they were considered natives.[35] In contrast, camel-owning nomads with no settled villages found themselves without a homeland and so were not acknowledged as natives anywhere.[36]

As noted by the chamber, from March 2003 to at least 14 July 2008, the date of the filing of the prosecution's application for the warrant of arrest for Al Bashir, a protracted armed conflict not of an international character within the meaning of Article 8(2)(f) of the Rome Statute existed in Darfur between the government of Sudan ('the GoS') and several organized armed groups, in particular the Sudanese Liberation Movement/Army ('the SLM/A') and the Justice and Equality Movement ('the JEM').[37] This campaign started soon after the attack on El Fasher airport in April 2003. The GoS issued a general call for the mobilization of the Janjaweed Militia in response to the activities of the SLM/A, the JEM, and other armed opposition groups in Darfur, and thereafter its forces, including the Sudanese armed forces and the allied Janjaweed Militia, the Sudanese police force, the National Intelligence and Security Service ('the NISS'), and the Humanitarian Aid Commission ('the HAC'), conducted a counter-insurgency campaign throughout the Darfur region against the said armed opposition groups.[38] The counter-insurgency campaign continued until the date of the filing of the prosecution application on 14 July 2008.[39]

A core component of the GoS counter-insurgency campaign was the unlawful attack on that part of the civilian population of Darfur – belonging largely to the Fur, Masalit and Zaghawa groups – perceived by the GoS as being close to the SLM/A, the JEM, and the other armed groups opposing the GoS in the ongoing armed conflict in Darfur.[40] As part of this core component, the GoS forces systematically committed acts of pillaging after the seizure of the towns and villages that were subject to their attacks,[41] including (1) the first attack on Kodoom on or about 15 August 2003; (2) the second attack on Kodoom on or about 31 August 2003; (3) the attack on Bindisi on or about 15 August 2003; (4) the aerial attack on Mukjar between August and September 2003;

32 See, generally, M. Mamdani, *Saviors and Survivors: Darfur, Politics and the War on Terror* (London: Verso, 2009).

33 ICC-02/05-01/09, Decision on the Prosecution's Application for a Warrant of Arrest Against Omar Hassan Ahmad Al Bashir, note 12 above, para. 70.

34 M. Mamdani, 'Who Has Been Fighting Whom in Darfur? (Part Two)', *Daily Monitor*, 31 March 2009.

35 *Ibid.*

36 *Ibid.*

37 ICC-02/05-01/09, Decision on the Prosecution's Application for a Warrant of Arrest against Omar Hassan Ahmad Al Bashir, note 12 above, paras. 61–2, 70.

38 *Ibid.*, paras. 66–7.

39 *Ibid.*, para. 75.

40 *Ibid.*, para. 76.

41 *Ibid.*, para. 77.

(5) the attack on Arawala on or about 10 December 2003; (66) the attack on Shattaya town and its surrounding villages (including Kailek) in February 2004; (7) the attack on Muhajenya on or about 8 October 2007: (8) the attacks on Saraf Jidad on 7, 12 and 24 January 2008; (9) the attack on Silea on 8 February 2008; (10) the attack on Sirba on 8 February 2008; (11) the attack on Abu Suruj on 8 February 2008; and (12) the attack on Jebel Moon between 18 and 22 February 2008.[42]

As a result of the above unlawful attacks, the GoS forces allegedly committed war crimes and crimes against humanity consisting of murder, extermination, forcible transfer, torture and rape.[43] Al Bashir, as the *de jure* and *de facto* president of the state of Sudan and commander-in-chief of the Sudanese armed forces from March 2003 to 14 July 2008, allegedly played an essential role in coordinating, with other high-ranking Sudanese political and military leaders, the design and implementation of the above-mentioned GoS counter-insurgency campaign.[44] In addition, he was allegedly in full control of all branches of the 'apparatus' of the state of Sudan, including the Sudanese armed forces and their allied Janjaweed Militia, the Sudanese police force, the NISS, and the HAC, and he used such control to secure the implementation of the common plan.[45]

The armed conflict in Darfur has attracted several actors in the region including the African Union (AU) and the UN hybrid peacekeeping force,[46] as well as the UN Security Council, which, as noted above and further discussed below, referred the situation in Darfur to the ICC.

2.2 Was the UN Security Council Referral of the Situation in Darfur to the ICC Discriminatory?

It is important to recall that Sudan signed the Rome Statute on 8 September 2000, but has not yet ratified it. However, this fact has not barred the ICC from investigating the crimes allegedly committed in Darfur because UN Security Council Resolution 1593 decided that 'the Government of Sudan and all other parties to the conflict in Darfur, *shall cooperate fully* with and provide any necessary assistance to the Court and the Prosecutor pursuant to this resolution' (emphasis added).[47] Clearly, the mandatory language used in Resolution 1593 – *shall cooperate fully* – obliges Sudan to cooperate fully with the court. However, in relation to non-state parties to the Rome Statute other than Sudan, as well as regional and international organizations, Resolution 1593, 'while recognizing that States not party to the Rome Statute have no obligation under the Statute, *urges all States* and concerned regional and other international organizations to cooperate fully' (emphasis

42 See Warrant of Arrest for Omar Hassan Ahmad Al Bashir, note 13 above.

43 ICC-02/05-01/09, Decision on the Prosecution's Application for a Warrant of Arrest against Omar Hassan Ahmad Al Bashir, note 12 above, paras. 78 and 109. For Human Rights Watch reports on alleged widespread abuses by the Sudanese military, allied militias and rebel forces in Darfur, see 'Darfur Destroyed' [online]. Available from: hrw.org/reports/2004/sudan0504/; 'If We Return, We Will Be Killed' [online]. Available from: hrw.org/backgrounder/africa/darfur1104/; and 'Targeting the Fur: Mass Killings in Darfur' [online]. Available from: at hrw.org/backgrounder/africa/darfur0105/.

44 Decision on the Prosecution's Application for a Warrant of Arrest against Omar Hassan Ahmad Al Bashir, note 12 above, para. 221.

45 *Ibid.*, para. 222.

46 See A. Abass, 'The United Nations, the African Union and the Darfur Crisis: Of Apology and Utopia', *Netherlands International Law Review*, 54(3) (2007), pp. 415–40; R.P. Barnidge, Jr., 'The United Nations and the African Union: Assessing a Partnership for Peace in Darfur', *Journal of Conflict and Security Law*, 14(1) (2009), pp. 93–113.

47 UN Security Council Resolution 1593, UN Doc. S/RES/1593, 2005, para. 2. For a discussion of the jurisdiction of the ICC over nationals of non-states parties, see D. Akande, 'The Jurisdiction of the International Criminal Court over Nationals of Non-Parties: Legal Basis and Limits', *Journal of International Criminal Justice*, 1(3) (2003), pp. 618–50.

added).[48] It is notable here that Resolution 1593 does not provide that non-state parties '*shall cooperate fully*' but instead uses non-mandatory language – simply 'urges' (i.e. recommends) such states and concerned organizations such as the AU and the UN to cooperate fully. The implication here is that while non-state parties are recommended to cooperate fully with the court, including cooperation required in the execution of the arrest warrant, they are not obliged to do so.

It is important to note that while the UN Security Council created a territorial basis for jurisdiction in Resolution 1593, namely Darfur, it added the nationality exception, included as a result of US insistence, which purports to limit the jurisdiction of the ICC (and other states apart from the state of nationality of the suspect) by deciding (paragraph 6) that

> nationals, current or former officials or personnel from a contributing State outside Sudan which is not a party to the Rome Statute of the International Criminal Court shall be subject to the exclusive jurisdiction of that contributing State for all alleged acts or omissions arising out of or related to operations in Sudan established or authorized by the Council or the African Union, unless such exclusive jurisdiction has been expressly waived by that contributing State.

The legality of this provision has been widely questioned.[49] Does it amount to a discriminatory referral (discriminatory investigation and prosecution)? If so, does this invalidate the entire referral, or can paragraph 6 (if it constitutes unacceptable discrimination at all) be severed from the Resolution? The Pre-Trial Chamber did not consider these questions, which were not raised before it. It is vital to note that non-discrimination and equality are fundamental components of international law and essential to the exercise and enjoyment of human rights. It is for this reason that the preamble and Articles 1(3) and 55 of the UN Charter prohibit discrimination. Since the UN Security Council has to act in accordance with the provisions of the UN Charter, its referrals to the ICC must not be discriminatory. This is consistent with the prohibition of discrimination in international treaties on several grounds including discrimination based on 'national origin'. Freedom from discrimination might give rise to obligations that concern or bind all states (obligations *erga omnes*), such as freedom from racial discrimination.[50] It is to be noted that discrimination constitutes any distinction, exclusion, restriction, or preference or other differential treatment that is directly or indirectly based on the internationally prohibited grounds of discrimination and that has the intention or effect of nullifying or impairing the recognition, enjoyment or exercise, on an equal footing, of human rights.[51]

---

48 *Ibid.*

49 E.g. Schabas, note 2 above, p. 51, noting that the Darfur situation 'comes to the Court via a defective Security Council resolution'.

50 See ICJ, *Barcelona Traction, Light and Power Company, Limited, Second Phase (Belgium* v *Spain), Judgment*, ICJ Reports 1970, 3, at pp. 32–4 (judgement of 5 February 1970). For a discussion of obligations *erga omnes*, see, generally, C.J. Tams, *Enforcing Obligations* Erga Omnes *in International Law* (Cambridge: Cambridge University Press, 2005).

51 For a similar definition, see International Convention on the Elimination of All Forms of Racial Discrimination (ICERD), UN Doc. A/6014 (1966), Article 1; Convention on Elimination of All Forms of Discrimination Against Women (CEDAW), UN Doc. A/34/46, Article 1; and International Convention on the Protection and Promotion of the Rights and Dignity of Persons with Disabilities, UN Doc. A/61/49 (2006), Article 2. Both the Human Rights Committee and the Committee on Economic, Social and Cultural Rights came to a similar interpretation respectively in General Comment No. 18, paras. 6 and 7; and General Comment No. 20, para. 7.

Clearly, under paragraph 6 of UN Security Council Resolution 1593, nationals of other states are excluded from the jurisdiction of the ICC even though they had participated in the Darfur conflict, and that is discriminatory. As the US representative Mrs Patterson observed:

> This resolution provides clear protections for United States persons. No United States person supporting the operations in the Sudan will be subjected to investigation or prosecution because of this resolution.[52]

This has the potential to affect the credibility and independence of the ICC.[53] Sudan has noted that UN Security Council resolution 1593 was 'unfortunate and ultimately defective since it exempted some parties and not others'.[54] The effect of paragraph 6 is an investigation and prosecution which clearly discriminates on the basis of nationality and can, in principle, give rise to a discriminatory prosecutorial policy contrary to treaty provisions binding upon virtually all UN member states, including the USA.[55] This is relevant where there is a reasonable basis to believe that individuals covered by paragraph 6 have committed crimes within the ICC's jurisdiction that have not been adequately dealt with at the national level and are of sufficient gravity to justify an investigation by the ICC.[56] Does the discriminatory nature of UN Security Council resolution 1593 mean that the resolution as a whole is invalid? This question is not addressed in the Rome Statute and remains debatable until the ICC decides this matter. William Schabas has noted that:

> Assuming that paragraph 6 of Resolution 1593 is illegal, the question of severability arises. If the impugned paragraph cannot be excised from the resolution, then the entire referral might be invalid.[57]

It is submitted that the normal consequence of such an unacceptable discriminatory provision is not that the resolution will not be in effect at all. Rather, such a discriminatory provision will generally be severable, in the sense that the resolution will be operative for all individuals alleged

52 Reports of the Secretary-General on the Sudan, 5158th Meeting, UN Doc. S/PV.5158, 31 March 2005 [online]. Available from: www.undemocracy.com/securitycouncil/meeting_5158.

53 *Ibid.* The Philippine ambassador noted: 'We also believe that the International Criminal Court (ICC) may be a casualty of resolution 1593 (2005). Operative paragraph 6 of the resolution is killing its credibility – softly, perhaps, but killing it nevertheless.... Operative paragraph 6 subtly subsumed the independence of the ICC into the political and diplomatic vagaries of the Security Council.'

54 United Nations, *Report of the Security Council Mission to Djibouti (on Somalia), the Sudan, Chad, the Democratic Republic of the Congo and Côte d'Ivoire, 31 May to 10 June 2008*, UN Doc S/2008/460 (15 July 2008), para. 60.

55 See, in particular, Geneva Convention for the Amelioration of the Condition of the Wounded and Sick in Armed Forces in the Field, 75 UNTS 31, entered into force 21 October 1950, Article 49; Geneva Convention for the Amelioration of the Condition of Wounded, Sick and Shipwrecked Members of Armed Forces at Sea, 75 UNTS 85, entered into force 21 October 1950, Article 50; Geneva Convention Relative to the Treatment of Prisoners of War, 75 UNTS 135, entered into force 21 October 1950, Article 129; Geneva Convention Relative to the Protection of Civilian Persons in Time of War, 75 UNTS 287, entered into force 21 October 1950, Article 146; Convention Against Torture and Other Cruel, Inhuman or Degrading Treatment or Punishment, GA Res. 39/46 (annex, 39 UN GAOR Supp. (No. 51) at 197, UN Doc. A/39/51 (1984)), entered into force 26 June 1987, Article 5.

56 G. Sluiter, 'Obtaining Cooperation from Sudan – Where Is the Law?', *Journal of International Criminal Justice*, 6(1) (2008), pp. 871–84, at p. 881.

57 Schabas, note 2 above, p. 157.

to have committed crimes in Darfur without benefit of the discriminatory paragraph (i.e. regardless of nationality).

3. Decision of the Pre-trial Chamber on the Application for a Warrant of Arrest Against Al Bashir

The chamber of the ICC which delivered the first warrant of arrest for Al Bashir on 4 March 2009 was composed of presiding Judge Akua Kuenyehia (Ghana), Judge Anita Ušacka (Latvia) and Judge Sylvia Steiner (Brazil). As noted above, the chamber found that there were reasonable grounds to believe that Al Bashir is criminally responsible for war crimes and crimes against humanity. Three aspects of the chamber's decision are considered below because of their importance in international law, namely heads of state immunity; the concept of indirect (co)-perpetration; and the chamber's finding with respect to genocide.

3.1 Official Capacity as a Head of State and Head of State Immunity

The term 'immunity' generally means that 'a court cannot entertain a suit, not that the defendant is immune from criminal liability altogether'.[58] While it is recognized that immunities are 'valuable in preventing interference with representatives, and thereby maintaining the conduct of international relations, they can also lead to serious injustice'.[59] This normally arises where a head of state or government, a member of government or parliament, or an elected representative or a government official relies on immunity which may attach to the official capacity to avoid criminal prosecution.

Generally, under customary international law, serving heads of state are accorded immunity from the criminal jurisdiction of foreign states.[60] Those immunities, as stated by the International Court of Justice (ICJ) in the *Arrest Warrant* case,[61] 'protect the individual concerned against any act of authority of another state which would hinder him or her in the performance of his or her duties'. Treaties may also confer immunity on serving heads of state when abroad – for example, as state representatives to international organizations[62] or special missions.[63] This immunity from criminal jurisdiction includes immunity from personal arrest or detention and extends even to cases

58 See I. Bantekas and S. Nash, *International Criminal Law*, 3rd edn (London: Cavendish, Routledge, 2007), p. 100, citing, *inter alia*, *Case Concerning the Arrest Warrant* of *11 April 2000 (Democratic Republic of Congo* v *Belgium)*, judgement, 14 February 2002 (hereafter '*Arrest Warrant* case'), ICJ Reports 2002, 3, 41 ILM 536 (2002), paras. 47–55.

59 R. Cryer *et al.*, *An Introduction to International Criminal Law and Procedure* (Cambridge: Cambridge University Press, 2007), p. 422.

60 For a discussion, see R. Van Alebeek, *The Immunity of States and Their Officials in International Criminal Law and International Human Rights Law* (Oxford: Oxford University Press, 2008), p. 169; H. Fox, *The Law of State Immunity* (Oxford: Oxford University Press, 2008), p. 667; International Law Commission, *Immunity of State Officials from Foreign Criminal Jurisdiction: Memorandum Prepared by the Secretariat*, UN Doc. A/CN.4/596 (31 March 2008), para. 146.

61 Bantekas and Nash, note 58, above, para. 54.

62 See Convention on the Privileges and Immunities of the United Nations, adopted by the UN General Assembly on 13 February 1946, 1 UNTS 15, Article IV.

63 See UN Convention on Special Missions, adopted by the UN General Assembly on 8 December 1969, entered into force on 21 June 1985, 1400 UNTS 231, Articles 21, 31 and 39.

where heads of state are suspected of having committed war crimes or crimes against humanity.[64] As noted by the ICJ:

> A Head of State enjoys in particular 'full immunity from criminal jurisdiction and inviolability' which protects him or her 'against any act of authority of another State which would hinder him or her in the performance of his or her duties'.[65]

However, serving heads of states parties to the Rome Statute are not immune from ICC jurisdiction because such states have agreed to an exception under Article 27(1) of the Rome Statute, which provides that the 'Statute shall apply equally to all persons without any distinction based on official capacity'. While discussing immunities enjoyed under international law by an incumbent or former minister for foreign affairs in the *Arrest Warrant* case, the ICJ held that the immunities enjoyed under international law by an incumbent or former minister for foreign affairs do not represent a bar to criminal prosecution in certain circumstances, including the following:

> [A]n incumbent or former Minister for Foreign Affairs may be subject to criminal proceedings before certain international criminal courts, where they have jurisdiction. Examples include the International Criminal Tribunal for the former Yugoslavia, and the International Criminal Tribunal for Rwanda, established pursuant to Security Council resolutions under Chapter VII of the United Nations Charter, and the future International Criminal Court created by the 1998 Rome Convention. The latter's Statute expressly provides, in Article 27, paragraph 2, that '[i]mmunities or special procedural rules which may attach to the official capacity of a person, whether under national or international law, shall not bar the Court from exercising its jurisdiction over such a person.'[66]

It makes sense to apply the above position to a head of state. Thus, serving heads of state parties to the Rome Statute cannot invoke immunity of heads of state because of Article 27. However, Sudan has not ratified the Rome Statute and so is not bound by Article 27. In the case of non-states parties to the Rome Statute such as Sudan, the question arises of whether Sudan is bound by the Rome Statute, including its Article 27. Does President Al Bashir enjoy immunity from arrest and prosecution as a head of state not party to the Rome Statute? Should Sudan as a non-state party to the Rome Statute be treated as a party to the Rome Statute (and thus bound by the provisions of the Rome Statute including Article 27) by virtue of the compulsory nature of the UN Security Council powers under Chapter VII of the UN Charter?

The Rome Statute cannot create obligation for a non-state party without its consent[67] and, as such, the statute cannot remove the official immunity enjoyed by a head of state of a non-state party. Indeed, under the Rome Statute, states parties to the Rome Statute must not act inconsistently with the state or diplomatic immunity obligations of non-state parties.[68] It must be recalled that under the UN Charter, Security Council resolutions adopted under Chapter VII are binding on all UN

---

64 See *Arrest Warrant* case, note 58 above, para. 58, applying the above position to incumbent ministers of foreign affairs. The same position must extend to the serving head of state.

65 *Certain Questions of Mutual Assistance in Criminal Matters (Djibouti* v *France)*, 2008 ICJ Reports, para. 170, quoting from *Arrest Warrant* case, note 58 above, para. 54.

66 *Arrest Warrant* case, note 58 above, para. 60.

67 Vienna Convention on the Law of Treaties (1969), 1155 UNTS 331. Article 34 provides: 'A treaty does not create either obligations or rights for a third State without its consent.'

68 Rome Statute, Article 98.

member states, including Sudan.[69] Although the ICC chamber applied Resolution 1593 to justify its jurisdiction over Al Bashir,[70] its interpretation of Resolution 1593 was broad. The chamber did not explicitly address the question of immunity. It only considered immunity implicitly when dealing with the question of jurisdiction. As a preliminary matter, the chamber considered summarily the question of whether the case against Al Bashir falls within the jurisdiction of the ICC. In answering this question in the affirmative, the chamber held that

> without prejudice to a further determination of the matter pursuant to article 19 of the Statute, the Chamber considers that the current position of Omar Al Bashir as Head of a state *which is not party* to the statute, has no effect on the Court's jurisdiction over the present case (emphasis added).[71]

In effect, Sudan was treated as a state party to the Rome Statute not by its consent but as a result of Resolution 1593. However, Resolution 1593 did not expressly deal with the question of immunity. It should be recalled that in its refusal to cooperate with the ICC Sudan has argued that it 'would never cooperate with the Court since it was not a signatory [*sic*; note that Sudan is a signatory but not a party] to the Rome Statute'.[72] The argument that Sudan is not a party to the Rome Statute is likely to be raised with respect to immunity if Al Bashir stands trial. Therefore, it could be argued that, since Sudan is not a party to the Rome Statute, its head of state's immunity in customary international law has not been affected by Article 27, as the Rome Statute cannot clearly bind a non-state party. Other states, acting collectively, cannot remove immunity by a treaty to which the state possessing the immunity under customary international law is not a party, when they cannot do this individually. Therefore, the fact that the ICC is an international court does not, *ipso facto*, mean that immunity cannot be invoked before it, as the ICC member states could not have transferred to an international organization the power to try persons whom, for want of jurisdiction, they could not try themselves, such as the head of state of a non-party.[73]

However, although Article 27 does not remove the head of state immunity of non-state parties to the Rome Statute, in the case of Al Bashir such immunity may be regarded as having been removed by UN Security Council Resolution 1593 that referred the situation in Darfur to the ICC under Chapter VII of the UN Charter. It is well established that the Security Council can withdraw immunity from anyone, and this is what it had done in establishing the *ad hoc* tribunals.[74] Although UN Security Council Resolution 1593 does not explicitly remove immunity enjoyed by the head of state, it could be argued that such immunity was removed implicitly on the basis of any of the following: (1) Security Council referral to the ICC means that all individuals investigated and prosecuted via the referral are bound by the provisions of the Rome Statute including Article

69 UN Charter, Articles 24(1), 25, and 103.

70 See ICC-02/05-01/09, Decision on the Prosecution's Application for a Warrant of Arrest Against Omar Hassan Ahmad Al Bashir, note 12 above, paras. 40 and 45.

71 *Ibid.*, para. 41.

72 United Nations, *Report of the Security Council Mission to Djibouti (on Somalia)*, note 54 above, para. 60. Sudan signed the Rome Statute on 8 September 2000.

73 See M. Milanovic, 'ICC Prosecutor Charges the President of Sudan with Genocide, Crimes Against Humanity and War Crimes in Darfur', *American Society of International Law Insights*, 12(15) (28 July 2008) [online]. Available from: http://www.asil.org/insights080728.cfm#_edn1.

74 Schabas, note 2 above, p. 232, citing *Milošević* (IT-02-54-PT), Decision on Preliminary Motions, 8 November 2001, paras. 26–34; *Taylor* (SCSL-2003-01-I), Decision on Immunity from Jurisdiction, 31 May 2004, para. 41.

27;[75] (2) that when the Security Council decided in Resolution 1593, operative paragraph 2, that the GoS of Sudan 'shall cooperate fully with and provide any necessary assistance to the Court and the Prosecutor pursuant to this resolution' that included a lifting of the immunity; (3) that Article 27 restates an already existing principle of customary international law concerning the exercise of jurisdiction by any international court. Thus, it applies with respect to every person enjoying immunities under customary international law, regardless of whether the state this person represents is a party to the Rome Statute.[76]

In reaching its decision on jurisdiction, the chamber advanced its reasons upon which its jurisdiction was based. The chamber noted that according to the preamble of the Rome Statute, one of the core goals of the statute is to put an end to impunity for the perpetrators of the most serious crimes of concern to the international community as a whole, which 'must not go unpunished'.[77] The chamber observed that in order to achieve this goal Article 27(1) and (2) of the Rome Statute provide for the following 'core principles':

i. 'This Statute shall apply equally to all persons without any distinction based on official capacity;'
ii. '[...] official capacity as a Head of State or Government, a member of Government or parliament, an elected representative or a government official shall in no case exempt a person from criminal responsibility under this Statute, nor shall it, in and of itself, constitute a ground for reduction of sentence;' and
iii. 'Immunities or special procedural rules which may attach to the official capacity of a person, whether under national or international law, shall not bar the Court from exercising its jurisdiction over such a person.'[78]

While putting an end to impunity is a legitimate goal, in itself it does not provide sufficient legal basis which can entitle the ICC to disregard immunities of serving heads of non-state parties. This goal is stated in the Rome Statute to which Sudan is clearly not a party and thus not bound by it. Arguably, the chamber's decision suggests that any claim to immunity by Al Bashir would be inconsistent with Sudan's obligation as a signatory state to the Rome Statute to 'refrain from acts which would defeat the object and purpose of a treaty',[79] which is to avoid impunity for those responsible for the most serious crimes. Similar but less detailed provisions can be found in the statutes of UN international criminal tribunals.[80]

---

75 By Article 1 of the Rome Statute: 'The jurisdiction and functioning of the Court shall be governed by the provisions of this Statute.'

76 P. Gaeta, 'Does President Al Bashir Enjoy Immunity from Arrest?', *Journal of International Criminal Justice*, 7(2) (2009), pp. 315–32, at pp. 322–3.

77 See ICC-02/05-01/09, Decision on the Prosecution's Application for a Warrant of Arrest against Omar Hassan Ahmad Al Bashir, note 12 above, para. 42, citing preamble of the Rome Statute, paras. 4 and 5.

78 *Ibid*., para. 43.

79 Vienna Convention, note 67 above, Art. 18.

80 See the Statute of the International Criminal Tribunal for the Former Yugoslavia, 32 ILM (1993) 1203, Article 7(2); the Statute of the International Tribunal for Rwanda, 33 *ILM* 1598, 1600 (1994), Article 6(2); and the Statute of the Special Court for Sierra Leone, Article 6(2) [online]. Available from: www.sc-sl.org/LinkClick.aspx?fileticket=uClnd1MJeEw%3d&tabid=200. These articles provide that '[t]he official position of any accused person, whether as Head of State or Government or as a responsible Government official, shall not relieve such person of criminal responsibility nor mitigate punishment.' See also Charter of the International Military Tribunal, 82 *UNTS* 280, entered into force 8 August 1945, Article 7, stating

However, the chamber did not make any analysis of Article 27(1) and (2) of the Rome Statute.[81] It is submitted that Article 27(2) of the Rome Statute simply restates an already existing principle of international law concerning the exercise of jurisdiction by any international criminal court. In this regard, it will be recalled that there are two categories of rules granting immunity from criminal responsibility, namely those accruing under *international law* and those provided for in *national* legislation.[82] Immunities accruing under international law may relate either to the conduct of state agents acting in their official capacity (so-called functional – *rationae materiae* or organic – immunities), or to protect the private or official acts carried out by some categories of state officials, such as heads of state and diplomats, accredited to a host country, while in office, as well as private or official acts performed prior to taking office, and they are possessed only as long as the official is in office (personal or *rationae personae* immunities).[83]

Both functional and personal immunities may be invoked by a state official before *foreign* courts, while national immunities involve exemption from national jurisdiction. However, immunities that exist in national or in international law (e.g. constitutional law and all rules of general and special international law such as those contained in the 1961 Vienna Convention on Diplomatic Relations) 'shall not bar the Court [ICC] from exercising jurisdiction'.[84] This confirms that in principle the ICC can indict, issue an arrest warrant for, and prosecute a serving head of state provided that the state is a party to the Rome Statute or, as in the case of Sudan, that the situation is referred to the ICC by the UN Security Council under Chapter VII of the UN Charter. Under Article 25 of the UN Charter, Sudan is obliged to accept and carry out decisions of the UN Security Council.[85] As noted by the chamber,

> by referring the Darfur situation to the Court, pursuant to article 13(b) of the Statute, the Security Council of the United Nations has also accepted that the investigation into the said situation, as well as any prosecution arising therefrom, will take place in accordance with the statutory framework provided for in the Statute, the Elements of Crimes and the Rules as a whole.[86]

By implication, the chamber took the view that the UN Security Council implicitly adopted Article 27 of the Rome Statute, and as such the ICC has jurisdiction over Al Bashir, notwithstanding his position as a serving head of state of a non-state party to the Rome Statute.

It should be noted that prosecuting serving heads of states by the ICC is consistent with the practice of other international criminal tribunals. The International Criminal Tribunal for the former Yugoslavia (ICTY) indicted Slobodan Milošević while he was still the head of state

---

that '[t]he official position of defendants, whether as Heads of State or responsible officials in Government Departments, shall not be considered as freeing them from responsibility or mitigating punishment.'

81 For a discussion of Article 27 of the Rome Statute, see O. Triffterer, 'Article 27: Irrelevance of Official Capacity', in Triffterer, note 2 above, pp. 779–93. See also D. Akande, 'International Law Immunities and the International Criminal Court', *American Journal of International Law*, 98(3) (2004), pp. 419–32.

82 Cassese, *International Criminal Law*, note 4 above, pp. 302–14.

83 *Ibid.*, pp. 302–4.

84 Triffterer, note 2 above, p. 791.

85 Article 25 provides: 'The Members of the United Nations agree to accept and carry out the decisions of the Security Council in accordance with the present Charter.' See also *Legal Consequences for States of the Continued Presence of South Africa in Namibia (South West Africa) Notwithstanding Security Council Resolution 276* (1970), ICJ Advisory Opinion of 21 June 1971, ICJ Reports 16.

86 See ICC-02/05-01/09, Decision on the Prosecution's Application for a Warrant of Arrest Against Omar Hassan Ahmad Al Bashir, note 12 above, para. 45.

of the Federal Republic of Yugoslavia.[87] Likewise, in June 2003, the Special Court for Sierra Leone (SCSL) indicted and issued an arrest warrant for Charles Taylor while he was president of neighbouring Liberia.[88] The SCSL held that 'the principle seems now well established that the sovereign equality of states does not prevent a Head of State from being prosecuted before an international criminal tribunal or court.'[89] It relied on passages in *Pinochet* and the *Arrest Warrant* case which make reference to the possibility of prosecution before international criminal courts where such courts have jurisdiction.[90] Nevertheless, in both of these cases (Milošević and Taylor), custody of the accused was only secured after they had been removed or stepped down from power. Thus, their trials commenced when they were former heads of states. As indicated in the *Arrest Warrant* case,[91] under international law serving heads of states are immune from the jurisdiction of *other states* and as such they may not be prosecuted in foreign national courts although they may be prosecuted before 'certain international tribunals' (since these are not organs of a particular state or group of states) where these have jurisdiction, and here the examples are given of such tribunals the ICTY, the International Criminal Tribunal for Rwanda (ICTR) and the ICC. In the case of genocide, the Genocide Convention[92] states that persons committing genocide, conspiracy to commit genocide, direct and public incitement to commit genocide, attempted genocide, and complicity in genocide 'shall be punished, whether they are constitutionally responsible rulers, public officials or private individuals'. In such cases, the Genocide Convention clearly lifts immunity. It is also significant to note that the ICJ implicitly admitted that under customary international law official status does not relieve responsibility for genocide.[93]

Although in the first decision to issue a warrant of arrest for Al Bashir, the majority of the chamber did not find reasonable grounds to believe that Al Bashir had committed genocide, there was consensus that there were reasonable grounds to believe that he was an indirect perpetrator (or according to the majority an indirect co-perpetrator) of war crimes and crimes against humanity, as shown in Section 3.3 below. Given that these are among the most serious crimes of concern to the international community as a whole, which 'must not go unpunished', it is understandable that official capacity as a head of state or government and the immunities which may attach to such capacity could not bar the ICC chamber from considering Al Bashir's alleged criminal responsibility under the Rome Statute at the stage of issuing a warrant of arrest. It is likely, however, that if the prosecution proceeds to the trial stage, the admissibility of the Al Bashir case or the jurisdiction of

87 *Indictment of Milošević and Others*, IT-99-37, 24 May 1999 [online]. Available from: www.un.org/icty/indictment/english/mil-ii990524e.htm. The same indictment also charged Milan Milutinović who, as president of Serbia, was its head of state.

88 *Prosecutor* v *Charles Taylor*, Immunity from Jurisdiction, No. SCSL-03-01-7, 31 May 2004. For a survey, see M. Frulli, 'The Question of Charles Taylor's Immunity: Still in Search of a Balanced Application of Personal Immunities?', *Journal of International Criminal Justice*, 2(4) (2004), pp. 1118–29.

89 *Prosecutor* v *Charles Taylor*, note 88 above, para. 52.

90 See *Regina* v *Bow Street Metropolitan Stipendiary Magistrate and Others, Ex Parte Pinochet* (No. 3) [1999]2 *All ER* 97; *Arrest Warrant* case, note 58 above, para. 61.

91 *Arrest Warrant* case, note 58 above, para. 61. For a comment, see A. Cassese, 'When May Senior State Officials Be Tried for International Crimes? Some Comments on the *Congo* v. *Belgium* Case', *European Journal of International Law*, 13(4) (2002), pp. 853–75. See also K.R. Gray, 'Case Concerning the Arrest Warrant of 11 April 2000 (*Democratic Republic of the Congo* v. *Belgium*)', *European Journal of International Law*, 13(3) (2002), pp. 723ff.

92 Article 4, 78 UNTS 277.

93 *Reservations to the Convention on the Prevention and Punishment of Genocide*, Advisory Opinion of 28 May 1951, *ICJ Reports* 1951, 15 at 24.

the ICC in the case would be challenged on the basis of Al Bashir's official capacity as head of state of a state not a party to the Rome Statute.[94] As noted by the Pre-Trial Chamber, its decision was 'without prejudice to a further determination of the matter pursuant to article 19 of the statute'.

3.2 Al Bashir's Criminal Responsibility as an Indirect Perpetrator, or as an Indirect Co-perpetrator

It should be recalled that in his application for the issuance of an arrest warrant against Al Bashir, the ICC prosecutor argued that Al Bashir did not physically or directly carry out the alleged crimes but committed them (indirectly) through members of the state apparatus, the army and the militia. This means that the application was based on the view that Al Bashir was an indirect perpetrator or an indirect co-perpetrator; of note is that this was the first time a prosecutor before an international tribunal has based a prosecution on the concept of indirect perpetration.[95] Indirect perpetration and indirect co-perpetration are provided for in Article 25(3)(a) of the Rome Statute, which recognizes that a person can commit a crime 'through another person' or 'jointly with another' in the following terms:

> In accordance with this Statute, a person shall be criminally responsible and liable for punishment for a crime within the jurisdiction of the Court if that person: Commits such a crime, whether as an individual, jointly with another or through another person, regardless of whether that other person is criminally responsible.

The chamber defined the notions of indirect perpetration and indirect co-perpetration. In relation to the notion of indirect perpetration,[96] the chamber referred to its decision on the confirmation of the charges in the *Katanga and Ngudjolo* case, where it highlighted that

> [t]he leader must use his control over the apparatus to execute crimes, which means that the leader, as the perpetrator behind the perpetrator, mobilises his authority and power within the organisation to secure compliance with his orders. Compliance must include the commission of any of the crimes under the jurisdiction of this Court.[97]

The chamber held that the notion of indirect co-perpetration is applicable when some or all of the co-perpetrators carry out their respective essential contributions to the common plan through another person.[98] It recalled that in these types of situations

94 Rome Statute, Articles 19(1), 19(2)(a) and 19(4).

95 For a discussion, see F. Jessberger and J. Geneuss, 'On the Application of a Theory of Indirect Perpetration in *Al Bashir*: German Doctrine at The Hague?', *Journal of International Criminal Justice*, 6(5) (2008), pp. 853–69.

96 See ICC-02/05-01/09, Decision on the Prosecution's Application for a Warrant of Arrest against Omar Hassan Ahmad Al Bashir, note 12 above, para. 211.

97 *The Prosecutor* v *Germain Katanga and Mathieu Ngudjolo Chui*, ICC-01/04-01/07-717, para. 514.

98 See ICC-02/05-01/09, Decision on the Prosecution's Application for a Warrant of Arrest Against Omar Hassan Ahmad Al Bashir, note 12 above, para. 213.

> [c]o-perpetration or joint commission through another person is nonetheless not possible if the suspects behaved without the concrete intent to bring about the objective elements of the crime and if there is a low and unaccepted probability that such would be a result of their activities.[99]

The majority found that there were reasonable grounds to believe that, soon after the April 2003 attack on the El Fasher airport, a common plan to carry out a counter-insurgency campaign against the SLM/A, the JEM, and other armed groups opposing the GoS in Darfur was agreed upon at the highest level of the GoS by Omar Al Bashir and other high-ranking Sudanese political and military leaders.[100] The chamber also found that there were reasonable grounds to believe that a 'core component' of such common plan was the unlawful attack on that part of the civilian population of Darfur – belonging largely to the Fur, Masalit and Zaghawa groups – perceived by the GoS as being close to the SLM/A, the JEM, and other armed groups opposing the GoS in the ongoing armed conflict in Darfur.[101] Furthermore, the majority found that there were reasonable grounds to believe that Omar Al Bashir and the other high-ranking Sudanese political and military leaders directed the branches of the 'apparatus' of the state of Sudan that they led, in a coordinated manner, in order to jointly implement the common plan.[102] In particular, the chamber found that there were reasonable grounds to believe that the common plan was, to a very important extent, implemented through state and local security committees in Darfur.[103] The chamber concluded that Al Bashir, as *de jure* and *de facto* president of the state of Sudan and commander-in-chief of the Sudanese Armed Forces, played an 'essential role' in coordinating the design and implementation of the common plan.[104]

In the alternative, the chamber found that there were reasonable grounds to believe that Al Bashir (1) played a role that went beyond coordinating the implementation of the common plan; (2) was in full control of all branches of the 'apparatus' of the state of Sudan, including the Sudanese armed forces and their allied Janjaweed Militia, the Sudanese police forces, the NISS, and the HAC; and (3) used such control to secure the implementation of the common plan.[105] As a result, the chamber found that there were reasonable grounds to believe that Al Bashir was criminally responsible as an indirect perpetrator, or as an indirect co-perpetrator,[106] under Article 25(3)(a) of the Rome Statute for:

i. intentionally directing attacks against a civilian population as such or against individual civilians not taking direct part in hostilities as a war crime, within the meaning of Article 8(2)(e)(i) of the Statute;

---

99 ICC-01/04-01/07-717, para. 537.

100 See ICC-02/05-01/09, Decision on the Prosecution's Application for a Warrant of Arrest against Omar Hassan Ahmad Al Bashir, note 12 above, para. 214.

101 *Ibid.*, para. 215.

102 *Ibid.*, para. 216.

103 *Ibid.*, paras. 217–20.

104 *Ibid.*, para. 221.

105 *Ibid.*, para. 222.

106 Judge Anita Ušacka dissented: 'I do not find any evidence which addresses the issue of the locus of control; it is unclear whether such control indeed rested fully with Omar Al Bashir, or whether it was shared by others such that each person had the power to frustrate the commission of the crime. For this reason, I would decline to find reasonable grounds to believe that Omar Al Bashir was responsible through co-perpetration and instead issue an arrest warrant based only on the mode of liability alleged by the Prosecution, indirect perpetration.' See Ušacka dissent, note 119 below, para. 104.

ii. pillage as a war crime, within the meaning of Article 8(2)(e)(v) of the Statute;
iii. murder as a crime against humanity, within the meaning of Article 7(l)(a) of the Statute;
iv. extermination as a crime against humanity, within the meaning of Article 7(l)(b) of the Statute;
v. forcible transfer as a crime against humanity, within the meaning of Article 7(1)(d) of the Statute;
vi. torture as a crime against humanity, within the meaning of Article 7(l)(f) of the Statute; and
vii. rape as a crime against humanity, within the meaning of Article 7(1)(g) of the Statute.[107]

The application of indirect perpetration (or indirect co-perpetration) in the Al Bashir case is a welcome development in line with the present trends because today, more than in the past, it is state officials, and in particular senior officials, that commit international crimes.[108] It is rare for such persons to commit such crimes directly; instead they order, plan, instigate, organize, aid and abet, culpably tolerate or acquiesce, or willingly or negligently fail to prevent or punish international crimes.[109] In any case, it is likely that international crimes by definition may involve senior state officials. This is the case, for example, with crimes against humanity defined in Article 7 of the Rome Statute as being committed as part of a 'widespread or systematic attack' directed against any civilian population, with knowledge of the attack. It is unlikely that an attack would be 'systematic or widespread' without some form of involvement of state officials or by an organized group. It is also the case that state officials would often avoid direct involvement in the commission of international crimes in order to avoid potential criminal prosecution. Thus, the best way to ensure accountability of such leaders is by holding them accountable either as indirect perpetrators or, when appropriate, as indirect co-perpetrators.

3.3 Insufficient Evidence to Prove Genocide

There has been considerable controversy over the question of whether or not genocide was committed in Darfur. A brief background is useful to understand the nature of this controversy. In September 2004, the US Secretary of State, Colin Powell, called upon the UN Security Council to initiate a full investigation in Darfur, claiming that 'genocide has occurred and may still be occurring in Darfur'.[110] In response to Secretary of State Powell's appeal, UN Security Council Resolution 1564 of 18 September 2004 requested that the Secretary General rapidly establish

> an international commission of inquiry in order immediately to investigate reports of violations of international humanitarian law and human rights law in Darfur by all parties, to determine also whether or not acts of genocide have occurred, and to identify the perpetrators of such violations with a view to ensuring that those responsible are held accountable.[111]

---

107 ICC-02/05-01/09, Decision on the Prosecution's Application for a Warrant of Arrest against Omar Hassan Ahmad Al Bashir, note 12 above, para. 249.

108 Cassese, *International Criminal Law*, note 4 above, p. 307.

109 *Ibid.*

110 Secretary of State Colin L. Powell, Text of Colin Powell Testimony to Senate Foreign Relations Committee, Washington, DC, 9 September 2004 [online]. Available from: www.voanews.com/english/archive/2004-09/a-2004-09-09-8-Text.cfm. See also S. Totten and E. Marcusen, 'The US Government Darfur Genocide Investigation', *Journal of Genocide Research*, 7(2) (2005), pp. 279–90.

111 UN Doc. S/RES/1564, 18 September 2004, para. 12.

The UN Secretary-General promptly created an International Commission of Inquiry ('the commission'), chaired by Professor Antonio Cassese, as called for in the above Security Council Resolution. The five-member commission included three African members from Ghana, South Africa and Egypt. The commission in its report to the Secretary-General on 25 January 2005 found that violations of international humanitarian law and human rights law had occurred and were continuing in Darfur and that the Sudanese justice system was unwilling and unable to address the crimes.[112] However, it disagreed with Secretary of State Powell, concluding that the violations that had been committed in the Darfur region of Sudan were not acts of genocide but rather crimes against humanity, essentially because it failed to find evidence of a state plan or policy to annihilate, in whole or in part, a group distinguished on racial, ethnic, national or religious ground.[113] The commission called for prosecution by the ICC.[114]

Notwithstanding the commission's view on genocide, the ICC prosecutor submitted that there were reasonable grounds to believe that President Al Bashir bears criminal responsibility for genocide.[115] Did the GoS and Al Bashir commit genocide? The answer to this question depends on whether or not the GoS and Al Bashir had intent to destroy, in whole or in part, a national, ethnical, racial or religious group. The former Senior Prosecuting Counsel at the ICTY and ICC noted that '[s]erious disagreement remains, however, as to whether Al Bashir and the Sudanese government intended actually to destroy, in part, the Fur, Masalit and Zaghawa peoples of Darfur'.[116] As shown below, this disagreement was manifested in the first Pre-Trial Chamber's decision in the Al Bashir case.

Genocide is defined in Article 6 of the Rome Statute.[117] This provision is essentially similar to Article II of the Genocide Convention.[118] By Article 6 of the Rome Statute, genocide means any of the following acts committed with 'intent to destroy, in whole or in part, a national, ethnical, racial or religious group':

---

112 See *Report of the International Commission of Inquiry on Violations of International Humanitarian Law and Human Rights Law in Darfur to the United Nations Secretary-General – Pursuant to Security Council Resolution 1564 of 18 September 2004*, 25 January 2004, UN Doc. S/2005/60 [online]. Available from: www.un.org/News/dh/sudan/com_inq_darfur.pdf (hereafter 'Commission of Inquiry'). For a comment on this report, see C. Byron, 'Comment on the Report of the International Commission of Inquiry on Darfur to the United Nations Secretary-General', *Human Rights Law Review*, 5(2) (2005), pp. 351–60; and the Contributions to the Symposium, 'The Commission of Inquiry on Darfur and Its Follow-Up: A Critical View', *Journal of International Criminal Justice*, 3(3) (2005), pp. 539ff.

113 Commission of Inquiry, note 112 above, paras. 489–522, 640–1. For comment, see the articles in a special issue of : *Fordham International Law Journal*, 31(4) (2008), on 'The Crisis in Darfur'; and W.A. Schabas, 'Darfur and the "Odious Scourge": The Commission of Inquiry's Findings on Genocide', *Leiden Journal of International Law*, 18(4) (2005), pp. 871–85.

114 Commission of Inquiry, note 112 above, para. 569.

115 ICC-02/05-01/09, Decision on the Prosecution's Application for a Warrant of Arrest Against Omar Hassan Ahmad Al Bashir, note 12 above, para. 1.

116 A.T. Cayley, 'The Prosecutor's Strategy in Seeking the Arrest of Sudanese President Al Bashir on Charges of Genocide,' *Journal of International Criminal Justice*, 6(5) (2008), pp. 829–40, at p. 840.

117 See W.A. Schabas, 'Article 6: Genocide', in Triffterer, note 2 above, pp. 143–57. For a comprehensive discussion of genocide in international law, see, generally, Schabas, *Genocide in International Law: The Crime of Crimes, 2nd ed.* (Cambridge: Cambridge University Press, 2009).

118 78 UNTS 277 (1951).

a. killing members of the group;
b. causing serious bodily or mental harm to members of the group;
c. deliberately inflicting on the group conditions of life calculated to bring about its physical destruction in whole or in part;
d. imposing measures intended to prevent births within the group;
e. forcibly transferring children of the group to another group.

Thus, the specific intent (*dolus specialis*) to destroy in whole or in part a national, ethnical, racial or religious group is an essential component of the definition of genocide. Accordingly, to prove genocide, it has to be shown that

> (i) an Accused possessed an *intent*, (ii) that intent consisted of the intent to *destroy*, (iii) the intent was to destroy *a group or a substantial part thereof* and (iv) the intent to destroy a group consisted of the intent to destroy the group *as such* (as distinguished from an intent to destroy a group of individuals within the group or substantial part thereof) (emphasis added).[119]

It is important to note that the ICC Elements of Crimes[120] on genocide add contextual elements as an objective point of reference for the determination of a realistic genocidal intent by providing:

> The Conduct [killing, causing serious bodily harm etc] took place in the context of a manifest pattern of similar conduct directed against that group or was conduct that could itself effect such destruction.

The above contextual element was incorporated by the chamber.[121] However, this remains a contentious issue because the ICC Elements of Crimes are not legally binding on the court.[122] The chamber found, by a majority of two to one,[123] that the materials provided by the prosecution failed to provide reasonable grounds to believe that the government of Sudan acted with a specific intent to destroy in whole or in part the Fur, Masalit and Zaghawa groups. The majority observed that:

> the Prosecution acknowledges that (i) it does not have any direct evidence in relation to Omar Al Bashir's alleged responsibility for the crime of genocide; and that therefore (ii) its allegations concerning genocide are solely based on certain inferences that, according to the Prosecution, can be drawn from the facts of the case.[124]

---

119 See Separate and Partly Dissenting Opinion of Judge Anita Ušacka, ICC-02/05-01/09, 4 March 2009, para. 36 (hereafter 'Ušacka dissent').

120 UN Doc. PCNICC/2000/1/Add.2 (2000).

121 For a discussion, see C. Kreß, 'The Crime of Genocide and Contextual Elements: A Comment on the ICC Pre-Trial Chamber's Decision in the Al Bashir Case', *Journal of International Criminal Justice*, 7(2) (2009), pp. 297–306; R. Cryer, 'The Definitions of International Crimes in the Al Bashir Arrest Warrant Decision', *Journal of International Criminal Justice*, 7(3) (2009), pp. 283–96, at pp. 289–96.

122 Ušacka dissent, note. 119 above, para. 17.

123 Judge Anita Ušacka dissented as noted in notes 106 and 119 above.

124 ICC-02/05-01/09, Decision on the Prosecution's Application for a Warrant of Arrest Against Omar Hassan Ahmad Al Bashir, note 12 above, para. 111.

Given that a specific intent to destroy in whole or in part the targeted group (national, ethnic, racial or religious) is an essential element of the crime of genocide,[125] the majority held that

> despite the particular seriousness of those war crimes and crimes against humanity that appeared to have been committed by GoS forces in Darfur between 2003 and 2008, a number of materials provided by the Prosecution point to the existence of several factors indicating that the commission of such crimes can reasonably be explained by reasons other than the existence of a GoS's genocidal intent to destroy in whole or in part the Fur, Masalit and Zaghawa groups.[126]

Consequently, the first warrant of arrest does not include any count for genocide. Nevertheless, the majority considered that if, as a result of the ongoing prosecution's investigation into the crimes allegedly committed by Al Bashir, 'additional evidence on the existence of a GoS's genocidal intent is gathered', the majority's conclusion would not prevent the prosecution from requesting, pursuant to Article 58(6) of the Statute, an amendment to the arrest warrant for Al Bashir so as to include the crime of genocide.[127] It is, however, unlikely that such evidence would be obtained on the basis of nationality, race or religion because, as the majority observed, there are no reasonable grounds to believe that nationality, race and/or religion are a distinctive feature of any of the three different groups (the Fur, the Masalit and the Zaghawa) allegedly targeted.[128] Indeed, the members of these three groups, as well as others in the region, appear to have Sudanese nationality, similar racial features and a shared Muslim origin.[129] The only possible ground is that each of the said three groups is a distinct ethnic group as each group has its own language, its own tribal customs, and its own traditional links to its lands.[130] As Cayley observed:

> It is difficult to cry government-led genocide in one breath and then explain in the next why 2 million Darfuris have sought refuge around the principal army garrisons of their province. One million Darfuris live in Khartoum where they have never been bothered during the entire course of the war. As Rony Brauman of *Médecins sans Frontières* points out, 'Can one seriously imagine Tutsis seeking refuge in areas controlled by the Rwandan army in 1994 or Jews seeking refuge with the Wehrmacht in 1943?[131]

However, in a partly dissenting opinion, Judge Anita Ušacka found reasonable grounds to issue an arrest warrant on the basis of the existence of reasonable grounds to believe that Al Bashir committed the crime of genocide.[132] There were two main reasons for her dissent from the majority. Firstly, unlike the majority, she looked at the target of the counter-insurgency campaign as being a

125 See Rome Statute, Article 6.

126 ICC-02/05-01/09, Decision on the Prosecution's Application for a Warrant of Arrest against Omar Hassan Ahmad Al Bashir, note 12 above, para. 204(v). But see Ušacka dissent, note 119 above; she was satisfied that there were reasonable grounds to issue an arrest warrant on the basis of the existence of reasonable grounds to believe that Al Bashir committed the crime of genocide.

127 See ICC-02/05-01/09, note 12 above, para. 207.

128 *Ibid.*, para. 136.

129 *Ibid.*

130 *Ibid.*, para. 137.

131 Cayley, note 116 above, p. 840, citing R. Brauman, 'The ICC's Bashir Indictment: Law against Peace', *World Politics Review*, 23 July 2008 [online]. Available from: http://www.worldpoliticsreview.com/Article.aspx?id=2471.

132 See Ušacka dissent, note 119 above.

single ethnic group of the 'African tribes', which in turn comprised smaller groups, including the Fur, Masalit and Zaghawa.[133] She noted that the Fur, Masalit and Zaghawa population was targeted as a unitary – though diverse – entity of 'African tribes', even though neither the perceived entity nor the Fur, Masalit and Zaghawa are in fact racially distinct from the perceived 'Arab' tribes.[134]

Secondly, she applied a lower evidentiary threshold as required at the arrest warrant stage. Trials at the ICC take three stages: (1) the issuance of a warrant of arrest or summons to appear under Article 58 of the Rome Statute; (2) the confirmation of the charges and committal of a person for trial under Article 61 of the Rome Statute; and (3) the conviction of an accused person under Article 66 of the Rome Statute. Significantly, different evidential standards must be met at each stage of the trial, and these are progressively higher. At the stage of issuing an arrest warrant or a summons to appear, the Pre-Trial Chamber need only be 'satisfied that there are *reasonable grounds to believe* that the person has committed a crime within the jurisdiction of the Court' (emphasis added).[135] In contrast, when deciding whether or not to confirm the charges, the chamber must determine whether there is '*sufficient evidence* to establish *substantial grounds to believe* that the person committed the crime charged' (emphasis added).[136] Finally, at the trial stage, the Trial Chamber must 'be convinced of the guilt of the accused *beyond a reasonable doubt*' (emphasis added) in order to convict an accused.[137]

Judge Ušacka decided that, given the preliminary nature of the proceedings at the arrest warrant stage, the prosecution need not demonstrate that genocidal intent is the only reasonable inference available on the evidence.[138] This is because this is 'tantamount to requiring the Prosecution to present sufficient evidence to allow the Chamber to be convinced of genocidal intent beyond reasonable doubt, a threshold which is not applicable at this stage, according to article 58 of the Statute'.[139] This appears to be a correct interpretation of the Rome Statute because, as noted above, all that is required in order to obtain an arrest warrant under Article 58 of the Rome Statute is for the chamber to be satisfied that '[t]here are *reasonable grounds to believe* that the person has committed a crime within the jurisdiction of the Court' (emphasis added).[140] The evidence which raises reasonable grounds to believe need not be at the same level as that necessary to justify a conviction or even to confirm the charge.[141] Judge Ušacka found the evidence submitted sufficient, concluding, *inter alia*, that Al Bashir 'possessed the intent to destroy the ethnic group of the "African tribes" as such'.[142] Although this is a wider understanding of a targeted group, it would raise the threshold for what amounts to a 'substantial' part of the group. Nonetheless, she acknowledged that

133 *Ibid.*, para. 26.

134 *Ibid.*, para. 25.

135 Rome Statute, Article 58(l)(a).

136 *Ibid.*, Article 61(7).

137 *Ibid.*, Article 66(3).

138 Ušacka dissent, note 119 above, paras. 32–4, 84.

139 *Ibid.*, para. 31.

140 Rome Statute, Article 58(1)(a).

141 See *The Prosecutor* v *Thomas Lubanga Dyilo*, Decision on the Prosecutor's Application for a Warrant of Arrest, Article 58, ICC-01/04-01/06-8-Corr, para. 12.

142 Ušacka dissent, note 119 above, para. 76.

> [a] Trial Chamber might later conclude that some evidence would not permit it to find, beyond a reasonable doubt, that Omar Al Bashir possessed genocidal intent. However, this is not the task of the Pre-Trial Chamber at the arrest warrant stage.[143]

It is implicit in the foregoing dissent that the majority were not satisfied that there were reasonable grounds to believe that Al Bashir committed genocide for two main reasons: (1) they failed to identify the targeted group, which Judge Ušacka identified as 'African tribes' targeted as the result of a perception of an affiliation between the Fur, Masalit and Zaghawa and the rebel groups as opposed to 'Arab tribes', and (2) the evidential standard applied by the majority at the pre-trial stage requiring the prosecution to demonstrate that genocidal intent was the only reasonable inference available on the evidence was higher than required. In effect, this standard went beyond proving that there were 'reasonable grounds to believe', as required at the pre-trial stage, and amounted, in substance, to requiring the prosecution to prove the charges of genocide at the pre-trial stage 'beyond reasonable doubt', although this standard applies at the trial stage.

As expected, the ICC prosecutor applied for leave to appeal[144] under Article 82(1)(d) of the Rome Statute,[145] and his application was granted to consider whether the correct standard of proof in the context of Article 58 of the Rome Statute requires that the *only* reasonable conclusion to be drawn from the evidence is the existence of reasonable grounds to believe that the person has committed a crime within the jurisdiction of the court.[146] This means that the prosecutor would be able to seek the addition of genocide charges to Bashir's arrest warrant. The decision of the Appeals Chamber in this regard would help to provide clarity on the law on proof by inference, particularly at the arrest warrant stage. In its judgement of 3 February 2010, the Appeals Chamber ruled that 'the Pre-Trial Chamber applied an erroneous standard of proof when evaluating the evidence submitted by the Prosecutor and, consequently, rejected his application for a warrant of arrest in respect of the crime of genocide' (judgement on the appeal of the Prosecutor against the 'Decision on the Prosecution's Application for a Warrant of Arrest against Omar Hassan Ahmad Al Bashir', ICC-02/05-01/09-OA, 3 February 2010, para. 41). The Appeals Chamber refused to direct the Pre-Trial Chamber to issue a new arrest warrant for the crime of genocide, but remanded the matter to the Pre-Trial Chamber for a new decision, this time using the correct standard of proof (ICC-02/05-01/09-OA, 3 February 2010, para. 42). The Pre-Trial Chamber reinstated the genocide charge on 12 July 2010 on the basis of the lower standard of proof identified by the Appeals Chamber (Second Decision on the Prosecution's Application for a Warrant of Arrest, ICC-02/05-01/09, 12 July 2010). This might create an additional obligation for states parties to the Genocide Convention to arrest Al Bashir because the Genocide Convention contains an implicit obligation to cooperate with competent international courts, including an obligation to arrest persons (whether they are constitutionally responsible rulers, public officials or private individuals) suspected of

143 *Ibid.*, para. 85.

144 Prosecution's Application for Leave to Appeal the Decision on the Prosecution's Application for a Warrant of Arrest Against Omar Hassan Ahmad Al Bashir, ICC-02/05-01/09-12.

145 Article 82(1)(d) provides: 'Either party may appeal any of the following decisions in accordance with the Rules of Procedure and Evidence: A decision that involves an issue that would significantly affect the fair and expeditious conduct of the proceedings or the outcome of the trial, and for which, in the opinion of the Pre-Trial or Trial Chamber, an immediate resolution by the Appeals Chamber may materially advance the proceedings'.

146 Decision on the Prosecutor's Application for Leave to Appeal the 'Decision on the Prosecution's Application for a Warrant of Arrest Against Omar Hassan Ahmad Al Bashir', No. ICC-02/05-01/09 (24 June 2009).

genocide.[147] There is no exception of immunity set out in the Genocide Convention. Thus the issue of head-of-state immunity for Al Bashir has no relevance to genocide charges under the Genocide Convention, whose object is to punish *all persons* committing genocide.

It is important to note that 137 states have ratified the Genocide Convention including some non-states parties to the Rome Statute such as the USA, China, Russia and Sudan. In the case of Sudan the Genocide Convention entered into force on 11 January 2004, after the entry into force of the Rome Statute. Sudan has not submitted any reservation or declaration to provisions in the Genocide Convention. If the Pre-Trial Chamber issues an arrest warrant for genocide against Al Bashir, Sudan would be obliged under Article VI of the Genocide Convention to ensure that he 'be tried by a competent tribunal of the State in the territory of which the act was committed, or by such international penal tribunal as may have jurisdiction with respect to those Contracting Parties which shall have accepted its jurisdiction'. Sudan would, therefore, have a choice between a national trial for genocide in Sudan or an international trial – such as before the ICC. Sudan's failure to institute national proceedings or to surrender Al Bashir for international trial may give rise to a dispute relating to Sudan's fulfilment of the Genocide Convention, which could be submitted to the ICJ at the request of any of parties to the dispute under Article IX of the Genocide Convention. In respect of other states not parties to the Rome Statute but parties to the Genocide Convention, such as the USA, China, and Russia, their duty under Article VI of the Genocide Convention would be to ensure that Al Bashir be tried either in Sudan (or another state party to the Genocide Convention) or before an international penal tribunal such as the ICC.

Certainly, as is well known, it is generally difficult to establish the crime of genocide because of the difficulty in proving intent to destroy a protected group as such. Save in the case of a confession (which is difficult to obtain), there will hardly be any direct evidence to prove the specific 'intent to destroy' a protected group in whole or in part. Indeed, the ICTY has so far been unable to establish genocide anywhere in Bosnia except in Srebrenica, where, in July 1995, Bosnian Serb forces massacred around 8,000 Bosnian Muslim men and boys.[148] Time will show whether genocide charges in the Al Bashir case are well founded, or founded at all. Although the majority did not find reasonable grounds to issue a warrant for genocide against Al Bashir in the first warrant of arrest, it remains a fact that the indictment for crimes against humanity and war crimes represents the recognition by the ICC of Al Bashir's alleged liability for some of the most serious crimes in international criminal law. While genocide is perceived to be the 'crime of crimes', crimes against humanity and war crimes can be as extremely serious as genocide.

3.4 Arresting Al Bashir Remains a Challenge

It remains to be seen whether Al Bashir will stand trial before the ICC since, under the Rome Statute, there are no 'trials in absentia'.[149] Yet, as is well known, the ICC has no police force or army to arrest Al Bashir. As noted above, the UN Security Council Resolution 1593 created a clear international legal obligation on Sudan to arrest Al Bashir. In operative paragraph 2, the Security Council

147 Genocide Convention, Articles IV and VI; ICJ, *The Application of the Convention on the Prevention and Punishment of the Crime of Genocide (Bosnia and Herzegovina* v *Serbia and Montenegro)* (judgement of 26 February 2007), p. 108 [online]. Available from: http://www.icj-cij.org/docket/files/91/13685.pdf#view=FitH&pagemode=none&search=%22stojanovic%22.

148 See *Prosecutor* v *Krstić*, IT-98-33, Trial Chamber, 2 August 2001; Appeals Chamber Judgement, 19 April 2004.

149 Rome Statute, Article 63(1), provides that '[t]he accused shall be present during the trial'.

> Decides that the Government of Sudan and all other parties to the conflict in Darfur shall cooperate fully with and provide any necessary assistance to the Court and the Prosecutor pursuant to this resolution and, while recognising that States not party to the Rome Statute have no obligation under the Statute, urges all States and concerned regional and other international organisations to cooperate fully.

Although the chamber rightly stressed that, pursuant to UN Security Council Resolution 1593, Sudan was obliged 'to cooperate fully with and provide any necessary assistance to the Court,'[150] such cooperation has not been forthcoming. It is highly unlikely that Sudan would cooperate with the ICC in the arrest and surrender of Al Bashir as long as he remains a head of state and commander-in-chief of the armed forces. Sudan has signalled that it has no plans to arrest Al-Bashir, but any of the states parties to the Rome Statute are obligated to arrest him if he travels there.[151] This means that he will find it increasingly difficult to travel freely to some states (especially states outside Africa and Arab states) without facing a real risk of arrest, a fact that is likely to affect his political future. There are, however, significant practical difficulties in securing his arrest as shown in the next section. If Al Bashir remains at large, the ICC will be prevented from exercising its functions and powers against him. In this regard, the chamber might ultimately be left with no alternative but to make a finding to the effect that Sudan has failed to comply and 'refer the matter ... to the Security Council'.[152] In that event the Security Council would act under the UN Charter to decide on the appropriate measures, which could include military action.[153]

As noted earlier above, UN Security Council Resolution 1593, para. 2, after rightly 'recognising that States not party to the Rome Statute have no obligation under the Statute', '*urges* all States and concerned regional and other international organisations to cooperate fully'. Does this mean that non-parties are obliged to cooperate with the court? It has been observed that the word 'urges' suggests 'nothing more than a recommendation or exhortation to take action'.[154] This view is supported by the fact that when the Security Council intends to create a mandatory legal obligation, its practice is to use mandatory language, such as 'member states shall' or 'requires'. It follows therefore that an urging to cooperate is manifestly not intended to create a legal obligation for non-state parties to the Rome Statute to arrest Al Bashir, if he travels within their territory.[155] It is a request for assistance. However, non-parties are not prohibited from arresting him but urged to do so on a voluntary basis. It follows therefore that while Sudan has a clear international legal

150 See ICC-02/05-01/09, Decision on the Prosecution's Application for a Warrant of Arrest Against Omar Hassan Ahmad Al Bashir, note 12 above, para. 247.

151 In July 2009, there were 110 states parties to the Rome Statute. A list of states parties is available at the ICC website: www.icc-cpi.int/Menus/ASP/states+parties/.

152 Rome Statute, Article 87(7) states: '[w]here a State Party fails to comply with a request to cooperate by the Court contrary to the provisions of this Statute, thereby preventing the Court from exercising its functions and powers under this Statute, the Court may make a finding to that effect and refer the matter to the Assembly of States Parties or, where the Security Council referred the matter to the Court, to the Security Council'.

153 UN Charter, Articles 41 and 42. Some commentators called for strong military action as early as 2005 'to protect black Africans in western Sudan'. See S.J. Udombana, 'When Neutrality Is a Sin: The Darfur Crisis and the Crisis of Humanitarian Intervention in Sudan', *Human Rights Quarterly*, 27(4) (2005), pp. 1149–99.

154 D. Akande, 'The Legal Nature of Security Council Referrals to the ICC and Its Impact on Al Bashir's Immunities', *Journal of International Criminal Justice*, 7(2) (2009), pp. 333–52, at p. 344.

155 *Ibid.*

obligation to arrest Al Bashir, all states, including non-state parties to the Rome statute, and regional and international organizations, are recommended to arrest and surrender Al Bashir to the ICC. But which state or regional organization would arrest Al Bashir? Immediate arrest would have been expected from the neighbouring states Al Bashir often visits or from the UN peacekeeping force in Sudan. However, it is highly unlikely that the UN peacekeeping force in Sudan will try to arrest Al Bashir for fear of possible violent reprisals and eviction from the country. Similarly, most African states and the League of Arab States are opposed to the warrant. The ICC prosecutor urged Sudan to arrest Al-Bashir and, failing that, called upon any other state to apprehend him.[156] It is open to speculation whether this would happen in the absence of cooperation from all states.

Indeed, since the ICC issued the warrant, Al Bashir has travelled to some Arab and African states including Qatar, Saudi Arabia, Egypt, Eritrea, Ethiopia, Libya and Zimbabwe (none of which are parties to the Rome Statute), possibly in an attempt to shore up regional support and show defiance to the ICC. Moreover, in July 2009, the African Union (AU) decided that,

> in view of the fact that the request by the African Union [to the UN Security Council to defer the proceedings initiated against President Al Bashir] has never been acted upon, the AU member states *shall not cooperate* pursuant to the provisions of Article 98 of the Rome Statute of the ICC relating to immunities, for the arrest and surrender of President Omar El Bashir of The Sudan [emphasis added].[157]

If the above resolution is implemented, it effectively allows Al Bashir to travel across Africa without fear of arrest and surrender to the ICC. The decision may be criticized on the basis that it pits the AU on the side of impunity against victims of atrocities, and that the text is in contradiction to international legal obligations of AU member states parties to the Rome Statute, whether or not such states agree with the indictment. States parties to the Rome Statute are obliged to 'cooperate fully' with the court in its investigation and prosecution of crimes of a person under Article 86 of the Rome Statute. This includes the obligation to cooperate fully in the execution of arrest warrants because without arrest and surrender the court would be unable to prosecute. However, there is some support for the view that, while the ICC arrest warrant is a lawful coercive act against an incumbent head of state, the ICC request to states parties to arrest and surrender President Al Bashir is patently at odds with Article 98(1) of the Rome Statute and it is an act *ultra vires*.[158] Accordingly, it has been argued that any state other than Sudan that enforces the warrant against Al Bashir would violate international rules recognizing the immunity from arrest for incumbent heads of state and thereby commit an international wrongful act with respect to Sudan.[159] According to this view, states parties to the Rome Statute are not bound to comply with the ICC request to arrest and surrender Al Bashir while he is still a serving head of state. This raises the question of

156 D. Charter, 'ICC Issues War Crimes Arrest Warrant for President Al-Bashir of Sudan', Times Online, 4 March 2009 [online]. Available from: www.timesonline.co.uk/tol/news/world/africa/article5845465.ece, quoting the prosecutor to have stated that '[a]s soon as Mr Al-Bashir travels in international airspace his plane could be intercepted and he could be arrested. That is what I expect.'

157 See Decision on the Meeting of African States Parties to the Rome Statute of the International Criminal Court (ICC), Doc.Assembly/AU/13(XIII), para. 10. In Security Council Resolution 1828, S/RES/1828 (31 July 2008), Preamble paras. 8 and 9, the council simply takes note of the request by the AU to defer the investigation under Article 16.

158 For a discussion, see Gaeta, note 76 above, p. 329.

159 *Ibid*., p. 332.

the relationship between Articles 27 and 98 of the Rome Statute. It would be useful for the ICC to address this in the future.

However, the above AU decision was no victory for Sudan or Al Bashir as it did not declare Al Bashir to be innocent. Besides, some African states parties to the Rome Statute, including Botswana and South Africa, have indicated that they would fulfil their international legal obligations by arresting Al Bashir if he were to enter their territory and surrender him to the ICC. Even so, although it is likely that there will be no immediate arrest and surrender of Al Bashir after the ICC's warrant, the issuing of the warrant is expected to put enormous pressure on the Sudanese regime and other African and Arab leaders to resolve Sudan's problems. Since the warrant was issued, the African Security Committee decided to carry out its own investigations and the AU set up the African Union High-Level Panel on Darfur.[160] In addition, it would make it more difficult for Al Bashir to travel freely to states parties to the Rome Statute and to the Genocide Convention including AU member states parties due to pressure for his arrest, as shown by the fact that he did not attend AU meetings in South Africa (in May 2009), Uganda (in July and October 2009), and Nigeria (in October 2009).[161]

It will also be difficult for Al Bashir to travel to non-states parties to the Rome Statute (for high-level events) outside the AU and the League of Arab member states. For example, despite official invitation, he was unable to attend the summit of the Organization of the Islamic Conference (OIC) in Turkey (in November 2009) after the European Union (EU) put pressure on the host Turkey either to stop Al-Bashir from attending the economic summit or arrest him upon arrival. Similarly, it will be difficult for him to attend UN organs or conferences convened by the UN outside Africa and Arab states, like the UN Conference on Climate Change in Copenhagen, Denmark, in December 2009, without facing a real risk of arrest. It should be noted, however, that Article 105(2) of the UN Charter provides that

> Representatives of the Members of the United Nations and officials of the Organization shall similarly enjoy such privileges and immunities as are necessary for the independent exercise of their functions in connection with the Organization.

This provision is elaborated by Article IV, Section 12 of the Convention on the Privileges and Immunities of the United Nations (1946),162 which provides:

> Representatives of Members to the principal and subsidiary organs of the United Nations and to conferences convened by the United Nations, shall, while exercising their functions and during the journey to and from the place of meeting, enjoy the following privileges and immunities:
>
> (a) Immunity from personal arrest or detention …

160 See *Darfur: The Quest for Peace, Justice and Reconciliation – Report of the African Union High-Level Panel on Darfur* (AUPD), October 2009, PSC/AHG/2(CCVII).

161 See R. Kagumire, 'Bashir Blocked but Is Museveni off the Hook?', *The Independent*, 29 July 2009; 'Sudan's Bashir Not Attending Uganda Summit', Sudan Tribune, 19 October 2009 [online]. Available from: http://www.sudantribune.com/spip.php?article32824; Amnesty International, 'Nigerian Government Must Arrest Sudanese President During Visit', 23 October 2009 [online]. Available from: http://www.amnesty.org/en/news-and-updates/news/nigerian-government-must-arrest-sudanese-president-during-visit-20091023. However, President Al Bashir has been able to visit some ICC States parties in Africa such as Chad (in July 2010) and Kenya (in August 2010) without arrest.

162 1 UNTS 15, 13 February 1946.

While it can be argued that this obligation to accord immunity is a UN Charter obligation (which cannot be waived by the UN Security Council) and thus prevails over any other inconsistent obligation (even if the UN Security Council were to explicitly provide that Al Bashir should be arrested at any UN conference) as a result of Article 103 of the UN Charter, the ICC states parties may in practice ignore this immunity and honour the ICC arrest warrant. Thus, it is possible that the warrant has led to Al Bashir's international stigmatization and isolation, which may be used by political competitors to demand regime change in the long run.

4. Conclusion

The analysis above allows us to make several concluding observations about the ICC warrant of arrest for President Al Bashir. The establishment of the ICC is a major step in the struggle against impunity. Given that there is currently no international court of human rights, the ICC can play an essential role by holding individuals responsible for international crimes within its jurisdiction without any distinction based on official capacity. The court's decision to issue a warrant of arrest for Al Bashir confirms this. Since the warrant was issued, there have been renewed efforts to address the question of accountability for serious crimes of international concern at the regional level in Africa, efforts which would be complementary to national jurisdiction and processes for fighting impunity. In this regard, it is important to note that the AU has considered the possibility of empowering the African Court of Justice and Human Rights with new powers to try persons for international crimes such as genocide, crimes against humanity and war crimes in a manner complementary to national jurisdiction.163 If this does indeed occur, the African Court will be the first regional human rights body to have criminal jurisdiction to pronounce itself on what has hitherto fallen within the purview of international criminal tribunals. This would be a positive development if the African Court receives full cooperation from all African states with respect to its additional criminal jurisdiction.

Following the ICC's investigations in Darfur, Sudan instituted some legal reforms ostensibly designed to improve domestic accountability. These include the establishment of the Special Criminal Court on the Events in Darfur in June 2005; the establishment of two additional special courts in November 2005, and numerous committees – the Judicial Investigations Committee, the Special Prosecutions Commissions, the Committee Against Rape, the Unit for Combating Violence Against Women and Children of the Ministry of Justice, and the Committee on Compensations – the establishment of the Specialized Prosecution for Crimes Against Humanity Office in Khartoum; and the reform of Sudan's criminal code to include international crimes such as crimes against humanity and war crimes. While such domestic institutions have the potential to prosecute international crimes, these courts have not conducted proceedings relevant to the ICC after four years.[164] Indeed, such courts cannot prosecute President Al Bashir while still in office given his immunity. Thus, reforms are essential within Sudan's legal system to ensure the effective

163 See Decision on the Implementation of the Assembly Decision on the Abuse of the Principle of Universal Jurisdiction – Doc. Assembly/AU/3 (XII) (February 2009), para. 9, requested: 'the [AU] Commission, in consultation with the African Commission on Human and Peoples' Rights, and the African Court on Human and Peoples' Rights, to examine the implications of the Court being empowered to try international crimes such as genocide, crimes against humanity and war crimes, and report thereon to the Assembly in 2010'.

164 See Ninth Report of the Prosecutor of the International Criminal Court to the UN Security Council Pursuant to UN Security Council Resolution 1593 (2005), paras. 52–63.

prosecution of all perpetrators of international crimes in Darfur. In this regard the establishment of a hybrid court deserves serious attention.[165]

Although the ICC's decision cannot be rightly considered as being 'political',[166] it must be noted that the prosecutor's decision to prosecute Al Bashir, a sitting head of state, is a 'profoundly political decision', since its consequence is a call for regime change.[167] As shown above, Al Bashir is the first sitting president to be indicted for war crimes and crimes against humanity by the ICC, a move that has certainly broken new ground in confirming that official capacity as a serving head of state and the immunity which may attach to such official capacity is not a bar to the ICC's investigation and prosecution. As noted above, the Pre-Trial Chamber did not examine in detail the question of immunities of state officials whose states are not party to the Rome Statute and the question of whether states parties to the Rome Statute can rely on Article 98 of the Rome Statute to justify non-cooperation with the ICC. This requires clarification in the future.

Despite the controversy arising from the issue of the warrant, it is an important step towards ensuring accountability for human rights violations in Sudan. For the millions of Darfuri victims of the conflict, this decision provides an independent legal recognition that there are 'reasonable grounds to believe' that Al Bashir (as an indirect perpetrator or an indirect co-perpetrator) is personally criminally responsible for the war crimes and crimes against humanity committed against them. However, his arrest and surrender to the ICC remains a challenge, as his trial depends on his presence before the ICC. It is certainly difficult to obtain Al Bashir's custody, and as such the warrant of arrest is likely to remain ink on paper, at least in the short run. The arrest of Al Bashir and his surrender to the ICC would possibly have been easier if the warrant of arrest remained sealed and only made public after Al Bashir had travelled outside African and Arab states.

The success of the ICC in the Sudan, and more particularly in securing the arrest and surrender of Al Bashir, remains to be seen given the lack of cooperation from Sudan and other states in the AU and Arab League. The ICC warrant was described by Sudan's UN ambassador as 'an attempt at regime change', and it was said that Sudan would not be bound by it.[168] It has been claimed that the ICC is 'one mechanism of neo-colonialist policy used by the West against free and independent countries'.[169] This has been largely based on the perception of 'who the ICC selects for investigation'. It is this selectivity that has given rise to the 'neo-colonial' charge against the ICC, a matter that affects its credibility. It is vital to note that the overall problem in international criminal prosecutions still affects the ICC: '[p]olitical considerations, power, and patronage will continue

---

165 See *Report of the African Union High-Level Panel on Darfur* (AUPD), note 160 above, paras. 322–33.

166 Following the issuance of the ICC arrest warrant for Al Bashir, the Sudanese minister of justice, Abdel Basit Sabdarat, told the news network Al-Jazeera that '[w]e will not deal with this court [the ICC] ... It has no jurisdiction, it is a political decision.' See Al Jazeera, 'World Reacts to Bashir Warrant', 5 March 2009 [online]. Available from: english.aljazeera.net/news/africa/2009/03/2009341438156231.html. See also Abdel Rahim El Siddig, 'Arrest Warrant Against Sitting Head of State Is Abuse of Law', *The New Vision*, 11 March 2009 [online]. Available from:www.newvision.co.ug/D/8/20/674250.

167 See W.A. Schabas, 'ICC Observers Exclusive Interview', 26 March 2009 [online]. Available from: http://iccobservers.wordpress.com/2009/03/26/icc-observers-exclusive-interview-william-schabas-professor-of-human-rights-law-and-director-of-the-irish-centre-for-human-rights-at-the-national-university-of-ireland-galway/.

168 M. Simons and N. Macfarquhar, 'Court Issues Arrest Warrant for Sudan's Leader', *New York Times*, 4 March 2009 [online]. Available from: www.nytimes.com/2009/03/05/world/africa/05court.html.

169 See BBC News, 'Arrest Warrant Draws Sudan Scorn', 5 March 2009 [online]. Available from: news.bbc.co.uk/1/hi/world/africa/7924982.stm, quoting Sudanese presidential aide Mustafa Othman Ismail.

to determine who is to be tried for international crimes and who not.'[170] In this respect, Professor Mahmood Mamdani has noted:

> Its name notwithstanding, the ICC is rapidly turning into a Western court to try African crimes against humanity. Even then, its approach is selective: It targets governments that are adversaries of the United States and ignores [the] U.S. allies, effectively conferring impunity on them.[171] The government of Sudan committed lesser atrocities in Darfur compared to what [the] US President George Bush committed in Iraq. Why didn't the ICC issue arrest warrants against Bush?[172]

If the ICC is really to have credibility, and particularly in its current investigations in Africa, it needs to do a lot more work by supporting local national processes of justice and working with them rather than being seen as some sort of alien imposition from outside. As a permanent judicial institution that aspires to be global in scope and universal in acceptance, the ICC needs to demonstrate that it is not a neo-colonial institution investigating crimes in a few weak states. This requires widening its scope of investigations and possible prosecutions of crimes committed by the nationals of the most powerful states falling within its jurisdiction, while at the same time acting independently in deciding cases before it.

If the indictment for Al Bashir is to be meaningful, it must be the case that what applies to Al Bashir also applies to the leaders of the most powerful governments when there are reasonable grounds to believe that they have committed crimes within the jurisdiction of the ICC and when, as has been the case in Sudan, the national institutions have shown unwillingness or inability to investigate and prosecute such crimes effectively. Al Bashir claims to be innocent[173] and insisted in his first interview since the arrest warrant was issued that

> What has been reported to have happened in Darfur did not actually happen at all.... What happened in Darfur was an insurgency. The state has the responsibility to fight the rebels.... Any talk about crimes committed inside Darfur is a hostile and organised media propaganda to tarnish the reputation of the government and is a part of the declared war against our government.[174]

In light of the above defence, he should not wait for the UN Security Council (an organ that is perceived by the GoS to be an instrument of American and British power)[175] to act under Articles

170 I. Brownlie, *Principles of Public International Law* 7th edn (Oxford: Oxford University Press, 2008), p. 604.

171 Mamdani, *Saviors and Survivors,* note 32 above, p. 284.

172 F. Kagolo and S. Akidi, 'Mamdani Raps Bashir Indictment', *The New Vision*, 26 August 2009 [online]. Available from: http://www.newvision.co.ug/D/8/13/692558.

173 See full transcript of Lindsey Hilsum's interview with Omar al-Bashir, president of Sudan, 17 October 2008, *Channel Four News* [online]. Available from: www.channel4.com/news/articles/politics/international_politics/interview+omar+albashir/2562362.

174 See BBC, 'Sudan Leader Denies Darfur Crimes', *BBC News*, 12 May 2009 [online]. Available from: http://news.bbc.co.uk/1/hi/world/africa/8046516.stm.

175 See A. de Waal, 'Darfur, the Court and Khartoum: The Politics of State Non-Cooperation', in N. Waddell and P. Clark (eds), *Courting Conflict? Justice, Peace and the ICC in Africa* (London: Royal African Society, 2008), p. 34. In an interview in August 2009, Al Bashir stated that the ICC 'is a tool to terrorize countries that the West thinks are disobedient'. See S. Dealey, 'Omar al-Bashir Q&A: "In Any War, Mistakes Happen on the Ground"', *Time*, 14 August 2009 [online]. Available from:http://www.time.com/time/world/article/0,8599,1916262,00.html.

41–42 of the UN Charter. He could voluntarily surrender himself to the ICC and defend himself, but this is highly unlikely since he does not respect the ICC as an independent court. On 9 March 2009, Al Bashir reportedly made public his disrespect for the ICC decision by stating:

> in reference to the ICC decision they can cancel it, or they can boil it and drink the water, we are ready for you.... Mark my words – *the Prosecutor, his court and all its members are under my shoes* [emphasis added].[176]

Given that the ICC lacks an independent enforcement mechanism for its warrants, the permanent members of the UN Security Council, particularly the USA and China, should affirm support for the ICC and insist that Sudan and states parties to the Rome Statute cooperate fully with the ICC as required by the UN Security Council, unless or until the Security Council defers the prosecutions in accordance with Article 16 of the Rome Statute.[177]

Finally, the indictment of Al Bashir by the ICC indicates that there are serious implications in indicting a sitting head of state – in fact, basically indicting an entire government structure – in the absence of effective measures and mechanisms in place to execute the warrant and to protect victims in whose name this is being primarily issued. Although there is no question as to whether there should be accountability for genocide, crimes against humanity and war crimes, it is essential to consider how accountability in terms of timing and process should be weighed against other relevant considerations such as the peace process and the withdrawal of essential humanitarian support necessary to live in dignity. In the context of Sudan, although there is yet no clear case for a deferral under Article 16 of the Rome Statute, the UN Security Council should seriously consider such a deferral in the future if the deferral is used to bring about broader and genuine accountability measures in Sudan, including genuine domestic prosecutions necessary to end impunity, and to end the armed conflict and crimes in the Darfur region. In doing so, the Security Council should seriously examine the 'grave concern' of the AU that the indictment 'continues to undermine the ongoing efforts aimed at facilitating the early resolution of the conflict in Darfur'.[178]

---

176 See Ninth Report of the Prosecutor of the International Criminal Court to the UN Security Council Pursuant to UN Security Council Resolution 1593 (2005), para. 35.

177 See International Crisis Group, *Sudan: Justice, Peace and the ICC*, Africa Report No. 152, 17 July 2009 [online]. Available from: http://www.crisisgroup.org/library/documents/africa/horn_of_africa/152_sudan_justice_peace_and_the_icc.pdf. See also M. Bergsmo and J. Pejic, 'Article 16: Deferral of Investigation or Prosecution', in Triffterer, note 2 above, p. 598. For a limited interpretation of Article 16, see D. Scheffer, 'The Security Council's Struggle over Darfur and International Justice', *The Jurist*, 20 August 2008 [online]. Available from: jurist.law.pitt.edu/forumy/2008/08/security-councils-struggle-over-darfur.php.

178 See Decision on the Meeting of African States Parties to the Rome Statute of the International Criminal Court (ICC), Doc.Assembly/AU/13(XIII), para. 3. See also African Union, Peace and Security Council, Communiqué, 175th Meeting, 5 March 2009, PSC/PR/ Comm (CLXXV).

Chapter 25

The Right to an Effective Remedy: Balancing Realism and Aspiration

Sonja B. Starr

1. Introduction

Of all the fundamental principles set forth in the UDHR,[1] few have been so transformed over the ensuing six decades as Article 8's 'right to an effective remedy'. During the drafting of the UDHR, the provision on remedies appears to have been essentially an afterthought.[2] Indeed, for decades thereafter, remedies did not occupy a prominent role in human rights discourse, and the content of the right to a remedy was little developed.[3] That has changed. The international human rights community has successfully pushed for creation of international remedial mechanisms, and international case-law and soft-law instruments have begun to establish principles governing reparations. This chapter reviews those developments and assesses the current state of the law of remedies.

The topic of remedies in human rights law vastly exceeds the scope of this short chapter. Following an initial, brief historical overview, the remainder of the chapter is therefore, by necessity, confined in several significant respects. First, the right to an effective remedy encompasses both a procedural component concerning the right to raise human rights concerns before courts and a substantive component concerning the actual relief to which the victim is entitled.[4] This chapter focuses only on the substantive aspect, sometimes referred to as the law of reparations. Second, this chapter focuses heavily on the decisions of international courts, rather than on domestic court decisions or voluntary governmental decisions to offer reparations. Although domestic actors are the most important frontline implementers of international human rights law,[5] international judicial opinion is likely to influence those actors' understanding of remedial requirements, making the international case law a logical starting point.[6] Third, the chapter does not focus specifically on

---

1 GA Res. 217A (III), UN Doc. A/810 at 71 (1948).

2 Erik Møse, Article 8, in G. Alfredsson and A. Eide (eds), *The Universal Declaration of Human Rights* (Dordrecht: Martinus Nijhoff, 1999), p. 188.

3 See Dinah Shelton, *Remedies in International Human Rights Law*, 2nd edn (Oxford: Oxford University Press, 2005), p. 467.

4 E.g. Office of the High Commissioner for Human Rights (OHCHR), Rule-of-Law Tools for Post-Conflict States: Reparations Programmes 6 (2008); Shelton, note 3 above, p. 7.

5 See Jeremy Sarkin, 'Reparations for Gross Human Rights Violations as an Outcome of Criminal Versus Civil Court Proceedings', in K. De Feyter *et al.* (eds), *Out of the Ashes: Reparation for Victims of Gross and Systematic Human Rights Violations* (Antwerp: Intersentia, 2005), p. 155, noting that victims far more commonly obtain reparations for human rights abuses in domestic courts.

6 See OHCHR, note 4 above, pp. 34–5, noting that international court decisions have 'often played a very important role in catalyzing the willingness of Governments to establish massive reparations programmes' domestically.

the special problems posed by reparations in the context of political transitions or reparations for historical injustices inflicted during past generations. Instead, it aims to identify remedial principles of more general application.

Sections 2 and 3 of this chapter briefly trace the evolution of the individual right to an effective remedy, and identify major types of remedies granted by international courts in human rights cases. Section 4 discusses the corrective, expressive, structural, and deterrent purposes of remedies and the effectiveness of current remedial practice in accomplishing them. Section 5 argues that human rights law, committed in theory to the 'full remedy' ideal but in practice often unable to realize it, is in need of a coherent set of principles governing the permissibility of remedial shortfall and the choice among 'second-best' remedies in situations involving strong competing interests. Concluding observations are made in Section 6.

2. The Right to an Effective Remedy: A Brief History

International law has long recognized the principle that violations of international obligations generate an obligation to make reparation. This basic principle – *ubi ius, ibi remedium*, or 'where there is a right, there is a remedy' – is firmly grounded in domestic law in both common-law and civil-law countries.[7] Prior to the post-war human rights movement, it was already well ingrained in the law of state responsibility. The classic formulation comes from the decision of the Permanent Court of International Justice (PCIJ) in 1928 in the *Chorzów Factory Case*: '[I]t is a principle of international law, and even a general conception of law, that *any breach of an engagement involves an obligation to make reparation*.'[8] The court further specified, in '[o]ne of the most oft-quoted passages in international law':[9]

> The essential principle … is that *reparation must, as far as possible, wipe out all consequences of the illegal act and reestablish the situation which would, in all probability, have existed if that act had not been committed.* [It must consist of r]estitution in kind, or, if this is not possible, payment of a sum corresponding to the value which a restitution in kind would bear.[10]

I refer to this principle as the 'full remedy rule', in that it permits no avoidable remedial shortfall: whatever damages cannot be corrected through restitution must, if at all possible, otherwise be fully compensated. The principle has repeatedly been reiterated by the International Court of Justice (ICJ),[11] and remains 'the cornerstone of international claims for reparations, whether presented by

---

7 E.g. *Marbury* v *Madison*, 5 U.S. (1 Cranch) 137, 163 (1803); William Blackstone, *Commentaries*, 3, *23; See Shelton, note 3 above, pp. 27–9, reviewing constitutional provisions and judicial holdings; Christine D. Gray, *Judicial Remedies in International Law* (Oxford: Clarendon Press, 1987), p. 8, discussing the civil law concepts of *damnum emergens* and *lucrum cessans*.

8 *Chorzów Factory* (Germany *v* Poland), 1928 P.C.I.J. (ser. A), at 46.

9 Dinah Shelton, 'Righting Wrongs: Reparations in the Articles on State Responsibility', *American Journal of International Law*, 96 (2002), pp. 833–56.

10 *Chorzów Factory*, 1928 P.C.I.J. at 47.

11 E.g. Armed Activities on the Territory of the Congo (Congo *v* Uganda), 2005 I.C.J. ¶ 259 (legality of foreign intervention); Legal Consequences of the Construction of a Wall in Occupied Palestinian Territory, Advisory Opinion, 43 I.L.M. 1009, ¶ 152 (2004); Avena Case (Mex. *v* U.S.), 2004 I.C.J. ¶¶ 119–21 (consular assistance to defendants).

states or other litigants'.[12] For instance, the International Law Commission's recent draft Articles on State Responsibility likewise require violators – in addition to ceasing the offending conduct[13] – to 'make full reparation' for 'any damage, whether material or moral'.[14]

Nonetheless, it was not until recent decades that the right to an *individual* remedy assumed a significant place in international human rights law. As noted above, this right was peripheral in the negotiations over the UDHR, with the proposal to add Article 8 only being introduced very late in the process. Article 8 occasioned little debate, however, suggesting that delegates considered its basic principle uncontroversial. This principle was understood as being procedural – it was a right of access to the courts, intended to curtail executive or legislative abuses of power.[15] Like other aspects of the UDHR, Article 8 emerged in part as a reaction to the experience of Nazi Germany, which had shown the dangers of unchecked power in the political branches.[16] It was also grounded in the Latin American concept of *amparo* (a judicial writ protecting individual rights) and in the US concepts of *habeas corpus* (protecting detainees' access to courts) and judicial review.[17] Article 8 thus specified a right to a *judicial* remedy, whereas subsequent treaties allowed decisions by other kinds of neutral adjudicators. Article 8 did not purport to specify types of substantive reparation.

Following the UDHR came a series of binding human rights treaties, each containing provisions establishing an individual right to an effective remedy.[18] These provisions directly govern remedies provided by national authorities, although they are sometimes invoked to support international courts' remedial decisions.[19] The treaties establishing the regional human rights courts in Europe, the Americas, and Africa also contain provisions specifically authorizing international judicial remedies.[20] None of these provisions offers much detailed guidance as to specific forms of reparation.

Indeed, the substantive aspect of the international right to a remedy remained largely undeveloped for decades, as international jurisprudence and scholarship focused principally on the elaboration of primary rules of state conduct.[21] The 1980s and 1990s, however, saw a shift in

12 Shelton, note 9 above, p. 836.

13 International Law Commission, Responsibility of States for Internationally Wrongful Acts, annexed to GA Res. 56/83, 12 December 2001 ('ILC Articles'), Art. 30.

14 *Ibid.*, Art. 31.

15 Møse, note 2 above, pp. 188–95.

16 Johannes Morinsk, *The Universal Declaration of Human Rights* (Philadelphia: University of Pennsylvania Press, 2000), pp. 48–9.

17 Møse, note 2 above, pp. 194–6.

18 E.g. International Covenant on Civil and Political Rights, Arts. 2(3), 9(5), and 14(6), 999 UNTS 171 ('ICCPR'); Convention on the Elimination of Racial Discrimination, Art. 6, 21 December 1965, 660 UNTS 195; Convention on the Elimination of Discrimination Against Women, Art. 2(c), UN Doc. A/34/46; Convention Against Torture and Other Cruel, Inhuman or Degrading Treatment or Punishment, Art. 14, UN Doc. A/39/51 (1984).

19 Shelton, note 3 above, p. 114.

20 American Convention on Human Rights, Art. 63(1), 1144 UNTS 123, entered into force 18 July 1978 ('American Convention'); European Convention for the Protection of Human Rights and Fundamental Freedoms, Art. 41, 213 UNTS 222, entered into force 3 September 1953, as amended by Protocols Nos 3, 5, and 8 ('European Convention'); Protocol to the African Charter on Human and Peoples' Rights on the Establishment of an African Court on Human and People's Rights, Art. 27(1), OAU Doc. OAU/LEG/EXP/AFCHPR/PROT (III), adopted 9 June 1998; Protocol on the Statute of the African Court of Justice and Human Rights, Art. 45, adopted 1 July 2008 (will supplant the 1998 protocol after its ratification by 15 states).

21 See Heidy Rombouts *et al.*, 'The Right to Reparation for Victims of Gross and Systematic Violations of Human Rights', in De Feyter *et al.*, note 5 above, p. 355.

the focus of the human rights movement towards enforcement, driven by the ever-starker disparity between the ambitious rhetoric of human rights instruments and the reality of widespread violation. During this period, a number of developments significantly advanced the substantive international law of remedies.

The first was the creation of several influential soft-law documents concerning remedies. The first of these was the 1985 Basic Principles on Justice for Victims of Crime and Abuse of Power,[22] which were 'founded, in part, on Article 8 of the Universal Declaration' and were 'the first international instrument to articulate victims' right to access justice and obtain reparation for their injuries'.[23] Subsequently, following an extensive drafting process led by Special Rapporteurs Theo Van Boven and Cherif Bassiouni, the United Nations (UN) Human Rights Commission produced a set of Basic Principles and Guidelines on the Right to a Remedy and Reparation for Victims of Violations of International Human Rights and Humanitarian Law.[24] The Principles are widely seen as fairly authoritative,[25] and set forth a right of reparation for human rights violations 'proportional to the gravity of the violations and the harms'.[26] This right includes restoration, so far as possible, of the *status quo ante*, and compensation for all damages.[27] Most recently, the UN Human Rights Committee issued a general comment affirming the individual right to a remedy and identifying various appropriate forms of reparation.[28]

Second, human rights advocates also began to bring domestic litigation grounded in innovative international law-based theories, and the resulting judgements helped to confirm the principle that victims of human rights violations are entitled to remedies. The seminal case was *Filartiga* v *Peña-Irala*, which was decided in a US court in 1980.[29] In Europe, many states have passed legislation allowing causes of action for violations of the European Convention.[30] Elsewhere, while domestic statutes allowing civil claims specifically for international human rights violations remain fairly rare, many states have other provisions not linked to international law specifically that can be invoked in human rights cases.[31] In some civil law countries, the *partie civile* system has also allowed victims to initiate criminal proceedings against human rights abusers and obtain reparations in the process.[32]

Third, major political transitions and civil conflicts throughout the world presented the question of how a post-transition or post-conflict government should confront past abuses. Among other approaches, a number of transitional states established claims commissions or other domestic

22 GA Res. 40/34, 29 November 1985, A/CONF.121/22/Rev.1.

23 Cherif Bassiouni, 'International Recognition of Victims' Rights', *Human Rights Law Review*, 6 (2006), pp. 203–79.

24 E/CN.4/2000/62, Annex (hereinafter 'Basic Principles'); see Dinah Shelton, 'The UN Principles and Guidelines on Reparations', in De Feyter *et al.*, note 5 above, pp. 14–18, describing drafting process.

25 Shelton, note 24 above, p. 31.

26 Basic Principles, note 24 above, ¶¶ 11, 15–16.

27 *Ibid.*, ¶¶ 21–3.

28 General Comment 31, 'The Nature of the General Legal Obligation Imposed on States Parties to the Covenant', CCPR/C/74/CRP.4/Rev/3 (5 May 2003).

29 630 F.2d 876 (2d Cir. 1980).

30 See Rombouts *et al.*, note 21 above, p. 427.

31 *Ibid.*, p. 422.

32 Sarkin, note 5 above, pp. 153–4.

reparations schemes designed to provide compensation or other assistance to individual victims and communities.[33]

Fourth, the 1980s and 1990s saw the growth of the historical reparations movement as well as a trend toward voluntary governmental apologies and sometimes restitution for both recent and historical wrongs.[34] These have included, for instance, reparations by Swiss banks and the German government for stolen property and coerced labour during the Holocaust,[35] US reparations for internment of Japanese-Americans,[36] and official apologies for abuses ranging from Japan's sexual enslavement of 'comfort women' to the US invasion of Hawaii.[37] Many of these developments were grounded more in moral or political claims than in clearly defined legal entitlements. Still, they supported the growing consensus that victims of human rights violations are entitled to symbolic and material reparation.

Fifth, in the late 1980s, the Inter-American Court of Human Rights (IACtHR) began to exercise its contentious jurisdiction. From the beginning, rather than deferring to state enforcement decisions as the European Court of Human Rights (ECtHR) did, it issued detailed remedial orders each time it found violations of the American Convention. The IACtHR has held that the remedial provision of its charter codifies the *Chorzów Factory* full-remedy rule.[38] As discussed further in the next section, the court has over time clearly established itself as the leader among international bodies in the development of creative, ambitious remedies.

Sixth, far more slowly, the ECtHR has begun to develop a somewhat more assertive law of remedies. The court's traditional practice has been to remand cases to national authorities for the adoption of an effective remedy. In doing so, the court invokes the full-remedy rule, admonishing the state party that the remedy must 'restore as far as possible the situation existing before the breach'.[39] Where domestic law does not provide for a full remedy, Article 41 provides that the court shall make up the difference by ordering 'just satisfaction'.[40] The court has increasingly asserted this power, particularly since its major reorganization in 1998.

Seventh, the UN Human Rights Committee has increasingly issued, along with its findings concerning violations of the International Covenant on Civil and Political Rights (ICCPR),[41] strongly worded statements concerning the state party's obligation to provide an effective remedy and identifying specific remedies that would suffice. It then demands follow-up reports concerning the state's provision of remedies. Although the committee lacks the power to make binding orders,

33 See OHCHR, note 4 above, pp. 19–21, describing several programmes; Shelton, note 3 above, p. 40, describing others.

34 E.g. John Torpey, 'Victims and Citizens', in De Feyter *et al.*, note 5 above, p. 41; Elazar Barkan, *The Guilt of Nations* (New York: W.W. Norton, 2000), p. ix, describing a 'new international morality'.

35 See Regula Ludi, 'Historical Reflections on Holocaust Reparations', in M. du Plessis and S. Peté (eds), *Repairing the Past? International Perspectives on Reparations for Gross Human Rights Abuses* (Antwerp: Intersentia, 2007), pp. 138–9.

36 *Ibid.*, pp. 42–3.

37 See Barkan, note 34 above, pp. 55–8 (discussing the Japanese apology) and 216–17 (discussing Hawaii).

38 E.g. Garrido and Baigorria Case, Inter-Am. Ct. H.R. (Ser. C), No. 39, ¶¶ 39–40 (1998); Durand and Ugarte Case, Inter-Am Ct. H.R. (Ser. C), No. 89, ¶ 24 (2001).

39 Lustig-Prean *v* United Kingdom, 29 Eur. Ct. H.R. 548, ¶ 22 (1999).

40 European Convention, note 20 above, Art. 41.

41 999 UNTS 171.

such statements point out existing obligations of international law and thus may be understood as something more than mere policy recommendations.[42]

Eighth, a more recent major development has been the establishment of the International Criminal Court (ICC) and its innovative victim reparations mechanisms. The ICC statute allows victims to receive reparations through a trust fund, which comes ultimately from two sources: seizures of perpetrators' assets[43] and supplementary contributions from states parties.[44] The ICC is just beginning its work and has not yet considered any victim reparations claims. Still, it is reasonable to expect it to contribute substantially to the future development of the substantive law of remedies.

Finally, the newest addition to the international remedial landscape is the nascent African regional human rights court, which is now in the process of being combined with the African Court of Justice and has not yet started hearing cases. The court will potentially also be an important new contributor to the law of remedies.

Meanwhile, human rights scholars have generally embraced the *Chorzów Factory* principles and have pushed for the development of stronger judicial remedies for rights violations.[45] In short, scholars and courts generally agree that victims of human rights violations have a right to an effective remedy that makes them whole for their injuries. As the following sections will illustrate, however, the actual remedies that courts order do not always effectively vindicate that principle.

3. Types of Remedies in International Courts

This section provides an overview of a number of kinds of reparations often ordered by international courts, including restitution, compensation, declaratory judgements, injunctions ordering structural or legislative reform, symbolic satisfaction including apologies, information, and collective assistance to victimized groups. In addition, international courts generally order states to cease ongoing violations – such orders are not included here because they are not truly remedial, but simply enforce the state's basic duty to respect human rights.

3.1 Restitution

Although compensation is much more widely granted, international courts uniformly assert that the *preferred* remedy for human rights violations is *restitutio in integrum*. This concept (often just called 'restitution') refers to specific relief designed actually to restore the victim as closely as possible to the position he or she would have occupied without the violation, rather than merely figuratively 'making her whole' through compensation. Human rights cases often involve irreversible harm, making full restitution unattainable. Still, some form of partial restitution can

42 See, generally, Martin Scheinin, 'The Human Rights Committee's Pronouncements on the Right to an Effective Remedy', in Nisuke Ando (ed.), *Towards Implementing Universal Human Rights* (Dordrecht: Martin Nijhoff, 2004), pp. 101–4.

43 See Rome Statute of the International Criminal Court, Arts. 77, 86–7, 93, 109.

44 See Pablo de Grieff and Marieke Wierda, 'The Trust Fund for Victims of the International Criminal Court', in De Feyter *et al.*, note 5 above, p. 228.

45 E.g. Shelton, note 3 above, p. 100; Rombouts *et al.*, note 21 above, pp. 363, 366; Shelton, note 9 above, p. 835; Naomi Rohrt-Arriaza, 'Reparations Decisions and Dilemmas', *Hastings International and Comparative Law Review*, 27 (2004), pp. 157–219; Salvatore Zappala, *Human Rights in International Criminal Proceedings* (Oxford: Oxford University Press, 2005), p. 150.

often be accomplished. For instance, stolen land or cultural property can be returned, or parents wrongfully denied access to their children can be provided access. Medical and psychological injuries can be partially alleviated by ordering appropriate health care.[46] The IACtHR has recognized interference with a victim's 'life plan' as a cognizable injury, and has accordingly required the state to provide victims and family members with special scholarships so as to help them put their lives back on track.[47]

Restitution can also include remedies granted to enforce the procedural rights of criminal defendants, such as vacatur of unlawfully obtained conviction and granting of retrials. The regional human rights courts occasionally order such remedies.[48] In their procedural case law, international criminal tribunals have likewise invoked the right to an effective remedy that corrects the effects of a breach.[49] In addition, the UN Human Rights Committee has consistently held that commutation of a death sentence is an essential remedy in any capital case involving violations of the ICCPR.[50]

The ECtHR has often stated that restitution is the preferred remedy in principle, but it virtually never orders it, as it has repeatedly held that it lacks the authority to do so. Rather, where restitution appears appropriate, the court simply finds a violation and leaves it to the state party to develop an appropriate remedy under the supervision of the Committee of Ministers.[51] Sometimes the court suggests specific remedies;[52] occasionally, it suggests that only *one* available remedy would be adequate.[53] Even then, though, the court generally does not actually *order* that remedy – although there are rare exceptions. The court, for instance, recently ordered the release of a seriously ill, pre-trial detainee who had been detained without sufficient cause and deprived of necessary medical treatment.[54] However, this order might simply be understood as requiring cessation of ongoing violations, rather than restitution. The text of Article 41 of the European Convention, which refers to 'just satisfaction', offers no clear basis for the court's repeated assertion that it lacks the power to order remedies other than compensation. Indeed, in a dissent from the Grand Chamber's recent decision in *Salduz* v *Turkey*, several judges recently argued that the assertion is unfounded. They argued that tribunals have the inherent authority to fashion remedies, that the European Convention does not confine the court's remedial authority to compensation, and that it should thus order restitution, the preferred form of compensation for international wrongs, when possible.[55] The court's refusal to order restitution is better explained by political or institutional concerns than by textual restrictions: the court considers itself relatively ill-equipped to fashion remedial orders to be implemented within domestic legal schemes, beyond simple orders of compensation. Its remedial

46 See Douglas Cassel, 'The Expanding Scope and Impact of Reparations Awarded by the Inter-American Court of Human Rights', in De Feyter *et al.*, note 5 above, pp. 202–3, discussing Inter-American Court cases.

47 See *Cantoral Benevides* v *Peru (Reparations)*, Serie C, no. 88, ¶ 60 (3 December 2001).

48 E.g. Castillo Petruzzi *et al.*, Case, 52 Inter-Am. Ct. H.R. (ser. C) (1999).

49 E.g. Prosecutor *v* Kajelijeli, ICTR 98-44A-A, judgement, ¶¶ 254–5 (23 May 2005); Prosecutor *v* Rwamakuba, ICTR-98-44-A, Decision on Appeal Against Decision on Appropriate Remedy, paras. 23–6 (13 September 2007).

50 Communication Nos. 210/1986 and 225/1987 (*Pratt and Morgan* v *Jamaica*), 6 April 1989, UN Doc. A/44/40, vol. II, 222, para. 15; see Scheinin, note 42 above, pp. 110–11.

51 See Shelton, note 3 above, p. 199.

52 E.g. *Intersplav* v *Ukraine*, 9 January 2007, ¶ 48 (recommending administrative change).

53 E.g. *Salduz* v *Turkey*, Application No. 36391/02, ¶ 72 (Grand Ch., 27 November 2008).

54 *Aleksanyan* v *Russia,* Application No. 46468/06, 22 December 2008, ¶¶ 239–40.

55 *Salduz*, note 53 above, Joint Concurring Opinion of Judges Rozakis, Spielman, Ziemele, and Lazarova Trajkovska.

deference is analogous to the 'margin of appreciation' the court gives to national authorities in the implementation of substantive convention rights – both reflect the subsidiarity principle.[56]

3.2 Compensation

Monetary compensation is, in practice, by far the most common international remedy for human rights violations. It is the only remedy, other than declaratory relief, regularly ordered by the ECtHR, and it is also regularly ordered by the IACtHR along with other remedies. Compensation is the remedy typically granted by domestic reparations schemes in transitional contexts, and by international claims commissions. It is also the primary remedy that the ICC statute contemplates being given to victims.

Like *restitutio in integrum*, compensation is designed to 'make the victim whole', and thus covers all meaningful harms that are not redressed through restitution. These include both pecuniary damages and non-pecuniary or 'moral' damages, such as pain and suffering, emotional distress, and, at the IACtHR, the previously discussed interruption of the victim's 'life plan'. Indeed, most of the damages in many cases are non-pecuniary.[57] Interest and court costs may also be included. Still, compensation orders in international courts tend to be modest, a point discussed further in Section 4.1.

3.3 Declaratory Relief

In the human rights context, declaratory relief typically simply refers to the court's finding that a violation was committed, and is thus provided in every case in which the applicant prevails. This kind of declaration is distinct from the familiar uses of declaratory remedies in domestic courts, which are generally forward-looking and are used to clarify the parties' ongoing legal rights. Mere findings of liability, without more, provide no material benefit to the victim; as remedies, they are purely symbolic.

Still, the ECtHR and IACtHR both have repeatedly held that such findings count as 'remedies' for non-pecuniary injuries. In practice, the IACtHR always also provides other remedies[58] – but the ECtHR sometimes does not. In *Golder* v *United Kingdom* in 1975, the court held that mere declaratory relief sufficed as 'adequate just satisfaction'.[59] The court has since followed *Golder* a number of times (albeit inconsistently), often over vociferous dissents.[60]

3.4 Structural Injunctions and Legislative Reforms

Beyond reparations benefiting the specific claimants, remedies in human rights cases can encompass broader measures designed to prevent similar violations in the future. The IACtHR is the unquestioned leader in devising such remedies. In cases involving individual murders or disappearances, for instance, it has ordered the creation of a nationwide genetic databank to

---

56 E.g. Laurence R. Helfer, 'Redesigning the European Court of Human Rights', *European Journal of International Law*, 19(1) (2008), pp. 125–59, at p. 128.

57 See Cassel, note 46 above, p. 199.

58 E.g. Case of the 'Street Children', 2001 Inter-Am. Ct. H.R. (ser. C), No. 77, ¶ 88 (26 May 2001).

59 1975 Eur. Ct. H.R. ¶ 46 and Disposition.

60 E.g. Nikolova *v* Bulgaria, 31 Eur. Ct. H.R. 3, ¶ O-12 (1999) (Bonello, J., dissenting) ('*Nikolova* Dissent'); Marckx *v* Belgium, 2 Eur. Ct. H.R. 330 (ser. A) (1979) (joint dissenting opinion of six judges).

identify missing persons,[61] broad human rights education programmes for the armed forces and police,[62] a comprehensive system of judicial records covering all government detainees,[63] and a new legislative provision criminalizing enforced disappearance.[64]

3.5 Apology and Other Symbolic Measures

As noted above, official state apology has taken on increased prominence in recent decades – one recent volume on the subject was in fact entitled *The Age of Apology*.[65] Most such apologies have been undertaken without legal coercion. Apologies, however, are a recognized form of 'satisfaction' under international law, and thus may be ordered by courts as a remedial measure.[66] The IACtHR has sometimes required apologies, often in the course of 'a public ceremony, where victims [also] officially receive awards of compensation'.[67] 'Satisfaction' may also encompass other symbolic measures, and in this context, too, the IACtHR has adopted a variety of creative remedies. For instance, it has often required the state to name a public space or school after a victim, to create a special memorial, or to establish a scholarship fund in the victim's name.[68]

3.6 Information and Investigation

Another type of remedial order concerns investigation of abuses and provision of information to victims and family members. The IACtHR has issued such orders in most of these cases.[69] They are particularly important in cases involving enforced disappearance, where silence concerning victims' fates exacerbates family members' pain. The court typically orders the state party to provide all known information to family members, to conduct investigations to fill in gaps, and to return remains of deceased victims wherever possible. Moreover, the court often specifies that states must open *criminal* investigations into abuses and, as appropriate, prosecute individuals who are guilty of international crimes.[70]

3.7 Collective Remedies

Finally, where an individual applicant's claim is part of a broader pattern of state abuse, international courts have sometimes ordered material measures designed to benefit a broader victimized community, such as the construction of roads and schools. The IACtHR has again taken the lead in

61 *Molina Theissen* case, 2004 Inter-Am Ct. H.R. (ser. C), No. 108, ¶¶ 90–1 (3 July 2005).

62 *Myrna Mack Chang* case, 2003 Inter-Am Ct. H.R. (ser. C), No. 101 (25 November 2003).

63 *Juan Humbérto Sanchez* case, 2003 Inter-Am. Ct. H.R. (ser. C), No. 99 (7 June 2003).

64 *Trujillo-Oroza* case, 2002 Inter-Am. Ct. H.R. (ser. C)., No. 92, ¶¶ 94–8. See also Cassel, note 46 above, pp. 205–6, listing other examples of legislative and administrative reforms ordered by the court.

65 Mark Gibney et al. (eds), *The Age of Apology: Facing up to the Past* (Philadelphia: University of Pennsylvania Press, 2008).

66 See ILC articles, note 13 above, Art. 37(2).

67 Cassel, note 46 above, p. 204.

68 *Ibid.* (citing cases).

69 *Ibid.*, p. 203.

70 Criminal prosecution itself is not generally considered to fall within the realm of 'reparation', and thus falls beyond this chapter's scope.

this regard with a variety of different orders.[71] In addition, the African Commission on Human and Peoples' Rights, which lacks the authority to issue binding remedies, has recommended a number of collective remedies, such as the clean-up of environmental pollution on indigenous lands.[72] These remedies, however, enforce provisions of the African Charter on Human and Peoples' Rights (ACHPR) governing collective rights, which distinguish the charter from most other major human rights treaties. Collective remedies are also authorized by the rules of procedure and evidence of the ICC, reflecting 'the fact that some crimes within the ICC statute have a collective or group element, such as the crime of genocide'.[73]

4. Purposes of Remedies

4.1 Corrective Justice

In international case law and human rights scholarship, the principal stated purpose of remedies is generally to require the perpetrator to make victims whole for their injuries. This objective, which is grounded in the idea of 'corrective justice', has a long pedigree in the law of state responsibility, in domestic public and private law, and in the case law of the human rights courts, as the discussion above illustrates. Corrective justice theories date back at least to the time of Aristotle, who described the objective as being to 'make the parties equal' by cancelling out the effects of a wrong.[74] Human rights scholars and advocates have widely embraced such theories.[75] Nonetheless, actual remedies in human rights cases often fail to vindicate corrective principles fully. In mass-abuse cases, it is commonplace to note that the *Chorzów* principle is merely an unrealizable ideal – full compensation for all victims, especially in poor countries, is a practical impossibility.[76] But remedies often fall short even in smaller-scale cases. In particular, the compensation orders entered by the ECtHR, discussed in Section 2.2, are often so minimal that it is hard to conceive of them, realistically, as making the victim whole. Recently, for instance, the ECtHR found Turkey responsible for detaining an applicant for an excessive time (seven years) pending criminal proceedings, without providing a way to challenge his detention; during these years, the applicant was repeatedly beaten and subjected to other conduct violating the convention's prohibition on 'inhuman or degrading treatment'. The court awarded the applicant 17,500 euros.[77] In another recent case, the court awarded a widow 20,000 euros for the death of her husband, which resulted from the Polish authorities' refusal to provide adequate medical care during his pre-trial detention.[78] Both these amounts seem to understate the injury suffered. These were large awards by European Court standards, however – compensation for less egregious injuries tends to be very modest indeed.

---

71 E.g. Mayagna (Sumo) Awas Tingni Community *v* Nicaragua, Serie. C, No. 78, ¶ 167 (31 May 2001); Rombouts *et al.*, note 21 above, pp. 408–9.

72 Social and Economic Rights Action Center *v* Nigeria, No. 155/96, 15th Annual Activity Report, Annex V; see Rombouts *et al.*, note 21 above, pp. 407–8.

73 Shelton, note 3 above, p. 234; see ICC Rules of Criminal Procedure and Evidence, Rule 97, PCNICC/2000/1/Add/1 (2 November 2000).

74 Aristotle, *The Ethics* (trans. J.A.K. Thomson, Harmondsworth: Penguin, 1955), p. 148.

75 E.g. Shelton, note 3 above, p.148 (citing Aristotle).

76 See note 111 below.

77 *Demirbaş and Others* v *Turkey*, Application Nos. 50973/06, 8672/07 and 8722/07 (December 2008).

78 *Dzieciak* v *Poland,* Application No. 77766/01 (December 2008).

Even more dubious than these small awards, from a corrective perspective, is the ECtHR's *Golder* line of precedent, which holds that declaratory relief alone can amount to an adequate remedy for non-pecuniary injuries. The court has consistently and appropriately recognized that non-pecuniary injuries are often the central part of the harm suffered in human rights cases. This recognition makes the *Golder* approach incomprehensible from a corrective justice perspective. If significant harm is done, then corrective justice requires the *perpetrator* to do something to repair that harm. The court's mere recognition of the violation does not amount to repair, and it does not require any action at all from the perpetrator. Moreover, even if a finding of liability can meaningfully be understood as a 'remedy', that finding presumably does not depend on the existence of the non-pecuniary harm in question – it would be entered even if the only harm suffered was pecuniary. Thus, the *Golder* approach functionally *ignores* non-pecuniary injury, and can hardly be said to correct it.

4.2 Expressive Goals

Remedies for human rights violators are often justified in terms of the message the remedy will send to the violator, the victim, and the community at large. For instance, recommending a range of measures to memorialize victims, the Sierra Leone Truth and Reconciliation Commission observed: 'Symbolic reparations . . . are a clear expression of recognition for the harm suffered. Symbolic reparations can preserve the memory of what happened [and] serve as a reminder that society must not let this happen again.'[79] The UN Office of the High Commissioner for Human Rights (OHCHR) has likewise argued that the key objective of transitional reparations programmes is to 'provide a measure of recognition to victims and thus to make a contribution to the full recovery of their dignity'.[80] More generally, as Dinah Shelton has argued, '[r]emedies express opprobrium to the wrongdoer' and thus 'affirm, reinforce, and reify the fundamental values of society'.[81] These arguments reflect an expressive approach to legal remedies.

Expressive legal remedies respond to 'expressive harms'. Expressive legal theories are premised on the idea that wrongful conduct can harm individuals not just because of its material consequences but because of what it *means* – often, because it signals disrespect for the victim's dignity or humanity, which are core human rights concerns. For instance, an individual who is beaten up in a bar fight may experience the same physical injuries as one who is beaten by government soldiers for belonging to a racial minority group, but the latter is likely to experience serious additional harm due to the government's expression of contempt. Moreover, other members of the group may suffer nearly comparable expressive injuries – even without feeling the assault's physical effects, they may acutely feel its meaning. Expressive remedies are to combat these harmful messages by affirming the victim's humanity and condemning the wrongdoer's conduct. As Elizabeth Anderson and Richard Pildes put it, 'expressive legal remedies matter because they express recognition of injury and reaffirmation of the underlying normative principles for how the relevant relationships are to be constituted.'[82] Such messages can have positive practical consequences in terms of preventing comparable abuses in the future. Studies show that the law can shape subsequent behaviour not just by causing potential wrongdoers to fear legal penalties (deterrence), but also,

79 *Witness to Truth: Report of the Sierra Leone Truth and Reconciliation Commission*, ch. 4, para. 27 (2004).

80 OHCHR, note 4 above, p. 30.

81 Shelton, note 3 above, p. 12.

82 Elizabeth S. Anderson and Richard H. Pildes, 'Expressive Theories of Law: A General Restatement', *University of Pennsylvania Law Review*, 148 (2000), pp. 1503–75, at p. 1529.

perhaps more effectively, by sending messages that influence social norms and attach stigma to wrongful conduct.[83] State actors, no less than private citizens, are subject to social influences, and promotion of rule-of-law social norms may influence them to comply.[84]

Many of the human rights remedies discussed in the previous section are entirely or principally expressive in character. A state apology, for instance, 'answers to the harm that injustice causes to the dignity of the victims' by communicating 'a moral recognition or acknowledgment of their human worth and dignity'.[85] Moreover, recent voluntary state apologies have created 'new atmosphere[s] of openness' and triggered 'a flurry of apologies' from civil society representatives for their roles in human rights abuses, amplifying the apology's social impact.[86]

Court-ordered apologies might be seen as insincere, clouding this message. Still, even court-ordered apologies appear to mean something to many victims of human rights abuses, who have sought them out in international and domestic litigation. The act of apologising, even if involuntarily, can serve as a morally appropriate moment of public shaming of the wrongdoer. Forcing a wrongdoer to apologise, even if insincerely, may be a way of inculcating human rights values in the wrongdoer himself – akin to the reasons parents force children to apologise – or in the community more broadly. Moreover, the relevant message may not be contained solely in the apology itself, but rather in the court's decision to order it, which reflects the judgement of the national or international community affirming the victim's dignity and condemning the violation.

Similarly, other kinds of symbolic remedies, such as the naming of public places or days of remembrance, often ordered by the IACtHR, are clearly designed to serve an expressive purpose: requiring the state to publicly honour the memory of victims. Such remedies can go beyond one-time apologies by providing a lasting testament to the victims' dignity and humanity and a reminder of the human costs of state abuses. Even if such memorials trigger no immediately noticeable shift in public values or state behaviour, they may nonetheless contribute to the development of respect for human rights in the long run.

Another objection to symbolic remedies, related but distinct from the insincerity objection, is that talk is cheap and easily forgotten. Even if apologies and public remembrances are sincere, they do not do anything practical for victims and are nearly costless for the state, making them a low-value expressive signal. Some scholars have even suggested that apologies are trivializing, even 'somewhat absurd, if not obscene', in the context of the most serious human rights violations such as crimes against humanity.[87] This objection is a serious one, and indeed, apologies may not always be effective expressive remedies. The value of any remedy is culturally and situationally dependent, and remedial orders should be tailored accordingly.[88]

---

83 E.g. Paul H. Robinson and John M. Darley, 'The Utility of Desert', *Northwestern University Law Review*, 91 (1997), pp. 453–99, at pp. 454–7, 470; Cass R. Sunstein, 'On the Expressive Function of Law', *University of Pennsylvania Law Review*, 144 (1996), pp. 2021–53, at pp. 2026–7.

84 See Ryan Goodman and Derek Jinks, 'How to Influence States: Socialization and Human Rights Law', *Duke Law Journal*, 54 (2004), pp. 621–703, at pp. 638–55.

85 Janna Thompson, 'Apology, Justice, and Respect: A Critical Defense of Political Apology', in Gibney *et al.*, note 65 above, pp. 31–44, at p. 34 (quoting Trudy Govier and Wilhelm Verwoerd, *The Practice of Public Apologies* (2002)).

86 Elazar Barkan and Alexander Karn, *Taking Wrongs Seriously* (Stanford, CA: Stanford University Press, 2006), p. 22.

87 Jean-Marc Coicaud and Jibecke Jönsson, 'Elements of a Road Map for a Politics of Apology', in Gibney et al., note 65 above, pp. 77–94, p. 83.

88 E.g. Alison Dundes Renteln, 'Apologies: A Cross-Cultural Analysis', in Gibney et al., note 65 above, pp. 61–76, at pp. 65–9, discussing cultural variation in meaning of apologies.

But if symbolic remedies do nothing for victims or even insult them, it is hard to see why, in so many cases, victims even of very serious abuses have pushed hard to get them. The IACtHR's innovative use of symbolic remedies has not really been the product of judicial ingenuity – rather, it has been driven by the litigation strategies of claimants and the political pressures applied by victims' advocates. Moreover, many of the court's remedial orders in contested cases have been modelled on the friendly settlements reached by parties in other cases, which often include apologies and other symbolic relief as core components.[89] This suggests that at least some victims of human rights abuses, in negotiating settlements, have been willing to sacrifice demands for greater material compensation in order to obtain public recognition of the violations. Likewise, South Africans 'turned out in large numbers to listen to perpetrators' apologies' in the Truth and Reconciliation Commission, suggesting that those words mattered to victims.[90]

Moreover, state resistance to symbolic satisfaction in many cases suggests that such remedies are not, indeed, costless or trivial to states. Official state apologies for wrongdoing – even in the 'age of apology' – remain rather exceptional, to say nothing of more extensive symbolic acceptances of responsibility. While some states have agreed to such measures, others have strongly resisted political pressure to accept responsibility or have even disregarded judicial orders.[91] As Michael Freeman put it, 'if apologies are cheap, . . . it is hard to explain why they are so rare.'[92]

Still, in addition to these 'merely' symbolic remedies, material reparation can also serve important expressive purposes. A court's order that the wrongdoer provide reparation is a way of publicly recognizing the wrongfulness of the underlying conduct. The corrective and expressive justifications for remedies are distinct – the former focuses on the inherent justice of the award itself, and the latter on the message it sends – but they are closely intertwined. The most effective expressive remedy will often be a corrective one, because such remedies are understood to 'restore' victims of wrongdoing to their 'rightful positions' and thus symbolize full respect for the victims' rights.[93]

Indeed, this interrelationship suggests that non-material, symbolic remedies may often be insufficient, taken alone, to express condemnation of the wrongdoing and respect for the victim. Judicial messages may 'ring hollow' unless at least some concrete steps are taken to repair the victim's injury.[94] The amount of the reparation may also matter. As Brandon Hamber observes concerning litigation over South African apartheid, 'money has come to take on a symbolic meaning itself. The settlements of the apartheid lawsuits need to be substantial . . . to register the extent of

---

89 See Cassel, note 46 above, p. 211.

90 Catherine Jenkins, 'Taking Apology Seriously', in du Plessis and Peté, note 35 above, p. 78 (quoting Rosalind Shaw).

91 *Ibid.*, pp. 71–2, noting the 'extreme reluctance of authors of political crimes to apologise in any form', and citing the example of former Rwandan Prime Minister Jean Kambanda, who refused to express regret at his sentencing hearing even when it might have helped him avoid a life sentence).

92 Michael Freeman, 'Back to the Future: The Historical Dimensions of Liberal Justice', in du Plessis and S. Peté, note 35 above, p. 50; see also Coicaud and Jönsson, note 87 above, p. 85, noting that powerful states are especially resistant to apologies.

93 See Lawrence Friedman, 'Reactive and Incompletely Theorized State Constitutional Decision-Making', *Mississippi Law Journal*, 77 (2007), pp. 265ff, at p. 286 (arguing that 'return to the status quo ante . . . recognises the expressive injury and reaffirms' the proper 'relationship between government and citizen').

94 *Ibid.*, p. 289; see Rhoda E. Howard-Hassmann and Anthony P. Lombardo, 'Words Require Action: African Elite Opinion About Apologies from the "West"', in Gibney et al., note 65 above, pp. 216–28, at p. 226.

the hurt.'[95] This point suggests a further serious drawback to the ECtHR's declaratory-relief-only approach in the *Golder* line of cases. Consider a hypothetical case posed by Anderson and Pildes:

> Suppose a defendant convicted of a vicious crime is brought before a judge for sentencing. The judge declares, 'Your crime is horrific and wrong, and the State condemns you for it,' and – then releases the convict without punishment. The outraged public would naturally think that the judge did not really mean what he said. . . . To condemn meaningfully requires not a mere utterance, even in the form of a stern lecture from the bench, but a practice of punishment socially understood to express condemnation effectively.[96]

Although this passage concerns criminal punishment, its logic applies to civil reparations for human rights abuses. 'Mere utterances' may be insufficient to express condemnation of the abuses and respect for the victim in a meaningful way.

On the other hand, in some human rights contexts, material reparation may itself carry a hollow or even negative expressive message. Some victims have criticized reparations as 'blood money' and refused to accept them, demanding criminal investigation of the underlying abuses instead.[97] More generally, money damages are often criticized for commodifying victims' suffering, essentially allowing states to pay a price to commit human rights abuses.[98]

The strength of these expressive objections may vary among different situations – where damage awards are culturally understood as expressive acts, they do not function as mere 'prices'. Generally, these concerns are more compelling when material reparations serve as the *sole* remedy for human rights abuses. Intuitively, compensation or material restitution is less likely to be seen as mere pricing – or worse, as blood money – when it is accompanied by remedies that send a strong and explicit message condemning the underlying misconduct. A potential model is provided by the IACtHR's complicated remedial orders, which generally combine material and symbolic relief and often also order states to undertake criminal investigations. Likewise, reparations at the ICC ought to largely avoid these criticisms, as they are accompanied by criminal punishment and thus should not be seen as allowing perpetrators to buy impunity.

4.3 Prevention of Repetition

Another major remedial objective is to prevent the violating state from committing similar violations in the future. This objective overlaps with the expressive goals discussed above, since expressive remedies seek in part to shame the perpetrator into accepting and complying with human rights norms. But this preventive purpose can be achieved in other more concrete ways as well. Again, the IACtHR has taken the lead in designing preventive remedies, including constitutional and legislative reforms and adoption of human rights training programmes for military and police personnel. Its transparency-oriented remedies, like requirements of investigation, may also serve this purpose – in addition to providing relief to family members seeking information, such measures also may serve to undercut the atmosphere of secrecy that allows human rights violations to flourish.

---

95 Brandon Hamber, 'The Dilemma of Reparations', in De Feyter *et al.*, note 5 above, p. 146; see Barkan, note 34 above, p. 27.

96 Anderson and Pildes, note 82 above, p. 1567.

97 OHCHR, note 4 above, pp. 12, 34; Hamber, note 95 above, p. 139; Barkan, note 34 above, pp. 24–5, 58.

98 See Shelton, note 3 above, at 290; Richard Abel, 'Civil Rights and Wrongs', *Loyola of Los Angeles Law Review*, 38(3) 2005, pp. 1421–34, at p. 1430, raising similar arguments in the domestic context.

At least in terms of getting these structural orders implemented in the first place, the IACtHR has enjoyed reasonable, if far from perfect, success.[99] It is much harder to measure the ultimate impact of such remedies in achieving lasting change in government behaviour. In other contexts, scholarly assessments of the effectiveness of human rights education and training are mixed, and such programmes are only useful if they are well designed and implemented.[100] Effective oversight of training programmes is essential,[101] and while the Inter-American Commission is an appropriate institution to provide this, scholars have noted in the past that its human rights education programmes have been under funded.[102] Still, the court's innovative structural remedies carry significant potential, in principle, to have a transformative effect on state behaviour, provided its orders are effectively carried out.

4.4 General Deterrence

A fourth remedial objective is general deterrence – that is, deterring potential human rights abusers generally (and not just the specific party involved in the case) by threatening the imposition of undesirable consequences. Although general deterrence is a common justification for civil damages in some domestic systems, especially that of the USA, it has played a relatively small role in judicial and scholarly discourse about reparations in the international human rights context. Still, it could, and perhaps should, be a more significant consideration. After all, the international human rights movement does not aim only to come to terms with the past, but also to contribute to the development of a better future. General deterrence is already a major theme in scholarship and jurisprudence in international criminal law, and this emphasizes the need to end the widespread expectation of impunity. But criminal punishment is not the only consequence that may deter potential violators. Notably, many human rights abuses are committed in pursuit of private financial gain. The prospect of ultimately being bankrupted by compensation awards might reduce this incentive.

There are a number of reasons for scepticism, however, about the prospect of achieving effective deterrence through civil reparations in human rights cases, particularly in international courts. First, international courts do not generally have the capacity to hear very large numbers of cases. Potential violators thus know that their odds of actually facing penalties are relatively low. Second, the deterrent capacity of money damages is particularly limited when those damages are imposed on the state itself rather than individual perpetrators of human rights abuses. As Dinah Shelton observes, states have comparatively deep pockets and can often easily absorb damage awards.[103] Certainly, it is hard to see how the small financial awards given by the ECtHR will have much deterrent effect on the behaviour of European states.

Shelton proposes that deterrence of states therefore requires much larger damage awards – punitive damages, set at levels often greatly exceeding the amount required to compensate the

99 See Cassel, note 46 above, p. 214, describing degree of compliance as 'surprising'; but see Eric A. Posner and John C. Yoo, 'Judicial Independence in International Tribunals', *California Law Review*, 93 (2005), pp. 1–74, at pp. 41–4, describing compliance difficulties.

100 See, generally, Mary O'Rawe, 'Human Rights, Transitional Societies, and Police Training', *St John's Journal of Legal Commentary*, 22 (2007), pp. 199ff, at pp. 212–17.

101 *Ibid.*

102 See Cecilia Medina, 'Toward Effectiveness in the Promotion of Human Rights in the Americas', *Transnational Law and Contemporary Problems*, 8 (1998), pp. 337–58, at p. 357.

103 See Shelton, note 3 above, pp. 14, 358.

victim.[104] This proposal is appealing, but it is not a panacea. Studies of deterrence in other contexts show that in shaping human behaviour, the probability of penalties is far more important than their magnitude,[105] and there is no reason to think this tendency to dismiss the prospect of low-probability punishments does not apply to state decision-makers. Moreover, as discussed below in Section 5, large damage awards against states impose considerable cost on innocent citizens. Finally, governments may simply not respond to financial incentives the way private individuals and corporations do, at least not predictably.[106] Governments have too many options for offsetting financial losses – they can raise taxes, shift money from other programmes, or even, simply, print money. Ultimately, governments may be more influenced by threats to their political power than to their treasuries.[107]

These observations suggest several guidelines for the use of reparations to achieve general deterrence. First, the reach and efficiency of a reparations system may be more important than the magnitude of the awards it grants – that is, reparations will have to be seen to be granted in a large number of cases in order to appreciably affect violators' incentives. In this respect, the European human rights system is by far the world's most effective. Many thousands of cases have now been heard by Strasbourg itself, not to mention the cases decided by domestic courts applying the European Convention.

Second, the relative difficulty of deterring states with financial awards argues for the development of remedial mechanisms that allow individual perpetrators of human rights abuses to be held civilly responsible. The ICC offers one venue for such claims,[108] but it can only hear relatively few cases, so mechanisms with broader reach are necessary. Domestic courts offer the most realistic prospect for dealing with large numbers of cases, but international courts could play a broader role – for instance, regional human rights courts could be empowered to seize the assets of individuals implicated in the state abuses they identify, or to order states to do so.

Finally, if states respond more to political than to financial pressures, they may be more deterred by symbolic remedies than by material reparations. As noted above, state leaders often resist such symbolic remedies, suggesting that they may impose significant political costs. Structural injunctions may likewise have some deterrent effect, as they may require the adoption of political reforms that states had previously resisted.

5. Permissible Remedial Shortfall and Second-Best Remedies

Although the discussion above suggests that international courts may need to become more ambitious and creative in their remedial approaches, it would be short-sighted to conclude that stronger remedies are always preferable. In crafting remedies, courts sometimes face strong competing interests, the possibility of non-compliance, and the risk that overly assertive remedies

104 *Ibid.*, pp. 14, 355–8.

105 See Dan M. Kahan, 'Social Influence, Social Meaning, and Deterrence', *Virginia Law Review*, 83(3) (1997), pp. 349–95, at p. 380 and n. 112 (citing studies).

106 Daryl J. Levinson, 'Making Government Pay: Markets, Politics, and the Allocation of Constitutional Costs', *University of Chicago Law Review*, 67(2) (2000), pp. 345–420, at pp. 361–2, 420.

107 *Ibid.*

108 See Sonja B. Starr, 'Extraordinary Crimes at Ordinary Times: International Justice Beyond Crisis Situations', *Northwestern University Law Review*, 101 (2007), pp. 1257–1314, at pp. 1287, 1295–6, arguing that ICC prosecutors should consider, in selecting cases, perpetrators' possession of substantial assets that could be seized.

will trigger a backlash against victims. Human rights case law and scholarship have not yet developed a systematic approach to handling these kinds of conflicts. Indeed, courts rarely confront these competing interests candidly, instead adopting *sub rosa* remedial compromises. This section discusses these problems and offers some thoughts on solutions.[109]

5.1 Justifications for Remedial Shortfall

There are a number of possible compelling reasons that the above-discussed remedial ideals might sometimes need to give way to some kind of compromise. The most obvious are situations in which fulfilling those ideals is simply impossible. The prototypical example is mass-abuse situations, in which the number of victims far outstrips available resources.[110] Scholars and advocates have widely accepted compromise remedies in such cases – indeed, impossibility has always been a built-in exception to the *Chorzów Factory* full-remedy rule.[111]

Despite this recognition, the human rights community has been too reluctant to acknowledge the need for similar compromises where ideal remedies are not impossible, but are undesirable because of strong competing interests. For instance, even in cases involving just one or a few claimants, orders for material reparations can impose large costs on states that will trade off with other state priorities. In many cases, especially in poor countries, this means that funding for social programmes will be cut, and other innocent citizens will suffer. Victims of human rights abuses often have serious material needs, but victims are not necessarily the neediest people in a society, and even if they are, concentrating a relatively large amount of assistance in the hands of just a few of those who need it might not be the best outcome from a distributive perspective. The need for reparative justice may legitimately trump these distributive concerns – this is a normative question that is beyond the scope of this chapter. But it would be hard to argue that it should be illegitimate, as a matter of international law, for courts at least to consider these kinds of competing interests when they craft remedial orders in human rights cases.

Another possible problem is that ambitious remedial orders may trigger societal resentment against the victims or the group to which they belong. This is especially a risk when it comes to remedies that demand noticeable trade-offs with social spending on behalf of other citizens, or those that go beyond what is necessary for corrective purposes in order to serve deterrent or other objectives. Such remedies risk being seen as 'windfalls' that exceed what the victims 'deserve'.

This perception may undermine the intended expressive message of the remedy. The expressive value of law turns on its perceived moral legitimacy,[112] which in turn depends in part on consistency with cultural intuitions concerning fairness. As Stephen Schulhofer argues, 'desert is essential to the stigmatizing effects of punishment.'[113] Likewise, Robinson and Darley argue that excessive punishment may have a net negative effect on compliance with law – the marginal deterrent benefit

---

109 For a more extensive discussion of these problems, see Sonja B. Starr, 'Rethinking "Effective Remedies": Remedial Deterrence in International Courts', *New York University Law Review*, 83 (2008), pp. 693–768.

110 See Shelton, note 3 above, at 389–90, 399.

111 E.g. *ibid.*, p. 399; Basic Principles, note 24 above, ¶ 18; OHCHR, note 4 above, pp. 28–9; de Grieff and Wierda, note 44 above, p. 233; Rombouts *et al.*, note 21 above, p. 459; Rohrt-Arriaza, note 45 above, p. 181.

112 E.g. Robinson and Darley, note 83 above, p. 457.

113 Stephen J. Schulhofer, 'Criminal Justice Discretion as a Regulatory System', *Journal of Legal Studies*, 17 (1988), pp. 43–82, at p. 68.

'is outweighed by the additional cost' to the 'law's moral credibility'.[114] Although these arguments focus on criminal punishment, their logic applies to the condemnatory message of civil remedies as well. Indeed, experience in US courts, where punitive damages are relatively common, suggests that the perceived excessive size of some punitive awards undermines their expressive message.[115]

Resentment of strong remedies may often be unjustified – the product of unappealing jealousy or sometimes bigotry – and it could be argued that courts should not cater to these tendencies by denying effective remedies to victims.[116] The problem, though, is that the victims themselves may ultimately be harmed by an escalation in hostility. If so, a lesser remedy may ultimately be more effective for victims, and it seems counterproductive for a court to ignore that fact.[117] Moreover, if the remedy's expressive message is undermined, it may encourage further human rights abuses, harming other future victims, and it is also legitimate to consider the interests of such innocent third parties.

Relatedly, courts also must consider whether a given remedial order outstrips their own institutional capacity to obtain execution. International courts have no police or military at their disposal, and compliance with their orders is ultimately dependent on the cooperation of state parties. Excessively ambitious remedial orders risk simply being disregarded, making them useless to the victims. Moreover, such non-compliance may undermine the credibility of the court and hurt its effectiveness more broadly, as other states see that its orders need not be taken seriously.[118]

The ECtHR's cautious remedial jurisprudence almost surely results in part from a fear of such consequences, and it is hard to say that the court is entirely wrong. Its deferential approaches have probably contributed to its success in obtaining nearly perfect compliance with its judgements. In this author's view, the court tends to err too much on the side of caution, especially today; as it has firmly established itself already, it would probably be safe for the court to experiment with more ambitious remedial approaches. On the other hand, for new courts such as the African Court on Human and Peoples' Rights (ACtHPR) or the ICC, a dose of that caution may be essential to consolidation of authority and long-run effectiveness.

When it comes to remedies granted to defendants in the criminal process, particularly strong competing interests may arise: the punishment of crime and protection of the public. Such remedies sometimes serve as windfalls that enable guilty defendants to escape punishment. In international criminal tribunals, this problem is especially serious, as the defendants are themselves accused of egregious human rights abuses and may pose a serious threat if set free.[119] Retrial, meanwhile, is often not a realistic option given the tremendous length and expense of trials.[120] Moreover, resentment and political backlash are important considerations in this context as well. Notably, at one time, in the *Barayagwiza* case, the Rwanda Tribunal attempted to release a defendant due to procedural violations. As a result, the government of Rwanda threatened to completely cease

---

114 Robinson and Darley, note 83 above, pp. 457–8.

115 Brent T. White, 'Say You're Sorry: Court-Ordered Apologies as a Civil Rights Remedy', *Cornell Law Review*, 91 (2006), pp. 1261ff, at pp. 1279–80.

116 See Shelton, note 3 above, p. 102.

117 See Paul Gewirtz, 'Remedies and Resistance', *Yale Law Journal*, 92 (1983), pp. 585ff, at p. 609, arguing that US courts in desegregation should consider the possible effects of white resistance for black victims.

118 See Shelton, note 3 above, p. 290; Starr, note 109 above, p. 724.

119 See Starr, note 109 above, p. 717.

120 *Ibid.*, p. 716.

cooperation with the tribunal, effectively shutting it down; the tribunal backed down and found an excuse to amend its order.[121]

5.2 Remedial Deterrence and Circumvention

While strengthening enforcement of the right to an effective remedy is generally desirable, rigid adherence to strict remedial rules may be self-defeating. When competing interests or institutional efficacy concerns make remedies overly costly to courts, resistance to candid interest-balancing may perversely make it less likely that victims of human rights violations will receive any remedy at all. If they are unable to avoid excessive remedial costs through a candid interest-balancing approach to remedies, courts may seek to avoid them covertly in one of two ways.

The first way is *sub rosa* dilution of the effective remedy requirement. If courts cannot admit openly that they cannot grant an otherwise-required remedy because of some strong competing interest, they may simply grant a lesser remedy and assert that that remedy *is* 'effective'. This may help to explain the ECtHR's sporadic practice, in the *Golder* line of cases, of simply defining down full or effective remedies to permit declaratory relief alone to suffice. Unfortunately, *Golder* sets the precedent that a judgement of condemnation amounts to full reparation for *all* non-pecuniary damages (no matter how severe) caused by human rights abuses, even *without* some special competing interest. And indeed, several national courts in Europe have followed that precedent.[122]

The second way is 'remedial deterrence': the high costs of the required remedy may deter courts from recognizing rights violations in the first place.[123] This results in an overkill response to competing interests: rather than search for an acceptable compromise remedy, courts grant no remedy at all. Courts can avoid remedial costs by adjusting doctrinal rules at various other stages of the proceedings: narrowing their substantive interpretations of rights, deeming violations non-prejudicial, or manipulating admissibility requirements or other procedural rules to avoid hearing the claim in the first place. These circumvention strategies have all been documented as results of strong remedial rules in domestic courts,[124] and international courts may well behave similarly. Indeed, I have argued elsewhere that remedial deterrence appears to have significantly impacted procedural rights jurisprudence at international criminal tribunals.[125] To avoid releasing accused war criminals, triggering political backlash, or incurring the massive costs of retrial, international criminal tribunals have adopted strikingly narrow interpretations of a number of procedural rights – for instance, they have tolerated many years' worth of prosecutorial delays without finding violations of the right to a speedy trial.[126] In the above-mentioned *Barayagwiza* case, the Rwanda Tribunal was forced to alter its assessment of the underlying rights violations in order to justify reversing its decision to release the accused.[127]

121 *Ibid.*, p. 717.

122 *Nikolova* dissent, note 60 above, referring to cases.

123 See Daryl J. Levinson, 'Rights Essentialism and Remedial Equilibration', *Columbia Law Review*, 99 (1999), pp. 857–940, coining this phrase.

124 E.g. *ibid.*; Richard H. Fallon, Jr., 'The Linkage Between Justiciability and Remedies – and Their Connections to Substantive Rights', *Virginia Law Review*, 92 (2006), pp. 633–705; J.A.E. Pottow, 'Constitutional Remedies in the Criminal Context: A Unified Approach to Section 24 (Part II)', *Criminal Law Quarterly*, 44 (2000), pp. 34ff, at p. 60.

125 Starr, note 109 above, pp. 710–30.

126 *Ibid.* p. 720–3.

127 *Ibid.*, pp. 717–18.

These circumvention strategies sacrifice judicial candour: rather than acknowledging the dilemma posed by strong competing interests, the court simply pretends an ineffective remedy is effective or manipulates its rights interpretations. Candour is broadly understood to be a vital part of the judicial function – the requirement that courts give honest reasons for decisions is a critical 'restraint on abuse of judicial power'.[128] Moreover, these covert compromises result in bad precedents for other courts and government actors by defining down the right to an effective remedy or the underlying substantive human rights. 'A subterfuge that compromises an ideal without saying so creates a risk that the ideal will be weakened, that people will come to think that the ideal *means* only what has been imperfectly realised.'[129]

5.3 An Interest-Balancing Approach to Remedies

How, then, should courts respond when they face difficult remedial dilemmas? There is no single easy answer – such judgements will depend on subjective normative considerations and on the specific circumstances. However, it is possible to identify some general guidelines.

First, wherever possible, intractable remedial dilemmas should be avoided by creativity in the institutional design of international courts, claims commissions, and domestic reparations schemes. Judges need to have at their disposal not just strong remedies, but remedies that they are willing to invoke and able to enforce. For instance, in international criminal tribunals, the stark costs of release and retrial could be avoided by giving the tribunals a more flexible array of remedial options for procedural violations. Retrial could be made more realistic via expedited procedures, rather than requiring a whole trial *de novo*. Or, as alternatives to retrial, tribunals could liberalize the standards for admission of new evidence on appeal or for reopening of trial proceedings while the appeal is pending. Tribunals could also lower hurdles for interlocutory appeals, allowing procedural problems to be addressed at an earlier stage when they can be remedied more easily.[130]

Second, where difficult remedial dilemmas cannot be avoided, courts should be empowered to balance competing interests candidly and search for acceptable compromises.[131] Such an approach would extend the approach human rights law already takes to mass-abuse situations, where full remedies are impossible, to smaller-scale cases, where full remedies are in principle possible but are in practice undesirable. Interest-balancing does not, however, mean wholly even-handed cost-benefit analysis. Rather, courts should give a heavy presumption in favour of remedying rights violations, and depart from that norm only when very strong countervailing considerations are present. As Paul Gewirtz has argued concerning interest-balancing in US constitutional remedies, 'the social benefit of the right and the interest in undoing effects of its violation must be given exceptional weight in the balance; otherwise the . . . allocation of rights would be subject to a *de novo* utilitarian re-evaluation in particular cases.'[132]

The case for interest balancing is particularly compelling in the context of cases involving large material awards that implicate serious distributive justice concerns. It is equally compelling in the case of injunctive remedies that involve broad structural reform, which sometimes present clear conflicts with third-party interests. For instance, consider the potential privacy concerns involved

128 David L. Shapiro, 'In Defense of Judicial Candor', *Harvard Law Review*, 100 (1987), pp. 731–50, at p. 737.

129 Gewirtz, note 117 above, p. 673.

130 See Starr, note 109 above, pp. 746–52.

131 *Ibid.*, pp. 752–66.

132 Gewirtz, note 117 above, p. 607.

in the creation of a nationwide genetic databank.[133] Such collateral costs may well be justified, but they should at least be considered explicitly, with remedial orders tailored to avoid unnecessary third-party harm–. In the genetic databank case, the IACtHR could have specified that participation be voluntary and that information privacy be protected.

On the other hand, an interest-balancing approach might often favour reliance on symbolic or collective remedies. Because symbolic remedies do not generally impose significant material costs, they raise fewer distributive concerns and may be less likely to promote resentment and non-compliance. To be sure, as discussed above, governments have sometimes resisted symbolic measures such as apologies – but many states have cooperated with requests for apologies, memorials, and the like, as the Inter-American system's friendly settlements illustrate,[134] and a court may well be able to predict what a given state's reaction will be.

Collective remedies, such as community programmes or infrastructure, in turn, offer a measure of reparation to large numbers of victims at once, and thus avoid disproportionate payouts to whichever victim happened to bring a claim. The OHCHR has criticized collective remedies because they are non-exclusive – any citizen might benefit from a road or a bridge, making them less directed at victims specifically and thus less 'reparative'.[135] But that very feature is an advantage from an interest-balancing perspective – it offers the prospect of assisting others in need as well as the victims, mitigating distributive justice concerns and making the remedy less likely to be met with resentment.

6. Conclusion

Six decades after its articulation in the UDHR, the right to an effective remedy remains a rapidly evolving component of human rights law – it enjoys broad support in principle, but its specific content has not been clearly defined. This is illustrated by the drastic differences in remedial approach between the European and Inter-American courts, two regional human rights courts with similar treaty mandates. Even wider variation is found among the multitude of other domestic and international courts and other remedial institutions. And every new institution with authority to grant reparations, such as the ICC and the African Court, offers the prospect of taking remedial doctrine in new and unexpected directions.

In a sense, this variation is appropriate – while many aspects of the law of remedies merit further elucidation, it is no disaster that the world lacks a uniform set of specific remedial principles. Remedies serve a variety of purposes – corrective, expressive, deterrent, and structural – and are granted in a vast variety of different cultural contexts and political circumstances. Not all victims of human rights abuses want the same remedies. Moreover, the competing interests at stake in each case will also vary widely, as will communities' normative judgements as to which interests to value more highly.

Courts should therefore avoid adopting excessively rigid remedial rules or practices. Designers of such courts should empower them with a flexible array of remedial options, so as to avoid forcing them, in cases raising strong competing interests, to make all-or-nothing choices between extremely costly remedies and no remedies at all. Moreover, courts should avoid boxing themselves in by creating inflexible remedial doctrine – either weakening their remedial authority unnecessarily (as

133 *Molina Theissen*, note 61 above,, pp. 43–4.

134 See Cassel, note 46 above, p. 214.

135 OHCHR, note 4 above, p. 26.

in the ECtHR's holdings that it lacks the power to grant restitution) or committing themselves to extremely strong remedial rules that they will not be able to follow through on.

Instead, courts should be willing to be creative in crafting remedial packages to serve a combination of remedial purposes, and they should be able to adjust as necessary where competing interests are sufficiently compelling. And they should be honest about the choices they are making, articulating reasoned justifications for any departures from their usual remedial practices. By following these principles, courts can best balance the far-reaching aspirations of the law of remedies with the pragmatic concerns that stand in the way of realizing those aspirations.

Chapter 26
Protecting Human Rights in Emergency Situations: The Example of the Right to Education

Vernor Muñoz Villalobos

1. Introduction

The focus of this chapter is on the protection of human rights in emergency situations, with particular reference to the right to education since education is not only a human right in itself but also 'an indispensable means of realizing other human rights'.[1] Thus, protecting the right to education in emergency situations can reinforce the protection of other human rights by creating a more favourable environment for the realization of human rights – for example, by empowering women, safeguarding children from exploitative and hazardous labour and sexual exploitation, promoting human rights and democracy, and protecting the environment.[2]

Six decades after the UDHR,[3] the commitment to realizing the human right to education has been a signal failure. It has seen the goals of Education for All[4] and the educational targets of the Millennium Development Goals[5] continually subsumed to the logic of economics, which, in turn, sees education as nothing more than an instrument of the market. This failure to conceptualize education as a human right not only impacts negatively, to a certain extent, on the progressive realization of the right to education but also impacts on the realization of other human rights since education contributes to realizing other human rights. For some, moreover, the consequence of this is a complete denial of the right to education.

For much of my mandate as United Nations (UN) Special Rapporteur on Education,[6] I have paid particular attention to groups of persons traditionally marginalized and particularly vulnerable to exclusion from education. In so doing, I have attempted to establish the causes and circumstances surrounding their exclusion and the challenges that must be faced in order to promote the realization of their right to education. It has become clear from this that there remains an urgent need to redouble efforts to safeguard the right to education for those people – especially children, adolescents and youths – who are denied any possibility of attending school or attaining an education as the result, direct or indirect, of an emergency situation impacting their community.

---

1 Committee on Economic, Social and Cultural Rights (CESCR), *General Comment 13: The Right to Education* (Twenty-First Session, 1999), UN Doc. E/C.12/1999/10 (1999), para. 1.

2 *Ibid.*

3 Universal Declaration of Human Rights, adopted 10 December 1948, UNGA Res 217 A(III).

4 Dakar Framework of Action on Education for All [online]. Available from: http://www.unesco.org/education/efa/ed_for_all/dakfram_eng.shtml [accessed 27 April 2009].

5 [online]. Available from: http://www.un.org/millenniumgoals/ [accessed 27 April 2009].

6 Mandate and documents relating to the United Nations Special Rapporteur on Education [online]. Available from: http://www2.ohchr.org/english/issues/education/rapporteur/index.htm [accessed 27 April 2009].

For the purposes of this chapter, 'emergency' refers to any crisis situation arising from natural causes (such as earthquake, tsunami, flood or hurricane), from armed conflict, which may be international (including military occupation) or internal (as defined in international humanitarian law), or from post-conflict situations that impair, interrupt, delay or deny the right to education, impede its development, or hold back its realization. Such situations put people's health and lives at risk and threaten or destroy public and private assets, limiting the capacity and resources to guarantee human rights and uphold social responsibilities. Recurrent and/or combined emergencies in impoverished regions may, of course, have a multiplier effect, with devastating consequences for school infrastructure, teaching and the educational opportunities generally of the children living in those regions.

Emergency situations are becoming increasingly frequent the world over.[7] However, the impact on each person directly involved in an emergency, while invariably brutal, may also vary, as will people's personal reactions. At no time should such situations entail suspension of domestic and international obligations to guarantee the human rights of all those affected. State institutions, the international community, organizations, and individuals that offer assistance when they arise, should be guided by those rights, rather than responding on the basis of often unwarranted and incorrect assumptions or financial risk. Further, those that do offer assistance should act with those impacted rather than for them.

Article 26 of the UDHR acknowledges that everyone has the right to education, which should be directed to the full development of the human personality and to the strengthening of respect for human rights and fundamental freedoms, and should further 'promote understanding, tolerance and friendship'. Education can and indeed should play a key role in promoting cooperation and human understanding. Yet we would do well to heed history and recognize that education can be of a kind that does not build peace but increases social and gender inequalities and may well fuel conflict. In this respect, it is likely, and necessary, that the debate on the role of education in generating conflict and also on the ways in which education can help build a lasting peace will continue.

Indeed, there is a disjunction between social, cultural and economic structures and educational activities carried out in times of emergency. There is an urgent need to close this gap because, although the impact of every emergency is different, there is one prevailing characteristic common to all: the interruption, degradation or destruction of education and educational systems.[8]

This chapter is divided into eight sections. Section 2 deals with the protection of education in emergencies, stressing the importance of education in emergency situations. Section 3 examines briefly the international legal and political framework for the protection of education in emergencies. Section 4 considers the role of donors in the implementation of the right to education in emergencies, while Section 5 considers the question of education providers in emergency situations, noting that there is no single agency to which states requiring educational assistance can turn in an emergency. Section 6 identifies groups that are more vulnerable to violations of the right to education in emergency situations. Section 7 considers selected issues on three aspects of the right to education, namely the curriculum, quality and shared learning, while Section 8 offers some recommendations.

---

7 According to the World Health Organization, the twentieth century was the most violent period in human history. E.G. Krug, *World Report on Violence and Health: Summary* (Geneva: World Health Organization, 2002).

8 M. Sinclair, *Planning Education in and After Emergencies* (Paris: UNESCO, 2002) [online]. Available from: http://www.unesco.org/iiep/PDF/Fund73.pdf [accessed 27 April 2009].

2. Education in Emergencies

There is a multiplicity of proposed definitions and conceptions of 'emergency' and the stages or time frames they reflect. The focus here will, however, be on the period from early response to an emergency to the initial stages of reconstruction, since it is during these stages that what are perhaps the worst violations of the right to education occur.[9] It is during this period that educational systems and opportunities are destroyed, that the limited attention paid by the humanitarian agencies involved, and the relative absence of clear programmatic principles, indicators or funding, are most clearly revealed.

The role and content of education in emergency situations are also a source of conceptual disagreement, especially where a distinction is being made between education in emergencies and education in non-emergency situations. An educational vision based firmly on respect for human rights, and more particularly the human right to education, will help clarify the conceptual issues.

2.1 Context

The consequences of brutal armed conflicts and of natural disasters for education have become increasingly visible. Either can strike in any region, often without warning. No state is exempt, and all have differing forms and levels of resources upon which they can draw to deal – or otherwise – with the consequences, and in all (now) the civilian population is the chief casualty. Statistics on conflict-related emergencies remain disturbingly vague, as most are based on estimates, which vary dramatically. In 2003, the UN Children's Fund (UNICEF) stated that 121 million children were affected by armed conflict,[10] yet, in 2000, the UN Educational, Scientific and Cultural Organization (UNESCO) had put the figure at 104 million.[11] A comprehensive review in 2004[12] estimated the number of children and adolescents affected by armed conflict and without access to formal education to be at least 27 million, most being internally displaced persons (90%). More generally, approximately half of children who receive no education live in states where there is or recently has been armed conflict and where, in some states, net school enrolment is below 50%.[13]

The number of refugee and displaced children receiving no education outside the camps of the Office of the United Nations High Commissioner for Refugees (UNHCR) remains unknown, as does the number of illiterate young people, adolescents and adults who have no educational opportunities. In 1998, hundreds of schools in Central America were damaged by Hurricane Mitch, and many others were turned into shelters. In Aceh, Indonesia, 1,000 teachers were lost after the tsunami in 2004, and 50& of schools were destroyed, leaving 140,000 elementary students and

9 Inter-Agency Network for Education in Emergencies (INEE), *Minimum Standards for Education in Emergencies, Chronic Crises and Early Reconstruction* (Paris: UNESCO, 2004), p. 8 [online]. Available from: http://www.ineesite.org/index.php/post/inee_handbook/ [accessed 27April 2009].

10 UNICEF, *The State of the World's Children* (New York: UNICEF, 2004) [online]. Available from: http://www.unicef.org/sowc07/docs/sowc07.pdf [accessed 27 April 2009].

11 UNESCO, *EFA Global Monitoring Report: Gender and Education for All: The Leap to Equality* (2003/4) [online]. Available from: http://www.portal.unesco.org/education/en/ev.php-URL_ID=23023&URL_DO=DO_TOPIC&URL_SECTION=201.html [accessed 27 April 2009].

12 L. Bethke and S. Braunschweig, *Global Survey on Education in Emergencies* (New York: Women's Commission for Refugee Women and Children, 2004).

13 See further UNHCR, Report of Special Rapporteur on the Right to Education, UN Doc. E/CN.4/2006/45 (2006).

20,000 junior high school students with nowhere to study. The tsunami destroyed 112 schools in Sri Lanka.[14]

Even though natural disasters are 'statistically less lethal' than conflicts, causing one-third of the number of deaths, natural disasters in the 1990s affected seven times the number of people affected by conflict.[15] Notably, natural disasters are on the rise, occurring three times as often in the 1990s as they did in the 1950s. There are no reliable data permitting a comparison of the impact of natural disasters and the impact of armed conflicts. There are reliable data, however, showing that around 90% of those affected by natural disasters live in states with limited capacity to cope with that impact.[16]

Statistics in themselves are not always sufficient to show the degradation and destruction of education systems when an emergency arises, particularly in the case of armed conflict when teachers, students and parents become the targets of violence. Few statistics record the impact of violence in schools themselves in times of conflict, despite reports that levels of teacher violence against students also intensify. Parents keep their children at home to avoid the risks involved in the trip to and from school and also to avoid falling victim to landmines. Further, during times of conflict, schools can become recruitment centres for children, who are forced to become soldiers, this in itself being a direct attack on children's education and lives.

The killing of students and teachers and the bombing and destruction of schools have escalated sharply over the past four years in terms of victims and brutality,[17] and in certain states, Afghanistan being a notable example, there is a clear gender dimension. Such attacks are directed against girls' schools, the sole intent being to intimidate and prevent girls from accessing education.[18]

It is my firm view that security in schools, meaning not only physical, psychological and emotional safety but also an uninterrupted education in conditions conducive to knowledge acquisition and character development, forms part of the right to education.[19] This means that states have a responsibility to punish perpetrators and devise effective methods of protection.

Emergencies impact particularly severely on people with disabilities. In her now well-known report, 'Impact of Armed Conflict on Children',[20] Graça Machel noted that, for every child killed, three are seriously injured or permanently disabled. More specifically, she found that armed conflict and political violence are the leading causes of injury and physical disability, and are primarily responsible for the desperate conditions of over 4 million children who currently live with disabilities and for the lack of basic services and/or minimum support. This lack of support

---

14 D. Burde, *Education in Crisis Situations: Mapping the Field* (Washington, DC: USAID, 2005), pp. 8–9 [online]. Available from: http://www.caii-dc.com/CAIIStaff/Dashboard_GIROAdminCAIIStaff/Dashboard_CAIIAdminDatabase/publications/Ed_Crisis_Final.pdf.

15 *Ibid.*, p. 9.

16 *Ibid.*, p. 8.

17 B. O'Malley, *Education Under Attack: A Global Study on Targeted Political and Military Violence Against Education Staff, Students, Teachers, Union and Government Officials, Aid Workers and Institutions* (Paris: UNESCO, 2007) [online]. Available from: http://www.unesco.org/education/attack/educationunderattack.pdf [accessed 27 April 2007].

18 R. Coomaraswamy, February 2008 [online]. Available from: http://www.un.org/children/conflict/english/12-feb-2008-statement-at-the-security-council-open-deb.html [accessed 27 April 2009].

19 UNHCR, 'Report of the Special Rapporteur on the Right to Education' (2005) E/CN.4/2005/50, para. 119.

20 G. Machel, *Impact of Armed Conflict on Children*, UN Doc. A/51/306 (2006) [online]. Available from: http://www.unicef.org/graca/a51-306_en.pdf [accessed 27 April 2009].

is compounded by broad economic decline and health problems that frequently accompany emergencies generally. The lack of clear statistical data on emergencies does not, and cannot, hide the clear fact that the impact of emergencies on education has been enormous.[21]

2.2 The Importance of Education in Emergencies

Learning encompasses our past and future at once; it is an aspect of life that comprehends everything that makes development possible. To learn is to adapt, to cooperate, and to transform our environment. It is the process by which people communicate, put forward ideas and bring them to fruition; learning is the organizing principle of every society. Nearly all communities affected by emergencies organize themselves rapidly. They identify representative leaders, provide assistance to their people, and determine priorities and needs:[22] these include education, which is always demanded by populations affected by emergencies.

Although I am opposed to the current tendency to treat education as no more than a tool, I recognize that, beyond the human rights imperative, education also provides physical, psychosocial and cognitive protection that can be both lifesaving and life-sustaining. Education offers safe spaces for learning, as well as the ability to identify and provide support for affected individuals, particularly children and adolescents. Education mitigates the psychosocial impact of conflict and disasters by giving a sense of normality, stability, structure and hope during a time of crisis, and provides essential building blocks for social reconstruction and future economic stability. Education can also directly save lives by protecting against exploitation and harm, including abduction, recruitment of children into armed groups, and sexual and gender-based violence. In addition, it provides the knowledge and skills to survive in a crisis through, for example, the dissemination of lifesaving information about landmine and cluster bomb safety, HIV/AIDS prevention, conflict resolution mechanisms and peace building.[23]

Humanitarian aid traditionally focuses on the three classic areas of food, health and shelter. Assistance, however, should be geared to people's overall needs and welfare, which as noted above, clearly implicates education. Aid that merely supplies calories for the stomach and water for the throat reduces people to things.[24] More searching questions should therefore be asked as to why education does not automatically form a fourth arm of humanitarian aid.

3. International Legal and Political Framework

The international legal and political framework of education in emergencies is the product of several global developments – the ever-increasing number of natural disasters, the changing nature of conflict and the fight against terrorism – and an unwavering perception of what education should be and the quality and kinds of education that should be available.

---

21 M. Sommers, *Youth: Care and Protection of Children in Emergencies: A Field Guide* (Washington, DC: Save the Children, 2001).

22 G. Martone, *Educating Children in Emergency Settings: An Unexpected Lifeline* (New York: International Rescue Committee, 2007).

23 INEE Minimum Standards for Education in Emergencies, Chronic Crises and Early Reconstruction (Paris: UNESCO, 2004), note 9 above.

24 T. Vaux, *The Selfish Altruist: Relief Work in Famine and War* (London: Earthscan Publications, 2001).

The obligation of states to respect, protect and fulfil the right to education endures throughout emergency situations. In addition, the right to education inheres in each person regardless of legal status, whether 'refugee', 'child soldier' or 'internally displaced'. This introduces a complexity, however, that has been previously anticipated;[25] although each person has the same right to education, few individuals have the same educational needs. Moreover, states have the primary responsibility in law for guaranteeing education, even if they lack the capacity needed to do so. This is why, since the international community's legal undertakings have been conceived to fully meet people's needs, these undertakings include the provision of educational cooperation, as provided for in Article 28(3) of the UN Convention on the Rights of the Child (CRC).[26]

Although states are, rhetorically, collectively committed to adopting a human rights perspective on the provision of education, these commitments have not translated frequently enough into collective responses to emergencies.

3.1 Legal Framework

The UDHR establishes, in Article 26, the right to free compulsory elementary education. Article 13 of the International Covenant on Economic, Social and Cultural Rights (ICESCR)[27] defines the scope of this right more precisely, requiring that education should be available to all who have not received or completed primary education. The CRC also obliges states to ensure, without discrimination of any kind, access to education for all children living in their territories.[28] Its Article 28 protects free compulsory primary education, urges states to develop accessible secondary education and other forms of education, and encourages international cooperation in educational matters. In support of this, it refers to the best interests of the child (Article 3) and the right to life and to survival and development to the maximum extent possible (Article 6).

The threat to each of these principles becomes more acute in times of emergency, and particular care and effort are needed to secure them. Special attention must also be paid to the real aims of education, which are interpreted by the Committee on the Rights of the Child (CRC) as transcending mere access to formal schooling and embracing a broad range of life experiences and learning processes that enable children, individually and collectively, to develop their personalities, talents and abilities and live a full and satisfying life within society.[29] Moreover, under Article 22 of the CRC, states are obliged to ensure that a child who is seeking refugee status receives appropriate protection and humanitarian assistance, and enjoys all rights as set forth in the convention. This includes the obligation to provide prompt and full access to education and rapid integration into the regular education system.[30] In addition, under Article 39 of the CRC, states should, *inter alia*, take all appropriate measures to promote physical and psychological recovery and social reintegration

25 UNCHR, 'Report of the Special Rapporteur on Education on the Right to Education of Persons with Disabilities', UN Doc. A/HRC/4/29 (2007).

26 Adopted 20 November 1989, entered into force 2 September 1990, GA Res. 44/25, 44 GOAR, Supp. (No. 49), UN Doc. A/44/49 at 166 (1989).

27 Adopted 16 December 1966 entered into force 3 January 1976, UNGA Res. 2200A (XXI), UN Doc. A/6316 (1966), 993 UNTS 3.

28 Committee on the Rights of the Child (CRC), Articles 2 and 28.

29 Committee on the Rights of the Child (CRC), *General Comment 1: The Aims of Education* (Twenty-Sixth Session), UN Doc. CRC /GC/2001/1(2001), para. 1. See also CRC, Article 29.

30 Committee on the Rights of the Child (CRC), *General Comment 6: Treatment of Unaccompanied and Separated Children Outside Their Country of Origin* (Thirty-Ninth Session), UN Doc. CRC/GC/2005/6 (2005), paras. 41–3.

of child victims of armed conflicts. Of particular importance is Article 38, which calls on states to respect and ensure respect for international humanitarian law in relation to children.

The Optional Protocol to the Convention on the Rights of the Child on the involvement of children in armed conflict[31] has the potential to reduce the number of children recruited into regular armies and irregular armed groups and to mitigate the implications for their educational opportunities.[32] It has been followed by several UN Security Council resolutions, most notably Resolution 1612 (2005),[33] which establishes a monitoring and reporting mechanism for children and armed conflict. However, the accountability mechanisms of the CRC[34] remain weak, for they provide for no more than state party reports. Nonetheless, the CRC has shown a special interest in, and commitment to, the issue of education in emergencies, as reflected in its guidelines for submission of reports, its written and oral questions, its recommendations, and the 2008 Day of General Discussion on education in emergencies.[35]

The Convention Relating to the Status of Refugees[36] also provides that refugee children should be accorded the same treatment as is accorded to nationals with respect to elementary education (Article 22(1)) and treatment no less favourable than that accorded to foreigners with respect to education other than elementary education (Article 22(2)). In 1993, the UNHCR adopted a policy on refugee children that includes the guiding principle that, in all actions concerning refugee children, the child's best interests should be given primary consideration.[37] Quality education is always in a child's best interests.

The UNHCR found it necessary, however, to gear much of its work towards the protection of displaced persons, despite the lack of specific mandate within its statute for such work.[38] The growing number of displaced persons and the lack of specific legal protection prompted the

31 Optional Protocol to the Convention on the Rights of the Child on the Involvement of Children in Armed Conflict (adopted 25 May 2000, entered into force 12 February 2002), UNGA Res. A/RES/54/262.

32 Protocols I Additional to the Geneva Conventions of August 1949, and Relating to the Protection of Victims of International Armed Conflicts (adopted 8 June 1977, entered into force 7 December 1978, UN Doc. A/32/144 Annex 1, 1125 UNTS no. 17512), and Protocol II Additional to the Geneva Conventions of August 1949 and Relating to the Protection of Victims of Non-International Armed Conflicts (adopted 8 June 1977, entered into force 7 December 1978, UN Doc. A/32/144 Annex II, 1125 UNTS no. 17513); the African Charter on the Rights and Welfare of the Child (adopted 1990, entered into force 29 November 1999, O.A.U. Doc. CAB/LEG/24.9/49); ILO Convention Concerning the Prohibition and Immediate Action for the Elimination of the Worst Forms of Child Labour Convention: C182 (adopted 17 June 1999, entered into force 19 November 2000); and the Rome Statute of the International Criminal Court (adopted 17 July 1998, entered into force 1 July 2002). Arts. 8.2.(b) (xxvi) and 8.2.(c) (vii) also seek to prohibit the recruitment of children into groups/and national forces.

33 UNSC Res. 1612 (26 July 2005), UN Doc S/RES/1612.

34 Details of the work of the CRC [online]. Available from: http://www2.ohchr.org/english/bodies/crc/comments.htm [accessed 27 April 2009].

35 See details of Discussion Day and subsequent recommendations [online]. Available from: http://www2.ohchr.org/English/bodies/crc/discussion2008.htm [accessed 27 April 2009].

36 Convention Relating to the Status of Refugees (adopted 28 July 1951, entered into force 22 April 1954), 189 UNTS 137.

37 United Nations High Commissioner for Human Rights, *Refugee Children: Guidelines on Protection and Care* (Geneva: 1994), p. 73 [online]. Available from: http://www.unhcr.org/cgi-bin/texis/vtx/protect/opendoc.pdf?tbl=PROTECTION&id=3b84c6c67 [accessed April 2009].

38 The General Assembly progressively granted competence to UN High Commissioner for Refugees on issues related to internally displaced populations, based on Article 9 of the Statute of the Office of the United Nations High Commissioner for Refugees, UNGA Res. 428 (1950) GAOR 325th Session.

development of the Guiding Principles on Internal Displacement (Guiding Principles),[39] on the basis of international humanitarian law and international human rights law. The Guiding Principles affirm the right to free compulsory education, and in particular the full and equal participation of women and girls (Principle 23). Although they are not legally binding, the Guiding Principles have been disseminated widely among states and international agencies and are increasingly being used to guide protection and assistance strategies.

Guidance does not, however, equate with responsibility and accountability mechanisms. Such mechanisms of greatest relevance to those member states the UN seek to assist, are poorly developed. In 2005, in an attempt to offset this lack of development, the Inter-Agency Standing Committee's Education Cluster[40] created a group which aimed to improve the predictability and accountability of response within the UN. Unfortunately, the UNHCR still lacks sufficient resources to perform the lead role it has accepted in certain components of that response.[41]

International humanitarian law establishes a regulatory framework protecting the right to education during armed conflicts. The Geneva Convention Relative to the Protection of Civilian Persons in Time of War[42] (GC IV) states that measures should be taken to ensure that children who are orphaned or separated from their families as a result of a war have access to education.[43] The 1977 Additional Protocol II[44] to the Geneva Conventions, applying as it does to non-international conflicts, is of the utmost relevance today as it covers the actions of non-state armed groups. Of particular relevance here is its Article 4,(3)(a), which asserts an obligation to provide children with the care and aid they require, and more specifically the right to receive education.[45]

Also of particular importance is Article 8 of the Statute of the International Criminal Court (ICC),[46] which states that all intentional attacks on buildings dedicated to education constitute war crimes and are therefore subject to the court's jurisdiction.[47] In 1999, the UN Security Council

---

39 Report of the Repesentative of the Secretary-General, Mr Francis M. Deng, submitted pursuant to Commission Resolution 1997/39: *Guiding Principles on Internal Displacement*, UN Doc. DE/CN.4/1998/53/Add.2 (1998).

40 See note 65 below.

41 In 2007, the UN High Commissioner for Refugees, issued 'Rôle du HCR dans l'appui a un renforcement de la réponse humanitaire aux situations de déplacement interne. Cadre politique et stratégie de mise en œuvre, UNHCR, EC/58/SC/CRP.18. (2007) [Guidance for UN Humanitarian and/or Resident Coordinators and Country Teams'].

42 Geneva Convention Relative to the Protection of Civilian Persons in Time of War (adopted 12 August 1948, entered into force 21 October 1950, 75 UNTS 287) (GC IV).

43 See also Art. 50 of GC IV and Art. 78 of Protocol I Additional to the Geneva Conventions of 12 August 1949 and relating to the Protection of Victims of International Armed Conflicts (adopted 8 June 1977, entered into force 7 December 1978, UN Doc. A/32/144 Annex I, 1125 UNS no. 17512).

44 Protocol II Additional to the Geneva Conventions of 12 August 1949 and relating to the Protection of Victims of Non-International Armed Conflicts (adopted 8 June 1977, entered into force 7 December 1978, UN Doc. A/32/144 Annex II, 1125 UNTS no. 17513).

45 International humanitarian law is applicable to all forms of conflicts, including those in the territories of states that have not ratified the Protocols Additional to the Geneva Conventions of 12 August 1949. See further J.-M. Henckaerts and L. Doswald-Beck, *Customary International Humanitarian Law* (Cambridge: Cambridge University Press, 2005), vol. 1, Rules, ICRC, p. 481.

46 Rome Statue of the International Criminal Court (adopted 17 July 1998, entered into force 1 July 2002, UN Doc. A/CONF. 183/9; 37 ILM 1002 (1998); 2187 UNTS 90.

47 *Ibid.*, Article 8.2.(a) (iv).

adopted Resolution 1261 (1999)[48] condemning all attacks on 'objects protected under international law', including schools, and calling on all parties concerned to put an end to such practices.[49]

Perhaps, case law with the greatest potential for impact is that of the International Criminal Court (ICC). Such case law is still very much in its infancy, but as it develops, it offers an opportunity to send a powerful message to those who continue to undermine the right to education: the impunity with which education has been attacked for so many years must now cease.[50]

3.2 International Political Responsibilities

The recognition given in Articles 4 and 28 of the CRC to the need for international cooperation in order to implement the right to education has not translated fully and clearly into political responsibilities for the international community. Nonetheless, the goal of education for all set up by the World Conference on Education for All (Jomtien),[51] held in Jomtien, Thailand, in 1990, certainly moved the language of human rights obligations towards a future responsibility concerning the establishment of minimum standards in basic education. Although Jomtien paid particular attention to groups vulnerable to exclusion from education, the focus on education in emergencies was scant.

The Dakar Framework for Action on Education for All (Dakar Framework)[52] was adopted at the World Education Forum (World Forum),[53] held in Dakar in 2000. The World Forum paid greater, albeit still insufficient, attention to the educational consequences of emergencies, placing special emphasis on children affected by conflict, natural disasters and instability. It also emphasized the need to conduct educational programmes in ways that promote mutual understanding, peace and tolerance, and that help to prevent violence and conflict. The date by which these needs should be met was set at 2015. There is an interesting statement in the Dakar Framework to the effect that 'no countries seriously committed to education for all will be thwarted in their achievement of this goal by a lack of resources.'[54] The implication is clear: any state desirous of ensuring primary education, but incapable of doing so, should be able to obtain the funds essential for that purpose.

In contrast to the political moves preceding them, the Millennium Development Goals[55] do not use the language of rights and state obligations. Instead, they assign educational goals to a development rather than a rights agenda. The effect has been to narrow the view of education

48 UNSC Res. 1261 (25 August 1999), UN Doc. S/RES/1261.

49 See also resolutions of Security Council (2000), UNSC Res. 1379 (20 November 2001) UN Doc. S/RES/1379, and UNSC Res. 1539 (22 April 2004) UN Doc. S/RES/1539.

50 The International Criminal Tribunal for the former Yugoslavia considers the destruction of school buildings to be a war crime. See further *The Prosecutor* v *Blaskic* (Trial Chamber), IT-95-14-T, 3 March 2000, para. 185 [online]. Available from: http://www.icty.org/x/cases/blaskic/tjug/en/bla-tj000303e.pdf [accessed 27 April 2009], and *The Prosecutor* v *Naletilic and Martinovic* (Trial Chamber), IT-98-38-T, 31 March 2003, paras. 603–5 [online]. Available from: http://www.icty.org/x/cases/naletilic_martinovic/tjug/en/nal-tj030331-e.pdf [accessed 27 April 2009].

51 World Conference on Education for All [online]. Available from: http://portal.unesco.org/education/en/ev.php-URL_ID=37612&URL_DO=DO_TOPIC&URL_SECTION=201.html [accessed 27 April 2009].

52 Text of Dakar Framework of Action on Education for All [online]. Available from: http://www.unesco.org/education/efa/ed_for_all/dakfram_eng.shtml [accessed 27 April 2009].

53 World Education Forum [online]. Available from: http://www.unesco.org/education/efa/wef_2000/ [accessed 27 April 2009].

54 Dakar Framework, note 52 above. para.10.

55 [online]. Available from: http://www.un.org/millenniumgoals/ [accessed 27 April 2009].

to that of a quantifiable access to a full primary education that is free, compulsory and of good quality by the year 2015 (Goal 2) and the promotion of gender parity by the year 2005 (Goal 3). This has also had the effect of diverting attention from other educational goals that are of specific and crucial importance in emergency situations. However, while political commitments on education are welcome, a commitment to long-term development goals is not effective in prioritizing education as a human right in emergencies, or in holding states accountable for violations.

In emergency situations, the obligation remains for states to ensure the right to education, even though they might lack the requisite will and/or capacity to do so. In recognition of this, a variety of actors – international non-governmental organizations (NGOs), national and international agencies and some donors – have attempted to partially shoulder this responsibility. They invariably do so within the, often severe, constraints of their specific mandates, agendas and resources. The recognition of the need for, and indeed the growing coordination among all the actors involved in education in emergencies, with delimited responsibilities and shared examples of best practices, has resulted in the creation of qualitative standards and indicators that, among other effects, broaden the legal and political framework in which these actors are expected to operate. Of these, perhaps, and more specifically, the Minimum Standards for Education in Emergencies, Chronic Crises and Early Reconstruction (INEE Minimum Standards),[56] developed by the Inter-Agency Network for Education in Emergencies (INEE),[57] stand out. These were drafted as a direct response to the neglect of education within humanitarian aid efforts. Indeed, at the time of their development even the 'Sphere Standards',[58] which had codified a system of principles of humanitarian aid, referred to human rights but omitted references to education.

The INEE Minimum Standards offer a harmonized framework of principles and paths of action to all actors who may be involved in the provision of education during emergencies, for them to coordinate their educational activities and, even more importantly, to promote the acceptance of responsibilities. These Minimum Standards need to be strengthened in this latter aspect, and the international community is urged here to redouble its efforts in working towards this goal.

Despite the growing awareness of the need for delivery of education in emergencies and the progress made in doing so, there still remains an enormous gap between the legal and political responsibilities of the international community and its action and funding priorities. The reasons for and consequences of this gap will be considered in the following section.

4. Donors' Action and Priorities

With notable exceptions, the international community is tolerant of violations of the right to education in emergencies. This is clear from the priorities for action detailed further below, and from the perception, which is directly challenged here, that education is a facet of development rather than a humanitarian activity, and even less a human right. By operating on that basis, states have fallen short of the responsibility enshrined in the international instruments which define the nature and the content of the right to education.

56 See note 9 above.

57 See further [online]. Available from: http://www.ineesite.org/ [accessed 27 April 2009].

58 See further [online]. Available from: http://www.sphereproject.org/.

4.1 Priorities for Action

UNICEF and UNESCO, the UN agencies that have assumed leadership for education in emergencies, are formally committed to the right to education. However, this commitment is not always matched by the educational strategies of large sectors of the international community, including other UN agencies, intergovernmental organizations, development banks, the private sector and civil society agencies.[59] Although some progress has been achieved, especially with the creation of the Inter-Agency Standing Committee's Education Cluster, education as a priority in humanitarian assistance will continue to remain beyond reach until this priority is recognized by all, including, primarily, governments.

4.2 Donors

Humanitarian assistance is under-funded, barely receiving two-thirds of sums identified as being needed and formally requested.[60] Consequently, when priorities are set, education in emergencies is not high on the list. In 2004, for example, only approximately 1.5% of the total humanitarian commitments were earmarked for educational programmes.[61] Further, estimates for the years 2001 to 2005 showed that the actual financial contributions made for education averaged 42% of real needs, as compared with 66% in all the other humanitarian sectors.[62]

There is a steady increase in the literature covering the challenges relating to the financing of education in emergencies, a selection of which is highlighted below. These challenges clearly indicate the need for monitoring, evaluation, dialogue and dissemination of best practices and innovations. Further, the provision of funding for education in times of emergency must be the result of a commitment to human rights, rather than of an exercise in risk avoidance.

The challenges relating to education in emergencies most frequently discussed include the following:

a. The lack of sufficient and suitable funding for education in general and the failure to honour formal commitments, despite the adoption of policies and the support of many donors who promote Education for All and the Millennium Development Goals.
b. The existence of a dominant paradigm of aid, based on the widely held premise that assistance is most effective in states with stronger policies and institutional adjustments.[63] Despite bilateral donors' emphasis on the importance of assisting the countries with the

---

59 'Report by the Director-General on Global Action Plan to Achieve the Education for All Goals' (March 2006), UN Doc. 174 EX/9, para. 8 [online]. Available from: http://unesdoc.unesco.org/images/0014/001442/144245e.pdf [accessed 27 April 2009].

60 Canadian International Development Agency and the Inter-Agency Network for Education in Emergencies, *Policy Roundtable in Emergencies, Fragile States and Reconstruction: Addressing Challenges and Exploring Alternatives* (New York: CIDA-INEE Policy Roundtable Report, 2006), p. 36 [online]. Available from: http://www.ineesite.org/index.php/post/policy_roundtable_2006/) [accessed 27 April 2007].

61 R. Winthrop and R. Mendenhall, ' Education in Emergencies: A Critical Factor in Achieving the Millennium Development Goals', in *Commonwealth Minister Reference Book* (London: Commonwealth Secretariat, 2006).

62 *Ibid*., p. 13.

63 M. McGillivray, *Aid Allocation and Fragile States* (World Institute for Development Economics Research, Finland. Background Paper for the Senior Level Forum on Development Effectiveness in Fragile States, London, 2005), pp. 13–14. *Ibid.*

most pressing needs, such states – also referred to as emergency-affected fragile states – receive approximately 43% less funding than they would need on the basis of the size of their population, their degree of poverty, and their level of political and institutional development. Also, their flows of aid have been twice as volatile as those of the low-income countries.[64]

c. Donors are reluctant to consider education as part of aid and humanitarian response, despite the fact that emergency situations can, and often do, last for many years.
d. The priorities of donors have moved from the financing of long-term development needs, to concentrate instead on humanitarian disaster relief. This frequently leads, as previously noted, to a focus on activities in the traditional fields of food, health and shelter.[65]
e. Lack of continuity in funding between the onset of an emergency and reconstruction (often divided into 'humanitarian phases' and 'development phases').
f. Limited evidence concerning the effectiveness and responsibility of the providers of education in emergencies.

The limited involvement of donors in the implementation of the right to education has hampered coordination, the development of partnerships, examination of alternative funding models and the building of risk-management capabilities. Currently, a number of worthy measures to tackle these questions are being taken, but there is a need for encouragement by way of a greater commitment by the international community as a whole.

5. Education Providers in Situations of Emergency

There is no single agency to which states requiring educational assistance can turn in an emergency. Nor is there a single funding mechanism for channelling financial resources. On the contrary, a plethora of actors take the stage, each with their own expertise, agenda and distinct priorities, mandates, capacities, spheres of influence, field presence and financial bases. They include both agencies and other bodies of the UN system, bilateral and multilateral donors, international and domestic NGOs, and affected communities. Very prominent are many NGOs and, of course, the Inter-Agency Network for Education in Emergencies. But we must ask, and answer honestly, whether this diffuse reaction to emergency situations is a sufficient indicator of an effective and appropriate collective response.

Education in emergencies enjoys a high level of awareness within the UN. UNESCO works in collaboration with UNHCR and UNICEF. UNHCR is responsible for refugee protection in emergencies and is the lead agency for the protection of internally displaced populations. UNICEF is the body responsible for children and adolescents. In addition, and often at the request of governments, UNICEF also pays particular attention to internally displaced populations and to returnees and their reintegration, since it is the lead agency for assistance in the provision of primary education in post-emergency situations. UNESCO has as its mandate to contribute to peace, security and development through education and intellectual cooperation. A major effort that it has deployed since its foundation has been to ensure the right to education of persons

64 *Ibid.*

65 Statement for endorsement by the UN Secretary-General, Symposium on 'Nutrition in the Context of Conflict and Crisis' (Standing Committee on Nutrition, Berlin, 2002) [online]. Available from: http://www.unscn.org/archives/scnnews24/ch04.htm [accessed 27 April 2009].

affected by armed conflicts through advocacy for a comprehensive understanding in the interests of peace. Although it has a wide-ranging mandate, UNESCO is painfully short of funds and other resources.

In general, the interventions of the agencies of the UN system are characterized by their concentration on primary education and by a concomitant lack of attention paid to tertiary education, particularly in fragile states. It is evident that coordination between the agencies is improving, but there is no clear division of labour, leading to the continuation of gaps, confusion and duplication. If the agencies of the UN are to fulfil their mandates more completely, they will need to be adequately financed by the member states. Also, they will need to revitalize their coordination efforts and raise the profile of the place occupied by education as a right in emergency situations.

Finally, although the World Bank has made important contributions to education in emergencies, it continues to be working outside the human rights framework. This reflects its strategy on education, which is to concentrate on support to education in the reconstruction stages following emergencies. Further, it identifies with the utilitarian concept of education as a tool for economic development, since it considers education, first and foremost, as a major factor in the achievement of the Millennium Development Goals. Together with the narrow focus on primary education, this demonstrates a degree of disregard for the Education for All agenda.

5.1 Inter-Agency Standing Committee's Education Cluster

The recent creation of the Inter-Agency Standing Committee's Education Cluster[66] is welcome, constituting as it does a first step towards the inclusion of education as a priority component of humanitarian response. There are currently high hopes for increased and more effective collaboration within the shared leadership of the UN agencies, especially UNICEF and international NGOs.

The Education Cluster must act to meet the need to ensure a greater responsibility in that response on the part of the international community, including the UN, donor agencies and states, and local and international NGOs. It should become the proper mechanism for determining the educational needs in emergency situations and responding to them in a coordinated manner, for which purpose it should use and develop the tools laid down by the INEE. The Education Cluster must also ensure that donors are in a position, and willing, to provide the funds needed to respond to any emergency, making available the resources necessary for education as a component of early response.

6. Affected Populations

Populations are not homogeneous and are variously impacted by emergencies. The challenges they encounter are equally varied and this variety should be reflected in specific education-related humanitarian responses.

Nonetheless, the potential that assistance may be differentiated or demarcated brings with it the risk of introducing in the provision of education an additional component of the

66 The Inter-Agency Education Cluster on Education was created by the Working Group of the Interagency Standing Committee in 2006. Further information on the Inter-Agency Standing Committee [online]. Available from: http://www.humanitarianinfo.org/iasc/pageloader.aspx [accessed 27 April 2009]. Further information on the Inter-Agency Education Cluster [online]. Available from: http://www.humanitarianreform.org/humanitarianreform/Default.aspx?tabid=115 [accessed 27 April 2009].

discrimination and inequality which these marginalized populations often experience even in times of peace. In times of emergency, such inequality and discrimination increases still further for marginalized groups, groups such as women and girls, persons with disabilities, persons living with HIV/AIDS, ethnic minorities, and indigenous and migrant communities. Such persons and communities suffer a double or, perhaps, multiple discrimination. Some of these groups are considered below.

6.1 Refugees and Returnees

The educational options for this population are determined, to a large degree, by the repatriation efforts led by UNHCR. The aim of bringing about successful repatriation and reintegration of returnees, both teachers and students, has led to an emphasis in the study plans on all those aspects that recall the country of origin. This approach is not, however, always possible, as the relevant teaching material is often unobtainable or unsuitable. Such materials may be, for example, a version of the curriculum as it existed before the conflict, and that may even have contributed to the conflict itself, or may be a mixture of the local model of the study plan plus innovations made to it by an NGO. Poor use of teaching materials may create problems relating to the accreditation of the teaching received, with refugees and/or returnees being accepted neither by the national education system of their host country nor by that of their country of origin, creating a source of social tension.

6.2 Internally Displaced Persons

Internally displaced persons are disproportionately denied their right to education, with estimates standing at approximately 90%. This may be due to a number or a combination of reasons: chronic lack of security, lack of an international agency specifically mandated to respond to their needs, lack of physical access to education providers, lack of political will in governments to allow education providers to offer such people real opportunities, or the simple reluctance of governments to commit themselves generally to fulfilment of the right.

6.3 Women and Girls

Gender parity in education is the focus of a global educational strategy that is obviously inadequate. In the context of emergencies, the relevant literature tends to concentrate on challenges other than parity: those created by the greater vulnerability of women and girls, including their problems of security, hygiene and the lack of adequate sanitary facilities within the educational institutions, as well as the shortage of female teachers and the fact that girls are also required to do housework.

The impact of emergencies on girls is more serious given that, historically, they have been the victims of exploitation and emotional and physical aggression, especially sexual aggression. For this reason it is of fundamental importance in early response to emergencies to develop appropriate curricula that can be adapted to their particular needs and rights. There is a need to go further in providing comprehensive protection for young and adolescent girls, guaranteeing their safety en route to and from school and an environment free of aggression, by means of strategies that will encourage them to stay in school. To achieve this goal, it is essential to work with women teachers.

6.4 Child Soldiers and Combatants

It is estimated that around 250,000 boys and girls worldwide have been recruited to serve not only as soldiers, but also in the detection of mines, or as spies, messengers and members of suicide missions.[67] A large proportion of international attention has been focused on their demobilization and reintegration, in line with international disarmament principles and the reintegration and demobilization standards laid down in the CRC. If such programmes are to be effective, there is a need to deal with the imbalance in the attention that donors pay to demobilization as compared with reintegration. Further, a rights-based approach is needed to ensure that all educational programmes deal with the multiple discrimination experienced by child soldiers, discrimination directed, among others, against adolescents, minorities and those with disabilities.

Formal and informal education, vocational training and social capacity-building, in general, have been identified by many former child soldiers or combatants as essential to their long-term well-being,[68] and their prioritization should be a guiding principle for assistance offered. Their participation in those processes should be fully guaranteed.

6.5 People with Disabilities

People with disabilities, of either sex and of all ages, and in most parts of the world, suffer from a pervasive and disproportionate denial of their right to education.[69] In emergencies, however, particularly during conflicts and the post-conflict period, their right to receive special support and care is not always recognized by communities or states.

6.6 Young People and Adolescents

The education of young people and adolescents has been traditionally disregarded by governments and the international community, since priority is always given to primary education. There are justifications for this emphasis, but the result should not be a total lack of attention to the other levels. However, there are an increasing number of experiments in accessible, realistic, relevant and flexible learning, promoted primarily by international NGOs that offer youngsters an alternative basic education. These initiatives have largely been ignored by governments and donors, possibly owing to their lack of emphasis on standardization.

6.7.1 Consultations with children My various consultations with children and adolescents who have lived through conflict situations point to certain similarities in educational experiences and hopes. It is evident, for example, that conflict has a serious impact on their enjoyment of the right to an education that is free of charge, compulsory, relevant and of good quality, especially for the children still living in the affected areas. As many of the children and adolescents indicated, access to education and whether or not children remain in school depend to a large extent on the cost of education to them, including uniforms, teaching materials, food and travel. This is a significant obstacle, since many of the children fled their communities of origin, together with their families,

67 Mireille Affa'a Mindzie, *Children Associated with Armed Forces* (Centre for Conflict Resolution, South Africa, 2008).

68 Information gathered during a visit in my capacity as Special Rapporteur to the Ivory Coast, by invitation of Save the Children International Alliance.

69 UNCHR, 'Report of the Special Rapporteur on Education on the Right to Education of Persons with Disabilities' (2007), A/HRC/4/29.

and now find themselves in conditions of extreme poverty. They also raised concerns regarding the extremely poor state of the school infrastructure, and some indicated that they had to walk long distances to reach school and in so doing were afraid of attack by armed groups.

When the children and adolescents were questioned regarding matters to do with the curriculum, without exception all expressed the hope that the study plans would contribute to strengthening the peace processes.

7. Curriculum, Quality and Shared Learning

The objectives of education for all set out in the Dakar Framework for Action clearly state that access to a quality education is a basic human right of the victims of conflicts and natural disasters. Since education plays a role in shielding people's life, dignity and security and also constitutes an area where all human rights converge, especially in emergencies, it is essential to focus on learning and learners. One reason for the difficulties in implementing the right to education is denial of this convergence of human rights, especially when it comes to groups that historically suffer social and economic discrimination. This not only results in the denial of the human right to education, but also damages its specific content, because knowledge not built upon personal development that is respectful of human rights is inferior knowledge.[70]

The quality of education implies a collective responsibility that includes respect for the individual nature of all persons; it implies respect for and empowerment of diversity, since any learning demands the recognition of the Other as a legitimate being. For this reason, the search for consensus and the recognition of differences constitute sources of education that are of crucial importance in the creation of cultures of peace.

The transition from emergency intervention to large-scale reconstruction provides unique opportunities for curriculum design and for improving the quality of learning. This requires generating data and minimum standards and proposes introducing innovative, flexible and dynamic assessment systems.[71] The development of the curriculum and the wide spectrum of teaching activities that this includes require democratic and participatory attitudes in teachers and students alike. These attitudes have to embrace all sectors of the community, and above all the groups that have historically been marginalized.

In conflict and post-conflict situations, the new curriculum development that is required must be based on a detailed analysis and an understanding of any role played by the previous education system in creating the conflict, such that the emergency itself may turn into an opportunity for qualitative change. In other words, the context of each emergency has to impact the pedagogical approach to education in particular and to social reconstruction processes in general.

An urgent task for governments has to be education for peaceful coexistence. Education for peace shares the same objective as human rights and should involve education as a whole, rather than as isolated components of the curriculum. It should make possible the understanding by all learners of the causes and consequences of emergencies. To date, scant attention has been paid to these principles.

70 UNCHR, 'Report of Special Rapporteur on the Right to Education', UN Doc. E/CN.4/2005/50 (2005).

71 J. Bernard, *With Peace in Mind: Assessment as a Tool for Cultivating the Quality of Education in Emergencies and Long-Term Reconstruction* (UNESCO, Basic Education Division, 2008).

8. Recommendations

The recommendations below are both general and specifically targeted. It is imperative that if education in emergencies is to take its proper position in the humanitarian response and subsequent reconstruction, all actors directly and indirectly affected must seek to work and learn collaboratively and in concert with one another at all times. These recommendations should be viewed with such collaboration in mind.

8.1 General Recommendations

The international community is urged to commit more wholeheartedly to the implementation of the right to education in emergencies. As a first step in this direction, it is recommended that this right be recognized by states, donors, multilateral agencies and organizations as an integral part of the humanitarian response to conflicts and natural disasters.

The following measures should be taken so as to guarantee the immediate priority of this right:

a. Greater emphasis must be placed on guaranteeing the right to education during emergency situations, in contrast to the current focus on post-conflict situations.
b. Increased action must be taken to bring to an end the impunity of persons and armed groups, including regular armies, who attack schools, students and teachers.
c. There is need for further research into the effectiveness of some of the measures prompted by the increase in violence against schools, teachers and students, such as armed responses in defence of communities and the promotion of resistance.
d. Although there is an increased interest in the allocation and effectiveness of assistance in emergency situations, greater attention should be paid to assigning more resources specifically to fragile states.
e. Prompt attention should be paid to the consequences of emergency situations for girls and female adolescents, and strategic measures developed to give physical and emotional protection in order to ensure their attendance at school.
f. Increased and more thorough research is needed into specific programmes for young people and adolescents, including the particular needs of persons with disabilities.
g. Greater attention to understanding and the development of education for peace is required.
h. There should be a shift away from the current emphasis on quantifiable, but often inaccurate, figures on, for example, school enrolment and dropout rates, and greater use of qualitative methodologies which will make it possible to determine the degree of psychosocial care required during emergencies.

8.2 Recommendations to States

The following recommendations are directed specifically at states, which should:

a. Develop a plan that prepares for education in emergencies, as part of their general educational programmes, to include specific measures for continuity of education at all levels and during all the phases of the emergency. Such a plan should include training for the teachers in various aspects of emergency situations.
b. Draw up a programme of studies that is adaptable, non-discriminatory, gender-sensitive

and of high quality, and that meets children's and young people's needs during emergency situations.

c. Ensure the involvement of children, parents and civil society in planning school activities, so that safe spaces are provided for students throughout the emergency.
d. Design and implement specific plans to avoid exploitation of girls and young women in the wake of emergencies.

8.3 Recommendations to Donors

The following recommendations are directed specifically at donors, who should.

a. Include education in all their humanitarian assistance plans and increase the education allocation to at least 4.2% of total humanitarian assistance, in line with need.[72]
b. Actively support the Inter-Agency Standing Committee's Education Cluster;
c. Use the Inter-Agency Network for Education in Emergencies Minimum Standards as a basis for the educational activities that are part of humanitarian response.

8.4 Recommendations to Intergovernmental Organizations and NGOs

The following recommendations are directed specifically at intergovernmental organizations and NGOs, which should:

a. guarantee that educational responses to emergencies are in line with the INEE Minimum Standards;
b. seek mechanisms to ensure greater and more effective NGO involvement in the Inter-Agency Standing Committee, with a view to improving the coordination of the humanitarian response in the area of education;
c. organize and coordinate efforts for the effective implementation of quality programmes of inclusive education during the emergency response.

9. Conclusion

As I revisit my 2008 thematic report on the 'Right to Education in Emergency Situations' for the purposes of this chapter, it is clear that in the intervening two years the welcome progress that has been made is insufficient: education continues to be relentlessly assailed in times of conflict and through natural disasters. It demands much greater effort at international, regional and national levels if it is to be protected in its own right and as an enabling right.[73]

In the Democratic Republic of Congo, for instance, a recent report details an education system that is 'catastrophically failing' its children due to conflict, economic decline, and corruption.[74] In India, the education of tens of thousands of children has allegedly been disrupted by Maoist

72 J. Dolan, *Last in Line, Last in School: How Donors Are Failing Children in Conflict-Affected Fragile States* (International Save the Children Alliance, 2007) [online]. Available from: http://www.savethechildren.org.uk/en/docs/last_in_line_long.pdf [accessed 27 April 2009].

73 See note 1 above.

74 Open Society Initiative for Southern Africa, *The Democratic Republic of Congo: Effective Delivery of Public Services in the Education Sector. A Discussion Paper* (2009) [online]. Available from: http://www.

bombing of remote government schools,[75] by the Maoists' recruitment of children in their armed forces,[76] and by the occupation and use of school buildings as outposts by government security forces.[77] In Colombia, educators, commonly seen as community leaders, purportedly bear the brunt of political violence.[78] In Gaza, Israeli blockades are severely restricting school supplies,[79] and in Iraq, in addition to a severely damaged educational infrastructure, staff and students in higher education are the direct targets of attack.[80]

The Philippines is experiencing recurrent typhoons and consequent mass displacement with schools acting as emergency shelters.[81] In Samoa, numerous schools have been destroyed as a result of a recent earthquake closely followed by a tsunami.[82] While states and other actors attempt to ameliorate the consequences of these disasters, every day of interrupted or denied education will affect each pupil's future.

The international human rights legal framework, within which this mere illustrative fraction of current situations is situated,[83] albeit imperfect, remains a valuable tool for states, educators and advocates keen to strengthen the protection of education in emergencies. Crucially, it is closely intertwined with international humanitarian and international criminal law. While the synergy between the three remains under-explored, it is suggested that, combined, the three contain few obvious technical 'gaps'[84] in protection, with international humanitarian law forbidding the targeting of education systems in times of conflict and international human rights law containing an obligation to respect, protect and fulfil the right to education at all times and notably, in situations of conflict, a 'duty to protect' the public[85] from attacks.[86] International criminal law goes some way

afrimap.org/english/images/report/AfriMAP-DRC-PublicServices-Educ-DD-EN.pdf [accessed 2 November 2009].

75 Human Rights Watch, *Sabotaged Schooling: Naxalite Attacks and Police Occupation of Schools in India's Bihar and Jharkhand States* (December 2009).

76 Human Rights Watch, *Dangerous Duty, Children and the Chhattisgarh Conflict* (2008) [online]. Available from:http://www.hrw.org/en/reports/2008/09/05/dangerous-duty [accessed 2 November 2009].

77 Human Rights Watch, note 75 above.

78 M. Novelli, *Colombia's Classroom Wars: Political Violence Against Education Sector Trade Unionists* (Brussels: Education International: 2009) [online]. Available from: http://download.ei-ie.org/Docs/WebDepot/EI_ColombiaStudy_eng_final_web.pdf [accessed 2 November 2009].

79 Human Rights Watch, Press release, 'Israel: Stop Blocking School Supplies' (October 2009) [online]. Available from: http://www.hrw.org/en/news/2009/10/09/israel-stop-blocking-school-supplies-entering-gaza-0 [accessed 2 November 2009].

80 H. Paanakker, 'Higher Education in Iraq Under Attack: An Explorative Study on the Political Violence Against Academics and the Higher Education System in the Conflict in Iraq' (master's thesis in International Development Studies, Graduate School of Social Sciences, University of Amsterdam, The Netherlands, 2009).

81 [online]. Available from: http://www.guardian.co.uk/world/2009/nov/01/philippines-hit-by-third-typhoon [accessed 2 November 2009].

82 [online]. Available from: http://www.infonews.co.nz/news.cfm?l=1&t=143&id=42798 [accessed 2 November 2009].

83 See further B. O'Malley, *Education Under Attack 2010* (forthcoming, UNESCO 2010).

84 See, however, G. Bart, 'Ambiguous Protection of Schools Under the Law of War: Time for Parity with Hospitals and Religious Buildings', *Georgetown Journal of International Law*, 40(2) (2009), pp. 405–46.

85 Which includes attacks on students and teachers.

86 See, for instance, B. Abramson, 'International Law and the Protection of Education Systems' (paper presented at seminar 'Education Under Attack', Paris, 28 September – 1 October 2009, in *Protecting Education from Attack: A State-of-the-Art Review* (Paris: UNESCO, forthcoming).

towards enhancing accountability. It remains evident, however, that this overarching framework would benefit from increased coherence, further particularization and a significantly raised profile among current and potential actors.

Most recent steps in this direction include the endorsement, by the heads of state of the African Union, of the Convention on the Protection and Assistance of Internally Displaced Persons in Africa,[87] the first legally binding instrument defining – on a continental scale – the responsibilities of states, armed groups and civil society to uprooted citizens.[88] More generally, government and non-government educators, the media, intergovernmental organizations, and human rights advocates are actively and jointly exploring avenues in which relevant research, monitoring, reporting,[89] prevention and response, and, critically, accountability may be improved.[90] Ideas currently being mooted include the development of internationally endorsed guidelines on the protection of education in times of emergency, a relevant general comment from the CRC, and engaging more actively with UN Security Council mechanisms and the ICC.

The tolerance by the international community of the violation of the right to education in times of emergency is under challenge. It is our collective responsibility to rise to this challenge and ensure that the principle of an education for all, enshrined in the UDHR, is fully protected in emergency situations.

87 African Union, *African Union Convention for the Protection and Assistance of Internally Displaced Persons in Africa ('Kampala Convention')*, 22 October 2009 (not yet in force) [online]. Available from: http://www.unhcr.org/refworld/docid/4ae572d82.html [accessed 2 November 2009].

88 Article 9.2(b): '[States Parties shall] …Provide internally displaced persons to the fullest extent practicable and with the least possible delay, with adequate humanitarian assistance, which shall include … education … and where appropriate, extend such assistance to local and host communities.'

89 See further Z. Coursen-Neff, *Monitoring and Reporting on Attacks on Education for Prevention, Early Warning, Rapid Response, and Accountability* (Human Rights Watch, forthcoming).

90 See recommendations emerging from seminar 'Protecting Education from Attack', note 86 above.

Chapter 27
Protect, Respect, and Remedy: The UN Framework for Business and Human Rights

John Gerard Ruggie

1. Introduction

The UDHR[1] of 1948 did not explicitly refer to the relationship between business and human rights. However, it provided in its preamble that 'every individual and every organ of society, keeping this Declaration constantly in mind, shall strive by teaching and education to promote respect for these rights and freedoms.' How can the existing international human rights system protect individuals and communities against corporate-related human rights harm? The international community is still in the early stages of adapting the human rights regime to provide more effective protection to individuals and communities against corporate-related human rights harm. This chapter, which I presented to the United Nations Human Rights Council in 2008 in my capacity as Special Representative of the Secretary-General for Business and Human Rights, and which the Council welcomed unanimously, presents a principles-based conceptual and policy framework intended to help achieve this aim. The framework comprises three core principles: the state duty to protect against human rights abuses by third parties, including business; the corporate responsibility to respect human rights; and the need for more effective access to remedies. The three principles form a complementary whole in that each supports the others in achieving sustainable progress.

Business is a major source of investment and job creation, and markets can be highly efficient means for allocating scarce resources. They constitute powerful forces capable of generating economic growth, reducing poverty, and increasing demand for the rule of law, thereby contributing to the realization of a broad spectrum of human rights. But markets work optimally only if they are embedded within rules, customs and institutions. Markets themselves require these to survive and thrive, while society needs them to manage the adverse effects of market dynamics and produce the public goods that markets under-supply. Indeed, history teaches us that markets pose the greatest risks – to society and business itself – when their scope and power far exceed the reach of the institutional underpinnings that allow them to function smoothly and ensure their political sustainability. This is such a time, and escalating charges of corporate-related human rights abuses are the canary in the coal mine, signalling that all is not well.

The root cause of the business and human rights predicament today lies in the governance gaps created by globalization – between the scope and impact of economic forces and actors, and the capacity of societies to manage their adverse consequences. These governance gaps provide the permissive environment for wrongful acts by companies of all kinds without adequate sanctioning or reparation. How to narrow and ultimately bridge the gaps in relation to human rights is our fundamental challenge. The business and human rights debate currently lacks an authoritative focal point. Claims and counter-claims proliferate, initiatives abound, and yet no effort reaches

1 GA Res. 217A (III), UN Doc. A/810 at 71 (1948).

significant scale. Amid this confusing mix, laggards – states as well as companies – continue to fly below the radar.

Some stakeholders believe that the solution lies in a limited list of human rights for which companies would have responsibility, while extending to companies, where they have influence, essentially the same range of responsibilities as states. For reasons this chapter spells out, the author does not share this view. Briefly, business can affect virtually all internationally recognized rights. Therefore, any limited list will almost certainly miss one or more rights that may turn out to be significant in a particular instance, thereby providing misleading guidance. At the same time, as economic actors, companies have unique responsibilities. If those responsibilities are entangled with state obligations, it makes it difficult if not impossible to tell who is responsible for what in practice. Hence, this chapter pursues the more promising path of addressing the specific responsibilities of companies in relation to all rights they may impact.

There is no single, silver-bullet solution to the institutional misalignments in the business and human rights domain. Instead, all social actors – states, businesses, and civil society – must learn to do many things differently. But those things must cohere and become cumulative, making it critically important to get the foundation right. Every stakeholder group, despite their other differences, has expressed the urgent need for a common conceptual and policy framework, a foundation on which thinking and action can build. Accordingly, in 2008, I proposed, and the United Nations (UN) Human Rights Council unanimously welcomed, the 'protect, respect and remedy' framework. It rests on differentiated but complementary responsibilities; the state duty to protect against human rights abuses by third parties, including business; the corporate responsibility to respect human rights; and the need for more effective access to remedies. Each principle is an essential component of the framework: the state duty to protect because it lies at the very core of the international human rights regime;[2] the corporate responsibility to respect because it is the basic expectation society has of business; and access to remedy, because even the most concerted efforts cannot prevent all abuse, while access to judicial redress is often problematic, and non-judicial means are limited in number, scope, and effectiveness. The three principles form a complementary whole in that each supports the others in achieving sustainable progress.

2. Protect, Respect and Remedy

The framing of policy challenges can have profound consequences for assigning responsibilities to relevant actors and determining whether the combination is capable of meeting the overall policy objectives. The business and human rights agenda remains hampered because it has not yet been framed in a way that fully reflects the complexities and dynamics of globalization and provides governments and other social actors with effective guidance.

2.1 The Challenge

How should we frame today's challenges in order to capture their essential attributes? As noted at the outset, our focus should be on ways to reduce or compensate for the governance gaps created by globalization, because they permit corporate-related human rights harm to occur even where none may be intended. Take the case of transnational corporations. Their legal rights have been

---

2 The duty to protect is well established in international law and must not be confused with the concept of the 'responsibility to protect' in the humanitarian intervention debate.

expanded significantly over the past generation. This has encouraged investment and trade flows, but it has also created instances of imbalances between firms and states that may be detrimental to human rights. The nearly 3,000 bilateral investment treaties currently in effect are a case in point. While providing legitimate protection to foreign investors, these treaties also permit those investors to take host states to binding international arbitration, including for alleged damages resulting from implementation of legislation to improve domestic social and environmental standards – even when the legislation applies uniformly to all businesses, foreign and domestic. A European mining company operating in South Africa recently challenged that country's black economic empowerment laws on these grounds.[3]

At the same time, the legal framework regulating transnational corporations operates much as it did long before the recent wave of globalization. A parent company and its subsidiaries continue to be construed as distinct legal entities. Therefore, the parent company is generally not liable for wrongs committed by a subsidiary, even where it is the sole shareholder, unless the subsidiary is under such close operational control by the parent that it can be seen as its mere agent. Furthermore, despite the transformative changes in the global economic landscape generated by offshore sourcing, purchasing goods and services even from sole suppliers remains an unrelated party transaction, and the buyer bears no legal liability for the acts of suppliers even where the buyer may be in part responsible for those acts. Factors such as these make it exceedingly difficult to hold the extended enterprise accountable for human rights harm. Each legally distinct corporate entity is subject to the laws of the countries in which it is based and operates. Yet, states, particularly some developing countries, may lack the institutional capacity to enforce national laws and regulations against transnational firms doing business in their territory even when the will is there, or they may feel constrained from doing so by having to compete internationally for investment. Home states of transnational firms may be reluctant to regulate against overseas harm by these firms because the permissible scope of national regulation with extraterritorial effect remains poorly understood, or out of concern that those firms might lose investment opportunities or relocate their headquarters.

This dynamic is hardly limited to transnational corporations. To attract investments and promote exports, governments may exempt national firms from certain legal and regulatory requirements or fail to adopt such standards in the first place. And what is the result? A survey of allegations of the worst cases of corporate-related human rights harm conducted in 2006 indicated that they occurred, predictably, where governance challenges were greatest: disproportionately in low-income countries; in countries that often had just emerged from or still were in conflict; and in countries where the rule of law was weak and levels of corruption high.[4] A significant fraction of the allegations involved companies being complicit in the acts of governments or armed factions.[5] A study conducted for my UN mandate by the Office of the UN High Commissioner for Human Rights (OHCHR) confirms these findings but also shows that adverse business impacts on human rights are not limited to these contexts.[6]

3 *Piero Foresti, Laura De Carli and Others* v *Republic of South Africa* (International Centre for Settlement of Investment Disputes, case No. ARB (AF)/07/1).

4 See Interim report of the Special Representative of the Secretary-General on the Issue of Human Rights and Transnational Corporations and Other Business Enterprises, UN Doc. E/CN.4/2006/97 (22 February 2006).

5 *Ibid.*

6 'Corporations and human rights: a survey of the scope and patterns of alleged corporate-related human rights abuse', Report of the Special Representative of the Secretary-General on the Issue of Human Rights and Transnational Corporations and Other Business Enterprises, Addendum 2, UN Document A/HRC/8/5/Add.2, 23 May 2008.

2.2 The Framework

In so far as governance gaps are at the root of the business and human rights predicament, effective responses must aim to reduce those gaps. But individual actions, whether by states or firms, may be too constrained by the competitive dynamics just described. Therefore, more coherent and concerted approaches are required. The framework of 'protect, respect, and remedy' can assist all social actors – governments, companies, and civil society – to reduce the adverse human rights consequences of these misalignments.[7]

Take first the state duty to protect. It has both legal and policy dimensions. It is now well established that international law provides that states have a duty to protect against human rights abuses by non-state actors, including by business, affecting persons within their territory or jurisdiction.[8] The specific language employed in the main UN human rights treaties varies, but all include two sets of obligations. First, the treaties commit states parties to refrain from violating the enumerated rights of persons within their territory and/or jurisdiction. Second, the treaties require states to 'ensure' (or some functionally equivalent verb) the enjoyment or realization of those rights by rights holders.[9] In turn, ensuring that rights holders enjoy their rights requires protection by states against other social actors, including businesses, which impede or negate those rights. Guidance from international human rights bodies suggests that the state duty to protect applies to all recognized rights that private parties are capable of impairing, and to all types of business enterprises.[10]

The state duty to protect is a standard of conduct, not result. That is, states are not held responsible for corporate-related human rights abuse *per se* but may be considered in breach of their obligations where they fail to take appropriate steps to prevent it and to investigate, punish and redress it when it occurs.[11] Within these parameters, states have discretion as to how to fulfil the duty. The main human rights treaties generally contemplate legislative, administrative and judicial measures. The UN treaty bodies have recommended to states such measures as adopting anti-discrimination legislation governing employment practices; consulting with communities before approving mining and logging projects; monitoring and addressing the human rights impacts of such projects; and encouraging businesses to develop codes of conduct that include human rights.

7 Multi-stakeholder initiatives, such as the Kimberley Process, reflect elements of all three principles; they were discussed at length in last year's report (UN Doc. A/HRC/4/35, paras. 52–61).

8 UN Docs A/HRC/4/35, and A/HRC/4/35/Add.1. Some states hold that this duty is limited to protecting persons who are within both their territory and jurisdiction.

9 For example, the International Covenant on Civil and Political Rights and the Convention on the Rights of the Child use 'respect and ensure', with 'respect' in the state context, meaning that the state must refrain from violating the rights. The Convention on the Rights of Persons with Disabilities requires states parties to 'ensure and promote', and to take appropriate measures to 'eliminate' abuse by private 'enterprises'. The International Convention on the Elimination of All Forms of Racial Discrimination requires that each state party 'shall prohibit and bring to an end … racial discrimination by any persons, group or organization'. The Convention on the Elimination of All Forms of Discrimination Against Women *requires* states parties 'to take all appropriate measures to eliminate discrimination against women by any person, organization or enterprise'. In the International Covenant on Economic, Social and Cultural Rights states parties undertake 'to take steps … achieving progressively the full realization of rights', while its rights-specific provisions, such as those dealing with labour, refer to states 'ensuring' those rights.

10 See A/HRC/8/5/Add.1 for a summary of the Special Representative's research on the UN human rights treaties and treaty body commentaries.

11 Corporate acts may be directly attributed to states in some circumstances, as where a state exercises such close control that the company is its mere agent.

The extraterritorial dimension of the duty to protect remains unsettled in international law. Current guidance from international human rights bodies suggests that states are not required to regulate the extraterritorial activities of businesses incorporated in their jurisdiction, but nor are they generally prohibited from doing so provided there is a recognized jurisdictional basis and that an overall reasonableness test is met. Within those parameters, some UN treaty bodies are encouraging home states to take steps to prevent abuse abroad by corporations within their jurisdiction.[12]

But there are also strong policy reasons for home states to encourage their companies to respect rights abroad, especially if a state itself is involved in the business venture – whether as owner, investor, insurer, procurer, or simply promoter. Such encouragement gets home states out of the untenable position of being associated with possible overseas corporate abuse. And it can provide much-needed support to host states that lack the capacity to implement fully an effective regulatory environment on their own. Moreover, there is an expanding web of potential corporate liability for international crimes, reflecting international standards but imposed through national courts.[13] As discussed in the next section, in some jurisdictions innovations in regulation and adjudication are moving toward greater recognition of the complex organizational forms characteristic of modern business enterprises.

It is often stressed that governments are the appropriate entities to make the difficult balancing decisions required to reconcile different societal needs. However, there are questions about whether governments have got the balance right. Many governments take a narrow approach to managing the business and human rights agenda.[14] It is often segregated within its own conceptual and (typically weak) institutional box – kept apart from, or heavily discounted in, other policy domains that shape business practices, including commercial policy, investment policy, securities regulation, and corporate governance. This inadequate domestic policy coherence is replicated internationally. Governments should not assume they are helping business by failing to provide adequate guidance for, or regulation of, the human rights impact of corporate activities. On the contrary, the less governments do the more they increase reputational and other risks to business. We elaborate further on these issues below.

The corporate responsibility to respect human rights is the second principle. It is recognized in such soft-law instruments as the Tripartite Declaration of Principles Concerning Multinational Enterprises and Social Policy,[15] and the Organisation for Economic Cooperation and Development (OECD) Guidelines for Multinational Enterprises.[16] It is invoked by the largest global business organizations in their submission to the mandate, which states that companies 'are expected to obey the law, even if it is not enforced, and to respect the principles of relevant international instruments where national law is absent'.[17] It is one of the commitments companies undertake in

12 E.g. CERD/C/USA/CO/6 (2008), para. 30; CESCR General Comment 19 (2008), para. 54.

13 UN Doc. A/HRC/4/35, paras. 19–32.

14 UN Doc. A/HRC/4/35/Add.3.

15 ILO Official Bulletin, Series A, No. 3 (2000).

16 See Organization for Economic Co-operation and Development, DAFFE/IME/WPG(2000)15/FINAL.

17 International Organization of Employers, International Chamber of Commerce, Business and Industry Advisory Committee to the Organisation for Economic Co-operation and Development (OECD), 'Business and Human Rights: The Role of Government in Weak Governance Zones', December 2006, para. 15 [online]. Available from: http://www.reports-and-materials.org/Role-of-Business-in-Weak-Governance-Zones-Dec-2006.pdf.

joining the UN Global Compact.[18] And indeed companies worldwide increasingly claim to respect human rights.[19]

To respect rights essentially means to act with due diligence to avoid infringing on the rights of others. Because companies can affect virtually all internationally recognized rights, they should consider the responsibility to respect in relation to all such rights, although some may require greater attention in particular contexts. There are situations in which companies may have additional responsibilities – for example, where they perform certain public functions, or because they have undertaken additional commitments voluntarily. But the responsibility to respect is the baseline expectation for all companies in all situations.

Yet, how do companies know they respect human rights? Do they have systems in place enabling them to support the claim with any degree of confidence? Most do not. What is required is due diligence – a process whereby companies not only ensure compliance with national laws but also manage the risk of human rights harm with a view to avoiding it.[20] The scope of human rights-related due diligence is determined by the context in which a company is operating, its activities, and the relationships associated with those activities.

Access to remedy is the third principle. Even where institutions operate optimally, disputes over the human rights impact of companies are likely to occur. Currently, access to formal judicial systems is often most difficult where the need is greatest. And non-judicial mechanisms are seriously underdeveloped – from the company level up through national and international levels. Section 5 below identifies criteria of effectiveness for grievance mechanisms and suggests ways to strengthen the current system.

3. The State Duty to Protect

The general nature of the duty to protect is well understood by human rights experts within governments and beyond. What seems less well internalized is the diverse array of policy domains through which states may fulfil this duty with respect to business activities, including how to foster a corporate culture respectful of human rights at home and abroad. This should be viewed as an urgent policy priority for governments – necessitated by the escalating exposure of people and communities to corporate-related abuses, and the growing exposure of companies to social risks they clearly cannot manage adequately on their own. The following discussion is not intended to insist on specific legislative or other policy actions, but to illustrate important issues and innovative approaches the author believes deserve serious consideration. Adjudication is addressed in Section 5 below.

3.1 Corporate Culture

Governments are uniquely placed to foster corporate cultures in which respecting rights is an integral part of doing business. This would reinforce steps companies themselves are asked to

18 See [online]. Available from: http://www.unglobalcompact.org/AboutTheGC/TheTenPrinciples/humanRights.html.

19 UN Docs A/HRC/4/35/Add.3, A/HRC/4/35/Add.4, and 'Human Rights Policies of Chinese Companies: Results from a Survey', [online]. Available from: http://www.business-humanrights.org/Documents/Ruggie-China-survey-Sep-2007.pdf.

20 A traditional definition of due diligence is 'the diligence reasonably expected from, and ordinarily exercised by, a person who seeks to satisfy a legal requirement or discharge an obligation'. *Black's Law Dictionary*, 8th edn (2006).

take to demonstrate their respect for rights, as described in Section 4 below. Two approaches are illustrated here.

First, governments can support and strengthen market pressures on companies to respect rights. Sustainability reporting can enable stakeholders to compare rights-related performance. Several states, sub-national authorities, and stock exchanges are calling for such disclosure.[21] Sweden requires independently ensured sustainability reports, using Global Reporting Initiative guidelines for its state-owned enterprises, and China recently issued an advisory opinion on this subject.[22] Some jurisdictions have gone further by redefining fiduciary duties. The recently revised United Kingdom (UK) Companies Act requires directors to 'have regard' to such matters as 'the impact of the company's operations on the community and the environment',[23] and regulators are increasingly rejecting company attempts to prevent shareholder proposals regarding human rights issues being considered at annual general meetings.[24]

Second, some states are beginning to use 'corporate culture' in deciding corporate criminal accountability.[25] They examine a company's policies, rules and practices to determine criminal liability and punishment, rather than basing accountability on the individual acts of employees or officers. These principles may be invoked at the liability stage, or during sentencing and in exercising prosecutorial discretion.[26] Both incentivize companies to have appropriate compliance systems.

In principle, inducing a rights-respecting corporate culture should be easier to achieve in state-owned enterprises (SOEs). Senior management in SOEs is typically appointed by and reports to state entities. Indeed, the state itself may be held responsible under international law for the internationally wrongful acts of its SOEs if they can be considered state organs or are acting on behalf, or under the orders, of the state. Beyond any legal obligations, human rights harm caused by SOEs reflects directly on the state's reputation, providing it with an incentive in the national interest to exercise greater oversight. Much the same is true of sovereign wealth funds and the human rights impacts of their investments.

3.2 Policy Alignment

The adverse effects of domestic policy incoherence include 'vertical' incoherence, in which governments take on human rights commitments without regard to implementation; and 'horizontal'

21 Among other examples, the Johannesburg Securities Exchange mandates sustainability reporting, as does France's law on new economic regulations.

22 'Guidelines for External Reporting by Swedish State-Owned Companies', adopted 29 November 2007 [online]. Available from: http://www.sweden.gov.se/sb/d/8194/a/93506; and 'Instructing Opinions About Central State-Owned Enterprises Fulfilling Social Responsibility', issued by China's State-Owned Asset Supervision and Administration Commission of the State Council, 4 January 2008.

23 Section 172 (1) (d) of the United Kingdom Companies Act (2006), which came into effect 1 October 2007.

24 'Trends in the Use of Corporate Law and Shareholder Activism to Increase Corporate Responsibility and Accountability for Human Rights', prepared for the Special Representative by the law firm Fried Frank [online]. Available from: http://www.business-humanrights.org/Documents/Fried-Frank-Memo-Dec-2007.pdf.

25 'Corporate Culture as a Basis for the Criminal Liability of Corporations', prepared for the Special Representative by the law firm Allens Arthur Robinson [online]. Available from: http://www.reports-and-materials.org/Allens-Arthur-Robinson-Corporate-Culture-paper-for-Ruggie-Feb-2008.pdf.

26 For examples of the former, see Section 12.3 of Australia's Criminal Code Act 1995 (Cth) and Article 102 of the Swiss Penal Code. For an example of the latter, see Chapter 8 of the *United States Federal Sentencing Guidelines Manual*: (2006) §8C2.5(b)(1).

incoherence, in which departments – such as trade, investment promotion, development, foreign affairs – work at cross-purposes with the state's human rights obligations and the agencies charged with implementing them. Two instances of this latter pattern are considered below: the first from host states, and the second from home states.

To attract foreign investment, host states offer protection through bilateral investment treaties and host government agreements. They promise to treat investors fairly, equitably, and without discrimination, and to make no unilateral changes to investment conditions. But investor protections have expanded with little regard to states' duties to protect, skewing the balance between the two. Consequently, host states can find it difficult to strengthen domestic social and environmental standards, including those related to human rights, without fear of foreign investor challenge, which can take place under binding international arbitration. This imbalance creates potential difficulties for all types of countries. Agreements between host governments and companies sometimes include promises to 'freeze' the existing regulatory regime for the project's duration, which can be a half-century for major infrastructure and extractive industries projects. During the investment's lifetime, even social and environmental regulatory changes that are applied equally to domestic companies can be challenged by foreign investors claiming exemption or compensation.

The imbalance is particularly problematic for developing countries. Our examination of nearly 90 contracts indicates that those signed with non-OECD countries constrain the host state's regulatory powers significantly more than those signed with OECD countries – and that country risk ratings alone do not seem to account for the variance.[27] Yet, it is precisely in developing countries that regulatory development may be most needed. When investment cases go to international arbitration they are generally treated as commercial disputes in which public interest considerations, including human rights, play little or no role. Additionally, arbitration processes are often conducted in strict confidentiality so that the public in the country facing a claim may not even know of its existence. Where human rights and other public interests are concerned, transparency should be a governing principle, without prejudice to legitimate commercial confidentiality. States, companies, the institutions supporting investments, and those designing arbitration procedures should work towards developing better means to balance investor interests and the needs of host states to discharge their human rights obligations.[28]

Now consider an example from the home state side. It concerns export credit agencies (ECAs), which finance or guarantee exports and investments in regions and sectors that may be too risky for the private sector alone. ECAs may be state agencies or privatized, but all are mandated by the state and perform a public function. Despite this state nexus, however, relatively few ECAs explicitly consider human rights at any stage of their involvement; indeed, in informal discussions, a number indicate they might require specific authority from their government overseers to do so.

On policy grounds alone, a strong case can be made that ECAs, representing not only commercial interests but also the broader public interest, should require clients to perform adequate due diligence on their potential human rights impacts. This would enable ECAs to flag up where serious human rights concerns would require greater oversight – and possibly indicate where state support should not proceed or continue. Closer alignment between a state's ECA and its official development agency is also desirable. A development agency may view the arrival of an ECA-supported private investment in a particular region of a country as reason to focus its own efforts elsewhere. But if the

27 See 'Stabilization clauses and human rights' [online]. Available from: http://www.reports-and-materials.org/Stabilization-Clauses-and-Human-Rights-11-Mar-2008.pdf.

28 Similar concerns have been raised regarding international and regional trade agreements, specifically about the state's ability to ensure access to essential services and protect the right to health. The Special Representative has not had the opportunity to conduct independent research on these trade-related issues.

investment has a large physical and social footprint, the chances are that it will generate pressures that local authorities may need help in managing – and which the home country development agency might be able to provide. This is but a small sample of issues where more effective policy alignment by states is required to support the business and human rights agenda.

3.3 The International Level

Effective guidance and support at the international level would help states achieve greater policy coherence. The human rights treaty bodies can play an important role in making recommendations to states on implementing their obligations to protect rights vis-à-vis corporate activities.[29] Special procedures mandate holders can also highlight relevant issues.[30] OHCHR can contribute to capacity-building in states that may lack the necessary tools by providing technical advice. States are encouraged to share information about challenges and best practices, thus promoting more consistent approaches and perhaps increasing their expectations of each other for protecting rights against corporate abuse. Peer learning would be facilitated by states including information about business in their reports for the universal periodic review. Where states lack the technical or financial resources to effectively regulate companies and monitor their compliance, assistance from other states with the relevant knowledge and experience offers an important means to strengthen the enforcement of human rights standards. Such partnerships could be particularly fruitful between states that have extensive trade and investment links, and between the home and host states of the same transnationals.

Finally, the OECD Guidelines are currently the most widely applicable set of government-endorsed standards related to corporate responsibility and human rights. Most recently updated in 2000, their current human rights provisions not only lack specificity, but in key respects have also fallen behind the voluntary standards of many companies and business organizations. Revision of the guidelines addressing these concerns would be timely.

3.4 Conflict Zones

It is well established that some of the most egregious human rights abuses, including those related to corporations, occur in conflict zones. The human rights regime cannot function as intended in the unique circumstances of sporadic or sustained violence, governance breakdown, and absence of the rule of law. Specific policy innovations are required to prevent corporate abuse, yet it seems that many states lag behind international institutions and responsible businesses in grappling with these difficult issues. State policies and practices – where they exist at all – are limited, fragmented and mostly unilateral. The use of UN Security Council sanctions targeting certain companies deemed to have contributed to conflicts in the Democratic Republic of the Congo, Sierra Leone and Liberia demonstrated a restraining effect. A recent report by the UN Secretary-General recommends that this enforcement tool be continued and improved.[31] But there is a need for more proactive policies

29 In June 2007, the Special Representative met with treaty body representatives to discuss their emerging guidance.

30 In June 2007, the Special Representative met with other human rights mandate holders to share experiences.

31 UN Doc. S/2008/18, particularly paras. 16–18. In some instances, the lists identifying individuals and companies for sanctions have been criticized on due process grounds.

to prevent harmful corporate involvement in conflict situations. As the UN Secretary-General notes, states need to do more to 'promote conflict-sensitive practices in their business sectors'.[32]

Home states could identify indicators to trigger alerts with respect to companies in conflict zones. They could then provide or facilitate access to information and advice – whether from home or their overseas embassies – to help businesses address the heightened human rights risks and ensure they act appropriately when engaging with local actors. There may be a point at which the home state would withdraw its support altogether. None of this detracts from host state duties to protect against all corporate abuse within their jurisdictions, including conflict zones.

In sum, the human rights regime rests upon the bedrock role of states. That is why the duty to protect is a core principle of the business and human rights framework. But meeting business and human rights challenges also requires the active participation of business directly. We now turn to the second principle.

4. The Corporate Responsibility to Respect

When it comes to the role companies themselves must play, the main focus in the debate has been on identifying a limited set of rights for which they may bear responsibility. For example, the draft norms on the responsibilities of transnational corporations and other business enterprises with regard to human rights generated intense discussions about whether its list of rights was too long or too short, and why some rights were included and others not. At the same time, the norms would have extended to companies essentially the entire range of duties that states have, separated only by the undefined concepts of 'primary' versus 'secondary' obligations and 'corporate sphere of influence'. This formula emphasizes precisely the wrong side of the equation: defining a limited list of rights linked to imprecise and expansive responsibilities, rather than defining the specific responsibilities of companies with regard to all rights.

The table below shows why any attempt to limit internationally recognized rights is inherently problematic. Drawn from more than 300 reports of alleged corporate-related human rights abuses, it makes a critical point: there are few if any internationally recognized rights that business cannot impact – or be perceived to impact – in some manner. Therefore, companies should consider all such rights. It may be useful for operational guidance purposes to map which rights companies have tended to affect most often in particular sectors or situations.[33] It is also helpful for companies to understand how human rights relate to their management functions – for example, human resources, security of assets and personnel, supply chains, and community engagement.[34] Both means of developing guidance should be pursued, but neither limits the rights companies should take into account.

The more difficult question of what precise responsibilities companies have in relation to rights has received far less attention. While corporations may be considered 'organs of society', they are specialized economic organs, not democratic public interest institutions. As such, their responsibilities cannot and should not simply mirror the duties of states. Accordingly, we have focused on identifying the distinctive responsibilities of companies in relation to human rights.

32 *Ibid.*, para. 20.

33 For example, the International Council on Mining and Metals conducted a study of 38 cases of allegations of human rights or related abuses involving mining companies in order to uncover patterns of human rights impacts. Second submission to the Special Representative, October 2006 [online]. Available from: http://www.icmm.com/newsdetail.php?rcd=119.

34 The companies in the Business Leaders Initiative on Human Rights (BLIHR) are developing this approach. See [online]. Available from: http://www.blihr.org.

Table 27.1 Business impact on human rights

	Labour rights	
Freedom of association	Right to equal pay for equal work	
Right to organize and participate in collective bargaining	Right to equality at work	
Right to non-discrimination	Right to just and favourable remuneration	
Abolition of slavery and forced labour	Right to a safe work environment	
Abolition of child labour	Right to rest and leisure	
Right to work	Right to family life	
	Non-labour rights	
Right to life, liberty and security of the person	Right of peaceful assembly	Right to an adequate standard of living (including food, clothing, and housing)
Freedom from torture or cruel, inhuman or degrading treatment	Right to marry and form a family	Right to physical and mental health; access to medical services
Equal recognition and protection under the law	Freedom of thought, conscience and religion	Right to education
Right to a fair trial	Right to hold opinions, freedom of information and expression	Right to participate in cultural life, the benefits of scientific progress, and protection of authorial interests
Right to self-determination	Right to political life	Right to social security
Freedom of movement	Right to privacy	

Source: This table is based on a study of 320 cases (from all regions and sectors) of alleged corporate-related human rights abuse reported on the Business and Human Rights Resource Centre website* from February 2005 to December 2007. Each case was coded for what right(s) the alleged abuse impacted, referencing the rights in the UDHR; International Covenant on Civil and Political Rights (ICCPR); International Covenant on Economic, Social and Cultural Rights (ICESCR); and International Labour Organization (ILO) core conventions.
*Available from: http://www.business-humanrights.org/Home.

4.1 Respecting Rights

In addition to compliance with national laws, the baseline responsibility of companies is to respect human rights. Failure to meet this responsibility can subject companies to the court of public opinion – comprising employees, communities, consumers, civil society, as well as investors – and occasionally to charges in actual courts. Whereas governments define the scope of legal compliance, the broader scope of the responsibility to respect is defined by social expectations – as part of what is sometimes called a company's social licence to operate.[35]

The corporate responsibility to respect exists independently of states' duties. Therefore, there is no need for the slippery distinction between 'primary' state and 'secondary' corporate obligations – which in any event would invite endless strategic gaming on the ground about who is responsible for what. Furthermore, because the responsibility to respect is a baseline expectation, a company cannot compensate for human rights harm by performing good deeds elsewhere. Finally, 'doing no harm' is not merely a passive responsibility for firms but may entail positive steps – for example, a workplace anti-discrimination policy might require the company to adopt specific recruitment and training programmes.

4.2 Due Diligence

To discharge the responsibility to respect requires due diligence. This concept describes the steps a company must take to become aware of, prevent and address adverse human rights impacts. Comparable processes are typically already embedded in companies because in many countries they are legally required to have information and control systems in place to assess and manage financial and related risks.[36] If companies are to carry out due diligence, what factors should be considered? The process inevitably will be inductive and fact-based, but the principles guiding it can be stated succinctly. Companies should consider three sets of factors. The first is the country contexts in which their business activities take place, to highlight any specific human rights challenges they may pose. The second is what human rights impacts their own activities may have within that context – for example, in their capacity as producers, service providers, employers, and neighbours. The third is whether they might contribute to abuse through the relationships connected to their activities, such as with business partners, suppliers, state agencies, and other non-state actors. How far or how deep this process must go will depend on circumstances.

For the substantive content of the due diligence process, companies should look, at a minimum, to the international bill of human rights and the core conventions of the ILO, because the principles they embody comprise the benchmarks against which other social actors judge the human rights impacts of companies. The basic human rights due diligence process should include the following.[37]

---

35 There are situations where national laws and international standards conflict. Further guidance for companies needs to be developed, but companies serious about seeking to resolve the dilemma are finding ways to honour the spirit of international standards.

36 'There are due diligence processes that a corporation must undertake to meet its general legal obligations that either accommodate or are at least amenable to consideration of human rights laws or standards.' Allens Arthur Robinson, 'Corporate Duty and Human Rights Under Australian Law', prepared for the Special Representative, p. 1 [online]. Available from: http://www.business-humanrights.org/Updates/Archive/SpecialRepPapers.

37 The principles are the same for all companies, although specific procedures may differ in small and medium-sized enterprises.

4.2.1 Policies Companies need to adopt a human rights policy. Broad aspirational language may be used to describe respect for human rights, but more detailed guidance in specific functional areas is necessary to give those commitments meaning.

4.2.2 Impact Assessments Many corporate human rights issues arise because companies fail to consider the potential implications of their activities before they begin. Companies must take proactive steps to understand how existing and proposed activities may affect human rights. The scale of human rights impact assessments will depend on the industry and national and local context.[38] While these assessments can be linked with other processes like risk assessments or environmental and social impact assessments, they should include explicit references to internationally recognized human rights. Based on the information uncovered, companies should refine their plans to address and avoid potential negative human rights impacts on an ongoing basis.

4.2.3 Integration The integration of human rights policies throughout a company may be the biggest challenge in fulfilling the corporate responsibility to respect. As in states, human rights considerations are often isolated within a company. That can lead to inconsistent or contradictory actions: product developers may not consider human rights implications; sales or procurement teams may not know the risks of entering into relationships with certain parties; and company lobbying may contradict commitments to human rights. Leadership from the top is essential to embed respect for human rights throughout a company, as is training to ensure consistency, as well as capacity to respond appropriately when unforeseen situations arise.[39]

4.2.4 Tracking performance Monitoring and auditing processes permit a company to track ongoing developments. The procedures may vary across sectors and even among company departments, but regular updates of human rights impact and performance are crucial. Tracking generates information needed to create appropriate incentives and disincentives for employees and ensure continuous improvement. Confidential means to report non-compliance, such as hotlines, can also provide useful feedback. As companies adopt and refine due diligence practices, industry and multi-stakeholder initiatives can promote sharing of information, improvement of tools, and standardization of metrics. The UN Compact is well-positioned to play such a role, enjoying a United Nations platform and reaching widely into the corporate community, including in developing countries.

4.3 Sphere of Influence

Sphere of influence was introduced into corporate social responsibility discourse by the UN Global Compact. It was intended as a spatial metaphor: the 'sphere' was expressed in concentric circles with company operations at the core, moving outward to suppliers, the community, and beyond, with the assumption that the 'influence' – and thus presumably the responsibility – of the company declines from one circle to the next. The draft norms later proposed the concept as a basis for attributing legal obligations to companies, using it as though it were analogous to the jurisdiction of states.

38 The Special Representative submitted a separate report on this subject in 2007 (UN Doc. A/HRC/4/74).

39 BLIHR, OHCHR, and the Global Compact, *A Guide for Integrating Human Rights into Business Management* [online]. Available from: www.ohchr.org/Documents/Publications/GuideHRBusinessen.pdf.

Sphere of influence remains a useful metaphor for companies in thinking about their human rights impacts beyond the workplace and in identifying opportunities to support human rights, which is what the UN Global Compact seeks to achieve.[40] But a more rigorous approach is required to define the parameters of the responsibility to respect and its due diligence component. To begin with, sphere of influence conflates two very different meanings of influence: one is impact, where the company's activities or relationships are causing human rights harm; the other is whatever leverage a company may have over actors that are causing harm. The first falls squarely within the responsibility to respect; the second may only do so in particular circumstances.

Anchoring corporate responsibility in the second meaning of influence requires assuming, in moral philosophy terms, that 'can implies ought'. But companies cannot be held responsible for the human rights impacts of every entity over which they may have some influence, because this would include cases in which they were not a causal agent, direct or indirect, of the harm in question. Nor is it desirable to have companies act whenever they have influence, particularly over governments. Asking companies to support human rights voluntarily where they have influence is one thing; but attributing responsibility to them on that basis alone is quite another. Moreover, influence can only be defined in relation to someone or something. Consequently, it is itself subject to influence: a government can deliberately fail to perform its duties in the hope or expectation that a company will yield to social pressures to promote or fulfil certain rights – again demonstrating why state duties and corporate responsibilities must be defined independently of one another.

Finally, the emphasis on proximity in the sphere of influence model can be misleading. Clearly, companies need to be concerned with their impact on workers and surrounding communities. But their activities can equally affect the rights of people far away from the source – as, for example, violations of privacy rights by Internet service providers can endanger dispersed end-users. Hence, it is not proximity that determines whether or not a human rights impact falls within the responsibility to respect, but rather the company's web of activities and relationships. In short, the scope of due diligence to meet the corporate responsibility to respect human rights is not a fixed sphere, nor is it based on influence. Rather, it depends on the potential and actual human rights impacts resulting from a company's business activities and the relationships connected to those activities.

4.4 Complicity

The corporate responsibility to respect human rights includes avoiding complicity. The concept has legal and non-legal pedigrees, and the implications of both are important for companies. Complicity refers to indirect involvement by companies in human rights abuses – where the actual harm is committed by another party, including governments and non-state actors. Due diligence can help a company avoid complicity.

The legal meaning of complicity has been spelled out most clearly in the area of aiding and abetting international crimes; that is, knowingly providing practical assistance or encouragement that has a substantial effect on the commission of a crime, as discussed in my 2007 report to the Human Rights Council.[41] The number of domestic jurisdictions in which charges for international crimes can be brought against corporations is increasing, and companies may also incur non-criminal liability for complicity in human rights abuses.

---

40 See [online]. Available from: http://www.unglobalcompact.org/AboutTheGC/TheTenPrinciples/index.html.

41 UN Doc. A/HRC/4/35, paras. 22–32.

In non-legal contexts, corporate complicity has become an important benchmark for social actors, including public and private investors, the UN Global Compact, campaigning organizations, and companies themselves. Claims of complicity can impose reputational costs and even lead to divestment, without legal liability being established.[42] In this context, allegations of complicity have included indirect violations of the broad spectrum of human rights – political, civil, economic, social, and cultural.

Owing to the relatively limited case history, especially in relation to companies rather than individuals, and given the substantial variations in definitions of complicity within and between the legal and non-legal spheres, it is not possible to specify definitive tests for what constitutes complicity in any given context. But companies should bear in mind the considerations set out below.

Mere presence in a country, paying taxes, or silence in the face of abuses is unlikely to amount to the practical assistance required for legal liability. However, acts of omission in narrow contexts have led to legal liability of individuals when the omission legitimized or encouraged the abuse.[43] Moreover, under international criminal law standards, practical assistance or encouragement need neither cause the actual abuse nor be related temporally or physically to the abuse. Similarly, deriving a benefit from a human rights abuse is not likely on its own to bring legal liability. Nevertheless, benefiting from abuses may carry negative implications for companies in the public perception. Legal interpretations of 'having knowledge' vary. When applied to companies, it might require that there be actual knowledge, or that the company 'should have known', that its actions or omissions would contribute to a human rights abuse. Knowledge may be inferred from both direct and circumstantial facts. The 'should have known' standard is what a company could reasonably be expected to know under the circumstances.

In international criminal law, complicity does not require knowledge of the specific abuse or a desire for it to have occurred, as long as there was knowledge of the contribution. Therefore, it may not matter that the company was merely carrying out normal business activities if those activities contributed to the abuse and the company was aware or should have been aware of its contribution. The fact that a company was following orders, fulfilling contractual obligations, or even complying with national law will not, alone, guarantee it legal protection.

In short, the relationship between complicity and due diligence is clear and compelling: companies can avoid complicity by employing the due diligence processes described above – which, as noted, apply not only to their own activities but also to the relationships connected with them.

5. Access to Remedies

Effective grievance mechanisms play an important role in the state duty to protect, in both its legal and policy dimensions, as well as in the corporate responsibility to respect. State regulation proscribing certain corporate conduct will have little impact without accompanying mechanisms to investigate, punish, and redress abuses. Equally, the corporate responsibility to respect requires a means for those who believe they have been harmed to bring this to the attention of the company

---

42 The Norwegian Government pension fund excludes and has divested from companies, including Wal-Mart, for complicity in human rights violations. Council on Ethics for the Government Pension Fund, annual reports 2006 and 2007 [online]. Available from: http://ww w.regjeringen.no/en/sub/Styrer-rad-utvalg/ethics_council/annual- reports.html?id=458699.

43 For example, International Criminal Tribunal for the Former Yugoslavia, Trial Chamber judgement *Kvocka et al.* (IT-98-30/1-T), 2 November 2001, paras. 257–61.

and seek remediation, without prejudice to legal channels available. Providing access to remedy does not presume that all allegations represent real abuses or bona fide complaints.

Expectations for states to take concrete steps to adjudicate corporate-related human rights harm are expanding. Treaty bodies increasingly recommend that states investigate and punish human rights abuse by corporations and provide access to redress for such abuse when it affects persons within their jurisdiction.[44] Redress could include compensation, restitution, guarantees of non-repetition, changes in relevant law and public apologies. As discussed earlier, regulators are also using new tools to hold corporations accountable under both civil and criminal law, focused on failures in organizational culture.

Non-judicial mechanisms play an important role alongside judicial processes. They may be particularly significant in a country where courts are unable, for whatever reason, to provide adequate and effective access to remedy. Yet they are also important in societies with well-functioning rule of law institutions, where they may provide a more immediate, accessible, affordable, and adaptable point of initial recourse. State-based, non-judicial mechanisms include agencies with oversight of particular standards (for example, health and safety); publicly funded mediation services, such as those handling labour rights disputes in the UK and South Africa; national human rights institutions; or mechanisms such as the OECD's National Contact Points.

Non-state mechanisms may be linked to industry-based or multi-industry organizations; to multi-stakeholder initiatives ensuring member compliance with standards; to project financiers requiring certain standards of clients; or to particular companies or projects. Non-state mechanisms must not undermine the strengthening of state institutions, particularly judicial mechanisms, but can offer additional opportunities for recourse and redress. Yet this patchwork of mechanisms remains incomplete and flawed. It must be improved in its parts and as a whole.

5.1 Judicial Mechanisms

Judicial mechanisms are often under-equipped to provide effective remedies for victims of corporate abuse. Victims face particular challenges when seeking personal compensation or reparation as opposed to more general sanction of the corporation through a fine or administrative remedies. They may lack a basis in domestic law on which to found a claim. Even if they can bring a case, political, economic or legal considerations may hamper enforcement.

Some complainants have sought remedy outside the state where the harm occurred, particularly through home state courts, but have faced extensive obstacles. Costs may be prohibitive, especially without legal aid; non-citizens may lack legal standing; and claims may be barred by statutes of limitations. Matters are further complicated if the claimant is seeking redress from a parent corporation for actions by a foreign subsidiary. In common law countries, the court may dismiss the case based on *forum non conveniens* grounds – essentially, that there is a more appropriate forum for it. Even the most independent judiciaries may be influenced by governments arguing for dismissal based on various 'matters of state'. These obstacles may deter claims or leave the victim with a remedy that is difficult to enforce.

The law is slowly evolving in response to some of these obstacles. In some jurisdictions, plaintiffs have brought cases against parent companies claiming that they should be held responsible for their

44 For instance, the Committee on the Rights of the Child increasingly recommends that states parties comply with Article 3 (4) of the Optional Protocol to the Convention on the Rights of the Child on the sale of children, child prostitution and child pornography, which requires them to take measures, where appropriate and, subject to national law, to establish criminal, civil or administrative liability of legal persons for treaty offences. See UN Doc. A/HRC/4/35/Add.1, para. 64.

own actions and omissions in relation to harm involving their foreign subsidiaries.[45] Elsewhere it is getting somewhat more difficult for defendant companies to have cases alleging harm abroad dismissed on the basis that there is a more appropriate forum.[46] And foreign plaintiffs are using the United States (US) Alien Tort Claims Act to sue even non-US companies for harm suffered abroad.[47] States should strengthen judicial capacity to hear complaints and enforce remedies against all corporations operating or based in their territory, while also protecting against frivolous claims. States should address obstacles to access to justice, including for foreign plaintiffs – especially where alleged abuses reach the level of widespread and systematic human rights violations.

5.2 Non-Judicial Grievance Mechanisms

Non-judicial mechanisms to address alleged breaches of human rights standards should meet certain principles to be credible and effective. Based on a year of multi-stakeholder and bilateral consultations conducted under my mandate,[48] we have found that, at a minimum, such mechanisms must be:

a. *Legitimate*: a mechanism must have clear, transparent and sufficiently independent governance structures to ensure that no party to a particular grievance process can interfere with the fair conduct of that process.
b. *Accessible*: a mechanism must be publicized to those who may wish to access it and provide adequate assistance for aggrieved parties who may face barriers to access, including language, literacy, awareness, finance, distance, or fear of reprisal.
c. *Predictable*: a mechanism must provide a clear and known procedure with a time frame for each stage and clarity on the types of process and outcome it can (and cannot) offer, as well as a means of monitoring the implementation of any outcome.
d. *Equitable*: a mechanism must ensure that aggrieved parties have reasonable access to sources of information, advice and expertise necessary to engage in a grievance process on fair and equitable terms.
e. *Rights-compatible*: a mechanism must ensure that its outcomes and remedies accord with internationally recognized human rights standards.
f. *Transparent*: a mechanism must provide sufficient transparency of process and outcome to meet the public interest concerns at stake and should presume transparency wherever possible; non-state mechanisms in particular should be transparent about the receipt of complaints and the key elements of their outcomes.

---

45 For example, *Connelly* v *RTZ Corporation plc and Others* [1998] AC 854, and *Lubbe* v *Cape plc* [2000] 4 All ER 268 (House of Lords, United Kingdom).

46 The European Court of Justice has confirmed that national courts in an EU member state may not dismiss actions against companies domiciled in that state on *forum non conveniens* grounds. *Owusu* v *Jackson* [2005] ECR-I-1283. And in Australia, defendants must now prove that the forum is 'clearly inappropriate'. *Voth* v *Manildra Flour Mills Pty. Ltd.* (1990) 171 C.L.R. 538 (H.C.A.).

47 More than 40 cases have been brought against companies under this statute since 1993, when the first was filed.

48 The process involved experts from all stakeholder groups and regions. These principles, based on more specific guidance developed for companies, apply across non-judicial mechanisms of different kinds. See [online]. Available from: http://www.business-humanrights.org/Links/Repository/308254/link_page_view.

5.3 Company-Level Grievance Mechanisms

Currently, the primary means through which grievances against companies play out are litigation and public campaigns. For a company to take a bet on winning lawsuits or successfully countering hostile campaigns is, at best, optimistic risk management. Companies should identify and address grievances early, before they escalate. An effective grievance mechanism is part of the corporate responsibility to respect. A company can provide a grievance mechanism directly and be integrally involved in its administration. This could include the use of external resources – possibly shared with other companies – such as hotlines for raising complaints, advisory services for complainants, or expert mediators. Or it may involve a wholly external mechanism. Whatever the form, the company should ensure that the process abides by the principles outlined above.

Where a company is directly involved in administering a mechanism, problems may arise if it acts as both defendant and judge. Therefore, the mechanism should focus on direct or mediated dialogue. It should be designed and overseen jointly with representatives of the groups who may need to access it. Care should be taken to redress imbalances in information and expertise between parties, enabling effective dialogue and sustainable solutions. These mechanisms should not negatively impact opportunities for complainants to seek recourse through state-based mechanisms, including the courts.

5.4 State-Based Non-Judicial Mechanisms

Our research indicates that out of the 85 recognized national human rights institutions (NHRIs) at least 40 are able to handle grievances related to the human rights performance of companies. Of these, 31 are accredited under the Paris Principles.[49] Some are limited to human rights abuses alleged against state-owned enterprises or private companies providing public services. Others can address grievances against any kind of company, but only with regard to specific kinds of human rights-related grievances, often discrimination. A third group – notably in Africa – admits grievances against all companies with regard to any human rights issue.[50]

The actual and potential importance of these institutions cannot be overstated. Where NHRIs are able to address grievances involving companies, they can provide a means to hold business accountable. NHRIs are particularly well positioned to provide processes – whether adjudicative or mediation-based – that are culturally appropriate, accessible, and expeditious. Even where they cannot themselves handle grievances, they can provide information and advice on other avenues of recourse to those seeking remedy. Through increased interchange of information, they could act as lynchpins within the wider system of grievance mechanisms, linking local, national and international levels across countries and regions. NHRIs that do not currently publicize information about their business-related work should do so.

The 40 states adhering to the OECD Guidelines for Multinational Enterprises must provide a National Contact Point (NCP), whose tasks include handling grievances. OECD provides procedural guidance, with individual NCPs having flexibility in the application of the guidelines. The NCPs are potentially an important vehicle for providing remedy. However, with a few exceptions, experience suggests that in practice they have too often failed to meet this potential. The housing of some NCPs

---

49 The Paris Principles relate to the status of national human rights institutions (NHRIs) and establish criteria for their composition, guarantees of independence and pluralism, competence, responsibilities, and methods of operation. See [online]. Available from: http://www.nhri.net/default.asp?PID=312&DID=0.

50 'Business and Human Rights: A Survey of NHRI Practices' [online]. Available from: http://www.business-humanrights.org/Gettingstarted/UNSpecialRepresentative .

primarily or wholly within government departments tasked with promoting business, trade and investment raises questions about conflicts of interest. NCPs often lack the resources to undertake adequate investigation of complaints and the training to provide effective mediation. There are typically no time frames for the commencement or completion of the process, and outcomes are often not publicly reported. In sum, many NCP processes appear to come up short when measured against the minimum principles set out in Section 5.2 above.

Certain NCPs, recognizing such shortfalls, have sought innovative solutions. Several have involved multiple government departments and created multi-stakeholder advisory groups. Perhaps most interesting is the decision of the Dutch government to reorganize its NCP such that a four-person, multi-stakeholder group handles grievances independent of, though supported administratively by, the government. Alternative suggestions have included placing NCPs under the legislative branch or within a NHRI. OECD and adhering states should consider these and other options for addressing current deficits, while preserving the important role of governments in raising awareness of the guidelines and providing incentives for corporate compliance and learning.

5.5 Multi-Stakeholder or Industry Initiatives and Financiers

For multi-stakeholder or industry initiatives aiming to advance human rights standards in the practices of their corporate members, a grievance mechanism provides an important check on performance. The same is true for financial institutions seeking to ensure compliance with human rights standards in the conduct of the projects they support. In the absence of an effective grievance mechanism, the credibility of such initiatives and institutions may be questioned. The Voluntary Principles on Security and Human Rights[51] recently faced this challenge, and I know of calls for other initiatives, including the Equator Principles,[52] to develop a grievance process. Furthermore, while many of these mechanisms require their corporate members or clients to have their own grievance processes as a first port of call, few set clear process standards for them. This risks encouraging tokenistic rather than effective processes at the operational level.

As the number of initiatives aimed at promoting standards increases, collaborative models for their grievance mechanisms will likely become more important. These could facilitate access for complainants by providing a single avenue for recourse to multiple organizations; marshal the collective leverage of organizations and their members to achieve solutions; and reduce the resource implications for the individual entities involved. The organizations concerned must remain responsible for ensuring that any such mechanism meets the minimum principles described above.

5.6 Gaps in Access

The foregoing describes a patchwork of grievance mechanisms at different levels of the international system, with different constituencies and processes. Yet, considerable numbers of individuals whose human rights are impacted by corporations lack access to any functioning mechanism that could provide remedy. This is due in part to a lack of awareness as to where these mechanisms are located, how they function, and what supporting resources exist. NHRIs, NGOs, academic institutions, governments and other actors could address this gap through improved information flows.

Yet, this is not solely about a lack of information. It also reflects intended and unintended limitations in the competence and coverage of existing mechanisms. Consequently, some actors have

51 [online]. Available from: http://www.fco.gov.uk/resources/en/pdf/pdf7/fco_voluntaryprinciples.

52 [online]. Available from: http://www.equator-principles.com/.

proposed the creation of a global ombudsman function that could receive and handle complaints. Such a mechanism would need to provide ready access without becoming a first port of call; offer effective processes without undermining the development of national mechanisms; provide timely responses while likely being located far from participants; and furnish appropriate solutions while dealing with different sectors, cultures and political contexts. It would need to show some early successes if faith in its capacity were not quickly to be undermined. To perform these tasks, any such function would need to be well resourced. Careful consideration should go into whether these criteria actually can and would be met before moving in this direction.

6. Conclusion

The current debate on the business and human rights agenda originated in the 1990s, as liberalization, technology, and innovations in corporate structure combined to expand prior limits on where and how businesses could operate globally. Many countries, including in the developing world, have been able to take advantage of this new economic landscape to increase prosperity and reduce poverty. But as has happened throughout history, rapid market expansion has also created governance gaps in numerous policy domains: gaps between the scope of economic activities and actors, and the capacity of political institutions to manage their adverse consequences. The area of business and human rights is one such domain.

In fact, progress has been made in the past decade, at least in some industries and by growing numbers of firms including public–private hybrids combining mandatory with voluntary measures, and industry and company self-regulation.[53] All have their strengths and shortcomings, but few would have been conceivable a mere decade ago. Likewise, there is an expanding web of potential corporate liability for international crimes, reflecting international standards but imposed through national courts. Governments have adopted a variety of measures, albeit gingerly to date, to promote a corporate culture respectful of human rights. Fragments of international institutional provisions exist with similar aims.

Without in any manner disparaging these steps, our fundamental problem is that there are too few of them, none has reached a scale commensurate with the challenges at hand, there is little cross-learning, and they do not cohere as parts of a more systemic response with cumulative effects. That is what needs fixing. And that is what the framework of 'protect, respect and remedy' is intended to help achieve. The UN is not a centralized command-and-control system that can impose its will on the world – indeed it has no 'will' apart from that with which member states endow it. But it can and must lead intellectually and by setting expectations and aspirations. The Human Rights Council can make a singular contribution to closing the governance gaps in business and human rights by supporting this framework, inviting its further elaboration, and fostering its uptake by all relevant social actors.

53 See 'Business and Human Rights: Mapping International Standards of Responsibility and Accountability for Corporate Acts', Report of the Special Representative of the Secretary-General on the issue of human rights and transnational corporations and other business enterprises, UN Document A/HRC/4/35, 19 February 2007.

PART V
'And Beyond'

Chapter 28
A Future for Human Rights Law

Robert McCorquodale

1. Introduction

> The GENERAL ASSEMBLY proclaims THIS UNIVERSAL DECLARATION OF HUMAN RIGHTS as a common standard of achievement for all peoples and all nations, to the end that every individual and every organ of society, keeping this Declaration constantly in mind, shall strive by teaching and education to promote respect for these rights and freedoms and by progressive measures, national and international, to secure their universal and effective recognition and observance, both among the peoples of Member States themselves and among the peoples of territories under their jurisdiction.[1]

On a cold Paris evening on 10 December 1948, just before midnight, the members of the General Assembly of the United Nations (UN) rose as one to give a standing ovation to Eleanor Roosevelt and the other members of the UN Human Rights Commission. This rare gesture of appreciation was because the commission had been the primary drafters of the UDHR, which had just been adopted by the General Assembly. As the then president of the General Assembly, Herbert Evatt of Australia, stated:

> [T]he adoption of the Declaration is a step forward in a great evolutionary process ... the first occasion on which the organised community of nations has made a declaration of human rights and fundamental freedoms. That document is backed by the authority of the body of opinion of the United Nations as a whole and millions of people, men, women and children all over the world who would turn to it for help, guidance and inspiration.[2]

Six decades after the adoption of the UDHR, it is valuable to reflect on where there may be a further 'evolutionary process' in the development of international human rights law.

While the authors of the various chapters in this book have expertly analysed many aspects of the development of international human rights law over the past six decades after the adoption of the UDHR, I aim, in this concluding chapter, to offer some thoughts on the future of international human rights legal protections based upon the terms and inspiration of the UDHR. I will do so in the context of the final words of the Preamble of the UDHR, which are set out above. These words indicate that 'every individual and every organ of society' is to promote respect for human rights, and they are to secure the 'universal and effective recognition and observance' of human rights. These words do not demand that only one 'organ of society' –the state – has the responsibility to protect human rights and

---

1 Universal Declaration of Human Rights, GA Res. 217A (III), UN Doc. A/810 at 71 (1948), Preamble.

2 Dr H.V. Evatt (Australia), Plenary Meetings of the General Assembly, 183rd Plenary Meeting (10 December 1948), p. 934.

to ensure their fulfilment. Rather, these words make clear that every person and every organ of society has these responsibilities.[3] Therefore, I will explore the possibilities that may arise in the future for human rights protections if international human rights law were to be inspired by the UDHR to extend legal obligations to individuals and other organs of society, that is, to non-state actors, and the impact that this could have on the universal and effective protection of human rights.

2. The State and the UDHR

There has been much debate about whether the UDHR – or parts of it – is legally binding on states under international law. There is no doubt, however, that most of its articles have been the direct inspiration for human rights found in international and regional human rights treaties, which create binding international legal obligations on those states that are parties to them, as well as in national legal protections. As every state has ratified at least one major international human rights treaty (albeit many with reservations), there is a consensus that human rights can and do create international legal obligations on states. This was confirmed by the Vienna Declaration on Human Rights, which stated that 'the promotion and protection of all human rights is a legitimate concern of the international community.'[4]

One part of this debate concerns whether all or some of the articles of the UDHR are binding on all states as a matter of customary international law. While this argument has rightly been treated with caution, recent developments have made this argument more tenable. On 18 June 2007, the UN Human Rights Council adopted a resolution for the creation of the Universal Periodic Review (UPR). This required every member state of the UN to be reviewed regularly for its compliance with human rights. The resolution stated that the basis for the review is the following:

a. The Charter of the United Nations;
b. The Universal Declaration of Human Rights;
c. Human rights instruments to which a State is party;
d. Voluntary pledges and commitments made by States, including those undertaken when presenting their candidatures for election to the Human Rights Council (hereinafter 'the Council').[5]

This resolution makes clear that one of the appropriate legal sources for questioning every state about its human rights record is the UDHR. Since the UPR began, many states have been questioned about human rights for which they have no treaty obligations. The only basis for the question (and the answers) could be customary international law obligations arising from the UDHR. There have been no objections by states that this is an improper or illegal basis. This implies that states have accepted that the UDHR is a legitimate and lawful basis for binding customary international legal obligations on all states.[6]

---

3 This responsibility is reiterated in the UN Declaration on the Right and Responsibility of Individuals, Groups and Organs of Society to Promote and Protect Universally Recognized Human Rights and Fundamental Freedoms, A/RES/53/144, adopted by the UN General Assembly on 8 March 1999.

4 Vienna Declaration and Programme of Action on Human Rights 1993, 32 ILM 1661 (1993), para. 4.

5 UN Human Rights Council Resolution 5/1, 18 June 2007 (A/HRC/5/21).

6 For comments on the UPR process see P. Sen (ed.), *Universal Periodic Review of Human Rights* (Commonwealth Secretariat, 2009), and F.D. Gaer, 'A Voice Not an Echo: Universal Periodic Review and the UN Treaty Body System', *Human Rights Law Review*, 7(1) (2007), pp. 109–39.

This development is consistent with the general acceptance by states that they have the obligation to respect, protect and fulfil international human rights legal obligations. These legal obligations of a state are not restricted to actions and inactions by state actors, such as the government, police, military and the courts, but also encompass actions by non-state actors within the territory of the state. For example, the state has been held responsible where it has failed to protect civilians from non-state armed opposition groups and from paramilitaries during internal armed conflict, and where it has not investigated the situation.[7] In addition, states have been held internationally legally responsible where employees of corporations have been dismissed or victimized for joining a trade union,[8] where the activities of non-state actors have caused pollution,[9] and for failures by the state to protect indigenous peoples' land from harm caused by development.[10] This position is based on the general obligations on states as rightly indicated by the Human Rights Committee (HRC):

> [T]he positive obligations on States Parties to ensure Covenant [the International Covenant on Civil and Political Rights] rights will only be fully discharged if individuals are protected by the State, not just against violations of Covenant rights by its agents, but also against acts committed by private persons or entities that would impair the enjoyment of Covenant rights in so far as they are amenable to application between private persons or entities. There may be circumstances in which a failure to ensure Covenant rights as required by article 2 [being the general obligations on a State] would give rise to violations by States Parties of those rights, as a result of States Parties' permitting or failing to take appropriate measures or to exercise due diligence to prevent, punish, investigate or redress the harm caused by such acts by private persons or entities.[11]

These views are essentially applicable for every major human rights treaty. A state is responsible, under international human rights law, for the actions of all those within its jurisdiction for violations of human rights.

---

7 E.g. *Vélásquez Rodriguez* v *Honduras* (1989), 28 ILM 294, and *Ergi* v *Turkey (1998), European Human Rights Reports*, 32, pp. 388ff.

8 *Young, James and Webster* v *UK* (1982), *European Human Rights Reports*, 4, pp. 38ff.

9 E.g. *Lopez Ostra* v *Spain* (1994), *European Human Rights Reports*, 20, pp. 277ff; *Guerra* v *Italy* (1998), *European Human Rights Reports*, 26, pp. 357ff. See also *Social and Economic Rights Action Centre and the Centre for Economic and Social Rights* v *Nigeria*, Communication No. 155/96 (2003) *International Human Rights Reports*, 10, 282 (African Commission on Human and Peoples' Rights, 27 October 2001), especially para. 59: '[Nigeria is in violation] of local people's rights to [...] health [...] and life [by] breaching its duty to protect the Ogoni people from damaging acts of oil companies'.

10 See *Yanomami Community* v *Brazil*, Case 7615, Resolution No. 12/85 (Inter-American Commission on Human Rights, 5 March 1985); *The Mayagna (Sumo) Awas Tingni Community* v *Nicaragua*, Series C, No. 79 (2001, 2003), *International Human Rights Reports*, 10, 758 (Inter-American Court of Human Rights, judgement of 31 August 2001), and *Hopu and Bessert* v *France*, Communication No. 549/1993, UN Doc CCPR/C/60/D/549/1993/Rev.1 (29 December 1997).

11 Human Rights Committee (HRC), *General Comment 31: Nature of the General Legal Obligation Imposed on States Parties to the Covenant*, UN Doc CCPR/C/21/Rev.1/Add.13 (29 March 2004) para. 8. The HRC also notes that some articles of the ICCPR address more directly the positive obligations of states in relation to the activities of non-state actors; see, for example, HRC, *General Comment 20: Article 7 (Prohibition of Torture, or Other Cruel, Inhuman or Degrading Treatment or Punishment)*, UN Doc HRI/GEN/1/Rev (10 March 1992), para. 4.

3. Beyond the State

However, the UDHR does not limit its concerns to state actions or state responsibility. It is not directed to states alone. It is directed to 'every individual and every organ of society'. It does not require – in contrast to human rights treaties – that it is for states solely to respect human rights and for states solely to secure the rights.

Indeed, during the drafting of the UDHR, a meeting of the UN Economic, Social and Cultural Organization (UNESCO) sought to clarify the philosophy of human rights. It obtained views from around the world about human rights. They concluded that, across all cultures, human rights could be 'seen as implicit in man's nature as an individual and as a member of society and to follow from the fundamental right to live'.[12] Their views were not dependent on the role of the state but reflected the broader idea of human rights within the context of neighbourhoods and societies, including in terms of duties to a neighbour.

This is a powerful idea about human rights. Under the UDHR, human rights are about protecting individuals (and groups) from oppressive power, primarily in the context of the communities and neighbourhoods within which they live. This idea of human rights for which 'every individual and every organ of society' is responsible is at the heart of the UDHR. However, this idea has generally been lost in the formulation of much of international human rights law, especially in the treaties. While the preambles of these treaties do refer to broader issues as to the philosophical basis of human rights, they ultimately focus on a single relationship between an individual and the state. Even the group rights, such as the right of self-determination, are largely restricted in exercise to individual means within most treaties. Thus, the human rights expressed in treaties are conceived in terms of a binary opposition between the individual and the state, with the individual being 'rights-bearing' solely in relation to the state.[13]

A number of scholars have noted how this construct of the state and the individual in human rights treaties is created in the form of an ideal of the European or Western centralized model of the state and of an autonomous self-interested individual, even though the model has limited utility elsewhere.[14] Dianne Otto has shown how this construction erases alternative experiences, particularly of those having communitarian traditions and of women, and reinforces the notion that some actions are 'private' and so not within the coverage of international human rights law.[15] Indeed,

> The narrow focus of human rights law on State responsibility is not only out of step with current power relations, but also tends to obscure them. The exclusive concern with national governments

---

12 The UNESCO Committee's report is found in J. Maritian, *Human Rights: Comments and Interpretations* (New York: Wingate, 1949). See also discussion in M.A. Glendon, *A World Made New: Eleanor Roosevelt and the Universal Declaration of Human Rights* (New York: Random House, 2001), Ch. 5.

13 The African Charter on Human and Peoples' Rights does make some attempt to reinstate this broader relationship of rights within societies other than the state, but this is often seen as an attempt by states to reduce their international legal obligations rather than to expand those entities which have human rights responsibilities.

14 E.g. M. Foucault, 'Two Lectures', in C. Gordon (ed.), *Power/Knowledge* (New York: Pantheon, 1980), p. 78; N. Tsagourias, *Jurisprudence of International Law: The Humanitarian Dimension* (Manchester: Manchester University Press, 2000); and L. Henkin, *International Law: Politics and Values* (Dordrecht: Martinus Nijhoff, 1995).

15 D. Otto, 'Rethinking Universals: Opening Transformative Possibilities in International Human Rights Law', *Australian Year Book of International Law*, 18 (1997), pp. 1ff.

> not only distorts the reality of the growing weakness of national-level authority, but also shields other actors from greater responsibility. The focus on State responsibility also creates a false sense of rigidity or inevitability about social and political hierarchies and existing inequities.[16]

One other consequence, as Philip Allott has astutely pointed out, is that:

> Human rights [have been] quickly appropriated by governments, embodied in treaties, made part of the stuff of primitive international relations, swept up into the maw of an international bureaucracy. The reality of the idea of human rights has been degraded. From being a source of ultimate anxiety for usurping holders of public social power, they were turned into bureaucratic small-change.[17]

What is lost in this narrow conception of human rights adopted by international human rights treaties is the broader concept of human rights found in the UDHR, which is about empowering humans in every situation and every relationship.

It is possible for the broader understanding of human rights in the UDHR to be carried forward in the future. This would mean that human rights' legal protections are not limited to the relationship with one institution, that is, the state, which is essentially a political institution. Instead, they are involved in every relationship that humans have: economic, social, cultural, religious, personal. This is not surprising as individuals, community leaders, groups and non-governmental organizations can all impact on the human rights of others. As the former president of the Czech Republic, Václav Havel, has noted:

> The exercise of power is determined by thousands of interactions between the world of the powerful and that of the powerless, all the more so because these worlds are never divided by a sharp line: everyone has a small part of himself in both.[18]

Sadly, the reality is that many people are oppressed by others who have more political, economic, social or cultural power, or power within personal relationships. It is this desire to assert human rights in the face of the potential of oppressive power in any form that is found in the UDHR. It is a responsibility on 'every individual and every organ of society' to protect these human rights in their daily lives. Indeed, Eleanor Roosevelt noted:

> Where after all, do universal human rights begin? In small places, close to home – so close and so small that they cannot be seen on any map of the world. Yet they are the world of the individual person: the neighborhood he [or she] lives in; the school or college he [or she] attends; the factory, farm or office where he [or she] works. Such are the places where every man, woman, or child seeks equal justice, equal opportunity, equal dignity without discrimination. Unless these rights have meaning there, they have little meaning anywhere. Without concerted citizen action to uphold them close to home, we shall look in vain for progress in the larger world.[19]

---

16 C. Jochnick, 'Confronting the Impunity of Non-State Actors: New Fields for the Promotion of Human Rights', 21 *Human Rights Quarterly*, 21(1) (1999), pp. 56–79 at p. 59.

17 P. Allott, *Eunomia* (Oxford: Oxford University Press, 1988), p. 288.

18 V. Havel, *Disturbing the Peace* (London: Faber, 1990), p. 182.

19 Eleanor Roosevelt, remarks at presentation of booklet on human rights, *In Your Hands,* to the Commission on Human Rights, New York, 27 March 1958.

Therefore, the future for human rights in terms of the UDHR is the extension of human rights legal responsibilities to other organs of society beyond the state and so to rights that are relevant to people's daily lives.

4. Non-State Actors and Human Rights

4.1 Corporations

Eleanor Roosevelt spoke of the need for human rights to be in the 'the factory, farm or office' where people work. Yet, despite many attempts and assertions, the reality is that international human rights law has not directly engaged in this area of economic activity. This is despite the fact that corporations own many factories, farms and offices, and that the majority of investment into developing states is by corporations.[20]

There have been a number of attempts at the national, regional and international levels to deal with the impacts on human rights of corporate activity through legal regulation. Most have not succeeded, largely through lack of political will by states or through strong resistance by corporations. Therefore, under current international human rights law, only states have direct international legal responsibility for the violation of human rights in factories, farms and offices. This is despite the clear evidence that corporations can and do violate human rights.

How international human rights law has dealt with this issue has largely been by expanding the scope of a state's responsibility for corporate activity, as shown above.[21] The current developments do not, so far, show a willingness to create any direct international legal obligations of corporations in relation to violations of human rights. For example, the framework crafted by John Ruggie, the Special Representative of the UN Secretary-General on the Issue of Human Rights and Transnational Corporations and Other Business Enterprises (the Ruggie framework), limits the responsibilities of corporations to 'social expectations' without legal remedies.[22] While this approach is a considerable advance in terms of accepting that corporations do have responsibilities in relation to all human rights, those responsibilities are only to 'promote respect for' human rights and not to 'secure their universal observance' in relation to corporations.

While there are many non-legal pressures on corporations not to violate human rights, nevertheless, if there are no international legal obligations on corporations operating around the world to protect human rights, it is very difficult to provide remedies and make human rights operate in every factory, farm and office as envisaged by the drafters of the UDHR. However, the remarkably swift acceptance of the Ruggie framework in recent years indicates that it is an area of considerable progressive development. So it is possible to foresee further developments in this area (perhaps similarly swift) towards imposing direct international legal obligations on corporations regarding human rights.

---

20 Foreign direct investment (i.e. mainly corporate investment) into developing states was about $US1,692 billion in 2007; see UNCTAD, *World Investment Report* (2008).

21 For a fuller discussion, see R. McCorquodale and P. Simons, 'Responsibility Beyond Borders: State Responsibility for Extraterritorial Violations by Corporations of International Human Rights Law', *Modern Law Review*, 70 (2007), pp. 598–625.

22 See UN Doc. A/HRC/ 8/5 of 7 April 2008, paras. 54–61; and UN Doc. A/HRC/11/13 of 22 April 2009. See also Chapter 27 in this volume.

4.2 International Organizations

Across the world, many factories, farms and offices are affected by the financial support of the international financial institutions. The decisions by the World Bank, the International Monetary Fund (IMF), the World Trade Organization (WTO), and other international organizations of states can have a significant impact on what infrastructure is built in a state and the governance of a territory. However, many of these international organizations expressly or implicitly consider that they do not have any direct responsibility for violations of human rights, even though they have international legal personality.

Some international organizations have clear territorial powers that are similar to state powers. Indeed,

> [T]he United Nations assumption of powers akin to those of sovereign States allows the conceptual leap toward a vision of the United Nations as not merely a benign promoter, but as a potential guarantor of human rights in places like Kosovo or East Timor.... [The mandates of recent UN peacekeeping missions] emphatically proclaimed the 'applicability' of human rights standards by stipulating that '[I]n exercising their functions, all persons undertaking public duties or holding public office [in the respective territories] shall observe internationally recognised human rights standards.'[23]

On this basis, the Ombudsperson in Kosovo considered that the UN peacekeeping mission in that territory (UNMIK) was effectively a 'surrogate State [which imposed] all ensuing obligations, including affirmative obligations to secure human rights to everyone within [its] jurisdiction'.[24] Thus, it is possible to consider that an international organization that is acting as a sovereign is subject to international human rights law obligations.

While some of the international organizations do not have sovereign powers, their activity can directly affect human rights. For example, decisions by international financial institutions to fund the building of dams that involve the large-scale forcible removal of people from their homes, the likely effect on the right to health of millions of people of decisions made by pharmaceutical corporations under a global trade treaty, and the decisions on distribution of food by refugee agencies can all have direct impacts on human rights.[25] In fact, there are instances where international organizations have acknowledged this, with the 'abundance of official training manuals and courses on the duty of UN personnel to protect and respect human rights [making] it quite clear that the UN itself sees that it, and its personnel, must respect international human rights'.[26]

It is, therefore, important that in the future international organizations have clear human rights legal responsibilities, for which there are direct remedies against them and not only against the states that constitute them. This would lead to a greater chance of securing universal human rights obligations.

---

23 F. Mégret and F. Hoffmann, 'The UN as a Human Rights Violator? Some Reflections on the United Nations Changing Human Rights Responsibilities', *Human Rights Quarterly*, 25 (2003), pp. 314–42, at pp. 333–4.

24 Ombudsperson Institution in Kosovo, Special Report No. 2 (27 October 2000): Available from: www.ombudspersonkosovo.org.

25 On trade and human rights issues, see, for example, A. Lang, 'Rethinking Trade and Human Rights', *Tulane Journal of International and Comparative Law*, 15 (2007), pp. 335–413.

26 A. Clapham, *Human Rights Obligations of Non-State Actors* (Oxford: Oxford University Press, 2006), p. 127.

4.3 Armed Opposition Groups

For many people the greatest threat to their human rights comes from those who are in opposition to the state, especially as there are more civilians than military personnel being killed in armed conflicts today. Yet, the actions by armed opposition groups (including terrorist groups) are not violations of international human rights law (though they may be violations of international humanitarian law and/or international criminal law) because those groups are non-state actors. Indeed, the structure of international human rights law 'presupposes and depends upon viable, effective states and accountable law enforcement bodies at the domestic level, which is not the case for many states'.[27] This ignores the reality that some states are not able to administer the territory in a way that protects those living in it, as in Colombia, where there are, or have been, substantial areas of territory that are not under the effective control of the state.

While there are understandable dangers in reducing the obligations of a state, it is possible to have joint obligations of both the state and the non-state actor. In many cases the armed opposition group seeks some international legitimacy and so may be prepared to accept international human rights legal obligations (and international humanitarian legal obligations). This broadening of obligations would assist the protection of those affected on the territory controlled by armed opposition groups and may open potential peace processes. Indeed, the International Criminal Tribunal for the Former Yugoslavia (ICTY) determined that

> A State-sovereignty-oriented approach [of international law] has been gradually supplanted by a human-being-oriented approach. Gradually the maxim of Roman law *hominum causa omne jus constitutum est* (all law is created for the benefit of human beings) has gained a firm foothold in the international community as well. It follows that in the area of armed conflict the distinction between interstate wars and civil wars is losing its validity as far as human beings are concerned. Why protect civilians from belligerent violence, or ban rape, torture or the wanton destruction of hospitals, churches, museums or private property, as well as proscribe weapons causing unnecessary suffering, when two sovereign states are engaged in war, and yet refrain from enacting the same bans or providing the same protection when armed violence has erupted 'only' within the territory of a sovereign state? If international law, while, of course, duly safeguarding the legitimate interests of states, must gradually turn to the protection of human beings, it is only natural that the aforementioned distinction should gradually lose its weight.[28]

If this broad conceptual approach is taken, then it is feasible that, over time, armed opposition groups will become subject to international human rights law. This may not be too distant in time, as the UN Security Council has already made clear that terrorists (who are non-state actors) are subject to international law. In Resolution 1373 (2001), paragraph 5, the UN Security Council unanimously declared that:

> [A]cts, methods, and practices of terrorism are contrary to the purposes and principles of the United Nations and that knowingly financing, planning and inciting terrorist acts are also contrary to the purposes and principles of the United Nations.

---

27 A. Goldsmith, 'Policing Weak States: Citizen Safety and State Responsibility', *Policing and Society*, 13 (2003), pp. 3–12, at p. 9.

28 *Prosecutor* v *Tadic*, Decision on the Defence Motion for Interlocutory Motion for Appeal on Jurisdiction, 2 October 1995, IT-94-1-AR72.

This paragraph does not expressly link the terrorist activities to a state's responsibility. Rather, it indicates that terrorist activities by themselves are a breach of international law, no matter who is undertaking those activities. As the resolution does not refer to crimes against humanity or other acknowledged areas of individual responsibility under international law, the UN Security Council must be asserting that terrorist actions *per se* give rise to individual international responsibility. So certain actions by non-state actors (if terrorist actions) are in breach of international law (and can modify that law) and, it must be assumed, give rise to international obligations of those non-state actors. It is thus possible to foresee that these obligations could extend to armed opposition groups in relation to human rights in the future.

4.4 Social Organizations

The UDHR is aimed at 'every organ of society'. In most societies there is an importance accorded to communities, collectives, groups and families, especially as humans possess a general communal quality. Almost every person is part of a group or groups and is seen as being part of a group or groups, from local collectives and neighbourhoods, to trade unions and non-governmental organizations (NGOs), and from religious and cultural organizations to linguistic and educational bodies. All individuals' identities, histories and engagements are usually affected by belonging to groups and by the communities within which they live. Indeed, the UDHR recognizes this in Article 29(1), which provides that '[e]veryone has duties to the community in which alone the free and full development of his personality is possible.'

These social groups can be vitally important in the upholding and protecting of human rights. Many of them have brought human rights cases to courts, provided widespread support and activism, and been able to enforce states' human rights legal obligations. Some international human rights treaties acknowledge the role of social groups, particularly the role of families. The Convention on the Rights of the Child (CRC)[29] provides in Article 5:

> States Parties shall respect the responsibilities, rights and duties of parents or, where applicable, the members of the extended family or community as provided for by local custom, legal guardians or other persons legally responsible for the child, to provide, in a manner consistent with the evolving capacities of the child, appropriate direction and guidance in the exercise by the child of the rights recognized in the present Convention.[30]

This respect for social groups and their traditions is an important aspect of human rights. However, these social groups can also be potential sources of oppression and violation of human rights, including where the conduct occurs in the shadow of family life. As Isaiah Berlin has noted:

> [M]utiny against the life of the barracks – suffocation in 'closed' societies – against the laws and institutions that are felt to be unjust or oppressive or corrupt or indifferent to some of the deepest aspirations of human beings, occurs in the history of every long-lived state and church and social order.[31]

29 1577 UNTS 3.

30 See also, for example, the African Charter of Human and Peoples' Rights 1981, Articles 17 and 18.

31 I. Berlin, *Crooked Timber of Humanity* (Princeton, NJ: Princeton University Press, 1991), p. 259.

Despite this, there is only very little in current international human rights law that makes such social groups responsible for human rights violations. For example, the Convention on the Elimination of Forms of Discrimination Against Women (CEDAW)[32] requires states to abolish social and cultural patterns and practices that discriminate against women, and Article 24(3) of the CRC makes clear that 'States Parties shall take all effective and appropriate measures with a view to abolishing traditional practices prejudicial to the health of children.'

The Convention on the Protection and Promotion of the Rights and Dignity of Persons with Disabilities[33] has taken this position one step further. Not only are there obligations in this treaty of states to adopt measures to 'combat stereotypes, prejudices and harmful practices relating to persons with disabilities' (Article 8(1)), but there is also a requirement that states raise social awareness and 'nurtur[e] receptiveness to the right of persons with disabilities' (Article 8(2)). This suggests 'truly a tidal attempt at engineering changes in attitude.... Persons with disabilities ... should not have to pay for their autonomy by being removed from the community, nor should they have to pay for living in the community by giving up their autonomy.'[34]

While these are important developments, so far, in the six decades of the UDHR, the legal responsibility is still placed on the state and not on the social group. It may be that the most effective method of preventing oppression and violations of human rights by a social group will be by state action and through extending the obligations of the state. However, there may eventually be horizontal applications of international human rights law, so that it applies to actions that violate international human rights law that are taken by a non-state actor against another non-state actor.

5. Application to Poverty

All human rights – civil, political, economic, social, cultural and group – will be affected by a future international human rights law that applies directly to non-state actors. This may also enable the protection of other aspects of the daily lives of many people that are not well protected by international human rights law at the moment. For example, poverty affects many people's lives and in many instances it is the actions of non-state actors, such as corporations, international organizations, armed opposition groups and social groups, which create the greatest impact on the lives of those in poverty, especially as the state is often very distant from their daily activities.[35] Yet vulnerability caused by poverty is not well protected currently in international human rights law.

This absence of poverty in human rights protections is a surprising situation considering that part of the inspiration for the drafting of the UDHR (as confirmed in its Preamble) was President Franklin Roosevelt's speech on the 'four freedoms', one of which was 'freedom from want'.[36] While freedom from poverty itself was not expressed as a human right, it was understood to be behind the creation of Article 25. Matthew Craven has observed in that regard that '[e]conomic,

32 UN Doc. A/34/46.

33 UN Doc A/61/49.

34 F. Mégret, 'The Disabilities Convention: Towards a Holistic Concept of Rights', *International Journal of Human Rights*, 12 (2008), pp. 261–78, at p. 268.

35 E.g. World Bank, *Voices of the Poor: Can Anyone Hear Us?* (Oxford: Oxford University Press/ World Bank, 2000).

36 This section is largely based on M. Baderin and R. McCorquodale, 'Poverty and the International Covenant on Economic, Social and Cultural Rights', in G. van Bueren (ed.), *Law's Duty to the Poor* (Oxford: Oxford University Press/UNESCO, forthcoming 2010).

social and cultural rights could be said to be an expression of Roosevelt's idea of 'freedom from want',[37] indicating that the need to address issues relating to poverty had been identified right from the beginning of human rights development at the international level.

Poverty is usually defined in economic terms, though it is better defined in capabilities terms, as the Committee on Economic, Social and Cultural Right states:

> In the recent past, poverty was often defined as insufficient income to buy a minimum basket of goods and services. Today, the term is usually understood more broadly as the lack of basic capabilities to live in dignity. This definition recognizes poverty's broader features, such as hunger, poor education, discrimination, vulnerability and social exclusion. The Committee notes that this understanding of poverty corresponds with numerous provisions of the Covenant. In the light of the International Bill of Rights [which includes the UDHR], poverty may be defined as a human condition characterized by sustained or chronic deprivation of the resources, capabilities, choices, security and power necessary for the enjoyment of an adequate standard of living and other civil, cultural, economic, political and social rights. While acknowledging that there is no universally accepted definition, the Committee endorses this multi-dimensional understanding of poverty, which reflects the indivisible and interdependent nature of all human rights.[38]

The adoption – on the 60th anniversary of the UDHR – of an Optional Protocol to the International Covenant on Economic, Social and Cultural Rights[39] should open the possibility of individual complaints in relation to poverty being articulated. As the committee itself noted:

> While the common theme underlying poor people's experiences is one of powerlessness, human rights can empower individuals and communities. The challenge is to connect the powerless with the empowering potential of human rights. Although human rights are not a panacea, they can help to equalise the distribution and exercise of power within and between societies.[40]

With so much of this power that affects people in poverty being in the hands of non-state actors, having an international human rights law that applied directly to non-state actors could enable empowerment of the poor.

So, there is the possibility that one of the underpinning foundations of the UDHR – to end poverty – may be able to have 'effective recognition and observance' (to use the words of the UDHR) through developments in international human rights law in the future. There should be similar impacts on other human rights protections.

6. Conclusion

The UDHR is a remarkable document, which was adopted just as the Cold War began. Six decades later, it is still a remarkable document that, as Amartya Sen has commented, 'has been quite pivotal in bringing discussion and debate to a very important subject, and its impact on reasoning and

37 M. Craven, *The International Covenant on Economic, Social and Cultural Rights: A Perspective on Its Development* (Oxford: Oxford University Press, 1995), p. 8.

38 ESCR Committee, 'Statement on Poverty and the International Covenant on Economic, Social and Cultural Rights' (2001) E/C.12/2001/10, paras. 7 and 8.

39 UN General Assembly Resolution A/RES/63/117 of 10 December 2008.

40 E/C.12/2001/10, note 38 above, para. 6.

actions in the world has been quite remarkable'.[41] Indeed, one of the effects of the UDHR has been to include human rights in everyday discourse at local, national, regional and international levels.

Human rights language is now found, for example, in climate change proposals, in trade negotiations and in armed conflict activity. While some of this language is problematic and can be harmful in terms of a dilution of the idea of human rights, it is evident that there is a pull towards human rights being recognized as relevant to daily life.[42] As Patricia Williams notes:

> [F]or the historically disempowered, the conferring of rights is symbolic of all the denied aspects of their humanity: rights imply a respect that places one in referential range of self and others, that elevates one's status from human body to social being.... 'Rights' feels new in the mouths of most black [and other oppressed] people. It is still deliciously empowering to say. It is the magic wand of inclusion and exclusion, of power and no power. The concept of rights, both positive and negative, is the maker of citizenship, our relation to others.[43]

This is an important power of human rights, albeit sometimes more in terms of rhetoric than reality. Human rights are only fully effective when they are lived reality.

There are aspects of the UDHR that have been lost in much of the debate about its impact. Its mission was not aimed solely at states or designed to create an international human rights law in which only states have legal obligations. Its intention was to ensure that 'every individual and every organ of society' has responsibilities to promote respect for human rights and 'secure [the] universal and effective recognition and observance' of human rights. This was an appeal beyond states. It was intended to affect non-state actors.

As shown here, non-state actors do violate human rights, but they do not currently have clear direct international human rights responsibilities. This limits human rights and affects the daily lives of many people around the world. It is therefore possible – indeed desirable – that the future development of human rights law will be inspired by the UDHR to extend the legal obligations of human rights clearly to non-state actors.

41 A. Sen, 'The Power of a Declaration: Making Human Rights Real', *The New Republic*, 4 February 2009, p. 240.

42 See J. von Bernstorff, 'The Changing Fortunes of the UDHR: Genesis and Symbolic Dimensions of the Turn to Rights in International Law', *European Journal of International Law*, 19(5) (2008), pp. 903–24; C. McCrudden, 'Human Dignity and Judicial Interpretation of Human Rights', *European Journal of International Law*, 19(4) (2008), pp. 655–724; and D. Kennedy, *The Dark Sides of Virtue: Reassessing International Humanitarianism* (Princeton, NJ: Princeton University Press, 2008).

43 P. Williams, *The Alchemy of Race and Rights* (Cambridge, MA: Harvard University Press, 1991), 164.

Index

For Product Safety Concerns and Information please contact our
EU representative GPSR@taylorandfrancis.com Taylor & Francis
Verlag GmbH, Kaufingerstraße 24, 80331 München, Germany